INTERNATIONAL LAW

DOCTRINE, PRACTICE, AND THEORY ⸎ SECOND EDITION

John H. Currie, FACULTY OF LAW (COMMON LAW), UNIVERSITY OF OTTAWA

Craig Forcese, FACULTY OF LAW (COMMON LAW), UNIVERSITY OF OTTAWA

Joanna Harrington, FACULTY OF LAW, UNIVERSITY OF ALBERTA

Valerie Oosterveld, FACULTY OF LAW, UNIVERSITY OF WESTERN ONTARIO

www.publicinternationallaw.ca

International Law: Doctrine, Practice, and Theory, second edition
© Irwin Law Inc, 2014

Published in 2014 by
Irwin Law
14 Duncan Street
Suite 206
Toronto, Ontario
M5H 3G8
www.irwinlaw.com

ISBN: 978-1-55221-357-5
e-book ISBN: 978-1-55221-358-2

Cover and interior design by Heather Raven

Cataloguing in Publication available from Library and Archives Canada

The publisher acknowledges the financial support of the Government of Canada through the Book Publishing Industry Development Program (BPIDP) for its publishing activities.

We acknowledge the assistance of the OMDC Book Fund, an initiative of Ontario Media Development Corporation.

Printed and bound in Canada.

3 4 5   20 19 18

SUMMARY TABLE OF CONTENTS

DETAILED TABLE OF CONTENTS

ACKNOWLEDGMENTS

This book was made possible through the hard work of several students over the past several years. Sincere thanks go to Adam Huff, Danna Ingleton, Koren Marriott, Lise Rivet, and Chloé Rousselle, all former students of the University of Ottawa; and Kathleen Burke, Joseph Cescon, Vera Dokter, Andrea Marlowe, Scott Robinson, and Kirsten Stefanik of the University of Western Ontario. The authors also thank the Law Foundation of Ontario and the Social Sciences and Humanities Research Council for their support of the authors' research activities, which have helped shape several chapters in this book.

The authors would also like to acknowledge, with gratitude, the team at Irwin Law, particularly Jeff Miller for his belief in, and close collaboration on, this project, as well as Lesley Steeve and Heather Raven for their help in the production of this book.

INTRODUCTION

OUR PROJECT

From all appearances, the early twenty-first century is a time of uncertainty for the world legal order. Since the publication of the first edition of this book, the fields of international law and international relations have been wracked by political upheavals and appalling levels of violence against civilians; a global financial crisis in 2008; a global pandemic in 2009; and environmental disasters such as the Gulf of Mexico oil spill in 2010. The Arab Spring movement has led to tumultuous changes in governments, while natural disasters, such as cyclone Nargis in Myanmar in 2008 or the massive earthquakes in Haiti, New Zealand, and Japan in 2010 and 2011, have placed new pressures on international law to facilitate inter-state cooperation in times of humanitarian crisis. World trade talks continue to stall, with some governments hoping to stimulate their economies either through protectionist measures or the conclusion of regional agreements, such as a desired Trans-Pacific Partnership or trans-Atlantic trade deals with an expanding European Union. While the growth of the Internet and social media has led to new means of providing support for social change, governments also face greater risks of information insecurity, as demonstrated in 2010 by the WikiLeaks release of hundreds of confidential US State Department cables. China's rise as a result of huge economic growth is also having an impact on world affairs, as is the growing influence of emerging leaders such as Brazil, India, and South Africa, but regional conflicts, including China's disputes with its neighbours in the East China and South China Seas, are heightening geopolitical insecurity. Nuclear insecurity is another contributing factor, while legal insecurity also exists, with questions arising as to whether current law is adequate to address the use of drones and new methods of cyberwarfare.

The attacks of September 11, 2001 (9/11) also continue to have an impact on both international law and international relations. Measured against the heady optimism that immediately followed the Cold War, international relations in the post-9/11 era have appeared tumultuous, divisive, and ominous. In the immediate aftermath of 9/11, unsettling new views on the exercise of hard power in foreign affairs gained sway, prompting some democratic states to embrace a doctrine of "pre-emptive self-defence" and the illegal resort to force in places like Iraq. Memoranda from government officials pushed the envelope in efforts to defend torture as a practice legitimated by the shadowy "war against terror." Attempts were also made to distort the provisions of the widely respected Geneva Conventions in order to consign unknown numbers of individuals, through rendition, to black holes into which no credible legal light was permitted to penetrate.

Meanwhile, older problems have assumed ominous new forms. Terrorists now destroy themselves to destroy others. Reports of nuclear ambitions in Iran, nuclear weapons testing in North Korea, and nuclear tensions between India and Pakistan cast a pall more alarming than the Cold War. Conflict flares in the Democratic Republic of Congo, sending refugees across international borders and internally displacing many more. Places like Somalia, rudderless and forgotten, evaporate from the world's consciousness until reports of Somali pirates threaten the world's reliance on international shipping. Sub-Saharan Africa as a whole confronts a virtual demographic collapse, with all its attendant social and political ramifications, under the weight of an HIV/AIDS crisis, while millions of people die preventable deaths or live unnecessarily difficult lives, pressed up against insurmountable social, political, and economic barriers of staggering injustice. The British science fiction writer Arthur C. Clarke predicted that, in 2001, we would be visiting the planets. In reality, in 2013, governments—notwithstanding the lessons of Srebrenica and Rwanda—are still debating the implementation of a "responsibility to protect" civilians and whether that responsibility should propel intervention in places like Syria, where countless individuals have died.

The horrors outlined above are different in scale but not in substance from those that have afflicted humanity for much of its existence: war, famine, hatred, disease, death. But there is another story—one of slow, incremental progress towards a less desperately barbaric human condition. Much of this progress is shockingly recent in a long history of human strife, yet enormous strides have been made in the last sixty years or so. These have included, to name but a few, the birth of a global public consciousness, perhaps best exemplified in the establishment of the United Nations and its affiliated institutions; the relegation of war, previously a legitimate instrument of international discourse, to the status of the ultimate offence against the international legal order; the recognition of universally defined human rights as an inalienable birthright of every individual; the termination of centuries of colonial domination and exploitation of the great majority of the world's population, and the recognition of their right of self-determination; and the dawning realization that our planet's resources are not infinite and that human activity must be carefully managed if we are to avoid destroying our own habitat.

These foundational developments have led, in the last generation and in particular since the end of the Cold War, to accelerated accomplishments, most of which have no precedents. To name a recent few: the creation of the World Trade Organization, which has significantly reduced barriers to the free flow of trade between states; the establishment of the first permanent International Criminal Court, which has jurisdiction to try the most serious international crimes; the continued, quiet spread of liberal democracy throughout Latin America, Eastern Europe, South Africa, and parts of Southeast Asia; the expansion of the European Union ever further eastward; the possibility, not yet entirely realized, of affordable HIV/AIDS medications for Africa; the spectacular emergence out of grinding poverty of large portions of East Asia; and the information revolution, knitting together a world community and fostering the coalescence of a worldwide public consciousness as never before.

To some, these may seem to be paltry, timid steps, and certainly no adequate countervails to the world's sufferings. As you review these materials, some of these accomplishments may indeed have foundered, whereas some challenges may have been resolved, and yet other successes and reversals may have emerged. What will likely remain constant, however, is uncertainty over whether "progress" is indeed being made. Is the world generally a happier, safer, more prosperous and sustainable place than before? Is it more just?

The answers to these questions likely depend on the perspective of the observer. Economists might point to measures of world economic activity. Public health experts might focus on the rate of infection for influenza, HIV, malaria, or any of dozens of other diseases. Human rights advocates might cite the waxing or waning propensity of states to torture. We, however, are professors of international law and observers of international relations. For us, the measure of progress lies not in any one statistic. Instead, it depends on the advancement of a particular process: the spread of rules, principles, and standards that effectively and justly govern the conduct of international relations, replace military and economic coercion with reliance on the rule of law, supplant despotism and corruption with good governance, and enable the world community truly to conceive of itself as such, in order to surmount — peaceably, cooperatively — the perils it confronts. Progress, in other words, is the development of a system of international law that enables the world community to deal expeditiously and constructively with life's crises.

How, then, would we assess the state of international law in the second decade of the twenty-first century? What mark would we assign it, as professional evaluators? Reluctantly, we would give it a "C": passable given its relative youth as a legal system; showing signs of promise and improvement; but not nearly living up to its potential, and often depressingly unfocused on the true tasks and challenges before it.

Certainly, we are not among those who contest the very existence or significance of something called "international law." Such a position should be implausible to anyone who has boarded a commercial flight to a foreign destination, confident that her airliner will not be shot down over foreign territory, that her passport will be honoured upon landing, and that her fundamental human rights will be respected during her visit. So, too, for anyone who engages in even the most mundane of daily activities, such as mailing a postcard abroad, receiving an overseas telephone call from a relative, or purchasing an imported good. In countless ways, international law quietly, unobtrusively, but nevertheless quite effectively, has a profound impact upon our daily existence. Even those of us who have no personal experience of war, torture, genocide, hijacking, slavery, colonial occupation, institutionalized racism, arbitrary detention, unchecked disease, runaway inflation, unsafe work conditions, famine, poisoned waterways — or any number of other evils — might pause to consider whether our charmed existence is mere historical accident and our own good luck, or whether it may, at least in part, be attributable to concerted efforts to address such issues by way of a global legal order and rules of international law.

We concede that, in the most politicized areas of international relations, international law's writ appears often to fall on deaf ears. Far too many are those who, notwithstanding international legal efforts, do indeed still experience the scourges listed above. However, to the extent international law remains inadequate or its dictates go ignored in key areas — war and conflict, the protection of human rights, the preservation of our environment — we contend this is often because of a Trojan horse that lurks at the very heart of the current system of international law itself: state sovereignty. As the introductory materials that follow will show, the international legal system as we know it was constructed principally in reaction to the emergence of the sovereign nation-state. International law's most fundamental elements are therefore aimed at respecting the sovereignty of states while, paradoxically, attempting to regulate their behaviour. The malaise of international law stems, in other words, not from its non-existence or irrelevance, but from its fundamental incoherence.

Incoherence is not unique to the international legal system. Anyone who has studied domestic systems of public law will be familiar with the apparent paradoxes of governance for and by the governed. However, domestic—or, as international lawyers call them, "municipal"—legal systems have two practical advantages over international law in either addressing or avoiding such paradoxes. First, they are usually products of clearly constituted, hierarchical sources of legal authority, which generally endow law-making bodies with clear jurisdiction to create positive legal obligations. Second, domestic law is usually enforced by courts and police forces, backed where necessary by the full coercive power of the state. It is true that, in any domestic system, there may be actors—economically or politically powerful individuals, corporations, or groups—capable of contesting, co-opting, or contorting domestic law, and of frustrating its enforcement. Most inhabitants of states, however, have little prospect of escaping the reach of domestic law. Municipal law, therefore, looks and feels like "the real thing": statutes and regulations, crime and punishment, breach and remedy.

This is not quite as true in the international arena. Where the typical domestic legal system is one of hierarchy with lawmakers enunciating enforceable norms for all, international law is the product of a mostly "horizontal" system: each state is in some sense a sovereign lawmaker, and no one state out-ranks another, at least in formal, legal terms. Even the international institutions that most resemble legislatures—the United Nations General Assembly, for instance—generally lack the law-making powers of state legislative branches and are more akin to discussion fora. The result is an excruciatingly complex process of international law-making that depends, on the one hand, on international agreements known as treaties (the content of which usually reflects the lowest common denominator of acceptability to the world's states); and, on the other, on an inchoate system of customary law derived, not from law-making judges as exist in common law jurisdictions, but from a perplexing exegesis of state practice and belief.

Moreover, this problematic law-making process is further hampered by the conceptual environment in which it takes place. That environment is not primarily conceived of as an international community with common needs and concerns; rather, the starting premise is the essential "separateness"—the sovereignty—of each member of the so-called international community. The law-making process thus has to contend with each state's assessment of its own national interests, which often displaces consideration of the greater, common good.

And this is not sovereignty's only challenge for international law. Even where international law exists—even incontestably—the horizontal system of equally sovereign states renders it virtually unenforceable in any way analogous to domestic law enforcement. Yes, states litigate in international venues, but only when they freely choose to do so—and many refuse. And a complaining state's success in an international legal forum is sometimes not closely correlated with a change in the offending state's behaviour. Remarkably, some individuals perpetrating serious international crimes now serve prison sentences. But the scope of these justiciable international crimes is narrow, and impunity remains the order of the day for many of the world's human rights abusers.

Is it useful, therefore, to study rules, fuzzy in their contours; sometimes dubious in their existence, utility, or wisdom; and often honoured in the breach? We believe the answer to that question is yes. It is true that, as Canada's minister of foreign affairs observed in 2002, international law is to law what Swiss cheese is to cheese: cheese, but full of holes.[1] However, we think—with apologies for abusing the metaphor—that there is still enough cheese there into which to sink one's teeth. As for the holes, they are egregious. But we believe that the very existence of these shortcomings makes the study of international law the more pressing. The most unnerving problems we face in the twenty-first century are global in scope. Global problems demand global solutions. And those solutions will only come if we can make of international law a truly robust system of problem solving. That is our task as professors and practitioners of international law. We urge that it be your project, too, today as students of international law, and tomorrow as practitioners. We want this book to be your first step along that path.

OUR PERSPECTIVE

We believe it also important in this introduction to establish our perspective in approaching this subject. We are each citizens of Canada, a classic "middle power" in international relations, and as such we are heavily influenced by middle power perspectives on international law.

A "middle power" has been described as "a state whose leaders consider that it cannot act alone effectively but may be able to have a systemic impact in a small group or through an international institution."[2] As such, Canadian policy-makers are generally receptive to international law, most particularly in the areas of institution building and international trade. Middle power approaches to international law appear preoccupied with two things: first, the levelling effect of the international rule of law (potentially constraining the dominance of great powers); and, second, the related process of favouring collective action over unilateralism. Taken together, these middle power approaches tend to validate the concept of international law more clearly than do the rather ambiguous great power stances, often much more hostile to international law.

We attach two caveats, one regret, and one disclaimer to these observations. First, we do not mean to suggest that international law generates universal or ready enthusiasm in middle powers in all instances. Canada, like many nations, has its *comprador* elite, inclined to accommodate great powers. In the Canadian context, this class sees an independent foreign policy as an expensive extravagance in a dependent economy. For this reason, promoting the concept of international law to middle power governments is usually not a hard sell. It is, however, sometimes extremely difficult to persuade policy-makers that middle

---

1   The Honourable Bill Graham, Minister of Foreign Affairs, "Notes for an Address on the Occasion of a Tribute to Professor Thomas Franck," New York, 5 October 2002 (copy on file with the authors). Minister Graham may have been inspired by a similar metaphor used by the well-known international legal scholar Anthony D'Amato to describe "a Swiss Cheese view of sovereignty: there's plenty of cheese, but there are holes in it (for human rights)": Anthony D'Amato, "Human Rights as Part of Customary International Law: A Plea for Change of Paradigms" (1995–96) 25 Ga J Int'l & Comp L 47 at 64.

2   Robert O Keohane, "Lilliputians' Dilemmas: Small States in International Politics" (1969) 23 International Organization 291 at 296.

powers can, or should, pursue a given course of action in the face of stiff resistance from great powers. On the abolition of landmines, the creation of the International Criminal Court, and opposition to the 2003 Iraq war, for example, Canada leaned into the wind blowing from some quarters and held its ground. If that wind were to reach a gale, it is by no means clear that Canada's appreciation of the appropriate balance between devotion to international law and loyalty to great power allies would remain unchanged.

Which brings us to our second caveat. We do not mean to suggest that middle powers enjoy some particular monopoly on virtue. As Professor Jack Goldsmith has observed, discussing Sweden:

> Middle powers show a greater devotion to international law and institutions than more powerful nations, because they can exercise power abroad most effectively in this fashion. But here, as before, it is important not to confuse internationalism with cosmopolitanism. Middle powers by definition have relatively little unilateral influence in politico-military issues. They focus their diplomatic and related foreign affairs resources where they can exert the most influence, especially against the major powers. Their commitments to international institutions associated with cosmopolitan charity thus have a structural explanation wholly apart from cosmopolitan sentiment.[3]

Third, our regret: the strong middle power focus on multilateralism sometimes becomes an end, rather than merely a means. This desire for a "seat at the table" as a goal in and of itself is open to criticism. However, in multilateral venues, middle powers magnify their influence relative to that which they would possess absent such institutions. This satisfying tendency may make middle powers particularly loath to partake in judicious unilateralism, even where warranted and entirely consistent with (and supportive of) international law.

Last, our disclaimer: a middle power approach—and our endorsement of it—should not be confused with a prickly "anti-Americanism." Like many of our American counterparts, we often have strong objections to the United States' administration's conduct of foreign affairs (and to similar conduct by other great powers). Nevertheless, we generally agree that if the world must have a hegemon, better the United States than most other candidates.

As middle power academics, we are, however, acutely suspicious of the value of hegemony itself. Great powers rise and great powers fall. Perhaps since 1815, and certainly since the late nineteenth century, two of the greatest hegemons have been the United Kingdom and the United States—both Anglo-Saxon powers. Canada is very much a product of the hegemony of these two states, and not surprisingly we have a great deal of sympathy for the international order they have fostered. Nevertheless, we are uneasy about an international order built around the transient great powers that history and circumstance create. The next great power—or perhaps, the current one—may in time prove significantly less receptive to normative ideas we believe should infuse international law. In such circumstances, the best therapy would seem to be a system of international law unfavourable to unalloyed hegemony.

---

3   Jack Goldsmith, "Liberal Democracy and Cosmopolitan Duty" (2003) 55 Stan L Rev 1667 at 1690–691.

For all these reasons, we intend this book to reflect a value-based approach to international law infused with support for the middle power position. A value-based normative vision of international law is, of course, fraught with hazard. Prominent "normative" approaches to international legal theory—not least the New Haven School associated with Yale University—have spawned criticism that their prescriptions reflect a "nationalist" (in the New Haven case, American) bias.[4] We do not, however, shy away from this peril. Lawyers have an obligation to promote just outcomes. In this book, we endorse values that we allow ourselves the luxury of believing are conducive to such outcomes.

To meet our objective we propose a normative metre stick, to be applied from time to time through the chapters that follow. This metre stick has both a procedural and a substantive dimension. Procedurally, we ask whether the doctrine, practice, and theory of various aspects of international law in fact stabilize international relations, smoothing away rough edges that might otherwise precipitate conflict. Substantively, we ask whether the doctrine, practice, and theory of various aspects of international law contribute to what we envisage should be its ultimate objective: do they make the world a better place? Sometimes we offer our own perspectives on these questions. In other instances, we raise issues or pose queries designed to prompt critical consideration of these matters by the reader.

USING THIS BOOK

The second edition of this book continues to use the subtitle "Doctrine, Practice, and Theory." We intend it to provide a solid grounding in all these aspects of the substance of international law. But we have also tried to include discussions throughout that provide context to the legal discussion or insight into how international law is actually practiced. For instance, readers will find text boxes (captioned "Law in Context") throughout this book that describe particular practical conundrums and controversies in international law and affairs. The purpose of these is to illustrate, and stimulate reflection on, some of the real world implications of the legal topic under discussion.

International law is also a constantly evolving area. To maintain the currency of this book, we have developed a website, found at www.publicinternationallaw.ca. Here, we have included various tools and aids and will add materials and discussions designed to keep this book current between editions.

---

4   See "McDougal's Jurisprudence: Utility, Influence, Controversy: Remarks by Oscar Schachter" (1985) 79 Am Soc Int'l L Proc 266 at 272–73.

PART I

THE INTERNATIONAL LEGAL "SYSTEM"

CHAPTER 1

THE CONCEPT OF INTERNATIONAL LAW IN CONTEXT

For many years, the study of international law in common law countries has been surprisingly ahistorical and markedly theory-poor.[1] Scholars of international law and international relations were traditionally preoccupied with what were viewed as monolithic states, sometimes ignoring the intra-state nuances emphasized by their domestically focused counterparts in the fields of domestic public law and political science. In its crudest form, international law was viewed as what states do, while international relations, in their crudest and most simplistic form, were viewed as manifestations of the whim of hegemonic states. Put these two approaches together and international law was what powerful states wanted it to be. For those taking this perspective, there was little need for theory or anything more than very short-term accounts of history.

Admittedly, there remains some truth to this view. International law often is the product of—rather than a restraint on—*realpolitik*. "The hell with international law," former US Secretary of State Dean Acheson reportedly said during the Cuban missile crisis. "It's just a series of precedents and decisions that have been made in the past."[2] "I don't care what international lawyers say," US President George W. Bush reportedly stated to his assembled advisors when questions about the use of force in Afghanistan arose in 2001, "we are going to kick some ass."[3] On the other hand, a state's ability to influence other states can be negatively affected by its perceived failure to abide by international law. US President Barack Obama acknowledged, upon his acceptance of the 2009 Nobel Peace Prize, that no state can "insist that others follow the rules of the road if we refuse to follow them ourselves."[4]

For this reason, it remains the case that powerful—even dominant—states do not always dictate outcomes in international relations. Witness the failure of the United States and the United Kingdom to secure a UN Security Council resolution authorizing (or, as some argued at the time, confirming prior authorization of) their invasion of Iraq in 2003. Nor is international law controlled by such states. If it were, the campaigns to create the

---

1 See, however, the recent contributions of Alexander Orakhelashvili, ed, *Research Handbook on the Theory and History of International Law* (Cheltenham: Edward Elgar, 2011); and Bardo Fassbender & Anne Peters, eds, *The Oxford Handbook of the History of International Law* (Oxford: Oxford University Press, 2012).

2 Cited in Wilhelm Grewe, "The Role of International Law in Diplomatic Practice" (1999) 1 J Hist Int'l L 22 at 26.

3 Richard A Clarke, *Against All Enemies: Inside America's War on Terror* (New York: Free Press, 2004) at 24.

4 Barack H Obama, "A Just and Lasting Peace," Nobel Lecture, Oslo, Norway, 10 December 2009, online: www.nobelprize.org/nobel_prizes/peace/laureates/2009/obama-lecture_en.html.

International Criminal Court[5] and ban the use of anti-personnel landmines[6] would have foundered in the face of opposition by the United States and China in both instances.

From this, we can conclude that international law and international relations are more nuanced than the crude, simplistic visions outlined above. Nuance is best understood, we believe, by investing some effort in examining history and theory so as to provide context. Accordingly, in this chapter we undertake three tasks: first, we offer a definition of international law, one that probes several different theoretical ways of understanding the concept; second, we provide an analytical history of international law, focusing on the emergence of sovereign states and the resulting legal developments; and, third, through the twin prisms of international legal theory and international relations theory, we examine the question: does international law matter?

A. DEFINING INTERNATIONAL LAW

1) International Law as the Law among States

"International law" is simple to define but difficult to explain. The actual expression "international law" is usually attributed to Jeremy Bentham, in his *Introduction to the Principles of Morals and Legislation* (1789). There, Bentham wrote that "mutual transactions between sovereigns" were the "subject of that branch of jurisprudence which may be properly and exclusively termed *international*." He then observed that "[t]he word *international*, it must be acknowledged, is a new one; though, it is hoped, sufficiently analogous and intelligible. It is calculated to express, in a more significant way, the branch of law which goes commonly under the name of the *law of nations*."[7] The "law of nations" is, therefore, the classical term for international law, and is the expression employed by its most famous early exponent, Dutch jurist Hugo Grotius.

These phrases—"law of nations" and "international law"—have an intuitive meaning: the law as between nations. However, the terms "international" and "nations" each obscure the traditional reach of international law. "International" is defined in the *Oxford English Dictionary* in the manner one might expect: "Existing, constituted, or carried on between different nations; pertaining to the relations between nations,"[8] whereas "international law" is defined as the law "under which nations are regarded as individual members of a common polity, bound by a common rule of agreement or custom."[9] In turn, the word "nation," upon which these definitions depend, has an ambiguous meaning. It may be defined as "a people or group of peoples; a political state." It may also be a "large aggregate of communities and individuals united by factors such as common descent,

---

5   *Rome Statute of the International Criminal Court*, 17 July 1998, 2187 UNTS 3, Can TS 2002 No 13, (1998) 37 ILM 2002, in force 1 July 2002.

6   *Convention on the Prohibition of the Use, Stockpiling, Production and Transfer of Anti-Personnel Mines and on Their Destruction*, 18 September 1997, 2056 UNTS 211, Can TS 1999 No 4, in force 1 March 1999 [*Landmines Convention*].

7   Jeremy Bentham, *An Introduction to the Principles of Morals and Legislation* (1789) (London: W Pickering, 1823), c XVII at para 2 [emphasis in the original].

8   *Oxford English Dictionary*, sv "international," online: www.oed.com [*OED*].

9   *Ibid*, sv "law, international law, the law of nations."

language, culture, history, or occupation of the same territory, so as to form a distinct people." Put another way, a "nation" may be a state, or it may not be. The French term *"nation"* also includes the dual meaning of its English counterpart: a broad human community or, alternatively, a political state.

The "State"—in French, *l'État*—in turn is defined by the *Oxford English Dictionary* as: "The body politic as organized for supreme civil rule and government; the political organization which is the basis of civil government. Hence: the supreme civil power or government of a country or nation; the group of people collectively engaged in exercising or administering this."[10] The *Oxford English Dictionary* also defines "state" as: "A community of people living in a defined territory and organized under its own government; a commonwealth, a nation."[11]

As for the distinction between state and nation, the two concepts are usually conflated. Thus, since the twentieth century, it has become commonplace to speak of "nation-states"—suggesting a coincidence between shared ethnicity, language, and culture, on the one hand, and the state, on the other. Indeed, the expression "nation-state" is defined by the *Oxford English Dictionary* as "[a]n independent political state formed from a people who share a common national identity (historically, culturally, or ethnically)" and "(more generally) any independent political state."[12] As we shall see, international law—and in particular, the twentieth-century doctrine requiring respect for the principle of self-determination—has tended to fuel this conflation of "state" and "nation," arguably contributing to much of the ethnic conflict and bloodshed of the immediate post-colonial and post–Cold War periods.

In its classic guise, however, international law was very definitely not the law governing relations between "nations" *cum* peoples. It was—and largely remains—the law among *states*, those centralized political institutions able to claim "sovereignty" over a fixed piece of territory. Thus, the renowned German jurist (and British law professor) Lassa Oppenheim defined the "Law of Nations or International Law (*Droit des gens, Völkerrecht*)" as "the name for the body of customary and conventional rules which are considered legally binding by civilised states in their intercourse with each other."[13] Similarly, *Starke's International Law* tells us that international law is "that body of rules which is composed for its greater part of the principles and rules of conduct which states feel themselves bound to observe, and therefore, do commonly observe in their relations with each other."[14] For these reasons, scholars have suggested that, in Bentham's era, the expression "interstatal" law, though perhaps less elegant, would have been a more accurate descriptor than "international" law.[15]

That said, it would be wrong to view international law exclusively as a code of behaviour governing state interaction. As *Starke's International Law* also explains, international law includes "rules of law relating to the functioning of international institutions or or-

10 *Ibid, sv* "state."

11 *Ibid.*

12 *Ibid, sv* "nation-state."

13 Lassa Oppenheim, *International Law: A Treatise*, vol 1 (London: Longmans, 1905) at 3, s 1.

14 Ivan A Shearer, ed, *Starke's International Law*, 11th ed (London: Butterworths, 1994) at 3.

15 See, for example, Arthur Nussbaum, *A Concise History of the Law of Nations* (New York: Macmillan, 1962) at 136 [Nussbaum].

ganizations, their relations with each other, and their relations with states and individuals" as well as "certain rules of law relating to individuals and non-state entities so far as the rights and duties of such individuals and non-state entities are the concern of the international community."[16] Over time, Oppenheim (and the scholars who revised his original work) also revised his definition to recognize that while the rules of international law are primarily those that govern the relations of states, "[i]nternational organizations and, to some extent, also individuals[,] may be subjects of rights conferred and duties imposed by international law."[17]

Put another way, international law is: the law among states; the law enunciating certain rights and obligations states have vis-à-vis non-state actors, such as individuals, international organizations, and other entities; and, to a more limited extent, the law imposing certain obligations on non-state actors in areas of concern to the international community. As these rights and obligations often affect the freedom of states to do what they will with respect to individuals or other non-state actors within their jurisdiction, international law is obviously now more than an interstatal code, or, in French, *droit interétatique*. Indeed, in some areas (but admittedly not all), international law comes to approximate a sort of "universal" law, purporting to establish baseline standards that states are required to observe in their domestic law or practice, and not merely in their interactions with other states.

2) Theoretical Accounts of International Law

While international law is not necessarily universal in application, an historical approach reveals that there is nothing new in conceiving of international law as "universal" law. Indeed, modern international law's infatuation with the goal of universality reflects a "back to the future" phenomenon. The jurists of early modern Europe, generally credited with inventing the discipline, had little doubt that there was a higher law binding states and their rulers. This vision of a higher code of conduct, which itself assumed a wide array of variants, usually goes under the name of "natural law."

a) International Law and Natural Law

Associated originally with Stoic philosophy in ancient Greece and Rome, natural law theory dates to ancient times. Stoics, such as the Roman lawyer and statesman Cicero, believed that certain fundamental, and shared, moral values underlie the legal systems of all peoples,[18] and to that extent are universal. These ancient concepts proved influential in medieval and, in turn, early modern Europe. In these periods, however, natural law generally took on a religious hue. Natural law was God's universal law, one that had obvious primacy over the temporal laws of human beings. As such, it proved influential in shaping the way governing elites behaved.[19]

---

16 Shearer, above note 14 at 3.

17 Sir Robert Jennings & Sir Arthur Watts, eds, *Oppenheim's International Law*, vol 1, 9th ed (London: Pearson Education, 1992) at 4, s 1.

18 *The Columbia Encyclopedia*, 6th ed (New York: Columbia University Press, 2001–2005).

19 See Harold Hongju Koh, "Review Essay: Why Do Nations Obey International Law?" (1997) 106 Yale LJ 2599 [Koh].

When Christianity ultimately fractured during the Reformation into its then-mutually antagonistic denominations, and the Enlightenment subsequently raised the banner of human reason and rationality, these religious foundations for universal principles again abated. As in antiquity, therefore, modern natural law theories tended to view the "laws of nature" as "universally applicable rules derived from right reason."[20] As one scholar has observed:

> Before the Reformation and the consequent confessionalisation, the law of nations was clearly rooted in the divine law administered by the church. Religious division did not completely destroy the general referral to this divine law, but a denominational church link was ruled out. Therefore, from this point on it became re-connected to a rational natural law, although it was based on the divine will (in a form neutral between denominations) well into the 18th Century.[21]

Thus, a modern definition describes natural law as a "doctrine that human affairs should be governed by ethical principles that are part of the very nature of things and that can be understood by reason."[22] Natural law theorists seek to understand why a law is as it is and whether that law is justified in its claim to authority.[23]

It is difficult to overstate the significance of the natural law approach to early international law. As Sir Frederick Pollock noted in 1922, "[w]ith regard to international law, it is notorious that all authorities down to the end of the eighteenth century, and almost all outside England to this day, have treated it as a body of doctrine derived from and justified by the Law of Nature."[24] Key among these authorities was Hugo Grotius, sometimes called the "father" of international law. Grotius, in his classic work *The Law of War and Peace* (1625), wrote:

> Natural right is the dictate of right reason, showing the moral turpitude, or moral necessity, of any act from its agreement or disagreement with a rational nature, and consequently that such an act is either forbidden or commanded by God, the author of nature. The actions, upon which such a dictate is given, are either binding or unlawful in themselves, and therefore necessarily understood to be commanded or forbidden by God. This mark distinguishes natural right, not only from human law, but from the law, which God himself has been pleased to reveal, called, by some, the voluntary divine right, which does not command or forbid things in themselves either binding or unlawful, but makes them unlawful by its prohibition, and binding by its command.[25]

Grotius then goes on to equate these natural rights and the laws of nature with the "laws of nations."

---

20 Nussbaum, above note 15 at 15.

21 Heinhard Stager, "From the International Law of Christianity to the International Law of the World Citizen" (2001) 3 J Hist Int'l L 180 at 184.

22 *The New Dictionary of Cultural Literacy*, 3d ed (Boston: Houghton Mifflin, 2002).

23 Robert P George, "Natural Law and International Order" in Robert P George, ed, *In Defence of Natural Law* (Oxford: Clarendon Press, 1999) at 228. See also Robert P George, "Natural Law" (2008) 31:1 Harv JL & Pub Pol'y 171.

24 Sir Frederick Pollock, *Essays in Law* (London: Macmillan, 1922) at 63.

25 Hugo Grotius, *Three Books Treating of the Rights of War & Peace* (London: MW for Thomas Basset, 1682) at 4.

Grotius's thinking was obviously heavily influenced by religious doctrine. Indeed, the content of what Grotius viewed as the law of nations in relation to war and peace was derived from biblical, as much as classical, sources. Still, he decoupled natural law from its religious underpinnings:

> Now the Law of Nature is so unalterable, that it cannot be changed even by God himself. For although the power of God is infinite, yet there are some things, to which it does not extend. Because the things so expressed would have no true meaning, but imply a contradiction. Thus two and two must make four, nor is it possible to be otherwise; nor, again, can what is really evil not be evil.[26]

Natural law theory, applied to international law, seemed to ensure that conceptions of justice, or at least morality, remained at the core of international obligations. Consider, however, the following Enlightenment-era refinement of natural law thinking by Swiss legal philosopher Emmerich de Vattel in his 1758 book, *Le Droit des Gens*:

The Law of Nations or Principles of the Law of Nature Applied to the Conduct and Affairs of Nations and Sovereigns

PRELIMINARIES

§ 3. Definition of the law of nations.
The Law of Nations is the science which teaches the rights subsisting between nations or states, and the obligations correspondent to those rights . . . .

§ 4. In what light nations or states are to be considered.
Nations being composed of men naturally free and independent, and who, before the establishment of civil societies, lived together in the state of nature, — *Nations*, or sovereign states, are to be considered as so many free persons living together in the state of nature.

It is a settled point with writers on the *natural* law, that all men inherit from *nature* a perfect *liberty* and *independence*, of which they cannot be deprived without their own consent. In a State, the individual citizens do not enjoy them *fully* and absolutely, because they have made a *partial* surrender of them to the sovereign. But the body of the nation, the State, remains absolutely free and independent with respect to all other men, and all *other* Nations, as long as it has not voluntarily submitted to them.

§ 5. To what laws nations are subject.
As men are subject to the laws of nature, — and as their union in civil society cannot have exempted them from the obligation to observe those laws, since by that union they do not cease to be men, — the entire nation, whose common will is but the result of the united wills of the citizens, remains subject to the *laws of nature*, and is bound to respect them in all her proceedings. And since right arises from obligation, as we have just observed (§3), the nation possesses also the same rights which nature has conferred upon men in order to enable them to perform their duties.

---

26 *Ibid* at 5.

§ 6. In what the law of nations originally consists.

We must therefore apply to nations the rules of the law of nature, in order to discover what their obligations are, and what their rights: consequently, the *law of Nations* is originally no other than the *law of Nature applied* to Nations. But as the application of a rule cannot be just and reasonable unless it be made in a manner suitable to the subject, we are not to imagine that the law of nations is precisely and in every case the same as the law of nature, with the difference only of the subjects to which it is applied, so as to allow of our substituting nations for individuals. A state or civil society is a subject very different from an individual of the human race; from which circumstance, pursuant to the law of nature itself, there result, in many cases, very different obligations and rights: since the same general rule, applied to two subjects, cannot produce exactly the same decisions, when the subjects are different; and a particular rule which is perfectly just with respect to one subject, is not applicable to another subject of a quite different nature. There are many cases, therefore, in which the *law of Nature* does not decide between state and state in the same manner as it would between man and man. We must therefore know how to accommodate the application of it to different subjects; and it is the art of thus applying it with a precision founded on right reason, that renders the *law of Nations* a distinct science.

§ 7. Definition of the necessary law of nations.

We call that the *Necessary Law of Nations* which consists in the application of the law of nature to *Nations*. It is *Necessary* because nations are *absolutely* bound to observe it. This law contains the precepts prescribed by the *law of nature* to *states*, on whom that law is not less obligatory than on individuals, since states are composed of men, their resolutions are taken by men, and the law of nature is binding on all men, under whatever relation they act. This is the law which Grotius, and those who follow him, call the *Internal law of Nations*, on account of its being obligatory on nations in point of conscience. Several writers term it the *Natural law of Nations*.

§ 8. It is immutable.

Since therefore the necessary law of nations consists in the application of the law of nature to states, — which law is immutable, as being founded on the nature of things, and particularly on the nature of man, — it follows that the *Necessary* law of nations is *immutable*.

§ 9. Nations can make no change in it, nor dispense with the obligations arising from it.

Whence, as this law is immutable, and the obligations that arise from it necessary and indispensable, nations can neither make any changes in it by their conventions, dispense with it in their own conduct, nor reciprocally release each other from the observance of it.

This is the principle by which we may distinguish *lawful* conventions or treaties from those that are not lawful, and innocent and rational customs from those that are unjust or censurable.

There are things, just *in themselves*, and allowed by the necessary law of nations, on which states may mutually agree with each other, and which they may consecrate and enforce by their manners and customs. There are others of an *indifferent nature*, respecting which, it rests at the option of nations to make in their treaties whatever agreements they please, or to introduce whatever custom or practice they think proper. But every treaty, every custom, which contravenes the injunctions or prohibitions of the *Necessary* law of nations is unlawful . . . .[27]

The modern natural-law lawyer continues to claim that all legal norms must be consistent with a set of moral constraints, the content of which is found in such concepts as the common good.[28] The notion of a higher body of principle that constrains more mundane rules in this way continues to animate at least some areas of international law.

b) From Natural Law to Natural Rights

Despite its early prominence in writings beginning in the sixteenth century, natural law leaves much to be desired as a theoretical basis for international law. First, it may be founded on a false premise: the presumption that human beings, and thus states, are rational and reasonable, and that the expression of this rationality will necessarily produce a common understanding of natural law's content. In addition, natural law is a very difficult concept on which to build a working legal order, one that must deal with the details of everyday life. True, in a domestic legal system with legislatures and judges, it is possible to imagine a system of jurisprudence and statute law informed by commonly held views about reason, justice, utility, or other such principles. Indeed, the notion of a "higher law" lies at the core of constitutionalism in the liberal democratic tradition, reflecting a variant of natural law thinking known as "natural rights." The following passage, from the American *Declaration of Independence* (1776), may be familiar:

> When in the Course of human events, it becomes necessary for one people to dissolve the political bands which have connected them with another, and to assume among the powers of the earth, the separate and equal station to which the Laws of Nature and of Nature's God entitle them, a decent respect to the opinions of mankind requires that they should declare the causes which impel them to the separation.
>
> We hold these truths to be self-evident, that all men are created equal, that they are endowed by their Creator with certain unalienable Rights, that among these are Life, Liberty and the pursuit of Happiness. — That to secure these rights, Governments are instituted among Men, deriving their just powers from the consent of the governed, — That whenever any Form of Government becomes destructive of these ends, it is the Right of the People to alter or to abolish it, and to institute new Government . . . .[29]

Consider likewise the following extract from the French *Declaration of the Rights of Man and of the Citizen* (1789):

> The representatives of the French people, organized as a National Assembly, believing that the ignorance, neglect, or contempt of the rights of man are the sole cause of public calamities and of the corruption of governments, have determined to set forth in a solemn declaration the natural, unalienable, and sacred rights of man, in order that this declaration,

---

27 Emmerich de Vattel, *Le Droit des Gens*, vol 3 (English trans) (1758; repr, Washington: Carnegie Institute of Washington, 1916).

28 See, for example, John M Finnis, *Natural Law and Natural Rights*, 2d ed (Oxford: Clarendon, 2011).

29 *Declaration of Independence*, 1776, US Const, Art I, s 8, cl 8 at paras 1–2.

being constantly before all the members of the Social body, shall remind them continually of their rights and duties; in order that the acts of the legislative power, as well as those of the executive power, may be compared at any moment with the objects and purposes of all political institutions and may thus be more respected, and, lastly, in order that the grievances of the citizens, based hereafter upon simple and incontestable principles, shall tend to the maintenance of the constitution and redound to the happiness of all.[30]

The vision articulated in both these documents—ultimately the progenitors (along with the *Magna Carta* (1215)) of constitutionalized guarantees of civil and political rights—is heavily informed by natural law thinking: the laws of nature are the origin of "natural," "inalienable," and "self-evident" rights.

In the American, European, and increasingly global legal traditions, these principles have been codified and articulated in great detail by legislatures and courts, giving them a "positive" legal force and tremendous, even foundational, legitimacy. Put another way, natural law thinking—the notion that there are principles higher than even the state itself, to which the state is subordinated—works in a "vertical" system of governance, where the state, acting through its legislatures and courts, can authoritatively declare and put these principles into operation. This process of codifying natural law concepts is facilitated in the democratic polities where, in the tradition of John Locke and other, similar political thinkers, the legitimacy of the state itself is a product of the consent of the citizenry. In this tradition, a failure to incorporate into the state's legal fabric these concepts that exist above and apart from the state and which limit the power of the state to do as it wishes, undermines the legitimacy of that state itself. Recall again the words of the American *Declaration of Independence* of 1776:

> Prudence, indeed, will dictate that Governments long established should not be changed for light and transient causes; and accordingly all experience hath shewn, that mankind are more disposed to suffer, while evils are sufferable, than to right themselves by abolishing the forms to which they are accustomed. But when a long train of abuses and usurpations, pursuing invariably the same Object evinces a design to reduce them under absolute Despotism, it is their right, it is their duty, to throw off such Government, and to provide new Guards for their future security.[31]

In this approach, the legitimacy, even continuity, of the state is conditional on acceptance of inalienable civil and political rights.

By comparison, in the international arena, there is no central lawmaker able to declare, definitively, that a given higher principle requires a certain course of action, or even to establish, authoritatively, that any such principle exists. International law is a "horizontal" system, with no formal hierarchical political structure empowered to impose principles. Thus, to the extent that international law is envisaged as a body of natural law principles separate and apart from domestic law, serious questions of effectiveness arise. Moreover, international law links communities with very different visions of the legitimacy of states.

---

30 *Declaration of the Rights of Man and of the Citizen*, 1789, preamble.
31 *Declaration of Independence*, 1776 at para 2.

The liberal, democratic notion that state legitimacy depends on the forbearance of the governed is clearly not universally shared.

c) Positivism and International Law

In this environment, natural law principles—premised on the notion that there is something out there above states that must be recognized even if states refuse to do so—have less traction. Thus, by the nineteenth and early twentieth centuries, adherence to the natural law account of international law had abated. In its place, international jurists deployed "positivism" to explain international law. Positivism is, in many respects, the antithesis of natural law, and in fact rose in prominence in the nineteenth century in reaction to natural law thinking. As the Mexico-United States General Claims Commission wrote in *North American Dredging Company of Texas (USA v Mexico)*:

> The law of nature may have been helpful, some three centuries ago, to build up a new law of nations, and the conception of inalienable rights of men and nature may have exercised a salutary influence, some one hundred and fifty years ago, on the development of modern democracy on both sides of the ocean; but they have failed as durable foundations of either municipal or international law and can not be used in the present day as substitutes for positive municipal law, on the one hand, and for positive international law, as recognized by nations and governments through their acts and statements, on the other hand.[32]

Although, as with natural law, positivism has its variants, its purer forms are generally characterized by three core suppositions.[33] First, true law is created only by a "laying down" of that law, at a discrete point in history. Second, this "laying down" must be performed by a sovereign entity. Third, such laws are effective, even if unjust when measured against some other, moral (or natural law) standard. Thus, for extreme positivists, law exists only to the extent that it is effectively imposed by a sovereign power,[34] and it persists as law even if viewed as unjust by some other measure.

In practice, positivism enhances the state-centrism of international law: as the state is the sole "sovereign" it must thus be the sole source of law. In this respect, positivism echoed Thomas Hobbes, who argued in *Leviathan* that positive laws were "those which have not been from eternity, but have been made laws by the will of those that have had the sovereign power over others."[35]

For a positivist, international law is nothing more than law that is adopted and applied by states. The content of international law depends, therefore, entirely on the voluntary adherence of states to international principles. As explained by the Permanent Court of International Justice in the famous *Lotus* case:

> International law governs relations between independent States. The rules of law binding upon States therefore emanate from their own free will as expressed in conventions

---

32 (1926), 4 RIAA 26 at 29–30.
33 See Stephen Hall, "The Persistent Spectre: Natural Law, International Order and the Limits of Legal Positivism" (2001) 12 EJIL 269 at 272 [Hall].
34 *Encyclopedia of Public International Law*, vol 3 (Amsterdam: North-Holland, 2000), "Positivism" at 1073 [*Encyclopedia*].
35 Thomas Hobbes, *Leviathan* (London: Andrew Crooke, 1651), c XXVI at para 7.

or by usages generally accepted as expressing principles of law and established in order to regulate the relations between those co-existing independent communities or with a view to the achievement of common aims. Restrictions upon the freedom of States cannot therefore be presumed.[36]

As noted above, however, positivism comes in many shades of grey. In its more moderate (and widely accepted) guise, positivism would limit the content of international law to those norms expressly or *implicitly* agreed to by states, usually in international treaties, but also through their consistent patterns of behaviour.

In contrast, in one of its most radical forms, positivism becomes less of a foundation for international law than a basis for denying its very existence. In his work, *The Province of Jurisprudence Determined* (1832), political philosopher John Austin ranked international law with the "rules of honour" and the "law set by fashion." Put another way, international law was not truly law, and was instead a species of morality. Austin's conclusions were driven in part by the horizontal nature of international law: in this view, binding law could only stem from the fear of coercion where a sovereign was disobeyed. Where, as with international law, there was no such powerful "super-sovereign" able to enforce its will against the purported subjects of international law—all of which were, after all, sovereign themselves—there could be no law. To the extent it existed, adherence to international "law" was prompted, not by sovereign command, but by fear of conflict between sovereigns: "[T]he law obtaining between nations is law (improperly so called) set by general opinion. The duties which it imposes are enforced by moral sanctions: by fear on the part of nations, or by fear on the part of sovereigns, of provoking general hostility, and incurring its probable evils, in case they shall violate maxims generally received and respected."[37]

This form of positivism, while not garnering widespread adherence by international lawyers or even states, continues to prove influential in some international legal and international relations thinking. Indeed, some positivists have continued to question international law's legitimacy into the modern period. Consider this summary:

> Hans Kelsen modified John Austin's rejection of international law as a system not enforced by sovereign command, claiming instead that international law constitutes a primitive form of law, based on self-help. H.L.A. Hart refined that challenge, arguing that international law lacks two features that he deemed central to the very concept of law: first, "the secondary rules of change and adjudication which provide for legislature and courts"; and second, "a unifying rule of recognition, specifying 'sources' of law and providing general criteria for the identification of its rules." Until actors within the international system internalize both a rule of recognition and secondary rules for orderly change and interpretation, Hart argued, international law will consist only of a set of primary rules with which nations will comply out of a sense of moral, not legal, obligation. In effect, Hart defined the very notion of "obedience" out of international law, for under his description, international rules are ones with which nations may conform or

---

36 *The Case of the SS "Lotus"* (1927), PCIJ (Ser A) No 10 at 18.

37 John Austin, *The Province of Jurisprudence Determined in Lectures on Jurisprudence or The Philosophy of Positive Law*, vol 1 (London: John Murray, 1873) 82 at 232.

comply, but never "obey," in the sense of internally accepting or incorporating those rules into national law.[38]

Such extreme positivist views have been critiqued on empirical grounds. Even in the absence of a sovereign lawmaker and law-enforcer, there clearly exists a body of rules and principles that states do abide by, usually in the belief they are obliged to do so. As one critic of Austinian positivism has observed:

> States continued to regard international law as real law, they continued to abide by its rules in the vast majority of cases, their diplomatic communications continued to bristle with claims and counter-claims of legal rights, and they continued to sign treaties by which they regarded themselves and other states as legally bound. This remained so notwithstanding the absence of an international sovereign, the absence of an independent political community subject to such a sovereign, the absence of any commands set by the former to the latter, and (usually) the absence of a factual power of coercion in case of a violation of the law.[39]

This point has been made repeatedly. As J.L. Brierly observed: "The best evidence for the existence of international law is that every actual State recognizes that it does exist and that it is itself under an obligation to observe it. States often violate international law, just as individuals often violate municipal law; but no more than individuals do states defend their actions by claiming that they are above the law."[40]

A similar observation was made in a 1904 international arbitration concerning a ship called the *Prometheus*:

> It was contended on behalf of the owners of the *Prometheus* that the term "law" as applied to this recognized system of principles and rules known as international law is an inexact expression, that there is, in other words, no such thing as international law; that there can be no such law binding upon all nations inasmuch as there is no sanction for such law, that is to say that there is no means by which obedience to such law can be imposed upon any given nation refusing obedience thereto. I do not concur in that contention. In my opinion a law may be established and become international, that is to say binding upon all nations, by the agreement of such nations to be bound thereby, although it may be impossible to enforce obedience thereto by any given nation party to that agreement. The resistance of a nation to a law to which it has agreed does not derogate from the authority of the law because that resistance cannot, perhaps, be overcome. Such resistance merely makes the resisting nation a breaker of the law to which it has given its adherence, but it leaves the law, to the establishment of which the resisting nation was a party, still subsisting. Could it be successfully contended that because any given person or body of persons possessed for the time being power to resist an established municipal law such law had no existence? The answer to such a contention would be that the law still existed, though it might not for the time being be possible to enforce obedience with it.[41]

---

38 Koh, above note 19 at 2616.
39 Hall, above note 33 at 281.
40 James L Brierly, *The Outlook for International Law* (Oxford: Clarendon Press, 1944) at 5.
41 *In the Matter of an Arbitration between the Osaka Shosen Kaisha and the Owners of the SS Prometheus* (1904) 2 Hong Kong L Rev 207 at 225.

Subsequently, in *The Law of Nations*, Brierly wrote:

> It has often been said that international law ought to be classified as a branch of ethics rather than of law. . . . [I]f international law is nothing but international morality, it is certainly not the whole of international morality, and it is difficult to see how we are to distinguish it from those other admittedly moral standards which we apply in forming our judgements on the conduct of states. . . . [Q]uestions of international law are invariably treated as legal questions by the foreign offices which conduct our international business, and in the courts, national or international, before which they are brought; legal forms and methods are used in diplomatic controversies and in judicial and arbitral proceedings, and authorities and precedents are cited in argument as a matter of course. . . . [W]hen a breach of international law is alleged by one party to a controversy, the act impugned is practically never defended by claiming the right of private judgment, which would be the natural defence if the issue concerned the morality of the act, but always by attempting to prove that no rule has been violated. . . .
>
>   . . . Most of the characteristics which differentiate international law from the law of the state and are often thought to throw doubt on its legal character, such, for instance, as its basis in custom, the fact that the submission of parties to the jurisdiction of courts is voluntary, the absence of regular processes either for creating or enforcing it, are familiar features of early [domestic] legal systems; and it is only in quite modern times . . . that to identify law with the will of the state has become even a plausible theory.[42]

Of course, these comments beg the question, "*why* do states obey?," especially given the absence of traditional enforcement mechanisms within the international legal system. By the end of the nineteenth century, several potential answers had been advanced:

> The first was an Austinian, positivistic realist strand, which suggests that nations never "obey" international law, because "it is not really law." The philosophical tradition of analyzing international law obligation had bifurcated into a Hobbesian utilitarian, rationalistic strand, which acknowledged that nations sometimes follow international law, but only when it serves their self-interest to do so, and a liberal Kantian strand, which assumed that nations generally obey international law, guided by a sense of moral and ethical obligation derived from considerations of natural law and justice. Bentham's international law writings suggested a fourth, process-based strand, which derived a nation's incentive to obey from the encouragement and prodding of other nations with whom it is engaged in a discursive legal process.[43]

We return to this question of whether and why states obey international law in Section C below on international law and international relations theory.

d) The Dilution of Positivism in Modern International Law

Positivism and natural law doctrines have been critiqued extensively. Both approaches to explaining international law have their flaws.

---

42 James L Brierly, *The Law of Nations*, 6th ed (New York: Oxford University Press, 1963) at 70–71 [Brierly, *Law of Nations*].

43 Koh, above note 19 at 2611.

With respect to positivism, it does not fully capture or explain the actual behaviour of states from the early to mid-twentieth century, and, as we shall see, it is difficult to reconcile with many of the actual doctrines of modern international law readily acknowledged by states. Moreover, whatever else it may be, positivism is a deeply conservative doctrine. If law is nothing more than the pronouncements of the sovereign, and the legitimacy of that law cannot be contested with non-positivistic conceptions of justice, law becomes a tool of power rather than a means to challenge or constrain the arbitrary exercise of that power by the sovereign. In the international context, if international law is simply what states hold it to be by their pronouncements and actions, it becomes descriptive rather than prescriptive — that is, rather than constraining state conduct, it legitimates that conduct, whatever it might be. For example, some scholars have argued that the positivist approach to international law greatly facilitated Eurocentric views of the international order in the nineteenth and early twentieth centuries. Consider the following comments:

> For positivists, the sovereign state was the foundation of the whole legal system, and their broad project was to reconstitute the entire framework of international law based on this premise. . . . [F]or positivists, the rules of international law were to be discovered, not by speculative inquiries into the nature of justice or teleology, but by a careful study of the actual behavior of states and the institutions and laws that those states created. . . .
>
> A further central feature of positivism was the distinction it made between civilized and uncivilized states. The naturalist notion that a single, universally applicable law governed a naturally constituted society of nations was completely repudiated by jurists of the mid-nineteenth century. . . .
>
> Positivist jurisprudence was so insistent on this distinction that any system of law that failed to acknowledge it was unacceptable. In crude terms, in the naturalist world, law was given; in the positivist world, law was created by human societies and institutions. Once the connection between "law" and "institutions" had been established, it followed from this premise that jurists could focus on the character of institutions, a shift that facilitated the racialization of law by delimiting the notion of law to very specific European institutions.[44]

Further, to the extent the Austinian objection to international law is predicated on the absence of formal enforcement mechanisms in international law, it is very much out of date. Some contemporary international legal regimes, addressing various subject matters, are indeed equipped with enforcement mechanisms of varying potency. Perhaps the most significant are the powers of the UN Security Council to maintain or restore international peace and security, as provided in Chapter VII of the UN Charter.[45] Other subject-matter-specific examples include the International Criminal Court and the World Trade Organization, illustrations to which we return later in these materials.

Another fundamental difficulty with exclusively positivist accounts of international law is their failure to reconcile, convincingly, the positivist requirement of state consent with the phenomenon of customary international law. Customary international law, an ancient

---

44 Antony Anghie, "Finding the Peripheries: Sovereignty and Colonialism in Nineteenth-Century International Law" (1999) 40 Harv Int'l LJ 1 at 13, 22, and 24–25.

45 Charter of the United Nations, 26 June 1945, Can TS 1945 No 7, in force 24 October 1945 [UN Charter].

concept and one of the primary sources of international law, is nominally predicated on state consent, and thus arguably consistent with at least soft-positivist theories. In theory, a uniform and consistent (that is, customary) pattern of behaviour by states may give rise to a binding legal obligation to continue to observe that same behaviour. State consent to the legally binding nature of that obligation is said to be implied in the very act of participating in the behaviour in the first place.

In practice, however, this is something of a legal fiction—while rules of customary international law are generally binding on all states, not all states in fact participate in the behaviour that generates them. Positivists would respond that those states not participating in the relevant rule-creating behaviour could nevertheless be said to have implicitly consented to the rules by acquiescing in that behaviour by others. But even this argument falls short. So prevalent is the notion that all states are bound by customary international law that this is considered to be a very hallmark of statehood. Thus, to be a state—even a new one—is to be bound by all existing customary international legal rules—including those in the creation of which one has had no opportunity either to participate or even acquiesce. This approach was confirmed in the massive decolonization process of the twentieth century, which saw scores of newly independent states admitted to the community of nations—but subject to its extant rules of customary international law.

To argue that new states "consent" (expressly or impliedly) to customary international law is, in the words of Sir Hersch Lauterpacht, "no more than a fiction resorted to in order to conceal the objectively binding force of international law as independent of the will of the particular State."[46] Brierly makes a similar point:

> *Implied* consent is not a philosophically sound explanation of customary law . . . a customary rule is observed, not because it has been consented to, but because it is believed to be binding, and whatever may be the explanation or the justification for that belief, its binding force does not depend, and is not felt by those who follow it to depend, on the approval of the individual or the state to which it is addressed. Further, in the practical administration of international law, states are continually treated as bound by principles which they cannot, except by the most strained construction of the facts, be said to have consented, and it is unreasonable, when we are seeking the true nature of international rules, to force the facts into a preconceived theory instead of finding a theory which will explain the facts as we have them.[47]

Thus, the universally binding character of general rules of customary international law is difficult to reconcile with a positivist explanation of international law. This is even more acutely the case where rules of international law are said to constitute *jus cogens* or *erga omnes* obligations, two concepts which we examine in Chapter 2, Section E.

Natural law's main flaws have been touched upon above, and as we have seen, explain in part its decline in the nineteenth century as an adequate account of international law. Essentially, because it has not historically been grounded in sources that have law-making authority—sovereign legislatures and courts—natural law has been perceived as lack-

---

46 Sir Hersch Lauterpacht, *Private Law Sources and Analogies of International Law* (Hamden, CN: Archon Books, 1927) at 53.

47 Brierly, *Law of Nations*, above note 42 at 52–53.

ing legitimacy. How can the law of nations comprise the scribbles of non-appointed, and unrepresentative, international jurists supposedly tapping into some higher form of human reason, particularly when these scholars give conflicting accounts of this natural law?

And yet, the influences of natural law—in particular, the claim that at least some rights and obligations are not susceptible to abrogation, curtailment, or amendment, even by sovereign states—have resurfaced in international law since the early to mid-twentieth century. Perhaps the most prominent example of this phenomenon has been the emergence of a body of international human rights law, premised on the inalienability of certain fundamental rights previously considered sacrosanct in only the domestic legal systems of certain states. How has this occurred, in a legal system still heavily influenced by positivist notions of the sovereignty of states and still largely "horizontal" in structure? The answer, we suggest, lies in the fact that natural law's chief disadvantages—its lack of legitimacy and clarity—have been partially transcended by the contemporary development of international institutions that, while not truly sovereign lawmakers, simulate domestic legislative bodies and courts. This institutional semblance gives the pronouncements of these bodies a measure both of concreteness and authority, which, while to a certain degree derivative of, nevertheless remain distinct from, the sovereign authority of their state members.

In many instances, these international institutions have "soft power," to borrow a concept developed by American political scientist Joseph Nye.[48] For Nye, these institutions lack the "hard power" and coercive apparatuses of states—such as armed forces—but possess a political and moral legitimacy that is influential in international relations. Moreover, they tend to encourage the emergence of normative principles that may ultimately crystallize into binding legal obligations. As we shall see in greater detail in Chapter 2, these principles are often aspirational and grounded in a sense of what states *should* do, rather than a bare assessment of what states *must* do. To that extent, it is more attuned to natural law thinking than positivism. For example, the Universal Declaration of Human Rights, a formally non-binding declaration of the UN General Assembly, clearly invokes natural law concepts in its preamble:

Universal Declaration of Human Rights, GA Res 217A (III)[49]

Whereas recognition of the inherent dignity and of the equal and inalienable rights of all members of the human family is the foundation of freedom, justice and peace in the world,

Whereas disregard and contempt for human rights have resulted in barbarous acts which have outraged the conscience of mankind, and the advent of a world in which human beings shall enjoy freedom of speech and belief and freedom from fear and want has been proclaimed as the highest aspiration of the common people,

Whereas it is essential, if man is not to be compelled to have recourse, as a last resort, to rebellion against tyranny and oppression, that human rights should be protected by the rule of law,

Whereas it is essential to promote the development of friendly relations between nations,

---

48 Joseph S Nye, *Soft Power: The Means to Success in World Politics* (New York: Public Affairs, 2004). See also Joseph S Nye, *The Future of Power* (New York: Public Affairs, 2011).

49 Reprinted in UN GAOR, 3d Sess, Part 1 at 71–77, UN Doc A/810 (1948).

Whereas the peoples of the United Nations have in the Charter reaffirmed their faith in fundamental human rights, in the dignity and worth of the human person and in the equal rights of men and women and have determined to promote social progress and better standards of life in larger freedom,

Whereas Member States have pledged themselves to achieve, in co-operation with the United Nations, the promotion of universal respect for and observance of human rights and fundamental freedoms,

Whereas a common understanding of these rights and freedoms is of the greatest importance for the full realization of this pledge,

Now, Therefore THE GENERAL ASSEMBLY proclaims THIS UNIVERSAL DECLARATION OF HUMAN RIGHTS as a common standard of achievement for all peoples and all nations, to the end that every individual and every organ of society, keeping this Declaration constantly in mind, shall strive by teaching and education to promote respect for these rights and freedoms and by progressive measures, national and international, to secure their universal and effective recognition and observance, both among the peoples of Member States themselves and among the peoples of territories under their jurisdiction.

While the Universal Declaration of Human Rights is a political text adopted by the General Assembly and thus not legally binding per se, it rapidly became the basis for further international legal developments in the field of human rights. As we shall see in Chapter 9, a number of its provisions were subsequently transformed into widely ratified, binding treaty obligations—by which states expressly agree to be bound, a positivist process. At the same time, a great many of the Declaration's provisions (but not all)[50] have come to be considered as reflective of general rules of customary international law, and thus universally binding, which as we have seen cannot readily be reconciled with positivist accounts of international law. Moreover, some internationally recognized human rights obligations have come to be viewed as so fundamental that their abrogation by states is considered impermissible (the doctrine of *jus cogens*)—a notion that clearly harkens back to natural law's immutable, inalienable laws of nature.

In other words, appreciation of the shortcomings of unbridled positivism, coupled with rehabilitation of the idea that there are certain fundamental, inalienable rights and obligations that must be respected—even by sovereign states—has led to a situation where both schools of thought are in fact operative in modern international law. Largely by virtue of the proliferation of permanent international institutions, which have provided fora both for distilling principled, values-based norms and for subsequently incorporating these norms into treaty law or customary state practice, international law has become theoretically "complex": no longer can it be explained by reference only to positivist or natural law theories.

---

50 Consider, for example, the right to asylum (article 14) and the right to own property (article 17) in the Declaration, neither of which was transformed into treaty obligations in the subsequently adopted International Covenant on Civil and Political Rights, 16 December 1966, 999 UNTS 171, Can TS 1976 No 47, (1967) 61 ILM 368, in force 23 March 1976, or in the International Covenant on Economic, Social and Cultural Rights, 16 December 1966, 993 UNTS 3, Can TS 1976 No 46, (1967) 6 ILM 360, in force 3 January 1976.

Moreover, as we shall see repeatedly throughout these materials, the alloying of natural law and positivist influences in modern international law has produced potent "universalizing" effects. Judicious resort to natural law principles serves to galvanize international public opinion (including that of states) in support of legal doctrines considered fundamental to the international legal order, whereas deployment of positivist processes (such as the negotiation, conclusion, and bringing into force of multilateral "law-making" treaties) fosters consensus on the precise delineation and operationalization of such doctrines. The result has been, in a limited but growing number of areas of international law, universal or near-universal concurrence with the rules in question. How international law arrived at this point, and whether these developments really matter, are concerns we address in the next two sections.

B. A CRITICAL HISTORY OF INTERNATIONAL LAW

1) Lurch and Lull: International Law's Episodic Development

A history of international law is generally divided into several implicit or explicit periods. A typical division, based on Wilhelm Grewe's *Epochs of International Law*, might be: the Spanish period, 1494–1648; the French period, 1648–1815; the English period, 1815–1919; the English-American period, 1919–1945; the period of American-Soviet rivalry, 1945–1989; and the post–Cold War period, 1989 to the present.[51] Other authorities propose similar categorizations.[52]

These epochs are effectively bookmarks in the history of (Euro-American) international relations. The names assigned to these epochs in Grewe's typology reflect the hegemonic state or states in the international relations of the period. The rupture point demarcating each of these periods is a pivotal event in world history, one that follows a crisis in international affairs. Thus, 1648 is the date of the Treaty of Westphalia, ending the Thirty Years' War; 1815 represents the end of the Napoleonic Wars, and the introduction of a new balance of power in Europe; 1919 is the date of the Treaty of Versailles, terminating World War I; 1945 is the year both Germany and Japan surrendered to the Allies, ending World War II; 1989 is the year the Berlin Wall tumbled, a symbolic end to the Cold War.

The fact that international law—in its broad contours, if not all its details—is often shaped by crises in international relations raises important theoretical questions, which we mention here but do not further explore in these materials. In international law, progress and change can be described as a process of "punctuated equilibrium." Niles Eldredge and Stephen Jay Gould coined this term in the 1970s as a theory of biological evolution.[53] It postulates that species may emerge very quickly, in large numbers, at particular points in geological history, followed by long periods of little change—equilibria. So in international law, sudden and often radical evolution in international legal doctrine

---

51   Wilhelm Grewe, *The Epochs of International Law*, trans by Michael Byers (Berlin: de Gruyter, 2000).

52   See, for example, *Encyclopedia*, above note 34, vol 2, "History of the Law of Nations 1648 to 1815" at 750; Antonio Cassese, *International Law*, 2d ed (New York: Oxford University Press, 2004). The key events in international legal history associated with different eras are described in John H Currie, *Public International Law*, 2d ed (Toronto: Irwin Law, 2008) at c 1, s B.

53   Niles Eldredge, *Fossils: The Evolution and Extinction of Species* (New York: HN Abrams, 1991).

may emerge quickly, precipitated by crises in international relations. At the risk of abusing by analogy Kuhn's already overused theory of scientific development,[54] these changes could be called "paradigm shifts." They are then followed by periods, often long, of relative stasis in international law.

If true, some might suggest that the post–Cold War era in international law ended on September 11, 2001. The crisis sparked by the terrorist attacks on New York and Washington could be argued to have propelled the international community in unexpected directions, producing new international norms that would more or less radically alter the international system, thus creating a new equilibrium. Whether such a fundamental shift has occurred or is still occurring, what the new norms might be, and where the new equilibrium would lie, remain contested issues.

2) Sovereignty and Its Discontents

While this chronological description provides important context to the study of international law, it is also important to understand the history of the concept of the sovereign state. As we shall now see, this is because our current system of international law is largely a by-product of the emergence of the sovereign state, and the evolution of both has therefore been closely intertwined.

a) Early Modern Europe

International law, in its modern guise, traces its origins to early modern Europe. Not coincidentally, this same period—the sixteenth and seventeenth centuries—saw the rise of "states," as the term is understood today. The evolution of the state as a form of sociopolitical organization, and of international law as a means of facilitating relations between these bodies, has been profoundly shaped by the concept of "sovereignty."

Early modern Europe was not moved by some peculiar genius to develop what has become international law. It is certainly true that rules governing relations between different "peoples" have existed even in the most distant antiquity and in all parts of the globe. Indeed, it seems fair to say that wherever social development reaches the point where one socially organized group of human beings views itself as distinct from another, "international" customs or rules must emerge if these groups of people are to interact.

The historical record is replete with such practices. Treaties, forms of diplomatic immunity, and principles governing war were all recognized in antiquity, both in Europe and elsewhere. Nevertheless, with the exception of some Roman *domestic* legal concepts that influenced, by analogy, early modern European jurists, few of these particular principles persisted as such as a basis for contemporary international law. Why, then, do most international lawyers trace the origins of modern international law to seventeenth-century Europe? Implicit in this query are in fact two questions: first, why *early modern* Europe; and, second, why Europe at all?

The simple answer to the first question is probably necessity. Early modern Europe was a civilization in crisis. The shared medieval worldview, centred on the Catholic Church and supported by such institutions as the Holy Roman Empire and the feudal structures

---

54 Thomas Kuhn, *The Structure of Scientific Revolutions* (Chicago: University of Chicago Press, 1962).

that cut across ethnic and linguistic lines, was in tatters. The discovery of the New World, the Renaissance and, perhaps most acutely, the Reformation, rent the relative unity of culture and thought in Europe. Politically, European peoples were increasingly herded into centralized and ethnically homogenized polities. These "states" were initially the product of monarchical ambitions. However, traditional rivalries between these centralizing monarchs and aristocratic houses were compounded by sectarian hostilities, fracturing Europe. The European wars of religion, and particularly the Thirty Years' War of 1618–1648, were the horrific consequence of royal geopolitical machinations and religious intolerance.

The Thirty Years' War began, in essence, as a civil war in the Holy Roman Empire. That central European polity—which as Voltaire famously observed was neither holy, nor Roman, nor an empire—was merely a confederation of mostly Germanic states, sharing certain weak federal structures by the seventeenth century. Moreover, it was a confederation of states divided between Protestant and Catholic princes. The Protestant rulers opposed the Catholic Hapsburg Emperor, and formed alliances with other, foreign states. The conflict ultimately embroiled most of Europe in a continental war driven less by religion than by the imperial ambitions of an emergent France and the fading hegemony of an overextended Spain.

The Thirty Years' War, probably the most disastrous war in European history until the twentieth century, culminated in the Treaty of Westphalia of 1648. While its importance has sometimes been overstated, the Treaty of Westphalia is as reasonable a "bright-line" starting point for the modern state system as any offered by history. The Treaty (really two settlements signed at Osnabrück and Münster in Westphalia) came close to being a "European collective agreement."[55] While its specific terms have long since become obsolete, they reflected a worldview that continues to echo in international law. Consider the following passages:

Treaty of Westphalia, 1648

LXIV.
And to prevent for the future any Differences arising in the Politick State, all and every one of the Electors, Princes and States of the Roman Empire, are so establish'd and confirm'd in their antient Rights, Prerogatives, Libertys, Privileges, free exercise of Territorial Right, as well Ecclesiastick, as Politick Lordships, Regales, by virtue of this present Transaction: that they never can or ought to be molested therein by any whomsoever upon any manner of pretence.

LXV.
They shall enjoy without contradiction, the Right of Suffrage in all Deliberations touching the Affairs of the Empire; but above all, when the Business in hand shall be the making or interpreting of Laws, the declaring of Wars, imposing of Taxes, levying or quartering of Soldiers, erecting new Fortifications in the Territorys of the States, or reinforcing the old Garisons; as also when a Peace of Alliance is to be concluded, and treated about, or the like, none of these, or the like things shall be acted for the future, without the Suffrage and Consent of the Free Assembly of all the States of the Empire: Above all, it shall

---

55 *Encyclopedia*, above note 34, vol 2, "History of the Law of Nations 1648 to 1815" at 750.

be free perpetually to each of the States of the Empire, to make Alliances with Strangers for their Preservation and Safety; provided, nevertheless, such Alliances be not against the Emperor, and the Empire, nor against the Publick Peace, and this Treaty, and without prejudice to the Oath by which every one is bound to the Emperor and the Empire. . . .

LXVII.

That as well as general as particular Diets, the free Towns, and other States of the Empire, shall have decisive Votes; they shall, without molestation, keep their Regales, Customs, annual Revenues, Libertys, Privileges to confiscate, to raise Taxes, and other Rights, lawfully obtain'd from the Emperor and Empire, or enjoy'd long before these Commotions, with a full Jurisdiction within the inclosure of their Walls, and their Territorys: making void at the same time, annulling and for the future prohibiting all Things, which by Reprisals, Arrests, stopping of Passages, and other prejudicial Acts, either during the War, under what pretext soever they have been done and attempted hitherto by private Authority, or may hereafter without any preceding formality of Right be non-interf'd. As for the rest, all laudable Customs of the sacred Roman Empire, the fundamental Constitutions and Laws, shall for the future be strictly observ'd, all the Confusions which time of War have, or could introduce, being remov'd and laid aside.

Thus, under the Treaty, the principalities of the Empire were entitled to make foreign alliances, albeit not against the Emperor himself. Meanwhile, other provisions gave these states substantial control over internal affairs. Read as a whole, the Treaty therefore extended a large measure of autonomy to over 300 member polities of the Empire. In part because of these provisions and in part because it led to the ascendancy of centralized France as the archetypical "state," the Treaty of Westphalia is often associated with the concept of sovereignty. It is, therefore, sometimes viewed as the progenitor of modern international law.[56] Though overstated, there is some truth to this view.

Sovereignty is a concept that continues to dominate and bedevil international law. While not exactly coincident in time with the Treaty of Westphalia, the association of sovereignty with "states" is also very much a product of early modern Europe. Indeed, the first reference to "sovereign state" identified by the *Oxford English Dictionary* is in Shakespeare's *King John* (1595): "I am too high-born to be propertied, To be a secondary at control, Or useful serving-man and instrument, To any sovereign state throughout the world."[57]

Medieval Europe, linked by a single, "universal" Church, could not conceive of any sort of secular, unlimited power. Even monarchs were bound by a natural law stemming from the divine order, and were often legally dependent on the Church.[58] As late as 1494, powerful secular rulers turned to the Pope to settle disputes between them. In that year, Spain and Portugal entered into the Treaty of Tordesillas, an attempt brokered by the Pope to partition the Americas between the two colonial powers. Some years later, Henry VIII, in his efforts to secure a divorce, asked for the Pope's dispensation, hardly the act of a fully sovereign head of state. The Pope's recalcitrance drove Henry to embrace the Protestant cause, thus contesting the authority of the Catholic Church.

---

56 See Nussbaum, above note 15 at 115.
57 *OED*, above note 8.
58 *Encyclopedia*, above note 34, vol 4, "Sovereignty" at 501.

Ultimately, the Reformation and the resulting schism in Christianity in northern Europe altered the sense of legal *communitas communitatum*, or legal "common roof," for all Europe. Though Aristotle used the expression "sovereign" in reference to a community's supreme authority,[59] the term's modern significance dates to efforts by (often, but not exclusively, Protestant) European rulers — like Henry VIII — to deny papal authority in favour of the autonomy of states. Niccolo Machiavelli responded to circumstances in divided Italy in *The Prince* (1513) by urging the pursuit by princes of secular authority through whatever means necessary. It was, however, the French scholar Jean Bodin, in his *Six livres de la république* (1576),[60] who responded to the divided politics of late sixteenth-century France, then rocked by sectarian strife, by articulating the first proto-modern concept of "sovereignty."

Bodin's "sovereignty" anticipated substantial power residing in a single individual — the monarch. "[T]he distinguishing mark of the sovereign," urged Bodin, is "that he cannot in any way be subject to the commands of another, for it is he who makes law for the subject, abrogates law already made, and amends obsolete law."[61] Sovereignty, for Bodin, had several dimensions, some which might be characterized as domestic powers and others as authority over foreign affairs. Thus, sovereignty included "the power to make law binding on all" the monarch's subjects and precluded appeals of the prince's decisions beyond the prince himself. But sovereignty also included the making of war and peace, the pre-eminent foreign relations issue of Bodin's (and, all too often, our) time and "one of the most important rights of sovereignty, since it brings in its train either the ruin or the salvation of the state."[62] Sovereignty thus meant autonomy in both internal affairs and international relations. These two features — autonomy in internal and foreign affairs — constitute the core of state sovereignty to our day.

Notably, however, Bodin's sovereignty was not absolute. Even Bodin's princes were subject to a higher, natural law — the laws of God — though Bodin was hostile to the notion that the Pope or any other earthly prince should serve as the vessel for this law. Even in this early iteration, therefore, sovereignty incorporated two, apparently irreconcilable, concepts: first, plenary power and autonomy; and second, subordination of this autonomy to a higher code of behaviour.

This tension is also reflected in the Treaty of Westphalia itself, which, as already noted, has iconic status in the history of international law. Consider the following provision:

Treaty of Westphalia, 1648

XXVIII.

That those of the Confession of Augsburg, and particularly the Inhabitants of Oppenheim, shall be put in possession again of their Churches, and Ecclesiastical Estates, as they were in the Year 1624 as also that all others of the said Confession of Augsburg, who shall demand it, shall have the free Exercise of their Religion, as well in publick Churches at the appointed Hours, as in private in their own Houses, or in others chosen for this purpose by their Ministers, or by those of their Neighbours, preaching the Word of God.

---

59 *Ibid* at 502.
60 Abridged and translated by MJ Hooley (Oxford: Blackwell, 1955), online: www.constitution.org/bodin/bodin_.htm.
61 *Ibid*, Book 1, c VIII, "Concerning Sovereignty."
62 *Ibid*, Book 1, c X, "The True Attributes of Sovereignty."

What this passage, and the Treaty as a whole, did was restore the "Peace of Augsburg," a settlement reached in the Empire in 1555 which provided the original legal basis for Lutheran Protestantism in the federation. The Treaty also extended this religious peace to Calvinism, thus broadening tolerance in much of the Empire to the federation's three great religious communities—Lutherans, Calvinists, and Catholics.

In sum, the Treaty of Westphalia at the same time extended virtual sovereignty to the princes and then constrained how that sovereignty could be exercised vis-à-vis the religious practices of the Empire's inhabitants. Put another way, even the archetypical expression of early modern state "sovereignty" contained restraints deeply inconsistent with unalloyed domestic autonomy.

Thus, sovereignty, even in its earliest iterations by jurists like Bodin or in treaties like the Treaty of Westphalia, was deeply compromised: autonomy was followed—or some-times, preceded—by important caveats on that autonomy.

b) Europe and the International Law of "Civilized" States

Our first question asked why modern international law originated in early modern Europe. The answer, outlined above, is necessity, born of collapsing universalistic world views. A fractured Europe partitioned itself into states and wielded the doctrine of sovereignty to regulate relations on a divided continent.

How then to explain that a development confined to this one particular part of the globe came to lie at the heart of the current global legal order? The simple answer is: European power. Just as Europeans were developing state-based structures of social or-ganization, they were also colonizing the so-called New World. The Americas, stripped of the better part of their indigenous inhabitants by germ and sword, "inherited" a European worldview. More than that, when mainly economic tensions between colonists and the European metropoles produced conflict between American colonies and European states in the seventeenth and eighteenth centuries, the rebellious colonists invoked European natural law concepts to justify the erection of new states, and then guarded the sovereign prerogatives of those states jealously. Consider US President Monroe's seventh annual message to Congress, on 2 December 1823 (the well-known "Monroe Doctrine"):

> [T]he American continents, by the free and independent condition which they have as-sumed and maintain, are henceforth not to be considered as subjects for future coloniz-ation by any European powers. . . . With the existing colonies or dependencies of any European power we have not interfered and shall not interfere. But with the Govern-ments who have declared their independence and maintain it, and whose independence we have, on great consideration and on just principles, acknowledged, we could not view any interposition for the purpose of oppressing them, or controlling in any other manner their destiny, by any European power in any other light than as the manifestation of an unfriendly disposition toward the United States.

By the early 1800s, with the conclusion of the Napoleonic Wars in Europe and the in-dependence of Latin America, international law remained a European system, albeit one that had spread to Europe's former colonies in the Americas. As Heinhard Steiger notes:

> By 1815 only sovereign states could participate in the law of nations order. The basic structure of the legal system from the previous epoch was indeed kept. At the same time,

however, the principle of sovereignty was made considerably more distinct. . . . A state was classed as a legal and political body governing a people, principally according to the new though unclear concept of the national state, in a defined territory, under a sovereign state power. This could only refer to a "civilised" state. Political bodies that were not considered civilised according to the aforementioned description were not members of the international legal system. Those states belonging to this circle, without question or examination, were those that in the previous epoch (until 1815) had already risen to the status of the sovereign European states, as well as the USA. It was therefore, in this respect, continuity on the basis of self-definition and own decision making. This circle was, however, capable of expansion, if, in the opinion of the civilised states, states outside this circle fulfilled the criteria.[63]

Notice the emphasis on "civilized states." By the early twentieth century, states were defined (rather intuitively) as politically centralized communities. Thus T.J. Lawrence, in his *The Principles of International Law* (1910), wrote that "*a state may be defined as a political community, the members of which are bound together by the tie of common subjection to some central authority, whose commands the bulk of them habitually obey.*"[64] But not all such political communities were states entitled to recognition at international law. Several other prerequisites had to be met, some of which persist to this day. Perhaps most perniciously, the "degree of civilization" of the political community was listed well into the twentieth century as among the criteria for deciding whether an entity qualified as a state at international law:

An African tribe is not a state in the sense in which the word is used in international law, although it may have a unified control under one chieftain, and may dominate and live on a certain territory. . . . It was formerly stated that only Christian powers could be the subjects of international law, since it was a group of Christian states which first formally bound themselves to respect its obligations. In 1856, however, Turkey was formally admitted into the family of civilized nations, by the Treaty of Paris; and in the latter half of the 19th century China and Japan were admitted.[65]

Civilization, of course, was to be measured against a European standard. Consider this discussion from F.E. Smith, *International Law* (1911):

It is difficult to indicate with precision the circumstances under which such admission [to the "family of nations"] takes place in the case of a nation formerly barbarous. . . . The assimilation of European ideas, the growth of humane habits, the frank attempt to break down the barriers of exclusion, all these will insensibly prepare the way. Japan has fully established her claim to be recognised as a subject of international law. She acceded to the Geneva Convention in 1886; European nations have abandoned their extraterritorial

63 Heinhard Steiger, *The Right to a Humane Environment* (Berlin: Schmidt, 1973) at 185.
64 Thomas J Lawrence, *The Principles of International Law* (London: MacMillan, 1910) at para 35 [emphasis in the original].
65 Elizabeth Fisher Read, *International Law and International Relations* (New York: American Foundation, 1925) at 12.

privileges in her territory; she has attained to a high standard of conduct in warfare, from which she has only once fallen away; she was a party to all the Conventions of the Second Peace Conference of 1907; her procedure at the Conference of London in 1908–9 was based upon a view of International Law which was marked by profound and careful study and a lofty sense of humanity; and since her war with Russia she has taken her place beyond question among the greater powers. In the case of China, there is more doubt, for it is not yet proved to what extent her troops can be brought to obey the rules of civilised war. In 1899, though summoned to the Peace Conference, she did not sign the Convention relative to the laws and customs of land warfare; but eight years later all hesitation in that respect had disappeared, and she was a party to all the Conventions of 1907. Precipitancy in admission is to be deprecated, and it is food for reflection that the Treaty of Paris in 1856 admitted Turkey to share in the advantages of the system of Europe, even though the Capitulations which exempted foreigners from Turkish jurisdiction were allowed to remain in force.[66]

It is difficult to read these prescriptions for membership in the "family of nations" as anything other than Eurocentric expressions of *realpolitik*. "Civilized nations" were those that acted like Europeans, fought like Europeans, and perhaps most importantly, matched Europeans in war, as had the Japanese in their 1905 conflict with Russia. Civilized nations entitled to be recognized as states acquired, by virtue of their statehood, sovereignty over their internal and external affairs, albeit limited by treaties in some instances. In comparison, "uncivilized" peoples who could not aspire to state status in international law were those which European states could conquer, and then incorporate into their domestic legal spheres, as colonies. Colonies are the antithesis of sovereign states. As one scholar notes,

> The insistence on a European model of statehood and the organization of the state, and the articulation in parochial terms of a "standard of civilization" which was itself applied in self-serving ways, were all conducive to the structuring and promotion of a great deal of inequality. . . . The Eurocentric system excluded from its purview entities that powerful recognized states were not willing to treat as "states," whether because they wished to dominate or colonize these entities, or because these did not closely resemble "states" as the category had come to be understood, or because they showed little acceptance of the organizing ideas of the system, or because they did not seem likely to uphold international legal obligations.[67]

Civilization, as an express prerequisite for statehood, has fallen away, most obviously in the post–World War II era. Colonialism has given way to a concept of self-determination of peoples. We will discuss this concept at length in Chapter 4. For our purposes here, self-determination does not reflect a radical rethinking of state-centrism in international law. It has not relaxed the requirement that non-European peoples structure their political organization in a European fashion in order to be considered states. It is not an enticement for former colonial populations to invent new political orders bearing little resemblance to that devised in Europe. Instead, it is an invitation to these societies to join the

---

66 Frederick E Smith (later first Earl of Birkenhead), *International Law*, 4th ed (London: JM Dent & Sons, 1911) at 35–36.

67 Benedict Kingsbury, "Sovereignty and Inequality" (1998) 9 EJIL 599 at 606–7.

community of sovereign states—and thus, implicitly, to emulate the European model. For this reason, virtually the entire inhabited world now is occupied by states meeting classical, European expectations:

> The Western model of the state became established globally as a structural equilibrium or a reference point. Once established, it came to dominate the normative and ontological landscape, and helped to delegitimize the possible alternatives. Non-European forms of political organization that might have attained widespread legitimacy as alternatives to the European-style sovereign state were subordinated and delegitimized as global models, a situation which for the time being remains unlikely to be reversed, however important such non-European forms are in contemporary politics.[68]

In sum, in early modernity, Europeans established a "world" order founded upon sovereign states for their own insular reasons. These rules excluded from full participation the better part of the world's peoples until about six decades ago. The exclusion of these communities was deeply connected with colonialism, which in turn was made possible by European military and economic supremacy. When colonialism became economically, militarily, and, ultimately, politically unsustainable, what replaced it was a global replication of the Eurocentric state model—complete with its many foibles.

In relation to this last point, take, for instance, the feminist critique of international law and its foundations:

> The structure of the international legal order reflects a male perspective and ensures its continued dominance. The primary subjects of international law are states and, increasingly, international organizations. In both states and international organizations the invisibility of women is striking. Power structures within governments are overwhelmingly masculine: women have significant positions of power in very few states, and in those where they do, their numbers are minuscule. Women are either unrepresented or underrepresented in the national and global decision-making processes.
>
> States are patriarchal structures not only because they exclude women from elite positions and decision-making roles, but also because they are based on the concentration of power in, and control by, an elite and the domestic legitimation of a monopoly over the use of force to maintain that control. This foundation is reinforced by international legal principles of sovereign equality, political independence and territorial integrity and the legitimation of force to defend those attributes. . . .
>
> The normative structure of international law has allowed issues of particular concern to women to be either ignored or undermined. For example, modern international law rests on and reproduces various dichotomies between the public and private spheres, and the "public" sphere is regarded as the province of international law. One such distinction is between public international law, the law governing the relations between nation-states, and private international law, the rules about conflicts between national legal systems. Another is the distinction between matters of international "public" concern and matters "private" to states that are considered within their domestic jurisdiction, in which the international community has no recognized legal interest. . . .

---

68 *Ibid* at 607.

[This] societal division into public and private spheres . . . relegates many matters of concern to women to the private area regarded as inappropriate for legal regulation. . . .[69]

If sovereignty was the product of a fractured Europe, and the Eurocentric (and patriarchal) state-based system of international law was, in turn, the product of European expansionism, does sovereignty have a legitimate role in contemporary international law? We ask that question repeatedly throughout these materials, and we often endorse positions that would further constrain state sovereignty.

Nevertheless, careful arguments can be made that sovereignty may still have a role to play in facilitating international relations between the disparate peoples that populate the planet. Recall that Westphalian sovereignty was (in part) an ideological cure for the bloody conflicts that raged in Europe when states sought to interfere in the affairs of other states. Human culture is still very diverse, and much that goes on in one state offends the sensibilities of the inhabitants of other states. International law has itself condemned some of these practices, once the sole domestic domain of sovereign states. Still, this international regulation is relatively limited (and often stiffly resisted). In this environment, it seems likely that sovereignty continues to have a stabilizing role. Consider the point of view of American diplomat Richard Haass, a former director of policy planning at the US Department of State:

> Sovereignty has been a source of stability for more than two centuries. It has fostered world order by establishing legal protections against external intervention and by offering a diplomatic foundation for the negotiation of international treaties, the formation of international organizations, and the development of international law. It has also provided a stable framework within which representative government and market economies could emerge in many nations. At the beginning of the twenty-first century, sovereignty remains an essential foundation for peace, democracy, and prosperity.[70]

As in previous centuries, the key question for the international community in the twenty-first century probably is not "whether sovereignty?" but instead "how much sovereignty?"

C. INTERNATIONAL LAW AND INTERNATIONAL RELATIONS THEORY

The final area to canvass before concluding this introductory chapter is the relationship between the study of international law and of international politics, and specifically international relations theory. Here, we engage with the question: Does international law matter in international relations?

---

69 Hilary Charlesworth, Christine Chinkin, & Shelley Wright, "Feminist Approaches to International Law" (1991) 85 AJIL 613 at 621–22, 625, and 644.

70 Richard N Haass, "Sovereignty: Existing Rights, Evolving Responsibilities" (Remarks delivered at the School of Foreign Service and the Mortara Center for International Studies, Georgetown University, 14 January 2003), in John H Jackson, "Sovereignty-Modern: A New Approach to an Outdated Concept" (2003) 97 AJIL 782 at 789.

1) The Challenge of International Relations Theory to International Law

International law and international relations scholarship have not always had a happy relationship, although the divide between some law schools and political science departments in this field is fading.[71] Nonetheless, international relations scholars — particularly those of the realist and rationalist schools — have queried forcefully international law's relevance in international affairs. In some respects, this critique echoes the extreme positivist objection to international law: If international law is simply what states do, then international law is at best a codified description of international politics.

Although there are offshoots and subdivisions,[72] consider the three main theoretical camps within the field of international relations, and the relationship of each to international law:

Realist theory . . . treat[s] states as the principal actors in international politics. States interact in an environment of anarchy, defined as the absence of any central government able to keep peace or enforce agreements. Security is their overriding goal, and self-help their guiding principle. Under these conditions, differences in power are usually sufficient to explain important events. Realists concentrate on interactions among major powers and on matters of war and peace. . . .

Realists do not conclude that international cooperation and international law are unlikely or unimportant: states will naturally cooperate when it advances their interests. They do assert, however, that political realities constrain the commitments states will accept, and that the interests of more powerful states set the terms of cooperation. As a corollary, realists believe that international rules and institutions have little, if any, independent effect on state behavior: they are mere ("epiphenomenal") artifacts of the underlying interest and power relationships, and will be changed or disregarded (at least on important issues) if those relationships change. . . .

Various forms of *liberal* IR [international relations] theory . . . insist on methodological individualism, viewing individuals and private groups as the fundamental actors in international (and domestic) politics. States are not insignificant, but their preferences are determined by domestic politics rather than assumed interests or material factors like relative power. . . . [I]nterstate politics are more complex and fluid than realists . . . assume: national preferences can vary widely and change unpredictably. It calls for careful attention to the domestic politics and constitutional structures of individual states. . . .

Constructivist theory . . . [argues that] international actors operate within a social context of shared subjective understandings and norms. . . . Even fundamental notions like the state, sovereignty and national interests are socially constructed. . . . In terms of legal

---

71   Resulting in such works as Jeffrey L Dunoff & Mark A Pollack, eds, *Interdisciplinary Perspectives on International Law and International Relations: The State of the Art* (Cambridge: Cambridge University Press, 2012).

72   For example, those who follow what is termed the "English School" in international relations theory would note its broad division between pluralist and solidarist approaches (with the English School label referring to scholars of various nationalities associated with the London School of Economics and Oxford University, among others). See further, Timothy Dunne et al, eds, *International Relations Theories: Discipline and Diversity*, 2d ed (Oxford: Oxford University Press, 2010).

doctrine, for constructivists all is subjective. . . . [N]ormative understandings vary with historical and political context. . . .[73]

At its base, constructivism asserts that states obey international law due to norms. In doing so, constructivism draws from critical theory, postmodernism, feminist theory, and sociological theories, among others. For constructivists, international law gives structure to the international system. States create and follow international law because of their moral and social commitment to the ideas embodied in international legal rules.

As the above extract suggests, realists have generally discounted the contribution of international law to international relations. As noted in a well-known 1993 article by Princeton University international law and relations scholar Anne-Marie Slaughter:

> Th[e] seasoned [realist] observers of the interwar period reacted against Wilsonian liberal internationalism, which presumed that the combination of democracy and international organization could vanquish war and power politics. They believed instead in the polarity of law and power, opposing one to the other as the respective emblems of the domestic versus the international realm, normative aspiration versus positive description, cooperation versus conflict, soft versus hard, idealist versus realist. Regardless of their domestic colors, states in the international realm were champions only of their own national interest. "Law," as understood in the domestic sense, had no place in this world. The only relevant laws were the "laws of politics," and politics was "a struggle for power." . . .
>
> This, then, was the Realist challenge to international lawyers: a challenge to establish the "relevance" of international law. International legal theorists had long grappled with the theoretical conundrum of the sources of international legal obligation — of law being simultaneously "of" and "above" the state. Yet the endless debates on this question nevertheless assumed that international legal rules, however derived, had some effect on state behavior, that law and power *interacted* in some way, rather than marking opposite ends of the domestic-international spectrum. Political Realists, by contrast, gave no quarter. Their challenge struck at the heart of the discipline, claiming that international law was but a collection of evanescent maxims or a "repository of legal rationalizations."[74]

This realist challenge had important implications for the way international law was perceived, especially in the United States. As Yale University law professor Harold Hongju Koh has explained:

> [T]he realists' Cold War disdain for the utopianism of international law helped trigger the odd estrangement between the fields of international law and international relations. Although the two fields cover much of the same intellectual territory, they began to evolve independently, pursuing different analytic missions, and reaching different conclusions about the influence of law in international affairs. Over time, the fields came to adopt an unspoken division of labor regarding the intellectual projects that they would pursue.

---

73 Kenneth W Abbott, "International Relations Theory, International Law, and the Regime Governing Atrocities in Internal Conflicts" (1999) 93 AJIL 361 at 364–67. See further Scott Burchill et al, *Theories of International Relations*, 4th ed (London: Palgrave Macmillan, 2009).

74 Anne-Marie Slaughter, "International Law and International Relations Theory: A Dual Agenda" (1993) 87 AJIL 205 at 207–8.

International relations scholars, suffused with realism, treated international law as naïve and virtually beneath discussion. International lawyers, meanwhile, shifted their gaze toward modest tasks: description of international legal norms; application of these norms to particular cases; and occasional prescription of what the rule of law should be. Legal scholars therefore largely avoided the difficult tasks of causal explanation and prediction.[75]

This division of labour may in part be an occupational hazard. As lawyers, we are not generally preoccupied with *explaining* state behaviour — we are more concerned with shaping it. Admittedly, an understanding of the former may assist in accomplishing the latter. However, law has a normative purpose. It is a value-driven enterprise: social engineering, not social science. This is plainly the case in domestic law, where values clearly animate legislation and jurisprudence. Modern domestic legal scholarship is rightly preoccupied with unearthing, critiquing, and, at times, replacing these values. Our task in studying international law should be no different.

For these reasons, international law and international relations theory have two very different projects. To the extent it provides insight into how international relations are conducted, international relations theory is of acute interest to international lawyers who are determined to "make their case." Yet, international relations theory generally provides no guidance on what that case should be. It does not always (or even often) answer the question: what values *should* animate the international community? For this reason, while cross-fertilization is vital, international lawyers should be wary of aligning their project too closely with that of their international relations peers.

That being said, international lawyers have not all folded their tents in response to the realist challenge, and some have mounted a spirited theoretical defence.[76] There is a good reason for this: international relations theorists (most notably within the realist camp) toss stones from a glass house. There is little doubt that powerful states — with power measured in both the "hard power" sense of military and economic might, and the more inchoate sense of "soft power" — have a disproportionate influence on international affairs. This is a reasonable insight of the realist school (and remains so even with US President Obama's encouragement of what he terms a "smart power" US foreign policy).

Yet the preoccupation of both positivist legal theory and the realist international relations scholarship with monolithic states misses much that actually occurs in international law and relations. States are not monolithic, as anyone with a passing knowledge of domestic politics will attest. States do not choose to conform to or ignore international law; human policy-makers do. And policy-makers are motivated by a diverse array of institutional and personal factors. Whether in Canada or France, the United States or the United Kingdom, disagreements often arise between government departments, between the executive, legislative and judicial branches, and between political parties whose representatives serve on foreign policy committees. Consider the (admittedly partisan and US-focused) comments of Samuel Berger, writing in *Foreign Affairs*:

> The real "clash of civilizations" is taking place within Washington. . . . It is not really a clash over discrete policy issues — the merits of the war in Iraq, the costs of the Kyoto

Protocol, or the level of spending on foreign aid, for example—but between diametrically opposed conceptions of America's role in the world. It is a battle fought between liberal internationalists in both parties who believe that our strength is usually greatest when we work in concert with allies in defense of shared values and interests, versus those who seem to believe that the United States should go it alone—or not go it at all.[77]

In parliamentary systems such as Canada's, departmental ideologies and objectives flavour international relations just as powerfully. The then Department of Foreign Affairs and International Trade (DFAIT) likely approached the 2002 deportation of Maher Arar by the United States to Syria very differently than did the Royal Canadian Mounted Police (RCMP) or the Canadian Security and Intelligence Service (CSIS). Even among lawyers who work for the federal government, the Department of Foreign Affairs, Trade and Development (as it is now known) and the Department of Justice sometimes take notoriously different approaches to international legal issues.

Moreover, in federal states—even those in which sub-national federal units, such as provinces and territories, play no formal or direct role in international affairs—foreign policy is often heavily influenced by regional factors and intergovernmental relations. Consider the likely influence of the views of British Columbia or the Atlantic provinces on Canada's approach to ocean issues; of energy-rich Alberta or coal-dependent Nova Scotia on Canada's willingness to withdraw from the Kyoto Protocol;[78] or of the separatist movement in Quebec and of self-governing Aboriginal communities on Canada's approach to the application of the doctrine of self-determination in international law.

Added to inter-institutional and intergovernmental conflicts within states are the vagaries of domestic politics and individual psychology. Leaders have different personalities and political convictions that shape their international conduct. Canada likely did not participate in the Iraq war of 2003 because the legacy-conscious Jean Chrétien was prime minister at the relevant time, instead of then Canadian Alliance (and later Conservative) Party leader Stephen Harper.[79] Similarly, with Stephen Harper as prime minister, Canada has taken a more overt stand in support of Israeli foreign policy than under previous governments.

Beyond this, layered onto the state system of international relations are international institutions, such as the United Nations. These bodies sometimes have autonomy of identity and action from state members, both in international law and in practice. Here, too, personality matters. UN Secretary-General Ban Ki-moon is a very different person than his predecessor, Kofi Annan, and this difference is reflected in the initiatives that each have championed. Louise Arbour, in her aggressive pursuit of war criminals as chief prosecutor of the International Criminal Tribunals for the Former Yugoslavia and Rwanda in the late 1990s, can be thanked for enhancing the effectiveness of the tribunal processes

---

77 Samuel R Berger, "Foreign Policy for a Democratic President" (2004) 83:3 *Foreign Affairs* 47 at 50.

78 Kyoto Protocol to the United Nations Framework Convention on Climate Change, 11 December 1997, 2303 UNTS 148, in force 16 February 2005 (entry into force for Canada 17 December 2002, withdrawal with effect 15 December 2012).

79 Stephen Harper, "The Canadian Alliance Refuses to be Neutral" *National Post* (21 March 2003) A13: "Today, the world is at war. A coalition of countries under the leadership of our key allies in Britain and the United States is leading a military intervention to disarm Saddam Hussein. Prime Minister Jean Chrétien is opposed to joining this multilateral coalition of nations. . . . This is a serious mistake."

in those regions. A different chief prosecutor, one perhaps more concerned with the political ramifications of indicting Serb leaders engaged in the Kosovo conflict, would have had a very different impact.[80]

International institutions, and the conferences they host, are also venues where non-state actors in the form of non-governmental organizations (NGOs) articulate views on international relations, sometimes in opposition to those taken by states. International institutions are not democratic in the sense of being directly representative of, and directly accountable to, a global citizenry. They do, however, negate the strict monopoly of states in international relations, providing a very different playing field than would exist in their absence. The Ottawa Process, which involved a crucial partnership between certain states and NGOs leading to the conclusion of the Landmines Convention[81] is a case in point. Again, personality played a role in this process, not least the personalities of Jodi Williams, the NGO campaigner ultimately awarded a Nobel Peace Prize for her efforts, and Canada's then-foreign affairs minister, Lloyd Axworthy.[82] To be at all useful, international relations theory—and international legal theory—must anticipate and explain the role of these non-state actors, and the psychologies of their human participants, in shaping the conduct of international relations and law.

Finally, culture and history matter. It is difficult to explain tensions between China and Taiwan without a frank appreciation of modern Chinese history. Indeed, it is very difficult to understand Chinese relations with the world as a whole without a full appreciation of the Chinese emphasis on "saving face" and what political scientist Peter Gries has called "face nationalism."[83] For its part, US foreign policy is very much coloured by that nation's historical identification with "life, liberty, and the pursuit of happiness" and its emphasis on individualism and market-based problem solving.[84] For many years, Canada's foreign policy was influenced by Canada's self-image as the "helpful fixer"—an historical and cultural product of the Pearson era in Canadian foreign policy. In the Canadian discourse, peacekeeping has been as much a symbol of Canada as its scarlet-clad Mounties and images of the Arctic. More recently, energy, trade, immigration, and military influence have appeared to be the driving forces behind Canada's foreign policy.

For all these reasons, a full understanding of international relations must not only grapple with intra-state politicking and the role played by non-state actors and international institutions in modern international relations, but must also account for the role of personality, as mediated by culture and history. While elements of this approach are found in liberal, and even more plainly, in constructivist international relations theory, no one theory seems to provide a fully satisfactory account of international relations.

---

80 See Michael Ignatieff, *Virtual War: Kosovo and Beyond* (Toronto: Viking, 2000) at 124 *et seq.*

81 Above note 6.

82 Lloyd Axworthy has described the unique nature of the Ottawa Process, and the role of personality and non-state actors, in Lloyd Axworthy, *Navigating a New World: Canada's Global Future* (Toronto: Alfred A Knopf Canada, 2003).

83 Peter Gries, "A 'China Threat'? Power and Passion in Chinese 'Face Nationalism'" (Fall 1999) 162:2 *World Affairs* 63.

84 For a discussion of the historical cultural tendencies in American foreign policy, see Walter Russell Mead, *Special Providence: American Foreign Policy and How It Changed the World* (New York: Alfred A Knopf, 2001).

2) Why International Law Matters

It has been said that "almost all nations observe almost all principles of international law and almost all of their obligations almost all of the time."[85] Given the above critique of the dominant theoretical camps within the field of international relations, how do international lawyers (and international relations scholars receptive to international law) answer this question: Why does international law matter in international relations?

By the late 1990s, there were at least five theoretical strands within the international legal literature as to whether international law mattered and, if so, why states obeyed it. Consider this 1998 summary by Yale University law professor Harold Koh:

> The first school of thought, the "realist" strand, suggests that nations never truly obey international law, but only conform their conduct to it when sufficiently coerced. Iraq, for example, "obeyed" international law when it withdrew from Kuwait and when it recently permitted United Nations weapons inspections. But in both cases, Iraq plainly acted in response to external sanctions, not internal compulsion. The second strand, rationalism . . . acknowledges that nations follow international law when it serves their self-interest to do so and sees such rationality as becoming embedded into institutions and regimes, such as the World Trade Organization or the international debt regime. Third, a liberal Kantian strand . . . assumes that nations obey international law, guided by a sense of moral obligation derived from considerations of fairness, democracy, and legitimacy that are embedded in their "liberal," domestic legal structures. Fourth, a communitarian Grotian strand . . . has identified, as a key causal factor, the commonality of values within "international society": a community that constructs national interests and identities. Fifth and finally, the legal process strand derives a nation's incentive to obey from the encouragement and prodding of other nations with which it is engaged in a discursive legal process. The traditional focus of international legal process theorists . . . has been on the horizontal legal process that occurs among nation-states while interacting within treaty regimes that operate on a global plane.[86]

Today's debates rage primarily between the rationalist and constructivist camps, or (broadly speaking) the interest-based and norm-based approaches.[87] Advocates of a rationalist approach tend to argue that international law is the result of states acting logically to maximize their interests.[88] These scholars rely on economics-based rational choice theory, and explain foreign policy as self-interested, goal-seeking behaviour (with self-interest extending beyond security issues that were the prime concern of traditional realists).[89]

---

85 Louis Henkin, *How Nations Behave: Law and Foreign Policy*, 2d ed (New York: Columbia University Press, 1979) at 47.

86 Harold Hongju Koh, "The 1998 Frankel Lecture: Bringing International Law Home" (1998) 35 Hous L Rev 623 at 634–35.

87 Oona Hathaway, "Between Power and Principles: An Integrated Theory of International Law" (2005) 72 U Chicago L Rev 469 at 472.

88 Jack L Goldsmith & Eric A Posner, *The Limits of International Law* (Oxford: Oxford University Press, 2005) at 3–5 [Goldsmith & Posner].

89 See further, Andrew T Guzman, *How International Law Works: A Rational Choice Theory* (Oxford: Oxford University Press, 2007).

Constructivists, by contrast, believe that states create and comply with international law not only because they expect a reward for doing so, but also because of their commitment (or the commitment of actors within the state) to the norms or ideas embodied in international law.[90] Fairness theory and legal process theory are variants of this normative approach.

Koh himself proposes a variant of the legal process theory. As summarized by other scholars, Koh urges that:

> [C]ompliance with international rules is not explained entirely by the functional benefits it provides but, rather, by the process of internalization of international legal norms into the internal value sets of domestic legal systems. This internalization occurs through a complex process of repeated interaction, norm enunciation and interpretation, which occurs in such varied contexts as transnational public law litigation in domestic courts, international commercial arbitration, and lobbying of legislatures by nongovernmental organizations.[91]

For many practitioners of international law, international law matters because those exercising influence in international relations believe it matters. Recent legal scholarship also opines that international law matters in a variety of ways by shifting decision-making authority from some actors to others, by setting benchmarks for private decision making, by shaping the interpretation of domestic law, and by providing categories through which actors see the world.[92] The importance of internalized expectations and values should not be understated. Politics is not often a question of brute force. The capacity to induce others to do as you wish — in other words, power — is sometimes (and perhaps often) a result of the legitimacy of the action sought, and less a product of coercion. This is true of domestic law as much as international law: people abide by domestic law because they share a common sense of the legitimacy of that law, not always or even generally because they fear punishment.

The importance of "legitimacy" as a tool for understanding international law should also not be underestimated. As the late Thomas Franck of New York University School of Law explained, compliance with international law is often secured by a belief in the legitimacy of the rule, which in turn requires a belief that the rule came into existence through the right process.[93] For Franck, it was the legitimacy of the process that "exerts a pull to compliance." Consider also the views of political scientist Joseph Nye:

> Power and legitimacy are not antithetical, but complementary. Humans are neither purely moral nor totally cynical. It is a political fact that the belief in right and wrong helps move people to act, and therefore legitimacy is a source of power. If a state's acts are perceived as illegitimate, the costs of a policy will be higher. States appeal to international

---

90 For a work that develops an "interactional" account of international law using constructivist work, as well as the legal theory of Lon Fuller, to elucidate the role of legitimacy in the practice of international law, see Jutta Brunnée & Stephen J. Toope, *Legitimacy and Legality in International Law: An Interactional Account* (Cambridge: Cambridge University Press, 2010).

91 Anne-Marie Slaughter, Andrew S Tulumello, & Stepan Wood, "International Law and International Relations Theory: A New Generation of Interdisciplinary Scholarship" (1998) 92 AJIL 367 at 381.

92 See, for example, Robert Howse & Ruti Teitel, "Beyond Compliance: Rethinking Why International Law Really Matters" (2010) 1:2 Global Policy 127–36.

93 Thomas M Franck, "Legitimacy in the International System" (1988) 82 AJIL 705 at 706.

law and organization to legitimize their own policies or delegitimize others, and that often shapes their tactics and outcomes.[94]

The appeal to international law to secure legitimacy can be illustrated by the decision of the United States, the United Kingdom, and others to form a "coalition of the willing" to invade Iraq in 2003. This action did not receive the explicit endorsement of the UN Security Council, the sole body capable of authorizing military force directed against another state in cases other than self-defence. Nevertheless, the coalition states pointed to a long list of UN Security Council resolutions on Iraq—including Resolution 1441 (2002)—in an effort to legitimize their acts. We return to this issue in detail in Chapter 14. For present purposes, consider the following extract from then-US Secretary of State Colin Powell's address to the UN Security Council of 3 February 2003, delivered just prior to the invasion:

Last 8 November, the Council passed Resolution 1441 (2002) by a unanimous vote. The purpose of that resolution was to disarm Iraq of its weapons of mass destruction. Iraq had already been found guilty of material breach of its obligations, stretching back over 16 previous resolutions and 12 years. Resolution 1441 (2002) was not dealing with an innocent party, but with a regime that the Council has repeatedly convicted over the years. Resolution 1441 (2002) gave Iraq one last chance to come into compliance or to face serious consequences. No Council member present and voting on that day had any illusions about the nature and intent of the resolution or what "serious consequences" meant if Iraq did not comply. . . .

[T]he information and intelligence we have gathered point to an active and systematic effort on the part of the Iraqi regime to keep key materials and people from the inspectors, in direct violation of Resolution 1441 (2002).

The pattern is not just one of reluctant cooperation. Nor is it merely a lack of cooperation. What we see is a deliberate campaign to prevent any meaningful inspection work.

Operative paragraph 4 of resolution 1441 (2002), which we lingered over so long last fall, clearly states that "false statements or omissions" in the declaration and a "failure by Iraq at any time to comply with, and cooperate fully in the implementation of this resolution shall constitute"—the facts speak for themselves—"a further material breach of Iraq's obligations." . . .

By this standard—the standard of this operative paragraph—I believe that Iraq is now in further material breach of its obligations. I believe that this conclusion is irrefutable and undeniable. Iraq has now placed itself in danger of the serious consequences called for in resolution 1441 (2002).

This body places itself in danger of irrelevance if it allows Iraq to continue to defy its will without responding effectively and immediately. . . .

Over three months ago, the Council recognized that Iraq continued to pose a threat to international peace and security, and that Iraq had been, and remained in material breach of its disarmament obligations. Today, Iraq still poses a threat, and Iraq still remains in material breach. Indeed, by its failure to seize its one last opportunity to come

---

94 Joseph S Nye, *Understanding International Conflicts: An Introduction to Theory and History*, 7th ed (New York: Pearson Longman, 2009) at 176 [Nye, *Understanding*]. But see Goldsmith & Posner, above note 88 at 26 (suggesting that states are unaffected by the legitimacy of a rule).

clean and disarm, Iraq has put itself in deeper material breach and closer to the day when it will face serious consequences for its continued defiance of the Council.

We have an obligation to our citizens—we have an obligation to this body—to see that our resolutions are complied with. We wrote resolution 1441 (2002) not in order to go to war. We wrote resolution 1441 (2002) to try to preserve the peace. We wrote resolution 1441 (2002) to give Iraq one last chance. Iraq is not so far taking that one last chance. We must not shrink from whatever is ahead of us. We must not fail in our duty and our responsibility to the citizens of the countries that are represented by this body.[95]

The Iraq war of 2003 is viewed by many as a prime example of non-compliance with international law. And yet, while the argument that Resolution 1441 (2002) and its predecessors could authorize the use of force in the way urged by the coalition is now widely accepted as having little substance, the Iraq conflict demonstrates that even the most powerful of states, in times of the greatest of crises, see virtue in using the parlance and discourse of international law to justify their actions. By speaking the language of international law, even great powers may end up acting in a fashion different than would otherwise have been the case. The United States and the United Kingdom still invaded Iraq, but they did so in a manner (and at a time) very different than might have been the case had their leaders and governments paid no attention to international law at all.

There is also a second reason why international law matters in international politics, one again identified by Nye: predictability.

> States are involved in conflicts with each other all the time. The vast range of international transactions, both public and private, includes trade, tourism, diplomatic missions, and contacts among peoples across national boundaries. As interdependence grows, those contacts grow and there are increasing opportunities for friction. International law allows governments to avoid conflict at a high level when such friction arises. For example, if an American tourist is arrested for smuggling drugs in Mexico, a British ship collides with a Norwegian ship in the North Sea, or a Japanese firm claims that an Indian company has infringed its patents, the governments may not want to spoil their other relations over these private collisions. Handling such issues by international law and agreed principles depoliticizes them and makes them predictable. Predictability is necessary for transactions to flourish and for the orderly handling of the conflicts that inevitably accompany them.[96]

International law, in other words, may sometimes take the high politics out of international relations, setting ground rules for otherwise uncertain encounters between states.

For both of these reasons—legitimacy and predictability—it is impossible to understand modern international relations without understanding the content of international law. In Chapter 2, we begin discussing the substance of that law.

---

95   UN Doc S/PV 4701 at 2, 7, 8, and 17 (3 February 2003).
96   Nye, *Understanding*, above note 94 at 175–76.

CHAPTER 2

SOURCES OF INTERNATIONAL LAW

A. GENERAL

In the preceding chapter, we defined international law both by focusing on its historical role as the law of sovereign states and by examining various theories advanced to explain it. In this chapter we ask the same question—what is international law?—from a doctrinal perspective. Specifically, here we examine where the rules of international law come from and in what circumstances they emerge; how one assesses whether a given norm really is a rule of international law; and how one determines which entities are bound by any given rule of international law.

The answers to these questions are not simple. As we have already seen, unlike domestic legal systems, there is no clear constitutional structure in the international sphere assigning a particular body an exclusive or even principal law-making role. Rather, in keeping with the predominant role still played by sovereign states in the international system, international law is generated by complex, decentralized processes. Moreover, when compared with most domestic legal systems, the international legal system is plagued by a paucity of dispute resolution mechanisms with the power to determine the content of international law in a general, binding manner. Thus, the content of international law is more readily contestable in international relations, and statements of principle are prone to protracted debates about their precise legal status and ambit. Adding to this complexity is the fact that not all states or other international actors are bound by the same rules of international law. Contrary to popular misconception, international law is not necessarily universal law.

What are the decentralized law-making processes referred to above? This is to ask about the sources of international law. Asked to list the sources of international law, state representatives and international legal scholars almost invariably point to Article 38(1) of the treaty establishing the International Court of Justice (ICJ), the Statute of the ICJ. We examine the ICJ—or World Court—at length in Chapter 3. For the present, consider the manner in which the sources of international law are described in Article 38(1). Is their description more consistent with positivist or natural law theories? Who, if anyone, appears to be the dominant player in "producing" each form of international law? What is the significance of the closing phrase of Article 38(1)(d)?

Statute of the International Court of Justice, 26 June 1945, Can TS 1945 No 7, in force 24 October 1945

Article 38

(1) The Court, whose function is to decide in accordance with international law such disputes as are submitted to it, shall apply:

(a) international conventions, whether general or particular, establishing rules expressly recognized by the contesting states;

(b) international custom, as evidence of a general practice accepted as law;

(c) the general principles of law recognized by civilized nations;

(d) subject to the provisions of Article 59 [which provides that the decision of the Court has no binding force except between the parties and in respect of that particular case], judicial decisions and the teachings of the most highly qualified publicists of the various nations, as subsidiary means for the determination of rules of law.

B. TREATIES

1) The Concept of Treaties

The best known source of international law is the "treaty," referred to in Article 38(1)(a) of the Statute of the ICJ as "international conventions, whether general or particular . . ." Examples include: the Charter of the United Nations[1] (the constitutive instrument of the UN); the International Covenant on Civil and Political Rights[2] and the International Covenant on Economic, Social and Cultural Rights[3] (the two most important multilateral human rights treaties); the Agreement between the United Nations and the Government of Sierra Leone on the Establishment of a Special Court for Sierra Leone[4] (providing for the prosecution of serious international crimes committed in Sierra Leone); the Canada-Israel Free Trade Agreement[5] (a bilateral agreement liberalizing trade between the two parties); and many others. At the time of writing, Canada is a party to approximately 2,500 treaties that are in force.

Treaties are, in some sense, international "contracts"[6] between states and/or certain international organizations, setting out rules that bind, as a matter of international law, the parties to them in their relations with one another. These agreements can be bilateral (between two parties) or multilateral (between more than two parties).[7] Treaties also go by various names, including: treaty, covenant, protocol, agreement, procès-verbal, exchange of notes, exchange of letters, joint communiqué, charter, statute, and more. Article 38(1)(a) of the Statute of the ICJ (itself a treaty, notwithstanding the use of "Statute" in its title) uses one of the most common terms to refer to a treaty as a source of international law, namely "convention." While historical, political, or other reasons may account for the

---

1   26 June 1945, Can TS 1945 No 7, in force 24 October 1945 [UN Charter].

2   16 December 1966, 999 UNTS 171, Can TS 1976 No 47, in force 23 March 1976 [ICCPR].

3   16 December 1996, 993 UNTS 3, Can TS 1976 No 46, in force 3 January 1976 [ICESR].

4   16 January 2002, 2178 UNTS 137, in force 12 April 2002.

5   31 July 1996, Can TS 1997 No 49, in force 1 January 1997. See also *Canada-Israel Free Trade Agreement Implementation Act*, SC 1996, c 33.

6   The domestic law notion of "contract" is used only by way of analogy here, and contracts in the strict sense should not be confused with treaties. An essential distinction between the two is that contracts are governed by domestic law whereas treaties are governed by international law.

7   A particular type of multilateral treaty, known as a "plurilateral" treaty, is recognized by some authors and in the practice of some states: see for example Anthony Aust, *Modern Treaty Law and Practice*, 2d ed (Cambridge: Cambridge University Press, 2007) at 139 ("The term 'plurilateral' . . . describes a treaty negotiated between a limited number of states with a particular interest in the subject matter").

use of a particular term as part of a treaty's title, the international legal effect of a treaty does not vary depending on the word used to designate it.

In domestic legal systems, the existence of a legally binding contract depends on a comprehensive body of law governing the creation, operation, and termination of contracts. So too in the international legal system: the creation, operation, and termination of treaties are governed by a body of international law known as "treaty law," or the "law of treaties." The most notable source of treaty law is itself a treaty: the Vienna Convention on the Law of Treaties (VCLT), which codifies the most important rules governing the formation, legal effects, and termination of treaties. While the VCLT lacks universal adherence by states—at the time of writing it has 113 states parties, not including key states such as the United States, France, and India—commentators and states themselves usually regard most of its provisions as reflecting rules of customary international law. We discuss customary international law in detail below. For present purposes, to the extent the VCLT reflects rules of customary international law, those rules are binding on all states regardless of whether they are, strictly speaking, parties to the VCLT. Most of the VCLT is thus a convenient reference point for the law of treaties binding on all states.

2) The Legal Essence of Treaties

In the above section we examined in general terms the concept of treaties. We turn now to a more detailed examination of the essential international legal requirements for treaties. In other words, what are the indispensable features of an agreement if it is to be considered a "treaty"? Consider first the following excerpt from the VCLT:

Vienna Convention on the Law of Treaties, 23 May 1969, 1155 UNTS 331, Can TS 1980 No 37, in force 27 January 1980

Article 1
Scope of the present Convention
The present Convention applies to treaties between States.

Article 2
Use of terms
1. For the purposes of the present Convention:
    (a) "treaty" means an international agreement concluded between States in written form and governed by international law, whether embodied in a single instrument or in two or more related instruments and whatever its particular designation; . . .

Article 3
International agreements not within the scope of the present Convention
The fact that the present Convention does not apply to international agreements concluded between States and other subjects of international law or between such other subjects of international law, or to international agreements not in written form, shall not affect:
    (a) the legal force of such agreements;
    (b) the application to them of any of the rules set forth in the present Convention to which they would be subject under international law independently of the Convention;

(c) the application of the Convention to the relations of States as between themselves under international agreements to which other subjects of international law are also parties.

. . .

Article 6
Capacity of States to conclude treaties
Every State possesses capacity to conclude treaties.

Beyond the fundamental requirement of an "international agreement . . . governed by international law," the foregoing articles raise two key issues: (1) who may be a party to an international agreement if it is to be considered a treaty, and (2) in order to constitute a treaty, must an agreement assume any particular form?

On the first of these issues, perhaps the most notable feature of the opening articles of the VCLT is their repeated reference to "states." Indeed, the very definition of "treaty" in Article 1(a) envisages an agreement between states, and not between states and other entities. This reflects the vast preponderance of treaty practice: historically, *only* states had the power to conclude treaties, and it remains the case that most treaties are still concluded between states alone. It is this practical reality that explains the focus placed by the drafters of the VCLT on the role of states in treaty formation.

However, that focus is somewhat misleading, as signalled by Article 3 of the VCLT above. In fact, modern international treaty law also contemplates that certain international organizations, also known as intergovernmental organizations, may become parties to treaties. Whether any particular international organization, such as the UN, has this ability or not largely depends on the nature and extent of the powers conferred upon it by the states establishing it. This is a point explored in greater detail in Chapter 3, where we consider the issue of international legal personality. However, the fact that states have clearly bestowed treaty-participation powers upon some international organizations prompted the conclusion in 1986 of a treaty dealing specifically with treaties to which international organizations are parties: the Vienna Convention on the Law of Treaties between States and International Organizations or between International Organizations.[8] The provisions of this treaty largely mirror those of the 1969 VCLT. While the 1986 treaty is not in force, most of its provisions reflect extant customary international law and thus their content is binding on states and relevant international organizations. (For ease of reference in the discussion that follows, we will refer only to states as being parties to treaties, although it should be remembered that many international organizations may also be parties to treaties.)

This, however, is the extent of international law's flexibility when it comes to the range of entities that may participate in treaties. Thus, international law does not recognize as a "treaty" an agreement between a state (or international organization) and an individual, corporation, or other non-state entity. Consider how, in the following case, the ICJ resists concluding that an agreement between a state and a non-state actor — in this case, an oil company — constitutes a treaty.

---

8   21 March 1986, UN Doc A/CONF.129/15 (not yet in force).

Anglo-Iranian Oil Co Case (Jurisdiction) (United Kingdom v Iran), Judgment, [1952] ICJ
Rep 93 at 111–12

[In 1951, the Government of Iran undertook a programme of nationalization of the country's oil industry. Anglo-Iranian Oil, an oil company incorporated in the United Kingdom but doing business in Iran, was adversely affected by this new policy. The UK brought the company's resulting claim against Iran to the ICJ. As Iran had only consented to the compulsory jurisdiction of the Court in respect of disputes arising out of treaties to which it was a party, a preliminary issue was whether the company's claim arose out of such a treaty. The UK claimed that an agreement concluded in 1933 between the company and Iran, pursuant to settlement of a prior dispute between the two states, was such a treaty, and that Iran's nationalization policy violated that treaty.]

The Court will now consider whether the settlement in 1933 of the dispute between the Government of the United Kingdom and the Government of Iran relating to the D'Arcy Concession, through the mediation of the Council of the League of Nations, resulted, as is claimed by the United Kingdom, in any agreement between the two Governments which may be regarded as a treaty or convention. . . .

The United Kingdom maintains that . . . the Government of Iran undertook certain treaty obligations towards the Government of the United Kingdom. It endeavours to establish those obligations by contending that the agreement signed by the Iranian Government with the Anglo-Persian Oil Company on April 29th, 1933, has a double character, the character of being at once a concessionary contract between the Iranian Government and the Company and a treaty between the two Governments. It is further argued by the United Kingdom that even if the settlement reached in 1933 only amounted to a tacit or an implied agreement, it must be considered to be within the meaning of the term "treaties or conventions". . . .

The Court cannot accept the view that the contract signed between the Iranian Government and the Anglo-Persian Oil Company has a double character. It is nothing more than a concessionary contract between a government and a foreign corporation. The United Kingdom Government is not a party to the contract; there is no privity of contract between the Government of Iran and the Government of the United Kingdom. Under the contract the Iranian Government cannot claim from the United Kingdom Government any rights which it may claim from the Company, nor can it be called upon to perform towards the United Kingdom Government any obligations which it is bound to perform towards the Company. The document bearing the signatures of the representatives of the Iranian Government and the Company has a single purpose: the purpose of regulating the relations between that Government and the Company in regard to the concession. It does not regulate in any way the relations between the two Governments. . . .

The second issue raised by the first several provisions of the VCLT is whether an agreement must assume any particular form to be considered a valid and binding treaty. Contrast Article 2(1)(a), which defines a treaty as an international agreement in "written form," with Article 3, which indicates that this limitation on the scope of the VCLT does not affect the legal force of agreements not in written form. This clearly suggests a degree of flexibility in treaty law generally with respect to the form a treaty may assume. Consider the following case.

Maritime Delimitation and Territorial Questions between Qatar and Bahrain, Jurisdiction and Admissibility, Judgment, [1994] ICJ Rep 112

[In 1976, Qatar and Bahrain agreed to third party mediation of their maritime boundary dispute by the King of Saudi Arabia. No progress was made until 1987, when the Saudi King sent letters in identical terms to each party proposing that "[a]ll the disputed matters shall be referred to the International Court of Justice, at The Hague, for a final ruling binding upon both parties, who shall have to execute its terms." This proposal was accepted in reply letters from the two heads of state. There nevertheless ensued two further years of unsuccessful negotiations on the specific formulation of the issues to be submitted to the Court. At a meeting in 1990, Qatar indicated, orally, that it could accept a previously proposed Bahraini formulation. Following the meeting, the foreign ministers of Bahrain, Qatar, and Saudi Arabia signed minutes recording that they had reaffirmed their prior agreement to submit the dispute to the Court, that they would continue to negotiate the formulation of the issues to be submitted to the Court for a defined period, and that failing agreement, "the parties may submit the matter to the International Court of Justice in accordance with the Bahraini formula, which has been accepted by Qatar." When the parties failed to agree on a formulation by the end of the defined period, Qatar submitted the dispute to the Court using the Bahraini formula.]

. . . 22. The Parties agree that the exchanges of letters of December 1987 constitute an international agreement with binding force in their mutual relations. Bahrain however maintains that the Minutes of 25 December 1990 were no more than a simple record of negotiations . . . ; that accordingly they did not rank as an international agreement and could not, therefore, serve as a basis for the jurisdiction of the Court.

23. The Court would observe, in the first place, that international agreements may take a number of forms and be given a diversity of names. Article 2, paragraph (1) (a), of the Vienna Convention on the Law of Treaties of 23 May 1969 provides that for the purposes of that Convention,

> "'treaty' means an international agreement concluded between States in written form and governed by international law, whether embodied in a single instrument or in two or more related instruments and whatever its particular designation."

Furthermore, as the Court said, in a case concerning a joint communiqué,

> "it knows of no rule of international law which might preclude a joint communiqué from constituting an international agreement to submit a dispute to arbitration or judicial settlement" (*Aegean Sea Continental Shelf* . . .)

In order to ascertain whether an agreement of that kind has been concluded, "the Court must have regard above all to its actual terms and to the particular circumstances in which it was drawn up" (*ibid.*). . . .

25. . . . [T]he 1990 Minutes include a reaffirmation of obligations previously entered into; they entrust King Fahd with the task of attempting to find a solution to the dispute during a period of six months; and, lastly, they address the circumstances under which the Court could be seised after May 1991. Accordingly, and contrary to the contentions of Bahrain,

the Minutes are not a simple record of a meeting . . .; they do not merely give an account of discussions and summarize points of agreement and disagreement. They enumerate the commitments to which the Parties have consented. They thus create rights and obligations in international law for the Parties. They constitute an international agreement.

26. Bahrain however maintains that the signatories of the Minutes never intended to conclude an agreement of this kind. . . .

27. The Court does not find it necessary to consider what might have been the intentions of the Foreign Minister of Bahrain or, for that matter, those of the Foreign Minister of Qatar. The two Ministers signed a text recording commitments accepted by their Governments, some of which were to be given immediate application. Having signed such a text, the Foreign Minister of Bahrain is not in a position subsequently to say that he intended to subscribe only to a "statement recording a political understanding", and not to an international agreement.

28. Bahrain however bases its contention, that no international agreement was concluded, also upon another argument. It maintains that the subsequent conduct of the Parties showed that they never considered the 1990 Minutes to be an agreement of this kind; and that not only was this the position of Bahrain, but it was also that of Qatar. Bahrain points out that Qatar waited until June 1991 before it applied to the United Nations Secretariat to register the Minutes of December 1990 under Article 102 of the Charter; and moreover that Bahrain objected to such registration. Bahrain also observes that, contrary to what is laid down in Article 17 of the Pact of the League of Arab States, Qatar did not file the 1990 Minutes with the General Secretariat of the League; nor did it follow the procedures required by its own Constitution for the conclusion of treaties. This conduct showed that Qatar, like Bahrain, never considered the 1990 Minutes to be an international agreement.

29. The Court would observe that an international agreement or treaty that has not been registered with the Secretariat of the United Nations may not, according to the provisions of Article 102 of the Charter, be invoked by the parties before any organ of the United Nations. Non-registration or late registration, on the other hand, does not have any consequence for the actual validity of the agreement, which remains no less binding upon the parties. The Court therefore cannot infer from the fact that Qatar did not apply for registration of the 1990 Minutes until six months after they were signed that Qatar considered, in December 1990, that those Minutes did not constitute an international agreement. The same conclusion follows as regards the non-registration of the text with the General Secretariat of the Arab League. Nor is there anything in the material before the Court which would justify deducing from any disregard by Qatar of its constitutional rules relating to the conclusion of treaties that it did not intend to conclude, and did not consider that it had concluded, an instrument of that kind; nor could any such intention, even if shown to exist, prevail over the actual terms of the instrument in question. Accordingly Bahrain's argument on these points also cannot be accepted.

30. The Court concludes that the Minutes of 25 December 1990, like the exchanges of letters of December 1987, constitute an international agreement creating rights and obligations for the Parties. . . .

Thus, a written record of an agreement, even if informally drawn up and not having the outward appearance of a formal treaty, can give rise to binding treaty relations. Can an exchange of oral statements do the same? Consider the following decision of the Permanent Court of International Justice (PCIJ), the ICJ's predecessor.

Legal Status of Eastern Greenland (Denmark v Norway) (1933), PCIJ (Ser A/B) No 53 at 70–71

[In 1931, Norway proclaimed sovereignty over Eastern Greenland. Denmark, itself claiming sovereignty over the whole of Greenland, instituted proceedings against Norway in the PCIJ, contending that Norway had "by treaty or otherwise herself recognized Danish sovereignty." In particular, the Danish government had, in the course of the peace negotiations following World War I, offered assurances to Norway that it (Denmark) would not object to the Norwegian claim to Spitzbergen. In return, the Danish government, through one of its ministers, had sought the assurance of the Norwegian foreign minister that Norway would not contest Denmark's claim to sovereignty over Greenland.]

. . . [It] can hardly be denied that what Denmark was asking of Norway ("not to make any difficulties in the settlement of the [Greenland] question") was equivalent to what she was indicating her readiness to concede in the Spitzbergen question (to refrain from opposing "the wishes of Norway in regard to the settlement of this question"). What Denmark desired to obtain from Norway was that the latter should do nothing to obstruct the Danish plans in regard to Greenland. The declaration which the Minister for Foreign Affairs gave on July 22nd, 1919, on behalf of the Norwegian Government, was definitely affirmative: "I told the Danish Minister today that the Norwegian Government would not make any difficulty in the settlement of this question."

The Court considers it beyond all dispute that a reply of this nature given by the Minister for Foreign Affairs on behalf of his Government in response to a request by the diplomatic representative of a foreign Power, in regard to a question falling within his province, is binding upon the country to which the Minister belongs. . . .

Consider the implications of treaty law's flexibility with respect to issues of form. For example, what are the consequences for the actions and statements of senior representatives of states and international organizations? Are there broader consequences for the certainty and predictability of the legal obligations states and international organizations owe to one another? Is there reason to believe that the content of those obligations would differ if the formal requirements for treaties were more exacting and, if so, would the differences be, in general, desirable? Is a state more likely to respect a legal obligation to which it has committed formally, or one that results from informal exchanges such as those considered in the foregoing cases?

In light of the foregoing materials, what are the essential attributes of a treaty?

3) Treaty-Making

a) The Flexibility of Treaty-Making Practice

In this section, we move from the legal characteristics of treaties to focus on the process by which most treaties are made. We will see that the VCLT contemplates a complex, multi-step process for the creation of treaties, including the accreditation of persons to conduct negotiations on behalf of each state; the negotiation, adoption, and authentication of a final version of a new treaty text; the signification of a state's consent to be bound by the treaty; and the entry into force of the treaty.

These formalities obviously have little application in the case of treaty obligations arising from the informal processes illustrated in the preceding section. Even in more deliberate treaty-making settings, moreover, many of the VCLT's treaty-making requirements are "default" practices subject to modification by mutual consent of the parties negotiating a treaty. Thus, it is not uncommon for the parties first to address and agree upon a number of matters related to the manner in which the eventual treaty is to be negotiated and brought into force. For example, in a multilateral context, the negotiating parties may agree that adoption of the text requires consensus or unanimity, rather than a two-thirds majority as provided in the VCLT. Of course, while the negotiating parties are free to agree to depart from elements of the treaty-making process described in the VCLT, the departure must not be so fundamental as to compromise the essential treaty elements reviewed in the previous section. If it is, the entire purpose of the enterprise—the conclusion of a valid and legally binding agreement—will be undermined.

Notwithstanding their largely provisional nature, the treaty-making provisions of the VCLT nevertheless provide a convenient set of default rules that will govern in the absence of special agreement by the negotiating parties to the contrary. They also reflect a particular body of treaty practice that has developed under the influence of international organizations such as the United Nations, which have been active in proposing treaty projects and providing fora in which states may negotiate them. One scholar has described the practice as follows:

> Neither the United Nations nor any of its specialized agencies was conceived as a legislative body. Their charters and governing instruments contemplated that their objectives would be carried out mainly through recommendations aimed at coordinating (or "harmonizing") the actions of their member states. The authority to impose mandatory rules was limited (with some exceptions) to the internal administration of the organization in question. . . . What was not fully realized at first is that the UN political bodies—though denied legislative power—could act like legislatures by adopting law-making treaties and declarations of law. Their recommendations did not have to remain merely requests or wishes if the collective will of governments supported more authoritative outcomes. . . .
>
> The most obvious instrument of lawmaking in the UN system is the multilateral "norm-creating" treaty. Hundreds of such treaties have been concluded; they were initiated, negotiated and adopted by UN organs or by international conferences under the aegis of a UN body. Their subjects have been as diverse as the functions of the UN organizations. Many deal with problems that are technical and seemingly arcane. Others are addressed to problems affecting ordinary people: health, food, education, human rights, pollution, transportation, television. . . .
>
> Their genesis in the UN system involves an apparent "democratization" of lawmaking markedly different from traditional treaty making and contemporary treaty negotiation by a few states. In the UN system the rule is that all member states have a right to participate

in the negotiation and adoption process. They generally do so on the basis of "sovereign equality." Decisions are usually taken by simple or two-thirds majority vote. . . .[9]

b) The Doctrine of Intertemporal Law Applied to Treaty-Making

Before proceeding to a detailed review of the VCLT's treaty-making process, however, let us voice a word of caution: like the rest of international law, the law of treaties has evolved. International law is replete with old treaties concluded in eras governed by different treaty rules. How then to assess the current status of these "legacy" treaties? The answer to this question is to rely on the doctrine of intertemporal law. We return to this concept in other contexts in Chapters 4 and 12. For present purposes, however, the doctrine of intertemporal law dictates that the validity of bygone treaty practice is to be assessed according to the law of treaties that governed at the time of that practice. Consider the following case:

> ### Case Concerning Right of Passage over Indian Territory (Portugal v India), Merits, [1960] ICJ Rep 6 at 37
>
> [Portugal relied upon an eighteenth-century treaty between itself and local Indian rulers (the Marathas) by which the latter had conferred sovereignty on Portugal over certain enclaves, as well as a right of passage to and from such enclaves. India objected to Portugal's reliance on the treaty, in part because India maintained it had not been validly concluded.]
>
> . . . India objects on various grounds that what is alleged to be the Treaty of 1779 was not validly entered into and never became in law a treaty binding upon the Marathas. The Court's attention has, in this connection, been drawn *inter alia* to the divergence between the different texts of the Treaty placed before the Court and to the absence of any text accepted as authentic by both parties and attested by them or by their duly authorized representatives. The Court does not consider it necessary to deal with these and other objections raised by India to the form of the Treaty and the procedure by means of which agreement upon its terms was reached. It is sufficient to state that the validity of a treaty concluded as long ago as the last quarter of the eighteenth century, in the conditions then prevailing in the Indian Peninsula, should not be judged upon the basis of practices and procedures which have since developed only gradually. The Marathas themselves regarded the Treaty of 1779 as valid and binding upon them, and gave effect to its provisions. The Treaty is frequently referred to as such in subsequent formal Maratha documents, including the two *sanads* of 1783 and 1785, which purport to have been issued in pursuance of the Treaty. The Marathas did not at any time cast any doubt upon the validity or binding character of the Treaty. . . .

c) The Treaty-Making Process under the Vienna Convention on the Law of Treaties

The obvious starting point in concluding a treaty is the negotiation of its terms. Individuals represent states at these negotiations. The first step is, therefore, to ensure that the right individuals are present and properly represent their sending states.

---

9   Oscar Schachter, "United Nations Law" (1994) 88 AJIL 1 at 1–2.

i) Accreditation of State Representatives

International law traditionally viewed a given individual as the appropriate agent of the state where that person possessed "full powers" — essentially, a document from a competent state authority designating an individual as competent to represent and exercise powers on behalf of the state in relation to an international issue or negotiation. The VCLT preserves the concept of "full powers," but also broadens the range of actors presumed to properly represent a state in a treaty negotiation context.

> **Vienna Convention on the Law of Treaties, 23 May 1969, 1155 UNTS 331, Can TS 1980 No 37, in force 27 January 1980**
>
> *Article 7*
>
> *Full powers*
>
> 1. A person is considered as representing a State for the purpose of adopting or authenticating the text of a treaty or for the purpose of expressing the consent of the State to be bound by a treaty if:
>
> > (a) he produces appropriate full powers; or
> >
> > (b) it appears from the practice of the States concerned or from other circumstances that their intention was to consider that person as representing the State for such purposes and to dispense with full powers.
>
> 2. In virtue of their functions and without having to produce full powers, the following are considered as representing their State:
>
> > (a) Heads of State, Heads of Government and Ministers for Foreign Affairs, for the purpose of performing all acts relating to the conclusion of a treaty;
> >
> > (b) heads of diplomatic missions, for the purpose of adopting the text of a treaty between the accrediting State and the State to which they are accredited;
> >
> > (c) representatives accredited by States to an international conference or to an international organization or one of its organs, for the purpose of adopting the text of a treaty in that conference, organization or organ.

Who determines Canada's representative in this treaty-making process? The answer to this question turns on which level and branch of government is constitutionally empowered to negotiate and bind Canada to an international treaty. Remarkably, treaty-making power is not squarely addressed in Canada's enacted constitution.[10] Section 132 of the *Constitution Act, 1867* does confer on Parliament and the Government of Canada the power to perform the obligations of Canada under treaties between the British Empire and other states, but that provision is now largely spent and does not in any event address the power to make treaties on behalf of Canada.[11] Nevertheless, judicial opinion[12]

---

10 By contrast, Australia's constitution, adopted after Canada's, does contain an express "external affairs" power: *An Act to Constitute the Commonwealth of Australia, 1990*, 63 & 64 Vict, c 12, s 51(xxix).

11 *Constitution Act, 1867*, 30 & 31 Vict, c 3, s 132.

12 *Reference re The Weekly Rest in Industrial Undertakings Act, The Minimum Wages Act, and The Limitation of Hours of Work Act*, [1936] SCR 461 at 488–89, Duff CJ, rev'd on other grounds *A-G Canada v A-G Ontario*, [1937] AC 326 (JCPC) [*Labour Conventions* case]. See also *Thomson v Thomson*, [1994] 3 SCR 551 at paras 112–14, L'Heureux-Dubé & McLachlin JJ.

confirms the widely held view that it is only the federal government that is empowered to enter into treaties on behalf of Canada.[13] That said, some provinces (most notably Quebec) regularly urge that they must have a role in treaty negotiations involving areas of provincial jurisdiction. The Quebec government describes its view this way:

> On matters within its jurisdiction, the Government of Québec hopes that a formal and predictable framework will ensure its participation within Canadian delegations during the deliberations or conferences of international organizations. In order to make this possible, Québec must be able to participate fully in all stages of . . . negotiations . . . relating to its responsibilities. . . . The approach outlined for international organizations must also serve as the model for the Government of Québec's participation in agreements which the federal government negotiates with other countries or groups of countries and which affect Québec's responsibilities.[14]

At the federal level, it is the executive branch of government that has the power to make or enter into treaties, as part of the prerogative power over the conduct of foreign affairs. In the words of Allan Gotlieb:

> [T]he power to make, or enter into, a treaty is possessed by the Crown. It is therefore a power that belongs to the executive branch of the Canadian Government, and not to the Parliament of Canada. The capacity of the Crown to enter into treaties derives from the common law of England which recognized in the sovereign a number of "prerogative" powers, some of which the Crown, both in England and Canada, has continued to possess to this day. . . .
>
> Prominent among the prerogative powers are those in the field of foreign affairs. . . . In Canada, as in England, these prerogative powers in the field of foreign affairs, including the treaty-making power, are exercised on the advice of the ministers of the Crown. This means, in effect, that the treaty-making power in Canada is exercised by the Governor-General in Council on the advice of the Canadian ministers, and in particular, the minister responsible for foreign relations [the minister of foreign affairs].[15]

Indeed, by an Act of Parliament, the minister of foreign affairs is given primacy in overseeing Canada's international relations. Section 10 of the *Department of Foreign Affairs and International Trade Act*, RSC 1985, c E-22, reads, in part, as follows:

---

13 See, for example, Hon Paul Martin Sr, Secretary of State for External Affairs, *Federalism and International Relations* (Ottawa: Queen's Printer, 1968) at 11–33; GL Morris, "The Treaty-Making Power: A Canadian Dilemma" (1967) 45 Can Bar Rev 478 at 484. For an overview of arguments advanced by some scholars in favour of a provincial treaty-making power, see Claude Emanuelli, *Droit international public: Contribution à l'étude du droit international selon une perspective canadienne*, 3e édition (Montréal: Wilson & Lafleur, 2010) at 92–94; but see Peter W Hogg, *Constitutional Law of Canada*, 5th ed (Toronto: Carswell, 2007), vol I at 342–43.

14 Ministère des Relations internationales (Québec), *Québec's International Policy: Working in Concert* (Québec: Government of Québec, 2006) at 28 and 30, online: http://www.mrifce.gouv.qc.ca/Content/documents/en/Politique.pdf.

15 Allan E Gotlieb, *Canadian Treaty-Making* (Toronto: Butterworths, 1968) at 4–5 [Gotlieb].

(1) The powers, duties and functions of the Minister extend to and include all matters over which Parliament has jurisdiction, not by law assigned to any other department, board or agency of the Government of Canada, relating to the conduct of the external affairs of Canada, including international trade and commerce and international development.

(2) In exercising his powers and carrying out his duties and functions under this Act, the Minister shall . . .

(c) conduct and manage international negotiations as they relate to Canada; . . .

(j) foster the development of international law and its application in Canada's external relations. . . .

The legal primacy of the foreign minister gives that person oversight over the treaty-negotiation process, but this does not capture fully the practice employed by Canada. First, other departments of government are often involved in treaty negotiations touching on their specific areas of responsibility. For example, Environment Canada may participate in treaty negotiations dealing with environmental issues, as will the Canada Revenue Agency in negotiations dealing with tax matters.[16] Similarly, several federal government departments played a role, in their respective areas of responsibility, in the negotiation of the North American Free Trade Agreement and the General Agreement on Tariffs and Trade.[17] In other words, while the Department of Foreign Affairs, Trade and Development as a general rule takes the lead in international treaty negotiations, other government departments contribute expertise as required. Second, treaty negotiations are almost invariably conducted by government officials, with ministers playing a less direct role, such as providing negotiating instructions and formally expressing consent to be bound by the treaty once it has been concluded.

In Canadian practice, the conferral of full powers to negotiate and conclude treaties binding on Canada "normally take[s] the form of an order of the Governor in Council authorizing the Prime Minister, a minister or another Canadian representative to participate in the negotiations (at the conference) and ultimately to conclude and sign the treaty on behalf of Canada."[18] For example, by Order-in-Council PC 1998-2287 (adopted 16 December 1998), the Governor General in Council—essentially the federal cabinet—authorized "the Minister of Foreign Affairs (a) to sign, on behalf of the Government of Canada, the Rome Statute of the International Criminal Court, 1998, or (b) to execute and issue an Instrument of Full Powers authorizing [officials] to sign, on behalf of the Government of Canada, the Rome Statute of the International Criminal Court, 1998."

What if the person purporting to represent Canada lacks the requisite full powers, or is not a person presumed to have such powers under Article 7 of the VCLT? Article 8 of the VCLT sets out a simple rule: "An act relating to the conclusion of a treaty performed by a

16 See Laura Barnett, *Canada's Approach to the Treaty-Making Process* (Ottawa: Library of Parliament, 2012) at 1.

17 North American Free Trade Agreement between the Government of Canada, the Government of the United Mexican States and the Government of the United States of America, 17 December 1992, Can TS 1994 No 2, (1993) 32 ILM 289, in force 1 January 1994 [NAFTA]; General Agreement on Tariffs and Trade, 30 October 1947, 55 UNTS 187, Can TS 1948 No 31, in force 1 January 1948 [GATT]. See Daniel Dupras, *International Treaties: Canadian Practice* (Ottawa: Library of Parliament, 2000).

18 Daniel Dupras, *Canada's International Obligations under the Leading International Conventions on the Control of Narcotic Drugs* (Ottawa: Library of Parliament, 1998), Appendix I at ii.

person who cannot be considered under article 7 as authorized to represent a State for that purpose is without legal effect unless afterwards confirmed by that State."

ii) Finalization of the Treaty Text

Once negotiations by properly accredited representatives are complete, the text of the treaty is usually "adopted"—the step by which the negotiating process is formally ended—and "authenticated"—the step by which the text is verified as an accurate expression of the outcome of the negotiations. The process of adoption and authentication is described in the following provisions of the VCLT.

Vienna Convention on the Law of Treaties, 23 May 1969, 1155 UNTS 331, Can TS 1980 No 37, in force 27 January 1980

Article 9
Adoption of the text
1. The adoption of the text of a treaty takes place by the consent of all the States participating in its drawing up except as provided in paragraph 2.

2. The adoption of the text of a treaty at an international conference takes place by the vote of two thirds of the States present and voting, unless by the same majority they shall decide to apply a different rule.

Article 10
Authentication of the text
The text of a treaty is established as authentic and definitive:
    (a) by such procedure as may be provided for in the text or agreed upon by the States participating in its drawing up; or
    (b) failing such procedure, by the signature, signature *ad referendum* or initialling by the representatives of those States of the text of the treaty or of the Final Act of a conference incorporating the text.

iii) Expression of Consent to Be Bound

Adoption and authentication do not in themselves bind the negotiating states to the new treaty. Rather, adoption and authentication are the means by which negotiating states signify their agreement *to* the terms of the treaty. A fundamentally important further step is then necessary before any negotiating (or other) state can also be said to be bound *by* the terms of the treaty so agreed: it must express its consent to be so bound. There are numerous forms in which consent to be bound may be expressed.

Vienna Convention on the Law of Treaties, 23 May 1969, 1155 UNTS 331, Can TS 1980 No 37, in force 27 January 1980

Article 11
Means of expressing consent to be bound by a treaty
The consent of a State to be bound by a treaty may be expressed by signature, exchange of instruments constituting a treaty, ratification, acceptance, approval or accession, or by any other means if so agreed.

Article 12

Consent to be bound by a treaty expressed by signature

1. The consent of a State to be bound by a treaty is expressed by the signature of its representative when:

    (a) the treaty provides that signature shall have that effect;

    (b) it is otherwise established that the negotiating States were agreed that signature should have that effect; or

    (c) the intention of the State to give that effect to the signature appears from the full powers of its representative or was expressed during the negotiation.

2. For the purposes of paragraph 1:

    (a) the initialling of a text constitutes a signature of the treaty when it is established that the negotiating States so agreed;

    (b) the signature *ad referendum* of a treaty by a representative, if confirmed by his State, constitutes a full signature of the treaty.

Article 13

Consent to be bound by a treaty expressed by an exchange of instruments constituting a treaty

The consent of States to be bound by a treaty constituted by instruments exchanged between them is expressed by that exchange when:

    (a) the instruments provide that their exchange shall have that effect; or

    (b) it is otherwise established that those States were agreed that the exchange of instruments should have that effect.

Article 14

Consent to be bound by a treaty expressed by ratification, acceptance or approval

1. The consent of a State to be bound by a treaty is expressed by ratification when:

    (a) the treaty provides for such consent to be expressed by means of ratification;

    (b) it is otherwise established that the negotiating States were agreed that ratification should be required;

    (c) the representative of the State has signed the treaty subject to ratification; or

    (d) the intention of the State to sign the treaty subject to ratification appears from the full powers of its representative or was expressed during the negotiation.

2. The consent of a State to be bound by a treaty is expressed by acceptance or approval under conditions similar to those which apply to ratification.

Article 15

Consent to be bound by a treaty expressed by accession

The consent of a State to be bound by a treaty is expressed by accession when:

    (a) the treaty provides that such consent may be expressed by that State by means of accession;

    (b) it is otherwise established that the negotiating States were agreed that such consent may be expressed by that State by means of accession; or

    (c) all the parties have subsequently agreed that such consent may be expressed by that State by means of accession.

Article 16

Exchange or deposit of instruments of ratification, acceptance, approval or accession

Unless the treaty otherwise provides, instruments of ratification, acceptance, approval or accession establish the consent of a State to be bound by a treaty upon:

(a) their exchange between the contracting States;

(b) their deposit with the depositary; or

(c) their notification to the contracting States or to the depositary, if so agreed. . . .

Note the reference in Article 11 to the manifold ways in which consent to be bound by a treaty may be expressed by a state: "signature, exchange of instruments constituting a treaty, ratification, acceptance, approval or accession, or by any other means if so agreed." The VCLT itself expresses no preference for one or other of these approaches. Articles 12 to 15 make clear that such preferences are for the treaty itself to specify, or the negotiating states to otherwise determine.

The vast majority of treaty practice suggests that the mechanisms by which consent to be bound is commonly expressed fall into three classes: (1) a single-stage expression of consent by a negotiating state; (2) a two-stage expression of consent by a negotiating state; and (3) a single-stage expression of consent by a state that did not participate in the treaty negotiations.

Signature is the classic single-stage expression of consent to be bound by a negotiating state—as long as the treaty allows for consent to be expressed by that means, the negotiating states were otherwise agreed on the point, or the signing state clearly intends it to have such effect. In such cases, the initialling or signing of the treaty by the appropriate state official is both the beginning and end of the process by which a state signals consent to be bound. The state is thenceforth a "party" to the treaty. This approach is most commonly used in the bilateral treaty context.

In many circumstances, however, a state's constitutional requirements and traditions preclude immediate assumption of an international obligation without consultation with or approval by, for instance, the state's legislative branch. For example, Article II(2) of the US Constitution provides that the US president "shall have Power, by and with the Advice and Consent of the Senate, to make Treaties, provided two thirds of the Senators present concur." Treaty ratification by the United States generally depends, therefore, on the "advice and consent" of the Senate, a legislative body (although the US president, acting alone, can enter into treaties deemed to be executive agreements). Similar constitutional provisions, requiring the involvement of either elected legislatures or regional representative bodies, can be found in Ireland and Germany, among other countries. Even where there are no such domestic constitutional constraints, moreover, a negotiating state may wish to analyze the treaty text, as adopted and authenticated, before taking the final step of binding itself to the treaty. This usually arises in the context of multilateral treaty negotiations.

To accommodate these realities, therefore, the negotiating states may agree to a two-stage process for expressing consent to be bound. For example, the treaty may provide for signature, as a preliminary expression of support in principle for the treaty; followed by an additional step, by which a state in fact expresses its consent to be bound by the treaty. Usually known as ratification (but sometimes also as acceptance or approval), the precise form this supplementary step takes is determined by each negotiating state's own traditions (subject, of course, to any constraints imposed by the treaty itself), although it most often assumes the form of an instrument of ratification, acceptance, or approval clearly expressing the state's consent to be bound. In this two-stage scenario, a state that has signed but not ratified (or accepted or approved) the treaty is referred to as a "signatory," whereas a state that has taken the added step of ratifying (or accepting or approving) is referred to as a "party" to the treaty. It is not uncommon to find mistaken references, for example in media reports, to "signatories" of a treaty when the author is in fact describing those states that have consented to be bound by it; in law, the correct term for such states would be "parties." We will return, below, to the legal consequences of being a signatory but not a party to a treaty.

Signature followed by ratification, acceptance, or approval is, however, a process traditionally open only to those states that originally negotiated the treaty. If a non-negotiating state wishes subsequently to become a party to the treaty, it is only able to do so if the parties, the treaty, or both, so permit. If so permitted, the non-negotiating state becomes a party to the treaty by way of "accession," a single-stage process by which the acceding state expresses its consent to be bound. The precise process by which one accedes to a treaty is often specified in the treaty itself, but usually it simply requires deposit of a duly executed instrument of accession that clearly communicates the acceding state's consent to be bound by the treaty.

Once issued domestically, a state's instrument of ratification, acceptance, approval, or accession is either deposited with, or notified to, the body identified for that purpose in the treaty (often, in the case of multilateral treaties, the Secretary-General of the United Nations). Alternatively—particularly in the case of bilateral treaties or multilateral treaties between a small number of states—such instruments may be exchanged between or notified to the other state(s). It is only at the point of deposit, exchange, or notification that a state has expressed its consent to be bound—and thus becomes a party to the treaty.

In Canada, there is no legal requirement that treaties be approved by Parliament (or the provincial legislatures) before Canada can express its consent to be bound by them. As noted above, in Canada, signifying consent to be bound by a treaty is a power exercised by the federal executive branch, operating pursuant to the royal prerogative power over the conduct of foreign affairs. As a result, the federal government may sign and ratify or accede to an international treaty, binding Canada as a matter of international law, without any recourse to Parliament.[19]

That said, the federal government used to consider it worthwhile and expedient to seek parliamentary endorsement of a treaty prior to binding Canada to it.[20] Historically, this entirely voluntary practice was reserved for "important" treaties, including "peace treaties; defence treaties (including those imposing military sanctions); treaties on the imposition of economic sanctions; treaties on Canada's territorial jurisdiction (land and maritime frontiers, air space and near-earth space); trade treaties; treaties resulting in public expenditures (economic and technical aid programs, food aid programs, devel-

---

19   Gotlieb, above note 15 at 14.

20   See Joanna Harrington, "Redressing the Democratic Deficit in Treaty Law Making: (Re-)Establishing a Role for Parliament" (2005) 50 McGill LJ 465.

oping country loan programs); and treaties pertaining to international organizations."[21] Various private members' bills introduced in (but never enacted into law by) Parliament have from time to time proposed making this practice mandatory, some even proposing a requirement of parliamentary committee review of all treaties before ratification.

Similar such statutory obligations now exist in the United Kingdom. Since November 2011, the *Constitutional Reform and Governance Act 2010* provides that most treaties requiring ratification are to be laid before the UK Parliament, accompanied by explanatory memoranda, for at least twenty-one sitting days.[22] The *Act* also gives legal effect to a resolution of the House of Commons or Lords that a treaty should not be ratified.[23] A similar statutory rule requiring parliamentary scrutiny of treaties was proposed in 1995 in Australia, but that jurisdiction opted instead for an administrative approach involving treaty scrutiny by a committee, known as the Joint Standing Committee on Treaties (JSCOT), composed of members of both Houses of the Australian Parliament.[24]

As the scope of the royal prerogative is subject to curtailment by an Act of Parliament, the Parliament of Canada certainly would have the constitutional authority to enact changes to the treaty-making process in Canada similar to those enacted in the United Kingdom. Indeed, the minority Conservative government elected in Canada in early 2006 indicated an intention to pursue such legislative proposals during its mandate. In 2008, however, the same government instead adopted an administrative policy requiring the tabling of treaties in the House of Commons.[25] Pursuant to the 2008 policy, the government will table the text of treaties "following their adoption by signature or otherwise"[26] and will observe a waiting period of twenty-one sitting days before expressing Canada's consent to be bound by them. The purpose of the waiting period is to allow parliamentarians to initiate debate and request votes on motions regarding the treaty. Yet, the policy provides for exceptions to the tabling and waiting-period requirements in cases deemed "appropriate" by the prime minister—for example, where ratification of a treaty is urgently required. Bilateral treaties that do not involve a two-step approval process may also be excluded from the scope of the policy (although many bilateral treaties on such matters as double taxation and social security are drafted according to a pre-approved template).[27] Further, as the policy has no legal force in itself, the government only undertakes to "consider" any concerns raised by opposition parties during the twenty-one-day tabling period, and retains the sole authority to decide whether or not to bind Canada to the treaty.[28]

---

21 Anne-Marie Jacomy-Millette, *L'introduction et l'application des traités internationaux au Canada* (Paris: LGDJ, 1971) at 114, cited in Dupras, above note 18. See also Gotlieb, above note 15 at 15 *et seq.*

22 (UK), 2010, c 25, Part 2, brought into force by *The Constitutional Reform and Governance Act 2010 (Commencement No 3) Order 2010*, SI 2010 No 2703 (c 125).

23 *Constitutional Reform and Governance Act 2010*, ibid, s 20.

24 See further Joanna Harrington, "Scrutiny and Approval: The Role for Westminster-Style Parliaments in Treaty-Making" (2006) 55 ICLQ 121. On subsequent British developments, see Jill Barrett, "United Kingdom and Parliamentary Scrutiny of Treaties: Recent Reforms" (2011) 60 ICLQ 225.

25 See Government of Canada, "Policy on Tabling Treaties in Parliament" (25 January 2008), online: www. treaty-accord.gc.ca/procedures.aspx.

26 *Ibid* at para 4.

27 *Ibid* at para 6.2(c) (extending the policy, in the case of treaties for which there is no two-step approval process, only to *multilateral* treaties).

28 *Ibid* at para 6.6(a).

Along with the absence of any statutory obligation, these provisos make it clear that the policy does not formally change the legal or constitutional locus of the treaty-making power in Canada. That power remains vested in the federal executive branch as an aspect of the royal prerogative power over the conduct of foreign affairs.

Until and unless any such changes are legislated, therefore, the domestic process in Canada for becoming party to a treaty usually only legally requires issuance of an order in council by the federal cabinet authorizing a government representative to express Canada's consent to be bound by the treaty. For example, Order-in-Council 2000-1072 (adopted 5 July 2000) authorized "the Minister of Foreign Affairs to sign, on behalf of the Government of Canada, an Instrument of Ratification with respect to the Rome Statute of the International Criminal Court." This raises issues with respect to democratic control of Canada's treaty obligations. What arguments can be made to defend the democratic sufficiency of concentration of the Canadian treaty-making power in the hands of the federal executive? What are the "democratic deficits" of the process?[29] Is it sufficient that the 2008 policy reiterates the long-standing federal government practice of delaying ratification of or accession to treaties until any federal legislation required to implement the treaty has been enacted by Parliament?[30] As suggested by this last question, full appreciation of democratic control over the assumption of treaty obligations by Canada must also take into account the rules surrounding the domestic legal effect of treaties within Canada, a subject to which we return below.

If a state fails to follow the steps set out in the treaty by which consent to be bound may be expressed, can it have any obligations under the treaty? Consider the following case.

North Sea Continental Shelf, Judgment, [1969] ICJ Rep 3

[The then Federal Republic of Germany (also known as West Germany), along with Denmark and the Netherlands, had previously agreed on a partial delimitation of the continental shelf lying off their respective coasts but were unable to agree on certain key segments of the delimitation. They accordingly sought a ruling from the Court as to the "principles and rules of international law" that should govern the delimitation. Denmark and the Netherlands were parties to the 1958 Convention on the Continental Shelf,[31] Article 6 of which set out certain rules governing such delimitations. West Germany had signed but not ratified the Convention, but Denmark and the Netherlands argued that Germany was bound by its provisions on the basis of conduct exhibiting acceptance of its terms.]

26. . . . Denmark and the Netherlands have both signed and ratified the Convention, and are parties to it, the former since 10 June 1964, the latter since 20 March 1966. The Federal Republic was one of the signatories of the Convention, but has never ratified it, and is consequently not a party.

27. It is admitted on behalf of Denmark and the Netherlands that in these circumstances the Convention cannot, as such, be binding on the Federal Republic, in the sense of the

---

29 See further Harrington, above note 20.

30 "Policy on Tabling Treaties in Parliament," above note 25 at para 6.2(b).

31 29 April 1958, 499 UNTS 311, Can TS 1970 No 4, in force 10 June 1964 [1958 Convention on the Continental Shelf].

Republic being contractually bound by it. But it is contended that the Convention, or the régime of the Convention, and in particular of Article 6, has become binding on the Federal Republic in another way—namely because, by conduct, by public statements and proclamations, and in other ways, the Republic has unilaterally assumed the obligations of the Convention; or has manifested its acceptance of the conventional régime; or has recognized it as being generally applicable to the delimitation of continental shelf areas. It has also been suggested that the Federal Republic had held itself out as so assuming, accepting or recognizing, in such a manner as to cause other States, and in particular Denmark and the Netherlands, to rely on the attitude thus taken up.

28. As regards these contentions, it is clear that only a very definite, very consistent course of conduct on the part of a State in the situation of the Federal Republic could justify the Court in upholding them; and, if this had existed—that is to say if there had been a real intention to manifest acceptance or recognition of the applicability of the conventional ré-gime—then it must be asked why it was that the Federal Republic did not take the obvious step of giving expression to this readiness by simply ratifying the Convention. In principle, when a number of States, including the one whose conduct is invoked, and those invoking it, have drawn up a convention specifically providing for a particular method by which the intention to become bound by the régime of the convention is to be manifested—namely by the carrying out of certain prescribed formalities (ratification, accession), it is not lightly to be presumed that a State which has not carried out these formalities, though at all times fully able and entitled to do so, has nevertheless somehow become bound in another way. Indeed if it were a question not of obligation but of rights,—if, that is to say, a State which, though entitled to do so, had not ratified or acceded, attempted to claim rights under the convention, on the basis of a declared willingness to be bound by it, or of conduct evincing acceptance of the conventional régime, it would simply be told that, not having become a party to the convention it could not claim any rights under it until the professed willing-ness and acceptance had been manifested in the prescribed form. . . .

30. Having regard to these considerations of principle, it appears to the Court that only the existence of a situation of estoppel could suffice to lend substance to this conten-tion,—that is to say if the Federal Republic were now precluded from denying the ap-plicability of the conventional régime, by reason of past conduct, declarations, etc., which not only clearly and consistently evinced acceptance of that régime, but also had caused Denmark or the Netherlands, in reliance on such conduct, detrimentally to change pos-ition or suffer some prejudice. Of this there is no evidence whatever in the present case.

31. In these circumstances it seems to the Court that little useful purpose would be served by passing in review and subjecting to detailed scrutiny the various acts relied on by Denmark and the Netherlands as being indicative of the Federal Republic's acceptance of the régime of Article 6. . . .

32. . . . [I]t appears to the Court that none of the elements invoked is decisive; each is ultimately negative or inconclusive; all are capable of varying interpretations or explana-tions. . . . [I]t would certainly not be possible to draw the positive inference that the Fed-eral Republic, though not a party to the Convention, had accepted the régime of Article 6 in a manner binding upon itself.

33. The dangers of the doctrine here advanced by Denmark and the Netherlands, if it had to be given general application in the international law field, hardly need stressing. . . .

The two-stage process of signifying consent to be bound implies that a gap in time will exist between a state's signature and its subsequent ratification, acceptance, or approval of a treaty. A gap in time may also exist between the expression of a state's consent to be bound by a treaty and the treaty's entry into force. This may happen, for example, where the treaty's entry into force is delayed pending the occurrence of some event, such as the deposit of a required number of instruments of ratification.

In the first of these cases, the state has signed the treaty but has not expressed its consent to be bound by it. In the second, the state has expressed its consent to be bound by the treaty but the treaty itself provides that it does not come into force for parties to it until some future point in time. In both cases, it might seem logical to conclude that the state does not yet have any obligations in relation to the prospective treaty regime. However, treaty law provides otherwise, as illustrated by this provision in the VCLT:

Vienna Convention on the Law of Treaties, 23 May 1969, 1155 UNTS 331, Can TS 1980 No 37, in force 27 January 1980

Article 18
Obligation not to defeat the object and purpose of a treaty prior to its entry into force
A State is obliged to refrain from acts which would defeat the object and purpose of a treaty when:
  (a) it has signed the treaty or has exchanged instruments constituting the treaty subject to ratification, acceptance or approval, until it shall have made its intention clear not to become a party to the treaty; or
  (b) it has expressed its consent to be bound by the treaty, pending the entry into force of the treaty and provided that such entry into force is not unduly delayed.

Consider the section on "Performance of Treaty Obligations" below.[32] What is the distinction between being obliged to perform a treaty and being obliged not to defeat its object and purpose? Would the consequences of a breach of each obligation be the same? Can there be situations where the two obligations are coterminous?

In reviewing the significance of Article 18, consider the following materials concerning the actions of the United States, Israel, and Sudan in relation to the International Criminal Court.

Rome Statute of the International Criminal Court, 17 July 1998, 2187 UNTS 3, Can TS 2002 No 13, in force 1 July 2002

Article 125
Signature, ratification, acceptance, approval or accession
1. This Statute shall be open for signature by all States in Rome, at the headquarters of the Food and Agriculture Organization of the United Nations, on 17 July 1998. There-

---

32 See Section B(6)(a), below.

after, it shall remain open for signature in Rome at the Ministry of Foreign Affairs of Italy until 17 October 1998. After that date, the Statute shall remain open for signature in New York, at United Nations Headquarters, until 31 December 2000.

2. This Statute is subject to ratification, acceptance or approval by signatory States. Instruments of ratification, acceptance or approval shall be deposited with the Secretary-General of the United Nations.

3. This Statute shall be open to accession by all States. Instruments of accession shall be deposited with the Secretary-General of the United Nations.

The United States signed the Rome Statute on 31 December 2000, in the last days of the Clinton administration. Subsequently, in a letter dated 6 May 2002, the US Under Secretary of State for Arms Control and International Security in the Bush administration informed the UN Secretary-General of the following:[33]

Dear Mr. Secretary-General:

This is to inform you, in connection with the Rome Statute of the International Criminal Court adopted on July 17, 1998, that the United States does not intend to become a party to the treaty. Accordingly, the United States has no legal obligations arising from its signature on December 31, 2000. The United States requests that its intention not to become a party, as expressed in this letter, be reflected in the depositary's status lists relating to this treaty.

Sincerely,
John R. Bolton

Israel sent a similar letter to the UN Secretary-General on 28 August 2002, as did Sudan on 26 August 2008.

During the period between 31 December 2000 (the date of the US signature of the Rome Statute) and Under Secretary Bolton's letter of 6 May 2002, it could be argued that the United States had an obligation to do nothing that would defeat the object and purpose of the Rome Statute—assuming that Article 18 reflects customary international law (recall that the United States is not a party to the VCLT and thus not directly bound by Article 18).[34] Does Under Secretary Bolton's letter support or undermine such an argument? Under what circumstances could it be argued that Under Secretary Bolton's letter was itself a violation of such an obligation?

d) Entry into Force, Provisional Application, and Registration of Treaties

As suggested above, the entry into force of a treaty may be delayed with the consent or agreement of the negotiating states. For example, where meaningful performance of a treaty would require participation by several states, the treaty may provide that it will only come into force once a certain threshold number of states have either ratified or acceded to the treaty. Another technique is to specify, in the treaty, a date upon which it will come into

---

33 US Department of State Archives, online: http://2001-2009.state.gov/r/pa/prs/ps/2002/9968.htm.

34 Note that the customary status of the principle laid down in article 18 remains uncertain: see, for example, Aust, above note 7 at 117–18. Note that Israel is also not a party to the VCLT, although Sudan is.

force so as to permit negotiating states to take the necessary steps in their domestic legal orders, before the treaty comes into force, to ensure their future performance of the treaty's obligations. The VCLT provides for such special agreements between the negotiating states regarding entry into force of the treaty, and also provides a fall-back rule in the event no such agreement exists. It is even possible for the negotiating states to agree to apply certain provisions of the treaty "provisionally"—that is, pending its actual entry into force.

The idea that a treaty may provide for the date or event which is to trigger its coming into force, its provisional application pending entry into force or, as seen above, the process by which states may express their consent to be bound by it, raises a curious question. How can a treaty that is not yet in force, or is not yet binding upon certain states, have such legal effects? Is it not circular to say that a treaty may create legal requirements before it is in force? The law of treaties also supplies a rule to resolve any such apparent circularity.

Vienna Convention on the Law of Treaties, 23 May 1969, 1155 UNTS 331, Can TS 1980 No 37, in force 27 January 1980

Article 24
Entry into force
1. A treaty enters into force in such manner and upon such date as it may provide or as the negotiating States may agree.

2. Failing any such provision or agreement, a treaty enters into force as soon as consent to be bound by the treaty has been established for all the negotiating States.

3. When the consent of a State to be bound by a treaty is established on a date after the treaty has come into force, the treaty enters into force for that State on that date, unless the treaty otherwise provides.

4. The provisions of a treaty regulating the authentication of its text, the establishment of the consent of States to be bound by the treaty, the manner or date of its entry into force, reservations, the functions of the depositary and other matters arising necessarily before the entry into force of the treaty apply from the time of the adoption of its text.

Article 25
Provisional application
1. A treaty or a part of a treaty is applied provisionally pending its entry into force if:
    (a) the treaty itself so provides; or
    (b) the negotiating States have in some other manner so agreed.

2. Unless the treaty otherwise provides or the negotiating States have otherwise agreed, the provisional application of a treaty or a part of a treaty with respect to a State shall be terminated if that State notifies the other States between which the treaty is being applied provisionally of its intention not to become a party to the treaty.
. . .

Article 80
Registration and publication of treaties
1. Treaties shall, after their entry into force, be transmitted to the Secretariat of the United Nations for registration or filing and recording, as the case may be, and for publication.

2. The designation of a depositary shall constitute authorization for it to perform the acts specified in the preceding paragraph.

Sensing a need to clarify the precise legal significance of provisional application, the International Law Commission (ILC) — a UN body of international legal experts charged with codifying or progressively developing international law (and the same body that drafted the VCLT) — decided in 2012 to study the topic further.[35] At the time of writing, such further study is still in its preliminary stages.[36]

The registration process is also anticipated in the UN Charter. Article 102 provides:

1. Every treaty and every international agreement entered into by any Member of the United Nations after the present Charter comes into force shall as soon as possible be registered with the Secretariat and published by it.

2. No party to any such treaty or international agreement which has not been registered in accordance with the provisions of paragraph 1 of this Article may invoke that treaty or agreement before any organ of the United Nations.

The prohibition in Article 102(2) barring reliance on an unregistered treaty "before any organ of the United Nations" would include reliance on such a treaty in proceedings before the ICJ. As suggested by this provision, treaty registration is obviously taken seriously in the UN system. In part, the incorporation of strong registration provisions in the UN Charter was an attempt to deter the making of secret treaties, which historically have been blamed for destabilizing the international order. A similar obligation was included in the earlier Covenant of the League of Nations because secret treaties of alliance were thought to have contributed to the outbreak of World War I.[37] However, note that the penalty for failure to register a treaty in accordance with the UN Charter falls short of imposing any consequences for the continuing validity of the treaty itself: see, for example, paragraph 29 of the *Qatar v Bahrain* case reproduced in Section B(2) above.

How effective a deterrent to secret treaties is an inability to invoke them before a UN organ? How likely is it that a party to such a treaty would ever seek to do so?

4) Reservations

Reservations raise some of the most perplexing issues in treaty law. A reservation, as defined by Article 2(1)(d) of the VCLT, is "a unilateral statement, however phrased or named, made by a State, when signing, ratifying, accepting, approving or acceding to a treaty, whereby it purports to exclude or to modify the legal effect of certain provisions

---

35 *Report of the International Law Commission*, UN GAOR, 67th Sess, Supp No 10 at c VII, paras 140–55, UN Doc A/67/10 (2012) [*ILC Report 2012*].

36 See Juan Manuel Gómez-Robledo, Special Rapporteur, "First report on the provisional application of treaties", UN Doc A/CN.4/664 (2013).

37 Covenant of the League of Nations, 28 April 1919, (1919) 13 AJIL Supp 128, in force 10 January 1920, art 18: "Every treaty or international engagement entered into hereafter by any Member of the League shall be forthwith registered with the Secretariat and shall as soon as possible be published by it. No such treaty or international engagement shall be binding until so registered."

of the treaty in their application to that State." Treaty law has traditionally been hostile to reservations. After all, the intended effect of a reservation is to change, unilaterally, the deal negotiated by states.

Until the mid-twentieth century, the prevailing view in international law was that reservations were impermissible unless agreed to by all the parties to a treaty. That view was relaxed in the following advisory opinion of the ICJ, and subsequently in the VCLT itself. Note the trade-off raised in the ICJ's reasoning below: reservations may encourage increased adherence to a treaty, albeit at the possible expense of its coherence and integrity. This is at once the promise and threat of reservations.

Reservations to the Convention on Genocide, Advisory Opinion, [1951] ICJ Rep 15 at 21–30

[The UN General Assembly sought an advisory opinion from the Court on the following questions:

"In so far as concerns the [1948] Convention on the Prevention and Punishment of the Crime of Genocide in the event of a State ratifying or acceding to the Convention subject to a reservation . . .

I. Can the reserving State be regarded as being a party to the Convention while still maintaining its reservation if the reservation is objected to by one or more of the parties to the Convention but not by others?

II. If the answer to Question I is in the affirmative, what is the effect of the reservation as between the reserving State and: (a) The parties which object to the reservation? (b) Those which accept it? . . ."]

. . . [T]he Court observes that [Question I] refers, not to the possibility of making reservations to the Genocide Convention, but solely to the question whether a contracting State which has made a reservation can, while still maintaining it, be regarded as being a party to the Convention, when there is a divergence of views between the contracting parties concerning this reservation, some accepting the reservation, others refusing to accept it.

It is well established that in its treaty relations a State cannot be bound without its consent, and that consequently no reservation can be effective against any State without its agreement thereto. It is also a generally recognized principle that a multilateral convention is the result of an agreement freely concluded upon its clauses and that consequently none of the contracting parties is entitled to frustrate or impair, by means of unilateral decisions or particular agreements, the purpose and *raison d'être* of the convention. To this principle was linked the notion of the integrity of the convention as adopted, a notion which in its traditional concept involved the proposition that no reservation was valid unless it was accepted by all the contracting parties without exception, as would have been the case if it had been stated during the negotiations.

This concept, which is directly inspired by the notion of contract, is of undisputed value as a principle. However, as regards the Genocide Convention, it is proper to refer to a variety of circumstances which would lead to a more flexible application of this principle. Among these circumstances may be noted the clearly universal character of the United Nations under whose auspices the Convention was concluded, and the very wide degree of participation envisaged by Article XI of the Convention. Extensive participation in conventions of this type has already given rise to greater flexibility in the international practice concerning multilateral conventions. More general resort to reservations, very great allowance made for tacit assent to reservations, the existence of practices which go so far as to admit that the author of reservations which have been rejected by certain contracting parties is nevertheless to be regarded as a party to the convention in relation to those contracting parties that have accepted the reservations—all these factors are manifestations of a new need for flexibility in the operation of multilateral conventions.

It must also be pointed out that although the Genocide Convention was finally approved unanimously, it is nevertheless the result of a series of majority votes. The majority principle, while facilitating the conclusion of multilateral conventions, may also make it necessary for certain States to make reservations. This observation is confirmed by the great number of reservations which have been made of recent years to multilateral conventions.

In this state of international practice, it could certainly not be inferred from the absence of an article providing for reservations in a multilateral convention that the contracting States are prohibited from making certain reservations. Account should also be taken of the fact that the absence of such an article or even the decision not to insert such an article can be explained by the desire not to invite a multiplicity of reservations. The character of a multilateral convention, its purpose, provisions, mode of preparation and adoption, are factors which must be considered in determining, in the absence of any express provision on the subject, the possibility of making reservations, as well as their validity and effect.

Although it was decided during the preparatory work not to insert a special article on reservations, it is none the less true that the faculty for States to make reservations was contemplated at successive stages of the drafting of the Convention. . . .

The Court recognizes that an understanding was reached within the General Assembly on the faculty to make reservations to the Genocide Convention and that it is permitted to conclude therefrom that States becoming parties to the Convention gave their assent thereto. It must now determine what kind of reservations may be made and what kind of objections may be taken to them.

The solution of these problems must be found in the special characteristics of the Genocide Convention. The origins and character of that Convention, the objects pursued by the General Assembly and the contracting parties, the relations which exist between the provisions of the Convention, *inter se*, and between those provisions and these objects, furnish elements of interpretation of the will of the General Assembly and the parties. The origins of the Convention show that it was the intention of the United Nations to condemn and punish genocide as "a crime under international law" involving a denial of the right of existence of entire human groups, a denial which shocks the conscience of mankind and results in great losses to humanity, and which is contrary to moral law and to the spirit and aims of the United Nations. . . . The first consequence arising from this conception is that the principles underlying the Convention are principles which are recognized by civilized nations as binding on States, even without any conventional obligation. A second consequence is the universal character both of the condemnation of genocide and of the co-operation required "in order to liberate mankind from such an odious scourge" (Preamble to the Convention). The Genocide Convention was therefore intended by the General Assembly and by the contracting parties to be definitely universal in scope. It was in fact approved on December 9th, 1948, by a resolution which was unanimously adopted by fifty-six States.

The objects of such a convention must also be considered. The Convention was manifestly adopted for a purely humanitarian and civilizing purpose. It is indeed difficult to imagine a convention that might have this dual character to a greater degree, since its object on the one hand is to safeguard the very existence of certain human groups and on the other to confirm and endorse the most elementary principles of morality. In such a convention the contracting States do not have any interests of their own; they merely have, one and all, a common interest, namely, the accomplishment of those high purposes which are the *raison d'être* of the convention. Consequently, in a convention of this type one cannot speak of individual advantages or disadvantages to States, or of the maintenance of a perfect contractual balance between rights and duties. The high ideals which inspired the Convention provide, by virtue of the common will of the parties, the foundation and measure of all its provisions.

The foregoing considerations, when applied to the question of reservations, and more particularly to the effects of objections to reservations, lead to the following conclusions.

The object and purpose of the Genocide Convention imply that it was the intention of the General Assembly and of the States which adopted it that as many States as possible should participate. The complete exclusion from the Convention of one or more States would not only restrict the scope of its application, but would detract from the authority of the moral and humanitarian principles which are its basis. It is inconceivable that the contracting parties readily contemplated that an objection to a minor reservation should produce such a result. But even less could the contracting parties have intended to sacrifice the very object of the Convention in favour of a vain desire to secure as many participants as possible. The object and purpose of the Convention thus limit both the freedom of making reservations and that of objecting to them. It follows that it is the compatibility of a reservation with the object and purpose of the Convention that must furnish the criterion for the attitude of a State in making the reservation on accession as well as for the appraisal by a State in objecting to the reservation. Such is the rule of conduct which must guide every State in the appraisal which it must make, individually and from its own standpoint, of the admissibility of any reservation.

Any other view would lead either to the acceptance of reservations which frustrate the purposes which the General Assembly and the contracting parties had in mind, or to recognition that the parties to the Convention have the power of excluding from it the author of a reservation, even a minor one, which may be quite compatible with those purposes.

It has nevertheless been argued that any State entitled to become a party to the Genocide Convention may do so while making any reservation it chooses by virtue of its sovereignty. The Court cannot share this view. It is obvious that so extreme an application of the idea of State sovereignty could lead to a complete disregard of the object and purpose of the Convention.

On the other hand, it has been argued that there exists a rule of international law subjecting the effect of a reservation to the express or tacit assent of all the contracting parties. This theory rests essentially on a contractual conception of the absolute integrity of the convention as adopted. This view, however, cannot prevail if, having regard to the character of the convention, its purpose and its mode of adoption, it can be established that the parties intended to derogate from that rule by admitting the faculty to make reservations thereto.

It does not appear, moreover, that the conception of the absolute integrity of a convention has been transformed into a rule of international law. The considerable part which tacit assent has always played in estimating the effect which is to be given to reservations scarcely permits one to state that such a rule exists, determining with sufficient precision the effect of objections made to reservations. In fact, the examples of objections made to reservations appear to be too rare in international practice to have given rise to such a rule. . . . The opinion of the Secretary-General of the United Nations himself is embodied in the following passage of his report of September 21st, 1950: "While it is universally recognized that the consent of the other governments concerned must be sought before they can be bound by the terms of a reservation, there has not been unanimity either as to the procedure to be followed by a depositary in obtaining the necessary consent or as to the legal effect of a State's objecting to a reservation."

It may, however, be asked whether the General Assembly of the United Nations, in approving the Genocide Convention, had in mind the practice according to which the Secretary-General, in exercising his functions as a depositary, did not regard a reservation as definitively accepted until it had been established that none of the other contracting States objected to it. If this were the case, it might be argued that the implied intention of the contracting parties was to make the effectiveness of any reservation to the Genocide Convention conditional on the assent of all the parties.

The Court does not consider that this view corresponds to reality. It must be pointed out, first of all, that the existence of an administrative practice does not in itself constitute a decisive factor in ascertaining what views the contracting States to the Genocide Convention may have had concerning the rights and duties resulting therefrom. It must also be pointed out that there existed among the American States members both of the United Nations and of the Organization of American States, a different practice which goes so far as to permit a reserving State to become a party irrespective of the nature of the reservations or of the objections raised by other contracting States. The preparatory work of the Convention contains nothing to justify the statement that the contracting States implicitly had any definite practice in mind. Nor is there any such indication in the subsequent attitude of the contracting States: neither the reservations made by certain States nor the position adopted by other States towards those reservations permit the conclusion that assent to one or the other of these practices had been given. Finally, it is not without interest to note, in view of the preference generally said to attach to an established practice, that the debate on reservations to multilateral treaties which took place in the Sixth Committee at the fifth session of the General Assembly reveals a profound divergence of views, some delegations being attached to the idea of the absolute integrity of the Convention, others favouring a more flexible practice which would bring about the participation of as many States as possible.

It results from the foregoing considerations that Question I, on account of its abstract character, cannot be given an absolute answer. The appraisal of a reservation and the effect of objections that might be made to it depend upon the particular circumstances of each individual case.

Having replied to Question I, the Court will now examine Question II. . . .

The considerations which form the basis of the Court's reply to Question I are to a large extent equally applicable here. As has been pointed out above, each State which is a party to the Convention is entitled to appraise the validity of the reservation, and it exercises this right individually and from its own standpoint. As no State can be bound by a reservation to which it has not consented, it necessarily follows that each State objecting to it will or will not, on the basis of its individual appraisal within the limits of the criterion of the object and purpose stated above, consider the reserving State to be a party to the Convention. In the ordinary course of events, such a decision will only affect the relationship between the State making the reservation and the objecting State; on the other hand, as will be pointed out later, such a decision might aim at the complete exclusion from the Convention in a case where it was expressed by the adoption of a position on the jurisdictional plane.

The disadvantages which result from this possible divergence of views—which an article concerning the making of reservations could have obviated—are real; they are mitigated by the common duty of the contracting States to be guided in their judgment by the compatibility or incompatibility of the reservation with the object and purpose of the Convention. It must clearly be assumed that the contracting States are desirous of preserving intact at least what is essential to the object of the Convention; should this desire be absent, it is quite clear that the Convention itself would be impaired both in its principle and in its application.

It may be that the divergence of views between parties as to the admissibility of a reservation will not in fact have any consequences. On the other hand, it may be that certain parties who consider that the assent given by other parties to a reservation is incompatible with the purpose of the Convention, will decide to adopt a position on the jurisdictional plane in respect of this divergence and to settle the dispute which thus arises either by special agreement or by the procedure laid down in Article IX of the Convention.

Finally, it may be that a State, whilst not claiming that a reservation is incompatible with the object and purpose of the Convention, will nevertheless object to it, but that an understanding between that State and the reserving State will have the effect that the Convention will enter into force between them, except for the clauses affected by the reservation. . . .

For these reasons,

THE COURT IS OF OPINION . . . ,

On Question I: by seven votes to five,

that a State which has made and maintained a reservation which has been objected to by one or more of the parties to the Convention but not by others, can be regarded as being a party to the Convention if the reservation is compatible with the object and purpose of the Convention; otherwise, that State cannot be regarded as being a party to the Convention.

On Question II: by seven votes to five,

(*a*) that if a party to the Convention objects to a reservation which it considers to be incompatible with the object and purpose of the Convention, it can in fact consider that the reserving State is not a party to the Convention;

(b) that if, on the other hand, a party accepts the reservation as being compatible with the object and purpose of the Convention, it can in fact consider that the reserving State is a party to the Convention; . . .

Concluded several years later, the VCLT adopted the ICJ's view that compatibility with a treaty's "object and purpose" is the factor controlling the permissibility and effect of reservations, and guiding state objections thereto. However, in doing so, the VCLT further opened the door to reservations. Consider the following articles and how they expand on the principles laid out in the *Reservations* opinion, above.

Vienna Convention on the Law of Treaties, 23 May 1969, 1155 UNTS 331, Can TS 1980 No 37, in force 27 January 1980

Article 19
Formulation of reservations
A State may, when signing, ratifying, accepting, approving or acceding to a treaty, formulate a reservation unless:
   (a) the reservation is prohibited by the treaty;
   (b) the treaty provides that only specified reservations, which do not include the reservation in question, may be made; or
   (c) in cases not falling under sub-paragraphs (a) and (b), the reservation is incompatible with the object and purpose of the treaty.

Article 20
Acceptance of and objection to reservations
1. A reservation expressly authorized by a treaty does not require any subsequent acceptance by the other contracting States unless the treaty so provides.

2. When it appears from the limited number of the negotiating States and the object and purpose of a treaty that the application of the treaty in its entirety between all the parties is an essential condition of the consent of each one to be bound by the treaty, a reservation requires acceptance by all the parties.

3. When a treaty is a constituent instrument of an international organization and unless it otherwise provides, a reservation requires the acceptance of the competent organ of that organization.

4. In cases not falling under the preceding paragraphs and unless the treaty otherwise provides:
   (a) acceptance by another contracting State of a reservation constitutes the reserving State a party to the treaty in relation to that other State if or when the treaty is in force for those States;
   (b) an objection by another contracting State to a reservation does not preclude the entry into force of the treaty as between the objecting and reserving States unless a contrary intention is definitely expressed by the objecting State;
   (c) an act expressing a State's consent to be bound by the treaty and containing a reservation is effective as soon as at least one other contracting State has accepted the reservation.

5. For the purposes of paragraphs 2 and 4 and unless the treaty otherwise provides, a reservation is considered to have been accepted by a State if it shall have raised no objection to the reservation by the end of a period of twelve months after it was notified of the reservation or by the date on which it expressed its consent to be bound by the treaty, whichever is later.

Article 21
Legal effects of reservations and of objections to reservations
1. A reservation established with regard to another party in accordance with articles 19, 20 and 23:

> (a) modifies for the reserving State in its relations with that other party the provisions of the treaty to which the reservation relates to the extent of the reservation; and
> (b) modifies those provisions to the same extent for that other party in its relations with the reserving State.

2. The reservation does not modify the provisions of the treaty for the other parties to the treaty *inter se.*

3. When a State objecting to a reservation has not opposed the entry into force of the treaty between itself and the reserving State, the provisions to which the reservation relates do not apply as between the two States to the extent of the reservation.

What is the practical difference between the legal effects contemplated in paragraphs 1 and 3 of Article 21? Can there be situations where it will make no practical difference whether responding states accept the reservation or object to it (without opposing the entry into force of the treaty between themselves and the reserving state)?

The reservation rules in the VCLT effectively enable a "bilateralization" of multilateral treaty regimes. Most multilateral treaties purport to extend the same rights to and impose the same obligations on all parties. However, where permitted, a state making a reservation may modify these rights and obligations as between itself and other parties which fail to object the entry into force of the treaty between themselves and the reserving state. The result is a customized treaty regime applicable between such states and the reserving state, but not between other non-reserving parties *inter se.* Rather, the latter remain bound, as between themselves, by the original, unreserved terms of the treaty.

LAW IN CONTEXT

Reservations to Human Rights Treaties

The bilateral "customizing" effect of reservations is particularly contentious in the human rights area, as reflected in the following "General Comment" from the UN Human Rights Committee (the treaty monitoring body established by the International Covenant on Civil and Political Rights,[38] which is discussed in Chapter 9). In grappling with the issue of reservations to the Covenant and its Protocols, the Committee confronted two principal questions: First, how exactly may one determine whether a given reservation runs counter

---

38 ICCPR, above note 2.

to the "object and purpose" of the Covenant? Second, who may legitimately determine this question in connection with human rights treaties? The Committee's non-legally binding, but potentially persuasive, General Comment to states parties reads as follows:

> **Human Rights Committee,** *General Comment 24: Issues relating to reservations made upon ratification or accession to the Covenant or the Optional Protocols thereto, or in relation to declarations under Article 41 of the Covenant,* UN Doc CCPR/C/21/Rev.1/Add.6 (1994)[39]
>
> 1. As of 1 November 1994, 46 of the 127 States parties to the International Covenant on Civil and Political Rights had, between them, entered 150 reservations of varying significance to their acceptance of the obligations of the Covenant. Some of these reservations exclude the duty to provide and guarantee particular rights in the Covenant. Others are couched in more general terms, often directed to ensuring the continued paramountcy of certain domestic legal provisions. Still others are directed at the competence of the Committee. The number of reservations, their content and their scope may undermine the effective implementation of the Covenant and tend to weaken respect for the obligations of States Parties. . . .
>
> 4. The possibility of entering reservations may encourage States which consider that they have difficulties in guaranteeing all the rights in the Covenant nonetheless to accept the generality of obligations in that instrument. Reservations may serve a useful function to enable States to adapt specific elements in their laws to the inherent rights of each person as articulated in the Covenant. However, it is desirable in principle that States accept the full range of obligations, because the human rights norms are the legal expression of the essential rights that every person is entitled to as a human being.
>
> 5. The Covenant neither prohibits reservations nor mentions any type of permitted reservation. . . .
>
> 6. The absence of a prohibition on reservations does not mean that any reservation is permitted. The matter of reservations under the Covenant . . . is governed by international law. Article 19(3) of the Vienna Convention on the Law of Treaties provides relevant guidance. . . .
>
> 7. In an instrument which articulates very many civil and political rights, each of the many articles, and indeed their interplay, secures the objectives of the Covenant. The object and purpose of the Covenant is to create legally binding standards for human rights by defining certain civil and political rights and placing them in a framework of obligations which are legally binding for those States which ratify; and to provide an efficacious supervisory machinery for the obligations undertaken. . . .
>
> [The Committee then sets out in detail the rights and articles of the Covenant to which reservations are impermissible because of their centrality to the above object and pur-

---

39 Reprinted in *Compilation of General Comments and General Recommendations Adopted by Human Rights Treaty Bodies,* UN Doc HRI/GEN/1/Rev.9 (27 May 2008), vol I at 210–17.

pose, before asking and answering the question, "Who may decide whether a reservation is impermissible?"]

16. The Committee finds it important to address which body has the legal authority to make determinations as to whether specific reservations are compatible with the object and purpose of the Covenant. As for international treaties in general, the International Court of Justice has indicated in the Reservations to the Genocide Convention Case (1951) that a State which objected to a reservation on the grounds of incompatibility with the object and purpose of a treaty could, through objecting, regard the treaty as not in effect as between itself and the reserving State. Article 20, paragraph 4, of the Vienna Convention on the Law of Treaties 1969 contains provisions most relevant to the present case on acceptance of and objection to reservations. This provides for the possibility of a State to object to a reservation made by another State. Article 21 deals with the legal effects of objections by States to reservations made by other States. . . .

17. As indicated above, it is the Vienna Convention on the Law of Treaties that provides the definition of reservations and also the application of the object and purpose test in the absence of other specific provisions. But the Committee believes that its provisions on the role of State objections in relation to reservations are inappropriate to address the problem of reservations to human rights treaties. Such treaties, and the Covenant specifically, are not a web of inter-State exchanges of mutual obligations. They concern the endowment of individuals with rights. The principle of inter-State reciprocity has no place, save perhaps in the limited context of reservations to declarations on the Committee's competence under article 41. And because the operation of the classic rules on reservations is so inadequate for the Covenant, States have often not seen any legal interest in or need to object to reservations. The absence of protest by States cannot imply that a reservation is either compatible or incompatible with the object and purpose of the Covenant. Objections have been occasional, made by some States but not others, and on grounds not always specified; when an objection is made, it often does not specify a legal consequence, or sometimes even indicates that the objecting party none the less does not regard the Covenant as not in effect as between the parties concerned. In short, the pattern is so unclear that it is not safe to assume that a non-objecting State thinks that a particular reservation is acceptable. In the view of the Committee, because of the special characteristics of the Covenant as a human rights treaty, it is open to question what effect objections have between States *inter se*. However, an objection to a reservation made by States may provide some guidance to the Committee in its interpretation as to its compatibility with the object and purpose of the Covenant.

18. It necessarily falls to the Committee to determine whether a specific reservation is compatible with the object and purpose of the Covenant. This is in part because, as indicated above, it is an inappropriate task for States parties in relation to human rights treaties, and in part because it is a task that the Committee cannot avoid in the performance of its functions. In order to know the scope of its duty to examine a State's compliance under article 40 or a communication under the first Optional Protocol, the Committee has necessarily to take a view on the compatibility of a reservation with the object and purpose of the Covenant and with general international law. Because of

the special character of a human rights treaty, the compatibility of a reservation with the object and purpose of the Covenant must be established objectively, by reference to legal principles, and the Committee is particularly well placed to perform this task. The normal consequence of an unacceptable reservation is not that the Covenant will not be in effect at all for a reserving party. Rather, such a reservation will generally be severable, in the sense that the Covenant will be operative for the reserving party without benefit of the reservation.

19. Reservations must be specific and transparent, so that the Committee, those under the jurisdiction of the reserving State and other States parties may be clear as to what obligations of human rights compliance have or have not been undertaken. Reservations may thus not be general, but must refer to a particular provision of the Covenant and indicate in precise terms its scope in relation thereto. When considering the compatibility of possible reservations with the object and purpose of the Covenant, States should also take into consideration the overall effect of a group of reservations, as well as the effect of each reservation on the integrity of the Covenant, which remains an essential consideration. States should not enter so many reservations that they are in effect accepting a limited number of human rights obligations, and not the Covenant as such. So that reservations do not lead to a perpetual non-attainment of international human rights standards, reservations should not systematically reduce the obligations undertaken only to those presently existing in less demanding standards of domestic law. . . .

20. States should institute procedures to ensure that each and every proposed reservation is compatible with the object and purpose of the Covenant. It is desirable for a State entering a reservation to indicate in precise terms the domestic legislation or practices which it believes to be incompatible with the Covenant obligation reserved; and to explain the time period it requires to render its own laws and practices compatible with the Covenant, or why it is unable to render its own laws and practices compatible with the Covenant. States should also ensure that the necessity for maintaining reservations is periodically reviewed, taking into account any observations and recommendations made by the Committee during examination of their reports. Reservations should be withdrawn at the earliest possible moment. Reports to the Committee should contain information on what action has been taken to review, reconsider or withdraw reservations.

The Human Rights Committee's approach to reservations, as expressed in General Comment 24, was controversial, and not all states parties to the Covenant creating the Committee agreed with the Committee's interpretation of the law. In a rare move, three states issued public statements criticizing the Committee's approach: France, the United Kingdom, and the United States.[40] All three states were of the view that General Comment 24 "appears to go much too far" (to use the American wording of the objection). The Committee's analysis in paragraphs 16 to 20 was said to be of particular concern since it would appear to

---

40   The views of the United Kingdom and the United States can be found in an annex appended to the Committee's annual report for 1995, while the views of France are found appended to its 1996 report: *Report of the Human Rights Committee*, UN GAOR, 50th Sess, Supp No 40, vol I, annex VI at 126–35, UN Doc A/50/40 (1996); *Report of the Human Rights Committee*, UN GAOR, 51st Sess, Supp No 40, vol I, annex VI at 104–6, UN Doc A/51/40 (1997).

dispense with the established procedures for determining the permissibility of reservations and divest states parties of any role in determining the meaning of their treaty obligations.[41] With respect to the matter of severability—mentioned in paragraph 18 above—the United Kingdom made clear its view that "severability would entail excising both the reservation *and the parts of the treaty to which it applies*," with any other solution considered "deeply contrary to principle."[42] However, some members of the ICJ (but not the Court itself) have since commented that the tenor of General Comment 24 is reflective of new trends emerging in treaty practice that move beyond the approach of the ICJ in its 1951 *Reservations* opinion with respect to the compatibility of reservations to human rights treaties.[43]

In its observations on General Comment 24, the United Kingdom also mentioned that the topic of reservations to treaties was a matter currently being studied by the ILC. In 2011, the ILC adopted a *Guide to Practice on Reservations to Treaties*.[44] While not purporting to amend the reservations scheme set out in the VCLT, the purpose of the ILC's *Guide* is to "to provide assistance to practitioners of international law, who are often faced with sensitive problems concerning, in particular, the validity and effects of reservations to treaties."[45] To what extent are the following provisions of the *Guide* compatible with the views of the Human Rights Committee (itself a "treaty monitoring body") as set out above?

International Law Commission, "Guide to Practice on Reservations to Treaties" in *Report of the International Law Commission*, UN GAOR, 66th Sess, Supp No 10, Addendum, UN Doc A/66/10/Add.1 (2011)

3.2.1 Competence of the treaty monitoring bodies to assess the permissibility of reservations
1. A treaty monitoring body may, for the purpose of discharging the functions entrusted to it, assess the permissibility of reservations formulated by a State or an international organization.

2. The assessment made by such a body in the exercise of this competence has no greater legal effect than that of the act which contains it.

. . . .

3.2.3 Consideration of the assessments of treaty monitoring bodies
States and international organizations that have formulated reservations to a treaty establishing a treaty monitoring body shall give consideration to that body's assessment of the permissibility of the reservations.

---

41 Observations of the United States of America, dated 28 March 1995, reprinted in *Report of the Human Rights Committee*, UN GAOR, 50th Sess, Supp No 40, vol I, annex VI at 126–27, UN Doc A/50/40 (1996).

42 Observations of the United Kingdom of Great Britain and Northern Ireland, dated 21 July 1995, reprinted in *Report of the Human Rights Committee*, UN GAOR, 50th Sess, Supp No 40, vol I, annex VI at 133, UN Doc A/50/40 (1996).

43 *Armed Activities on the Territory of the Congo (New Application: 2002) (Democratic Republic of the Congo v Rwanda)*, Jurisdiction and Admissibility, Judgment, [2006] ICJ Rep 6 at 58–59 (dissenting opinion of Judge Koroma) and 69 (joint separate opinion of Judges Higgins, Kooijmans, Elaraby, Owada, and Simma).

44 Reprinted in *Report of the International Law Commission*, UN GAOR, 66th Sess, Supp No 10, Addendum, UN Doc A/66/10/Add.1 (2011) [*ILC Report 2011 Addendum*].

45 *Ibid* at 34.

3.2.4 Bodies competent to assess the permissibility of reservations in the event of the establishment of a treaty monitoring body

When a treaty establishes a treaty monitoring body, the competence of that body is without prejudice to the competence of the contracting States or contracting organizations to assess the permissibility of reservations to that treaty, or to that of dispute settlement bodies competent to interpret or apply the treaty.

Some recent treaties have solved the reservation problem simply by banning the practice entirely. Consider Article 19 of the convention that prohibits the use, stockpiling, production, and transfer of anti-personnel mines: "The Articles of this Convention shall not be subject to reservations."[46] Other treaties are less absolute in prohibiting reservations, but do signal which reservations are or are not permissible. Consider the following provision of the International Convention on the Elimination of All Forms of Racial Discrimination:

Article 20

1. The Secretary-General of the United Nations shall receive and circulate to all States which are or may become Parties to this Convention reservations made by States at the time of ratification or accession. Any State which objects to the reservation shall, within a period of ninety days from the date of the said communication, notify the Secretary-General that it does not accept it.

2. A reservation incompatible with the object and purpose of this Convention shall not be permitted, nor shall a reservation the effect of which would inhibit the operation of any of the bodies established by this Convention be allowed. A reservation shall be considered incompatible or inhibitive if at least two-thirds of the States Parties to this Convention object to it.[47]

In most cases, however, determining whether a reservation is contrary to the object and purpose of a treaty is a difficult and uncoordinated undertaking. As rather mildly noted in the *Restatement of the Law, Third, Foreign Relations Law of the United States*,[48] reference to the object and purpose of a treaty, which ostensibly provides an objective standard for assessing the validity of a reservation, "introduces an element of uncertainty and possible disagreement."[49] On this issue, the ILC *Guide to Practice on Reservations to Treaties* states that "[a] reservation is incompatible with the object and purpose of the treaty if it affects an essential element of the treaty that is necessary to its general tenor, in such a way that the reservation impairs the *raison d'être* of the treaty."[50] The *Guide* also directs practitioners to apply the usual rules of treaty interpretation, which we review below,

---

46   Convention on the Prohibition of the Use, Stockpiling, Production and Transfer of Anti-Personnel Mines and on Their Destruction, 18 September 1997, 2056 UNTS 211, Can TS 1999 No 4, in force 1 March 1999.

47   International Convention on the Elimination of All Forms of Racial Discrimination, 7 March 1966, 660 UNTS 195, Can TS 1970 No 28, in force 4 January 1969.

48   American Law Institute, *Restatement of the Law, Third, Foreign Relations Law of the United States* (St Paul, MN: American Law Institute Publishers, 1987) [*Third Restatement*].

49   *Ibid* at para 313, comment c.

50   *ILC Report 2011 Addendum*, above note 44 at 18, clause 3.1.5.

in determining a treaty's object and purpose.[51] Does such guidance reduce the potential for uncertainty and disagreement in evaluating the validity of reservations?

What if a reservation is incompatible with the object and purpose of a treaty and, therefore, invalid? Does the state formulating the reservation become a party to the treaty without the benefit of the reservation, or does it not become a party at all? In the context of human rights treaties, the Human Rights Committee has taken the former position (see paragraph 18 of General Comment 24, reproduced above, and recall the British objection). Controversially, the ILC's *Guide* presumes that such an outcome applies to treaties generally, "[u]nless the author of the invalid reservation has expressed a contrary intention or such an intention is otherwise established."[52] Is this approach consistent with the answer given by the ICJ to Question I in the 1951 *Reservations* opinion?

5) Amendment and Modification of Treaties

While a reservation is a unilateral act by which a party to a treaty seeks to alter the scope of its rights and obligations vis-à-vis other parties, the law of treaties also allows for changes to treaty terms by mutual consent among the parties. This is a very straightforward undertaking in the case of a bilateral treaty. As long as both parties to the treaty agree to change its terms, their mutual rights and obligations under the treaty are "amended" accordingly. In the case of multilateral treaties, however, there are varying degrees of complexity to the process.

A proposal to change the terms of a multilateral treaty for potentially all parties is referred to as a proposal for "amendment." Unless the treaty provides otherwise, the process for concluding an amendment is the same as the process for concluding the original treaty itself. Thus, while all parties are entitled to participate in the process of amendment, the concurrence of all parties is usually not required before the treaty may be amended (recall, for example, the two-thirds rule for adoption of multilateral treaties, which is often also applied to treaty amendments). Similarly, once the amendment is adopted, not all parties to the original treaty are necessarily bound by it. Rather, the amendment only binds, and is only operative as between, those parties that express their consent to be bound by it. The remaining parties continue to be bound by the provisions of the unamended treaty in their relations with one another and with parties to the amended treaty. A treaty amending an earlier treaty is often named a protocol.

Thus, the process and effect of amending a treaty are essentially the same as concluding an entirely new treaty with somewhat different terms. In either case, the mutual rights and obligations of any two states are governed by the treaty to which they are both party. If they are both party to two treaties with inconsistent terms, their mutual rights and obligations are governed by the more recently concluded treaty.

A less elaborate process is "modification" of a multilateral treaty between some of the parties only. This is generally accomplished by agreement between the relevant parties and is permissible as long as the modification does not impede achievement of the

---

51   *Ibid*, clause 3.1.5.1.

52   *Ibid* at 26, clause 4.5.3(2).

treaty's object and purpose or otherwise affect the rights and obligations of parties not participating in the modification.

The following provisions of the VCLT codify the process for the amendment and modification of treaties. Why is compatibility with the object and purpose of a treaty a condition precedent of a valid modification whereas it is not in the case of amendment? Consider the similarities in effect of modification of, and acceptance of reservations to, treaties.

Vienna Convention on the Law of Treaties, 23 May 1969, 1155 UNTS 331, Can TS 1980 No 37, in force 27 January 1980

Article 39
General rule regarding the amendment of treaties
A treaty may be amended by agreement between the parties. The rules laid down in Part II apply to such an agreement except in so far as the treaty may otherwise provide.

Article 40
Amendment of multilateral treaties
1. Unless the treaty otherwise provides, the amendment of multilateral treaties shall be governed by the following paragraphs.

2. Any proposal to amend a multilateral treaty as between all the parties must be notified to all the contracting States, each one of which shall have the right to take part in:
    (a) the decision as to the action to be taken in regard to such proposal;
    (b) the negotiation and conclusion of any agreement for the amendment of the treaty.

3. Every State entitled to become a party to the treaty shall also be entitled to become a party to the treaty as amended.

4. The amending agreement does not bind any State already a party to the treaty which does not become a party to the amending agreement; article 30, paragraph 4(b), applies in relation to such State.

5. Any State which becomes a party to the treaty after the entry into force of the amending agreement shall, failing an expression of a different intention by that State:
    (a) be considered as a party to the treaty as amended; and
    (b) be considered as a party to the unamended treaty in relation to any party to the treaty not bound by the amending agreement.

Article 41
Agreements to modify multilateral treaties between certain of the parties only
1. Two or more of the parties to a multilateral treaty may conclude an agreement to modify the treaty as between themselves alone if:
    (a) the possibility of such a modification is provided for by the treaty; or
    (b) the modification in question is not prohibited by the treaty and:
        (i) does not affect the enjoyment by the other parties of their rights under the treaty or the performance of their obligations;
        (ii) does not relate to a provision, derogation from which is incompatible with the effective execution of the object and purpose of the treaty as a whole.

2. Unless in a case falling under paragraph 1(a) the treaty otherwise provides, the parties in question shall notify the other parties of their intention to conclude the agreement and of the modification to the treaty for which it provides.

6) Treaty Rights and Obligations

a) Performance of Treaty Obligations

Obviously, the precise obligations and rights created by a treaty are determined by the articles of that treaty itself. The VCLT does, however, set out general rules on the legal consequences of being a party to a treaty. By far the most important of these is the doctrine of *pacta sunt servanda*—the rule that pacts must be performed in good faith. It is this rule that imbues treaties with their binding legal effect. While it is articulated in the VCLT, the rule is also universally recognized by states and international lawyers alike as one of the most fundamental rules of customary international law. What is the significance of that fact for the view that treaties are a positivist source of international law?

As a corollary to the foundational doctrine of *pacta sunt servanda*, treaty law also provides that a state's internal laws do not excuse its failure to perform its treaty obligations. It is therefore conceivable that a state could have inconsistent, competing legal obligations—those under the law of treaties and those under its domestic law.

Vienna Convention on the Law of Treaties, 23 May 1969, 1155 UNTS 331, Can TS 1980 No 37, in force 27 January 1980

Article 26
Pacta sunt servanda
Every treaty in force is binding upon the parties to it and must be performed by them in good faith.

Article 27
Internal law and observance of treaties
A party may not invoke the provisions of its internal law as justification for its failure to perform a treaty. This rule is without prejudice to article 46 [discussed later, and which permits a state to invalidate its consent to a treaty if it was given in manifest violation of a rule of its internal law of fundamental importance].

***Treatment of Polish Nationals*, Advisory Opinion (1932), PCIJ (Ser A/B) No 44 at 24**

[Danzig was a "Free City" established pursuant to one of the peace treaties concluding World War I. A dispute arose between Poland and Danzig with respect to the latter's treatment of Polish nationals, leading to a request for an opinion on whether that treatment could be justified by reference to the Constitution of Danzig.]

. . . It should however be observed that, while on the one hand, according to generally accepted principles, a State cannot rely, as against another State, on the provisions of the latter's Constitution, but only on international law and international obligations duly accepted, on the other hand and conversely, a State cannot adduce as against another State its own Constitution with a view to evading obligations incumbent upon it under international law or treaties in force. Applying these principles to the present case, it results that the question of the treatment of Polish nationals or other persons of Polish origin or speech must be settled exclusively on the bases of the rules of international law and the treaty provisions in force between Poland and Danzig.

Article 27 of the VCLT raises real issues for states in which one branch of government has the power to make treaties and another has the power to perform them. In Canada, for example, the executive branch has the power to make treaties but not the power to implement them where doing so requires changes to Canadian law—the latter process being the constitutional preserve of the law-making branch. The situation is fraught with even more difficulty in federal states where legislative power is partitioned between levels of government. For example, in Canada, either Parliament or the provincial legislatures may, depending on the subject matter of the treaty, have exclusive constitutional author-ity to enact law necessary for the performance of the treaty. We return to this complex issue below in considering the interaction of treaty and domestic law in Canada. For present purposes, however, the rule in Article 27 means that the Canadian government must be careful in undertaking treaty commitments in order to avoid situations in which Parliament or the provincial legislatures may not cooperate in the performance of those obligations, as suggested by the following study of Canada's treaty-making practice:

Laura Barnett, "Canada's Approach to the Treaty-Making Process" (Ottawa: Library of Parliament, 2012) at 3–4, 6–7 (footnotes omitted)

. . . Canada cannot ratify an international treaty until measures are in place to ensure that the terms of the treaty are enforceable in Canadian law.

There are two ways for this task to be accomplished. In some cases it is abundantly clear that domestic legislation must be put in place in order to implement the terms of an international treaty. If so, the ministers concerned give instructions for an implementa-tion bill to be drafted. After receiving Cabinet approval, the bill is tabled in Parliament and goes through the parliamentary legislative process. . . . Although it is rare for an implementing Act not to be passed by Parliament, this can happen. For example, in 1988 the Senate refused to pass the proposed Canada-United States Free Trade Agreement Implementation Act, thereby triggering an election. A similar bill was passed shortly afterwards by a new Parliament.

By contrast, many treaties and international conventions, particularly international human rights treaties and foreign investment promotion and protection agreements, do not necessarily require specific legislation for implementation. In such cases, the govern-ment will state that domestic legislation is already consistent with Canada's international obligations or that the object of the treaty does not require new statutory provisions. Thus ratification can proceed without specific implementing legislation. In this case, prior to ratification, government officials will conduct a review of existing legislation to deter-mine whether any amendments or new legislation are needed to comply with the treaty. In doing so, officials from the Department of Justice Canada consult with other federal departments and agencies, the provinces and territories, and non-governmental organ-izations to determine whether existing legislation is in conformity with the international treaty, as well as whether the government may have to enter a reservation or statement of understanding to the treaty to clarify Canada's position on certain issues. Where provincial or territorial legislation is implicated, the executive will not ratify the treaty until all Canadian jurisdictions have indicated that they support ratification.

. . .

No discussion of Canada's compliance with its international treaty obligations is complete without an examination of the role of the provinces. Although the federal government has sole authority to negotiate, sign and ratify international treaties, many treaties nonetheless deal with matters that fall under provincial jurisdiction. In Canada, Parliament and the provincial legislative assemblies may pass legislation in areas where they have jurisdiction under the Constitution of Canada. This division of legislative power is provided for mainly in sections 91 and 92 of the Constitution Act, 1867. While provincial consent is not required for ratification, the federal government nonetheless has a policy of consulting with the provinces before signing treaties that touch on matters of provincial jurisdiction.

As well, although the federal government is the only level of government responsible to the international community for compliance with the treaties that it signs, it cannot enforce compliance with international treaties in areas beyond its jurisdiction. In the 1937 Labour Conventions Case the Privy Council held that the federal government cannot use the need to comply with international treaties as justification for encroaching on areas of provincial jurisdiction. Whenever a treaty concerns an area of provincial jurisdiction, the relevant provisions may be implemented only by the provincial legislative assemblies. Thus, treaty implementation and compliance are an area of federal, provincial and territorial responsibility.

Yet, despite Canada's constitutional arrangement, articles 26 and 27 of the Vienna Convention on the Law of Treaties still hold the federal government accountable to the international community for making best efforts to implement international treaties in Canada. Once a treaty has been ratified, there is a presumption that Canada will comply with it in good faith. One example of the federal government's ongoing obligation to comply with its international obligations arose in Ariel Hollis Waldman v. Canada. In this case, a UN treaty body criticized Ontario's funding of a separate Catholic school system, turning to the federal government for this violation of the equality provision of the *International Covenant on Civil and Political Rights*– even though this preferential treatment is entrenched in section 93 of the Constitution Act, 1867. Another more recent example involves the NAFTA and the federal government's obligation to pay compensation to forest products company AbitibiBowater due to actions taken by the Government of Newfoundland and Labrador.

In order to limit Canada's liability where a treaty concerns an area of provincial legislative jurisdiction, some treaties contain a "federal state clause." To varying degrees, depending on the purpose of the treaty and the wording of its articles, the clause informs all the parties that the Government of Canada may have certain difficulties in implementing the treaty because to do so it will have to secure the cooperation of the Canadian provinces. By including this clause the government commits itself to performing only those international obligations that come within federal jurisdiction, and to make best efforts to get provincial compliance. By contrast, some provinces have implemented legislation specifically intended to give some international treaties effect in provincial law. . . .

[*Reproduced with the permission of the Library of Parliament, 2013.*]

b) The Scope of Treaty Obligations

The VCLT also includes rules on the scope of treaties, both temporally and geographically. Consider the following provisions:

> **Vienna Convention on the Law of Treaties, 23 May 1969, 1155 UNTS 331, Can TS 1980 No 37, in force 27 January 1980**
>
> *Article 28*
> *Non-retroactivity of treaties*
> Unless a different intention appears from the treaty or is otherwise established, its provisions do not bind a party in relation to any act or fact which took place or any situation which ceased to exist before the date of the entry into force of the treaty with respect to that party.
>
> *Article 29*
> *Territorial scope of treaties*
> Unless a different intention appears from the treaty or is otherwise established, a treaty is binding upon each party in respect of its entire territory.

One potentially complex question is whether a treaty may ever grant rights or impose obligations on a third state—one that is not a party to the treaty. As seen in the *North Sea Continental Shelf* judgment above, international law is generally hostile to the notion that a treaty may impose obligations on non-parties, even when a state has taken the first step towards becoming a party by signing the treaty subject to subsequent ratification. Consider, however, the following decision of the Permanent Court of International Justice, which discusses the very limited circumstances in which treaty provisions may in fact be relevant for non-parties.

> **Case of the Free Zones of Upper Savoy and the District of Gex (France v Switzerland) (1932), PCIJ (Ser A/B) No 46 at 141–48**
>
> [At issue was Article 435 of the Treaty of Versailles,[53] to which France was a party but Switzerland was not. France had purported to abrogate unilaterally, pursuant to Article 435, the status of certain customs-free zones along the French-Swiss border.]
>
> . . . Article 435, paragraph 2, as such, does not involve the abolition of the free zones. But, even were it otherwise, it is certain that, in any case, Article 435 of the Treaty of Versailles is not binding upon Switzerland, who is not a Party to that Treaty, except to the extent to which that country accepted it. That extent is determined by the note of the Federal Council of May 5th, 1919. . . . It is by that instrument, and by it alone, that Switzerland has acquiesced in the provision of Article 435; and she did so under certain conditions and reservations, set out in the said note, which states, *inter alia*: "The Federal Council would not wish that its acceptance of the above wording . . . should lead to the conclusion that it would agree to the suppression of a system intended to give neighbouring territory the benefit of a special régime which is appropriate to the geographical and economical

---

53   28 June 1919, (1919) 13 AJIL Supp 151, in force 20 January 1920.

situation and which has been well tested." And again: "In the opinion of the Federal Council, the question is not the modification of the customs system of the zones as set up by the treaties mentioned above, but only the regulation in a manner more appropriate to the economic conditions of the present day of the terms of the exchange of goods between the regions in question."

No reservation could be more explicit. . . .

The Court, therefore, reaches the conclusion that Article 435, paragraph 2, of the Treaty of Versailles, with its Annexes, has not abrogated the régime of the free zones as between France and Switzerland. . . .

[The Court went on to consider whether the Treaty of Paris of 1814 (concluding the Napoleonic wars) conferred any positive rights on Switzerland vis-à-vis France with respect to maintenance of at least one of the free zones ("Gex"). Several states, including France, were parties to the Treaty of Paris, but Switzerland, again, was not.]

Pursuant to Article 6 of the Treaty of Paris of May 30th, 1814, the Powers assembled at the Congress of Vienna addressed to Switzerland, on March 20th, 1815, a "Declaration" to the effect that "as soon as the Helvetic Diet shall have duly and formally acceded to the stipulations in the present instrument, an act shall be prepared containing the acknowledgment and the guarantee, on the part of all the Powers, of the perpetual neutrality of Switzerland, in her new frontiers" [and] "that the road which leads from Geneva into Switzerland by Versoy, shall at all times be free".

The proposal thus made to Switzerland by the Powers was accepted by the Federal Diet by means of the "act of acceptance" of May 27th, 1815. . . .

It follows . . . that the creation of the Gex zone forms part of a territorial arrangement in favour of Switzerland, made as a result of an agreement between that country and the Powers, including France, which agreement confers on this zone the character of a contract to which Switzerland is a Party. . . .

The Court, having reached this conclusion simply on the basis of an examination of the situation of fact in regard to this case, need not consider the legal nature of the Gex zone from the point of view of whether it constitutes a stipulation in favour of a third Party.

But were the matter also to be envisaged from this aspect, the following observations should be made:

It cannot be lightly presumed that stipulations favourable to a third State have been adopted with the object of creating an actual right in its favour. There is however nothing to prevent the will of sovereign States from having this object and this effect. The question of the existence of a right acquired under an instrument drawn between other States is therefore one to be decided in each particular case: it must be ascertained whether the States which have stipulated in favour of a third State meant to create for that State an actual right which the latter has accepted as such. . . .

The general rule that the effect of treaty provisions does not extend to non-parties — and the limited exceptions to it — are codified in the VCLT. Note how the following provisions distinguish between the extension of rights and obligations to non-parties (or "third states"). Assuming the general rule is that a treaty can create neither rights nor obligations for non-parties without their consent, what is the basis for such a distinction?

Vienna Convention on the Law of Treaties, 23 May 1969, 1155 UNTS 331, Can TS 1980 No 37, in force 27 January 1980

Article 2
Use of terms
1. For the purposes of the present Convention:

   . . .

   (h) "third State" means a State not a party to the treaty;

   . . .

Article 34
General rule regarding third States
A treaty does not create either obligations or rights for a third State without its consent.

Article 35
Treaties providing for obligations for third States
An obligation arises for a third State from a provision of a treaty if the parties to the treaty intend the provision to be the means of establishing the obligation and the third State expressly accepts that obligation in writing.

Article 36
Treaties providing for rights for third States
1. A right arises for a third State from a provision of a treaty if the parties to the treaty intend the provision to accord that right either to the third State, or to a group of States to which it belongs, or to all States, and the third State assents thereto. Its assent shall be presumed so long as the contrary is not indicated, unless the treaty otherwise provides.

2. A State exercising a right in accordance with paragraph 1 shall comply with the conditions for its exercise provided for in the treaty or established in conformity with the treaty.

Article 37
Revocation or modification of obligations or rights of third States
1. When an obligation has arisen for a third State in conformity with article 35, the obligation may be revoked or modified only with the consent of the parties to the treaty and of the third State, unless it is established that they had otherwise agreed.

2. When a right has arisen for a third State in conformity with article 36, the right may not be revoked or modified by the parties if it is established that the right was intended not to be revocable or subject to modification without the consent of the third State.

Article 38
Rules in a treaty becoming binding on third States through international custom
Nothing in articles 34 to 37 precludes a rule set forth in a treaty from becoming binding upon a third State as a customary rule of international law, recognized as such.

As Article 38 suggests, caution is called for in applying the rules governing the legal obligations of non-parties to treaties. Recall that, in some instances, a provision codified in a treaty may also reflect a rule of customary international law which, as we shall see below, is a body of international law presumed to be binding on all states. In such circumstances, a non-party to the treaty may not be bound by the treaty provision per se, but will generally be bound by the corresponding rule of customary international law.

7) Treaty Interpretation

If a state is to perform its obligations or exercise its rights under a treaty, the precise content of those rights and obligations must be established. For this reason, the terms of a treaty, like those of a contract or statutory enactment, must be interpreted. The VCLT contains a series of short but important rules on treaty interpretation.

Vienna Convention on the Law of Treaties, 23 May 1969, 1155 UNTS 331, Can TS 1980 No 37, in force 27 January 1980

Article 31
General rule of interpretation
1. A treaty shall be interpreted in good faith in accordance with the ordinary meaning to be given to the terms of the treaty in their context and in the light of its object and purpose.

2. The context for the purpose of the interpretation of a treaty shall comprise, in addition to the text, including its preamble and annexes:
   (a) any agreement relating to the treaty which was made between all the parties in connexion with the conclusion of the treaty;
   (b) any instrument which was made by one or more parties in connexion with the conclusion of the treaty and accepted by the other parties as an instrument related to the treaty.

3. There shall be taken into account, together with the context:
   (a) any subsequent agreement between the parties regarding the interpretation of the treaty or the application of its provisions;
   (b) any subsequent practice in the application of the treaty which establishes the agreement of the parties regarding its interpretation;
   (c) any relevant rules of international law applicable in the relations between the parties.

4. A special meaning shall be given to a term if it is established that the parties so intended.

Article 32
Supplementary means of interpretation
Recourse may be had to supplementary means of interpretation, including the preparatory work of the treaty and the circumstances of its conclusion, in order to confirm the meaning resulting from the application of article 31, or to determine the meaning when the interpretation according to article 31:
   (a) leaves the meaning ambiguous or obscure; or
   (b) leads to a result which is manifestly absurd or unreasonable.

Article 33

Interpretation of treaties authenticated in two or more languages

1. When a treaty has been authenticated in two or more languages, the text is equally authoritative in each language, unless the treaty provides or the parties agree that, in case of divergence, a particular text shall prevail.

2. A version of the treaty in a language other than one of those in which the text was authenticated shall be considered an authentic text only if the treaty so provides or the parties so agree.

3. The terms of the treaty are presumed to have the same meaning in each authentic text.

4. Except where a particular text prevails in accordance with paragraph 1, when a comparison of the authentic texts discloses a difference of meaning which the application of articles 31 and 32 does not remove, the meaning which best reconciles the texts, having regard to the object and purpose of the treaty, shall be adopted.

These rules give clear primacy to the words of the treaty itself in the interpretation exercise, but note the range of factors, other than the words themselves, that may be considered in determining their ordinary meaning. Particularly relevant are the treaty's context, the object and purpose of the treaty, and any subsequent practice or agreements between the parties relevant to interpretation of the treaty's terms. In difficult cases, it may be permissible to go still further afield and rely upon such external evidence as the preparatory work (or *travaux préparatoires*) produced during the negotiation and drafting of the treaty. The International Law Commission (ILC) had this to say about the relationship between the various factors referred to in the interpretation provisions of the VCLT (which, it will be recalled, the ILC had drafted):

"Draft Articles on the Law of Treaties with Commentaries" in *Reports of the International Law Commission*, **UN GAOR, 21st Sess, Supp No 9 at 20–99, UN Doc A/6309/Rev.1 (1966)**

(8) . . . [A]rticle [31] is entitled "General rule of interpretation" in the singular, not "General *rules*" in the plural, because the Commission desired to emphasize that the process of interpretation is a unity and that the provisions of the article form a single, closely integrated rule. In the same way the word "context" in the opening phrase of paragraph 2 is designed to link all the elements of interpretation mentioned in this paragraph to the word "context" in the first paragraph and thereby incorporate them in the provision contained in that paragraph. Equally, the opening phrase of paragraph 3 "There shall be taken into account *together with the context*" is designed to incorporate in paragraph 1 the elements of interpretation set out in paragraph 3. If the provision in paragraph 4 . . . is of a different character, the word "special" serves to indicate its relation to the rule in paragraph 1. . . .

(9) . . . [Thus,] the article, when read as a whole, cannot properly be regarded as laying down a legal hierarchy of norms for the interpretation of treaties.

(11) The article as already indicated is based on the view that the text must be presumed to be the authentic expression of the intentions of the parties; and that, in consequence, the starting point of interpretation is the elucidation of the meaning of the

text, not an investigation *ab initio* into the intentions of the parties. . . . Moreover, the jurisprudence of the International Court contains many pronouncements from which it is permissible to conclude that the textual approach to treaty interpretation is regarded by it as established law. In particular, the Court has more than once stressed that it is not the function of interpretation to revise treaties or to read into them what they do not, expressly or by implication, contain.

(12) *Paragraph 1* contains three separate principles. The first—interpretation in good faith—flows directly from the rule *pacta sunt servanda*. The second principle is the very essence of the textual approach: the parties are to be presumed to have that intention which appears from the ordinary meaning of the terms used by them. The third principle is one both of common sense and good faith; the ordinary meaning of a term is not to be determined in the abstract but in the context of the treaty and in the light of its object and purpose. . . .

(13) *Paragraph 2* seeks to define what is comprised in the "context" for the purposes of the interpretation of the treaty. That the preamble forms part of a treaty for purposes of interpretation is too well settled to require comment, as is also the case with documents which are specifically made annexes to the treaty. The question is how far other documents connected with the treaty are to be regarded as forming part of the "context" for the purposes of interpretation. Paragraph 2 proposes that two classes of documents should be so regarded: *(a)* any agreement relating to the treaty which was made between all the parties in connexion with the conclusion of the treaty; and *(b)* any instrument which was made in connexion with the conclusion of the treaty and accepted by the other parties as an instrument related to the treaty.

The principle on which this provision is based is that a unilateral document cannot be regarded as forming part of the "context" within the meaning of article [31] unless not only was it made in connexion with the conclusion of the treaty but its relation to the treaty was accepted in the same manner by the other parties. On the other hand, the fact that these two classes of documents are recognized in paragraph 2 as forming part of the "context" does not mean that they are necessarily to be considered as an integral part of the treaty. Whether they are an actual part of the treaty depends on the intention of the parties in each case. What is proposed in paragraph 2 is that, for purposes of interpreting the treaty, these categories of documents should not be treated as mere evidence to which recourse may be had for the purpose of resolving an ambiguity or obscurity, but as part of the context for the purpose of arriving at the ordinary meaning of the terms of the treaty.

(14) *Paragraph 3(a)* specifies as a further authentic element of interpretation to be taken into account together with the context any subsequent agreement between the parties regarding the interpretation of the treaty. A question of fact may sometimes arise as to whether an understanding reached during the negotiations concerning the meaning of a provision was or was not intended to constitute an agreed basis for its interpretation. But it is well settled that when an agreement as to the interpretation of a provision is established as having been reached before or at the time of the conclusion of the treaty, it is to be regarded as forming part of the treaty. . . . Similarly, an agreement as to the interpretation of a provision reached after the conclusion of the treaty represents an authentic interpretation by the parties which must be read into the treaty for purposes of its interpretation.

(15) *Paragraph 3(b)* then similarly specifies as an element to be taken into account together with the context: "any subsequent practice in the application of the treaty which establishes the understanding of the parties regarding its interpretation". The importance of such subsequent practice in the application of the treaty, as an element of interpretation, is obvious; for it constitutes objective evidence of the understanding of the parties as to the meaning of the treaty. Recourse to it as a means of interpretation is well-established in the jurisprudence of international tribunals. . . .

(19) . . . [T]he Commission decided to specify in article [32] that recourse to further means of interpretation, including preparatory work, is permissible for the purpose of confirming the meaning resulting from the application of article [31] and for the purpose of determining the meaning when the interpretation according to article [31]:

(a) Leaves the meaning ambiguous or obscure; or

(b) Leads to a result which is manifestly absurd or unreasonable.

The word "supplementary" emphasizes that article [32] does not provide for alternative, autonomous, means of interpretation but only for means to aid an interpretation governed by the principles contained in article [31]. Sub-paragraph *(a)* admits the use of these means for the purpose of deciding the meaning in cases where there is no clear meaning. Sub-paragraph *(b)* does the same in cases where interpretation according to article [31] gives a meaning which is "manifestly absurd or unreasonable." The Court has recognized this exception to the rule that the ordinary meaning of the terms must prevail. On the other hand, the comparative rarity of the cases in which it has done so suggest that it regards this exception as limited to cases where the absurd or unreasonable character of the "ordinary" meaning is manifest. The Commission considered that the exception must be strictly limited, if it is not to weaken unduly the authority of the ordinary meaning of the terms. Sub-paragraph *(b)* is accordingly confined to cases where interpretation under article [31] gives a result which is manifestly absurd or unreasonable. . . .

It should be noted that, at the time of writing, the ILC is in the early stages of considering the matter of subsequent agreements and subsequent practice in relation to the interpretation of treaties, with a view to elucidating the ways in which adjudicative bodies in fact make use of such agreements and practice in interpreting treaties.[54]

Recall our earlier examination, in Section B(3)(b) above, of the doctrine of intertemporal law and its effect on questions related to the treaty-making process. The doctrine also has implications for the interpretation of treaties, as illustrated in the following case.

Rights of Nationals of the United States of America in Morocco (France v United States of America), Judgment, [1952] ICJ Rep 176 at 189

[A treaty concluded between the United States and Morocco in 1836 provided that, in the case of "any dispute" between citizens of the United States in Morocco, jurisdiction to resolve the dispute would rest with the American consul in Morocco rather than with the

---

54 See *ILC Report 2012*, above note 35, c X, para 240; Georg Nolte, Special Rapporteur, "First report on subsequent agreements and subsequent practice in relation to treaty interpretation", UN Doc A/CN.4/660 (2013).

local authorities. At issue was whether "any dispute" should be read to include civil and criminal, or only civil, disputes. France represented Morocco in the proceedings given that, at the time, Morocco was a French protectorate.]

. . . It is argued that Article 20 should be construed as giving consular jurisdiction over all disputes, civil and criminal, between United States citizens and protégés. France, on the other hand, contends that the word "dispute" is limited to civil cases. It has been argued that this word in its ordinary and natural sense would be confined to civil disputes, and that crimes are offences against the State and not disputes between private individuals.

The Treaty of 1836 replaced an earlier treaty between the United States and Morocco which was concluded in 1787. The two treaties were substantially identical in terms and Articles 20 and 21 are the same in both. Accordingly, in construing the provisions of Article 20—and, in particular, the expression "shall have any dispute with each other"—it is necessary to take into account the meaning of the word "dispute" at the times when the two treaties were concluded. For this purpose it is possible to look at the way in which the word "dispute" or its French counterpart was used in the different treaties concluded by Morocco: e.g., with France in 1631 and 1682, with Great Britain in 1721, 1750, 1751, 1760 and 1801. It is clear that in these instances the word was used to cover both civil and criminal disputes.

It is also necessary to take into account that, at the times of these two treaties, the clear-cut distinction between civil and criminal matters had not yet been developed in Morocco.

Accordingly, it is necessary to construe the word "dispute", as used in Article 20, as referring both to civil disputes and to criminal disputes, in so far as they relate to breaches of the criminal law committed by a United States citizen or protégé upon another United States citizen or protégé. . . .

However, the doctrine of intertemporal law must be applied with caution when interpreting a treaty:

Aegean Sea Continental Shelf (Greece v Turkey), Judgment, [1978] ICJ Rep 3

[At issue was whether the parties had agreed to submit their dispute over the extent of their respective continental shelves to the Court. Greece relied upon the 1928 General Act for the Pacific Settlement of International Disputes,[55] to which both Greece and Turkey were parties, as a basis for the Court's jurisdiction. Turkey objected on the basis that Greece, in acceding to the General Act, had formulated a reservation excluding "disputes relating to the territorial status of Greece."]

. . . 69. The Greek Government maintains that a restrictive view has to be taken of the meaning of the expression "disputes relating to the territorial status of Greece" in reservation *(b)* by reason of the historical context in which that expression was incorporated into the reservation. . . .

---

55 26 September 1928, 93 LNTS 343, in force 16 August 1929, later amended by the Revised General Act for the Pacific Settlement of International Disputes, 28 April 1949, 71 UNTS 101, in force 20 September 1950 (neither Greece nor Turkey became parties to the Revised General Act).

74. In the opinion of the Court, the historical evidence adduced by Greece does not suffice to establish that the expression "territorial status" was used in the League of Nations period, and in particular in the General Act of 1928, in the special, restricted, sense contended for by Greece. The evidence seems rather to confirm that the expression "territorial status" was used in its ordinary, generic sense of any matters properly to be considered as relating to the integrity and legal régime of a State's territory. . . .

77. The Greek Government, however, has advanced a further historical argument by which it seeks to convince the Court that there can be no question of the applicability of reservation *(b)* with respect to the present dispute. This is that the very idea of the continental shelf was wholly unknown in 1928 when the General Act was concluded, and in 1931 when Greece acceded to the Act. . . . Once it is established that the expression "the territorial status of Greece" was used in Greece's instrument of accession as a generic term denoting any matters comprised within the concept of territorial status under general international law, the presumption necessarily arises that its meaning was intended to follow the evolution of the law and to correspond with the meaning attached to the expression by the law in force at any given time. This presumption, in the view of the Court, is even more compelling when it is recalled that the 1928 Act was a convention for the pacific settlement of disputes designed to be of the most general kind and of continuing duration, for it hardly seems conceivable that in such a convention terms like "domestic jurisdiction" and "territorial status" were intended to have a fixed content regardless of the subsequent evolution of international law. . . .

Dispute Regarding Navigational and Related Rights (Costa Rica v Nicaragua), Judgment, [2009] ICJ Rep 213

[The parties disagreed over the interpretation of an 1858 treaty between them that permitted Costa Rica to make navigational use, for purposes of "comercio" (commerce), of a portion of the San Juan River forming part of Nicaraguan territory. One of the points of contention was whether the word "comercio" should be limited to its 1858 meaning which, according to Nicaragua, would have included trade in goods but not services such as the transport of persons.]

63. . . . It is true that the terms used in a treaty must be interpreted in light of what is determined to have been the parties' common intention, which is, by definition, contemporaneous with the treaty's conclusion. That may lead a court seised of a dispute, or the parties themselves, when they seek to determine the meaning of a treaty for purposes of good-faith compliance with it, to ascertain the meaning a term had when the treaty was drafted, since doing so can shed light on the parties' common intention. The Court has so proceeded in certain cases requiring it to interpret a term whose meaning had evolved since the conclusion of the treaty at issue, and in those cases the Court adhered to the original meaning (to this effect, see, for example, the Judgment of 27 August 1952 in the case concerning *Rights of Nationals of the United States of America in Morocco (France v. United States of America)*). . . .

64. This does not however signify that, where a term's meaning is no longer the same as it was at the date of conclusion, no account should ever be taken of its meaning at the time when the treaty is to be interpreted for purposes of applying it.

On the one hand, the subsequent practice of the parties, within the meaning of Article 31(3)*(b)* of the Vienna Convention, can result in a departure from the original intent on the basis of a tacit agreement between the parties. On the other hand, there are situations in which the parties' intent upon conclusion of the treaty was, or may be presumed to have been, to give the terms used—or some of them—a meaning or content capable of evolving, not one fixed once and for all, so as to make allowance for, among other things, developments in international law. In such instances it is indeed in order to respect the parties' common intention at the time the treaty was concluded, not to depart from it, that account should be taken of the meaning acquired by the terms in question upon each occasion on which the treaty is to be applied. . . .

65. A good illustration of this reasoning is found in the Judgment handed down by the Court on 18 December 1978 in the case concerning *Aegean Sea Continental Shelf (Greece v. Turkey)*. . . .

66. . . . [T]he Court's reasoning in that case . . . is founded on the idea that, where the parties have used generic terms in a treaty, the parties necessarily having been aware that the meaning of the terms was likely to evolve over time, and where the treaty has been entered into for a very long period or is "of continuing duration", the parties must be presumed, as a general rule, to have intended those terms to have an evolving meaning.

67. This is so in the present case in respect of the term "comercio" as used in Article VI of the 1858 Treaty. First, this is a generic term, referring to a class of activity. Second, the 1858 Treaty was entered into for an unlimited duration; from the outset it was intended to create a legal régime characterized by its perpetuity. . . .

70. The Court concludes from the foregoing that the terms by which the extent of Costa Rica's right of free navigation has been defined, including in particular the term "comercio", must be understood to have the meaning they bear on each occasion on which the Treaty is to be applied, and not necessarily their original meaning. Thus, even assuming that the notion of "commerce" does not have the same meaning today as it did in the mid-nineteenth century, it is the present meaning which must be accepted for purposes of applying the Treaty.

71. Accordingly, the Court finds that the right of free navigation in question applies to the transport of persons as well as the transport of goods, as the activity of transporting persons can be commercial in nature nowadays. This is the case if the carrier engages in the activity for profit-making purposes.

8) Invalidity, Suspension, and Termination of Treaties

a) General

There are a number of rules of treaty law that permit states to evade treaty obligations to which they would otherwise be bound. Those rules fall into two broad conceptual categories. Those relating to *invalidity* question whether binding treaty obligations were ever validly created in the first place. Those relating to *suspension* or *termination* proceed from the assumption that valid treaty obligations were created but that they should now be considered inoperative, either temporarily or permanently. The VCLT includes many detailed rules governing both categories.

Obviously, rules that permit states to evade treaty obligations pose a threat to the stability of the system of mutual legal obligation upon which treaty law is built. The overall tone of the VCLT's invalidity, suspension, and termination provisions therefore reflects treaty law's general hostility towards such rules. Articles 42 and 43 provide the starting point. Note how Article 42 envisages that the Convention's rules constitute the *exclusive* means of challenging the validity of a treaty, whereas suspension or termination of a treaty may take place either pursuant to the VCLT *or* to the provisions of the treaty itself.[56] What is the logic behind this distinction? Article 43 serves as a reminder that treaties are not the only sources of international legal obligation that may bind states.

In the following articles, reference is made to "denunciation" and "withdrawal." These terms both relate to a unilateral act of repudiation of a treaty by a party with a view to terminating its obligations under the treaty. Denunciation is used in the bilateral context (and if successful brings about not only the termination of the denouncing party's obligations under the treaty, but the treaty itself); whereas withdrawal is used in the multilateral context (and if successful terminates the withdrawing party's obligations, but not necessarily the treaty itself).

Vienna Convention on the Law of Treaties, 23 May 1969, 1155 UNTS 33, Can TS 1980 No 37, in force 27 January 1980

Article 42
Validity and continuance in force of treaties
1. The validity of a treaty or of the consent of a State to be bound by a treaty may be impeached only through the application of the present Convention.

2. The termination of a treaty, its denunciation or the withdrawal of a party, may take place only as a result of the application of the provisions of the treaty or of the present Convention. The same rule applies to suspension of the operation of a treaty.

Article 43
Obligations imposed by international law independently of a treaty
The invalidity, termination or denunciation of a treaty, the withdrawal of a party from it, or the suspension of its operation, as a result of the application of the present Convention or of the provisions of the treaty, shall not in any way impair the duty of any State to fulfil any obligation embodied in the treaty to which it would be subject under international law independently of the treaty.

b) Invalidity of Treaties
Articles 46 to 53 of the VCLT set out the exhaustive bases upon which a treaty, or a state's consent to be bound by it, may be considered invalid.

Articles 46 and 47 address situations where the alleged invalidity flows from domestic legal constraints. Note the distinction between Article 46 (which sets out the limited

---

56 See also Articles 54 and 57.

circumstances in which conflict with domestic law arrests the valid *creation* of legal obligations) and Article 27 (which, as we have seen, provides that conflict with domestic law does not excuse failure to *perform* treaty obligations). Article 47, which deals with the effects of limits on a state representative's authority to express consent to be bound by a treaty, must be read along with Articles 7 and 8, relating to full powers.

By contrast, Articles 48 to 52 deal with "external" bases of invalidity. Below we examine some caselaw relating to invalidity based on error and coercion of states, but there is very little state practice relating to the effects of fraud, bribery, and coercion of state representatives on the validity of treaties. These provisions nevertheless seem sensible and perhaps self-evident corollaries of the proposition that treaty obligations arise as a result of a state's freely expressed consent to be bound by such obligations.

Article 53 also renders invalid treaties that, while properly concluded, conflict with higher principles of international law—so-called *jus cogens* or peremptory norms. *Jus cogens* rules of international law are discussed in greater detail in Section E of this chapter.

Consider the different language used in Articles 46 to 53 to describe the effect of each of the situations addressed in those articles. Note, for example, that some situations allow a state to "invoke" the situation as "invalidating its consent," whereas others simply render the treaty "void." What important option does the former category confer on the state whose consent to be bound is in issue? Consider also the practical significance of each category in a multilateral context.

Vienna Convention on the Law of Treaties, 23 May 1969, 1155 UNTS 331, Can TS 1980 No 37, in force 27 January 1980

Article 46
Provisions of internal law regarding competence to conclude treaties
1. A State may not invoke the fact that its consent to be bound by a treaty has been expressed in violation of a provision of its internal law regarding competence to conclude treaties as invalidating its consent unless that violation was manifest and concerned a rule of its internal law of fundamental importance.

2. A violation is manifest if it would be objectively evident to any State conducting itself in the matter in accordance with normal practice and in good faith.

Article 47
Specific restrictions on authority to express the consent of a State
If the authority of a representative to express the consent of a State to be bound by a particular treaty has been made subject to a specific restriction, his omission to observe that restriction may not be invoked as invalidating the consent expressed by him unless the restriction was notified to the other negotiating States prior to his expressing such consent.

Article 48
Error
1. A State may invoke an error in a treaty as invalidating its consent to be bound by the treaty if the error relates to a fact or situation which was assumed by that State to exist at the time when the treaty was concluded and formed an essential basis of its consent to be bound by the treaty.

2. Paragraph 1 shall not apply if the State in question contributed by its own conduct to the error or if the circumstances were such as to put that State on notice of a possible error.

3. An error relating only to the wording of the text of a treaty does not affect its validity; article 79 then applies.

Article 49
Fraud
If a State has been induced to conclude a treaty by the fraudulent conduct of another negotiating State, the State may invoke the fraud as invalidating its consent to be bound by the treaty.

Article 50
Corruption of a representative of a State
If the expression of a State's consent to be bound by a treaty has been procured through the corruption of its representative directly or indirectly by another negotiating State, the State may invoke such corruption as invalidating its consent to be bound by the treaty.

Article 51
Coercion of a representative of a State
The expression of a State's consent to be bound by a treaty which has been procured by the coercion of its representative through acts or threats directed against him shall be without any legal effect.

Article 52
Coercion of a State by the threat or use of force
A treaty is void if its conclusion has been procured by the threat or use of force in viola-tion of the principles of international law embodied in the Charter of the United Nations.

Article 53
Treaties conflicting with a peremptory norm of general international law (jus cogens)
A treaty is void if, at the time of its conclusion, it conflicts with a peremptory norm of general international law. For the purposes of the present Convention, a peremptory norm of general international law is a norm accepted and recognized by the international community of States as a whole as a norm from which no derogation is permitted and which can be modified only by a subsequent norm of general international law having the same character.

The error justification for invalidating a treaty is not an easy claim to prove, especially where the state making the argument is partially to blame for the mistake. Consider the following case by way of analogy:

Case Concerning the Temple of Preah Vihear (Cambodia v Thailand), Merits, Judgment, [1962] ICJ Rep 6 at 57

[The parties disputed sovereignty over the precincts of the Temple at Preah Vihear, which is located close to the Thai-Cambodian border. A 1904 Treaty had provided that the boundary between Thailand and Cambodia was to follow the watershed between the two countries, to be plotted by a mixed boundary commission. Maps were duly completed and sent to Thailand, one of which showed the Preah Vihear district on the Cambodian side of the boundary. It later emerged that truly following the watershed would have placed Preah Vihear within Thai territory. The Court nevertheless found on various grounds that sovereignty over Preah Vihear belonged to Cambodia. In a separate concurring opinion, Judge Fitzmaurice specifically addressed the Thai argument that any consent to Cambodian sovereignty it may have exhibited was vitiated by the fact that the map on which it relied was in error.]

Separate Opinion of Sir Gerald Fitzmaurice
. . . In the interests of the stability of contracts, the principle of error as vitiating consent is usually applied somewhat strictly; and I consider that this approach is also the correct one in international law, in the interests of the stability of treaties, and of frontier lines established by treaty or other forms of agreement. That there was (as I think) an error in the map by reference to the true watershed line does not necessarily mean that Thailand was herself under any misapprehension, nor that, if she was, she can, in law, now plead the fact. . . .

It was the Siamese Government itself which, with the assent, and actually at the suggestion of the Siamese members of the Mixed Commission, formally requested that the work of preparing the maps of the frontier areas should be carried out by the French topographical officers. . . .

It is apparent, therefore, that no one on the Siamese side could have been under any misapprehension as to the provenance of these maps. Furthermore, it is evident that the Siamese authorities deliberately left the whole thing to the French elements involved, and thus accepted the risk that the maps might prove inaccurate in some respects. Consequently, it was for them to verify the results, if they wished to do so, in whatever way was most appropriate in the circumstances, e.g. by consulting neutral experts. If they did not (for whatever reasons) wish to do this, then they had to abide by these results. The formal request for extra copies for the use of the provincial Governors shows that, in any event, the case was not one of a mere passive reception of these maps by the Siamese authorities.

The explanation of all this, there can be no reasonable doubt, is that, in effect, everyone on the Siamese side relied on the skill and good faith of the French topographical officers producing the maps. There can equally be no doubt that the latter acted in complete good faith, used all their skill, and fully believed that the watershed in the Preah Vihear region ran as indicated by the Annex I line. One may sympathize with Siam's lack of topographical and cartographical expertise at this time, but one is dealing with sovereign independent States to whom certain rules of law apply; and it remains the fact that, in the absence of any question of lack of good faith, the legal effect of reliance on the skill of an expert is that one must abide by the results—in short, a principle akin to that of *caveat emptor* is relevant. . . . [T]he Siamese authorities, knowing the character and provenance of the map, being in a position to consult their Commissioners who had received it, or experts of their own choice, made no objection, and raised no query, in relation to a line which was clearly intended to represent and constitute the line of the frontier in this region, and which anyone looking at it must have seen at once placed Preah Vihear on the Cambodian side of the line. Today Thailand says the map was erroneous and that she was under a misapprehension about it. But the Siamese authorities of that date plainly accepted the risk that just such an error as this might in time be discovered: and whoever does that, must be held thereby also, and in advance, to have accepted such errors as do in fact eventually come to light. . . .

The reference in Article 52 of the VCLT to the "threat or use of force" is an obvious allusion to Article 2(4) of the UN Charter, which reads: "All Members shall refrain in their international relations from the threat or use of force against the territorial integrity or political independence of any state, or in any other manner inconsistent with the Purposes of the United Nations." The scope of Article 2(4) is discussed at length in Chapter 14. For present purposes, however, on what basis would a peace treaty or other agreement terminating hostilities between two states be considered valid? Consider the importance of the words other than "threat or use of force" used in Article 52.

When the "threat or use of force" language was debated in relation to Article 52 of the VCLT, some states took the view that extreme forms of economic coercion should also be covered. However, this view was opposed by a minority of key states, including the United States.[57] As a compromise, the negotiating states adopted the Declaration on the Prohibition of the Threat or Use of Economic or Political Coercion in Concluding a Treaty,[58] condemning the "threat or use of pressure in any form, whether military, political or economic . . . in violation of the principles of the sovereign equality of States and freedom of consent." Shortly thereafter, in 1970, the UN General Assembly adopted the Friendly Relations Declaration,[59] which provides that "[n]o State may use or encourage the use of economic . . . measures to coerce another State in order to obtain from it the subordination of the exercise of its sovereign rights and to secure from it advantages of any kind." These documents, while not binding international legal instruments in their own right, may reflect the emergence of customary principles of international law.[60] Even if so, however, would it necessarily follow that treaties procured by economic or political coercion would automatically be void? Should the concept of coercion of states, as used in Article 52, be expanded? If so, how should the threshold degree of economic or other pressure required to constitute coercion and thereby void a treaty be defined? What, if any, effect would such an expansion have on the validity of treaties generally?

Recently, at least one scholar has pointed to Article 52 in arguing that some of the agreements entered into by the Federal Republic of Yugoslavia in relation to the settle-

---

57 See Jon Hink, "The Republic of Palau and the United States: Self-Determination Becomes the Price of Free Association" (1990) 78 Cal L Rev 915 at 962 *et seq.*

58 *Official Records of the United Nations Conference on the Law of Treaties,* 1st and 2d Sess, UN Doc A/CONF.39/1/Add. 2 (1971).

59 *Declaration on Principles of International Law Concerning Friendly Relations and Co-operation among States in Accordance with the Charter of the United Nations,* GA Res 2625 (XXV), UN Doc A/RES/2625/XXV, UN GAOR, 25th Sess, Supp No 28 at 121–24, UN Doc A/8028 Corr 1 (1970); (1970) 9 ILM 1292 [Friendly Relations Declaration].

60 The International Court of Justice continues to recognize that the Friendly Relations Declaration reflects customary international law: *Accordance with International Law of the Unilateral Declaration of Independence in Respect of Kosovo,* Advisory Opinion, [2010] ICJ Rep 403 at para 80.

ment of the Kosovo conflict were coerced and thus void.[61] In the case that follows, however, the ICJ took a cautious approach to Article 52.

Fisheries Jurisdiction (United Kingdom v Iceland), Jurisdiction of the Court, Judgment, [1973] ICJ Rep 3

[Iceland purported to increase the breadth of the exclusive fisheries zone along its coast from 12 to 50 nautical miles. The United Kingdom objected and submitted the matter to the ICJ pursuant to a 1961 agreement with Iceland that disputes over fisheries jurisdiction would be referred to the Court. In disputing the ICJ's jurisdiction, Iceland pointed to official correspondence indicating that: "The 1961 Exchange of Notes took place under extremely difficult circumstances, when the British Royal Navy had been using force to oppose the 12-mile fishery limit established by the Icelandic Government in 1958." Iceland suggested that these circumstances might constitute improper duress, vitiating the treaty. The ICJ rejected this argument as follows.]

24. . . . [T]his statement [cited above] could be interpreted as a veiled charge of duress purportedly rendering the Exchange of Notes void *ab initio*, and it was dealt with as such by the United Kingdom in its Memorial. There can be little doubt, as is implied in the Charter of the United Nations and recognized in Article 52 of the Vienna Convention on the Law of Treaties, that under contemporary international law an agreement concluded under the threat or use of force is void. It is equally clear that a court cannot consider an accusation of this serious nature on the basis of a vague general charge unfortified by evidence in its support. The history of the negotiations which led up to the 1961 Exchange of Notes reveals that these instruments were freely negotiated by the interested parties on the basis of perfect equality and freedom of decision on both sides. No fact has been brought to the attention of the Court from any quarter suggesting the slightest doubt on this matter.

Where the invalidity of a treaty is established, Article 69 of the VCLT provides that it is void and has no legal force. Further, if acts have been performed in reliance upon the treaty: (a) each party may require any other party to establish as far as possible in their mutual relations the position that would have existed if the acts had not been performed; and (b) acts performed in good faith before the invalidity was invoked are not rendered unlawful by reason only of the invalidity of the treaty. This detrimental reliance concept does not extend to states that, through their own acts of fraud, corruption, or coercion, create the circumstances giving rise to the invalidity.

c) Termination and Suspension of the Operation of Treaties

i) *Termination or Suspension by Consent*

A treaty validly brought into force may subsequently be terminated or suspended in certain circumstances. Exactly when and in what circumstances this may occur is usually a matter agreed to by the parties themselves. For example, the treaty itself may expressly

---

61 Enrico Milano, "Security Council Action in the Balkans: Reviewing the Legality of Kosovo's Territorial Status" (2003) 14 EJIL 999.

or by implication provide for its termination or suspension, or permit unilateral denunciation of or withdrawal from the treaty by one of the parties. Even where the treaty does not address these matters, the parties may subsequently consent, either expressly or by necessary implication, to its termination or suspension. Note how the following provisions of the VCLT, while accommodating consensual termination, suspension, denunciation, or withdrawal, nevertheless seek to ensure respect for the intentions of the parties and (at least in the multilateral context) the rights of remaining parties to the treaty.

Vienna Convention on the Law of Treaties, 23 May 1969, 1155 UNTS 331, Can TS 1980 No 37, in force 27 January 1980

Article 54
Termination of or withdrawal from a treaty under its provisions or by consent of the parties
The termination of a treaty or the withdrawal of a party may take place:
    (a) in conformity with the provisions of the treaty; or
    (b) at any time by consent of all the parties after consultation with the other contracting States.

Article 55
Reduction of the parties to a multilateral treaty below the number necessary for its entry into force
Unless the treaty otherwise provides, a multilateral treaty does not terminate by reason only of the fact that the number of the parties falls below the number necessary for its entry into force.

Article 56
Denunciation of or withdrawal from a treaty containing no provision regarding termination, denunciation or withdrawal
1. A treaty which contains no provision regarding its termination and which does not provide for denunciation or withdrawal is not subject to denunciation or withdrawal unless:
    (a) it is established that the parties intended to admit the possibility of denunciation or withdrawal; or
    (b) a right of denunciation or withdrawal may be implied by the nature of the treaty.

2. A party shall give not less than twelve months' notice of its intention to denounce or withdraw from a treaty under paragraph 1.

Article 57
Suspension of the operation of a treaty under its provisions or by consent of the parties
The operation of a treaty in regard to all the parties or to a particular party may be suspended:
    (a) in conformity with the provisions of the treaty; or
    (b) at any time by consent of all the parties after consultation with the other contracting States.

Article 58
Suspension of the operation of a multilateral treaty by agreement between certain of the parties only
1. Two or more parties to a multilateral treaty may conclude an agreement to suspend the operation of provisions of the treaty, temporarily and as between themselves alone, if:

(a) the possibility of such a suspension is provided for by the treaty; or

(b) the suspension in question is not prohibited by the treaty and:

(i) does not affect the enjoyment by the other parties of their rights under the treaty or the performance of their obligations;

(ii) is not incompatible with the object and purpose of the treaty.

2. Unless in a case falling under paragraph 1(a) the treaty otherwise provides, the parties in question shall notify the other parties of their intention to conclude the agreement and of those provisions of the treaty the operation of which they intend to suspend.

Article 59
Termination or suspension of the operation of a treaty implied by conclusion of a later treaty
1. A treaty shall be considered as terminated if all the parties to it conclude a later treaty relating to the same subject-matter and:

(a) it appears from the later treaty or is otherwise established that the parties intended that the matter should be governed by that treaty; or

(b) the provisions of the later treaty are so far incompatible with those of the earlier one that the two treaties are not capable of being applied at the same time.

2. The earlier treaty shall be considered as only suspended in operation if it appears from the later treaty or is otherwise established that such was the intention of the parties.

LAW IN CONTEXT

Withdrawal from Human Rights Treaties

In Article 56, the VCLT suggests that a power of withdrawal or denunciation may be implied. In the human rights area, efforts to withdraw on the basis of an implied right to do so may be firmly resisted. Consider the following discussion, focusing on North Korea's attempt to withdraw from a key human rights convention.

Philippe Kirsch, "Canadian Practice in International Law at the Department of Foreign Affairs in 1996–1997" (1997) 35 Can YB Int'l Law 349 at 369–71

Treaties

Denunciation of Treaties
. . . [A] good case can be made that the "denunciation" of the [International] Covenant [on Civil and Political Rights (ICCPR)] by the [Democratic People's Republic of Korea] (DPRK) is of no legal effect and that it remains bound by its provisions. We note, however, that the issue of whether or not the ICCPR is subject to denunciation has not been subject to a clear pronouncement in international law or jurisprudence. Furthermore, in the absence of a precedent—and other states' reactions to it—there is no extant state practice on this point.

The Process of "Denunciation" at International Law
Neither of the Covenants (ICCPR or ICESCR) contains an express provision for denunciation by a State Party. Accordingly, denunciation would have to proceed in accordance with

the international law of treaties. The Vienna Convention on the Law of Treaties [VCLT] contains the following provision: . . . [Article 56 is reproduced.]

Canada and South Korea are parties to the VCLT, while the DPRK is not. Its provisions are, however, widely regarded as reflecting the customary international law of treaties. Two questions therefore arise from the absence of a denunciation clause in the ICCPR.

Did the Parties intend to admit the possibility of denunciation or withdrawal?

The intent of states parties, where not expressly stated, may be deduced from a number of circumstances. . . . [A] review of the purposes of the ICCPR—as expressed in the preamble—can provide a useful insight into the intention of the State Parties concerning their own ability to revoke the ICCPR's provisions. In our view, the references in the preamble to "the obligation of States under the Charter of the United Nations to promote universal respect for, and observance of, human rights and fundamental freedoms" as well as the references to "inherent dignity" and "equal and inalienable rights" and to the goals of the Universal Declaration are evidence of the Parties' acknowledgement of the fundamental and irrevocable nature of these rights.

The First Optional Protocol to the ICCPR, which expressly and with procedural detail provides for denunciation, usefully illustrates the point that, where the Parties do intend to allow for denunciation, they will do so expressly.

Finally, the absence of a precedent for the denunciation of the ICCPR or ICESCR by a State Party suggests that state practice . . . argues against the availability of denunciation.

Is a right of denunciation "implied by the nature of the treaty"?

In our view, the nature of the ICCPR seems to preclude such an implication, which is more readily made in the context of instruments that regulate the conduct of State Parties as between themselves, usually based on mutual concessions, such as a mutual legal assistance treaty, the GATT, or an oil exploration agreement. The Covenants, on the other hand, oblige State Parties unilaterally to protect and implement the fundamental rights of persons, the existence of which is already recognized as customary international law and cannot thus be denied. Finally, academic views on the denunciability of the Covenants confirm that their "nature" would appear to preclude the implication that these treaties are denounceable. . . .

A further analogy concerning the "nature" of the ICCPR can be drawn in respect of its own derogation provisions. The Covenant provides for derogability only of certain of its provisions, and then only in "times of emergency which threatens the life of the nation." As a result, even armed conflict, or the exercise of a State's right at international law to the use of force in self-defence, cannot operate to vitiate certain central provisions of the ICCPR. . . . It would therefore be difficult to argue that unilateral denunciation by a State Party—in a fit of political pique at that—could achieve the same end. . . .

Conclusion

In conclusion, there are strong arguments in favour of the view that the ICCPR is not an instrument that can be denounced unilaterally by a State Party. Moreover, it should be noted that the substantive provisions of the ICCPR—in particular those tracking the Universal Declaration and/or the expressly nonderogable rights, but not the reporting obligations—have entered into customary international law. Accordingly, even if the denunciation of the ICCPR by the DPRK were to be of legal effect, the DPRK would remain under an obligation at international law not to contravene its provisions.

Absent consent, the VCLT also allows a party to invoke, unilaterally, certain very limited grounds for termination or suspension of its treaty obligations, as we shall now see.

ii) Termination or Suspension in Response to a Breach

Termination or suspension may serve as a self-help remedy for one or more parties to a treaty in response to its breach by another. Naturally, permitting such retaliatory measures is more complicated in the case of a multilateral treaty, as outlined in the following provisions of the VCLT. What is the rationale behind the exception set out in Article 60(5)?

Vienna Convention on the Law of Treaties, 23 May 1969, 1155 UNTS 331, Can TS 1980 No 37, in force 27 January 1980

Article 60
Termination or suspension of the operation of a treaty as a consequence of its breach

1. A material breach of a bilateral treaty by one of the parties entitles the other to invoke the breach as a ground for terminating the treaty or suspending its operation in whole or in part.

2. A material breach of a multilateral treaty by one of the parties entitles:
    (a) the other parties by unanimous agreement to suspend the operation of the treaty in whole or in part or to terminate it either:
        (i) in the relations between themselves and the defaulting State, or
        (ii) as between all the parties;

    (b) a party specially affected by the breach to invoke it as a ground for suspending the operation of the treaty in whole or in part in the relations between itself and the defaulting State;
    (c) any party other than the defaulting State to invoke the breach as a ground for suspending the operation of the treaty in whole or in part with respect to itself if the treaty is of such a character that a material breach of its provisions by one party radically changes the position of every party with respect to the further performance of its obligations under the treaty.

3. A material breach of a treaty, for the purposes of this article, consists in:
    (a) a repudiation of the treaty not sanctioned by the present Convention; or
    (b) the violation of a provision essential to the accomplishment of the object or purpose of the treaty.

4. The foregoing paragraphs are without prejudice to any provision in the treaty applicable in the event of a breach.

5. Paragraphs 1 to 3 do not apply to provisions relating to the protection of the human person contained in treaties of a humanitarian character, in particular to provisions prohibiting any form of reprisals against persons protected by such treaties.

The principles codified in Article 60 were considered in a case before the ICJ concerning apartheid-era South Africa's behaviour in Namibia.

Legal Consequences for States of the Continued Presence of South Africa in Namibia (South West Africa) Notwithstanding Security Council Resolution 276 (1970), Advisory Opinion, [1971] ICJ Rep 16

[Following World War I, South West Africa (later Namibia) was deemed, by the League of Nations, incapable of governing itself. The League therefore granted South Africa a "Mandate" (a form of trusteeship) over South West Africa. Following the demise of the League, South Africa contended that the Mandate had lapsed and that it was free to dispose of South West Africa as it wished. The Court rejected that contention in a 1950 advisory opinion[62] and in a 1962 preliminary ruling on applications brought by Ethiopia and Liberia (cited in the extract below).[63] South Africa nevertheless persisted in occupying Namibia, prompting the General Assembly to adopt a resolution[64] terminating the Mandate on the basis that South Africa had fundamentally breached its Mandate obligations. The UN Security Council asked the ICJ for its opinion on the legality of this move.]

94. In examining this action of the General Assembly it is appropriate to have regard to the general principles of international law regulating termination of a treaty relationship on account of breach. For even if the mandate is viewed as having the character of an institution, as is maintained, it depends on those international agreements which created the system and regulated its application. As the Court indicated in 1962 "this Mandate, like practically all other similar Mandates" was "a special type of instrument composite in nature and instituting a novel international regime. It incorporates a definite agreement . . ." (*I.C.J. Reports 1962*, p. 331). The Court stated conclusively in that Judgment that the Mandate ". . . in fact and in law, is an international agreement having the character of a treaty or convention" (*I.C.J. Reports 1962*, p. 330). The rules laid down by the Vienna Convention on the Law of Treaties concerning termination of a treaty relationship on account of breach (adopted without a dissenting vote) may in many respects be considered as a codification of existing customary law on the subject. In the light of these rules, only a material breach of a treaty justifies termination, such breach being defined as:

    (a) a repudiation of the treaty not sanctioned by the present Convention; or

    (b) the violation of a provision essential to the accomplishment of the object or purpose of the treaty (Art. 60, para. 3).

95. General Assembly resolution 2145 (XXI) determines that both forms of material breach had occurred in this case. By stressing that South Africa "has, in fact, disavowed the Mandate", the General Assembly declared in fact that it had repudiated it. The resolution in question is therefore to be viewed as the exercise of the right to terminate a rela-

---

62 *International Status of South-West Africa*, Advisory Opinion, [1950] ICJ Rep 128.

63 *South West Africa Cases (Ethiopia v South Africa; Liberia v South Africa)*, Preliminary Objections, Judgment, [1962] ICJ Rep 319.

64 *Question of South West Africa*, GA Res 2145 (XXI), reprinted in UN GAOR, 21st Sess, Supp No 16 at 2–3, UN Doc A/6316 (1966).

tionship in case of a deliberate and persistent violation of obligations which destroys the very object and purpose of that relationship.

96. It has been contended that the Covenant of the League of Nations did not confer on the Council of the League power to terminate a mandate for misconduct of the mandatory and that no such power could therefore be exercised by the United Nations, since it could not derive from the League greater powers than the latter itself had. For this objection to prevail it would be necessary to show that the mandates system, as established under the League, excluded the application of the general principle of law that a right of termination on account of breach must be presumed to exist in respect of all treaties, except as regards provisions relating to the protection of the human person contained in treaties of a humanitarian character (as indicated in Art, 60, para. 5, of the Vienna Convention). The silence of a treaty as to the existence of such a right cannot be interpreted as implying the exclusion of a right which has its source outside of the treaty, in general international law, and is dependent on the occurrence of circumstances which are not normally envisaged when a treaty is concluded. . . .

iii) Termination or Suspension in Response to Impossibility

What happens if it becomes impossible to fulfill one's treaty obligations? The answer depends, in the law of treaties, on what one means by "impossible."

Vienna Convention on the Law of Treaties, 23 May 1969, 1155 UNTS 331, Can TS 1980 No 37, in force 27 January 1980

Article 61
Supervening impossibility of performance
1. A party may invoke the impossibility of performing a treaty as a ground for terminating or withdrawing from it if the impossibility results from the permanent disappearance or destruction of an object indispensable for the execution of the treaty. If the impossibility is temporary, it may be invoked only as a ground for suspending the operation of the treaty.

2. Impossibility of performance may not be invoked by a party as a ground for terminating, withdrawing from or suspending the operation of a treaty if the impossibility is the result of a breach by that party either of an obligation under the treaty or of any other international obligation owed to any other party to the treaty.

As the case that follows suggests, the grounds for invoking impossibility of performance as a basis for terminating or suspending a treaty are applied strictly.

Gabčíkovo-Nagymaros Project (Hungary v Slovakia), Judgment, [1997] ICJ Rep 7

. . . 15. The present case arose out of the signature, on 16 September 1977, by the Hungarian People's Republic and the Czechoslovak People's Republic [Slovakia's predecessor state], of a treaty "concerning the construction and operation of the Gabčíkovo-Nagymaros System of Locks" (hereinafter called the "1977 Treaty"). . . .

It provides for the construction and operation of a System of Locks by the parties as a "joint investment." . . .

The joint investment was . . . essentially aimed at the production of hydroelectricity, the improvement of navigation on the relevant section of the Danube and the protection of the areas along the banks against flooding. At the same time, by the terms of the Treaty, the contracting parties undertook to ensure that the quality of water in the Danube was not impaired as a result of the Project, and that compliance with the obligations for the protection of nature arising in connection with the construction and operation of the System of Locks would be observed. . . .

22. As a result of intense criticism which the Project had generated in Hungary, the Hungarian Government decided on 13 May 1989 to suspend the works at Nagymaros pending the completion of various studies which the competent authorities were to finish before 31 July 1989. On 21 July 1989, the Hungarian Government extended the suspension of the works at Nagymaros until 31 October 1989, and, in addition, suspended the works at Dunakiliti until the same date. Lastly, on 27 October 1989, Hungary decided to abandon the works at Nagymaros and to maintain the status quo at Dunakiliti.

23. During this period, negotiations . . . continued between the two parties but to no avail, and, on 19 May 1992, the Hungarian Government transmitted to the Czechoslovak Government a Note Verbale terminating the 1977 Treaty with effect from 25 May 1992. . . .

102. [In defending its actions,] Hungary . . . relied on the principle of the impossibility of performance as reflected in Article 61 of the Vienna Convention on the Law of Treaties. Hungary's interpretation of the wording of Article 61 is, however, not in conformity with the terms of that Article, nor with the intentions of the Diplomatic Conference which adopted the Convention. Article 61, paragraph 1, requires the "permanent disappearance or destruction of an object indispensable for the execution" of the treaty to justify the termination of a treaty on grounds of impossibility of performance. During the conference, a proposal was made to extend the scope of the article by including in it cases such as the impossibility to make certain payments because of serious financial difficulties. . . . Although it was recognized that such situations could lead to a preclusion of the wrongfulness of non-performance by a party of its treaty obligations, the participating States were not prepared to consider such situations to be a ground for terminating or suspending a treaty, and preferred to limit themselves to a narrower concept.

103. Hungary contended that the essential object of the [1977] Treaty—an economic joint investment which was consistent with environmental protection and which was operated by the two contracting parties jointly—had permanently disappeared and that the Treaty had thus become impossible to perform. It is not necessary for the Court to determine whether the term "object" in Article 61 can also be understood to embrace a legal régime as in any event, even if that were the case, it would have to conclude that in this instance that régime had not definitively ceased to exist. The 1977 Treaty . . . actually made available to the parties the necessary means to proceed at any time, by negotiation, to the required readjustments between economic imperatives and ecological imperatives. The Court would add that, if the joint exploitation of the investment was no longer possible, this was originally because Hungary did not carry out most of the works for which it was responsible under the 1977 Treaty; Article 61, paragraph 2, of the Vienna Convention expressly provides that impossibility of performance may not be invoked for the termination of a treaty by a party to that treaty when it results from that party's own breach of an obligation flowing from that treaty.

What is the reason for the strict treatment of impossibility as a basis for termination or suspension of treaty obligations? Are there situations in which this strict approach might lead to injustice or hardship for a state or its people? Reconsider these questions after reading the materials in the next subsection on fundamental changes of circumstances.

iv) Termination or Suspension in Response to Fundamental Changes of Circumstances
While it may not be impossible, in the strict sense of Article 61, for a party to perform its obligations under a treaty, doing so may in some cases require steps that are simply unacceptable to that party. What are the dangers of permitting unilateral termination, suspension, or withdrawal in such circumstances? Consider how Article 62 addresses this tension.

Vienna Convention on the Law of Treaties, 23 May 1969, 1155 UNTS 331, Can TS 1980 No 37, in force 27 January 1980

Article 62
Fundamental change of circumstances
1. A fundamental change of circumstances which has occurred with regard to those existing at the time of the conclusion of a treaty, and which was not foreseen by the parties, may not be invoked as a ground for terminating or withdrawing from the treaty unless:
    (a) the existence of those circumstances constituted an essential basis of the consent of the parties to be bound by the treaty; and
    (b) the effect of the change is radically to transform the extent of obligations still to be performed under the treaty.

2. A fundamental change of circumstances may not be invoked as a ground for terminating or withdrawing from a treaty:
    (a) if the treaty establishes a boundary; or
    (b) if the fundamental change is the result of a breach by the party invoking it either of an obligation under the treaty or of any other international obligation owed to any other party to the treaty.

3. If, under the foregoing paragraphs, a party may invoke a fundamental change of circumstances as a ground for terminating or withdrawing from a treaty it may also invoke the change as a ground for suspending the operation of the treaty.

Does Article 62 lean towards protecting the interests of the party wishing to terminate or suspend its obligations, or those of the other parties to the treaty, in such a case? Consider the manner in which the rules relating to fundamental changes of circumstances were applied by the ICJ in the following cases.

Fisheries Jurisdiction (United Kingdom v Iceland), **Jurisdiction of the Court, Judgment, [1973] ICJ Rep 3**

[Iceland purported to increase the breadth of the exclusive fisheries zone off its coasts from twelve to fifty nautical miles. The United Kingdom objected and submitted the matter to the ICJ pursuant to a 1961 agreement with Iceland that disputes over Iceland's fisheries jurisdiction would be referred to the Court. Iceland contended that that agreement was no longer in force given various changes in circumstances since its making. The ICJ rejected this argument as follows.]

34. It is possible that today Iceland may find that some of the motives which induced it to enter into the 1961 Exchange of Notes have become less compelling or have disappeared altogether. But this is not a ground justifying the repudiation of those parts of the agreement the object and purpose of which have remained unchanged. . . .

35. In his letter of 29 May 1972 to the Registrar, the Minister for Foreign Affairs of Iceland refers to "the changed circumstances resulting from the ever-increasing exploitation of the fishery resources in the seas surrounding Iceland". . . .

36. In these statements the Government of Iceland is basing itself on the principle of termination of a treaty by reason of change of circumstances. International law admits that a fundamental change in the circumstances which determined the parties to accept a treaty, if it has resulted in a radical transformation of the extent of the obligations imposed by it, may, under certain conditions, afford the party affected a ground for invoking the termination or suspension of the treaty. This principle, and the conditions and exceptions to which it is subject, have been embodied in Article 62 of the Vienna Convention on the Law of Treaties, which may in many respects be considered as a codification of existing customary law on the subject of the termination of a treaty relationship on account of change of circumstances.

37. One of the basic requirements embodied in that Article is that the change of circumstances must have been a fundamental one. In this respect the Government of Iceland has, with regard to developments in fishing techniques, referred . . . to the increased exploitation of the fishery resources in the seas surrounding Iceland and to the danger of still further exploitation because of an increase in the catching capacity of fishing fleets. The Icelandic statements recall the exceptional dependence of that country on its fishing for its existence and economic development. In his letter of 29 May 1972 the Minister stated:

> "The Government of Iceland, considering that the vital interests of the people of Iceland are involved, respectfully informs the Court that it is not willing to confer jurisdiction on the Court in any case involving the extent of the fishery limits of Iceland. . . ."

38. The invocation by Iceland of its "vital interests," which were not made the subject of an express reservation to the acceptance of the jurisdictional obligation under the 1961 Exchange of Notes, must be interpreted, in the context of the assertion of changed circumstances, as an indication by Iceland of the reason why it regards as fundamental the changes which in its view have taken place in previously existing fishing techniques. This interpretation would correspond to the traditional view that the changes of circumstances which must be regarded as fundamental or vital are those which imperil the existence or vital development of one of the parties. . . .

40. . . . But the alleged changes could not affect in the least the obligation to submit to the Court's jurisdiction, which is the only issue at the present stage of the proceedings. It follows that the apprehended dangers for the vital interests of Iceland, resulting from chan-

ges in fishing techniques, cannot constitute a fundamental change with respect to the lapse or subsistence of the compromissory clause establishing the Court's jurisdiction. . . .

43. Moreover, in order that a change of circumstances may give rise to a ground for invoking the termination of a treaty it is also necessary that it should have resulted in a radical transformation of the extent of the obligations still to be performed. The change must have increased the burden of the obligations to be executed to the extent of rendering the performance something essentially different from that originally undertaken. In respect of the obligation with which the Court is here concerned, this condition is wholly unsatisfied; the change of circumstances alleged by Iceland cannot be said to have transformed radically the extent of the jurisdictional obligation which is imposed in the 1961 Exchange of Notes. The compromissory clause enabled either of the parties to submit to the Court any dispute between them relating to an extension of Icelandic fisheries jurisdiction in the waters above its continental shelf beyond the 12-mile limit. The present dispute is exactly of the character anticipated in the compromissory clause of the Exchange of Notes. Not only has the jurisdictional obligation not been radically transformed in its extent; it has remained precisely what it was in 1961. . . .

Separate Opinion of Sir Gerald Fitzmaurice

. . . 17. With regard to the question of "changed circumstances" I have nothing to add to what is stated in paragraphs 35–43 of the Court's Judgment, except to emphasize that in my opinion the only change that could possibly be relevant (if at all) would be some change relating directly to the, so to speak, operability of the jurisdictional clause itself—not to such things as developments in fishery techniques or in Iceland's situation relative to fisheries. These would indeed be matters that would militate for, not against, adjudication. But as regards the jurisdictional clause itself, the only "change" that has occurred is the purported extension of Icelandic fishery limits. This however is the absolute *reverse* of the type of change to which the doctrine of "changed circumstances" relates, namely one never contemplated by the Parties: it is in fact the actual change they did contemplate, and specified as the one that would give rise to the obligation to have recourse to adjudication. . . .

Gabčíkovo-Nagymaros Project (Hungary v Slovakia), Judgment, [1997] ICJ Rep 7

[This case concerned a treaty providing for the construction and operation of a series of dams on the Danube river, as set out in the excerpt appearing above in Section B(8)(c)(iii).]

104. Hungary further argued that it was entitled to invoke a number of events which, cumulatively, would have constituted a fundamental change of circumstances. In this respect it specified profound changes of a political nature, the Project's diminishing economic viability, the progress of environmental knowledge and the development of new norms and prescriptions of international environmental law. . . .

The prevailing political situation was certainly relevant for the conclusion of the 1977 Treaty. But the Court will recall that the Treaty provided for a joint investment programme for the production of energy, the control of floods and the improvement of navigation on the Danube. In the Court's view, the prevalent political conditions were thus not so closely linked to the object and purpose of the Treaty that they constituted an essential basis of the consent of the parties and, in changing, radically altered the extent of the obligations still to be performed. The same holds good for the economic system in force at the time of the conclusion of the 1977 Treaty. Besides, even though the estimated profitability of the Project might have appeared less in 1992 than in 1977, it does not appear from the record before the Court that it was bound to diminish to such an extent that the treaty obligations of the parties would have been radically transformed as a result.

The Court does not consider that new developments in the state of environmental knowledge and of environmental law can be said to have been completely unforeseen. What is more, the formulation of [the 1977 Treaty], designed to accommodate change, made it possible for the parties to take account of such developments and to apply them when implementing those treaty provisions.

The changed circumstances advanced by Hungary are, in the Court's view, not of such a nature, either individually or collectively, that their effect would radically transform the extent of the obligations still to be performed in order to accomplish the Project. A fundamental change of circumstances must have been unforeseen; the existence of the circumstances at the time of the Treaty's conclusion must have constituted an essential basis of the consent of the parties to be bound by the Treaty. The negative and conditional wording of Article 62 of the Vienna Convention on the Law of Treaties is a clear indication moreover that the stability of treaty relations requires that the plea of fundamental change of circumstances be applied only in exceptional cases. . . .

International treaty law's reluctance to allow even extreme circumstances to serve as a basis for suspending or terminating otherwise valid treaty relations is also illustrated in the ILC's Draft Articles on the Effects of Armed Conflicts on Treaties.[65] The "general principle" that lies at the heart of these Draft Articles is that even "an armed conflict does not *ipso facto* terminate or suspend the operation of treaties."[66]

v) Automatic Termination Due to Emergence of Conflicting Peremptory Norms

All of the foregoing bases for termination or suspension of treaty obligations require some action by at least one of the parties to the treaty. However, the VCLT also anticipates one instance where a treaty will terminate automatically:

Vienna Convention on the Law of Treaties, 23 May 1969, 1155 UNTS 331, Can TS 1980 No 37, in force 27 January 1980

Article 64
Emergence of a new peremptory norm of general international law (jus cogens)
If a new peremptory norm of general international law emerges, any existing treaty which is in conflict with that norm becomes void and terminates.

Article 64 is a logical corollary of the definition of peremptory norms as rules of higher law (known as *jus cogens* rules—a matter to which we return in Section E of this chapter)

---

65   Reprinted in *Report of the International Law Commission*, UN GAOR, 66th Sess, Supp No 10 at c VI, UN Doc A/66/10 (2011) [*ILC Report 2011*].

66   *Ibid* at 175, art 3.

and of the rule, articulated in Article 53, that treaties conflicting with such peremptory norms at the time of their conclusion are void.

vi) Consequences of Termination and Suspension

In general, termination of a treaty does not have retroactive effects (thus further underlining the distinction between invalidity and termination of a treaty). Similarly, the suspension of treaty obligations has time-limited effects.

Vienna Convention on the Law of Treaties, 23 May 1969, 1155 UNTS 331, Can TS 1980 No 37, in force 27 January 1980

Article 70
Consequences of the termination of a treaty
1. Unless the treaty otherwise provides or the parties otherwise agree, the termination of a treaty under its provisions or in accordance with the present Convention:
    (a) releases the parties from any obligation further to perform the treaty;
    (b) does not affect any right, obligation or legal situation of the parties created through the execution of the treaty prior to its termination.

2. If a State denounces or withdraws from a multilateral treaty, paragraph 1 applies in the relations between that State and each of the other parties to the treaty from the date when such denunciation or withdrawal takes effect.

Article 71
Consequences of the invalidity of a treaty which conflicts with a peremptory norm of general international law
. . . 2. In the case of a treaty which becomes void and terminates under article 64, the termination of the treaty:
    (a) releases the parties from any obligation further to perform the treaty;
    (b) does not affect any right, obligation or legal situation of the parties created through the execution of the treaty prior to its termination; provided that those rights, obligations or situations may thereafter be maintained only to the extent that their maintenance is not in itself in conflict with the new peremptory norm of general international law.

Article 72
Consequences of the suspension of the operation of a treaty
1. Unless the treaty otherwise provides or the parties otherwise agree, the suspension of the operation of a treaty under its provisions or in accordance with the present Convention:
    (a) releases the parties between which the operation of the treaty is suspended from the obligation to perform the treaty in their mutual relations during the period of the suspension;
    (b) does not otherwise affect the legal relations between the parties established by the treaty.

2. During the period of the suspension the parties shall refrain from acts tending to obstruct the resumption of the operation of the treaty.

C. CUSTOMARY INTERNATIONAL LAW

1) General Customary International Law

a) The Nature of Customary International Law

Recall that Article 38(1)(b) of the Statute of the International Court of Justice lists "international custom, as evidence of a general practice accepted as law" as one of the sources of international law that the ICJ may rely upon. Custom is the oldest source of rules in the international legal system, but also a source of evolution in the international legal system as practices adapt to new or changing circumstances. Perhaps the most remarkable feature of rules of "general" customary international law is that, once established, these rules are universally binding on all states (subject to very limited exceptions described below). The processes by which customary international law is formed, therefore, are of critical interest to states. Those processes are driven by the very nature of customary international law, which one international legal scholar has defined in the following way:

> Custom in its legal sense means something more than mere habit or usage; it is a usage felt by those who follow it to be an obligatory one. There must be present a feeling that, if the usage is departed from, some form of sanction will probably, or at any rate ought to, fall on the transgressor. Evidence that a custom in this sense exists in the international sphere can be found only by examining the practice of states; that is to say, we must look at what states do in their relations with one another and attempt to understand why they do it, and in particular whether they recognize an obligation to adopt a certain course, or, in the words of Article 38, we must examine whether the alleged custom shows "a general practice accepted as law."[67]

Doctrinally, therefore, the existence of customary international law requires two elements: (1) widespread and uniform state practice; and (2) accompanying *opinio juris*, or a belief on the part of states that their practice is mandatory as a matter of law. Consider the importance of each of these elements in the Permanent Court of International Justice's search for relevant customary international law in the following case.

The Case of the SS "Lotus" (France v Turkey), (1927) PCIJ (Ser A) No 10 at 18, 27–28, 30, and 32

[This case arose from a collision on the high seas between two ships, one French and the other Turkish. The Turkish vessel sank, killing eight passengers and crew members. The French ship was also badly damaged but managed to reach the nearby port of Constantinople (now Istanbul), where Turkish authorities arrested and charged one of its officers with involuntary manslaughter. The French officer was ultimately tried and convicted of various offences relating to the collision under Turkish law in a Turkish court. France brought a claim against Turkey claiming that Turkey's actions had violated a customary international law limitation on state jurisdiction in cases of high seas collision.]

---

67   James L Brierly, *The Law of Nations: An Introduction to the International Law of Peace*, 6th ed (Oxford: Clarendon Press, 1963) at 59–60.

. . . International law governs relations between independent States. The rules of law binding upon States therefore emanate from their own free will as expressed in conventions or by usages generally accepted as expressing principles of law and established in order to regulate the relations between these co-existing independent communities or with a view to the achievement of common aims. Restrictions upon the independence of States cannot therefore be presumed. . . .

It only remains to examine the third argument advanced by the French Government and to ascertain whether a rule specially applying to collision cases has grown up, according to which criminal proceedings regarding such cases come exclusively within the jurisdiction of the State whose flag is flown [by the vessel on which the offence occurred].

In this connection, the Agent for the French Government has drawn the Court's attention to the fact that questions of jurisdiction in collision cases, which frequently arise before civil courts, are but rarely encountered in the practice of criminal courts. He deduces from this that, in practice, prosecutions only occur before the courts of the State whose flag is flown and that that circumstance is proof of a tacit consent on the part of States and, consequently, shows what positive international law is in collision cases.

In the Court's opinion, this conclusion is not warranted. Even if the rarity of the judicial decisions to be found among the reported cases were sufficient to prove in point of fact the circumstance alleged by the Agent for the French Government, it would merely show that States had often, in practice, abstained from instituting criminal proceedings, and not that they recognized themselves as being obliged to do so; for only if such abstention were based on their being conscious of having a duty to abstain would it be possible to speak of an international custom. The alleged fact does not allow one to infer that States have been conscious of having such a duty; on the other hand, as will presently be seen, there are other circumstances calculated to show that the contrary is true. . . .

The conclusion at which the Court has therefore arrived is that there is no rule of international law in regard to collision cases to the effect that criminal proceedings are exclusively within the jurisdiction of the State whose flag is flown. . . .

FOR THESE REASONS,

The Court, having heard both Parties, gives, by the President's casting vote—the votes being equally divided—judgment to the effect

(1) that . . . Turkey, by instituting criminal proceedings in pursuance of Turkish law against Lieutenant Demons, officer of the watch on board the *Lotus* at the time of the collision, has not acted in conflict with the principles of international law. . . .

b) The Dual Elements of Customary International Law

i) State Practice

What constitutes sufficient state practice to give rise to a rule of customary international law? Consider the following cases.

Fisheries Case (United Kingdom v Norway), Judgment, [1951] ICJ Rep 116 at 129–30 and 138–39

[Norway contended that it was entitled, on the basis of historic practice, to use straight baselines as the starting point for measuring the breadth of its territorial sea and thus enclose certain coastal waters as its internal waters. In 1933, the United Kingdom objected to this practice, claiming that customary international law obliged Norway to use baselines that followed the low-water mark along its highly indented coasts.]

. . . The Court will confine itself at this stage to noting that . . . several States have deemed it necessary to follow the straight base-lines method and that they have not encountered objections of principle by other States. This method consists of selecting appropriate points on the low-water mark and drawing straight lines between them. This has been done, not only in the case of well-defined bays, but also in cases of minor curvatures of the coast line where it was solely a question of giving a simpler form to the belt of territorial waters. . . .

From the standpoint of international law, it is now necessary to consider whether the application of the Norwegian system encountered any opposition from foreign States.

Norway has been in a position to argue without any contradiction that neither the promulgation of her delimitation Decrees in 1869 and in 1889, nor their application, gave rise to any opposition on the part of foreign States. Since, moreover, these Decrees constitute, as has been shown above, the application of a well-defined and uniform system, it is indeed this system itself which would reap the benefit of general toleration, the basis of an historical consolidation which would make it enforceable as against all States.

The general toleration of foreign States with regard to the Norwegian practice is an unchallenged fact. For a period of more than sixty years the United Kingdom Government itself in no way contested it. . . . It would appear that it was only in its Memorandum of July 27th, 1933, that the United Kingdom made a formal and definite protest on this point.

The United Kingdom Government has argued that the Norwegian system of delimitation was not known to it and that the system therefore lacked the notoriety essential to provide the basis of an historic title enforceable against it. The Court is unable to accept this view. As a coastal State on the North Sea, greatly interested in the fisheries in this area, as a maritime Power traditionally concerned with the law of the sea and concerned particularly to defend the freedom of the seas, the United Kingdom could not have been ignorant of the Decree of 1869 which had at once provoked a request for explanations by the French Government. Nor, knowing of it, could it have been under any misapprehension as to the significance of its terms, which clearly described it as constituting the application of a system. . . .

The Court notes that in respect of a situation which could only be strengthened with the passage of time, the United Kingdom Government refrained from formulating reservations.

The notoriety of the facts, the general toleration of the international community, Great Britain's position in the North Sea, her own interest in the question, and her prolonged abstention would in any case warrant Norway's enforcement of her system against the United Kingdom.

The Court is thus led to conclude that the method of straight lines, established in the Norwegian system, was imposed by the peculiar geography of the Norwegian coast; that even before the dispute arose, this method had been consolidated by a constant and suf- ficiently long practice, in the face of which the attitude of governments bears witness to the fact that they did not consider it to be contrary to international law. . . .

What striking feature characterizes the "practice" of states (other than Norway and the "several states [that] follow[ed] the straight baselines method" at that time) relied upon by the ICJ in the *Fisheries Case* to find that the use of straight baselines was consist- ent with customary international law? The United Kingdom has since made use of straight baselines with respect to its indented coastline in Scotland. The following case considers the significance of a particular form of state practice—treaty practice—in evaluating the emergence or crystallization of a new rule of customary international law.

North Sea Continental Shelf, Judgment, [1969] ICJ Rep 3

[The then Federal Republic of Germany (West Germany), along with Denmark and the Netherlands, had previously agreed on a partial delimitation of their respective contin- ental shelves but were unable to agree on certain remaining segments of the delimita- tion. They accordingly sought a ruling from the Court as to the "principles and rules of international law" that should govern the delimitation. Denmark and the Netherlands were parties to the 1958 Convention on the Continental Shelf,[68] adopted in Geneva, in which Article 6 sets out certain rules governing such delimitations. Germany was not, however, a party to that Convention, leading the Court to address the content of custom- ary international law on the issue.]

. . . 26. . . . Denmark and the Netherlands contend [that Article 6 of the Convention on the Continental Shelf] represent[s] the accepted rule of general international law on the subject of continental shelf delimitation, as it exists independently of the Convention. . . . The Convention received 46 signatures and, up-to-date, there have been 39 ratifications or accessions. It came into force on 10 June 1964, having received the 22 ratifications or accessions required for that purpose (Article 11), and was therefore in force at the time when the various delimitations of continental shelf boundaries described earlier . . . took place between the Parties. . . . Denmark and the Netherlands have both signed and rati- fied the Convention, and are parties to it, the former since 10 June 1964, the latter since 20 March 1966. The Federal Republic was one of the signatories of the Convention, but has never ratified it, and is consequently not a party. . . .

61. . . . Denmark and the Netherlands themselves in the course of the oral hearing . . . had not in fact contended that the delimitation article (Article 6) of the Convention "em- bodied already received rules of customary law in the sense that the Convention was merely declaratory of existing rules." Their contention was, rather, that although prior to the Conference [during which the Convention was negotiated], continental shelf law was only in the formative stage, and State practice lacked uniformity, yet "the process of

---

68   1958 Convention on the Continental Shelf, above note 31.

the definition and consolidation of the emerging customary law took place through the work of the International Law Commission, the reaction of governments to that work and the proceedings of the Geneva Conference"; and this emerging customary law became "crystallized in the adoption of the Continental Shelf Convention by the Conference".

62. Whatever validity this contention may have in respect of at least certain parts of the Convention, the Court cannot accept it as regards the delimitation provision (Article 6), the relevant parts of which were adopted almost unchanged from the draft of the International Law Commission that formed the basis of discussion at the Conference. The status of the rule in the Convention therefore depends mainly on the processes that led the Commission to propose it. . . . [T]he principle of equidistance, as it now figures in Article 6 of the Convention, was proposed by the Commission with considerable hesitation, somewhat on an experimental basis, at most *de lege ferenda*, and not at all *de lege lata* or as an emerging rule of customary international law. This is clearly not the sort of foundation on which Article 6 of the Convention could be said to have reflected or crystallized such a rule.

63. The foregoing conclusion receives significant confirmation from the fact that Article 6 is one of those in respect of which, under the reservations article of the Convention (Article 12) reservations may be made by any State on signing, ratifying or acceding,—for, speaking generally, it is a characteristic of purely conventional rules and obligations that, in regard to them, some faculty of making unilateral reservations may, within certain limits, be admitted;—whereas this cannot be so in the case of general or customary law rules and obligations which, by their very nature, must have equal force for all members of the international community, and cannot therefore be the subject of any right of unilateral exclusion exercisable at will by any one of them in its own favour. Consequently, it is to be expected that when, for whatever reason, rules or obligations of this order are embodied, or are intended to be reflected in certain provisions of a convention, such provisions will figure amongst those in respect of which a right of unilateral reservation is not conferred, or is excluded. . . .

69. In the light of these various considerations, the Court reaches the conclusion that the Geneva Convention did not embody or crystallize any pre-existing or emergent rule of customary law. . . .

70. The Court must now proceed to the last stage in the argument put forward on behalf of Denmark and the Netherlands. This is to the effect that even if there was at the date of the Geneva Convention no rule of customary international law in favour of the equidistance principle, and no such rule was crystallized in Article 6 of the Convention, nevertheless such a rule has come into being since the Convention, partly because of its own impact, partly on the basis of subsequent State practice,—and that this rule, being now a rule of customary international law binding on all States, including therefore the Federal Republic, should be declared applicable to the delimitation of the boundaries between the Parties' respective continental shelf areas in the North Sea.

71. In so far as this contention is based on the view that Article 6 of the Convention has had the influence, and has produced the effect, described, it clearly involves treating that Article as a norm-creating provision which has constituted the foundation of, or has gen-

erated a rule which, while only conventional or contractual in its origin, has since passed into the general *corpus* of international law, and is now accepted as such by the *opinio juris*, so as to have become binding even for countries which have never, and do not, become parties to the Convention. There is no doubt that this process is a perfectly possible one and does from time to time occur: it constitutes indeed one of the recognized methods by which new rules of customary international law may be formed. At the same time this result is not lightly to be regarded as having been attained.

72. It would in the first place be necessary that the provision concerned should, at all events potentially, be of a fundamentally norm-creating character such as could be regarded as forming the basis of a general rule of law. . . . [H]aving regard to the relationship of . . . Article [6] to other provisions of the Convention, this must be open to some doubt. In the first place, Article 6 is so framed as to put second the obligation to make use of the equidistance method, causing it to come after a primary obligation to effect delimitation by agreement. Such a primary obligation constitutes an unusual preface to what is claimed to be a potential general rule of law. . . .

73. With respect to the other elements usually regarded as necessary before a conventional rule can be considered to have become a general rule of international law, it might be that, even without the passage of any considerable period of time, a very widespread and representative participation in the convention might suffice of itself, provided it included that of States whose interests were specially affected. In the present case however, the Court notes that, even if allowance is made for the existence of a number of States to whom participation in the Geneva Convention is not open, or which, by reason for instance of being land-locked States, would have no interest in becoming parties to it, the number of ratifications and accessions so far secured is, though respectable, hardly sufficient. That non-ratification may sometimes be due to factors other than active disapproval of the convention concerned can hardly constitute a basis on which positive acceptance of its principles can be implied: the reasons are speculative, but the facts remain.

74. As regards the time element, the Court notes that it is over ten years since the Convention was signed, but that it is even now less than five since it came into force in June 1964, and that when the present proceedings were brought it was less than three years, while less than one had elapsed at the time when the respective negotiations between the Federal Republic and the other two Parties for a complete delimitation broke down on the question of the application of the equidistance principle. Although the passage of only a short period of time is not necessarily, or of itself, a bar to the formation of a new rule of customary international law on the basis of what was originally a purely conventional rule, an indispensable requirement would be that within the period in question, short though it might be, State practice, including that of States whose interests are specially affected, should have been both extensive and virtually uniform in the sense of the provision invoked;—and should moreover have occurred in such a way as to show a general recognition that a rule of law or legal obligation is involved.

In *North Sea Continental Shelf*, the ICJ "counted heads" in assessing the extent of state practice, noting the number of countries which had used the Article 6 "equidistance" method of continental shelf delimitation. Some of its language suggests, however, that not all states are equal in assessing the significance of their practice to the emergence of a rule of customary international law. In particular, the ICJ suggested that the practice of "[s]tates whose interests were specially affected" — in this case, coastal states — weighs more heavily in the calculation than that of other — in this case, landlocked — states. In his dissenting opinion, Judge Lachs underscored this point, and then commented on how general and representative state practice must be to evidence a rule of customary international law:

> [A] mathematical computation, important as it is in itself, should be supplemented by, so to speak, a spectral analysis of the representativity of the States parties to the Convention.
>
> For in the world today an essential factor in the formation of a new rule of general international law is to be taken into account: namely that States with different political, economic and legal systems, States of all continents, participate in the process. No more can a general rule of international law be established by the fiat of one or of a few, or — as it was once claimed — by the consensus of European States only. . . .
>
> All this leads to the conclusion that the principles and rules enshrined in the Convention, and in particular the equidistance rule, have been accepted not only by those States which are parties to the Convention on the Continental Shelf, but also by those which have subsequently followed it in agreements, or in their legislation, or have acquiesced in it when faced with legislative acts of other States affecting them. This can be viewed as evidence of a practice widespread enough to satisfy the criteria for a general rule of law.
>
> For to become binding, a rule or principle of international law need not pass the test of universal acceptance. This is reflected in several statements of the Court, e.g.: "generally . . . adopted in the practice of States" (*Fisheries Judgment, I.C.J. Reports 1951*, p. 128). Not all States have, as I indicated earlier in a different context, an opportunity or possibility of applying a given rule. The evidence should be sought in the behaviour of a great number of States, possibly the majority of States, in any case the great majority of the interested States.
>
> Thus this test cannot be, nor is it, one endowed with any absolute character: it is of its very nature relative. Criteria of frequency, continuity and uniformity are involved. However, not all potential rules are susceptible to verification by all these criteria. Frequency may be invoked only in situations where there are many and successive opportunities to apply a rule. This is not the case with delimitation, which is a one-time act. Furthermore, as it produces lasting consequences, it invariably implies an intention to satisfy the criterion of continuity.
>
> As for uniformity, "too much importance need not be attached to" a "few uncertainties or contradictions, real and apparent" (*Fisheries, Judgment, I.C.J. Reports 1951*, p. 138). . . .[69]

The ICJ elaborated on the latter point in the case that follows.

---

[69] *North Sea Continental Shelf*, Judgment, [1969] ICJ Rep 3 at 227–29.

Military and Paramilitary Activities in and against Nicaragua (Nicaragua v United States of America), **Merits, Judgment, [1986] ICJ Rep 14**

[Nicaragua claimed that the United States had unlawfully used force against it contrary to Article 2(4) of the UN Charter. As the United States had excluded from the scope of the Court's jurisdiction any dispute arising under a multilateral treaty unless all affected parties to the treaty were also parties to the proceedings before the Court (which they were not), the Court had to consider whether the Article 2(4) prohibition also existed as a matter of customary international law. In discussing the requirements of customary international law, the Court addressed the significance of state practice inconsistent with the purported customary rule.]

184. The Court notes that there is in fact evidence, to be examined below, of a considerable degree of agreement between the Parties as to the content of the customary international law relating to the non-use of force and non-intervention. This concurrence of their views does not however dispense the Court from having itself to ascertain what rules of customary international law are applicable. The mere fact that States declare their recognition of certain rules is not sufficient for the Court to consider these as being part of customary international law, and as applicable as such to those States. Bound as it is by Article 38 of its Statute to apply, *inter alia*, international custom "as evidence of a general practice accepted as law", the Court may not disregard the essential role played by general practice. Where two States agree to incorporate a particular rule in a treaty, their agreement suffices to make that rule a legal one, binding upon them; but in the field of customary international law, the shared view of the Parties as to the content of what they regard as the rule is not enough. The Court must satisfy itself that the existence of the rule in the *opinio juris* of States is confirmed by practice. . . .

186. It is not to be expected that in the practice of States the application of the rules in question should have been perfect, in the sense that States should have refrained, with complete consistency, from the use of force or from intervention in each other's internal affairs. The Court does not consider that, for a rule to be established as customary, the corresponding practice must be in absolutely rigorous conformity with the rule. In order to deduce the existence of customary rules, the Court deems it sufficient that the conduct of States should, in general, be consistent with such rules, and that instances of State conduct inconsistent with a given rule should generally have been treated as breaches of that rule, not as indications of the recognition of a new rule. If a State acts in a way *prima facie* incompatible with a recognized rule, but defends its conduct by appealing to exceptions or justifications contained within the rule itself, then whether or not the State's conduct is in fact justifiable on that basis, the significance of that attitude is to confirm rather than to weaken the rule. . . .

ii) Opinio Juris

As suggested above, even very widespread and consistent state practice does not of itself give rise to rules of customary international law. In addition, evidence of a specific motivation for such state practice is required, as illustrated in the following further excerpt from the *North Sea Continental Shelf* judgment.

North Sea Continental Shelf, Judgment, [1969] ICJ Rep 3

[Denmark and the Netherlands urged that Article 6 of the 1958 Convention on the Continental Shelf,[70] adopted in Geneva, which prescribed a method of delimitation, had become customary international law binding upon the Federal Republic of Germany (West Germany). Having concluded that there was insufficient state practice to support this argument, the ICJ turned to the issue of *opinio juris.*]

75. The Court must now consider whether State practice in the matter of continental shelf delimitation has, subsequent to the Geneva Convention [occurred in such a way as to show a general recognition that a rule of law or legal obligation is involved]. Leaving aside cases which, for various reasons, the Court does not consider to be reliable guides as precedents, such as delimitations effected between the present Parties themselves, or not relating to international boundaries, some fifteen cases have been cited in the course of the present proceedings, occurring mostly since the signature of the 1958 Geneva Convention, in which continental shelf boundaries have been delimited according to the equidistance principle — in the majority of the cases by agreement, in a few others unilaterally — or else the delimitation was foreshadowed but has not yet been carried out. . . . But even if these various cases constituted more than a very small proportion of those potentially calling for delimitation in the world as a whole, the Court would not think it necessary to enumerate or evaluate them separately, since there are, *a priori,* several grounds which deprive them of weight as precedents in the present context.

76. To begin with, over half the States concerned, whether acting unilaterally or conjointly, were or shortly became parties to the Geneva Convention, and were therefore presumably, so far as they were concerned, acting actually or potentially in the application of the Convention. From their action no inference could legitimately be drawn as to the existence of a rule of customary international law in favour of the equidistance principle. As regards those States, on the other hand, which were not, and have not become parties to the Convention, the basis of their action can only be problematical and must remain entirely speculative. Clearly, they were not applying the Convention. But from that no inference could justifiably be drawn that they believed themselves to be applying a mandatory rule of customary international law. There is not a shred of evidence that they did and . . . there is no lack of other reasons for using the equidistance method, so that acting, or agreeing to act in a certain way, does not of itself demonstrate anything of a juridical nature.

77. The essential point in this connection — and it seems necessary to stress it — is that even if these instances of action by non-parties to the Convention were much more numerous than they in fact are, they would not, even in the aggregate, suffice in themselves to constitute the *opinio juris;* — for, in order to achieve this result, two conditions must be fulfilled. Not only must the acts concerned amount to a settled practice, but they must also be such, or be carried out in such a way, as to be evidence of a belief that this practice is rendered obligatory by the existence of a rule of law requiring it. The need for such a belief, i.e., the existence of a subjective element, is implicit in the very notion of the *opinio juris sive necessitatis.* The States concerned must therefore feel that they are conforming to

---

70 1958 Convention on the Continental Shelf, above note 31.

what amounts to a legal obligation. The frequency, or even habitual character of the acts is not in itself enough. There are many international acts, e.g., in the field of ceremonial [*sic*] and protocol, which are performed almost invariably, but which are motivated only by considerations of courtesy, convenience or tradition, and not by any sense of legal duty.

78. In this respect the Court follows the view adopted by the Permanent Court of International Justice in the *Lotus* case. . . . [T]he position [here] is simply that in certain cases — not a great number — the States concerned agreed to draw or did draw the boundaries concerned according to the principle of equidistance. There is no evidence that they so acted because they felt legally compelled to draw them in this way by reason of a rule of customary law obliging them to do so — especially considering that they might have been motivated by other obvious factors. . . .

81. The Court accordingly concludes that if the Geneva Convention was not in its origins or inception declaratory of a mandatory rule of customary international law enjoining the use of the equidistance principle for the delimitation of continental shelf areas between adjacent States, neither has its subsequent effect been constitutive of such a rule; and that State practice up-to-date has equally been insufficient for the purpose. . . .

The ICJ's insistence on proof of *opinio juris* over and above evidence of widespread and uniform state practice raises the important question of how one establishes a state's motivation for behaving in particular ways. In fact, states often explicitly explain their reasons for engaging in certain actions and comment extensively on the content of their (and others') international legal obligations. For example, in *Military and Paramilitary Activities in and against Nicaragua*,[71] the ICJ concluded that the *opinio juris* of states in relation to the customary prohibition on the use of force "may, though with all due caution, be deduced from, *inter alia*, the attitude of the Parties and the attitude of States towards certain General Assembly resolutions . . . ."[72] These resolutions, as well as other international instruments expressing the views of states, supported the existence of a customary ban on the use of force in international relations.

The ICJ's reliance on "certain" General Assembly resolutions prompts a word of caution: General Assembly resolutions do not per se create binding international law. That said, some resolutions, depending on whether they are adopted by consensus or (in the case of a vote) supported by a significant majority of member states, may either influence or reflect international law in several ways. First, as the ICJ concluded in the *Nicaragua* case, they may be *evidence* of *opinio juris* that confirms the existence of a rule of customary international law. Second, they may be invoked as an authoritative interpretation of a binding treaty obligation, such as those set out in the UN Charter. Third, they may be regarded as assessments of general principles of law accepted by states,[73] a third source of international law anticipated in Article 38(1)(c) of the Statute of the ICJ, discussed in Section D(1) below. And in all of these various ways, General Assembly resolutions may influence the subsequent practice and *opinio juris* of states and, thus, the future content

---

71 Merits, Judgment, [1986] ICJ Rep 14 [*Nicaragua* case].
72 *Ibid* at para 188.
73 Schachter, above note 9 at 3.

of customary international law. We discuss the broader role of the General Assembly at greater length in Chapter 3.

In the *Nicaragua* case, the ICJ also considered whether there existed in customary international law a principle of non-intervention in the internal affairs of sovereign states. In doing so, it had to address the problem of mixed state practice, specifically the failure of many states to follow this rule. The United States, for instance, has a long history of interfering in the internal affairs of Latin American states. We have already seen how the ICJ addressed this issue, in connection with the customary prohibition on the use of force, by taking a somewhat relaxed view of the requirement of consistent state practice. Consider how the ICJ also dealt with the issue, in connection with the customary prohibition on intervention, through a nuanced application of the *opinio juris* concept.

Military and Paramilitary Activities in and against Nicaragua (Nicaragua v United States of America), Merits, Judgment, [1986] ICJ Rep 14

202. The principle of non-intervention involves the right of every sovereign State to conduct its affairs without outside interference; though examples of trespass against this principle are not infrequent, the Court considers that it is part and parcel of customary international law. As the Court has observed: "Between independent States, respect for territorial sovereignty is an essential foundation of international relations" . . . and international law requires political integrity also to be respected. Expressions of an *opinio juris* regarding the existence of the principle of non-intervention in customary international law are numerous and not difficult to find. . . . The existence in the *opinio juris* of States of the principle of non-intervention is backed by established and substantial practice. . . .

205. Notwithstanding the multiplicity of declarations by States accepting the principle of non-intervention, there remain[s the] question . . . is the practice sufficiently in conformity with it for this to be a rule of customary international law ? . . .

206. . . . There have been in recent years a number of instances of foreign intervention for the benefit of forces opposed to the government of another State. . . . [The Court] has to consider whether there might be indications of a practice illustrative of belief in a kind of general right for States to intervene, directly or indirectly, with or without armed force, in support of an internal opposition in another State, whose cause appeared particularly worthy by reason of the political and moral values with which it was identified. For such a general right to come into existence would involve a fundamental modification of the customary law principle of non-intervention.

207. In considering the instances of the conduct above described, the Court has to emphasize that, as was observed in the *North Sea Continental Shelf* cases, for a new customary rule to be formed, not only must the acts concerned "amount to a settled practice," but they must be accompanied by the *opinio juris sive necessitatis*. Either the States taking such action or other States in a position to react to it, must have behaved so that their conduct is

> "evidence of a belief that this practice is rendered obligatory by the existence of a rule of law requiring it. The need for such a belief, i.e., the existence of a subjective element, is implicit in the very notion of the *opinio juris sive necessitatis*."

... The significance for the Court of cases of State conduct prima facie inconsistent with the principle of non-intervention lies in the nature of the ground offered as justification. Reliance by a State on a novel right or an unprecedented exception to the principle might, if shared in principle by other States, tend towards a modification of customary international law. In fact however the Court finds that States have not justified their conduct by reference to a new right of intervention or a new exception to the principle of its prohibition. The United States authorities have on some occasions clearly stated their grounds for intervening in the affairs of a foreign State for reasons connected with, for example, the domestic policies of that country, its ideology, the level of its armaments, or the direction of its foreign policy. But these were statements of international policy, and not an assertion of rules of existing international law.

208. In particular, as regards the conduct towards Nicaragua which is the subject of the present case, the United States has not claimed that its intervention, which it justified in this way on the political level, was also justified on the legal level, alleging the exercise of a new right of intervention regarded by the United States as existing in such circumstances. ...

209. The Court ... finds that no such general right of intervention, in support of an opposition within another State, exists in contemporary international law. ...

c) Methodological Difficulties

The twin criteria of state practice and *opinio juris* employed to determine the existence of a rule of customary international law are difficult to apply in practice. As Judge Tanaka, dissenting in *North Sea Continental Shelf*, noted:

The formation of a customary law in a given society, be it municipal or international, is a complex psychological and sociological process, and therefore, it is not an easy matter to decide. The first factor of customary law, which can be called its *corpus*, constitutes a usage or a continuous repetition of the same kind of acts; in customary international law State practice is required. It represents a quantitative factor of customary law. The second factor of customary law, which can be called its *animus*, constitutes *opinio juris sive necessitatis* by which a simple usage can be transformed into a custom with the binding power. It represents a qualitative factor of customary law.

   To decide whether these two factors in the formative process of a customary law exist or not, is a delicate and difficult matter. The repetition, the number of examples of State practice, the duration of time required for the generation of customary law cannot be mathematically and uniformly decided. Each fact requires to be evaluated relatively according to the different occasions and circumstances. ...

   ... [S]o far as the qualitative factor, namely *opinio juris sive necessitatis* is concerned, it is extremely difficult to get evidence of its existence in concrete cases. This factor, relating to internal motivation and being of a psychological nature, cannot be ascertained very easily, particularly when diverse legislative and executive organs of a government participate in an internal process of decision-making in respect of ratification or other State acts. There is no other way than to ascertain the existence of *opinio juris* from the fact of the external existence of a certain custom and its necessity felt in the international community, rather than to seek evidence as to the subjective motives for each example of State practice, which is something which is impossible of achievement. . . .

In short, the process of generation of a customary law is relative in its manner . . . The time factor, namely the duration of custom, is relative; the same with [the] factor of number, namely State practice. Not only must each factor generating a customary law be appraised according to the occasion and circumstances, but the formation as a whole must be considered as an organic and dynamic process. We must not scrutinize formalistically the conditions required for customary law and forget the social necessity, namely the importance of the aims and purposes to be realized by the customary law in question. . . .[74]

Ultimately, measuring state practice is a quasi-empirical exercise. Doctrine demands that states be tabulated according to whether they engage or acquiesce in a given practice or not. This empirical approach to state practice raises important quandaries. First, what constitutes proper evidence of state practice? The influential *Restatement of the Law, Third, Foreign Relations Law of the United States* offers the following illustrative list:

"Practice of states" . . . includes diplomatic acts and instructions as well as public measures and other governmental acts and official statements of policy, whether they are unilateral or undertaken in cooperation with other states, for example in organizations such as the Organization for Economic Cooperation and Development (OECD). Inaction may constitute state practice, as when a state acquiesces in acts of another state that affect its legal rights.[75]

Applying this broad conception of state practice in the context of human rights law, the *Restatement* lists the following as "practice accepted as building customary human rights law":

. . . virtually universal adherence to the United Nations Charter and its human rights provisions, and virtually universal and frequently reiterated acceptance of the Universal Declaration of Human Rights even if only in principle; virtually universal participation of states in the preparation and adoption of international agreements recognizing human rights principles generally, or particular rights; the adoption of human rights principles by states in regional organizations in Europe, Latin America, and Africa . . . ; general support by states for United Nations resolutions declaring, recognizing, invoking, and applying international human rights principles in international law; action by states to conform their national law or practice to standards or principles declared by international bodies, and the incorporation of human rights provisions, directly or by reference, in national constitutions and laws; invocation of human rights principles in national policy, in diplomatic practice, in international organization activities and actions; and other diplomatic communications or action by states reflecting the view that certain practices violate international human rights law, including condemnation and other adverse state reactions to violations by other states.[76]

---

74 *North Sea Continental Shelf*, above note 69 at 175–76 and 178.
75 *Third Restatement*, above note 48 at para 102, Comment b.
76 *Ibid* at para 701, n 2.

This list of indicia may be less insightful than may at first be apparent. For example, some of these elements—such as condemnation of violations—might be taken as much as evidence of *opinio juris* as state practice. In addition, how does one evaluate inconsistent diplomatic acts, official statements, or other government acts? What if the executive, judicial, and legislative branches of a given state pursue different paths? And what if states say one thing in their public pronouncements and yet do another? Most states publicly condemn torture—and yet, consider the following:

> A survey of Amnesty International's research files from 1997 to mid-2000 found that the organization had received reports of torture or ill-treatment by agents of the state in over 150 countries during the period. In more than 70 countries the victims included political prisoners, but ordinary criminals and criminal suspects had reportedly been victims of torture or ill-treatment in over 130 countries. People had reportedly died as a result of torture in over 80 countries. These figures related only to actions by state agents and did not include abuses by armed political groups and private individuals that can be assimilated to the notion of torture or ill-treatment.[77]

Despite these depressing statistics, the prohibition of torture is widely regarded by state representatives and jurists as customary international law, likely of a *jus cogens* character.

The frequent disconnect between doctrine and empirical reality in customary international law has prompted many critiques of the state practice concept and the materials used to prove it:

> There is little agreement about which types of national actions count as state practice. Policy statements, national legislation, and diplomatic correspondence are the least controversial sources. Treaties—especially multilateral treaties, but also bilateral ones—are often used as evidence of CIL [customary international law], but in an inconsistent and undertheorized way. The writings of jurists are a common but highly tendentious source of CIL. Even more controversially, United Nations General Assembly Resolutions and other nonbinding statements and resolutions by multilateral bodies are often viewed as evidence of CIL. Those who study and use CIL—courts, arbitrators, diplomats, politicians, scholars—invoke these sources selectively.[78]

Adding to the methodological problems associated with customary international law is the issue of how one quantifies state practice. Certainly, as the cases above suggest, the ICJ has readily acknowledged that practice need not be universal or perfectly consistent, but it must be sufficiently "general," "widespread," "uniform," and "settled." What precisely do these terms mean, and how does one quantify the "sufficiency" threshold? Moreover, ascertaining the actual practice of almost 200 states is an arduous task, rarely undertaken. As one respected textbook on international law puts the matter:

---

77 Amnesty International, *Combating Torture: A Manual for Action* (London: Amnesty International, 2003) at 2.

78 Jack Goldsmith & Eric Posner, "Theory of Customary International Law" (1999) 66 U Chi L Rev 1113 at 1117.

> The difficulties involved in extracting a customary rule or principle of international law from a mass of heterogeneous documentation of state practice, state judicial decisions, diplomatic history, etc., are not to be minimized. . . . Not only, also, is the documentation itself frequently defective or incomplete, but the practice of some states is documented less adequately than that of other states.[79]

Likely for these very reasons, critics have charged that customary international law "is usually based on a highly selective survey of state practice that includes only major powers and interested nations."[80]

Perhaps even more problematic is the *opinio juris* concept. Consider the following critique:

> The *opinio juris* requirement raises more problems. Courts and scholars sometimes infer it from the existence of a widespread behavioral regularity. But this makes *opinio juris* redundant with the state practice requirement, which, by assumption, is insufficient by itself to establish CIL. To avoid this problem, courts and scholars sometimes require independent evidence of *opinio juris*, such as a statement by an important government official, ratification of a treaty that contains a norm similar to the CIL norm in question, or an attitude of approval toward a General Assembly Resolution. The appropriate conditions for the use of such evidence are unsettled. In addition, there is no convincing explanation of the process by which a voluntary behavioral regularity transforms itself into a binding legal obligation. *Opinio juris* is described as the psychological component of CIL because it refers to an attitude that nations supposedly have toward a behavioral regularity. The idea of *opinio juris* is mysterious because the legal obligation is created by a nation's belief in the existence of the legal obligation. *Opinio juris* is really a conclusion about a practice's status as international law; it does not explain *how* a widespread and uniform practice becomes law.[81]

Even taken at face value, however, none of these critiques are particularly surprising. Rather, they are merely symptomatic of the inherently elusive nature of customary law in general and of customary international law in particular. As observed by Judge Tanaka in the excerpt reproduced above, the formation of customary law is a complex psychological and sociological process. Why would the relationship between state practice and *opinio juris*, not to mention the means by which either element is ascertained or quantified, be any less complex? The fact remains that customary international law is a powerful normative concept universally recognized by states, notwithstanding the inevitable methodological difficulties associated with its operationalization.

How are these difficulties overcome? In practice, claims of customary international legal status for a given principle are often supported by reference to the scholarly writings of international jurists and decisions of international tribunals. Rarely do these sources themselves delve into the full empirical record in an effort to tease out the state practice and *opinio juris* supportive of customary status. They tend, instead, to "sample" the em-

---

79 Ivan A Shearer, ed, *Starke's International Law*, 11th ed (Toronto: Butterworths, 1994) at 36.
80 Goldsmith & Posner, above note 78.
81 *Ibid* at 1117–118.

pirical record in a manner considered representative of broader trends, and to cite the writings of other scholars and international tribunals, in order to determine whether a principle is indeed "accepted" as customary international law. Even the ICJ has on occasion been accused of behaving like a common law court, positing previously unrecognized rules of customary international law rather than rigorously demonstrating state practice and *opinio juris* in support of such rules. Meanwhile, non-governmental groups (particularly in the international human rights area) have been effective in advocating the universality and obligatory nature of particular norms, thereby enhancing such norms' claims to customary international legal status.

If this is the true "political economy" of customary international law,[82] two observations stem from it. First, the oft-repeated doctrinal position — that customary international law depends on state practice coupled with *opinio juris* — oversimplifies the manner in which such law actually emerges. Second, the importance of scholarly and judicial writings in influencing the emergence of customary international norms implies an important role for what international relations scholars call an "epistemic community" — a network of experts who influence the conduct of international affairs and the content of international law.

Recall that "judicial decisions and the teachings of the most highly qualified publicists of the various nations" is listed in Article 38(1)(d) of the Statute of the ICJ as a "subsidiary means" by which the Court may determine rules of law. What is the formal distinction between "sources" of law and "subsidiary means" for its determination? Consider whether this formal distinction has any *practical* meaning when it comes to determining whether a given rule of law does or does not exist. What conclusions can be drawn as to the relative importance of the practice and *opinio juris* of states, on the one hand, and of the views of the broader epistemic community, on the other, to the emergence or ascertainment of a rule of customary international law?

Perhaps signalling an appreciation of the need for greater clarity regarding the means by which customary international law emerges and can be identified, the ILC added the topic of "Formation and Evidence of Customary International Law" to its programme of work in 2012.[83]

d) Interaction of Treaty and Customary International Law

We have already seen, in our review of the *North Sea Continental Shelf* cases, that the treaty practice of states may constitute state practice or *opinio juris* that either crystallizes incipient, or gives rise to wholly new, customary international law. These are but two of the many complex ways in which customary international law may interact with treaties. For example, treaties may also codify customary international law, distilling into treaty form pre-existing law, or *lex lata*. Conversely, treaties may contradict existing customary international law. In those circumstances, as between parties to the treaty, the treaty will generally prevail, whereas obligations sourced in customary international law between a party and a non-party, or between two non-parties to the treaty, remain unaffected.

---

82   See, for example, Donald J Kochan, "The Political Economy of the Production of Customary International Law: The Role of Non-governmental Organizations in U.S. Courts" (2004) 22 Berkeley J Int'l L 240.

83   See *ILC Report 2012*, above note 35, c VIII, paras 156–202.

However, as the number of parties to the treaty grows, and as state practice and *opinio juris* become increasingly aligned with the terms of the treaty, the content of customary international law may itself, in time, be affected.

This latter possibility suggests that similar or even identical treaty and customary international law may coexist in parallel. Consider the discussion of this matter in the excerpt from the *Nicaragua* case below. At issue at this point in the case was whether a customary bar on the use of force persisted given a similar prohibition in the UN Charter. This was relevant because the United States had not consented unconditionally to the Court's jurisdiction over disputes arising under the UN Charter or other multilateral treaties.

> ### *Military and Paramilitary Activities in and against Nicaragua (Nicaragua v United States of America)*, Merits, Judgment, [1986] ICJ Rep 14
>
> 175. The Court does not consider that, in the areas of law relevant to the present dispute, it can be claimed that all the customary rules which may be invoked have a content exactly identical to that of the rules contained in the treaties which cannot be applied by virtue of the United States reservation. On a number of points, the areas governed by the two sources of law do not exactly overlap, and the substantive rules in which they are framed are not identical in content. But in addition, even if a treaty norm and a customary norm relevant to the present dispute were to have exactly the same content, this would not be a reason for the Court to take the view that the operation of the treaty process must necessarily deprive the customary norm of its separate applicability. Nor can the multilateral treaty reservation be interpreted as meaning that, once applicable to a given dispute, it would exclude the application of any rule of customary international law the content of which was the same as, or analogous to, that of the treaty-law rule which had caused the reservation to become effective. . . .
>
> 177. . . . The existence of identical rules in international treaty law and customary law has been clearly recognized by the Court in the *North Sea Continental Shelf* cases. To a large extent, those cases turned on the question whether a rule enshrined in a treaty also existed as a customary rule, either because the treaty had merely codified the custom, or caused it to "crystallize," or because it had influenced its subsequent adoption. The Court found that this identity of content in treaty law and in customary international law did not exist in the case of the rule invoked, which appeared in one article of the treaty, but did not suggest that such identity was debarred as a matter of principle: on the contrary, it considered it to be clear that certain other articles of the treaty in question "were . . . regarded as reflecting, or as crystallizing, received or at least emergent rules of customary international law." . . . More generally, there are no grounds for holding that when customary international law is comprised of rules identical to those of treaty law, the latter "supervenes" the former, so that the customary international law has no further existence of its own.
>
> 178. There are a number of reasons for considering that, even if two norms belonging to two sources of international law appear identical in content, and even if the States in question are bound by these rules both on the level of treaty-law and on that of customary international law, these norms retain a separate existence. This is so from the standpoint

of their applicability. In a legal dispute affecting two States, one of them may argue that the applicability of a treaty rule to its own conduct depends on the other State's conduct in respect of the application of other rules, on other subjects, also included in the same treaty. For example, if a State exercises its right to terminate or suspend the operation of a treaty on the ground of the violation by the other party of a "provision essential to the accomplishment of the object or purpose of the treaty" (in the words of Art. 60, para. 3 *(b)*, of the Vienna Convention on the Law of Treaties), it is exempted, vis-à-vis the other State, from a rule of treaty-law because of the breach by that other State of a different rule of treaty-law. But if the two rules in question also exist as rules of customary international law, the failure of the one State to apply the one rule does not justify the other State in declining to apply the other rule. Rules which are identical in treaty law and in customary international law are also distinguishable by reference to the methods of interpretation and application. A State may accept a rule contained in a treaty not simply because it favours the application of the rule itself, but also because the treaty establishes what that State regards as desirable institutions or mechanisms to ensure implementation of the rule. Thus, if that rule parallels a rule of customary international law, two rules of the same content are subject to separate treatment as regards the organs competent to verify their implementation, depending on whether they are customary rules or treaty rules. The present dispute illustrates this point.

179. It will therefore be clear that customary international law continues to exist and to apply, separately from international treaty law, even where the two categories of law have an identical content. Consequently, in ascertaining the content of the customary international law applicable to the present dispute, the Court must satisfy itself that the Parties are bound by the customary rules in question; but the Court is in no way bound to uphold these rules only in so far as they differ from the treaty rules which it is prevented by the United States reservation from applying in the present dispute. . . .

2) Exceptions to the Universality of Customary International Law

Thus far, we have described rules of customary international law as being universally binding on all states. There are three exceptions to this general position: first, and as seen above, a treaty rule that is inconsistent with a rule of customary international law will generally prevail, as between parties to that treaty; second, rules of "regional" customary international law may displace, as between states within the relevant region, rules of general customary international law; and third, so-called persistent objectors may unilaterally escape the reach of customary international law. We deal with the latter two exceptions in the following subsections.

a) Regional Customary International Law

Sometimes customary practices arise as between a limited number of states rather than the international community as a whole. The following cases explain the circumstances in which such "regional" practices have law-making effects.

Colombian-Peruvian Asylum Case, Judgment, [1950] ICJ Rep 266

[A Peruvian dissident and fugitive was granted asylum as a political refugee in the Colombian embassy in Lima, Peru. Colombia claimed that it had a unilateral right to grant such "diplomatic asylum" within Latin America. However, the granting of asylum interfered with Peru's territorial jurisdiction vis-à-vis its own national.]

. . . The Colombian Government has . . . invoked . . . an alleged regional or local custom peculiar to Latin-American States.

The Party which relies on a custom of this kind must prove that this custom is established in such a manner that it has become binding on the other Party. The Colombian Government must prove that the rule invoked by it is in accordance with a constant and uniform usage practised by the States in question, and that this usage is the expression of a right appertaining to the State granting asylum and a duty incumbent on the territorial State. This follows from Article 38 of the Statute of the Court, which refers to international custom "as evidence of a general practice accepted as law". . . .

It is particularly the Montevideo Convention of 1933 which Counsel for the Colombian Government has . . . relied on in this connexion. It is contended that this Convention has merely codified principles which were already recognized by Latin-American custom, and that it is valid against Peru as a proof of customary law. The limited number of States which have ratified this Convention reveals the weakness of this argument. . . .

Finally, the Colombian Government has referred to a large number of particular cases in which diplomatic asylum was in fact granted and respected. But it has not shown that the alleged rule of unilateral and definitive qualification was invoked or—if in some cases it was in fact invoked—that it was, apart from conventional stipulations, exercised by the States granting asylum as a right appertaining to them and respected by the territorial States as a duty incumbent on them and not merely for reasons of political expediency. The facts brought to the knowledge of the Court disclose so much uncertainty and contradiction, so much fluctuation and discrepancy in the exercise of diplomatic asylum and in the official views expressed on various occasions, there has been so much inconsistency in the rapid succession of conventions on asylum, ratified by some States and rejected by others, and the practice has been so much influenced by considerations of political expediency in the various cases, that it is not possible to discern in all this any constant and uniform usage, accepted as law, with regard to the alleged rule of unilateral and definitive qualification of the offence.

The Court cannot therefore find that the Colombian Government has proved the existence of such a custom. But even if it could be supposed that such a custom existed between certain Latin-American States only, it could not be invoked against Peru which, far from having by its attitude adhered to it, has, on the contrary, repudiated it by refraining from ratifying the Montevideo Conventions of 1933 and 1939, which were the first to include a rule concerning the qualification of the offence in matters of diplomatic asylum. . . .

Notice that the ICJ's approach to regional customary international law in the *Colombian-Peruvian Asylum Case* applies the same basic criteria to regional custom as to general custom: state practice and accompanying *opinio juris*. Nevertheless, one difference between the universal and the regional doctrines relates to the legal significance accorded silence by a state. In general customary international law, mere silence or inaction by a state in the face of practice by other states is generally considered acquiescence in that practice. In turn, this acquiescence is itself considered a form of state practice confirming the existence of a corresponding rule of customary international law. The rule for regional practice, however, is different: a state taking no position on the practice is excluded from the ambit of its potential binding effect. The reason for the distinction is logical: general or universal customary international law is just that, general or universal. Regional customary international law, on the other hand, applies only to a subset of states. How else to determine the membership of that subset than to rely on the express state practice and *opinio juris* of its potential members? Or consider the matter from a slightly different angle: silence in the face of both general state practice and differing regional state practice can only be construed as acquiescence in either one or the other of them. International law favours the universalizing effects of the former.

One other issue is raised by the *Asylum Case*: should we take the ICJ's focus on a "Latin American practice" as an indication that regional customary international law requires a sizable subset of the world's countries? The case that follows suggests not.

Case Concerning Right of Passage over Indian Territory (Portugal v India), **Merits, Judgment, [1960] ICJ Rep 6 at 39–44**

[Portugal claimed that it had enjoyed, for at least a century, a right of free passage over Indian territory between various enclaves under Portuguese sovereignty. The government of India suspended this right of passage in 1954 as a security measure in the face of civil unrest over the continuing Portuguese presence on the Indian subcontinent. Portugal maintained that the suspension violated a rule of regional customary international law, applicable between it and India, which curtailed India's general customary legal right to control passage over its own territory.]

. . . For the purpose of determining whether Portugal has established the right of passage claimed by it, the Court must have regard to what happened during the British and post-British periods. During these periods, there had developed between the Portuguese and the territorial sovereign with regard to passage to the enclaves a practice upon which Portugal relies for the purpose of establishing the right of passage claimed by it.

With regard to Portugal's claim of a right of passage as formulated by it on the basis of local custom, it is objected on behalf of India that no local custom could be established between only two States. It is difficult to see why the number of States between which a local custom may be established on the basis of long practice must necessarily be larger than two. The Court sees no reason why long continued practice between two States accepted by them as regulating their relations should not form the basis of mutual rights and obligations between the two States. . . .

It is common ground between the Parties that the passage of private persons and civil officials was not subject to any restrictions, beyond routine control, during these periods. There is nothing on the record to indicate the contrary.

Goods in general, that is to say, all merchandise other than arms and ammunition, also passed freely between . . . the enclaves during the periods in question, subject only, at certain times, to customs regulations and such regulation and control as were necessitated by considerations of security or revenue. The general prohibition of the transit of goods during the Second World War and prohibitions imposed upon the transit of salt and, on certain occasions, upon that of liquor and materials for the distillation of liquor, were specific measures necessitated by the considerations just referred to. The scope and purpose of each prohibition were clearly defined. In all other cases the passage of goods was free. No authorization or licence was required.

The Court, therefore, concludes that, with regard to private persons, civil officials and goods in general there existed during the British and post-British periods a constant and uniform practice allowing free passage between Daman and the enclaves. This practice having continued over a period extending beyond a century and a quarter unaffected by the change of regime in respect of the intervening territory which occurred when India became independent, the Court is, in view of all the circumstances of the case, satisfied that that practice was accepted as law by the Parties and has given rise to a right and a correlative obligation. . . .

[However], during the British and post-British periods, Portuguese armed forces and armed police did not pass between . . . the enclaves as of right and . . . , after 1878, such passage could only take place with previous authorization by the British and later by India, accorded either under a reciprocal arrangement already agreed to, or in individual cases. Having regard to the special circumstances of the case, this necessity for authorization before passage could take place constitutes, in the view of the Court, a negation of passage as of right. The practice predicates that the territorial sovereign had the discretionary power to withdraw or to refuse permission. It is argued that permission was always granted, but this does not, in the opinion of the Court, affect the legal position. There is nothing in the record to show that grant of permission was incumbent on the British or on India as an obligation. . . .

There was thus established a clear distinction between the practice permitting free passage of private persons, civil officials and goods in general, and the practice requiring previous authorization, as in the case of armed forces, armed police, and arms and ammunition. . . .

The Court is here dealing with a concrete case having special features. Historically the case goes back to a period when, and relates to a region in which, the relations between neighbouring States were not regulated by precisely formulated rules but were governed largely by practice. Where therefore the Court finds a practice clearly established between two States which was accepted by the Parties as governing the relations between them, the Court must attribute decisive effect to that practice for the purpose of determining their specific rights and obligations. Such a particular practice must prevail over any general rules. . . .

[The Court went on to apply the regional customary rule permitting free non-military passage, but found that this rule had not been violated by India in the circumstances of the case.]

Reflecting the fact that the formation of "regional" customary international law does not necessarily require the participation of more than two states — or, for that matter, of states co-located in a given "region" — regional customary international law is also sometimes referred to as "local" or "special" customary international law.

Recalling that treaties need not assume any particular form or be reduced to writing, is there any difference between a rule of regional customary international law between two states and a bilateral treaty between them?

b) Persistent Objectors

Put simply, a persistent objector is a state that has actively and consistently denied the existence or applicability to it of a rule of customary international law since the emergence of that rule. The effect of this is to escape the binding effect of the rule. The justification for the concept, and its key requirements, have been described by one commentator as follows:

> Because sovereign autonomy is a fundamental principle of international law, a corollary doctrine developed that a state which persistently objects to an emerging norm is not bound by the norm once it gains the status of customary international law. There are two conditions a state must fulfill in order to opt out of the new customary rule. First, the state must object when the rule is in its nascent stage, and continue to object afterwards. Evidence of objection must be clear, and the objector state must rebut a presumption of acceptance. Silence or failure to object is interpreted as consent. Second, the objection must be consistent. A state may not object some of the time, apply the rule at other times, and still be a persistent objector.[84]

Note in particular the requirement of objection "when the rule is in its nascent stage." What is the significance of this for recently established states? Note also the requirement of consistency. What is the likelihood of a state maintaining an objection (and resisting pressure to conform) to a rule of customary international law over an extended period of time?

While most jurists and states appear to accept the existence of the persistent objector rule, judicial decisions relying on it are few and far between.[85] One example is the Anglo-Norwegian *Fisheries Case*, which we examined above. In that case, the United Kingdom argued that a rule of customary international law prevented Norway from enclosing, as internal waters, bays with mouths wider than ten nautical miles. While the Court dismissed this particular argument on the basis that no such rule of customary international law existed, it went further, stating: "In any event the ten-mile rule would appear to be inapplicable as against Norway inasmuch as she has always opposed any attempt to apply it to the Norwegian coast."[86]

Recall also the Court's rejection of the applicability to Peru of any regional customary law of asylum in Latin America in the *Asylum Case*:

> [E]ven if it could be supposed that such a custom existed between certain Latin-American States only, it could not be invoked against Peru which, far from having by its attitude adhered to it, has, on the contrary, repudiated it by refraining from ratifying the Monte-

---

84   Lynn Loschin, "The Persistent Objector and Customary Human Rights Law: A Proposed Analytical Framework" (1996) 2 UC Davis J Int'l L & Pol'y 147 at 150–51.

85   See Jonathan Charney, "The Persistent Objector Rule and the Development of Customary International Law" (1985) 56 Brit YB Int'l L 1.

86   *Fisheries Case (United Kingdom v Norway)*, Judgment, [1951] ICJ Rep 116 at 131.

video Conventions of 1933 and 1939, which were the first to include a rule concerning the qualification of the offence in matters of diplomatic asylum.[87]

The concept of persistent objection raises a difficult question related to our earlier discussion of customary international law and its formation. What if, instead of one solitary persistent objector, there are several? What if these several are amongst the most influential states in the international community? How many such persistent objectors does it take before a norm is barred from evolving into customary international law at all? After all, state practice must be sufficiently widespread and general for a customary principle to emerge. Further, there is language in the cases we have considered that suggests that the practice of states most directly affected by a given norm may be given greater weight in assessing whether customary international law has crystallized.

Just as the criteria of generality, uniformity, and consistency of state practice are malleable, there are no clear answers to the foregoing questions. Yet they are of considerable practical importance in a number of areas. Consider, for example, how these issues were engaged in the ICJ's 1996 advisory opinion on the legality of nuclear weapons.[88] In that case, the UN General Assembly had requested an advisory opinion from the Court on the following question: "Is the threat or use of nuclear weapons in any circumstances permitted under international law?"

The Court concluded that the threat or use of nuclear weapons would, in most cases, be illegal. It justified its conclusion with reference to various principles of international humanitarian and environmental law, as well as principles relating to the use of force by states. However, the Court declined to rule whether such threat or use of force would be lawful or unlawful in an "extreme circumstance of self-defence, in which the very survival of a State would be at stake."

On this issue, the United States had argued:

> . . . customary law could not be created over the objection of the nuclear-weapon States, which are the States whose interests are most specifically affected. Nor could customary law be created by abstaining from the use of nuclear weapons for humanitarian, political or military reasons, rather than from a belief that such abstention is required by law. Among the most important indicators of State practice in this area are the international agreements that regulate but do not prohibit nuclear weapons by the major military powers, and the official views expressed by States on this question.[89]

The United States thus urged that the dissent of the nuclear power states should suffice to preclude the emergence of a customary rule barring the use of nuclear weapons. This position was not addressed in the majority's opinion, but was embraced by dissenting judge Schwebel, vice-president of the ICJ, as follows:

---

87 *Colombian-Peruvian Asylum Case*, Judgment, [1950] ICJ Rep 266 at 277–78 [*Asylum Case*].

88 *Legality of the Threat or Use of Nuclear Weapons*, Advisory Opinion, [1996] ICJ Rep 226 [*Nuclear Weapons* case].

89 "Letter dated 20 June 1995 from the Acting Legal Adviser to the Department of State, together with Written Statement of the Government of the United States of America" in *Nuclear Weapons* case, *ibid*.

This nuclear practice is not a practice of a lone and secondary persistent objector. This is not a practice of a pariah Government crying out in the wilderness of otherwise adverse international opinion. This is the practice of five of the world's major Powers, of the permanent Members of the Security Council, significantly supported for almost 50 years by their allies and other States sheltering under their nuclear umbrellas. That is to say, it is the practice of States—and a practice supported by a large and weighty number of other States—that together represent the bulk of the world's military and economic and financial and technological power and a very large proportion of its population. This practice has been recognized, accommodated and in some measure accepted by the international community. . . .[90]

Consider that the 1968 Treaty on Non-Proliferation of Nuclear Weapons regulates nuclear weaponry.[91] Under this treaty, only five states—the United States, the United Kingdom, France, China, and Russia—are entitled to possess nuclear weapons but are (along with other states parties) "to pursue negotiations in good faith on effective measures relating to cessation of the nuclear arms race at an early date and to nuclear disarmament." The 185 or so other states parties, meanwhile, are barred from acquiring nuclear weapons. In these circumstances, is it reasonable that the position taken by the five "official" nuclear weapons states should govern, thus precluding the emergence of a customary bar on the threat or use of nuclear weapons? Alternatively, are these five states more directly affected by the threat or use of nuclear weapons than other states, such that their state practice and *opinio juris* should be given greater weight in ascertaining the content of customary international law on this issue? Or should the five official nuclear weapons states (along with a handful of "unofficial" nuclear states) simply be considered persistent objectors to a rule of customary international law reflected in the state practice and *opinio juris* of the great majority of the world's states?

D. OTHER SOURCES OF INTERNATIONAL LAW

In addition to treaties and customary international law, Article 38(1) of the Statute of the ICJ also refers to "general principles of law recognized by civilized nations" and "judicial decisions and the teachings of the most highly qualified publicists of the various nations, as subsidiary means for the determination of rules of law."

We have already discussed judicial decisions and the teachings of publicists. As noted, doctrine dictates that these writings are subsidiary sources of international law, meant to elucidate—but not create—its content. As also noted, the methodological challenges posed by customary international law in particular may elevate judicial decisions and legal literature to a higher, more influential plane than the strict language of Article 38(1)(d) would seem to allow.

The category of "general principles of law" requires lengthier discussion.

---

90 *Nuclear Weapons* case, above note 88 at 312.
91 1 July 1968, 729 UNTS 161, Can TS 1970 No 7, in force 5 March 1970.

1) General Principles of Law

What are "general principles of law recognized by civilized nations"? Some jurists have urged that the reference to "general principles" means general principles of *international* law; however, this interpretation seems suspect and even circular. What value would be added by listing, as an independent source of international law, general principles of international law? Presumably, general principles of international law would already exist in either treaty or customary form, in which case they would *already* be sources of international law.

A more plausible, useful, and hence widely accepted understanding of "general principles" ties this concept to basic legal principles commonly found in *domestic* legal systems. Consider the following case.

International Status of South-West Africa, Advisory Opinion, [1950] ICJ Rep 128

[Following the First World War, South Africa was granted a "Mandate" over South West Africa (later Namibia), which at the time was deemed a territory incapable of governing itself. The nature and terms of the Mandate were specified in Article 22 of the Covenant of the League of Nations,[92] which referred to the "principle that the well-being and development of such peoples [that is, those inhabiting the mandate territories] form a sacred trust of civilization." Following the demise of the League of Nations, South Africa contended that the Mandate had lapsed and that it was free to dispose of South West Africa as it wished. With the UN serving as the post-1945 successor to the League, the General Assembly sought an advisory opinion from the ICJ on the status of South West Africa. The Court rejected the South African position and advised that the Mandate had survived the dissolution of the League. In a separate, concurring judgment, Judge McNair referred explicitly to the role of "general principles of law" in resolving the case.]

Separate Opinion of Judge McNair:

. . . What is the duty of an international tribunal when confronted with a new legal institution the object and terminology of which are reminiscent of the rules and institutions of private law? To what extent is it useful or necessary to examine what may at first sight appear to be relevant analogies in private law systems and draw help and inspiration from them? International law has recruited and continues to recruit many of its rules and institutions from private systems of law. Article 38(1)*(c)* of the Statute of the Court bears witness that this process is still active, and it will be noted that this article authorizes the Court to "apply . . . *(c)* the general principles of law recognized by civilized nations." The way in which international law borrows from this source is not by means of importing private law institutions "lock, stock and barrel", ready-made and fully equipped with a set of rules. It would be difficult to reconcile such a process with the application of "the general principles of law." In my opinion, the true view of the duty of international tribunals in this matter is to regard any features or terminology which are reminiscent of the rules and institutions of private law as an indication of policy and principles rather than as directly importing these rules and institutions. I quote a sentence from a judgment by Chief Justice Innes in the decision of the Supreme Court of South Africa in *Rex* v. *Christian*, South African Law Reports [1924], Appellate Division, 101, 112:

---

92 28 June 1919, (1919) 13 AJIL Supp 128, in force 10 January 1920, as amended.

"Article 22 [of the Covenant] describes the administration of the territories and peoples with which it deals as a tutelage to be exercised by the governing Power as mandatory on behalf of the League. Those terms were probably employed, not in their strict legal sense, but as indicating the policy which the governing authority should pursue. The relationship between the League and the mandatory could not with any legal accuracy be described as that of principal and agent."

Let us then seek to discover the underlying policy and principles of Article 22 and of the Mandates. No technical significance can be attached to the words "sacred trust of civilization," but they are an apt description of the policy of the authors of the Mandates System, and the words "sacred trust" were not used here for the first time in relation to dependent peoples. . . . Any English lawyer who was instructed to prepare the legal instruments required to give effect to the policy of Article 22 would inevitably be reminded of, and influenced by, the trust of English and American law, though he would soon realize the need of much adaptation for the purposes of the new international institution. Professor Brierly's opinion . . . that the governing principle of the Mandates System is to be found in the trust . . . [is] here very much in point, and it is worth noting that the historical basis of the legal enforcement of the English trust is that it was something which was binding upon the conscience of the trustee; that is why it was legally enforced. It also seems probable that the conception of the Mandates System owes something to the French *tutelle*.

Nearly every legal system possesses some institution whereby the property (and sometimes the persons) of those who are not *sui juris*, such as a minor or a lunatic, can be entrusted to some responsible person as a trustee or *tuteur* or *curateur*. The Anglo-American trust serves this purpose, and another purpose even more closely akin to the Mandates System, namely, the vesting of property in trustees, and its management by them in order that the public or some class of the public may derive benefit or that some public purpose may be served. The trust has frequently been used to protect the weak and the dependent, in cases where there is "great might on the one side and unmight on the other," and the English courts have for many centuries pursued a vigorous policy in the administration and enforcement of trusts.

There are three general principles which are common to all these institutions:

(a) that the control of the trustee, *tuteur* or *curateur* over the property is limited in one way or another; he is not in the position of the normal complete owner, who can do what he likes with his own, because he is precluded from administering the property for his own personal benefit;
(b) that the trustee, *tuteur* or *curateur* is under some kind of legal obligation, based on confidence and conscience, to carry out the trust or mission confided to him for the benefit of some other person or for some public purpose;
(c) that any attempt by one of these persons to absorb the property entrusted to him into his own patrimony would be illegal and would be prevented by the law.

These are some of the general principles of private law which throw light upon this new institution, and I am convinced that in its future development the law governing the trust is a source from which much can be derived. . . .

In his reasoning, Judge McNair urges that "nearly every legal system" possessed a trust or trust-like concept. Yet, he cites examples only from the Anglo-American common law and the French civil law systems. How should we read this juxtaposition of statements: a claim of near-universal recognition of a principle in domestic legal systems, and a review of only a handful of these systems? Is there any basis in the phrase "general principles of law recognized by civilized nations" for such a selective approach?

Consider also the reasoning of Lord Asquith of Bishopstone (a British Law Lord), sitting as an arbitrator in *In the Matter of an Arbitration Between Petroleum Development (Trucial Coast) Ltd and the Sheikh of Abu Dhabi.*[93] At issue was the proper interpretation of an oil concession contract between the Sheikh of Abu Dhabi and an oil company. The contract did not prescribe the law to be applied in analyzing its terms, but simply specified that the agreement was to be interpreted "in a fashion consistent with reason." Lord Asquith took this phrase to demand "the application of principles rooted in the good sense and common practice of the generality of civilised nations—a sort of 'modern law of nature.'" He then held that "English municipal law is inapplicable *as such*," but that "some of its rules are . . . so firmly grounded in reason, as to form part of this broad body of jurisprudence—this 'modern law of nature.'"[94] Lord Asquith was less inclined to include the law of Abu Dhabi in this "modern law of nature." In his words, "[t]he Sheikh administers a purely discretionary justice with the assistance of the Koran; and it would be fanciful to suggest that in this very primitive region there is any settled body of legal principles applicable to the construction of modern commercial instruments."[95]

When Judge McNair and Lord Asquith wrote their decisions in the 1950s, there were roughly sixty states in the world, and the British and French empires (among others) still exercised sovereignty over most of Africa and Asia. Would Judge McNair's and Lord Asquith's surveys of legal systems, if conducted today, suffice for purposes of establishing "general principles" within the meaning of Article 38(1)(c)? Would such an analysis require an empirical survey of all domestic legal systems, or merely those of the more influential European, American, African, and Asian states?

Several points help address these questions. First, caution should be exercised in reading too much into the phrase "civilized nations." This reference in the Statute of the ICJ is actually a carry-over from the treaty establishing the ICJ's predecessor, the Permanent Court of International Justice (PCIJ). Its invocation of "civilized nations" therefore reflects the parlance of the late nineteenth and early twentieth centuries rather than the doctrinal scope of "general principles." At most, "civilized nations" might be taken to refer to "states with well-developed legal systems."[96] Consider also the position of Judge Ammoun, in his separate opinion in the *North Sea Continental Shelf* judgment:

> It is important . . . to observe that the form of words of Article 38, paragraph 1*(c)*, of the Statute, referring to "the general principles of law recognized by civilized nations", is inapplicable in the form in which it is set down, since the term "civilized nations" is

93 Reprinted in (1952) 1 ICLQ 247–61 [*Abu Dhabi* case].

94 *Ibid* at 251.

95 *Ibid* at 250–51.

96 See Christopher A Ford, "Judicial Discretion in International Jurisprudence: Article 38(1)(c) and 'General Principles of Law'" (1994) 5 Duke J Comp & Int'l L 35 at 65.

incompatible with the relevant provisions of the United Nations Charter and the consequences thereof is an ill-advised limitation of the notion of general principles of law. . . .

The discrimination between civilized nations and uncivilized nations . . . is the legacy of the period, now passed away, of colonialism, and of the time long-past when a
limited number of Powers established the rules, of custom or of treaty-law, of a European
law applied in relation to the whole community of nations. . . .

Thus it is that certain nations . . . which did not form part of the limited concert of
States which did the law-making, up to the first decades of the 20th century, for the whole
of the international community, today participate in the determination or elaboration of
the general principles of law. . . .

. . . [I]t is to be borne in mind . . . that the general principles of law . . . are nothing
other than the norms common to the different legislations of the world, united by the
identity of the legal reason therefor . . . transposed from the internal legal system to the
international legal system . . .

The criterion of the distinction between civilized nations and those which are allegedly not so has thus been a political criterion, — power politics, — and anything but an
ethical or legal one. . . .

It is the common underlying principle of national rules in all latitudes which explains
and justifies their annexation into public international law. Thus the general principles of
law, when they effect a synthesis and digest of the [domestic] law of the nations — of all the
nations — seem closer than other sources of law to international morality. By being incorporated in the law of nations, they strip off any tincture of nationalism, so as to represent,
like the principle of equity, the purest moral values. Thus borne along by these values upon
the path of development, international law approaches more and more closely to unity.[97]

Judge Ammoun's position raises a second issue, one also touched upon in the questions noted above: how "general" must the occurrence of principles of law in domestic
legal systems be in order to constitute "general principles of law recognized by civilized
nations"? Two approaches to this issue are reflected in the academic literature as well as
the jurisprudence.

The first, consistent with Judge Ammoun's position, is comparativism. In its most rigid
form, comparativism involves a massive comparative law undertaking, teasing common
principles from as many domestic legal systems as possible. For example, in the *Case
Concerning Right of Passage over Indian Territory*, discussed above, Portugal researched
the domestic jurisprudence of sixty-four states in an effort to discern a general principle
relating to rights of passage. It submitted that the domestic law of sixty-one countries
recognized such a right and therefore that "the municipal laws of the civilized nations are
unanimous."[98]

A review of the domestic legal practices of the world's states is obviously an arduous
undertaking. An intermediate comparativist approach is, therefore, to survey a represent-

---

97 *North Sea Continental Shelf*, above note 69 at 134–35 (separate opinion of Judge Fouad Ammoun).
98 *Right of Passage over Indian Territory (Portugal v India)*, Merits, Judgment, [1960] ICJ Rep 6 at 11–12 (Portuguese final submissions). The ICJ did not pronounce on this issue, deciding the matter with reference to
customary international law.

ative sample of the world's legal systems. Scholars and decision makers endorsing this methodology have, in the words of one commentator:

> aspired to judge the universality of a proposition, not against a census of municipal systems, but by looking to whether it received the support of a representative sample of the different types of socio-economic organization—such as, for example, the leading states of each of the world's capitalist, socialist and "non-aligned" blocs. Such a standard of "system-representative" support would find propositions general to the extent they gained support from suitably representative states of the principal systemic ordering of countries.[99]

Judge McNair could be considered to have undertaken a limited form of such an analysis in his opinion in the *International Status of South-West Africa* case, above. Of course, this "systems" approach raises its own methodological quandaries: What is a representative sample of the world's legal systems? What criteria are to be used to distinguish between "systems"? Which states are to be considered representative of each legal system? Should greater weight be given to systems used in a great many states, or in states with very large populations? And so on.

The second broad approach to the "generality" issue is manifested in the categorist school. Categorists reject the comparative project, instead invoking as general principles those domestic norms that are, in the eye of the decision maker, inherently good and necessary ingredients of any functioning legal system. The categorist approach is, therefore, much like that of Lord Asquith in the *Abu Dhabi* case.[100] The critique of this position is obvious: "Whereas the comparativist approach possessed a relatively straightforward, if cumbersome, process by which to evaluate the general acceptance of a particular principle, categoricism placed itself solely at the mercy of the decision maker."[101] That decision maker may be prone to view her or his own domestic legal tradition as manifesting many good ideas necessary for the proper functioning of a legal system.

Notwithstanding these uncertainties, "general principles" have been applied in practice to fill lacunae in international law: gaps not otherwise filled by treaties or customary international law that would, if not filled, greatly impede the utility of international law as a sensible dispute-resolution system. One well-respected jurist puts it this way:

> Tribunals have not adopted a mechanical system of borrowing from domestic law. Rather they have employed elements or adapted modes of general legal reasoning as well as comparative law analogies in order to make a coherent body of rules for application by international judicial process. It is difficult for state practice to generate the evolution of the rules of procedure and evidence as well as the substantive law that a court must employ. An international tribunal chooses, edits, and adapts elements from other developed systems. The result is a body of international law the content of which has been influenced by domestic law but which is still its own creation.[102]

---

99 Ford, above note 96 at 69.

100 *Abu Dhabi* case, above note 93.

101 Ford, above note 96 at 73.

102 James Crawford, *Brownlie's Principles of Public International Law*, 8th ed (Oxford: Oxford University Press, 2012) at 35.

Used in this modest way, general principles are a necessary ingredient of international law. Applied with due regard for the requirement that they be "general[ly] . . . recognized," disputes over their legitimacy can be minimized or avoided.

2) Unilateral Declarations

The discussion above covers the sources of international law listed in Article 38(1) of the Statute of the ICJ. There is, however, at least one other way in which states may bind themselves in international law, and that is by unilateral declarations.

Nuclear Tests (Australia v France), Judgment, [1974] ICJ Rep 253

[Australia, and New Zealand in a companion case ([1974] ICJ Rep 457), sought an order from the Court requiring France to cease atmospheric nuclear testing in the South Pacific based on statements made by the French president, prime minister, and minister of defence. France refused to recognize the Court's jurisdiction or to participate in the proceedings.]

34. It will be convenient to take the statements . . . in chronological order. The first statement is contained in the communiqué issued by the Office of the President of the French Republic on 8 June 1974, shortly before the commencement of the 1974 series of French nuclear tests:

> "The Decree reintroducing the security measures in the South Pacific nuclear test zone has been published in the Official Journal of 8 June 1974.
>
> The Office of the President of the Republic takes this opportunity of stating that in view of the stage reached in carrying out the French nuclear defence programme France will be in a position to pass on to the stage of underground explosions as soon as the series of tests planned for this summer is completed."

A copy of the communiqué was transmitted with a Note dated 11 June 1974 from the French Embassy in Canberra to the Australian Department of Foreign Affairs, and as already mentioned, the text of the communiqué was brought to the attention of the Court in the course of the oral proceedings.

35. In addition to this, the Court cannot fail to take note of a reference to a document made by counsel at a public hearing in the proceedings, parallel to this case, instituted by New Zealand . . . [that indicated] that on 10 June 1974 the French Embassy in Wellington sent a Note to the New Zealand Ministry of Foreign Affairs, containing a passage . . . which, in the translation used by New Zealand, runs as follows:

> "France, at the point which has been reached in the execution of its programme of defence by nuclear means, will be in a position to move to the stage of underground tests, as soon as the test series planned for this summer is completed.
>
> Thus the atmospheric tests which are soon to be carried out will, in the normal course of events, be the last of this type. . . ."

37. The next statement to be considered . . . will be that made on 25 July [1974] at a press conference given by the President of the Republic, when he said:

". . . on this question of nuclear tests, you know that the Prime Minister had publicly expressed himself in the National Assembly in his speech introducing the Government's programme. He had indicated that French nuclear testing would continue. I had myself made it clear that this round of atmospheric tests would be the last, and so the members of the Government were completely informed of our intentions in this respect. . . ."

40. On 11 October 1974, the [French] Minister of Defence held a press conference during which he stated twice, in almost identical terms, that there would not be any atmospheric tests in 1975 and that France was ready to proceed to underground tests. When the comment was made that he had not added "in the normal course of events", he agreed that he had not. This latter point is relevant in view of the passage from the Note of 10 June 1974 from the French Embassy in Wellington to the Ministry of Foreign Affairs of New Zealand, quoted in paragraph 35 above. . . .

41. In view of the foregoing, the Court finds that France made public its intention to cease the conduct of atmospheric nuclear tests following the conclusion of the 1974 series of tests. The Court must in particular take into consideration the President's statement of 25 July 1974 (paragraph 37 above) followed by the Defence Minister's statement on 11 October 1974 (paragraph 40). These reveal that the official statements made on behalf of France concerning future nuclear testing are not subject to whatever proviso, if any, was implied by the expression "in the normal course of events [*normalement*]" . . . .

43. It is well recognized that declarations made by way of unilateral acts, concerning legal or factual situations, may have the effect of creating legal obligations. Declarations of this kind may be, and often are, very specific. When it is the intention of the State making the declaration that it should become bound according to its terms, that intention confers on the declaration the character of a legal undertaking, the State being thenceforth legally required to follow a course of conduct consistent with the declaration. An undertaking of this kind, if given publicly, and with an intent to be bound, even though not made within the context of international negotiations, is binding. In these circumstances, nothing in the nature of a *quid pro quo* nor any subsequent acceptance of the declaration, nor even any reply or reaction from other States, is required for the declaration to take effect, since such a requirement would be inconsistent with the strictly unilateral nature of the juridical act by which the pronouncement by the State was made.

44. Of course, not all unilateral acts imply obligation; but a State may choose to take up a certain position in relation to a particular matter with the intention of being bound — the intention is to be ascertained by interpretation of the act. When States make statements by which their freedom of action is to be limited, a restrictive interpretation is called for.

45. With regard to the question of form, it should be observed that this is not a domain in which international law imposes any special or strict requirements. Whether a statement is made orally or in writing makes no essential difference, for such statements made in particular circumstances may create commitments in international law, which does not require that they should be couched in written form. Thus the question of form is not

decisive. . . . [Quoting from an earlier ICJ judgment, the Court then concluded:] [T]he sole relevant question is whether the language employed in any given declaration does reveal a clear intention. . . .

46. One of the basic principles governing the creation and performance of legal obligations, whatever their source, is the principle of good faith. Trust and confidence are inherent in international co-operation, in particular in an age when this co-operation in many fields is becoming increasingly essential. Just as the very rule of *pacta sunt servanda* in the law of treaties is based on good faith, so also is the binding character of an international obligation assumed by unilateral declaration. Thus interested States may take cognizance of unilateral declarations and place confidence in them, and are entitled to require that the obligation thus created be respected. . . .

49. Of the statements by the French Government now before the Court, the most essential are clearly those made by the President of the Republic. There can be no doubt, in view of his functions, that his public communications or statements, oral or written, as Head of State, are in international relations acts of the French State. His statements, and those of members of the French Government acting under his authority, up to the last statement made by the Minister of Defence (of 11 October 1974), constitute a whole. Thus, in whatever form these statements were expressed, they must be held to constitute an engagement of the State, having regard to their intention and to the circumstances in which they were made.

50. The unilateral statements of the French authorities were made outside the Court, publicly and *erga omnes*, even though the first of them was communicated to the Government of Australia. As was observed above, to have legal effect, there was no need for these statements to be addressed to a particular State, nor was acceptance by any other State required. The general nature and characteristics of these statements are decisive for the evaluation of the legal implications, and it is to the interpretation of the statements that the Court must now proceed. The Court is entitled to presume, at the outset, that these statements were not made *in vacuo*, but in relation to the tests which constitute the very object of the present proceedings, although France has not appeared in the case.

51. In announcing that the 1974 series of atmospheric tests would be the last, the French Government conveyed to the world at large, including the Applicant, its intention effectively to terminate these tests. It was bound to assume that other States might take note of these statements and rely on their being effective. The validity of these statements and their legal consequences must be considered within the general framework of the security of international intercourse, and the confidence and trust which are so essential in the relations among States. It is from the actual substance of these statements, and from the circumstances attending their making, that the legal implications of the unilateral act must be deduced. The objects of these statements are clear and they were addressed to the international community as a whole, and the Court holds that they constitute an undertaking possessing legal effect. The Court considers that the President of the Republic, in deciding upon the effective cessation of atmospheric tests, gave an undertaking to the international community to which his words were addressed. It is true that the French Government has consistently maintained, for example in a Note dated 7 Febru-

ary 1973 from the French Ambassador in Canberra to the Prime Minister and Minister for Foreign Affairs of Australia, that it "has the conviction that its nuclear experiments have not violated any rule of international law", nor did France recognize that it was bound by any rule of international law to terminate its tests, but this does not affect the legal consequences of the statements examined above. The Court finds that the unilateral undertaking resulting from these statements cannot be interpreted as having been made in implicit reliance on an arbitrary power of reconsideration. The Court finds further that the French Government has undertaken an obligation the precise nature and limits of which must be understood in accordance with the actual terms in which they have been publicly expressed.

52. Thus the Court faces a situation in which the objective of the Applicant has in effect been accomplished, inasmuch as the Court finds that France has undertaken the obligation to hold no further nuclear tests in the atmosphere in the South Pacific. . . .

62. For these reasons, THE COURT, by nine votes to six, finds that the claim of Australia no longer has any object and that the Court is therefore not called upon to give a decision thereon. . . .

The concept of binding unilateral declarations is appealing at one level. Why not compel a state to meet promises it makes publicly? The practical reality is more difficult. Who can bind the state by a unilateral declaration — only the head of state and members of the government acting under her authority, as in the *Nuclear Tests* cases, or would some lesser official suffice? What basis is there for finding an intention to create legally binding obligations absent an explicit statement of such intent? Can a state ever retract a unilateral declaration? Why shouldn't a second, equally emphatic unilateral declaration that counters a first one be equally binding? How realistic is it to think that any state intends to bind itself irrevocably and in perpetuity without saying so explicitly?

In Canadian and Anglo-American domestic contract law, some of these difficulties are at least partially resolved by the concept of detrimental reliance, pursuant to which a unilateral promise may become binding only if it induces someone to rely upon it to their detriment. The Court in the *Nuclear Tests* cases emphasized the public nature of the French statements, which meant that "other States might take note of these statements and rely on their being effective."[103] However, the Court did not insist on evidence of *actual*, much less *detrimental*, reliance, prompting critiques like this one:

[T]he World Court has created a potentially open-ended basis for state responsibility — the "contort" [combining contract and tort] of making a unilateral promise. The Court has even suggested that an informal, internal statement might give rise to such liability, even without a showing of substantial detrimental reliance by another state. . . . Enforcement of gratuitous promises in the absence of reliance . . . potentially expos[es] states to liability for every utterance, no matter how contradictory. To control the gratuitous promise doctrine, the Court or an appropriate law-making convention should clarify that gratuitous promises that do *not* induce reliance are binding only when made with clear intent to be bound.

---

103 *Nuclear Tests (Australia v France)*, Judgment, [1974] ICJ Rep 253 at para 51 [*Nuclear Tests* cases].

That intent could be demonstrated by a writing signed by a high-ranking state official, or perhaps even by ratification through the state's normal constitutional processes.[104]

Given the uncertainties raised by unilateral declarations, it is not surprising that the ICJ signalled restraint in relying on such declarations in the subsequent *Frontier Dispute*. In that matter, Burkina Faso and Mali submitted a border dispute to adjudication by the ICJ. One issue was whether a statement made by Mali's head of state, which related to the disputed border but was conveyed outside of negotiations over the dispute, had legal significance. A Chamber of the Court made the following comments:

> 39. [S]uch declarations "concerning legal or factual situations" may indeed "have the effect of creating legal obligations" for the State on whose behalf they are made, as the Court observed in the *Nuclear Tests* cases. . . . But the Court also made clear in those cases that it is only "when it is the intention of the State making the declaration that it should become bound according to its terms" that "that intention confers on the declaration the character of a legal undertaking. " . . . Thus it all depends on the intention of the State in question, and the Court emphasized that it is for the Court to "form its own view of the meaning and scope intended by the author of a unilateral declaration which may create a legal obligation." . . .
>
> 40. In order to assess the intentions of the author of a unilateral act, account must be taken of all the factual circumstances in which the act occurred. For example, in the *Nuclear Tests* cases, the Court took the view that since the applicant States were not the only ones concerned at the possible continuance of atmospheric testing by the French Government, that Government's unilateral declarations had "conveyed to the world at large, including the Applicant, its intention effectively to terminate these tests" . . . . In the particular circumstances of those cases, the French Government could not express an intention to be bound otherwise than by unilateral declarations. It is difficult to see how it could have accepted the terms of a negotiated solution with each of the applicants without thereby jeopardizing its contention that its conduct was lawful. The circumstances of the present case are radically different. Here, there was nothing to hinder the Parties from manifesting an intention to accept the binding character of the conclusions of [the body trying to mediate a border settlement] by the normal method: a formal agreement on the basis of reciprocity. Since no agreement of this kind was concluded between the Parties, the Chamber finds that there are no grounds to interpret the declaration made by Mali's head of State . . . as a unilateral act with legal implications in regard to the present case.[105]

From this reasoning, two propositions may be gleaned: first, the state must clearly *intend* to bind itself by the unilateral declaration, having regard to all the surrounding factual circumstances. Second, the Court will be reluctant to discern any such intent where the subject matter of the declaration is readily amenable to the more usual process of negotiation and conclusion of an agreement between the interested states. The failure of the states concerned to conclude such an agreement militates against an inference of intent, on the part of the declaring state, to undertake legal obligations. By contrast, the

---

104 Geoffrey R Watson, "The Death of Treaty" (1994) 55 Ohio St LJ 781 at 814.
105 *Frontier Dispute (Burkina Faso v Mali)*, Judgment, [1986] ICJ Rep 554 at paras 39–40 [*Frontier Dispute*].

absence of an agreement may not be relevant in this way in circumstances where the state makes a promise affecting the interests of the international community at large, or a significant number of states. In such a case, the lack of agreement is just as likely the result of practical difficulties inherent in the conclusion of broad multilateral agreements as it is evidence of the absence of intent by the declaring state to undertake legal obligations.

In April 2010, US President Barack Obama declared before the world's media that the United States was "explicitly committing not to use nuclear weapons against non-nuclear states that are in compliance with the Nuclear Non-Proliferation Treaty [NPT], even if they attacked the United States with biological or chemical weapons or launched a crippling cyber attack."[106] The US president's announcement accompanied the release of the country's *Nuclear Posture Review Report*, which stated that "the United States is now prepared to strengthen its long-standing 'negative security assurance' by declaring that the United States will not use or threaten to use nuclear weapons against non-nuclear weapons states that are party to the NPT and in compliance with their nuclear non-proliferation obligations."[107] In light of the materials reviewed above, did these statements create international legal obligations that are binding on the United States?

Given the highly fact-sensitive nature of the criteria articulated by the ICJ in the *Nuclear Tests* and *Frontier* cases, exactly when unilateral declarations may give rise to binding legal obligations remains difficult to determine on an *a priori* basis. It should nevertheless be noted that the International Law Commission, at the invitation of the UN General Assembly, has formulated a set of guiding principles to provide assistance in this regard:

"Guiding Principles Applicable to Unilateral Declarations of States Capable of Creating Legal Obligations" in *Report of the International Law Commission*, UN GAOR, 61st Sess, Supp No 10 at c IX.D.1, UN Doc A/61/10 (2006)

1. Declarations publicly made and manifesting the will to be bound may have the effect of creating legal obligations. When the conditions for this are met, the binding character of such declarations is based on good faith; States concerned may then take them into consideration and rely on them; such States are entitled to require that such obligations be respected;

2. Any State possesses capacity to undertake legal obligations through unilateral declarations;

3. To determine the legal effects of such declarations, it is necessary to take account of their content, of all the factual circumstances in which they were made, and of the reactions to which they gave rise;

4. A unilateral declaration binds the State internationally only if it is made by an authority vested with the power to do so. By virtue of their functions, heads of State, heads of Government and ministers for foreign affairs are competent to formulate such declara-

---

106 David E Sanger & Peter Baker, "Obama Limits When U.S. Would Use Nuclear Weapons," *New York Times* (5 April 2010) A1.

107 US Department of Defense, *Nuclear Posture Review Report* (April 2010) at viii & 15, online: www.defense.gov/npr/docs/2010%20Nuclear%20Posture%20Review%20Report.pdf.

tions. Other persons representing the State in specified areas may be authorized to bind it, through their declarations, in areas falling within their competence;

5. Unilateral declarations may be formulated orally or in writing;

6. Unilateral declarations may be addressed to the international community as a whole, to one or several States or to other entities;

7. A unilateral declaration entails obligations for the formulating State only if it is stated in clear and specific terms. In the case of doubt as to the scope of the obligations resulting from such a declaration, such obligations must be interpreted in a restrictive manner. In interpreting the content of such obligations, weight shall be given first and foremost to the text of the declaration, together with the context and the circumstances in which it was formulated;

8. A unilateral declaration which is in conflict with a peremptory norm of general international law is void;

9. No obligation may result for other States from the unilateral declaration of a State. However, the other State or States concerned may incur obligations in relation to such a unilateral declaration to the extent that they clearly accepted such a declaration;

10. A unilateral declaration that has created legal obligations for the State making the declaration cannot be revoked arbitrarily. In assessing whether a revocation would be arbitrary, consideration should be given to:
 (i) Any specific terms of the declaration relating to revocation;
 (ii) The extent to which those to whom the obligations are owed have relied on such obligations;
 (iii) The extent to which there has been a fundamental change in the circumstances.

Is Guiding Principle 10 consistent with the ICJ's reasoning in the *Nuclear Tests* cases? In finding that France had not included an implicit power of arbitrary reconsideration when making its unilateral declarations, did the ICJ suggest that it would not have been free to do so?

3) "Soft Law" and Other Influences on the Development of International Law

More elusive than the foregoing formal sources of international law is the so-termed concept of "soft law," which refers to principles of a political, practical, humanitarian, or moral nature that can influence state behaviour, but that do not, strictly speaking, correspond to extant legal obligations or rights. The use of soft law at the international level is similar to the use by domestic courts of non-legally binding materials, such as policy statements, guidelines, manuals, and handbooks, to guide the exercise of statutory discretion,[108] although there is greater scope for soft law to play an influential role on the international legal plane. As one commentator has explained:

---

108 See for example *Thamotharem v Canada (Minister of Citizenship and Immigration)*, 2007 FCA 198 at paras 55–64, Evans JA.

In many fields of international law—such as environment, human rights, trade, and arms control—important principles and nonbinding norms are contained in resolutions or other decisions of states and intergovernmental organizations. International conferences are increasingly important sources of declarations that are nonbinding (except for any rules of customary international law included), that are intended to influence the behavior of states and non-state actors. . . .

Nonbinding legal instruments are negotiated by governments for several reasons. Such instruments may be a first step toward the negotiation of subsequent, binding agreements. Many of the legal instruments that extend specific human rights to groups or set forth new human rights began as nonbinding instruments. . . .

States and other actors may prefer nonbinding instruments because they can be more easily adapted to changing circumstances. In some cases, countries may negotiate framework agreements, which, although binding, contain provisions that are not expressed in obligatory language. The framework agreements may give countries considerable flexibility in implementing the treaty. Often such agreements lead to protocols, which contain specific binding obligations. . . .

In other cases, nonbinding legal instruments may be largely hortatory because it would be difficult to reach binding agreement on precise legal norms. These instruments, be they intergovernmental conference declarations or other forms, still affect policy and expectations about how others will behave. . . .

This trend to formulate nonbinding legal instruments is likely to increase more rapidly than the negotiation of formal international conventions. This is because agreement is usually easier to achieve, the transaction costs for governments and even nongovernmental organizations are lower, the opportunity to set forth detailed strategies is greater, and the ability to respond to rapid changes in scientific understanding or economic or social conditions is better.[109]

The manuals and guidance notes prepared by expert bodies as diverse as the UN Refugee Agency (UNHCR) and the International Civil Aviation Organization (ICAO) may be considered influential soft law instruments. So too might some of the work of the International Law Commission (ILC), although many of its reports may also be considered akin to the writings of highly qualified publicists. Composed of thirty-four experts, the ILC was established by the UN General Assembly in 1947 and charged, under the terms of its governing statute, with "the promotion of the progressive development of international law and its codification." "Progressive development" is defined as "the preparation of draft conventions on subjects which have not yet been regulated by international law or in regard to which the law has not yet been sufficiently developed in the practice of States." Codification means "the more precise formulation and systematization of rules of international law in fields where there already has been extensive State practice, precedent and doctrine."[110]

---

109 Edith Brown Weiss, "The President's Message," *American Society of International Law Newsletter* (September 1995). See further Dinah Shelton, *Commitment and Compliance: The Role of Non-binding Norms in the International Legal System* (Oxford: Oxford University Press, 2003).

110 See article 15 of the Statute of the International Law Commission, found in the annex to *Establishment of an International Law Commission*, GA Res 174(II), reprinted in UN GAOR, 2nd Sess at 105–110, UN Doc A/519 (1947).

In its "progressive development" role, the ILC is often a source of potentially influential soft law principles that may lead to the conclusion of a new treaty or the emergence of rules of customary international law. In its codification role, the ILC's work has been influential in ascertaining and reducing principles of customary international law to written, and sometimes treaty, form. In this way, its work provides evidence of existing law, with one former ILC member having noted that: "The Commission's success is further marked by the frequency with which states have accepted the codification conventions as evidence of existing law—recognizing their rules and citing them as law long before the conventions have entered into force."[111] The VCLT is an example of this phenomenon, as is the work of the ILC on state responsibility, discussed in Chapter 12.

It should be noted, however, that there is no exclusivity to the club of potential contributors to the vast body of soft law that informs, and sometimes becomes, binding international law. Governments, international organizations, non-governmental organizations, other civil society groups, scholars, think-tanks, litigants, parliamentarians, and many others are often the source of memoranda of understanding, resolutions, submissions, studies, opinions, reports, guidelines, and so on that, as indicated in the excerpt above, are intended to influence, *inter alia*, the behaviour of states. To the extent they do so, they may play an indirect role, filtered through the formal international law-making processes we have reviewed in this chapter, in shaping international law itself.

E. THE CONCEPTS OF *JUS COGENS* NORMS AND *ERGA OMNES* OBLIGATIONS

Before leaving the topic of sources of international law, we turn briefly to two important concepts that have already been mentioned in passing in the first two chapters of this book and to which we will return periodically throughout the remainder of these materials. Both concepts —*jus cogens* rules and *erga omnes* obligations—have to do with the characteristics of certain special rules of international law, whether these rules emanate from treaty, custom, or some other source of international law.

Put simply, a rule of *jus cogens* (also known as a peremptory norm) is a higher principle of international law from which no derogation is permitted, except by a rule that has also achieved *jus cogens* status. This notion is articulated in Article 53 of the VCLT:

> A treaty is void if, at the time of its conclusion, it conflicts with a peremptory norm of general international law. For the purposes of the present Convention, a peremptory norm of general international law is a norm accepted and recognized by the international community of States as a whole as a norm from which no derogation is permitted and which can be modified only by a subsequent norm of general international law having the same character.

Despite its obvious potency, the *jus cogens* concept is poorly developed in international law. One consequence of this is that some states, most notably France, have not given their full support to the VCLT because of its *jus cogens* provisions. While the idea of higher,

---

111 Bernhard Graefrath, "The International Law Commission Tomorrow: Improving Its Organization and Methods Of Work" (1991) 85 AJIL 595.

peremptory law is generally accepted, there is no readily accepted test for ascertaining whether a rule has achieved *jus cogens* status, and hence no general agreement on which rules of international law fall within this category. Consider the following critique:

> One major difficulty is related to the identification of norms of *jus cogens*. First, should this function of identification be performed solely by multilateral law-making conventions, or may a norm of *jus cogens* evolve through the same process as in the case of customary rules of international law? Article 64 of the Vienna Convention on the Law of Treaties provides that "if a new peremptory norm of general international law emerges, any existing treaty which is in conflict with that norm becomes void and terminates." The word "emerges" shows that it was contemplated that a norm of *jus cogens* could be one of customary international law. . . . Second, there is a lack of consensus as to what, at present, are norms of *jus cogens*.[112]

On this second issue, *Restatement of the Law, Third, Foreign Relations Law of the United States* says this:

> Although the concept of *jus cogens* is now accepted, its content is not agreed. There is general agreement that the principles of the United Nations Charter prohibiting the use of force are *jus cogens*. . . . It has been suggested that norms that create "international crimes" and obligate all states to proceed against violations are also peremptory. . . . Such norms might include rules prohibiting genocide, slave trade and slavery, apartheid and other gross violations of human rights, and perhaps attacks on diplomats.[113]

Consider also the view of the International Law Commission expressed in its commentaries to its 2001 "Draft Articles on State Responsibility for Internationally Wrongful Acts," discussed in Chapter 12:

> . . . it is generally agreed that the prohibition of aggression is to be regarded as peremptory. This is supported, for example, by the Commission's commentary to what was to become article 53 [of the Vienna Convention on the Law of Treaties], uncontradicted statements by Governments in the course of the Vienna Conference on the Law of Treaties, the submissions of both parties in *Military and Paramilitary Activities* [*in and against Nicaragua*] and the Court's own position in that case. There also seems to be widespread agreement with other examples listed in the Commission's commentary to article 53: viz. the prohibitions against slavery and the slave trade, genocide, and racial discrimination and apartheid. These practices have been prohibited in widely ratified international treaties and conventions admitting of no exception. There was general agreement among Governments as to the peremptory character of these prohibitions at the Vienna Conference. As to the peremptory character of the prohibition against genocide, this is supported by a number of decisions by national and international courts. . . .
>
> Although not specifically listed in the Commission's commentary to article 53 of the 1969 Vienna Convention, the peremptory character of certain other norms seems also to

---

112 Shearer, above note 79 at 49.
113 *Third Restatement*, above note 48 at para 102, comment 6.

be generally accepted. This applies to the prohibition against torture as defined in article 1 of the Convention against Torture and Other Cruel, Inhuman or Degrading Treatment or Punishment. The peremptory character of this prohibition has been confirmed by decisions of international and national bodies. In the light of the description by the ICJ of the basic rules of international humanitarian law applicable in armed conflict as "intransgressible" in character, it would also seem justified to treat these as peremptory. Finally, the obligation to respect the right of self-determination deserves to be mentioned. As the Court noted in the *East Timor* case, "[t]he principle of self-determination . . . is one of the essential principles of contemporary international law", which gives rise to an obligation to the international community as a whole to permit and respect its exercise.[114]

The concept of *erga omnes* obligations is beset by even greater uncertainty. An obligation *erga omnes* is a duty that "all States can be held to have a legal interest" in protecting.[115] In other words, a violation of an *erga omnes* obligation is a violation of an obligation owed to all members of the international community, not simply to one or several states. In *dicta* in the *Barcelona Traction* case, the ICJ listed examples of obligations *erga omnes*: the bans on aggression and genocide and rules concerning "basic rights" of human beings, including the prohibition of slavery and racial discrimination.[116] More recently, the ICJ has opined that the right of self-determination, and some rules of international humanitarian law, also give rise to obligations *erga omnes*, as the following extract shows.

Legal Consequences of the Construction of a Wall in the Occupied Palestinian Territory, Advisory Opinion, [2004] ICJ Rep 136

[In 2003, the UN General Assembly asked the Court for an advisory opinion on the following question: "What are the legal consequences arising from the construction of the wall being built by Israel, the occupying Power, in the Occupied Palestinian Territory, including in and around East Jerusalem, as described in the report of the Secretary-General, considering the rules and principles of international law, including the Fourth Geneva Convention of 1949, and relevant Security Council and General Assembly resolutions?" The Court concluded that "the construction of the wall being built by Israel, the occupying Power, in the Occupied Palestinian Territory, including in and around East Jerusalem, and its associated régime, are contrary to international law." It then addressed the question of the consequences of this violation for Israel and other states. In so doing, it raised the issue of obligations *erga omnes*.]

155. The Court would observe that the obligations violated by Israel include certain obligations *erga omnes*. As the Court indicated in the *Barcelona Traction* case, such obligations are by their very nature "the concern of all States" and, "In view of the importance of the rights involved, all States can be held to have a legal interest in their protection"

---

114 International Law Commission, "Commentaries to the Draft Articles on Responsibility of States for Internationally Wrongful Acts," 53d Sess (2001) at 112–13.

115 *Barcelona Traction, Light and Power Company, Ltd*, Second Phase, Judgment, [1970] ICJ Rep 3 at 32 [*Barcelona Traction* case].

116 *Ibid.* See also Maurizo Ragazzi, *The Concept of International Obligations* Erga Omnes (Oxford: Clarendon Press, 1997) at 139.

. . . . The obligations *erga omnes* violated by Israel are the obligation to respect the right of the Palestinian people to self-determination, and certain of its obligations under international humanitarian law.

156. As regards the first of these, the Court has already observed . . . that in the *East Timor* case, it described as "irreproachable" the assertion that "the right of peoples to self-determination, as it evolved from the Charter and from United Nations practice, has an *erga omnes* character" (*I.C.J. Reports 1995*, p. 102, para. 29). The Court would also recall that under the terms of General Assembly resolution 2625 (XXV), already mentioned above (see paragraph 88),

> "Every State has the duty to promote, through joint and separate action, realization of the principle of equal rights and self-determination of peoples, in accordance with the provisions of the Charter, and to render assistance to the United Nations in carrying out the responsibilities entrusted to it by the Charter regarding the implementation of the principle . . ."

157. With regard to international humanitarian law, the Court recalls that in its Advisory Opinion on the *Legality of the Threat or Use of Nuclear Weapons* it stated that "a great many rules of humanitarian law applicable in armed conflict are so fundamental to the respect of the human person and 'elementary considerations of humanity' . . . ", that they are "to be observed by all States whether or not they have ratified the conventions that contain them, because they constitute intransgressible principles of international customary law" . . . In the Court's view, these rules incorporate obligations which are essentially of an *erga omnes* character.

158. The Court would also emphasize that Article 1 of the Fourth Geneva Convention, a provision common to the four Geneva Conventions, provides that "The High Contracting Parties undertake to respect and to ensure respect for the present Convention in all circumstances." It follows from that provision that every State party to that Convention, whether or not it is a party to a specific conflict, is under an obligation to ensure that the requirements of the instruments in question are complied with.

159. Given the character and the importance of the rights and obligations involved, the Court is of the view that all States are under an obligation not to recognize the illegal situation resulting from the construction of the wall in the Occupied Palestinian Territory, including in and around East Jerusalem. They are also under an obligation not to render aid or assistance in maintaining the situation created by such construction. It is also for all States, while respecting the United Nations Charter and international law, to see to it that any impediment, resulting from the construction of the wall, to the exercise by the Palestinian people of its right to self-determination is brought to an end. In addition, all the States parties to the Geneva Convention relative to the Protection of Civilian Persons in Time of War of 12 August 1949 are under an obligation, while respecting the United Nations Charter and international law, to ensure compliance by Israel with international humanitarian law as embodied in that Convention.

The human rights area, in particular, contains several claims that certain rights entail *erga omnes* obligations. In *Barcelona Traction*, the ICJ listed the bars on slavery and racial discrimination as two examples of *erga omnes* obligations relating to the "principles and rules concerning the basic rights of human beings."[117] It did not assert, however, that these were the only human rights principles having *erga omnes* status. More recent sources expand this list. Thus, the *Third Restatement* lists, as additional *erga omnes* obligations, the prohibition of: murder or disappearing of individuals; torture or other cruel, inhuman, or degrading treatment or punishment; prolonged arbitrary detention; and a "consistent pattern of gross violations of internationally recognized human rights."[118] The well-respected *Institut de Droit international* (Institute of International Law) went even further in 1989 in resolving that the international obligation to ensure the observance of human rights is an *erga omnes* obligation. In the Institute's opinion, which was based on the considered views of its expert membership, this obligation "is incumbent upon every State in relation to the international community as a whole, and every State has a legal interest in the protection of human rights."[119]

Perhaps more fundamental still than the difficulty of identifying which rules of international law are of an *erga omnes* character is that of giving concrete, practical effect to such a character. As we have seen above, in theory an *erga omnes* obligation is one that all states have an interest in protecting. We have also seen that, in its advisory opinion on the *Legal Consequences of the Construction of a Wall*, the ICJ attempted to give substance to this theoretical interest by finding that all states had certain correlative duties not to recognize, aid, or assist in Israel's breach of its *erga omnes* obligations and, "while respecting the *United Nations Charter* and international law," to ensure Israel's compliance with such obligations. However, the difficulty with articulating rules that "all states" have an interest and indeed a duty to see respected is that there is, as yet, no such coordinated entity as "all states." The more difficult issue, therefore, is whether obligations owed to "all states" or to "the international community as a whole" can also be considered obligations owed to each and every state individually. This has important practical implications for the enforceability of such rules, a topic to which we will return in greater detail in Chapter 12 on the topic of state responsibility for internationally wrongful acts.

Like *jus cogens* norms, moreover, it is not at all certain how exactly a given principle achieves *erga omnes* stature. States do sometimes take the lead in advocating the existence of one or the other of these types of norms. As with international law generally, the field is crowded with scholars, advocacy groups, or others advancing claims concerning the "higher" status of given international legal rules. At some point, these views may infuse more formal international discourse, finding their way into the rhetoric (and occasionally, the behaviour) of states or the judgments of international tribunals. In this way, they may take on concrete legal significance with powerful normative effects.

---

117 *Barcelona Traction* case, above note 115 at 32.

118 *Third Restatement*, above note 48, s 702.

119 Institute of International Law, "The Protection of Human Rights and the Principle of Non-intervention in Internal Affairs of States," Resolution 1989-III, adopted at Saint-Jacques-de-Compostelle, art 1, online: www.idi-iil.org/idiE/resolutionsE/1989_comp_03_en.PDF.

F. THE INTERACTION OF INTERNATIONAL AND CANADIAN DOMESTIC LAW

1) The International/Domestic Legal Juncture

So far in this chapter we have focused on the processes by which international law is created—or, looking at it slightly differently, how one determines the existence and extent of international legal rights and obligations. This "law of sources" is inherently international in nature and outlook, in the sense that it defines the law that applies directly to subjects of international law within the international legal system itself.

However, as we shall see in Chapter 3, the "subjects of international law" are for the most part limited to states and certain international organizations (that is, intergovernmental organizations established by agreement among states). So of what relevance is international law to other entities, such as individuals, corporations, and even governmental organs within states (such as courts or regulatory bodies or municipalities)? The answer to this question is complicated by the fact that most such entities are already subject to national, or "domestic," legal systems. For example, Canadian courts are established pursuant to Canadian law and thus bound to apply that law. Similarly, Canadian residents are subject to various federal, provincial (or territorial), and municipal laws originating within the Canadian legal system. Canadian nationals abroad may be subject to certain rules of Canadian law as well as rules established by the domestic legal system of the state in which they are living, doing business, or visiting. So the question of the relevance of international law to most entities other than states and international organizations often comes down to the relevance of international law to or within the domestic legal system(s) to which such entities are already subject. To put it more concretely: the relevance of international law to, say, a Canadian court or resident usually turns on the extent to which the Canadian legal system takes notice of, or gives domestic legal effect to, international law.

It is at this juncture of international and domestic law that some of the more peculiar effects of the notion of state sovereignty are in evidence. From the perspective of the international legal system—on the "international plane"—states are positively obligated to fulfill their international legal obligations emanating from the formal sources we have reviewed above. In addition, much of international law looks to domestic law and policy for its implementation and enforcement. Yet, being sovereign, states are generally free to structure their internal affairs, including their domestic legal systems, as they see fit. While performing one's international legal obligations may require adaptations to one's domestic law (recall, for example, the rule in Article 27 of the VCLT), international law does not generally dictate *how* such adaptation is to occur. Thus states are afforded a large measure of discretion not only in how to structure their domestic legal systems but also in how those systems interact with the international legal system.

As a result, virtually every state has its own set of rules governing how its domestic legal system will treat international law generally as well as that particular state's international legal obligations specifically. These "reception" rules are, of course, rules of domestic rather than international law, and they tend to vary from state to state. While it would therefore be a gargantuan task to address this topic comprehensively, we propose to close this chapter on the sources of international law by examining how those sources may be, or become, relevant in the Canadian domestic context specifically. For example, can a litigant in a Canadian courtroom invoke Canada's treaty obligations as part of her case? Can a Canadian court rely on customary international law in disposing of a claim?

2) Canadian Domestic Law's Treatment of Treaties

a) Monism, Dualism, and the Canadian Requirement of Treaty Transformation

Above we saw that once a treaty is concluded, a state has signified its proper consent to be bound by it, and it comes into force, the state is legally bound by the treaty as a matter of international law. As also suggested above, however, it is not necessarily true that the treaty automatically becomes binding within the state's *domestic* legal system. Some states—including, notably, those with a domestic legal system that follows the British parliamentary tradition—emphasize the separation between the international and domestic spheres of law. They take what is known as a "dualist" approach, at least to treaty law: treaty law does not become enforceable before domestic courts unless it is first "transformed" into domestic law by a domestic law-making process—usually the enactment of treaty "implementing" legislation by a domestic legislature. Some states take the opposite, or "monist" view, and consider international treaty law automatically "incorporated" into domestic law without any need for domestic legislative transformation.

Hersch Lauterpacht, *Oppenheim's International Law*, vol 1 (8th ed, 1955) at 37–39

20. According to what may be called the dualistic view, the Law of Nations and the Municipal Law of the several States are essentially different from each other. They differ, first, as regards their sources. The sources of Municipal Law are custom grown up within the boundaries of the States concerned and statutes enacted by the law-giving authority. The sources of International Law are custom grown up among States and law-making treaties concluded by them.

The Law of Nations and Municipal Law differ, secondly, regarding the relations they regulate. Municipal Law regulates relations between the individuals under the sway of a State and the relations between the State and the individual. International Law, on the other hand, regulates relations between States.

The Law of Nations and Municipal Law differ, thirdly, with regard to the substance of their law: whereas Municipal Law is a law of a sovereign over individuals subjected to his sway, the Law of Nations is a law not above, but between, sovereign States, and is therefore a weaker law.

If the Law of Nations and Municipal Law differ as demonstrated, the Law of Nations can neither as a body nor in parts be *per se* a part of Municipal Law. Just as Municipal Law lacks the power of altering or creating rules of International Law, so the latter lacks absolutely the power of altering or creating rules of Municipal Law. If, according to the Municipal Law of an individual State, the Law of Nations as a body or in parts is considered to be part of the law of the land, this can only be so either by municipal custom or by statute, and then the respective rules of the Law of Nations have by adoption become at the same time rules of Municipal Law. Wherever and whenever such total or partial adoption has not taken place, municipal courts cannot be considered to be bound by International Law, because it has, *per se*, no power over municipal courts. And if it happens that a rule of Municipal Law is in indubitable conflict with a rule of the Law of Nations, municipal courts must apply the former.

21. The above dualistic view is opposed by what may conveniently be called the monistic doctrine. The latter rejects all three premises of the dualists. It denies, in the first instance, that the subjects of the two systems of law are essentially different and maintains that in both it is ultimately the conduct of the individuals which is regulated by law, the only difference being that in the international sphere the consequences of such conduct are attributed to the State. Secondly, it asserts that in both spheres law is essentially a command binding upon the subjects of the law independently of their will. Thirdly, it maintains that International Law and Municipal Law, far from being essentially different, must be regarded as manifestations of a single conception of law. This is so not only for the terminological reason that it would be improper to give the same designation of law to two fundamentally different sets of rules governing the same conduct. The main reason for the essential identity of the two spheres of law is, it is maintained, that some of the fundamental notions of International Law cannot be comprehended without the assumption of a superior legal order from which the various systems of Municipal Law are, in a sense, derived by way of delegation. It is International Law which determines the jurisdictional limits of the personal and territorial competence of States. Similarly, it is only by reference to a higher legal rule in relation to which they are all equal, that the equality and independence of a number of sovereign States can be conceived. Failing that superior legal order, the science of law would be confronted with the spectacle of some sixty [now almost 200] sovereign States each claiming to be the absolutely highest and underived authority. It is admitted that municipal courts may be bound by the law of their States to enforce statutes which are contrary to International Law. But this, it may be said, merely shows that, in view of the weakness of International Law and organisation, States admit and tolerate what is actually a conflict of duties within the same legal system—a phenomenon not altogether unknown in other spheres of Municipal Law. In any case, from the point of view of International Law the validity of a pronouncement of a municipal court is in such case purely provisional. It still leaves intact the international responsibility of the State. It is a well recognised rule that a State is internationally responsible for the decisions of its courts, even if given in conformity with the law of the State concerned, whenever that law happens to be contrary to International Law. . . .

Canada, in keeping with its predominantly British constitutional heritage, has traditionally taken a dualist approach to treaty law. When Canada signs and ratifies a human rights treaty, for instance, Canadian law relating to human rights does not change automatically. If pre-existing Canadian law were inconsistent with the treaty's requirements but left unchanged by Canadian legislators, Canada would be acting illegally from an *international* legal perspective, but would be doing nothing wrong from a *domestic* legal perspective. The treaty-based human rights obligation only becomes part of Canadian law if it is received by statute of Parliament or a legislature (or, arguably, by binding common law precedent).[120] Consider the following decision of the Supreme Court of Canada.

---

120 This statement assumes that the treaty-based obligation does not also exist in customary international law. We discuss the domestic effect of customary international law in Section F(3) of this chapter. It

Capital Cities Communications Inc v Canadian Radio-Television Commission, [1978] 2 SCR 141 at 171–89

[American television broadcasters challenged a CRTC decision permitting substitution of commercial advertisements in signals originating in the United States. The challenge was based in part on an apparent conflict between the CRTC decision, issued pursuant to the *Broadcasting Act*, and the terms of the Inter-American Radio Communications Convention,[121] to which Canada and the United States are parties.]

The judgment of Laskin C.J. and Martland, Judson, Ritchie, Spence and Dickson JJ. was delivered by the Chief Justice:

. . . Counsel for the appellants made a number of submissions connected with Canada's adherence as a party to the Inter-American Radio Communications Convention of 1937 to which the United States was also a party. The submissions . . . were as follows: (1) The Commission was an agent of the Canadian Government and as such bound by the terms of the Convention; (2) the *Broadcasting Act* should be interpreted in the light of the Convention, or in such a way as not to violate Canada's international obligations thereunder. . . .

Turning to the appellants' submissions in the order in which they were made, I am unable to appreciate how it can be said that the Commission is an agent or arm of the Canadian Government and as such bound by the Convention provisions in the same way as the Government. There is nothing in the *Broadcasting Act*, nor was our attention directed to any other legislation which would give the Commission any other status than that of a federal regulatory agency established with defined statutory powers. There is nothing to show that it derives any authority from the Convention or that the Convention, *per se*, qualifies the regulatory authority conferred upon the Commission by the *Broadcasting Act*. Indeed, if the contention of the appellants has any force under its first submission it can only relate to the obligations of Canada under the Convention towards other ratifying signatories. There would be no domestic, internal consequences unless they arose from implementing legislation giving the Convention a legal effect within Canada.

The second submission asks this Court to say that the provisions of the *Broadcasting Act* are ambiguous in so far as they relate to the powers of the Commission, and that as an aid to their construction resort should be had to the terms of the Convention. I do not find any ambiguity that would require resort to the Convention, which is, in any event, nowhere mentioned in the *Broadcasting Act*; and certainly the Convention *per se* cannot prevail against the express stipulations of the Act. . . .

[Chief Justice Laskin went on to conclude that the wording of the existing legislation failed to implement the relevant provisions of the Convention in such a way as to provide a basis for the broadcasters' claim.]

The judgment of Pigeon, Beetz and de Grandpré JJ. was delivered by Pigeon J. (dissenting):

---

must also be noted that many human rights treaties also contain obligations to promote, encourage, and educate — obligations that can be implemented domestically through policy and administrative action, rather than legislation.

121 13 December 1937, (1941) 35 AJIL Supp 56, in force 17 April 1939.

. . . I cannot agree that the Commission may properly issue authorizations in violation of Canada's treaty obligations. Its duty is to implement the policy established by Parliament. While this policy makes no reference to Canada's treaty obligations, it is an integral part of the national structure that external affairs are the responsibility of the Federal Government. It is an oversimplification to say that treaties are of no legal effect unless implemented by legislation. In this connection I would refer to the judgment of the English Court of Appeal in *Post Office v. Estuary Radio Ltd.*, [[1968] 2 Q.B. 740] [where] Diplock L.J. said (at pp. 756–7):

> . . . there is a presumption that the Crown did not intend to break an international treaty . . . , and if there is any ambiguity in the Order in Council, it should be resolved so as to accord with the provisions of the Convention in so far as that is a plausible meaning of the express words of the order. . . .

Applying those principles, I would say that, on the appeal from the decision of the Commission, judicial notice ought to be taken that, by virtue of the Convention the appellants had a legal interest entitled to protection in the use of their assigned channels, for broadcasts in an area extending into Canada. Therefore the Commission could not validly authorize an interference with this interest in violation of the Convention signed by Canada. . . .

What important Anglo-Canadian constitutional principle undergirds the general proposition that treaties must be transformed before they have domestic legal effect in Canada? (Recall which branch of government has the power to make treaties that bind Canada internationally; and then consider which branch of government generally has the power to make law.) Are the arguments made by Pigeon J in favour of a different rule convincing?

As it happens, the position of the majority in *Capital Cities Communications Inc v Canadian Radio-Television Commission* may overstate somewhat the applicable rule. Consider the following case's qualification of the requirement for legislative implementation, depending on the type of treaty involved:

Francis v Canada, [1956] SCR 618 at 629

[Francis was an Indian within the meaning of the *Indian Act*, residing on the St. Regis Indian Reserve in Quebec. He purchased various household appliances in the United States and paid import duties and taxes, under protest, in order to get them into Canada. He then applied for the return of the monies on the basis that he was exempt from import duties and taxes due to Article III of the Treaty of Amity, Commerce and Navigation of 1794 between the United Kingdom and the United States, also known as the Jay Treaty.]

The judgment of Kerwin C.J., Taschereau and Fauteux JJ. was delivered by the Chief Justice:

. . . The Jay Treaty was not a Treaty of Peace and it is clear that in Canada such rights and privileges as are here advanced of subjects of a contracting party to a treaty are enforceable by the Courts only where the treaty has been implemented or sanctioned by legislation. This is an adaptation of the language of Lamont J., speaking for himself and

Cannon J. in *Arrow River & Tributaries Slide & Boom Co. Ltd v. Pigeon Timber Co. Ltd.* [[1932] S.C.R. 495], and is justified by a continuous line of authority in England. . . . It has been held that no rights under a treaty of cession can be enforced in the Courts except in so far as they have been incorporated in municipal law. . . .

[The chief justice then reviewed various pieces of legislation and concluded that none implemented the relevant terms of the Jay Treaty.]

The appeal should be dismissed with costs.

The judgment of Rand and Cartwright JJ. was delivered by Rand J.:

. . . The contention is put as follows: art. 3 [of the Jay Treaty] effects the enactment of substantive law not requiring statutory confirmation as being a provision in a treaty of peace, the making of which is in the exercise of the prerogative including, here, a legislative function. . . .

A peace treaty in its primary and legitimate meaning is a treaty concluding a war, "an agreement" — in the words of Sir William Scott in the *Eliza Ann and others* [((1873) 1 Dods. 244, 248] — "to waive all discussion concerning the respective rights to the parties and to bury in oblivion all the original causes of the war." The Treaty of Paris, 1783 was of that nature; it recognized the independence of the United States, fixed boundaries, secured the property of former and continuing subjects and citizens in both countries against prosecution and against confiscation of their property, provided for the withdrawal of British troops from the lands of and border points in the United States and for other matters not germane here.

The question of the Indians, however, was left untouched, and during the years that followed they presented both governments with problems of reconciliation. . . . These, with the events developing in Europe and the need of both for the restoration of trade, induced a common desire to remove these frictions, which eventuated in the treaty of 1794. . . .

Assuming, then, a broader authority under the prerogative in negotiating a peace treaty, neither the causes nor the purposes of the treaty of 1794 bring it within that category.

A treaty is primarily an executive act establishing relationships between what are recognized as two or more independent states acting in sovereign capacities; but as will be seen, its implementation may call for both legislative and judicial action. Speaking generally, provisions that give recognition to incidents of sovereignty or deal with matters in exclusively sovereign aspects, do not require legislative confirmation: for example, the recognition of independence, the establishment of boundaries and, in a treaty of peace, the transfer of sovereignty over property, are deemed executed and the treaty becomes the muniment or evidence of the political or proprietary title. Stipulations for future social or commercial relations assume a state of peace: when peace is broken by war, by reason of the impossibility of their exercise, they are deemed to be abrogated as upon a failure of the condition on which they depend. But provisions may expressly or impliedly break in upon these general considerations; the terms may contemplate continuance or suspension during a state of war. The interpretation is according to the rules that govern that of instruments generally; from the entire circumstantial background, the nature of the matters dealt with and the objects in view, we gather the intention of the parties as expressed in the language used. When such matters touch individuals, the judicial organ must act but a result that brought about non-concurrence between the judicial and the executive branches, say as to abrogation, and apart from any question of an international adjudication, would, to say the least, be undesirable.

Except as to diplomatic status and certain immunities and to belligerent rights, treaty provisions affecting matters within the scope of municipal law, that is, which purport to change existing law or restrict the future action of the legislature, including, under our constitution, the participation of the Crown, and in the absence of a constitutional provision declaring the treaty itself to be law of the state, as in the United States, must be supplemented by statutory action. . . .

To the enactment of fiscal provisions, certainly in the case of a treaty not a peace treaty, the prerogative does not extend, and only by legislation can customs duties be imposed or removed or can the condition under which goods may be brought into this country be affected. I agree, therefore, with Cameron J. in holding that legislation was necessary to bring within municipal law the exemption of the clause in question. . . . For over a century, then, there has been no statutory provision in this country giving effect to that clause of the article. . . .

The appeal must therefore be dismissed. . . .

[Justices Kellock and Abbott delivered a concurring judgment rejecting Francis's claim on the basis that no exemption from customs duties or taxes was provided for in the *Indian Act*.]

Thus, in a few cases, the subject-matter of a treaty may come within existing implementation powers held by the federal executive branch of government, obviating the need for statutory implementation by the legislative branch. In others, performance of the treaty may require no change to domestic law at all—either because the necessary legal framework already exists in current legislation or common law, or because the treaty's terms do not relate to domestic legal matters in any event. In such cases there is, again, no need for legislative implementation.[122]

b) Canadian Legislative Jurisdiction and Treaty Transformation

Turning to those treaties that do require legislative implementation in Canada, an important question arises from Canada's federal structure. Which body or bodies—Parliament or the provincial legislatures—perform(s) the act of transformation? The answer to this question depends on Canada's constitutional division of legislative powers, a point made in the *Labour Conventions* case:

---

122 Note, however, that the judgment in *Francis* did not satisfy Aboriginal peoples in Canada, who have brought subsequent claims, both domestically and internationally, without success, to give domestic effect to the Jay Treaty's provisions. See, for example, *Mitchell v Minister of National Revenue*, 2001 SCC 33, [2001] 1 SCR 91; *Mitchell v Canada*, Report No 61/08, Case 12.435 in [2008] *Annual Report of the Inter-American Commission on Human Rights* at c III.C.5, OAS Doc OEA/Ser.L/V/II.134, Doc 5, rev 1 (25 February 2009).

Attorney-General for Canada v Attorney-General for Ontario; Reference Re Weekly Rest in Industrial Undertakings Act, Minimum Wages Act and Limitation of Hours of Work Act, [1937] AC 326 at 350–54 (JCPC) [*Labour Conventions* case]

[This reference concerned the authority of the Parliament of Canada to enact three statutes implementing conventions adopted by the International Labour Organization in 1919, 1921, and 1928, and ratified by the Canadian government in 1935. The two principal issues raised were (1) whether the federal executive had the exclusive power to conclude treaties on behalf of Canada; and (2) whether the federal Parliament had exclusive authority to implement treaties by way of legislation, even where the subject-matter of the treaty fell under a provincial head of legislative jurisdiction provided for in section 92 of the *Constitution Act, 1867*.[123] The Supreme Court of Canada held that the federal executive had the treaty-making power but was evenly divided on the second issue, which was then brought before the Judicial Committee of the Privy Council.]

Lord Atkin:

. . . [T]he validity of the legislation can only depend upon ss. 91 and 92. Now it had to be admitted that normally this legislation came within the classes of subjects by s. 92 assigned exclusively to the Legislatures of the Provinces, namely — property and civil rights in the Province. . . . How, then, can the legislation be within the legislative powers given by s. 91 to the Dominion Parliament? It is not within the enumerated classes of subjects in s. 91: and it appears to be expressly excluded from the general powers given by the first words of the section. . . .

For the purposes of ss. 91 and 92, i.e., the distribution of legislative powers between the Dominion and the Provinces, there is no such thing as treaty legislation as such. The distribution is based on classes of subjects; and as a treaty deals with a particular class of subjects so will the legislative power of performing it be ascertained. No one can doubt that this distribution is one of the most essential conditions, probably the most essential condition, in the inter-provincial compact to which the British North America Act gives effect. If the position of Lower Canada, now Quebec, alone were considered, the existence of her separate jurisprudence as to both property and civil rights might be said to depend upon loyal adherence to her constitutional right to the exclusive competence of her own Legislature in these matters. Nor is it of less importance for the other Provinces, though their law may be based on English jurisprudence, to preserve their own right to legislate for themselves in respect of local conditions which may vary by as great a distance as separates the Atlantic from the Pacific. It would be remarkable that while the Dominion could not initiate legislation, however desirable, which affected civil rights in the Provinces, yet its Government not responsible to the Provinces nor controlled by Provincial Parliaments need only agree with a foreign country to enact such legislation, and its Parliament would be forthwith clothed with authority to affect Provincial rights to the full extent of such agreement. Such a result would appear to undermine the constitutional safeguards of Provincial constitutional autonomy.

---

123 Above note 11.

It follows from what has been said that no further legislative competence is obtained by the Dominion from its accession to international status, and the consequent increase in the scope of its executive functions. It is true, as pointed out in the judgment of the Chief Justice, that as the executive is now clothed with the powers of making treaties so the Parliament of Canada, to which the executive is responsible, has imposed upon it responsibilities in connection with such treaties, for if it were to disapprove of them they would either not be made or the Ministers would meet their constitutional fate. But this is true of all executive functions in their relation to Parliament. There is no existing constitutional ground for stretching the competence of the Dominion Parliament so that it becomes enlarged to keep pace with enlarged functions of the Dominion executive. If the new functions affect the classes of subjects enumerated in s. 92 legislation to support the new functions is in the competence of the Provincial Legislatures only. If they do not, the competence of the Dominion Legislature is declared by s. 91 and existed *ab origine*. In other words, the Dominion cannot, merely by making promises to foreign countries, clothe itself with legislative authority inconsistent with the constitution which gave it birth. . . .

It must not be thought that the result of this decision is that Canada is incompetent to legislate in performance of treaty obligations. In totality of legislative powers, Dominion and Provincial together, she is fully equipped. But the legislative powers remain distributed, and if in the exercise of her new functions derived from her new international status Canada incurs obligations they must, so far as legislation be concerned, when they deal with Provincial classes of subjects, be dealt with by the totality of powers, in other words by co-operation between the Dominion and the Provinces. While the ship of state now sails on larger ventures and into foreign waters she still retains the watertight compartments which are an essential part of her original structure. The Supreme Court was equally divided and therefore the formal judgment could only state the opinions of the three judges on either side. Their Lordships are of opinion that the answer to the three questions should be that the Act in each case is *ultra vires* of the Parliament of Canada, and they will humbly advise His Majesty accordingly.

What challenges are posed by the Judicial Committee of the Privy Council's rejection of a parliamentary power to enact "treaty legislation" that would mirror the federal executive's exclusive authority to make treaties? Are such challenges justified by the risks that recognition of such a power would pose to provincial spheres of legislative jurisdiction?

c) The Direct Significance of Treaties in Canadian Law

Given Canada's dualist approach to treaty law, of what significance are a treaty's terms, as such, in Canadian law? As seen above, the answer has traditionally been none. Either the treaty has been transformed into Canadian law, in which case it is the transforming legislation (or other domestic implementing source) that "speaks" within the Canadian legal system; or it has not, in which case the treaty may have significance internationally but not domestically. However, in recent years, the Supreme Court of Canada has indicated that treaties do indeed have some limited, direct effects of their own in Canadian law. Initially confined to treaties that had been legislatively implemented, these direct effects have still more recently been extended by the Court to *unimplemented* treaties to which Canada is a party. We consider these two lines of authority in the next two subsections.

i) Significance of a Legislatively Implemented Treaty

Transforming a treaty entails the making of domestic law that corresponds to or implements the terms and obligations of the treaty. What role then remains for the treaty itself? As the following cases suggest, the treaty may have an interpretive function.

National Corn Growers Assn v Canada (Import Tribunal), [1990] 2 SCR 1324

[At issue was a potential inconsistency between section 42 of the *Special Import Measures Act* (SIMA), RSC 1985, c S-15, and a corresponding provision under the General Agreement on Tariffs and Trade (GATT),[124] to which Canada was a party. The issue was whether the Canadian Import Tribunal was bound to interpret section 42 as enacted, or whether it could have recourse to the corresponding GATT obligation to assist in its interpretation of section 42.]

The judgment of La Forest, L'Heureux-Dubé, Gonthier and McLachlin JJ. was delivered by Gonthier J.:

. . . 73. The first issue to be decided is whether it was patently unreasonable for the Tribunal to make reference to the *GATT* for the purpose of interpreting *SIMA*. In turning to that issue, I note that it was not disputed in either of the courts below that the Canadian legislation was designed to implement Canada's *GATT* obligations. . . .

74. The first comment I wish to make is that I share the appellants' view that in circumstances where the domestic legislation is unclear it is reasonable to examine any underlying international agreement. In interpreting legislation which has been enacted with a view towards implementing international obligations, as is the case here, it is reasonable for a tribunal to examine the domestic law in the context of the relevant agreement to clarify any uncertainty. Indeed where the text of the domestic law lends itself to it, one should also strive to expound an interpretation which is consonant with the relevant international obligations.

75. Second, and more specifically, it is reasonable to make reference to an international agreement at the very outset of the inquiry to determine if there is any ambiguity, even latent, in the domestic legislation. The Court of Appeal's suggestion that recourse to an international treaty is only available where the provision of the domestic legislation is ambiguous on its face is to be rejected. As I. Brownlie has stated at p. 51 of *Principles of Public International Law* (3rd ed. 1979):

> If the convention may be used on the correct principle that the statute is intended to implement the convention then, it follows, the latter becomes a proper aid to interpretation, and, more especially, may reveal a latent ambiguity in the text of the statute even if this was "clear in itself". Moreover, the principle or presumption that the Crown does not intend to break an international treaty must have the corollary that the text of the international instrument is a primary source of meaning or "interpretation". The courts have lately accepted the need to refer to the relevant treaty even in the absence of ambiguity in the legislative text when taken in isolation.

. . .

---

124 GATT, above note 17.

76. Having found that the rules of statutory interpretation allow consideration of an underlying agreement at the preliminary stage of determining if the domestic legislation contains an ambiguity, I do not hesitate to conclude in this case that the Tribunal did not act unreasonably in consulting the *GATT*. . . .

The reasons of Dickson C.J. and Lamer C.J. and Wilson J. were delivered by Wilson J.:

1. I have had the benefit of reading the reasons of my colleague Justice Gonthier. I am in agreement that this Court should not interfere with the Canadian Import Tribunal's interpretation of s. 42 of the *Special Import Measures Act*. . . . But I have reached this conclusion for somewhat different reasons from those advanced by my colleague. . . .

31. . . . I do not think that it is this Court's role on an application for judicial review to look beyond the Tribunal's statute to determine whether the Tribunal's interpretation of that statute is consistent with Canada's international obligations. If the interpretation is not consistent with Canada's obligations under the *GATT*, then it is for the legislature to address this matter. Until such time as the courts in this country are given the responsibility of enforcing the *GATT*, I do not think that they should begin to analyze the merits of a tribunal's interpretation of the Act in light of the *GATT*. Courts have no particular expertise in the interpretation of international trade agreements and, in my view, they should not get into the business of trying to explain the significance of the Kennedy and Tokyo Rounds of negotiations (or the ongoing Uruguay Round of talks) for the *GATT*, let alone for the "proper" interpretation of the Act. . . .

Pushpanathan v Canada (Minister of Citizenship and Immigration), [1998] 1 SCR 982

[The appellant claimed refugee status under certain provisions of the *Immigration Act*, RSC 1985, c I-2, as amended, which were designed to give domestic legal effect to Canada's obligations under the Convention Relating to the Status of Refugees.[125] His claim was denied on the basis of the exclusion clause in Article 1F(c) of the convention, which provides that refugee status does not apply to a person who "has been guilty of acts contrary to the purposes and principles of the United Nations." The appellant had previously been convicted of conspiracy to traffic in a narcotic. At issue was the correct interpretation of the expression "acts contrary to the purposes and principles of the United Nations," and in particular which rules of interpretation would apply.]

The judgment of L'Heureux-Dubé, Gonthier, McLachlin and Bastarache JJ. was delivered by Bastarache J.:

. . . 51. . . . Since the purpose of the Act incorporating Article 1F(c) is to implement the underlying Convention, the Court must adopt an interpretation consistent with Canada's obligations under the Convention. The wording of the Convention and the rules of treaty interpretation will therefore be applied to determine the meaning of Article 1F(c) in domestic law. . . .

52. Those [interpretation] rules are succinctly articulated in the Vienna Convention on the Law of Treaties. . . .

---

125 28 July 1951, 189 UNTS 137, Can TS 1969 No 6, in force 22 April 1954.

55. In my view, the Federal Court of Appeal erred in dismissing the objects and purposes of the treaty, and in according virtually no weight to the indications provided in the *travaux préparatoires.* As will be seen later, the legislative history of Article 1F indicates that the signatories to the Convention wished to ascribe a special meaning to the words "purposes and principles of the United Nations" in the context of the Convention. . . . The extremely general words in Article 1F(c) are not so unambiguous as to foreclose examination of other indications of the proper scope of the provision. An examination of the purpose and context of the treaty as a whole, as well as the purpose of the individual provision in question as suggested by the *travaux préparatoires,* provide helpful interpretative guidelines.

[After reviewing this history, Bastarache J concluded that the appellant's participation in a conspiracy to traffic in a narcotic was not a violation of Article 1F(c), and the matter was returned to the competent authorities for reconsideration.]

If, as the foregoing cases hold, Canadian courts may rely directly on treaties as well as on international rules of treaty interpretation (at least in interpreting domestic implementing legislation), just how dualist is Canada's domestic legal approach to treaty law? Consider the same question in light of the materials in the next section.

ii) Significance of a Legislatively Unimplemented Treaty

As discussed above, the *Capital Cities* case stands for the proposition that, where a relevant legislative body fails to transform a treaty into Canadian law, that treaty is not a source of law that can be applied by Canadian courts.

Looked at from one perspective, dualism is a sensible doctrine. Recall that in Canadian law and practice, it is the federal executive that is empowered to negotiate and enter into international treaties. If these international legal obligations agreed to by the executive had immediate and direct force of law within Canada, the executive's treaty-making power would be tantamount to a domestic legislative power, contrary to important constitutional principles relating to the separation (and division) of powers. By expressing Canada's consent to be bound by an international treaty requiring, for instance, extended patent protection, the executive would effectively legislate a matter otherwise governed by an Act of Parliament, in this case the *Patent Act*, RSC 1985, c P-4. The federal executive could also avoid the division of legislative powers in the *Constitution Act, 1867* by employing its treaty-making power to, in effect, legislate in provincial areas of jurisdiction. For example, most human rights treaties are concerned with matters falling within provincial legislative jurisdiction.

On the other hand, where the legislative branch fails fully to harmonize domestic law with treaty law (something that is surprisingly common), the result is an unfortunate legal schizophrenia: Canada is bound by the treaty as a matter of international law, and yet domestic actors — including the federal government that undertook the treaty obligation — need not abide by the treaty as a matter of domestic law. This perplexing situation is particularly controversial where the treaty in question relates to the rights of individuals. Consider the following case in which the Supreme Court of Canada departed from a strict dualist approach.

Baker v Canada (Minister of Citizenship and Immigration), [1999] 2 SCR 817

[The appellant, a Jamaican national with Canadian-born dependent children, was ordered deported from Canada. She applied for an exemption, under section 114(2) of the *Immigration Act*, RSC 1985, c I-2 and related regulations, based on humanitarian and compassionate (H & C) considerations, including the effect of her possible departure on her Canadian-born children. The application was denied. Judicial review was denied in the Federal Court, but on appeal, Canada's highest court was asked: "Given that the *Immigration Act* does not expressly incorporate the language of Canada's international obligations with respect to the International Convention on the Rights of the Child, must federal immigration authorities treat the best interests of the child as a primary consideration in assessing an applicant under section 114 (2) of the *Immigration Act*?" The majority disposed of the appeal on the basis that the original decision suffered from a reasonable apprehension of bias, but went on, in the excerpts that follow, to consider the effect of the Convention on the Rights of the Child[126] on the interpretation of section 114(2) of the *Immigration Act* and related regulations.]

L'Heureux-Dubé J. (Gonthier, McLachlin, Bastarache and Binnie JJ. concurring):

67. Determining whether the approach taken by the immigration officer was within the boundaries set out by the words of the statute and the values of administrative law requires a contextual approach, as is taken to statutory interpretation generally. . . . In my opinion, a reasonable exercise of the power conferred by the section requires close attention to the interests and needs of children. Children's rights, and attention to their interests, are central humanitarian and compassionate values in Canadian society. Indications of children's interests as important considerations governing the manner in which H & C powers should be exercised may be found, for example, in the purposes of the Act, in international instruments, and in the guidelines for making H & C decisions published by the Minister herself. . . .

69. Another indicator of the importance of considering the interests of children when making a compassionate and humanitarian decision is the ratification by Canada of the *Convention on the Rights of the Child*, and the recognition of the importance of children's rights and the best interests of children in other international instruments ratified by Canada. International treaties and conventions are not part of Canadian law unless they have been implemented by statute: *Francis v. The Queen*, [1956] S.C.R. 618, at p. 621; *Capital Cities Communications Inc. v. Canadian Radio-Television Commission*, [1978] 2 S.C.R. 141, at pp. 172–73. I agree with the respondent and the Court of Appeal that the Convention has not been implemented by Parliament. Its provisions therefore have no direct application within Canadian law.

70. Nevertheless, the values reflected in international human rights law may help inform the contextual approach to statutory interpretation and judicial review. As stated in R. Sullivan, *Driedger on the Construction of Statutes* (3rd ed. 1994), at p. 330:

> [T]he legislature is presumed to respect the values and principles enshrined in international law, both customary and conventional. These constitute a part of the legal

---

126 20 November 1989, 1577 UNTS 3, Can TS 1992 No 3, in force 2 September 1990.

context in which legislation is enacted and read. *In so far as possible, therefore, interpretations that reflect these values and principles are preferred.* [Emphasis added.]

The important role of international human rights law as an aid in interpreting domestic law has also been emphasized in other common law countries: see, for example, *Tavita v. Minister of Immigration*, [1994] 2 N.Z.L.R. 257 (C.A.), at p. 266; *Vishaka v. Rajasthan*, [1997] 3 L.R.C. 361 (S.C. India), at p. 367. It is also a critical influence on the interpretation of the scope of the rights included in the *Charter*: *Slaight Communications*, [[1989] 1 S.C.R. 1038]; *R. v. Keegstra*, [1990] 3 S.C.R. 697.

71. The values and principles of the Convention recognize the importance of being attentive to the rights and best interests of children when decisions are made that relate to and affect their future. In addition, the preamble, recalling the Universal Declaration of Human Rights, recognizes that "childhood is entitled to special care and assistance." A similar emphasis on the importance of placing considerable value on the protection of children and their needs and interests is also contained in other international instruments. The United Nations Declaration of the Rights of the Child (1959), in its preamble, states that the child "needs special safeguards and care." The principles of the Convention and other international instruments place special importance on protections for children and childhood, and on particular consideration of their interests, needs, and rights. They help show the values that are central in determining whether this decision was a reasonable exercise of the H & C power. . . .

Iacobucci J. (Cory J. concurring):

78. I agree with L'Heureux-Dubé J.'s reasons and disposition of this appeal, except to the extent that my colleague addresses the effect of international law on the exercise of ministerial discretion pursuant to s. 114(2) of the *Immigration Act*. . . . The certified question at issue in this appeal concerns whether federal immigration authorities must treat the best interests of the child as a primary consideration in assessing an application for humanitarian and compassionate consideration under s. 114(2) of the Act, given that the legislation does not implement the provisions contained in the *Convention of the Rights of the Child* . . . , a multilateral convention to which Canada is party. In my opinion, the certified question should be answered in the negative.

79. It is a matter of well-settled law that an international convention ratified by the executive branch of government is of no force or effect within the Canadian legal system until such time as its provisions have been incorporated into domestic law by way of implementing legislation: *Capital Cities Communications Inc. v. Canadian Radio-Television Commission*. . . . I do not agree with the approach adopted by my colleague, wherein reference is made to the underlying values of an unimplemented international treaty in the course of the contextual approach to statutory interpretation and administrative law, because such an approach is not in accordance with the Court's jurisprudence concerning the status of international law within the domestic legal system.

80. In my view, one should proceed with caution in deciding matters of this nature, lest we adversely affect the balance maintained by our Parliamentary tradition, or inadvertently grant the executive the power to bind citizens without the necessity of involving the legislative branch. I do not share my colleague's confidence that the Court's

precedent in *Capital Cities, supra,* survives intact following the adoption of a principle of law which permits reference to an unincorporated convention during the process of statutory interpretation. Instead, the result will be that the appellant is able to achieve indirectly what cannot be achieved directly, namely, to give force and effect within the domestic legal system to international obligations undertaken by the executive alone that have yet to be subject to the democratic will of Parliament.

81. The primacy accorded to the rights of children in the Convention, assuming for the sake of argument that the factual circumstances of this appeal are included within the scope of the relevant provisions, is irrelevant unless and until such provisions are the subject of legislation enacted by Parliament. In answering the certified question in the negative, I am mindful that the result may well have been different had my colleague concluded that the appellant's claim fell within the ambit of rights protected by the *Canadian Charter of Rights and Freedoms.* Had this been the case, the Court would have had an opportunity to consider the application of the interpretive presumption, established by the Court's decision in *Slaight Communications Inc. v. Davidson,* [*supra*], and confirmed in subsequent jurisprudence, that administrative discretion involving *Charter* rights be exercised in accordance with similar international human rights norms.

For some, the majority in *Baker* took a cautious approach by relying on the "values reflected in international human rights law," but others question how one can distinguish such values from the relevant treaty-based rules themselves. What is the difference between relying on the value "of being attentive to the . . . best interests of children" and relying on the treaty obligation to consider the best interests of children? Is this a distinction without a difference, as suggested by Iacobucci J?

Since *Baker,* the Court has come to use much less circumspect language in describing the potential effects of Canada's international (including treaty) obligations on its understanding of domestic law. For example, in *R v Hape,* the majority described the following rule of "Conformity with International Law as an Interpretive Principle of Domestic Law":

It is a well-established principle of statutory interpretation that legislation will be presumed to conform to international law. The presumption of conformity is based on the rule of judicial policy that, as a matter of law, courts will strive to avoid constructions of domestic law pursuant to which the state would be in violation of its international obligations, unless the wording of the statute clearly compels that result. . . . [T]he presumption has two aspects. First, the legislature is presumed to act in compliance with Canada's obligations as a signatory of [or more accurately a party to] international treaties and as a member of the international community. In deciding between possible interpretations, courts will avoid a construction that would place Canada in breach of those obligations. The second aspect is that the legislature is presumed to comply with the values and principles of customary and conventional international law. Those values and principles form part of the context in which statutes are enacted, and courts will therefore prefer a construction that reflects them. The presumption is rebuttable, however. Parliamentary sovereignty requires courts to give effect to a statute that demonstrates an unequivocal legislative intent to default on an international obligation. . . .

. . . The presumption applies equally to customary international law and treaty obligations.[127]

It would therefore seem that the interpretive relevance of treaties in Canadian law may turn less on whether they have been the subject of domestic implementing legislation than on whether Canada has become a party to them — such that they form part of Canada's "international obligations."

In a more recent pronouncement, however, the Supreme Court of Canada appears to have added some nuance to the "presumption of conformity" articulated in *Hape*. In *Merck Frosst Canada Ltd v Canada (Health)*,[128] the Court was required to interpret the trade secrets exemption under the federal *Access to Information Act*, RSC 1985, c A-1. One party argued that, in the absence of a definition of "trade secrets" in the Act, this term should be interpreted in a manner consistent with the trade secrets provisions of the North American Free Trade Agreement (NAFTA),[129] to which Canada is a party. Justice Cromwell for the majority responded to this submission as follows:

> I accept, of course, that to the extent possible domestic legislation should be interpreted so that it is consistent with Canada's international obligations. . . . However, Canada is not necessarily required to adopt the treaty definition of "trade secrets" into its access to information law in order to fulfill its treaty obligations. These obligations could be fulfilled in other ways. As the respondent notes, Canada has opted to address these obligations in the pharmaceutical context by focussing on protecting parties against commercial use of their trade secrets by others. The amendments to the *Food and Drug Regulations* in 1995 and 2006 reflect this approach. . . . This choice of approach . . . undermines Merck's argument that Parliament intended the definition of "trade secret" in s. 20(1)(a) [of the *Access to Information Act*] to mirror the NAFTA definition.[130]

Is there a difference between interpreting legislation to "conform to international law" and doing so only insofar as necessary to permit Canada to fulfill its international obligations?

In light of the rules set out in *Hape* and *Merck Frosst*, what role remains for the traditional requirement of transformation before treaties may have domestic legal effect in Canada?

3) Canadian Domestic Law's Treatment of Customary International Law

As seen above, Canada traditionally takes a dualist approach to treaty law, requiring that the provisions of an international treaty be transformed into Canadian law prior to having domestic legal effect. Canada's approach to customary international law is very different.

---

127 *R v Hape*, 2007 SCC 26, [2007] 2 SCR 232 at paras 53–54. For application of the *Baker* values approach to an (incorrectly) identified rule of customary international law, see *114957 Canada Ltée (Spraytech, Société d'arrosage) v Hudson (Town)*, 2001 SCC 40, [2001] 2 SCR 241 at paras 30–32; such an approach was unnecessary if rules of customary international law are automatically part of domestic law.

128 *Merck Frosst Canada Ltd v Canada (Health)*, 2012 SCC 3, [2012] 1 SCR 23 [*Merck Frosst*].

129 NAFTA, above note 17, art 1711.

130 *Merck Frosst*, above note 128 at para 117.

Here, it is generally accepted that Canada takes a monist approach, such that the rules of customary international law are presumed automatically to form part of the common law. Note, however, that this presumption of direct incorporation of customary international law into domestic common law can always be displaced by irreconcilably contrary Canadian statute law or binding precedent.

In *Jose Pereira E Hijos SA v Canada (Attorney General)*, the Federal Court Trial Division (now known simply as the Federal Court) wrote:

> The principles concerning the application of international law in our courts are well settled. . . . One may sum those up in the following terms: accepted principles of customary international law are recognized and are applied in Canadian courts, as part of the domestic law unless, of course, they are in conflict with domestic law. In construing domestic law, whether statutory or common law, the courts will seek to avoid construction or application that would conflict with the accepted principles of international law.[131]

Similar comments were made in *Bouzari v Iran* by the Ontario Court of Appeal:

> As acknowledged by the Attorney General in this case, customary rules of international law are directly incorporated into Canadian domestic law unless explicitly ousted by contrary legislation. So far as possible, domestic legislation should be interpreted consistently with those obligations. This is even more so where the obligation is a peremptory norm of customary international law, or jus cogens. . . .
>
> However, . . . whether Canada's obligations arise pursuant to treaty or to customary international law, it is open to Canada to legislate contrary to them. Such legislation would determine Canada's domestic law although it would put Canada in breach of its international obligations.[132]

Still more recently, LeBel J, speaking for the majority of the Supreme Court of Canada in *R v Hape*, had the following to say on the relationship between customary international and Canadian law:

> The English tradition follows an adoptionist approach to the reception of customary international law. Prohibitive rules of international custom may be incorporated directly into domestic law through the common law, without the need for legislative action. According to the doctrine of adoption, the courts may adopt rules of customary international law as common law rules in order to base their decisions upon them, provided there is no valid legislation that clearly conflicts with the customary rule. . . . Although it has long been recognized in English common law, the doctrine received its strongest endorsement in the landmark case of Trendtex Trading Corp. v. Central Bank of Nigeria, [1977] 1 Q.B. 529 (C.A.). Lord Denning considered both the doctrine of adoption and the doctrine of transformation. . . . In his opinion, the doctrine of adoption represents the correct approach in English law. Rules of international law are incorporated automatically, as they evolve, unless they conflict with legislation. . . .

---

131 [1997] 2 FC 84 at para 20.
132 (2004) 71 OR (3d) 675 at paras 65–66, leave to appeal to SCC refused, [2005] 1 SCR vi.

Despite th[is] Court's silence in some recent cases, the doctrine of adoption has never been rejected in Canada. Indeed, there is a long line of cases in which the Court has either formally accepted it or at least applied it. In my view, following the common law tradition, it appears that the doctrine of adoption operates in Canada such that prohibitive rules of customary international law should be incorporated into domestic law in the absence of conflicting legislation. The automatic incorporation of such rules is justified on the basis that international custom, as the law of nations, is also the law of Canada unless, in a valid exercise of its sovereignty, Canada declares that its law is to the contrary. Parliamentary sovereignty dictates that a legislature may violate international law, but that it must do so expressly. Absent an express derogation, the courts may look to prohibitive rules of customary international law to aid in the interpretation of Canadian law and the development of the common law.[133]

Is the Supreme Court's description of the "doctrine of adoption" clear? Is a rule that provides for the "automatic incorporation" of customary international law the same as a rule that says that customary international law "should be incorporated"? Or as a rule that says courts "may adopt" customary international law? Is adoption or incorporation of customary international law in domestic law the same as looking to it "to aid in the interpretation of Canadian law and the development of the common law"?

Consider the "presumption of conformity" described above in discussing the domestic legal effect of unimplemented treaties. How, if at all, does that presumption differ in its effect from the "doctrine of adoption" applicable to customary international law?

4) The Relevance of International Law in Interpreting the *Canadian Charter of Rights and Freedoms*

Early on in its jurisprudence interpreting the *Canadian Charter of Rights and Freedoms*,[134] the Supreme Court of Canada noted the close connection between the fundamental rights protected in the *Charter* and international human rights law. While not finding that the *Charter* implemented, as such, Canada's numerous international human rights treaty undertakings, the Supreme Court clearly indicated that the latter would frame its interpretation of *Charter* guarantees. The following passage in particular, cited in the Supreme Court's majority judgment in *Slaight Communications Inc v Davidson*, suggests a robust role for Canada's human rights treaty obligations:

The content of Canada's international human rights obligations is . . . an important indicia of the meaning of the "full benefit of the *Charter*'s protection." . . . [T]he *Charter* should generally be presumed to provide protection at least as great as that afforded by similar provisions in international human rights documents which Canada has ratified.[135]

---

133 *R v Hape*, above note 127 at paras 36 and 39.
134 Part I of the *Constitution Act, 1982*, being Schedule B to the *Canada Act 1982* (UK), 1982, c 11 [*Charter*].
135 *Reference Re Public Service Employee Relations Act (Alta)*, [1987] 1 SCR 313 at 349, Dickson CJ dissenting, cited with approval by the majority in *Slaight Communications Inc v Davidson*, [1989] 1 SCR 1038 at 1056.

Considering that this rule was said to apply to human rights treaties that Canada has ratified (as distinct from implemented), what are its implications? Recall that all law in Canada must be consistent with the Canadian Constitution, including the *Charter*. Is there any legal reason for which Canada's untransformed human rights treaty obligations should have greater domestic legal effect than its other untransformed treaty obligations? A related question, of course, is whether Canada *has* any untransformed human rights treaty obligations. In this regard it is notable that the Canadian government relies expressly on the *Charter*—in addition to federal and provincial statutes, caselaw, policy, and administrative practice—when reporting on Canada's implementation efforts to international human rights treaty-monitoring bodies.

While the *Slaight Communications* "minimum content" approach prevailed for several years, the Court signalled a considerable shift in attitude towards the relevance of Canada's international human rights obligations in *Charter* interpretation in the following case.

Suresh v Canada (Minister of Citizenship and Immigration), 2002 SCC 1, [2002] 1 SCR 3

[The appellant, a Convention refugee from Sri Lanka, was ordered deported by the minister of citizenship and immigration pursuant to section 53(1)(b) of the *Immigration Act*, RSC 1985, c I-2. The stated reason for the deportation order was that he was a danger to the security of Canada. This in turn was based on his alleged membership in the Liberation Tigers of Tamil Eelam, an organization believed to be engaged in terrorist activity in Sri Lanka and whose members are subject to torture in Sri Lanka. The appellant applied for judicial review of the order and challenged section 53(1)(b) of the *Immigration Act* on the basis that it violated the *Charter*.]

The Court:

. . . 43. Section 53 of the *Immigration Act* permits deportation "to a country where the person's life or freedom would be threatened." The question is whether such deportation violates s. 7 of the *Charter*. Torture is defined in Article 1 of the CAT [Convention Against Torture, to which Canada is a party] as including the unlawful use of psychological or physical techniques to intentionally inflict severe pain and suffering on another, when such pain or suffering is inflicted by or with the consent of public officials. . . .

44. Section 7 of the *Charter* guarantees "[e]veryone . . . the right to life, liberty and security of the person and the right not to be deprived thereof except in accordance with the principles of fundamental justice." It is conceded that "everyone" includes refugees and that deportation to torture may deprive a refugee of liberty, security and perhaps life. The only question is whether this deprivation is in accordance with the principles of fundamental justice. If it is not, s. 7 is violated and, barring justification of the violation under s. 1 of the *Charter*, deportation to torture is unconstitutional. . . .

59. . . . The provisions of the *Immigration Act* dealing with deportation must be considered in their international context: *Pushpanathan, supra*. Similarly, the principles of fundamental justice expressed in s. 7 of the *Charter* and the limits on rights that may be justified under s. 1 of the *Charter* cannot be considered in isolation from the international norms which they reflect. A complete understanding of the Act and the *Charter* requires consideration of the international perspective.

60. International treaty norms are not, strictly speaking, binding in Canada unless they have been incorporated into Canadian law by enactment. However, in seeking the meaning of the Canadian Constitution, the courts may be informed by international law. Our concern is not with Canada's international obligations *qua* obligations; rather, our concern is with the principles of fundamental justice. We look to international law as evidence of these principles and not as controlling in itself. . . .

66. Deportation to torture is prohibited by both the ICCPR [International Covenant on Civil and Political Rights], which Canada ratified in 1976, and the CAT, which Canada ratified in 1987. . . . While the provisions of the ICCPR do not themselves specifically address the permissibility of a state's expelling a person to face torture elsewhere, *General Comment 20* to the ICCPR makes clear that Article 7 is intended to cover that scenario, explaining that ". . . States parties must not expose individuals to the danger of torture . . . upon return to another country by way of their extradition, expulsion or refoulement." . . .

68. The CAT takes the same stand. . . . The CAT's import is clear: a state is not to expel a person to face torture, which includes both the physical and mental infliction of pain and suffering, elsewhere.

69. Robertson J.A., however, held that the CAT's clear proscription of deportation to torture must defer to Article 33(2) of the *Refugee Convention*, which permits a country to return (*refouler*) a refugee who is a danger to the country's security. . . .

72. In our view, the prohibition in the ICCPR and the CAT on returning a refugee to face a risk of torture reflects the prevailing international norm. Article 33 of the *Refugee Convention* protects, in a limited way, refugees from threats to life and freedom from all sources. By contrast, the CAT protects everyone, without derogation, from state-sponsored torture. Moreover, the *Refugee Convention* itself expresses a "profound concern for refugees" and its principal purpose is to "assure refugees the widest possible exercise of . . . fundamental rights and freedoms" (Preamble). This negates the suggestion that the provisions of the *Refugee Convention* should be used to deny rights that other legal instruments make universally available to everyone. . . .

75. We conclude that . . . international law rejects deportation to torture, even where national security interests are at stake. This is the norm which best informs the content of the principles of fundamental justice under s. 7 of the *Charter*. . . .

76. The Canadian rejection of torture is reflected in the international conventions to which Canada is a party. The Canadian and international perspectives in turn inform our constitutional norms. The rejection of state action leading to torture generally, and deportation to torture specifically, is virtually categoric. Indeed, both domestic and international jurisprudence suggest that torture is so abhorrent that it will almost always be disproportionate to interests on the other side of the balance, even security interests. This suggests that, barring extraordinary circumstances, deportation to torture will generally violate the principles of fundamental justice protected by s. 7 of the *Charter*. . . .

78. We do not exclude the possibility that in exceptional circumstances, deportation to face torture might be justified, either as a consequence of the balancing process mandated by s. 7 of the *Charter* or under s. 1. . . . Insofar as Canada is unable to deport a person where there are substantial grounds to believe he or she would be tortured on return, this is not because Article 3 of the CAT directly constrains the actions of the Canadian government, but because the fundamental justice balance under s. 7 of the *Charter*

generally precludes deportation to torture when applied on a case-by-case basis. We may predict that it will rarely be struck in favour of expulsion where there is a serious risk of torture. However, as the matter is one of balance, precise prediction is elusive. The ambit of an exceptional discretion to deport to torture, if any, must await future cases.

79. In these circumstances, s. 53(1)(b) does not violate s. 7 of the *Charter*. What is at issue is not the legislation, but the Minister's obligation to exercise the discretion s. 53 confers in a constitutional manner. . . .

[The Supreme Court concluded that some of the procedures followed in Suresh's case did not meet the required constitutional standards. Thus, the appellant was entitled to a new deportation hearing.]

Note that the Convention Against Torture[136] categorically rejects deportation to a danger of being subjected to torture, even where national security interests are at stake. Yet, in *Suresh* the Supreme Court of Canada stated, in *obiter*, that section 7 of the *Charter* may not prohibit such deportation "in exceptional circumstances." This is a clear indication that, while treaties may "inform" *Charter* interpretation, they are, to use the Supreme Court's own words, "not . . . controlling." If not a one-off result explained by its immediate post-9/11 context, the *Suresh* approach could be interpreted as a repudiation of the "minimum content" approach previously espoused in *Slaight Communications*.

Yet the Supreme Court of Canada has vacillated on this issue. For example, in *R v Hape*, a majority of the Court stated:

This Court has also looked to international law to assist it in interpreting the *Charter*. Whenever possible, it has sought to ensure consistency between its interpretation of the *Charter*, on the one hand, and Canada's international obligations and the relevant principles of international law, on the other. . . .

In interpreting the scope of application of the *Charter*, the courts should seek to ensure compliance with Canada's binding obligations under international law where the express words are capable of supporting such a construction.[137]

Further, in *Health Services*[138]—decided, incidentally, one day after *Hape*—a majority of the Court appeared to resuscitate the *Slaight Communications* rule, stating that:

[T]he *Charter* should be presumed to provide at least as great a level of protection as is found in the international human rights documents that Canada has ratified.[139]

---

136 Convention Against Torture and Other Cruel, Inhuman or Degrading Treatment or Punishment, 10 December 1984, 1465 UNTS 85, Can TS 1987 No 36, in force 26 June 1987.

137 *R v Hape*, above note 127 at paras 55–56.

138 *Health Services and Support—Facilities Subsector Bargaining Assn v British Columbia*, 2007 SCC 27, [2007] 2 SCR 391.

139 *Ibid* at para 70. See also *Divito v Canada (Public Safety and Emergency Preparedness)*, 2013 SCC 47 at paras 23–25, where a majority of the Court quoted this passage from *Health Services* with approval and held that the rights protected by the ICCPR, above note 2, "provide a minimum level of protection in interpreting the . . . rights under the *Charter*."

Comparing these two rulings, released within a day of one another, is there a difference between ensuring "compliance" with Canada's "binding obligations under international law" when construing the *Charter*, and presuming that the *Charter* provides "at least as great a level of protection as is found in the international human rights documents that Canada has ratified"? Could "compliance" potentially impose upper limits, in addition to lower bounds, on *Charter* interpretation? Could consideration of all of Canada's binding obligations under international law lead to different results than considering only "the international human rights documents that Canada has ratified"?

In light of the foregoing materials, what is the rule governing the use of international law in construing the *Charter*? How does that rule differ, it at all, from the rules governing the use of international law in interpreting Canadian statutory and common law?

CHAPTER 3

INTERNATIONAL LEGAL PERSONS

Having discussed the ways in which international law is made and ascertained, we turn now to a consideration of those entities which have formal roles to play in the international legal system. The classic, doctrinal approach to this topic is to focus on the "subjects" of international law, namely, those entities created or regulated directly by international law. For reasons expressed in Chapter 1, the state is chief among these "subjects." Certain international (that is, intergovernmental) organizations are also now recognized as subjects of international law. However, as we shall see, the difficulty with the concept of subjects is that it suggests an all-or-nothing approach to identifying the relevant players in the international legal system. The reality is more complex. Entities other than states have widely divergent entitlements and obligations under distinct areas of international law, as well as differing capacities on the international legal plane. In other words, they have varying degrees of international legal personality or subjecthood.

In this chapter, we go beyond the classic approach of describing the subjects of international law and focus on the extent to which those entities with the greatest degree of international legal personality—states and international organizations—have formal roles to play on the international stage, either as subjects of international legal obligations, beneficiaries of international legal rights, or as agents with legal standing or capacity to participate in and influence the conduct of international legal relations. This focus will also allow us to examine in some detail the nature and lifecycle of states, as well as the character and functioning of international organizations. In subsequent chapters, we will examine the more restricted international legal personality of other players on the international stage.

A. STATES AS ULTIMATE INTERNATIONAL LEGAL PERSONS

The state is the key subject of international law and the key actor in international relations, thus enjoying the ultimate degree of international legal personality. Chapters 1 and 2 underscore the importance of states as authors of the rules of international law. However, states can also be considered as products of international law in the sense that the law provides criteria for determining whether a given entity constitutes a state. After all, not all collectivities of human beings are states, with all the international legal capacities, rights, and obligations flowing from such status. We begin by focusing on these international legal prerequisites for statehood.

1) Prerequisites of Statehood in International Law

a) Overview

Article 1 of the 1933 Convention on the Rights and Duties of States, concluded in Montevideo, Uruguay, provides a useful starting point for describing the prerequisites of statehood: "The state as a person of international law should possess the following qualifications: a) a permanent population; b) a defined territory; c) government; and d) capacity to enter into relations with the other states."[1]

Only a handful of states are parties to the Montevideo Convention. Nevertheless, Article 1, with its list of prerequisites for statehood, is commonly considered to reflect customary international law. Consider how the four prerequisites of statehood have been defined by the influential *Restatement of the Law, Third, Foreign Relations Law of the United States:*

> *Permanent population.* To be a state an entity must have a population that is significant and permanent. . . . An entity that has a significant number of permanent inhabitants in its territory satisfies the requirement even if large numbers of nomads move in and out of the territory.

> *Defined territory.* An entity may satisfy the territorial requirement for statehood even if its boundaries have not been finally settled, if one or more of its boundaries are disputed, or if some of its territory is claimed by another state. An entity does not necessarily cease to be a state even if all of its territory has been occupied by a foreign power or if it has otherwise lost control of its territory temporarily.

> *Government.* A state need not have any particular form of government, but there must be some authority exercising governmental functions and able to represent the entity in international relations.

> *Capacity to conduct international relations.* An entity is not a state unless it has competence, within its own constitutional system, to conduct international relations with other states, as well as the political, technical, and financial capabilities to do so. . . . States do not cease to be states because they have agreed not to engage in certain international activities or have delegated authority to do so to a "supranational" entity, e.g., the European Communities.[2]

Note that, while the Charter of the United Nations (UN Charter) specifies requirements for becoming a member of that body and limits membership to states, it does not establish criteria for statehood itself:

Charter of the United Nations, 26 June 1945, Can TS 1945 No 7, in force 24 October 1945

Article 3

The original Members of the United Nations shall be the states which, having participated in the United Nations Conference on International Organization at San Francisco,

---

1   Convention on Rights and Duties of States adopted by the Seventh International Conference of American States, 26 December 1933, 165 LNTS 19, in force 26 December 1934 (also known as the Montevideo Convention on the Rights and Duties of States).

2   American Law Institute, *Restatement of the Law, Third, Foreign Relations Law of the United States* (St Paul, MN: American Law Institute Publishers, 1987) at para 201 [*Third Restatement*].

or having previously signed the Declaration by United Nations of 1 January 1942, sign the present Charter and ratify it in accordance with Article 110.

Article 4

1. Membership in the United Nations is open to all other peace-loving states which accept the obligations contained in the present Charter and, in the judgment of the Organization, are able and willing to carry out these obligations.

2. The admission of any such state to membership in the United Nations will be effected by a decision of the General Assembly upon the recommendation of the Security Council.

On their face, the legal requirements for statehood and the UN membership rules are straightforward. In practice, there are shades of grey. There are, at present, 193 UN member states and another dozen entities working towards a possible future claim for membership.[3] As for observer states, the Holy See—being the government of the Catholic Church in Rome with a global spiritual remit that is not limited to the territory of Vatican City—has been considered a non-member permanent observer "state" of the United Nations since 1964. According to the United Nations, such status "is based purely on practice, and there are no provisions for it in the United Nations Charter."[4] The benefits of this status are as follows, as described by one critic:

> Privileges of Non-Member State Permanent Observers include the ability to sign and ratify UN-sponsored treaties, to participate in world conferences with full voting rights, to take part in discussions and decisions in the General Assembly, and to participate in various UN agencies, commissions, and committees. . . .
>
> The Holy See has voted and actively participated in several UN world conferences, which rank among the foremost forums for international lawmaking. The UN generally grants widespread state access to participation at international conferences. General Assembly resolutions convening world conferences have invited "all States" to participate "in full, with full voting rights." . . . Unlike non-governmental organizations, "states" have the ability to prevent consensus and stall the conference process.[5]

The Holy See's status as an observer state participating in international conferences has generated controversy, in large measure because of its views on abortion and women's reproductive rights. Consider the following condemnation from the Center for Reproductive Rights, a US-based non-governmental group using the law to advance reproductive freedom as a fundamental human right:

---

3   As an example of the shades of grey, the US State Department considers there to be 195 independent states in the world—a tally that includes the Holy See and Kosovo as states: US State Department, Bureau of Intelligence and Research, "Independent States in the World" (3 January 2012), online: www.state.gov/s/inr/rls/4250.htm

4   United Nations, "About Permanent Observers" online: www.un.org/en/members/aboutpermobservers.shtml.

5   Center for Reproductive Rights, *The Holy See at the United Nations: An Obstacle to Women's Reproductive Health and Rights* (August 2000) at 3 and 5, online: www.crlp.org/pdf/pub_bp_holyseeattheun.pdf.

During the development of consensus agreements at recent world conferences, the Holy See has joined forces with a small group of conservative governments and radical, right wing organizations. They have attempted to intervene and obstruct the goal of reaching consensus on legal, policy, and program reforms needed to further women's sexual and reproductive health and rights. Many of the reactionary policies pursued by the Holy See ultimately have the effect of denying women their human rights. The views advocated by the Holy See at the UN touch on issues that include the role of women in society, HIV/AIDS, contraception, abortion, sexual and reproductive health services, and adolescents.[6]

The Center has underscored its concerns with the Holy See's policies by challenging its claim to statehood:

Because the Holy See exists to govern the Roman Catholic Church worldwide, beyond the limits of the Vatican City, its legitimacy as a state is questionable. The Holy See has itself stated that its mission at the UN is "of a religious and moral character." In addition, the Holy See does not meet international legal definitions of statehood. According to the Montevideo Convention on the Rights and Duties of States, "[t]he State as a person of international law should possess the following qualifications: a) a permanent population; b) a defined territory; c) government; and d) capacity to enter into relations with the other states." These four factual criteria for determining statehood are founded on principles agreed upon by a host of international law scholars and are consistent with the foreign relations laws of some nations.

The Holy See does not meet all four of the criteria in the Montevideo definition. Other than the nominal population of the Vatican City, the Holy See does not have a "permanent population." Rather, it governs a large group of voluntary religious followers who reside as citizens in other states. Similarly, the Holy See does not possess a "defined territory" other than the Vatican City, which serves only to host a small collection of religious and administrative buildings. As to the "government" criterion, the Holy See is itself the government of the Roman Catholic Church and, by definition, of the Vatican City. It cannot therefore be regarded as an entity that possesses a government. The only characteristic of a modern state that is attributable to the Holy See is its capacity to enter into relations with other states. The Holy See is party to international treaties, and it receives foreign envoys.[7]

There is a non-governmental group campaign contesting the Holy See's status as a state and its role at the United Nations,[8] and the position taken by these groups has found some support in the academic legal literature.[9]

---

6   *Ibid* at 5.

7   *Ibid* at 3 (footnotes omitted).

8   See Catholics for Choice, *The Catholic Church at the United Nations: Church or State?* (Washington, DC: Catholics for Choice, 2013), online: www.catholicsforchoice.org/topics/politics/documents/CFC_See_Change_2013.pdf

9   Yasmin Abdullah, "The Holy See at United Nations Conferences: State or Church?" (1996) 96 Colum L Rev 1835. See also Cedric Ryngaert, "The Legal Status of the Holy See" (2011) 3:3 Goettingen J Int'l L 829–59.

The Holy See has defended its status, relying mostly on historical justifications and its regular diplomatic relations with states rather than on a strict application of all the Montevideo criteria:

> Since the late Middle Ages, no one has contested the international legitimacy of the Holy See; neither the Soviets in the recent past, nor the Chinese today. There is no doubt about the Holy See's full belonging to the international community. A single statistic is enough: in 1978, when Pope John Paul II was elected Supreme Pontiff, the Holy See had diplomatic relations with 84 countries; today, this number has risen to 172.
>
> The Holy See, which enjoys international juridical status, is thus presented as a — *sovereign and independent moral authority* — and as such takes part in international relations. Within nations its action as a moral authority, aims at furthering an ethic of relations between the different protagonists of the international community.[10]

The only other UN non-member permanent observer state at the time of writing is Palestine. Consider the following excerpt from the UN General Assembly resolution that granted such status in November 2012:

Status of Palestine in the United Nations, GA Res 67/19, UN Doc A/RES/67/19 (2012), to be reprinted in UN GAOR, 67th Sess, Supp No 49, UN Doc A/67/49 (2013)

The General Assembly, . . .

Recalling its resolution 181 (II) of 29 November 1947 [recommending termination of the United Kingdom's Mandate for Palestine and the establishment in its stead of two independent states, one Arab and one Jewish], . . .

Reaffirming also its resolutions 43/176 of 15 December 1988 and 66/17 of 30 November 2011 and all relevant resolutions regarding the peaceful settlement of the question of Palestine, which, inter alia, stress the need for the withdrawal of Israel from the Palestinian territory occupied since 1967, including East Jerusalem, the realization of the inalienable rights of the Palestinian people, primarily the right to self-determination and the right to their independent State, a just resolution of the problem of the Palestine refugees in conformity with resolution 194 (III) of 11 December 1948 and the complete cessation of all Israeli settlement activities in the Occupied Palestinian Territory, including East Jerusalem, . . .

Recalling its resolutions 3210 (XXIX) of 14 October 1974 and 3237 (XXIX) of 22 November 1974, by which, respectively, the Palestine Liberation Organization was invited to participate in the deliberations of the General Assembly as the representative of the Palestinian people and was granted observer status,

Recalling also its resolution 43/177 of 15 December 1988, by which it, inter alia, acknowledged the proclamation of the State of Palestine by the Palestine National Council on 15 November 1988 and decided that the designation "Palestine" should be used in place of the designation "Palestine Liberation Organization" in the United Nations sys-

---

10   Archbishop Jean-Louis Tauran, "The Presence of the Holy See in the International Organizations" (A lecture delivered at the Catholic University of the Sacred Heart in Milan, 22 April 2002), reprinted in *L'Osservatore Romano* (Weekly Edition in English) (22 May 2002) at 8.

tem, without prejudice to the observer status and functions of the Palestine Liberation Organization within the United Nations system,

Taking into consideration that the Executive Committee of the Palestine Liberation Organization, in accordance with a decision by the Palestine National Council, is entrusted with the powers and responsibilities of the Provisional Government of the State of Palestine, . . .

Reaffirming its commitment, in accordance with international law, to the two-State solution of an independent, sovereign, democratic, viable and contiguous State of Palestine living side by side with Israel in peace and security on the basis of the pre-1967 borders,

Bearing in mind the mutual recognition of 9 September 1993 between the Government of the State of Israel and the Palestine Liberation Organization, the representative of the Palestinian people, . . .

Commending the Palestinian National Authority's 2009 plan for constructing the institutions of an independent Palestinian State within a two-year period, and welcoming the positive assessments in this regard about readiness for statehood by the World Bank, the United Nations and the International Monetary Fund and as reflected in the Ad Hoc Liaison Committee Chair conclusions of April 2011 and subsequent Chair conclusions, which determined that the Palestinian Authority is above the threshold for a functioning State in key sectors studied,

Recognizing that full membership is enjoyed by Palestine in the United Nations Educational, Scientific and Cultural Organization, the Economic and Social Commission for Western Asia and the Group of Asia-Pacific States and that Palestine is also a full member of the League of Arab States, the Movement of Non-Aligned Countries, the Organization of Islamic Cooperation and the Group of 77 and China,

Recognizing also that, to date, 132 States Members of the United Nations have accorded recognition to the State of Palestine,

Taking note of the 11 November 2011 report of the Security Council Committee on the Admission of New Members, . . .

1. *Reaffirms* the right of the Palestinian people to self-determination and to independence in their State of Palestine on the Palestinian territory occupied since 1967;

2. *Decides* to accord to Palestine non-member observer State status in the United Nations, without prejudice to the acquired rights, privileges and role of the Palestine Liberation Organization in the United Nations as the representative of the Palestinian people, in accordance with the relevant resolutions and practice;

3. *Expresses the hope* that the Security Council will consider favourably the application submitted on 23 September 2011 by the State of Palestine for admission to full membership in the United Nations;

4. *Affirms* its determination to contribute to the achievement of the inalienable rights of the Palestinian people and the attainment of a peaceful settlement in the Middle East that ends the occupation that began in 1967 and fulfils the vision of two States: an independent, sovereign, democratic, contiguous and viable State of Palestine living side by side in peace and security with Israel on the basis of the pre-1967 borders. . . .

Note the hope expressed in operative paragraph 3 of resolution 67/19 that the Security Council will favourably consider Palestine's bid for full membership in the UN, and consider again the importance of the procedural requirements for admission to full UN membership set out in Article 4(2) of the UN Charter. As the UN Charter limits full UN membership to states, but does not address the requirements of permanent observer status — a status held by several non-state entities — of what value is resolution 67/19 in determining whether Palestine is a state under international law? In reflecting on this question, note the various factors considered in the report of the Security Council's Committee on the Admission of New Members, to which reference is made in the preamble of resolution 67/19:

Report of the Committee on the Admission of New Members Concerning the Application of Palestine for Admission to Membership in the United Nations, UN Doc S/2011/705 (11 November 2011)

3. [T]he Presidency of the Security Council . . . convened five informal meetings of the Committee . . . to carefully consider whether Palestine met the specific criteria for admission to membership contained in Article 4 of the Charter of the United Nations. . . .

4. In the course of the meetings of the Committee, differing views were expressed. . . .

5. It was stated that the criteria set out in Article 4 of the Charter were the only factors that could be taken into consideration in the Committee's deliberations. . . .

6. It was also asserted that the Committee's work, whatever its outcome, should be mindful of the broader political context. The view was expressed that a two-State solution via a negotiated settlement remained the only option for a long-term sustainable peace and that final status issues had to be resolved through negotiations. Support was expressed for a two-State solution based on pre-1967 borders, resulting from political negotiations, leading to an independent State of Palestine with East Jerusalem as its capital. It was stressed that Palestine's right to self-determination and recognition is not contrary to Israel's right to exist.

7. It was stated that the Committee's work should not harm the prospects of the resumption of peace talks, particularly in the light of the Quartet statement on 23 September 2011 that had set out a clear timetable for the resumption of negotiations. Similarly, it was stated that the prospect of negotiations should not delay the Security Council's consideration of Palestine's application. It was stated that Palestine's application was neither detrimental to the political process nor an alternative to negotiations. It was also stated that the Palestinian application would not bring the parties closer to peace. It was further stated that the question of the recognition of Palestinian statehood could not and should not be subject to the outcome of negotiations between the Palestinians and Israelis, and that, otherwise, Palestinian statehood would be made dependent on the approval of Israel, which would grant the occupying Power a right of veto over the right to self-determination of the Palestinian people, which has been recognized by the General Assembly as an inalienable right since 1974. Concerns were raised in relation to Israel's continued settlement activities. The view was expressed that those activities were considered illegal under international law and were an obstacle to a comprehensive peace.

8. In relation to the application of Palestine . . . , attention was drawn to the letter received by the Secretary-General from the President of Palestine on 23 September 2011, which contained a declaration — made in a formal instrument — stating that the State of Palestine was a peace-loving nation; that it accepted the obligations contained in the Charter of the United Nations; and that it solemnly undertook to fulfil them.

9. On the criterion of statehood, reference was made to the 1933 Montevideo Convention on the Rights and Duties of States, which declares that a State as a person of international law should possess a permanent population, a defined territory, a government and the capacity to enter into relations with other States.

10. With regard to the requirements of a permanent population and a defined territory, the view was expressed that Palestine fulfilled these criteria. It was stressed that the lack of precisely settled borders was not an obstacle to statehood.

11. Questions were raised, however, regarding Palestine's control over its territory, in view of the fact that Hamas[11] was the de facto authority in the Gaza Strip. It was affirmed that the Israeli occupation was a factor preventing the Palestinian government from exercising full control over its territory. However, the view was expressed that occupation by a foreign Power did not imply that the sovereignty of an occupied territory was to be transferred to the occupying Power.

12. With regard to the requirement of a government, the view was expressed that Palestine fulfilled this criterion. However, it was stated that Hamas was in control of 40 per cent of the population of Palestine; therefore the Palestinian Authority could not be considered to have effective government control over the claimed territory. It was stressed that the Palestine Liberation Organization, and not Hamas, was the legitimate representative of the Palestinian people.

13. Reference was made to reports of the World Bank, the International Monetary Fund and the Ad Hoc Liaison Committee for the Coordination of the International Assistance to Palestinians, which had concluded that Palestine's governmental functions were now sufficient for the functioning of a State.

14. With regard to the requirement that a State have the capacity to enter into relations with other States, the view was expressed that Palestine fulfilled this criterion. It was recalled that Palestine had been accepted into membership in the Non-Aligned Movement, the Organization of Islamic Cooperation, the Economic and Social Commission for Western Asia, the Group of 77 and the United Nations Educational, Scientific and Cultural Organization. In addition, over 130 States had recognized Palestine as an independent sovereign State. Questions were raised, however, regarding the authority of the Palestinian Authority to engage in relations with other States, since under the Oslo Accords the Palestinian Authority could not engage in foreign relations.

---

11 [Hamas is a Palestinian Islamist organization that emerged from the Muslim Brotherhood in 1987, and gained control over the Gaza Strip in 2007. Hamas is a listed entity, as that term is used in section 83.05(1) of Canada's *Criminal Code*, RSC 1985, c C-46, as amended.]

15. With regard to the requirement that an applicant be "peace-loving", the view was expressed that Palestine fulfilled this criterion in view of its commitment to the achievement of a just, lasting and comprehensive resolution of the Israeli-Palestinian conflict. It was further stated that Palestine's fulfilment of this criterion was also evident in its commitment to resuming negotiations on all final status issues on the basis of the internationally endorsed terms of reference, relevant United Nations resolutions, the Madrid principles, the Arab Peace Initiative and the Quartet road map.

16. Questions were raised as to whether Palestine was indeed a peace-loving State, since Hamas refused to renounce terrorism and violence, and had the stated aim of destroying Israel. Reference was made, on the other hand, to the Advisory Opinion of the International Court of Justice on Namibia, of 1971, which stated that the only acts that could be attributable to a State were those of the State's recognized authority.

17. With regard to the requirement that an applicant accept the obligations contained in the Charter and be able and willing to carry out those obligations, the view was expressed that Palestine fulfilled these criteria, as was evident, inter alia, from the solemn declaration to this effect contained in its application. It was recalled that in 1948, when considering the application of Israel for membership, it had been argued that Israel's solemn pledge to carry out its obligations under the Charter was sufficient to meet this criterion.

18. The view was also expressed that the Charter required more than a verbal commitment by an applicant to carry out its Charter obligations; an applicant had to show a commitment to the peaceful settlement of disputes and to refrain from the threat or the use of force in the conduct of its international relations. In this connection, it was stressed that Hamas had not accepted these obligations.

19. The view was expressed that the Committee should recommend to the Council that Palestine be admitted to membership in the United Nations. A different view was expressed that the membership application could not be supported at this time and an abstention was envisaged in the event of a vote. Yet another view expressed was that there were serious questions about the application, that the applicant did not meet the requirements for membership and that a favourable recommendation to the General Assembly would not be supported.

20. Further, it was suggested that, as an intermediate step, the General Assembly should adopt a resolution by which Palestine would be made an Observer State.

21. In summing up the debate at the 110th meeting of the Committee, the Chair stated that the Committee was unable to make a unanimous recommendation to the Security Council. . . .

As noted above, the UN Charter expressly limits membership in the United Nations to states. On this basis, it is generally assumed that admission to UN membership furnishes conclusive proof of statehood. In light of the range of factors considered in the above report, does the converse hold true? What legal conclusions, if any, regarding an entity's statehood can be drawn from its failure to secure UN membership?

Applying the legal criteria for statehood, are the Holy See or Palestine states? Consider the importance, under the fourth criterion of capacity to enter into relations with other states, of the fact that most states have established relations with both entities of a sort usually reserved for states. While we consider the concept of "recognition of states" in a subsequent section, it would be difficult to overstate the practical and legal significance of a demonstrated ability to satisfy the fourth criterion of statehood. If enough states treat another entity like a state by entering into relations with it on that basis, for all practical purposes it acquires the international legal personality of a state. Of course, as we discuss below, the converse may also be true.

Moreover, critiques of the Holy See's and Palestine's claims to statehood do not adequately address the fact that international law does not impose rigid or arbitrary quantitative criteria when it comes to the Montevideo requirements. There must be *some* territory, *some* permanent population, *some* effective government and *enough* independence to enter into international relations. Measured against these relaxed standards, do the Holy See or Palestine meet the international legal definition of a state?

All this is not to say that the test for statehood is always easy to meet. The concept of "effective government" and capacity to enter into foreign relations raise occasional difficulties. How stringently should the requirements of "effective government" and "capacity to enter into relations with other states" be applied? Have they changed over time? Are they applied differently when considering a new candidate for statehood, as opposed to situations where effective government or foreign relations capacity in an established state evaporate? We consider some difficult cases raising these issues in the next two subsections.

b) Difficult Cases: Effective Government

Aaland Islands Case, (1920) League of Nations OJ Special Supp No 3 at 3

[The Council of the League of Nations was asked to assess the status and future of the Aaland Islands, which had historic ties to Finland, Sweden, and Russia. The Council referred the matter to an ad hoc group of jurists, as the Permanent Court of International Justice had not yet been established. A preliminary matter to be determined by the jurists was the date at which Finland emerged as an independent state in the aftermath of the Russian revolution.]

... [F]or a considerable time the conditions required for the formation of a sovereign state did not exist. In the midst of revolution and anarchy, certain elements essential to the existence of a state, even some elements of fact, were lacking for a fairly considerable period. Political and social life was disorganized: the authorities were not strong enough to assert themselves; civil war was rife; further, the Diet, the legality of which had been disputed by a large section of the people had been dispersed by the revolutionary party, and the Government had been chased from the capital and forcibly prevented from carrying out its duties: the armed camps and the police were divided into opposing forces, and Russian troops, and after a time Germans also, took part in the civil war between the inhabitants and between the Red and White Finnish troops. It is, therefore, difficult to say at what exact date the Finnish Republic, in the legal sense of the term, actually became a definitely constituted sovereign state. This certainly did not take place until a stable political organization had been created, and until the public authorities had become strong enough to assert themselves throughout the territories of the state without the assistance of foreign troops. It would appear that it was in May 1918, that the civil war ended and that the foreign troops began to leave the country, so that from that time onwards it was possible to reestablish order and normal political and social life, little by little.

[The League of Nations ultimately concluded that Finland should retain sovereignty over the islands, but that they should be treated as an autonomous zone.]

The *Aaland Islands Case* applies a strict test for effective government: no statehood is achieved until public authorities are "strong enough to assert themselves throughout the territories of the state without the assistance of foreign troops." In 1960, the newly independent Congo became a member of the United Nations. As noted above, UN membership is limited to states. Was the Congo a "state" in 1960? Consider the state of its government at that time, as described by Professor James Crawford of the University of Cambridge:

> The situation in the Congo after independence . . . involved the following factors:
> - The absence of any effective preparation for independence. . . .
> - The existence of various secessionary movements, at least one of which (in Katanga) was inspired by foreign interests and led to civil war.
> - The division of the central government, shortly after independence, into two factions, both claiming to be the lawful government.
> - The reintroduction . . . of Belgian troops shortly after independence, under claim of humanitarian intervention.
> - The immediate and continuing need, because of the effective bankruptcy of the Congolese authorities, for international aid on a large scale.
> - The introduction of United Nations forces shortly after independence to restore order and prevent civil war. . . .
>
> Anything less like effective government it would be hard to imagine.[12]

The Congo's difficult "birth," and its subsequent political troubles, raise the question: should the criterion of "effective government" be relaxed where the putative state is a former colony engaged in a protracted and contested process of decolonization? Alternatively, given that all states are juridically equal in international law, should we insist on an *Aaland Islands* standard in all cases? Applying the latter standard, neither the Congo nor, more recently, Croatia or Bosnia and Herzegovina could be viewed as states at the point of their recognition as such by the United Nations or other states. Did the international community err in recognizing these entities as states?

There are strong policy reasons for quickly recognizing the transition of a proto-state to full statehood, even in the absence of fully consolidated governmental authority. An entity that is not a state inherits none of the international legal rights or obligations associated with statehood, such as state obligations to respect international human rights or humanitarian law and to refrain from using force against its neighbours, or the right to

---

12 James Crawford, *The Creation of States in International Law*, 2d ed (Oxford: Oxford University Press, 2006) at 56–57.

be free from interference by its neighbours in its internal affairs. The result of prolonged uncertainty as to the status of a Congo, a Bosnia, or a Croatia could be chaos.

Having achieved statehood, what happens when a fragile post-colonial government topples? Consider a phenomenon much in the public eye in the twenty-first century: so-called failed, or collapsed, states.

Sebastian von Einsiedel, "Policy Responses to State Failure"[13]

1. WHAT IS A FAILED STATE AND WHY DO STATES COLLAPSE?

What are failed states?

. . . There is no agreement in the scholarly literature on the definition of failed states and various definitions can be viewed in contrast to the different concepts of the state. The most often cited . . . definition was offered by William Zartman for whom collapse means "that the basic functions of the state are no longer performed." A collapsing state therefore is one that maintains few or no functioning state institutions, has lost its power to confer identity, can no longer assure security, and has lost its legitimacy. . . .

There is no doubt, of course, that state failure dramatically increases the likelihood of civil war and it is worth looking briefly at the interrelationship of the two phenomena. The weakening of state institutions increases the likelihood of violent conflict in several ways. First, the erosion of state authorities sharpens the security dilemma for minority groups within a state. Second, Snyder has argued that in weak states ethnic concepts of nationalism . . . are more likely to prevail than civic concepts of nationalism. . . . Third, the weaker the state, the greater the incentives for regional leaders to exploit the power vacuum. This may take the form of "state capture," an advanced form of corruption, or outright warlordism as seen in Afghanistan prior to the Taliban and Somalia today. . . .

Why do states fail?

Ignatieff has assembled a list of causes of why states collapse:

> Sometimes the cause is colonial legacy; sometimes it is maladministration by an in-
> digenous elite; sometimes, failure is a legacy first of interference by outside powers,
> and then abandonment. . . . [A]nd most important[ly], many failed and failing states
> are poor and have suffered from the steadily more adverse terms of trade in a global-
> ized economy.

This list shows that causes for state failure can be located at many levels: the system level, the state level and at the level of individual leaders. These various theories on root causes for state failure are not necessarily mutually exclusive but should be seen as complementary explanatory models.

Among the most often mentioned root causes of state collapse is the legacy of colonialism. Apart from the creation of colonial borders creating unviable entities prone to eth-

---

13 Sebastian von Einsiedel, "Policy Responses to State Failure" in Simon Chesterman et al, eds, *Making States Work: State Failure and the Crisis of Governance* (Tokyo: United Nations University Press, 2005) at 13–35. Reprinted with permission.

nic conflict, the imposition of colonial rule brought along the destruction of traditional social structures without replacing them with Western constitutional and institutional structures and an effective identity as a new state. Pointing to the wave of state failure in Africa in the 1990s, several authors go further and argue that the European model of the sovereign nation-state is simply the wrong institution for that continent. They claim that Africa's demography (sparse population in rural areas), geography (poor communication lines and trade routes), political culture and heritage (characterized by political control over people instead of land, multiple layers of sovereignty), and social structure (built around family relationships and spiritual authority) are incompatible with the state model imposed by the European colonizers. According to Jeffrey Herbst the etiquette of sovereignty that newly independent African states were granted was nothing but a "legal fiction." The sanctity of boundaries that came along with the grant of sovereignty removed the threat of secession and with it incentives for leaders to reach accommodation with disaffected populations. Arguing along the same lines, Christopher Clapham differentiates between those African countries with a tradition of precolonial statehood (such as southern Uganda, Ethiopia, Eritrea, southern Ghana and Rwanda) and those without (such as Somalia, northern Uganda, southern Sudan, Liberia, Sierra Leone) and argues that the former "are far better able to survive (and even learn from) the experience of bad government." Furthermore, insurgent movements derived from societies from the former group of countries have been far more likely to set up effective structures of government, even amidst the chaos resulting from the defeat of their incumbent rivals.

While accepting the importance of the colonialist experience for the understanding of Africa's ongoing malaise, Zartman and others reject the reasoning of Clapham and Herbst, that modern sovereign states are simply the wrong institutions for Africa. Zartman argues that "no common theme or characteristic runs through the cases of collapse that would indicate that collapse was the result either of the same 'Western-style' malfunction in the state or of particularly badly adapted Western institutions." Zartman affirms that "there is no typical 'African state' especially adapted to African circumstances, or specifically derived from a precolonial proto-institution; rather is there a set of functions that need to be performed for the coherence and the effectiveness of the polity—anywhere." Liberia could serve as an interesting case study in this respect. It has a long history of independence and did not experience a typical foreign colonial rule yet experienced one of the worst cases of state collapse in the 1990s. . . .

[Still other] authors . . . view the present incidence of state collapse as largely a function of the major powers' withdrawal of interest and resources from weak states after the end of the Cold War. This sudden end of outside support, which took place against the background of a structural economic crisis in the developing world starting in the early 1980s, left the leaders of many shadow states without resources to distribute to their followers and to maintain a strong, functioning army. Increasingly, this meant that states lost the monopoly over violence. . . .

How should international law treat failed states? Should they be considered stripped of their status as states? The answer is probably no. One scholar puts it this way:

Arguably, a completely non-functioning government indicates the disappearance of several of the indicia of statehood, such as plenary authority over a territory and population and the ability to enter into relations with other States.

... Yet, a State is not necessarily extinguished by substantial changes in territory, population, or government, or in some cases by all three. ... [T]here is a strong presumption in favor of the continuance, and against the extinction, of an established State. Extensive civil strife and the breakdown of order through foreign invasion have not affected the personalities of established States. Such States have also been immune to extinction because of revolution and prolonged anarchy. ...

Given the strong presumption in favor of retaining international personality, and taking into account recognition and the views of the entity concerned, failed States do not appear to have forfeited their status as States. ... The fundamental problem is the breakdown of effective government; the other indices of statehood remain in place. Yet, this scenario alone does not appear to have led to a loss of statehood. Territory and population remain in place, and the international community continues to treat these States as States, thereby recognizing that these States remain sovereign entities.[14]

c) Difficult Cases: Capacity to Enter into Foreign Relations

The capacity of a state to enter into foreign relations — often referred to as its "independence" — can be a highly politicized question, especially where a state surrenders some of its autonomy in foreign (or even domestic) affairs to another state or entity. Consider the following materials.

***Customs Régime Between Germany and Austria*, Advisory Opinion (1931), PCIJ (Ser A/B) No 41**

[After World War I, the peace treaty with Austria (signed at Saint-Germain in 1919) provided that the "independence of Austria is inalienable otherwise than with the consent of the Council of the League of Nations." In Protocol 1 to that treaty, Austria also agreed to abstain from "granting to any State a special regime or exclusive advantages calculated to threaten [Austria's economic] independence." In 1931, Austria subsequently agreed to negotiate a treaty with Germany to "assimilate the tariff and economic policies" of the two states—that is, to establish a customs union. In response, the Council of the League of Nations asked the Permanent Court of International Justice for an advisory opinion on whether such a treaty between Germany and Austria would violate either the Treaty of Saint-Germain or its Protocol. In answering this question, the Court had to consider the meaning of "independence."]

The Court:

... [T]he independence of Austria, according to Article 88 of the Treaty of Saint-Germain, must be understood to mean the continued existence of Austria within her present frontiers as a separate State with sole right of decision in all matters economic, political, financial or other with the result that that independence is violated, as soon as there is any violation thereof, either in the economic, political, or any other field, these different aspects of independence being in practice one and indivisible.

---

14 Ruth E Gordon, "Some Legal Problems with Trusteeship" (1995) 28 Cornell Int'l LJ 301 at 335–37.

If by the regime contemplated by the Austro-German Protocol of 1931 Austria does not alienate her independence, the Council's consent on this matter is obviously not necessary. In the other event, however, it is essential.

By "alienation," as mentioned in Article 88, must be understood any voluntary act by the Austrian State which would cause it to lose its independence or which would modify its independence in that its sovereign will would be subordinated to the will of another Power or particular group of Powers, or would even be replaced by such will. . . .

It can scarcely be denied that the establishment of this [customs union] does not in itself constitute an act alienating Austria's independence, for Austria does not thereby cease, within her own frontiers, to be a separate State, with its own government and administration; and, in view . . . of the possibility of denouncing the treaty, it may be said that legally Austria retains the possibility of exercising her independence. . . .

[The Court thus concluded that the proposed customs union was consistent with the maintenance of Austria's independence and, hence, with Article 88 of the Treaty of Saint-Germain. The Court nevertheless went on to conclude that the proposed arrangement was inconsistent with Protocol 1 because it was a "special regime" that would grant "exclusive advantages" to Germany and that was, moreover, calculated to threaten Austria's economic independence. Judge Anzilotti, concurring in the outcome, appended a separate opinion in which he commented as follows:]

. . . The independence of Austria within the meaning of Article 88 is nothing else but the existence of Austria, within the frontiers laid down by the Treaty of Saint-Germain, as a separate State and not subject to the authority of any other State or group of States. Independence as thus understood is really no more than the normal condition of States according to international law; it may also be described as sovereignty (*suprema potestas*), *or external sovereignty, by which is meant that the State has over it no other authority than that of international law.*

The conception of independence, regarded as the normal characteristic of States as subjects of international law, cannot be better defined than by comparing it with the exceptional and, to some extent, abnormal class of States known as "dependent States." These are States subject to the authority of one or more other States. The idea of dependence therefore necessarily implies a relation between a superior State (suzerain, protector, etc.) and an inferior or subject State (vassal, protégé, etc.); the relation between the State which can legally impose its will and the State which is legally compelled to submit to that will. Where there is no such relation of superiority and subordination, it is impossible to speak of dependence within the meaning of international law.

It follows that the legal conception of independence has nothing to do with a State's subordination to international law or with the numerous and constantly increasing states of *de facto* dependence which characterize the relation of one country to other countries.

It also follows that the restrictions upon a State's liberty, whether arising out of ordinary international law or contractual engagements, do not as such in the least affect its independence. As long as these restrictions do not place the State under the legal authority of another State, the former remains an independent State however extensive and burdensome those obligations may be.

This is obviously the standpoint of the Treaty of Saint-Germain when it proclaims the independence of Austria despite the many serious restrictions it imposes upon her freedom in the economic, military and other spheres. These restrictions do not put Austria under the authority of the other contracting States, which means that Austria is an independent State within the meaning of international law. . . .

The Court and Judge Anzilotti draw a distinction between ordinary treaties and other international legal obligations, which by their nature limit a state's freedom of action in particular spheres; and, on the other hand, treaties or other international legal obligations that go further and place a state under the legal authority of another state. Only the latter are inconsistent with a state's independence. As the following case demonstrates, however, it is not always easy to distinguish the two.

Case Concerning Rights of Nationals of the United States of America in Morocco (France v United States of America), Judgment, [1952] ICJ Rep 176

[A treaty was concluded between the United States and Morocco in 1836 on certain consular and trade issues. At issue, in part, was whether the establishment of the French Protectorate over Morocco by a subsequent treaty concluded on 30 March 1912, between France and Morocco, affected the 1836 US-Moroccan agreement.]

. . . It is not disputed by the French Government that Morocco, even under the Protectorate, has retained its personality as a State in international law. The rights of France in Morocco are defined by the Protectorate Treaty of 1912. . . .

Under this Treaty, Morocco remained a sovereign State but it made an arrangement of a contractual character whereby France undertook to exercise certain sovereign powers in the name and on behalf of Morocco, and, in principle, all of the international relations of Morocco. France, in the exercise of this function, is bound not only by the provisions of the Treaty . . . , but also by all treaty obligations to which Morocco had been subject before the Protectorate and which have not since been terminated or suspended by arrangement with the interested States. . . .

Considering that the capacity to enter into relations with states is a key criterion of statehood, how would you reconcile Morocco's assignment of the conduct of its international relations to France with its continued existence as a state? Are all protectorates by their nature disqualified from statehood?

One of the most controversial claims of statehood based on alleged independence arose during the apartheid era in South Africa. During that period, the South African government forcibly displaced black South Africans to territorial enclaves known as "Bantu homelands" or "Bantustans," creating the Bantustan states of Transkei, Bophuthatswana, Venda, and Ciskei between 1976 and 1981. One scholar described the policy as follows:

The bantustans marked the formalization of South African racism. . . . The bantustan policy effected the expulsion of black South Africans from developed urban areas — except on limited terms of benefit to whites — and from some eighty-seven percent of all land in the nation, including all of the most fertile and mineral rich property. Black "citizenship" was imposed in the bantustans, with the logical consequence that blacks were stripped of the rights of citizens in the newly constructed white South Africa.[15]

The international community resisted South Africa's claims that these Bantustans constituted states. As part of a 1976 program of action against apartheid, the General Assembly adopted a number of resolutions, including the following:

The So-called Independent Transkei and Other Bantustans, GA Res 31/6 A, UN Doc A/ RES/31/6A (1976)[16]

The General Assembly,

Recalling its resolution 3411 D (XXX) of 28 November 1975 condemning the establishment of bantustans by the racist régime of South Africa,

Taking note that the racist régime of South Africa declared the sham "independence" of the Transkei on 26 October 1976,

Having considered the report of the Special Committee against *Apartheid* and its special reports,

1. *Strongly condemns* the establishment of bantustans as designed to consolidate the inhuman policies of *apartheid*, to destroy the territorial integrity of the country, to perpetuate white minority domination and to dispossess the African people of South Africa of their inalienable rights;

2. *Rejects* the declaration of "independence" of the Transkei and declares it invalid;

3. *Calls upon* all Governments to deny any form of recognition to the so-called independent Transkei and to refrain from having any dealings with the so-called independent Transkei or other bantustans;

4. *Requests* all States to take effective measures to prohibit all individuals, corporations and other institutions under their jurisdiction from having any dealings with the so-called independent Transkei or other bantustans.

Were the Bantustan states truly states? This very question was addressed by the courts of one of these "homelands" in *S v Banda*.[17] At issue was whether members of the Bophuthatswana military could be charged with treason after mounting a coup attempt. The defendants argued that, as Bophuthatswana was not a true state, there could be no charge of treason. The court disagreed, citing the criteria in the Montevideo Convention and observing that Bophuthatswana met each.[18]

---

15   Richard T Ford, "Law's Territory (A History of Jurisdiction)" (1999) 97 Mich L Rev 843 at 914.

16   Reprinted in UN GAOR, 31st Sess, Supp No 39, vol I at 10–11, UN Doc A/31/39 (1977). The General Assembly had earlier condemned South Africa's establishment of the Bantustans and the forcible removal of people to those areas in *Establishment of Bantustans*, GA Res 2775 E (XXVI), reprinted in UN GAOR, 25th Sess, Supp No 29 at 42–43, UN Doc A/8429 (1971).

17   [1989] (4) SALR 519 at 529–31 (Bophuthatswana General Division).

18   See Thomas Grant, "Defining Statehood: The *Montevideo Convention* and its Discontents" (1999) 37 Colum J Transnat'l L 403 at n 126.

Did the Bantustans actually meet the criteria for statehood? While controversy exists in relation to these elements, the Bantustans arguably had a defined territory and a permanent population. They also had governments, albeit highly unstable ones. But as for a capacity to enter into foreign relations, the answer depends on what is meant by capacity. If capacity hinges purely on *de jure* constitutional or legal independence from another state, the Bantustans might have qualified as they did have such formal authority in law. Consider the following:

> Bophuthatswana became independent on 6 December, 1977 pursuant to the [South African] *Status of Boputhatswana Act (No. 89) 1977*. Section 1 states that Bophuthatswana is "declared to be a sovereign and independent State and shall cease to be part of the Republic of South Africa." The latter will accordingly "cease to exercise any authority over the said territory." The *Republic of Bophuthatswana Constitution Act (No. 18) 1977* declares in section 1(1) that Bophuthatswana "is a sovereign independent state and a republic which accepts the principles of democracy and an economy based on private and communal ownership and free enterprise."[19]

Doctrinal international law singles out this *de jure* capacity as an important consideration in assessing the capacity to enter into foreign relations. As the *Restatement of the Law, Third, Foreign Relations Law of the United States* puts it, the entity must have "competence, within its own constitutional system, to conduct international relations with other states, as well as the political, technical, and financial capabilities to do so."[20]

On the other hand, an exclusive focus on *de jure* capacity would be fraught with evident difficulties. In the Bantustan case, South African influence over governance in the Bantustans was dramatic especially in the financial area, belying any claims that the entities were actually independent. To be "independent," and thus meet the "capacity" criterion, a state must surely be more than the puppet of another state. As one scholar notes, independence does not exist where there is "foreign control overbearing the decision-making of the entity concerned on a wide range of matters and doing so systematically and on a continuing basis."[21]

Consider a second difficulty: what if the entity asserting statehood is attempting to secede from an existing state? As part of that attempt, it promulgates its own laws and constitution authorizing it to enter into foreign relations. That law and the capacity it authorizes are contested by the original state, which resists the secession and claims that under the constitutional law that governs the original state—including the secessionist region—both the secession and the secessionist region's foreign relations law are illicit. Such a scenario is not so fantastic for Canadian observers, attuned to the occasionally fractious relationship between Quebec and the rest of Canada. If it were to occur, would it be accurate to say that the secessionist region had the "competence within its own constitutional system" to conduct international relations?

---

19   Nii Lante Wallace-Bruce, *Claims to Statehood in International Law* (New York: Carlton Press, 1994) at 119.
20   *Third Restatement*, above note 2.
21   James Crawford, *Brownlie's Principles of Public International Law*, 8th ed (Oxford: Oxford University Press, 2012) at 130 [*Brownlie's Principles*] [emphasis in original].

In this circumstance, the actual behaviour of the international community in entering into relations (or not) with the putative state would be influential, and perhaps dispositive, of the statehood question. In the case of the Bantustans, even if they exercised power independently, their capacity to enter into foreign relations would have been disputed, as they would have had no opportunity to exercise it. No state other than South Africa recognized the Bantustans as states, and indeed some states strictly avoided any act that could be construed as recognition of the Bantustans. Diplomatic officials from Canada and the United States, for example, refused to enter the Bantustans. In this fashion, the Bantustans were effectively barred from entering into relations with states other than South Africa. In these circumstances, no matter what formal capacity might be asserted, the willingness (or otherwise) of other states to give effect to that capacity by entering into relations with the putative state will be a powerful determinant of the reality or validity of that capacity.

Consider also the controversy over the independence and "statehood" of Taiwan. Some writers argue that Taiwan meets all the requirements for statehood, including a capacity to enter into foreign relations. As one observer put the matter in 1995: "The Taiwanese government's capacity to carry on relations with other states is abundantly clear. It has full diplomatic relations with twenty-nine states. It enters into treaties with these governments and through agreements with them, effectively signs on to multilateral treaties."[22] This passage obviously relies on Taiwan's *de facto* capacity to enter into international relations, albeit with a relatively small number of states. If the practices of twenty-nine states are relevant in assessing Taiwan's capacity to enter into foreign relations, what is one to make of the views of the vast majority of states that refuse to do so notwithstanding Taiwan's persistent efforts in that regard? Note also that commentators who disagree that Taiwan is capable of statehood often point to the island's *de jure* lack of sovereignty in their arguments: "Although politically separated from the Chinese mainland for slightly more than fifty years, Taiwan remains under the sovereignty of China. Even though Taiwan may arguably satisfy the requirement of separateness in the sense that it is maintaining a separate legal order different from that of the mainland, it clearly does not fulfil the requirement of sovereignty."[23] Ultimately, views as to whether Taiwan is a state of its own, distinct from China, depend on an ideological choice in favour of a one China or two Chinas policy.

Canada's position on the issue of Taiwanese statehood was articulated by the Department of Foreign Affairs and International Trade in April 2003, in the context of a case before the Quebec Superior Court. At issue was whether Taiwan was a state, and thus entitled to state immunity under Canadian law; a topic discussed further in Chapter 8. The department explained its position as follows:

> This is in response to your letter of March 19, 2003, in which you requested that a certificate be issued by the Minister or his authorized person under s. 14 of the *State Immunity Act* to establish whether "Taiwan" is a foreign state for the purposes of that Act.

---

22 Cheri Attix, "Between the Devil and the Deep Blue Sea: Are Taiwan's Trading Partners Implying Recognition of Taiwanese Statehood?" (1995) 25 Cal W Int'l LJ 357 at 368.

23 Jianming Shen, "Sovereignty, Statehood, Self-determination, and the Issue of Taiwan" (2000) 15 Am U Int'l L Rev 1101 at 1138–139.

I wish to inform you that the Department cannot respond positively to your request and no such certificate will be issued at this time. Canada has a one-China policy which recognizes the People's Republic of China, with its government located in Beijing, and it has full diplomatic relations with that government. Canada does not have diplomatic relations with "Taiwan" or the "Republic of China."[24]

Notwithstanding the Canadian government's position, the Court concluded in favour of statehood for Taiwan, relying on a mechanical application of the Montevideo Convention criteria:

Parent v Singapore Airlines Ltd, [2003] JQ no 18068 (SC)

¶56 The proof in the present case is conclusive in relation to the four constitutive elements of a state: (1) The island of Taiwan is a defined territory; (2) the island of Taiwan is occupied by a permanent population; (3) an effective government exists in Taiwan and (4) the government of Taiwan enters into relations with other states.

¶57 This reality is notably confirmed elsewhere:
- on the occasion of a declaration made by the Foreign Affairs minister, the Honourable Paul Martin [Sr.], during a speech in Banff entitled "Canada and the Pacific" and reproduced in *The Canadian Yearbook of International Law*, volume VI, 1968:

  We consider that the isolation of Communist China from a large part of normal international relations is dangerous. We are prepared to accept the reality of the victory in mainland China in 1949 . . . . We consider, however, that the effective political independence of Taiwan is a political reality too.

  — The Honourable Paul Martin

- in the conclusion of the text by author D. Barry Kirkham, "The International Legal Status of Formosa," in *The Canadian Yearbook of International Law*:

  Thus, it would appear that the presumption against statehood created by universal non-recognition is capable of being rebutted. It is a strong presumption and the evidence to rebut it would have to be voluminous and cogent. In the case of Formosa evidence is of that sort. The island has been completely independent of any foreign control for seventeen odd years; it has its own government and army; it easily passes all the traditional tests of international law for statehood. The only disabilities are the lack of recognition of a Formosan state, the claims of its own government to be the government of another state of which Formosa is allegedly a part, and its somewhat murky beginnings resulting from political upheaval following the war. None of these disabilities, however, are deemed sufficient to override those factors pointing to Formosan statehood. Thus the conclusion is reached that by international law Formosa has achieved statehood and is accordingly entitled to the rights and subject to the obligations of a state.

---

24 *Parent v Singapore Airlines Ltd*, [2003] JQ no 18068 at para 25 (SC).

- as well as in the *Annuaire français de droit international:*

> Eighteen million inhabitants live on a demarcated territory and are administered by a government whose authority is well established. The island enjoys a political, administrative and social organization similar to that of a state. If the notion of a state stems from effectiveness, Taiwan has all the attributes of a state.

¶58 The Court therefore concludes, for the purposes of the present case, that [Taiwan] has the right to benefit from the immunity anticipated by the law.

Was it appropriate for the Quebec Superior Court to draw conclusions regarding Taiwan's *legal* status from the then Canadian foreign minister's 1968 reference to the "effective *political* independence of Taiwan" as a "*political* reality"? Is it relevant that from 1993 to 2007, the Taipei government was unsuccessful in its various attempts to join the UN as the Republic of China or Taiwan,[25] resulting in its discontinuance of the effort in 2008?

As the discussion above suggests, both formal and factual capacity to enter into international relations are relevant in assessing statehood. This makes the "capacity" criterion a troublesome "chicken-and-egg" concept: capacity to enter into foreign relations is a prerequisite of statehood established, in part, by the successful exercise of such capacity; and yet, the successful exercise of this capacity depends on the willingness of other states to treat the entity as a state and thus enter into such relations with it in the first place. This brings us to an issue that we have so far been skirting: the role of recognition.

2) Recognition of States and Governments

a) Recognition of States

We have suggested at several points above that recognition of an entity as a state by other states is a *practical* necessity for that entity's ability to enjoy one of the chief characteristics of statehood—the capacity to enter into foreign relations. What, however, is the doctrinal significance of recognition by other states? Is such recognition a *legal* necessity for the emergence of a state in international law? Consider the following passage from the *Restatement of the Law, Third, Foreign Relations Law of the United States:*

> 1. *Statehood and recognition.* The literature of international law reflects disagreement as to the significance of the recognition of statehood. Under the "declaratory" theory, an entity that satisfies the requirements of [the Montevideo Convention] is a state with all the corresponding capacities, rights, and duties, and other states have the duty to treat it as such. Recognition by other states is merely "declaratory," confirming that the entity is a state, and expressing the intent to treat it as a state. Another view has been that recognition by other states is "constitutive," i.e., that an entity is not a state in international law unless it is generally recognized as such by other states.[26]

---

25 See further, the transcript of the debate in the General Assembly in 2007: UN Doc A/62/PV.2 at 2–27 (21 September 2007) & UN Doc A/62/PV.3 at 1–12 (21 September 2007).

26 *Third Restatement*, above note 2 at para 202.

The "declaratory" view—probably the prevailing position in modern international legal scholarship—considers satisfaction of the Montevideo Convention criteria as objectively sufficient to constitute the state in law, regardless of positions taken by other states. Recognition by other states, when it comes, is simply an acknowledgement of that legal reality. In contrast, for constitutivists, an entity is not a state under international law until, in addition to satisfying the Montevideo Convention criteria, it is recognized as such by other states. One scholar describes the constitutivist view this way:

> . . . [T]he constitutivist model regards statehood as entirely contingent on recognition by preexisting states. Forcefully stated, "A State is, and becomes, an International Person through recognition only and exclusively." The virtues of this view are twofold: First, it appears to comport better with the traditional conception of international law as *"jus gentium voluntarium*—nothing more than voluntary or consensual behavior, manifest in the practice of states." . . . Second, an entity that lacks recognition by other states remains, in practice, a non-entity. This is because the inquiry into statehood reduces in practice to questions about whether an entity does or should enjoy the incidents of statehood; and these questions, in turn, depend on whether existing states choose to extend these privileges. For this reason, the constitutivist model may at first blush appear more pragmatic than the declaratory model.[27]

Still, constitutivism has its own flaws. Not least, it leaves important doctrinal issues unresolved. For example, how many states must extend recognition in order to elevate an entity to statehood? What if some states actively refuse recognition of an entity? To illustrate, many Arab states have actively and persistently refused to recognize the state of Israel, even though it clearly satisfies the Montevideo Convention criteria. If, under the constitutive model, their refusal to recognize nonetheless sufficed to bar Israel from statehood, the result would be legal incoherence. For instance, the equally sovereign will of other states that had extended recognition would be thwarted. To address this difficulty, one might posit statehood vis-à-vis certain (recognizing) states but not others, although such a form of "relative statehood" seems scarcely reconcilable with reality or with the fundamental international legal principle of the sovereign equality of all states. It would also introduce other profound legal incoherencies of its own: if Israel were not a state vis-à-vis non-recognizing states, it would not owe such states key international legal duties (for example, the duty imposed on states by the UN Charter to refrain from the threat or use of force against other states). Even states refusing to recognize Israel do not go that far.

Some of these difficulties might be resolved by establishing clear thresholds defining the number of recognitions required in order to achieve statehood. Other problems would, however, remain. Constitutivism—because it makes existing states the gatekeepers of statehood—would introduce a vigorous political element into the legal equation of statehood. Historically, constitutivism was associated with a now antiquated view of statehood, one that insisted that entities demonstrate a sufficient level of "civilization" before being "accorded" statehood. The result was a highly select international community composed of

---

27 Robert D Sloane, "The Changing Face of Recognition in International Law: A Case Study of Tibet" (2002) 16 Emory Int'l L Rev 107 at 116–17.

states reflecting a Eurocentric conception of civilization, and the relegation of other human communities to legal categories amenable to exploitation and colonial domination.

As the example of Israel illustrates, politics remain an inevitable consideration in state recognition practices to this day. The question is whether to imbue such political considerations with juridical consequences. Consider the following once "secret" memorandum, illustrating Canada's own recognition practices:

Memorandum from Acting Secretary of State for External Affairs to Cabinet, Ottawa, 1 November 1952[28]

RECOGNITION OF VIETNAM, LAOS AND CAMBODIA

... When it previously considered this question on February 23, 1950, the Cabinet agreed with the recommendation that "recognition be not extended at this time to the Indochinese states," although some encouragement to the French and to the new states was given in a sympathetic reference to their establishment in a statement to the House. Since then, the French have continued to urge Canada to extend recognition to the three states and the question has been frequently under review in the Department. Indochina continues to be one of the most critical soft spots in Asia which the Communists are probing. The struggle being waged by the French and Indochinese to hold them in check is relentless and costly. In the context of the cold war, particularly of its intensification in Asia, there is now some political urgency for Canada to reconsider its stand on Indochina. ...

3. The United Kingdom, in extending recognition early in 1950, employed the following formula:

> His Majesty's Government in the United Kingdom recognizes the status of Vietnam as an Associate State within the French Union in accordance with the terms of the Agreement dated March 8, 1949, between President Auriol and His Majesty Bao Dai and recognizes the Government of His Majesty Bao Dai as the Government of that state.

This formula was adopted by a number of other states including Australia, New Zealand and the Union of South Africa, and falls considerably short of full recognition of a sovereign state and government. The United States extended "diplomatic recognition" without qualification or explanation.

4. *Factors for recognition*

The military forecast for 1953 points to a continued stalemate in Indochina. There is reliable evidence that France is facing grave difficulties in supporting major military efforts in both Europe and Indochina and in maintaining its position in North Africa. If present trends continue, they may in the long run weaken the French Union's ability and determination to continue resistance in Indochina. Accordingly, any encouragement which can be given to the Franco Vietnamese forces to hold on would be desirable.

5. The opinion is widely held in France that it is getting the short end of the stick in its NATO association; while the French alone must bear the responsibility of safeguarding

---

28 Reprinted in *Documents on Canadian External Relations*, vol 18, No 1008.

western strategic interests in Indochina, they are being asked to make increased efforts to meet NATO commitments, to approve German rearmament and to work harder toward European unity—under the shadow of severe criticism of their colonial policy on Tunisia and Morocco. Anything Canada could do at this time to improve French morale would no doubt be of assistance in helping them to bear these burdens.

6. Thirty-three governments have thus far recognized the Government of Bao Dai. The list includes the majority of Canada's NATO colleagues, who, would no doubt welcome Canadian recognition as moral support for France, and ultimately for NATO. Such a move would contribute towards a manifestation of the political solidarity of the democracies on cold war problems in Asia.

7. In the Council for Technical Co-operation of the Colombo Plan, Canada has in effect had direct dealings with representatives of Vietnam, Laos, and Cambodia, now full members of the Council. Canada has also voted in favour of the admission of these three states to a number of the United Nations Specialized Agencies. Whereas neither of these actions necessarily constitutes recognition by Canada, they have likely been interpreted by the states concerned as indicating a possible trend in that direction. Moreover, at the present session of the General Assembly, Canada will, if the issue is raised, support the admission to the United Nations of these three states. This might be interpreted as constituting implied recognition by Canada.

8. *Factors against recognition*
Vietnam, Laos and Cambodia do not fulfil the customary legal requirements for the recognition of states. Nor do their governments fulfil the customary legal requirements for the recognition of governments. Since the signing of the 1949 agreements, whereby France granted considerable independence in domestic matters but retained a large measure of control over foreign affairs, defence and finance, there has been little change in the basis of this relationship; and in practice the three states cannot be considered as independent. The present indications are that this situation is likely to continue for some time to come.

9. The strongest argument against recognition is the negative attitude of the other non-Communist states of Asia (excluding South Korea and Thailand) and of the Middle East (excluding Jordan). Their refusal to recognize the Indochinese states seems to be based primarily on distrust of French intentions. Canadian action at this time to recognize the states of Vietnam, Laos and Cambodia and their governments might attract unfavourable attention in a number of other Asian and Middle East States, particularly in India and Pakistan, and might weaken our advantageous position as a "neutral" on colonial questions. The undesirable "white versus Asian" alignment, already too prevalent in the Commonwealth, might recur on this issue.

10. Recognition would probably mean little to the governments concerned, unless it were accompanied with more concrete assistance.

11. *Recommendations*
In essence the question of recognizing the states of Vietnam, Laos and Cambodia and their governments is one in which our reluctance to recognize governments, which do not fulfil the customary legal requirements and which are frowned upon by most of the

neighbouring countries in Asia, must be weighed against our desire to assist a NATO colleague, sorely tried by foreign and domestic problems, and to bolster such limited independence as the governments themselves now possess. My opinion is that the political factors, in particular the NATO considerations, override the legal and other objections. I am therefore recommending that Canada extend recognition to Vietnam, Laos and Cambodia.

12. My recommendation is qualified by the suggestion that we grant recognition in accordance with the formula adopted by the United Kingdom and other states, that is, that Canada recognize each of the Indochinese states as "an Associate State within the French Union in accordance with the terms of the Agreement dated March 8, 1949, between President Auriol and His Majesty Bao Dai and recognizes the Government of His Majesty Bao Dai as the government of that state." Recognition would then not constitute recognition, in the usual sense of the word, of three new, fully sovereign states in the international community and of fully independent governments, but would only constitute a recognition of treaty arrangements.

13. Moreover, careful consideration should be given to the timing of a notification of Canadian recognition. In order to minimize the undesirable effect of such recognition in friendly Asian countries, the announcement might be timed so as not to coincide with the results of voting in the General Assembly on issues, on which Canada might be obliged to take a stand opposite to that of friendly Asian countries, especially India and Pakistan.

The Canadian approach to recognition as a result of the collapsing French colonies in Southeast Asia was clearly guided by considerations of *realpolitik*. Consider also more recent examples of the politics of state recognition. On 26 August 2008, Russia recognized the independent statehood of the breakaway Georgian provinces of South Ossetia and Abkhazia.[29] In statements made by the Russian president, and by Russia's representative in the UN Security Council, these acts of recognition were justified on the basis of Georgia's history of violent attempts to assert control over the provinces (including Georgia's August 2008 offensive in South Ossetia), the alleged genocide of the South Ossetian and Abkhazian peoples by Georgia, the "freely expressed will of the Ossetian and Abkhaz peoples" to be independent of Georgia, and their "right to decide their destiny by themselves."[30] Some commentators also drew comparisons to the recognition of Kosovo by Western states, discussed below.[31]

To date, few states have joined Russia in recognizing the independence of South Ossetia and Abkhazia. Instead, the Russian acts of recognition have been widely condemned by many states and regional organizations (including the European Union, the OSCE, NATO, and the G7) on the basis that they are inconsistent with the obligation to respect Georgia's political and territorial integrity; the duty not to intervene in Georgia's domes-

---

29 Clifford J Levy, "Russia Backs Independence of Georgian Enclaves," *New York Times* (26 August 2008).

30 Government of Russia, Statement by President of Russia Dmitry Medvedev (26 August 2008), online: http://archive.kremlin.ru/eng/speeches/2008/08/26/1543_type82912_205752.shtml.

31 But see, "South Ossetia is not Kosovo," *The Economist* (28 August 2008) 1.

tic affairs; and UN Security Council resolutions affirming the sovereignty, independence, and territorial integrity of Georgia within its internationally recognized borders. Most of these states and organizations had already condemned, on the same grounds, the large-scale military operation undertaken by Russia on Georgian territory, beginning on 8 August 2008, in purported support of South Ossetia's and Abkhazia's right of self-determination. This brief war prompted Georgia to institute proceedings against Russia in the International Court of Justice (ICJ) under the International Convention on the Elimination of All Forms of Racial Discrimination[32] (discussed further in Section B(2)(v) below). While active hostilities between Russian and Georgian troops ceased in early October 2008, Russia maintains a considerable troop presence in South Ossetia and Abkhazia.

Another controversy arose following the 2008 unilateral declaration of independence by Kosovo, a long-time province of Serbia. States varied enormously in their responses to this declaration and their preparedness to recognize Kosovo as a new state. As described by one analyst in 2011:

> Only 75 out of 192 states have recognized the new state. Though the International Court of Justice ruled that Kosovo's declaration of independence was not illegal under international law [a matter discussed in Chapter 4], about two thirds of the international community is reluctant to establish formal contacts. Most recently, Oman, Guinea Bissau, and Qatar established diplomatic relations.
>
> The EU is divided: Greece, Romania, Spain, Cyprus, and Slovakia rejected a joint EU decision on Kosovo's status. Africa, South America, the Middle East, and Asia simply do not have Kosovo on their radar.
>
> Legally, there is no fixed number of recognitions at which a country becomes internationally accepted. For UN membership, the Security Council must agree. Admission, however, is difficult at the moment because Russia or China would likely use their veto power. Russian UN envoy Vitaly Churkin has already made clear that Moscow will not allow the cancelation of UN Resolution 1244, which confirms Serbia's territorial integrity. At the same time, however, Russia has recognized the independence of Georgia's breakaway regions Abkhazia and South Ossetia.[33]

The typically political nature of state recognition practices makes constitutivism an unattractive legal theory of statehood. As one scholar puts it:

> At the theoretical level . . . to reduce the international law of recognition to a pure matter of political will eviscerates its status as law. . . . "[S]ome concession to the *realpolitik* of international relations is essential if international law is to be taken seriously as a framework for actual state behavior" but at the same time, "establishment of a meaningful international law of peace and security requires the collective denial of recognition of

---

32 7 March 1966, 660 UNTS 195, Can TS 1970 No 28, in force 4 January 1969.
33 Martin Waehlisch & Behar Xharra, "Three Years After Independence, Kosovo Struggles for Recognition," *Radio Free Europe* (17 February 2011), online: www.rferl.org/content/commentary_kosovo_third_anniversary/2312109.html. As of 1 January 2013, that number had risen to 91 out of 193 UN Member States, according to the President of the Republic of Kosovo, Atifeti Jahjaga, online: www.president-ksgov.net/?page=2,54.

the fruits of illegal acts; otherwise, violations of international law are permitted to create rights in international law."[34]

Put another way, a pure declaratory position naively resists acknowledging the essential role played by states in actually extending the benefits of statehood. An entity that fails to attract state recognition is, like the South African Bantustans, factually incapable of entering into international relations. On the other hand, a pure constitutivist position would allow existing states to play political games by denying statehood to entities that, by every objective measure, should be accorded that status. The result could be both inequitable and potentially destabilizing.

Is there a middle ground between these two equally unpalatable poles? One possibility would be to constrain the political discretion of states to extend or withhold recognition by requiring them to apply reasonable and relatively objective criteria to such decisions. Many states do apply criteria drawn from the four factors listed in the Montevideo Convention. Others have gone further. Consider the approach to recognition employed by the European Community (now the European Union) in relation to states emerging from the former Soviet Bloc in the 1990s:

Declaration on the "Guidelines on the Recognition of New States in Eastern Europe and in the Soviet Union" (16 December 1991), (1992) 31 ILM 1486–487

In compliance with the European Council's request, Ministers have assessed developments in Eastern Europe and the Soviet Union with a view to elaborating an approach regarding relations with new states.

In this connection they have adopted the following guidelines on the formal recognition of new states in Eastern Europe and in the Soviet Union:

The Community and its Member States confirm their attachment to the principles of the Helsinki Final Act and the Charter of Paris, in particular the principle of self-determination. They affirm their readiness to recognize, subject to the normal standards of international practice and the political realities in each case, those new States which, following the historic changes in the region, have constituted themselves on a democratic basis, have accepted the appropriate international obligations and have committed themselves in good faith to a peaceful process and to negotiations.

Therefore, they adopt a common position on the process of recognition of these new States, which requires:

- respect for the provisions of the Charter of the United Nations and the commitments subscribed to in the Final Act of Helsinki and in the Charter of Paris, especially with regard to the rule of law, democracy and human rights
- guarantees for the rights of ethnic and national groups and minorities in accordance with the commitments subscribed to in the framework of the CSCE[35]

---

34 Sloane, above note 27 at 117–18.
35 The Conference on Security and Cooperation in Europe (CSCE), now the Organization for Security and Cooperation in Europe (OSCE), was established as part of the 1975 Helsinki process. The Conference reflected a then *détente* between the Western and Soviet Bloc and incorporated human rights, security,

- respect for the inviolability of all frontiers which can only be changed by peaceful means and by common agreement
- acceptance of all relevant commitments with regard to disarmament and nuclear non-proliferation as well as to security and regional stability
- commitment to settle by agreement, including where appropriate by recourse to arbitration, all questions concerning State succession and regional disputes.

The Community and its Member States will not recognize entities which are the result of aggression. They would take account of the effects of recognition on neighbouring States.

The commitment to these principles opens the way to recognition by the Community and its Member States and to the establishment of diplomatic relations. It could be laid down in agreements.

The European approach to recognition—while it has not always been applied consistently—has important implications. First, the experience in Eastern Europe "seems to point towards a trend to attempt to constitute states through the process of recognition."[36] Second, the European recognition criteria, if widely adopted, would effectively impose new criteria for statehood tied to such considerations as respect for human rights. This would be true either because of the re-emergence of a constitutivist approach or simply as a practical matter because state recognition is required if the would-be state is to partake in international relations. One commentator makes this observation:

> It now seems that the "political realities" have gained primacy over the inclinations to maintain consistency by applying accepted criteria to test the fact of statehood. This should not be seen as necessarily a negative development. The application of the traditional criteria as the test for statehood and therefore the rationale behind recognition was largely amoral. How a government came to be in effective control over its territory was, for the most part, not considered to be a relevant factor. The adoption of conditions leading to recognition is an attempt to introduce a greater moral dimension.[37]

b) Recognition of Governments

Recognition of states should not be confused with recognition of governments. While recognition of states relates to the emergence of new states on the international scene, recognition of governments relates to the new governments of *existing* states. Like state recognition, whether to recognize a particular government in an existing state is a political decision

---

and economic cooperation provisions through declaratory statements of political intent and commitment found in a non-binding Final Act. In November 1990, following the adoption of the Charter of Paris, the CSCE was converted into the more permanent OSCE, headed by a Council of Foreign Ministers. The OSCE includes all European countries, Canada, and the United States.

36 Roland Rich, "Recognition of States: The Collapse of Yugoslavia and the Soviet Union" (1993) 4 EJIL 36 at 65. See also Karen Knop, "The 'Righting' of Recognition: Recognition of States in Eastern Europe and the Soviet Union" in Yves LeBouthillier et al, eds, *Selected Papers in International Law: Contribution of the Canadian Council on International Law* (The Hague: Kluwer, 1999) 261.

37 Rich, above note 36 at 64.

made by other states. Unlike state recognition, however, recognition of governments has no formal or legal significance for the existence of the state itself.[38] One scholar puts it this way:

> To specify legal criteria for governmental recognition proves even more theoretically difficult [than for state recognition], for two principal reasons: the debate over whether governmental recognition is indeed a legal question at all (or whether, by contrast, it is properly understood as purely political); and second, the question of the meaning of "recognition." Recognition generally lies within the discretion of sovereigns. Most scholars and statesmen agree that international law does not provide unequivocal criteria that establish a duty of recognition under certain circumstances. The conventional view is that "recognition, as a public act of state, is an optional and political act and there is no legal duty in this regard." Decisions to recognize or refuse recognition to governments remain sovereign prerogatives, exercised "in accordance with [each state's] policy objectives and ideologies."[39]

Recognition of governments does, however, raise significant international legal issues that are not directly related to the ascertainment of statehood per se. For instance, as discussed in the introduction and in greater detail below, one of the core attributes of all states is sovereignty, which has as one of its corollaries the international legal rule that states are not to interfere in the internal affairs of other states. How can this rule be reconciled with the act, by one state, of recognizing or refusing to recognize the government of another? Is such a decision not inherently a pronouncement on the validity of a sovereign state's political order? Recognizing this difficulty and sensitive to a long history of US interference in the internal affairs of Latin American states, Mexico proposed the "Estrada Doctrine" of government recognition in 1930:

Estrada Doctrine of Recognition, (1931) 25 AJIL Supp 203

Declaration of Señor Don Genaro Estrada, Secretary of Foreign Relations of Mexico, published in the press on September 27, 1930, relating to the express recognition of governments.

Because of changes which have occurred in the régimes of some South American countries, the Government of Mexico has once more been obliged to put into effect, for its own part, the so-called theory of the "recognition" of governments.

It is a well-known fact that some years ago Mexico suffered, as few nations have, from the consequences of that doctrine, which allows foreign governments to pass upon the legitimacy or illegitimacy of the régime existing in another country, with the result that situations arise in which the legal qualifications or national status of governments or authorities are apparently made subject to the opinion of foreigners.

Ever since the Great War, the doctrine of so-called "recognitions" has been applied in particular to the nations of this continent, although in well-known cases of change of régime occurring in European countries the governments of the nations have not made

---

38 We therefore raise it here only for purposes of distinguishing it from the recognition of states.
39 Sloane, above note 27 at 120.

express declarations of recognition; consequently, the system has been changing into a special practice applicable to the Latin American Republics.

After a very careful study of the subject, the Government of Mexico has transmitted instructions to its Ministers or Chargés d'Affaires in the countries affected by the recent political crises, informing them that the Mexican Government is issuing no declarations in the sense of grants of recognition, since that nation considers that such a course is an insulting practice and one which, in addition to the fact that, it offends the sovereignty of other nations, implies that judgment of some sort may be passed upon the internal affairs of those nations by other governments, inasmuch as the latter assume . . . an attitude of criticism, when they decide, favourably or unfavourably, as to the legal qualifications of foreign régimes.

Therefore, the Government of Mexico confines itself to the maintenance or withdrawal, as it may deem advisable, of its diplomatic agents, and to the continued acceptance, also when it may deem advisable, of such similar accredited diplomatic agents as the respective nations may have in Mexico; and in so doing, it does not pronounce judgment, either precipitately or a posteriori, regarding the right of foreign nations to accept, maintain or replace their governments or authorities. Naturally, in so far as concerns the usual formulas for accrediting and receiving agents and for the exchange of signed letters of Heads of Governments and Chancellors, the Mexican Government will continue to use the same formulas accepted up to the present time by international law and diplomatic law.

The Estrada Doctrine represents the most common approach in modern international relations to the issue of recognition of governments. Essentially, it prescribes that there shall be no such recognition at all, such that no adverse inferences may be drawn from a state's failure to endorse any particular foreign government. But consider the consequences of such a hands-off policy. Should states not distinguish between governments that abide by international and domestic law and those that establish repressive regimes or come to power by undemocratic means? Contrast the Estrada Doctrine with the approach proposed in the 1920s by Dr Julio Tobar Donoso, a former minister of foreign affairs of Ecuador: "The American Republics for the sake of their good name and credit apart from other humanitarian or altruistic considerations, should intervene indirectly in the internal dissensions of the Republics of the Continent. Such intervention might consist at least in the non-recognition of *de facto*, revolutionary governments created contrary to the constitution."[40]

As international society moves towards a global consciousness and as our understanding of the ambit of the "internal" affairs of states evolves, the Tobar Doctrine may have more appeal than does the Estrada approach. Estrada would compel silence on the governmental legitimacy of the Islamic fundamentalist Taliban regime in Afghanistan, the *de facto* government of that state from 1996 to 2001. Tobar would not. When asked whether Canada would make a firm commitment to not extend recognition to the Taliban, then Canadian Minister of Foreign Affairs Lloyd Axworthy advised the House of Commons that "in any recognition we would take into account the values, the stands and the behaviour

---

40   Cited in Philip Marshall Brown, "The Legal Effects of Recognition" (1950) 44 Am J Int'l L 617 at 621.

of the recipient state."[41] Yet, in the end, in accordance with its practice (since 1988) of adhering to the Estrada Doctrine, Canada was silent on recognition of the Taliban. But, like most states, it also did not have diplomatic relations with the group. Consider also the approach urged by the US Senate, in a 1999 resolution:

> *Resolved, That it is the sense of the Senate that* —
>
> (1) the President should instruct the United States Representative to the United Nations to use all appropriate means to prevent any Taliban-led government in Afghanistan from obtaining the seat in the United Nations General Assembly reserved for Afghanistan so long as gross violations of internationally recognized human rights against women and girls persist; and
>
> (2) the United States should refuse to recognize any government in Afghanistan which is not taking actions to achieve the following goals in Afghanistan:
>
> (A) The effective participation of women in all civil, economic, and social life.
>
> (B) The right of women to work.
>
> (C) The right of women and girls to an education without discrimination and the reopening of schools to women and girls at all levels of education.
>
> (D) The freedom of movement of women and girls.
>
> (E) Equal access of women and girls to health facilities.
>
> (F) Equal access of women and girls to humanitarian aid.[42]

The issue raised by section 2 of this resolution is whether any such refusal to recognize the Taliban government would, in itself, have any practical or legal effect. Refusal to recognize a would-be state may, as we have seen above, have some significance for its chances of acceding to statehood. No such significance would attach to recognition (or "non-recognition") of a new government in an existing state, however. At most, such a statement would merely signal political approval or disapproval of the regime, which admittedly might play some role in encouraging it to abide by, for instance, international human rights standards. However, as suggested in section 1 of the US Senate resolution, states have other means at their disposal by which to achieve this same end, means that do not expose them to criticism for interfering in the domestic affairs of other states. For example, as the actual practice of most states in relation to the Taliban *de facto* government shows, many states following the Estrada Doctrine nevertheless choose to express their disapproval of a foreign government by curtailing or refusing to maintain diplomatic or other relations with it:

> [The Estrada Doctrine] still accommodates expression of disapproval toward a given government, but this is done by refusal to establish diplomatic relations, a purely optional step in any event. Moreover, the United States, though sometimes cited as an exception to this policy, parallels the shift seen in the practice of many States: "In recent years, U.S. practice has been to de-emphasize and avoid the use of recognition in cases of changes of government and to concern ourselves with the question of whether we wish to have

---

41 Canada, House of Commons, 35th Parliament, Debates (30 September 1996) at 4863 (Lloyd Axworthy).

42 US, S Res 68, "A resolution expressing the sense of the Senate regarding the treatment of women and girls by the Taliban in Afghanistan," 106th Cong, 1999.

diplomatic relations with the new governments." To an extent, then, the earlier function of recognizing—or not recognizing—governments has been folded into the institution of diplomatic relations.[43]

Avoiding recognition or non-recognition of "governments" per se also affords diplomatic flexibility where states wish to express political support for an internal opposition movement that has not yet consolidated effective control of a state that has descended into civil conflict. For example, in December 2012, the United States "recognized the Syrian Opposition Council as *the* legitimate representative of the Syrian people" and invited the Opposition Council to establish ties with Washington.[44] Note the careful use of the term "representative" rather than "government." Such a move was expressly tied to the US desire to see the incumbent Syrian government of Bashar al-Assad, widely condemned for atrocities perpetrated against Syrian civilians yet still in power, replaced.

Such practices, then, allow states to avoid the direct intrusion into the ostensibly internal affairs of other states entailed by recognition (or not) of their governments, while still expressing indirect approval or disapproval of their governments themselves. For present purposes, however, such practices have no direct effect on the legal existence of the states putatively controlled by such governments.

3) Changes in States and Governments

What are the international legal consequences of the emergence of a new state on the international scene, or of a new government displacing an old one within an existing state? These are distinct issues which raise the doctrines of state succession and state continuity respectively.

a) State Succession

Broadly speaking, state succession is the body of international law dealing with the consequences of the demise and emergence of states. What legal obligations and rights does a new state have when it first emerges, and what happens to those of an existing state that merges with another state or otherwise ceases to exist?

With respect to customary international legal rights and obligations, the answer is straightforward: customary international law is presumptively binding on all states, old and new. Further, as we have already seen above, for a state to escape the universally binding effect of a rule of customary international law, it must persistently object to that rule from the time of the rule's inception. Thus, where a rule of customary international law already exists at the time of emergence of a new state, that state is in no position to be a persistent objector and will be bound by the rule along with all other states.

The situation with respect to treaty rights and obligations is somewhat more complex, as we shall now see.

---

43   Crawford, above note 12 at 152.
44   William J Burns, US Deputy Secretary of State, "Remarks to the Friends of the Syrian People," delivered in Marrakech, Morocco, 12 December 2012, online: www.state.gov/s/d/2012/201818.htm [emphasis in original].

i) Succession and Treaties

The Vienna Convention on Succession of States in Respect of Treaties, concluded in 1978 based on a draft convention prepared by the International Law Commission, provides a starting point for our examination of state succession to treaty rights and obligations (although it should be noted at the outset that the Convention has few states parties). Consider the following provisions.

> **Vienna Convention on Succession of States in Respect of Treaties, 23 August 1978, 146 UNTS 3, in force 6 November 1996**
>
> *Article 2*
> *Use of terms*
> 1. For the purposes of the present Convention . . .
>   (f) "newly independent State" means a successor State the territory of which immediately before the date of the succession of States was a dependent territory for the international relations of which the predecessor State was responsible. . . .
>
> *Article 8*
> *Agreements for the devolution of treaty obligations or rights from a predecessor State to a successor State*
> 1. The obligations or rights of a predecessor State under treaties in force in respect of a territory at the date of a succession of States do not become the obligations or rights of the successor State towards other States parties to those treaties by reason only of the fact that the predecessor State and the successor State have concluded an agreement providing that such obligations or rights shall devolve upon the successor State. . . .
>
> *Article 9*
> *Unilateral declaration by a successor State regarding treaties of the predecessor State*
> 1. Obligations or rights under treaties in force in respect of a territory at the date of a succession of States do not become the obligations or rights of the successor State . . . by reason only of the fact that the successor State has made a unilateral declaration providing for the continuance in force of the treaties in respect of its territory. . . .
>
> *Article 11*
> *Boundary regimes*
> A succession of States does not as such affect:
>   (a) a boundary established by a treaty; or
>   (b) obligations and rights established by a treaty and relating to the regime of a boundary.
>
> *Article 12*
> *Other territorial regimes*
> 1. A succession of States does not as such affect:
>   (a) obligations relating to the use of any territory, or to restrictions upon its use, established by a treaty for the benefit of any territory of a foreign State and considered as attaching to the territories in question. . . .

3. The provisions of the present article do not apply to treaty obligations of the predecessor State providing for the establishment of foreign military bases on the territory to which the succession of States relates. . . .

Article 15
Succession in respect of part of territory

When part of the territory of a State . . . becomes part of the territory of another State:

(a) treaties of the predecessor State cease to be in force in respect of the territory to which the succession of States . . . ; and

(b) treaties of the successor State are in force in respect of the territory to which the succession of States relates . . . ; unless it appears from the treaty or is otherwise established that the application of the treaty to that territory would be incompatible with the object and purpose of the treaty or would radically change the conditions for its operation.

Article 16
Position in respect of the treaties of the predecessor State

A newly independent State is not bound to maintain in force, or to become a party to, any treaty by reason only of the fact that at the date of the succession of States the treaty was in force in respect of the territory to which the succession of States relates. . . .

Article 17
Participation in treaties in force at the date of the succession of States

1. Subject to paragraphs 2 and 3, a newly independent State may, by a notification of succession, establish its status as a party to any multilateral treaty which at the date of the succession of States was in force in respect of the territory to which the succession of States relates.

2. Paragraph 1 does not apply if it appears from the treaty or is otherwise established that the application of the treaty in respect of the newly independent State would be incompatible with the object and purpose of the treaty or would radically change the conditions for its operation.

3. When, under the terms of the treaty or by reason of the limited number of the negotiating States and the object and purpose of the treaty, the participation of any other State in the treaty must be considered as requiring the consent of all the parties, the newly independent State may establish its status as a party to the treaty only with such consent. . . .

Article 24
Conditions under which a treaty is considered as being in force in the case of a succession of States

1. A bilateral treaty which at the date of a succession of States was in force in respect of the territory to which the succession of States relates is considered as being in force between a newly independent State and the other State party when:

(a) they expressly so agree; or

(b) by reason of their conduct they are to be considered as having so agreed. . . .

Article 31

Effects of a uniting of States in respect of treaties in force at the date of the succession of States

1. When two or more States unite and so form one successor State, any treaty in force at the date of the succession of States in respect of any of them continues in force in respect of the successor State unless:

(a) the successor State and the other State party or States parties otherwise agree; or

(b) it appears from the treaty or is otherwise established that the application of the treaty in respect of the successor State would be incompatible with the object and purpose of the treaty or would radically change the conditions for its operation.

2. Any treaty continuing in force in conformity with paragraph 1 shall apply only in respect of the part of the territory of the successor State in respect of which the treaty was in force at the date of the succession of States unless:

(a) in the case of a multilateral treaty not falling within the category mentioned in article 17, paragraph 3, the successor State makes a notification that the treaty shall apply in respect of its entire territory;

(b) in the case of a multilateral treaty falling within the category mentioned in article 17, paragraph 3, the successor State and the other States parties otherwise agree; or

(c) in the case of a bilateral treaty, the successor State and the other State party otherwise agree.

3. Paragraph 2(a) does not apply if it appears from the treaty or is otherwise established that the application of the treaty in respect of the entire territory of the successor State would be incompatible with the object and purpose of the treaty or would radically change the conditions for its operation. . . .

Article 34

Succession of States in cases of separation of parts of a State

1. When a part or parts of the territory of a State separate to form one or more States, whether or not the predecessor State continues to exist:

(a) any treaty in force at the date of the succession of States in respect of the entire territory of the predecessor State continues in force in respect of each successor State so formed;

(b) any treaty in force at the date of the succession of States in respect only of that part of the territory of the predecessor State which has become a successor State continues in force in respect of that successor State alone.

2. Paragraph 1 does not apply if:

(a) the States concerned otherwise agree; or

(b) it appears from the treaty or is otherwise established that the application of the treaty in respect of the successor State would be incompatible with the object and purpose of the treaty or would radically change the conditions for its operation. . . .

The expression "newly independent State," as defined in the Vienna Convention on Succession of States in Respect of Treaties, is a euphemism for former colonies. With respect to these former colonies, Article 16 of the Convention adopts a "non-transmissibility" or "clean slate" approach to treaty obligations entered into by the predecessor state.

In other words, former colonies are not automatically parties to treaties entered into by their former colonial rulers.

In contrast, Articles 31 and 34 of the Convention apply a different rule, referred to as the "transmissibility" approach, with respect to new states other than former colonies. However, the transmissibility approach is not widely accepted by the international community and likely does not reflect customary international law. Instead, the "clean slate" approach appears to be much more widely accepted as the rule applicable to *all* types of new states.

Another controversial distinction introduced by the Convention between the position of newly independent states and other new states is the ability of the former unilaterally to declare themselves parties to certain multilateral treaties to which their former colonial rulers were parties (see Article 17). By contrast, Article 9 sets out the general rule for other new states, namely that such unilateral declarations do not suffice in themselves to "transmit" the treaties of the predecessor to the successor state. Given the essentially contractual nature of the law of treaties, it is in fact this latter rule that is generally considered applicable in customary international law to all new states without distinction. As one commentator states:

> When a new state emerges it is not bound by the treaties of the predecessor sovereign by virtue of a principle of state succession. . . . [A]s a matter of general principle a new state, *ex hypothesi* a non-party, cannot be bound by a treaty, and in addition other parties to a treaty are not bound to accept a new party, as it were, by operation of law. . . .
>
> The rule of non-transmissibility applies both to secession of 'newly independent states' . . . and to other appearances of new states by the union or dissolution of states. The distinctions drawn by. . . the Vienna Convention on Succession of States in Respect of Treaties are not reflected in the practice of states.[45]

Likely for these reasons, the Vienna Convention on Succession of States in Respect of Treaties has only twenty-two parties at the time of writing, although the remainder of its provisions are largely uncontroversial and likely correspond in large measure to customary international law.

The dominant rule of non-transmissibility does not necessarily mean that a new state may never become a party to a treaty ratified or acceded to by a predecessor state. Rather, it really only means that this does not happen automatically, as an inherent consequence of succession. Once established, a new state would be free to become a party to the treaty in accordance with its terms and the general law of treaties. In some cases, particularly with respect to bilateral, regional, or defence treaties, or treaties constituting intergovernmental organizations, this might require the consent, tacit or otherwise, of other parties to the treaty. In other cases, however, such as multilateral "law-making" treaties that remain open to new parties, the new state need merely communicate its intention, in some appropriate way, to become bound by the treaty.

Note also how the non-transmissibility rule is tempered, in Articles 11 and 12 of the Vienna Convention on Succession of States in Respect of Treaties, in the case of treaties dealing with boundary or other "territorial" regimes. Both these exceptions to the non-

---

45 *Brownlie's Principles*, above note 21 at 438.

transmissibility rule are well established in customary international law, as illustrated in the following decisions of the International Court of Justice.

Gabčíkovo-Nagymaros Project (Hungary/Slovakia), Judgment, [1997] ICJ Rep 7

. . . The present case arose out of the signature, on 16 September 1977, by the Hungarian People's Republic and the Czechoslovak People's Republic, of a treaty "concerning the construction and operation of the Gabčíkovo-Nagymaros System of Locks" (hereinafter called the "1977 Treaty"). . . . The 1977 Treaty entered into force on 30 June 1978. It provides for the construction and operation of a System of Locks by the parties as a "joint investment." . . . The joint investment was . . . essentially aimed at the production of hydroelectricity, the improvement of navigation on the relevant section of the Danube and the protection of the areas along the banks against flooding. . . .

On 1 January 1993 Slovakia became an independent State. . . .

The Court must . . . turn to the question whether Slovakia became a party to the 1977 Treaty as successor to Czechoslovakia. . . .

According to Hungary, "There is no rule of international law which provides for automatic succession to bilateral treaties on the disappearance of a party" and such a treaty will not survive unless another State succeeds to it by express agreement between that State and the remaining party. . . .

Hungary claimed that there was no rule of succession which could operate in the present case to override the absence of consent. Referring to Article 34 of the Vienna Convention of 23 August 1978 on Succession of States in respect of Treaties, in which "a rule of automatic succession to all treaties is provided for," based on the principle of continuity, Hungary argued not only that it never signed or ratified the Convention, but that the "concept of automatic succession" contained in that Article was not and is not, and has never been accepted as, a statement of general international law. . . .

Slovakia acknowledged that there was no agreement on succession to the Treaty between itself and Hungary. It relied instead, in the first place, on the "general rule of continuity which applies in the case of dissolution"; it argued, secondly, that the Treaty is one "attaching to [the] territory" within the meaning of Article 12 of the 1978 Vienna Convention, and that it contains provisions relating to a boundary. . . .

The Court does not find it necessary for the purposes of the present case to enter into a discussion of whether or not Article 34 of the 1978 Convention reflects the state of customary international law. More relevant to its present analysis is the particular nature and character of the 1977 Treaty. An examination of this Treaty confirms that, aside from its undoubted nature as a joint investment, its major elements were the proposed construction and joint operation of a large, integrated and indivisible complex of structures and installations on specific parts of the respective territories of Hungary and Czechoslovakia along the Danube. The Treaty also established the navigational régime for an important sector of an international waterway, in particular the relocation of the main international shipping lane to the bypass canal. In so doing, it inescapably created a situation in which the interests of other users of the Danube were affected. . . .

In its Commentary on the Draft Articles on Succession of States in respect of Treaties, adopted at its twenty-sixth session, the International Law Commission identified "treaties of a territorial character" as having been regarded both in traditional doctrine and in modern opinion as unaffected by a succession of States. ... The draft text of Article 12, which reflects this principle, was subsequently adopted unchanged in the 1978 Vienna Convention. The Court considers that Article 12 reflects a rule of customary international law; it notes that neither of the Parties disputed this. Moreover, the Commission indicated that "treaties concerning water rights or navigation on rivers are commonly regarded as candidates for inclusion in the category of territorial treaties." ... Taking all these factors into account, the Court finds that the content of the 1977 Treaty indicates that it must be regarded as establishing a territorial régime within the meaning of Article 12 of 1978 Vienna Convention. It created rights and obligations "attaching to" the parts of the Danube to which it relates; thus the Treaty itself cannot be affected by a succession of States. The Court therefore concludes that the 1977 Treaty became binding upon Slovakia on 1 January 1993. ...

Territorial Dispute (Libyan Arab Jamahiriya/Chad), Judgment, [1994] ICJ Rep 6

[A border dispute arose between Libya and Chad. At issue, in part, was the impact of the 1955 Treaty of Friendship and Good Neighbourliness between France (as predecessor to its former colony, Chad) and Libya on the dispute.]

... [T]he Treaty must, in the view of the Court, be taken to have determined a permanent frontier. There is nothing in the 1955 Treaty to indicate that the boundary agreed was to be provisional or temporary; on the contrary it bears all the hallmarks of finality. The establishment of this boundary is a fact which, from the outset, has had a legal life of its own, independently of the fate of the 1955 Treaty. Once agreed, the boundary stands, for any other approach would vitiate the fundamental principle of the stability of boundaries, the importance of which has been repeatedly emphasized by the Court (*Temple of Preah Vihear*, I.C.J. Reports 1962, p. 34; *Aegean Sea Continental Shelf*, I.C.J. Reports 1978, p. 36).

73. A boundary established by treaty thus achieves a permanence which the treaty itself does not necessarily enjoy. The treaty can cease to be in force without in any way affecting the continuance of the boundary. In this instance the Parties have not exercised their option to terminate the Treaty, but whether or not the option be exercised, the boundary remains. This is not to say that two States may not by mutual agreement vary the border between them; such a result can of course be achieved by mutual consent, but when a boundary has been the subject of agreement, the continued existence of that boundary is not dependent upon the continuing life of the treaty under which the boundary is agreed.

In *Gabčíkovo-Nagymaros*, the Court clearly held that the treaty itself survived the succession between Czechoslovakia and Slovakia. Was this the case in the *Libya/Chad Territorial Dispute* excerpted immediately above? Consider the significance of the Court's observation that "the Parties have not exercised their option to terminate the Treaty." In fact, the *Libya/Chad* judgment appears to apply two transmissibility rules in the case of state succession: the transmissibility of treaty provisions establishing a boundary, and the transmissibility of the boundary itself, independent of the subsequent fate of the treaty.

The rule applied in the *Libya/Chad Territorial Dispute* and reflected in Article 11 of the 1978 Vienna Convention concerns the transmissibility of international boundary regimes. However, the underlying notion that land borders should, in the interests of stability, be transmissible is captured also in the doctrine of *uti possidetis juris*. The principle of *uti possidetis juris* has been applied in order to elevate former colonial administrative borders (that is, those separating different colonial territories administered by a single colonial power) to international boundaries when those different territories achieve independence. At one level, this doctrine seems grossly unfair: why should the often arbitrary administrative borders drawn up by a colonial power bind its decolonized successors? The answer, put simply, is to avoid the chaos that would otherwise be produced. Consider the following ICJ case:

Frontier Dispute (Burkina Faso/Republic of Mali), Judgment, [1986] ICJ Rep 554

[Burkina Faso and Mali, both former colonies of France, submitted their boundary dispute to adjudication before a chamber of the International Court of Justice.]

19. The characteristic feature of the legal context of the frontier determination to be undertaken by the Chamber is that both States involved derive their existence from the process of decolonization which has been unfolding in Africa during the past 30 years. Their territories, and that of Niger, were formerly part of the French colonies which were grouped together under the name of French West Africa (AOF) [Afrique occidentale française]. Considering only the situation which prevailed immediately before the accession to independence of the two States, and disregarding previous administrative changes, it can be said that Burkina Faso corresponds to the colony of Upper Volta, and the Republic of Mali to the colony of Sudan (formerly French Sudan). It is to be supposed that the Parties drew inspiration from the principle expressly stated in the well-known resolution (AGH/Res. 16 (I)), adopted at the first session of the Conference of African Heads of State and Government, meeting in Cairo in 1964, whereby the Conference solemnly declared that all member States of the Organization of African Unity "solemnly . . . pledge themselves to respect the frontiers existing on their achievement of national independence," inasmuch as, in the preamble to their Special Agreement, they stated that the settlement of the dispute by the Chamber must be "based in particular on respect for the principle of the intangibility of frontiers inherited from colonization." It is clear from this text, and from the pleadings and oral arguments of the Parties, that they are in agreement as regards both the applicable law and the starting-point for the legal reasoning which is to lead to the determination of the frontier between their territories in the disputed area.

20. Since the two Parties have, as noted above, expressly requested the Chamber to resolve their dispute on the basis, in particular, of the "principle of the intangibility of frontiers inherited from colonization," the Chamber cannot disregard the principle of *uti possidetis juris*, the application of which gives rise to this respect for intangibility of frontiers. Although there is no need, for the purposes of the present case, to show that this is a firmly established principle of international law where decolonization is concerned, the Chamber nonetheless wishes to emphasize its general scope, in view of its exceptional importance for the African continent and for the two Parties. In this connection it should be noted that the principle of *uti possidetis* seems to have been first invoked and applied

in Spanish America, inasmuch as this was the continent which first witnessed the phenomenon of decolonization involving the formation of a number of sovereign States on territory formerly belonging to a single metropolitan State. Nevertheless the principle is not a special rule which pertains solely to one specific system of international law. It is a general principle, which is logically connected with the phenomenon of the obtaining of independence, wherever it occurs. Its obvious purpose is to prevent the independence and stability of new States being endangered by fratricidal struggles provoked by the challenging of frontiers following the withdrawal of the administering power.

21. It was for this reason that, as soon as the phenomenon of decolonization characteristic of the situation in Spanish America in the 19th century subsequently appeared in Africa in the 20th century, the principle of *uti possidetis*, in the sense described above, fell to be applied. The fact that the new African States have respected the administrative boundaries and frontiers established by the colonial powers must be seen not as a mere practice contributing to the gradual emergence of a principle of customary international law, limited in its impact to the African continent as it had previously been to Spanish America, but as the application in Africa of a rule of general scope.

22. The elements of *uti possidetis* were latent in the many declarations made by African leaders in the dawn of independence. These declarations confirmed the maintenance of the territorial status quo at the time of independence, and stated the principle of respect both for the frontiers deriving from international agreements, and for those resulting from mere internal administrative divisions. . . .

23. There are several different aspects to this principle, in its well-known application in Spanish America. The first aspect, emphasized by the Latin genitive *juris*, is found in the pre-eminence accorded to legal title over effective possession as a basis of sovereignty. Its purpose, at the time of the achievement of independence by the former Spanish colonies of America, was to scotch any designs which non-American colonizing powers might have on regions which had been assigned by the former metropolitan State to one division or another, but which were still uninhabited or unexplored. However, there is more to the principle of *uti possidetis* than this particular aspect. The essence of the principle lies in its primary aim of securing respect for the territorial boundaries at the moment when independence is achieved. Such territorial boundaries might be no more than delimitations between different administrative divisions or colonies all subject to the same sovereign. In that case, the application of the principle of *uti possidetis* resulted in administrative boundaries being transformed into international frontiers in the full sense of the term. This is true both of the States which took shape in the regions of South America which were dependent on the Spanish Crown, and of the States Parties to the present case, which took shape within the vast territories of French West Africa. *Uti possidetis*, as a principle which upgraded former administrative delimitations, established during the colonial period, to international frontiers, is therefore a principle of a general kind which is logically connected with this form of decolonization wherever it occurs. . . .

25. However, it may be wondered how the time-hallowed principle has been able to withstand the new approaches to international law as expressed in Africa, where the successive attainment of independence and the emergence of new States have been ac-

companied by a certain questioning of traditional international law. At first sight this principle conflicts outright with another one, the right of peoples to self-determination. In fact, however, the maintenance of the territorial status quo in Africa is often seen as the wisest course, to preserve what has been achieved by peoples who have struggled for their independence, and to avoid a disruption which would deprive the continent of the gains achieved by much sacrifice. The essential requirement of stability in order to survive, to develop and gradually to consolidate their independence in all fields, has induced African States judiciously to consent to the respecting of colonial frontiers, and to take account of it in the interpretation of the principle of self-determination of peoples.

26. Thus the principle of *uti possidetis* has kept its place among the most important legal principles, despite the apparent contradiction which explained its coexistence alongside the new norms. Indeed it was by deliberate choice that African States selected, among all the classic principles, that of *uti possidetis*. This remains an undeniable fact. . . . By becoming independent, a new State acquires sovereignty with the territorial base and boundaries left to it by the colonial power. This is part of the ordinary operation of the machinery of State succession. International law—and consequently the principle of *uti possidetis*—applies to the new State (as a State) not with retroactive effect, but immediately and from that moment onwards. It applies to the State as it is, i.e., to the "photograph" of the territorial situation then existing. The principle of *uti possidetis* freezes the territorial title; it stops the clock, but does not put back the hands. . . .

The principle of *uti possidetis juris* now has resonance outside of the Latin American and African decolonization experience. Consider the following discussion:

If the principle of *uti possidetis* has now been clearly recognized as a rule of international law applicable generally with regard to the phenomenon of decolonization, it remains to be determined whether it is a principle applicable to all situations of independence, irrespective of the factual situation. This issue, as to whether *uti possidetis* applies beyond the decolonization context, has come to the fore only in recent years, but with some force, as the Yugoslav and USSR examples demonstrate.

The Yugoslav Arbitration Commission took a clear view on this question. In Opinion No. 2, it was stressed that "it is well established that, whatever the circumstances, the right to self-determination must not involve changes to existing frontiers at the time of independence (*uti possidetis juris*) except where the states concerned agree otherwise." More directly, the Commission held in Opinion No. 3 that

except where otherwise agreed, the former boundaries become frontiers protected by international law. This conclusion follows from the principle of respect for the territorial status quo and in particular from the principle of *uti possidetis*. *Uti possidetis*, though initially applied in settling decolonization issues in America and Africa, is today recognized as a general principle, as stated by the International Court of Justice in its Judgment of 22 December 1986 in the case between *Burkina Faso and Mali (Frontier Dispute)*. . . .[46]

---

46 Malcolm N Shaw, "Peoples, Territorialism and Boundaries" (1997) 8 EJIL 478 at 495–96.

Should territorial and boundary treaties be the only exceptions to the non-transmissibility rule? As the judgments above suggest, these exceptions are well-established in state practice and *opinio juris* due to concerns about the destabilizing impact of non-transmissibility where state territory is at issue: if agreements concerning borders do not survive succession, boundary disputes and even conflict may arise whenever a new state emerges. However, is there not an equally compelling argument to be made that, if a new state is not bound by the human rights treaty obligations of its predecessor, the result may be instability and human suffering? Consider the views and conclusions of this commentator:

> Within the wider area of State succession, the subject of State succession in respect of human rights treaties is of particular interest. From a policy point of view, its importance lies in the fact that massive human rights violations often occur precisely during the periods of political instability which tend to accompany State succession. In such circumstances there is an urgent need to know the precise extent of the international obligations which are incumbent on the successor State. This applies not only to the primary obligations (the international human rights standards which are in force) but also to the secondary obligations (the reporting obligations, the complaints procedures and, more generally, the rules of accountability). . . .
>
> State practice during the 1990s strongly supports the view that obligations arising from a human rights treaty are not affected by a succession of States. This applies to all obligations undertaken by the predecessor State, including any reservations, declarations and derogations made by it. The continuity of these obligations occurs *ipso jure*. The successor State is under no obligation to issue confirmations to anyone. Consent from the other States parties is not required. Individuals residing within a given territory therefore remain entitled to the rights granted to them under a human rights treaty. They cannot be deprived of the protection of these rights by virtue of the fact that another State has assumed responsibility for the territory in which they find themselves. It follows that human rights treaties have a similar "localized" character as treaties establishing boundaries and other territorial regimes.[47]

ii) Succession and State Property and Debts

Succession of states with respect to state property and debts is a somewhat uncertain area of international law, although an attempt to clarify the situation was made in the Vienna Convention on the Succession of States in Respect of State Property, Archives and State Debts. This treaty, based on a set of draft articles prepared by the International Law Commission, is controversial in part and, with only seven states parties, is not yet in force. Consider the following provisions:

---

47 Menno T Kamminga, "State Succession in Respect of Human Rights Treaties" (1996) 7 EJIL 469 at 470 and 482–83.

Vienna Convention on Succession of States in Respect of State Property, Archives and Debts, 8 April 1983, UN Doc A/CONF.117/4, (1983) 22 ILM 306 (not yet in force)

PART II
STATE PROPERTY

Article 14
Transfer of part of the territory of a State
1. When part of the territory of a State is transferred by that State to another State, the passing of State property of the predecessor State to the successor State is to be settled by agreement between them.

2. In the absence of such an agreement:
(a) immovable State property of the predecessor State situated in the territory to which the succession of States relates shall pass to the successor State;
(b) movable State property of the predecessor State connected with the activity of the predecessor State in respect of the territory to which the succession of States relates shall pass to the successor State.

Article 15
Newly independent State
1. When the successor State is a newly independent State:
(a) immovable State property of the predecessor State situated in the territory to which the succession of States relates shall pass to the successor State;
(b) immovable property, having belonged to the territory to which the succession of States relates, situated outside it and having become State property of the predecessor State during the period of dependence, shall pass to the successor State;
(c) immovable State property of the predecessor State other than that mentioned in subparagraph (b) and situated outside the territory to which the succession of States relates, to the creation of which the dependent territory has contributed, shall pass to the successor State in proportion to the contribution of the dependent territory;
(d) movable State property of the predecessor State connected with the activity of the predecessor State in respect of the territory to which the succession of States relates shall pass to the successor State;
(e) movable property, having belonged to the territory to which the succession of States relates and having become State property of the predecessor State during the period of dependence, shall pass to the successor State;
(f) movable State property of the predecessor State, other than the property mentioned in subparagraphs (d) and (e), to the creation of which the dependent territory has contributed, shall pass to the successor State in proportion to the contribution of the dependent territory. . . .

4. Agreements concluded between the predecessor State and the newly independent State to determine succession to State property of the predecessor State otherwise than by the application of [the above provisions] shall not infringe the principle of the permanent sovereignty of every people over its wealth and natural resources.

Article 16
Uniting of States

When two or more States unite and so form one successor State, the State property of the predecessor States shall pass to the successor State.

Article 17
Separation of part or parts of the territory of a State

1. When part or parts of the territory of a State separate from that State and form a successor State, and unless the predecessor State and the successor State otherwise agree:

(a) immovable State property of the predecessor State situated in the territory to which the succession of States relates shall pass to the successor State;

(b) movable State property of the predecessor State connected with the activity of the predecessor State in respect of the territory to which the succession of States relates shall pass to the successor State;

(c) movable State property of the predecessor State, other than that mentioned in subparagraph (b), shall pass to the successor State in an equitable proportion. . . .

Article 18
Dissolution of a State

1. When a State dissolves and ceases to exist and the parts of the territory of the predecessor State form two or more successor States, and unless the successor States concerned otherwise agree:

(a) immovable State property of the predecessor State shall pass to the successor State in the territory of which it is situated;

(b) immovable State property of the predecessor State situated outside its territory shall pass to the successor States in equitable proportions;

(c) movable State property of the predecessor State connected with the activity of the predecessor State in respect of the territories to which the succession of States relates shall pass to the successor State concerned;

(d) movable State property of the predecessor State, other than that mentioned in subparagraph (c), shall pass to the successor States in equitable proportions. . . .

PART IV
STATE DEBTS

Article 33
State debt

. . . "State debt" means any financial obligation of a predecessor State arising in conformity with international law towards another State, an international organization or any other subject of international law. . . .

Article 37
Transfer of part of the territory of a State

1. When part of the territory of a State is transferred by that State to another State, the passing of the State debt of the predecessor State to the successor State is to be settled by agreement between them.

2. In the absence of such an agreement, the State debt of the predecessor State shall pass to the successor State in an equitable proportion, taking into account, in particular, the property, rights and interests which pass to the successor State in relation to that State debt.

Article 38
Newly independent State
1. When the successor State is a newly independent State, no State debt of the predecessor State shall pass to the newly independent State, unless an agreement between them provides otherwise in view of the link between the State debt of the predecessor State connected with its activity in the territory to which the succession of States relates and the property, rights and interests which pass to the newly independent State.

2. The agreement referred to in paragraph 1 shall not infringe the principle of the permanent sovereignty of every people over its wealth and natural resources, nor shall its implementation endanger the fundamental economic equilibria of the newly independent State.

Article 39
Uniting of States
When two or more States unite and so form one successor State, the State debt of the predecessor States shall pass to the successor State.

Article 40
Separation of part or parts of the territory of a State
1. When part or parts of the territory of a State separate from that State and form a State, and unless the predecessor State and the successor State otherwise agree, the State debt of the predecessor State shall pass to the successor State in an equitable proportion, taking into account, in particular, the property, rights and interests which pass to the successor State in relation to that State debt.

2. Paragraph 1 applies when part of the territory of a State separates from that State and unites with another State.

Article 41
Dissolution of a State
When a State dissolves and ceases to exist and the parts of the territory of the predecessor State form two or more successor States, and unless the successor States otherwise agree, the State debt of the predecessor State shall pass to the successor States in equitable proportions, taking into account, in particular, the property, rights and interests which pass to the successor States in relation to that State debt.

At the time of writing, only seven states—mostly successor states to the former Yugoslavia and the former Soviet Union—have ratified the 1983 Vienna Convention. A key reason for its apparent rejection by the vast majority of states appears to be, again, the different succession regime it propounds in respect of newly independent states.

The partition of property and debts became an acute concern in the 1990s, with the dissolution of the Soviet Union and the collapse of Yugoslavia. One commentator notes the outcome of the prolonged negotiation over this issue in relation to the former Socialist Federal Republic of Yugoslavia (SFRY), as follows:

> The Agreement on Succession Issues marks the end of more than nine years of struggle over the distribution of the property, assets, and liabilities of the former SFRY. The resolution accepted by the parties represents a carefully drafted compromise that strikes a balance between the conflicting interests of the five Yugoslav successor states, by determining their rights and obligations on the basis of the—all too often rudimentary—rules of the law of state succession and the principle of equity. . . .
>
> Furthermore, the adoption of the Succession Agreement has helped more closely to identify both the merits and the shortcomings of the 1983 Vienna Convention on State Succession in Respect of State Property, Archives and Debts. Although the Agreement makes no direct reference to the 1983 Convention, many of its provisions were implemented, first, in the practice of the Badinter Commission and international monetary institutions and, subsequently, in the Succession Agreement itself. The Agreement relies to a great extent on the provisions of the Convention that govern the dissolution of a state, in particular, the principles enshrined in Articles 18 (State Property), 31 (Archives), and 41 (Debts). But the Agreement has also brought about some striking novelties and modifications of those provisions. These include the strong protection of a nation's cultural heritage in the context of state succession, the codification of the "final beneficiary rule" in the context of localized debts, and extensive protection of acquired rights, especially in a postconflict environment.[48]

This passage, and the failure of the 1983 Vienna Convention to attract widespread state support, suggest that the law of state succession with respect to state property and debts remains in a considerable state of flux.

b) State Continuity

State continuity focuses on the international legal implications of changes in government rather than the consequences of the emergence or disappearance of states. At its most basic, state continuity means that states persist even when their governments change. This is a simple corollary of the legal position that international legal personality resides in the state rather than in its government of the day. Moreover, this is so whether or not the change in government is legal under a state's municipal law, including its constitutional law. A critical consequence of this is that a domestically illicit government, even one that is not recognized by other states, may continue to incur international legal obligations on behalf of the state, as long as it effectively governs. The result, of course, is that state governments effectively bind, at international law, successor governments. Consider the outcome of the following arbitration:

---

48 Carsten Stahn, "The Agreement on Succession Issues of the Former Socialist Federal Republic of Yugoslavia" (2002) 96 AJIL 379 at 396–97.

Aguilar-Amory and Royal Bank of Canada Claims (Great Britain v Costa Rica) (1923), **1 RIAA 375 (Tinoco Arbitration)**

OPINION AND AWARD OF WILLIAM H. TAFT, SOLE ARBITRATOR.

Washington, D.C., October 18, 1923.

In January, 1917, the Government of Costa Rica, under President Alfredo Gonzalez was overthrown by Frederico Tinoco, the Secretary of War. Gonzalez fled. Tinoco assumed power, called an election, and established a new constitution in June, 1917. His government continued until August, 1919, when Tinoco retired, and left the country. His government fell in September following. After a provisional government under one Barquero, the old constitution was restored and elections held under it. . . .

On the 22nd of August, 1922, the Constitutional Congress of the restored Costa Rican Government passed a law known as Law of Nullities No. 41. It invalidated all contracts between the executive power and private persons, made with or without approval of the legislative power between January 27, 1917 and September 2, 1919, covering the period of the Tinoco government. . . .

The claim of Great Britain is that the Royal Bank of Canada and the Central Costa Rica Petroleum Company are British corporations whose shares are owned by British subjects; that the Banco Internacional of Costa Rica and the Government of Costa Rica are both indebted to the Royal Bank in the sum of 998,000 colones, evidenced by 998 one thousand colones bills held by the Bank; that the Central Costa Rica Petroleum Company owns, by due assignment, a grant by the Tinoco government in 1918 of the right to explore for and exploit oil deposits in Costa Rica, and that both the indebtedness and the concession have been annulled without right by the Law of Nullities and should be excepted from its operation. She asks an award that she is entitled on behalf of her subjects to have the claim of the bank paid, and the concession recognized and given effect by the Costa Rican Government.

The Government of Costa Rica denies its liability for the acts or obligations of the Tinoco government and maintains that the Law of Nullities was a legitimate exercise of its legislative governing power. It further denies the validity of such claims on the merits, unaffected by the Law of Nullities. . . .

Coming now to the general issues applicable to both claims, Great Britain contends, first, that the Tinoco government was the only government of Costa Rica *de facto* and de jure for two years and nine months; that during that time there was no other government disputing its sovereignty, that it was in peaceful administration of the whole country, with the acquiescence of its people.

Second, that the succeeding government could not by legislative decree avoid responsibility for acts of that government affecting British subjects, or appropriate or confiscate rights and property by that government except in violation of international law; that the act of Nullities is as to British interests, therefore itself a nullity, and is to be disregarded, with the consequence that the contracts validly made with the Tinoco government must be performed by the present Costa Rican Government, and that the property which has been invaded or the rights nullified must be restored.

To these contentions the Costa Rican Government answers: First, that the Tinoco government was not a de facto or de jure government according to the rules of international law. This raises an issue of fact.

Second, that the contracts and obligations of the Tinoco government, set up by Great Britain on behalf of its subjects, are void, and do not create a legal obligation, because the government of Tinoco and its acts were in violation of the constitution of Costa Rica of 1871.

Third, that Great Britain is estopped by the fact that it did not recognize the Tinoco government during its incumbency, to claim on behalf of its subjects that Tinoco's was a government which could confer rights binding on its successor. . . .

Dr. John Bassett Moore, now a member of the Permanent Court of International Justice, in his *Digest of International Law*, Volume I, p. 249, announces the general principle which has had such universal acquiescence as to become well settled international law:

> Changes in the government or the internal policy of a state do not as a rule affect its position in international law. A monarchy may be transformed into a republic or a republic into a monarchy; absolute principles may be substituted for constitutional, or the reverse; but, though the government changes, the nation remains, with rights and obligations unimpaired. . . .
>
> The principle of the continuity of states has important results. The state is bound by engagements entered into by governments that have ceased to exist; the restored government is generally liable for the acts of the usurper. The governments of Louis XVIII and Louis Philippe so far as practicable indemnified the citizens of foreign states for losses caused by the government of Napoleon; and the King of the Two Cicilies made compensation to citizens of the United States for the wrongful acts of Murat.

Again Dr. Moore says:

> The origin and organization of government are questions generally of internal discussion and decision. Foreign powers deal with the existing *de facto* government, when sufficiently established to give reasonable assurance of its permanence, and of the acquiescence of those who constitute the state in its ability to maintain itself, and discharge its internal duties and its external obligations.

The same principle is announced in Professor Borchard's new work on *The Diplomatic Protection of Citizens Abroad*:

> Considering the characteristics and attributes of the *de facto* government, a general government *de facto* having completely taken the place of the regularly constituted authorities in the state binds the nation. So far as its international obligations are concerned, it represents the state. It succeeds to the debts of the regular government it has displaced and transmits its own obligations to succeeding titular governments. Its loans and contracts bind the state and the state is responsible for the governmental acts of the *de facto* authorities. In general its treaties are valid obligations of the state. It may alienate the national territory and the judgments of its courts are admitted to be effective after its authority has ceased. An exception to these rules has occasionally been noted in the practice of some of the states of Latin America, which declare null and void the acts of a usurping *de facto* intermediary government, when the regular

government it has displaced succeeds in restoring its control. Nevertheless, acts validly undertaken in the name of the state and having an international character cannot lightly be repudiated and foreign governments generally insist on their binding force. The legality or constitutional legitimacy of a *de facto* government is without importance internationally so far as the matter of representing the state is concerned. . . .

. . . First what are the facts to be gathered from the documents and evidence submitted by the two parties as to the *de facto* character of the Tinoco government?

In January, 1917, Frederico A. Tinoco was Secretary of War under Alfredo Gonzalez, the then President of Costa Rica. . . . Tinoco used the army and navy to seize the government, assume the provisional headship of the Republic and become Commander-in-Chief of the army. . . . Tinoco constituted a provisional government at once and summoned the people to an election for deputies. . . . At the same time he directed an election to take place for the Presidency. . . . Some 61,000 votes were cast for Tinoco and 259 for another candidate. Tinoco then was inaugurated as the President. . . . A new constitution was adopted June 8, 1917, supplanting the constitution of 1871. For a full two years Tinoco and the legislative assembly under him peaceably administered the affairs of the Government of Costa Rica, and there was no disorder of a revolutionary character during that interval. No other government of any kind asserted power in the country. . . .

Though Tinoco came in with popular approval, the result of his two years administration of the law was to rouse opposition to him. Conspiracies outside of the country were projected to organize a force to attack him. . . . [However,] there is no substantial evidence that Tinoco was not in actual and peaceable administration without resistance or conflict or contest by anyone until a few months before the time when he retired and resigned. . . .

. . . I must hold that from the evidence the Tinoco government was an actual sovereign government.

But it is urged that many leading Powers refused to recognize the Tinoco government, and that recognition by other nations is the chief and best evidence of the birth, existence and continuity of succession of a government. Undoubtedly recognition by other Powers is an important evidential factor in establishing proof of the existence of a government in the society of nations. What are the facts as to this? The Tinoco government was recognized by [20 states]. . . .

What were the circumstances as to the other nations? . . .

[The arbitrator then reviewed the position of the United States, which was to deny recognition, in emphatic terms, of the Tinoco government.] Probably because of the leadership of the United States in respect to a matter of this kind, her then Allies in the war, Great Britain, France and Italy declined to recognize the Tinoco government. . . .

The merits of the policy of the United States in this non-recognition it is not for the arbitrator to discuss, for the reason that in his consideration of this case, he is necessarily controlled by principles of international law, and however justified as a national policy non-recognition on such a ground may be, it certainly has not been acquiesced in by all the nations of the world, which is a condition precedent to considering it as a postulate of international law.

. . . Such non-recognition . . . cannot outweigh the evidence disclosed by this record before me as to the *de facto* character of Tinoco's government, according to the standard set by international law.

Second, it is ably and earnestly argued on behalf of Costa Rica that the Tinoco government cannot be considered a *de facto* government, because it was not established and maintained in accord with the constitution of Costa Rica of 1871. To hold that a government which establishes itself and maintains a peaceful administration, with the acquiescence of the people for a substantial period of time, does not become a *de facto* government unless it conforms to a previous constitution would be to hold that within the rules of international law a revolution contrary to the fundamental law of the existing government cannot establish a new government. This cannot be, and is not, true. The change by revolution upsets the rule of the authorities in power under the then existing fundamental law, and sets aside the fundamental law in so far as the change of rule makes it necessary. To speak of a revolution creating a *de facto* government, which conforms to the limitations of the old constitution is to use a contradiction in terms. The same government continues internationally, but not the internal law of its being. The issue is not whether the new government assumes power or conducts its administration under constitutional limitations established by the people during the incumbency of the government it has overthrown. The question is, has it really established itself in such a way that all within its influence recognize its control, and that there is no opposing force assuming to be a government in its place? Is it discharging its functions as a government usually does, respected within its own jurisdiction? . . .

Third, it is further objected by Costa Rica that Great Britain by her failure to recognize the Tinoco government is estopped now to urge claims of her subjects dependent upon the acts and contracts of the Tinoco government. The evidential weight of such non-recognition against the claim of its de facto character I have already considered and admitted. The contention here goes further and precludes a government which did not recognize a *de facto* government from appearing in an international tribunal in behalf of its nationals to claim any rights based on the acts of such government.

. . . Here the executive of Great Britain takes the position that the Tinoco government which it did not recognize, was nevertheless a de facto government that could create rights in British subjects which it now seeks to protect. Of course, as already emphasized, its failure to recognize the *de facto* government can be used against it as evidence to disprove the character it now attributes to that government, but this does not bar it from changing its position. . . .

The failure to recognize the *de facto* government did not lead the succeeding government to change its position in any way upon the faith of it. Non-recognition may have aided the succeeding government to come into power; but subsequent presentation of claims based on the *de facto existence* of the previous government and its dealings does not work an injury to the succeeding government in the nature of a fraud or breach of faith. An equitable estoppel to prove the truth must rest on previous conduct of the person to be estopped, which has led the person claiming the estoppel into a position in which the truth will injure him. There is no such case here.

There are other estoppels recognized in municipal law than those which rest on equitable considerations. They are based on public policy. It may be urged that it would be in the interest of the stability of governments and the orderly adjustment of international relations, and so a proper rule of international law, that a government in recognizing or refusing to recognize a government claiming admission to the society of nations should thereafter be held to an attitude consistent with its deliberate conclusion on this issue. Arguments for and against such a rule occur to me; but it suffices to say that I have not been cited to text writers of authority or to decisions of significance indicating a general acquiescence of nations in such a rule. Without this, it cannot be applied here as a principle of international law.

A consideration of the issues before us, therefore, recurs to the merits of the two claims. The decision of them must be governed by the answer to the question whether the claims would have been good against the Tinoco government as a government, unaffected by the Law of Nullities and unaffected by the Costa Rican Constitution of 1871. . . .

The outcome of the arbitration on its merits is described in the extract below:

Great Britain v Costa Rica, (1923–1924) 2 Annual Digest of Public International Law Cases 176–77

Held: (a) In respect of the Banking Transactions: . . . The transactions in question, which in themselves did not constitute transactions of an ordinary nature and which were "full of irregularities," were made at a time when the popularity of the Tinoco Government had disappeared, and when the political and military movement aiming at the overthrow of that Government was gaining strength. The payments made by the bank were either in favour of Frederico Tinoco himself "for expenses of representation of the Chief of the State in his approaching trip abroad," or to his brother as salary and expenses in respect of a diplomatic post to which the latter was appointed by Tinoco. "The case of the Royal Bank depends not on "the mere form of the transaction but upon the good faith" of the bank in the payment of money for the real use of the Costa Rican Government under the Tinoco régime. It must make out its case of actual furnishing of money to the government for its legitimate use. It has not done so. [It] knew that this money was to be used by the retiring president, F. Tinoco, for his personal support after he had taken refuge in a foreign country. It could not hold his own government [responsible] for the money paid to him for this purpose." The position was essentially the same in respect to the payments made to Tinoco's brother. The Royal Bank of Canada cannot be deemed to have proved that the payments were made for legitimate, governmental use. Its claim must fail.

(b In respect of the Concession: . . . The concession was granted by a body without power to grant it. The vital clause (Article X) of the concession involved exemptions from taxation and limitations of future taxation. According to the Constitution obtaining at the time of the Tinoco Government, the power to grant such exemptions was vested in the Congress (composed of the Chamber of Deputies and the Senate). But the concession was granted by the Chamber of Deputies and approved by the President. It is impossible to reject the clause in question and hold the remainder of the concession valid. "That article is too vital an element in its value. The contract cannot be made over by this tribunal for the parties." . . .

The *Tinoco Arbitration* is well-known for its holding that even an illegal government may bind a state to international obligations. It is also notable, though less well-known, for its conclusion on the merits that, even so, the foreign companies allegedly injured by the subsequent government's repudiation of deals entered into by the Tinoco government received no or modest recovery. We look at each of these issues in turn.

First, the concept that a state may be bound by obligations entered into by an illicit government may seem unfair, but consider the consequences if the rule were otherwise. The following determination of the Inter-American Court of Human Rights provides an illustration:

Velásquez Rodríguez Case, Judgment of 29 July 1988, (1988) Inter-Am Ct HR (Ser C) No 4

[Petitioners made claims against the Honduran government after several students were "disappeared" by armed men in civilian clothing. At issue, in part, was whether these men were state agents such as to engage the responsibility of the Honduran state. In the course of its reasoning, the Inter-American Court of Human Rights commented on the implications of a change of government for issues of state responsibility.]

182. The Court is convinced, and has so found, that the disappearance of Manfredo Velásquez was carried out by agents who acted under cover of public authority. However, even had that fact not been proven, the failure of the State apparatus to act, which is clearly proven, is a failure on the part of Honduras to fulfill the duties it assumed under Article 1 (1) of the [American Convention on Human Rights[49]], which obligated it to ensure Manfredo Velásquez the free and full exercise of his human rights.

183. The Court notes that the legal order of Honduras does not authorize such acts and that internal law defines them as crimes. The Court also recognizes that not all levels of the Government of Honduras were necessarily aware of those acts, nor is there any evidence that such acts were the result of official orders. Nevertheless, those circumstances are irrelevant for the purposes of establishing whether Honduras is responsible under international law for the violations of human rights perpetrated within the practice of disappearances.

184. According to the principle of the continuity of the State in international law, responsibility exists both independently of changes of government over a period of time and continuously from the time of the act that creates responsibility to the time when the act is declared illegal. The foregoing is also valid in the area of human rights although, from an ethical or political point of view, the attitude of the new government may be much more respectful of those rights than that of the government in power when the violations occurred.

185. The Court, therefore, concludes that the facts found in this proceeding show that the State of Honduras is responsible for the involuntary disappearance of Angel Manfredo Velásquez Rodríguez. Thus, Honduras has violated Articles 7, 5 and 4 of the Convention.

There may be a limit to the notion that illegitimate governments bind their states: where a state's effective government is in place due to a violation of *international*—and

---

49   22 November 1969, 1144 UNTS 144, in force 18 July 1978.

not merely *domestic*—law, the state may continue but the actions of its *de facto* government may not necessarily incur international legal obligations on its behalf. For example, in modern international law, it is, as a general rule, impermissible for one state to seek to install a particular government in another state. To do so would constitute intervention in the internal affairs of that other state, contrary to the principles of the sovereign equality and independence of states. What happens when these rules are breached? While there is little clear, recent practice upon which to rely, it is at least arguable that the actions of a "puppet" regime installed by a foreign state may not be binding on the "victim" state. The principle *ex injuria jus non oritur* provides that acts which are contrary to international law cannot become a source of rights for a wrongdoer since to grant recognition to an illegal act or situation would tend to perpetuate it and be of benefit to the state which has acted illegally.[50]

Applying this standard, should Iraq be considered bound by contracts entered into by transitional Iraqi governments following the March 2003 invasion of the country by "Coalition" forces from the United States, the United Kingdom, and Australia? Does the answer differ if specifically considering agreements concluded or other liabilities incurred from April 2003 until the June 2004 transfer of "sovereignty" by the occupying Coalition Provisional Authority? International law regulating armed conflict has rules governing changes to domestic law by occupying powers that may help answer this question. Consider Article 43 of the 1907 Hague Regulations, found in the Annex to the 1907 (Hague) Convention (IV) respecting the Laws and Customs of War on Land:[51]

> The authority of the legitimate power having in fact passed into the hands of the occupant, the latter shall take all the measures in his power to restore, and ensure, as far as possible, public order and safety, while respecting, unless absolutely prevented, the laws in force in the country.

The Fourth Geneva Convention of 1949 contains similar, albeit more detailed, provisions.[52] Pointing to these provisions, commentators expressed concern that foreign investment laws in Iraq, promulgated by the Coalition Provisional Authority, are internationally illegal. Consider the following news report:

> The US-led provisional authority in Iraq may be breaking international law by selling state assets, experts have warned, raising the prospect that contracts signed now by foreign investors could be scrapped by a future Iraqi government.
>
> International businesspeople attending a conference in London this week heard that some orders issued by the US-led Coalition Provisional Authority (CPA) might be in breach of the 1907 Hague Regulations and the Fourth Geneva Convention. . . .
>
> International law obliges occupying powers to respect laws already in force in a country "unless absolutely prevented" from doing so.

---

50 Sir Robert Jennings & Sir Arthur Watts, eds, *Oppenheim's International Law*, 9th ed, vol I (London: Pearson, 1992) at 184, s 54.

51 18 October 1907, BTS 1910 No 9, 1 Bevans 631, in force 16 January 1910.

52 Geneva Convention Relative to the Protection of Civilian Persons in Time of War (Geneva Convention IV), 12 August 1949, 75 UNTS 287, Can TS 1965 No 20, in force 21 October 1950.

According to international law experts, that throws doubt on the legality of the CPA's September 19[, 2003] order opening the Iraqi economy to foreign investment. In what amounted to a blueprint for transforming Iraq into a market economy, Order 39 permitted full foreign ownership of a wide range of state-owned Iraqi assets, barring natural resources such as oil.

However, such sweeping economic reform may not be legal, as the UK government was privately warned by its chief law officer in the first days of the war. In his private advice, later leaked to the press, Lord Goldsmith wrote that "the imposition of major structural economic reforms would not be authorised by international law."[53]

Should it always be the case that obligations entered into by an occupying or puppet regime are inapplicable to the "host" state as a matter of international law? Afghanistan, for example, ratified the 1984 Convention against Torture and Other Cruel, Inhuman or Degrading Treatment or Punishment[54] in 1987. At that time, the Afghan government was widely considered a Soviet puppet. Does that mean that the Taliban government, when it came to power in Afghanistan in the mid-1990s, could disclaim obligations under the Convention against Torture by arguing that the treaty was entered into by an internationally illegitimate government? What arguments of law and principle can be made in support of the contention that the *ex injuria jus non oritur* concept should not extend to international human rights obligations undertaken by an internationally illegitimate government? Considering that the content of much of international human rights law exists as a matter of customary international law, would such an exception be relevant?

Consider now the second aspect of the *Tinoco Arbitration*: the conclusion on the merits that the two foreign companies should obtain no or limited recovery because they were or should have been alive to the shady nature of the transactions in question. This conclusion appears to be based on domestic Costa Rican law. The related issue — whether foreign investors should be able to collect on debts incurred by illegitimate regimes — remains uncertain in international law. As one commentator suggests:

> One possibility . . . might be to develop a system under which third parties dealing with a grossly unrepresentative regime would be required to take the risk of doing so. This would apply both to States and to private parties, including corporations. It would put them on notice that if they wish to deal with a regime lacking in any legitimacy or popular support, they would take the risk of the review of the transaction by a subsequent representative government.[55]

Consider the following argument in support of such a doctrine of odious debts:

---

53 Thomas Catan, "Iraq Business Deals May Be Invalid, Law Experts Warn," *Financial Times* (London edition) (29 October 2003) 14.

54 10 December 1984, 1465 UNTS 85, Can TS 1987 No 36, in force 26 June 1987 [Convention against Torture].

55 James Crawford, "Democracy and International Law" (1993) 64 Brit YB Int'l L 113 at 139.

Patricia Adams, Probe International, "The Doctrine of Odious Debts: Using the Law to Cancel Illegitimate Debts"[56]

In the 1920s, a Russian professor of law named Alexander Sack, who was teaching in Paris, published the most extensive and the most important treatises on the treatment of state debts. Professor Sack was then, and he remains to this day, the world's preeminent legal scholar on the treatment of public debts. He wrote in a politically tumultuous time, when colonial territories were becoming independent, when monarchies were becoming republics, and when military rulers were being replaced by civilians. Borders were constantly changing and new ideologies of socialism, communism and fascism were overthrowing old orders.

Professor Sack was no radical. So that international commerce and trade did not break down, Sack believed that government debts should be repaid when a new government or new sovereign came to power. His argument? Sack believed that these debts represent obligations of the state. He defined the state to be the territory, rather than a specific governmental structure.

With one exception. Sack believed that debts not created in the interests of the state, should not be bound to this general rule. Some debts, he said, were odious.

And he defined an odious debt this way: "If a despotic power incurs a debt not for the needs or in the interest of the State, but to strengthen its despotic regime, to repress the population that fights against it, etc., this debt is odious for the population of all the State."

He went on. "This debt is not an obligation for the nation; it is a regime's debt." Sack called it "a personal debt of the power that has incurred it." When this power falls, that debt "consequently . . . falls with the fall of this power."

According to Alexander Sack, these "odious" debts could not encumber the territory of the State, because such debts do not fulfill the conditions that determine the legality of the debts of the State. And here is the pivotal point of Sack's doctrine: "the debts of the state must be incurred and the funds from it employed for the needs and in the interests of the State," in order to be considered legally enforceable. . . .

Professor Sack was . . . [even] more specific. "When a government incurs debts to subjugate the population of a part of its territory or to colonize it with members of the dominant nationality, etc., these debts are odious to the indigenous population of that part of the territory of the debtor State."

Sack also considered a debt odious when, "the loans [are] incurred by members of the government or by persons or groups associated with the government to serve interests manifestly personal—interests that are unrelated to the interests of the State." A bribe is an example of a manifestly personal interest.

Now, in order for a debt to be deemed "odious," Sack said that the lender must also be aware that the loan is "contrary to the interests of the nation."

In this case, Professor Sack said, "the creditors have committed a hostile act" against the people. They can't therefore expect that a nation freed from a despotic power will assume the 'odious' debts, which he called "personal debts of that power."

---

56   A paper presented at the Conference on Illegitimate Debts organized by the German Jubilee Network, 21–30 June 2002. Reprinted with permission.

For creditors to expect any protection for their loans to foreign states, their loans must be utilized for the needs and interests of the state; otherwise the loans belonged to the power which contracted them, and were therefore . . . debts of the regime.

To avoid abuse of the doctrine by self-serving interpretation, Sack proposed that a new government be required to prove that the debts it inherited from a previous regime did not serve the public interest and that the creditors were aware of this. Following these proofs, the onus would be on the creditors to show that the funds were utilized for the benefit of the territory. If the creditors could not do so, before an international tribunal, or "in the opinion of competent and impartial representatives of the family of nations," the debt would be unenforceable.

. . . [T]his doctrine is more than just legal theory, it is legal practice.

The cases that Professor Sack based his doctrine on will be of great interest to you.

Let me turn to the case of the Cuban debts. After the Americans won Cuba from Spain in the Spanish-American War of 1898, the Spanish argued in the peace negotiations that the Cuban debts should be assumed by the Americans. The Spanish argued the prevailing principle of international law: that state obligations belong to a land and its people, not to a regime.

The Americans replied that the so-called "Cuban debt," "imposed upon the people of Cuba without their consent and by force of arms" was indeed one of the main reasons Cubans were struggling for their independence.

Furthermore, the Americans added, much of the borrowing was designed to crush attempts by the Cuban population to revolt against Spanish domination, and was spent in a manner contrary to Cuba's interest. "They are debts created by the Government of Spain, for its own purposes and through its own agents, in whose creation Cuba had no voice."

"The debt was contracted by Spain for national purposes, which in some cases were alien and in others actually averse to the interest of Cuba . . . in reality the greater part of it was contracted for the purpose of supporting a Spanish army in Cuba."

The Americans had little sympathy for the lenders. "The creditors," they said, "from the beginning, took the chances of the investment."

The United States never acknowledged liability for the Cuban debt, nor did they assume any Spanish debts. The holders of the so-called "Cuban debt" never collected fully on their claims.

About 20 years later, and still before Alexander Sack defined the Doctrine of Odious Debts, another very important case occurred. This case involved the Royal Bank of Canada, a private commercial bank from my country, which made a loan to the outgoing dictator of Costa Rica, President Tinoco. [The author reviews the *Tinoco Arbitration*'s conclusion on the merits, summarized above.]

Alexander Sack based his Doctrine of Odious Debts on these and many other cases. But what became of this legal principle over the next 60 years? Though the Doctrine of Odious Debts has been buried in the tomes of law libraries, its principles have not gone completely unnoticed. In fact they have nagged lenders for decades. In 1982, lawyers at The First National Bank of Chicago wrote in a professional journal, "The consequences of a change of sovereignty for loan agreements may depend in part on the use of the loan proceeds by the predecessor state. If the debt of the predecessor is deemed to be "odious,"" i.e., the debt proceeds are used against the interests of the local populace, then the debt may not be chargeable to the successor."

Although bank loan agreements usually say what the loan is intended for, the lawyers went on, the use described is often too general to ensure that the loan benefited the people and so too general to guarantee loan enforcement. Moreover, the loan documents rarely restrict the money's use.

"Commercial banks should be alert to the dangers of such doctrines," the First National Bank lawyers warned. "Because successor governments have invoked doctrines based on an 'odious' or 'hostile' use of proceeds, lenders should describe with specificity the uses of the loan proceeds and, if possible, bind the borrower by representation, warranty, and covenant to those uses." . . .

[A]n extensive study on the odious debts doctrine has just been completed by a legal team at McGill University. . . .

"The conclusion from the investigation is that the doctrine may be coherently defined, has a lengthy history in international relations, is relatively well supported under international law, and can be modified with relative ease to accommodate some of the problematic aspects that may be held against it." . . .

There are three necessary conditions for a debt to be considered odious, they say: 1) the debt must not have received the consent of the nation; 2) the funds borrowed must have been contracted and spent in a manner that is contrary to the interests of the nation; and 3) the creditor must be aware of these facts.

The McGill legal team also proposes a number of fora for challenging odious debts, including the International Court of Justice, international arbitration, and domestic courts . . . and recommends that World Bank loans might provide the best test cases for an odious debts challenge. . . .

Is the case of the Cuban debts, referred to above, an instance of change of government or of state succession? Which of these two legal contexts forms the basis of the advice given by the lawyers representing First National Bank? The authors of the McGill study acknowledge that "most of the state practice cited in this study [relates to] cases of state succession."[57] Is state practice in the state succession context — most of which, according to the McGill study, predates World War II — relevant to establishing the existence of an odious debts doctrine in a change of government context? Should it be, given the overarching policy concern that public debts be incurred in the interests of the population? Or, considering the issue from the perspective of the creditor, is the fact that a predecessor state often survives a state succession, whereas a change of government by definition extinguishes the prior government, a relevant consideration?

Given the malleability of the notion of "public interest" — particularly in the context of changes of government — what effect might recognition of an odious debts doctrine have on the ability of states (including developing states) to obtain foreign loans or attract foreign investment?

---

57 Centre for International Sustainable Development Law, "Advancing the Odious Debt Doctrine," CISDL Working Paper (11 March 2003) at 47, online: http://cisdl.org/public/docs/pdf/Odious_Debt_Study.pdf.

4) Key Corollaries of Statehood

As we shall see throughout these materials, once an entity is a state, it is the pre-eminent subject of international law. It has, as a consequence, the full range of international legal obligations, rights, and capacities associated with statehood. Some of these rights, obligations, and capacities are core precepts of international law that flow from the nature of states and the very structure of the international legal system. Others might be considered "derivative," in the sense that they exist by virtue of the will of states, harnessed through the law-making processes we have reviewed in Chapter 2. Rules in the former category could not be changed without fundamentally affecting the nature of the international legal system itself; rules in the latter could. In this section, it is the former category that interests us. Here we briefly examine some of these core precepts of international law that attach so fundamentally to states that they can rightly be considered "corollaries" of statehood. Because of the fundamental nature of these precepts, they will also necessarily arise and be considered at greater length in other contexts in these materials.

As one of its first projects, the International Law Commission (ILC) was asked to prepare what became the "Draft Declaration on Rights and Duties of States" — a text commended to states and jurists by the UN General Assembly in 1949.[58] While the receipt of the draft declaration by the General Assembly has not led to the drafting of a treaty,[59] and the declaration is not in its own right legally binding, it has had a "long-term effect on the development of international law."[60] It is also fair to say that many of its provisions reflect core precepts of modern international law in the sense referred to above, and can thus serve as starting points for our overview.

a) Sovereignty

The first two articles of the 1949 Draft Declaration on Rights and Duties of States read as follows:

Article 1

Every State has the right to independence and hence to exercise freely, without dictation by any other State, all its legal powers, including the choice of its own form of government.

Article 2

Every State has the right to exercise jurisdiction over its territory and over all persons and things therein, subject to the immunities recognized by international law.

These two articles articulate a doctrine of sovereignty. The definition of "sovereignty," and its centrality to international law, were discussed at length in Chapter 1. In the specific

---

58 *Declaration on Rights and Duties of States*, GA Res 375 (IV), reprinted in UN GAOR, 4th Sess at 66–67, UN Doc A/1251 (1949).

59 Indeed, the General Assembly decided to postpone further consideration of the draft declaration in 1951: *Draft Declaration on Rights and Duties of States*, GA Res 596 (VI), reprinted in UN GAOR, 6th Sess, Supp No 20 at 83–84, UN Doc A/2119 (1951).

60 Bernhard Graefrath, "The International Law Commission Tomorrow: Improving Its Organization and Methods of Work" (1991) 85 AJIL 595.

context of the relations between states, the arbitrator in the *Island of Palmas Case* (discussed at greater length in Chapter 4) described sovereignty in this manner:

> Sovereignty in the relations between States signifies independence. Independence in regard to a portion of the globe is the right to exercise therein, to the exclusion of any other State, the functions of a State. The development of the national organization of States during the last few centuries and, as a corollary, the development of international law, have established this principle of the exclusive competence of the State in regard to its own territory in such a way as to make it the point of departure in settling most questions that concern international relations . . . .[61]

b) Sovereign Equality

Article 5 of the 1949 Draft Declaration on Rights and Duties of States provides that "Every State has the right to equality in law with every other State."[62] This concept of "sovereign equality" runs throughout modern international law. Article 2(1) of the UN Charter, for instance, provides that the UN and its members shall act in accordance with "the principle of the sovereign equality of all its Members." The General Assembly's "Friendly Relations Declaration"—widely considered to reflect customary international law—proposes the following, precise meaning of "sovereign equality":

> *Declaration on Principles of International Law Concerning Friendly Relations and Co-operation in accordance with the Charter of the United Nations* **GA Res 2625 (XXV), UN Doc A/RES/2625/XXV (1970)**[63]
>
> *The principle of sovereign equality of States:*
> All States enjoy sovereign equality. They have equal rights and duties and are equal members of the international community, notwithstanding differences of an economic, social, political or other nature.
>
> In particular, sovereign equality includes the following elements:
> (a) States are judicially equal;
> (b) Each State enjoys the rights inherent in full sovereignty;
> (c) Each State has the duty to respect the personality of other States;
> (d) The territorial integrity and political independence of the State are inviolable;
> (e) Each State has the right freely to choose and develop its political, social, economic and cultural systems;
> (f) Each State has the duty to comply fully and in good faith with its international obligations and to live in peace with other States.

Sovereign equality may be a doctrinal requirement of international law, but what is the reality? One commentator offers this view:

---

61 *Island of Palmas Case (Netherlands v United States)* (1928), 2 RIAA 829 at 838.
62 Above note 58, art 5.
63 Reprinted in UN GAOR, 25th Sess, Supp No 28 at 121–24, UN Doc A/8028 Corr 1 (1970); (1970) 9 ILM 1292.

Legal equality is . . . vital to the international legal system composed of approximately 190 nation-states. Referred to as "sovereign equality" in this context, legal equality in international law enables weaker states to enter into treaties with powerful states with the expectation that the treaties will be upheld. Sovereign equality also provides states with equal votes in many international organizations and ensures them the equal benefit of essential privileges such as diplomatic immunity for their representatives abroad.

But . . . there are limits to the concept of sovereign equality in international law. Some of these limits are legally formalized: there are only five permanent, veto-holding members of the U.N. Security Council, for example. Similarly, the votes of certain economically powerful states are accorded greater weight than those of other member states of the World Bank and International Monetary Fund. These formal differences are often the results of disparities in negotiating power among the states that established these organizations. In most treaty negotiations, weak states attach greater value to the stability offered by conventional instruments than powerful states and are therefore often willing to make significant concessions in order to secure a legal regime. And powerful states, with their greater resources and broader range of activities and interests, are better able to link bargaining issues and negotiating arenas strategically so as to offer incentives—and disincentives—across and among a wider range of topics, thereby constraining the options of less powerful states in ways that are subtle yet often extremely effective.[64]

The factual and sometimes formal imbalance of power among states colours the outcomes of most international legal relations, including international treaty negotiations. This is not to say that the most powerful states always get their way, as suggested by the ultimately successful negotiation of conventions banning land mines or establishing the International Criminal Court in the face of opposition from powerful states (discussed in Chapter 1). But treaties may demonstrate systemic biases favouring the interests of powerful nations. Take, for example, the international trade law regime. The agreements constituting the World Trade Organization include stringent rules on intellectual property, barring piracy of patents and the like. Notably, most patent holders are corporations and other nationals of developed countries. Meanwhile, international trade law has been woefully unsuccessful in reining in highly protectionist agricultural policies and subsidies in these developed nations. Agriculture is an area in which less developed nations could enjoy true comparative advantages. Contrasting the vigour with which intellectual property is protected with the desultory approach of trade law to agriculture, the systemic bias in favour of developed countries seems clear.

Formal "sovereign equality" gives all UN member states an equal voice in the General Assembly, an equal right to participate in negotiating multilateral treaties, an equal right to insist on the privileges and immunities attaching to states, and so on. Looked at from the perspective of *realpolitik*, however, it does not ensure equal ability of states to avail themselves of these formal attributes of sovereignty, much less ensure that outcomes are equitable. Consider the following issues: (1) Do guarantees of formal equality in even the most sophisticated domestic legal systems fare any better? (2) What would be the consequences of abandoning the formal notion of sovereign equality and reflecting, in

---

64 Michael Byers, "Introduction: Power, Obligation, and Customary International Law" (2001) 11 Duke J Comp & Int'l L 81 at 82.

international legal doctrine, the factual inequalities between states? (3) What would be the principal challenges in seeking to develop international legal doctrines that favour equitable outcomes and substantive sovereign equality? (4) Is the entrenchment of formal sovereign equality a first step or an impediment along that path?

c) The Duty of Non-Intervention

A logical consequence of the sovereignty and equality of all states is a state's entitlement to be free from intervention, by other states, in its sovereign sphere of influence, and a concomitant duty to refrain from intervening in that of others. The 1949 Draft Declaration on Rights and Duties of States[65] states it thus:

> *Article 3*
> Every State has the duty to refrain from intervention in the internal or external affairs of any other State.

> *Article 4*
> Every State has the duty to refrain from fomenting civil strife in the territory of another State, and to prevent the organization within its territory of activities calculated to foment such civil strife.

The duty of non-intervention in the domestic affairs of states is a concept reflected in many hortatory UN General Assembly declarations. We have already noted the General Assembly's influential Friendly Relations Declaration. This instrument expands on the foregoing terse statement of the duty of non-intervention in the following way:

> *Declaration on Principles of International Law Concerning Friendly Relations and Cooperation in accordance with the Charter of the United Nations,* **GA Res 2625 (XXV), UN Doc A/RES/2625/XXV (1970)**[66]

> *The principle concerning the duty not to intervene in matters within the domestic jurisdiction of any State, in accordance with the Charter:*

> No State or group of States has the right to intervene, directly or indirectly, for any reason whatever, in the internal or external affairs of any other State. Consequently, armed intervention and all other forms of interference or attempted threats against the personality of the State or against its political, economic and cultural elements, are in violation of international law.

> No State may use or encourage the use of economic, political or any other type of measures to coerce another State in order to obtain from it the subordination of the exercise of its sovereign rights and to secure from it advantages of any kind. Also, no State shall organize, assist, foment, finance, incite or tolerate subversive, terrorist or armed activities directed towards the violent overthrow of the regime of another State, or interfere in civil strife in another State.

---

65 Above note 58.
66 Reprinted in UN GAOR, 25th Sess, Supp No 28 at 121–24, UN Doc A/8028 Corr 1 (1970); (1970) 9 ILM 1292.

The use of force to deprive peoples of their national identity constitutes a violation of their inalienable rights and of the principle of non-intervention.

Every State has an inalienable right to choose its political, economic, social and cultural systems, without interference in any form by another State.

What is the significance of the Friendly Relations Declaration's use of the expressions "coerce" and "subordination of the exercise of its sovereign rights" in connection with the "use of economic, political, or any other type of measures" against another state?

While, as noted above, the Friendly Relations Declaration is not in itself a legally binding instrument, it is nevertheless widely considered reflective of customary international law. Consider these observations by the International Court of Justice in the *Nicaragua* case:

Military and Paramilitary Activities in and against Nicaragua (Nicaragua v United States of America), Merits, Judgment, [1986] ICJ Rep 14

[This case involved a claim by Nicaragua that the United States had been intervening in its internal affairs, including through the use of force, contrary to principles of customary international law reflected in the UN Charter.]

188. The Court thus finds that both Parties take the view that the principles as to the use of force incorporated in the United Nations Charter correspond, in essentials, to those found in customary international law. The Parties thus both take the view that the fundamental principle in this area is expressed in the terms employed in Article 2, paragraph 4, of the United Nations Charter. They therefore accept a treaty-law obligation to refrain in their international relations from the threat or use of force against the territorial integrity or political independence of any State, or in any other manner inconsistent with the purposes of the United Nations. The Court has however to be satisfied that there exists in customary international law an *opinio juris* as to the binding character of such abstention. This *opinio juris* may, though with all due caution, be deduced from, inter alia, the attitude of the Parties and the attitude of States towards certain General Assembly resolutions, and particularly resolution 2625 (XXV) entitled "Declaration on Principles of International Law concerning Friendly Relations and Co-operation among States in accordance with the Charter of the United Nations". The effect of consent to the text of such resolutions cannot be understood as merely that of a "reiteration or elucidation" of the treaty commitment undertaken in the Charter. On the contrary, it may be understood as an acceptance of the validity of the rule or set of rules declared by the resolution by themselves. The principle of non-use of force, for example, may thus be regarded as a principle of customary international law, . . .

202. The principle of non-intervention involves the right of every sovereign State to conduct its affairs without outside interference; though examples of trespass against this principle are not infrequent, the Court considers that it is part and parcel of customary international law. As the Court has observed: "Between independent States, respect for territorial sovereignty is an essential foundation of international relations" . . . , and international law requires political integrity also to be respected. Expressions of an *opinio juris* regarding the existence of the principle of non-intervention in customary international

law are numerous and not difficult to find. Of course, statements whereby States avow their recognition of the principles of international law set forth in the United Nations Charter cannot strictly be interpreted as applying to the principle of non-intervention by States in the internal and external affairs of other States, since this principle is not, as such, spelt out in the Charter. But it was never intended that the Charter should embody written confirmation of every essential principle of international law in force. The existence in the *opinio juris* of States of the principle of non-intervention is backed by established and substantial practice. It has moreover been presented as a corollary of the principle of the sovereign equality of States. A particular instance of this is General Assembly resolution 2625 (XXV), the Declaration on the Principles of International Law concerning Friendly Relations and Co-operation among States. In the Corfu Channel case, when a State claimed a right of intervention in order to secure evidence in the territory of another State for submission to an international tribunal . . . the Court observed that:

> the alleged right of intervention [is] the manifestation of a policy of force, such as has, in the past, given rise to most serious abuses and such as cannot, whatever be the present defects in international organization, find a place in international law. Intervention is perhaps still less admissible in the particular form it would take here; for, from the nature of things, it would be reserved for the most powerful States, and might easily lead to perverting the administration of international justice itself. . . .

203. The principle has since been reflected in numerous declarations adopted by international organizations and conferences in which the United States and Nicaragua have participated, e.g., General Assembly resolution 2131 (XX), the Declaration on the Inadmissibility of Intervention in the Domestic Affairs of States and the Protection of their Independence and Sovereignty.

. . . [I]n view of the generally accepted formulations, the principle forbids all States or groups of States to intervene directly or indirectly in internal or external affairs of other States. A prohibited intervention must accordingly be one bearing on matters in which each State is permitted, by the principle of State sovereignty, to decide freely. One of these is the choice of a political, economic, social and cultural system, and the formulation of foreign policy. Intervention is wrongful when it uses methods of coercion in regard to such choices, which must remain free ones. The element of coercion, which defines and indeed forms the very essence of, prohibited intervention, is particularly obvious in the case of an intervention which uses force, either in the direct form of military action, or in the indirect form of support for subversive or terrorist armed activities within another State. . . . These forms of action are therefore wrongful in the light of both the principle of non-use of force, and that of non-intervention. . . .

[The Court went on to observe that there was no exception to the bar on intervention in the sovereign affairs of a state where the intervening state objected to "the domestic policies of that country, its ideology, the level of its armaments, or the direction of its foreign policy."]

A particular and fundamental aspect of the duty not to intervene in the domestic affairs of other states is the obligation to refrain from using force against their territorial integrity or political independence. The 1949 Draft Declaration on Rights and Duties of States[67] contains several articles dealing broadly with this obligation, as follows:

Article 8

Every State has the duty to settle its disputes with other States by peaceful means in such a manner that international peace and security, and justice, are not endangered.

Article 9

Every State has the duty to refrain from resorting to war as an instrument of national policy, and to refrain from the threat or use of force against the territorial integrity or political independence of another State in any other manner inconsistent with international law and order.

Article 10

Every State has the duty to refrain from giving assistance to any State which is acting in violation of article 9, or against which the United Nations is taking preventive or enforcement action.

Article 11

Every State has the duty to refrain from recognizing any territorial acquisition by another State acting in violation of article 9.

These prohibitions are all replicated, in one form or another, in international law. Article 2(4) of the UN Charter contains the key prohibition on the use of force in international relations: "All Members shall refrain in their international relations from the threat or use of force against the territorial integrity or political independence of any state, or in any other manner inconsistent with the Purposes of the United Nations." The UN General Assembly's Friendly Relations Declaration develops this basic principle in the following way:

***Declaration on Principles of International Law Concerning Friendly Relations and Co-operation in accordance with the Charter of the United Nations, GA Res 2625 (XXV), UN Doc A/RES/2625/XXV (1970)**[68]*

The principle that States shall refrain in their international relations from the threat or use of force against the territorial integrity or political independence of any State, or in any other manner inconsistent with the purpose of the United Nations:

Every State has the duty to refrain in its international relations from the threat or use of force against the territorial integrity or political independence of any State, or in any other manner inconsistent with the purposes of the United Nations. Such a threat or use of force constitutes a violation of international law and the Charter of the United Nations and shall never be employed as a means of settling international issues.

A war of aggression constitutes a crime against the peace, for which there is responsibility under international law.

67　Above note 58.

68　Reprinted in UN GAOR, 25th Sess, Supp No 28 at 121–24, UN Doc A/8028 Corr 1 (1970); (1970) 9 ILM 1292.

In accordance with the purposes and principles of the United Nations, States have the duty to refrain from propaganda for wars of aggression.

Every State has the duty to refrain from the threat or use of force to violate the existing international boundaries of another State or as a means of solving international disputes, including territorial disputes and problems concerning frontiers of States. . . .

States have a duty to refrain from acts of reprisal involving the use of force.

Every State has the duty to refrain from any forcible action which deprives peoples referred to in the elaboration of the principle of equal rights and self-determination of their right to self-determination and freedom and independence.

Every State has the duty to refrain from organizing or encouraging the organization of irregular forces or armed bands including mercenaries, for incursion into the territory of another State.

Every State has the duty to refrain from organizing, instigating, assisting or participating in acts of civil strife or terrorist acts in another State or acquiescing in organized activities within its territory directed towards the commission of such acts, when the acts referred to in the present paragraph involve a threat or use of force.

The territory of a State shall not be the object of military occupation resulting from the use of force in contravention of the provisions of the Charter. The territory of a State shall not be the object of acquisition by another State resulting from the threat or use of force. No territorial acquisition resulting from the threat or use of force shall be recognized as legal. Nothing in the foregoing shall be construed as affecting:

(a) Provisions of the Charter or any international agreement prior to the Charter régime and valid under international law; or

(b) The powers of the Security Council under the Charter. . . .

As with the Friendly Relations Declaration's more general provisions on non-intervention, the ICJ in the *Nicaragua* case found that "the adoption by States of this text affords an indication of their *opinio juris* as to customary international law on the question."[69] We will return to a more detailed examination of the prohibition of the use of force by states, and its exceptions, in Chapter 14.

d) The Duty to Respect International Law

The precise content of a state's international legal rights and duties are set out in the treaties to which it is a party, in customary international law, and in other sources of international legal obligation, as reviewed in Chapter 2. Undergirding all of these detailed rights and duties, however, and giving them legal significance, is the fundamental principle that states are obliged to observe these rules, a point captured (in relation to treaties) by the principle *pacta sunt servanda*, discussed in Chapter 2, and (more generally) in the 1949 Draft Declaration on Rights and Duties of States,[70] as follows:

---

69   *Military and Paramilitary Activities in and against Nicaragua (Nicaragua v United States of America)*, Merits, Judgment, [1986] ICJ Rep 14 at para 191 [*Nicaragua*].

70   Above note 58.

Article 13

Every State has the duty to carry out in good faith its obligations arising from treaties and other sources of international law, and it may not invoke provisions in its constitution or its laws as an excuse for failure to perform this duty.

Article 14

Every State has the duty to conduct its relations with other States in accordance with international law and with the principle that the sovereignty of each State is subject to the supremacy of international law.

The principle that states must respect international law may seem self-evident (at least to international lawyers), in that states can be presumed not to have articulated international "law" which they do not consider binding. However, the express statement of the principle serves as an important reminder that, in international law, sovereignty entails freedom from subjection to the sovereign will of other states but not from international law itself. Viewed from a slightly different angle, in modern international law, sovereignty flows from, is defined by, and depends upon, international law. States are accordingly not free to disregard its strictures without endangering their sovereignty and, hence, a key attribute of their statehood.

e) Protection of International Human Rights

The 1949 Draft Declaration on Rights and Duties of States[71] indicates, in Article 6, that: "Every State has the duty to treat all persons under its jurisdiction with respect for human rights and fundamental freedoms, without distinction as to race, sex, language, or religion." Article 1(3) of the UN Charter lists, as one of the purposes of the United Nations, "promoting and encouraging respect for human rights and for fundamental freedoms for all without distinction as to race, sex, language, or religion." Article 55 of the UN Charter, meanwhile, pledges the UN to promote "universal respect for, and observance of, human rights and fundamental freedoms for all without distinction as to race, sex, language, or religion."

From these tentative and somewhat vague beginnings to the subsequent adoption of the Universal Declaration of Human Rights[72] and the many human rights treaties that have followed, a vast body of highly detailed international human rights law has developed. Much of this law is sourced in both conventional and customary international law, the latter being presumptively binding upon all states. The overall effect of these legal developments has been a fundamental redefinition, in international law, of the relationship between states and the people under their jurisdiction. In the process, the scope of a state's "sovereign affairs" has been radically altered and the very concept of sovereignty itself affected. There are even strains entering the international legal discourse of states (for example, as seen above in our discussion of state recognition, or in the evolving "Responsibility to Protect" concept, discussed in Chapter 14) that suggest that respect for certain fundamental human rights is linked to a state's enjoyment of sovereignty.

We explore some of these linkages at greater length in subsequent chapters dealing with international human rights law and the use of force by states. For present purposes,

---

71   *Ibid.*
72   GA Res. 217 (III) (1948), reprinted in UN GAOR, 3rd Sess, Part 1 at 71–77, UN Doc A/810 (1948).

it may fairly be stated that to be a state necessarily entails, in modern international law, an obligation to respect and protect human rights.

B. INTERNATIONAL ORGANIZATIONS

We now turn to the second major type of actor in international law: the international (or intergovernmental) organization. First, we examine the international legal personality of international organizations—and specifically the United Nations (UN). Second, as it is the pre-eminent international organization, we examine the UN system in some detail, reviewing the UN Charter and then the role of the International Court of Justice (ICJ) as the "principal judicial organ" of the UN system.

1) The International Legal Personality of International Organizations

If international law is the "law of nations," what is the role of international organizations? Are they, like states, capable of both making, and being regulated by, international law? Do they have international legal rights and obligations in their own right, distinct from those imposed on their member states? In other words, do international organizations have international legal personality that clothes them with "standing" in the international legal system? The answer is "sometimes." Consider the following advisory opinion of the International Court of Justice.

> *Reparation for Injuries Suffered in the Service of the United Nations*, **Advisory Opinion,** **[1949] ICJ Rep 174**
>
> [Several UN personnel were killed in UN service in the territory of the newly established state of Israel. At the time, Israel had not yet been admitted to membership in the UN. The General Assembly asked the International Court of Justice for an advisory opinion on the possibility of the UN seeking reparations from Israel for the deaths.]
>
> . . . The first question asked of the Court is as follows:
>
>> In the event of an agent of the United Nations in the performance of his duties suffering injury in circumstances involving the responsibility of a State, has the United Nations, as an Organization, the capacity to bring an international claim against the responsible *de jure* or *de facto* government with a view to obtaining the reparation due in respect of the damage caused (a) to the United Nations, (b) to the victim or to persons entitled through him?
>
> . . . Competence to bring an international claim is, for those possessing it, the capacity to resort to the customary methods recognized by international law for the establishment, the presentation and the settlement of claims. Among these methods may be mentioned protest, request for an enquiry, negotiation, and request for submission to an arbitral tribunal or to the Court in so far as this may be authorized by the Statute [of the ICJ].
>
> This capacity certainly belongs to the State; a State can bring an international claim against another State. Such a claim takes the form of a claim between two political entities, equal in law, similar in form, and both the direct subjects of international law. . . .

But, in the international sphere, has the Organization such a nature as involves the capacity to bring an international claim? In order to answer this question, the Court must first enquire whether the Charter has given the Organization such a position that it possesses, in regard to its Members, rights which it is entitled to ask them to respect. In other words, does the Organization possess international personality? This is no doubt a doctrinal expression, which has sometimes given rise to controversy. But it will be used here to mean that if the Organization is recognized as having that personality, it is an entity capable of availing itself of obligations incumbent upon its Members.

To answer this question, which is not settled by the actual terms of the Charter, we must consider what characteristics it was intended thereby to give to the Organization.

The subjects of law in any legal system are not necessarily identical in their nature or in the extent of their rights, and their nature depends upon the needs of the community. Throughout its history, the development of international law has been influenced by the requirements of international life, and the progressive increase in the collective activities of States has already given rise to instances of action upon the international plane by certain entities which are not States. This development culminated in the establishment in June 1945 of an international organization whose purposes and principles are specified in the Charter of the United Nations. But to achieve these ends the attribution of international personality is indispensable.

The Charter has not been content to make the Organization created by it merely a centre 'for harmonizing the actions of nations in the attainment of these common ends' (Article I, para. 4). It has equipped that centre with organs, and has given it special tasks. It has defined the position of the Members in relation to the Organization by requiring them to give it every assistance in any action undertaken by it (Article 2, para. 5), and to accept and carry out the decisions of the Security Council; by authorizing the General Assembly to make recommendations to the Members; by giving the Organization legal capacity and privileges and immunities in the territory of each of its Members; and by providing for the conclusion of agreements between the Organization and its Members. Practice—in particular the conclusion of conventions to which the Organization is a party—has confirmed this character of the Organization, which occupies a position in certain respects in detachment from its Members, and which is under a duty to remind them, if need be, of certain obligations. It must be added that the Organization is a political body, charged with political tasks of an important character, and covering a wide field namely, the maintenance of international peace and security, the development of friendly relations among nations, and the achievement of international co-operation in the solution of problems of an economic, social, cultural or humanitarian character (Article 1); and in dealing with its Members it employs political means. The Convention on the Privileges and Immunities of the United Nations of 1946 creates rights and duties between each of the signatories and the Organization (see, in particular, Section 35).[73]

---

73 [Section 35 of the Convention on the Privileges and Immunities of the United Nations, 13 February 1946, 1 UNTS 15, in force 17 September 1946, provides: "This convention shall continue in force as between the United Nations and every Member which has deposited an instrument of accession for so long as that Member remains a Member of the United Nations, or until a revised general convention has been approved by the General Assembly and that Member has become a party to this revised convention."]

It is difficult to see how such a convention could operate except upon the international plane and as between parties possessing international personality.

In the opinion of the Court, the Organization was intended to exercise and enjoy, and is in fact exercising and enjoying, functions and rights which can only be explained on the basis of the possession of a large measure of international personality and the capacity to operate upon an international plane. It is at present the supreme type of international organization, and it could not carry out the intentions of its founders if it was devoid of international personality. It must be acknowledged that its Members, by entrusting certain functions to it, with the attendant duties and responsibilities, have clothed it with the competence required to enable those functions to be effectively discharged.

Accordingly, the Court has come to the conclusion that the Organization is an international person. That is not the same thing as saying that it is a State, which it certainly is not, or that its legal personality and rights and duties are the same as those of a State. Still less is it the same thing as saying that it is "a super-State," whatever that expression may mean. It does not even imply that all its rights and duties must be upon the international plane, any more than all the rights and duties of a State must be upon that plane. What it does mean is that it is a subject of international law and capable of possessing international rights and duties, and that it has capacity to maintain its rights by bringing international claims.

The next question is whether the sum of the international rights of the Organization comprises the right to bring the kind of international claim described in the Request for this Opinion. That is a claim against a State to obtain reparation in respect of the damage caused by the injury of an agent of the Organization in the course of the performance of his duties. Whereas a State possesses the totality of international rights and duties recognized by international law, the rights and duties of an entity such as the Organization must depend upon its purposes and functions as specified or implied in its constituent documents and developed in practice. The functions of the Organization are of such a character that they could not be effectively discharged if they involved the concurrent action, on the international plane, of fifty-eight or more Foreign Offices, and the Court concludes that the Members have endowed the Organization with capacity to bring international claims when necessitated by the discharge of its functions. . . .

The question remains whether the Organization has "the capacity to bring an international claim against the responsible de jure or de facto government . . ." when the defendant State is not a member of the Organization. . . .

On this point, the Court's opinion is that fifty States, representing the vast majority of the members of the international community, had the power, in conformity with international law, to bring into being an entity possessing objective international personality, and not merely personality recognized by them alone, together with capacity to bring international claims. . . .

The United Nations, like most international organizations, was established by multilateral treaty, the UN Charter. How did the Court go about answering the question of whether the United Nations had sufficient international legal personality to bring a claim against a state given that, in the Court's own words, the issue was "not settled by the actual terms of the Charter"? What were the key factors leading it to the conclusion that the United

Nations had, in fact, such capacity? Will the application of this analysis to other international organizations necessarily lead to the same result? Note the Court's observation that the "subjects of law in any legal system are not necessarily identical in their nature or in the extent of their rights." This could be said to be particularly true of international organizations, given the wide variation in their nature, structure, objects, and capacities, as defined in their constitutive treaties and by the practice of their members.

Finally, consider the Court's conclusion that the UN had the international legal capacity to bring a claim against a non-member state. Recalling again that the UN is the creature of a multilateral treaty, how can this conclusion be reconciled with the basic rule of treaty law that treaties do not create obligations for non-parties without their consent?

2) The United Nations System

a) Overview

As suggested above, the best-known and most influential international organization is, of course, the United Nations. Consider the following brief overview of the UN, prepared by that body's Department of Public Information:

The UN in Brief: How the UN Works, online: www.un.org/Overview/uninbrief/about. shtml

The United Nations was established on 24 October 1945 by 51 countries committed to preserving peace through international cooperation and collective security. Today, nearly every nation in the world belongs to the UN: membership totals 193 countries.

When States become Members of the United Nations, they agree to accept the obligations of the UN Charter, an international treaty that sets out basic principles of international relations. According to the Charter, the UN has four purposes: to maintain international peace and security; to develop friendly relations among nations; to cooperate in solving international problems and in promoting respect for human rights; [and] to be a centre for harmonizing the actions of nations.

The United Nations is not a world government and it does not make laws. It does, however, provide the means to help resolve international conflicts and formulate policies on matters affecting all of us. At the UN, all the Member States — large and small, rich and poor, with differing political views and social systems — have a voice and a vote in this process.

The United Nations has six main organs. Five of them — the General Assembly, the Security Council, the Economic and Social Council, the Trusteeship Council and the Secretariat — are based at UN Headquarters in New York. The sixth, the International Court of Justice, is located at The Hague in the Netherlands.

The General Assembly

All UN Member States are represented in the General Assembly — a "parliament of nations" which meets regularly and in special sessions to consider the world's most pressing problems. Each Member State has one vote. Decisions on such key issues as international peace and security, admitting new members and the UN budget are decided by two-thirds majority. Other matters are decided by simple majority. In recent years, a special effort has been made to reach decisions through consensus, rather than by taking a formal vote. The Assembly cannot force action by any State, but its recommendations are an important indication of world opinion and represent the moral authority of the community of nations.

The Assembly holds its annual regular session from September to December. When necessary, it may resume its session or hold a special or emergency session on subjects of particular concern. Its work is also carried out by its six Main Committees, other subsidiary bodies and the UN Secretariat. . . .

The Security Council

The UN Charter gives primary responsibility for maintaining international peace and security to the Security Council, which may meet whenever peace is threatened. Under the Charter, all Member States are obligated to carry out the Council's decisions.

The Council is made up of 15 members. Five of them are permanent members: China, France, Russian Federation, United Kingdom and United States. The other 10 are elected by the General Assembly for two-year terms. Member States are considering changes in the composition and methods of work of the Council so that it better reflects current political and economic realities.

The adoption of a Council decision requires nine votes in favour. Except in case of a vote on procedural matters, the Council cannot adopt a decision if one of the permanent members casts a veto.

When the Council examines a complaint concerning a threat to international peace, it first explores ways of reaching agreement by peaceful means. It may set forth principles for a peaceful settlement or undertake mediation. When a disputes leads to fighting, the Council seeks to bring it to an end. It may send peacekeeping forces to supervise a truce and keep opposing forces apart.

The Council can take measures to enforce its decisions. It may impose economic sanctions or an arms embargo. In some occasions, the Council has authorized Member States to take "all available means," including collective military action, to ensure that its decisions are carried out. The Council also recommends to the General Assembly a candidate for the post of Secretary-General and proposes the admission of new United Nations Member States.

The Economic and Social Council

The Economic and Social Council, under the overall authority of the General Assembly, co-ordinates the economic and social work of the United Nations and the UN family of organizations. As the central forum for discussing international economic and social issues and for formulating policy recommendations, the Council plays a key role in fostering international cooperation for development. It also consults with non-governmental organizations (NGOs), thereby maintaining a vital link between the United Nations and civil society.

The Council has 54 members, elected by the General Assembly for three-year terms. It meets throughout the year and holds a major session in July, during which a high-level meeting of Ministers discusses major economic, social and humanitarian issues.

The Council's subsidiary bodies meet regularly and report back to it. These bodies focus on such issues as social development, the status of women, crime prevention, narcotic drugs and sustainable development. Five regional commissions promote economic development and cooperation in their respective regions.

The Trusteeship Council

The Trusteeship Council was established to provide international supervision to 11 Trust Territories administered by seven Member States, and guarantee that appropriate steps were taken to prepare such Territories for autonomy or independence.

By 1994, all Trust Territories had achieved autonomy or independence, either as autonomous States or by joining neighbouring independent countries. The last to do so was the Trust Territory of the Pacific Islands (Palau), administered by the United States, which became the 185th Member State of the United Nations.

Having achieved its task, the Trusteeship Council, which is now made of the five permanent members of the Security Council, amended its rules of procedure and will meet as and when occasion may require. . . .

The International Court of Justice

The International Court of Justice, also known as the World Court, is the main judicial organ of the UN. Its 15 judges are elected by the General Assembly and the Security Council, voting independently and concurrently. The Court decides disputes between countries, based on the voluntary participation of the States concerned. If a State agrees to participate in a proceeding, it is obligated to comply with the Court's decision. The Court also gives advisory opinions to the United Nations and its specialized agencies.

The Secretariat

The Secretariat carries out the substantive and administrative work of the United Nations as directed by the General Assembly, the Security Council and the other organs. At its head is the Secretary-General, who provides overall administrative guidance.

The Secretariat consists of departments and offices with a total staff of about 44,000 under the regular budget, drawn from some 180 countries. Duty stations include UN Headquarters in New York, as well as UN offices in Geneva, Vienna, Nairobi and other locations.

The UN System

The International Monetary Fund, the World Bank and 13 other independent organizations known as "specialized agencies" are linked to the UN through cooperative agreements. These agencies, among them the World Health Organization and the International Civil Aviation Organization, are autonomous bodies created by intergovernmental agreement. They have wide-ranging international responsibilities in the economic, social, cultural, educational, health and related fields. Some of them, like the International Labour Organization and the Universal Postal Union, are older than the UN itself.

In addition, a number of UN offices, programmes and funds—such as the Office of the UN High Commissioner for Refugees (UNHCR), the UN Development Programme

(UNDP) and the UN Children's Fund (UNICEF)—work to improve the economic and social condition of people around the world. They report to the General Assembly or the Economic and Social Council.

All these organizations have their own governing bodies, budgets and secretariats. Together with the United Nations, they are known as the UN family, or the UN system. Together, they provide technical assistance and other forms of practical help in virtually all economic and social areas. . . .

In the remainder of this chapter, we examine in greater detail key UN institutions, with particular reference to the UN Charter. We begin with the preamble and first two articles of the UN Charter, which set out many important substantive legal concepts, followed by those portions of the UN Charter dealing with the composition, organs and key functions of the United Nations.

b) Purposes and Principles

Charter of the United Nations, 26 June 1945, Can TS 1945 No 7, in force 24 October 1945

WE THE PEOPLES OF THE UNITED NATIONS DETERMINED to save succeeding generations from the scourge of war, which twice in our lifetime has brought untold sorrow to mankind, and to reaffirm faith in fundamental human rights, in the dignity and worth of the human person, in the equal rights of men and women and of nations large and small, and to establish conditions under which justice and respect for the obligations arising from treaties and other sources of international law can be maintained, and to promote social progress and better standards of life in larger freedom,

AND FOR THESE ENDS to practice tolerance and live together in peace with one another as good neighbours, and to unite our strength to maintain international peace and security, and to ensure, by the acceptance of principles and the institution of methods, that armed force shall not be used, save in the common interest, and to employ international machinery for the promotion of the economic and social advancement of all peoples,

HAVE RESOLVED TO COMBINE OUR EFFORTS TO ACCOMPLISH THESE AIMS. Accordingly, our respective Governments, through representatives assembled in the city of San Francisco, who have exhibited their full powers found to be in good and due form, have agreed to the present Charter of the United Nations and do hereby establish an international organization to be known as the United Nations.

CHAPTER I
PURPOSES AND PRINCIPLES

Article 1
The Purposes of the United Nations are:

1. To maintain international peace and security, and to that end: to take effective collective measures for the prevention and removal of threats to the peace, and for the suppression of acts of aggression or other breaches of the peace, and to bring about by peaceful means, and in conformity with the principles of justice and international law, adjustment

or settlement of international disputes or situations which might lead to a breach of the peace;

2. To develop friendly relations among nations based on respect for the principle of equal rights and self-determination of peoples, and to take other appropriate measures to strengthen universal peace;

3. To achieve international co-operation in solving international problems of an economic, social, cultural, or humanitarian character, and in promoting and encouraging respect for human rights and for fundamental freedoms for all without distinction as to race, sex, language, or religion; and

4. To be a centre for harmonizing the actions of nations in the attainment of these common ends.

Article 2

The Organization and its Members, in pursuit of the Purposes stated in Article 1, shall act in accordance with the following Principles.

1. The Organization is based on the principle of the sovereign equality of all its Members.

2. All Members, in order to ensure to all of them the rights and benefits resulting from membership, shall fulfill in good faith the obligations assumed by them in accordance with the present Charter.

3. All Members shall settle their international disputes by peaceful means in such a manner that international peace and security, and justice, are not endangered.

4. All Members shall refrain in their international relations from the threat or use of force against the territorial integrity or political independence of any state, or in any other manner inconsistent with the Purposes of the United Nations.

5. All Members shall give the United Nations every assistance in any action it takes in accordance with the present Charter, and shall refrain from giving assistance to any state against which the United Nations is taking preventive or enforcement action.

6. The Organization shall ensure that states which are not Members of the United Nations act in accordance with these Principles so far as may be necessary for the maintenance of international peace and security.

7. Nothing contained in the present Charter shall authorize the United Nations to intervene in matters which are essentially within the domestic jurisdiction of any state or shall require the Members to submit such matters to settlement under the present Charter; but this principle shall not prejudice the application of enforcement measures under Chapter VII.

The "Purposes and Principles" found in Articles 1 and 2 "are designed to provide a guide for the conduct of the UN organs in a fairly flexible manner."[74] These Articles appear

---

74 Bruno Simma et al, eds, *The Charter of the United Nations: A Commentary*, 3d ed, vols I & II (Oxford: Oxford University Press, 2012) at 108.

to express the political aspirations of, and objectives for, the United Nations, rather than impose specific obligations and duties. It is disputable, therefore, whether the purposes articulated in Article 1 are legally binding. That said, the purposes articulated in paragraphs 1 to 3 of Article 1 refer to concepts that clearly are rooted in international law: the settlement of international disputes through peaceful means; respect for sovereign equality and self-determination of peoples; and the protection of human rights.

Moreover, some of these—such as the duty to settle disputes peacefully and to respect sovereign equality—take the form, in Article 2, of specific obligations imposed on member states or the United Nations itself. These and some of the other substantive obligations imposed by Article 2 are discussed more fully elsewhere in this book. For present purposes, however, take note of paragraphs 6 and 7 of Article 2. In particular, is paragraph 6 compatible with the basic rule of treaty law that treaties do not create obligations for non-parties without their consent? If not, what obligations does paragraph 6 impose on non-members of the United Nations, and do such obligations exist as a matter of customary international law in any event? With respect to paragraph 7, is it significant that the implied duty of non-intervention appears only to apply to the United Nations rather than to member states also? In reflecting on these questions, consider the combined effect of the opening phrase, and paragraph 1, of Article 2.

The balance of the UN Charter deals with the mechanics of the United Nations as an international organization.

c) Membership

Charter of the United Nations, 26 June 1945, Can TS 1945 No 7, in force 24 October 1945

CHAPTER II
MEMBERSHIP

Article 3
The original Members of the United Nations shall be the states which, having participated in the United Nations Conference on International Organization at San Francisco, or having previously signed the Declaration by United Nations of 1 January 1942, sign the present Charter and ratify it in accordance with Article 110.

Article 4
1. Membership in the United Nations is open to other peace-loving states which accept the obligations contained in the present Charter and, in the judgment of the Organization, are able and willing to carry out these obligations.

2. The admission of any such state to membership in the United Nations will be effected by a decision of the General Assembly upon the recommendation of the Security Council.

From its inception, the intent of the UN Charter's framers was to make the United Nations as universal an organization as possible, subject to certain criteria for membership set out in Article 4. On 26 June 1945, the fifty participants at the San Francisco Conference signed the UN Charter. Notably, two of these entities—India and the Philippines—subsequently ratified the UN Charter and became members (on 30 and 24 October 1945, respectively) before they were fully independent.[75] Similarly, the Byelorussian and Ukrainian Soviet Socialist Republics became original UN members—at the insistence of the USSR—even though they were constituent units of the USSR from 1922 until their emergence as the independent states of Belarus and Ukraine respectively upon the dissolution of the USSR in 1991. In other words, original membership in the United Nations did not hinge on strict adherence to the classic prerequisites for statehood reviewed above.[76]

Article 4 governs the admission of non-original members of the United Nations. It imposes five conditions. The entity must be (1) a state that is (2) peace-loving and (3) accepts the obligations contained in the UN Charter. It must also be (4) capable of carrying out these obligations and (5) willing to do so.[77] In some instances, satisfaction of the first requirement—that an entity be a state—was a contested issue. As commentators have explained: "Between 1946 and 1962, the statehood of applicants was repeatedly called into question during admission procedures for an alleged lack mainly of independent government but sometimes also of a sufficiently defined territory."[78] Entities were judged to lack an independent government as a result of foreign occupation, military occupation, a special relationship with a former colonial power, or factual dependence, but statehood was also disputed in the absence of sufficiently defined borders or where neighbouring states had made claims to the territory of the applicant entity.[79]

Since the 1960s, the Article 4 criteria have been applied liberally, with the decolonization of mostly developing states leading to a broadening of the spectrum of statehood and the admission of entities with what traditionally would have been considered weak claims to statehood. As commentators have noted: "The concept of conditional universality, thus, seemed to have largely been replaced by a concept of automatic admission."[80] Many "newly decolonized States were admitted without the criteria contained in Art[icle] 4(1) even being mentioned" and "[t]he admission of new member States thus became a mere procedural formality."[81] Since 1945, the number of states has burgeoned, and there are now 193 UN members.

It would be wrong, however, to suggest that every entity with a claim to statehood can readily obtain UN membership. We have already discussed three entities with a plausible claim to statehood that are not members of the United Nations: Taiwan, the Holy See, and Palestine (although, as noted above, the latter two have been granted UN observer status). Consider other entities not members of the United Nations which might have a claim to statehood: Abkhazia (part of Georgia); Cabinda (part of Angola); Jubaland (part of Somalia); Kosovo (discussed above); Kurdistan (part of Iraq and Turkey); Nagorno-Karabakh (part of Azerbaijan); Northern Cyprus; Puntland (part of Somalia); Somaliland

---

75 India achieved independence from the UK on 15 August 1947 and the Philippines achieved independence from the US on 4 July 1946.

76 See Wallace-Bruce, above note 19 at 59.

77 See *Conditions of Admission of a State to Membership in the United Nations* (Article 4 of the Charter), Advisory Opinion, [1949] ICJ Rep 56 [*Conditions of Admission Advisory Opinion*].

78 Simma et al, above note 74 at 346.

79 See *ibid* at 346 for examples where each factor was invoked.

80 *Ibid* at 343.

81 *Ibid* at 345.

(part of Somalia); South Ossetia (part of Georgia); Transdniestria (part of Moldavia); and the Western Sahara. How is it that these entities are not member states of the United Nations, a body aiming for universal membership?

In many of these cases, the answer is that the entity either has not satisfied, or has not been recognized by UN member states as satisfying, the international legal criteria for statehood. These two possibilities are of course not the same thing, as we have seen in our review of the central role played by politics in state recognition. In its very first advisory opinion, the International Court of Justice implied that Article 4 limits the grounds upon which a member state of the United Nations may rely in resisting a membership application.[82] However, the procedure for admission established in the UN Charter effectively elevates politics over law. Article 4(2) requires that a new member be admitted by a decision of the General Assembly upon the recommendation of the Security Council. If sufficient numbers of states participating in these two highly politicized organs decline to act, no membership is extended. Take the case of Taiwan's efforts to attain UN membership from 1993 to 2007, as described in this 1995 *New York Times* article:

> There is an inevitability to autumn's arrival in New York. Green leaves turn brown and carpet Central Park. Diplomatic cavalcades clog midtown Manhattan once the United Nations convenes its General Assembly. And Taiwan tries to get back into the United Nations while China works just as hard to keep it out.
>
> Today, China amassed enough support for the third year in a row to delete from the General Assembly's agenda a proposal that Taiwan's lack of representation be considered.[83]

Even if Taiwan had managed to place its membership on the agenda of the General Assembly, remember that the formal membership process contemplated in Article 4 requires a recommendation for membership by the Security Council.[84] China is a permanent member of that organ, and may therefore veto Security Council decisions, as discussed later in this chapter.

Charter of the United Nations, 26 June 1945, Can TS 1945 No 7, in force 24 October 1945

Article 5
A Member of the United Nations against which preventive or enforcement action has been taken by the Security Council may be suspended from the exercise of the rights and privileges of membership by the General Assembly upon the recommendation of the Security Council. The exercise of these rights and privileges may be restored by the Security Council.

---

82 *Conditions of Admission Advisory Opinion*, above note 77.
83 Christopher Wren, "Taiwan Again Tries to Join U.N., and Again China Bars Door," *New York Times* (21 September 1995) 5.
84 See *Competence of the General Assembly for the Admission of a State to the United Nations*, Advisory Opinion, [1950] ICJ Rep 4, affirming this requirement.

Article 6

A Member of the United Nations which has persistently violated the Principles contained in the present Charter may be expelled from the Organization by the General Assembly upon the recommendation of the Security Council.

No state has ever been expelled from the United Nations. Despite the absence of any express provision allowing unilateral withdrawals, Indonesia withdrew from the United Nations in 1965, but resumed participation in 1966. For its part, apartheid-era South Africa was prevented from participating in UN debates and the activities of the General Assembly between 1974 and 1993, after a finding by the Assembly's Credentials Committee that the then-government of South Africa was not representative of all its people.[85] If this standard of government representativeness were applied consistently, how many UN members would be entitled to participate in the General Assembly?

To say that no state has ever been expelled requires some nuance in the case of the former Yugoslavia. Security Council Resolution 777 (1992) of 19 September 1992 reads in part:

The Security Council, . . .

Considering that the State formerly known as the Socialist Federal Republic of Yugoslavia has ceased to exist,

Recalling in particular resolution 757 (1992) which notes that "the claim by the Federal Republic of Yugoslavia (Serbia and Montenegro) to continue automatically the membership of the former Socialist Federal Republic of Yugoslavia in the United Nations has not been generally accepted,"

1. Considers that the Federal Republic of Yugoslavia (Serbia and Montenegro) cannot continue automatically the membership of the former Socialist Federal Republic of Yugoslavia in the United Nations; and therefore recommends to the General Assembly that it decide that the Federal Republic of Yugoslavia (Serbia and Montenegro) should apply for membership in the United Nations and that it shall not participate in the work of the General Assembly. . . .[86]

In September 1992, the General Assembly adopted resolution 47/1, which reads in part:

The General Assembly,

Having received the recommendation of the Security Council of 19 September 1992 that the Federal Republic of Yugoslavia (Serbia and Montenegro) should apply for membership in the United Nations and that it shall not participate in the work of the General Assembly,

1. Considers that the Federal Republic of Yugoslavia (Serbia and Montenegro) cannot continue automatically the membership of the former Socialist Federal Republic of Yugoslavia in the United Nations; and therefore decides that the Federal Republic of Yugoslavia (Serb-

---

85   Ivan A Shearer, *Starke's International Law*, 11th ed (Toronto: Butterworths, 1994) at 571.

86   SC Resolution 777 (1992), adopted 19 September 1992, UN Doc S/RES/777 (1992).

ia and Montenegro) should apply for membership in the United Nations and that it shall not participate in the work of the General Assembly. . . .[87]

What was the legal authority for these resolutions, and what were their legal implications? As one commentator has stated, the General Assembly resolution "appears to recognize a temporary and shadowy status of a state subject to continuing obligations of membership such as amenability to the decisions of the Security Council and to the jurisdiction of the International Court of Justice" — a view incidentally affirmed by the ICJ itself[88] — "but unable to exercise the normal rights of membership."[89] Consider the interpretation of the resolution's effect offered by the Under-Secretary-General and Legal Counsel of the United Nations:

> While the General Assembly has stated unequivocally that the Federal Republic of Yugoslavia (Serbia and Montenegro) cannot automatically continue the membership of the former Socialist Federal Republic of Yugoslavia in the United Nations and that the Federal Republic of Yugoslavia (Serbia and Montenegro) should apply for membership in the United Nations, the *only* practical consequence that the resolution draws is that the Federal Republic of Yugoslavia (Serbia and Montenegro) shall not participate in the work of the General Assembly. It is clear, therefore, that representatives of the Federal Republic of Yugoslavia (Serbia and Montenegro) can no longer participate in the work of the General Assembly, its subsidiary organs, nor conferences and meetings convened by it.
>
> On the other hand, the resolution neither terminates nor suspends Yugoslavia's membership in the Organization. Consequently, the seat and nameplate remain as before, but in Assembly bodies representatives of the Federal Republic of Yugoslavia (Serbia and Montenegro) cannot sit behind the sign "Yugoslavia." Yugoslav missions at United Nations Headquarters and offices may continue to function and may receive and circulate documents. At Headquarters, the Secretariat will continue to fly the flag of the old Yugoslavia as it is the last flag of Yugoslavia used by the Secretariat. The resolution does not take away the right of Yugoslavia to participate in the work of organs other than Assembly bodies. The admission to the United Nations of a new Yugoslavia under Article 4 of the Charter will terminate the situation created by resolution 47/1. . . .[90]

In fact, following elections that ousted Slobodan Milosevic from power, the Federal Republic of Yugoslavia (subsequently renamed Serbia and Montenegro) was admitted to UN membership on 1 November 2000.[91] More recently still, only five weeks after its accession to independence in accordance with the constitution of Serbia and Montenegro,

---

87   *Recommendation of the Security Council of 19 September 1992*, GA Res 47/1, UN Doc A/RES/47/1 (1992), reprinted in UN GAOR, 47th Sess, Supp No 49, vol I at 12, UN Doc A/47/49 (1993).

88   *Application of the Convention on the Prevention and Punishment of the Crime of Genocide (Bosnia and Herzegovina v Yugoslavia (Serbia and Montenegro))*, Provisional Measures, Order of 8 April 1993, [1993] ICJ Rep 3 [*Application of the Genocide Convention Case — Provisional Measures*].

89   Shearer, above note 85 at 71.

90   *Application of the Genocide Convention Case — Provisional Measures*, above note 88 at para 17 [emphasis added].

91   See *Admission of the Federal Republic of Yugoslavia to membership in the United Nations*, GA Res 55/12, UN Doc A/RES/55/12 (2000), reprinted in UN GAOR, 55th Sess, Supp No 49, vol I at 28, UN Doc

Montenegro was admitted in its own right as the 192nd member of the United Nations.[92] Serbia continues the membership of the former Serbia and Montenegro.

d) Principal Organs

Charter of the United Nations, 26 June 1945, Can TS 1945 No 7, in force 24 October 1945

CHAPTER III
ORGANS

Article 7
1. There are established as the principal organs of the United Nations: a General Assembly, a Security Council, an Economic and Social Council, a Trusteeship Council, an International Court of Justice, and a Secretariat.

2. Such subsidiary organs as may be found necessary may be established in accordance with the present Charter.

Article 8
The United Nations shall place no restrictions on the eligibility of men and women to participate in any capacity and under conditions of equality in its principal and subsidiary organs.

i) General Assembly

Charter of the United Nations, 26 June 1945, Can TS 1945 No 7, in force 24 October 1945

CHAPTER IV
THE GENERAL ASSEMBLY

Article 9
1. The General Assembly shall consist of all the Members of the United Nations. . . .

Article 20
The General Assembly shall meet in regular annual sessions and in such special sessions as occasion may require. Special sessions shall be convoked by the Secretary-General at the request of the Security Council or of a majority of the Members of the United Nations.

The General Assembly is the only UN principal organ in which each state member is a permanent participant. While it may have some of the outward trappings of a world "parliament," the individuals who sit in the General Assembly and its committees are usually diplomats representing their sending states rather than elected representatives directly

---

A/55/49 (2000), acting on the recommendation of the Security Council found in Resolution 1326 (2000), adopted 31 October 2000, UN Doc S/RES/1326 (2000).

92 See *Admission of the Republic of Montenegro to Membership in the United* Nations, GA Res 60/264, UN Doc A/RES/60/264 (2006), reprinted in UN GAOR, 60th Sess, Supp No 49, vol III at 17, UN Doc A/60/49 (2006), acting on the recommendation of the Security Council found in Resolution 1691 (2006), adopted 22 June 2006, UN Doc S/RES/1691 (2006).

answerable to an electorate. Moreover, the General Assembly does not have law-making power and cannot enact "Acts of Parliament." It is also devoid of any notion of proportional representation by population. China, the state with the largest population, has the same, single vote as does Tuvalu, the state with the smallest population. Consider the following provisions of the UN Charter, reflecting this formal equality of member states:

Charter of the United Nations, 26 June 1945, Can TS 1945 No 7, in force 24 October 1945

Voting

Article 18

1. Each member of the General Assembly shall have one vote.

2. Decisions of the General Assembly on important questions shall be made by a two-thirds majority of the members present and voting. These questions shall include: recommendations with respect to the maintenance of international peace and security, the election of the non-permanent members of the Security Council, the election of the members of the Economic and Social Council, the election of members of the Trusteeship Council in accordance with paragraph 1 of Article 86, the admission of new Members to the United Nations, the suspension of the rights and privileges of membership, the expulsion of Members, questions relating to the operation of the trusteeship system, and budgetary questions.

3. Decisions on other questions, including the determination of additional categories of questions to be decided by a two-thirds majority, shall be made by a majority of the members present and voting.

The "one state, one vote" approach to General Assembly voting is different from that adopted in some other institutions. At the World Bank, for example, votes are weighted with reference to the financial subscription each state has made to the body, with more voting power flowing to those who have made the greatest financial contribution. The one state, one vote approach in the General Assembly also differs from that adopted with respect to the Security Council where certain states have been given the power to veto resolutions.

Note the distinction drawn in Article 18 between decisions on "important questions" and decisions on "other questions": the former requires the support of two-thirds of voting members, while the latter requires a simple majority. The list of "important questions" in Article 18(2) requiring two-thirds support is not exhaustive, and indeed Article 18(3) anticipates that other matters may be added to that list. In fact, the General Assembly's Rules of Procedure do include several supplemental matters requiring two-thirds support. In any General Assembly vote, support is measured with reference to those countries actually voting for or against, and not with reference to those countries that abstain either actively or by failing to appear for a vote. Even a minority of member states may make a decision if those states together constitute the requisite simple or two-thirds majority of states present and voting.[93]

---

93 See Rule 86 of the *Rules of Procedure of the General Assembly*, UN Doc A/520/Rev 17 (2008), and Simma et al, above note 74 at 625–26.

Notwithstanding these rules, the practice at the General Assembly often does not hinge on voting. Observers of the United Nations note that "[t]he vast majority of the General Assembly's more recent decisions have been adopted without a vote."[94] But this practice of adoption without a formal vote, to encourage the appearance of decision making by consensus, "has an impact on the way negotiations are conducted and the results achieved. The agreed text will almost certainly be the lowest common denominator of the interests of those who have participated in the negotiations."[95] In his 2005 report, *In Larger Freedom: Towards Development, Security and Human Rights for All*, the UN Secretary-General echoed this concern:

> 159. In recent years, the number of General Assembly resolutions approved by consensus has increased steadily. That would be good if it reflected a genuine unity of purpose among Member States in responding to global challenges. But unfortunately, consensus (often interpreted as requiring unanimity) has become an end in itself. It is sought first within each regional group and then at the level of the whole. This has not proved an effective way of reconciling the interests of Member States. Rather, it prompts the Assembly to retreat into generalities, abandoning any serious effort to take action. Such real debates as there are tend to focus on process rather than substance and many so-called decisions simply reflect the lowest common denominator of widely different opinions.[96]

In at least some instances, the consensus approach has been adopted to avoid the prickly problem of states that are in arrears in their payments to the United Nations, and thus technically stripped of their vote. Consider the implications of Article 19:

Charter of the United Nations, 26 June 1945, Can TS 1945 No 7, in force 24 October 1945

Article 19
A Member of the United Nations which is in arrears in the payment of its financial contributions to the Organization shall have no vote in the General Assembly if the amount of its arrears equals or exceeds the amount of the contributions due from it for the preceding two full years. The General Assembly may, nevertheless, permit such a Member to vote if it is satisfied that the failure to pay is due to conditions beyond the control of the Member.

The UN Charter says relatively little on the financing of the organization. Article 17 provides that the "General Assembly shall consider and approve the budget of the Organization" and that the "expenses of the Organization shall be borne by the Members as apportioned by the General Assembly." In Article 18, "budgetary questions" are among those requiring a two-thirds vote. In practice, contributions are scaled. In the "scale of assessments" in place for 2012, the United States is (by far) the most important contributor, covering 22 percent of the UN regular operating budget. Canada ranks seventh, providing

---

94 Simma et al, *ibid* at 627 and 633.
95 *Ibid* at 633.
96 *In Larger Freedom: Towards Development, Security and Human Rights for All: Report of the Secretary-General*, UN Doc A/59/2005 at para 159 (21 March 2005) [*In Larger Freedom*].

3.207 percent.[97] While Canada has a policy of paying its assessed contributions in full and on time, many other states are in arrears at any given point in time.

The US share of UN funding has been controversial in that country. The United States used to be significantly in arrears on its contributions, which caused significant budgetary difficulties within the United Nations. In 1999, this problem was substantially alleviated by the Helms-Biden legislation,[98] which authorized the payment of US$926 million in arrears, subject to certain conditions such as a reduction in US contributions from 25 to 22 percent of the UN's regular budget and from 31 to 26 percent of the peacekeeping budget. The legislation provides for the release of money in instalments calculated to amount to "more than the minimum amount required for [the United States] to avoid losing its vote in the General Assembly . . . under the provision[s] of Article 19 of the Charter."[99]

As of January 2013, twenty-two UN member states were in arrears under the terms of Article 19.[100] However, five of these states (Central African Republic, Comoros, Guinea-Bissau, Sao Tome and Principe, and Somalia) were granted permission to vote, the General Assembly having concluded that their failure to pay was due to conditions beyond their control.[101] Several states subsequently made payments to address their arrears such that by March 2013, only the following six states in arrears were not able to vote: Dominican Republic, Marshall Islands, Sierra Leone, Vanuatu, Venezuela, and Zimbabwe.

Charter of the United Nations, 26 June 1945, Can TS 1945 No 7, in force 24 October 1945

Article 10

The General Assembly may discuss any questions or any matters within the scope of the present Charter or relating to the powers and functions of any organs provided for in the present Charter, and, except as provided in Article 12, may make recommendations to the Members of the United Nations or to the Security Council or to both on any such questions or matters.

As Article 10 suggests, the General Assembly is not a legislative body. As we have already explored, it is not a formal source of international law, although its resolutions may sometimes evidence and influence the development of customary international law or lead to the negotiation of new treaties. The General Assembly "is essentially a deliberative body, with powers of discussion, investigation, review, supervision and criticism in relation to the work of the United Nations as a whole . . . and of the various other organs of world government provided for in the Charter including the specialised agencies."[102]

---

97 See *Assessment of Member States' Contributions to the United Nations Regular Budget for 2012*, UN Doc ST/ADM/SER.B/853 (27 December 2011).

98 The Helms-Biden agreement is contained in the Foreign Affairs Reform and Restructuring Act of 1998, HR 1757, 105th Cong (1998).

99 United Nations, *Press Briefing by Under-Secretary-General for Management* (22 December 1999).

100 *Letter dated 15 January 2013 from the Secretary-General to the President of the General Assembly*, UN Doc A/67/693 (15 January 2013).

101 *Scale of assessments for the apportionment of the expenses of the United Nations: requests under Article 19 of the Charter*, GA Res 67/2 (2012), reprinted in UN GAOR, 67th Sess, Supp No 49, UN Doc A/67/49 (2012).

102 Shearer, above note 85 at 572.

The General Assembly may, however, make binding decisions in certain organizational or administrative areas proper to the United Nations itself. These include its decisions on admission, suspension, and expulsion of members under Articles 4 and 5; its role in approving amendments to the UN Charter in Articles 108 and 109; the election of members to assorted organs and committees in Articles 23, 61, and 97; and its budgetary function in Article 17.

Nevertheless, for the most part, the General Assembly is limited under Article 10 to "a general power of discussion and recommendation,"[103] which "also encompasses a right to investigate."[104] In practice, the General Assembly exercises its recommendation function through "resolutions" or "declarations." Resolution is the broadest term, used to describe the manner in which the Assembly expresses its collective will in terms of specific recommendations (and sometimes observations or reminders). The term "declaration"—or more rarely, "charter"—is typically reserved for those resolutions that purport to reflect political or legal principles of general significance.[105]

The UN Charter includes illustrative references to subject-areas in relation to which the General Assembly may exercise its discussion and recommendation powers. For instance, Article 11 specifies that the "General Assembly may consider the general principles of co-operation in the maintenance of international peace and security, including the principles governing disarmament and the regulation of armaments." It "may make recommendations with regard to such principles to the Members or to the Security Council or to both." Further, it "may call the attention of the Security Council to situations which are likely to endanger international peace and security." Likewise, Article 14 indicates that the General Assembly "may recommend measures for the peaceful adjustment of any situation, regardless of origin, which it deems likely to impair the general welfare or friendly relations among nations, including situations resulting from a violation of the provisions of the present Charter setting forth the Purposes and Principles of the United Nations."

These more specific powers of discussion and recommendation do not constrain the general power set out in Article 10. A constraint does exist, however, in Article 12, which reads: "While the Security Council is exercising in respect of any dispute or situation the functions assigned to it in the present Charter, the General Assembly shall not make any recommendation with regard to that dispute or situation unless the Security Council so requests."

As we discuss below, the Security Council has primary responsibility in the area of international peace and security. Article 12 permits the Security Council to preclude a General Assembly recommendation on a given international peace and security matter where the Council is seized of the question. The ICJ, however, has emphasized an evolving interpretation of Article 12 in its advisory opinion on the Israeli wall in the Occupied Palestinian Territory:

---

103 See Simma et al, above note 74 at 463.
104 *Ibid* at 464.
105 *Ibid* at 478–79.

Legal Consequences of the Construction of a Wall in the Occupied Palestinian Territory,
Advisory Opinion, [2004] ICJ Rep 136

[In 2003, the UN General Assembly asked the Court for an advisory opinion on the following question: "What are the legal consequences arising from the construction of the wall
being built by Israel, the occupying Power, in the Occupied Palestinian Territory, including in and around East Jerusalem, as described in the report of the Secretary-General,
considering the rules and principles of international law, including the Fourth Geneva
Convention of 1949,[106] and relevant Security Council and General Assembly resolutions?"]

24. . . . Israel has alleged that, given the active engagement of the Security Council with
the situation in the Middle East, including the Palestinian question, the General Assembly acted *ultra vires* under the Charter when it requested an advisory opinion on the
legal consequences of the construction of the wall in the Occupied Palestinian Territory.

25. . . . A request for an advisory opinion is not in itself a "recommendation" by the General Assembly "with regard to [a] dispute or situation". It has however been argued in this
case that the adoption by the General Assembly of resolution ES-10/14 was *ultra vires* as
not in accordance with Article 12 [of the UN Charter]. The Court thus considers that it is
appropriate for it to examine the significance of that Article, having regard to the relevant
texts and the practice of the United Nations.

26. Under Article 24 of the Charter the Security Council has "primary responsibility for
the maintenance of international peace and security." In that regard it can impose on
States "an explicit obligation of compliance if for example it issues an order or command
. . . under Chapter VII" and can, to that end, "require enforcement by coercive action." . . .
However, the Court would emphasize that Article 24 refers to a primary, but not necessarily exclusive, competence. The General Assembly does have the power, *inter alia*,
under Article 14 of the Charter, to "recommend measures for the peaceful adjustment"
of various situations. . . . "[T]he only limitation which Article 14 imposes on the General
Assembly is the restriction found in Article 12, namely, that the Assembly should not
recommend measures while the Security Council is dealing with the same matter unless
the Council requests it to do so." . . .

27. As regards the practice of the United Nations, both the General Assembly and the Security Council initially interpreted and applied Article 12 to the effect that the Assembly
could not make a recommendation on a question concerning the maintenance of international peace and security while the matter remained on the Council's agenda. . . . However, this interpretation of Article 12 has evolved subsequently. . . . Indeed, the Court notes
that there has been an increasing tendency over time for the General Assembly and the
Security Council to deal in parallel with the same matter concerning the maintenance of
international peace and security. . . . It is often the case that, while the Security Council
has tended to focus on the aspects of such matters related to international peace and
security, the General Assembly has taken a broader view, considering also their humanitarian, social and economic aspects.

---

106 Above note 52.

28. The Court considers that the accepted practice of the General Assembly, as it has evolved, is consistent with Article 12, paragraph 1, of the Charter. The Court is accordingly of the view that the General Assembly, in adopting resolution ES-10/14, seeking an advisory opinion from the Court, did not contravene the provisions of Article 12, paragraph 1, of the Charter. The Court concludes that by submitting that request the General Assembly did not exceed its competence. . . .

In a subsequent advisory opinion, the Court has reiterated its narrow understanding of the limiting effects of Article 12, adding that: "The limit which the Charter places upon the General Assembly . . . in Article 12 . . . restricts the power of the General Assembly to make recommendations following a discussion, not its power to engage in such a discussion."[107]

The General Assembly is also assigned several specific responsibilities by the UN Charter, not least those in Articles 13 and 15:

Charter of the United Nations, 26 June 1945, Can TS 1945 No 7, in force 24 October 1945

Article 13

1. The General Assembly shall initiate studies and make recommendations for the purpose of:

  a. promoting international co-operation in the political field and encouraging the progressive development of international law and its codification;

  b. promoting international co-operation in the economic, social, cultural, educational, and health fields, and assisting in the realization of human rights and fundamental freedoms for all without distinction as to race, sex, language, or religion. . . .

Article 15

1. The General Assembly shall receive and consider annual and special reports from the Security Council; these reports shall include an account of the measures that the Security Council has decided upon or taken to maintain international peace and security.

2. The General Assembly shall receive and consider reports from the other organs of the United Nations.

Article 13 is the point of departure for the UN's vast role in facilitating the codification of international law. We have already discussed the role of the International Law Commission, a committee of experts established by the General Assembly in 1947 and charged with "the promotion of the progressive development of international law and its codification." The ILC was created as an explicit expression of "the need for giving effect to Article 13" of the UN Charter.[108]

---

107 *Accordance with International Law of the Unilateral Declaration of Independence in Respect of Kosovo,* Advisory Opinion, [2010] ICJ Rep 403 at para 40.

108 *Establishment of an International Law Commission,* GA Res. 174(II), UN Doc A/RES/174(II) (1947), reprinted in UN GAOR, 2d Sess at 105–10, UN Doc A/519 (1948).

Article 13 should be read in conjunction with Articles 21 and 22. These two provisions empower the General Assembly to put in place the administrative structure necessary to accomplish its tasks. Article 21 provides that the "General Assembly shall adopt its own rules of procedure." The General Assembly has, in fact, adopted detailed rules of procedure[109] that include reference to its all-important committees, where most of the detailed business of the General Assembly is conducted: First Committee (disarmament and international security); Second Committee (economic and financial); Third Committee (social, humanitarian, and cultural); Fourth Committee (special political and decolonization); Fifth Committee (administrative and budgetary); and Sixth Committee (legal). Article 22, for its part, stipulates that the "General Assembly may establish such subsidiary organs as it deems necessary for the performance of its functions." While many of the organizations that are part of the UN system are organized through the UN Economic and Social Council, discussed below, or established by separate treaty, Article 22 is an important constituting provision for many of the agencies that together comprise the United Nations. Notable subsidiary bodies created by the General Assembly pursuant to Article 22 include: the UN Children's Fund (UNICEF); the UN Development Programme (UNDP); the UN Environment Program (UNEP); the Office of the UN High Commissioner for Refugees (UNHCR); and in 2006, the UN Human Rights Council (to replace the former UN Commission on Human Rights).

Similarly, Article 15 should be read in conjunction with Article 24(3): "The Security Council shall submit annual and, when necessary, special reports to the General Assembly for its consideration." Does this apparent accountability regime somehow subordinate the Security Council to the General Assembly? Consider these observations:

> The simple wording of Arts. 15 (1) and 24 (3) of the Charter seems to speak for the subordination of the SC to the GA, and a right of supervision and control for the latter. However, the origin of this provision has to be taken into account. . . . [T]he GA's right to approve or disapprove the SC's report was discussed at the San Francisco Conference but not accepted.
>
> Subsequent practice clearly shows that the GA exercised very little control in the first years of the Organization. For many years, such a right of control was neither claimed nor exercised. However, over the last twenty years, the GA has shown a tendency to assert a stronger position *vis-à-vis* the SC.
>
> Yet, according to Art. 15 (1) of the Charter, the GA does not possess a right to control the activities that lie within the SC's main responsibilities under the Charter. This indicates that the SC, when acting within its responsibilities to maintain international peace and security, has a sovereign freedom of decision, at least as far as the GA is concerned.[110]

We now shift our focus to the Security Council, with its "sovereign freedom of decision."

---

109 *Rules of Procedure of the General Assembly*, UN Doc A/520/Rev.17 (2008).
110 Simma et al, above note 74 at 570.

ii) Security Council

Charter of the United Nations, 26 June 1945, Can TS 1945 No 7, in force 24 October 1945

Composition

Article 23

1. The Security Council shall consist of fifteen Members of the United Nations. The Republic of China, France, the Union of Soviet Socialist Republics, the United Kingdom of Great Britain and Northern Ireland, and the United States of America shall be permanent members of the Security Council. The General Assembly shall elect ten other Members of the United Nations to be nonpermanent members of the Security Council, due regard being specially paid, in the first instance to the contribution of Members of the United Nations to the maintenance of international peace and security and to the other purposes of the Organization, and also to equitable geographical distribution.

2. The non-permanent members of the Security Council shall be elected for a term of two years. . . . A retiring member shall not be eligible for immediate re-election.

3. Each member of the Security Council shall have one representative.

Article 23 makes obvious that the Security Council is not an organ in which every UN member state is directly represented at any one time. That said, the UN Charter does open the door to (non-voting) participation by states with a special interest in a matter before the Council. Article 31 provides that "Any Member of the United Nations which is not a member of the Security Council may participate, without vote, in the discussion of any question brought before the Security Council whenever the latter considers that the interests of that Member are specially affected." Article 32 similarly provides that "Any Member of the United Nations which is not a member of the Security Council or any state which is not a Member of the United Nations, if it is a party to a dispute under consideration by the Security Council, shall be invited to participate, without vote, in the discussion relating to the dispute. The Security Council shall lay down such conditions as it deems just for the participation of a state which is not a Member of the United Nations."

These modest provisos do not, however, dispel concerns about the non-representative nature of the actual membership of the Security Council. The composition of that body is probably the most controversial component of the UN Charter. The five permanent members listed in Article 23 (and commonly referred to as the "P5") were obviously the pre-eminent powers of the immediate post–World War II era. While that period has now passed, these five states retain their permanent seats on the Security Council. Meanwhile, the other 188 members of the contemporary United Nations vie for election to the remaining ten Security Council seats, and, if successful, hold this position for only two years.

Pursuant to Article 18(2), the election of the non-permanent members of the Security Council is one of those "important matters" requiring a two-thirds vote of the General Assembly. Article 23(1) specifies two criteria for selection: first, the contribution of members of the United Nations to the maintenance of international peace and security and to the other purposes of the Organization; and, second, equitable geographical distribution.

To give effect to the latter criterion, the General Assembly introduced in a 1963 resolution the following formula for non-permanent member selection:

> ... the ten non-permanent members of the Security Council shall be elected according to the following pattern:
> (a) Five from African and Asian states;
> (b) One from Eastern European States;
> (c) Two from Latin American States;
> (d) Two from Western European and other States.[111]

Within these categories, who gets elected is a matter of intense politics. David Malone, then a senior Canadian diplomat with many years of UN experience, described the process this way in 2000:

> ... [J]ockeying for seats is intense. Jockeying is nowhere more intense than within the Western European and Other Group (WEOG), which comprises members of the European Union (EU), Norway, a number of small European nations (Liechtenstein, Malta, Andorra, San Marino), the United States, Canada, Australia, and New Zealand. Its members, in an effort at preemption, are announcing their candidacies further and further in advance. For example, Canada announced its campaign for the 1999–2000 term in 1994, Greece has announced its candidacy for a term in 2005-2006, and Austria has already announced for 2009–2010. Most of the other regional groups have, by and large, managed to produce agreed slates of candidates in the past (although Asia in 1996 and Africa in 1993 proved exceptions) .... [112]

What strategies contribute to success? Simple "contribution ... to the maintenance of international peace and security and to the other purposes of the Organization" is no guarantee of support:

> *Broad national reputation is a poor guide to the likely success of Security Council* candidates. What group of countries seems more admirable to international observers than Scandinavia? Yet Sweden was beaten for a term in 1993–1994 (in a close race with New Zealand and Spain). Likewise, Australia has contributed much to international cooperation and peace since the inception of the UN in 1945. ... But it too was beaten for a term (in 1997–1998 by a now successful Sweden and by Portugal, the latter not noted for its international credentials and lumbered with a reputation as an appalling colonial power until the 1974 revolution) .... [113]

That said:

---

111 *Question of Equitable Representation on the Security Council and the Economic and Social Council*, GA Res 1991 (XVIII) A (1963), reprinted in UN GAOR, 18th Sess, Supp No 15 at 21–22, UN Doc A/5515 (1964).

112 David M Malone, "Eyes on the Prize: The Quest for Nonpermanent Seats on the UN Security Council" (2000) 6:1 Global Governance 3 at 3–4.

113 *Ibid* at 7 [italics in original]. In 2012, Australia was successful in its bid for a 2013–2015 term.

Convincing themes can help a campaign. The substantive attention span of many member states is not impressive. Candidates need to develop one or two themes on which they can hammer away consistently over the months (and, increasingly, years) of a campaign. Canada in 1998 stressed its close connections to most member states through shared membership in a number of non-universal organizations—the Commonwealth, La Francophonie, the Organization of American States (OAS), and the Organization for Security and Cooperation in Europe (OSCE). And it highlighted its credentials as a committed and innovative leader in UN peacekeeping. Canada also articulated a program for its Council membership that heavily emphasized the promotion of human security and humanitarian action as opposed to the state-security perspective through which the Council had traditionally viewed its work. In a fairly clear attack on the Permanent Five (the UN equivalent of running against city hall), Canada campaigned aggressively for greater Council openness, transparency, and accountability. Another theme that proved popular was its argument that the EU had been seriously overrepresented in the Council since 1994, winning all four non-permanent WEOG memberships on top of its two permanent ones. (This is about as close to "negative campaigning" as this generally high-minded contest witnessed.)[114]

Summarizing his conclusions, Malone writes:

. . . The strongest country does not necessarily win. A considerable sympathy vote from other, often disenfranchised small countries can be courted successfully by less prominent General Assembly members, even though this contradicts the guidance set out in Article 23:1 of the UN Charter. Article 23:1 places emphasis "in the first instance" on the contribution of member states to the maintenance of peace and security and to the other purposes of the organization and only secondarily on "equitable geographic distribution." Issues of personality, the risk of overbearing national attitudes, generous approaches to development assistance, rapacious and careless pursuit of national standing in the UN (and elsewhere), the size of campaign budgets, and the nature of the campaign platform are all relevant. No outcomes are assured . . . .[115]

In 2010, Canada failed to secure a Security Council seat, in a series of events described this way by one author:

For the first time since 1946, Canada failed in its decennial bid for a two-year term on the UN Security Council. The Prime Minister personally made Canada's case in two speeches to the General Assembly, to no avail. Canada fell 21 votes short of Foreign Affairs estimates before the vote, and 13 votes short of the two-thirds majority required to win the election on the first ballot. On the second round, Canada's support collapsed, and Foreign Affairs Minister Lawrence Cannon withdrew our candidacy.[116]

---

114 *Ibid* at 8 [emphasis in original].
115 *Ibid* at 18.
116 Adam Chapnick, "Canada's Failed Campaign for the UN Security Council: 10 Unanswered Questions", *Policy Options* (February 2011) at 58.

There was probably no single and simple reason for this failure, although commentators were quick to point fingers at controversial aspects of the Canadian government's foreign policy, especially its unstinting support of Israel and perceived reductions in aid to African states. Other factors likely also included Canada's tardiness in launching its campaign (perhaps attributable to a turnover of foreign ministers and domestic political distractions related to a minority parliamentary situation), as well as a host of (often unrelated) foreign relations irritants that undermined Canadian support among key voting blocs. Put another way, the outcome reflected the domestic and international politics of the moment.

Security Council reform is among the most intractable issues facing the United Nations. In his 2005 report, *In Larger Freedom: Towards Development, Security and Human Rights for All*, the UN Secretary-General proposed the following:

> 169. . . . The Security Council must be broadly representative of the realities of power in today's world. I therefore support the position set out in the report of the High-level Panel on Threats, Challenges and Change (A/59/565) concerning the reforms of the Security Council, namely:
>
> > (a) They should, in honouring Article 23 of the Charter, increase the involvement in decision-making of those who contribute most to the United Nations financially, militarily and diplomatically, specifically in terms of contributions to United Nations assessed budgets, participation in mandated peace operations, contributions to voluntary activities of the United Nations in the areas of security and development, and diplomatic activities in support of United Nations objectives and mandates. Among developed countries, achieving or making substantial progress towards the internationally agreed level of 0.7 per cent of GNP for ODA [Official Development Assistance] should be considered an important criterion of contribution;
> >
> > (b) They should bring into the decision-making process countries more representative of the broader membership, especially of the developing world;
> >
> > (c) They should not impair the effectiveness of the Security Council;
> >
> > (d) They should increase the democratic and accountable nature of the body.
>
> 170. I urge Member States to consider the two options, models A and B, proposed in that report (see box 5), or any other viable proposals in terms of size and balance that have emerged on the basis of either model. Member States should agree to take a decision on this important issue before the summit in September 2005. It would be very preferable for Member States to take this vital decision by consensus, but if they are unable to reach consensus this must not become an excuse for postponing action.[117]

---

117 *In Larger Freedom*, above note 96 at paras 169–70. Reprinted with permission.

Box 5

Security Council reform: models A and B

Model A provides for six new permanent seats, with no veto being created, and three new two-year term non-permanent seats, divided among the major regional areas as follows:

Regional area	No. of States	Permanent seats (continuing)	Proposed new permanent seats	Proposed two-year seats (non-renewable)	Total
Africa	53	0	2	4	6
Asia and Pacific	56	1	2	3	6
Europe	47	3	1	2	6
Americas	35	1	1	4	6
Totals model A	**191**	**5**	**6**	**13**	**24**

Model B provides for no new permanent seats but creates a new category of eight four-year renewable-term seats and one new two-year non-permanent (and non-renewable) seat, divided among the major regional areas as follows:

Regional area	No. of States	Permanent seats (continuing)	Proposed four-year renewable seats	Proposed two-year seats (non-renewable)	Total
Africa	53	0	2	4	6
Asia and Pacific	56	1	2	3	6
Europe	47	3	2	1	6
Americas	35	1	2	3	6
Totals model B	**191**	**5**	**8**	**11**	**24**

In fact, member states were unable to reach agreement, by consensus or otherwise, on reform of the structure of the Security Council either before or during the 2005 World Summit and any such reform seems unlikely in the immediate future. Consider that, under Articles 108 and 109, amendments to the Charter require the concurrence of two-thirds of the members of the United Nations, including all of the permanent members of the Security Council.

Charter of the United Nations, 26 June 1945, Can TS 1945 No 7, in force 24 October 1945

Voting

Article 27

1. Each member of the Security Council shall have one vote.

2. Decisions of the Security Council on procedural matters shall be made by an affirmative vote of nine members.

3. Decisions of the Security Council on all other matters shall be made by an affirmative vote of nine members including the concurring votes of the permanent members; provided that, in decisions under Chapter VI [pacific settlement of disputes], and under paragraph 3 of Article 52 [pacific settlement of disputes under regional arrangements], a party to a dispute shall abstain from voting.

The most jarring distinction between Security Council practices and those of the General Assembly is in the area of voting. As Article 27 indicates, each member of the Council—whether permanent or non-permanent—has one vote and decisions are taken by an affirmative vote of nine members. However, Article 27 also requires the "concurring votes of the permanent members" in relation to non-procedural matters. From this requirement flows the veto wielded by each of the P5: failure to secure the "concurring votes" of all of them effectively vetoes the resolution under consideration. Note the nuanced language of Article 27, which requires the "concurring," as distinct from the "affirmative," votes of the permanent members. Is this subtle difference significant? The matter is not without ambiguity and no guidance is provided in the Security Council's Rules of Procedure.[118]

Security Council practice, however, confirms the distinction: a "concurring" vote may be either an affirmative vote *or* an abstaining vote. In other words, a permanent member that abstains does not thereby veto the resolution under consideration, as confirmed by the ICJ after reviewing the practice of the Council:

> . . . the proceedings of the Security Council extending over a long period supply abundant evidence that [Council] presidential rulings and the positions taken by members of the Council, in particular its permanent members, have consistently and uniformly interpreted the practice of voluntary abstention by a permanent member as not constituting a bar to the adoption of resolutions. By abstaining, a member does not signify its objection to the approval of what is being proposed; in order to prevent the adoption of a resolution requiring unanimity of the permanent members, a permanent member has only to cast a negative vote. This procedure followed by the Security Council . . . has been generally accepted by Members of the United Nations and evidences a general practice of that Organization.[119]

Between the UN's creation in 1945 and 2012, the veto was exercised 269 times, according to the following breakdown: China (9); France (18); United Kingdom (32); United States (83); Russian Federation (128). In the Council's early years, Russia (then the Soviet Union) wielded the veto most frequently—113 times by the end of 1975. Yet, between 1976 and 2012, the United States exercised its veto seventy-one times, as compared to fifty-three times by all other permanent members combined.[120] It is also notable that all the P5 members appear now to be more judicious in their use of the veto than in prior periods: the number of vetoes has been relatively modest since the 1990s.

Setting aside simple protection of one's own national interests, are there any circumstances in which it would be appropriate for a permanent member to veto a resolution that otherwise had the support of at least nine other members of the Security Council?

---

118 *Provisional Rules of Procedure of the Security Council*, UN Doc S/96/Rev.7 (1983).

119 *Legal Consequences for States of the Continued Presence of South Africa in Namibia (South West Africa) Notwithstanding Security Council Resolution 276 (1970)*, Advisory Opinion, [1971] ICJ Rep 16 at 22.

120 See Global Policy Forum, "Changing Patterns in the Use of the Veto in the Security Council" (August 2012), online: www.globalpolicy.org/images/pdfs/Changing_Patterns_in_the_Use_of_the_Veto_as_of_August_2012.pdf. These statistics exclude forty-three vetoes used to block nominees for Secretary-General during closed sessions of the Security Council.

Reflect on the possible rationales for requiring both a super-majority as well as the "concurring" votes of the P5 for non-procedural decisions of the Council. Understanding the extraordinary powers of the Security Council may assist in that reflection.

Charter of the United Nations, 26 June 1945, Can TS 1945 No 7, in force 24 October 1945

Functions and Powers

Article 24

1. In order to ensure prompt and effective action by the United Nations, its Members confer on the Security Council primary responsibility for the maintenance of international peace and security, and agree that in carrying out its duties under this responsibility the Security Council acts on their behalf.

2. In discharging these duties the Security Council shall act in accordance with the Purposes and Principles of the United Nations. The specific powers granted to the Security Council for the discharge of these duties are laid down in Chapters VI, VII, VIII, and XII....

CHAPTER VI
PACIFIC SETTLEMENT OF DISPUTES

Article 33

1. The parties to any dispute, the continuance of which is likely to endanger the maintenance of international peace and security, shall, first of all, seek a solution by negotiation, enquiry, mediation, conciliation, arbitration, judicial settlement, resort to regional agencies or arrangements, or other peaceful means of their own choice.

2. The Security Council shall, when it deems necessary, call upon the parties to settle their dispute by such means.

Article 34

The Security Council may investigate any dispute, or any situation which might lead to international friction or give rise to a dispute, in order to determine whether the continuance of the dispute or situation is likely to endanger the maintenance of international peace and security....

Article 36

1. The Security Council may, at any stage of a dispute of the nature referred to in Article 33 or of a situation of like nature, recommend appropriate procedures or methods of adjustment.

2. The Security Council should take into consideration any procedures for the settlement of the dispute which have already been adopted by the parties.

3. In making recommendations under this Article the Security Council should also take into consideration that legal disputes should as a general rule be referred by the parties to the International Court of Justice in accordance with the provisions of the Statute of the Court.

Article 37

1. Should the parties to a dispute of the nature referred to in Article 33 fail to settle it by the means indicated in that Article, they shall refer it to the Security Council.

2. If the Security Council deems that the continuance of the dispute is in fact likely to endanger the maintenance of international peace and security, it shall decide whether to take action under Article 36 or to recommend such terms of settlement as it may consider appropriate.

Article 38

Without prejudice to the provisions of Articles 33 to 37, the Security Council may, if all the parties to any dispute so request, make recommendations to the parties with a view to a pacific settlement of the dispute.

CHAPTER VII
ACTION WITH RESPECT TO THREATS TO THE PEACE, BREACHES OF THE PEACE, AND ACTS OF AGGRESSION

Article 39

The Security Council shall determine the existence of any threat to the peace, breach of the peace, or act of aggression and shall make recommendations, or decide what measures shall be taken in accordance with Articles 41 and 42, to maintain or restore international peace and security.

Article 40

In order to prevent an aggravation of the situation, the Security Council may, before making the recommendations or deciding upon the measures provided for in Article 39, call upon the parties concerned to comply with such provisional measures as it deems necessary or desirable. Such provisional measures shall be without prejudice to the rights, claims, or position of the parties concerned. The Security Council shall duly take account of failure to comply with such provisional measures.

Article 41

The Security Council may decide what measures not involving the use of armed force are to be employed to give effect to its decisions, and it may call upon the Members of the United Nations to apply such measures. These may include complete or partial interruption of economic relations and of rail, sea, air, postal, telegraphic, radio, and other means of communication, and the severance of diplomatic relations.

Article 42

Should the Security Council consider that measures provided for in Article 41 would be inadequate or have proved to be inadequate, it may take such action by air, sea, or land forces as may be necessary to maintain or restore international peace and security. Such action may include demonstrations, blockade, and other operations by air, sea, or land forces of Members of the United Nations.

The Security Council's functions pursuant to Chapter VI are relatively modest. Consider the following commentary:

[The Council's] powers of calling upon the parties to settle disputes by peaceful means (article 33) or of recommending procedures or methods of adjustment (article 26) or of recommending terms of settlement (articles 37 and 38) are recommendatory only, and limited to disputes which are likely to endanger peace and security. It has no such powers with regard to all disputes, although it may investigate any dispute to see if it is likely to endanger peace and security (article 34). . . . The Security Council can under article 34 investigate "situations" which may lead to international friction or give rise to a dispute to see if they are likely to endanger peace and security, but its only other express power with regard to a "situation" is the power under article 36 of recommending procedures or methods of adjustment for a "situation" likely to endanger peace and security.[121]

Despite these seemingly modest powers, Chapter VI provides an arguable basis for Security Council authorization of peacekeeping, a term coined to describe a type of military action that is consent based and tries to maintain or preserve peace with a minimal use of force or a show of force. Peacekeeping is sometimes called a "Chapter VI and ½" activity because it is not formally anticipated by the terms of the UN Charter and lies somewhere between the Chapter VI regime for conflict prevention and the peaceful settlement of disputes and Chapter VII powers for addressing threats to or breaches of the peace. Clearly Chapter VII provides a legal basis for coercive military action, but as one commentator has observed: "Where the situation is not yet so urgent, i.e. where there is no immediate threat to the peace, the Council could also act under Chapter VI."[122]

Two conceptual reports prepared by the UN Secretary-General in 1992 and 1995[123] envisioned three roles for a UN peacekeeping operation, namely, "conflict prevention, conflict management during conflict, and post conflict peace-building.[124] As explained by then Secretary-General Boutros Boutros-Ghali in the 1992 report, *An Agenda for Peace*, "peace-keeping" refers to "the deployment of a United Nations presence in the field, hitherto with the consent of all the parties concerned, normally involving United Nations military and/or police personnel and frequently civilians as well. Peace-keeping is a technique that expands the possibilities for both the prevention of conflict and the making of peace."[125] By contrast, "peacemaking" was defined as "action to bring hostile parties to agreement, essentially through such peaceful means as those foreseen in Chapter VI of the Charter of the United Nations."[126] It was further added that:

34. Between the tasks of seeking to prevent conflict and keeping the peace lies the responsibility to try to bring hostile parties to agreement by peaceful means. Chapter VI of the Charter sets forth a comprehensive list of such means for the resolution of conflict.

---

121 Shearer, above note 85 at 581–82.

122 Simma et al, above note 74 at 1186.

123 *An Agenda for Peace: Preventive diplomacy, peacemaking and peace-keeping: Report of the Secretary-General pursuant to the statement adopted by the Summit Meeting of the Security Council on 31 January 1992*, UN Doc A/47/277-S/24111 (17 June 1992) and *Supplement to an Agenda for Peace: Position Paper of the Secretary-General on the Occasion of the Fiftieth Anniversary of the United Nations*, UN Doc A/50/60-S/1995/1 (3 January 1995).

124 Simma et al, above note 74 at 1182.

125 *An Agenda for Peace*, above note 123 at para 20.

126 *Ibid* at para 20.

These have been amplified in various declarations adopted by the General Assembly, . . . They have also been the subject of various resolutions of the General Assembly, including resolution 44/21 of 15 November 1989 on enhancing international peace, security and international cooperation in all its aspects in accordance with the Charter of the United Nations. The United Nations has had wide experience in the application of these peaceful means. If conflicts have gone unresolved, it is not because techniques for peaceful settlement were unknown or inadequate. The fault lies first in the lack of political will of parties to seek a solution to their differences through such means as are suggested in Chapter VI of the Charter, and second, in the lack of leverage at the disposal of a third party if this is the procedure chosen. The indifference of the international community to a problem, or the marginalization of it, can also thwart the possibilities of solution. We must look primarily to these areas if we hope to enhance the capacity of the Organization for achieving peaceful settlements.[127]

The United Nations has since established a Peacebuilding Commission to bring together relevant actors, share best practices, and focus attention on the reconstruction and institution-building efforts necessary for recovery from conflict.[128]

In contrast to Chapter VI, Chapter VII enumerates the most potent Security Council powers. First, under Article 39, the Council is empowered to determine the existence of "any threat to the peace, breach of the peace, or act of aggression"—all expressions that are undefined in the UN Charter. Second, under Article 40, it may call upon the parties concerned to comply with provisional measures designed to forestall the threat to international peace and security. Third, under Article 41, it may decide upon measures short of force—such as economic or other sanctions—to maintain or restore international peace and security. Fourth, under Articles 39 and 42, where the Security Council considers that measures short of force would be inadequate, it may authorize or impose measures involving the use of military force, again with a view to maintaining or restoring international peace and security. As discussed in greater detail in Chapter 14, the situations contemplated in Articles 39, 42 and 51—the latter relating to self-defence—are the only clear instances in which armed force may lawfully be used between states in international law.

The scope of the Security Council's power to impose measures under Chapter VII is substantial. While we consider in detail its specific power to authorize or impose the use of force in Chapter 14, consider the following comments on its establishment of the International Criminal Tribunal for the Former Yugoslavia (ICTY).

Prosecutor v Duško Tadić, Case No IT-94-1-A, (1995) 35 ILM 32, ICTY Appeals Chamber

[The Tribunal was established by resolution of the UN Security Council, acting under Chapter VII, to try war crimes, crimes against humanity, and genocide committed in the territory of the former Yugoslavia since 1991. In this case, the defendant, Duško Tadić, challenged the Security Council's authority under the UN Charter to establish such a judicial body. Amongst others, his argument was that this power did not flow from Chapter VII.]

---

127 *Ibid* at para 34.
128 *The Peacebuilding Commission*, GA Res 60/180, UN Doc A/RES/60/180 (2005), reprinted in UN GAOR, 60th Sess, Supp No 49, vol I at 96–98, UN Doc A/60/49 (2006).

28. . . . It is clear from [Article 39] that the Security Council plays a pivotal role and exercises a very wide discretion. . . . But this does not mean that its powers are unlimited. The Security Council is an organ of an international organization, established by a treaty which serves as a constitutional framework for that organization. The Security Council is thus subjected to certain constitutional limitations, however broad its powers under the constitution may be. Those powers cannot, in any case, go beyond the limits of the jurisdiction of the Organization at large, not to mention other specific limitations or those which may derive from the internal division of power within the Organization. In any case, neither the text nor the spirit of the *Charter conceives of the Security Council as legibus solutus (unbound by law).*

In particular, Article 24, after declaring, in paragraph 1, that the Members of the United Nations "confer on the Security Council primary responsibility for the maintenance of international peace and security," imposes on it, in paragraph 3, the obligation to report annually (or more frequently) to the General Assembly, and provides, more importantly, in paragraph 2, that: "In discharging these duties the Security Council shall act in accordance with the Purposes and Principles of the United Nations. The specific powers granted to the Security Council for the discharge of these duties are laid down in Chapters VI, VII, VIII, and XII." (Id., Art. 24(2).)

The Charter thus speaks the language of specific powers, not of absolute fiat.

29. What is the extent of the powers of the Security Council under Article 39 and the limits thereon, if any?

The Security Council plays the central role in the application of both parts of the Article. It is the Security Council that makes the determination that there exists one of the situations justifying the use of the "exceptional powers" of Chapter VII. And it is also the Security Council that chooses the reaction to such a situation: it either makes recommendations (i.e., opts not to use the exceptional powers but to continue to operate under Chapter VI) or decides to use the exceptional powers by ordering measures to be taken in accordance with Articles 41 and 42 with a view to maintaining or restoring international peace and security.

The situations justifying resort to the powers provided for in Chapter VII are a "threat to the peace," a "breach of the peace" or an "act of aggression." While the "act of aggression" is more amenable to a legal determination, the "threat to the peace" is more of a political concept. But the determination that there exists such a threat is not a totally unfettered discretion, as it has to remain, at the very least, within the limits of the Purposes and Principles of the Charter.

30. It is not necessary for the purposes of the present decision to examine any further the question of the limits of the discretion of the Security Council in determining the existence of a "threat to the peace." . . .

[One reason for this] is that an armed conflict (or a series of armed conflicts) has been taking place in the territory of the former Yugoslavia since long before the decision of the Security Council to establish this International Tribunal. If it is considered an international armed conflict, there is no doubt that it falls within the literal sense of the words "breach of the peace" (between the parties or, at the very least, as a "threat to the peace" of others). But even if it were considered merely as an "internal armed conflict," it would still constitute a "threat to the peace" according to the settled practice of the Security Council and the common understanding of the United Nations membership in general. Indeed, the practice of the Security Council is rich with cases of civil war or internal strife which it classified as a "threat to the peace" and dealt with under Chapter VII, with the encouragement or even at the behest of the General Assembly, such as the Congo crisis at the beginning of the 1960s and, more recently, Liberia and Somalia. It can thus be said that there is a common understanding, manifested by the "subsequent practice" of the membership of the United Nations at large, that the "threat to the peace" of Article 39 may include, as one of its species, internal armed conflicts. . . .

31. Once the Security Council determines that a particular situation poses a threat to the peace or that there exists a breach of the peace or an act of aggression, it enjoys a wide margin of discretion in choosing the course of action: as noted above . . . it can either continue, in spite of its determination, to act via recommendations, i.e., as if it were still within Chapter VI ("Pacific Settlement of Disputes") or it can exercise its exceptional powers under Chapter VII. In the words of Article 39, it would then "decide what measures shall be taken in accordance with Articles 41 and 42, to maintain or restore international peace and security." (United Nations Charter, art. 39.)

A question arises in this respect as to whether the choice of the Security Council is limited to the measures provided for in Articles 41 and 42 of the Charter (as the language of Article 39 suggests), or whether it has even larger discretion in the form of general powers to maintain and restore international peace and security under Chapter VII at large. In the latter case, one of course does not have to locate every measure decided by the Security Council under Chapter VII within the confines of Articles 41 and 42, or possibly Article 40. In any case, under both interpretations, the Security Council has a broad discretion in deciding on the course of action and evaluating the appropriateness of the measures to be taken. The language of Article 39 is quite clear as to the channelling of the very broad and exceptional powers of the Security Council under Chapter VII through Articles 41 and 42. These two Articles leave to the Security Council such a wide choice as not to warrant searching, on functional or other grounds, for even wider and more general powers than those already expressly provided for in the Charter.

These powers are coercive vis-à-vis the culprit State or entity. But they are also mandatory vis-à-vis the other Member States, who are under an obligation to cooperate with the Organization (Article 2, paragraph 5, Articles 25, 48) and with one another (Article 49), in the implementation of the action or measures decided by the Security Council. . . .

32. As with the determination of the existence of a threat to the peace, a breach of the peace or an act of aggression, the Security Council has a very wide margin of discretion under Article 39 to choose the appropriate course of action and to evaluate the suitability of the measures chosen, as well as their potential contribution to the restoration or maintenance of peace. But here again, this discretion is not unfettered; moreover, it is limited to the measures provided for in Articles 41 and 42. Indeed, in the case at hand, this last point serves as a basis for the Appellant's contention of invalidity of the establishment of the International Tribunal. . . .

33. The establishment of an international criminal tribunal is not expressly mentioned

among the enforcement measures provided for in Chapter VII, and more particularly in Articles 41 and 42.

Obviously, the establishment of the International Tribunal is not a measure under Article 42, as these are measures of a military nature, implying the use of armed force. Nor can it be considered a "provisional measure" under Article 40. These measures, as their denomination indicates, are intended to act as a "holding operation," producing a "standstill" or a "cooling-off" effect, "without prejudice to the rights, claims or position of the parties concerned." (United Nations Charter, art. 40.) They are akin to emergency police action rather than to the activity of a judicial organ dispensing justice according to law. . . .

34. *Prima facie*, the International Tribunal matches perfectly the description in Article 41 of "measures not involving the use of force." Appellant, however, has argued before both the Trial Chamber and this Appeals Chamber, that: ". . . It is clear that the establishment of a war crimes tribunal was not intended. The examples mentioned in this article focus upon economic and political measures and do not in any way suggest judicial measures.". . .

35. [This] argument does not stand by its own language. . . . It is evident that the measures set out in Article 41 are merely illustrative examples which obviously do not exclude other measures. All the Article requires is that they do not involve "the use of force." It is a negative definition. . . .

In sum, the establishment of the International Tribunal falls squarely within the powers of the Security Council under Article 41.

In the last two decades, the circumstances viewed by the Security Council as constituting a threat to international peace and security have expanded. Consider these observations:

Since the beginning of the 1990s, the understanding of what constitutes a "threat to the peace" has broadened considerably from the narrow concept of the absence of the use of armed force, to the wider concept of situations that may lead to the use of armed force. This shift from a purely formal to a substantive meaning of "threat to the peace" was marked in a statement by the president of the Council at the conclusion of its meeting on January 31, 1992. . . . Speaking on behalf of the members of the Council, the president declared that "the absence of war and military conflicts amongst States does not in itself ensure international peace and security. The non-military sources of instability in the economic, social, humanitarian and ecological fields have become threats to peace and security." . . .

Since 1992, a wide variety of situations has been classified as a "threat to the peace" by both the Security Council and the General Assembly. These include the proliferation and development of weapons of mass destruction (as well as their means of delivery), acts of international terrorism, the use of mercenaries, emergency situations, and the violent disintegration of states. Thus, a common understanding, manifested by the "subsequent practice" of the membership of the United Nations at large, can be said to have emerged that the "threat to the peace" of Article 39 may include certain situations *per se*.[129]

---

129 Stefan Talmon, "The Security Council as World Legislature" (2005) 99 AJIL 175 at 180–81.

The Security Council has also shifted the manner in which it addresses certain threats to peace and security. In the immediate aftermath of the terrorist attacks of September 11, 2001, the Council adopted Resolution 1373 (2001) pursuant to Chapter VII. Among other things, the resolution decided that all states shall:

Criminalize the wilful provision or collection, by any means, directly or indirectly, of funds by their nationals or in their territories with the intention that the funds should be used, or in the knowledge that they are to be used, in order to carry out terrorist acts . . .[130]

Consider also Security Council Resolution 1540 (2004), again adopted under Chapter VII, which decided that:

all States, in accordance with their national procedures, shall adopt and enforce appropriate effective laws which prohibit any non-State actor to manufacture, acquire, possess, develop, transport, transfer or use nuclear, chemical or biological weapons and their means of delivery, in particular for terrorist purposes, as well as attempts to engage in any of the foregoing activities, participate in them as an accomplice, assist or finance them.[131]

These resolutions are far more detailed than the classic Chapter VII resolutions of the past imposing sanctions or authorizing the use of force. Further, they go beyond requiring or authorizing certain economic or military measures. Rather, they resemble legislative enactments requiring, in turn, legislative action at the domestic level. Consider again the conclusion of the Appeals Chamber in *Tadić* that the only limitation on the measures the Security Council may impose under Article 41 is that they not involve the use of force.[132] What are the potential consequences for the sovereignty of states of such a holding?

Evaluating the significance of the Security Council's Chapter VII powers also requires consideration of the legal effects of Security Council decisions on states. Note that in *Tadić*,[133] the Appeals Chamber concluded that Chapter VII decisions are "mandatory vis-à-vis the other Member States, who are under an obligation to cooperate with the Organization (Article 2, paragraph 5, Articles 25, 48) and with one another (Article 49)." Consider the language of these provisions, as well as that of Article 103:

Charter of the United Nations, 26 June 1945, Can TS 1945 No 7, in force 24 October 1945

Article 25
The Members of the United Nations agree to accept and carry out the decisions of the Security Council in accordance with the present Charter. . . .

Article 48
1. The action required to carry out the decisions of the Security Council for the maintenance of international peace and security shall be taken by all the Members of the United Nations or by some of them, as the Security Council may determine.

---

130 SC Resolution 1373 (2011), adopted 28 September 2001, UN Doc S/RES/1373 (2001) at para 1(b).
131 SC Resolution 1540 (2004), adopted 28 April 2004, UN Doc S/RES/1540 (2004) at para 2.
132 *Prosecutor v Duško Tadić*, Case No IT-94-1-A, (1995) 35 ILM 32 (ICTY Appeals Chamber).
133 *Ibid* at para 31.

2. Such decisions shall be carried out by the Members of the United Nations directly and through their action in the appropriate international agencies of which they are members.

Article 49

The Members of the United Nations shall join in affording mutual assistance in carrying out the measures decided upon by the Security Council. . . .

Article 103

In the event of a conflict between the obligations of the Members of the United Nations under the present Charter and their obligations under any other international agreement, their obligations under the present Charter shall prevail.

The ICJ considered the combined significance of Articles 25 and 103 in an early phase of the *Aerial Incident at Lockerbie Case*.[134] The United States and the United Kingdom had demanded that Libya extradite two Libyan nationals suspected of causing the explosion of Pan American Flight 103 on 21 December 1988, over Lockerbie, Scotland. Libya maintained that its obligation to extradite—or not—should be governed by the terms of the Convention for the Suppression of Unlawful Acts against the Safety of Civil Aviation (Montreal Convention).[135] Libya sought an indication of provisional measures from the Court against the United States and the United Kingdom to protect its rights under the Montreal Convention. Shortly after the Court heard argument from the parties, but before it rendered its decision, the Security Council invoked Chapter VII of the UN Charter, having determined that Libya's continued failure to deliver the suspected terrorists constituted a threat to international peace and security. Accordingly, in Resolution 748 (1992), the Council decided that Libya must comply with the extradition requests of the United States and the United Kingdom.[136]

One question that thus arose was the impact of Resolution 748 (1992) on Libya's request for provisional measures by the Court. The ICJ rejected the Libyan request. Specifically, the Court indicated that:

[B]oth Libya and the United States, as Members of the United Nations, are obliged to accept and carry out the decisions of the Security Council in accordance with Article 25 of the Charter; [and] in accordance with Article 103 of the Charter, the obligations of the Parties in that respect prevail over their obligations under any other international agreement, including the Montreal Convention.[137]

Read together, the UN Charter provisions make the Security Council the world's most potent international organ. Indeed, the Security Council appears to view even non-UN members as bound by its decisions. For example, in response to apartheid-era South Africa's continued occupation of Namibia after its League of Nations mandate had been

---

134 *Questions of Interpretation and Application of the 1971 Montreal Convention arising from the Aerial Incident at Lockerbie (Libyan Arab Jamahiriya v United States of America)*, Provisional Measures, Order of 14 April 1992, [1992] ICJ Rep 114 [*Aerial Incident at Lockerbie—Provisional Measures*].
135 23 September 1971, 974 UNTS 178, Can TS 1973 No 6, in force 26 January 1973.
136 SC Resolution 748 (1992), adopted 31 March 1992, UN Doc S/RES/748 (1992) at para 1.
137 *Aerial Incident at Lockerbie—Provisional Measures*, above note 134 at 15.

terminated, the Council adopted Resolution 276 (1970), strongly condemning South Africa's refusal to withdraw and calling upon "all states" to refrain from any dealings with the Government of South Africa.[138] In its advisory opinion addressing the legal implications of Resolution 276 (1970), the ICJ examined whether the binding force of the Security Council's decision extended to both UN member and non-member states. It concluded that, as a matter of treaty law, it did not, as non-member states were not technically bound by Article 25 of the UN Charter to carry out the decisions of the Security Council. However, the General Assembly's prior termination of South Africa's mandate for Namibia made South Africa's continued presence in Namibia illegal, creating an obligation *erga omnes*—on all states—not to enter into relations with South Africa concerning Namibia. In other words, even though the Security Council's decision was not, in itself, technically binding on non-member states, they were bound to give it effect due to an independent legal obligation.[139] Since then, the Security Council has often employed all-encompassing and authoritative language purporting to require "all states" to refrain from various activities.

If the Security Council's jurisdiction under the UN Charter is pliable and expanding, and its authority binding on member states, are there any effective legal constraints on the Council? Although the matter is subject to debate, there is no clear practice or authority establishing any such constraints, leading to comments such as the following:

> *Respect for International Law:* . . . when acting under Chapter VII, the SC is normally not bound to respect international law apart from the Charter itself; in particular, it need not delve into lengthy discussions on the position of the parties under general international law. . . . This decision by the Charter to allow the SC to disregard international law when taking enforcement action cannot be set aside simply by reference to ideas such as the rule of law or the notion of a legal community. . . . The latter concepts are external to the Charter. . . .[140]

> *Human rights and humanitarian law:* . . . Art. 1(3) requires the UN to 'promot[e] and encourag[e] respect for human rights and for fundamental freedoms for all'. The SC is thus not allowed to disregard human rights and humanitarian law when taking enforcement action. Some commentators have gone further and interpreted this as an obligation . . . Yet this would seem to neglect the purposive character of the clause . . . Art. 3(1) establishes guidelines for the exercise of Chapter VII powers. It is then up to the SC to strike the concrete balance between humanitarian and human rights concerns and the goal of maintaining peace.[141]

Perhaps the only extra-Charter legal constraints on the Security Council's powers are peremptory norms of international law (*jus cogens* norms), although at least one group

---

138 SC Resolution 276 (1970), adopted 30 January 1970, UN Doc S/RES/276 (1970) at paras 1 & 5.

139 *Legal Consequences for States of the Continued Presence of South Africa in Namibia (South-West Africa) Notwithstanding Security Council Resolution 276 (1970)*, Advisory Opinion, [1971] ICJ Rep 16. For a full argument that Security Council resolutions cannot be considered binding on non-members, see Jericho Nkala, *The United Nations, International Law, and the Rhodesian Independence Crisis* (Oxford: Clarendon Press, 1985).

140 Simma et al, above note 74 at 1257 (footnotes omitted).

141 *Ibid* at 1258 (footnotes omitted).

of commentators has opined that the "general acceptance of a superiority of peremp-tory norms is open to doubt."[142] Some argue that Article 1(1) of the UN Charter "grants the SC a general exemption from all international legal norms, including those that later developed into peremptory ones."[143] Others, including members of the International Law Commission, argue that if "the United Nations Charter is not above *jus cogens*, then it also cannot transfer a power to contradict *jus cogens* to bodies that receive their jurisdiction from the Charter."[144] Consider too the views of Judge ad hoc Lauterpacht in his separate opinion in a 1993 proceeding in the *Application of the Genocide Convention Case*:

> The concept of *jus cogens* operates as a concept superior to both customary international law and treaty. The relief which Article 103 of the Charter may give the Security Council in case of conflict between one of its decisions and an operative treaty obligation can-not—as a matter of simple hierarchy of norms—extend to a conflict between a Security Council resolution and *jus cogens*. Indeed, one only has to state the opposite proposi-tion thus—that a Security Council resolution may even require participation in geno-cide—for its unacceptability to be apparent.
>
> . . . Nor should one overlook the significance of the provision in Article 24(2) of the Charter that, in discharging its duties to maintain international peace and security, the Security Council shall act in accordance with the Purposes and Principles of the United Nations. Amongst the Purposes set out in Article 1(3) of the Charter is that of achieving international co-operation "in promoting and encouraging respect for human rights and for fundamental freedoms for all without distinction as to race, sex, language or religion."
>
> . . . Now, it is not to be contemplated that the Security Council would ever deliberately adopt a resolution clearly and deliberately flouting a rule of *jus cogens* or violation of hu-man rights.[145]

While *jus cogens* norms may constrain Security Council powers, it is uncertain how such constraints could ever be enforced given that the International Court of Justice lacks an express power of judicial review in relation to Security Council determinations and decisions. This issue is addressed below, in subsection (v).

---

142 *Ibid* at 1259.

143 *Ibid* at 1260.

144 *Fragmentation of International Law: Difficulties arising from the Diversification and Expansion of Interna-tional Law: Report of the Study Group of the International Law Commission: Finalized by Martti Kosken-niemi*, UN Doc A/CN.4/L.682 (13 April 2006) at para 360.

145 *Application of the Convention on the Prevention and Punishment of the Crime of Genocide (Bosnia and Herzegovina v Yugoslavia (Serbia and Montenegro))*, Provisional Measures, Order of 13 September 1993, [1993] ICJ Rep 325 at 440, para 100, Judge ad hoc Lauterpacht.

iii) Economic and Social Council

Charter of the United Nations, 26 June 1945, Can TS 1945 No 7, in force 24 October 1945

CHAPTER IX
INTERNATIONAL ECONOMIC AND SOCIAL COOPERATION

Article 55
With a view to the creation of conditions of stability and well-being which are necessary for peaceful and friendly relations among nations based on respect for the principle of equal rights and self-determination of peoples, the United Nations shall promote:
a. higher standards of living, full employment, and conditions of economic and social progress and development;
b. solutions of international economic, social, health, and related problems; and international cultural and educational co-operation; and
c. universal respect for, and observance of, human rights and fundamental freedoms for all without distinction as to race, sex, language, or religion.

Article 56
All Members pledge themselves to take joint and separate action in co-operation with the Organization for the achievement of the purposes set forth in Article 55.

Article 57
The various specialized agencies, established by intergovernmental agreement and having wide international responsibilities, as defined in their basic instruments, in economic, social, cultural, educational, health, and related fields, shall be brought into relationship with the United Nations in accordance with the provisions of Article 63. . . .

Article 60
Responsibility for the discharge of the functions of the Organization set forth in this Chapter shall be vested in the General Assembly and, under the authority of the General Assembly, in the Economic and Social Council, which shall have for this purpose the powers set forth in Chapter X.

Articles 55 and 56 reflect a view, held by the framers of the UN Charter, that "peace needs to be secured by economic and social welfare and by the realization of human rights and that the Organization and its members should cooperate to this end."[146] Article 55, and its opening words, are particularly "noteworthy, as it establishes a link between peace and security, economic and social matters, as well as human rights."[147] We discuss Articles 55 and 56 in greater detail in Chapter 9. Here we focus on the organizational implications of Chapter IX of the UN Charter.

Article 57 refers to Article 63 of the UN Charter, which entitles the Economic and Social Council (ECOSOC) to "enter into agreements with any of the agencies referred to in Article 57, defining the terms on which the agency concerned shall be brought into

---

146 Simma et al, above note 74 at 1537.
147 *Ibid* at 1540.

relationship with the United Nations" and to "co-ordinate the activities of the specialized agencies through consultation with and recommendations to such agencies and through recommendations to the General Assembly and to the Members of the United Nations." These specialized agencies include the International Labour Organization (ILO), the Food and Agriculture Organization (FAO), the International Monetary Fund (IMF), the World Bank, the World Health Organization (WHO), and others.

The General Assembly has "responsibility for the discharge" of the UN Charter's Chapter IX functions, pursuant to Article 60, but so does ECOSOC, acting under the Assembly's authority and in accordance with the powers granted to it in Chapter X of the UN Charter.

Charter of the United Nations, 26 June 1945, Can TS 1945 No 7, in force 24 October 1945

CHAPTER X
THE ECONOMIC AND SOCIAL COUNCIL

Composition
Article 61
1. The Economic and Social Council shall consist of fifty-four Members of the United Nations elected by the General Assembly.

2. Subject to the provisions of paragraph 3, eighteen members of the Economic and Social Council shall be elected each year for a term of three years. A retiring member shall be eligible for immediate re-election. . . .

4. Each member of the Economic and Social Council shall have one representative. . . .

Voting
Article 67
1. Each member of the Economic and Social Council shall have one vote.

2. Decisions of the Economic and Social Council shall be made by a majority of the members present and voting.

ECOSOC members are elected from the membership of the United Nations in keeping with a principle of equitable geographical representation. Thus, each of the five regional groupings in the United Nations, described above in relation to the Security Council, is to have a number of seats on ECOSOC that is proportional to the size of its representation in the General Assembly.[148] In practice, fourteen seats are allocated to African states, eleven to Asian states, six to Eastern European states, ten to Latin American and Caribbean states, and thirteen to Western European and other states.

---

148 *Ibid* at 1674.

Charter of the United Nations, 26 June 1945, Can TS 1945 No 7, in force 24 October 1945

Functions and Powers
Article 62
1. The Economic and Social Council may make or initiate studies and reports with respect to international economic, social, cultural, educational, health, and related matters and may make recommendations with respect to any such matters to the General Assembly, to the Members of the United Nations, and to the specialized agencies concerned.

2. It may make recommendations for the purpose of promoting respect for, and observance of, human rights and fundamental freedoms for all.

3. It may prepare draft conventions for submission to the General Assembly, with respect to matters falling within its competence.

4. It may call, in accordance with the rules prescribed by the United Nations, international conferences on matters falling within its competence. . . .

Procedure
Article 68
The Economic and Social Council shall set up commissions in economic and social fields and for the promotion of human rights, and such other commissions as may be required for the performance of its functions.

ECOSOC "is regarded as the principal UN organ for discussing and addressing international economic and social issues as well as making recommendations to the member States, the GA and specialized organs on issues that are within their mandates."[149] ECOSOC also serves as the central mechanism for system-wide coordination on these issues within the United Nations. However, like other principal organs, ECOSOC has attracted the attention of reformers and in 2005, the member states agreed to reform and strengthen ECOSOC as follows:

2005 World Summit Outcome, **GA Res 60/1, UN Doc A/RES/60/1 (2005)**[150]

Economic and Social Council

155. We reaffirm the role that the Charter and the General Assembly have vested in the Economic and Social Council and recognize the need for a more effective Economic and Social Council as a principal body for coordination, policy review, policy dialogue and recommendations on issues of economic and social development, as well as for implementation of the international development goals agreed at the major United Nations conferences and summits, including the Millennium Development Goals. To achieve these objectives, the Council should:

(a) Promote global dialogue and partnership on global policies and trends in the economic, social, environmental and humanitarian fields. For this purpose, the Council

---

149 *Ibid* at 1679.
150 Reprinted in UN GAOR, 60th Sess, Supp No 49, vol I at 3–25, UN Doc A/60/49 (2005).

should serve as a quality platform for high-level engagement among Member States and with the international financial institutions, the private sector and civil society on emerging global trends, policies and action and develop its ability to respond better and more rapidly to developments in the international economic, environmental and social fields;

(b) Hold a biennial high-level Development Cooperation Forum to review trends in international development cooperation, including strategies, policies and financing, promote greater coherence among the development activities of different development partners and strengthen the links between the normative and operational work of the United Nations;

(c) Ensure follow-up of the outcomes of the major United Nations conferences and summits, including the internationally agreed development goals, and hold annual ministerial-level substantive reviews to assess progress, drawing on its functional and regional commissions and other international institutions, in accordance with their respective mandates;

(d) Support and complement international efforts aimed at addressing humanitarian emergencies, including natural disasters, in order to promote an improved, coordinated response from the United Nations;

(e) Play a major role in the overall coordination of funds, programmes and agencies, ensuring coherence among them and avoiding duplication of mandates and activities.

156. We stress that in order to fully perform the above functions, the organization of work, the agenda and the current methods of work of the Economic and Social Council should be adapted.

Recognizing the need for a more effective ECOSOC, these tasks were further developed in a General Assembly resolution adopted in 2006, aimed at "Strengthening the Economic and Social Council."[151] However, critics have said "that this was not a real reform, above all because of a lack of concrete obligations for the member States and of concrete measures."[152] In accordance with the terms of the 2006 resolution, a review session was held in June 2011 where the member states took note of the recommendations for reform, but could report no further progress.[153]

---

151 GA Res 61/16, UN Doc A/RES/61/16 (2006), reprinted in UN GAOR, 61st Sess, Supp No 49, vol I at 18–21, UN Doc A/61/49 (2007).

152 Simma et al, above note 74 at 1665.

153 *Review of the implementation of General Assembly resolution 61/16 on the strengthening of the Economic and Social Council*, GA Res 65/285, UN Doc A/RES/65/285 (2011), reprinted in UN GAOR, 65th Sess, Supp No 49, vol III at 72, UN Doc A/65/49 (2012).

iv) Secretariat

Charter of the United Nations, 26 June 1945, Can TS 1945 No 7, in force 24 October 1945

CHAPTER XV
THE SECRETARIAT

Article 97
The Secretariat shall comprise a Secretary-General and such staff as the Organization may require. The Secretary-General shall be appointed by the General Assembly upon the recommendation of the Security Council. He shall be the chief administrative officer of the Organization.

Article 98
The Secretary-General shall act in that capacity in all meetings of the General Assembly, of the Security Council, of the Economic and Social Council, and of the Trusteeship Council, and shall perform such other functions as are entrusted to him by these organs. The Secretary-General shall make an annual report to the General Assembly on the work of the Organization.

Article 99
The Secretary-General may bring to the attention of the Security Council any matter which in his opinion may threaten the maintenance of international peace and security.

Article 100
1. In the performance of their duties the Secretary-General and the staff shall not seek or receive instructions from any government or from any other authority external to the Organization. They shall refrain from any action which might reflect on their position as international officials responsible only to the Organization.

2. Each Member of the United Nations undertakes to respect the exclusively international character of the responsibilities of the Secretary-General and the staff and not to seek to influence them in the discharge of their responsibilities.

The Secretary-General is the public face of the United Nations, with administrative and political functions. To date, the position has been occupied exclusively by men. The position is not, however, analogous to that of a head of state or government. As the "chief administrative officer" for the United Nations, the Secretary-General's functions are supportive in nature but with a measure of independence. The Secretary-General coordinates the actions of the Secretariat and the other principal organs of the United Nations (other than the International Court of Justice), coordinates meetings and monitors implementation, calls special sessions of the General Assembly, oversees preparation of the UN's budget and its financial administration, and carries out other such functions. However, the role has evolved, and by the end of the 1990s, the office had also been entrusted with the civilian oversight of the territories of Kosovo and East Timor. Broad responsibilities in the civilian area were also entrusted to the Secretary-General in Afghanistan and Iraq in the 2000s.

The Secretary-General also has a political role, using his good offices and mediation functions to resolve disputes, and serving as a "norm entrepreneur" to advance new principles.[154] In practice, the various organs referred to in Article 98 have "entrusted" the Secretary-General with other functions, performed typically in an independent fashion. However, as explained by one commentator: "the SG and the Secretariat are set up to play two distinct roles. One is as a service staff to facilitate the effective functioning of the UN. . . . The other role is to administer the Organization in such a way as to advance its stated goals — which, at any particular moment, may or may not coincide with the interests of any particular member."[155]

Articles 99 and 100 serve to enhance the Secretary-General's political role and capacity for independent initiative. Consider the General Assembly's interpretation of the Secretary-General's peace and security powers in its 1991 *Declaration on Fact-finding by the United Nations in the Field of the Maintenance of International Peace and Security*:

> 28. The Secretary-General should monitor the state of international peace and security regularly and systematically in order to provide early warning of disputes or situations which might threaten international peace and security. The Secretary-General may bring relevant information to the attention of the Security Council and, where appropriate, of the General Assembly.

> 29. To this end, the Secretary-General should make full use of the information-gathering capabilities of the Secretariat and keep under review the improvement of these capabilities.[156]

These highly political functions render observance of the conditions of independence imposed upon the Secretary-General and his staff by Article 100 all the more important.

v) International Court of Justice

Charter of the United Nations, 26 June 1945, Can TS 1945 No 7, in force 24 October 1945

CHAPTER XIV
THE INTERNATIONAL COURT OF JUSTICE

Article 92
The International Court of Justice shall be the principal judicial organ of the United Nations. It shall function in accordance with the annexed Statute, which is based upon the Statute of the Permanent Court of International Justice and forms an integral part of the present Charter.

Article 93
1. All Members of the United Nations are *ipso facto* parties to the Statute of the International Court of Justice.

---

154 See further, Ian Johnstone, "The Secretary-General as Norm Entrepreneur" in Simon Chesterman, ed, *Secretary or General? The UN Secretary-General in World Politics* (Cambridge: Cambridge University Press, 2007) at 123.

155 Simma et al, above note 74 at 1993.

156 GA Res 46/59, UN Doc A/RES/46/59 (1991), reprinted in UN GAOR, 46th Sess, Supp No 49, vol I at 290–91, UN Doc A/46/49 (1992).

2. A state which is not a Member of the United Nations may become a party to the Statute of the International Court of Justice on conditions to be determined in each case by the General Assembly upon the recommendation of the Security Council.

The Permanent Court of International Justice (PCIJ) was the judicial organ established by the League of Nations for the resolution of disputes between states in accordance with international law. The International Court of Justice (ICJ) is the judicial organ established by the UN Charter and serves as the PCIJ's successor. As the above articles indicate, the ICJ is an organ of the United Nations, established by the Charter. Essential to understanding its functioning, however, is the additional treaty expanding on the role of the ICJ, known as the Statute of the International Court of Justice,[157] which is annexed to and incorporated by reference into the UN Charter. According to the Court itself:

The International Court of Justice is the principal judicial organ of the United Nations. Its seat is at the Peace Palace in The Hague (Netherlands). It began work in 1946, when it replaced the Permanent Court of International Justice which had functioned in the Peace Palace since 1922. It operates under a Statute largely similar to that of its predecessor, which is an integral part of the Charter of the United Nations.[158]

aa. Composition

The Statute of the International Court of Justice sets out the composition of the Court:

Statute of the International Court of Justice, 26 June 1945, Can TS 1945 No 7, in force 24 October 1945

Article 2
The Court shall be composed of a body of independent judges, elected regardless of their nationality from among persons of high moral character, who possess the qualifications required in their respective countries for appointment to the highest judicial offices, or are jurisconsults of recognized competence in international law.

Article 3
1. The Court shall consist of fifteen members, no two of whom may be nationals of the same state.

2. A person who for the purposes of membership in the Court could be regarded as a national of more than one state shall be deemed to be a national of the one in which he ordinarily exercises civil and political rights.

Article 4
1. The members of the Court shall be elected by the General Assembly and by the Security Council from a list of persons nominated by the national groups in the Permanent Court of Arbitration, in accordance with the following provisions.

---

157 Statute of the International Court of Justice, 26 June 1945, Can TS 1945 No 7, in force 24 October 1945 (ICJ Statute).

158 International Court of Justice, "The Court at a Glance" (10 December 2012), online: http://www.icj-cij.org/presscom/en/inotice.pdf.

2. In the case of Members of the United Nations not represented in the Permanent Court of Arbitration, candidates shall be nominated by national groups appointed for this purpose by their governments under the same conditions as those prescribed for members of the Permanent Court of Arbitration by Article 44 of the Convention of The Hague of 1907 for the pacific settlement of international disputes.

3. The conditions under which a state which is a party to the present Statute but is not a Member of the United Nations may participate in electing the members of the Court shall, in the absence of a special agreement, be laid down by the General Assembly upon recommendation of the Security Council. . . .

Article 13
1. The members of the Court shall be elected for nine years and may be re-elected; provided, however, that of the judges elected at the first election, the terms of five judges shall expire at the end of three years and the terms of five more judges shall expire at the end of six years. . . .

Article 31
1. Judges of the nationality of each of the parties shall retain their right to sit in the case before the Court.

Consider also the following summary, by the Court, of the qualifications of ICJ judges:

The judges must possess the qualifications required in their respective countries for appointment to the highest judicial offices, or be jurists of recognized competence in international law [Article 2]. The composition of the Court has also to reflect the main forms of civilization and the principal legal systems of the world [Article 9].

When the Court does not include a judge possessing the nationality of a State party to a case, that State may appoint a person to sit as a judge *ad hoc* for the purpose of the case [Article 31]. . . .[159]

bb. Function

As the ICJ notes, "the Court has a dual role: to settle in accordance with international law the legal disputes submitted to it by States, and to give advisory opinions on legal questions referred to it by duly authorized international organs and agencies."[160]

Under Article 34 of the ICJ Statute, only states may be parties to a contentious case — that is, a legal dispute — before the Court. Consider the following discussion:

The International Court of Justice, 5th ed (The Hague: International Court of Justice, 2004) at 35–36

It is the function of the ICJ to decide in accordance with international law disputes of a legal nature that are submitted to it by States. In doing so it is helping to achieve one of the primary aims of the United Nations, which, according to the Charter, is to bring

---

159 *Ibid.*
160 *Ibid.*

about the settlement of disputes by peaceful means and in conformity with the principles of justice and international law.

An international legal dispute is, as the PCIJ put it, "A disagreement on a question of law or fact, a conflict, a clash of legal views or of interests." Such a dispute between opposing parties may eventually lead to contentious proceedings before an international tribunal. It is conceivable that such proceedings could be between a State on the one hand and an international organization, a collectivity or an individual on the other. Within their respective fields of jurisdiction, institutions such as the Court of Justice of the European Communities in Luxembourg or the European Court of Human Rights in Strasbourg would be entitled to hear such disputes. This is not the case, however, with the ICJ, to which no case can be submitted unless both applicant and respondent are States. Despite various proposals and even the existence of a treaty providing for the possibility of proceedings before the Court between an international agency and a State, neither the United Nations nor any of its specialized agencies can be a party in contentious proceedings before the ICJ. As for private interests, these can only form the subject of proceedings in the International Court of Justice if a State, relying on international law, takes up the case of one of its nationals and invokes against another State the wrongs which its national claims to have suffered at the latter's hands, the dispute thus becoming one between States . . . . Like any other court, the ICJ can only operate within the constitutional limits that have been laid down for it. Hardly a day passes without the Registry receiving written or oral applications from private persons. However heart-rending, however well founded such applications may be, the ICJ is unable to entertain them and a standard reply is always sent: "Under Article 34 of the Statute, only States may be parties in cases before the Court."

Note that the ICJ is not the only forum in which states may settle their disputes. Article 95 of the UN Charter makes this clear: "Nothing in the present Charter shall prevent Members of the United Nations from entrusting the solution of their differences to other tribunals by virtue of agreements already in existence or which may be concluded in the future."

Even though UN member states are, pursuant to Article 93 of the UN Charter, automatically parties to the ICJ Statute, this does *not* in itself give the ICJ jurisdiction in relation to any dispute between these states. For this reason, in almost every contentious case coming before the ICJ, the question of its jurisdiction arises. Critically, the ICJ's jurisdiction in contentious cases depends on consent of the parties, manifested in one or more of three different ways:

The International Court of Justice, 5th ed (The Hague: International Court of Justice, 2004) at 36–46

A fundamental principle governing the settlement of international disputes is that the jurisdiction of an international tribunal depends in the last resort on the consent of the States concerned. Accordingly, no sovereign State can be made a party in proceedings before the Court unless it has in some manner or other consented thereto. It must have agreed that the dispute or the class of disputes in question should be dealt with by the

Court. It is this agreement that determines the jurisdiction of the Court so far as the particular dispute is concerned—the Court's jurisdiction *ratione materiae*. It is true that Article 36 of the Charter provides that the Security Council, which may at any stage of a dispute recommend appropriate procedures or methods of adjustment, is to "take into consideration that legal disputes should as a general rule be referred by the parties to the International Court of Justice." In the *Corfu Channel* case, however, the ICJ did not consider a recommendation by the Security Council to this effect sufficient to confer jurisdiction on the Court independently of the wishes of the parties to the dispute.

Special agreements

The way in which States manifest consent to their disputes of a legal nature being decided by the ICJ is defined in Article 36 of the Statute. Paragraph 1 thereof provides: "The jurisdiction of the Court comprises all cases which the parties refer to it and all matters specially provided for in the Charter of the United Nations or in treaties and conventions in force."

The first possibility envisaged here is where the parties bilaterally agree to submit an already existing dispute to the ICJ and thus to recognize its jurisdiction over that particular case. Such an agreement conferring jurisdiction on the Court is known as a "special agreement" or *"compromis"* [its traditional French designation]. Once such a special agreement has been lodged with the Court, the latter can entertain the case. . . .

It can also happen that a dispute is brought before the Court while at the time of the institution of the proceedings only one of the disputing States has validly recognized its jurisdiction over the case in question and the other has not, and that this latter State recognizes the Court's jurisdiction subsequently; this is a fairly rare situation and is known as *forum prorogatum*. . . . It has also happened 14 times that a State has instituted proceedings in the ICJ whilst recognizing that the opposing party has not recognized the Court's jurisdiction and inviting it to do so: to date, there has only been one instance where a State against whom an application has been filed has accepted such an invitation. . . .

Treaties and conventions

The second possibility envisaged in Article 36, paragraph 1, of the Statute is where treaties or conventions in force confer jurisdiction on the Court. It has become a general international practice to include in international agreements—both bilateral and multilateral—provisions, known as jurisdictional clauses, providing that disputes of a given class shall or may be submitted to one or more methods for the pacific settlement of disputes. Numerous clauses of this kind have provided and still provide for recourse to conciliation, mediation or arbitration; others provide for recourse to the Court, either immediately or after the failure of other means of pacific settlement. Accordingly, the States signatory to such agreements may, if a dispute of the kind envisaged in the jurisdictional clause of the treaty arises between them, either institute proceedings against the other party or parties by filing a unilateral application, or conclude a special agreement with such party or parties providing for the issue to be referred to the ICJ. The wording of such jurisdictional clauses varies from one treaty to another. Model jurisdictional clauses have been prepared by, *inter alia*, the Institute of International Law (1956). Jurisdictional clauses are to be found in treaties or conventions

- having as their object the pacific settlement of disputes between two or more States and providing in particular for the submission to judicial decision of specified classes of conflicts between States subject sometimes to certain exceptions;
- having an object other than the pacific settlement of disputes, in which case the jurisdictional clause of the treaty or convention in question will refer solely to disputes concerning the interpretation or application of the treaty or convention or only some of its provisions (e.g., disputes where the issue relates to a peremptory rule of international law—*jus cogens*). Such clauses may be included in the body of the text or in a protocol annexed to the treaty. They may likewise be compulsory or optional and may be open to reservations or not.

Nowadays such jurisdictional clauses confer jurisdiction on the ICJ. Those that were drawn up before the creation of the United Nations conferred it on the PCIJ. In order to prevent these from losing their effectiveness, the present Statute provides that the ICJ is to be substituted for the PCIJ. Provided that the agreement to which they relate is still in force and that the States concerned are parties to the Statute of the ICJ, any dispute that arises can be submitted to the ICJ in the same way as it could have been to the PCIJ. The few hundred treaties or conventions that confer jurisdiction on the Court in this way will normally have been registered with the Secretariat of the League or the United Nations and will appear in the collections of treaties published by those two Organizations. In addition, the PCIJ and the ICJ have published lists of and extracts from such treaties and conventions. It is not always easy to determine which of them are still in force. They probably number some 400 or so, some being bilateral, involving about 60 States, and others multilateral, involving a greater number of States.

Declarations Accepting the Compulsory Jurisdiction of the Court
A third means of consent to the Court's jurisdiction is described in paragraphs 2 and 3 of Article 36 of the Statute:

> 2. The States parties to the present Statute may at any time declare that they recognize as compulsory *ipso facto* and without special agreement, in relation to any other State accepting the same obligation, the jurisdiction of the Court in all legal disputes concerning: (a) the interpretation of a treaty; (b) any question of international law; (c) the existence of any fact which, if established, would constitute a breach of an international obligation; (d) the nature or extent of the reparation to be made for the breach of an international obligation.

> 3. The declarations referred to above may be made unconditionally or on condition of reciprocity on the part of several or certain States, or for a certain time.

This system, based on what has been known since the days of the PCIJ as the "optional clause", has led to the creation of a group of States who stand as it were in the same position towards the Court as the inhabitants of a country stand towards the courts of that country. Each State belonging to this group has in principle the right to bring any one or more other States belonging to the group before the Court by filing an application instituting proceedings with the Court, and, conversely, it has undertaken to appear before the Court should proceedings be instituted against it by one or more such other

States. This is why such declarations are known as "declarations of acceptance of the compulsory jurisdiction of the Court".[161]

These declarations, which take the form of a unilateral act of the State concerned, are deposited with the Secretary-General of the United Nations and are generally signed by the foreign minister of the State concerned or by its representative to the United Nations. They are published in the *United Nations Treaty Series* and in the *I.C.J. Yearbook*. Despite solemn appeals by the General Assembly of the United Nations . . . , by the Secretary-General of the United Nations . . . and by the Institute of International Law (1959), they are fewer in number than had been hoped. In July 2004 there were only 65, from the following regional groups: Africa 20; Latin America and the Caribbean 13; Asia 5; Europe and other States 27. It must be added that 13 other States that had at one time recognized the compulsory jurisdiction of the ICJ have withdrawn their declarations, 8 of them after they had been made respondents in proceedings before the Court. As with treaties or conventions, the Statute provides that declarations that refer to the PCIJ shall be regarded as applying to the ICJ. Seven of these were still in force in 2004, but 11 countries that had at one time recognized the compulsory jurisdiction of the PCIJ never did so in respect of the ICJ. . . .

Matters are further complicated by reservations to the acceptances of compulsory jurisdiction which serve to limit their scope. Such reservations are to be found in most such declarations (51 out of the 65 in force in July 2004). They usually recapitulate some of the wording of paragraphs 2 and 3 of Article 36, including especially points (a), (b), (c) and (d) (17 declarations). The declarations are made for a specific period, generally for five years and normally with a provision for tacit renewal and usually provide for the declarations to be terminated by simple notice, such notice to take effect after a specified time or immediately.

The most frequently employed reservations relate to disputes—

- for which another means of peaceful settlement is provided;
- arising before a certain date or concerning situations or facts anterior to that date, generally the date on which the State making the declaration first accepted the Court's compulsory jurisdiction;
- relating to matters falling within the domestic jurisdiction of the declaratory State, as determined by international law or by the State making the declaration itself;
- arising during or out of hostilities;
- with certain States: as between members of the Commonwealth or with States with which the State making the declaration does not have diplomatic relations;
- for the specific purpose of which the other party appears to have made its declaration of acceptance of compulsory jurisdiction;
- where the other party has accepted the Court's compulsory jurisdiction only a short time before the filing of the application (e.g., less than a year);
- concerning certain multilateral treaties;
- concerning certain aspects of the law of the sea.[162]

---

161 [Canada's most recent declaration, published in 1776 UNTS 9, was deposited on 10 May 1994, replacing a previous declaration made 10 September 1985.]

162 [Canada, for example, does not accept jurisdiction for "disputes arising out of or concerning conservation and management measures taken by Canada with respect to vessels fishing in the NAFO Regula-

The two most important of these reservations, that relating to other methods of pacific settlement, which is found in 39 declarations, and that relating to matters of domestic jurisdiction, which is found in 26 declarations, correspond to Article 95 and Article 2 (7) of the United Nations Charter respectively. These provide that nothing in the Charter:

"shall prevent Members of the United Nations from entrusting the solution of their differences to other tribunals by virtue of agreements already in existence or which may be concluded in the future";

"shall authorize the United Nations to intervene in matters which are essentially within the domestic jurisdiction of any State."

With regard to the latter, it is indisputable that every sovereign State has, under international law, what is known as its reserved domain, and it would be inconceivable for the ICJ to decide issues relating thereto. Nevertheless, as the PCIJ made clear in one of its first decisions, "The question whether a certain matter is or is not solely within the jurisdiction of a State is an essentially relative question; it depends upon the development of international relations."

This is no doubt one of the reasons why certain States have excluded from their recognition of the compulsory jurisdiction of the ICJ questions falling essentially within their field of domestic jurisdiction as "determined" by the State concerned or which such State "considers" essentially within its domestic jurisdiction. Such a reservation operates automatically: it is sufficient for a government relying upon such a reservation to declare that a question in relation to which proceedings have been brought against it in the ICJ falls within its domestic jurisdiction for the Court to be deprived of jurisdiction over the case. Ten countries originally employed such a formula in their declarations accepting the compulsory jurisdiction of the Court. The reservation was invoked in the *Certain Norwegian Loans* and *Interhandel* cases. The ICJ upheld the objection based on this reservation in the former case and did not deal with it in the latter case since it upheld an objection based on other grounds. Some Members of the Court expressed the opinion that such a reservation was contrary to the Statute, so that, according to certain judges, the reservation as such was null and void, whereas, according to others, the whole declaration accepting compulsory jurisdiction was null and void (1957, 1959). Following this, the Institute of International Law (1959) and various statesmen and jurists called upon those governments that had included such a reservation in their declaration to withdraw it. Certain States did so. In July 2004, five declarations included a clause of this kind (Liberia, Malawi, Mexico, Philippines, Sudan).

The importance of such reservations is increased by the condition of reciprocity, which expressly or by implication attaches to all declarations of acceptance of the Court's compulsory jurisdiction. This means that where a dispute arises between two or more States that have made a declaration, the reservations made by any of them can be relied upon against it by all the others. In other words, the Court's jurisdiction over the case is restricted to those classes of dispute that have not been excluded by any of them. If, for instance, there are two States, one of which has accepted the compulsory jurisdiction of the Court only in respect of disputes arising after the date of its acceptance of such compulsory

---

tory Area, as defined in the Convention on Future Multilateral Co-operation in the Northwest Atlantic Fisheries, 1978, and the enforcement of such measures."]

jurisdiction, such date being 1 February 1924, and the other State has excluded disputes relating to situations or facts prior to 21 August 1928, the ICJ, irrespective of which State was the applicant, would have jurisdiction only to hear cases arising after this latter date.

In recent years, the docket of the Court has burgeoned — although it is not clear whether the spike in activity in the late 1990s was simply an aberration, as some observers conclude.[163] Whatever the case, the constraints placed upon the ICJ's jurisdiction and the widespread unwillingness of states to accept its compulsory jurisdiction have undermined its full potential as an instrument for the peaceful settlement of disputes. In his 2005 report on UN reform, the UN Secretary-General urged states to rethink their approach to the ICJ:

> The International Court of Justice lies at the centre of the international system for adjudicating disputes among States. In recent years, the Court's docket has grown significantly and a number of disputes have been settled, but resources remain scarce. There is a need to consider means to strengthen the work of the Court. I urge those States that have not yet done so to consider recognizing the compulsory jurisdiction of the Court — generally if possible or, failing that, at least in specific situations. . . .[164]

The difficulties caused by the consensual nature of the ICJ's jurisdiction — and the extent to which the ICJ itself has been cautious in its approach to jurisdiction — are illustrated in the recent dispute between Russia and Georgia over South Ossetia and Abkhazia, mentioned above. In April 2011, the ICJ dismissed a complaint brought by Georgia in relation to Russia's conduct in these two secessionist regions of Georgia.[165] The complaint was grounded in the International Convention on the Elimination of All Forms of Racial Discrimination,[166] and alleged, *inter alia*, that Russia has engaged in, sponsored, defended, and supported racial discrimination in the secessionist regions. Georgia asserted that the ICJ had jurisdiction over the dispute by virtue of Article 22 of the Convention, which provides: "Any dispute between two or more States Parties with respect to the interpretation or application of this Convention, which is not settled by negotiation or by the procedures expressly provided for in this Convention, shall, at the request of any of the parties to the dispute, be referred to the International Court of Justice for decision, unless the disputants agree to another mode of settlement." Both Georgia and Russia were, at the relevant time, parties to the Convention.

In declining jurisdiction, the Court held that the phrase "which is not settled by negotiation" imposed a precondition on the matter being adjudicated by the ICJ. It found that Georgia had not negotiated on the question of racial discrimination with Russia (applying an arguably narrow understanding of what constitutes negotiation), and concluded that the ICJ was, therefore, without jurisdiction in the matter. In arriving at this position, the ICJ relied on a highly technical "ordinary meaning" interpretation that rested, essentially, on a redundancy argument: if the disputed phrase did not impose a precondition, its presence would be meaningless, as a dispute "which is not settled" is simply a dispute

---

163 See Eric Posner, *The Perils of Global Legalism* (Chicago: University of Chicago Press, 2009).
164 *In Larger Freedom*, above note 96 at para 139.
165 *Application of the International Convention on the Elimination of All Forms of Racial Discrimination (Georgia v Russian Federation)*, Preliminary Objections, Judgment, [2011] ICJ Rep 70.
166 Above note 32.

and the phrase would be an unnecessary modifier of the word "dispute." This approach is a failure of imagination, if nothing else: the phrase "dispute which is not settled by negotiations" could equally be viewed not as creating a precondition to jurisdiction, but as a mootness provision. That is, the ICJ has jurisdiction only to the extent that the dispute remains extant, and not where it has been rendered academic by resolution through negotiation. The latter approach would have kept the matter alive at the ICJ.

Presumably, even with the reasoning adopted by the ICJ, it would be open to Georgia to invite negotiations, the failure of which would potentially reignite the case. But this requirement comes at the cost of delaying the resolution of a dispute that has already precipitated one war.

Once (or more correctly, "if") the ICJ has jurisdiction over a dispute, recall that under Article 38 of the ICJ Statute, the Court is to apply the sources of international law: treaties, customary international law, general principles of law, and, as a subsidiary aid to determining the content of international law, jurisprudence and scholarly writings.

ICJ decisions in contentious cases are binding on the states parties to the case. Article 94 of the UN Charter reads:

> 1. Each Member of the United Nations undertakes to comply with the decision of the International Court of Justice in any case to which it is a party.
>
> 2. If any party to a case fails to perform the obligations incumbent upon it under a judgment rendered by the Court, the other party may have recourse to the Security Council, which may, if it deems necessary, make recommendations or decide upon measures to be taken to give to the judgment.

Whether states meet this obligation to comply with ICJ decisions is another issue. One 2004 study estimated the rate of full compliance with ICJ decisions at 80 percent between 1946 and 1987 and 60 percent between 1987 and 2004. In other cases, there was at least partial compliance, suggesting that full compliance figures do not fully capture responses to ICJ decisions.[167] Figures by other observers are more pessimistic. Eric Posner, in his 2009 critique of the ICJ, estimated compliance rates as 83 percent in 1946–1965; 20 percent in 1966–1985; and 29 percent in 1986–2004.[168]

As well as deciding contentious cases between states, the Court may give advisory opinions. Article 96 of the UN Charter reads:

> 1. The General Assembly or the Security Council may request the International Court of Justice to give an advisory opinion on any legal question.
>
> 2. Other organs of the United Nations and specialized agencies, which may at any time be so authorized by the General Assembly, may also request advisory opinions of the Court on legal questions arising within the scope of their activities.

Article 65 of the ICJ Statute adds: "The Court may give an advisory opinion on any legal

---

167 Colter Paulson, "Compliance with Final Judgments of the International Court of Justice since 1987" (2004) 93 AJIL 434.
168 Posner, above note 163.

question at the request of whatever body may be authorized by or in accordance with the Charter of the United Nations to make such a request." Consider the following discussion of advisory opinions and their procedures:

The International Court of Justice, 5th ed (The Hague: International Court of Justice, 2004) at 79–90

Since States alone have capacity to appear before the Court, public international organizations cannot as such be parties to any contentious proceedings, nor, indeed, to any case properly so called. It has been proposed from time to time that they be given this power, but nothing so far has come of this. If a question arises concerning the interpretation or implementation of their constitutions or of conventions adopted in pursuance thereof, it is for their member States to bring contentious proceedings in the ICJ; in such a case the organization concerned is informed of the proceedings by the Registrar and receives copies of the pleadings *(Appeal Relating to the Jurisdiction of the ICAO Council, Aerial Incident of 3 July 1988, Questions of Interpretation and Application of the 1971 Montreal Convention arising from the Aerial Incident at Lockerbie)*. All that it can then do is to furnish the Court with relevant information. Public international organizations may also furnish information in other circumstances, either on their own initiative or at the request of the parties or of the Court itself. The constitutions of some (e.g., FAO, UNESCO, WHO, ICAO, ITU, WIPO) or agreements between them and the United Nations stipulate that where they are requested to furnish information they are obliged to do so. The Rules of Court provide that time-limits for doing so may be imposed and that the parties to the case may comment on the information furnished. Only ICAO has furnished such written comments in the case concerning the *Aerial Incident of 3 July 1988*.

Advisory opinions are given to public international organizations

A special procedure, the advisory procedure, is, however, available to public international organizations and to them alone. Certain organs and agencies, at present 22 in number, have the right to ask the Court for an advisory opinion on a legal question.
- Through the effect of Article 96 of the Charter of the United Nations, the General Assembly and Security Council have as it were inherited with respect to the ICJ a power which the Covenant of the League of Nations previously conferred on the Assembly and Council of the League with respect to the PCIJ. In the time of the League, only the Council availed itself of this power, which then extended to "any dispute or question." Since 1947 it has applied to "any legal question" and it is above all the General Assembly of the United Nations that has made use of it, the Security Council having only once requested an advisory opinion.
- Four other United Nations organs have been authorized by General Assembly resolutions to request advisory opinions of the Court with respect to "legal questions arising within the scope of their activities," which represents an innovation as compared with the time of the League of Nations and the PCIJ, and two of those organs have availed themselves of the opportunity to do so.
- Sixteen specialized agencies, or entities assimilated thereto, are authorized by the General Assembly, in pursuance of agreements governing their relationship with the

United Nations, to ask the ICJ for advisory opinions "on legal questions arising within the scope of their activities." Here again, this represents an innovation by comparison with the time of the PCIJ, which, although it gave advisory opinions concerning the ILO, did so at the request of the Council of the League. Up to the present, however, only three agencies have availed themselves of this opportunity to ask the Court for an advisory opinion (UNESCO, IMO and WHO).

The precise circumstances in which each agency may avail itself of the Court's advisory jurisdiction are specified either in its constitutive act, constitution or statute . . . or in such particular instruments as its headquarters agreement or the convention governing its privileges and immunities. Advisory opinions may be requested relating to the interpretation of these texts or of the Charter of the United Nations, and may concern disagreements between —

- two or more organs or agencies *inter se* (e.g., the United Nations Economic and Social Council may submit to the Court "legal questions concerning mutual relations of the United Nations and specialized agencies") which is a rather theoretical possibility since the entities entitled to seek advisory opinions have in general the same member States;
- an organ or agency and one or more of its staff members;
- an organ or agency and one or more of its member States;
- two or more States Members of the same organ or agency *inter se*. . . .

Comparatively little use . . . has been made of the system of advisory opinions. The ICJ has delivered somewhat fewer opinions than its predecessor: 25 from 1948 to July 2004, against 27 from 1922 to 1935. It delivered about the same number of opinions up to and including 1956 (11) as it has done since that time (14). This decrease is to be explained by the fact that many more opinions relating to the consequences of the First World War were requested of the PCIJ (21) than were requested of the ICJ with respect to the consequences of the Second World War (3). Cases relating to decolonization (5) have not been sufficiently numerous to make up for this.

Procedure in respect of advisory opinions is based on that in contentious proceedings

The Court's procedure in advisory proceedings, although having distinctive features resulting from the special nature and object of the Court's advisory function, as just described, is based on the provisions in the Statute and Rules relating to contentious proceedings, to the extent that it recognizes them to be applicable.

Request for advisory opinion

Advisory proceedings begin with the filing of a written request for an advisory opinion. After suitable discussion, the organ or agency seeking the opinion will have embodied the question or questions to be submitted in a resolution or decision. . . .

Characteristics of advisory opinions

It is of the essence of the Court's advisory opinions that they are advisory, i.e., that, unlike the Court's judgments, they have no binding effect. The requesting organ, agency or organization remains free to give effect to the opinion by any means open to it, or not to do so. It is only in a few specific cases that it is stipulated beforehand that an opinion shall have binding force (e.g., conventions on the privileges and immunities of the United Nations . . . , its specialized agencies and the IAEA, and the host agreement between the United Nations and the United States). The Court's advisory function is herein different from its function in contentious cases, and is also to be distinguished from the role played by the supreme court of certain countries as an interpreter of those countries' constitutions. It remains nevertheless that the authority and prestige of the Court attach to its advisory opinions and that where the organ or agency concerned endorses that opinion, that decision is as it were sanctioned by international law.

At the time of writing, there have only been two ICJ advisory opinions since July 2004, styled as: *Accordance with International Law of the Unilateral Declaration of Independence in Respect of Kosovo*[169] and *Judgment No 2867 of the Administrative Tribunal of the International Labour Organization upon a Complaint Filed against the International Fund for Agricultural Development.*[170]

Given the dispute resolution and advisory functions of the ICJ, is there any possibility that this "principal judicial organ" of the UN system could also perform a judicial review role? For example, may the ICJ review Security Council resolutions to ensure they comply with the UN Charter? The question is not clearly settled, with strong views having been expressed on both sides.

In the *Application of the Genocide Convention* case, Judge ad hoc Lauterpacht observed that "the Court's power of judicial review is limited." All the same:

> That the Court has some power of this kind can hardly be doubted, though there can be no less doubt that it does not embrace any right of the Court to substitute its discretion for that of the Security Council in determining the existence of a threat to the peace, a breach of the peace or an act of aggression, or the political steps to be taken following such a determination. But the Court, as the principal judicial organ of the United Nations, is entitled, indeed bound, to ensure the rule of law within the United Nations system and, in cases properly brought before it, to insist on adherence by all United Nations organs to the rules governing their operation.[171]

President Schwebel, dissenting in the *Lockerbie* case, was much less open to a judicial review function for the ICJ:

Questions of Interpretation and Application of the 1971 Montreal Convention arising from the Aerial Incident at Lockerbie (Libyan Arab Jamahiriya v United Kingdom), Preliminary Objections, Judgment, [1998] ICJ Rep 9

[Recall that the United States and the United Kingdom had demanded that Libya extradite two Libyan nationals suspected of causing the explosion of Pan American Flight

---

169 Above note 107.

170 *Judgment No 2867 of the Administrative Tribunal of the International Labour Organization upon a Complaint Filed against the International Fund for Agricultural Development*, Advisory Opinion, ICJ General List No 146, 1 February 2012.

171 Above note 134 at para 99.

103 on 21 December 1988, over Lockerbie, Scotland. Libya maintained that its obligation to extradite—or not—should be governed by the terms of the Montreal Convention.[172] However, Security Council Resolution 748 (1992),[173] issued after the case was brought by Libya before the ICJ, required that Libya comply with the extradition requests of the United States and the United Kingdom. The question that thus arose was whether Resolution 748 (1992) rendered Libya's invocation of its rights under the Montreal Convention moot. Implicit in this question was whether the Court had the power to supervene or judicially review a Security Council resolution adopted under Chapter VII. In its preliminary decision on jurisdiction, the majority of the Court avoided this question by concluding that Resolution 748 (1992) post-dated the date at which the case was brought by Libya. As such, it could not affect the Court's jurisdiction, which was to be measured according to the date the case was brought. However, President Schwebel, in his dissenting opinion, addressed the judicial review issue, as follows:]

[With the majority's decision] the Court may have opened itself, not only in this but in future cases, to appearing to offer to recalcitrant States a means to parry and frustrate decisions of the Security Council by way of appeal to the Court. . . .

That last spectre raises the question of whether the Court is empowered to exercise judicial review of the decisions of the Security Council, a question as to which I think it right to express my current views. The Court is not generally so empowered, and it is particularly without power to overrule or undercut decisions of the Security Council made by it in pursuance of its authority under Articles 39, 41 and 42 of the Charter to determine the existence of any threat to the peace, breach of the peace, or act of aggression and to decide upon responsive measures to be taken to maintain or restore international peace and security.

The Court more than once has disclaimed possessing a power of judicial review. . . . It should be noted that the Court made these holdings in advisory proceedings, in which the Security Council and the General Assembly are entitled to request the Court's opinion "on any legal question." The authority of the Court to respond to such questions, and, in the course of so doing, to pass upon relevant resolutions of the Security Council and General Assembly, is not disputed. Nevertheless, if the Court could hold as it did in advisory proceedings, a fortiori in contentious proceedings the Court can hardly be entitled to invent, assert and apply powers of judicial review. . . .

The texts of the Charter of the United Nations and of the Statute of the Court furnish no shred of support for a conclusion that the Court possesses a power of judicial review in general, or a power to supervene the decisions of the Security Council in particular. On the contrary, by the absence of any such provision, and by according the Security Council "primary responsibility for the maintenance of international peace and security," the Charter and the Statute import the contrary. So extraordinary a power as that of judicial review is not ordinarily to be implied and never has been on the international plane. If the Court were to generate such a power, the Security Council would no longer be primary in its assigned responsibilities, because if the Court could overrule, negate, modify—or, as in this case, hold as proposed that decisions of the Security Council are not "opposable" to the principal object State of those decisions and to the object of its

172 Above note 135.
173 Above note 136.

sanctions—it would be the Court and not the Council that would exercise, or purport to exercise, the dispositive and hence primary authority.

The drafters of the Charter above all resolved to accord the Security Council alone extraordinary powers. They did so in order to further realization of the first Purpose of the United Nations,

> To maintain international peace and security, and to that end: to take effective collective measures for the prevention and removal of threats to the peace, and for the suppression of acts of aggression or other breaches of the peace, and to bring about by peaceful means, and in conformity with the principles of justice and international law, adjustment or settlement of international disputes or situations which might lead to a breach of the peace.

. . . [Articles 24 and 25]—the very heart of the Charter's design for the maintenance of international peace—manifest the plenitude of the powers of the Security Council, which are elaborated by the provisions of Chapters VI, VII, and VIII of the Charter. They also demonstrate that the Security Council is subject to the rule of law; it shall act in accordance with the Purposes and Principles of the United Nations and its decisions must be adopted in accordance with the Charter. At the same time, as Article 103 imports, it may lawfully decide upon measures which may in the interests of the maintenance or restoration of international peace and security derogate from the rights of a State under international law. The first Purpose of the United Nations quoted above also so indicates, for the reference to the principles of justice and international law designedly relates only to adjustment or settlement by peaceful means, and not to the taking of effective collective measures for the prevention and removal of threats to and breaches of the peace. It was deliberately so provided to ensure that the vital duty of preventing and removing threats to and breaches of the peace would not be limited by existing law. . . .

It does not follow from the facts that the decisions of the Security Council must be in accordance with the Charter and that the International Court of Justice is the principal judicial organ of the United Nations, that the Court is empowered to ensure that the Council's decisions do accord with the Charter. To hold that it does so follow is a monumental non sequitur, which overlooks the truth that, in many legal systems, national and international, the subjection of the acts of an organ to law by no means entails subjection of the legality of its actions to judicial review. In many cases, the system relies not upon judicial review but on self-censorship by the organ concerned or by its members or on review by another political organ.

Judicial review could have been provided for at San Francisco, in full or lesser measure, directly or indirectly, but both directly and indirectly it was not in any measure contemplated or enacted. . . . Proposals which in restricted measure would have accorded the Court a degree of authority, by way of advisory proceedings, to pass upon the legality of proposed resolutions of the Security Council in the sphere of peaceful settlement—what came to be Chapter VI of the Charter—were not accepted. What was never proposed, considered, or, so far as the records reveal, even imagined, was that the International Court of Justice would be entrusted with, or would develop, a power of judicial review at large, or a power to supervene, modify, negate or confine the applicability of resolutions of the Security Council whether directly or in the guise of interpretation. . . .

The conclusions to which the *travaux préparatoires* and text of the Charter lead are that the Court was not and was not meant to be invested with a power of judicial review of the legality or effects of decisions of the Security Council. Only the Security Council can determine what is a threat to or breach of the peace or act of aggression under Article 39, and under Article 39 only it can "decide what measures shall be taken . . . to maintain or restore international peace and security." Two States at variance in the interpretation of the Charter may submit a dispute to the Court, but that facility does not empower the Court to set aside or second-guess the determinations of the Security Council under Article 39. Contentious cases may come before the Court that call for its passing upon questions of law raised by Council decisions and for interpreting pertinent Council resolutions. But that power cannot be equated with an authority to review and confute the decisions of the Security Council.

It may of course be maintained that the Charter is a living instrument; that the present-day interpreters of the Charter are not bound by the intentions of its drafters of 50 years ago; that the Court has interpreted the powers of the United Nations constructively in other respects, and could take a constructive view of its own powers in respect of judicial review or some variation of it. The difficulty with this approach is that for the Court to engraft upon the Charter régime a power to review, and revise the reach of, resolutions of the Security Council would not be evolutionary but revolutionary. It would be not a development but a departure, and a great and grave departure. It would not be a development even arguably derived from the terms or structure of the Charter and Statute. It would not be a development arising out of customary international law, which has no principle of or provision for judicial review. It would not be a development drawn from the general principles of law. Judicial review, in varying forms, is found in a number of democratic polities, most famously that of the United States, where it was developed by the Supreme Court itself. But it is by no means a universal or even general principle of government or law. It is hardly found outside the democratic world and is not uniformly found in it. Where it exists internationally, as in the European Union, it is expressly provided for by treaty in specific terms. The United Nations is far from being a government, or an international organization comparable in its integration to the European Union, and it is not democratic.

The conclusion that the Court cannot judicially review or revise the resolutions of the Security Council is buttressed by the fact that only States may be parties in cases before the Court. The Security Council cannot be a party. For the Court to adjudge the legality of the Council's decisions in a proceeding brought by one State against another would be for the Court to adjudicate the Council's rights without giving the Council a hearing, which would run counter to fundamental judicial principles. . . . Any such judgment could not bind the Council, because, by the terms of Article 59 of the Statute, the decision of the Court has no binding force except between the parties and in respect of that particular case.

At the same time, a judgment of the Court which held resolutions of the Security Council adopted under Chapter VII of the Charter not to bind or to be "opposable" to a State, despite the terms of Article 25 of the Charter, would seriously prejudice the effectiveness of the Council's resolutions and subvert the integrity of the Charter. Such a holding would be tantamount to a judgment that the resolutions of the Security Council were *ultra vires*, at any rate in relation to that State. That could set the stage for an extraordinary confrontation between the Court and the Security Council. It could give rise to the question, is a holding by the Court that the Council has acted *ultra vires* a holding which of itself is *ultra vires?*

For some 45 years, the world rightly criticized stalemate in the Security Council. With the end of the Cold War, the Security Council has taken great strides towards performing as it was empowered to perform. That in turn has given rise to the complaint by some Members of the United Nations that they lack influence over the Council's decision-making. However understandable that complaint may be, it cannot furnish the Court with the legal authority to supervene the resolutions of the Security Council. The argument that it does is a purely political argument; the complaints that give rise to it should be addressed to and by the United Nations in its consideration of the reform of the Security Council. It is not an argument that can be heard in a court of law.

Consider the General Assembly's power to request advisory opinions, under Article 96 of the Charter, in conjunction with its power, under Article 10, to discuss any matter "relating to the powers and functions of any organs provided for in the present Charter." Bearing in mind that the ICJ has held that "[a] request for an advisory opinion is not in itself a 'recommendation' by the General Assembly" within the meaning of Article 12 of the UN Charter,[174] is there any legal reason for which the General Assembly could not request an advisory opinion of the Court on the legality, or consistency with the Charter, of a Security Council resolution? Would such an advisory opinion have any legal effect on the validity of such a resolution?

---

174 See *Legal Consequences of the Construction of a Wall in the Occupied Palestinian Territory*, Advisory Opinion, [2004] ICJ Rep 136 at para 25; *Accordance with International Law of the Unilateral Declaration of Independence in Respect of Kosovo*, Advisory Opinion, above note 107 at para 24.

STATE JURISDICTION

INTRODUCTION

In this Part, we examine the nature and extent of state jurisdiction over territory, persons, property, and transactions. Before doing so, we begin with a few definitional considerations.

Our title to this Part is "state jurisdiction." In the chapters that follow, we will also employ the expressions "sovereignty" and "sovereign title" when referring to the relationship between states and certain types of territory. Recall that, in international law, sovereignty is essentially autonomy from other states in both domestic matters and foreign relations. Used in relation to territory, it means autonomous control of that territory.

The difference between "jurisdiction" and "sovereignty" is a matter of degree rather than of kind. One observer has defined "jurisdiction" this way: "Jurisdiction is an aspect of sovereignty: it refers to a state's competence under international law to regulate the conduct of natural and juridical persons[, which] . . . includes the activity of all branches of government: legislative, executive and judicial."[1] In areas where states enjoy the full sum of these various jurisdictional competencies to the exclusion of all other states, they are said to be "sovereign." In other words, sovereignty is used by international lawyers as shorthand for full and exclusive jurisdiction. Yet, full and exclusive jurisdiction should not be confused with "absolute" sovereignty—which, as we have seen elsewhere in these materials, is (and probably always has been) a myth. From the earliest point in the modern state system, states have constrained their sovereignty through international law. As a result, full and exclusive state jurisdiction always falls short of absolute sovereignty. We explore this issue in some detail in Part III, where we examine specific limitations imposed by international law on state jurisdiction.

In the first three chapters of this Part, we focus on the jurisdictional relationship between states and territory. It is common to think of state jurisdiction as at its zenith, approximating sovereignty, in relation to territory. However, to say that sovereignty may be exercised by states over territory is not to say that *all* territory is subject to this plenary form of jurisdiction. Of course, by "territory," we mean more than land territory and refer to all spaces that may be occupied, visited, or explored by humankind. Territory in this sense, in modern international law, is controlled by states to varying degrees, depending on the class of territory at issue. Speaking generally, international law recognizes several such classes.

---

1   James Crawford, *Brownlie's Principles of Public International Law*, 8th ed (Oxford: Oxford University Press, 2012) at 456.

First, there is territory that corresponds to the physical or geographic state itself. This territory—typically comprising land, inland waterways, a thin band of sea along a state's coasts (if any), and the airspace above all of these—is controlled by the state to the exclusion of other states. This is the territory over which the state is said to enjoy sovereignty. Second, so-called *res nullius* territory may, in principle, be legally subjected to the exclusive jurisdictional control (that is, sovereignty) of a state, but is not currently subject to such control by any state. Third, *res communis* territory is not and may not be legally subjected to any state's exclusive jurisdictional control, but may be used and enjoyed by every state for its own purposes. Finally, a variant of the *res communis* category introduced in the last quarter of the twentieth century is territory constituting the so-called common heritage of mankind, since rephrased as "humankind." Such territory can neither be subjected to any state's exclusive jurisdictional control nor exploited unilaterally by any state, its resources being reserved for the benefit of humanity as a whole.

In this Part, we do not organize our discussion of the jurisdictional relationship between states and territory according to these legal categories. Instead, we apply a more intuitive distinction, examining jurisdiction over territory according to its different geographical manifestations: land, water, airspace, and outer space. Our twin focus will be how states acquire jurisdiction over such spaces as well as the legal scope of this jurisdiction.

In the final chapter of this Part, we consider the non-geographical dimensions of the jurisdiction of states; that is, the jurisdictional relationship between states and persons, property, and transactions.

CHAPTER 4

STATE JURISDICTION OVER LAND TERRITORY

With very few exceptions, all of the Earth's landmasses are subject to the full and exclusive jurisdiction, or sovereignty, of one state or another. We employ readily the expressions "sovereignty," "sovereign title," or "territorial sovereignty" to describe the typical jurisdictional relationship between states and land. Consider the following description of these concepts: "The essence of territorial sovereignty is contained in the notion of title. This term relates to both the factual and legal conditions under which territory is deemed to belong to one particular authority or another. . . . [T]he word 'title' comprehends both any evidence which may establish the existence of a right and the actual source of that right."[2] As we have already examined the meaning of sovereignty elsewhere, in this chapter we focus on the various international legal principles governing acquisition of sovereign title to land.

A. INTERTEMPORAL LAW AND SOVEREIGN TITLE TO LAND

How is it that states acquire sovereignty over land? One observer has noted that the international legal rules on state acquisition of territory "have often (although not always) had the effect of legitimising the results of the exercise of power."[3] This should come as no surprise, given that a principal source of international law, as we have seen, is the practice of states accompanied by a conviction in its legality. As a result, the answer to the question posed above has, along with the practice and *opinio juris* of states, changed over time, such that some previously lawful modes of territorial acquisition are now rejected in modern international law. Indeed, it is probably not an overstatement to say that many claims made by states to at least some of their territory are predicated in part on past acts of acquisition that, if committed today, would be regarded as illegitimate in modern law. Acquisition by conquest is a key example. However, retroactively reversing the results of these now unlawful means of territorial acquisition would, to put it mildly, be immensely difficult. It would, moreover, be inconsistent with the general practice and *opinio juris* of states on the matter, and hence with international law. Understanding the international law of territorial title requires, therefore, an appreciation of a concept we have already introduced: intertemporal law. The concept, in relation to sovereignty over territory, has been described as follows:

> One of the most important results of this universalization of international law [after the Treaty of Westphalia] has been the doctrine of intertemporal law. . . . The doctrine of intertemporal law [was] defined, in the . . . Island *of Palmas* arbitration, as follows: ". . . a

---

2   Malcolm N Shaw, *International Law*, 6th ed (Cambridge: Cambridge University Press, 2008) at 490.
3   *Ibid* at 489.

juridical fact must be appreciated in the light of the law contemporary with it, and not of the law in force at the time when a dispute in regard to it arises or falls to be settled." The doctrine is more fully stated, however, by Judge Huber later in the same case:

> As regards the question which of different legal systems prevailing at successive periods is to be applied in a particular case (the so-called intertemporal law), a distinction must be made between the creation of rights and the existence of rights. The same principle which subjects the act creative of a right to the law in force at the time the right arises, demands that the existence of the right, in other words its continued manifestation, shall follow the conditions required by the evolution of law.

There are therefore two elements, the first of which is that acts should be judged in the light of the law contemporary with their creation, and the second of which is that rights acquired in a valid manner according to the law contemporaneous with that creation may be lost if not maintained in accordance with the changes brought about by the development of international law. The first element of the doctrine of intertemporal law would seem to have been widely accepted in international law. . . . The second element — namely, that the mere acquisition of rights at the time of their creation is not enough, but that they must be maintained according to the evolution of international law — has aroused a good deal of controversy among the experts. . . .[4]

The doctrine of intertemporal law therefore accepts that history may not be rewritten every time the law changes, and that what are today perceived as yesterday's wrongs cannot now be undone without engendering profound instability and risking widespread conflict. Such instability and conflict would, moreover, likely be perpetual, as international law will, of course, continue to evolve.

As a result, the doctrine of intertemporal law has its critics. It has been condemned as a "political handmaiden to the politics of power of the imperial states who set out on a worldwide conquest of territory."[5] It could also be seen as one of those rules referred to above that have "the effect of legitimising the results of the exercise of power."[6] Yet, is this necessarily so? Consider the "second element" mentioned above. Why would intertemporal law not legalize the maintenance today of a colonial empire if that empire was first established at a time when it was internationally lawful to do so? Is the doctrine merely a guarantee against retroactive application of modern law, or are its effects more complex?

As we proceed through the materials on acquisition of sovereignty over land, consider the extent to which the doctrine of intertemporal law is a "handmaiden to the politics of power" or is, rather, a more nuanced conceptual tool designed to prevent historic events from producing modern chaos.

---

4   TO Elias, "The Doctrine of Intertemporal Law" (1980) 74 Am J Int'l L 285. See also Article 13 of the ILC Articles on State Responsibility for Internationally Wrongful Acts, discussed in Section D of Chapter 12.

5   Joshua Castellino & Steve Allen, *Title to Territory in International Law* (Burlington, VT: Ashgate, 2003) at 3.

6   A John Simmons, "On the Territorial Rights of States" (2001) 35 Philosophical Issues (Supp to Noûs) 300 at 321, n 13.

In the following sections, we subdivide the means by which sovereignty over land may be acquired into several categories, beginning with acquisition of legal sovereignty through "political" events.

B. ACQUISITION OF TERRITORIAL SOVEREIGNTY THROUGH POLITICAL EVENTS

1) The Relevance of Historical Context

Since its earliest days, international law has provided rules on what acts legitimately give a people sovereignty over land. Classic "political" methods by which states have asserted legal territorial sovereignty have included discovery (whether or not followed by effective occupation), effective occupation, prescription, cession, and conquest. While effective possession or occupation has always been, and continues to be, the key basis in international law for asserting sovereign title to land, it should be noted that the legal doctrines governing the *means* by which this possession is established—and the nature and extent of the occupation required or permitted—have shifted with time. However, as seen above, even those means that are now discredited—such as discovery and conquest—continue to have relevance in modern international law through application of the doctrine of intertemporal law. It is thus necessary to understand both those bases of title that have been discredited in modern international law, as well as those that today receive its approval. We review each in turn below.

Before doing so, it is important to recognize that most now-obsolete bases for asserting sovereignty over territory were legally constructed in such a way as to legitimize land acquisition by the powerful. This approach was abetted by a heavily ethnocentric approach to defining the legal concepts of statehood and sovereignty. Consider, for example, the following comments on the early use of international law as a vehicle for colonialism in Africa:

> Early international legal doctrine itself appeared to sanction colonization, the acquisition of territory by a recognized state and the imposition of its sovereignty over such territory. Such taking could occur as occupation, subjugation, or cession. In reality, the colonization of Africa utilized any of the three methods, or a combination thereof, although according to international law at the time only occupation was purportedly legal, since no recognized states existed in Africa. . . .
>
> Without much knowledge about the continent, early European jurists and publicists had decided that much of Africa was a no-man's land that could be brought under legal occupation. Territories inhabited by "persons who are not recognized as belonging to the great family of states to whom the international law applies," or "savage, barbarous tribes" belonged as of right upon discovery to the "civilized and Christian nation." . . .
>
> . . . Rules of "international law" exclusively crafted and employed by Europeans to extend their domination of other parts of the world could not have any legality in Africa, particularly if the effect of their application meant the loss of sovereignty. A Lagos paper captured the African interpretation of the legality of the Act of Berlin in sharp condemnatory language: "the world has, perhaps, never witnessed a robbery on so large a scale. Africa is helpless to prevent it. . . . It is on the cards that this 'Christian' business can only end, at no distant date, in the annihilation of the natives."

Wars of conquest and fraudulent treaties with African rulers and societies were the agencies for the effective imposition of European sovereignty. Occupation met with "tough resistance" almost everywhere as wars of "invasion or pacification" were "dark with slaughter and destruction."[7]

This legal heritage has had profound consequences for the structure of the international community, and its reverberations continue to be felt to this day in the evolution of the rules concerning the enjoyment of sovereignty over land. The materials that follow will, therefore, illustrate the deep-seated European ethnocentrism of international law that we first pointed out in Chapter 1. However, we will also see how modern international law has developed new rules that seek, in limited ways, to undo at least some of the results of European expansionism.

2) The Doctrine of Discovery

The doctrine of discovery is probably the best-known means by which (European) states laid claim to territories not already possessed by another (typically European) sovereign. The term "discovery" literally referred to the discovery of territory previously unknown to the Europeans making the discovery, most notably in the Americas. Such territory—while rarely ever empty of peoples—was regarded in law as *terra nullius* or empty land. This legal sleight of hand was accomplished through a definition of *terra nullius* that discounted the legal relevance of human societies that were not constituted on the early modern European model (a topic to which we return in the next section).

The acquisition of sovereignty via discovery was often accompanied by a symbolic act, such as the planting of a cross or flag. Sometimes, it involved the erection of a monument bearing the royal symbol of a European monarch and enclosing "a formal document stating that possession of the territory had been assumed."[8]

Consider the following discussion of discovery:

> Discovery, in the sense of bare sighting or physical discovery and as a mode of acquisition of territorial rights, was acknowledged by eminent writers on the law of nations . . . during the fifteenth and sixteenth centuries. But as a source of title it still stood on shaky grounds, since it failed to receive the approval of [other] respected jurists . . . and was contrary to state practice and the Roman Law from which rules of international law were deduced. As it could not stand independently, it was accorded at most the status of an inchoate title which had to be perfected by some other evidence [such as actual possession]. . . . With respect to the effect of inchoate title, it is believed by writers that other states are precluded from occupying the territory concerned during the time reasonably necessary for perfecting inchoate title.[9]

---

7   Makau W Mutua, "Why Redraw the Map of Africa: A Moral and Legal Inquiry" (1995) 16 Mich J Int'l L 1113 at 1128 and 1130–31. Reprinted with permission.

8   Surya Sharma, *Territorial Acquisition Disputes and International Law* (Leiden: Martinus Nijhoff Publishers, 1997) at 47.

9   *Ibid* at 40.

Certainly, as we shall see, this view of discovery as conferring nothing more than "inchoate" title contingent on some subsequent form of occupation prevailed as of the mid-nineteenth century. Other sources appeared to have accorded discovery more than mere "inchoate" legal significance, while still adverting to the significance of subsequent possession. For example, in the landmark case of *Johnson v M'Intosh*,[10] the US Supreme Court relied on the doctrine of discovery to ground European title in the Americas, urging that the "discovery" of North America by Europeans "gave to the nation making the discovery the sole right of acquiring the soil from the natives and establishing settlements upon it."[11] Any prior claim to territory by indigenous peoples could be discounted, given European ambitions and attitudes of racial and cultural superiority, as explained by Chief Justice Marshall:

> On the discovery of this immense continent, the great nations of Europe were eager to appropriate to themselves so much of it as they could respectively acquire. Its vast extent offered an ample field to the ambition and enterprise of all; and the character and religion of its inhabitants afforded an apology for considering them as a people over whom the superior genius of Europe might claim an ascendancy. The potentates of the old world found no difficulty in convincing themselves that they made ample compensation to the inhabitants of the new, by bestowing on them civilization and Christianity, in exchange for unlimited independence. But, as they were all in pursuit of nearly the same object, it was necessary, in order to avoid conflicting settlements, and consequent war with each other, to establish a principle, which all should acknowledge as the law by which the right of acquisition, which they all asserted, should be regulated as between themselves. This principle was, that discovery gave title to the government by whose subjects, or by whose authority, it was made, against all other European governments, which title might be consummated by possession.[12]

Consider the following critique of this approach:

> Discovery provided the necessary rhetoric for a nation to stake out its own boundaries in unoccupied areas to resolve competing claims over territory. . . . [T]he discovery doctrine acted as a template to obtain recognition of territorial sovereignty and receive equal respect from States in order to protect one's right to the territory. But the discovery of new lands did not always match the conceptual framework.
>
> The Americas provide an apt example, because much of these territories were inhabited by native peoples. In order to make the doctrine of discovery fit the situation presented, a fiction developed in the law of nations that treated native inhabitants as sub-human. Through such treatment, the discoverers were entitled to view the lands as "vacant" (*terra nullius*). The rationale driving this assumption was that natives were governed by custom, rather than the rules of law, and therefore lacked organization to put land to proprietary use.

---

10 21 US 543 (1823).
11 *Ibid* at 573.
12 *Ibid* at 572–73.

On the North American continent, discovery received a twist of American legal in-genuity in *Johnson v. M'Intosh*. In that case, Chief Justice Marshall applied the doctrine of discovery to justify the acquisition of territorial sovereignty based on native "savagery." Importantly, however, he also muddied the distinction between the international law definition of sovereignty and common law property concepts of ownership that gave "ac-quisition of title" to the discoverer. . . .

So, in North American law, *Johnson* has come to mean that not only territory, but land title, is acquired by discovery, although the original occupants retain a preferential right to occupy the land. By asserting that international law supported discovery as the basis of land title, and associating property concepts with territorial sovereignty, Marshall tailored the law of nations to fit the domestic circumstances he sought to address, namely, the numerous conflicts between Indians and the emerging society over territory.[13]

In modern international law, very little (if any) role is left for discovery in establishing sovereign title to land. As a practical matter, there is little land left to be "discovered." In effect, all of the world's land surface is either divided amongst the world's states or is currently insulated from claims of sovereign title. (Antarctica falls in the latter category, as discussed below.) Further, it is now well-established in international law that discovery gives rise to no, or at best an inchoate, title. This attenuates, but (due to intertemporal effects) does not entirely obliterate, its significance in modern international law.

3) Effective Occupation

The doctrine of discovery, such as it was, was only relevant in cases where land previ-ously unknown to Europeans first came to their attention. This limitation, together with the "inchoate" nature of the sovereign claims it purported to support, gave rise to the complementary and much more important doctrine of "effective occupation" of land said to be *terra nullius*.[14] Consider the discussion of effective occupation in the following case.

Island of Palmas Case (Netherlands v United States) (1928), 2 RIAA 829

[In 1925, a dispute arose between the United States and the Netherlands concerning sovereignty over the Island of Palmas, near the Philippines. The Philippines had been ceded to the United States by Spain after the Spanish-American War in 1898. The United States, as the inheritor of Spanish rights in the area, claimed that the Island of Palmas had been included in the Spanish cession. The Netherlands argued that the island had come under Dutch sovereignty from 1677 at the latest, through the operations of the Dutch East India Company. The matter was submitted to arbitration, the parties agree-ing that: "The sole duty of the Arbitrator shall be to determine whether the Island of Pal-mas (or Miangas) in its entirety forms a part of territory belonging to the United States of America or of Netherlands territory."]

---

13   Glen St Louis, "The Tangled Web of Sovereignty and Self-Governance: Canada's Obligation to the Cree Nation in Consideration of Quebec's Threats to Secede" (1996) 14 Berkeley J Int'l L 380 at 388–90.

14   James Crawford, *Brownlie's Principles of Public International Law*, 8th ed (Oxford: Oxford University Press, 2012) at 223 [*Brownlie's Principles*].

Huber, Arbitrator:

. . . The United States, as successor to the rights of Spain over the Philippines, bases its title in the first place on discovery. The existence of sovereignty thus acquired is, in the American view, confirmed not merely by the most reliable cartographers and authors, but also by treaty, in particular by the Treaty of Munster, of 1648, to which Spain and the Netherlands are themselves Contracting Parties. As, according to the same argument, nothing has occurred of a nature, in international law, to cause the acquired title to disappear, this latter title was intact at the moment when, by the Treaty of December 10th, 1898, Spain ceded the Philippines to the United States. In these circumstances, it is, in the American view, unnecessary to establish facts showing the actual display of sovereignty precisely over the Island of Palmas (or Miangas). . . .

According to the Netherlands Government, on the other hand, the fact of discovery by Spain is not proved, nor yet any other form of acquisition, and even if Spain had at any moment had a title, such title had been lost. . . .

The Netherlands Government's main argument endeavors to show that the Netherlands, represented for this purpose in the first period of colonization by the East India Company, have possessed and exercised rights of sovereignty from 1677, or probably from a date prior even to 1648, to the present day. This sovereignty arose out of conventions entered into with native princes of the Island of Sangi (the main island of Talautse (Sangi) Isles), establishing the suzerainty of the Netherlands over the territories of these princes, including Palmas (or Miangas). The state of affairs thus set up is claimed to be validated by international treaties. . . .

In the first place the Arbitrator deems it necessary to make some general remarks on sovereignty in its relation to territory. . . .

Sovereignty in the relations between States signifies independence. Independence in regard to a portion of the globe is the right to exercise therein, to the exclusion of any other State, the functions of a State. The development of the national organization of States during the last few centuries and, as a corollary, the development of international law, have established this principle of the exclusive competence of the State in regard to its own territory in such a way as to make it the point of departure in settling most questions that concern international relations. . . .

If a dispute arises as to the sovereignty over a portion of territory, it is customary to examine which of the States claiming sovereignty possesses a title — cession, conquest, occupation, etc. — superior to that which the other State might possibly bring forward against it. However, if the contestation is based on the fact that the other Party has actually displayed sovereignty, it cannot be sufficient to establish the title by which territorial sovereignty was validly acquired at a certain moment; it must also be shown that the territorial sovereignty has continued to exist and did exist at the moment which for the decision of the dispute must be considered as critical. This demonstration consists in the actual display of State activities, such as belongs only to the territorial sovereign.

Titles of acquisition of territorial sovereignty in present-day international law are either based on an act of effective apprehension, such as occupation or conquest, or, like cession, presuppose the ceding and the cessionary Powers or at least one of them, have the faculty of effectively disposing of the ceded territory. . . . It seems therefore natural that an element which is essential for the constitution of sovereignty should not be lacking in its continuation. So true is this, that practice, as well as doctrine, recognizes . . . that the continuous and peaceful display of territorial sovereignty (peaceful in relation to other States) is as good as a title. The growing insistence with which international law, ever since the middle of the 18th century, has demanded that the occupation shall be effective would be inconceivable, if effectiveness were required only for the act of acquisition and not equally for the maintenance of the right. If the effectiveness has above all been insisted on in regard to occupation, this is because the question rarely arises in connection with territories in which there is already an established order of things. . . .

Territorial sovereignty, as has already been said, involves the exclusive right to display the activities of a State. This right has a corollary, a duty: the obligation to protect within the territory the rights of other States, in particular their right to integrity and inviolability in peace and in war, together with the rights which each State may claim for its nationals in foreign territory. Without manifesting its territorial sovereignty in a manner corresponding to circumstances, the State cannot fulfil this duty. Territorial sovereignty cannot limit itself to its negative side, i.e. to excluding the activities of other States. . . .

The principle that continuous and peaceful display of the functions of State within a given region is a constituent element of territorial sovereignty is not only based on the conditions of the formation of independent States and their boundaries (as shown by the experience of political history) . . . [but also] on an international jurisprudence and doctrine widely accepted. . . .

Manifestations of territorial sovereignty assume, it is true, different forms, according to conditions of time and place. Although continuous in principle, sovereignty cannot be exercised in fact at every moment on every point of a territory. The intermittence and discontinuity compatible with the maintenance of the right necessarily differ according as inhabited or uninhabited regions are involved, or regions enclosed within territories in which sovereignty is incontestably displayed or again regions accessible from, for instance, the high seas. . . .

The title alleged by the United States of America as constituting the immediate foundation of its claim is that of cession, brought about by the Treaty of Paris, which cession transferred all rights of sovereignty which Spain may have possessed in the region indicated in Article III of the said Treaty and therefore also those concerning the Island of Palmas (or Miangas).

It is evident that Spain could not transfer more rights than she herself possessed. . . .

As pointed out above, the United States bases its claim, as successor of Spain, in the first place on discovery. . . .

The documents supplied to the Arbitrator with regard to the discovery of the island in question consist in the first place of a communication made by the Spanish Government to the United States Government as to researches in the archives concerning expeditions and discoveries in the Moluccas, the "Talaos" Islands, the Palos Islands and the Marianes. . . .

The above mentioned communication of the Spanish Government does not give any details as to the date of the expedition, the navigators or the circumstances in which the observations were made; it is not supported by extracts from the original reports on which it is based, nor accompanied by reproductions of the maps therein mentioned. . . .

In any case for the purpose of the present affair it may be admitted that the original title derived from discovery belonged to Spain. . . .

The fact that the island was originally called, not, as customarily, by a native name, but by a name borrowed from a European language, and referring to the vegetation, serves perhaps to show that no landing was made or that the island was uninhabited at the time of discovery. Indeed, the reports on record which concern the discovery of the Island of Palmas state only that an island was "seen," which island, according to the geographical data, is probably identical with that in dispute. No mention is made of landing or of contact with the natives. And in any case no signs of taking possession or of administration by Spain have been shown or even alleged to exist until the very recent date to which the reports of Captain Malone and M. Alvarez, of 1919, contained in the United States Memorandum, relate.

It is admitted by both sides that international law underwent profound modifications between the end of the Middle-Ages and the end of the 19th century, as regards the rights of discovery and acquisition of uninhabited regions or regions inhabited by savages or semi-civilized peoples. Both Parties are also agreed that a juridical fact must be appreciated in the light of the law contemporary with it, and not of the law in force at the time when a dispute in regard to it rises or falls to be settled. The effect of discovery by Spain is therefore to be determined by the rules of international law in force in the first half of the 16th century — or (to take the earliest date) in the first quarter of it, i.e., at the time when the Portuguese or Spaniards made their appearance in the Sea of Celebes.

If the view most favorable to the American arguments is adopted — with every reservation as to the soundness of such view — that is to say, if we consider as positive law at the period in question the rule that discovery as such, i.e. the mere fact of seeing land, without any act, even symbolical, of taking possession, involved *ipso jure* territorial sovereignty and not merely an "inchoate title," a *jus ad rem* [right to a thing], to be completed eventually by an actual and durable taking of possession within a reasonable time, the question arises whether sovereignty yet existed at the critical date, i.e. the moment of conclusion and coming into force of the Treaty of Paris.

As regards the question which of different legal systems prevailing at successive periods is to be applied in a particular case (the so-called intertemporal law), a distinction must be made between the creation of rights and the existence of rights. The same principle which subjects the act creative of a right to the law in force at the time the right arises, demands that the existence of the right, in other words its continued manifestation, shall follow the conditions required by the evolution of law. International law in the 19th century, having regard to the fact that most parts of the globe were under the sovereignty of states members of the community of nations, and that territories without a master had become relatively few, took account of a tendency already existing and especially developed since the middle of the 18th century, and laid down the principle that occupation, to constitute a claim to territorial sovereignty, must be effective, that is, offer certain guarantees to other States and their nationals. It seems therefore incompatible with this rule of positive law that there should be regions which are neither under the effective sovereignty of a State, nor without a master, but which are reserved for the exclusive influence of one State, in virtue solely of a title of acquisition which is no longer recognized by existing law, even if such a title ever conferred territorial sovereignty. For these reasons, discovery alone, without any subsequent act, cannot at the present time suffice to prove sovereignty over the Island of Palmas (or Miangas); and in so far as there is no sovereignty, the question of an abandonment properly speaking of sovereignty by one State in order that the sovereignty of another may take its place does not arise.

If on the other hand the view is adopted that discovery does not create a definitive title of sovereignty, but only an "inchoate" title, such a title exists, it is true, without external manifestation. However, according to the view that has prevailed at any rate since the 19th century, an inchoate title of discovery must be completed within a reasonable period by the effective occupation of the region claimed to be discovered. This principle must be applied in the present case, for the reasons given above in regard to the rules determining which of successive legal systems is to be applied (the so-called intertemporal law). Now, no act of occupation nor, except as to a recent period, any exercise of sovereignty at Palmas by Spain has been alleged. But even admitting that the Spanish title still existed as inchoate in 1898 and must be considered as included in the cession under Article III of the Treaty of Paris, an inchoate title could not prevail over the continuous and peaceful display of authority by another State; for such display may prevail even over a prior, definitive title put forward by another State. This point will be considered, when the Netherlands argument has been examined and the allegations of either Party as to the display of their authority can be compared. . . .

As it is not proved that Spain, at the beginning of 1648 or in June 1714, was in possession of the Island of Palmas (or Miangas), there is no proof that Spain acquired by the Treaty of Munster or the Treaty of Utrecht a title to sovereignty over the island which, in accordance with the said Treaties, and as long as they hold good, could have been modified by the Netherlands only in agreement with Spain.

It is, therefore, unnecessary to consider whether subsequently Spain by any express or conclusive action, abandoned the right, which the said Treaties may have conferred upon her in regard to Palmas (or Miangas). Moreover even if she had acquired a title she never intended to abandon, it would remain to be seen whether continuous and peaceful display of sovereignty by any other Power at a later period might not have superseded even conventional rights.

It appears further to be evident that Treaties concluded by Spain with third Powers recognizing her sovereignty over the "Philippines" could not be binding upon the Netherlands and as such Treaties do not mention the island in dispute, they are not available even as indirect evidence.

We thus come back to the question whether, failing any Treaty which, as between the States concerned, decides unequivocally what is the situation as regards the island, the existence of territorial sovereignty is established with sufficient soundness by other facts.

Although the United States Government does not take up the position that Spanish sovereignty must be recognized because it was actually exercised, the American Counter-Case none the less states that "there is at least some evidence of Spanish activities in the Island." In these circumstances it is necessary to consider whether and to what extent the territorial sovereignty of Spain was manifested in or in regard to the Island of Palmas (or Miangas). . . .

Apart from the facts already referred to concerning the period of discovery, . . . the documents laid before the Arbitration contain no trace of Spanish activities of any kind specifically on the Island of Palmas.

Neither is there any official document mentioning the Island of Palmas as belonging to an administrative or judicial district of the former Spanish government in the Philippines. . . .

. . . It has been explained above that in the exercise of territorial sovereignty there are necessarily gaps, intermittence in time and discontinuity in space. This phenomenon will be particularly noticeable in the case of colonial territories, partly uninhabited or as yet partly unsubdued. The fact that a State cannot prove display of sovereignty as regards such a portion of territory cannot forthwith be interpreted as showing that sovereignty is inexistent. Each case must be appreciated in accordance with the particular circumstances. . . .

As regards the territory forming the subject of the present dispute, it must be remembered that [it] is a somewhat isolated island, and therefore a territory clearly delimited and individualized. It is moreover an island permanently inhabited, occupied by a population sufficiently numerous for it to be impossible that acts of administration could be lacking for very long periods. The memoranda of both Parties assert that there is communication by boat and even with native craft between the Island of Palmas (or Miangas) and neighboring regions. The inability in such a case to indicate any acts of public administration makes it difficult to imagine the actual display of sovereignty, even if the sovereignty be regarded as confined within such narrow limits as would be supposed for a small island inhabited exclusively by natives.

The Netherlands' arguments contend that the East India Company established Dutch sovereignty over the Island of Palmas (or Miangas) as early as the 17th century, by means of conventions with the princes of Tabukan (Taboekan) and Taruna (Taroena), two native chieftains of the Island of Sangi (Groot Sangihe), the principal Island of the Talautse Isles (Sangi Islands), and that sovereignty has been displayed during the past two centuries. . . .

Even the oldest contract, dated 1677, contains clauses binding the vassal of the East India Company to refuse to admit the nationals of other States, in particular Spain, into his territories, and to tolerate no religion other than Protestantism, reformed according to the doctrine of the Synod of Dordrecht. Similar provisions are to be found in the other contracts of the 17th and 18th centuries. If both Spain and the Netherlands had in reality displayed their sovereignty over Palmas (or Miangas), it would seem that, during so long a period, collisions between the two Powers must almost inevitably have occurred. . . .

The United States base their claim on the titles of discovery, of recognition by treaty and of contiguity, i.e. titles relating to acts or circumstances leading to the acquisition of sovereignty; they have however not established the fact that sovereignty so acquired was effectively displayed at any time. . . .

The title of discovery . . . would . . . exist only as an inchoate title, as a claim to establish sovereignty by effective occupation. . . .

[The outcome of the case, and the conclusion that the Netherlands possessed sovereignty over Palmas by prescription, is reproduced in a subsequent section.]

Effective occupation seems a much more plausible basis upon which to assert sovereign title than discovery, as the former relies on ongoing *factual* displays of sovereign authority (rather than isolated, symbolic acts, often remote in time) as the *legal* basis for status as the territorial sovereign. The focus of effective occupation is to determine which state is displaying the attributes of statehood with respect to a certain piece of land at a particular, relevant point in time—the "critical date." It is much less concerned with which state may have been doing so at some other point in time. What was the "critical date" in evaluating the claim of effective occupation in the *Island of Palmas Case?* What is the effect of applying the intertemporal rule to the claim of (1) discovery and (2) effective occupation?

The International Court of Justice (ICJ) has more recently considered the importance of the critical date, as well as evidence of *effectivités*—that is, official administrative acts—in assessing a claim to sovereignty based on effective occupation:

Territorial and Maritime Dispute (Nicaragua v Colombia), ICJ General List No 124, 19 November 2012

[Nicaragua and Colombia disputed sovereignty over several islands lying between their respective coasts in the Caribbean Sea. Having considered and rejected the contentions of the parties that sovereignty over the disputed islands could be established on the basis of applicable treaty provisions or the *uti possidetis juris* doctrine (discussed in Chapter 3), the Court went on to consider Colombia's claim to sovereignty on the basis of effective occupation:]

(a) *Critical date*

67. The Court recalls that, in the context of a dispute related to sovereignty over land, such as present one, the date upon which the dispute crystallized is of significance. Its significance lies in distinguishing between those acts à titre de *souverain* occurring prior to the date when the dispute crystallized, which should be taken into consideration for the purpose of establishing or ascertaining sovereignty, and those acts occurring after that date, "which are in general meaningless for that purpose, having been carried out by a State which, already having claims to assert in a legal dispute, could have taken those actions strictly with the aim of buttressing those claims" (*Territorial and Maritime Dispute between Nicaragua and Honduras in the Caribbean Sea (Nicaragua v. Honduras), Judgment, I.C.J. Reports 2007 (II),* pp. 697-698, para. 117).

68. As the Court explained in the *Indonesia/Malaysia* case: "it cannot take into consideration acts having taken place after the date on which the dispute between the Parties crystallized unless such acts are a normal continuation of prior acts and are not undertaken for the purpose of improving the legal position of the Party which relies on them" (*Sovereignty over Pulau Ligitan and Pulau Sipadan (Indonesia/Malaysia), Judgment, I.C.J. Reports 2002,* p. 682, para. 135). . . .

71. The Court observes that there is no indication that there was a dispute before the 1969 exchange of Notes [between the parties]. . . . Indeed, the Notes can be seen as the manifestation of a difference of views between the Parties regarding sovereignty over certain maritime features in the south-western Caribbean. Moreover, Colombia does not seem to contest the critical date put forward by Nicaragua. In light of the above, the Court concludes that 12 June 1969, the date of Nicaragua's Note in response to Colombia's Note of 4 June 1969 . . . , is the critical date for the purposes of appraising *effectivités* in the present case.

(b) *Consideration of* effectivités

72. The Court notes that it is Colombia's submission that *effectivités* confirm its prior title to the maritime features in dispute. By contrast, Nicaragua has not provided any evidence that it has acted à titre de *souverain* in relation to these features and its claim for sovereignty relies largely on the principle of *uti possidetis juris*. . . .

80. The Court recalls that acts and activities considered to be performed à titre de *souverain* are in particular, but not limited to, legislative acts or acts of administrative control, acts relating to the application and enforcement of criminal or civil law, acts regulating immigration, acts regulating fishing and other economic activities, naval patrols as well as search and rescue operations . . . . It further recalls that "sovereignty over minor maritime features . . . may be established on the basis of a relatively modest display of State powers in terms of quality and quantity" . . . . Finally, a significant element to be taken into account is the extent to which any acts à titre de *souverain* in relation to disputed islands have been carried out by another State with a competing claim to sovereignty. As the Permanent Court of International Justice stated in its Judgment in the *Legal Status of Eastern Greenland* case: "It is impossible to read the records of the decisions in cases as to territorial sovereignty without observing that in many cases the tribunal has been satisfied with very little in the way of the actual exercise of sovereign rights, provided that the other State could not make out a superior claim. This is particularly true in the case of claims to sovereignty over areas in thinly populated or unsettled countries." . . .

81. The Court notes that although the majority of the acts à titre de *souverain* referred to by Colombia were exercised in the maritime area which encompasses all the disputed features, a number of them were undertaken specifically in relation to the maritime features in dispute. Colombia has indeed acted à titre de *souverain* in respect of both the maritime area surrounding the disputed features and the maritime features themselves. . . .

82. [The Court proceeds to consider the different categories of *effectivités* engaged in by Colombia, noting numerous instances of activities relating to public administration and legislation, regulation of economic activities, public works, law enforcement, naval and search and rescue operations, and consular representation.]

83. Colombia's activities à titre de *souverain* with regard to [the disputed islands], in particular, legislation relating to territorial organization, regulation of fishing activities and related measures of enforcement, maintenance of lighthouses and buoys, and naval visits, continued after the critical date. The Court considers that these activities are a normal continuation of prior acts à titre de *souverain*. The Court may therefore take these activities into consideration for the purposes of the present case . . . .

84. It has thus been established that for many decades Colombia continuously and consistently acted à titre de *souverain* in respect of the maritime features in dispute. This exercise of sovereign authority was public and there is no evidence that it met with any protest from Nicaragua prior to the critical date. Moreover, the evidence of Colombia's acts of administration with respect to the islands is in contrast to the absence of any evidence of acts à titre de *souverain* on the part of Nicaragua. The Court concludes that the

facts reviewed above provide very strong support for Colombia's claim of sovereignty over the maritime features in dispute. . . .

103. Having considered the entirety of the arguments and evidence put forward by the Parties, the Court concludes that Colombia, and not Nicaragua, has sovereignty over the [disputed] islands. . . .

Effective occupation therefore constitutes a potent basis for asserting sovereign title to land in international law. A few caveats are, however, in order.

First, the distinction between discovery—by which title purportedly flows from some historic, symbolic act—and effective occupation hinges on the meaning attributed to "effective." How much occupation must there be, and how must it be manifested, for title to be established? Doctrinally, effective occupation requires the continuous and peaceful display of state functions, accompanied by the requisite intent to establish permanent and exclusive control, as observed by the Permanent Court of International Justice in the *Legal Status of Eastern Greenland* case: "[A] claim to sovereignty based not upon some particular act or title such as a treaty of cession but merely upon continued display of authority, involves two elements each of which must be shown to exist: the intention and will to act as sovereign, and some actual exercise or display of such authority."[15]

Settlement and close physical control by the claiming state were once key considerations. However, the nature and degree of state functions that must be displayed depends, as indicated in the *Island of Palmas Case*, on the nature of the territory. Decisions from the early twentieth century even suggest that, at least in certain circumstances, little actual control need be exercised. Consider the following example:

Clipperton Island Case (France v Mexico) (1931), 2 RIAA 1105 [translation]

[The King of Italy was asked to decide a dispute between France and Mexico concerning sovereignty over a coral atoll in the eastern Pacific Ocean known as Clipperton Island. The remote island had been proclaimed part of France in 1858 but France did not take much action to assert its sovereignty until Mexico asserted a claim in 1897.]

. . . It is beyond doubt that by immemorial usage having the force of law, besides the *animus occupandi*, the actual, and not the nominal, taking of possession is a necessary condition of occupation. This taking of possession consists in the act, or series of acts, by which the occupying state reduces to its possession the territory in question and takes steps to exercise exclusive authority there. Strictly speaking, and in ordinary cases, that only takes place when the state establishes in the territory itself an organization capable of making its laws respected. But this step is, properly speaking, but a means of procedure to the taking of possession, and, therefore, is not identical with the latter. There may also be cases where it is unnecessary to have recourse to this method. Thus, if a territory, by virtue of the fact that it was completely uninhabited, is, from the first moment when the occupying state makes its appearance there, at the absolute and undisputed disposition of that state, from that moment the taking of possession must be considered as accomplished, and the occupation is thereby completed. . . .

---

15 *(Denmark v Norway)* (1933), PCIJ (Ser A/B) No 53 at 45–46.

The regularity of the French occupation has also been questioned because the other Powers were not notified of it. But it must be observed that the precise obligation to make such notification is contained in Art. 34 of the Act of Berlin cited above, which, as before mentioned, is not applicable to the present case. There is good reason to think that the notoriety given to the act, by whatever means, sufficed at the time, and that France provoked that notoriety by publishing the said act in the manner above indicated.

It follows from these premises that Clipperton Island was legitimately acquired by France on November 17, 1858. There is no reason to suppose that France has subsequently lost her right by *derelictio*, since she never had the animus of abandoning the island, and the fact that she has not exercised her authority there in a positive manner does not imply the forfeiture of an acquisition already definitively perfected.

For these reasons, we decide, as arbiter, that the sovereignty over Clipperton Island belongs to France, dating from November 17, 1858.

The *Clipperton Island* case applies a relaxed effective occupation test where land is uninhabited. This seems to imply that effective occupation might also be a valid basis for establishing sovereign title to *inhabited* lands, as long as sufficient actual control and sovereign intent are displayed. But how would such a position fit with the generally accepted doctrinal view that effective occupation can be used to acquire title only over unoccupied land (*terra nullius*)?

This question brings us to a second caveat concerning effective occupation as a basis of sovereign title. Its answer depends critically on the precise legal content of the *terra nullius* concept. Rather than its literal meaning — empty land, connoting the absence of any inhabitants at all — *terra nullius* has been defined in international law to mean land which is not occupied by a socially and politically organized people.[16] This may seem innocuous enough in an age when virtually all land territory is subject to occupation by one of almost 200 equally sovereign entities sharing a broadly similar, European-derived form of social and political organization — statehood. In the late nineteenth century, however, the view emerged that the type of social and political organization required to avoid relegation of inhabited territory to the status of *terra nullius* had to approximate that of European-style states. The proliferation of this view had, as its result, that effective occupation — like discovery — could be applied by those peoples part of the European world system (that is, those that had constituted themselves as "states") to acquire the lands of those peoples who were not part of this system. Consider the following description:

> Initially employed to designate territory that was "empty" and therefore free for colonization, [*terra nullius*] gradually took on racist overtones and until recently was determined to refer to territory on which people were not socially or politically organized. . . . This subtle change from its original meaning enabled the acquisition of much land in international legal history. In addition, once this land had been acquired, boundary lines were then drawn to demarcate ownership, and via the doctrine of *uti possidetis* those boundary lines have come to be recognized as the building blocks of the international community of states. . . . To further validate this creation, international law brings into play the rule governing intertemporal law by which actions committed in a previous era are buffered

---

16 See *Western Sahara*, Advisory Opinion, [1975] ICJ Rep 12 at 31–33 (reproduced below).

from scrutiny against more modern norms and principles. Thus while the woes of colonialism are well documented, the international legal system is precluded from raising legal questions about the manner in which colonialism functioned.[17]

Effective occupation replaced simple discovery as the basis for European claims over (non-European) territory by the nineteenth century at least in part because it responded to new conditions of colonialism. In fact, having defined the *terra nullius* concept in a manner that excluded the legal rights of most non-European societies, Europeans were then free to apply the concept of effective occupation to claim sovereignty over lands where their *animus possidendi* might exist, but actual possession was absent.

Elements of the African experience provide a case in point both of nominal invocation of effective occupation and the disregard by European powers of its essential qualities. In the late nineteenth century, European states engaged in their "scramble for Africa." On the African continent—"discovered" long before—the history of discovery was muddled with overlapping claims. In the words of one set of analysts, "by the late nineteenth century, the emerging and re-emerging powers were only too aware that unsubstantiated territorial claims deprived them of their imperial ambitions."[18] Effective occupation presented a means of settling contending European claims to territory without resorting to war between European states. In practice, however, securing actual control of African territories was often very difficult for the European powers, not least because of their vulnerability to tropical disease and the presence of existing inhabitants.

The solution was to invoke effective occupation while tempering its requirements, an approach adopted at the Berlin Conference in 1884. The Conference was convened between the European powers with the explicit purpose of distributing spheres of European influence in Africa, and produced the General Act of Berlin of 1885. Much of the General Act resolves specific territorial disputes between the European powers. The Act also contained, however, rules on the acquisition of new territory, as follows:

Article 34
Any Power which henceforth takes possession of a tract of land on the coasts of the African continent outside of its present possessions, or which, being hitherto without such possessions, shall acquire them, as well as the Power which assumes a Protectorate there, shall accompany the respective act with a notification thereof, addressed to the other Signatory Powers of the present Act, in order to enable them, if need be, to make good any claims of their own.

Article 35
The Signatory Powers of the present Act recognize the obligation to insure the establishment of authority in the regions occupied by them on the coasts of the African continent sufficient to protect existing rights, and, as the case may be, freedom of trade and of transit under the conditions agreed upon.

---

17   J Castellino & S Allen, eds, *Title to Territory in International Law: A Temporal Analysis* (Aldershot, Hampshire: Ashgate, 2003) at 3.
18   *Ibid* at 101.

Article 35 is, in effect, a requirement of effective occupation for at least coastal regions. It triggered a notice requirement and an obligation to facilitate trade. But that coastal occupation also allowed the projection of territorial claims—or at least spheres of influence—well beyond the territory actually occupied. In the result, as one set of commentators observes, "the powers in Africa replicated the approach adopted by the Iberians in the New World. . . . they claimed the entire continent before it was effectively occupied."[19] Full-scale incorporation of the interior regions into colonial empires then followed in the early twentieth century.

As has already been suggested, the interests of indigenous peoples did not figure in the nineteenth-century "effective occupation" analysis. As one commentator puts it, speaking of Africa: "Once European powers had agreed on 'spheres of influence,' effective occupation was achieved through wars of conquest or fraudulent treaties of 'protection' with rulers of precolonial African states and communities."[20]

This is reflective of a more general discounting, in nineteenth- and early twentieth-century international law, of the relevance of indigenous inhabitants. Note the absence of any discussion of the legal effects of indigenous interests in the *Island of Palmas Case* above. Consider also the notable absence of any discussion of indigenous interests in the following decision from the early twentieth century. Consider whether the test of effective occupation hinged on effectiveness vis-à-vis the *inhabitants* of the territory or, rather, vis-à-vis other *states*.

Legal Status of Eastern Greenland (Denmark v Norway) (1933), PCIJ (Ser A/B) No 53

[In 1931, Norway proclaimed sovereignty over Eastern Greenland. Denmark, itself claiming sovereignty over the whole of Greenland, instituted proceedings against Norway. At issue was whether Denmark had established sovereignty over the territory at the time of the Norwegian claim through effective occupation.]

. . . The Danish submission in the written pleading, that the Norwegian occupation of July 10th, 1931, is invalid, is founded upon the contention that the area occupied was at the time of the occupation subject to Danish sovereignty; that the area is part of Greenland, and at the time of the occupation Danish sovereignty existed over all Greenland; consequently it could not be occupied by another Power.

In support of this contention, the Danish Government advances two propositions. The first is that the sovereignty which Denmark now enjoys over Greenland has existed for a long time, has been continuously and peacefully exercised and, until the present dispute, has not been contested by any Power. . . .

The Norwegian submissions are that Denmark possessed no sovereignty over the area which Norway occupied on July 10th, 1931, and that at the time of the occupation the area was *terra nullius*. Her contention is that the area lay outside the limits of the Danish colonies in Greenland and that Danish sovereignty extended no further than the limits of these colonies. . . .

---

19 *Ibid* at 103.
20 Makau W Mutua, "Putting Humpty Dumpty Back Together Again: The Dilemmas of the Post-Colonial African State" (1995) 21 Brooklyn J Int'l L 505 at 518.

The first Danish argument is that the Norwegian occupation of part of the East coast of Greenland is invalid because Denmark has claimed and exercised sovereign rights over Greenland as a whole for a long time and has obtained thereby a valid title to sovereignty. The date at which such Danish sovereignty must have existed in order to render the Norwegian occupation invalid is the date at which the occupation took place, viz., July 10th, 1931.

The Danish claim is not founded upon any particular act of occupation but alleges — to use the phrase employed in the *Palmas Island* decision of the Permanent Court of Arbitration, April 4th, 1928 — a title "founded on the peaceful and continuous display of State authority over the island." It is based upon the view that Denmark now enjoys all the rights which the King of Denmark and Norway enjoyed over Greenland up till 1814. Both the existence and the extent of these rights must therefore be considered, as well as the Danish claim to sovereignty since that date. . . .

Before proceeding to consider in detail the evidence submitted to the Court, it may be well to state that a claim to sovereignty based not upon some particular act or title such as a treaty of cession but merely upon continued display of authority, involves two elements each of which must be shown to exist: the intention and will to act as sovereign, and some actual exercise or display of such authority.

Another circumstance which must be taken into account by any tribunal . . . is that up to 1931 there was no claim by any Power other than Denmark to the sovereignty over Greenland. Indeed, up till 1921, no Power disputed the Danish claim to sovereignty.

It is impossible to read the records of the decisions in cases as to territorial sovereignty without observing that in many cases the tribunal has been satisfied with very little in the way of the actual exercise of sovereign rights, provided that the other State could not make out a superior claim. This is particularly true in the case of claims to sovereignty over areas in thinly populated or unsettled countries. . . .

After the founding of Hans Egede's colonies in 1721, there is in part at least of Greenland a manifestation and exercise of sovereign rights. Consequently, both the elements necessary to establish a valid title to sovereignty — the intention and the exercise — were present, but the question arises as to how far the operation of these elements extended.

The King's pretensions to sovereignty which existed at the time of the foundation of the colonies are sufficient to demonstrate the intention, and, as said above, these were not limited to any particular part of the country.

Was the exercise of sovereign rights such as to confer a valid title to sovereignty over the whole country? The founding of the colonies was accompanied by the grant of a monopoly of the trade, and before long legislation was found to be necessary to protect and enforce the monopoly. . . . Legislation is one of the most obvious forms of the exercise of sovereign power, and it is clear that the operation of these enactments was not restricted to the limits of the colonies. It therefore follows that the sovereign right in virtue of which the enactments were issued cannot have been restricted to the limits of the colonies. . . .

The conclusion to which the Court is led is that, bearing in mind the absence of any claim to sovereignty by another Power, and the Arctic and inaccessible character of the uncolonized parts of the country, the King of Denmark and Norway displayed during the period from the founding of the colonies by Hans Egede in 1721 up to 1814 his authority to an extent sufficient to give his country a valid claim to sovereignty, and that his rights over Greenland were not limited to the colonized area. . . .

In order to establish the Danish contention that Denmark has exercised in fact sovereignty over all Greenland for a long time, Counsel for Denmark have laid stress on the long series of conventions — mostly commercial in character — which have been concluded by Denmark and in which, with the concurrence of the other contracting Party, a stipulation has been inserted to the effect that the convention shall not apply to Greenland. . . .

The importance of these treaties is that they show a willingness on the part of the States with which Denmark has contracted to admit her right to exclude Greenland. To some of these treaties, Norway has herself been a Party, and these must be dealt with later because they are relied on by Denmark as constituting binding admissions by Norway that Greenland is subject to Danish sovereignty. For the purpose of the present argument, the importance of these conventions, with whatever States they have been concluded, is due to the support which they lend to the Danish argument that Denmark possesses sovereignty over Greenland as a whole. . . .

To the extent that these treaties constitute evidence of recognition of her sovereignty over Greenland in general, Denmark is entitled to rely upon them.

These treaties may also be regarded as demonstrating sufficiently Denmark's will and intention to exercise sovereignty over Greenland. . . .

In view of the above facts, when taken in conjunction with the legislation she had enacted applicable to Greenland generally, the numerous treaties in which Denmark, with the concurrence of the other contracting Party, provided for the non-application of the treaty to Greenland in general, and the absence of all claim to sovereignty over Greenland by any other Power, Denmark must be regarded as having displayed during this period of 1814 to 1915 her authority over the uncolonized part of the country to a degree sufficient to confer a valid title to . . . sovereignty. . . .

The Legal Status of Eastern Greenland case was invoked by the ICJ in the more recent case of *Sovereignty over Pedra Branca/Pulau Batu Puteh, Middle Rocks and South Ledge*.[21] At issue was sovereign title to certain islands in the area of the Straits of Singapore. In deciding this issue, the Court noted the observation in Eastern Greenland that "up to 1931 there was no claim by any Power other than Denmark to the sovereignty over Greenland. Indeed, up till 1921, no Power disputed the Danish claim to sovereignty."[22] It then concluded:

If this conclusion was valid with reference to the thinly populated and unsettled territory of Eastern Greenland, it should also apply to the present case involving a tiny uninhabited and uninhabitable island, to which no claim of sovereignty had been made by any other Power throughout the years from the early sixteenth century until the middle of the nineteenth century. . . . The Court further recalls that, as expounded in the Eastern Greenland case . . . , international law is satisfied with varying degrees in the display of State authority, depending on the specific circumstances of each case.[23]

As this passage suggests, in *Eastern Greenland*, the Permanent Court had imposed a very undemanding test for effective occupation and had done so in a fashion seemingly

---

21   (Malaysia/Singapore), Judgment, [2008] ICJ Rep 12.
22   *Ibid* at para 64.
23   *Ibid* at para 66.

indifferent to the actual presence of an indigenous population. (In another extract from the *Eastern Greenland* case reproduced below, note the extent to which an indigenous presence was explicitly deemed irrelevant.) On this issue, would the *Eastern Greenland* case be decided the same way under today's international law? Compare the treatment given the *terra nullius* concept in *Eastern Greenland* with the approach taken in the following decision of the ICJ.

Western Sahara, Advisory Opinion, [1975] ICJ Rep 12

[Western Sahara is a region in west Africa which was inhabited by a largely nomadic, indigenous population at the time it was colonized by Spain in the late nineteenth century. When Spain moved to decolonize Western Sahara in the 1970s, controversy arose over the legal status of the territory; specifically, neighbouring Mauritania and Morocco each made claims of sovereignty to the region on the basis of historical and cultural ties. These claims were disputed by the Sahrawi inhabitants of Western Sahara, who invoked their right of self-determination. In 1974, Spain agreed to hold a popular referendum to decide the future status of Western Sahara before leaving the territory. Morocco and Mauritania opposed any referendum in which the Sahrawis could choose independence. In December 1974, at Morocco's request, the UN General Assembly asked the ICJ for an advisory opinion to determine the nature of the ties that existed between the Western Sahara and Morocco and Mauritania. A lengthier extract from the opinion is found in the section below on self-determination. The extract reproduced here sets out the Court's response to the question: "Was Western Sahara . . . at the time of colonization by Spain a territory belonging to no one (*terra nullius*)?"]

79. Turning to Question I, the Court observes that the request specifically locates the question in the context of "the time of colonization by Spain," and it therefore seems clear that the words "Was Western Sahara . . . a territory belonging to no one (*terra nullius*)?" have to be interpreted by reference to the law in force at that period. The expression "*terra nullius*" was a legal term of art employed in connection with "occupation" as one of the accepted legal methods of acquiring sovereignty over territory. "Occupation" being legally an original means of peaceably acquiring sovereignty over territory otherwise than by cession or succession, it was a cardinal condition of a valid "occupation" that the territory should be *terra nullius*—a territory belonging to no-one—at the time of the act alleged to constitute the "occupation" (cf. *Legal Status of Eastern Greenland*, P.C.I.J., Series A/B, No. 53, pp. 44 f. and 63 f.). In the view of the Court, therefore, a determination that Western Sahara was a "*terra nullius*" at the time of colonization by Spain would be possible only if it were established that at that time the territory belonged to no-one in the sense that it was then open to acquisition through the legal process of "occupation."

80. Whatever differences of opinion there may have been among jurists, the State practice of the relevant period indicates that territories inhabited by tribes or peoples having a social and political organization were not regarded as *terrae nullius*. It shows that in the case of such territories the acquisition of sovereignty was not generally considered as effected unilaterally through "occupation" of *terra nullius* by original title but through agreements concluded with local rulers. On occasion, it is true, the word "occupation"

was used in a non-technical sense denoting simply acquisition of sovereignty; but that did not signify that the acquisition of sovereignty through such agreements with authorities of the country was regarded as an "occupation" of a "*terra nullius*" in the proper sense of these terms. On the contrary, such agreements with local rulers, whether or not considered as an actual "cession" of the territory, were regarded as derivative roots of title, and not original titles obtained by occupation of *terrae nullius*.

According to the Court in *Western Sahara*, what is the "proper sense" of the term "*terra nullius*"? Is it limited to land without any inhabitants at all? If not, what sort of human presence would be required to remove a particular piece of land territory from the ambit of the concept? Would any form of social and political organization do? In answering these questions, consider the legal significance of the expression "*belonging* to no one."

To this recent elucidation of the *terra nullius* concept, we must add a third caveat to the observation that effective occupation is the most potent basis for asserting sovereign title to land in modern international law. To have legal effects, occupation must not only be effective; it must also not violate other rules of international law. As we shall see in subsequent sections, it is this added requirement that explains why colonial or foreign military occupation, as effective as they may be, are not sources of sovereign title in modern international law.

LAW IN CONTEXT

Antarctica: Frozen *Terra Nullius*

Antarctica is the Earth's only significant landmass yet to be incorporated into the sovereign territory of a state. This is not to say that no states have laid claim to portions of that continent. Indeed, there are many claims, some overlapping, as illustrated in Figure 4.1.

Many of these territorial claims are based on some combination of discovery and effective occupation. Consider, for instance, the Australian claim:

> Australia is among seven nations that have claimed territory in Antarctica. These claims are based on discovery and effective occupation of the claimed area, and are legal according to each nation's laws. Three countries—the United Kingdom, Chile and Argentina—have overlapping claims in the Antarctic.
>
> Some countries explicitly recognise these claims, some have a policy of not recognising any claims in Antarctica, and others reserve the right to make a claim of their own.
>
> . . . Australian Antarctic Territory covers nearly 5.9 million square kilometres, about 42% of Antarctica and nearly 80% of the total area of Australia itself.
>
> The Australian claim is based on a long historical association with this part of Antarctica. Australia's Douglas Mawson (later Sir Douglas Mawson) led a group of Australians and New Zealanders in the 1911 to 1914 Australasian Antarctic Expedition, which had bases at Commonwealth Bay, south of Tasmania, and the Shackleton Ice Shelf south of Perth. This expedition explored extensively along the coast near the bases.
>
> Mawson also led the British, Australian and New Zealand Antarctic Research Expedition (BANZARE) of 1929 to 1931. During this expedition Mawson claimed what is now Australian Antarctic Territory as British sovereign territory. Early in 1933, Britain

asserted sovereign rights over the claimed territory and placed the territory under the authority of the Commonwealth of Australia.

Sovereignty over the Territory was transferred from Britain to Australia under the *Australian Antarctic Territory Acceptance Act 1933*, which came into effect in 1936. . . .[24]

Figure 4.1: Antarctic Territorial Claims[25]

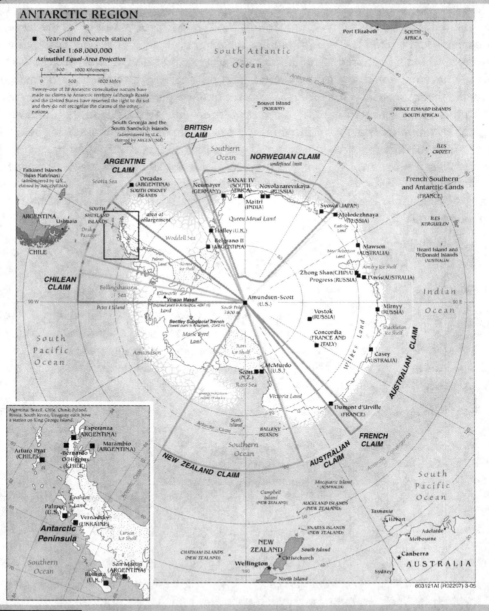

---

24 Australian Government, Department of Sustainability, Environment, Water, Population and Communities, Australian Antarctic Division, "Antarctic Territorial Claims" (6 June 2002), online: www.antarctica.gov.au/antarctic-law-and-treaty/our-treaty-obligations/antarctic-territorial-claims.

25 Map reprinted from *CIA World Factbook, 2006* (Washington, DC: Central Intelligence Agency, 2006).

Other key states—including the United States—have declined to make territorial claims to the Antarctic (although reserving the right to do so) and have refused to recognize the legitimacy of other states' territorial ambitions on the continent. As one commentator notes, most of these claims "are of rather dubious quality."[26]

In any event, state assertions of territorial sovereignty have been suspended by the Antarctic Treaty of 1959,[27] with all claimant states, and over thirty other states, becoming parties to an enhanced Antarctic Treaty system.[28] Preserving the continent as a demilitarized zone dedicated to scientific research, the treaty "freezes" territorial claims:

Article IV

1. Nothing contained in the present Treaty shall be interpreted as:

a. a renunciation by any Contracting Party of previously asserted rights of or claims to territorial sovereignty in Antarctica;

b. a renunciation or diminution by any Contracting Party of any basis of claim to territorial sovereignty in Antarctica which it may have whether as a result of its activities or those of its nationals in Antarctica, or otherwise;

c. prejudicing the position of any Contracting Party as regards its recognition or nonrecognition of any other State's rights of or claim or basis of claim to territorial sovereignty in Antarctica.

2. No acts or activities taking place while the present Treaty is in force shall constitute a basis for asserting, supporting or denying a claim to territorial sovereignty in Antarctica or create any rights of sovereignty in Antarctica. No new claim, or enlargement of an existing claim, to territorial sovereignty in Antarctica shall be asserted while the present Treaty is in force. . . .

Article VI

The provisions of the present Treaty shall apply to the area south of 60 degrees South Latitude, including all ice shelves, but nothing in the present Treaty shall prejudice or in any way affect the rights, or the exercise of the rights, of any State under international law with regard to the high seas within that area.

4) Prescription

While effective occupation as a source of sovereign title applies in relation to *terra nullius*, a similar concept applies in relation to land which already belongs to another sovereign. International law thus recognizes "prescriptive" title, an occupation-based concept analogous to the adverse possession doctrine found in most common law property systems. One commentator describes it this way:

. . . prescription denotes a process of acquiring a title to territory by a long, continued and uninterrupted possession. It, in fact, operates as a modality of transfer of a previously appropriated land mass from one territorial entity to another, and its policy justification

---

26 Shaw, above note 1 at 536.

27 1 December 1959, 402 UNTS 71, in force 23 June 1961.

28 See further, Secretariat of the Antarctic Treaty, online: www.ats.aq/index_e.htm.

is the concern with the maintenance of world order . . . and stability of territorial titles through time. . . .[29]

Acquisition of title by prescription depends on several pre-requisites: possession must be peaceful and sufficiently continuous, public, and lengthy.[30] Consider the following extract from the *Island of Palmas Case*.

Island of Palmas Case (Netherlands v United States) (1928), 2 RIAA 829

[Recall that the arbitrator was prepared to accept, for the sake of argument (but without deciding), that Spain could have established original title to Palmas by discovery.]

. . . The Netherlands . . . found their claim to sovereignty essentially on the title of peaceful and continuous display of State authority over the island. Since this title would in international law prevail over a title of acquisition of sovereignty not followed by actual display of State authority, it is necessary to ascertain in the first place, whether the contention of the Netherlands is sufficiently established by evidence, and if so, for what period of time.

The acts of indirect or direct display of Netherlands sovereignty at Palmas (or Miangas), especially in the 18th and early 19th centuries are not numerous, and there are considerable gaps in the evidence of continuous display. But apart from the consideration that the manifestations of sovereignty over a small and distant island, inhabited only by natives, cannot be expected to be frequent, it is not necessary that the display of sovereignty should go back to a very far distant period. It may suffice that such display existed in 1898, and had already existed as continuous and peaceful before that date long enough to enable any Power who might have considered herself as possessing sovereignty over the island, or having a claim to sovereignty, to have, according to local conditions, a reasonable possibility for ascertaining the existence of a state of things contrary to her real or alleged rights.

It is not necessary that the display of sovereignty should be established as having begun at a precise epoch; it suffices that it had existed at the critical period preceding the year 1898. It is quite natural that the establishment of sovereignty may be the outcome of a slow evolution, of a progressive intensification of State control. This is particularly the case, if sovereignty is acquired by the establishment of the suzerainty of a colonial Power over a native State, and in regard to outlying possessions of such a vassal State.

Now the evidence relating to the period after the middle of the 19th century makes it clear that the Netherlands Indian Government considered the island distinctly as a part of its possessions and that, in the years immediately preceding 1898, an intensification of display of sovereignty took place.

Since the moment when the Spaniards, in withdrawing from the Moluccas in 1666, made express reservations as to the maintenance of their sovereign rights, up to the contestation made by the United States in 1906, no contestation or other action whatever or protest against the exercise of territorial rights by the Netherlands over the Talautse

---

29   Sharma, above note 7 at 107–8.
30   *Ibid* at 110.

(Sangi) Isles and their dependencies (Miangas included) has been recorded. The peaceful character of the display of Netherlands sovereignty for the entire period to which the evidence concerning acts of display relates (1700–1906) must be admitted.

As to the conditions of acquisition of sovereignty by way of continuous and peaceful display of State authority (so-called prescription), some of which have been discussed in the United States Counter-Memorandum, the following must be said:

The display has been open and public, that is to say that it was in conformity with usages as to exercise of sovereignty over colonial States.

There can further be no doubt that the Netherlands exercised the State authority over the Sangi States as sovereign in their own right, not under a derived or precarious title.

The conditions of acquisition of sovereignty by the Netherlands are therefore to be considered as fulfilled. It remains now to be seen whether the United States as successors of Spain are in a position to bring forward an equivalent or stronger title. This is to be answered in the negative.

. . . An inchoate title [i.e. that of the United States, based on Spanish discovery, but with no effective occupation] . . . cannot prevail over a definite title founded on continuous and peaceful display of sovereignty. . . .

The Netherlands title of sovereignty, acquired by continuous and peaceful display of State authority during a long period of time going probably back beyond the year 1700, therefore holds good.

For these reasons the Arbitrator . . . decides that: The Island of Palmas (or Miangas) forms in its entirety a part of Netherlands territory.

Now consider how the ICJ approaches the question of prescriptive title in a more recent case. Notice the attention paid to the indigenous population, in contrast to the approach taken in the *Island of Palmas Case*.

Kasikili/Sedudu Island (Botswana v Namibia), Judgment, [1999] ICJ Rep 1045

[On 1 July 1890, Germany and Great Britain entered into a treaty that delimited their spheres of influence in southwest Africa. During the century that followed, these territories experienced various changes in status. Eventually, the independent Republic of Botswana came into being on 30 September 1966, on the territory of the former British Bechuanaland Protectorate, while the former German territory now known as Namibia became independent on 21 March 1990. Soon after Namibia's independence, differences arose between the two states concerning the location of the boundary around Kasikili/Sedudu Island. The Caprivi mentioned in the excerpt below forms part of Namibia.]

90. Namibia . . . claims title to Kasikili/Sedudu Island, not only on the basis of the 1890 Treaty but also, in the alternative, on the basis of the doctrine of prescription. Namibia argues that

> by virtue of continuous and exclusive occupation and use of Kasikili Island and exercise of sovereign jurisdiction over it from the beginning of the century, with full knowledge, acceptance and acquiescence by the governing authorities in Bechuanaland and Botswana, Namibia has prescriptive title to the Island.

94. According to Namibia, four conditions must be fulfilled to enable possession by a State to mature into a prescriptive title:

1. The possession of the . . . state must be exercised *à titre de souverain*.
2. The possession must be peaceful and uninterrupted.
3. The possession must be public.
4. The possession must endure for a certain length of time.

Namibia alleges that in the present case Germany was in peaceful possession of the Island from before the beginning of the century and exercised sovereignty over it from the time of the establishment of the first colonial station in the Caprivi in 1909, all in full view and with the full knowledge of the Bechuanaland authorities at Kasane, only a kilometre or two from the Island. It states that this peaceful and public possession of the Island, *à titre de souverain*, was continued without interruption by Germany's successor until accession of the territory to independence. Finally, it notes that, after itself becoming independent in 1966, Botswana, which was aware of the facts, remained silent for almost two further decades.

In support of its allegations, Namibia emphasizes the importance of the presence on the Island of Masubia people from the Eastern Caprivi "from the beginning of the colonial period at least, and probably a good deal further back than that." It asserts that

> [c]olonial records of German, British and South African authorities and the testimony of members of the Masubia community in the Kasika district before the JTTE [Joint Team of Technical Experts] conclusively show that the Masubia people of Eastern Caprivi have occupied and used Kasikili Island since time immemorial.

and points out that "[t]he Masubia of the Caprivi Strip have used and occupied Kasikili Island as a part of their lands and their lives." Although Namibia admits that, in order to establish sovereignty by operation of prescription, acquiescence and recognition, it must show more than the use of the disputed territory by private individuals for their private ends, it maintains that:

> Namibia's predecessors exercised continuous authority and jurisdiction over Kasikili Island. From 1909 until the termination of the Mandate in 1966, German, Bechuanaland and South African officials consistently governed the Eastern Caprivi through Masubia chiefs, whose jurisdiction extended to Kasikili Island. After termination of the Mandate, South Africa, under pressure from the liberation struggle, increasingly exerted direct power in the area until Namibia's independence on 21 March 1990.

Namibia states that the authority exercised over Kasikili Island by its predecessors was implemented

> [f]or the most part . . . through the modality of "indirect rule," using the chiefs and political institutions of the Masubia to carry out the directives of the ruling power, under the control and supervision of officials of that power

and that

> [a]lthough indirect rule was manifested in a variety of ways, its essence was that the acts of administration of the colonial authorities and those of the traditional authorities were acts of a single entity: the colonial government.

According to Namibia, this situation

> prevailed without any objection, reservation or protest from Botswana or its predecessors in interest for almost a century until 1984, when Botswana first made formal claim to the Island in private meetings with the South African government.

In support of its argument concerning prescription, Namibia also invokes the incident between a patrol boat of the South African Defence Force and a unit of the Botswana Defence Force in October 1984, which, in its view, indicated that South Africa was exercising jurisdiction over the Island by conducting military patrols in the southern channel. It also refers to a number of official maps of the Caprivi portraying the Island as part of Namibia from the beginning of the century, as well as to the concurrence of the British authorities.

95. Although it considers the doctrine of prescription inapplicable in this case for the reasons referred to earlier, Botswana accepts the criteria for acquiring prescriptive title as set out by Namibia; it argues, however, that those criteria have not been satisfied by Namibia and its predecessors. Botswana asserts, in substance, that "there is no credible evidence that either Namibia or its predecessors exercised State authority in respect of Kasikili/Sedudu" and that even if peaceful, public and continuous possession of the Island by the people of Caprivi had been proved, it could not have been *à titre de souverain*.

Botswana does not dispute that people from the Caprivi used Kasikili/Sedudu Island at times for agricultural purposes; but it maintains that so did people living on the other side of the Chobe, in Bechuanaland, and denies that there was ever any village or permanent settlement on the Island. Botswana emphasizes that in any case "[t]he acts of private persons cannot generate title unless those acts are subsequently ratified by the State"; that no evidence has been offered to the effect that the Masubia chiefs had authority to engage in title-generating activities for the benefit of Germany or its successors; and that evidence is also lacking of any "genuine belief" in the existence of title on the part of Germany and its successors.

With regard to patrolling by South Africa, Botswana asserts that this involved at the very most anti-guerrilla operations, which cannot be classified as an exercise of jurisdiction; it claims that the incident of 1984 could not constitute evidence of peaceful possession for the purposes of prescription. Finally, Botswana denies that the map evidence has any value in this case; it maintains that this evidence is contradictory and confused and that the authorities of Bechuanaland and Botswana never recognized or acquiesced in the maps showing the boundary in the southern channel.

96. The Parties agree between themselves that acquisitive prescription is recognized in international law and they further agree on the conditions under which title to territory may be acquired by prescription, but their views differ on whether those conditions are satisfied in this case. Their disagreement relates primarily to the legal inferences which may be drawn from the presence on Kasikili/Sedudu Island of the Masubia of Eastern Caprivi: while Namibia bases its argument primarily on that presence, considered in the light of the concept of "indirect rule," to claim that its predecessors exercised title-generating State authority over the Island, Botswana sees this as simply a "private" activity, without any relevance in the eyes of international law.

97. For present purposes, the Court need not concern itself with the status of acquisitive prescription in international law or with the conditions for acquiring title to territory by prescription. It considers, for the reasons set out below, that the conditions cited by Namibia itself are not satisfied in this case and that Namibia's argument on acquisitive prescription therefore cannot be accepted.

98. . . . [E]ven if links of allegiance may have existed between the Masubia and the Caprivi authorities, it has not been established that the members of this tribe occupied the Island *à titre de souverain*, i.e., that they were exercising functions of State authority there on behalf of those authorities. Indeed, the evidence shows that the Masubia used the Island intermittently, according to the seasons and their needs, for exclusively agricultural purposes; this use, which began prior to the establishment of any colonial administration in the Caprivi Strip, seems to have subsequently continued without being linked to territorial claims on the part of the Authority administering the Caprivi. Admittedly, when, in 1947–1948, the question of the boundary in the region arose for the first time between the local authorities of Bechuanaland Protectorate and of South Africa, the Chobe's "main channel" around the Island was said to be the northern channel, but the South African authorities relied on the presence of the Masubia on the Island in order to maintain that they had title based on prescription. However, from then on the Bechuanaland authorities took the position that the boundary was located in the northern channel and that the Island was part of the Protectorate; after some hesitation, they declined to satisfy South Africa's claims to the Island, while at the same time recognizing the need to protect the interests of the Caprivi tribes. The Court infers from this, first, that for Bechuanaland, the activities of the Masubia on the Island were an independent issue from that of title to the Island and, second, that, as soon as South Africa officially claimed title, Bechuanaland did not accept that claim, which precluded acquiescence on its part.

99. In the Court's view, Namibia has not established with the necessary degree of precision and certainty that acts of State authority capable of providing alternative justification for prescriptive title, in accordance with the conditions set out by Namibia, were carried out by its predecessors or by itself with regard to Kasikili/Sedudu Island. . . .

Note also the ICJ's position in *Sovereignty over Pulau Ligitan and Pulau Sipadan.*[31] At issue in that case was whether Indonesia or Malaysia had the better claim to two islands. Among other things, Indonesia urged that the waters around the islands had traditionally been used by Indonesian fishers. However, the Court viewed this use as irrelevant to the claim, noting that "activities by private persons cannot be seen as *effectivités* if they do not take place on the basis of official regulations or under governmental authority."[32]

Note how these decisions give primacy to state-based forms of prescriptive occupation: the requirement that occupation be *à titre de souverain*. Unless they are present as agents of the state, simple occupation by non-state actors is irrelevant, even if these people are connected in some manner to one of the disputing states. Consider the implications of this rule for cases involving former colonies like Botswana and Namibia. Since,

---

31 (Indonesia/Malaysia), Judgment, [2002] ICJ Rep 618.
32 *Ibid* at para 140.

in the colonial context, the "state" was the colonial power, what does the state-centric "*à titre de souverain*" requirement mean for the relevance of the actions of the colonized peoples? Under what limited circumstances would their actions be relevant in resolving a claim of sovereign title to land based on prescription? Consider also whether there are any consequences of this approach for the concept of *terra nullius.* Revisit the questions posed following the excerpt from the *Western Sahara* advisory opinion reproduced in the preceding section.

Does official, continuous, lengthy, peaceful, and open possession of land previously under another state's control always result in acquisition of prescriptive title to that land? Consider the ICJ's approach to this issue in resolving a territorial dispute between Cameroon and Nigeria:

Land and Maritime Boundary between Cameroon and Nigeria (Cameroon v Nigeria: Equatorial Guinea intervening), Judgment, [2002] ICJ Rep 303

[Cameroon and Nigeria disputed, *inter alia,* sovereign title to certain lands and villages in the area of Lake Chad (which lies close to their border in the north). The Court first found that the boundary in the relevant area had already been established by international agreement among predecessor colonial powers, the effects of which were binding upon the disputing parties as successor states. That agreed delimitation gave title to the disputed lands and villages to Cameroon. The Court then turned to consider an alternative argument put forward by Nigeria in support of its claim to title to the disputed areas:]

62. . . . Nigeria contends that its claim rests on three bases, which each apply both individually and jointly and one of which would be sufficient on its own:

(1) long occupation by Nigeria and by Nigerian nationals constituting an historical consolidation of title;

(2) effective administration by Nigeria, acting as sovereign and an absence of protest; and

(3) manifestations of sovereignty by Nigeria together with the acquiescence by Cameroon in Nigerian sovereignty . . . .

Among the components of the historical consolidation of its title over the disputed areas, Nigeria cites: (1) the attitude and affiliations of the population [and] the Nigerian nationality of the inhabitants of those villages; (2) the existence of historical links with Nigeria in the area, and in particular the maintenance of the system of traditional chiefs . . . ; (3) the exercise of authority by the traditional chiefs, which is claimed to be still an important element within the State structure of modern Nigeria; (4) the long settlement of Nigerian nationals in the area; and (5) the peaceful administration of the disputed villages by the Federal Government of Nigeria . . . . Nigeria contends that Cameroon acquiesced in the peaceful exercise of Nigerian sovereignty over the disputed areas and that that acquiescence constitutes a major element in the process of historical consolidation of title. . . .

63. For its part, Cameroon contends that, as the holder of a conventional territorial title to the disputed areas, it does not have to demonstrate the effective exercise of its sovereignty over those areas, since a valid conventional title prevails over any *effectivités* to the contrary. Hence, no form of historical consolidation can prevail over a conventional territor-

ial title in the absence of clear consent on the part of the holder of that title to the cession of part of its territory. . . . Cameroon states that it has never acquiesced in the modification of its conventional boundary with Nigeria; it argues that acquiescence in a boundary change must, in order to bind a State, be the act of competent authorities and that in this regard the attitude of the central authorities must prevail over that of the local ones . . . .

64. . . . Nigeria's claim based on the theory of historical consolidation of title and on the acquiescence of Cameroon must be assessed by reference to [the] initial determination of the Court [regarding the pre-existing frontier delimitation]. During the oral pleadings Cameroon's assertion that Nigerian *effectivités* were *contra legem* was dismissed by Nigeria as "completely question-begging and circular". The Court notes, however, that now that it has made its findings that the frontier in Lake Chad was delimited long before . . . , it necessarily follows that any Nigerian *effectivités* are indeed to be evaluated for their legal consequences as acts *contra legem*.

65. The Court will now examine Nigeria's argument based on historical consolidation of title. . . . The Court . . . observes that nothing in the [Court's prior jurisprudence] allows land occupation to prevail over an established treaty title. Moreover, the facts and circumstances put forward by Nigeria with respect to the Lake Chad villages concern a period of some 20 years, which is in any event far too short, even according to the theory relied on by it. Nigeria's arguments on this point cannot therefore be upheld.

66. Nigeria further states that the peaceful possession on which it relies, coupled with acts of administration, represents a manifestation of sovereignty . . . .

67. In this regard, it may be observed that the gradual settling of Nigerians in the villages was followed in turn by support provided by the Ngala Local Government in Nigeria, along with a degree of administration and supervision. . . . Some of these activities—the organization of public health and education facilities, policing, the administration of justice—could normally be considered to be acts *à titre de souverain*. The Court notes, however, that, as there was a pre-existing title held by Cameroon in this area of the lake, the pertinent legal test is whether there was thus evidenced acquiescence by Cameroon in the passing of title from itself to Nigeria.

68. . . . The Court has already ruled on a number of occasions on the legal relationship between *"effectivités"* and titles. In the *Frontier Dispute (Burkina Faso/Republic of Mali)* case, it pointed out that . . . :

> Where the act does not correspond to the law, where the territory which is the subject of the dispute is effectively administered by a State other than the one possessing the legal title, preference should be given to the holder of the title. In the event that the *effectivité* does not co-exist with any legal title, it must invariably be taken into consideration. . . .

It is this first eventuality here envisaged by the Court, and not the second, which corresponds to the situation obtaining in the present case. Thus Cameroon held the legal title to territory lying to the east of the boundary as fixed by the applicable instruments . . . . Hence the conduct of Cameroon in that territory has pertinence only for the question of whether it acquiesced in the establishment of a change in treaty title . . . .

[The Court then reviewed the evidence relating to Cameroon's conduct in the disputed areas and concluded:]

70. The Court finds that the above events, taken together, show that there was no acquiescence by Cameroon in the abandonment of its title in the area in favour of Nigeria. Accordingly, the Court concludes that the situation was essentially one where the *effectivités* adduced by Nigeria did not correspond to the law, and that accordingly "preference should be given to the holder of the title" . . . . The Court therefore concludes that, as regards the Settlements situated to the east of the frontier confirmed in the Henderson-Fleuriau Exchange of Notes of 1931, sovereignty has continued to lie with Cameroon . . . .

We return to the importance of acquiescence, in potentially displacing prior bases of title to sovereignty, in Section C below.

LAW IN CONTEXT

Canadian Sovereignty Claims in the Arctic

Canada is the second largest state in the world, but approximately 40 percent of its land-mass lies north of the permafrost line—the point at which ground remains frozen year-round. If Canada's north is measured from the tree line northwards, Canada has more Arctic land than any of the other seven Arctic states.[33] This region is, however, sparsely populated and climatically difficult, particularly in the High Arctic (comprising the Queen Elizabeth Islands). Historically, Canada has taken steps to bolster its claim to the region by pursuing a conscious policy of effective occupation, fearing that failure to assert its presence and contest the unauthorized presence of foreign nationals could undermine its sovereignty claim.

Consider the following discussion of these efforts, including the now notorious re-settlement of Inuit to the High Arctic at places like Grise Fiord:

Concern for Arctic sovereignty initially arose in 1880 when the arctic islands were transferred from Great Britain to Canada, ostensibly "to prevent the United States from claiming them." U.S. whalers wintering over posed the next threat, but perhaps more serious was the claim of the Danish explorer, Knud Rasmussen, that Greenland Eskimos had a right to hunt on Ellesmere Island because it was a "No Man's Land." Subsequent attempts to declare and enforce sovereign rights are well known: the Eastern Arctic Patrol, raising the flag on remote arctic islands, public declarations, establishing RCMP posts, arduous sled patrols, issuing licences to explorers, and enforcing game laws. The first formal challenge was settled in 1930 when Canada's title over the entire archipelago was formally recognized by Norway—after payment of $67,000 to Norwegian explorer Otto Sverdrup for his discovery of three major islands west of Ellesmere. At that point, the federal government's Northern Advisory Board formally announced that Canada's title was secure.

Still, various government actions continued to reflect concerns, despite public assurances to the contrary. In 1934, for example, 22 Cape Dorset Inuit were relocated to

---

Dundas Harbour where there was reported to be better hunting and trapping. They were assisted by families from Pangnirtung and Pond Inlet, and a Hudson's Bay Company trader. All were promised that they could return in two years if not satisfied with conditions. . . .

Two years later, conditions proved unsatisfactory, and the Inuit from Pangnirtung were transported home. The remainder were taken to Arctic Bay for a year, then on to Fort Ross where they stayed until the post closed in 1947; in the end, they were settled at Spence Bay.

If the 1934 "experiment in acclimatization," as it was then called, ended in failure, why was it attempted again only seven years later [at places like Grise Fiord on Ellesmere Island]? . . .

Following the Norwegian challenge in 1930, the Canadian government was particularly concerned that other discoveries might lead to further claims, unless the area was regularly patrolled, visited by Canadian scientific expeditions, and/or occupied by Canadian Inuit. . . .

In the immediate postwar years, the concern to protect sovereign claims was intense, particularly in the Privy Council Office and Department of External Affairs. Until such time as sovereignty was assured beyond all reasonable doubt, the accepted policy was to avoid public statements which might create an opportunity for direct challenge. In addition, some believed that public assertion of Canada's claims would only imply doubts as to their validity. . . .

While the debate continued in Ottawa, [United States Air Force] Intelligence was studying the possibility of claiming uninhabited regions in Grantland (northern Ellesmere), and on Prince Patrick and Melville Islands, on the legal premise that "sovereignty cannot be claimed without a degree of effective occupation, colonization, and use." . . . In the end, it was decided that this strategy would only be implemented should Canada refuse to co-operate in a time of crisis. Instead, the intelligence report suggested that Canada be assured "that the United States has no intention, now or in future, of claiming sovereignty over any section of the Canadian Arctic."

Canada's counter-strategy to a potential threat was to use the joint defence agreements from 1947 onward to gain evidence of U.S. acceptance of Canada's sovereign title. At the same time, it became government policy to promote the "Canadianization" of all U.S. military operations by assuming responsibility for air bases and weather stations; utilizing the RCAF for mapping, reconnaissance, and rescue and supply missions; promoting Canadian arctic scientific expeditions; and encouraging the use of Canadian goods and personnel by U.S. contractors. . . .

[A] 1958 [Canadian report stated] that "Canadian title appears secure provided adequate steps are taken to maintain Canadian activities there and, in pace with increasing international interest in the Arctic, to augment these activities to provide evidence of continuing effective occupation." Of greater relevance is the 1956 report on sovereignty and Ellesmere Island. Included is a list of Canadian activities since 1950 that implied "effective occupation" and exertion of authority. Among the items were:

- Six families of eskimo colonists were landed at Craig Harbour in August, 1953.
- In August, 1953 an R.C.M.P. detachment was opened at Alexandra Fiord.
- Seven Eskimo took up residence in August, 1953 at Alexandra Fiord.

These references confirm that Inuit settlement was considered an important factor in maintaining sovereign control over Ellesmere.

In the case of Grise Fiord and the aborted plans for Alexandra Fiord, concern for sovereignty was unquestionably the primary motive behind the initial idea and the selection of the site. . . . Without that motive, there would be no perceived benefit to relocate southern Inuit to such a distant and alien environment. There would have been no experiment, no hardship, and no expensive costs in returning the Inuit to their traditional homelands. Concern for sovereignty was the primary motive in determining when and where resettlement should occur. . . .[34]

The Grise Fiord resettlement inflicted massive hardship on the new town's population:

The government treated the resettlement as a human experiment; it wanted to determine if Inuit from a (comparatively) southern part of the Arctic could survive further north than any existing Inuit community. Provisions and equipment—such as rifles, fishing gear and material to repair tents—were withheld so that the resettled Inuit would not become dependent on government assistance. The Inuit survived the first winter—their first experience with total darkness that lasts several months—in substandard tents.[35]

At the urging of the Royal Commission on Aboriginal Peoples, the government compensated the relocatees and their descendants in the mid-1990s and formally apologized for the relocation in 2010.[36]

Consider whether the presence of Inuit would be legally relevant were the Canadian claim to some portion of the territory of the High Arctic to be contested. Would this Inuit presence demonstrate the required occupation *à titre de souverain*? Does the answer to this question depend on whether the Inuit were present in a particular place as a result of relocation by the Canadian government?

Canada's Department of Foreign Affairs and International Trade takes pains to note that Canada's claim of sovereignty over Arctic land is not, for the most part, contested:

First of all, Canada has no "claim" of sovereignty over the Arctic Archipelago. Canadian sovereignty is an accepted fact. There is no dispute about the ownership of the lands and islands of the Canadian Arctic Archipelago. . . . [T]hey belong to Canada.

Without delving too deeply into the legal history, the salient points are as follows: the legal title to the Arctic islands belonging to Great Britain was formally transferred to Canada by means of an Imperial Order-in-Council in 1880. In 1895, by its own order-in-council, Canada explicitly established the boundaries of its northern possessions, which included all islands up to latitude 83 1/4 north, i.e., the northern-most point of Ellesmere Island. This order-in-council enclosed all the islands southward from that latitude as part of Canada. . . .

34 Shelagh Grant, "A Case of Compounded Error: The Inuit Resettlement Project, 1953, and the Government Response, 1990" (1991) 19 *Northern Perspectives* 1.

35 Stephen Hazell, "The High Arctic Resettlement Experiment: A Question of Fundamental Justice" (1991) 19 *Northern Perspectives* 1.

36 Government of Canada, Aboriginal Affairs and Northern Development Canada, News Release, "Government of Canada Apologizes for Relocation of Inuit Families to the High Arctic," No 2-3398 (18 August 2010).

Prime Minister Trudeau could advise Parliament in May 1969 that Canada's sovereignty over the Arctic "is well established and that there is no dispute concerning this matter. No country has asserted a competing claim, no country now challenges Canada's sovereignty on any other basis; and many countries have indicated in many ways the recognition of Canada's sovereignty over these areas." In 1971 the then-Director-General of the Legal Bureau of the Department of External Affairs . . . emphasized that "Canada is aware of no challenge to its sovereignty over the mainland and islands of the Canadian Arctic." This remains true today, thirty years later. Only tiny Hans Island, . . . in Kennedy Channel exactly half-way between Ellesmere Island and Greenland, remains in dispute.

All this means that the land areas of Canada's Arctic Archipelago are undisputed parts of Canada. This is true whether the islands are inhabited or not. Should persons travel to the islands and, without Canada's lawful permission, take from them any wildlife, or minerals, or fresh water, or archaeological relics or if they leave their wastes and garbage, then they are breaching the laws of Canada and they can be prosecuted. Canada's legal sovereignty does not somehow evaporate simply because there are no Canadians on the island in question.[37]

Consider the one land dispute, mentioned above, that does persist in the Canadian Arctic (although it was reportedly nearing settlement at the time of writing).[38] In 2005, Canada and Denmark renewed (very publicly) a disagreement concerning sovereign title to a tiny island in the High Arctic called Hans Island. In reviewing the following synopsis from Canada's Department of Foreign Affairs and International Trade, consider whether Minister Graham's visit had anything to do with the *effectivités* concept noted above. Would it be given legal weight in a court of law?

Hans Island is a tiny, one-quarter square mile uninhabitable island in the Kennedy Channel between Ellesmere Island and Greenland. It is part of the sovereign territory of Canada. Canada's sovereignty over Hans Island is longstanding and based on a solid foundation in international law. However, Denmark also claims title over the island.

Though there have been many visits to the island by Canadian officials, including a Canadian Ranger patrol earlier this year, Minister of National Defence Bill Graham's visit to the island in mid-July, 2005 attracted a great deal of media attention on this issue.

Foreign Affairs Minister Pettigrew met with his Danish counterpart Minister Moller on the margins of the United Nations General Assembly in September 2005 to discuss a wide range of issues including Hans Island. They released a joint statement which affirmed the excellent bilateral relations between our two countries and contained a commitment to seek to achieve a long-term solution to this dispute.

. . . [S]ince the maritime delimitation in Kennedy Channel was settled by a treaty between Canada and Denmark in 1973, the dispute is strictly over Hans Island and not about the waters or seabed around it.[39]

---

37 Michael Leir, "Canadian Practice in International Law at the Department of Foreign Affairs in 1999–2000: Canada's Sovereignty in Changing Arctic Waters" (2001) 39 Can YB Int'l Law 485 at 486–87.

38 See Government of Canada, Foreign Affairs and International Trade Canada, News Release, "Canada and Kingdom of Denmark Reach Tentative Agreement on Lincoln Sea Boundary" (28 November 2012).

39 Government of Canada, Department of Foreign Affairs and International Trade, Legal Affairs Bureau,

5) Subjugation: Conquest and Annexation

Historically, conquest of territory followed by annexation was a key means of obtaining title to that territory. An international law treatise from the early twentieth century described acquisition of title by conquest as follows: "Conquest is the permanent absorption of all or part of the territory of a defeated enemy. A title resting upon conquest is not complete until the conqueror has satisfied two requirements. In the first place, he must possess the material strength to make his conquest good, and in the second, he must have, and exhibit, the intention of appropriation."[40]

Another mid-twentieth century scholar had this to say:

> Conquest is the taking possession of enemy territory through military force in time of war. Conquest alone does not *ipso facto* make the conquering State the sovereign of the conquered territory, although such territory comes through conquest for the time under the sway of the conqueror. Conquest is only a mode of acquisition if the conqueror, after having firmly established the conquest, formally annexes the territory. Such annexation makes the enemy State cease to exist, and thereby brings the war to an end. And as such ending of war is named subjugation, it is conquest followed by subjugation, and not conquest alone, which gives a title and is a mode of acquiring territory.[41]

Notice the emphasis on "states" engaged in conquest and subjugation. Conquest, even when permitted by international law, apparently could not transfer sovereignty where the conquering people was not considered a "state" within the meaning of the term in the European world legal order. Consider the view of the Permanent Court of International Justice in the *Eastern Greenland* case:

Legal Status of Eastern Greenland (Denmark v Norway) (1933), PCIJ (Ser A/B) No 53

In the period when the early Nordic colonies founded by Eric the Red in the 10th century in Greenland were in existence, the modern notions as to territorial sovereignty had not come into being. . . . [Nevertheless,] [s]o far as it is possible to apply modern terminology to the rights and pretensions of the kings of Norway in Greenland in the 13th and 14th centuries, the Court holds that at that date these rights amounted to sovereignty and that they were not limited to the two settlements.

It has been argued on behalf of Norway that after the disappearance of the two Nordic settlements, Norwegian sovereignty was lost and Greenland became a *terra nullius*.

Conquest and voluntary abandonment are the grounds on which this view is put forward. The word "conquest" is not an appropriate phrase, even if it is assumed that it was fighting with the Eskimos which led to the downfall of the settlements. Conquest only operates as a cause of loss of sovereignty when there is war between two States and by reason of the defeat of one of them sovereignty over territory passes from the loser

---

Examples of Current Issues of International Law of Particular Importance to Canada (2005) at 4 [on file with the authors].

40 JE Wylie, *Smith's International Law*, 4th ed (London: JM Dent, 1911) at 187.

41 Hersch Lauterpacht, *Oppenheim's International Law*, vol I, 8th ed (Harlow, Essex: Longman, 1955) at 566.

to the victorious State. The principle does not apply in a case where a settlement has been established in a distant country and its inhabitants are massacred by the aboriginal population. . . .

Acquisition of territory by conquest and annexation is no longer permissible. Recall Articles 2(3) and 2(4) of the UN Charter:[42]

Article 2
The Organization and its Members, in pursuit of the Purposes stated in Article 1, shall act in accordance with the following Principles. . . .

3. All Members shall settle their international disputes by peaceful means in such a manner that international peace and security, and justice, are not endangered.

4. All Members shall refrain in their international relations from the threat or use of force against the territorial integrity or political independence of any state, or in any other manner inconsistent with the Purposes of the United Nations. . . .

The UN Security Council has reaffirmed that territory may not be acquired by conquest. In Resolution 242 (1967), the Security Council emphasized "the inadmissibility of the acquisition of territory by war"[43] in the context of the Arab-Israeli conflict. In response to the Iraqi invasion of Kuwait in 1990, the Security Council decided in Resolution 662 (1990) that the Iraqi annexation of Kuwait "under any form and whatever pretext has no legal validity, and is considered null and void."[44] Further, all states were called upon "not to recognize that annexation and to refrain from any action or dealing that might be interpreted as an indirect recognition of the annexation."[45]

Note also the "Declaration on Principles of International Law Concerning Friendly Relations and Co-Operation among States in accordance with the Charter of the United Nations."[46] This key General Assembly resolution, the content of which is widely viewed as reflecting customary international law, reads in part:

Every State has the duty to refrain from the threat or use of force to violate the existing international boundaries of another State or as a means of solving international disputes, including territorial disputes and problems concerning frontiers of States. . . .

Every State has the duty to refrain from any forcible action which deprives peoples referred to in the elaboration of the principle of equal rights and self-determination of their right to self-determination and freedom and independence. . . .

The territory of a State shall not be the object of military occupation resulting from the use of force in contravention of the provisions of the Charter. The territory of a State shall not be the object of acquisition by another State resulting from the threat or use of

---

42 Charter of the United Nations, 26 June 1945, Can TS 1945 No 7, in force 24 October 1945 [UN Charter].
43 SC Resolution 242(1967), adopted 22 November 1967, UN Doc S/RES/242(1967) at preamb, para 2.
44 SC Resolution 662(1990), adopted 9 August 1990, UN Doc S/RES/662(1990) at para 1.
45 *Ibid* at para 2.
46 GA Res 2625(XXV), UN Doc A/RES/2625/XXV, reprinted in UN GAOR, 25th Sess, Supp No 28 at 121–24, UN Doc A/8082 Corr 1 (1970) [Friendly Relations Declaration].

force. No territorial acquisition resulting from the threat or use of force shall be recognized as legal. . . .

While acquisition of territory by force would now be illegal, this evolution in international law does not make past conquests unlawful. Recall that the doctrine of intertemporal law precludes the retroactive application of modern rules of law. For this reason:

> That international law has since legislated a ban on the process of acquisition by which title was acquired is not alone determinative of the current legal status of the continued fact of possession. In order to determine that status, lawyers first must ascertain which law governs—the law in force at the time of acquisition or the law in force today.
>   . . . Professor Robert Jennings writes:
>
>> Where, then, stands this law of conquest today? The first observation to be made is that, unless the rule of the intertemporal law is to be totally rejected—and there is neither authority nor reason to do this—old titles by conquest must still remain valid. . . .

> According to Jennings, the current disposition of vast territories would be thrown into doubt, if the view were accepted that changes in the rules governing territorial acquisition had retroactive effect on acquisitions accomplished under older rules. Jennings argues that for political reasons such doubt must be avoided. Legal foundation for the result Jennings reaches is furnished by his prescription of how to apply intertemporal law.[47]

6) Self-Determination

Our focus to this point has been the means by which sovereign title to territory may be acquired by pre-existing states. In this section, we turn to a more recent international legal phenomenon that may also, in some cases, result in the acquisition of territory by a state. However, it stands out because it more frequently results in the acquisition of sovereignty over territory by an entity that achieves statehood only at the moment of such acquisition. This phenomenon is the exercise by a people, not already constituting a state, of its right of self-determination.

The *principle* of self-determination is found in several important international legal instruments. For example, Article 1(2) of the UN Charter lists as one of the purposes of the United Nations the development of "friendly relations among nations based on respect for the principle of equal rights and self-determination of peoples." Article 55 charges the United Nations with promoting economic and social progress, solutions to economic, social and health problems, and human rights, all with a view to "the creation of conditions of stability and well-being which are necessary for peaceful and friendly relations among nations based on respect for the principle of equal rights and self-determination of peoples."

---

47   Thomas D Grant, "A Panel of Experts for Chechnya: Purposes and Prospects in Light of International Law" (1999) 40 Va J Int'l L 115 at 167.

Several key international human rights treaties also invoke a *right* of self-determination of peoples. Common Article 1 of both the International Covenant on Civil and Political Rights[48] and the International Covenant on Economic, Social and Cultural Rights[49] reads:

1. All peoples have the right of self-determination. By virtue of that right they freely determine their political status and freely pursue their economic, social and cultural development.

2. All peoples may, for their own ends, freely dispose of their natural wealth and resources without prejudice to any obligations arising out of international economic cooperation, based upon the principle of mutual benefit, and international law. In no case may a people be deprived of its own means of subsistence.

3. The States Parties to the present Covenant, including those having responsibility for the administration of Non-Self-Governing and Trust Territories, shall promote the realization of the right of self-determination, and shall respect that right, in conformity with the provisions of the Charter of the United Nations.

The following regional human rights treaty, discussed at greater length in Chapter 9, is even more emphatic:

African Charter of Human and Peoples' Rights, 27 June 1981, 1520 UNTS 245, in force 21 October 1986

Article 19
All peoples shall be equal; they shall enjoy the same respect and shall have the same rights. Nothing shall justify the domination of a people by another.

Article 20
1. All peoples shall have the right to existence. They shall have the unquestionable and inalienable right to self-determination. They shall freely determine their political status and shall pursue their economic and social development according to the policy they have freely chosen.

2. Colonized or oppressed peoples shall have the right to free themselves from the bonds of domination by resorting to any means recognized by the international community.

3. All peoples shall have the right to the assistance of the States parties to the present Charter in their liberation struggle against foreign domination, be it political, economic or cultural.

Article 21
1. All peoples shall freely dispose of their wealth and natural resources. This right shall be exercised in the exclusive interest of the people. In no case shall a people be deprived of it.

---

48   16 December 1966, 999 UNTS 171, Can TS 1976 No 47, in force 23 March 1976.
49   16 December 1966, 993 UNTS 3, Can TS 1976 No 46, in force 3 January 1976.

2. In case of spoliation the dispossessed people shall have the right to the lawful recovery of its property as well as to an adequate compensation.

3. The free disposal of wealth and natural resources shall be exercised without prejudice to the obligation of promoting international economic cooperation based on mutual respect, equitable exchange and the principles of international law.

4. States parties to the present Charter shall individually and collectively exercise the right to free disposal of their wealth and natural resources with a view to strengthening African unity and solidarity.

5. States parties to the present Charter shall undertake to eliminate all forms of foreign economic exploitation particularly that practiced by international monopolies so as to enable their peoples to fully benefit from the advantages derived from their national resources.

Article 22
1. All peoples shall have the right to their economic, social and cultural development with due regard to their freedom and identity and in the equal enjoyment of the common heritage of mankind.

2. States shall have the duty, individually or collectively, to ensure the exercise of the right to development.

The 1993 Vienna Declaration and Programme of Action,[50] being the outcome document of a UN World Conference on Human Rights, also reaffirmed the importance of self-determination in the human rights context:

2. All peoples have the right of self-determination. By virtue of that right they freely determine their political status, and freely pursue their economic, social and cultural development.

Taking into account the particular situation of peoples under colonial or other forms of alien domination or foreign occupation, the World Conference on Human Rights recognizes the right of peoples to take any legitimate action, in accordance with the Charter of the United Nations, to realize their inalienable right of self-determination. The World Conference on Human Rights considers the denial of the right of self-determination as a violation of human rights and underlines the importance of the effective realization of this right.

In accordance with the Declaration on Principles of International Law concerning Friendly Relations and Cooperation Among States in accordance with the Charter of the United Nations, this shall not be construed as authorizing or encouraging any action which would dismember or impair, totally or in part, the territorial integrity or political unity of sovereign and independent States conducting themselves in compliance with the principle of equal rights and self-determination of peoples and thus possessed of a Government representing the whole people belonging to the territory without distinction of any kind.

---

50   UN Doc A/CONF.157/23 (12 July 1993).

The UN General Assembly has also pronounced itself on self-determination and decolonization issues repeatedly, including in the Declaration on the Granting of Independence to Colonial Countries and Peoples[51] and the 1970 Friendly Relations Declaration.[52]

As some of these materials suggest, the right of self-determination was twentieth century international law's reaction to colonization. Consider the ICJ's account of the emergence of this right in the following case excerpts.

Legal Consequences for States of the Continued Presence of South Africa in Namibia (South West Africa) notwithstanding Security Council Resolution 276 (1970), **Advisory Opinion, [1971] ICJ Rep 16**

[Following World War I, South Africa was granted a mandate over South West Africa (later Namibia), which at the time was deemed incapable of governing itself. The nature and terms of the mandate were specified in Article 22 of the Covenant of the League of Nations.[53] Following the League's demise, South Africa contended that the mandate had lapsed and that it was free to dispose of South West Africa as it wished. The Court, in an earlier advisory opinion ([1950] ICJ Rep 128) rejected that contention. South Africa nevertheless persisted in occupying Namibia, prompting the Security Council to adopt Resolution 276 (1970), which declared South Africa's continued presence in Namibia illegal. The Security Council then sought the Court's opinion on the legal consequences of South Africa's continuing refusal to comply with Resolution 276 (1970). One of the issues addressed by the Court concerned the legality of General Assembly Resolution 2145 (XXI), by which the General Assembly purported to terminate South Africa's mandate over Namibia due to the fundamental breach by South Africa of its obligations under the mandate.]

. . . [T]he subsequent [post-1919] development of international law in regard to non-self-governing territories, as enshrined in the Charter of the United Nations, made the principle of self-determination applicable to all of [the mandatory powers]. The concept of the sacred trust was confirmed and expanded to all "territories whose peoples have not yet attained a full measure of self-government" (Art. 73). Thus it clearly embraced territories under a colonial regime. Obviously the sacred trust continued to apply to League of Nations mandated territories on which an international status had been conferred earlier. A further important stage in this development was the Declaration on the Granting of Independence to Colonial Countries and Peoples (General Assembly resolution 1514 (XV) of 14 December 1960), which embraces all peoples and territories which "have not yet attained independence." Nor is it possible to leave out of account the political history of mandated territories in general. All those which did not acquire independence, excluding Namibia, were placed under trusteeship. Today, only two out of fifteen, excluding Namibia, remain under United Nations tutelage. This is but a manifestation of the general development which has led to the birth of so many new States.

---

51 GA Res 1514(XV), UN Doc. A/RES/1514(XV), reprinted in UN GAOR, 15th Sess, Supp No 16 at 66–67, UN Doc A/4684 (1960).

52 Above note 45.

53 28 April 1919, (1919) 13 Am J Int'l L Supp 128, in force 10 January 1920, as amended.

53. All these considerations are germane to the Court's evaluation of the present case. Mindful as it is of the primary necessity of interpreting an instrument in accordance with the intentions of the parties at the time of its conclusion, the Court is bound to take into account the fact that the concepts embodied in Article 22 of the Covenant—"the strenuous conditions of the modern world" and "the well-being and development" of the peoples concerned—were not static, but were by definition evolutionary, as also, therefore, was the concept of the "sacred trust." The parties to the Covenant must consequently be deemed to have accepted them as such. That is why, viewing the institutions of 1919, the Court must take into consideration the changes which have occurred in the supervening half-century, and its interpretation cannot remain unaffected by the subsequent development of law, through the Charter of the United Nations and by way of customary law. Moreover, an international instrument has to be interpreted and applied within the framework of the entire legal system prevailing at the time of the interpretation. In the domain to which the present proceedings relate, the last fifty years, as indicated above, have brought important developments. These developments leave little doubt that the ultimate objective of the sacred trust was the self-determination and independence of the peoples concerned. In this domain, as elsewhere, the *corpus iuris gentium* [law of nations] has been considerably enriched, and this the Court, if it is faithfully to discharge its functions, may not ignore. . . .

[The Court concluded that the continued presence of South Africa in Namibia being illegal, South Africa was under an obligation to withdraw its administration from Namibia immediately and thus put an end to its occupation of the territory. It also held that the UN member states were under an obligation to recognize the illegality of South Africa's presence in Namibia and the invalidity of its acts on behalf of or concerning Namibia, and to refrain from any acts and in particular any dealings with the Government of South Africa implying recognition of the legality of, or lending support or assistance to, such presence and administration.]

Western Sahara, **Advisory Opinion, [1975] ICJ Rep 12**

[As Spain moved to decolonize Western Sahara, controversy arose over the legal status of the territory. Both Mauritania and Morocco made claims to the region on the basis of historical and cultural ties. These claims were resisted by the occupants of Western Sahara. At the urging of Morocco, the UN General Assembly therefore requested an advisory opinion from the International Court of Justice. Question II asked: "What were the legal ties between this territory and the Kingdom of Morocco and the Mauritanian entity?" Discussing the rights of these two states as well as those of the inhabitants of Western Sahara, the Court considered the principle of self-determination of peoples.]

54. The Charter of the United Nations, in Article 1, paragraph 2, indicates, as one of the purposes of the United Nations: "To develop friendly relations among nations based on respect for the principle of equal rights and self-determination of peoples . . ." This purpose is further developed in Articles 55 and 56 of the Charter. Those provisions have direct and particular relevance for non-self-governing territories, which are dealt with in Chapter XI of the Charter. As the Court stated in its Advisory Opinion of 21 June 1971

on *The Legal Consequences for States of the Continued Presence of South Africa in Namibia (South West Africa) notwithstanding Security Council Resolution 276 (1970):*

> the subsequent development of international law in regard to non-self-governing territories, as enshrined in the Charter of the United Nations, made the principle of self-determination applicable to all of them (I.C.J. Reports 1971, p. 31).

55. The principle of self-determination as a right of peoples, and its application for the purpose of bringing all colonial situations to a speedy end, were enunciated in the Declaration on the Granting of Independence to Colonial Countries and Peoples, General Assembly resolution 1514 (XV). In this resolution the General Assembly proclaims "the necessity of bringing to a speedy and unconditional end colonialism in all its forms and manifestations." To this end the resolution provides *inter alia*:

> 2. All peoples have the right to self-determination; by virtue of that right they freely determine their political status and freely pursue their economic, social and cultural development.

> . . .

> 5. Immediate steps shall be taken, in Trust and Non-Self-Governing Territories or all other territories which have not yet attained independence, to transfer all powers to the peoples of those territories, without any conditions or reservations, in accordance with their freely expressed will and desire, without any distinction as to race, creed or colour, in order to enable them to enjoy complete independence and freedom.

> 6. Any attempt aimed at the partial or total disruption of the national unity and the territorial integrity of a country is incompatible with the purpose and principles of the Charter of the United Nations.

The above provisions, in particular paragraph 2, thus confirm and emphasize that the application of the right of self-determination requires a free and genuine expression of the will of the peoples concerned. . . .

57. General Assembly resolution 1514 (XV) provided the basis for the process of decolonization which has resulted since 1960 in the creation of many States which are today Members of the United Nations. It is complemented in certain of its aspects by General Assembly resolution 1541 (XV), which has been invoked in the present proceedings. The latter resolution contemplates for non-self-governing territories more than one possibility, namely:

> (a) emergence as a sovereign independent State;
> (b) free association with an independent State; or
> (c) integration with an independent State.

At the same time, certain of its provisions give effect to the essential feature of the right of self-determination as established in resolution 1514(XV). Thus principle VII of resolution 1541 (XV) declares that: "Free association should be the result of a free and voluntary choice by the peoples of the territory concerned expressed through informed and democratic processes." Again, principle IX of resolution 1541 (XV) declares that:

Integration should have come about in the following circumstances:

(b) The integration should be the result of the freely expressed wishes of the territory's peoples acting with full knowledge of the change in their status, their wishes having been expressed through informed and democratic processes, impartially conducted and based on universal adult suffrage. The United Nations could, when it deems it necessary, supervise these processes.

58. General Assembly resolution 2625 (XXV), "Declaration on Principles of International Law concerning Friendly Relations and Co-operation among States in accordance with the Charter of the United Nations,"—to which reference was also made in the proceedings—mentions other possibilities besides independence, association or integration. But in doing so it reiterates the basic need to take account of the wishes of the people concerned:

> The establishment of a sovereign and independent State, the free association or integration with an independent State or the emergence into any other political status freely determined by a people constitute modes of implementing the right of self-determination by that people.

Resolution 2625 (XXV) further provides that:

> Every State has the duty to promote, through joint and separate action, realization of the principle of equal rights and self-determination of peoples in accordance with the provisions of the Charter, and to render assistance to the United Nations in carrying out the responsibilities entrusted to it by the Charter regarding the implementation of the principle, in order:
>
> (b) To bring a speedy end to colonialism, having due regard to the freely expressed will of the peoples concerned. . . .

In the end, the Court did not find legal ties between Western Sahara, Mauritania, or Morocco of such a nature as might affect the application of General Assembly resolution 1514 (XV) to the decolonization of Western Sahara. Specifically, these ties did not displace the right to exercise self-determination through the free and genuine expression of the will of the people of the territory.

Since *Western Sahara*, the ICJ has invested the concept of self-determination with potent legal significance. Consider its views in the following decision:

East Timor Case (Portugal v Australia), Judgment, [1995] ICJ Rep 90

[East Timor, a former Portuguese colony, was invaded and occupied by Indonesia in 1975, sparking resistance and, in turn, brutal repression. In 1989, Australia negotiated a treaty with Indonesia creating a "zone of cooperation" in the area between the "Indonesian Province of East Timor" and northern Australia. Portugal brought proceedings against Australia, arguing that this treaty constituted a failure by Australia to recognize Portugal as the only legitimate administering authority of East Timor as well as an infringement of the rights of the East Timorese to self-determination. Australia objected to the jurisdiction of the Court, arguing that Indonesia was a necessary party to the dispute and that, to reach a determination on the merits, the Court would have to rule on the legitimacy of Indonesia's claim to East Timor. The Court agreed that this was the case, and held that it did not have jurisdiction. In doing so, it commented as follows on the nature of the right to self-determination:]

29. . . . In the Court's view, Portugal's assertion that the right of peoples to self-determination, as it evolved from the Charter and from United Nations practice, has an *erga omnes* character, is irreproachable. The principle of self-determination of peoples has been recognized by the United Nations Charter and in the jurisprudence of the Court . . . ; it is one of the essential principles of contemporary international law. However, the Court considers that the *erga omnes* character of a norm and the rule of consent to jurisdiction are two different things. Whatever the nature of the obligations invoked, the Court could not rule on the lawfulness of the conduct of a State when its judgment would imply an evaluation of the lawfulness of the conduct of another State which is not a party to the case. Where this is so, the Court cannot act, even if the right in question is a right *erga omnes*. . . .

The Court repeated its views on the fundamental nature of self-determination in its advisory opinion on the wall being built by Israel in the Occupied Palestinian Territory. Consider its analysis:

Legal Consequences of the Construction of a Wall in the Occupied Palestinian Territory, Advisory Opinion, [2004] ICJ Rep 136

[In 2003, the UN General Assembly asked the Court for an advisory opinion in response to the question: "What are the legal consequences arising from the construction of the wall being built by Israel, the occupying Power, in the Occupied Palestinian Territory, including in and around East Jerusalem, as described in the report of the Secretary-General, considering the rules and principles of international law . . .?" In its answer, the Court addressed whether the Palestinian people enjoyed a right of self-determination and the implications thereof for the legality of the wall.]

. . . 70. Palestine was part of the Ottoman Empire. At the end of the First World War, a class "A" Mandate for Palestine was entrusted to Great Britain by the League of Nations. . . .

The Court recalls that in its Advisory Opinion on the *International Status of South West Africa*, speaking of mandates in general, it observed that "The Mandate was created, in the interest of the inhabitants of the territory, and of humanity in general, as an international institution with an international object—a sacred trust of civilization." . . . The Court also held in this regard that "two principles were considered to be of paramount importance: the principle of non-annexation and the principle that the well-being and development of . . . peoples [not yet able to govern themselves] form[ed] 'a sacred trust of civilization.'" . . .

71. In 1947 the United Kingdom announced its intention to complete evacuation of the mandated territory. . . . In the meantime, the General Assembly had on 29 November 1947 adopted resolution 181 (II) on the future government of Palestine, which "*Recom-*

mends to the United Kingdom . . . and to all other Members of the United Nations the adoption and implementation . . . of the Plan of Partition" of the territory, as set forth in the resolution, between two independent States, one Arab, the other Jewish, as well as the creation of a special international régime for the City of Jerusalem. The Arab population of Palestine and the Arab States rejected this plan, contending that it was unbalanced; on 14 May 1948, Israel proclaimed its independence on the strength of the General Assembly resolution; armed conflict then broke out between Israel and a number of Arab States and the Plan of Partition was not implemented.

72. By resolution 62 (1948) of 16 November 1948, the Security Council decided that "an armistice shall be established in all sectors of Palestine" and called upon the parties directly involved in the conflict to seek agreement to this end. In conformity with this decision, general armistice agreements were concluded in 1949 between Israel and the neighbouring States through mediation by the United Nations. . . . [One such agreement] fixed the armistice demarcation line between Israeli and Arab forces (often later called the "Green Line" owing to the colour used for it on maps; hereinafter the "Green Line). . . . It was agreed . . . that these provisions would not be "interpreted as prejudicing, in any sense, an ultimate political settlement between the Parties." It was also stated that "the Armistice Demarcation Lines . . . [were] agreed upon by the Parties without prejudice to future territorial settlements or boundary lines or to claims of either Party relating thereto." . . .

73. In the 1967 armed conflict, Israeli forces occupied all the territories which had constituted Palestine under British Mandate (including those known as the West Bank, lying to the east of the Green Line).

74. On 22 November 1967, the Security Council unanimously adopted resolution 242 (1967), which emphasized the inadmissibility of acquisition of territory by war and called for the "Withdrawal of Israel armed forces from territories occupied in the recent conflict," and "Termination of all claims or states of belligerency." . . .

85. Lastly, it should be noted that the construction of the wall has been accompanied by the creation of a new administrative régime. Thus in October 2003 the Israeli Defence Forces issued Orders establishing the part of the West Bank lying between the Green Line and the wall as a "Closed Area." Residents of this area may no longer remain in it, nor may non-residents enter it, unless holding a permit or identity card issued by the Israeli authorities. According to the report of the Secretary-General, most residents have received permits for a limited period. Israeli citizens, Israeli permanent residents and those eligible to immigrate to Israel in accordance with the Law of Return may remain in, or move freely to, from and within the Closed Area without a permit. Access to and exit from the Closed Area can only be made through access gates, which are opened infrequently and for short periods.

[After reviewing the instruments excerpted above, as well as its prior jurisprudence on self-determination, the Court continued:]

118. . . . [T]he Court observes that the existence of a "Palestinian people" is no longer in issue. Such existence has moreover been recognized by Israel in the exchange of letters

of 9 September 1993 between Mr. Yasser Arafat, President of the Palestine Liberation Organization (PLO) and Mr. Yitzhak Rabin, Israeli Prime Minister. In that correspondence, the President of the PLO recognized "the right of the State of Israel to exist in peace and security" and made various other commitments. In reply, the Israeli Prime Minister informed him that, in the light of those commitments, "the Government of Israel has decided to recognize the PLO as the representative of the Palestinian people." The Israeli-Palestinian Interim Agreement on the West Bank and the Gaza Strip of 28 September 1995 also refers a number of times to the Palestinian people and its "legitimate rights" (Preamble, paras. 4, 7, 8; Article II, para. 2; Article III, paras. 1 and 3; Article XXII, para. 2). The Court considers that those rights include the right to self-determination, as the General Assembly has moreover recognized on a number of occasions (see, for example, resolution 58/163 of 22 December 2003).

119. The Court notes that the route of the wall as fixed by the Israeli Government includes within the "Closed Area" . . . some 80 per cent of the settlers living in the Occupied Palestinian Territory. Moreover, it is apparent . . . that the wall's sinuous route has been traced in such a way as to include within that area the great majority of the Israeli settlements in the occupied Palestinian Territory (including East Jerusalem). . . .

120. . . . The Court concludes [on the basis of international humanitarian law and Security Council resolutions] that the Israeli settlements in the Occupied Palestinian Territory (including East Jerusalem) have been established in breach of international law.

121. Whilst the Court notes the assurance given by Israel that the construction of the wall does not amount to annexation and that the wall is of a temporary nature . . . , it nevertheless cannot remain indifferent to certain fears expressed to it that the route of the wall will prejudge the future frontier between Israel and Palestine, and the fear that Israel may integrate the settlements and their means of access. The Court considers that the construction of the wall and its associated régime create a "*fait accompli*" on the ground that could well become permanent, in which case, and notwithstanding the formal characterization of the wall by Israel, it would be tantamount to *de facto* annexation.

122. The Court recalls moreover that, according to the report of the Secretary-General, the planned route would incorporate in the area between the Green Line and the wall more than 16 per cent of the territory of the West Bank. Around 80 per cent of the settlers living in the Occupied Palestinian Territory, that is 320,000 individuals, would reside in that area, as well as 237,000 Palestinians. Moreover, as a result of the construction of the wall, around 160,000 other Palestinians would reside in almost completely encircled communities. . . .

In other terms, the route chosen for the wall gives expression *in loco* to the illegal measures taken by Israel with regard to Jerusalem and the settlements, as deplored by the Security Council. . . . There is also a risk of further alterations to the demographic composition of the Occupied Palestinian Territory resulting from the construction of the wall inasmuch as it is contributing . . . to the departure of Palestinian populations from certain areas. That construction, along with measures taken previously, thus severely impedes the exercise by the Palestinian people of its right to self-determination, and is therefore a breach of Israel's obligation to respect that right. . . .

149. The Court notes that Israel is first obliged to comply with the international obligations it has breached by the construction of the wall in the Occupied Palestinian Territory. . . . Consequently, Israel is bound to comply with its obligation to respect the right of the Palestinian people to self-determination. . . .

155. The Court would observe that the obligations violated by Israel include certain obligations *erga omnes.* As the Court indicated in the *Barcelona Traction* case, such obligations are by their very nature "the concern of all States" and, "In view of the importance of the rights involved, all States can be held to have a legal interest in their protection." . . . The obligations *erga omnes* violated by Israel [include] the obligation to respect the right of the Palestinian people to self-determination. . . .

156. As regards [this obligation], the Court has already observed . . . that in the *East Timor* case, it described as "irreproachable" the assertion that "the right of peoples to self-determination, as it evolved from the Charter and from United Nations practice, has an *erga omnes* character". . . The Court would also recall that under the terms of General Assembly resolution 2625 (XXV), already mentioned above (see paragraph 88),

> Every State has the duty to promote, through joint and separate action, realization of the principle of equal rights and self-determination of peoples, in accordance with the provisions of the Charter, and to render assistance to the United Nations in carrying out the responsibilities entrusted to it by the Charter regarding the implementation of the principle. . . .

159. Given the character and the importance of the rights and obligations involved, the Court is of the view that all States are under an obligation not to recognize the illegal situation resulting from the construction of the wall in the Occupied Palestinian Territory, including in and around East Jerusalem. They are also under an obligation not to render aid or assistance in maintaining the situation created by such construction. It is also for all States, while respecting the United Nations Charter and international law, to see to it that any impediment, resulting from the construction of the wall, to the exercise by the Palestinian people of its right to self-determination is brought to an end. . .

162. The Court has reached the conclusion that the construction of the wall by Israel in the Occupied Palestinian Territory is contrary to international law and has stated the legal consequences that are to be drawn from that illegality. The Court considers itself bound to add that this construction must be placed in a more general context. Since 1947, the year when General Assembly resolution 181 (II) was adopted and the Mandate for Palestine was terminated, there has been a succession of armed conflicts, acts of indiscriminate violence and repressive measures on the former mandated territory. . . . Illegal actions and unilateral decisions have been taken on all sides, whereas, in the Court's view, this tragic situation can be brought to an end only through implementation in good faith of all relevant Security Council resolutions, in particular resolutions 242 (1967) and 338 (1973). The "Roadmap" approved by Security Council resolution 1515 (2003) represents the most recent of efforts to initiate negotiations to this end. The Court considers that it has a duty to draw the attention of the General Assembly, to which the present Opinion is addressed, to the need for these efforts to be encouraged with a view

to achieving as soon as possible, on the basis of international law, a negotiated solution to the outstanding problems and the establishment of a Palestinian State, existing side by side with Israel and its other neighbours, with peace and security for all in the region.

Given these treaty provisions, resolutions, and judicial decisions, what exactly is "self-determination"? Despite ready acceptance of self-determination as an international legal right, there is remarkable uncertainty as to the conditions, modalities, and consequences of its exercise. Consider the following comments:

> There still remains some difficulty as to what the expression "self-determination" itself means, or includes. Some writers decline to treat it as a right of an absolute nature, stressing that it must be considered within the context of the people or group demanding to exercise it. Presumably it connotes freedom of choice to be exercised by a dependent people through a plebiscite or some other method of ascertainment of the people's wishes. Another difficult problem is to determine which communities of human beings constitute "peoples" . . . for the purpose of enjoying the right of self-determination. Aspects such as common territory, common language, and common political aims may have to be considered. *Semble*, there must normally be a territorial unit corresponding to the people to which the right may be regarded as attaching. Beyond this, there is the problem of whether, and, if so, to what extent the right of self-determination will permit secession of part of the territory of a state. An unqualified right to secession, as a derivative of the right of self-determination, could lead to disruption of state systems. In part for this reason, it is controversial according to the most recent practice and weight of opinion whether minority indigenous peoples, or tribal groups in certain countries, e.g. Canada and Australia, are "peoples" entitled to self-determination.[54]

Note the reference in the above passage to self-determination and indigenous peoples. There remain few international instruments defining the rights of indigenous peoples per se. One of these is the International Labour Organization's Convention No 169 Concerning Indigenous and Tribal Peoples in Independent Countries,[55] which entered into force in 1991, but to which Canada is not a party. In relation to land rights, this treaty provides, *inter alia*:

> *Article 14*
> 1. The rights of ownership and possession of the peoples concerned over the lands which they traditionally occupy shall be recognised. In addition, measures shall be taken in appropriate cases to safeguard the right of the peoples concerned to use lands not exclusively occupied by them, but to which they have traditionally had access for their subsistence and traditional activities. Particular attention shall be paid to the situation of nomadic peoples and shifting cultivators in this respect.
>
> 2. Governments shall take steps as necessary to identify the lands which the peoples concerned traditionally occupy, and to guarantee effective protection of their rights of ownership and possession.

---

54 Ivan A Shearer, *Starke's International Law*, 11th ed (Toronto: Butterworths, 1994) at 113.
55 27 June 1989, 1650 UNTS 383, in force 5 September 1991.

3. Adequate procedures shall be established within the national legal system to resolve land claims by the peoples concerned.

Article 15

1. The rights of the peoples concerned to the natural resources pertaining to their lands shall be specially safeguarded. These rights include the right of these peoples to participate in the use, management and conservation of these resources. . . .

ILO Convention No 169 includes, however, no reference to "self-determination" as such, to the disappointment of many indigenous peoples, and by 2013, the convention had attracted only twenty-two ratifications, mostly in Latin America.

By comparison, consider the following provisions of the United Nations Declaration on the Rights of Indigenous Peoples, adopted by the UN General Assembly in September 2007:

United Nations Declaration on the Rights of Indigenous Peoples, GA Res 61/295 (2007)[56]

The General Assembly,

. . .

Acknowledging that the Charter of the United Nations, the International Covenant on Economic, Social and Cultural Rights and the International Covenant on Civil and Political Rights, as well as the Vienna Declaration and Programme of Action, affirm the fundamental importance of the right to self-determination of all peoples, by virtue of which they freely determine their political status and freely pursue their economic, social and cultural development,

Bearing in mind that nothing in this Declaration may be used to deny any peoples their right of self-determination, exercised in conformity with international law,

Convinced that the recognition of the rights of indigenous peoples in this Declaration will enhance harmonious and cooperative relations between the State and indigenous peoples . . . ,

Recognizing that the situation of indigenous peoples varies from region to region and from country to country and that the significance of national and regional particularities and various historical and cultural backgrounds should be taken into consideration,

Solemnly proclaims the following United Nations Declaration on the Rights of Indigenous Peoples as a standard of achievement to be pursued in a spirit of partnership and mutual respect,

. . .

Article 3

Indigenous peoples have the right to self-determination. By virtue of that right they freely determine their political status and freely pursue their economic, social and cultural development.

---

56 GA Res 61/295, UN Doc A/RES/61/295, reprinted in UN GAOR, 61st Sess, Supp No 49, vol III at 15–25, UN Doc A/61/49 (2007).

Article 4

Indigenous peoples, in exercising their right to self-determination, have the right to autonomy or self-government in matters relating to their internal and local affairs, as well as ways and means for financing their autonomous functions.

Article 5

Indigenous peoples have the right to maintain and strengthen their distinct political, legal, economic, social and cultural institutions, while retaining their right to participate fully, if they so choose, in the political, economic, social and cultural life of the State.

. . .

Article 9

Indigenous peoples and individuals have the right to belong to an indigenous community or nation, in accordance with the traditions and customs of the community or nation concerned. No discrimination of any kind may arise from the exercise of such a right.

Article 10

Indigenous peoples shall not be forcibly removed from their lands or territories. No relocation shall take place without the free, prior and informed consent of the indigenous peoples concerned and after agreement on just and fair compensation and, where possible, with the option of return.

. . .

Article 19

States shall consult and cooperate in good faith with the indigenous peoples concerned through their own representative institutions in order to obtain their free, prior and informed consent before adopting and implementing legislative or administrative measures that may affect them.

. . .

Article 25

Indigenous peoples have the right to maintain and strengthen their distinctive spiritual relationship with their traditionally owned or otherwise occupied and used lands, territories, waters and coastal seas and other resources and to uphold their responsibilities to future generations in this regard.

Article 26

1. Indigenous peoples have the right to the lands, territories and resources which they have traditionally owned, occupied or otherwise used or acquired.

2. Indigenous peoples have the right to own, use, develop and control the lands, territories and resources that they possess by reason of traditional ownership or other traditional occupation or use, as well as those which they have otherwise acquired.

3. States shall give legal recognition and protection to these lands, territories and resources. Such recognition shall be conducted with due respect to the customs, traditions and land tenure systems of the indigenous peoples concerned.

Article 27

States shall establish and implement, in conjunction with indigenous peoples concerned, a fair, independent, impartial, open and transparent process, giving due recognition to indigenous peoples' laws, traditions, customs and land tenure systems, to recognize and adjudicate the rights of indigenous peoples pertaining to their lands, territories and re-sources, including those which were traditionally owned or otherwise occupied or used. Indigenous peoples shall have the right to participate in this process.

Article 28

1. Indigenous peoples have the right to redress, by means that can include restitution or, when this is not possible, just, fair and equitable compensation, for the lands, territories and resources which they have traditionally owned or otherwise occupied or used, and which have been confiscated, taken, occupied, used or damaged without their free, prior and informed consent.

2. Unless otherwise freely agreed upon by the peoples concerned, compensation shall take the form of lands, territories and resources equal in quality, size and legal status or of monetary compensation or other appropriate redress.

. . .

Article 46

1. Nothing in this Declaration may be interpreted as implying for any State, people, group or person any right to engage in any activity or to perform any act contrary to the Char-ter of the United Nations or construed as authorizing or encouraging any action which would dismember or impair, totally or in part, the territorial integrity or political unity of sovereign and independent States.

2. In the exercise of the rights enunciated in the present Declaration, human rights and fundamental freedoms of all shall be respected. The exercise of the rights set forth in this Declaration shall be subject only to such limitations as are determined by law and in accordance with international human rights obligations. Any such limitations shall be non-discriminatory and strictly necessary solely for the purpose of securing due recogni-tion and respect for the rights and freedoms of others and for meeting the just and most compelling requirements of a democratic society. . . .

The Declaration's provisions on self-determination were controversial for some states, as were the provisions on lands, territories, and resources, and the provisions requir-ing free, prior, and informed consent rather than consultation. Negotiations reportedly reached a breakthrough in 2004 with the inclusion of a proposed preambular require-ment that the right of self-determination be exercised in accordance with principles of international law. Such a reference to "principles of international law" was apparently viewed by many states as ensuring that recognition of the right of self-determination of indigenous peoples would not threaten the territorial integrity of states fulfilling their international human rights obligations.[57] Yet, by 2007, in order to secure the declaration's

---

57 "Rights & Democracy Applauds Canadian Government Stand on Self-Determination for Canada's In-digenous Peoples," *Canadian Corporate Newswire* (20 September 2004).

adoption by the greatest number of states, a more robust operative paragraph had to be included in the final version of the Declaration (see Article 46(1) above). Canada, along with Australia, New Zealand, and the United States, voted against the adoption of the Declaration in the General Assembly. In explaining its position, Canada stated:

> . . . Canada's position has remained consistent and based on principle. We have stated publicly that Canada has significant concerns with respect to the wording of the current text, including the provisions on lands, territories and resources; on free, prior and informed consent when used as a veto; on self- government without recognition of the importance of negotiations; on intellectual property; on military issues; and on the need to achieve an appropriate balance between the rights and obligations of indigenous peoples, Member States and third parties. . . .[58]

On 12 November 2010, Canada announced that it would henceforth support the Declaration as an "aspirational document" and a "non-legally binding document that does not reflect customary international law nor change Canadian laws." While expressly noting that the above concerns "are well known and remain," the government also stated "[w]e are now confident that Canada can interpret the principles expressed in the Declaration in a manner that is consistent with our Constitution and legal framework."[59] The United States expressed support for the Declaration a month later, while Australia and New Zealand reversed their positions in 2009 and 2010 respectively.

Does Article 3 of the Declaration suggest that indigenous peoples have the right to sovereignty in international law? Consider in particular Article 4, as well as the Declaration's provisions relating to land and territories. Do any of these suggest a right for indigenous peoples to accede to sovereignty and establish separate states on such lands? Or, in light of Article 46 of the Declaration, does "self-determination" as used in this instrument refer to a right exercisable *within* existing states — a form of "internal" self-determination?

The core legal elements of self-determination, as well as the distinction between so-called internal and external self-determination, were considered at length in the following decision of the Supreme Court of Canada.

Reference Re Secession of Quebec, [1998] 2 SCR 217

[The defeat of the second referendum on Quebec independence in 1995 by only the closest of margins prompted the Government of Canada to ask the Supreme Court for its opinion on the application of the international law of self-determination to the potential secession of a sub-national unit such as Quebec from Canada.]

The Court:

. . . The questions posed by the Governor in Council by way of Order in Council P.C. 1996-1497, dated September 30, 1996, read as follows:

---

58 Canada's statement is recorded in the transcript of the General Assembly's 107th Plenary Meeting, held on 13 September 2007, UN Doc A/61/PV.107 at 12–13.

59 Canada, Department of Aboriginal Affairs and Northern Development, "Canada's Statement of Support on the United Nations Declaration on the Rights of Indigenous Peoples" (12 November 2010), online: www.aadnc-aandc.gc.ca/eng/1309374239861/1309374546142.

. . . 2. Does international law give the National Assembly, legislature or government of Quebec the right to effect the secession of Quebec from Canada unilaterally? In this regard, is there a right to self-determination under international law that would give the National Assembly, legislature or government of Quebec the right to effect the secession of Quebec from Canada unilaterally? . . .

(1) Secession at International Law

111. It is clear that international law does not specifically grant component parts of sovereign states the legal right to secede unilaterally from their "parent" state. This is acknowledged by the experts who provided their opinions on behalf of both the *amicus curiae* and the Attorney General of Canada.[60] Given the lack of specific authorization for unilateral secession, proponents of the existence of such a right at international law are therefore left to attempt to found their argument (i) on the proposition that unilateral secession is not specifically prohibited and that what is not specifically prohibited is inferentially permitted; or (ii) on the implied duty of states to recognize the legitimacy of secession brought about by the exercise of the well-established international law right of "a people" to self-determination. The *amicus curiae* addressed the right of self-determination, but submitted that it was not applicable to the circumstances of Quebec within the Canadian federation, irrespective of the existence or non-existence of a referendum result in favour of secession. We agree on this point with the *amicus curiae*, for reasons that we will briefly develop.

(a) Absence of a Specific Prohibition

112. International law contains neither a right of unilateral secession nor the explicit denial of such a right, although such a denial is, to some extent, implicit in the exceptional circumstances required for secession to be permitted under the right of a people to self-determination, e.g., the right of secession that arises in the exceptional situation of an oppressed or colonial people, discussed below. As will be seen, international law places great importance on the territorial integrity of nation states and, by and large, leaves the creation of a new state to be determined by the domestic law of the existing state of which the seceding entity presently forms a part (R. Y. Jennings, *The Acquisition of Territory in International Law* (1963), at pp. 8–9). Where, as here, unilateral secession would be incompatible with the domestic Constitution, international law is likely to accept that conclusion subject to the right of peoples to self-determination, a topic to which we now turn.

(b) The Right of a People to Self-determination

113. While international law generally regulates the conduct of nation states, it does, in some specific circumstances, also recognize the "rights" of entities other than nation states — such as the right of a people to self-determination.

---

60 [The expert opinions provided by James Crawford, Luzius Wildhaber, George Abi Saab, Thomas Franck, Rosalyn Higgins, Alain Pellet, Malcolm Shaw, Christian Tomuschat, and Christine Chinkin can be found in Anne F Bayefsky, ed, *Self-Determination in International Law: Quebec and Lessons Learned: Legal Opinions* (The Hague: Kluwer Law International, 2000).]

114. The existence of the right of a people to self-determination is now so widely recognized in international conventions that the principle has acquired a status beyond "convention" and is considered a general principle of international law. (A. Cassese, *Self-determination of peoples: A legal reappraisal* (1995), at pp. 171–72; K. Doehring, "Self-Determination," in B. Simma, ed., *The Charter of the United Nations: A Commentary* (1994), at p. 70.). . . .

117. This basic principle of self-determination has been carried forward and addressed in so many U.N. conventions and resolutions that, as noted by Doehring, *supra*, at p. 60:

> The sheer number of resolutions concerning the right of self-determination makes their enumeration impossible. . . .

122. As will be seen, international law expects that the right to self-determination will be exercised by peoples within the framework of existing sovereign states and consistently with the maintenance of the territorial integrity of those states. Where this is not possible, in the exceptional circumstances discussed below, a right of secession may arise.

(i) Defining "Peoples"

123. International law grants the right to self-determination to "peoples." Accordingly, access to the right requires the threshold step of characterizing as a people the group seeking self-determination. However, as the right to self-determination has developed by virtue of a combination of international agreements and conventions, coupled with state practice, with little formal elaboration of the definition of "peoples," the result has been that the precise meaning of the term "people" remains somewhat uncertain.

124. It is clear that "a people" may include only a portion of the population of an existing state. The right to self-determination has developed largely as a human right, and is generally used in documents that simultaneously contain references to "nation" and "state." The juxtaposition of these terms is indicative that the reference to "people" does not necessarily mean the entirety of a state's population. To restrict the definition of the term to the population of existing states would render the granting of a right to self-determination largely duplicative, given the parallel emphasis within the majority of the source documents on the need to protect the territorial integrity of existing states, and would frustrate its remedial purpose.

125. While much of the Quebec population certainly shares many of the characteristics (such as a common language and culture) that would be considered in determining whether a specific group is a "people," as do other groups within Quebec and/or Canada, it is not necessary to explore this legal characterization to resolve Question 2 appropriately. Similarly, it is not necessary for the Court to determine whether, should a Quebec people exist within the definition of public international law, such a people encompasses the entirety of the provincial population or just a portion thereof. Nor is it necessary to examine the position of the aboriginal population within Quebec. As the following discussion of the scope of the right to self-determination will make clear, whatever be the correct application of the definition of people(s) in this context, their right of self-determination cannot in the present circumstances be said to ground a right to unilateral secession.

(ii) Scope of the Right to Self-determination

126. The recognized sources of international law establish that the right to self-determination of a people is normally fulfilled through internal self-determination—a people's pursuit of its political, economic, social and cultural development within the framework of an existing state. A right to external self-determination (which in this case potentially takes the form of the assertion of a right to unilateral secession) arises in only the most extreme of cases and, even then, under carefully defined circumstances. External self-determination can be defined as in the following statement from the Declaration on Friendly Relations as

> [t]he establishment of a sovereign and independent State, the free association or integration with an independent State or the emergence into any other political status freely determined by a people constitute modes of implementing the right of self-determination by that people.

127. The international law principle of self-determination has evolved within a framework of respect for the territorial integrity of existing states. The various international documents that support the existence of a people's right to self-determination also contain parallel statements supportive of the conclusion that the exercise of such a right must be sufficiently limited to prevent threats to an existing state's territorial integrity or the stability of relations between sovereign states.

128. The Declaration on Friendly Relations, the Vienna Declaration and the Declaration on the Occasion of the Fiftieth Anniversary of the United Nations are specific. They state, immediately after affirming a people's right to determine political, economic, social and cultural issues, that such rights are not to

> be construed as authorizing or encouraging any action that would dismember or impair, totally or in part, the territorial integrity or political unity of sovereign and independent States conducting themselves in compliance with the principle of equal rights and self-determination of peoples and thus possessed of a Government representing the whole people belonging to the territory without distinction. . . . [Emphasis added.]

129. Similarly, while the concluding document of the Vienna Meeting in 1989 of the Conference on Security and Co-operation in Europe on the follow-up to the Helsinki Final Act again refers to peoples having the right to determine "their internal and *external* political status" (emphasis added), that statement is immediately followed by express recognition that the participating states will at all times act, as stated in the Helsinki Final Act, "in conformity with the purposes and principles of the Charter of the United Nations and with the relevant norms of international law, *including those relating to territorial integrity of States*" [Emphasis added]. Principle 5 of the concluding document states that the participating states (including Canada):

> . . . confirm their commitment strictly and effectively to observe the principle of the territorial integrity of States. They will refrain from any violation of this principle and thus from any action aimed by direct or indirect means, in contravention of the purposes and principles of the Charter of the United Nations, other obligations under

international law or the provisions of the [Helsinki] Final Act, at violating the territorial integrity, political independence or the unity of a State. *No actions or situations in contravention of this principle will be recognized as legal by the participating States.* [Emphasis added.]

Accordingly, the reference in the Helsinki Final Act to a people determining its external political status is interpreted to mean the expression of a people's external political status through the government of the existing state, save in the exceptional circumstances discussed below. As noted by Cassese, supra, at p. 287, given the history and textual structure of this document, its reference to external self-determination simply means that "no territorial or other change can be brought about by the central authorities of a State that is contrary to the will of the whole people of that State."

130. While the International Covenant on Economic, Social and Cultural Rights and the International Covenant on Civil and Political Rights do not specifically refer to the protection of territorial integrity, they both define the ambit of the right to self-determination in terms that are normally attainable within the framework of an existing state. There is no necessary incompatibility between the maintenance of the territorial integrity of existing states, including Canada, and the right of a "people" to achieve a full measure of self-determination. A state whose government represents the whole of the people or peoples resident within its territory, on a basis of equality and without discrimination, and respects the principles of self-determination in its own internal arrangements, is entitled to the protection under international law of its territorial integrity.

(iii) Colonial and Oppressed Peoples

131. Accordingly, the general state of international law with respect to the right to self-determination is that the right operates within the overriding protection granted to the territorial integrity of "parent" states. However, as noted by Cassese, *supra*, at p. 334, there are certain defined contexts within which the right to the self-determination of peoples does allow that right to be exercised "externally," which, in the context of this Reference, would potentially mean secession:

> ... the right to external self-determination, which entails the possibility of choosing (or restoring) independence, has only been bestowed upon two classes of peoples (those under colonial rule or foreign occupation), based upon the assumption that both classes make up entities that are inherently distinct from the colonialist Power and the occupant Power and that their 'territorial integrity', all but destroyed by the colonialist or occupying Power, should be fully restored. . . .

132. The right of colonial peoples to exercise their right to self-determination by breaking away from the "imperial" power is now undisputed, but is irrelevant to this Reference.

133. The other clear case where a right to external self-determination accrues is where a people is subject to alien subjugation, domination or exploitation outside a colonial context. This recognition finds its roots in the Declaration on Friendly Relations:

> Every State has the duty to promote, through joint and separate action, realization of the principle of equal rights and self-determination of peoples, in accordance with the

provisions of the Charter, and to render assistance to the United Nations in carrying out the responsibilities entrusted to it by the Charter regarding the implementation of the principle, in order:

(a) To promote friendly relations and co-operation among States; and

(b) To bring a speedy end to colonialism, having due regard to the freely expressed will of the peoples concerned;

and bearing in mind that subjection of peoples to alien subjugation, domination and exploitation constitutes a violation of the principle, as well as a denial of fundamental human rights, and is contrary to the Charter.

134. A number of commentators have further asserted that the right to self-determination may ground a right to unilateral secession in a third circumstance. Although this third circumstance has been described in several ways, the underlying proposition is that, when a people is blocked from the meaningful exercise of its right to self-determination internally, it is entitled, as a last resort, to exercise it by secession. The Vienna Declaration requirement that governments represent "the whole people belonging to the territory without distinction of any kind" adds credence to the assertion that such a complete blockage may potentially give rise to a right of secession.

135. Clearly, such a circumstance parallels the other two recognized situations in that the ability of a people to exercise its right to self-determination internally is somehow being totally frustrated. While it remains unclear whether this third proposition actually reflects an established international law standard, it is unnecessary for present purposes to make that determination. Even assuming that the third circumstance is sufficient to create a right to unilateral secession under international law, the current Quebec context cannot be said to approach such a threshold. As stated by the *amicus curiae*, Addendum to the factum of the *amicus curiae*, at paras. 15–16:

[Translation] 15. The Quebec people is not the victim of attacks on its physical existence or integrity, or of a massive violation of its fundamental rights. The Quebec people is manifestly not, in the opinion of the *amicus curiae*, an oppressed people.

16. For close to 40 of the last 50 years, the Prime Minister of Canada has been a Quebecer. During this period, Quebecers have held from time to time all the most important positions in the federal Cabinet. During the 8 years prior to June 1997, the Prime Minister and the Leader of the Official Opposition in the House of Commons were both Quebecers. At present, the Prime Minister of Canada, the Right Honourable Chief Justice and two other members of the Court, the Chief of Staff of the Canadian Armed Forces and the Canadian ambassador to the United States, not to mention the Deputy Secretary-General of the United Nations, are all Quebecers. The international achievements of Quebecers in most fields of human endeavour are too numerous to list. Since the dynamism of the Quebec people has been directed toward the business sector, it has been clearly successful in Quebec, the rest of Canada and abroad.

136. The population of Quebec cannot plausibly be said to be denied access to government. Quebecers occupy prominent positions within the government of Canada. Residents of the province freely make political choices and pursue economic, social and

cultural development within Quebec, across Canada, and throughout the world. The population of Quebec is equitably represented in legislative, executive and judicial institutions. In short, to reflect the phraseology of the international documents that address the right to self-determination of peoples, Canada is a "sovereign and independent state conducting itself in compliance with the principle of equal rights and self-determination of peoples and thus possessed of a government representing the whole people belonging to the territory without distinction."

137. The continuing failure to reach agreement on amendments to the Constitution, while a matter of concern, does not amount to a denial of self-determination. In the absence of amendments to the Canadian Constitution, we must look at the constitutional arrangements presently in effect, and we cannot conclude under current circumstances that those arrangements place Quebecers in a disadvantaged position within the scope of the international law rule.

138. In summary, the international law right to self-determination only generates, at best, a right to external self-determination in situations of former colonies; where a people is oppressed, as for example under foreign military occupation; or where a definable group is denied meaningful access to government to pursue their political, economic, social and cultural development. In all three situations, the people in question are entitled to a right to external self-determination because they have been denied the ability to exert internally their right to self-determination. Such exceptional circumstances are manifestly inapplicable to Quebec under existing conditions. Accordingly, neither the population of the province of Quebec, even if characterized in terms of "people" or "peoples," nor its representative institutions, the National Assembly, the legislature or government of Quebec, possess a right, under international law, to secede unilaterally from Canada. . . .

140. As stated, an argument advanced by the *amicus curiae* on this branch of the Reference was that, while international law may not ground a positive right to unilateral secession in the context of Quebec, international law equally does not prohibit secession and, in fact, international recognition would be conferred on such a political reality if it emerged, for example, via effective control of the territory of what is now the province of Quebec.

141. It is true that international law may well, depending on the circumstances, adapt to recognize a political and/or factual reality, regardless of the legality of the steps leading to its creation. However, as mentioned at the outset, effectivity, as such, does not have any real applicability to Question 2, which asks whether a right to unilateral secession exists. . . .

The Supreme Court of Canada's view of the legal right of self-determination appears to be broadly supported. Referring to the Court's opinion as well as other state practice and *opinio juris*, Professor James Crawford submits that the following summary of the law of self-determination is "supported by current practice":

1) International law recognizes the principle of self-determination.
2) It is, however, not a right applicable just to any group of people desiring political independence or self-government. Like sovereignty, it is a legal principle. . . . It applies as a matter of right only after the unit of self-determination has been determined.

3) The units to which the principle applies are in general those territories established and recognized as separate political units; in particular it applies to the following: (a) trust and mandated territories, and territories treated as non-self-governing under Chapter XI of the Charter; (b) States, excluding for the purposes of the self-determination rule those parts of States which are themselves self-determination units as defined; (c) other territories forming distinct political-geographical areas, whose inhabitants are arbitrarily excluded from any share in the government either of the region or of the State to which they belong, with the result that the territory becomes in effect, with respect to the remainder of the State, non-self-governing; and (d) any other territories or situations to which self-determination is applied by the parties as an appropriate solution.

4) Where a self-determination unit is not already a State, it[s people] has a right of self-determination: that is, a right to choose its own political organization . . . without coercion and on a basis of equality.

5) Self-determination can result either in the independence of the self-determining unit as a separate State, or in its incorporation into or association with another State on a basis of political equality for the people of the unit.

6) By definition, matters of self-determination are not within the domestic jurisdiction of the metropolitan State.

7) Where a self-determination unit is a State, the principle of self-determination is represented by the rule against intervention in the internal affairs of that State, and in particular in the choice of the form of government of the State.[61]

In evaluating the Supreme Court of Canada's opinion on the interaction of the law and the politics of external self-determination, consider the outcome of the disputes in the four cases in which the ICJ has confirmed the existence of a legal right to self-determination — *Namibia*, *Western Sahara*, *East Timor*, and the *Israeli Wall* case. Namibia gained independence from South Africa in 1990, twenty-five years after the UN General Assembly terminated South Africa's mandate, nineteen years after the ICJ's decision affirming this termination and after a long guerrilla war and various UN-brokered agreements. East Timor became an independent state in 2002, twenty-seven years after the Indonesian invasion of the island and following decades of severe oppression and resistance, a tumultuous referendum on the region's future in 1999, further conflict, a multinational military intervention and the deployment of a transitional UN administration. The Israeli-Palestinian issue remains unresolved, and indeed the ICJ's advisory opinion has been rejected by Israel and coolly received by its allies. Finally, Morocco remains the occupying power in Western Sahara decades after the ICJ decision and the Moroccan invasion. A guerrilla war contesting Moroccan control ended in 1991 with a UN-brokered ceasefire, but the planned referendum on Western Sahara's future has been repeatedly postponed since then, stalling on the question of which inhabitants of the territory should be entitled to vote.

More recently, the issue of self-determination has arisen in relation to the attempt by Kosovo to establish itself as a separate state in 2008. Consider the following extract from

---

61 James Crawford, *The Creation of States in International Law*, 2d ed (Oxford: Clarendon Press, 2006) at 127–28.

the ICJ's advisory opinion on the legality of Kosovo's unilateral declaration of independence from Serbia in 2008:

Accordance with International Law of the Unilateral Declaration of Independence in Respect of Kosovo, **Advisory Opinion, [2010] ICJ Rep 403**

[In this opinion, the International Court of Justice began by making clear that the 2008 declaration of independence by Kosovo had to be considered within its factual context. This led the Court to consider the relevant characteristics of the framework put in place by Security Council resolution 1244 (1999) to ensure the interim administration of Kosovo, as well as the regulations promulgated thereunder by the United Nations Mission in Kosovo (UNMIK). The Court then considered the developments relating to the so-called final status process in the years preceding Kosovo's declaration of independence, before turning to the events of 17 February 2008:]

IV. THE QUESTION WHETHER THE DECLARATION OF INDEPENDENCE IS IN ACCORDANCE WITH INTERNATIONAL LAW

78. The Court now turns to the substance of the request submitted by the General Assembly. The Court recalls that it has been asked by the General Assembly to assess the accordance of the declaration of independence of 17 February 2008 with "international law" (resolution 63/3 of the General Assembly, 8 October 2008). The Court will first turn its attention to certain questions concerning the lawfulness of declarations of independence under general international law, against the background of which the question posed falls to be considered, and Security Council resolution 1244 (1999) is to be understood and applied. . . .

79. During the eighteenth, nineteenth and early twentieth centuries, there were numerous instances of declarations of independence, often strenuously opposed by the State from which independence was being declared. Sometimes a declaration resulted in the creation of a new State, at others it did not. In no case, however, does the practice of States as a whole suggest that the act of promulgating the declaration was regarded as contrary to international law. On the contrary, State practice during this period points clearly to the conclusion that international law contained no prohibition of declarations of independence. During the second half of the twentieth century, the international law of self-determination developed in such a way as to create a right to independence for the peoples of non-self-governing territories and peoples subject to alien subjugation, domination and exploitation. . . . A great many new States have come into existence as a result of the exercise of this right. There were, however, also instances of declarations of independence outside this context. The practice of States in these latter cases does not point to the emergence in international law of a new rule prohibiting the making of a declaration of independence in such cases.

80. Several participants in the proceedings before the Court have contended that a prohibition of unilateral declarations of independence is implicit in the principle of territorial integrity. The Court recalls that the principle of territorial integrity is an important part of the international legal order and is enshrined in the Charter of the United Nations, in

particular in Article 2, paragraph 4, which provides that: "All Members shall refrain in their international relations from the threat or use of force against the territorial integrity or political independence of any State, or in any other manner inconsistent with the Purposes of the United Nations." In General Assembly resolution 2625 (XXV), entitled "Declaration on Principles of International Law concerning Friendly Relations and Co-operation among States in Accordance with the Charter of the United Nations", which reflects customary international law, the General Assembly reiterated "[t]he principle that States shall refrain in their international relations from the threat or use of force against the territorial integrity or political independence of any State". This resolution then enumerated various obligations incumbent upon States to refrain from violating the territorial integrity of other sovereign States. In the same vein, the Final Act of the Helsinki Conference on Security and Co-operation in Europe of 1 August 1975 (the Helsinki Conference) stipulated that "[t]he participating States will respect the territorial integrity of each of the participating States" (Art. IV). Thus, the scope of the principle of territorial integrity is confined to the sphere of relations between States.

81. Several participants have invoked resolutions of the Security Council condemning particular declarations of independence: see, *inter alia*, Security Council resolutions 216 (1965) and 217 (1965), concerning Southern Rhodesia; Security Council resolution 541 (1983), concerning northern Cyprus; and Security Council resolution 787 (1992), concerning the Republika Srpska. The Court notes, however, that in all of those instances the Security Council was making a determination as regards the concrete situation existing at the time that those declarations of independence were made; the illegality attached to the declarations of independence thus stemmed not from the unilateral character of these declarations as such, but from the fact that they were, or would have been, connected with the unlawful use of force or other egregious violations of norms of general international law, in particular those of a peremptory character *(jus cogens)*. In the context of Kosovo, the Security Council has never taken this position. The exceptional character of the resolutions enumerated above appears to the Court to confirm that no general prohibition against unilateral declarations of independence may be inferred from the practice of the Security Council.

82. A number of participants in the present proceedings have claimed, although in almost every instance only as a secondary argument, that the population of Kosovo has the right to create an independent State either as a manifestation of a right to self-determination or pursuant to what they described as a right of "remedial secession" in the face of the situation in Kosovo. The Court has already noted (see paragraph 79 above) that one of the major developments of international law during the second half of the twentieth century has been the evolution of the right of self-determination. Whether, outside the context of non-self-governing territories and peoples subject to alien subjugation, domination and exploitation, the international law of self-determination confers upon part of the population of an existing State a right to separate from that State is, however, a subject on which radically different views were expressed by those taking part in the proceedings and expressing a position on the question. Similar differences existed regarding whether international law provides for a right of "remedial secession" and, if so, in what circumstances. There was also a sharp difference of views as to whether the cir-

cumstances which some participants maintained would give rise to a right of "remedial secession" were actually present in Kosovo.

83. The Court considers that it is not necessary to resolve these questions in the present case. The General Assembly has requested the Court's opinion only on whether or not the declaration of independence is in accordance with international law. Debates regarding the extent of the right of self-determination and the existence of any right of "remedial secession", however, concern the right to separate from a State. As the Court has already noted . . . , and as almost all participants agreed, that issue is beyond the scope of the question posed by the General Assembly. To answer that question, the Court need only determine whether the declaration of independence violated either general international law or the *lex specialis* created by Security Council resolution 1244 (1999).

84. For the reasons already given, the Court considers that general international law contains no applicable prohibition of declarations of independence. Accordingly, it concludes that the declaration of independence of 17 February 2008 did not violate general international law. Having arrived at that conclusion, the Court now turns to the legal relevance of Security Council resolution 1244, adopted on 10 June 1999.

[The Court went on to conclude that the declaration of independence of 17 February 2008 did not violate Security Council resolution 1244 (1999), either, such that "the adoption of that declaration did not violate any applicable rule of international law."]

Does the ICJ's technical approach to the question addressed to it do much to elucidate the law governing self-determination? Note the Court's reference to the "radically different views [expressed] by those taking part in the proceedings" on "[w]hether, outside the context of non-self-governing territories and peoples subject to alien subjugation, domination and exploitation, the international law of self-determination confers upon part of the population of an existing State a right to separate from that State" or "whether international law provides for a right of 'remedial secession.'" While the Court purports not to resolve issues related to self-determination in this case, what are the implications of its observations regarding the divergent views of states for the customary status of a right of self-determination outside the colonial and alien subjugation contexts?

7) Other Modes of Territorial Transfer

The other key forms of transfer of territorial sovereignty through political events are cession, renunciation, and abandonment. Unlike conquest, these three processes remain valid bases for the transfer of sovereign title to territory. Consider the following description of cession, which essentially entails the transfer of territory by agreement: "A right to territory may be conferred by treaty, provided the transferee takes it in accordance with the treaty. An actual transfer is not required. The date on which title changes will normally be the date on which the treaty comes into force."[62]

---

62 *Brownlie's Principles*, above note 13 at 226–27.

Consider also these comments: "The cession of a territory may be voluntary, or it may be under compulsion as a result of a war conducted successfully by the state to which the territory is ceded. . . . A cession by treaty is void where the conclusion of the treaty has been procured by the threat or use of force in violation of the principles of international law embodied in the United Nations Charter."[63]

Recall also Articles 49 to 52 of the Vienna Convention on the Law of Treaties, which, as we have seen in Chapter 2, provide for the invalidity of treaties brought about by fraud, corruption, coercion, or the threat or use of force in violation of the UN Charter.

What is the current legal effect of fraudulent or coerced treaties of cession that pre-date these modern instruments? Again, the doctrine of intertemporal law requires us to consider the state of international law at the time of conclusion of such treaties. While the prohibition of coercion by force in customary international law likely only dates back to the third or fourth decade of the twentieth century, rules precluding the validity of treaties procured by fraud or non-military coercion may have existed much earlier at customary international law. Consider the following description of the African experience:

> Even when conquests. . . were not undertaken [in Africa], effective colonial rule was im-posed by "treaties of protection" between African rulers and European powers, usually after a war, through coercion, intimidation, deceit, or any combination thereof. . . .
>
> It is difficult, if not impossible, to sustain the legality of the "treaties of protection" even under extant European law at the time. Treaty law was clear about who could enter into a treaty and what conditions gave it binding authority. Only states had treaty-making power by virtue of their sovereignty. A treaty had to have the mutual consent of the con-tracting parties and that consent had to be real and given under absolute freedom for the treaty's validity, provided that defeat in war and the subsequent cession of territory under duress did not invalidate a treaty. Even if consent was real among the parties, a treaty was not binding if the "consent was given in error, or under a delusion produced by a fraud." Invalidity extended to treaties obtained by intimidation. Many of the treaties of protection were obtained by intimidation, fraud, mistake or error because the parties misunder-stood each other, or without real or mutual consent. In addition, the treaties were invalid because European law did not recognize African political entities as states, with treaty-making power, and the rulers of those entities as heads of state; they were mere "chiefs" of "tribes." Such treaties would certainly be illegal if judged by the principles of current treaty law which is based on the Vienna Convention on the Law of Treaties. One African scholar has argued that these principles, which existed then, invalidated the "treaties."[64]

Despite their often unsavoury pedigrees, colonial treaties of cession continue to have modern international legal consequences. Consider the following excerpt from a decision of the ICJ that we have already considered in the context of prescriptive title, above.

---

63   Shearer, above note 53 at 153.
64   Mutua, above note 6 at 1131 and 1133.

Land and Maritime Boundary between Cameroon and Nigeria (Cameroon v Nigeria: Equatorial Guinea Intervening), Judgment, [2002] ICJ Rep 303

[Cameroon instituted proceedings against Nigeria in 1994 concerning a dispute relating to sovereignty over the Bakassi Peninsula in the Gulf of Guinea. Cameroon took the position that the Anglo-German Agreement of 11 March 1913 fixed the course of the relevant boundary, placing the Bakassi Peninsula on the German side of the boundary (and thus in modern Cameroon). It was, however, recognized that during the 1880s, European states had entered into many treaties with local rulers, with Great Britain alone having concluded some 350 treaties with the local chiefs of the Niger delta. Among these was a treaty concluded with the Kings and Chiefs of Old Calabar in 1884; however, this treaty did not specify the territory to which the British Crown was to extend "gracious favour and protection," nor did it indicate the territories over which each of the Kings and Chiefs exercised his powers. Before the International Court of Justice, Nigeria argued that this treaty only conferred limited rights on Great Britain and in no way transferred sovereignty to Great Britain over the territories of the Kings and Chiefs of Old Calabar. Thus, since Great Britain did not have sovereignty over those territories in 1913, it could not have ceded them to a third party, namely Germany, in the Anglo-German Agreement of 11 March 1913:]

204. Nigeria has contended that the very title of the 1884 Treaty and the reference in Article I to the undertaking of "protection," shows that Britain had no entitlement to do more than protect, and in particular had no entitlement to cede the territory concerned to third States. . . .

205. The Court calls attention to the fact that the international legal status of a "Treaty of Protection" entered into under the law obtaining at the time cannot be deduced from its title alone. Some treaties of protection were entered into with entities which retained thereunder a previously existing sovereignty under international law. This was the case whether the protected party was henceforth termed "protectorat" (as in the case of Morocco, Tunisia and Madagascar (1885; 1895) in their treaty relations with France) or "a protected State" (as in the case of Bahrain and Qatar in their treaty relations with Great Britain). In sub-Saharan Africa, however, treaties termed "treaties of protection" were entered into not with States, but rather with important indigenous rulers exercising local rule over identifiable areas of territory. In relation to a treaty of this kind in another part of the world, Max Huber, sitting as sole arbitrator in the *Island of Palmas* case, explained that such a treaty

> is not an agreement between equals; it is rather a form of internal organisation of a colonial territory, on the basis of autonomy of the natives . . . And thus suzerainty over the native States becomes the basis of territorial sovereignty as towards other members of the community of nations. (RIIA, Vol. II, pp. 858–59.)

The Court points out that these concepts also found expression in the *Western Sahara* Advisory Opinion. There the Court stated that in territories that were not *terra nullius*, but were inhabited by tribes or people having a social and political organization, "agreements concluded with local rulers . . . were regarded as derivative roots of title"

(*Western Sahara, Advisory Opinion*, I.C.J. Reports 1975, p. 39, para. 80). Even if this mode of acquisition does not reflect current international law, the principle of inter-temporal law requires that the legal consequences of the treaties concluded at that time in the Niger delta be given effect today, in the present dispute. . . .

207. In the view of the Court many factors point to the 1884 Treaty signed with the Kings and Chiefs of Old Calabar as not establishing an international protectorate. It was one of a multitude in a region where the local Rulers were not regarded as States. Indeed, apart from the parallel declarations of various lesser Chiefs agreeing to be bound by the 1884 Treaty, there is not even convincing evidence of a central federal power. There appears in Old Calabar rather to have been individual town-ships, headed by Chiefs, who regarded themselves as owing a general allegiance to more important Kings and Chiefs. Further, from the outset Britain regarded itself as administering the territories comprised in the 1884 Treaty, and not just protecting them. Consul Johnston reported in 1888 that "the country between the boundary of Lagos and the German boundary of Cameroons" was "administered by Her Majesty's Consular Officers, under various Orders in Council." The fact that a delegation was sent to London by the Kings and Chiefs of Old Calabar in 1913 to discuss matters of land tenure cannot be considered as implying international personality. It simply confirms the British administration by indirect rule.

Nigeria itself has been unable to point to any role, in matters relevant to the present case, played by the Kings and Chiefs of Old Calabar after the conclusion of the 1884 Treaty. In responding to a question of a Member of the Court Nigeria stated "It is not pos-sible to say with clarity and certainty what happened to the international legal personality of the Kings and Chiefs of Old Calabar after 1885." . . .

208. As to when the Kings and Chiefs ceased to exist as a separate entity, Nigeria told the Court it "is not a question susceptible of a clear-cut answer." . . .

Moreover, the Court has been presented with no evidence of any protest in 1913 by the Kings and Chiefs of Old Calabar; nor of any action by them to pass territory to Nigeria as it emerged to independence in 1960.

209. The Court thus concludes that, under the law at the time, Great Britain was in a pos-ition in 1913 to determine its boundaries with Germany in respect of Nigeria, including in the southern section.

In what respects do the propositions of late-nineteenth century treaty law relied on by the Court in this case differ from those asserted by W Mutua in the quotation appearing immediately above the case excerpt? Note that the Court did not consider the current views of the local population, many of whom considered themselves Nigerian. This fact contrib-uted to Nigeria's delay in relinquishing control over the Bakassi Peninsula until 2008.[65]

If cession depends on a treaty followed by actual transfer of control, may territory be transferred without such an agreement? Consider the concepts of renunciation and

---

65 "Nigeria Cedes Bakassi to Cameroon," *BBC News* (14 August 2008), online: http://news.bbc.co.uk/2/hi/africa/7559895.stm.

abandonment, both instances where a state unilaterally repudiates its title to territory. In the case of renunciation, the mantle of sovereignty devolves directly from the renouncing state to another state. In the case of abandonment, no other state immediately assumes sovereignty and the land is said to revert to *terra nullius*. Consider this discussion:

> It is possible for states to renounce title over territory in circumstances in which the subject-matter does not thereby become *terra nullius*. This distinguishes renunciation from abandonment. Furthermore, there is no element of reciprocity, and no commitment to transfer, as in the case of a treaty of cession. Renunciation may be recognition that another state now has title or an agreement to confer a power of disposition to be exercised by another state or a group of states. . . .
>
> . . . Abandonment refers to a situation where a state is held to have surrendered its title, converting the territory to *res nullius*, before another state establishes its own title by way of lawful allocation or effective occupation. In the case of abandonment, there is no usurpation of sovereignty since there are no contemporaneous competing claims . . . But because of the need to maintain stability and to avoid temptations to "squatting," abandonment is not to be presumed. Accordingly, very little evidence of *effectivités* will be required to prove maintenance of title, particularly in regard to remote and uninhabited areas.[66]

C. ACQUISITION OR LOSS OF SOVEREIGN TERRITORY BY REASON OF GEOMORPHOLOGY

Political events giving rise to sovereign title over territory are the most important means by which states acquire land. In rare instances, however, geographical configurations, and changes thereto, may affect the extent of a state's territory. Here, we discuss briefly accretion and its opposite, erosion, as well as the role, if any, played by the concept of geographic "contiguity."

The legal significance of accretion and erosion has been described as follows:

> Title by accretion occurs where new territory is added, mainly through natural causes, which can be fluvial action or otherwise (e.g. wind blown sand), to territory already under the sovereignty of the acquiring state. No formal act or assertion of title is necessary. It is immaterial whether the process of accretion has been gradual or imperceptible, as in the normal case of alluvial deposits or alluvial formation of islands, or whether it has been produced by a sudden and abrupt transfer of soil, provided that this has been embedded, and was not in any event identifiable as originating from another location.[67]

While likely correct as a statement of general international law, caution should be exercised in assuming there is never any distinction between the legal effects of accretion (or erosion) that is sudden versus gradual. For example, in the *Chamizal Arbitration (USA v Mexico)*,[68] such a distinction was important. Under a treaty of 1848, part of the Rio Grande

---

66 *Brownlie's Principles*, above note 13 at 228–30 and 233.
67 Shearer, above note 53 at 152–53.
68 (1911) 5 Am J Int'l L 782 (International Boundary Commission).

was made a boundary between the United States and Mexico. By 1911, the river's course had changed, producing a swath of land—called the Chamizal Tract—between the old and the new river courses. While the tract lay on the United States side of the new river course, both states claimed sovereignty over it. When the matter was put to arbitration, the Commission relied on treaty provisions to decide that the part of the tract produced by a gradual process of accretion belonged to the United States, but the portion suddenly created by a flood in 1864 belonged to Mexico.

A different type of geographic theory does not rely on geographical change but rather on the geographical relationship between a claimed piece of land and one over which sovereignty is established by one of the bases of title reviewed above. One author describes this type of geographic theory thus:

> Considerations of contiguity and geographical unity come to the fore when the disputed territory is uninhabited, barren or uncharted. . . . The principles are simply a part of judicial reasoning, but have significance in other respects. State activity as evidence of sovereignty need not press uniformly on every part of territory. Associated with this is the presumption of peripheral possession based on state activity, for example, on the coast of a barren territory. . . . [I]n giving effect to principles of geographical unity in *Eastern Greenland*, and thus concluding that somewhat localized Danish activity gave title over the whole of Greenland, the Permanent Court was not swayed [by] the significance of unity isolated from the context of effective occupation.[69]

"Contiguity" is sometimes asserted as a basis for sovereignty over claimed land, such as an island, on the mere basis of its proximity to existing sovereign territory. As suggested in the passage above, however, such an argument far overstates the significance of contiguity. As observed by the arbitrator in the *Island of Palmas Case*:[70]

> Although States have in certain circumstances maintained that islands relatively close to their shores belonged to them in virtue of their geographical situation, it is impossible to show the existence of a rule of positive international law to the effect that islands situated outside territorial waters should belong to a State from the mere fact that its territory forms the *terra firma* (nearest continent or island of considerable size).
>
> Nor is this principle of contiguity admissible as a legal method of deciding questions of territorial sovereignty; for it is wholly lacking in precision and would in its application lead to arbitrary results. This would be especially true in a case such as that of the island in question, which is not relatively close to one single continent, but forms part of a large archipelago in which strict delimitations between the different parts are not naturally obvious. . . .
>
> The title of contiguity, understood as a basis of territorial sovereignty, has no foundation in international law.

The one clear circumstance in which contiguity has a limited formal role to play in determining sovereignty over land relates to islands lying immediately off a state's coasts,

---

69 *Brownlie's Principles*, above note 13 at 237.
70 *Island of Palmas Case (Netherlands v United States)*, (1928) 2 RIAA 829.

within what is known as the "territorial sea" (that is, a twelve-nautical-mile wide belt of sea, discussed in detail in Chapter 5). An arbitral panel in a dispute concerning a fringe of islands off the Yemeni and Eritrean coasts noted the following:

> There is a strong presumption that islands within the twelve-mile coastal belt will belong to the coastal state, unless there is a fully-established case to the contrary (as, for example, in the case of the Channel Islands). But there is no like presumption outside the coastal belt, where the ownership of the islands is plainly at issue. . . . And even if there were a presumption of coastal-state sovereignty over islands falling within the twelve-mile territorial sea of a coastal belt island, it would be no more than a presumption, capable of being rebutted by evidence of a superior title.[71]

This last sentence provides some insight into the overall legal relevance of the "theory" of contiguity. At its highest, it provides nothing more than a rebuttable presumption of title over islands lying within a coastal state's territorial sea. Outside of that context, contiguity is not truly a "theory" at all and certainly no basis of title. At best, it is merely one factor among many which may or may not be relevant in assessing the geographical extent of a state's claim to sovereignty over land territory on one of the established bases of title reviewed above.

D. THE EFFECT OF RECOGNITION, ACQUIESCENCE, AND ESTOPPEL

Actions by a state that are inconsistent with its claim to sovereign title to land may undermine its legal basis for such a claim. Consider the concepts of "recognition," "acquiescence," and "estoppel" in this context:

> Recognition is a positive act by a state accepting a particular situation and, even though it may be implied from all the relevant circumstances, it is nevertheless an affirmation of the existence of a specific factual state of affairs, even if that accepted situation is inconsistent with the term in a treaty. Acquiescence, on the other hand, occurs in circumstances where a protest is called for and does not happen or does not happen in time in the circumstances. In other words, a situation arises which would seem to require a response denoting disagreement and, since this does not transpire, the state making no objection is understood to have accepted the new situation. The idea of estoppel in general is that a party which has made or consented to a particular statement upon which another party relies in subsequent activity to its detriment or the other's benefit cannot thereupon change its position.[72]

Acquiescence may be an important consideration in a claim grounded in prescription, discussed above. Thus, in *Sovereignty over Pedra Branca/Pulau Batu Puteh, Middle Rocks and South Ledge (Malaysia/Singapore)*, the ICJ described the concept of "acquiescence" in a territorial dispute in this manner:

---

71   *Eritrea v Yemen* (2001), 114 ILR 1 at 124–25 (PCA) (Award of the Arbitral Tribunal in the First Stage of the Proceedings: Territorial Sovereignty and Scope of the Dispute).

72   Shaw, above note 1 at 516.

Under certain circumstances, sovereignty over territory might pass as a result of the failure of the State which has sovereignty to respond to conduct à titre de *souverain* of the other State or . . . to concrete manifestations of the display of territorial sovereignty by the other State. . . . Such manifestations of the display of sovereignty may call for a response if they are not to be opposable to the State in question. The absence of reaction may well amount to acquiescence. The concept of acquiescence "is equivalent to tacit recognition manifested by unilateral conduct which the other party may interpret as consent . . .". That is to say, silence may also speak, but only if the conduct of the other State calls for a response.

. . . Critical for the Court's assessment of the conduct of the Parties is the central importance in international law and relations of State sovereignty over territory and of the stability and certainty of that sovereignty. Because of that, any passing of sovereignty over territory on the basis of the conduct of the Parties, as set out above, must be manifested clearly and without any doubt by that conduct and the relevant facts. That is especially so if what may be involved, in the case of one of the Parties, is in effect the abandonment of sovereignty over part of its territory.[73]

Much turns on the exact facts of each case. In the *Pedra Branca/Pulau Batu Putech* case, the Court considered that there had been acquiescence in behaviour that grounded a prescriptive claim:

. . . Without being exhaustive, the Court recalls their [Singapore's and its colonial predecessor, the United Kingdom's] investigation of marine accidents, their control over visits, Singapore's installation of naval communication equipment and its reclamation plans, all of which include acts *à titre de souverain*, the bulk of them after 1953. Malaysia and its predecessors did not respond in any way to that conduct, or the other conduct with that character identified earlier in this Judgment, of all of which (but for the installation of the naval communication equipment) it had notice.

. . . And, when official visits (in the 1970s for instance) were made, they were subject to express Singapore permission. Malaysia's official maps of the 1960s and 1970s also indicate an appreciation by it that Singapore had sovereignty. Those maps, like the conduct of both Parties which the Court has briefly recalled, are fully consistent with the final matter the Court recalls. It is the clearly stated position of the Acting Secretary of the [Malaysian] State of Johor in 1953 that Johor did not claim ownership of Pedra Branca/Pulau Batu Puteh. That statement has major significance.

. . . The Court is of the opinion that the relevant facts, including the conduct of the Parties, previously reviewed and summarized in the two preceding paragraphs, reflect a convergent evolution of the positions of the Parties regarding title to Pedra Branca/Pulau Batu Puteh. The Court concludes, especially by reference to the conduct of Singapore and its predecessors *à titre de souverain*, taken together with the conduct of Malaysia and its predecessors including their failure to respond to the conduct of Singapore and its predecessors, that by 1980 sovereignty over Pedra Branca/Pulau Batu Puteh had passed to Singapore.[74]

---

73 Above note 20 at paras 121–22.
74 *Ibid* at paras 274–76.

Consider also the following illustration of the way in which recognition of or acquiescence in a state's claim of sovereignty over land can give rise to an estoppel against a subsequent, contrary claim:

Case Concerning the Temple of Preah Vihear (Cambodia v Thailand), Merits, Judgment, [1962] ICJ Rep 6

[The parties disputed sovereignty over the precincts of the Temple at Preah Vihear, located along the Thai-Cambodian border which had been established by treaty in 1904. Under the treaty, the boundary was to follow the watershed between the two countries and a mixed boundary commission was established to map the precise course of the watershed. Maps were duly completed and published in 1907. Copies of the maps, one of which showed the Preah Vihear district on the Cambodian side of the boundary, were sent to Thailand. In fact, although the map purported to follow the watershed line as required by the treaty, it did not, since truly following the watershed would have placed the Temple precincts within Thai territory. The Court nevertheless found on various grounds, including the following, that sovereignty over Preah Vihear belonged to Cambodia:]

. . . The Court has considered the evidence furnished by Thailand of acts of an administrative character performed by her officials at or relative to Preah Vihear. France, and subsequently Cambodia, in view of her title founded on the Treaty of 1904, performed only a very few routine acts of administration in this small, deserted area. It was specifically admitted by Thailand in the course of the oral hearing that if Cambodia acquired sovereignty over the Temple area by virtue of the frontier settlement of 1904, she did not subsequently abandon it, nor did Thailand subsequently obtain it by any process of acquisitive prescription. Thailand's acts on the ground were therefore put forward as evidence of conduct as sovereign, sufficient to negative any suggestion that, under the 1904 Treaty settlement, Thailand accepted a delimitation having the effect of attributing the sovereignty over Preah Vihear to Cambodia. It is therefore from this standpoint that the Court must consider and evaluate these acts. The real question is whether they sufficed to efface or cancel out the clear impression of acceptance of the frontier line at Preah Vihear to be derived from the various considerations already discussed.

With one or two important exceptions to be mentioned presently, the acts concerned were exclusively the acts of local, provincial, authorities. To the extent that these activities took place, it is not clear that they had reference to the summit of Mount Preah Vihear and the Temple area itself, rather than to places somewhere in the vicinity. But however that may be, the Court finds it difficult to regard such local acts as overriding and negativing the consistent and undeviating attitude of the central Siamese authorities to the frontier line as mapped.

In this connection, much the most significant episode consisted of the visit paid to the Temple in 1930 by Prince Damrong, formerly Minister of the Interior, and at this time President of the Royal Institute of Siam, charged with duties in connection with the National Library and with archaeological monuments. The visit was part of an archaeological tour made by the Prince with the permission of the King of Siam, and it clearly had a quasi-official character. When the Prince arrived at Preah Vihear, he was officially received there by the French Resident for the adjoining Cambodian province, on behalf of the Resident Superior, with the French flag flying. The Prince could not possibly have failed to see the implications of a reception of this character. A clearer affirmation of title on the French Indo-Chinese side can scarcely be imagined. It demanded a reaction. Thailand did nothing. Furthermore, when Prince Damrong on his return to Bangkok sent the French Resident some photographs of the occasion, he used language which seems to admit that France, through her Resident, had acted as the host country.

The explanations regarding Prince Damrong's visit given on behalf of Thailand have not been found convincing by the Court. Looking at the incident as a whole, it appears to have amounted to a tacit recognition by Siam of the sovereignty of Cambodia (under French Protectorate) over Preah Vihear, through a failure to react in any way, on an occasion that called for a reaction in order to affirm or preserve title in the face of an obvious rival claim. What seems clear is that either Siam did not in fact believe she had any title—and this would be wholly consistent with her attitude all along, and thereafter, to the Annex I map and line—or else she decided not to assert it, which again means that she accepted the French claim, or accepted the frontier at Preah Vihear as it was drawn on the map. . . .

The remaining relevant facts must now be stated. In February 1949, not long after the conclusion of the proceedings of the Franco-Siamese Conciliation Commission, in the course of which, as has been seen, Thailand did not raise the question of Preah Vihear, France addressed a Note to the Government of Thailand stating that a report had been received of the stationing of four Siamese keepers at the Temple, and asking for information. There was no reply to this Note, nor to a follow-up Note of March 1949. In May 1949, France sent a further Note, setting out briefly, but quite explicitly, the grounds on which she considered Preah Vihear to be in Cambodia, and pointing out that a map produced by Thailand herself had recognized this fact. The withdrawal of the keepers was requested. Although there was an error in this Note, the significance of the latter was that it contained an unequivocal assertion of sovereignty. This French Note also received no reply. In July 1950, a further Note was sent. This too remained unanswered.

In these circumstances Cambodia, on attaining her independence in 1953, proposed, for her part, to send keepers or guards to the Temple, in the assertion or maintenance of her position. However, finding that Thai keepers were already there, the Cambodian keepers withdrew, and Cambodia sent a Note dated January 1954 to the Government of Thailand asking for information. This received a mere acknowledgment, but no explanation. Nor was there, even then, any formal affirmation of Thailand's claim. At the end of March 1954, the Government of Cambodia, drawing attention to the fact that no substantive reply to its previous Note had been received, notified the Government of Thailand that it now proposed to replace the previously withdrawn Cambodian keepers or guards by some Cambodian troops. In this Note Cambodia specifically referred to the justification of the Cambodian claim contained in the French Note of May 1949. This Cambodian Note also was not answered. However, the Cambodian troops were not in fact sent; and in June 1954, Cambodia addressed to Thailand a further Note stating that, as information had been received to the effect that Thai troops were already in occupation, the despatch of the Cambodian troops had been suspended in order not to aggravate the situation. The Note went on to ask that Thailand should either withdraw her troops or furnish Cambodia with her views on the matter. This Note equally received no reply. But the Thai "troops" (the Court understands that they are in fact a police force) remained. Again, therefore, it would seem that Thailand, while taking certain local action, was not prepared to deny the French and Cambodian claim at the diplomatic level.

No further diplomatic correspondence was produced to the Court; but eventually, in 1958, a conference was held at Bangkok between Thailand and Cambodia, to discuss various territorial matters in dispute between the Parties, including that of Preah Vihear. The representative of Thailand having declined to discuss the legal aspects of the matter, the negotiations broke down and Cambodia instituted the present proceedings.

The Court will now state the conclusions it draws from the facts as above set out.

Even if there were any doubt as to Siam's acceptance of the map in 1908, and hence of the frontier indicated thereon, the Court would consider, in the light of the subsequent course of events, that Thailand is now precluded by her conduct from asserting that she did not accept it. She has, for fifty years, enjoyed such benefits as the Treaty of 1904 conferred on her, if only the benefit of a stable frontier. France, and through her Cambodia, relied on Thailand's acceptance of the map. . . . [I]t is immaterial whether or not this reliance was based on a belief that the map was correct. It is not now open to Thailand, while continuing to claim and enjoy the benefits of the settlement, to deny that she was ever a consenting party to it. . . .

In an unusual development, Cambodia returned to the Court in 2011 seeking an "interpretation" of the 1962 judgment in the *Temple of Preah Vihear* case. At issue was the Thai refusal to vacate the promontory on which the temple sat. Thailand argued that while the 1962 judgment established sovereignty over the temple itself, the decision did not address its claim to the surrounding land. The Court disagreed with Thailand in a 2013 judgment, finding that Cambodia had sovereignty over the whole disputed territory and that Thailand was required to withdraw its personnel from the region.[75]

---

75 *Request for Interpretation of the Judgment of 15 June 1962 in the Case Concerning the Temple of Preah Vihear (Cambodia v Thailand)*, Judgment, ICJ General List No 151, 11 November 2013.

CHAPTER 5

STATE JURISDICTION OVER WATER

Over 70 percent of the Earth's surface is covered with water. Human beings obviously do not inhabit this "territory" in the same way as they do land. Yet, the oceans, rivers, and lakes of the world are an important source of resources, both biotic and mineral. They also provide fundamentally important means of transportation that are vital to travel, trade, and security. States therefore have an intense interest in the jurisdictional regimes applicable to the water regions of the world.

In our discussion of state jurisdiction over water, we first examine "inland" waterways and then turn to oceans.

A. INLAND WATERWAYS

Inland waterways are those bodies of water or watercourses, such as lakes and rivers, that are enclosed by land. It is difficult to extract generic rules of international law from the many legal regimes that govern the world's inland waterways. Most significant rivers and lakes that are bounded by more than one state are regulated by treaty, the specific terms of which vary. Consider, for example, comments made by the International Court of Justice in a recent case concerning rights of navigation along one particular inland waterway:

Dispute Regarding Navigational and Related Rights (Costa Rica v Nicaragua), Judgment, [2009] ICJ Rep 213

32. According to Costa Rica, its right of free navigation on the part of the San Juan river that is in dispute derives on the one hand from certain treaty provisions in force between the Parties, primarily but not exclusively the Treaty of Limits of 15 April 1858, and on the other hand from the rules of general international law that are applicable, even in the absence of treaty provisions, to navigation on "international rivers". The San Juan is said to fall into this category, at least as regards the section whose course follows the border, with Costa Rica thus possessing a customary right of free navigation in its capacity as a riparian State.

33. According to Nicaragua, on the contrary, the San Juan is not an "international river", since it flows entirely within the territory of a single country by virtue of the provisions of the 1858 Treaty of Limits, which establish the border in such a way that no part of the river falls under the sovereignty of a State other than Nicaragua. Moreover, Nicaragua challenges the existence of a general régime that might be applicable, under customary international law, to rivers whose course, or one of whose banks, constitutes the border between two States, and more widely to "international rivers". Lastly, according to Nic-

aragua, even if such a régime were to exist, it would be superseded in this case by the treaty provisions which define the status of the San Juan river and govern the riparian States' right of navigation. It is these special provisions which should be applied in order to settle the present dispute, in any event that part of it relating to the right of navigation on the river.

34. The Court does not consider that it is required to take a position in this case on whether and to what extent there exists, in customary international law, a régime applicable to navigation on "international rivers", either of universal scope or of a regional nature covering the geographical area in which the San Juan is situated. Nor does it consider, as a result, that it is required to settle the question of whether the San Juan falls into the category of "international rivers", as Costa Rica maintains, or is a national river which includes an international element, that being the argument of Nicaragua.

35. Indeed, even if categorization as an "international river" would be legally relevant in respect of navigation, in that it would entail the application of rules of customary international law to that question, such rules could only be operative, at the very most, in the absence of any treaty provisions that had the effect of excluding them, in particular because those provisions were intended to define completely the régime applicable to navigation, by the riparian States on a specific river or a section of it.

36. That is precisely the case in this instance. The 1858 Treaty of Limits completely defines the rules applicable to the section of the San Juan river that is in dispute in respect of navigation. Interpreted in the light of the other treaty provisions in force between the Parties, and in accordance with the arbitral or judicial decisions rendered on it, that Treaty is sufficient to settle the question of the extent of Costa Rica's right of free navigation which is now before the Court. Consequently, the Court has no need to consider whether, if these provisions did not exist, Costa Rica could nevertheless have relied for this purpose on rules derived from international, universal or regional custom. . . .

Given the situation-specific nature of most inland waterway legal regimes, we can only make a few general observations about the international law governing these regimes, and then turn to one specific example: the Canada-US inland waterways regime.

1) General Observations

In simple terms, inland waterways can be divided into three categories: those that are entirely within the territory of a single state; those that flow from one state to another; and those that lie or flow along a border between states. Inland waterways completely enclosed by a single state present relatively few difficulties in international law: "Where a river lies wholly within the territory of one state, it belongs entirely to that state, and generally speaking no other state is entitled to rights of navigation on it."[1] In other words, such inland waterways are part of a state's sovereign territory in much the same way as its land territory. The state enjoys plenary jurisdiction over these waterways.

---

1   Ivan A Shearer, *Starke's International Law*, 11th ed (Toronto: Butterworths, 1994) at 175.

Rivers and lakes that straddle or demarcate international borders cause greater complications. Consider this discussion of navigation rights:

> Also where a river passes through several states, each state owns that part of the river which runs through its territory, but controversy has centred round the question of the rights of riparian and other states to navigate along the whole length of the river. Several writers on international law . . . have been of the opinion that there is a general right of passage for all states along such international rivers, but this view has never been generally accepted in practice, and is certainly not recognized as a customary principle of international law. . . . [S]uch measures of freedom of navigation as become established on international waterways [are] almost entirely the creation of treaty.[2]

Water in international inland waterways is also a key resource, use of which may cause frictions between states. Consider these observations:

> It is believed that there is a general readiness of states to admit that any . . . use or diversion [of,] or interference [with, water flow] by one riparian state injuring the free navigability of a navigable international waterway to the detriment of a co-riparian state is a breach of international law. Short of this, it is perhaps only possible to say that there is a duty on a riparian state not, by any use of the river waters under its control to cause grievous or irreparable damage of an economic character on other riparian states, for example pollution, which might reasonably have been prevented. . . . Where the rivers concerned form part of a drainage basin, each riparian state is entitled to a reasonable and equitable share in the beneficial uses of the waters of the basin, a principle applied in numerous treaties.[3]

The International Law Commission has attempted to give effect to some of these general principles, with its efforts reflected in the following treaty:

Convention on the Law of the Non-navigational Uses of International Watercourses, 21 May 1997, UN Doc A/51/869 (not yet in force)

PART II.
GENERAL PRINCIPLES

Article 5
Equitable and reasonable utilization and participation
1. Watercourse States shall in their respective territories utilize an international watercourse in an equitable and reasonable manner. In particular, an international watercourse shall be used and developed by watercourse States with a view to attaining optimal and sustainable utilization thereof and benefits therefrom, taking into account the interests of the watercourse States concerned, consistent with adequate protection of the watercourse.

---

2   *Ibid.*
3   *Ibid* at 177.

2. Watercourse States shall participate in the use, development and protection of an international watercourse in an equitable and reasonable manner. Such participation includes both the right to utilize the watercourse and the duty to cooperate in the protection and development thereof, as provided in the present Convention.

Article 6
Factors relevant to equitable and reasonable utilization

1. Utilization of an international watercourse in an equitable and reasonable manner within the meaning of article 5 requires taking into account all relevant factors and circumstances, including:

(a) Geographic, hydrographic, hydrological, climatic, ecological and other factors of a natural character;

(b) The social and economic needs of the watercourse States concerned;

(c) The population dependent on the watercourse in each watercourse State;

(d) The effects of the use or uses of the watercourses in one watercourse State on other watercourse States;

(e) Existing and potential uses of the watercourse;

(f) Conservation, protection, development and economy of use of the water resources of the watercourse and the costs of measures taken to that effect;

(g) The availability of alternatives, of comparable value, to a particular planned or existing use.

2. In the application of article 5 or paragraph 1 of this article, watercourse States concerned shall, when the need arises, enter into consultations in a spirit of cooperation.

3. The weight to be given to each factor is to be determined by its importance in comparison with that of other relevant factors. In determining what is a reasonable and equitable use, all relevant factors are to be considered together and a conclusion reached on the basis of the whole.

Article 7
Obligation not to cause significant harm

1. Watercourse States shall, in utilizing an international watercourse in their territories, take all appropriate measures to prevent the causing of significant harm to other watercourse States.

2. Where significant harm nevertheless is caused to another watercourse State, the States whose use causes such harm shall, in the absence of agreement to such use, take all appropriate measures, having due regard for the provisions of articles 5 and 6, in consultation with the affected State, to eliminate or mitigate such harm and, where appropriate, to discuss the question of compensation.

Article 8
General obligation to cooperate

1. Watercourse States shall cooperate on the basis of sovereign equality, territorial integrity, mutual benefit and good faith in order to attain optimal utilization and adequate protection of an international watercourse.

2. In determining the manner of such cooperation, watercourse States may consider the establishment of joint mechanisms or commissions, as deemed necessary by them, to facilitate cooperation on relevant measures and procedures in the light of experience gained through cooperation in existing joint mechanisms and commissions in various regions.

The Convention on the Law of the Non-navigational Uses of International Watercourses was adopted by the UN General Assembly and opened for signature in 1997. By 2012 it had only secured twenty-nine of the thirty-five ratifications or accessions needed to bring it into force. It would appear that the majority of states prefer to regulate their obligations with respect to international watercourses by way of more specific bilateral or regional agreements.

LAW IN CONTEXT

Inland Waterways and Conflict

No state can survive without access to fresh water. In many regions of the world, such water is in scarce supply. These include regions already prone to violence. Consider the following discussion of the Jordan, Tigris-Euphrates, and Indus River basins:

> [T]he three river systems remain divided among competing political entities. The Jordan River basin flows through Israel, Jordan, Syria and Palestinian territory; the Tigris-Euphrates system passes through Iran, Iraq, Syria, Turkey, and areas occupied by the Kurdish population; and the Indus is shared among Afghanistan, China, India, Pakistan and Kashmir (some of whose inhabitants seek to become independent). These countries and regions are deeply divided along political, religious, ethnic and ideological lines. Disputes over water are therefore likely to be intensified by historical grievances and animosities. . . . Each of the three river systems . . . harbors a significant risk of violent conflict. This risk stems from the fact that the demand for water is growing while the supply is not, and from the failure of the riparians in those systems to establish an integrated basin-wide regime for the equitable distribution of shared resources. As population grows, and the need for water and food rises in tandem, each of the riparians will seek to maximize its utilization of the available supplies. When the actions of any one of these states results in a declining supply for any of the others, the conditions are set for an interbasin clash over the distribution of water. . . . The leaders of these countries are expected to provide the basic necessities of human life, especially water and food; if they fail in this, they lose their mandate to rule and can expect rising political unrest. In such circumstances, leaders usually respond in one of two ways: they attempt to stifle internal dissent through repressive measures, or they try to channel the discontent against external enemies, who are held responsible for the deprivation. The first approach can lead to civil war; the second, to interstate conflict.[4]

---

4   Michael Klare, *Resource Wars: The New Landscape of Global Conflict* (New York: Metropolitan Books, 2001) at 162 and 189.

The underdeveloped state of customary international law on the question of water re-source sharing does not help defuse the volatile situation in these river basins. In 2004, the UN Secretary-General's High-level Panel on Threats, Challenges, and Change recognized this problem, noting that "[m]ore legal mechanisms are necessary in the area of natural resources, fights over which have often been an obstacle to peace" and urging that: "The United Nations should work with national authorities, international financial institutions, civil society organizations and the private sector to develop norms governing the man-agement of natural resources for countries emerging from or at risk of conflict. . . . There should also be a focus on the development of rules, for example through the International Law Commission, for the use of transboundary resources, such as water."[5]

The International Law Commission in fact completed, in 2008, a set of draft articles dealing with transboundary aquifer (groundwater) systems.[6] At the time of writing, the UN General Assembly is still considering whether to proceed with the elaboration of a multilateral convention on the basis of these draft articles.[7]

Where rivers or lakes lie between two states, it is necessary to designate at exactly which points in the waterway the border lies. Again, this is a matter generally settled by treaty. Consider the terms of the Israeli-Jordan Peace Treaty of 1994, fixing the border be-tween these two states along the Jordan and Yarmouk Rivers:

> A) The boundary Line shall follow the middle of the main course of the flow of the Jordan and Yarmouk Rivers. B) The boundary line shall follow natural changes (accretion or ero-sion) in the course of the rivers unless otherwise agreed. Artificial changes in or of the course of the rivers shall not affect the location of the boundary unless otherwise agreed. No artificial changes may be made except by agreement between both Parties. C) In the event of a future sudden natural change in or of the course of the rivers (avulsion or cut-ting of new bed) the Joint Boundary Commission (Article 3 below) shall meet as soon as possible, to decide on necessary measures, which may include physical restoration of the prior location of the river course. . . . E) Adjustment to the boundary line in any of the rivers due to natural changes (accretion or erosion) shall be carried out whenever it is deemed necessary by the Boundary Commission or once every five years.

The approach adopted is a typical one, and may therefore reflect the default custom-ary international legal position:

> In general, where there is a navigable channel, the boundary will follow the middle line of that channel. . . . Where there is no such channel, the boundary line will, in general, be the middle line of the river itself or of its principal arm. These respective boundary lines would continue as median lines (and so would shift also) if the river itself changed course

---

5 *A More Secure World: Our Shared Responsibility: Report of the Secretary-General's High-level Panel on Threats, Challenges and Change*, UN Doc A/59/565 at 8–99 (2 December 2004) at paras 91–93 [*A More Secure World*].

6 International Law Commission, "Draft Articles on the Law of Transboundary Aquifers" in *Report of the In-ternational Law Commission*, UN GAOR, 63rd Sess, Supp No 10, c IV at para 53, UN Doc A/63/10 (2008).

7 See *The Law of Transboundary Aquifers*, GA Res 66/104, UN Doc A/RES/66/104, reprinted in UN GAOR, 66th Sess, Supp No 49, vol I at 594, UN Doc A/66/49 (2011).

as a result of gradual accretion on one bank or degradation of the other bank. Where, however, the river changed course suddenly and left its original bed for a new channel, the international boundary would continue to be the middle of the deserted river bed.[8]

2) The Canada-US Waterways Regime

The Canada-US waterways regime is governed principally by a 1909 treaty,[9] the key provisions of which are:

> **Treaty between the United States and Great Britain Relating to Boundary Waters, and Questions Arising between the United States and Canada, 11 January 1909, 36 US Stat 2448, UKTS 1910 No 23, in force 5 May 1910 [Canada-US Boundary Waters Treaty]**
>
> *Preliminary Article*
> For the purpose of this treaty boundary waters are defined as the waters from main shore to main shore of the lakes and rivers and connecting waterways, or the portions thereof, along which the international boundary between the United States and the Dominion of Canada passes, including all bays, arms, and inlets thereof, but not including tributary waters which in their natural channels would flow into such lakes, rivers, and waterways, or waters flowing from such lakes, rivers, and waterways, or the waters of rivers flowing across the boundary.
>
> *Article I*
> The High Contracting Parties agree that the navigation of all navigable boundary waters shall forever continue free and open for the purposes of commerce to the inhabitants and to the ships, vessels, and boats of both countries equally, subject, however, to any laws and regulations of either country, within its own territory, not inconsistent with such privilege of free navigation and applying equally and without discrimination to the inhabitants, ships, vessels, and boats of both countries. . . .
>
> *Article II*
> Each of the High Contracting Parties reserves to itself or [the states or provinces] . . . the exclusive jurisdiction and control over the use and diversion, whether temporary or permanent, of all waters on its own side of the line which in their natural channels would flow across the boundary or into boundary waters; but it is agreed that any interference with or diversion from their natural channel of such waters on either side of the boundary, resulting in any injury on the other side of the boundary, shall give rise to the same rights and entitle the injured parties to the same legal remedies as if such injury took place in the country where such diversion or interference occurs. . . . It is understood however, that neither of the High Contracting Parties intends by the foregoing provision to surrender any right, which it may have, to object to any interference with or diversions of waters on the other side of the boundary the effect of which would be productive of material injury to the navigation interests on its own side of the boundary.

---

8   Malcolm N Shaw, *International Law*, 6th ed (Cambridge: Cambridge University Press, 2008) at 531.
9   See also *International Boundary Waters Treaty Act*, RSC 1985, c I-17.

Article III

It is agreed that . . . no further or other uses or obstructions or diversions, whether temporary or permanent, of boundary waters on either side of the line, affecting the natural level or flow of boundary waters on the other side of the line shall be made except by authority of the United States or the Dominion of Canada within their respective jurisdictions and with the approval, as hereinafter provided, of a joint commission, to be known as the International Joint Commission.

The foregoing provisions are not intended to limit or interfere with the existing rights of the Government of the United States on the one side and the Government of the Dominion of Canada on the other, to undertake and carry on governmental works in boundary waters for the deepening of channels, the construction of breakwaters, the improvement of harbours, and other governmental works for the benefit of commerce and navigation, provided that such works are wholly on its own side of the line and do not materially affect the level or flow of the boundary waters on the other, nor are such provisions intended to interfere with the ordinary use of such waters for domestic and sanitary purposes.

Article IV

The High Contracting Parties agree that, except in cases provided for by special agreement between them, they will not permit the construction or maintenance on their respective sides of the boundary of any remedial or protective works or any dams or other obstructions in waters flowing from boundary waters or in waters at a lower level than the boundary in rivers flowing across the boundary, the effect of which is to raise the natural level of waters on the other side of the boundary unless the construction or maintenance thereof is approved by the aforesaid International Joint Commission.

It is further agreed that the waters herein defined as boundary waters and waters flowing across the boundary shall not be polluted on either side to the injury of health or property on the other. . . .

Article VII

The High Contracting Parties agree to establish and maintain an International Joint Commission of the United States and Canada composed of six commissioners, three on the part of the United States appointed by the President thereof, and three on the part of the United Kingdom appointed by His Majesty on the recommendation of the Governor in Council of the Dominion of Canada.

Article VIII

This International Joint Commission shall have jurisdiction over and shall pass upon all cases involving the use or obstruction or diversion of the waters with respect to which under Article III or IV of this Treaty the approval shall be governed by the following rules of principles which are adopted by the High Contracting Parties for this purpose:

The High Contracting Parties shall have, each on its own side of the boundary, equal and similar rights in the use of the waters hereinbefore defined as boundary waters.

The following order of precedence shall be observed among the various uses enumerated hereinafter for these waters, and no use shall be permitted which tends materially to conflict with or restrain any other use which is given preference over it in this order of precedence:

1. Uses for domestic and sanitary purposes;
2. Uses for navigation, including the service of canals for the purposes of navigation;
3. Uses for power and for irrigation purposes. . . .

The majority of the Commissioners shall have power to render a decision. In case the Commission is evenly divided upon any question or matter presented to it for decision, separate reports shall be made by the Commissioners on each side to their own Government. The High Contracting Parties shall thereupon endeavour to agree upon an adjustment of the question or matter of difference, and if an agreement is reached between them, it shall be reduced to writing in the form of a protocol, and shall be communicated to the Commissioners, who shall take such further proceedings as may be necessary to carry out such agreement. . . .

Article X

Any questions or matters of difference arising between the High Contracting Parties involving the rights, obligations, or interests of the United States or of the Dominion of Canada either in relation to each other or to their respective inhabitants, may be referred for decision to the International Joint Commission by the consent of the two Parties, it being understood that on the part of the United States any such action will be by and with the advice and consent of the Senate, and on the part of His Majesty's Government with the consent of the Governor General in Council. . . .

Consider the following opinion, given by the Canadian Department of Foreign Affairs and International Trade in August 2011, on whether Canada or the United States surrendered any sovereignty to the International Joint Commission (IJC) established pursuant to Article VII of the above treaty:

Alan H Kessel, "Canadian Practice in International Law at the Department of Foreign Affairs and International Trade in 2010–2011" (2011) 49 Can YB Int'l Law 381 at 392–93

. . . [W]e can see no merit in the following statement which asserts that both Canada and the USA somehow gave up their sovereign power to the IJC in the sense of providing resources to enforce the IJC's Orders:

> Canada and the United States gave up part of their sovereign power to the IJC when they signed the Boundary Waters Treaty, and anything that flows from IJC Orders is for the two governments to provide resources to enforce the Orders. Thus the 1914 Orders and subsequent supplementary orders led to not just one of quasi-judicial enforcer who but also participates in actual day-to-day operations in Lake Superior and (Lake Ontario as per 1952 and 1956 Orders) outflow regulation. These responsibilities cannot be delegated to provincial or municipal agencies, and definitely not to utilities (self-regulating).

Certainly both countries desired the IJC to issue orders of approval to manage jointly-held bodies of water rather than each country unilaterally doing so as they did prior to the conclusion of the Treaty. The IJC is an institution that is neither a creature of Canada nor the USA and as such has played a highly useful role in managing the two nations' shared water resources. But in the matter of providing resources in the form of personnel or financial support, the IJC has no compulsive authority to demand either from the two governments. The negotiating history of the Boundary Waters treaty illustrates again and again that the USA Administration was quite cautious in the authority given to the IJC and as illustrated by Article X, would only provide an arbitral authority to the IJC if the USA Senate provided its advice and consent, thereby ensuring it would never take place. There is no language in the treaty that would enable us to conclude that the USA legislative branch surrendered any of its appropriation power to the IJC, let alone to the USA Administration on the IJC's behalf.

We also contest the suggestion that the IJC is a *quasi-judicial* enforcer. In fact, . . . the IJC's orders of Approval are not enforceable at all in either Canadian or US Courts, which is an essential characteristic of a quasi-judicial act. They can become enforceable in Canadian courts if a parallel license is issued by the Minister under the regime of the [*International Boundary Waters Treaty Act*] but then it is the license being enforced, not the Order of Approval. In the USA, enforcement is tied to a license issued by the USA Federal Energy Regulatory Commission (FERC) without which IJC Orders in the USA have no practical legal effect. Therefore, to describe them as quasi-judicial, is simply in error.[10]

[Reprinted with permission of the Publisher from Canadian Yearbook of International Law, Volume 49 edited by John Currie © University of British Columbia Press 2011. All rights reserved by the Publisher.]

As to the scope of the free navigation provisions found in Article I of the Canada-US Boundary Waters Treaty, consider the following legal opinion from the Canadian Department of Foreign Affairs in March 2000:

Michael Leir, "Canadian Practice in International Law at the Department of Foreign Affairs in 1999–2000" (2000) 38 Can YB Int'l Law 331 at 348–50

The right of freedom of navigation on international watercourses is a right long recognized by international law. In North America, the United States and Great Britain historically entered into a series of treaties governing the boundaries between Canada and the United States and their respective rights concerning international or boundary waters. In these treaties the primacy of the principle of navigation has been constantly highlighted. . . .

The factual test of what is inconsistent with the principle of free navigation requires an understanding of what is contained in the principle. Nowhere in the treaties is there to be found a definition of the principle or its corollary, the interference with the freedom of navigation. It would be safe to say that the construction of a physical barrier that prevented the movement by shipping along a boundary water would interfere with the freedom of navigation. However, it is harder to gauge whether the effects of laws and regulations on the economic viability of merchant shipping, for example, would interfere with freedom of navigation. *Black's Law Dictionary* . . . defines "navigable" as: ". . . capable of allowing vessels or vehicles to pass, and thereby usable for travel or commerce." Courts have traditionally noted that the question of whether a body of water was navigable or not is a question of fact. Article I of the BWT [Boundary Waters Treaty] contains a further level of analysis. The Parties shall ensure navigation of navigable boundary waters for the purposes of commerce. At the time of the drafting of the Treaty the right of

---

10　The International Joint Commission maintains an official website at: www.ijc.org.

free navigation for the purposes of commerce was of the utmost importance, navigation by water being the main medium of communication at the time. This would envisage the carriage of goods and passengers by boat. . . .

Although there are differences between the European and North American experiences, one can draw parallels between the two. The history of the often multilateral European international river regime and the bilateral US-Canadian experience with the Great Lakes, while having some differences, share many similarities and common themes. Both place the freedom of navigation in a position of preeminence above other interests.

Both state that municipal laws and regulations cannot interfere with the freedom of navigation. Finally, both link the freedom of navigation with the freedom of commerce and extend the freedom of navigation beyond mere passage. Bela Vitanyi, a leading commentator on the law of international river navigation, analyses leading commentators' definitions of the freedom of navigation and its essential elements:

> Consequently, freedom of navigation seems to include the following elements:
> (a) Freedom of traffic, which means free movement of vessels as well as freedom to carry goods and passengers. This freedom includes freedom of transit. It also implies freedom to enter ports and use their equipment;
> (b) Free exercise of the shipping trade, which includes freedom to engage in the usual commercial activities of shipping companies. . . .
> (c) Freedom of freight. . . .

The Helsinki Rules on the Uses of International Rivers, International Law Association, 1966, are also extremely helpful in fleshing out the meaning and scope of the freedom of navigation as well as the degree to which municipal law can affect it. . . . Article XIV of the Rules defines the freedom of navigation for the purposes of the Rules:

> Article XIV—"Free navigation," as the term is used in this Chapter, includes the following freedoms of vessels of a riparian State on a basis of equality:
> (a) freedom of movement on the entire navigable course of the river or lake;
> (b) freedom to enter ports and to make use of plants and docks; and
> (c) freedom to transport goods and passengers, either directly or through transshipment, between the territory of another riparian State and between the territory of a riparian State and the open sea.

Article XV then sets out the rule regarding the applicability of municipal law to the freedom as set out in articles ("rights of police" in this context is a broad term encompassing all "policing" of the waterway concerned and would include laws and regulation pertaining to safety, health etc.):

> Article XV—A riparian State may exercise rights of police, including but not limited to the protection of public safety and health, over that portion of the river or lake subject to its jurisdiction, provided the exercise of such rights does not unreasonably interfere with the enjoyment of the rights of free navigation defined in Articles XIII and XIV.
>
> Comment: The right of free navigation is subject to the right of the State to enact and enforce within its territory reasonable measures which are necessary to police effectively its territory. Similarly, customs, public health and precautions against dis-

eases fall within this area of regulation. Such measures must be applied to all the co-riparian States on a basis of absolute equality and must not unreasonably impede freedom of navigation.

. . . [T]he Rules for the present analysis serve as an important interpretive tool for explaining Article I of the Boundary Waters Treaty which contains provisions protecting the freedom of navigation from interference by riparian States' laws and regulations.

It is clear from the above discussion that interference with the freedom of navigation is not limited solely to physical obstructions or other impediments to maritime trade. The emphasis on the freedom of commerce within the idea of freedom of navigation, Article I of the BWT's statement regarding laws and regulations, and academic commentary all clearly show that the freedom of navigation also provides for freedom from municipal laws and regulations, even those normally valid and with good purpose, if they interfere unreasonably with the freedom of navigation.

Notwithstanding a long-standing treaty relationship, joint Canada-US inland waterways management does generate occasional disputes, as illustrated by this 2005 description of cases from North Dakota:

There are a number of closely-related water projects under construction or consideration in North Dakota that have created serious concerns for the governments of Manitoba and Canada, along with some states and NGOs in the United States. The Northwest Area Water Supply project (NAWS) is designed to pipe water from the Missouri River system to municipalities across the continental divide in North Dakota and within the Red River/ Hudson Bay system. The interbasin transfer of water and concerns about the adequacy of the federal environmental assessment have prompted Manitoba to seek judicial review in United States Federal Court, supported by Canada, NGOs and the State of Missouri filing as *amici*. The Federal Court's initial decision largely favoured the Plaintiffs, but is presently under appeal.

The controversial Devil's Lake state project finally began operation in August 2005 after law suits from local environmentalists and the province of Manitoba were dismissed and following difficult bilateral negotiations between Canada and the United States culminating in a Joint Statement outlining an agreed process to resolve the issue. The process will include a rapid biota assessment that will lead towards the adoption of a permanent mitigation technology. The project takes water from this flood-prone lake and transfers it to the Red River system. Devil's Lake lies within the Red River system but has no natural outlet and also has very poor quality water.

Lastly, a congressionally-mandated study to examine future water needs of the Red River Valley in North Dakota is causing concern because of its over-emphasis on interbasin water transfers (proposing for study transfers both from the Missouri River and Lake of the Woods systems to the Red River valley). The study is a matter of considerable concern for Missouri, Minnesota, Manitoba and Canada. A significant water transfer from the Lake of the Woods would have direct implications for the Boundary Waters Treaty and the International Joint Commission.[11]

---

11 Department of Foreign Affairs, *Examples of Current Issues of International Law of Particular Importance to Canada* (October 2005) at 7.

Also controversial have been proposed US water diversions from the Great Lakes for use in the increasingly parched American mid- and south-west. In December 2005, Ontario, Quebec, and the eight Great Lakes US states of Illinois, Indiana, Michigan, Minnesota, New York, Ohio, Pennsylvania, and Wisconsin entered into a political compact and agreement to harmonize their approach to water management issues and also committing each jurisdiction to introduce laws barring water diversions in most instances.[12]

B. OCEANS

International law has traditionally disallowed state claims of sovereignty over the world's oceans, largely due to the economic and military interests of powerful seafaring states. With the exception of a thin margin along the coasts of states, almost all marine spaces were considered the "high seas," a *res communis* domain over which no state could assert sovereignty. That basic paradigm remains essentially unchanged in the modern law of the sea, although since the mid-twentieth century, a progressively wider margin of coastal waters has been subjected to a number of forms of jurisdictional control by coastal states. In this section, we focus on the extent and nature of these various coastal zones of state control before turning to the international legal regime applicable to the high seas. Figure 5.1 portrays the principal ocean zones recognized in the modern law of the sea, and the extent of state jurisdiction over each as defined in the 1982 United Nations Convention on the Law of the Sea (UNCLOS)[13]—a widely ratified multilateral treaty codifying much of the general law of the sea.

Figure 5.1: Ocean Zones under the UN Convention on the Law of the Sea

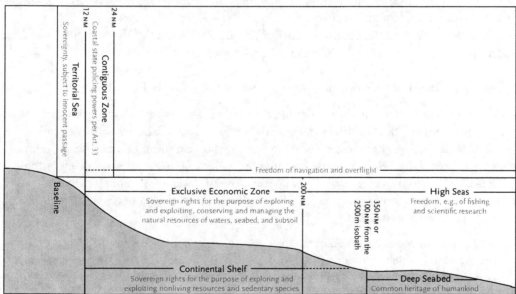

12   Great Lakes-St. Lawrence River Basin Sustainable Water Resources Compact and Great Lakes-St. Lawrence River Basin Sustainable Water Agreement (13 December 2005), online: www.glslregionalbody. org/GLSLRBAgreements.aspx.

13   10 December 1982, 1833 UNTS 3, (1982) 21 ILM 1261, in force 16 November 1994, entry into force for Canada 7 November 2003.

1) Baselines, Internal Waters, and the Territorial Sea

a) Measurement

As suggested above, the modern law of the sea permits coastal states to exercise various types of jurisdictional control over a number of coastal strips or "zones." Some of these zones, and their accompanying jurisdictional regimes, overlap. The breadth of each zone is typically defined by reference to a starting point and an endpoint. The starting point for most zones is the state's coast (although some zones begin where another zone ends), whereas zone endpoints are usually expressed in terms of distance from the state's coast. Thus, the state's coast typically acts as a "baseline" for measurement of the breadth of coastal zones.

There are two principal legal issues related to the concept of "baselines." The first is how to define a state's "coast." Given that oceans have tides, should the high or low water mark, or something in between, be taken as the "coast"? The second, more difficult issue is whether and when it is permissible to depart from the physical line of the state's coast and use some other baseline for purposes of measuring the extent of a state's coastal zones. For example, along a highly irregular coastline dotted with inlets and fjords, is it permissible for a state to simplify the measurement of its coastal zones by using "straight baselines" which approximate the overall contours of its coast rather than following its every twist and turn? To ask the question may appear to answer it, but there are issues other than geometrical expediency at stake. If permissible, "straight baselines" will, by definition, extend the reach of a state's coastal zones, and hence the jurisdiction associated with each such zone, further seaward. In addition, a straight baseline raises the question of the status of the waters lying on the *landward* side—that is, between the actual coast itself and the straight baseline.

Consider how the International Court of Justice approached these various issues associated with the concept of baselines in the following case:

Fisheries Case (United Kingdom v Norway), Judgment, [1951] ICJ Rep 116

[Norway contended that it was entitled to use straight baselines as the starting point from which to measure the breadth of its territorial sea and coastal fisheries zone. Beginning in 1933, the United Kingdom objected to this practice, claiming that customary international law obliged Norway to use baselines that followed the low-water mark left by the tides. The United Kingdom also contended that, even if the use of straight baselines were permissible at customary international law, such baselines could not exceed a maximum of 10 nautical miles in length.]

. . . The coastal zone concerned in the dispute is of considerable length. . . . The coast of the mainland, which, without taking any account of fjords, bays and minor indentations, is over 1,500 kilometres in length, is of a very distinctive configuration. Very broken along its whole length, it constantly opens out into indentations often penetrating for great distances inland. . . . To the west, the land configuration stretches out into the sea: the large and small islands, mountainous in character, the islets, rocks and reefs, some always above water, others emerging only at low tide, are in truth but an extension of the Norwegian mainland. The number of insular formations, large and small, which make up the "skjaergaard" [rocky rampart], is estimated by the Norwegian Government to be one hundred and twenty thousand. . . .

Within the "skjaergaard," almost every island has its large and its small bays; countless arms of the sea, straits, channels and mere waterways serve as a means of communication for the local population which inhabits the islands as it does the mainland. The coast of the mainland does not constitute, as it does in practically all other countries, a clear dividing line between land and sea. What matters, what really constitutes the Norwegian coast line, is the outer line of the "skjaergaard." . . .

Such are the realities which must be borne in mind in appraising the validity of the United Kingdom contention that the limits of the Norwegian fisheries zone laid down in the 1935 Decree are contrary to international law.

The Parties being in agreement on the figure of 4 miles for the breadth of the territorial sea, the problem which arises is from what baseline this breadth is to be reckoned. . . .

The Court has no difficulty in finding that, for the purpose of measuring the breadth of the territorial sea, it is the low-water mark as opposed to the high-water mark, or the mean between the two tides, which has generally been adopted in the practice of States. This criterion is the most favourable to the coastal State and clearly shows the character of territorial waters as appurtenant to the land territory. . . .

The Parties also agree that in the case of a low-tide elevation (drying rock) the outer edge at low water of this low-tide elevation may be taken into account as a base-point for calculating the breadth of the territorial sea. . . .

The Court finds itself obliged to decide whether the relevant low-water mark is that of the mainland or of the "skjaergaard." Since the mainland is bordered in its western sector by the "skjaergaard," which constitutes a whole with the mainland, it is the outer line of the "skjaergaard" which must be taken into account in delimiting the belt of Norwegian territorial waters. This solution is dictated by geographic realities.

Three methods have been contemplated to effect the application of the low-water mark rule. The simplest would appear to be the method of the *tracé parallèle*, which consists of drawing the outer limit of the belt of territorial waters by following the coast in all its sinuosities. This method may be applied without difficulty to an ordinary coast, which is not too broken. Where a coast is deeply indented and cut into, as is that of Eastern Finnmark, or where it is bordered by an archipelago such as the "skjaergaard" along the western sector of the coast here in question, the base-line becomes independent of the low-water mark, and can only be determined by means of a geometrical construction. In such circumstances the line of the low-water mark can no longer be put forward as a rule requiring the coastline to be followed in all its sinuosities. Nor can one characterize as exceptions to the rule the very many derogations which would be necessitated by such a rugged coast: the rule would disappear under the exceptions. Such a coast, viewed as a whole, calls for the application of a different method; that is, the method of base-lines which, within reasonable limits, may depart from the physical line of the coast. . . .

The principle that the belt of territorial waters must follow the general direction of the coast makes it possible to fix certain criteria valid for any delimitation of the territorial sea; these criteria will be elucidated later. The Court will confine itself at this stage to noting that, in order to apply this principle, several States have deemed it necessary to follow the straight base-lines method and that they have not encountered objections of principle by other States. This method consists of selecting appropriate points on the low-water mark and drawing straight lines between them. This has been done, not only in the case of well-defined bays, but also in cases of minor curvatures of the coast line where it was solely a question of giving a simpler form to the belt of territorial waters.

It has been contended, on behalf of the United Kingdom, that Norway may draw straight lines only across bays. The Court is unable to share this view. If the belt of territorial waters must follow the outer line of the "skjaergaard," and if the method of straight base-lines must be admitted in certain cases, there is no valid reason to draw them only across bays, as in Eastern Finnmark, and not also to draw them between islands, islets and rocks, across the sea areas separating them, even when such areas do not fall within the conception of a bay. It is sufficient that they should be situated between the island formations of the "skjaergaard," *inter fauces terrarum*. . . .

The Court now comes to the question of the length of the base-lines drawn across the waters lying between the various formations of the "skjaergaard." . . .

In this connection, the practice of States does not justify the formulation of any general rule of law. The attempts that have been made to subject groups of islands or coastal archipelagoes to conditions analogous to the limitations concerning bays (distance between the islands not exceeding twice the breadth of the territorial waters, or ten or twelve sea miles), have not got beyond the stage of proposals. . . .

Consequently, the Court is unable to share the view of the United Kingdom Government, that "Norway, in the matter of base-lines, now claims recognition of an exceptional system." As will be shown later, all that the Court can see therein is the application of general international law to a specific case. . . .

Thus the Court, confining itself for the moment to the Conclusions of the United Kingdom, finds that the Norwegian Government in fixing the base-lines for the delimitation of the Norwegian fisheries zone by the 1935 Decree has not violated international law. . . .

When the Court issued its judgment in the *Fisheries Case*, there was no multilateral treaty generally governing the concept of baselines. That situation has now changed.

United Nations Convention on the Law of the Sea, 10 December 1982, 1833 UNTS 3, in force 16 November 1994

Article 5
Normal baseline
Except where otherwise provided in this Convention, the normal baseline for measuring the breadth of the territorial sea is the low-water line along the coast as marked on large-scale charts officially recognized by the coastal State.

Article 6
Reefs
In the case of islands situated on atolls or of islands having fringing reefs, the baseline for measuring the breadth of the territorial sea is the seaward low-water line of the reef, as shown by the appropriate symbol on charts officially recognized by the coastal State.

Article 7

Straight baselines

1. In localities where the coastline is deeply indented and cut into, or if there is a fringe of islands along the coast in its immediate vicinity, the method of straight baselines joining appropriate points may be employed in drawing the baseline from which the breadth of the territorial sea is measured.

2. Where because of the presence of a delta and other natural conditions the coastline is highly unstable, the appropriate points may be selected along the furthest seaward extent of the low-water line and, notwithstanding subsequent regression of the low-water line, the straight baselines shall remain effective until changed by the coastal State in accordance with this Convention.

3. The drawing of straight baselines must not depart to any appreciable extent from the general direction of the coast, and the sea areas lying within the lines must be sufficiently closely linked to the land domain to be subject to the regime of internal waters.

4. Straight baselines shall not be drawn to and from low-tide elevations, unless lighthouses or similar installations which are permanently above sea level have been built on them or except in instances where the drawing of baselines to and from such elevations has received general international recognition.

5. Where the method of straight baselines is applicable under paragraph 1, account may be taken, in determining particular baselines, of economic interests peculiar to the region concerned, the reality and the importance of which are clearly evidenced by long usage.

6. The system of straight baselines may not be applied by a State in such a manner as to cut off the territorial sea of another State from the high seas or an exclusive economic zone. . . .

Article 9

Mouths of Rivers

If a river flows directly into the sea, the baseline shall be a straight line across the mouth of the river between points on the low-water line of its banks.

Article 10

Bays

1. This article relates only to bays the coasts of which belong to a single State.

2. For the purposes of this Convention, a bay is a well-marked indentation whose penetration is in such proportion to the width of its mouth as to contain land-locked waters and constitute more than a mere curvature of the coast. An indentation shall not, however, be regarded as a bay unless its area is as large as, or larger than, that of the semi-circle whose diameter is a line drawn across the mouth of that indentation.

3. For the purpose of measurement, the area of an indentation is that lying between the low-water mark around the shore of the indentation and a line joining the low-water mark of its natural entrance points. Where, because of the presence of islands, an indentation

has more than one mouth, the semicircle shall be drawn on a line as long as the sum total of the lengths of the lines across the different mouths. Islands within an indentation shall be included as if they were part of the water area of the indentation.

4. If the distance between the low-water marks of the natural entrance points of a bay does not exceed 24 nautical miles, a closing line may be drawn between these two low-water marks, and the waters enclosed thereby shall be considered as internal waters.

5. Where the distance between the low-water marks of the natural entrance points of a bay exceeds 24 nautical miles, a straight baseline of 24 nautical miles shall be drawn within the bay in such a manner as to enclose the maximum area of water that is possible with a line of that length.

6. The foregoing provisions do not apply to so-called "historic" bays, or in any case where the system of straight baselines provided for in article 7 is applied.

Article 11
Ports
For the purpose of delimiting the territorial sea, the outermost permanent harbour works which form an integral part of the harbour system are regarded as forming part of the coast. Off-shore installations and artificial islands shall not be considered as permanent harbour works.

Article 12
Roadsteads
Roadsteads which are normally used for the loading, unloading and anchoring of ships, and which would otherwise be situated wholly or partly outside the outer limit of the territorial sea, are included in the territorial sea.

Article 13
Low-tide elevations
1. A low-tide elevation is a naturally formed area of land which is surrounded by and above water at low tide but submerged at high tide. Where a low-tide elevation is situated wholly or partly at a distance not exceeding the breadth of the territorial sea from the mainland or an island, the low-water line on that elevation may be used as the baseline for measuring the breadth of the territorial sea.

2. Where a low-tide elevation is wholly situated at a distance exceeding the breadth of the territorial sea from the mainland or an island, it has no territorial sea of its own.

Article 14
Combination of methods for determining baselines
The coastal State may determine baselines in turn by any of the methods provided for in the foregoing articles to suit different conditions.

"Historic bays" are bodies of water that greatly exceed in size a standard bay but which, because of an historic and close relationship between these waters and the state in question, are subject to the full sovereignty of that state. The result is that the mouths of such bays are closed off with a straight baseline. A Canadian example is Hudson (historically

"Hudson's") Bay. Consider this 1974 position from Canada's then Department of External Affairs:

> Canada's claim to Hudson Bay as historic water dates from the British Government's grant in 1670 to the Hudson's Bay Company of title to the Hudson Bay and the surrounding territories. . . .
>
> The status of the waters of Hudson Bay and Hudson Strait was described in these terms by the Minister of Northern Affairs and Natural Resources on November 14, 1957 in reply to a question in the House of Commons: "The waters of Hudson Bay are Canadian waters by historic title in accordance with the universally accepted international law doctrine applying to historic bays. Canada regards as inland waters all the waters west of a line drawn across the entrance to Hudson Strait from Button Island to Hatton Head on Resolution Island." . . .
>
> Canada has similar historic claims to the waters of the Gulf of St. Lawrence (Prime Minister St. Laurent referred to this claim in the House of Commons on February 8, 1949 in reporting on the progress of negotiations for the union of Newfoundland with Canada when he said that it was Canada's intention to contend and to seek acquiescence in the contention that the Gulf of St. Lawrence "shall become an inland sea") . . . , the Bay of Fundy, Dixon Entrance, Hecate Strait and Queen Charlotte Sound on the British Columbia coast.[14]

Marine waters lying on the landward side of any straight baseline, including one drawn across the mouth of an historic bay, are considered a state's internal waters. Ocean lying on the seaward side of a baseline, to a maximum distance of 12 nautical miles, is known as the territorial sea:

United Nations Convention on the Law of the Sea, 10 December 1982, 1833 UNTS 3, in force 16 November 1994

Article 3
Breadth of the territorial sea
Every State has the right to establish the breadth of its territorial sea up to a limit not exceeding 12 nautical miles, measured from baselines determined in accordance with this Convention.

Article 4
Outer limit of the territorial sea
The outer limit of the territorial sea is the line every point of which is at a distance from the nearest point of the baseline equal to the breadth of the territorial sea. . . .

Article 8
Internal waters
1. Except as provided in Part IV [relating to archipelagic states], waters on the landward side of the baseline of the territorial sea form part of the internal waters of the State. . . .

---

14 Edward G Lee, "Canadian Practice in International Law during 1973 as Reflected Mainly in Public Correspondence and Statements of the Department of External Affairs" (1974) 12 Can YB Int'l Law 272 at 278–79.

Article 60
Artificial islands, installations and structures in the exclusive economic zone

. . .

8. Artificial islands, installations and structures do not possess the status of islands. They have no territorial sea of their own, and their presence does not affect the delimitation of the territorial sea, the exclusive economic zone or the continental shelf.

Article 121
Regime of Islands
1. An island is a naturally formed area of land, surrounded by water, which is above water at high tide.

2. . . . . [T]he territorial sea . . . of an island [is] determined in accordance with the provisions of this Convention applicable to other land territory. . . .

Once baselines are established (by whatever method), it is possible to imagine that two states proximate to one another across a strait may have overlapping claims to territorial sea. This possibility will arise where the strait, as measured from the respective baselines of the two coastal states, is less than 24 nautical miles in width. Similarly, in the case of two adjacent states whose land border meets the sea at a point where the coastline is concave, perpendicular measurement of the breadth of their respective territorial seas may result in overlapping claims. How is the extent of the territorial sea of each state established in such circumstances? Article 15 of UNCLOS provides:

> Where the coasts of two States are opposite or adjacent to each other, neither of the two States is entitled, failing agreement between them to the contrary, to extend its territorial sea beyond the median line every point of which is equidistant from the nearest points on the baselines from which the breadth of the territorial seas of each of the two States is measured. The above provision does not apply, however, where it is necessary by reason of historic title or other special circumstances to delimit the territorial seas of the two States in a way which is at variance therewith.

b) Nature of State Jurisdiction over Internal Waters and the Territorial Sea

Notably, different levels of control are exercised by the coastal state over internal waters and the territorial sea, although both are considered part of the coastal state's sovereign territory. Essentially, internal waters are subject to the full sovereign control of the coastal state in the same way as is its land territory. The exception to this is when a new straight baseline is established that "has the effect of enclosing as internal waters areas which had not previously been considered as such," in which case the ships of other states enjoy "a right to innocent passage" through those internal waters. As we shall see in the following provisions, however, this right to innocent passage is more generally applicable within the territorial sea, and thus acts as a constraint on the otherwise sovereign jurisdiction of the coastal state over its territorial sea.

LAW IN CONTEXT

State Control over Ports

A ship lying at anchor in port will generally be within a state's internal waters. Are foreign ships entitled as a matter of right to enter these port waters? Consider the view of the Canadian Department of Foreign Affairs and International Trade, expressed in a legal memorandum prepared in 2000:

Access to Ports

. . . A port is part of the internal waters of a State. As the editors of *Oppenheim* state at 572: "Internal waters are legally equivalent to a state's land, and are entirely subject to its territorial sovereignty." As a result, one would expect that a coastal state has a clear right to exclude vessels from its ports absent an agreement to the contrary. This view is supported by one group of writers, including Churchill and Lowe, and O'Connell. A second group of writers, including Colombos, favours the view that, generally, States have an obligation to provide access to their international ports. . . .

As stated above, Churchill and Lowe favour the view that a State has a right to exclude vessels from its ports subject to some exceptions. They put the point this way:

> The existence of sovereignty over internal waters and the absence of any general right of innocent passage through them logically implies the absence of any right in customary international law for foreign ships to enter a State's ports or other internal waters.

These authors note that, as a matter of practice, the international ports of States are presumed to be open to international merchant traffic but conclude that this presumption has not acquired the status of a right in customary law. Even if it had such a status, the right would be subject to at least three types of restrictions. First, a coastal State is entitled to nominate those of its ports that are open to international traffic. Second, a State may close a port to protect its vital interests without thereby violating customary international law. Third, a State may prescribe conditions for access to its ports and may limit access by particular types of vessels, e.g. tankers, nuclear powered vessels and fishing vessels. . . .

The second group of authors argues for a more general right of access to ports. For example, Colombos states as follows:

> 181 General principles applicable to ports—The right of sovereignty recognized to a State should not, in fact, be construed as conferring upon it an unlimited power to prohibit the use of its ports and harbours to foreign nationals. This would imply a neglect of its duties for the promotion of international intercourse, navigation and trade which customary international law imposes upon it. It is submitted that the general principles applicable to ports . . . are . . . as follows: (i) in time of peace, commercial ports must be left open to international traffic. The liberty of access to ports granted to foreign vessels implies their right to load and unload their cargoes. . . .

In sum, we conclude that the law applicable to the right of a coastal state to exclude particular vessels on a case-by-case basis from its ports is not completely clear. The authorities do support the following propositions. First, subject to specific treaty obligations and entry in cases of distress, a coastal state may close its ports to all international commercial traffic. Second, a coastal state may decide to exclude certain classes of vessels on a non-discriminatory basis. For example, subject to existing treaty commitments and trade obligations, Canada might exclude from its ports all vessels containing wastes or hazardous wastes. Canada might also require more extensive prior notification of imports of wastes than are currently provided for under [the *Canadian Environmental Protection Act*, SC 1999, c 33]. Finally, the balance of opinion amongst the learned authors is that a State has an even more extensive right to exclude vessels from its ports. This view is based upon the coastal State's full sovereignty over its ports. . . . This general position is of course subject to the terms of any applicable bilateral or multilateral treaty.[15]

Consider the scope of the right of innocent passage, and the corresponding limitations on coastal state jurisdiction over foreign ships in the territorial sea:

United Nations Convention on the Law of the Sea, 10 December 1982, 1833 UNTS 3, in force 16 November 1994

Article 17
Right of innocent passage
Subject to this Convention, ships of all States, whether coastal or land-locked, enjoy the right of innocent passage through the territorial sea.

Article 18
Meaning of passage
1. Passage means navigation through the territorial sea for the purpose of:
    (a) traversing that sea without entering internal waters or calling at a roadstead or port facility outside internal waters; or
    (b) proceeding to or from internal waters or a call at such roadstead or port facility.

2. Passage shall be continuous and expeditious. However, passage includes stopping and anchoring, but only in so far as the same are incidental to ordinary navigation or are rendered necessary by force majeure or distress or for the purpose of rendering assistance to persons, ships or aircraft in danger or distress.

Article 19
Meaning of innocent passage
1. Passage is innocent so long as it is not prejudicial to the peace, good order or security of the coastal State. Such passage shall take place in conformity with this Convention and with other rules of international law.

2. Passage of a foreign ship shall be considered to be prejudicial to the peace, good order or security of the coastal State if in the territorial sea it engages in any of the following activities:

---

15 Michael Leir, "Canadian Practice in International Law at the Department of Foreign Affairs in 1999–2000" (2000) 38 Can YB Int'l Law 331 at 355–57.

(a) any threat or use of force against the sovereignty, territorial integrity or political independence of the coastal State, or in any other manner in violation of the principles of international law embodied in the Charter of the United Nations;

(b) any exercise or practice with weapons of any kind;

(c) any act aimed at collecting information to the prejudice of the defence or security of the coastal State;

(d) any act of propaganda aimed at affecting the defence or security of the coastal State;

(e) the launching, landing or taking on board of any aircraft;

(f) the launching, landing or taking on board of any military device;

(g) the loading or unloading of any commodity, currency or person contrary to the customs, fiscal, immigration or sanitary laws and regulations of the coastal State;

(h) any act of wilful and serious pollution contrary to this Convention;

(i) any fishing activities;

(j) the carrying out of research or survey activities;

(k) any act aimed at interfering with any systems of communication or any other facilities or installations of the coastal State;

(l) any other activity not having a direct bearing on passage.

Article 20
Submarines and other underwater vehicles
In the territorial sea, submarines and other underwater vehicles are required to navigate on the surface and to show their flag.

Article 21
Laws and regulations of the coastal State relating to innocent passage
1. The coastal State may adopt laws and regulations, in conformity with the provisions of this Convention and other rules of international law, relating to innocent passage through the territorial sea, in respect of all or any of the following:

(a) the safety of navigation and the regulation of maritime traffic;

(b) the protection of navigational aids and facilities and other facilities or installations;

(c) the protection of cables and pipelines;

(d) the conservation of the living resources of the sea;

(e) the prevention of infringement of the fisheries laws and regulations of the coastal State;

(f) the preservation of the environment of the coastal State and the prevention, reduction and control of pollution thereof;

(g) marine scientific research and hydrographic surveys;

(h) the prevention of infringement of the customs, fiscal, immigration or sanitary laws and regulations of the coastal State.

2. Such laws and regulations shall not apply to the design, construction, manning or equipment of foreign ships unless they are giving effect to generally accepted international rules or standards. . . .

4. Foreign ships exercising the right of innocent passage through the territorial sea shall comply with all such laws and regulations and all generally accepted international regulations relating to the prevention of collisions at sea. . . .

Article 22
Sea lanes and traffic separation schemes in the territorial sea
1. The coastal State may, where necessary having regard to the safety of navigation, require foreign ships exercising the right of innocent passage through its territorial sea to use such sea lanes and traffic separation schemes as it may designate or prescribe for the regulation of the passage of ships.

2. In particular, tankers, nuclear-powered ships and ships carrying nuclear or other inherently dangerous or noxious substances or materials may be required to confine their passage to such sea lanes. . . .

Article 24
Duties of the coastal State
1. The coastal State shall not hamper the innocent passage of foreign ships through the territorial sea except in accordance with this Convention. In particular, in the application of this Convention or of any laws or regulations adopted in conformity with this Convention, the coastal State shall not:
　　(a) impose requirements on foreign ships which have the practical effect of denying or impairing the right of innocent passage; or
　　(b) discriminate in form or in fact against the ships of any State or against ships carrying cargoes to, from or on behalf of any State. . . .

Article 25
Rights of protection of the coastal State
1. The coastal State may take the necessary steps in its territorial sea to prevent passage which is not innocent.

2. In the case of ships proceeding to internal waters or a call at a port facility outside internal waters, the coastal State also has the right to take the necessary steps to prevent any breach of the conditions to which admission of those ships to internal waters or such a call is subject.

3. The coastal State may, without discrimination in form or in fact among foreign ships, suspend temporarily in specified areas of its territorial sea the innocent passage of foreign ships if such suspension is essential for the protection of its security, including weapons exercises. Such suspension shall take effect only after having been duly published.

Article 26
Charges which may be levied upon foreign ships
1. No charge may be levied upon foreign ships by reason only of their passage through the territorial sea.

2. Charges may be levied upon a foreign ship passing through the territorial sea as payment only for specific services rendered to the ship. These charges shall be levied without discrimination.

Innocent passage relates to the means by which the ship's passage is undertaken, as Article 19 suggests, and is a right. Note particularly the limitations on measures that may be taken by the coastal state to interfere with this right enjoyed by other states in its territorial sea (Articles 24 and 26). However, as suggested by Article 25, the right is strictly defined and hinges critically on the condition of "innocence" as defined by Article 19 of UNCLOS.

Consider the importance of the right of innocent passage through the territorial sea. Why have coastal states been willing to agree to such a dramatic incursion into their territorial sovereignty?

The foregoing provisions apply to "all ships." Thus, warships, like other vessels, are entitled to innocent passage, so long as they too respect the standards of "innocence." However, the Convention also includes some additional, detailed rules for warships:

United Nations Convention on the Law of the Sea, 10 December 1982, 1833 UNTS 3, in force 16 November 1994

Article 29
Definition of warships
For the purposes of this Convention, "warship" means a ship belonging to the armed forces of a State bearing the external marks distinguishing such ships of its nationality, under the command of an officer duly commissioned by the government of the State and whose name appears in the appropriate service list or its equivalent, and manned by a crew which is under regular armed forces discipline.

Article 30
Non-compliance by warships with the laws and regulations of the coastal State
If any warship does not comply with the laws and regulations of the coastal State concerning passage through the territorial sea and disregards any request for compliance therewith which is made to it, the coastal State may require it to leave the territorial sea immediately.

Article 31
Responsibility of the flag State for damage caused by a warship or other government ship operated for non-commercial purposes
The flag State shall bear international responsibility for any loss or damage to the coastal State resulting from the non-compliance by a warship or other government ship operated for non-commercial purposes with the laws and regulations of the coastal State concerning passage through the territorial sea or with the provisions of this Convention or other rules of international law.

Article 32
Immunities of warships and other government ships operated for non-commercial purposes
With such exceptions as are contained in [articles 17 through 26] and in articles 30 and 31, nothing in this Convention affects the immunities of warships and other government ships operated for non-commercial purposes.

Article 32 preserves the customary international legal position that foreign warships and non-commercial state vessels enjoy absolute immunity from coastal state enforcement jurisdiction. In effect, this means that unless the foreign state waives its immunity in respect of its vessel, the coastal state may not exercise any jurisdiction over persons or events occurring thereon. (We discuss state immunities at greater length in Chapter 8.) No similar immunity exists for other foreign ships. That said, as might be expected from the limited capacity of coastal states to interfere with the right of innocent passage, their jurisdiction in relation to events occurring on board foreign ships in the territorial sea is also limited:

United Nations Convention on the Law of the Sea, 10 December 1982, 1833 UNTS 3, in force 16 November 1994

Article 27
Criminal jurisdiction on board a foreign ship
1. The criminal jurisdiction of the coastal State should not be exercised on board a foreign ship passing through the territorial sea to arrest any person or to conduct any investigation in connection with any crime committed on board the ship during its passage, save only in the following cases:
    (a) if the consequences of the crime extend to the coastal State;
    (b) if the crime is of a kind to disturb the peace of the country or the good order of the territorial sea;
    (c) if the assistance of the local authorities has been requested by the master of the ship or by a diplomatic agent or consular officer of the flag State; or
    (d) if such measures are necessary for the suppression of illicit traffic in narcotic drugs or psychotropic substances.

2. The above provisions do not affect the right of the coastal State to take any steps authorized by its laws for the purpose of an arrest or investigation on board a foreign ship passing through the territorial sea after leaving internal waters. . . .

5. Except as provided in Part XII [dealing with Protection and Preservation of the Marine Environment] or with respect to violations of laws and regulations adopted in accordance with Part V [dealing with the Exclusive Economic Zone], the coastal State may not take any steps on board a foreign ship passing through the territorial sea to arrest any person or to conduct any investigation in connection with any crime committed before the ship entered the territorial sea, if the ship, proceeding from a foreign port, is only passing through the territorial sea without entering internal waters.

Article 28
Civil jurisdiction in relation to foreign ships
1. The coastal State should not stop or divert a foreign ship passing through the territorial sea for the purpose of exercising civil jurisdiction in relation to a person on board the ship.

2. The coastal State may not levy execution against or arrest the ship for the purpose of any civil proceedings, save only in respect of obligations or liabilities assumed or incurred by the ship itself in the course or for the purpose of its voyage through the waters of the coastal State.

3. Paragraph 2 is without prejudice to the right of the coastal State, in accordance with its laws, to levy execution against or to arrest, for the purpose of any civil proceedings, a

foreign ship lying in the territorial sea, or passing through the territorial sea after leaving internal waters.

As can be seen from these provisions, the exercise of enforcement jurisdiction by the coastal state over vessels in its territorial sea is the exception rather than the rule. While no similar restrictions exist in respect of foreign non-government vessels lying in internal waters, in practice many states follow the same rules in that situation. This does not mean, however, that foreign vessels are unregulated. As a general rule, jurisdiction is to be exercised over ships by their "flag state"—being the state in which they are registered.

2) International Straits

Before moving beyond the territorial sea, we examine briefly the special rules developed to deal with what are known as "international straits"—essentially, narrow ocean passages used for shipping and other forms of international transit that would, barring special rules, be captured by the regular rules set out above.

Even before the adoption of UNCLOS, international straits were subject to a special legal regime. Consider the following excerpt from the first contentious case decided by the International Court of Justice:

Corfu Channel Case (United Kingdom v Albania), Merits, [1949] ICJ Rep 4

[The Corfu Channel, lying between mainland Albania and the Greek island of Corfu, passes through the Albanian territorial sea. It had long been used by the United Kingdom and other states to pass from one area of the Mediterranean to another, notwithstanding the availability of other routes and longstanding Albanian claims that it had the right to control transit through the Channel. At the time this dispute arose, Albania was in a state of war with Greece and had warned the United Kingdom that it would no longer tolerate British transit through the Channel. Several British warships nevertheless transited the Channel and, in doing so, struck a minefield. There was no direct evidence that the mines had been laid by Albania. The British Navy subsequently returned and swept the Channel for mines. The United Kingdom then took action against Albania in the International Court of Justice for damages caused by the incident. Albania counterclaimed for violations of its sovereignty. The following excerpt from the judgment deals only with the latter issue.]

. . . The Court will now consider the Albanian contention that the United Kingdom Government violated Albanian sovereignty by sending the warships through this Strait without the previous authorization of the Albanian Government.

It is, in the opinion of the Court, generally recognized and in accordance with international custom that States in time of peace have a right to send their warships through straits used for international navigation between two parts of the high seas without the previous authorization of a coastal State, provided that the passage is innocent. Unless otherwise prescribed in an international convention, there is no right for a coastal State to prohibit such passage through straits in time of peace.

The Albanian Government does not dispute that the North Corfu Channel is a strait in the geographical sense; but it denies that this Channel belongs to the class of international highways through which a right of passage exists, on the grounds that it is only of secondary importance and not even a necessary route between two parts of the high seas, and that it is used almost exclusively for local traffic to and from the ports of Corfu and Saranda.

It may be asked whether the test is to be found in the volume of traffic passing through the Strait or in its greater or lesser importance for international navigation. But in the opinion of the Court the decisive criterion is rather its geographical situation as connecting two parts of the high seas and the fact of its being used for international navigation. Nor can it be decisive that this Strait is not a necessary route between two parts of the high seas, but only an alternative passage between the Aegean and the Adriatic Seas. It has nevertheless been a useful route for international maritime traffic. . . .

One fact of particular importance is that the North Corfu Channel constitutes a frontier between Albania and Greece, that a part of it is wholly within the territorial waters of these States, and that the Strait is of special importance to Greece by reason of the traffic to and from the port of Corfu.

Having regard to these various considerations, the Court has arrived at the conclusion that the North Corfu Channel should be considered as belonging to the class of international highways through which passage cannot be prohibited by a coastal State in time of peace. . . .

The special status of international straits is preserved—and in some cases enhanced—by UNCLOS. Note the differences between the applicability and nature of the right of passage through international straits recognized in the *Corfu Channel Case* and the following UNCLOS provisions respectively:

United Nations Convention on the Law of the Sea, 10 December 1982, 1833 UNTS 3, in force 16 November 1994

PART III
STRAITS USED FOR INTERNATIONAL NAVIGATION

Section 1: General Provisions

. . .

Article 36
High seas routes or routes through exclusive economic zones through straits used for international navigation
This Part does not apply to a strait used for international navigation if there exists through the strait a route through the high seas or through an exclusive economic zone of similar convenience with respect to navigational and hydrographical characteristics. . . .

Section 2: Transit Passage

Article 37
Scope of this section
This section applies to straits which are used for international navigation between one part of the high seas or an exclusive economic zone and another part of the high seas or an exclusive economic zone.

Article 38
Right of transit passage
1. In straits referred to in article 37, all ships and aircraft enjoy the right of transit passage, which shall not be impeded; except that, if the strait is formed by an island of a State bordering the strait and its mainland, transit passage shall not apply if there exists seaward of the island a route through the high seas or through an exclusive economic zone of similar convenience with respect to navigational and hydrographical characteristics.

2. Transit passage means the exercise in accordance with this Part of the freedom of navigation and overflight solely for the purpose of continuous and expeditious transit of the strait between one part of the high seas or an exclusive economic zone and another part of the high seas or an exclusive economic zone. However, the requirement of continuous and expeditious transit does not preclude passage through the strait for the purpose of entering, leaving or returning from a State bordering the strait, subject to the conditions of entry to that State. . . .

Article 39
Duties of ships and aircraft during transit passage
1. Ships and aircraft, while exercising the right of transit passage, shall:
    (a) proceed without delay through or over the strait;
    (b) refrain from any threat or use of force against the sovereignty, territorial integrity or political independence of States bordering the strait, or in any other manner in violation of the principles of international law embodied in the Charter of the United Nations;
    (c) refrain from any activities other than those incident to their normal modes of continuous and expeditious transit unless rendered necessary by force majeure or by distress;
    (d) comply with other relevant provisions of this Part.

2. Ships in transit passage shall:
    (a) comply with generally accepted international regulations, procedures and practices for safety at sea, including the International Regulations for Preventing Collisions at Sea;
    (b) comply with generally accepted international regulations, procedures and practices for the prevention, reduction and control of pollution from ships.

3. Aircraft in transit passage shall:
    (a) observe the Rules of the Air established by the International Civil Aviation Organization as they apply to civil aircraft; state aircraft will normally comply with such safety measures and will at all times operate with due regard for the safety of navigation;

(b) at all times monitor the radio frequency assigned by the competent internationally designated air traffic control authority or the appropriate international distress radio frequency.

Article 40
Research and survey activities
During transit passage, foreign ships, including marine scientific research and hydrographic survey ships, may not carry out any research or survey activities without the prior authorization of the States bordering straits.

Article 41
Sea lanes and traffic separation schemes in straits used for international navigation
1. In conformity with this Part, States bordering straits may designate sea lanes and prescribe traffic separation schemes for navigation in straits where necessary to promote the safe passage of ships.

2. Such States may, when circumstances require, and after giving due publicity thereto, substitute other sea lanes or traffic separation schemes for any sea lanes or traffic separation schemes previously designated or prescribed by them. . . .

Article 42
Laws and regulations of States bordering straits relating to transit passage
1. Subject to the provisions of this section, States bordering straits may adopt laws and regulations relating to transit passage through straits, in respect of all or any of the following:
    (a) the safety of navigation and the regulation of maritime traffic, as provided in article 41;
    (b) the prevention, reduction and control of pollution, by giving effect to applicable international regulations regarding the discharge of oil, oily wastes and other noxious substances in the strait;
    (c) with respect to fishing vessels, the prevention of fishing, including the stowage of fishing gear;
    (d) the loading or unloading of any commodity, currency or person in contravention of the customs, fiscal, immigration or sanitary laws and regulations of States bordering straits.

2. Such laws and regulations shall not discriminate in form or in fact among foreign ships or in their application have the practical effect of denying, hampering or impairing the right of transit passage as defined in this section.

3. States bordering straits shall give due publicity to all such laws and regulations.

4. Foreign ships exercising the right of transit passage shall comply with such laws and regulations.

5. The flag State of a ship or the State of registry of an aircraft entitled to sovereign immunity which acts in a manner contrary to such laws and regulations or other provisions of this Part shall bear international responsibility for any loss or damage which results to States bordering straits. . . .

Article 44

Duties of States bordering straits

States bordering straits shall not hamper transit passage and shall give appropriate publicity to any danger to navigation or overflight within or over the strait of which they have knowledge. There shall be no suspension of transit passage.

Section 3: Innocent Passage

Article 45

Innocent passage

1. The regime of innocent passage, in accordance with [Articles 17 through 32] shall apply in straits used for international navigation:

   (a) excluded from the application of the regime of transit passage under article 38, paragraph 1; or

   (b) between a part of the high seas or an exclusive economic zone and the territorial sea of a foreign State.

2. There shall be no suspension of innocent passage through such straits.

What are the essential differences between the UNCLOS regimes for innocent passage and transit passage through international straits? Is there any condition of innocence attached to the latter? May coastal states prevent or suspend the latter? What is the purpose of a transit passage regime that differs from innocent passage?

Before leaving this discussion of international straits, consider how the concepts of baselines, internal waters, the territorial sea, and international straits have implications for Canadian assertions of control over Arctic waters—particularly at a time when climate change is having a significant impact on the Arctic:

Donald M McRae, "Arctic Sovereignty: What Is at Stake?" (2007) 64(1) Behind the Headlines 1–23 (Canadian Institute for International Affairs)

Canada's Arctic consists of land, water and ice, sometimes permanently frozen, increasingly not. In 1907 Senator Poirier advocated that Canada's Arctic claim should extend from the mainland of Canada up to the North Pole, bounded by sector lines—the 141st meridian of west longitude to the west and the 60th meridian of west longitude to the east—which would form an apex at the North Pole. This is what is known as the sector claim in the Arctic. Although Poirier may well have been concerned only with the land within that sector, the sector claim has often been seen as a claim to sovereignty over land and waters. Certainly any discussion of Canada's Arctic sovereignty relates to the islands and waters lying north of the Canadian mainland, what is often referred to as the Canadian Arctic archipelago.

At the time of Senator Poirier's speech there was uncertainty about sovereignty over islands in the Arctic, but by the end of the 1930s any dispute over the islands within the Poirier sector, had abated. . . . With the exception of Hans Island, a small island in the Kennedy Channel between Greenland and Ellesmere Island whose sovereignty is disputed between Denmark and Canada, there is no challenge to Canada's sovereignty over the islands of the Arctic. . . .

Although the issue of sovereignty over the land is quite clear, the situation in respect of the waters is more complicated. . . .

Canada's Arctic Archipelago and the Northwest Passage

One basis for a sovereignty claim over the waters between the islands of the Canadian archipelago is that they are the internal waters of Canada on the basis of historic title. Such a claim involves treating Canada's rights to sovereignty over the lands, established through historic, effective occupation and control, as rights to sovereignty over the waters as well. Claims to treat waters as internal by reason of historic title are not unknown around the world. The basis for Canada's now uncontested claim that the waters of Hudson's Bay are internal waters rests in part on such a claim. And some support for an historic claim to the waters of the Arctic archipelago rests on the practice of the Inuit who for centuries occupied the land and ice, making no distinction between the frozen land and the frozen sea. . . .

The objective among supporters of the sector and the historic title claims was to ensure that the waters of the Canadian Arctic archipelago would be subject to full Canadian sovereignty. This would mean that the waters of the Northwest Passage would be subject to Canadian jurisdiction and control. Ships navigating through the Passage would be able to do so only if permitted by Canadian law and they could navigate only in accordance with Canadian law.

Control over the Northwest Passage lies at the heart of the Canadian Arctic sovereignty issue.

In 1963 Ivan Head wrote, "It is highly unlikely that uninterrupted surface passage from the Labrador Sea to either the Arctic Ocean or the Beaufort Sea, or *vice versa*, will ever be a reality. Future demands for the right of innocent passage through the archipelago are speculative to a degree." Transits of the Passage had been few, and they had generally been Canadian.

Some 6 years later the illusion was shattered when the voyage of the SS *Manhattan* awakened Canada to the possibility that there would be commercial shipping through the Northwest Passage. In fact, the Manhattan voyages demonstrated that commercial shipping was not feasible at that time, but it opened eyes to the enormous potential for environmental damage if oil tankers were eventually to transit Arctic waters, and it reawakened interest in the debate over sovereignty over the waters of the Arctic.

Although in 1970 Canada's claims to jurisdiction over the waters off its coast were not as extensive as they are today, at the very least any transit of the Northwest Passage involved passage through the territorial sea of Canada. But, of course, if those waters were territorial sea, there would be a right of innocent passage through them. And while it may have been possible at that time for the coastal state to establish laws to protect against marine pollution in the territorial sea, the extent of that authority was unclear.

There was a further problem. Linking as it does the North Atlantic and the North Pacific oceans, a sea route through the Northwest Passage might be regarded in law as an international strait through which there would also be a right of passage that would be more onerous for the coastal state than the right of innocent passage in the territorial sea. The events surrounding the Manhattan voyage took place at a particularly inopportune time. The negotiations for what was ultimately to become the 1982 Convention on the Law of the Sea were getting underway and major shipping states and states with large navies were talking of rights of transit through international straits that would be greater than "innocent passage". A right of "transit passage" was beginning to emerge.

In the wake of the *Manhattan* incident the Canadian government under Prime Minister Trudeau decided on a different strategy. Instead of asserting an all-purpose sovereignty claim, it enacted the Arctic Waters Pollution Prevention Act [RSC 1985, c A-12] under which jurisdiction out to 100 miles from the coast for pollution prevention purposes was asserted. Essentially, Canada was claiming the authority to control shipping in the Northwest Passage, indeed throughout the waters of the Arctic archipelago and beyond, according to its own standards, including the right if necessary to prohibit shipping in those waters. This novel unilateral assertion of jurisdiction was protested by the United States and by some European countries, but the opposition was not as widespread or as vociferous as might have been anticipated. States seemed to understand the problem Canada was seeking to deal with and there was some sympathy for it.

There followed a substantial campaign by Canada in a variety of multilateral fora to gain international acceptance of its right to regulate the unique Arctic marine environment. Ultimately that campaign met with success. The 1982 [United Nations] Convention on the Law of the Sea contains a provision known as the "arctic exception", Article 234, which permits coastal states to regulate to prevent, reduce or control marine pollution in ice-covered areas within its exclusive economic zone - that is within 200 nautical miles of its coast. The inclusion of Article 234 in the Convention was widely seen and understood by states to be a vindication of Canada's Arctic Waters Pollution Prevention Act. Indeed while the Act extended only to 100 nautical miles . . . , Article 234 permitted the exercise of jurisdiction out to 200 nautical miles.

There is, however, an important limitation in respect of Article 234. It does not apply to warships or to other government ships. This meant that the environmental strategy adopted following the voyage of the *SS Manhattan* resulting in the Arctic exception went only part way towards ensuring that Canada would be able to regulate to preserve the Arctic environment to deal with the consequences of navigation through the Northwest Passage.

The fact that Canada's authority was only partial was brought home in 1985 with the voyage of the US icebreaker *Polar Sea* into the waters of the Northwest Passage without Canada's prior consent. This put the issue of sovereignty back in the limelight. The United States appeared to assume that it could transit Canadian waters without Canada's consent, seemingly a clear challenge to Canada's claim to sovereignty over the waters of the Canadian Arctic archipelago.

By now there were few options left for Canada to preserve its legal position in respect of the Northwest Passage. What had to be done was to clarify its position on sovereignty over the waters. If the waters of the Arctic archipelago were internal waters of Canada, then Canada had full rights to regulate shipping in those waters, including warships and other government vessels of foreign states, and if necessary to exclude them from those waters.

The measure adopted by Canada to confirm sovereignty over the waters of the Canadian Arctic archipelago was known as the drawing of "straight baselines" . . . .

Thus, on 10 September 1985, Secretary of State Joe Clark announced that the government was confirming Canada's sovereignty over the waters of the Arctic archipelago by enclosing the archipelago with straight baselines. In a stirring speech to the House of Commons, Minister Clark stated, "Canada's sovereignty in the Arctic is indivisible. It embraces land, sea and ice. It extends without interruption to the seaward facing coasts of the Arctic islands. These Islands are joined and not divided by the waters between them."

Canada's actions resulted in protests by the United States and by the European Community. However, the Reagan administration in the United States seemed less interested in pressing its legal position and more interested in finding a way to cooperate with Canada. Thus, in 1988 the Arctic Cooperation Agreement was entered into between Canada and the United States under which the United States pledged that, "all navigation by US icebreakers within waters claimed by Canada to be internal will be undertaken with the consent of the Government of Canada."[16] Both parties, however, reserved their legal positions on the law of the sea, implicitly protecting their respective positions on the legal status of the waters of the Northwest Passage.

With the promulgation of straight baselines around the Arctic archipelago Canada has essentially done all it can do legally to cement its claim that the waters of the archipelago are the internal waters of Canada. As internal waters, the waters of the Northwest Passage are completely under Canadian sovereignty. They could never become an international strait. Thus whether vessels are permitted through the Northwest Passage and under what conditions would be decided in accordance with Canadian law.

Not all states accept that these are the internal waters of Canada, but no state has decided to take Canada to court over the matter. In fact, there is nothing stopping them from unilaterally doing so. In 1970, when Canada adopted the Arctic Waters Pollution Prevention Act, the government modified its acceptance of the compulsory jurisdiction of the International Court of Justice so that no state could challenge the international validity of the legislation without Canada's consent. In 1985, when straight baselines were drawn for the Arctic archipelago, Canada again modified its acceptance of the jurisdiction of the International Court, this time opening itself to challenge by other states without first seeking Canada's consent.

Thus if the United Kingdom wanted to challenge Canada's position on the Northwest Passage, it could bring a case against Canada tomorrow in the International Court of Justice and Canada would be forced to defend that case. The United States, however, could not bring such a claim since it no longer accepts the compulsory jurisdiction of the Court. . . .

Challenges to Canada's Sovereignty Claim

What, in legal terms, does a challenge to Canada's Arctic sovereignty mean? Canada's sovereignty over the land is unchallengeable so, with the exception of Hans Island, land is not in issue. Two things could be challenged. First, Canada's claim that the waters of the Canadian Arctic archipelago are the internal waters of Canada could be challenged.

---

16 [Agreement between the Government of Canada and the Government of the United States of America on Arctic Cooperation, 11 January 1988, 1852 UNTS 59, Can TS 1988 No 29, in force 11 January 1988, art 3.]

Second, a claim could be made that the waters of the Northwest Passage have the status of an "international strait" with a consequent right for international shipping to pass through those waters. . . .

Internal Waters

Predicting the outcome of litigation is a hazardous business in international law, particularly when one is dealing with an area that is in a sense unique with little in terms of prior authority to assist in the prediction. The combination of the sheer size of the area involved, the fact that it is comprised of land and frozen sea, the fact that Inuit have for centuries used the land and water is if they were interchangeable, all go to make examples of the use of straight baselines elsewhere in the world useful but not entirely on point.

At the same time, these differences are elements of strength in the Canadian position. The fact that the areas concerned are far larger than other areas where straight baselines are normally drawn is counterbalanced by the uniqueness of the interrelationship of sea, land and ice, and patterns of usage by indigenous peoples add to the particularity of the area. All of these factors go to support Canada's claim to use the straight baseline method to define and enclose the area. And straight baselines are more than an assertion that the waters of the Arctic archipelago are internal waters. They are also an important step in consolidating the claim that these are Canadian internal waters by virtue of historic title.

Since Canada was not a party to the 1982 [United Nations] Convention on the Law of the Sea when it drew straight baselines, the status of the waters enclosed by the baselines has to be measured at the time of the drawing of the baselines, not at the later date when Canada became a party to the Convention. Thus, Canada is not affected by Articles 8 and 35 of the 1982 Law of the Sea Convention. According to these Articles if the drawing of straight baselines encloses, as internal, waters through which previously a right of passage existed, then that right of passage remains even after the drawing of straight baselines. There was no such customary international law rule binding on Canada when it drew the baselines and so the waters enclosed by straight baselines are not affected.

Canada, then, has a strong legal argument to support the claim that the waters of the Arctic archipelago are the internal waters of Canada and thus subject to full Canadian sovereignty. If the matter were challenged before an international tribunal, Canada would have a good chance of winning. If it did, Canada's claim to permit or not to permit shipping through the Northwest Passage and to set standards for such shipping would be unassailable.

International Strait

The second possible challenge to Canada's arctic sovereignty is the claim that the waters of the Northwest Passage constitute an international strait. This is a critical issue, because the right of transit passage through international straits under the 1982 [United Nations] Convention on the Law of the Sea limits substantially the ability of the coastal state to control shipping exercising the right of passage.

It is difficult to deny that the Northwest Passage meets the geographic test for an international strait — it joins the waters of the Labrador Sea with the waters of the Beaufort Sea, or more broadly, it is a link between the Atlantic and Pacific Oceans. However, the key question is whether it meets the functional test. Are the waters of the Northwest Passage waters that are "used for international navigation"? The usage test is derived from the decision of the International Court of Justice in the 1949 *Corfu Channel Case*. There, the Court concluded that the Corfu Channel was an international strait. It was "used for international navigation" and in one recorded year there had been almost 3000 ships using the Channel.

If the *Corfu Channel Case* sets the standard of the volume of shipping required to meet the test of whether the waters are "used for international navigation" then the Northwest Passage clearly does not constitute an international strait. There have been approximately 100 surface transits of the Northwest Passage over the past 100 years, the vast majority by Canadian vessels. International navigation has been extremely limited. Moreover, with one or two exceptions all of the international transits have been with Canadian assent and in many cases with Canadian ice-breaking support.

There is one potentially important qualification to this. While the surface transits are known, much less is known about transit by submarines. It is assumed that they occur but it is not clear whether they occur under Canadian authority and with the consent of the Government of Canada or whether they are transits of which Canada knows little. If, in fact, they have been frequent and without Canadian knowledge or consent, then it might be possible to show that the Northwest Passage has been "used for international navigation" and that in practice submarines have been exercising a right of transit passage. One assumption is that most submarine transits would have been by US vessels and that they are in some way authorized under defence arrangements between Canada and the United States. But, again, there is no solid information about this and there are sufficient conflicting statements by former members of the Canadian military to indicate that this is an area of potential difficulty for the future.

A further argument about the term "used for international navigation" is that it could mean "capable of being used for international navigation". This appears to be the position adhered to by the United States. However, no support for this interpretation can be found in the *Corfu Channel Case*, and it seems to be contradicted by the express wording of the 1982 Convention itself. In defining an international strait, Article 37 of the Convention refers to "straits which are used for international navigation". The plain meaning of that phrase is that the reference is to straits that are actually used for international navigation, not waters that could potentially be used for international navigation.

Thus, should any state decide at the present time to challenge Canada's claim that the waters of the Northwest Passage are the internal waters of Canada or seek to assert that the Northwest Passage constitutes an international strait, they would be met with arguments that are legally sound and that would have a good chance of success. Nevertheless, this is to some extent uncharted territory and there remains a possibility that Canada could lose on either of those claims, or that the situation could change and that Canada's legal position would be less secure in the future.

What could cause such a change? As far as the internal waters claim is concerned nothing short of express abandonment of that claim by Canada can affect it. Either the waters of the Canadian Arctic archipelago are the internal waters of Canada or they are not. But the claim that the waters of the Northwest Passage constitute an international strait could be strengthened if the strait came to be used for international navigation. If the passage of foreign ships through the Northwest Passage increased, the argument that the waters are not "used for international navigation" would diminish and over time the claim that the test for an international strait was not met by the Northwest Passage would be difficult to maintain, particularly if passage were occurring without Canada's consent.

The difficult question is what kind of increase in international shipping would be necessary to turn the Northwest Passage into an international strait? Opinions are divided on this. On the one extreme, there is little support for the view that a single unauthorized transit of the Northwest Passage could transform the waters into an international strait. At the other extreme, it seems unlikely that the volume of shipping that existed in the Corfu Channel would be necessary, and indeed significantly less might be sufficient in the particular context of the remote and inhospitable arctic waters.

Certainly, if over a period of years there were international shipping through the Northwest Passage without any attempt by Canada to regulate that shipping, the waters could become an international strait. And the greater the volume of shipping, the greater the likelihood that this would occur. The challenge for Canada is to ensure that all transits of the Northwest Passage are with its knowledge and consent. . . .

What would be the consequences for Canada if it were to lose a challenge to its claim that the waters are the internal waters of Canada through which no right of passage exists? . . .

[W]hile a determination that the waters of the Canadian Arctic archipelago were not the internal waters of Canada would no doubt be perceived as a major loss to Canadian sovereignty, in practical terms the situation would be much as it is today. Canada would regulate commercial shipping through the Arctic Waters Pollution Prevention Act, and rely on its bilateral arrangement with the United States, the 1988 Arctic Cooperation Agreement, to cover US icebreakers — effectively covering all US government surface vessels that are likely to enter Arctic waters. The situation with respect to submarines would remain as obscure as it is today.

What if Canada were to lose a challenge to its position that the waters of the Northwest Passage do not constitute an international strait? . . .

[I]n this respect again, although it would be widely perceived as a significant sovereignty loss, the fact that the Northwest Passage constituted an international strait would have little impact on Canada's legal authority to regulate commercial shipping. And, once again, the situation with respect to warships and government vessels would depend on bilateral arrangements with other governments. The Arctic Cooperation Agreement would be significant here as well.

Having said this, there are two aspects that would still remain problematic. The first is the continued applicability of Article 234. That provision applies to "ice-covered areas" and it refers to them as areas, where particularly severe climatic conditions and the presence of ice covering such areas for most of the year create obstructions or exceptional hazards to navigation and pollution of the marine environment could cause major harm to or irreversible disturbance of the ecological balance.

If the ice recedes so that the Northwest Passage is no longer covered with ice for most of the year, can Article 234 still be applied? Certainly the susceptibility to major harm and irreversible ecological damage is unlikely to change, but would the other precondition for the application of Article 234 — that the area be ice-covered for most of the year — be lost? While this may not occur for some time, it indicates the precariousness of relying simply on Article 234 as a justification for Canadian authority to regulate shipping in the Arctic.

The second concern relates to submarine passage. If submarines are in fact passing through the Northwest Passage outside of the defence arrangements that Canada has with the United States or not otherwise known to or authorized by Canada, this remains a potential problem for Canada's claim that the waters of the Northwest Passage are not "used for international navigation" and hence not an international strait. . . .

Conclusion

The claim that Canada's Arctic sovereignty is under threat is a broad claim. And as a symbolic statement that Canadian governments should pay more attention to a vital part of Canada, it has an important role to play in Canadian political debate. But the "threat" if it can be called that, is much narrower in scope than the term Arctic sovereignty would imply. It is not about a threat to sovereignty over land or to Canada's rights over the waters of the Arctic archipelago more generally, or to Canada's rights to the marine and mineral resources of the waters or the seabed. All of these are intact and not challenged, nor are they challengeable.

The fundamental question is whether shipping through the Northwest Passage is to be regulated by Canada in accordance with standards that Canada itself determines, or whether Canada is limited in what it can do by having to comply with generally accepted international standards. This is simply another way of putting the question, are the waters of the Northwest Passage the internal waters of Canada or do they constitute an international strait? In fact, some would contend that it is incorrect to characterize the question as a sovereignty issue at all. There are many international straits around the world subject to the rules of transit passage, but the adjacent coastal states do not consider that the existence of the strait has somehow impaired their sovereignty.

Nevertheless, the issue in respect of transit through the Northwest Passage has been framed in Canada in sovereignty terms, and it is unlikely that the terminology will be abandoned. And there is no doubt that many Canadians would feel that their sovereignty had been diminished if shipping through the Northwest Passage could not be regulated according to standards set by Canada, regardless of what international lawyers might say about the meaning of sovereignty. . . .

Consider the following summary of the Government of Canada's position on these issues, and of steps being taken to address them, provided by the Legal Bureau of the Department of Foreign Affairs and International Trade in 2009:

Alan H Kessel, "Canadian Practice in International Law at the Department of Foreign Affairs and International Trade in 2008–2009" (2009) 47 Can YB Int'l Law 411 at 422–23

The "Northwest Passage"

No one disputes that the various waterways known as the "Northwest Passage" are Canadian. The issue is the legal status of these waters—control over foreign navigation. These waters are internal waters of Canada, which means Canada has an unfettered right to regulate as it would in land territory. The United States agrees the waters are Canadian, but contends that a "strait used for international navigation" runs through them, giving foreign vessels a right of transit. Through the 1988 *Arctic Cooperation Agreement* Canada and the US have agreed to disagree without prejudice to either position. The US asks for permission for its icebreakers to enter these waters, and Canada grants this permission.

Canada permits navigation in its internal waters, including the "Northwest Passage", providing ships respect Canadian conditions and controls related to safety, security, the environment, and Inuit interests. Ice conditions remain extremely variable and the "Northwest Passage" is unlikely to attract routine transits in the short to medium term.

Shipping Controls in the Canadian Arctic

On June 11, 2009 Bill C-3 (An Act to Amend the *Arctic Waters Pollution Prevention Act*) amending the definition "arctic waters"—to extend the geographic application of the AWPPA to the outer limit of Canada's EEZ north of 60—received Royal Assent. The right to exercise strict pollution prevention measures in ice-covered waters out to a maximum of 200 nautical miles is codified in Article 234 of the *United Nations Convention on the Law of the Sea* (UNCLOS).

Canada is currently in the process of developing the necessary regulations to formally establish the Northern Canada Vessel Traffic Services (NORDREG) zone with mandatory ship reporting requirements. The proposed regulations, expected to be in place for the 2010 shipping season, will replace the current voluntary system, which enjoys a high degree of compliance. These regulations are expected to be in place for the 2010 shipping season. Mandatory reporting to NORDREG will enhance the safety and security of vessels navigating in Arctic waters, and will provide better tools for pollution prevention in these waters.

[*Reprinted with permission of the Publisher from Canadian Yearbook of International Law, Volume 47 edited by Don McRae © University of British Columbia Press 2009. All rights reserved by the Publisher.*]

The coming into force of the NORDREG regime in July 2010[17] has prompted complaints by several states, including the United States, that Canada has no authority to impose such mandatory measures on foreign shipping without first seeking approval of the International Maritime Organization (IMO)—the UN specialized agency with responsibility for the safety and security of shipping and the prevention of marine pollution by ships. Consider the Government of Canada's position with respect to such complaints:

Alan H Kessel, "Canadian Practice in International Law at the Department of Foreign Affairs and International Trade in 2010–11" (2011) 49 Can YB Int'l Law 481 at 417–18

Article 234 of UNCLOS provides for the right of coastal States to adopt and enforce non-discriminatory laws and regulations for the prevention, reduction and control of marine pollution from vessels in ice-covered areas within the limits of the Exclusive Economic Zone (EEZ). Article 234 permits States to enact these laws and regulations without seeking prior IMO approval. Accompanying the right to enact such laws is a general obligation under Article 192 to protect and preserve the marine environment.

---

17   *Northern Canada Vessel Traffic Services Zone Regulations*, SOR 210/127, in force 1 July 2010.

Article 234 can be compared and contrasted with other provisions in the Convention dealing with the protection of the marine environment such as Article 211, paragraphs 5 and 6 which require the coastal State to conform to "generally accepted international rules and standards established through the competent international organization." In contrast, no such requirement is included in Article 234, which establishes its own *sui generis* code for appropriate unilateral coastal State measures. Article 234 overrides Article 211 in ice-covered areas. The uniqueness of Article 234 is apparent by the fact that it was not included within other sections dealing with the protection of the marine environment; rather, it stands distinct, as the only Article in Section 8 of Part XII [of UNCLOS].

Article 234 provides a complete legal justification in international law for NORDREG. Further, NORDREG is consistent with SOLAS [the International Convention for the Safety of Life at Sea – the principal convention administered by the IMO] Chapter V, Regulation 11.4, which provides that "Ship reporting systems not submitted to the Organization for adoption do not necessarily need to comply with this regulation" and Regulation 12, which provides that "use of VTS may only be made mandatory in sea areas within the territorial sea," qualified by "nothing in this regulation shall prejudice the rights and duties of governments under international law. . ." Canada's rights and duties under Article 234 of UNCLOS take precedence over the 12NM [nautical mile] limitation.

3) Archipelagic Waters

The ability to enclose with straight baselines "fringes of islands" (such as Canada's Arctic archipelago or those along the Norwegian coast) allows a coastal state to claim the waters between those islands as internal waters rather than as territorial sea (which would be subject to rights of innocent or, in the case of some international straits, transit passage). This raises questions as to how a state, composed entirely of islands—an archipelagic state—may establish its baselines, and as to the status of the waters between its constituent islands. Examples include Indonesia and the Philippines. Can a state that is a geographic archipelago simply enclose the waters between its islands with straight baselines and declare them internal waters? This was a much-debated issue at the diplomatic conference at which UNCLOS was negotiated. The issue was made the more complicated by the fact that important sea traffic lanes pass between the islands of several archipelagic states. Consider the compromise that was adopted, which required the creation of the *sui generis* regime of "archipelagic waters":

United Nations Convention on the Law of the Sea, 10 December 1982, 1833 UNTS 3, in force 16 November 1994

PART IV
ARCHIPELAGIC STATES

Article 46
Use of terms
For the purposes of this Convention:

(a) "archipelagic State" means a State constituted wholly by one or more archipelagos and may include other islands;

(b) "archipelago" means a group of islands, including parts of islands, interconnecting waters and other natural features which are so closely interrelated that such islands, waters and other natural features form an intrinsic geographical, economic and political entity, or which historically have been regarded as such.

Article 47
Archipelagic baselines

1. An archipelagic State may draw straight archipelagic baselines joining the outermost points of the outermost islands and drying reefs of the archipelago provided that within such baselines are included the main islands and an area in which the ratio of the area of the water to the area of the land, including atolls, is between 1 to 1 and 9 to 1.

2. The length of such baselines shall not exceed 100 nautical miles, except that up to 3 per cent of the total number of baselines enclosing any archipelago may exceed that length, up to a maximum length of 125 nautical miles.

3. The drawing of such baselines shall not depart to any appreciable extent from the general configuration of the archipelago.

4. Such baselines shall not be drawn to and from low-tide elevations, unless lighthouses or similar installations which are permanently above sea level have been built on them or where a low-tide elevation is situated wholly or partly at a distance not exceeding the breadth of the territorial sea from the nearest island. . . .

Article 48
Measurement of the breadth of the territorial sea, the contiguous zone, the exclusive economic zone and the continental shelf

The breadth of the territorial sea, the contiguous zone, the exclusive economic zone and the continental shelf shall be measured from archipelagic baselines drawn in accordance with article 47.

Article 49
Legal status of archipelagic waters, of the air space over archipelagic waters and of their bed and subsoil

1. The sovereignty of an archipelagic State extends to the waters enclosed by the archipelagic baselines drawn in accordance with article 47, described as archipelagic waters, regardless of their depth or distance from the coast.

2. This sovereignty extends to the air space over the archipelagic waters, as well as to their bed and subsoil, and the resources contained therein.

3. This sovereignty is exercised subject to this Part.

4. The regime of archipelagic sea lanes passage established in this Part shall not in other respects affect the status of the archipelagic waters, including the sea lanes, or the exercise by the archipelagic State of its sovereignty over such waters and their air space, bed and subsoil, and the resources contained therein.

Article 50
Delimitation of internal waters
Within its archipelagic waters, the archipelagic State may draw closing lines for the delimitation of internal waters, in accordance with articles 9, 10 and 11.

. . .

Article 52
Right of innocent passage
1. Subject to article 53 and without prejudice to article 50, ships of all States enjoy the right of innocent passage through archipelagic waters, in accordance with [Articles 17–32].

2. The archipelagic State may, without discrimination in form or in fact among foreign ships, suspend temporarily in specified areas of its archipelagic waters the innocent passage of foreign ships if such suspension is essential for the protection of its security. Such suspension shall take effect only after having been duly published.

Article 53
Right of archipelagic sea lanes passage
1. An archipelagic State may designate sea lanes and air routes thereabove, suitable for the continuous and expeditious passage of foreign ships and aircraft through or over its archipelagic waters and the adjacent territorial sea.

2. All ships and aircraft enjoy the right of archipelagic sea lanes passage in such sea lanes and air routes.

3. Archipelagic sea lanes passage means the exercise in accordance with this Convention of the rights of navigation and overflight in the normal mode solely for the purpose of continuous, expeditious and unobstructed transit between one part of the high seas or an exclusive economic zone and another part of the high seas or an exclusive economic zone.

4. Such sea lanes and air routes shall traverse the archipelagic waters and the adjacent territorial sea and shall include all normal passage routes used as routes for international navigation or overflight through or over archipelagic waters and, within such routes, so far as ships are concerned, all normal navigational channels, provided that duplication of routes of similar convenience between the same entry and exit points shall not be necessary. . . .

11. Ships in archipelagic sea lanes passage shall respect applicable sea lanes and traffic separation schemes established in accordance with this article.

12. If an archipelagic State does not designate sea lanes or air routes, the right of archipelagic sea lanes passage may be exercised through the routes normally used for internal navigation.

Article 54
Duties of ships and aircraft during their passage, research and survey activities, duties of the archipelagic State and laws and regulations of the archipelagic State relating to archipelagic sea lanes passage
Articles 39, 40, 42 and 44 apply *mutatis mutandis* to archipelagic sea lanes passage.

Given that states are considered to enjoy sovereignty over their territorial sea (including the airspace above and seabed and subsoil below it), how is the archipelagic waters regime in UNCLOS more advantageous to archipelagic states than if they simply had to establish baselines and their territorial sea in the same way as other states? Compare the maximum permissible breadth of the territorial sea with the maximum length of archipelagic straight baselines permitted by Article 47.

4) The Contiguous Zone

We now turn to another coastal zone, namely the contiguous zone as defined in Article 33 of UNCLOS:

United Nations Convention on the Law of the Sea, 10 December 1982, 1833 UNTS 3, in force 16 November 1994

Article 33

Contiguous Zone

1. In a zone contiguous to its territorial sea, described as the contiguous zone, the coastal State may exercise the control necessary to:

    (a) prevent infringement of its customs, fiscal, immigration or sanitary laws and regulations within its territory or territorial sea;

    (b) punish infringement of the above laws and regulations committed within its territory or territorial sea.

2. The contiguous zone may not extend beyond 24 nautical miles from the baselines from which the breadth of the territorial sea is measured.

In considering the nature of a coastal state's jurisdiction over this contiguous zone, it is important to bear in mind that traditional customary international law gave a coastal state no special jurisdictional rights over the oceans beyond its territorial sea at all. All such waters were considered the "high seas"—being a maritime area in which all states enjoyed precisely the same rights and freedoms. That legal situation has now changed, of course, with the advent of the contiguous zone and the other zones reviewed below. The key difference between all such zones and the territorial sea is that, in the latter, the presumptive starting point is the sovereignty of the coastal state, subject only to such limitations as are imposed by international law (such as the obligation to respect the right of innocent passage). By contrast, in coastal zones beyond the territorial sea, the presumptive starting point is the absence of any special coastal state jurisdiction other than that specifically granted by international law.

Considered in this light, a coastal state's jurisdiction over its contiguous zone as such is very limited. What is the purpose of recognizing such jurisdiction if its scope is limited to infringements of certain coastal state laws committed in the coastal state's territory or territorial sea? The following excerpt from Canada's *Oceans Act* may assist in answering this question:

Oceans Act, SC 1996, c 31

Contiguous zone of Canada

10. The contiguous zone of Canada consists of an area of the sea that has as its inner limit the outer limit of the territorial sea of Canada and as its outer limit the line every point of which is at a distance of 24 nautical miles from the nearest point of the baselines of the territorial sea of Canada, but does not include an area of the sea that forms part of the territorial sea of another state or in which another state has sovereign rights.

Prevention in contiguous zone of infringement of federal laws

11. A person who is responsible for the enforcement of a federal law that is a customs, fiscal, immigration or sanitary law and who has reasonable grounds to believe that a person in the contiguous zone of Canada would, if that person were to enter Canada, commit an offence under that law may, subject to Canada's international obligations, prevent the entry of that person into Canada or the commission of the offence and, for greater certainty, section 25 of the *Criminal Code* applies in respect of the exercise by a person of any powers under this section.

Enforcement in contiguous zone of federal laws

12. (1) Where there are reasonable grounds to believe that a person has committed an offence in Canada in respect of a federal law that is a customs, fiscal, immigration or sanitary law, every power of arrest, entry, search or seizure or other power that could be exercised in Canada in respect of that offence may also be exercised in the contiguous zone of Canada.

Limitation

(2) A power of arrest referred to in subsection (1) shall not be exercised in the contiguous zone of Canada on board any ship registered outside Canada without the consent of the Attorney General of Canada.

5) Fisheries Zones and Exclusive Economic Zones

A coastal state may have strong interests in exploiting the living and non-living resources of the ocean well beyond its territorial sea. These interests have grown steadily over the past several decades with the advent of deep sea fisheries, on-board refrigeration, and new marine resource exploitation technologies. The contiguous zone concept does not, however, provide any basis for such resource exploitation beyond the territorial sea. Customary international law thus developed the concept of a "fisheries zone" in which the coastal state enjoys preferential jurisdiction over the harvesting of living marine resources. Consider the following judgment describing the emergence of this legal construct:

Fisheries Jurisdiction Case (United Kingdom of Great Britain and Northern Ireland v Iceland), Merits, [1974] ICJ Rep 3

[In 1972, Iceland purported to establish an exclusive fisheries zone 50 nautical miles in breadth. The United Kingdom objected on the basis that customary international law did not permit the declaration of such a maritime zone, as well as on the basis of a 1961

Exchange of Notes with Iceland. Note that at the time of this decision, the maximum breadth of the territorial sea was uncertain at customary international law.]

51. . . . The question of the breadth of the territorial sea and that of the extent of the coastal State's fishery jurisdiction were left unsettled at the 1958 Conference [on the Law of the Sea]. These questions were referred to the Second Conference on the Law of the Sea, held in 1960. Furthermore, the question of the extent of the fisheries jurisdiction of the coastal State, which had constituted a serious obstacle to the reaching of an agreement at the 1958 Conference, became gradually separated from the notion of the territorial sea. This was a development which reflected the increasing importance of fishery resources for all States.

52. The 1960 Conference failed by one vote to adopt a text governing the two questions of the breadth of the territorial sea and the extent of fishery rights. However, after that Conference the law evolved through the practice of States on the basis of the debates and near-agreements at the Conference. Two concepts have crystallized as customary law in recent years arising out of the general consensus revealed at that Conference. The first is the concept of the fishery zone, the area in which a State may claim exclusive fishery jurisdiction independently of its territorial sea; the extension of that fishery zone up to a 12-mile limit from the baselines appears now to be generally accepted. The second is the concept of preferential rights of fishing in adjacent waters in favour of the coastal State in a situation of special dependence on its coastal fisheries, this preference operating in regard to other States concerned in the exploitation of the same fisheries, and to be implemented in the way indicated in paragraph 57 below.

53. In recent years the question of extending the coastal State's fisheries jurisdiction has come increasingly to the forefront. The Court is aware that a number of States has asserted an extension of fishery limits. The Court is also aware of present endeavours, pursued under the auspices of the United Nations, to achieve in a third Conference on the Law of the Sea the further codification and progressive development of this branch of the law, as it is of various proposals and preparatory documents produced in this framework, which must be regarded as manifestations of the views and opinions of individual States and as vehicles of their aspirations, rather than as expressing principles of existing law. The very fact of convening the third Conference on the Law of the Sea evidences a manifest desire on the part of all States to proceed to the codification of that law on a universal basis, including the question of fisheries and conservation of the living resources of the sea. . . . In the circumstances, the Court, as a court of law, cannot render judgment *sub specie legis ferendae*, or anticipate the law before the legislator has laid it down.

54. The concept of a 12-mile fishery zone, referred to in paragraph 52 above, as a tertium genus [third category] between the territorial sea and the high seas, has been accepted with regard to Iceland in the substantive provisions of the 1961 Exchange of Notes, and the United Kingdom has also applied the same fishery limit to its own coastal waters since 1964; therefore this matter is no longer in dispute between the Parties. At the same time, the concept of preferential rights, a notion that necessarily implies the existence of other legal rights in respect of which that preference operates, has been admitted by the Applicant to be relevant to the solution of the present dispute. Moreover, the Ap-

plicant has expressly recognized Iceland's preferential rights in the disputed waters and at the same time has invoked its own historic fishing rights in these same waters, on the ground that reasonable regard must be had to such traditional rights by the coastal State. . . .

55. The concept of preferential rights for the coastal State in a situation of special dependence on coastal fisheries originated in proposals submitted by Iceland at the Geneva Conference of 1958. Its delegation drew attention to the problem which would arise when, in spite of adequate fisheries conservation measures, the yield ceased to be sufficient to satisfy the requirements of all those who were interested in fishing in a given area. Iceland contended that in such a case, when a catch-limitation becomes necessary, special consideration should be given to the coastal State whose population is overwhelmingly dependent on the fishing resources in its adjacent waters.

56. An Icelandic proposal embodying these ideas failed to obtain the majority required, but a resolution was adopted at the 1958 Conference concerning the situation of countries or territories whose people are overwhelmingly dependent upon coastal fisheries for their livelihood or economic development. This resolution, after "recognizing that such situations call for exceptional measures befitting particular needs" recommended that:

> . . . where, for the purpose of conservation, it becomes necessary to limit the total catch of a stock or stocks of fish in an area of the high seas adjacent to the territorial sea of a coastal State, any other States fishing in that area should collaborate with the coastal State to secure just treatment of such situation, by establishing agreed measures which shall recognize any preferential requirements of the coastal State resulting from its dependence upon the fishery concerned while having regard to the interests of the other States.

The resolution further recommended that "appropriate conciliation and arbitral procedures shall be established for the settlement of any disagreement."

57. At the Plenary Meetings of the 1960 Conference the concept of preferential rights was embodied in a joint amendment presented by Brazil, Cuba and Uruguay which was subsequently incorporated by a substantial vote into a joint United States-Canadian proposal concerning a 6-mile territorial sea and an additional 6-mile fishing zone, thus totalling a 12-mile exclusive fishing zone, subject to a phasing-out period. This amendment provided, independently of the exclusive fishing zone, that the coastal State had:

> . . . the faculty of claiming preferential fishing rights in any area of the high seas adjacent to its exclusive fishing zone when it is scientifically established that a special situation or condition makes the exploitation of the living resources of the high seas in that area of fundamental importance to the economic development of the coastal State or the feeding of its population.

It also provided that:

> A special situation or condition may be deemed to exist when:
> (a) The fisheries and the economic development of the coastal State or the feeding of its population are so manifestly interrelated that, in consequence, that State is

greatly dependent on the living resources of the high seas in the area in respect of which preferential fishing is being claimed;

(b) It becomes necessary to limit the total catch of a stock or stocks of fish in such areas . . .

58. State practice on the subject of fisheries reveals an increasing and widespread acceptance of the concept of preferential rights for coastal States, particularly in favour of countries or territories in a situation of special dependence on coastal fisheries. Both the 1958 Resolution and the 1960 joint amendment concerning preferential rights were approved by a large majority of the Conferences, thus showing overwhelming support for the idea that in certain special situations it was fair to recognize that the coastal State had preferential fishing rights. After these Conferences, the preferential rights of the coastal State were recognized in various bilateral and multilateral international agreements. . . .

60. The preferential rights of the coastal State come into play only at the moment when an intensification in the exploitation of fishery resources makes it imperative to introduce some system of catch-limitation and sharing of those resources, to preserve the fish stocks in the interests of their rational and economic exploitation. This situation appears to have been reached in the present case. . . .

62. The concept of preferential rights is not compatible with the exclusion of all fishing activities of other States. A coastal State entitled to preferential rights is not free, unilaterally and according to its own uncontrolled discretion, to determine the extent of those rights. The characterization of the coastal State's rights as preferential implies a certain priority, but cannot imply the extinction of the concurrent rights of other States, and particularly of a State which, like the Applicant, has for many years been engaged in fishing in the waters in question, such fishing activity being important to the economy of the country concerned. The coastal State has to take into account and pay regard to the position of such other States, particularly when they have established an economic dependence on the same fishing grounds. Accordingly, the fact that Iceland is entitled to claim preferential rights does not suffice to justify its claim unilaterally to exclude the Applicant's fishing vessels from all fishing activity in the waters beyond the limits agreed to in the 1961 Exchange of Notes. . . .

72. . . . [E]ven if the Court holds that Iceland's extension of its fishery limits is not opposable to the Applicant, this does not mean that the Applicant is under no obligation to Iceland with respect to fishing in the disputed waters in the 12-mile to 50-mile zone. On the contrary, both States have an obligation to take full account of each other's rights and of any fishery conservation measures the necessity of which is shown to exist in those waters. It is one of the advances in maritime international law, resulting from the intensification of fishing, that the former *laissez faire* treatment of the living resources of the sea in the high seas has been replaced by a recognition of a duty to have due regard to the rights of other States and the needs of conservation for the benefit of all. Consequently, both Parties have the obligation to keep under review the fishery resources in the disputed waters and to examine together, in the light of scientific and other available information, the measures required for the conservation and development, and equitable exploitation, of those resources, taking into account any international agreement in force between them. . . .

As have many other states, Canada has defined a number of fisheries zones along its coasts.[18] As foreshadowed by the Court in the *Fisheries Jurisdiction Case*, however, the somewhat ambiguous notion of a "preferential" fisheries zone has been overtaken by the exclusive economic zone (EEZ), an innovation resulting from the Third Conference on the Law of the Sea now codified in UNCLOS:

United Nations Convention on the Law of the Sea, 10 December 1982, 1833 UNTS 3, in force 16 November 1994

Article 55
Specific legal regime of the exclusive economic zone
The exclusive economic zone is an area beyond and adjacent to the territorial sea, subject to the specific legal regime established in this Part, under which the rights and jurisdiction of the coastal State and the rights and freedoms of other States are governed by the relevant provisions of this Convention.

Article 56
Rights, jurisdiction and duties of the coastal State in the exclusive economic zone
1. In the exclusive economic zone, the coastal State has:
    (a) sovereign rights for the purpose of exploring and exploiting, conserving and managing the natural resources, whether living or non-living, of the waters superjacent to the sea-bed and of the sea-bed and its subsoil, and with regard to other activities for the economic exploitation and exploration of the zone, such as the production of energy from the water, currents and winds;
    (b) jurisdiction as provided for in the relevant provisions of this Convention with regard to:
        (i) the establishment and use of artificial islands, installations and structures;
        (ii) marine scientific research;
        (iii) the protection and preservation of the marine environment;
    (c) other rights and duties provided for in this Convention.

2. In exercising its rights and performing its duties under this Convention in the exclusive economic zone, the coastal State shall have due regard to the rights and duties of other States and shall act in a manner compatible with the provisions of this Convention.

3. The rights set out in this article with respect to the sea-bed and subsoil shall be exercised in accordance with Part VI [relating to the continental shelf].

Article 57
Breadth of the exclusive economic zone
The exclusive economic zone shall not extend beyond 200 nautical miles from the baselines from which the breadth of the territorial sea is measured.

---

18 See *Oceans Act*, SC 1996, c 31; see also *Fishing Zones of Canada (Zones 1, 2 and 3) Order*, CRC, c 1547; *Fishing Zones of Canada (Zones 4 and 5) Order*, CRC, c 1548; and *Fishing Zones of Canada (Zone 6) Order*, CRC, c 1549.

Article 58

Rights and duties of other States in the exclusive economic zone

1. In the exclusive economic zone all States, whether coastal or land-locked, enjoy, subject to the relevant provisions of this Convention, the freedoms ... of navigation and over-flight and of the laying of submarine cables and pipelines, and other internationally lawful uses of the sea related to these freedoms, such as those associated with the operation of ships, aircraft and submarine cables and pipelines, and compatible with the other provisions of this Convention.

2. Articles 88 to 115 [relating to the high seas] and other pertinent rules of international law apply to the exclusive economic zone in so far as they are not incompatible with this Part.

3. In exercising their rights and performing their duties under this Convention in the exclusive economic zone, States shall have due regard to the rights and duties of the coastal State and shall comply with the laws and regulations adopted by the coastal State in accordance with the provisions of this Convention and other rules of international law in so far as they are not incompatible with this Part. . . .

Article 60

Artificial islands, installations and structures in the exclusive economic zone

1. In the exclusive economic zone, the coastal State shall have the exclusive right to construct and to authorize and regulate the construction, operation and use of:

(a) artificial islands;

(b) installations and structures for the purposes provided for in article 56 and other economic purposes;

(c) installations and structures which may interfere with the exercise of the rights of the coastal State in the zone.

2. The coastal State shall have exclusive jurisdiction over such artificial islands, installations and structures, including jurisdiction with regard to customs, fiscal, health, safety and immigration laws and regulations.

3. Due notice must be given of the construction of such artificial islands, installations or structures, and permanent means for giving warning of their presence must be maintained. Any installations or structures which are abandoned or disused shall be removed to ensure safety of navigation, taking into account any generally accepted international standards established in this regard by the competent international organization. Such removal shall also have due regard to fishing, the protection of the marine environment and the rights and duties of other States. Appropriate publicity shall be given to the depth, position and dimensions of any installations or structures not entirely removed.

4. The coastal State may, where necessary, establish reasonable safety zones around such artificial islands, installations and structures in which it may take appropriate measures to ensure the safety both of navigation and of the artificial islands, installations and structures. . . .

8. Artificial islands, installations and structures do not possess the status of islands. They have no territorial sea of their own, and their presence does not affect the delimitation of the territorial sea, the exclusive economic zone or the continental shelf.

Article 61
Conservation of the living resources
1. The coastal State shall determine the allowable catch of the living resources in its exclusive economic zone.

2. The coastal State, taking into account the best scientific evidence available to it, shall ensure through proper conservation and management measures that the maintenance of the living resources in the exclusive economic zone is not endangered by over-exploitation. . . .

Article 62
Utilization of the living resources
1. The coastal State shall promote the objective of optimum utilization of the living resources in the exclusive economic zone without prejudice to article 61.

2. The coastal State shall determine its capacity to harvest the living resources of the exclusive economic zone. Where the coastal State does not have the capacity to harvest the entire allowable catch, it shall, through agreements or other arrangements and pursuant to the terms, conditions, laws and regulations referred to in paragraph 4, give other States access to the surplus of the allowable catch, having particular regard to the provisions of articles 69 and 70, especially in relation to the developing States mentioned therein.

3. In giving access to other States to its exclusive economic zone under this article the coastal State shall take into account all relevant factors, including, inter alia, the significance of the living resources of the area to the economy of the coastal State concerned and its other national interests, the provisions of articles 69 and 70, the requirements of developing States in the subregion or region in harvesting part of the surplus and the need to minimize economic dislocation in States whose nationals have habitually fished in the zone or which have made substantial efforts in research and identification of stocks.

4. Nationals of other States fishing in the exclusive economic zone shall comply with the conservation measures and with the other terms and conditions established in the laws and regulations of the coastal State. . . .

Article 65
Marine mammals
Nothing in this Part restricts the right of a coastal State or the competence of an international organization, as appropriate, to prohibit, limit or regulate the exploitation of marine mammals more strictly than provided for in this Part. States shall cooperate with a view to the conservation of marine mammals and in the case of cetaceans shall in particular work through the appropriate international organizations for their conservation, management and study.[19]

. . .

---

19 At the time of writing, proceedings instituted by Australia against Japan are pending before the International Court of Justice, alleging that Japan has breached its obligations under the International Convention for the Regulation of Whaling, 2 December 1946, 161 UNTS 74, in force 10 November 1948.

Article 69
Right of land-locked States
1. Land-locked States shall have the right to participate, on an equitable basis, in the exploitation of an appropriate part of the surplus of the living resources of the exclusive economic zones of coastal States of the same subregion or region, taking into account the relevant economic and geographical circumstances of all the States concerned and in conformity with the provisions of this article and of articles 61 and 62.

2. The terms and modalities of such participation shall be established by the States concerned through bilateral, subregional or regional agreements taking into account, *inter alia*:
(a) the need to avoid effects detrimental to fishing communities or fishing industries of the coastal State;
(b) the extent to which the land-locked State, in accordance with the provisions of this article, is participating or is entitled to participate under existing bilateral, subregional or regional agreements in the exploitation of living resources of the exclusive economic zones of other coastal States;
(c) the extent to which other land-locked States and geographically disadvantaged States are participating in the exploitation of the living resources of the exclusive economic zone of the coastal State and the consequent need to avoid a particular burden for any single coastal State or a part of it;
(d) the nutritional needs of the populations of the respective States.

3. When the harvesting capacity of a coastal State approaches a point which would enable it to harvest the entire allowable catch of the living resources in its exclusive economic zone, the coastal State and other States concerned shall co-operate in the establishment of equitable arrangements on a bilateral, subregional or regional basis to allow for participation of developing land-locked States of the same subregion or region in the exploitation of the living resources of the exclusive economic zones of coastal States of the subregion or region, as may be appropriate in the circumstances and on terms satisfactory to all parties. In the implementation of this provision the factors mentioned in paragraph 2 shall also be taken into account. . . .

Article 70
Right of geographically disadvantaged States
1. Geographically disadvantaged States shall have the right to participate, on an equitable basis, in the exploitation of an appropriate part of the surplus of the living resources of the exclusive economic zones of coastal States of the same subregion or region, taking into account the relevant economic and geographical circumstances of all the States concerned and in conformity with the provisions of this article and of articles 61 and 62.

2. For the purposes of this Part, "geographically disadvantaged States" means coastal States, including States bordering enclosed or semi-enclosed seas, whose geographical situation makes them dependent upon the exploitation of the living resources of the exclusive economic zones of other States in the subregion or region for adequate supplies of fish for the nutritional purposes of their populations or parts thereof, and coastal States which can claim no exclusive economic zones of their own.

3. The terms and modalities of such participation shall be established by the States concerned through bilateral, subregional or regional agreements taking into account, *inter alia*:

(a) the need to avoid effects detrimental to fishing communities or fishing industries of the coastal State;

(b) the extent to which the geographically disadvantaged State, in accordance with the provisions of this article, is participating or is entitled to participate under existing bilateral, subregional or regional agreements in the exploitation of living resources of the exclusive economic zones of other coastal States;

(c) the extent to which other geographically disadvantaged States and landlocked States are participating in the exploitation of the living resources of the exclusive economic zone of the coastal State and the consequent need to avoid a particular burden for any single coastal State or a part of it;

(d) the nutritional needs of the populations of the respective States.

4. When the harvesting capacity of a coastal State approaches a point which would enable it to harvest the entire allowable catch of the living resources in its exclusive economic zone, the coastal State and other States concerned shall co-operate in the establishment of equitable arrangements on a bilateral, subregional or regional basis to allow for participation of developing geographically disadvantaged States of the same subregion or region in the exploitation of the living resources of the exclusive economic zones of coastal States of the subregion or region, as may be appropriate in the circumstances and on terms satisfactory to all parties. In the implementation of this provision the factors mentioned in paragraph 3 shall also be taken into account. . . .

Article 71
Non-applicability of articles 69 and 70

The provisions of articles 69 and 70 do not apply in the case of a coastal State whose economy is overwhelmingly dependent on the exploitation of the living resources of its exclusive economic zone. . . .

Article 73
Enforcement of laws and regulations of the coastal State

1. The coastal State may, in the exercise of its sovereign rights to explore, exploit, conserve and manage the living resources in the exclusive economic zone, take such measures, including boarding, inspection, arrest and judicial proceedings, as may be necessary to ensure compliance with the laws and regulations adopted by it in conformity with this Convention.

2. Arrested vessels and their crews shall be promptly released upon the posting of reasonable bond or other security.

3. Coastal State penalties for violations of fisheries laws and regulations in the exclusive economic zone may not include imprisonment, in the absence of agreements to the contrary by the States concerned, or any other form of corporal punishment.

4. In cases of arrest or detention of foreign vessels the coastal State shall promptly notify the flag State, through appropriate channels, of the action taken and of any penalties subsequently imposed. . . .

Article 121
Regime of islands
1. An island is a naturally formed area of land, surrounded by water, which is above water at high tide.

2. Except as provided for in paragraph 3, the territorial sea, the contiguous zone, the exclusive economic zone and the continental shelf of an island are determined in accordance with the provisions of this Convention applicable to other land territory.

3. Rocks which cannot sustain human habitation or economic life of their own shall have no exclusive economic zone or continental shelf.

Given the breadth of this EEZ, it is easy to imagine circumstances where the EEZ claims of coastal states will overlap. Article 74 of UNCLOS anticipates this problem and (rather unhelpfully) specifies that any conflict over EEZ zones shall be resolved by agreement in order to achieve an "equitable solution":

Article 74
Delimitation of the exclusive economic zone between States with opposite or adjacent coasts
1. The delimitation of the exclusive economic zone between States with opposite or adjacent coasts shall be effected by agreement on the basis of international law, as referred to in Article 38 of the Statute of the International Court of Justice, in order to achieve an equitable solution.

2. If no agreement can be reached within a reasonable period of time, the States concerned shall resort to the procedures provided for in Part XV.

3. Pending agreement as provided for in paragraph 1, the States concerned, in a spirit of understanding and cooperation, shall make every effort to enter into provisional arrangements of a practical nature and, during this transitional period, not to jeopardize or hamper the reaching of the final agreement. Such arrangements shall be without prejudice to the final delimitation.

4. Where there is an agreement in force between the States concerned, questions relating to the delimitation of the exclusive economic zone shall be determined in accordance with the provisions of that agreement.

An important body of jurisprudence resulting from ICJ and arbitral decisions delimiting conflicting EEZs (and continental shelves, discussed below) now exists. How much guidance have international tribunals actually provided on reaching such equitable solutions? Consider this view published in 1993:

. . . [N]o normative principle of international law has developed that would mandate the specific location of any maritime boundary line. The state practice varies substantially. Due to the unlimited geographic and other circumstances that influence the settlements, no binding rule that would be sufficiently determinative to enable one to predict the location of a maritime boundary with any degree of precision is likely to evolve in the near future. . . . Furthermore, an *opinio juris* supporting a definitive norm certainly is absent.[20]

Consider, however, the following contrary view, expressed in 2001 by then president of the ICJ, Judge Guillaume:

Speech by HE Judge Gilbert Guillaume, President of the International Court of Justice, to the Sixth Committee of the General Assembly of the United Nations, 31 October 2001[21]

. . . As regards the delimitation of the continental shelf and the exclusive economic zone, the Court has also gradually established a case law which is now authoritative. . . .

As you know, in 1969, in the *North Sea Continental Shelf* case, the Court initially inclined towards a delimitation of that shelf in accordance with "equitable principles, and taking account of all the relevant circumstances." Next, in the case between Tunisia and Libya concerning a similar delimitation, it recalled that the delimitation must be achieved on the basis of equitable principles. The same approach was adopted in the *Gulf of Maine* case. These decisions were not without influence on the solution adopted by the Conference on the Law of the Sea. Thus, [UNCLOS], in Articles 74 and 83, provides for "States to effect delimitation by agreement on the basis of international law . . . in order to achieve an equitable solution."

At this stage, case law and treaty law had become so unpredictable that there was extensive debate within the doctrine on whether there still existed a law of delimitations or whether, in the name of equity, we were not ending up with arbitrary solutions. Sensitive to these criticisms, in subsequent years the Court proceeded to develop its case law in the direction of greater certainty.

That development was begun in the *Continental Shelf* case between the Libyan Arab Jamahiriya and Malta, in which the Court took the equidistance line as the point of departure for delimitation and moved it northwards, having regard to the equitable principles to be applied in the case, namely, the general configuration of the coasts and their different lengths. Thus, equidistance was reinstated as a provisional line open to possible correction in order to achieve an equitable result.

A new stage was then reached with the Judgment delivered on 14 June 1993 in the case between Denmark and Norway concerning the maritime delimitation in the area between Greenland and Jan Mayen.

In that case, the delimitation of the continental shelf fell to be effected in accordance with the 1958 Geneva Convention [on the Continental Shelf] (equidistance/special circumstances), whereas the fishing zones were to be effected in accordance with customary law (equitable solution, having regard to relevant factors). The Court stressed that, in both cases, an equitable result must be reached. It added that, as regards the fishing zones, delimitation had to proceed on the basis of equitable principles. In order to achieve

---

20 Jonathan Charney & Lewis Alexander, *International Maritime Boundaries*, vol 1 (Boston: Martinus Nijhoff Publishers, 1993) at xlii.

21 Online: www.icj-cij.org/court/index.php?pr=81&pt=3&p1=1&p2=3&p3=1&PHPSESSID=.

this, it held that it was appropriate to start from the equidistance line, subsequently making all the necessary corrections to it, having regard to the relevant factors. . . .

Thus, the law on maritime delimitations was completely reunified. Whether it be for the territorial sea, the continental shelf or the fishing zone, it is an equitable result that must be achieved. Such a result may be achieved by first identifying the equidistance line, then correcting that line to take into account special circumstances or relevant factors, which are both essentially geographical in nature.

This solution of principle, arrived at in the case concerning Jan Mayen/Greenland, was applicable thenceforth with regard to the delimitation of the continental shelf and the fishing zones of States with opposite coasts. It remained to be seen whether the same applied in the case of adjacent coasts.

The Court ruled affirmatively on the matter in the case between Qatar and Bahrain. In that case, the parties had conferred on the Court the task of drawing a single maritime line simultaneously dividing both the continental shelf and the exclusive economic zone. In order to do so, but on this occasion dealing with adjacent rather than opposite coasts, the Court again decided that an equidistance line should first be provisionally drawn, consideration then being given as to whether there were relevant circumstances leading to an adjustment of that line. . . .

. . . [I]t is encouraging to note that the law of maritime delimitations, by means of these developments in the Court's case law, has reached a new level of unity and certainty, whilst conserving the necessary flexibility. . . .

In all cases, the Court, as States also do, must first determine provisionally the equidistance line. It must then ask itself whether there are special or relevant circumstances requiring this line to be adjusted with a view to achieving equitable results.

The legal rule is now clear. However, each case nonetheless remains an individual one, in which the different circumstances invoked by the parties must be weighed with care. . . .

The Court subsequently applied this same method in its 2002 judgment concerning the *Land and Maritime Boundary between Cameroon and Nigeria*.[22] Consider also the following extract from a more recent ICJ judgment, which suggests a uniform, multiple stage approach to maritime delimitation:

Maritime Delimitation in the Black Sea (Romania v Ukraine), Judgment, [2009] ICJ Rep 61

115. When called upon to delimit the continental shelf or exclusive economic zones, or to draw a single delimitation line, the Court proceeds in defined stages.

116. These separate stages . . . have in recent decades been specified with precision. First, the Court will establish a provisional delimitation line, using methods that are geometrically objective and also appropriate for the geography of the area in which the delimitation is to take place. So far as delimitation between adjacent coasts is concerned, an equidistance line will be drawn unless there are compelling reasons that make this

---

22 (*Cameroon v Nigeria; Equatorial Guinea Intervening*), Judgment, [2002] ICJ Rep 303.

unfeasible in the particular case. . . . So far as opposite coasts are concerned, the provisional delimitation line will consist of a median line between the two coasts. No legal consequences flow from the use of the terms "median line" and "equidistance line" since the method of delimitation is the same for both.

117. Equidistance and median lines are to be constructed from the most appropriate points on the coasts of the two States concerned, with particular attention being paid to those protuberant coastal points situate nearest to the area to the delimited. The Court considers elsewhere . . . the extent to which the Court may, when constructing a single-purpose delimitation line, deviate from the base points selected by the Parties for their territorial seas. When construction of a provisional equidistance line between adjacent States is called for, the Court will have in mind considerations relating to both Parties' coastlines when choosing its own base points for this purpose. The line thus adopted is heavily dependent on the physical geography and the most seaward points of the two coasts.

118. In keeping with its settled jurisprudence on maritime delimitation, the first stage of the Court's approach is to establish the provisional equidistance line. At this initial stage of the construction of the provisional equidistance line the Court is not yet concerned with any relevant circumstances that may obtain and the line is plotted on strictly geometrical criteria on the basis of objective data. . . .

120. The course of the final line should result in an equitable solution (Articles 74 and 83 of UNCLOS). Therefore, the Court will at the next, second stage consider whether there are factors calling for the adjustment or shifting of the provisional equidistance line in order to achieve an equitable result . . . . The Court has also made clear that when the line to be drawn covers several zones of coincident jurisdictions, "the so-called equitable principles/relevant circumstances method may usefully be applied, as in these maritime zones this method is also suited to achieving an equitable result". . . .

121. This is the second part of the delimitation exercise to which the Court will turn, having first established the provisional equidistance line.

122. Finally, and at a third stage, the Court will verify that the line (a provisional equidistance line which may or may not have been adjusted by taking into account the relevant circumstances) does not, as it stands, lead to an inequitable result by reason of any marked disproportion between the ratio of the respective coastal lengths and the ratio between the relevant maritime area of each State by reference to the delimitation line. . . . A final check for an equitable outcome entails a confirmation that no great disproportionality of maritime areas is evident by comparison to the ratio of coastal lengths.

   This is not to suggest that these respective areas should be proportionate to coastal lengths — as the Court has said "the sharing out of the area is therefore the consequence of the delimitation, not vice versa".

The ICJ again endorsed this method in its 2012 judgment in *Territorial and Maritime Dispute (Nicaragua v Colombia)*.[23]

---

23 ICJ, General List No 124, 19 November 2012.

LAW IN CONTEXT

Uncertainty in Maritime Boundary Delimitation and Conflict

The relatively new rules on EEZs—with the prospect of lucrative state jurisdiction over natural resources extending considerable distances out to sea—present a real possibility of conflict. By 1998, "of more than 400 potential maritime boundaries, only about 160 [had] been formally agreed."[24] Further, some of the ocean and subsoil captured by these prospective maritime boundaries are resource rich, fuelling concern about discord between states. Consider the situation in the South China Sea:

> The South China Sea is rich in natural resources such as oil and natural gas. These resources have garnered attention throughout the Asia-Pacific region. Asia's economic growth rates have been among the highest in the world, and this economic growth will be accompanied by an increasing demand for energy. Between now and 2025, oil consumption in developing Asian countries is expected to rise by 3.0 percent annually on average, with more than one-third of this increase coming from China alone. If this growth rate is maintained, oil demand for these nations will increase from about 14.5 million barrels per day in 2000 to nearly 29.8 million barrels per day by 2025. . . .
>
> Competing territorial claims over the South China Sea and its resources are numerous, with the most contentious revolving around the Paracel Islands and Spratly Islands. However, ownership of virtually all of the South China Sea is contested. The disputed areas often involve oil and natural gas resources:

- Indonesia's ownership of the natural gas-rich fields offshore of the Natuna Islands was undisputed until China released an official map with unclear maritime boundaries indicating that Chinese-claimed waters in the South China Sea may extend into the waters around the Natuna Islands. Indonesia responded by choosing the Natuna Islands region as the site of its largest military exercises to date in 1996. . . .
- The Philippines' Malampaya and Camago natural gas and condensate fields are in Chinese-claimed waters. . . .
- Many of Malaysia's natural gas fields located offshore Sarawak also fall under the Chinese claim . . . In July 2002, a new oil discovery . . . about 100 miles offshore from Sabah on the island of Borneo rekindled interest in a latent dispute between Malaysia and Brunei over offshore rights. Brunei had asserted a 200-mile exclusive economic zone (EEZ) off its coastline in 2000. Negotiations between the two governments to resolve the issue are continuing. . . .
- Maritime boundaries in the natural gas-rich Gulf of Thailand portion of the South China Sea have not all been clearly defined. Several companies have signed exploration agreements but have been unable to drill in a disputed zone between Cambodia and Thailand. . . .

> Most of these claims are historical, but they are also based upon internationally accepted principles extending territorial claims offshore onto a country's continental shelf, as well as the 1982 United Nations Convention on the Law of the Sea. . . .

---

24 Victor Prescott & Clive Schofield, *The Maritime Political Boundaries of the World*, 2d ed (Boston: Martinus Nijhoff Publishers, 2005) at 1.

All of the Spratly Islands claimants have occupied some of the islands, and/or stationed troops and built fortified structures on the reefs. Brunei, which does not claim any of the Spratly Islands, has not occupied any of them, but has declared an Exclusive Economic Zone that includes Louisa Reef.

Military skirmishes have occurred numerous times over the past two decades. The most serious occurred in 1974, when China invaded and captured the Paracel Islands from Vietnam, and in 1988, when the Chinese and Vietnamese navies clashed at Johnson Reef in the Spratly Islands, sinking several Vietnamese boats and killing over 70 sailors.[25]

The dispute over the South China Sea remained a heated issue at the time of this writing. In 2012, China and the Philippines accused each other of intrusions into areas over which each has laid claim, and positioned vessels in the contested waters in what the BBC called a "maritime standoff." Subsequently, China created "Sansha city," a body that purports to exercise authority over Chinese territory in the region, prompting protests from Vietnam and the Philippines.[26] In 2013, a Philippine coast guard vessel pursued a Taiwanese fishing boat in disputed waters, firing live ammunition, killing a fisherman, and prompting stern diplomatic exchanges between the Philippines and Taiwan.[27]

As noted previously, the UN Secretary General's High-level Panel on Threats, Challenges and Change urged in 2004 that "[m]ore legal mechanisms are necessary in the area of natural resources, fights over which have often been an obstacle to peace" and suggested that there should be "a focus on the development of rules, for example through the International Law Commission, for the use of transboundary resources."[28]

Exclusive economic zone may be somewhat of a misnomer. Note the rights enjoyed by other states in the zone; such rights are not limited to non-economic uses of the EEZ. In particular, UNCLOS has developed and given substance to the somewhat amorphous concept of "preferential but not absolute" fishing rights of coastal states recognized by the ICJ in the *Fisheries Jurisdiction Case*. Note in particular the distinctions drawn between the rights of developed and developing states, and the provisions providing for the particular needs of landlocked and "geographically disadvantaged" states. In what circumstances, and to what degree, do coastal states truly enjoy *exclusive* rights of exploitation of the economic resources of their EEZ?

UNCLOS also imposes certain environmental management requirements on the coastal state with respect to its EEZ. Consider the connection between these obligations and the obligation of the coastal state to "promote the objective of optimum utilization of the living resources" of the EEZ. Is "optimum utilization" adequately defined in the foregoing provisions? Note that other provisions of UNCLOS address environmental pro-

---

25 US Energy Information Administration, *Country Analysis Briefs: The South China Sea*, online: www.eia. doe.gov/emeu/cabs/schina.html.

26 British Broadcasting Service, "Q&A: South China Sea Dispute," *BBC News* (15 May 2013) online: www. bbc.co.uk/news/world-asia-pacific-13748349. For a discussion of the Chinese claims, see the several articles contained in the Agora section of (2013) 107 AJIL 124.

27 Associated Press, "Fisherman's Shooting Sparks South China Sea Tensions," *Financial Times* (10 May 2013) online: www.ft.com/intl/cms/s/0/cb7c452a-b946-11e2-bc57-00144feabdc0.html#axzz2jhv70TaO.

28 *A More Secure World*, above note 5 at paras 91–93.

tection of the high seas and of the marine environment generally. Finally, note the jurisdiction vested in the coastal state to legislate and enforce laws relating to the regime of the EEZ.

Although the EEZ was an innovation in the law of the sea introduced by UNCLOS, it rapidly permeated customary international law, even before UNCLOS itself came into force in 1994:

Continental Shelf (Libyan Arab Jamahiriya/Malta), Judgment, [1985] ICJ Rep 13

[This case involved a dispute between the parties over the delimitation of their respective continental shelves. In the context of that dispute, the Court also addressed the customary international legal status of the exclusive economic zone.]

31. . . . . [T]he question arises of the relationship, both within the context of the 1982 Convention and generally, between the legal concept of the continental shelf and that of the exclusive economic zone. Malta relies on the genesis of the exclusive economic zone concept, and its inclusion in the 1982 Convention, as confirming the importance of the "distance principle" in the law of the continental shelf. . . . Malta has submitted that, in the present delimitation, account must be taken of . . . the provisions of the Convention concerning the exclusive economic zone. Malta's opinion is based on the statement made on this point by the Court itself in its 1982 Judgment . . . that the exclusive economic zone "may be regarded as part of modern international law" (I.C.J. Reports 1982, p. 48, para. 47 and p. 74, para. 100). . . .

32. Libya, on the other hand, points out that this case is concerned only with the delimitation of the continental shelf, and emphasizes that the 1982 Convention has not yet come into force and is not binding as between the Parties to the present case. . . . It is Libya's contention that the continental shelf has not been absorbed by the concept of the exclusive economic zone under present international law; and that the establishment of fishery zones and exclusive economic zones has not changed the law of maritime zone delimitation, or given more prominence to the criterion of distance from the coast. It also argues that, whereas the rights of the coastal State over its continental shelf are inherent and *ab initio*, rights over the exclusive economic zone exist only in so far as the coastal State chooses to proclaim such a zone. . . .

33. In the view of the Court, even though the present case relates only to the delimitation of the continental shelf and not to that of the exclusive economic zone, the principles and rules underlying the latter concept cannot be left out of consideration. As the 1982 Convention demonstrates, the two institutions — continental shelf and exclusive economic zone — are linked together in modern law. Since the rights enjoyed by a State over its continental shelf would also be possessed by it over the sea-bed and subsoil of any exclusive economic zone which it might proclaim, one of the relevant circumstances to be taken into account for the delimitation of the continental shelf of a State is the legally permissible extent of the exclusive economic zone appertaining to that same State. This does not mean that the concept of the continental shelf has been absorbed by that of the exclusive economic zone; it does however signify that greater importance must be attributed to elements, such as distance from the coast, which are common to both concepts.

34. . . . It is in the Court's view incontestable that . . . the institution of the exclusive economic zone, with its rule on entitlement by reason of distance, is shown by the practice of States to have become a part of customary law; in any case, Libya itself seemed to recognize this fact when, at one stage during the negotiation of the Special Agreement, it proposed that the extent of the exclusive economic zone be included in the reference to the Court. Although the institutions of the continental shelf and the exclusive economic zone are different and distinct, the rights which the exclusive economic zone entails over the sea-bed of the zone are defined by reference to the regime laid down for the continental shelf. Although there can be a continental shelf where there is no exclusive economic zone, there cannot be an exclusive economic zone without a corresponding continental shelf. It follows that, for juridical and practical reasons, the distance criterion must now apply to the continental shelf as well as to the exclusive economic zone; and this quite apart from the provision as to distance in paragraph 1 of Article 76. . . .

We now turn to the regime of the continental shelf, which is intimately connected to that of the EEZ.

6) The Continental Shelf

The EEZ includes the subsoil, seabed, and the living resources in the column of water above it. However, there is an even more detailed regime that governs the seabed and subsoil of the continental shelf:

United Nations Convention on the Law of the Sea, 10 December 1982, 1833 UNTS 3, in force 16 November 1994

Article 76
Definition of the continental shelf
1. The continental shelf of a coastal State comprises the sea-bed and subsoil of the submarine areas that extend beyond its territorial sea throughout the natural prolongation of its land territory to the outer edge of the continental margin, or to a distance of 200 nautical miles from the baselines from which the breadth of the territorial sea is measured where the outer edge of the continental margin does not extend up to that distance.

2. The continental shelf of a coastal State shall not extend beyond the limits provided for in paragraphs 4 to 6.

3. The continental margin comprises the submerged prolongation of the land mass of the coastal State, and consists of the sea-bed and subsoil of the shelf, the slope and the rise. It does not include the deep ocean floor with its oceanic ridges or the subsoil thereof. . . .

5. The fixed points comprising the line of the outer limits of the continental shelf on the sea-bed, . . . either shall not exceed 350 nautical miles from the baselines from which the breadth of the territorial sea is measured or shall not exceed 100 nautical miles from the 2,500 metre isobath, which is a line connecting the depth of 2,500 metres.

6. Notwithstanding the provisions of paragraph 5, on submarine ridges, the outer limit of the continental shelf shall not exceed 350 nautical miles from the baselines from which

the breadth of the territorial sea is measured. This paragraph does not apply to submarine elevations that are natural components of the continental margin, such as its plateaux, rises, caps, banks and spurs. . . .

8. Information on the limits of the continental shelf beyond 200 nautical miles from the baselines from which the breadth of the territorial sea is measured shall be submitted by the coastal State to the Commission on the Limits of the Continental Shelf set up under Annex II [of UNCLOS] on the basis of equitable geographical representation. The Commission shall make recommendations to coastal States on matters related to the establishment of the outer limits of their continental shelf. The limits of the shelf established by a coastal State on the basis of these recommendations shall be final and binding. . . .

Article 77
Rights of the coastal State over the continental shelf
1. The coastal State exercises over the continental shelf sovereign rights for the purpose of exploring it and exploiting its natural resources.

2. The rights referred to in paragraph 1 are exclusive in the sense that if the coastal State does not explore the continental shelf or exploit its natural resources, no one may undertake these activities without the express consent of the coastal State.

3. The rights of the coastal State over the continental shelf do not depend on occupation, effective or notional, or on any express proclamation.

4. The natural resources referred to in this Part consist of the mineral and other non-living resources of the sea-bed and subsoil together with living organisms belonging to sedentary species, that is to say, organisms which, at the harvestable stage, either are immobile on or under the sea-bed or are unable to move except in constant physical contact with the sea-bed or the subsoil.

Article 78
Legal status of the superjacent waters and air space and the rights and freedoms of other States
1. The rights of the coastal State over the continental shelf do not affect the legal status of the superjacent waters or of the air space above those waters.

2. The exercise of the rights of the coastal State over the continental shelf must not infringe or result in any unjustifiable interference with navigation and other rights and freedoms of other States as provided for in [UNCLOS] . . .

Article 79
Submarine cables and pipelines on the continental shelf
1. All States are entitled to lay submarine cables and pipelines on the continental shelf, in accordance with the provisions of this article.

2. Subject to its right to take reasonable measures for the exploration of the continental shelf, the exploitation of its natural resources and the prevention, reduction and control of pollution from pipelines, the coastal State may not impede the laying or maintenance of such cables or pipelines.

3. The delineation of the course for the laying of such pipelines on the continental shelf

is subject to the consent of the coastal State. . . .

Article 80
Artificial islands, installations and structures on the continental shelf
Article 60 applies *mutatis mutandis* to artificial islands, installations and structures on the continental shelf.

Article 81
Drilling on the continental shelf
The coastal State shall have the exclusive right to authorize and regulate drilling on the continental shelf for all purposes.

Article 82
Payments and contributions with respect to the exploitation of the continental shelf beyond 200 nautical miles
1. The coastal State shall make payments or contributions in kind in respect of the exploitation of the non-living resources of the continental shelf beyond 200 nautical miles from the baselines from which the breadth of the territorial sea is measured.

2. The payments and contributions shall be made annually with respect to all production at a site after the first five years of production at that site. For the sixth year, the rate of payment or contribution shall be 1 per cent of the value or volume of production at the site. The rate shall increase by 1 per cent for each subsequent year until the twelfth year and shall remain at 7 per cent thereafter. Production does not include resources used in connection with exploitation.

3. A developing State which is a net importer of a mineral resource produced from its continental shelf is exempt from making such payments or contributions in respect of that mineral resource.

4. The payments or contributions shall be made through the [International Sea Bed] Authority [established by UNCLOS], which shall distribute them to States Parties to this Convention, on the basis of equitable sharing criteria, taking into account the interests and needs of developing States, particularly the least developed and the land-locked among them.

Continental shelf rights need not be "claimed" by the coastal state in the same way as it must claim an EEZ. As suggested in the excerpt from *Libya v Malta* reproduced above, the coastal state's rights in its continental shelf flow inherently from its sovereignty over its adjacent land territory. Indeed, the continental shelf is generally considered the "natural prolongation" of the state's land territory, as suggested by the following proclamation made in 1945:

Truman Proclamation on the Continental Shelf, Presidential Proclamation No 2667, 28 September 1945, 10 Fed Reg 12303

Policy of the United States with Respect to the Natural Resources of the Subsoil and Sea Bed of the Continental Shelf

Whereas the Government of the United States of America, aware of the long range world-wide need for new sources of petroleum and other minerals, holds the view that efforts to discover and make available new supplies of these resources should be encouraged; and

Whereas its competent experts are of the opinion that such resources underlie many parts of the continental shelf off the coasts of the United States of America, and that with modern technological progress their utilisation is already practicable or will become so at an early date; and

Whereas recognized jurisdiction over these resources is required in the interest of their conservation and prudent utilisation when and as development is undertaken; and

Whereas it is the view of the Government of the United States that the exercise of jurisdiction over the natural resources of the subsoil and sea bed of the continental shelf by the contiguous nation is reasonable and just, since the effectiveness of measures to utilise or conserve these resources would be contingent upon cooperation and protection from shore, since the continental shelf may be regarded as an extension of the land mass of the coastal nation and thus naturally appurtenant to it, since these resources frequently form a seaward extension of a pool or deposit lying within the territory, and since self-protection compels the coastal nation to keep close watch over activities off its shores which are of their nature necessary for utilisation of these resources;

NOW THEREFORE I, HARRY S. TRUMAN, President of the United States of America, do hereby proclaim the following policy of the United States of America with respect to the natural resources of the subsoil and sea bed of the continental shelf.

Having concern for the urgency of conserving and prudently utilizing its natural resources, the Government of the United States regards the natural resources of the subsoil and sea bed of the continental shelf beneath the high seas but contiguous to the coasts of the United States as appertaining to the United States, subject to its jurisdiction and control. In cases where the continental shelf extends to the shores of another State, or is shared with an adjacent State, the boundary shall be determined by the United States and the State concerned in accordance with equitable principles. The character as high seas of the waters above the continental shelf and the right to their free and unimpeded navigation are in no way thus affected.

Notice how Article 76 of UNCLOS provides that a state's continental shelf is presumed to extend at least 200 nautical miles from its baselines. This is so whether or not the actual physical shelf extends that far. This "distance method" for defining the extent of the continental shelf is a departure from the method employed in the 1958 (Geneva) Convention on the Continental Shelf,[29] to which fifty-eight states (including Canada) are parties.[30] Article 1 of the 1958 treaty provides:

Article 1

For the purpose of these articles, the term "continental shelf" is used as referring,

(a) to the seabed and subsoil of the submarine areas adjacent to the coast but outside the area of the territorial sea, to a depth of 200 metres or, beyond that limit, to where

---

29 29 April 1958, 499 UNTS 311, Can TS 1970 No. 4, in force 10 June 1964.

30 While the 1958 treaty remains in force, its provisions are displaced, as between UNCLOS states parties, pursuant to Article 311(1) of UNCLOS.

the depth of the superjacent waters admits of the exploitation of the natural resources of the said areas;

(b) to the seabed and subsoil of similar submarine areas adjacent to the coasts of islands.

While a coastal state's continental shelf rights are inherent and therefore need not be claimed, UNCLOS provides that a state's continental shelf may extend beyond the default 200 nautical mile limit. A coastal state's claim to such an enlarged continental shelf, subject to the ultimate limits established in Article 76, must be vetted by the Commission on the Limits of the Continental Shelf, established by Annex II of UNCLOS. The size of continental shelves over which states might thus lay claim is vast. In the case of Canada, which is due to submit its claim to the Commission by 2013 (ten years following its ratification of UNCLOS), the potential area of the continental shelf extending beyond the 200 nautical mile entitlement has been estimated at roughly the area of all the prairie provinces combined.

Again, along with such extensive potential outer limits to the continental shelf, there is a substantial risk of overlapping claims. Consider these facts:

> [T]here are 151 coastal States, all with sovereign rights to the adjacent sea and shelf. Under the Convention, those rights cover a total area of about 60 million [square] km or around 20 percent of the world's oceans within the 200-nautical-mile (M) limit. But there is perhaps an additional 5 percent (15 million [square] km) which lies beyond the 200 M limit, to which sovereign rights may also extend under the terms of the Convention. Up to 54 coastal States may be able to claim extensions of their continental shelf beyond 200 M.[31]

And again, UNCLOS deploys an "equitable" dispute settlement standard, set out in Article 83 as follows: "The delimitation of the continental shelf between States with opposite or adjacent coasts shall be effected by agreement on the basis of international law, as referred to in Article 38 of the Statute of the International Court of Justice, in order to achieve an equitable solution."

Contrast the nature of the continental shelf resources that may be exclusively exploited by the coastal state with those that come within the EEZ regime. Compare also the exclusivity of the coastal state's rights of resource exploitation in its continental shelf with that applicable in its EEZ. In what limited circumstances is the coastal state obliged to "share" the fruits of exploitation of its continental shelf resources? The fact that any such sharing is required at all is a matter of some controversy, and is linked to the controversial resource exploitation regime established by UNCLOS over the deep seabed, which we examine in Section 8 below.

7) The High Seas

As we have seen, coastal states enjoy full sovereignty over their internal waters; sovereignty subject to certain jurisdictional limitations in their 12-nautical-mile territorial sea

---

31 Peter Cook & Chris Carleton, *Continental Shelf Limits: The Scientific and Legal Interface* (Oxford: Oxford University Press, 2000) at 3.

(as well as in their archipelagic waters, where relevant); limited law enforcement jurisdiction over their contiguous zone, extending to 24 nautical miles from their baselines; jurisdictional control over the resources in the water column out to 200 nautical miles from their baselines; and exclusive rights to the resources of the subsoil and seabed of their continental shelf to a potentially much greater distance. Beyond the outer limits of the territorial seas and EEZs lie the high seas; and beyond their continental shelves lies the deep seabed. In this section we consider the legal regime applicable in the high seas:

United Nations Convention on the Law of the Sea, 10 December 1982, 1833 UNTS 3, in force 16 November 1994

PART VII
HIGH SEAS

Section 1. General Provisions

Article 86
Application of the provisions of this Part
The provisions of this Part apply to all parts of the sea that are not included in the exclusive economic zone, in the territorial sea or in the internal waters of a State, or in the archipelagic waters of an archipelagic State. This article does not entail any abridgement of the freedoms enjoyed by all States in the exclusive economic zone in accordance with article 58.

Article 87
Freedom of the high seas
1. The high seas are open to all States, whether coastal or land-locked. Freedom of the high seas is exercised under the conditions laid down by this Convention and by other rules of international law. It comprises, inter alia, both for coastal and land-locked States:
    (a) freedom of navigation;
    (b) freedom of overflight;
    (c) freedom to lay submarine cables and pipelines, subject to Part VI;
    (d) freedom to construct artificial islands and other installations permitted under international law, subject to Part VI;
    (e) freedom of fishing, subject to the conditions laid down in section 2;
    (f) freedom of scientific research, subject to Parts VI and XIII.

2. These freedoms shall be exercised by all States with due regard for the interests of other States in their exercise of the freedom of the high seas, and also with due regard for the rights under this Convention with respect to activities in the Area.

Article 88
Reservation of the high seas for peaceful purposes
The high seas shall be reserved for peaceful purposes.

Article 89
Invalidity of claims of sovereignty over the high seas
No State may validly purport to subject any part of the high seas to its sovereignty.

Article 90
Right of navigation
Every State, whether coastal or land-locked, has the right to sail ships flying its flag on the high seas.

Article 91
Nationality of ships
1. Every State shall fix the conditions for the grant of its nationality to ships, for the registration of ships in its territory, and for the right to fly its flag. Ships have the nationality of the State whose flag they are entitled to fly. There must exist a genuine link between the State and the ship. . . .

Article 92
Status of ships
1. Ships shall sail under the flag of one State only and, save in exceptional cases expressly provided for in international treaties or in this Convention, shall be subject to its exclusive jurisdiction on the high seas. A ship may not change its flag during a voyage or while in a port of call, save in the case of a real transfer of ownership or change of registry.

2. A ship which sails under the flags of two or more States, using them according to convenience, may not claim any of the nationalities in question with respect to any other State, and may be assimilated to a ship without nationality. . . .

Article 94
Duties of the flag State
1. Every State shall effectively exercise its jurisdiction and control in administrative, technical and social matters over ships flying its flag.

2. In particular every State shall:
   (a) maintain a register of ships containing the names and particulars of ships flying its flag, except those which are excluded from generally accepted international regulations on account of their small size; and
   (b) assume jurisdiction under its internal law over each ship flying its flag and its master, officers and crew in respect of administrative, technical and social matters concerning the ship.

3. Every State shall take such measures for ships flying its flag as are necessary to ensure safety at sea with regard, inter alia, to:
   (a) the construction, equipment and seaworthiness of ships;
   (b) the manning of ships, labour conditions and the training of crews, taking into account the applicable international instruments;
   (c) the use of signals, the maintenance of communications and the prevention of collisions. . . .

Article 95
Immunity of warships on the high seas
Warships on the high seas have complete immunity from the jurisdiction of any State other than the flag State.

Article 96
Immunity of ships used only on government non-commercial service
Ships owned or operated by a State and used only on government non-commercial service shall, on the high seas, have complete immunity from the jurisdiction of any State other than the flag State.

Article 97
Penal jurisdiction in matters of collision or any other incident of navigation
1. In the event of a collision or any other incident of navigation concerning a ship on the high seas, involving the penal or disciplinary responsibility of the master or of any other person in the service of the ship, no penal or disciplinary proceedings may be instituted against such person except before the judicial or administrative authorities either of the flag State or of the State of which such person is a national.

2. In disciplinary matters, the State which has issued a master's certificate or a certificate of competence or licence shall alone be competent, after due legal process, to pronounce the withdrawal of such certificates, even if the holder is not a national of the State which issued them.

3. No arrest or detention of the ship, even as a measure of investigation, shall be ordered by any authorities other than those of the flag State. . . .

Article 100
Duty to co-operate in the repression of piracy
All States shall co-operate to the fullest possible extent in the repression of piracy on the high seas or in any other place outside the jurisdiction of any State.

Article 101
Definition of piracy
Piracy consists of any of the following acts:
> (a) any illegal acts of violence or detention, or any act of depredation, committed for private ends by the crew or the passengers of a private ship or a private aircraft, and directed:
>> (i) on the high seas, against another ship or aircraft, or against persons or property on board such ship or aircraft;
>> (ii) against a ship, aircraft, persons or property in a place outside the jurisdiction of any State;
> (b) any act of voluntary participation in the operation of a ship or of an aircraft with knowledge of facts making it a pirate ship or aircraft;
> (c) any act of inciting or of intentionally facilitating an act described in subparagraph (a) or (b). . . .

Article 105
Seizure of a pirate ship or aircraft
On the high seas, or in any other place outside the jurisdiction of any State, every State may seize a pirate ship or aircraft, or a ship or aircraft taken by piracy and under the control of pirates, and arrest the persons and seize the property on board. The courts of the State which carried out the seizure may decide upon the penalties to be imposed, and

may also determine the action to be taken with regard to the ships, aircraft or property, subject to the rights of third parties acting in good faith. . . .

Article 107
Ships and aircraft which are entitled to seize on account of piracy
A seizure on account of piracy may be carried out only by warships or military aircraft, or other ships or aircraft clearly marked and identifiable as being on government service and authorized to that effect. . . .

Article 110
Right of visit
1. Except where acts of interference derive from powers conferred by treaty, a warship which encounters on the high seas a foreign ship, other than a ship entitled to complete immunity in accordance with articles 95 and 96, is not justified in boarding it unless there is reasonable ground for suspecting that:

(a) the ship is engaged in piracy;
(b) the ship is engaged in the slave trade;
(c) the ship is engaged in unauthorized broadcasting . . . ;
(d) the ship is without nationality; or
(e) though flying a foreign flag or refusing to show its flag, the ship is, in reality, of the same nationality as the warship. . . .

2. In the cases provided for in paragraph 1, the warship may proceed to verify the ship's right to fly its flag. To this end, it may send a boat under the command of an officer to the suspected ship. If suspicion remains after the documents have been checked, it may proceed to a further examination on board the ship, which must be carried out with all possible consideration.

3. If the suspicions prove to be unfounded, and provided that the ship boarded has not committed any act justifying them, it shall be compensated for any loss or damage that may have been sustained.

4. These provisions apply *mutatis mutandis* to military aircraft.

5. These provisions also apply to any other duly authorized ships or aircraft clearly marked and identifiable as being on government service.

Article 111
Right of hot pursuit
1. The hot pursuit of a foreign ship may be undertaken when the competent authorities of the coastal State have good reason to believe that the ship has violated the laws and regulations of that State. Such pursuit must be commenced when the foreign ship or one of its boats is within the internal waters, the archipelagic waters, the territorial sea or the contiguous zone of the pursuing State, and may only be continued outside the territorial sea or the contiguous zone if the pursuit has not been interrupted. It is not necessary that, at the time when the foreign ship within the territorial sea or the contiguous zone receives the order to stop, the ship giving the order should likewise be within the territorial sea or the contiguous zone. If the foreign ship is within a contiguous zone, as defined in

article 33, the pursuit may only be undertaken if there has been a violation of the rights for the protection of which the zone was established.

2. The right of hot pursuit shall apply *mutatis mutandis* to violations in the exclusive economic zone or on the continental shelf, including safety zones around continental shelf installations, of the laws and regulations of the coastal State applicable in accordance with this Convention to the exclusive economic zone or the continental shelf, including such safety zones.

3. The right of hot pursuit ceases as soon as the ship pursued enters the territorial sea of its own State or of a third State. . . .

5. The right of hot pursuit may be exercised only by warships or military aircraft, or other ships or aircraft clearly marked and identifiable as being on government service and authorized to that effect. . . .

The high seas are *res communis* — territory that may not be subject to claims of state sovereignty. However, this concept and the various freedoms of the high seas recognized in UNCLOS, and in customary international law, do not make of the high seas a lawless zone. Rather, as illustrated in the provisions above, all vessels on the high seas are required to have a nationality and each state is vested with the responsibility — and jurisdiction — to regulate the activities of those vessels bearing its nationality. As a general rule, this "flag state" jurisdiction over vessels on the high seas is considered exclusive.

LAW IN CONTEXT

Flags of Convenience and the "Lawless" Seas

Article 91 of UNCLOS specifies that there "must exist a genuine link between the State and the ship" for that state to extend nationality to the ship. However, a "genuine link" can be established through compliance with a state's domestic registration procedure,[32] allowing so-called open registry states to extend their nationality or flag to virtually all comers. These states are sometimes called "flag-of-convenience" states. The Institute of Shipping Economics and Logistics (ISL) reported in 2010 that "[t]oday, 70% of the world merchant fleets tonnage is flagged out, e.g., not registered in the country of domicile of the owner. More than one third of this tonnage is registered in one of the two major open registries, namely Panama and Liberia."[33]

As Article 94 of UNCLOS indicates, flag states have a vital role to play in regulating ships to ensure seaworthiness and proper labour standards, especially on the high seas where no other state may generally assume jurisdiction. Many flag-of-convenience states are, however, notoriously ineffectual in performing these duties. Consider these observations from the International Transport Workers' Federation:

32 *The M/V Saiga (No 2) Case* (Saint Vincent and the Grenadines v Guinea), Judgment of 1 July 1999 (1999), 38 ILM 1323 (International Tribunal for the Law of the Sea) at paras 62–65 and 75–88.

33 Institute of Shipping Economics and Logistics, "Comment: World Merchant Fleet by Ownership Patterns" (2010) 54:7 *Shipping Statistics & Market Review* 5.

In nearly 55 years of campaigning against FOCs [flags of convenience] the ITF has developed a network of inspectors to investigate suspect ships. Their reports reveal a catalogue of abuse of seafarers:

- Very low wages
- Poor on-board conditions
- Inadequate food and clean drinking water
- Long periods of work without proper rest leading to stress and fatigue. . . .

Many FOC vessels are older than the average age of the rest of the world fleet. Tens of thousands of seafarers endure miserable, life-threatening conditions on sub-standard vessels. Many of the detentions by Port State Control authorities involve aging and badly maintained FOC vessels that should never have sailed. Many of these ships have been referred to as "floating coffins."

Casualties are higher among FOC vessels. In 2001, 63 percent of all losses in absolute tonnage terms were accounted for by just thirteen FOC registers. The top five registers in terms of numbers of ships lost were all FOCs: Panama, Cyprus, St Vincent, Cambodia, and Malta.[34]

While some are satisfied that registration establishes a sufficient "genuine link," others are not. A United Nations Convention on Conditions for the Registration of Ships proposes a number of measures designed to "ensur[e] or, as the case may be, strengthen the genuine link between a State and ships flying its flag, . . . in order to exercise effectively its jurisdiction and control over such ships with regard to identification and accountability of shipowners and operators as well as with regard to administrative, technical, economic and social matters."[35] Under this convention, a flagging state must introduce laws on ship ownership providing for the participation "by that State or its nationals as owners of ships flying its flag or in the ownership of such ships . . . sufficient to permit the flag State to exercise effectively its jurisdiction and control over ships flying its flag", and/or "observe the principle that a satisfactory part of the complement consisting of officers and crew of ships flying its flag be nationals or persons domiciled or lawfully in permanent residence in that State."[36] Further, "[t]he State of registration, before entering a ship in its register of ships, shall ensure that the shipowning company or a subsidiary shipowning company is established and/or has its principal place of business within its territory in accordance with its laws and regulations."[37] If the company does not meet this requirement, it must at least have a representative domiciled in the registering state amenable to legal process. The ship's owners must be in a position "to meet the financial obligations that may arise from the operation of such a ship to cover risks which are normally insured in international maritime transportation in respect of damage to third parties."[38] This convention is not,

34   International Transport Workers' Federation, *What Do FOC's Mean to Seafarers?* (undated), online: www.itfglobal.org/flags-convenience/flags-convenien-184.cfm. See further, Deirdre Fitzpatrick & Michael Anderson, eds, *Seafarers' Rights* (Oxford: Oxford University Press, 2005).
35   7 February 1986, UN Doc TD/RS/CONF/19/Add.1, not in force, art 1.
36   *Ibid*, arts 7–9.
37   *Ibid*, art 10(1).
38   *Ibid*, art 10(3).

however, in force, having failed so far to secure the required threshold of ratifications of "40 States, the combined tonnage of which amounts to at least 25 percent of the world tonnage." At the time of writing, only fifteen states have become parties to the treaty. It is notable, however, that in 2005, Liberia (with roughly 11 percent of the world's tonnage) became one of them.

What are the exceptions to the rule of exclusive flag state jurisdiction on the high seas? What is the justification for each? Note the right of hot pursuit, which temporarily "extends" a coastal state's enforcement jurisdiction onto the high seas in the limited circumstances described in Article 111. What measures are pursuing states entitled to take if they are unable to apprehend the fleeing ship before it enters the territorial sea of another state? Consider the following arbitral decision concerning just such a situation involving a Canadian vessel fleeing an American coast guard vessel:

Claim of the British Ship "I'm Alone" v United States (1933), 3 RIAA 1609

[The *I'm Alone* was a Canadian-registered vessel that was sunk on the high seas by an American coast guard vessel after two days of hot pursuit. An arbitration commission was established by the parties to deal with the resulting international claims.]

. . . The third question is based upon the assumption that the United States Government has the right of hot pursuit in the circumstances. . . . The question is whether, in the circumstances, the Government of the United States was legally justified in sinking the *I'm Alone*. . . .

On the assumptions stated in the question, the United States might . . . use necessary and reasonable force for the purpose of effecting the objects of boarding, searching, seizing and bringing into port the suspected vessel; and if sinking should occur incidentally, as a result of the exercise of necessary and reasonable force for such purpose, the pursuing vessel might be entirely blameless. But the Commissioners think that . . . the admittedly intentional sinking of the suspected vessel was not justified . . . by any principle of international law. . . .

LAW IN CONTEXT

Terrorism and the High Seas

Since September 11, 2001, maritime security has become a key preoccupation. Consider this discussion from the 2005 US National Strategy for Maritime Security:

Non-state terrorist groups that exploit open borders challenge the sovereignty of nations and have an increasingly damaging effect on international affairs. . . . Successful attacks in the maritime domain provide opportunities to cause significant disruption to regional and global economies. . . . Some terrorist groups have used shipping as a means of conveyance for positioning their agents, logistical support, and generating revenue. . . .

Terrorists have indicated a strong desire to use WMD [weapons of mass destruction]. This prospect creates a more complex and perilous security situation, further aggravated by countries that are unable to account for or adequately secure their stockpiles of such weapons and associated materials. This circumstance, coupled with increased access to the technology needed to build and employ those weapons, increases the possibility that a terrorist attack involving WMD could occur. . . .

Terrorists can also develop effective attack capabilities relatively quickly using a variety of platforms, including explosives-laden suicide boats and light aircraft; merchant and cruise ships as kinetic weapons to ram another vessel, warship, port facility, or offshore platform; commercial vessels as launch platforms for missile attacks; underwater swimmers to infiltrate ports; and unmanned underwater explosive delivery vehicles. . . . Terrorists can also take advantage of a vessel's legitimate cargo, such as chemicals, petroleum, or liquefied natural gas, as the explosive component of an attack. Vessels can be used to transport powerful conventional explosives or WMD for detonation in a port or alongside an offshore facility.[39]

One response to this threat has been the Proliferation Security Initiative (PSI). Pursuant to the PSI, participating states agree to use their own laws and coordinate their activities to interdict shipments of dangerous technology to suspect states and non-state actors. It does not, however, change the rules of international law:

The initiative does not empower countries to do anything that they previously could not do. Most importantly, PSI does not grant governments any new legal authority to conduct interdictions in international waters or airspace. Such interdictions may take place, but they must be confined to what is currently permissible under international law. For example, a ship can be stopped in international waters if it is not flying a national flag or properly registered. It cannot be stopped simply because it is suspected of transporting WMD or related goods. PSI is primarily intended to encourage participating countries to take greater advantage of their own existing national laws to intercept threatening trade passing through their territories and where they have jurisdiction to act. . . .[40]

At the heart of the PSI are reciprocal, bilateral "ship boarding" agreements between the United States and key ship registry nations, including the world's most important flagging states, Panama and Liberia. These agreements anticipate (but do not require automatic) reciprocal authorization from each state to board the other's commercial ships on the high seas in order to interdict movement of dangerous material and weapons. Put another way, participants signal preparedness in the agreements to delegate their jurisdiction under international law to regulate shipping flying their flag. Since the United States is one of the few states with a true "blue water" navy able to conduct interdictions on the high seas, the PSI ship boarding agreements provide it with the means to seek (and receive) from flagging states proxy authority to regulate their shipping in international waters.

Another response to potential maritime terrorist (and other) threats is the recent extension of the North American Aerospace Defense Command (NORAD) Agreement be-

---

39 US Government, *The National Strategy for Maritime Security* (September 2005), online: www.ise.gov/sites/default/files/0509%20National%20Strategy%20for%20Maritime%20Security.pdf.

40 Arms Control Association, *The Proliferation Security Initiative (PSI) at a Glance* (2012), online: www.armscontrol.org/factsheets/PSI.

tween Canada and the United States to add a maritime surveillance mission to NORAD's traditional aerospace warning and control missions, as follows:

1. The primary missions of NORAD in the future shall be to provide:

. . .

c. Maritime warning for North America.

2. For the purposes of this Agreement:

. . .

c. "Maritime warning" consists of processing, assessing, and disseminating intelligence and information related to the respective maritime areas and internal waterways of, and the maritime approaches to, Canada and the United States, and warning of maritime threats to, or attacks against North America utilizing mutual support arrangements with other commands and agencies, to enable identification, validation, and response by national commands and agencies responsible for maritime defense and security. Through these tasks NORAD shall develop a comprehensive shared understanding of maritime activities to better identify potential maritime threats to North American security. Maritime surveillance and control shall continue to be exercised by national commands and, as appropriate, coordinated bilaterally.[41]

Note that this mission is not limited to the maritime areas and internal waterways of the participating states, but extends also to the "maritime approaches" to each country.

8) The Deep Seabed

The final maritime area to examine is the deep seabed—identified in law as the seabed and subsoil of the ocean floor beyond the limits of national jurisdiction, i.e. beyond the limits of the continental shelf as defined according to Article 76 of UNCLOS. Traditionally, the deep seabed was considered part of the *res communis* regime of the high seas, and thus open to exploration and exploitation by any state. As scientific and technological advances enhanced the prospects for such exploration and exploitation, pressure emerged to establish a special legal regime that would level the playing field between developed and developing states. This idea proved highly controversial. Consider this 1969 UN General Assembly resolution and its voting pattern:

> *Question of the reservation exclusively for peaceful purposes of the sea-bed and the ocean floor, and the subsoil thereof, underlying the high seas beyond the limits of present national jurisdiction, and the use of their resources in the interests of mankind,* **GA Res 2574 (XXIX) D, adopted 15 December 1969**[42]
>
> *The General Assembly,*
>   *Recalling* its resolution 2467 A (XXIII) of 21 December 1968 to the effect that the exploitation of the resources of the sea-bed and the ocean floor, and the subsoil thereof,

---

41 Agreement between the Government of Canada and the Government of the United States of America on the North American Aerospace Defense Command, 28 April 2006, Can TS 2006 No 6, in force 12 May 2006.

42 Reprinted in UN GAOR, 24th Sess, Supp No 30 at 11, UN Doc A/7630 (1970).

beyond the limits of national jurisdiction, should be carried out for the benefit of mankind as a whole, irrespective of the geographical location of States, taking into account the special interests and needs of the developing countries,

Convinced that it is essential, for the achievement of this purpose, that such activities be carried out under an international regime, including appropriate international machinery,

Noting that this matter is under consideration by the Committee on the Peaceful Uses of the Sea-Bed and the Ocean Floor beyond the Limits of National Jurisdiction,

Recalling its resolution 2340 (XXII) of 18 December 1967 on the importance of preserving the sea-bed and the ocean floor, and the subsoil thereof, beyond the limits of national jurisdiction, from actions and uses which might be detrimental to the common interests of mankind,

Declares that, pending the establishment of the aforementioned international regime:

(a) States and persons, physical or juridical, are bound to refrain from all activities of exploitation of the resources of the area of the sea-bed and ocean floor, and the subsoil thereof, beyond the limits of national jurisdiction;

(b) No claim to any part of that area or its resources shall be recognized.

Adopted by a recorded vote of 62–28–28 (with eight states recorded as absent):

In favour: Afghanistan, Algeria, Argentina, Barbados, Bolivia, Brazil, Burundi, Central African Republic, Ceylon, Chad, Chile, Colombia, Congo (Brazzaville), Congo (Democratic Republic of), Costa Rica, Cyprus, Dahomey, Dominican Republic, Ecuador, Ethiopia, Finland, Guatemala, Guinea, Guyana, Haiti, Honduras, India, Iraq, Jamaica, Jordan, Kenya, Kuwait, Lesotho, Malaysia, Maldives, Mali, Mauritania, Mauritius, Mexico, Morocco, Nepal, Nicaragua, Niger, Pakistan, Panama, Paraguay, Peru, Rwanda, Singapore, Somalia, Southern Yemen, Sweden, Thailand, Trinidad and Tobago, Tunisia, Uganda, United Republic of Tanzania, Uruguay, Venezuela, Yemen, Yugoslavia, Zambia.

Against: Australia, Austria, Belgium, Bulgaria, Byelorussia, Canada, Czechoslovakia, Denmark, France, Ghana, Hungary, Iceland, Ireland, Italy, Japan, Luxembourg, Malta, Mongolia, Netherlands, New Zealand, Norway, Poland, Portugal, South Africa, Ukraine, USSR, United Kingdom, United States.

Abstaining: Burma, China, Cuba, El Salvador, Greece, Indonesia, Iran, Israel, Ivory Coast, Laos, Lebanon, Liberia, Libya, Madagascar, Malawi, Nigeria, Philippines, Romania, Saudi Arabia, Sierra Leone, Spain, Sudan, Swaziland, Syria, Togo, Turkey, United Arab Republic, Upper Volta.

Absent: Albania, Botswana, Cambodia, Cameroon, Equatorial Guinea, Gabon, Gambia, Senegal.[43]

Following protracted and difficult negotiations, the following UNCLOS provisions attempted to establish this "international regime."

---

43 UN Doc A/PV.1833 (15 December 1969).

United Nations Convention on the Law of the Sea, 10 December 1982, 1833 UNTS 3, in force 16 November 1994

Article 1
Use of terms and scope
1. For the purposes of this Convention:
(1) "Area" means the seabed and ocean floor and subsoil thereof beyond the limits of national jurisdiction;
(2) "Authority" means the International Seabed Authority;
(3) "activities in the Area" means all activities of exploration for, and exploitation of, the resources of the Area. . . .

PART XI
THE AREA

Section 1. General Provisions

Article 133
Use of terms
For the purposes of this Part:
(a) "resources" means all solid, liquid or gaseous mineral resources in situ in the Area at or beneath the sea-bed, including polymetallic nodules;
(b) resources, when recovered from the Area, are referred to as "minerals." . . .

Article 135
Legal status of the superjacent waters and air space
Neither this Part nor any rights granted or exercised pursuant thereto shall affect the legal status of the waters superjacent to the Area or that of the air space above those waters.

Section 2. Principles Governing the Area

Article 136
Common heritage of mankind
The Area and its resources are the common heritage of mankind.

Article 137
Legal status of the Area and its resources
1. No State shall claim or exercise sovereignty or sovereign rights over any part of the Area or its resources, nor shall any State or natural or juridical person appropriate any part thereof. No such claim or exercise of sovereignty or sovereign rights nor such appropriation shall be recognized.

2. All rights in the resources of the Area are vested in mankind as a whole on whose behalf the Authority shall act. These resources are not subject to alienation. The minerals recovered from the Area, however, may only be alienated in accordance with this Part and the rules, regulations and procedures of the Authority.

3. No State or natural or juridical person shall claim, acquire or exercise rights with respect to the minerals recovered from the Area except in accordance with this Part.

Otherwise, no such claim, acquisition or exercise of such rights shall be recognized.
. . .

Article 139
Responsibility to ensure compliance and liability for damage
1. States Parties shall have the responsibility to ensure that activities in the Area, whether carried out by States Parties, or state enterprises or natural or juridical persons which possess the nationality of States Parties or are effectively controlled by them or their nationals, shall be carried out in conformity with this Part. The same responsibility applies to international organizations for activities in the Area carried out by such organizations. . . .

Article 140
Benefit of mankind
1. Activities in the Area shall, as specifically provided for in this Part, be carried out for the benefit of mankind as a whole, irrespective of the geographical location of States, whether coastal or land-locked, and taking into particular consideration the interests and needs of developing States . . .

2. The Authority shall provide for the equitable sharing of financial and other economic benefits derived from activities in the Area through any appropriate mechanism on a non-discriminatory basis, in accordance with article 160, paragraph 2 (f)(i).

Article 141
Use of the Area exclusively for peaceful purposes
The Area shall be open to use exclusively for peaceful purposes by all States, whether coastal or land-locked, without discrimination and without prejudice to the other provisions of this Part.

Article 142
Rights and legitimate interests of coastal States
1. Activities in the Area, with respect to resource deposits in the Area which lie across limits of national jurisdiction, shall be conducted with due regard to the rights and legitimate interests of any coastal State across whose jurisdiction such deposits lie. . . .

Article 143
Marine scientific research
1. Marine scientific research in the Area shall be carried out exclusively for peaceful purposes and for the benefit of mankind as a whole in accordance with Part XIII. . . .

Article 144
Transfer of technology
1. The Authority shall take measures in accordance with this Convention:
    (a) to acquire technology and scientific knowledge relating to activities in the Area; and
    (b) to promote and encourage the transfer to developing States of such technology and scientific knowledge so that all States Parties benefit therefrom.

2. To this end the Authority and States Parties shall co-operate in promoting the transfer of technology and scientific knowledge relating to activities in the Area so that the

Enterprise and all States Parties may benefit therefrom. In particular they shall initiate and promote:

(a) programmes for the transfer of technology to the Enterprise and to developing States with regard to activities in the Area, including, inter alia, facilitating the access of the Enterprise and of developing States to the relevant technology, under fair and reasonable terms and conditions;

(b) measures directed towards the advancement of the technology of the Enterprise and the domestic technology of developing States, particularly by providing opportunities to personnel from the Enterprise and from developing States for training in marine science and technology and for their full participation in activities in the Area. . . .

Article 148

Participation of developing States in activities in the Area

The effective participation of developing States in activities in the Area shall be promoted as specifically provided for in this Part, having due regard to their special interests and needs, and in particular to the special need of the landlocked and geographically disadvantaged among them to overcome obstacles arising from their disadvantaged location, including remoteness from the Area and difficulty of access to and from it. . . .

Section 3: Development of Resources of the Area

. . .

Article 153

System of exploration and exploitation

1. Activities in the Area shall be organized, carried out and controlled by the Authority on behalf of mankind as a whole in accordance with this article as well as other relevant provisions of this Part and the relevant Annexes, and the rules, regulations and procedures of the Authority. . . .

The regime envisioned for the deep seabed proved sufficiently unpalatable to many developed states that, without further action, it was clear that many of them would not ratify UNCLOS. It was only after the negotiation of an additional agreement amending the deep seabed regime that many developed states chose to ratify UNCLOS, prompting its coming into force in November 1994. Consider the following provisions of the additional agreement and how they affect the "common heritage of humankind" regime originally contemplated for the deep seabed by UNCLOS:

Agreement relating to the Implementation of Part XI of the United Nations Convention on the Law of the Sea of 10 December 1982, 28 July 1994, 183 UNTS 3, in force 28 July 1996

The States Parties to this Agreement,

. . . *Reaffirming* that the seabed and ocean floor and subsoil thereof, beyond the limits of national jurisdiction (hereinafter referred to as "the Area"), as well as the resources of the Area, are the common heritage of mankind, . . .

Noting the political and economic changes, including market-oriented approaches, affecting the implementation of Part XI,

Wishing to facilitate universal participation in the Convention, . . .

Have agreed as follows:

Article 1
Implementation of Part XI

1. The States Parties to this Agreement undertake to implement Part XI in accordance with this Agreement.

2. The Annex forms an integral part of this Agreement.

Article 2
Relationship between this Agreement and Part XI

1. The provisions of this Agreement and Part XI shall be interpreted and applied together as a single instrument. In the event of any inconsistency between this Agreement and Part XI, the provisions of this Agreement shall prevail. . . .

Annex

Section 1. Costs to States Parties and Institutional Arrangements

1. The International Seabed Authority (hereinafter referred to as "the Authority") is the organization through which States Parties to the Convention shall, in accordance with the regime for the Area established in Part XI and this Agreement, organize and control activities in the Area, particularly with a view to administering the resources of the Area. . . .

2. In order to minimize costs to States Parties, all organs and subsidiary bodies to be established under the Convention and this Agreement shall be cost-effective. This principle shall also apply to the frequency, duration and scheduling of meetings.

3. The setting up and the functioning of the organs and subsidiary bodies of the Authority shall be based on an evolutionary approach, taking into account the functional needs of the organs and subsidiary bodies concerned in order that they may discharge effectively their respective responsibilities at various stages of the development of activities in the Area. . . .

Section 2: The Enterprise

1. The Secretariat of the Authority shall perform the functions of the Enterprise until it begins to operate independently of the Secretariat. . . .

2. The Enterprise shall conduct its initial deep seabed mining operations through joint ventures. . . .

Section 5. Transfer of Technology

1. In addition to the provisions of article 144 of the Convention, transfer of technology for the purposes of Part XI shall be governed by the following principles:

   (a) The Enterprise, and developing States wishing to obtain deep seabed mining technology, shall seek to obtain such technology on fair and reasonable commercial terms and conditions on the open market, or through joint-venture arrangements;

(b) If the Enterprise or developing States are unable to obtain deep seabed mining technology, the Authority may request all or any of the contractors and their respective sponsoring State or States to cooperate with it in facilitating the acquisition of deep seabed mining technology by the Enterprise or its joint venture, or by a developing State or States seeking to acquire such technology on fair and reasonable commercial terms and conditions, consistent with the effective protection of intellectual property rights. States Parties undertake to cooperate fully and effectively with the Authority for this purpose and to ensure that contractors sponsored by them also cooperate fully with the Authority;

(c) As a general rule, States Parties shall promote international technical and scientific cooperation with regard to activities in the Area either between the parties concerned or by developing training, technical assistance and scientific cooperation programmes in marine science and technology and the protection and preservation of the marine environment. . . .

Section 6. Production Policy

1. The production policy of the Authority shall be based on the following principles:

(a) Development of the resources of the Area shall take place in accordance with sound commercial principles;

(b) The provisions of the General Agreement on Tariffs and Trade, its relevant codes and successor or superseding agreements shall apply with respect to activities in the Area;

(c) In particular, there shall be no subsidization of activities in the Area except as may be permitted under the agreements referred to in subparagraph (b). Subsidization for the purpose of these principles shall be defined in terms of the agreements referred to in subparagraph (b);

(d) There shall be no discrimination between minerals derived from the Area and from other sources. There shall be no preferential access to markets for such minerals or for imports of commodities produced from such minerals . . .

Section 7. Economic Assistance

1. The policy of the Authority of assisting developing countries which suffer serious adverse effects on their export earnings or economies resulting from a reduction in the price of an affected mineral or in the volume of exports of that mineral, to the extent that such reduction is caused by activities in the Area, shall be based on the following principles:

(a) The Authority shall establish an economic assistance fund from a portion of the funds of the Authority which exceeds those necessary to cover the administrative expenses of the Authority. . . .

(b) Developing land-based producer States whose economies have been determined to be seriously affected by the production of minerals from the deep seabed shall be assisted from the economic assistance fund of the Authority;

(c) The Authority shall provide assistance from the fund to affected developing land-based producer States, where appropriate, in cooperation with existing global or regional development institutions which have the infrastructure and expertise to carry out such assistance programmes. . . .

To what extent are the provisions of the Implementation Agreement consistent with the original "common heritage of humankind" concept articulated in Part XI of UNCLOS?

Given the widespread ratification of both the Implementation Agreement and UNCLOS, and their subsequent coming into force, it could be argued that the legal regime for the deep seabed has become customary international law and, hence, presumptively binding on all states, including non-parties. However, some states, most notably the United States, have persistently objected to this internationalized regime concerning the resources of the deep seabed. Just how the views of such states may be reconciled with what appears to be an emergent customary international law regime remains to be seen as there remains an element of the theoretical to the issue. Consider the following commentary:

> Both the Area itself, which comprises about sixty per cent of the whole sea bed, and its resources (limited by article 133 to mineral resources) are the "common heritage of mankind." As such they are not susceptible of unilateral national appropriation. Rights in the Area and to its resources can be obtained only in accordance with the provisions of the Convention, which is to say, only with the authorization of the International Sea Bed Authority established by the 1982 Convention ([UNCLOS], art. 137).
>
> All activities in the Area, which in principle may be conducted both by the Authority itself through its mining arm, the "Enterprise," and by commercial operators are to be carried out for the benefit of mankind as a whole, taking into particular consideration the interests of developing states and peoples who have not attained self-governing status. . . .
>
> The "common heritage" will be exploited for the benefit of "mankind as a whole" and not simply of the industrialized States, in a number of ways. The collection and distribution among States—in particular, developing States and peoples—of payments made to the Authority by the commercial operators and perhaps later by the Enterprise is the most obvious. The Convention does not stipulate the manner in which the financial benefits are to be shared out; only that the sharing should be "equitable" ([UNCLOS], art. 140). Precise rules will be decided upon by the Authority. In fact some States will, in effect, have a preferential claim on the monies. These are the developing States that suffer adverse effects on their export earnings or economies as a result of falls in mineral prices caused by sea bed mining, for whose benefit the Convention requires the Authority to establish a system of economic assistance. But it seems clear that the financial benefits of sea bed exploitation are likely to be modest and not immediate. Commercial mining is still some way off. . . .[44]

Mineral deposits on the surface of the ocean floor are more difficult to collect because of the depths and pressures involved. To date, the activities of the Authority in the Area have been exploratory in character,[45] with seventeen contracts for exploration having been granted in areas of the Indian, Atlantic, and Pacific Oceans. As work moves into the exploitation phase, the Authority is developing financial arrangements between the licensees, while also developing a comprehensive "mining code" to regulate the prospecting, exploration, and exploitation of marine minerals in the deep seabed.

---

44 RR Churchill & AV Lowe, *The Law of the Sea*, 3d ed (Manchester: Manchester University Press, 1999) at 238–53.

45 Up-to-date information on exploratory activities can be obtained from the official website of the International Seabed Authority, online: www.isa.org.jm/en/scientific/exploration.

STATE JURISDICTION OVER AIR AND SPACE

We continue this part on the jurisdictional relationship between states and territory with a brief examination of air and space law. Both airspace and outer space present theoretical and practical difficulties for international law. Not least, neither is inhabited in any sort of permanent way. Indeed, until relatively recently, neither was a domain in which human beings were active. Technological developments in the twentieth century made both air and space flight possible, rapidly making state jurisdiction over the Earth's atmosphere and areas beyond an important legal issue.

A. AIRSPACE

Consider this overview of early approaches to air law:

> There were a variety of theories prior to the First World War with regard to the status of the airspace above states and territorial waters but the outbreak of that conflict, with its recognition of the security implications of use of the air, changed this and the approach that then prevailed, with little dissension, was based upon the extension of state sovereignty upwards into airspace. . . . [T]he international law rules protecting sovereignty of states apply to the airspace as they do to the land below.[1]

The International Court of Justice (ICJ) recognized the concept of state sovereignty over airspace in the *Nicaragua* decision.[2] There, it concluded that the United States had conducted numerous unauthorized overflights of Nicaragua. It viewed these transits as inconsistent with international law, observing that: "The principle of respect for territorial sovereignty is . . . directly infringed by the unauthorized overflight of a state's territory by aircraft belonging to or under the control of the government of another state."[3]

The critical concept, of course, is "unauthorized." In a world where international air navigation is commonplace, an international legal regime has developed to facilitate the

---

1 Malcolm N Shaw, *International Law*, 6th ed (Cambridge: Cambridge University Press, 2008) at 541–42. See also (Paris) Convention Relating to the Regulation of Aerial Navigation (with Additional Protocol), 13 October 1919, 11 LNTS 173, in force 29 March 1922, ratified by His Majesty on behalf of the British Empire in 1922 and later denounced by Canada in 1947 when Canada became a party to the Chicago Convention: *Johannesson v Municipality of West St Paul*, [1952] 1 SCR 292 at 307, 310, 316, and 322–23.

2 *Military and Paramilitary Activities in and against Nicaragua (Nicaragua v United States of America)*, Merits, [1986] ICJ Rep 14 [*Nicaragua*].

3 *Ibid* at para 251.

movement of civil aircraft through state airspace. Consider the key terms of the near-universally ratified Chicago Convention on International Civil Aviation.

(Chicago) Convention on International Civil Aviation, 7 December 1944, 15 UNTS 295, Can TS 1994 No 36, in force 4 April 1947

Article 1
Sovereignty
The contracting States recognize that every State has complete and exclusive sovereignty over the airspace above its territory.

Article 2
Territory
For the purposes of this Convention the territory of a State shall be deemed to be the land areas and territorial waters adjacent thereto under the sovereignty, suzerainty, protection or mandate of such State.

Article 3
Civil and state aircraft
(a) This Convention shall be applicable only to civil aircraft, and shall not be applicable to state aircraft.

(b) Aircraft used in military, customs and police services shall be deemed to be state aircraft.

(c) No state aircraft of a contracting State shall fly over the territory of another State or land thereon without authorization by special agreement or otherwise, and in accordance with the terms thereof.

(d) The contracting States undertake, when issuing regulations for their state aircraft, that they will have due regard for the safety of navigation of civil aircraft. . . .

Article 3bis[4]
(a) The contracting States recognize that every State must refrain from resorting to the use of weapons against civil aircraft in flight and that, in case of interception, the lives of persons on board and the safety of aircraft must not be endangered. This provision shall not be interpreted as modifying in any way the rights and obligations of States set forth in the Charter of the United Nations.

(b) The contracting States recognize that every State, in the exercise of its sovereignty, is entitled to require the landing at some designated airport of a civil aircraft flying above its territory without authority or if there are reasonable grounds to conclude that it is being used for any purpose inconsistent with the aims of this Convention; it may also give such aircraft any other instructions to put an end to such violations. For this purpose, the contracting States may resort to any appropriate means consistent with relevant rules of international law, including the relevant provisions of this Convention, specifically para-

---

4   This article was inserted into the Chicago Convention pursuant to an amendment that took effect on 1 October 1998: see Protocol relating to an amendment to the Convention on International Civil Aviation (Article 3*bis*), 10 May 1984, 2122 UNTS 337, Can TS 1998 No 55, in force 1 October 1998. Note that, at the time of writing, the United States is not a party to this protocol.

graph (a) of this Article. Each contracting State agrees to publish its regulations in force regarding the interception of civil aircraft.

(c) Every civil aircraft shall comply with an order given in conformity with paragraph (b) of this Article. To this end each contracting State shall establish all necessary provisions in its national laws or regulations to make such compliance mandatory for any civil aircraft registered in that State or operated by an operator who has his principal place of business or permanent residence in that State. Each contracting State shall make any violation of such applicable laws or regulations punishable by severe penalties and shall submit the case to its competent authorities in accordance with its laws or regulations.

(d) Each contracting State shall take appropriate measures to prohibit the deliberate use of any civil aircraft registered in that State or operated by an operator who has his principal place of business or permanent residence in that State for any purpose inconsistent with the aims of this Convention. This provision shall not affect paragraph (a) or derogate from paragraphs (b) and (c) of this Article. . . .

Article 5
Right of non-scheduled flight
Each contracting State agrees that all aircraft of the other contracting States, being aircraft not engaged in scheduled international air services shall have the right, subject to the observance of the terms of this Convention, to make flights into or in transit non-stop across its territory and to make stops for non-traffic purposes without the necessity of obtaining prior permission, and subject to the right of the State flown over to require landing. Each contracting State nevertheless reserves the right, for reasons of safety of flight, to require aircraft desiring to proceed over regions which are inaccessible or without adequate air navigation facilities to follow prescribed routes, or to obtain special permission for such flights.

Such aircraft, if engaged in the carriage of passengers, cargo, or mail for remuneration or hire on other than scheduled international air services, shall also, subject to the provisions of Article 7, have the privilege of taking on or discharging passengers, cargo, or mail, subject to the right of any State where such embarkation or discharge takes place to impose such regulations, conditions or limitations at it may consider desirable.

Article 6
Scheduled air services
No scheduled international air service may be operated over or into the territory of a contracting State, except with the special permission or other authorization of that State, and in accordance with the terms of such permission or authorization. . . .

Article 9
Prohibited areas
(a) Each contracting State may, for reasons of military necessity or public safety, restrict or prohibit uniformly the aircraft of other States from flying over certain areas of its territory, provided that no distinction in this respect is made between the aircraft of the State whose territory is involved, engaged in international scheduled airline services, and the aircraft of the other contracting States likewise engaged. Such prohibited areas shall be of reasonable extent and location so as not to interfere unnecessarily with air naviga-

tion. Descriptions of such prohibited areas in the territory of a contracting State, as well as any subsequent alterations therein, shall be communicated as soon as possible to the other contracting States and to the International Civil Aviation Organization.

(b) Each contracting State reserves also the right, in exceptional circumstances or during a period of emergency, or in the interest of public safety, and with immediate effect, temporarily to restrict or prohibit flying over the whole or any part of its territory, on condition that such restriction or prohibition shall be applicable without distinction of nationality to aircraft of all other States.

(c) Each contracting State, under such regulations as it may prescribe, may require any aircraft entering the areas contemplated in subparagraphs (a) or (b) above to effect a landing as soon as practicable thereafter at some designated airport within its territory. . . .

The specialized UN agency that oversees civilian aviation is the International Civil Aviation Organization (ICAO), based in Montreal.[5] Pursuant to Article 44 of the Chicago Convention:

The aims and objectives of the Organization are to develop the principles and techniques of international air navigation and to foster the planning and development of international air transport so as to:

(a) Insure the safe and orderly growth of international civil aviation throughout the world;

(b) Encourage the arts of aircraft design and operation for peaceful purposes;

(c) Encourage the development of airways, airports, and air navigation facilities for international civil aviation;

(d) Meet the needs of the peoples of the world for safe, regular, efficient and economical air transport;

(e) Prevent economic waste caused by unreasonable competition;

(f) Insure that the rights of contracting States are fully respected and that every contracting State has a fair opportunity to operate international airlines;

(g) Avoid discrimination between contracting States;

(h) Promote safety of flight in international air navigation;

(i) Promote generally the development of all aspects of international civil aeronautics.

LAW IN CONTEXT

Use of Force against Civilian Airliners

States closely guard their airspace. Since World War II, there have been several instances in which military jets have downed civilian airliners, including the following:[6]

---

5   See further, Michael Milde, *International Air Law and ICAO*, 2d ed (The Hague: Eleven International Publishers, 2012).

6   See an earlier edition of Malcolm N Shaw, *International Law*, 5th ed (Cambridge: Cambridge University Press, 2003) at 473–78.

- 1955: An airliner operated by El Al Israel Airlines (El Al Flight 402) was shot down by Bulgarian fighters after it intruded into Bulgarian airspace. A case brought by Israel was dismissed by the ICJ for want of jurisdiction.[7]

- 1973: A Libyan Arab Airlines airliner (Flight 114) intruding over the Israeli-occupied Sinai Peninsula was downed by Israeli jets, prompting condemnation of Israel's actions and, ultimately, an apology and payment of compensation by Israel.

- 1983: The Soviet Union shot down a Korean Airlines aircraft (KAL Flight 007) in sensitive Soviet airspace, killing all 269 persons on board. The Soviets purportedly believed that the aircraft was spying. Their actions were condemned by the ICAO and prompted the adoption of Article 3bis of the Chicago Convention, barring the use of "weapons" against civilian aircraft. Note that Article 3bis does not preclude the use of force, only the use of weapons. This language thus permits interception of civilian aircraft, so long as weapons are not then employed against the aircraft itself. Consider, however, the last sentence of paragraph (a) of Article 3bis. Is this prohibition absolute? Is an obligation to "refrain from" using weapons the same as an obligation not to use weapons? Given the treaty basis of this prohibition, would it preclude a state from using weapons against civilian aircraft possessing that state's own nationality?

- 1988: The American warship USS Vincennes, on operations in the Persian Gulf, downed Iran Air Flight 655 with a missile following misidentification of the aircraft. All 290 persons on board were killed. Although not a case of defending sovereign airspace, the United States defended its actions on the basis of a right of self-defence, coupled with misidentification of the aircraft as being military in nature. Iran brought a case against the United States in the ICJ that was later discontinued.[8]

- 1996: The Cuban Air Force shot down two of three small civilian aircraft over international waters, killing four Cuban-Americans on a mission to assist those wanting to leave Cuba. The Cuban actions prompted a stern rebuke from the ICAO that was later endorsed by the UN Security Council.[9]

- 2001: Directly following the September 11, 2001 attacks on the World Trade Center and the Pentagon, the United States ordered all civilian aircraft in its airspace to land and forbade entry into its airspace by incoming international air traffic. In the years following these events, several states have reportedly adopted policies that would allow state officials, as a last resort, to shoot down "rogue" civilian aircraft—that is, civilian aircraft under the control of individuals intending to use them as a weapon against targets on the surface.[10]

---

7 *Case concerning the Aerial Incident of July 27, 1955 (Israel v Bulgaria)*, Preliminary Objections, [1959] ICJ Rep 127.

8 *Aerial Incident of 3 July 1988 (Islamic Republic of Iran v United States of America)*, Order, [1996] ICJ Rep 9.

9 SC Resolution 1067 (1996), adopted 26 July 1996, UN Doc S/RES/1067 (1996). The relatives of the victims also brought a case against Cuba to the relevant inter-American human rights body: see *Armando Alejandre Jr v Cuba*, Report No 86/99, Case 11.589, *Annual Report of the Inter-American Commission on Human Rights 1999*, OAS Doc OEA/Ser.L/V/11.106 Doc 6 rev at III.C.5 (13 April 1990).

10 See Robin F Holman, "The Rogue Civil Airliner and International Human Rights Law: An Argument for a Proportionality of Effects Analysis within the Right to Life" (2010) 48 Can YB Int'l Law 39 at 40.

In the same way as the column of airspace over a state's sovereign territory is included in that sovereign territory, the airspace over the oceans beyond states' territorial seas is governed by essentially the same rules as the high seas. Note, for instance, the references to freedom of "overflight" in the provisions of the 1982 United Nations Convention on the Law of the Sea (UNCLOS), reviewed in Chapter 5.

In addition to guidelines adopted within the ICAO, a network of bilateral treaties on air services and air transport, as well as multilateral treaties on such matters as liability for loss[11] and the commission of crimes on and against aircraft,[12] constitute further aspects of international air law.

B. OUTER SPACE

International law is not limited in its application to the Earth. With the advent of space exploration in the mid-twentieth century, the international community turned its attention to whether and how "outer space" and "celestial bodies" were to be integrated into the state-based international legal system. The main issues were control over outer space itself, as well as entitlement to any resources that might be found there.

With respect to control over outer space itself, the doctrine employed for airspace (i.e., that states enjoy sovereignty in the airspace over their territories to an undefined height) obviously made little sense in an era in which satellites could be expected to orbit the Earth in abundant quantities. The issue, however, was how to define the upward extent of states' sovereign airspace and, hence, the lower extent of any different regime that would apply in outer space. In fact, the exact height where sovereign airspace ends and outer space begins remains uncertain in international law. Some states take the view that outer space begins at the point above which aircraft cannot fly.[13] An alternative view is that it begins at the altitude of the lowest viable satellite orbit.[14] Wherever the boundary lies, international law has imposed a *res communis* regime on outer space: no portion of outer space, including any celestial bodies, may be appropriated by any state as part of its sovereign territory.

The second issue—entitlement to the resources of outer space—has proven more intractable. In an early resolution, the UN General Assembly declared that: "The exploration and use of outer space shall be carried on for the benefit and in the interests of all mankind."[15] This statement, while somewhat ambiguous, nevertheless carries echoes of

11 See (Montreal) Convention for the Unification of Certain Rules for International Carriage by Air, 28 May 1999, 2242 UNTS 350, in force 4 November 2003, as amended 30 June 2009.

12 See (Tokyo) Convention on Offences and Certain Other Acts Committed on Board Aircraft, 14 September 1963, 704 UNTS 219, Can TS 1970 No 5, in force 4 December 1969; (Hague) Convention for the Suppression of Unlawful Seizure of Aircraft, 16 December 1970, 860 UNTS 105, Can TS 1972 No 23, in force 14 October 1971; (Montreal) Convention for the Suppression of Unlawful Acts against the Safety of Civil Aviation, 23 September 1971, 974 UNTS 177, Can TS 1973 No 6, in force 26 January 1973.

13 Shaw, above note 1 at 543, n 308 (discussing the British position).

14 James Crawford, *Brownlie's Principles of Public International Law*, 8th ed (Oxford: Oxford University Press, 2012) at 349.

15 *Declaration of Legal Principles Governing the Activities of States in the Exploration and Use of Outer Space*, GA Res 1962 (XVIII), UN Doc A/RES/1962 (XVIII), reprinted in UN GAOR, 18th Sess, Supp No 15 at 15–16, UN Doc A/5515 (1963), preamble.

the "common heritage of humankind" concept developed in respect of the resources of the deep seabed in UNCLOS. On the other hand, it could be argued that unilateral state exploitation of resources found in outer space is, at least in some indirect ways, of "benefit [to] and in the interests of all mankind."

Five multilateral treaties have been developed to address various issues of space law. The first—the so-called Outer Space Treaty[16]—is the most important, as it has been ratified by 101 states as of 2013, including all major space-faring states. By contrast, the so-called Moon Treaty[17] has far fewer parties: only fifteen as of 2013, none of which has a significant space program. Consider how each of these treaties approaches the issues identified above:

Treaty on Principles Governing the Activities of States in the Exploration and Use of Outer Space, Including the Moon and Other Celestial Bodies, 27 January 1967, 610 UNTS 205, Can TS 1976 No. 19, in force 10 October 1967

Article I

The exploration and use of outer space, including the moon and other celestial bodies, shall be carried out for the benefit and in the interests of all countries, irrespective of their degree of economic or scientific development, and shall be the province of all mankind.

Outer space, including the moon and other celestial bodies, shall be free for exploration and use by all States without discrimination of any kind, on a basis of equality and in accordance with international law, and there shall be free access to all areas of celestial bodies.

There shall be freedom of scientific investigation in outer space, including the moon and other celestial bodies, and States shall facilitate and encourage international cooperation in such investigation.

Article II

Outer space, including the moon and other celestial bodies, is not subject to national appropriation by claim of sovereignty, by means of use or occupation, or by any other means.

Article III

States Parties to the Treaty shall carry on activities in the exploration and use of outer space, including the moon and other celestial bodies, in accordance with international law, including the Charter of the United Nations, in the interest of maintaining international peace and security and promoting international co-operation and understanding.

Article IV

States Parties to the Treaty undertake not to place in orbit around the earth any objects carrying nuclear weapons or any other kinds of weapons of mass destruction, instal such weapons on celestial bodies, or station such weapons in outer space in any other manner.

---

16 Treaty on Principles Governing the Activities of States in the Exploration and Use of Outer Space, including the Moon and Other Celestial Bodies, 27 January 1967, 610 UNTS 205, Can TS 1967 No 19, in force 10 October 1967 [Outer Space Treaty].

17 Agreement Governing the Activities of States on the Moon and other Celestial Bodies, 5 December 1979, 1363 UNTS 3, in force 11 July 1984 [Moon Treaty]. Canada is not a party to this treaty.

The moon and other celestial bodies shall be used by all States Parties to the Treaty exclusively for peaceful purposes. The establishment of military bases, installations and fortifications, the testing of any type of weapons and the conduct of military manoeuvres on celestial bodies shall be forbidden. The use of military personnel for scientific research or for any other peaceful purposes shall not be prohibited. The use of any equipment or facility necessary for peaceful exploration of the moon and other celestial bodies shall also not be prohibited. . . .

Article VIII

A State Party to the Treaty on whose registry an object launched into outer space is carried shall retain jurisdiction and control over such object, and over any personnel thereof, while in outer space or on a celestial body. Ownership of objects launched into outer space, including objects landed or constructed on a celestial body, and of their component parts, is not affected by their presence in outer space or on a celestial body or by their return to the Earth. Such objects or component parts found beyond the limits of the State Party to the Treaty on whose registry they are carried shall be returned to that State Party, which shall, upon request, furnish identifying data prior to their return.

Agreement Governing the Activities of States on the Moon and other Celestial Bodies, 5 December 1979, 1363 UNTS 3, in force 11 July 1984

Article 1

1. The provisions of this Agreement relating to the moon shall also apply to other celestial bodies within the solar system, other than the earth, except in so far as specific legal norms enter into force with respect to any of these celestial bodies. . . .

Article 4

1. The exploration and use of the moon shall be the province of all mankind and shall be carried out for the benefit and in the interests of all countries, irrespective of their degree of economic or scientific development. Due regard shall be paid to the interests of present and future generations as well as to the need to promote higher standards of living and conditions of economic and social progress and development in accordance with the Charter of the United Nations. . . .

Article 6

1. There shall be freedom of scientific investigation on the moon by all States Parties without discrimination of any kind, on the basis of equality and in accordance with international law. . . .

Article 11

1. The moon and its natural resources are the common heritage of mankind, which finds its expression in the provisions of this Agreement and in particular in paragraph 5 of this article.

2. The moon is not subject to national appropriation by any claim of sovereignty, by means of use or occupation, or by any other means.

3. Neither the surface nor the subsurface of the moon, nor any part thereof or natural resources in place, shall become property of any State, international intergovernmental

or non-governmental organization, national organization or non-governmental entity or of any natural person. The placement of personnel, space vehicles, equipment, facilities, stations and installations on or below the surface of the moon, including structures connected with its surface or subsurface, shall not create a right of ownership over the surface or the subsurface of the moon or any areas thereof. The foregoing provisions are without prejudice to the international régime referred to in paragraph 5 of this article.

4. States Parties have the right to exploration and use of the moon without discrimination of any kind, on a basis of equality and in accordance with international law and the terms of this Agreement.

5. States Parties to this Agreement hereby undertake to establish an international régime, including appropriate procedures, to govern the exploitation of the natural resources of the moon as such exploitation is about to become feasible. . . .

7. The main purposes of the international régime to be established shall include:
   (a) The orderly and safe development of the natural resources of the moon;
   (b) The rational management of those resources;
   (c) The expansion of opportunities in the use of those resources;
   (d) An equitable sharing by all States Parties in the benefits derived from those resources, whereby the interests and needs of the developing countries, as well as the efforts of those countries which have contributed either directly or indirectly to the exploration of the moon, shall be given special consideration.

The common name given to the second of the above treaties — the "Moon Treaty" — is a misnomer given the provisions of Article 1. In any case, the paucity of state ratifications of the Moon Treaty suggests that at least some of its provisions are rejected by many states, including those most likely to go to the moon or other bodies in our solar system. Moreover, the "international regime" foreseen in Article 11(5) remains to be established.

How would you interpret Article 1 of the Outer Space Treaty, in particular its provisions that the "use of outer space, including the moon and other celestial bodies, shall be carried out for the benefit and in the interests of all countries" and that "[o]uter space, including the moon and other celestial bodies, shall be free for exploration and use by all States"? Are these provisions properly understood as imposing a common heritage of humankind regime on the exploitation of resources of the moon and other celestial bodies, as suggested by Article 11 of the Moon Treaty? Can they be interpreted differently? Does the failure of the Moon Treaty to attract a significant number of parties have any significance for the correct interpretation of the Outer Space Treaty? Consider the importance of this issue in light of the following principle set out in the 2010 National Space Policy of the United States:

> A robust and competitive commercial space sector is vital to continued progress in space. The United States is committed to encouraging and facilitating the growth of a U.S. commercial space sector that supports U.S. needs, is globally competitive, and advances U.S. leadership in the generation of new markets and innovation-driven entrepreneurship.[18]

---

18 National Space Policy of the United States of America, 28 June 2010 at 3, online: www.whitehouse.gov/sites/default/files/national_space_policy_6-28-10.pdf.

In any event, economically viable exploitation of the resources of the moon and the other "celestial bodies" of our solar system remains a hypothetical possibility at the time of writing.

The three remaining multilateral space law treaties of significance concern the rescue and return of astronauts, the registration and return of objects launched into space, and liability for damage caused by space objects.[19] In 1978, a Soviet nuclear-powered satellite known as Cosmos-954 crashed in the Northwest Territories, scattering much radioactive debris. The USSR (as it was then called) eventually paid the sum of $3 million to Canada in full and final settlement of Canada's claim arising from the associated cleanup costs.[20]

The United Nations has been active in fostering the development by states of an international legal regime for the peaceful uses of outer space. Consider the following action plan, adopted by resolution at the Third United Nations Conference on the Exploration and Peaceful Uses of Outer Space held in Vienna in 1999, which gives some idea of the range of issues currently being pursued by states with respect to outer space:

The Space Millennium: Vienna Declaration on Space and Human Development, in *Report of the Third United Nations Conference on the Exploration and Peaceful Uses of Outer Space,* **UN Doc A/CONF.184/6 at 6–19 (18 October 1999)**

The States participating in the Third United Nations Conference on the Exploration and Peaceful Uses of Outer Space (UNISPACE III), held in Vienna from 19 to 30 July 1999. . . .

1. Declare the following as the nucleus of a strategy to address global challenges in the future:

(a) Protecting the Earth's environment and managing its resources: action should be taken:

   (i) To develop a comprehensive, worldwide, environmental monitoring strategy for long-term global observations by building on existing space and ground capabilities, through the coordination of the activities of various entities and organizations involved in such efforts;

   (ii) To improve the management of the Earth's natural resources by increasing and facilitating the research and operational use of remote sensing data, enhancing the coordination of remote sensing systems and increasing access to, and the affordability of, imagery;

   (iii) To develop and implement the Integrated Global Observing Strategy so as to enable access to and the use of space-based and other Earth observation data;

   (iv) To enhance weather and climate forecasting by expanding international cooperation in the field of meteorological satellite applications;

---

19 Agreement on the Rescue of Astronauts, the Return of Astronauts and the Return of Objects Launched into Outer Space, 22 April 1968, 672 UNTS 120, Can TS 1975 No 6, in force 3 December 1968; Convention on the International Liability for Damage Caused by Space Objects, 29 March 1972, 961 UNTS 188, Can TS 1975 No 7, in force 1 September 1972; Convention on Registration of Objects Launched into Outer Space, 12 November 974, 1023 UNTS 15, Can TS 1976 No 36, in force 15 September 1976.

20 Protocol between the Government of Canada and the Government of the Union of Soviet Socialist Republics, 2 April 1981, Can TS 1981 No 8, in force 2 April 1981.

(v) To ensure, to the extent possible, that all space activities, in particular those which may have harmful effects on the local and global environment, are carried out in a manner that limits such effects and to take appropriate measures to achieve that objective;

(b) Using space applications for human security, development and welfare: action should be taken:

(i) To improve public health services by expanding and coordinating space-based services for telemedicine and for controlling infectious diseases;

(ii) To implement an integrated, global system, especially through international cooperation, to manage natural disaster mitigation, relief and prevention efforts, especially of an international nature, through Earth observation, communications and other space-based services, making maximum use of existing capabilities and filling gaps in worldwide satellite coverage;

(iii) To promote literacy and enhance rural education by improving and coordinating educational programmes and satellite-related infrastructure;

(iv) To improve knowledge-sharing by giving more importance to the promotion of universal access to space-based communication services and by devising efficient policies, infrastructure, standards and applications development projects;

(v) To improve the efficiency and security of transport, search and rescue, geodesy and other activities by promoting the enhancement of, universal access to and compatibility of space-based navigation and positioning systems;

(vi) To assist States, especially developing countries, in applying the results of space research with a view to promoting the sustainable development of all peoples;

(c) Advancing scientific knowledge of space and protecting the space environment: action should be taken:

(i) To improve the scientific knowledge of near and outer space by promoting cooperative activities in such areas as astronomy, space biology and medicine, space physics, the study of near-Earth objects and planetary exploration;

(ii) To improve the protection of the near-Earth space and outer space environments through further research in and implementation of mitigation measures for space debris;

(iii) To improve the international coordination of activities related to near-Earth objects, harmonizing the worldwide efforts directed at identification, follow-up observation and orbit prediction, while at the same time giving consideration to developing a common strategy that would include future activities related to near-Earth objects;

(iv) To protect the near and outer space environments through further research on designs, safety measures and procedures associated with the use of nuclear power sources in outer space;

(v) To ensure that all users of space consider the possible consequences of their activities, whether ongoing or planned, before further irreversible actions are taken affecting future utilization of near-Earth space or outer space, especially in areas such as astronomy, Earth observation and remote sensing, as well as global positioning and navigation systems, where unwanted emissions have become an issue of concern as they interfere with bands in the electromagnetic spectrum already used for those applications;

(d) Enhancing education and training opportunities and ensuring public awareness of the importance of space activities. . . .

(e) Strengthening and repositioning of space activities in the United Nations system: action should be taken:

   (i)   To reaffirm the role of the Committee on the Peaceful Uses of Outer Space, its two subcommittees and its secretariat in leading global efforts for the exploration and peaceful use of outer space relating to significant global issues;

   (ii) To assist in the improvement of the capacity-building process in developing countries and countries with economies in transition by emphasizing the development and transfer of knowledge and skills, by ensuring sustainable funding mechanisms for the regional centres for space science and technology education, affiliated to the United Nations, by enhancing support for the United Nations Programme on Space Applications through the provision of adequate resources, and by participating in the implementation of the new strategy of the Programme arising from UNISPACE III; . . .

   (iv) To promote the efforts of the Committee on the Peaceful Uses of Outer Space in the development of space law by inviting States to ratify or accede to, and inviting intergovernmental organizations to declare acceptance of, the outer space treaties developed by the Committee and by considering the further development of space law to meet the needs of the international community, taking into particular account the needs of developing countries and countries with economies in transition; . . .

(f) Promoting international cooperation: action should be taken to follow up the decision by the States participating in UNISPACE III:

   . . .

   (ii) To establish a special voluntary United Nations fund for the purpose of implementing the recommendations of UNISPACE III . . . ;

   (iii) To adopt measures aimed at identifying new and innovative sources of financing at the international level, including in the private sector, in order to support the implementation of the recommendations of UNISPACE III in developing countries . . . ;

. . .

4. Recommend to the General Assembly that it review and evaluate, within existing resources, the implementation of the recommendations of UNISPACE III after a period of five years. . . .

A five-year review of the implementation of these recommendations was conducted by the UN Committee on the Peaceful Uses of Outer Space (COPUOS) in 2004.[21]

As suggested in paragraph 1(c)(ii) of the above action plan, one issue of concern to states relates to the ever-increasing accumulation of space debris orbiting the Earth, such as defunct satellites, hardware from space missions, and fragments caused by explosions. Experts estimate that there are over 300,000 objects of orbital debris with a diameter

---

21 *Review of the Implementation of the Recommendations of the Third United Nations Conference on the Exploration and Peaceful Uses of Outer Space: Note by the Secretary-General*, UN Doc A/59/174 (23 July 2004).

larger than one centimetre, as well as several million that are smaller in size.[22] Space debris poses "a significant, constant, and indiscriminate threat to all spacecraft,"[23] including functioning satellites, which are crucial for a range of communications, navigational, financial, and other key activities. According to the Canadian research partnership known as Space Security Index, "[t]ravelling at speeds of up to 7.8 kilometers (km) per second, even small pieces of space debris can destroy or severely disable a satellite upon impact."[24] The annual growth rate of new debris decreased in the 1990s due to efforts by states to mitigate debris, but that rate has increased again in the recent years with the 2007 Anti-Satellite Weapon (ASAT) test conducted by China (intentionally destroying one of its own satellites), the 2008 destruction by the United States of a failed satellite, and the 2009 accidental collision of a defunct Russian and an operational US satellite.[25]

One response to the threat posed by space debris is to increase space surveillance capabilities, an objective of the United States' Space Surveillance Network (to which Canada contributes since the launch of its Sapphire satellite in 2013.)[26] On the regulatory front, states adopted Space Debris Mitigation Guidelines in 2008. These guidelines aim to limit the creation of space debris in the near term, as well as over the longer term. The following is an excerpt from these Guidelines:

Space Debris Mitigation Guidelines in *Report of the Committee on the Peaceful Uses of Outer Space*, UN GAOR 62nd Sess, Supp No 20, Annex at 48–50, UN Doc A/62/20 (2007)

Guideline 1: Limit debris released during normal operations
Space systems should be designed not to release debris during normal operations. If this is not feasible, the effect of any release of debris on the outer space environment should be minimized . . . .

Guideline 2: Minimize the potential for break-ups during operational phases
Spacecraft and launch vehicle orbital stages should be designed to avoid failure modes which may lead to accidental break-ups. In cases where a condition leading to such a failure is detected, disposal and passivation measures should be planned and executed to avoid break-ups. . . .

Guideline 3: Limit the probability of accidental collision in orbit
In developing the design and mission profile of spacecraft and launch vehicle stages, the probability of accidental collision with known objects during the system's launch phase and orbital lifetime should be estimated and limited. If available orbital data indicate a

22 Cesar Jaramillo, ed, *Space Security Index 2012* (Waterloo, ON: Project Ploughshares, 2012) at 11, online: www.spacesecurity.org/SpaceSecurityReport2012.pdf.
23 *Ibid.*
24 *Ibid.*
25 *Ibid.* See also United Nations, "Space Debris: Orbiting Debris Threatens Sustainable Use of Outer Space" (2008), online: www.un.org/en/events/tenstories/08/spacedebris.shtml; Joseph S Imburgia, "Space Debris and Its Threat to National Security: A Proposal for a Binding International Agreement to Clean Up the Junk" (2011) 44 Vanderbilt J Int'l L 589.
26 See National Defence Canada, News Release, "The Canadian Sapphire Satellite is Successfully Launched" (25 February 2013), online: http://nouvelles.gc.ca/web/article-eng.do?nid=722619.

potential collision, adjustment of the launch time or an on-orbit avoidance manoeuvre should be considered . . . .

Guideline 4: Avoid intentional destruction and other harmful activities
Recognizing than an increased risk of collision could pose a threat to space operations, the intentional destruction of any on-orbit spacecraft and launch vehicle orbital stages or other harmful activities that generate long-lived debris should be avoided.

When intentional break-ups are necessary, they should be conducted at sufficiently low altitudes to limit the orbital lifetime of resulting fragments . . . .

Guideline 6: Limit the long-term presence of spacecraft and launch vehicle orbital stages in the low-Earth orbit (LEO) region after the end of their mission
Spacecraft and launch vehicle orbital stages that have terminated their operational phases in orbits that pass through the LEO region should be removed from orbit in a controlled fashion. If this is not possible, they should be disposed of in orbits that avoid their long-term presence in the LEO region. . . .

Guideline 7: Limit the long-term interference of spacecraft and launch vehicle orbital stages with the geosynchronous Earth orbit (GEO) region after the end of their mission
Spacecraft and launch vehicle orbital stages that have terminated their operational phases in orbits that pass through the GEO region should be left in orbits that avoid their long-term interference with the GEO region. . . .

These Space Debris Mitigation Guidelines are voluntary, and states and international organizations active in space—including the European Union, China, Japan, Russia, and the United States—have also developed domestic debris mitigation standards.[27] What status do the Space Debris Mitigation Guidelines have under international law? Does the fact that these Guidelines "are not universally or regularly followed" affect your analysis?[28]

27 *Space Security Index 2012*, above note 22 at 11.
28 *Ibid.*

CHAPTER 7

STATE JURISDICTION OVER PERSONS, CONDUCT, AND EVENTS

A. INTRODUCTION

State jurisdiction over territory should not be confused with state jurisdiction over persons, conduct, and events within (or outside) that territory. While the effects of these different types of jurisdiction will sometimes coincide, there is not always a complete correspondence between them.

By "state jurisdiction over persons, conduct, and events," we mean a state's power to regulate or control persons, conduct, and events, or to subject them to the power of the state. Such state jurisdiction is commonly expressed in the form of domestic public law provisions (for example, criminal, administrative, or constitutional law) that purport to apply to persons and their activities. In other instances, state jurisdiction may come in the form of domestic private law statutes or common law principles governing civil liability between persons or civil relationships arising out of property or transactions. In both cases, such state jurisdiction is often exercised with respect to persons, conduct, and events *within* the state's sovereign territory. However, this is not always the case, such that international law provides rules on when it is acceptable for any given state to impose this liability or control over persons or dealings *abroad*. As the Supreme Court of Canada has explained:

> Where a dispute is wholly contained within the territory of one state, jurisdiction is not an issue. However, disputes and events commonly have implications for more than one state, and competing claims for jurisdiction can arise on grounds other than territoriality, which are, of course, extraterritorial in nature.[1]

In order to understand the international legal boundaries for the exercise of state jurisdiction over persons, conduct, and events, it is important to make a definitional distinction. State jurisdiction may be subdivided into "enforcement jurisdiction"—the capacity to *enforce* rules or take coercive action—and "prescriptive jurisdiction"—the capacity to *make* rules regulating persons or their conduct. As we shall see, the permissible extent of a state's *enforcement* jurisdiction is very narrowly circumscribed in international law, and is closely tied to its sovereign territory. On the other hand, states have substantial, though not unlimited, latitude to *prescribe* conduct beyond their borders. Note that some commentators identify "adjudicative or judicial jurisdiction" as a third division, with some

---

1   *R v Hape*, 2007 SCC 26, [2007] 2 SCR 292 at para 60 [*Hape*].

judicial support;[2] but other, authoritative voices subsume adjudicative jurisdiction within the two categories of prescriptive and enforcement jurisdiction.[3] The discussion below follows the latter, two-category approach.

B. ENFORCEMENT JURISDICTION

Consider the implications of the following case for the extent of a state's enforcement jurisdiction:

> ### The Case of the SS "Lotus" (France v Turkey) (1927), PCIJ (Ser A) No 10 at 18–19 [Lotus Case]
>
> [This case arose from a collision on the high seas between two ships, one French, the other Turkish. The Turkish vessel sank, killing eight passengers and crew members. The French steamer was also badly damaged but managed to put into the nearby port of Constantinople (now Istanbul), where Turkish authorities arrested and charged one of its officers with involuntary manslaughter. The French officer was ultimately tried and convicted of various offences relating to the collision under Turkish law in a Turkish court. France brought a claim against Turkey claiming that it had exceeded its jurisdiction in so acting. As part of its argument, France contended that there was a rule of customary international law that forbade Turkey from prosecuting a foreign national for criminal acts occurring outside Turkish territory.]
>
> . . . [I]t is not a question of stating principles which would permit Turkey to take criminal proceedings, but of formulating the principles, if any, which might have been violated by such proceedings.
>
> This way of stating the question is also dictated by the very nature and existing conditions of international law.
>
> International law governs relations between independent States. The rules of law binding upon States therefore emanate from their own free will as expressed in conventions or by usages generally accepted as expressing principles of law and established in order to regulate the relations between these co-existing independent communities or with a view to the achievement of common aims. Restrictions upon the independence of States cannot therefore be presumed.
>
> Now the first and foremost restriction imposed by international law upon a State is that—failing the existence of a permissive rule to the contrary—it may not exercise its power in any form in the territory of another State. In this sense jurisdiction is certainly

---

2   See Steve Coughlan et al, "Global Reach, Local Grasp: Constructing Extraterritorial Jurisdiction in the Age of Globalization" (2007) 6 CJLT 29 at 32, cited with support in *Hape*, above note 1 at paras 58 and 65.

3   See, for example, Vaughan Lowe & Christopher Staker, "Jurisdiction" in Malcolm D Evans, ed, *International Law*, 3rd ed (Oxford: Oxford University Press, 2010) at 313 ("It is doubtful whether it is necessary to separate out this type of jurisdiction. . . . [A]ll of this can be analyzed in terms of prescriptive and enforcement jurisdiction. It seems unnecessary to introduce a separate category of 'jurisdiction to adjudicate'. . . .") See also James Crawford, *Brownlie's Principles of Public International Law* (Oxford: Oxford University Press, 2012) at 456 [*Brownlie's Principles*].

territorial; it cannot be exercised by a State outside its territory except by virtue of a permissive rule derived from international custom or from a convention. . . .

[The Court then went on to consider the rules of international law related to prescriptive jurisdiction. That portion of the judgment is reproduced below in Section C: Prescriptive Jurisdiction.]

The *Lotus Case* reflects the generally accepted position in international law that a state may not, as a general rule, *enforce* its laws or take other coercive action outside of its sovereign territory.[4] We say "as a general rule" because, as suggested in the *Lotus Case*, there may be specific exceptions that permit the extraterritorial exercise of such jurisdiction. Indeed, we have already seen in Chapter 5 some such exceptions in our examination of the enforcement powers of states on the high seas or in other maritime zones outside their territorial sea. Similar "permissive rules" of enforcement jurisdiction apply aboard aircraft or spacecraft when they are not within any state's sovereign territory. In contrast, the general prohibition on extraterritorial enforcement jurisdiction is at its most absolute when it comes to the exercise of such jurisdiction within another state's territory: "The governing principle of enforcement jurisdiction is that a state cannot take measures on the territory of another state by way of enforcement of its laws without the consent of the latter."[5]

What happens if a state fails to honour this rule? What if one state's agents apprehend a fugitive within another state's borders and then remove that person to face judicial proceedings before its own courts, without the other state's consent? Such an action would constitute an undoubted violation of the restrictions placed by international law on the extent of a state's enforcement jurisdiction. Does this mean, however, that international law requires the domestic courts of the apprehending state to decline to hear the case? Consider the following cases from several states:

Attorney-General of the Government of Israel v Eichmann (1961), 36 ILR 5 (Dist Ct Jerusalem)

[Adolf Eichmann was a German Nazi and the head of the Jewish Office of the German Gestapo. As such, he was a key organizer of the Holocaust. Eichmann was apprehended in Argentina in 1960 by persons acting on behalf of the Israeli government, and removed to Israel without the consent of the Argentine government. In Israel, he was put on trial before a domestic Israeli court for his role in the Holocaust.]

Adolf Eichmann has been arraigned before this Court on charges of unsurpassed gravity—crimes against the Jewish people, crimes against humanity, and war crimes. The period of the crimes ascribed to him, and their historical background, is that of the Hitler régime in Germany and in Europe. . . .

---

4 This position, as expressed in the final paragraph of the excerpt from the *Lotus Case* reproduced above, was endorsed by the Supreme Court of Canada in *Hape*, above note 1 at para 65.

5 *Brownlie's Principles*, above note 3 at 479. For example, states enforce their own laws on military bases they establish on the territory of foreign (host) states, with the consent of those host states; the terms of such consent are usually detailed in a Status of Forces Agreement (SOFA) between the sending and host states.

The . . . contention of learned defence counsel was that the trial of the accused in Israel following upon his kidnapping in a foreign land, is in conflict with international law and takes away the jurisdiction of this Court. Counsel argued that the accused, who had resided in Argentina under an assumed name, was kidnapped on May 11, 1960, by agents of the State of Israel and forcibly brought to Israel. . . . He summed up his submission by contending that the Court ought not to lend its support to an illegal act of the State, and that in these circumstances the State of Israel has no jurisdiction to try the accused. . . .

[However, i]t is an established rule of law that a person being tried for an offence against the laws of a State may not oppose his trial by reason of the illegality of his arrest or of the means whereby he was brought within the jurisdiction of that State. The courts in England, the United States and Israel have constantly held that the circumstances of the arrest and the mode of bringing of the accused into the territory of the State have no relevance to his trial, and they have consistently refused in all instances to enter upon an examination of these circumstances.

[The Court then reviewed British caselaw affirming the foregoing statement of the law.]

Before turning . . . to American precedents, we would dwell briefly on the import of the judgments we have reviewed above from the point of view of international law. The question which poses itself from this point of view is—whether the principle . . . that the accused may not challenge his trial by reason of the illegality of his arrest or of the means whereby he was brought to the jurisdiction, is limited to the illegality of those means in the sense of the municipal law of the country in question, or whether the principle is general and also applies to the use of means which are a violation of international law, namely, a violation of the sovereignty of a foreign State. The recently published article by O'Higgins . . . is devoted to an analysis of these [English] judgments . . . from this point of view. The learned author's conclusion is as follows . . .

> A British court will probably exercise jurisdiction over a criminal brought before it as the result of a violation of international law. There is, however, no precedent which binds any British court to adopt this view.

This careful appraisal is based on the learned author's view that most English precedents do not in practice deal with cases of violation of international law. . . .

American case law on this question is more unequivocal. . . . American precedents expressly establish that it makes no difference whether or not the measures whereby the accused was brought into the jurisdiction were unlawful in point of municipal law or of international law and they are all unanimous that the Court will not enter into an examination of this question, which is not relevant to the trial of the accused. The *ratio* of this rule is that the right to plead violation of the sovereignty of a State is the exclusive right of that State. Only a sovereign State may raise the plea or waive it, and the accused has no right to take over the rights of that State. The same principle has also found expression in English judgments. . . .

This principle was well explained by Travers . . . The learned author, who supports the doctrine as crystallized in the United States, says

. . . [Editor's translation] There are two reasons [for this doctrine].

First, the arrested individual has no standing to speak on behalf of the foreign state; he or she is not its representative.

Second, the foreign state may, in the exercise of its sovereignty, make any concession it considers appropriate and is free to waive any unlawful acts. Its silence amounts to such waiver, at least presumptively.

Considerable importance attaches to this statement in the present case, in view of the settlement of the dispute between Argentina and Israel. Whatever we may think of the general legal problem, now that the Governments of Argentina and Israel have issued their joint communiqué of August 3, 1960, to the effect that both Governments have decided to regard as closed the "incident" whereby the sovereignty of Argentina was infringed, there certainly remains to the accused in this case no right to base himself on the "infringed sovereignty" of the State of Argentina. The indictment in this case was filed after Argentina had exonerated Israel of violation of her sovereignty and there was no longer any breach of international law. In these circumstances the accused cannot presume to speak, as it were, on behalf of Argentina and claim rights which that sovereign State had waived. . . .

By the joint decision of the Governments of Argentina and Israel of August 3, 1960, "to regard as closed the incident that arose out of the action taken by the citizens of Israel, which infringed the fundamental rights of the State of Argentina," the country whose sovereignty was violated has waived its claims, including the claim for the return of the accused, and any violation of international law which might have been involved in the "incident" in question has been "cured." According to the principles of international law no doubt can therefore be cast on the jurisdiction of Israel to bring the accused to trial after August 3, 1960. After that date, no cause remained, in respect of a violation of international law, which could have served to support a plea against his trial in Israel.

[Having thus rejected his objections to the Court's jurisdiction, the District Court proceeded to convict Eichmann of the majority of the crimes for which he was indicted. The judgment was upheld on appeal.]

Argentina did lodge a complaint about the violation of its sovereignty with Israel, and with the UN Security Council,[6] leading the latter to adopt a resolution requesting Israel "to make appropriate reparation" while also recognizing "the concern of people in all countries that Eichmann should be brought to appropriate justice for the crimes of which he is accused."[7] What if, rather than declaring the matter closed six weeks later, Argentina had continued to protest? Would the "uncured" violation of international law matter? Consider the following position:

---

6   See *Letter dated 15 June 1960 from the Representative of Argentina addressed to the President of the Security Council*, UN Doc S/4336 (15 June 1960).

7   SC Resolution 138 (1960), adopted 23 June 1960, UN Doc S/RES/138 (1960) at preambular para 5 and operative para 2.

United States v Alvarez-Machain, 504 US 655, 112 S Ct 2188 (1992)

[Alvarez-Machain was abducted from Mexico and flown to the United States by persons acting on instructions from the US Drug Enforcement Administration (DEA). Upon arrival in Texas, he was arrested by DEA officials on charges that he had participated in the kidnapping, torture, and murder of a DEA agent serving in Mexico. Alvarez-Machain was brought to trial in Los Angeles, despite vigorous protests from Mexico with respect to the violation of its territorial sovereignty. Mexico also complained that the United States should have made use of an existing bilateral extradition treaty between the two states. The case came before the US Supreme Court as a result of a challenge by Alvarez-Machain to the validity of the criminal proceedings in the American courts that followed upon his illegal kidnapping.]

CHIEF JUSTICE REHNQUIST delivered the opinion of the Court.

The issue in this case is whether a criminal defendant, abducted to the United States from a nation with which it has an extradition treaty, thereby acquires a defense to the jurisdiction of this country's courts. We hold that he does not, and that he may be tried in federal district court for violations of the criminal law of the United States. . . .

In *Ker v. Illinois*, 119 U.S. 436 [7 S. Ct. 225] (1886) . . . , we addressed the issue of a defendant brought before the court by way of a forcible abduction. Frederick Ker had been tried and convicted in an Illinois court for larceny; his presence before the court was procured by means of forcible abduction from Peru. . . . We rejected Ker's due process argument . . . , holding in line with "the highest authorities" that "such forcible abduction is no sufficient reason why the party should not answer when brought within the jurisdiction of the court which has the right to try him for such an offence, and presents no valid objection to his trial in such court." . . .

The only differences between *Ker* and the present case are that *Ker* was decided on the premise that there was no governmental involvement in the abduction . . . ; and Peru, from which Ker was abducted, did not object to his prosecution. Respondent finds these differences to be dispositive . . . , contending that they show that respondent's prosecution . . . violates the implied terms of a valid extradition treaty. The Government, on the other hand, argues that [there is an] "exception" to the rule in *Ker* only when an extradition treaty is invoked, and the terms of the treaty provide that its breach will limit the jurisdiction of a court. . . . Therefore, our first inquiry must be whether the abduction of respondent from Mexico violated the Extradition Treaty between the United States and Mexico. If we conclude that the Treaty does not prohibit respondent's abduction, the rule in *Ker* applies, and the court need not inquire as to how respondent came before it.

. . . The [Extradition] Treaty says nothing about the obligations of the United States and Mexico to refrain from forcible abductions of people from the territory of the other nation, or the consequences under the Treaty if such an abduction occurs. . . .

The history of negotiation and practice under the Treaty also fails to show that abductions outside of the Treaty constitute a violation of the Treaty. As the Solicitor General notes, the Mexican Government was made aware, as early as 1906, of the *Ker* doctrine, and the United States' position that it applied to forcible abductions made outside of the terms of the United States-Mexico Extradition Treaty. Nonetheless, the current version of the Treaty, signed in 1978, does not attempt to establish a rule that would in any way curtail the effect of *Ker*. Moreover, although language which would grant individuals exactly the right sought by respondent had been considered and drafted as early as 1935 by a prominent group of legal scholars sponsored by the faculty of Harvard Law School, no such clause appears in the current Treaty.

Thus, the language of the Treaty, in the context of its history, does not support the proposition that the Treaty prohibits abductions outside of its terms. The remaining question, therefore, is whether the Treaty should be interpreted so as to include an implied term prohibiting prosecution where the defendant's presence is obtained by means other than those established by the Treaty. . . .

Respondent contends that the Treaty must be interpreted against the backdrop of customary international law, and that international abductions are "so clearly prohibited in international law" that there was no reason to include such a clause in the Treaty itself. . . . The international censure of international abductions is further evidenced, according to respondent, by the United Nations Charter and the Charter of the Organization of American States. . . . Respondent does not argue that these sources of international law provide an independent basis for the right respondent asserts not to be tried in the United States, but rather that they should inform the interpretation of the Treaty terms. . . .

[T]he difficulty with the support respondent garners from international law is that none of it relates to the practice of nations in relation to extradition treaties. . . . In the instant case, respondent would imply terms in the Extradition Treaty from the practice of nations with regards to international law more generally. Respondent would have us find that the Treaty acts as a prohibition against a violation of the general principle of international law that one government may not "exercise its police power in the territory of another state." . . . There are many actions which could be taken by a nation that would violate this principle, including waging war, but it cannot seriously be contended that an invasion of the United States by Mexico would violate the terms of the Extradition Treaty between the two nations. . . .

In sum, to infer from this Treaty and its terms that it prohibits all means of gaining the presence of an individual outside of its terms goes beyond established precedent and practice. . . . [T]o imply from the terms of this Treaty that it prohibits obtaining the presence of an individual by means outside of the procedures the Treaty establishes requires a much larger inferential leap, with only the most general of international law principles to support it. The general principles cited by respondent simply fail to persuade us that we should imply in the United States-Mexico Extradition Treaty a term prohibiting international abductions.

Respondent . . . may be correct that respondent's abduction was "shocking" . . . , and that it may be in violation of general international law principles. Mexico has protested the abduction of respondent through diplomatic notes . . . , and the decision of whether respondent should be returned to Mexico, as a matter outside of the Treaty, is a matter for the Executive Branch. We conclude, however, that respondent's abduction was not in violation of the Extradition Treaty between the United States and Mexico, and therefore the rule of *Ker v. Illinois* is fully applicable to this case. The fact of respondent's forcible abduction does not therefore prohibit his trial in a court in the United States for violations of the criminal laws of the United States. . . .

The . . . case is remanded for further proceedings consistent with this opinion.

JUSTICE STEVENS, with whom JUSTICE BLACKMUN and JUSTICE O'CONNOR join, dissenting:

. . . The law of nations [on the issue of forcible apprehension abroad] has not changed. Thus, a leading treatise explains:

> A State must not perform acts of sovereignty in the territory of another State. . . .
>
> It is . . . a breach of International Law for a State to send its agents to the territory of another State to apprehend persons accused of having committed a crime. Apart from other satisfaction, the first duty of the offending State is to hand over the person in question to the State in whose territory he was apprehended. (*Oppenheim's International Law* 295, and n. 1, H. Lauterpacht, 8th ed., 1955).

Commenting on the precise issue raised by this case, the chief reporter for the American Law Institute's Restatement of Foreign Relations [stated]:

> When done without consent of the foreign government, abducting a person from a foreign country is a gross violation of international law and gross disrespect for a norm high in the opinion of mankind. It is a blatant violation of the territorial integrity of another state; it eviscerates the extradition system (established by a comprehensive network of treaties involving virtually all states).

. . . A critical flaw pervades the Court's entire opinion. It fails to differentiate between the conduct of private citizens, which does not violate any treaty obligation, and conduct expressly authorized by the Executive Branch of the Government, which unquestionably constitutes a flagrant violation of international law, and in my opinion, also constitutes a breach of our treaty obligations. . . .

As the Court observes at the outset of its opinion, there is reason to believe that respondent participated in an especially brutal murder of an American law enforcement agent. That fact, if true, may explain the Executive's intense interest in punishing respondent in our courts. Such an explanation, however, provides no justification for disregarding the Rule of Law that this Court has a duty to uphold. . . .

The significance of this Court's precedents is illustrated by a recent decision of the Court of Appeal of the Republic of South Africa. Based largely on its understanding of the import of this Court's cases — including our decision in *Ker* — that court held that the prosecution of a defendant kidnapped by agents of South Africa in another country must be dismissed. *S v. Ebrahim*, S. Afr. L. Rep. (Apr.–June 1991) [[1991] 2 S Afr LR 553]. The Court of Appeal of South Africa — indeed, I suspect most courts throughout the civilized world — will be deeply disturbed by the "monstrous" decision the Court announces today. For every nation that has an interest in preserving the Rule of Law is affected, directly or indirectly, by a decision of this character. As Thomas Paine warned, an "avidity to punish is always dangerous to liberty" because it leads a nation "to stretch, to misinterpret, and to misapply even the best of laws." To counter that tendency, he reminds us:

> He that would make his own liberty secure must guard even his enemy from oppression; for if he violates this duty he establishes a precedent that will reach to himself.

I respectfully dissent.

The majority judgment in *Alvarez-Machain* and its support for a rule of *male captus, bene detentus* [wrongly captured, properly detained] has attracted much criticism,[8] as its practical effect is domestic permission for an extraterritorial extension of US police powers that goes against well-established principles of international law. Would a rule of international law prohibiting a domestic court from exercising jurisdiction over a defendant whose presence had been secured by a violation of another state's territorial sovereignty be desirable? Would it be effective in curtailing such violations? Would a refusal by the Israeli or American courts respectively to try Eichmann and Alvarez-Machain have been in the interests of the rule of law? Consider the "abuse of process" approach that has developed in the law of the United Kingdom since the British cases cited in the Israeli court's decision in *Eichmann*:

R v Horseferry Road Magistrates' Court, ex parte Bennett, [1994] 1 AC 42 at 61–68 (HL)

[The English police traced a New Zealand citizen, suspected of having committed crimes in England, to South Africa. No extradition treaty existed between South Africa and the United Kingdom, but special arrangements could be made under the applicable extradition statute. Having taken the decision not to use the extradition process, the English police colluded with the South African police to force Bennett's return to England under the pretext of a deportation to New Zealand via England. Bennett later contested the jurisdiction of the British courts as serving to perpetuate an abuse of process, relying in part on the minority's dissenting opinion in *Alvarez-Machain*.]

LORD GRIFFITHS: . . . Your Lordships are now invited to extend the concept of abuse of process a stage further. In the present case there is no suggestion that the appellant cannot have a fair trial, nor could it be suggested that it would have been unfair to try him if he had been returned to this country through extradition procedures. If the court is to have the power to interfere with the prosecution in the present circumstances it must be because the judiciary accept a responsibility for the maintenance of the rule of law that embraces a willingness to oversee executive action and to refuse to countenance behaviour that threatens either basic human rights or the rule of law.

My Lords, I have no doubt that the judiciary should accept this responsibility in the field of criminal law. The great growth of administrative law during the latter half of this century has occurred because of the recognition by the judiciary and Parliament alike that it is the function of the High Court to ensure that executive action is exercised responsibly and as Parliament intended. So also should it be in the field of criminal law and if it comes to the attention of the court that there has been a serious abuse of power it should, in my view, express its disapproval by refusing to act upon it.

Let us consider the position in the context of extradition. Extradition procedures are designed not only to ensure that criminals are returned from one country to another but also to protect the rights of those who are accused of crimes by the requesting country.

---

8   See, for example, Rosemary Rayfuse, "International Abductions and the United States Supreme Court: The Law of the Jungle Reigns" (1993) 42 ICLQ 882–97. See also "Agora: International Kidnapping" (1992) 86 AJIL 736–56.

. . . If a practice developed in which the police or prosecuting authorities of this country ignored extradition procedures and secured the return of an accused by a mere request to police colleagues in another country they would be flouting the extradition procedures and depriving the accused of the safeguards built into the extradition process for his benefit. It is to my mind unthinkable that in such circumstances the court should declare itself to be powerless and stand idly by. . . .

The courts, of course, have no power to apply direct discipline to the police or the prosecuting authorities, but they can refuse to allow them to take advantage of abuse of power by regarding their behaviour as an abuse of process and thus preventing a prosecution.

In my view your Lordships should now declare that where process of law is available to return an accused to this country through extradition procedures our courts will refuse to try him if he has been forcibly brought within our jurisdiction in disregard of those procedures by a process to which our own police, prosecuting or other executive authorities have been a knowing party.

If extradition is not available very different considerations will arise on which I express no opinion. . . .

I would answer the certified question as follows. The High Court in the exercise of its supervisory jurisdiction has power to inquire into the circumstances by which a person has been brought within the jurisdiction and if satisfied that it was in disregard of extradition procedures it may stay the prosecution and order the release of the accused. . . .

LORD BRIDGE OF HARWICH: . . . In this country and in Scotland the mainstream of authority, as the careful review in the speech of my noble and learned friend, Lord Griffiths, shows, appears to give a negative answer to the question posed, holding that the courts have no power to examine the circumstances in which a prisoner was brought within the jurisdiction. I fully recognise the cogency of the arguments which can be adduced in support of this view, sustained as they are by the public interest in the prosecution and punishment of crime. But none of the previous authorities is binding on your Lordships' House and, if there is another important principle of law which ought to influence the answer to the question posed, then your Lordships are at liberty, indeed under a duty, to examine it and, if it transpires that this is an area where two valid principles of law come into conflict, it must, in my opinion, be for your Lordships to decide as a matter of principle which of the two conflicting principles of law ought to prevail.

. . . Whatever differences there may be between the legal systems of South Africa, the United States, New Zealand and this country, many of the basic principles to which they seek to give effect stem from common roots. There is, I think, no principle more basic to any proper system of law than the maintenance of the rule of law itself. When it is shown that the law enforcement agency responsible for bringing a prosecution has only been enabled to do so by participating in violations of international law and of the laws of another state in order to secure the presence of the accused within the territorial jurisdiction of the court, I think that respect for the rule of law demands that the court take cognisance of that circumstance. To hold that the court may turn a blind eye to executive lawlessness beyond the frontiers of its own jurisdiction is, to my mind, an insular and unacceptable view. Having then taken cognisance of the lawlessness it would again appear to me to be a wholly inadequate response for the court to hold that the only remedy lies in civil proceedings at the suit of the defendant or in disciplinary or criminal proceedings against the individual officers of the law enforcement agency who were concerned in the illegal action taken. Since the prosecution could never have been brought if the defendant had not been illegally abducted, the whole proceeding is tainted. If a resident in another country is properly extradited here, the time when the prosecution commences is the time when the authorities here set the extradition process in motion. By parity of reasoning, if the authorities, instead of proceeding by way of extradition, have resorted to abduction, that is the effective commencement of the prosecution process and is the illegal foundation on which it rests. It is apt, in my view, to describe these circumstances . . . as an "abuse of the criminal jurisdiction in general" or indeed, in the language of Mansfield J. in *United States v. Toscanino*, 500 F.2d 267, as a "degradation" of the court's criminal process. To hold that in these circumstances the court may decline to exercise its jurisdiction on the ground that its process has been abused may be an extension of the doctrine of abuse of process but is, in my view, a wholly proper and necessary one.

For these reasons and for the reasons given in the speech of my noble and learned friend, Lord Griffiths, with which I fully agree, I would allow the appeal. . . .

Note the repeated references in *Alvarez-Machain* and *ex parte Bennett* to extradition. Extradition is a process of surrender, on request, of persons accused or convicted of a crime to the jurisdiction of the requesting state. In other words, it is the process by which a requested state exercises its (territorial) enforcement jurisdiction over an individual so as to achieve the transfer of that individual to a requesting state's enforcement jurisdiction. This process is typically governed by a bilateral treaty between the requested and requesting states, subject to their human rights obligations,[9] although extradition can be arranged on an *ad hoc* basis in the absence of a treaty framework. Extradition can also be the subject of a regional arrangement.[10] While the terms of extradition treaties may vary, the General Assembly has proposed a "model" extradition treaty to be used as a guide for drafting new extradition treaties and thus encourage uniformity. Consider some of the model treaty's key components:

Model Treaty on Extradition, GA Res 45/116 (1990), subsequently amended by GA Res 52/88 (1997)[11]

Article 1
Obligation to extradite
Each Party agrees to extradite to the other, upon request and subject to the provisions of the present Treaty, any person who is wanted in the requesting State for prosecution for

---

9 See, for example, Joanna Harrington, "The Role for Human Rights in Canadian Extradition Law" (2005) 43 Can YB Int'l Law 45–100.

10 See, for example, European Convention on Extradition, 13 December 1957, 359 UNTS 273, ETS No 24, in force 18 April 1960, as amended; Inter-American Convention on Extradition, 25 February 1981, 1752 UNTS 177, OASTS No 60, in force 28 March 1992. See also the European Council Framework Decision of 13 June 2002 on the European Arrest Warrant and the Surrender Procedures Between Member States (2002/584/JHA), OJ No L 190/1.

11 *Model Treaty on Extradition*, GA Res. 45/166, UN Doc. A/RES/45/166 (1990), reprinted in UN GAOR, 45th Sess, Supp No 49, vol I at 211–15, UN Doc A/45/49 (1991), as amended by *International Coopera-*

an extraditable offence or for the imposition or enforcement of a sentence in respect of such an offence.

Article 2
Extraditable offences

1. For the purposes of the present Treaty, extraditable offences are offences that are punishable under the laws of both Parties by imprisonment or other deprivation of liberty for a maximum period of at least [one/two] year(s), or by a more severe penalty. Where the request for extradition relates to a person who is wanted for the enforcement of a sentence of imprisonment or other deprivation of liberty imposed for such an offence, extradition shall be granted only if a period of at least [four/six] months of such sentence remains to be served.

2. In determining whether an offence is an offence punishable under the laws of both Parties, it shall not matter whether:

(a) The laws of the Parties place the acts or omissions constituting the offence within the same category of offence or denominate the offence by the same terminology;

(b) Under the laws of the Parties the constituent elements of the offence differ, it being understood that the totality of the acts or omissions as presented by the requesting State shall be taken into account. . . .

Article 3
Mandatory grounds for refusal

Extradition shall not be granted in any of the following circumstances:

(a) If the offence for which extradition is requested is regarded by the requested State as an offence of a political nature. Reference to an offence of a political nature shall not include any offence in respect of which the Parties have assumed an obligation, pursuant to any multilateral convention, to take prosecutorial action where they do not extradite, or any other offence that the Parties have agreed is not an offence of a political character for the purposes of extradition;

(b) If the requested State has substantial grounds for believing that the request for extradition has been made for the purpose of prosecuting or punishing a person on account of that person's race, religion, nationality, ethnic origin, political opinions, sex or status, or that that person's position may be prejudiced for any of those reasons;

(c) If the offence for which extradition is requested is an offence under military law, which is not also an offence under ordinary criminal law;

(d) If there has been a final judgement rendered against the person in the requested State in respect of the offence for which the person's extradition is requested;

(e) If the person whose extradition is requested has, under the law of either Party, become immune from prosecution or punishment for any reason, including lapse of time or amnesty;

(f) If the person whose extradition is requested has been or would be subjected in the requesting State to torture or cruel, inhuman or degrading treatment or punishment or if that person has not received or would not receive the minimum guarantees in criminal

tion in Criminal Matters, GA Res 52/88, A/RES/52/88 (1997), reprinted in UN GAOR, 52nd Sess, Supp No 49, vol I at 213–15, UN Doc A/52/88 (1998) [footnotes and commentary omitted].

proceedings, as contained in the International Covenant on Civil and Political Rights, article 14;

(g) If the judgement of the requesting State has been rendered in absentia, the convicted person has not had sufficient notice of the trial or the opportunity to arrange for his or her defence and he has not had or will not have the opportunity to have the case retried in his or her presence.

Article 4
Optional grounds for refusal
Extradition may be refused in any of the following circumstances:

(a) If the person whose extradition is requested is a national of the requested State. Where extradition is refused on this ground, the requested State shall, if the other State so requests, submit the case to its competent authorities with a view to taking appropriate action against the person in respect of the offence for which extradition had been requested;

(b) If the competent authorities of the requested State have decided either not to institute or to terminate proceedings against the person for the offence in respect of which extradition is requested;

(c) If a prosecution in respect of the offence for which extradition is requested is pending in the requested State against the person whose extradition is requested;

(d) If the offence for which extradition is requested carries the death penalty under the law of the requesting State, unless that State gives such assurance as the requested State considers sufficient that the death penalty will not be imposed or, if imposed, will not be carried out. Where extradition is refused on this ground, the requested State shall, if the other State so requests, submit the case to its competent authorities with a view to taking appropriate action against the person in respect of the offence for which extradition had been requested;

(e) If the offence for which extradition is requested has been committed outside the territory of either Party and the law of the requested State does not provide for jurisdiction over such an offence committed outside its territory in comparable circumstances;

(f) If the offence for which extradition is requested is regarded under the law of the requested State as having been committed in whole or in part within that State. Where extradition is refused on this ground, the requested State shall, if the other State so requests, submit the case to its competent authorities with a view to taking appropriate action against the person for the offence for which extradition had been requested;

(g) If the person whose extradition is requested has been sentenced or would be liable to be tried or sentenced in the requesting State by an extraordinary or ad hoc court or tribunal;

(h) If the requested State, while also taking into account the nature of the offence and the interests of the requesting State, considers that, in the circumstances of the case, the extradition of that person would be incompatible with humanitarian considerations in view of age, health or other personal circumstances of that person. . . .

Several complaints concerning both extradition and deportation (when the latter is used as a means of disguised extradition) have been lodged with the UN Human Rights

Committee, the treaty monitoring body established by the International Covenant on Civil and Political Rights.[12] In 2003, the Committee found Canada in violation of its international human rights obligations for having deported, rather than extradited, a wanted American fugitive who had escaped from prison after being convicted of murder and sentenced to death. The Committee noted that the extradition process, and its associated safeguards, served to protect an individual's fundamental rights. With respect to the safeguard of an assurance, referenced above in Article 4(d) of the Model Extradition Treaty, the Committee concluded: "That for countries that *have* abolished the death penalty, there is an obligation not to expose a person to a real risk of its application. Thus, they may not remove, either by deportation or extradition, individuals from their jurisdiction if it may be reasonably anticipated that they will be sentenced to death, without ensuring that the death sentence would not be carried out."[13]

C. PRESCRIPTIVE JURISDICTION

1) General

We turn now to "prescriptive" jurisdiction, also called legislative jurisdiction, referring as it does to a state's power to make rules to regulate or prescribe conduct. Here, the permissible extent of a state's jurisdiction is more expansive than with enforcement jurisdiction, and lawfully extends in a number of instances beyond a state's borders. Consider the comments of the Permanent Court of International Justice in the *Lotus Case*:

> *The Case of the SS "Lotus" (France v Turkey)* (1927), PCIJ (Ser A) No 10 at 19–20 and 32 [*Lotus Case*]

> [After holding that a state's enforcement jurisdiction is strictly territorial, as seen in the extract above, the Court continued:]

> It does not, however, follow that international law prohibits a State from exercising jurisdiction in its own territory, in respect of any case which relates to acts which have taken place abroad, and in which it cannot rely on some permissive rule of international law. Such a view would only be tenable if international law contained a general prohibition to States to extend the application of their laws and the jurisdiction of their courts to persons, property and acts outside their territory, and if, as an exception to this general prohibition, it allowed States to do so in certain specific cases. But this is certainly not the case under international law as it stands at present. Far from laying down a general prohibition to the effect that States may not extend the application of their laws and the jurisdiction of their courts to persons, property and acts outside their territory, it leaves

---

12 16 December 1966, 999 UNTS 171, Can TS 1976 No 47, in force 23 March 1976, art 28.

13 *Judge v Canada*, Communication No 829/1998, UN Doc CCPR/C/78/D/829/1998, reprinted in *Report of the Human Rights Committee*, UN GAOR, 58th Sess, Supp No 40, vol 2, Annex VG, UN Doc A/58/40 (2003); (2004) 42 ILM 214 at para 10.4 [emphasis in original]. See also Joanna Harrington, "The Absent Dialogue: Extradition and the International Covenant on Civil and Political Rights" (2006) 32 Queen's LJ 82. National courts, including the Supreme Court of Canada, have also found extradition to face the death penalty to be barred on human rights grounds: see *United States v Burns*, 2001 SCC 7, [2001] 1 SCR 283.

them in this respect a wide measure of discretion, which is only limited in certain cases by prohibitive rules; as regards other cases, every State remains free to adopt the principles which it regards as best and most suitable. . . .

In these circumstances all that can be required of a State is that it should not overstep the limits which international law places upon its jurisdiction; within these limits, its title to exercise jurisdiction rests in its sovereignty.

It follows from the foregoing that the contention of the French Government to the effect that Turkey must in each case be able to cite a rule of international law authorizing her to exercise jurisdiction [over an event that took place outside her territory, but where the defendant is now within it], is opposed to . . . generally accepted international law. . . . [T]his contention would apply in regard to civil as well as to criminal cases, and would be applicable on conditions of absolute reciprocity . . . ; in practice, it would therefore in many cases result in paralysing the action of the courts, owing to the impossibility of citing a universally accepted rule on which to support the exercise of their jurisdiction.

Nevertheless, it has to be seen whether the foregoing considerations really apply as regards criminal jurisdiction, or whether this jurisdiction is governed by a different principle: this might be the outcome of the close connection which for a long time existed between the conception of supreme criminal jurisdiction and that of a State, and also by the especial importance of criminal jurisdiction from the point of view of the individual.

Though it is true that in all systems of law the principle of the territorial character of criminal law is fundamental, it is equally true that all or nearly all these systems of law extend their action to offences committed outside the territory of the State which adopts them, and they do so in ways which vary from State to State. The territoriality of criminal law, therefore, is not an absolute principle of international law and by no means coincides with territorial sovereignty. . . .

FOR THESE REASONS,

The Court, having heard both Parties, gives, by the President's casting vote — the votes being equally divided —, judgment to the effect

(1) that . . . Turkey, by instituting criminal proceedings in pursuance of Turkish law against Lieutenant Demons, officer of the watch on board the *Lotus* at the time of the collision, has not acted in conflict with the principles of international law. . . .

According to the *Lotus Case*, the starting presumption for the exercise by states of extraterritorial *prescriptive* jurisdiction is precisely the opposite of that for their exercise of extraterritorial *enforcement* jurisdiction. Rather than a general prohibition subject to exceptions (as with the latter), in the case of prescriptive jurisdiction there is no general prohibition, although there are certain limits imposed by international law. Is there an explanation for this difference of approach? Consider the practical implications of extraterritorial enforcement jurisdiction for the fundamental obligation of states to refrain from forcible interference with the territorial integrity of other states, introduced in Chapter 3 and explored in detail in Chapter 14.

The different starting point for prescriptive jurisdiction is reflected in the diversity of bases or principles upon which states in fact premise the exercise of such jurisdiction. Broadly speaking, the bulk of state practice can be classified according to the five following categories: (1) matters connected to state territory; (2) where the perpetrator is a national of the state; (3) where the victim is a national of the state; (4) where the essential interests of the state are engaged; or (5) where the act is one that gives rise to universal jurisdiction for all states. More difficult, however, is to identify the precise limitations placed by international law on the exercise by states of prescriptive jurisdiction in each of these situations. Consider this overview from Canada's Department of Foreign Affairs and International Trade:

Colleen Swords, "Canadian Practice in International Law at the Department of Foreign Affairs in 2001–2" (2002) 40 Can YB Int'l Law 469 at 494–95

The starting point is the proposition that prescriptive jurisdiction is territorial. However, this area of the law is still unsettled and the territorial theory has been refined to accommodate some of the modern jurisdictional conflicts. While the territorial theory remains the best foundation for the law, it has been accepted that states may exercise extraterritorial prescriptive jurisdiction under certain circumstances. An important element for the exercise of jurisdiction is that a significant portion of an activity take place in the territory of the state claiming jurisdiction. There should be a "real and substantial link" between the subject matter of jurisdiction and the territorial base.

Since commentators still disagree on the appropriateness of various principles underlying extraterritorial prescriptive jurisdiction, their categorizations of principles often differ from each other but usually include at least variants of the following:

Nationality: It is generally recognized that a state may exercise jurisdiction over its nationals, wherever they are located.

Effects: The "effects doctrine," or "objective territoriality principle," holds that a state may have jurisdiction in respect to conduct outside its territory that has an effect inside its territory. The principle has been used extensively in the area of antitrust and competition policy enforcement, with the result that there is considerable, if not always consistent, commentary and domestic jurisprudence on the limits of this doctrine.

Universality: Some crimes are considered so heinous as to justify universal jurisdiction by states over the perpetrators. These include crimes such as piracy, slavery, war crimes, air hijacking, etc. In the postwar era, the international community has generally identified such crimes by adoption of international conventions.

Passive Personality: This is still controversial, but some states assert jurisdiction over non-nationals when the victim is a national outside the territory of the state.

Protective: It is accepted that states may exercise jurisdiction over non-nationals outside the state if their conduct constitutes a threat to the security of the state. This principle is rarely used by common law jurisdictions.

The federal government of Canada can and does exercise extraterritorial prescriptive jurisdiction. Accordingly, Canada does not object to the assertion of extraterritorial jurisdiction *per se*. Indeed, Canada asserted extraterritorial jurisdiction in several statutes including the *Criminal Code* (aircraft hijacking, hostage taking, crimes against humanity, etc.), the *Arctic Waters Pollution Act* of 1970, the *Coastal Fisheries Protection Act* (1995 seizure of the Spanish fishing trawler *Estai*), the *Competition Act*, the *United Nations Act*, and the *Special Economic Measures Act*. What Canada does oppose is conflict created by such assertions of jurisdiction. More specifically, Canada opposes extraterritorial measures that contradict or undermine the laws or clearly enunciated policies of another state exercising concurrent jurisdiction on a territorial basis over the same conduct. As a corollary, Canadian policy is not to impose extraterritorial jurisdiction which could create such conflict with the laws or policies of states exercising territorial jurisdiction.

[Reprinted with permission of the Publisher from Canadian Yearbook of International Law, Volume 40 edited by Don McRae © University of British Columbia Press 2002. All rights reserved by the Publisher.]

We turn now to a detailed discussion of each of the five bases or principles upon which states tend to exercise their prescriptive jurisdiction over persons, conduct, and events.[14] That discussion reveals some of the limits imposed by international law on the exercise of such jurisdiction by states.

2) The Territorial Principle and Matters Connected to State Territory

States obviously have prescriptive jurisdiction in relation to persons, conduct, and events taking place wholly within their territorial limits.[15] However, states may also have prescriptive jurisdiction where an event is only partially connected to that territory. Canadian criminal law, for instance, would likely apply where someone standing on the Canadian banks of the St. Lawrence shoots someone on the American side of the river, even though not all elements of the crime were concluded in Canada. Consider the views of the Supreme Court of Canada on the issue of partial territorial connection, which has much relevance in a globalized world with frequent cross-border conduct, including crime:

Libman v The Queen, [1985] 2 SCR 178

[This case involved an international fraud ring in which individuals in Canada fraudulently solicited investments by Americans in supposed gold mining operations in Costa Rica. American investors made payments to offices located in Costa Rica and Panama, where Libman and his associates collected the proceeds. When Libman was charged in Canada with fraud, he argued that no fraud could be complete until the American investors had been deprived of their funds, which occurred either in the United States, Costa Rica, or Panama, but not in Canada. Libman therefore argued that the Canadian *Criminal Code*, RSC 1985, c C-46, did not apply to his alleged acts.]

The judgment of the Court was delivered by

---

14 The terms "bases of jurisdiction" and "principles of jurisdiction" mean the same thing: Lowe & Staker, above note 3 at 320.

15 This form of jurisdiction is rooted in the concept that a state must have defined territory and permanent population: Bernard H Oxman, "Jurisdiction of States" in Rüdiger Wolfrum, ed, *The Max Planck Encyclopedia of Public International Law*, vol VI (Oxford: Oxford University Press, 2012) at 546–57, para 11. See also Lowe & Staker, above note 3 at 320 ("The territorial principle is a corollary of the sovereignty of a State over its territory.").

LA FOREST J.: — . . .

65. As noted earlier, the territorial principle in criminal law was developed by the courts to respond to two practical considerations, first, that a country has generally little direct concern for the actions of malefactors abroad; and secondly, that other states may legitimately take umbrage if a country attempts to regulate matters taking place wholly or substantially within their territories. For these reasons the courts adopted a presumption against the application of laws beyond the realm, a presumption later codified in this country in s. 5(2) [now s. 6(2)] of the *Criminal Code*.

66. While, we saw, there were occasional strong expressions of the territorial doctrine, particularly in earlier times, the fact is that the courts never applied the doctrine rigidly. To have done so . . . would have meant that a state could not apply its laws to offences whose elements occurred in several countries. This would have provided an easy escape for international criminals. What the courts sought to do, albeit in ways that were sometimes rather unsophisticated and at times inconsistent with the expressed *rationales* in earlier cases, was to give the principle an interpretation consistent with its underlying *rationale*. They did not, and indeed were not really invited to deal with transactions in other countries that had no domestic impact. But Canadian courts (like those in England and other countries for that matter) frequently took jurisdiction over transnational offences that occurred partly in Canada where they felt this country had a legitimate interest in doing so. Interestingly, s. 5(2) of the *Code* expresses the territorial principle in a manner that rather reflects its purpose. That provision does not say that criminal law is confined to Canadian territory; it says rather that no person "shall be convicted in Canada for an offence committed outside of Canada."

67. This country has a legitimate interest in prosecuting persons for activities that take place abroad but have an unlawful consequence here. . . . Indeed, from an early period the English courts have recognized such an interest in other countries. . . . The protection of the public in this country is widely acknowledged to be a legitimate purpose of criminal law, and one moreover that another nation could not easily say offended the dictates of comity.

68. But the courts did not confine themselves to taking jurisdiction over transnational offences whose impact was felt within the country. As early as 1883 they also took jurisdiction in cases where the victim and hence the impact was abroad. In the early cases, there was a tendency to justify this in terms of the links that connected the act to the jurisdiction. In doing so they foreshadowed modern academic writing on the subject, which points out that a similar approach prevails in both public and private international law. . . .

69 Starting with *Ellis* in England, the courts began to use another test: that an offence takes place where its gist or gravamen occurs. This approach was particularly prevalent in Canada. It is possible to explain many of the cases on this basis which, at a superficial level, may seem rational. The location of the offence according to this approach also corresponds to the place where the fruits of the wrongful scheme are obtained, so one can easily be led into thinking that is where the wrongful act takes place. But whatever value the notion of the gist of an offence may have for other purposes, it has little relevance

in this context. The offence of fraud, for example, consists not only of obtaining money, goods or other property; it also requires that they have been obtained by fraud. Both elements must be proved. Similarly in the offence of obtaining property by false pretences, no matter how much one insists that the gist of the offence is the obtaining, the offence can only take place if the property is obtained by false pretences. What is more I see no overriding policy reason that would favour the place of obtaining the goods. There are many cases, it is true, where this is also the place where the impact is felt, but that is not necessarily so. . . . Nor will it necessarily be the place where the harm is felt. . . .

70. Sometimes the gist or gravamen test is associated (though the two may be looked at separately) with the "completion of the offence" or terminatory test, as in the present case, for example. This seems more prevalent in England, at least in the eyes of some academics. . . . That test may have the advantage of removing criminal liability for acts that take place after the offence as defined is completed, but it also has the result of removing from consideration earlier acts constituting the offence, here the fraudulent activities alleged to have occurred in Toronto.

71. It also ignores the fact that the fruits of the transaction were obtained in Canada as contemplated by the scheme. Their delivery here was not accidental or irrelevant. It was an integral part of the scheme. While it may not in strictness constitute part of the offence, it is, I think, relevant in considering whether a transaction falls outside Canadian territory. For in considering that question we must, in my view, take into account all relevant facts that take place in Canada that may legitimately give this country an interest in prosecuting the offence. One must then consider whether there is anything in those facts that offends international comity. . . . [T]he law would be lame indeed if its strictures could be avoided by the simple artifice of going outside the country to obtain the fruits of a scheme that was hatched in and largely put into effect in Canada. In this case, the whole operation of obtaining the proceeds of the fraud outside the country was a mere sham and should be treated as such. . . .

74. I might summarize my approach to the limits of territoriality in this way. As I see it, all that is necessary to make an offence subject to the jurisdiction of our courts is that a significant portion of the activities constituting that offence took place in Canada. As it is put by modern academics, it is sufficient that there be a "real and substantial link" between an offence and this country, a test well known in public and private international law. . . . [T]his does not require legislation. It was the courts after all that defined the manner in which the doctrine of territoriality applied, and the test proposed simply amounts to a revival of the earlier way of formulating the principle. It is in fact the test that best reconciles all the cases. . . .

76. Just what may constitute a real and substantial link in a particular case, I need not explore. There were ample links here. The outer limits of the test may, however, well be coterminous with the requirements of international comity.

77. As I have already noted, in some of the early cases the English courts tended to express a narrow view of the territorial application of English law so as to ensure that they did not unduly infringe on the jurisdiction of other states. However, even as early as the

late 19th century, following the invention and development of modern means of communication, they began to exercise criminal jurisdiction over transnational transactions as long as a significant part of the chain of action occurred in England. Since then means of communications have proliferated at an accelerating pace and the common interests of states have grown proportionately. Under these circumstances, the notion of comity, which means no more nor less than "kindly and considerate behaviour towards others," has also evolved. How considerate is it of the interests of the United States in this case to permit criminals based in this country to prey on its citizens? How does it conform to its interests or to ours for us to permit such activities when law enforcement agencies in both countries have developed cooperative schemes to prevent and prosecute those engaged in such activities? To ask these questions is to answer them. No issue of comity is involved here. In this regard, I make mine the words of Lord Diplock in *Treacy v. Director of Public Prosecutions* cited earlier. . . . [W]e should not be indifferent to the protection of the public in other countries. In a shrinking world, we are all our brother's keepers. In the criminal arena this is underlined by the international cooperative schemes that have been developed among national law enforcement bodies.

78. For these reasons, I have no difficulty in holding on the facts agreed upon for the purposes of this appeal, that the counts of fraud with which the appellant is charged may properly be prosecuted in Canada, and I see nothing in the requirements of international comity that would dictate that this country refrain from exercising its jurisdiction. Since these fraudulent activities took place in Canada, it follows . . . that the conspiracy count may also be proceeded with in Canada. . . .

Aside from its discussion of the territorial principle of jurisdiction, does the judgment in *Libman* suggest elements of the outer limits of a state's lawful exercise of prescriptive jurisdiction under international law?

Usually, the territorial principle of jurisdiction is invoked by a state to justify the application of its prescriptive jurisdiction to persons or events having a connection to its territory. Consider now a variation on this theme: an attempt by the government of a state to *deny* itself prescriptive jurisdiction over events connected to territory over which the state in question exercises *de facto* control but not sovereign title:

Rasul v Bush, 542 US 466, 124 S Ct 2686 (2004)

[Following the terrorist attacks of September 11, 2001, US armed forces were sent to Afghanistan to conduct a military campaign against al-Qaida and the Taliban regime, then the *de facto* government of Afghanistan. A number of non-US nationals were captured during the conflict and held in a military detention and interrogation facility located at the Guantanamo Bay Naval Base in Cuba, including the petitioners in this landmark case. The United States occupies the Guantanamo base under a lease and treaty with Cuba that recognizes Cuba's "ultimate sovereignty." However, the lease gives the United States "complete jurisdiction and control" provided it does not abandon the leased areas. The petitioners wished to challenge the legality of their detention. A preliminary issue was whether US *habeas corpus* law applied to executive detention of foreign nationals outside sovereign US territory (but in territory subject to its "complete jurisdiction and control").]

JUSTICE STEVENS delivered the opinion of the Court (Rehnquist C.J, Scalia, and Thomas JJ. dissenting):

... Habeas corpus is ... "a writ antecedent to statute, ... throwing its root deep into the genius of our common law.". ... The writ appeared in English law several centuries ago, became "an integral part of our common-law heritage" by the time the Colonies achieved independence ... and received explicit recognition in the Constitution, which forbids suspension of "the Privilege of the Writ of Habeas Corpus ... unless when in Cases of Rebellion or Invasion the public Safety may require it." ...

As it has evolved over the past two centuries, the habeas statute clearly has expanded habeas corpus "beyond the limits that obtained during the 17th and 18th centuries.". ... But "[a]t its historical core, the writ of habeas corpus has served as a means of reviewing the legality of Executive detention, and it is in that context that its protections have been strongest." ... As Justice Jackson wrote in an opinion respecting the availability of habeas corpus to aliens held in U.S. custody:

> Executive imprisonment has been considered oppressive and lawless since John, at Runnymede, pledged that no free man should be imprisoned, dispossessed, outlawed, or exiled save by the judgment of his peers or by the law of the land. The judges of England developed the writ of habeas corpus largely to preserve these immunities from executive restraint. ...

Consistent with the historic purpose of the writ, this Court has recognized the federal courts' power to review applications for habeas relief in a wide variety of cases involving Executive detention, in wartime as well as in times of peace. ...

The question now before us is whether the habeas statute confers a right to judicial review of the legality of Executive detention of aliens in a territory over which the United States exercises plenary and exclusive jurisdiction, but not "ultimate sovereignty." ...

... [R]espondents contend that we can discern a limit on [the applicable habeas statute] through application of the "longstanding principle of American law" that congressional legislation is presumed not to have extraterritorial application unless such intent is clearly manifested. Whatever traction the presumption against extraterritoriality might have in other contexts, it certainly has no application to the operation of the habeas statute with respect to persons detained within "the territorial jurisdiction" of the United States. ... By the express terms of its agreements with Cuba, the United States exercises "complete jurisdiction and control" over the Guantanamo Bay Naval Base, and may continue to exercise such control permanently if it so chooses. Respondents themselves concede that the habeas statute would create federal-court jurisdiction over the claims of an American citizen held at the base. ... Considering that the statute draws no distinction between Americans and aliens held in federal custody, there is little reason to think that Congress intended the geographical coverage of the statute to vary depending on the detainee's citizenship. Aliens held at the base, no less than American citizens, are entitled to invoke the federal courts' authority under [the habeas statute].

Application of the habeas statute to persons detained at the base is consistent with the historical reach of the writ of habeas corpus. At common law, courts exercised habeas jurisdiction over the claims of aliens detained within sovereign territory of the realm, ...

as well as the claims of persons detained in the so-called "exempt jurisdictions," where ordinary writs did not run, and all other dominions under the sovereign's control. As Lord Mansfield wrote in 1759, even if a territory was "no part of the realm," there was "no doubt" as to the court's power to issue writs of habeas corpus if the territory was "under the subjection of the Crown." . . . Later cases confirmed that the reach of the writ depended not on formal notions of territorial sovereignty, but rather on the practical question of "the exact extent and nature of the jurisdiction or dominion exercised in fact by the Crown." . . .

In the end, the answer to the question presented is clear. Petitioners contend that they are being held in federal custody in violation of the laws of the United States. No party questions the District Court's jurisdiction over petitioners' custodians. . . . [The *habeas* statute], by its terms, requires nothing more. We therefore hold that [it] confers on the District Court jurisdiction to hear petitioners' habeas corpus challenges to the legality of their detention at the Guantanamo Bay Naval Base.

In addition to invoking the District Court's jurisdiction under [the habeas statute], the *Al Odah* petitioners' complaint invoked the court's jurisdiction under . . . the federal question statute, as well as . . . the *Alien Tort Statute*. . . .

[N]othing in . . . any of our other cases categorically excludes aliens detained in military custody outside the United States from the "privilege of litigation" in U.S. courts. . . . The courts of the United States have traditionally been open to nonresident aliens. . . . And indeed, [the *Alien Tort Statute*] explicitly confers the privilege of suing for an actionable "tort . . . committed in violation of the law of nations or a treaty of the United States" on aliens alone. The fact that petitioners in these cases are being held in military custody is immaterial to the question of the District Court's jurisdiction over their nonhabeas statutory claims.

Whether and what further proceedings may become necessary after respondents make their response to the merits of petitioners' claims are matters that we need not address now. What is presently at stake is only whether the federal courts have jurisdiction to determine the legality of the Executive's potentially indefinite detention of individuals who claim to be wholly innocent of wrongdoing. Answering that question in the affirmative, we reverse the judgment of the Court of Appeals and remand for the District Court to consider in the first instance the merits of petitioners' claims.

It is so ordered.

These approaches seem sensible. Where there is a "real and substantial link" — in the words of the Supreme Court of Canada — between a given act and a state's territory, or territory under its *de facto* control, the state should be able to exercise its prescriptive jurisdiction. However, what if the connection between the act in question and a state's territory is more remote? What if the entire event or transaction takes place outside the territory under a state's sovereignty or control, but nevertheless has an effect within that state? Consider this overview of the controversial "effects doctrine" adopted by US courts:

The basic rule of extraterritorial application of U.S. commercial laws, otherwise referred to as the "effects doctrine," was formulated by Judge Learned Hand in *United States v. Aluminum Company of America*. Here, Learned Hand applied U.S. antitrust laws to extraterritorial commercial events, despite a lack of any express Congressional intent to make the statute applicable extra-territorially. Under the effects doctrine, the *Sherman Act* [a competition law statute] subjects extraterritorial commercial conduct that has a substantial, direct, and foreseeable effect on U.S. domestic or foreign commerce to liability in federal courts. The Supreme Court's decision in *Hartford Fire Insurance Company v. California* is the modern judicial endorsement of this doctrine. While an earlier Supreme Court case had held that legislation is territorial in scope unless there is an express intention to the contrary, subsequent case law has eroded this principle, replacing it with the effects doctrine. Congress has also enacted statutes with an explicit extraterritorial mandate, often leading to controversies with its trading partners. For example, the *Cuban Liberty and Democratic Solidarity ("LIBERTAD") Act*, also know as the *Helms-Burton Act*, imposed penalties upon business managers, (irrespective of their territorial location), for "trafficking'" in properties belonging to U.S. citizens expropriated by Cuba. After protests by Canadians and Europeans about the propriety and legality of these extraterritorial penalties, and the attendant secondary boycotts under international law, the President of the United States suspended their application. In addition, France and Great Britain enacted blocking legislation to impede the provisions of the *Helms-Burton Act*. Such expansive extraterritorial applications of U.S. laws have therefore not been without fallout from U.S. trading partners.[16]

As the above passage suggests, Canada (among others) has responded vigorously to American assertions of prescriptive jurisdiction over commercial and other transactions taking place in Canada that have no links to the United States other than their "effects" on US interests or US foreign policy objectives. In fact, in 1984, Parliament enacted the *Foreign Extraterritorial Measures Act* in an attempt to counter such US measures.[17] Consider some of this statute's key provisions:

Foreign Extraterritorial Measures Act, RSC 1985, c F-29

3. (1) Where, in the opinion of the Attorney General of Canada, a foreign tribunal has exercised, is exercising or is proposing or likely to exercise jurisdiction or powers of a kind or in a manner that has adversely affected or is likely to adversely affect significant Canadian interests in relation to international trade or commerce involving a business carried on in whole or in part in Canada or that otherwise has infringed or is likely to infringe Canadian sovereignty, or jurisdiction or powers that is or are related to the enforcement of a foreign trade law or a provision of a foreign trade law set out in the schedule, the Attorney General of Canada may, by order, prohibit or restrict

(a) the production before or the disclosure or identification to, or for the purposes of, a foreign tribunal of records that, at any time while the order is in force, are in Canada or are in the possession or under the control of a Canadian citizen or a person resident in Canada;

---

16 James Thuo Gathii, "Torture, Extraterritoriality, Terrorism, and International Law" (2003) 67 Alta L Rev 335 at 364.

17 See further, William C Graham, "The Foreign Extraterritorial Measures Act" (1985–1986) 11 Can Bus LJ 410–44.

(b) the doing of any act in Canada, in relation to records that, at any time while the order is in force, are in Canada or are in the possession or under the control of a Canadian citizen or a person resident in Canada, that will, or is likely to, result in the records, or information as to the contents of the records or from which the records might be identified, being produced before or disclosed or identified to, or for the purposes of, a foreign tribunal; and

(c) the giving by a person, at a time when that person is a Canadian citizen or a resident of Canada, of information before, or for the purposes of, a foreign tribunal in relation to, or in relation to the contents or identification of, records that, at any time while the order is in force, are or were in Canada or under the control of a Canadian citizen or a person resident in Canada. . . .

5. (1) Where, in the opinion of the Attorney General of Canada, a foreign state or foreign tribunal has taken or is proposing or is likely to take measures affecting international trade or commerce of a kind or in a manner that has adversely affected or is likely to adversely affect significant Canadian interests in relation to international trade or commerce involving business carried on in whole or in part in Canada or that otherwise has infringed or is likely to infringe Canadian sovereignty, the Attorney General of Canada may, with the concurrence of the Minister of Foreign Affairs, by order,

(a) require any person in Canada to give notice to him of such measures, or of any directives, instructions, intimations of policy or other communications relating to such measures from a person who is in a position to direct or influence the policies of the person in Canada; or

(b) prohibit any person in Canada from complying with such measures, or with any directives, instructions, intimations of policy or other communications relating to such measures from a person who is in a position to direct or influence the policies of the person in Canada. . . .

7. (1) Every person who contravenes an order made under section 3 or 5 that is directed to the person and that has been served on the person in accordance with section 6 is guilty of an offence and liable

(a) on conviction on indictment,

    (i) in the case of a corporation, to a fine not exceeding $1,500,000, and

    (ii) in the case of an individual, to a fine not exceeding $150,000 or to imprisonment for a term not exceeding five years, or to both; or

(b) on summary conviction,

    (i) in the case of a corporation, to a fine not exceeding $150,000, and

    (ii) in the case of an individual, to a fine not exceeding $15,000 or to imprisonment for a term not exceeding two years, or to both. . . .

7.1 Any judgment given under the law of the United States entitled *Cuban Liberty and Democratic Solidarity (LIBERTAD) Act of 1996* shall not be recognized or enforceable in any manner in Canada.

What does enactment of the *Foreign Extraterritorial Measures Act* by Canada, and the enactment of similar statutes by several other states, in response to American invocation of the "effects doctrine" tell you about the general limits placed by international law on the exercise of prescriptive jurisdiction by states?

3) Nationality Principle of Jurisdiction

a) Introduction

A second circumstance in which states may assert prescriptive jurisdiction over persons, conduct, and events is where there is a link of nationality between the regulating state and the regulated person or object. We have already seen, for example, that a state is entitled (and indeed, required) to exercise prescriptive jurisdiction over vessels having its national-ity—that is, those vessels registered in that state and flying its flag. Similar rules apply to aircraft and space vehicles.

The nationality principle extends prescriptive jurisdiction over the conduct of a state's nationals while outside the territory of that state.[18] As one commentator describes it, "under this principle, jurisdiction is assumed by the state of which the person against whom proceedings are taken, is a national."[19]

The critical issue here, of course, is how one establishes who or what is a national of a given state. While each state's domestic legal system may take different approaches to this question, international law also provides certain broad guidelines. We look at this international law of nationality in relation first to individuals and then with respect to corporations. In reviewing these materials, consider whether the international legal rules pertaining to the nationality of individuals and corporations provide further guidance as to the international legal limits on the prescriptive jurisdiction of states. Does a common theme begin to emerge with respect to the limits we have examined in the context of the territorial principle of prescriptive jurisdiction?

b) Nationality of Individuals

It may be surprising that international law provides little guidance concerning the nation-ality of individuals, thus allowing states much latitude. As explained by the Permanent Court of International Justice in a 1923 advisory opinion, nationality falls within a domain of legal competence reserved to a state's internal law, although it may be limited by a state's treaty obligations. The Court opined: "in the present state of international law, questions of nationality are . . . in principle within the reserved domain [of states]."[20] This position finds affirmation in Article 1 of the 1930 Convention on Certain Questions Relat-ing to the Conflict of Nationality Laws (Hague Convention), which provides: "It is for each State to determine under its own law who are its nationals. This law shall be recognized by other States in so far as it is consistent with international conventions, international custom, and the principles of law generally recognized with regard to nationality."[21] While not particularly significant in its own right because of the limited number of parties to the

---

18 This principle stems from the concept that a state must have a permanent population: Oxman, above note 15 at para 11.

19 Ivan A Shearer, *Starke's International Law*, 11th ed (Toronto: Butterworths, 1994) at 210.

20 *Nationality Decrees Issued in Tunis and Morocco (French Zone)*, Advisory Opinion (1923), PCIJ (Ser B) No 4 at 24.

21 12 April 1930, 179 LNTS 89, Can TS 1937 No 7, in force 1 July 1937, denunciated by Canada 15 May 1996.

Hague Convention, Article 1 likely reflects the fundamental starting point with respect to the customary international law of nationality.

In practice, the domestic laws of states tend to base nationality on birth in the territory of the state (*jus soli*), on descent from nationals of the state (*jus sanguinis*), or both. Nationality may also be acquired after birth in many states through "naturalization." Canada currently provides for all of these means of acquiring Canadian citizenship, as provided in the *Citizenship Act*, RSC 1985, c C-29:

> 3. (1) Subject to this Act, a person is a citizen if
> (a) the person was born in Canada after February 14, 1977;
> (b) the person was born outside Canada after February 14, 1977 and at the time of his birth one of his parents, other than a parent who adopted him, was a citizen;
> (c) the person has been granted or acquired citizenship [through the process of naturalization set out in the Act] and, in the case of a person who is fourteen years of age or over on the day that he is granted citizenship, he has taken the oath of citizenship. . . .

Still, there is an outer limit to the deference international law accords states in determining their own nationality rules. A state's approach may be challenged "where there is insufficient connection between the State of nationality and the individual or where nationality has been improperly conferred."[22] In addition, discriminatory denials of nationality may also be challenged on human rights grounds.[23] Article 1 of the 1930 Hague Convention itself notes that nationality decisions inconsistent with "international conventions, international custom and the principles of law generally recognized with regard to nationality" need not be recognized by other states.

The International Court of Justice's decision in the *Nottebohm Case* provides the clearest pronouncement on the extent of a state's discretion, under international law, to award nationality:

Nottebohm Case (Liechtenstein v Guatemala), **Second Phase, Judgment, [1955] ICJ Rep 4**

[Nottebohm was a German national by birth but moved to Guatemala in 1905 where he established a home, a business, and a family. He lived there for thirty-four years before travelling briefly to Lichtenstein in 1939, where he applied for and was granted Liechtensteinian nationality. Under German law, obtaining another state's nationality automatically entailed loss of German nationality. Nottebohm then returned to Guatemala until 1943, when he was detained and deported and his property was seized without compensation on the basis that he was an enemy national. Guatemala was at that time in a state of belligerency with Germany, which entitled Guatemala to take certain extraordinary steps with respect to belligerent nationals and their property. Liechtenstein espoused Nottebohm's claim for compensation against Guatemala before the International Court of Justice. Guatemala objected to the admissibility of the claim on the basis that it re-

---

22 C John R Dugard, "First Report on Diplomatic Protection," UN Doc A/CN.4/506, reprinted in [2000] 2 ILC YB 205–46 at para 98.

23 See, for example, Human Rights Council, *The Right to a Nationality: Women and Children*, HRC Res 20/4, UN Doc A/HRC/20/4 (2012), reprinted in *Report of the Human Rights Council*, UN GAOR, 67th Sess, Supp No 53 at 141–43, UN Doc A/67/53 (2012).

fused to recognize Nottebohm's Liechtensteinian nationality and, hence, Liechtenstein's standing to espouse his claim.]

[T]he Court must consider whether such an act of granting nationality by Liechtenstein directly entails an obligation on the part of Guatemala to recognize its effect, namely, Liechtenstein's right to exercise its protection. In other words, it must be determined whether that unilateral act by Liechtenstein is one which can be relied upon against Guatemala in regard to the exercise of protection. The Court will deal with this question without considering that of the validity of Nottebohm's naturalization according to the law of Liechtenstein.

It is for Liechtenstein, as it is for every sovereign State, to settle by its own legislation the rules relating to the acquisition of its nationality, and to confer that nationality by naturalization granted by its own organs in accordance with that legislation. It is not necessary to determine whether international law imposes any limitations on its freedom of decision in this domain. Furthermore, nationality has its most immediate, its most far-reaching and, for most people, its only effects within the legal system of the State conferring it. Nationality serves above all to determine that the person upon whom it is conferred enjoys the rights and is bound by the obligations which the law of the State in question grants to or imposes on its nationals. This is implied in the wider concept that nationality is within the domestic jurisdiction of the State.

But the issue which the Court must decide is not one which pertains to the legal system of Liechtenstein. It does not depend on the law or on the decision of Liechtenstein whether that State is entitled to exercise its protection, in the case under consideration. To exercise protection, to apply to the Court, is to place oneself on the plane of international law. It is international law which determines whether a State is entitled to exercise protection and to seise the Court. . . .

According to the practice of States, to arbitral and judicial decisions and to the opinions of writers, nationality is a legal bond having as its basis a social fact of attachment, a genuine connection of existence, interests and sentiments, together with the existence of reciprocal rights and duties. It may be said to constitute the juridical expression of the fact that the individual upon whom it is conferred, either directly by the law or as the result of an act of the authorities, is in fact more closely connected with the population of the State conferring nationality than with that of any other State. Conferred by a State, it only entitles that State to exercise protection vis-à-vis another State, if it constitutes a translation into juridical terms of the individual's connection with the State which has made him its national.

Diplomatic protection and protection by means of international judicial proceedings constitute measures for the defence of the rights of the State. As the Permanent Court of International Justice has said and has repeated, "by taking up the case of one of its subjects and by resorting to diplomatic action or international judicial proceedings on his behalf, a State is in reality asserting its own rights — its right to ensure, in the person of its subjects, respect for the rules of international law" (P.C.I.J., Series A, No. 2, p. 12, and Series A/B, Nos. 20–21, p. 17).

Since this is the character which nationality must present when it is invoked to furnish the State which has granted it with a title to the exercise of protection and to the institution of international judicial proceedings, the Court must ascertain whether the nationality granted to Nottebohm by means of naturalization is of this character or, in other words, whether the factual connection between Nottebohm and Liechtenstein in the period preceding, contemporaneous with and following his naturalization appears to be sufficiently close, so preponderant in relation to any connection which may have existed between him and any other State, that it is possible to regard the nationality conferred upon him as real and effective, as the exact juridical expression of a social fact of a connection which existed previously or came into existence thereafter.

Naturalization is not a matter to be taken lightly. To seek and to obtain it is not something that happens frequently in the life of a human being. It involves his breaking of a bond of allegiance and his establishment of a new bond of allegiance. It may have far-reaching consequences and involve profound changes in the destiny of the individual who obtains it. It concerns him personally, and to consider it only from the point of view of its repercussions with regard to his property would be to misunderstand its profound significance. In order to appraise its international effect, it is impossible to disregard the circumstances in which it was conferred, the serious character which attaches to it, the real and effective, and not merely the verbal preference of the individual seeking it for the country which grants it to him.

At the time of his naturalization does Nottebohm appear to have been more closely attached by his tradition, his establishment, his interests, his activities, his family ties, his intentions for the near future to Liechtenstein than to any other State? . . .

The essential facts are as follows:

At the date when he applied for naturalization Nottebohm had been a German national from the time of his birth. He had always retained his connections with members of his family who had remained in Germany and he had always had business connections with that country. His country had been at war for more than a month, and there is nothing to indicate that the application for naturalization then made by Nottebohm was motivated by any desire to dissociate himself from the Government of his country.

He had been settled in Guatemala for 34 years. He had carried on his activities there. It was the main seat of his interests. He returned there shortly after his naturalization, and it remained the centre of his interests and of his business activities. He stayed there until his removal as a result of war measures in 1943. He subsequently attempted to return there, and he now complains of Guatemala's refusal to admit him. There, too, were several members of his family who sought to safeguard his interests.

In contrast, his actual connections with Liechtenstein were extremely tenuous. No settled abode, no prolonged residence in that country at the time of his application for naturalization: the application indicates that he was paying a visit there and confirms the transient character of this visit by its request that the naturalization proceedings should be initiated and concluded without delay. No intention of settling there was shown at that time or realized in the ensuing weeks, months or years — on the contrary, he returned to Guatemala very shortly after his naturalization and showed every intention of remaining there. If Nottebohm went to Liechtenstein in 1946, this was because of the refusal of Guatemala to admit him. No indication is given of the grounds warranting the waiver of the condition of residence, required by the 1934 Nationality Law, which waiver was implicitly granted to him. There is no allegation of any economic interests or of any activities exercised or to be exercised in Liechtenstein, and no manifestation of any intention whatsoever to transfer all or some of his interests and his business activities to Liechtenstein. It is unnecessary in this connection to attribute much importance to the promise to pay the taxes levied at the time of his naturalization. The only links to be discovered between the Principality and Nottebohm are the short sojourns already referred to and the presence in Vaduz of one of his brothers: but his brother's presence is referred to in his application for naturalization only as a reference to his good conduct. Furthermore, other members of his family have asserted Nottebohm's desire to spend his old age in Guatemala.

These facts clearly establish, on the one hand, the absence of any bond of attachment between Nottebohm and Liechtenstein and, on the other hand, the existence of a long-standing and close connection between him and Guatemala, a link which his naturalization in no way weakened. That naturalization was not based on any real prior connection with Liechtenstein, nor did it in any way alter the manner of life of the person upon whom it was conferred in exceptional circumstances of speed and accommodation. In both respects, it was lacking in the genuineness requisite to an act of such importance, if it is to be entitled to be respected by a State in the position of Guatemala. It was granted without regard to the concept of nationality adopted in international relations.

Naturalization was asked for not so much for the purpose of obtaining a legal recognition of Nottebohm's membership in fact in the population of Liechtenstein, as it was to enable him to substitute for his status as a national of a belligerent State that of a national of a neutral State, with the sole aim of thus coming within the protection of Liechtenstein but not of becoming wedded to its traditions, its interests, its way of life or of assuming the obligations — other than fiscal obligations — and exercising the rights pertaining to the status thus acquired.

Guatemala is under no obligation to recognize a nationality granted in such circumstances. Liechtenstein consequently is not entitled to extend its protection to Nottebohm vis-à-vis Guatemala and its claim must, for this reason, be held to be inadmissible. . . .

Does *Nottebohm* hold that Liechtenstein was not entitled, under international law, to grant its nationality to Nottebohm? Or does it assert a more limited principle? Perhaps *Nottebohm* should be read as a reaction to efforts to manipulate the consequences of the laws of war.[24]

Nottebohm has been interpreted as requiring the existence of a real and effective link between a person and a state extending nationality to that person before that nationality may be relied upon against another state, even in instances where the person does not also have the nationality of that other state: "The *Nottebohm* case is seen as authority for the position that there should be an 'effective' or 'genuine' link between the individual and the State of nationality, not only in the case of dual or plural nationality (where such a requirement is generally accepted), but also where the national possesses only one nationality."[25]

---

24 See Robert D Sloane, "Breaking the Genuine Link: The Contemporary International Regulation of Nationality" (2009) 50 Harv Int'l LJ 1.

25 Dugard, above note 22 at para 106.

A potential peril with such an approach is the possibility that expatriates living in a state of which they are not a national may see the international value of their nationality dissipate as their connection to their state of nationality fades. This possibility may be partially addressed by treating birth in, or descent from nationals of, the state of nationality as an enduring "effective or genuine link" with that state, but this does not deal with cases where one's sole nationality is the result of naturalization or where state laws do not confer nationality based on birth alone. The ultimate result of living abroad from one's state of nationality in such cases could be effective "statelessness."

Statelessness raises a number of problems in international law and has prompted attempts to limit the occurrence of the phenomenon. We start from the position that there is a generally recognized human right to acquire a nationality.[26] Second, while to date they have attracted only a modest number of ratifications, two multilateral treaties specifically attempt to limit statelessness: the Convention relating to the Status of Stateless Persons[27] and the Convention on the Reduction of Statelessness.[28] Among other things, the latter treaty provides that "[a] Contracting State shall not deprive a person of his nationality if such deprivation would render him stateless."[29] Would this provision require a contracting state to recognize the (foreign) nationality of a person having no genuine or effective link to her only state of nationality? Had Guatemala and Liechtenstein been parties to such a provision, would it have required Guatemala to recognize Nottebohm's Liechtensteinian nationality (bearing in mind that German law provided for the automatic loss of German nationality upon obtaining the nationality of any other state)? Or, assuming Germany had been a party to such a provision, would it rather have been incumbent on Germany not to deprive Nottebohm of his German nationality?

The United States-Italian Conciliation Commission, established after World War II, rejected a "dissipating nationality" interpretation of the *Nottebohm* test in the *Flegenheimer Case*.[30] Albert Flegenheimer was born in Germany in 1890, but claimed to have US citizenship given that his father had become a naturalized US citizen before that date. Like other German Jews, Flegenheimer was divested of his German citizenship by the Nazi regime in 1933. At issue before the Commission was whether Flegenheimer was a US national for the purposes of compensation under the terms of the post–World War II peace treaty between the United States and Italy. Such compensation was said to be owed in respect of a 1941 sale made under duress by Flegenheimer of shares in an Italian company to an Italian national.

The Italian government claimed that Flegenheimer could not be considered a US national. For various reasons, the Commission agreed. However, it rejected the Italian argument that in the absence of the pertinent treaty provisions, Flegenheimer's case would fail due to the theory of effective nationality. In the Commission's words:

---

26 See Convention on the Rights of the Child, 20 November 1989, 1577 UNTS 3, Can TS 1992 No 3, in force 2 September 1990, art 7. See also HRC Res 20/4, above note 23.

27 28 September 1954, 360 UNTS 117, in force 6 June 1960. As of July 2013, this treaty has seventy-seven states parties; Canada is not a party.

28 30 August 1961, 989 UNTS 175, Can TS 1978 No 32, in force 13 December 1975. As of July 2013, this treaty has fifty-one states parties, including Canada.

29 *Ibid*, art 8.

30 Decision No 182 of 20 September 1958, 14 RIAA 327.

But when a person is vested with only one nationality, which is attributed to him or her either *jure sanguinis* or *jure soli*, or by a valid naturalization entailing the positive loss of the former nationality, the theory of effective nationality cannot be applied without the risk of causing confusion. . . . [T]he persons by the thousands who, because of the facility of travel in the modern world, possess the positive legal nationality of a State, but live in foreign States where they are domiciled and where their family and business centre is located, would be exposed to non-recognition, at the international level, of the nationality with which they are undeniably vested by virtue of the laws of their national State, if this doctrine were to be generalized.[31]

c) Nationality of Corporations

Corporations are legal entities created pursuant to the domestic laws of states. Even a "multinational" or "transnational" corporation is simply a series of corporate entities, incorporated pursuant to the laws of several states, which are usually controlled or owned by a controlling "parent" corporation incorporated in another state. State (and treaty) practice on the nationality of corporations varies. Some states emphasize the extent to which a company is connected to a state in deciding whether to treat it as a national of that state. On the other hand, public international law has long accepted that a corporation's nationality may be based simply on the state of incorporation and/or the state where the corporation's head office is located. Consider the reasoning of the ICJ in the following case:

Barcelona Traction, Light and Power Company, Limited (Belgium v Spain), Second Phase, Judgment, [1970] ICJ Rep 3

[Barcelona Traction was a holding company incorporated in Canada, where it had its head office. It had formed a number of subsidiary companies, some pursuant to Canadian law but others pursuant to Spanish law, to carry on business in Spain. A large percentage of Barcelona Traction's share capital was owned by Belgian nationals. Due to a number of financial restrictions imposed by the Spanish government on Barcelona Traction's assets in Spain, the company was eventually declared bankrupt by a Spanish court. Belgium then brought a claim against Spain on behalf of the Belgian shareholders, alleging that Spain had caused the bankruptcy and consequent losses for those shareholders. Spain raised a preliminary objection to the claim on the basis that any injury sustained was to the company, a Canadian national, which Belgium had no standing to represent. One of the issues to be addressed by the Court, therefore, was the nationality of the company.]

70. In allocating corporate entities to States for purposes of diplomatic protection, international law is based, but only to a limited extent, on an analogy with the rules governing the nationality of individuals. The traditional rule attributes the right of diplomatic protection of a corporate entity to the State under the laws of which it is incorporated and in whose territory it has its registered office. These two criteria have been confirmed by long practice and by numerous international instruments. This notwithstanding, further or different links are at times said to be required in order that a right of diplomatic

---

31 *Ibid* at 377.

protection should exist. Indeed, it has been the practice of some States to give a company incorporated under their law diplomatic protection solely when it has its seat (siege social) or management or centre of control in their territory, or when a majority or a substantial proportion of the shares has been owned by nationals of the State concerned. Only then, it has been held, does there exist between the corporation and the State in question a genuine connection of the kind familiar from other branches of international law. However, in the particular field of the diplomatic protection of corporate entities, no absolute test of the "genuine connection" has found general acceptance. Such tests as have been applied are of a relative nature, and sometimes links with one State have had to be weighed against those with another. In this connection reference has been made to the *Nottebohm* case. In fact the Parties made frequent reference to it in the course of the proceedings. However, given both the legal and factual aspects of protection in the present case the Court is of the opinion that there can be no analogy with the issues raised or the decision given in that case.

71. In the present case, it is not disputed that the company was incorporated in Canada and has its registered office in that country. The incorporation of the company under the law of Canada was an act of free choice. Not only did the founders of the company seek its incorporation under Canadian law but it has remained under that law for a period of over 50 years. It has maintained in Canada its registered office, its accounts and its share registers. Board meetings were held there for many years; it has been listed in the records of the Canadian tax authorities. Thus a close and permanent connection has been established, fortified by the passage of over half a century. This connection is in no way weakened by the fact that the company engaged from the very outset in commercial activities outside Canada, for that was its declared object. Barcelona Traction's links with Canada are thus manifold.

72. Furthermore, the Canadian nationality of the company has received general recognition. Prior to the institution of proceedings before the Court, three other governments apart from that of Canada (those of the United Kingdom, the United States and Belgium) made representations concerning the treatment accorded to Barcelona Traction by the Spanish authorities. The United Kingdom Government intervened on behalf of bondholders and of shareholders. Several representations were also made by the United States Government, but not on behalf of the Barcelona Traction company as such.

73. Both Governments acted at certain stages in close co-operation with the Canadian Government. An agreement was reached in 1950 on the setting-up of an independent committee of experts. While the Belgian and Canadian Governments contemplated a committee composed of Belgian, Canadian and Spanish members, the Spanish Government suggested a committee composed of British, Canadian and Spanish members. This was agreed to by the Canadian and United Kingdom Governments, and the task of the committee was, in particular, to establish the monies imported into Spain by Barcelona Traction or any of its subsidiaries, to determine and appraise the materials and services brought into the country, to determine and appraise the amounts withdrawn from Spain by Barcelona Traction or any of its subsidiaries, and to compute the profits earned in Spain by Barcelona Traction or any of its subsidiaries and the amounts susceptible of being withdrawn from the country at 31 December 1949.

74. As to the Belgian Government, its earlier action was also undertaken in close co-operation with the Canadian Government. The Belgian Government admitted the Canadian character of the company in the course of the present proceedings. It explicitly stated that Barcelona Traction was a company of neither Spanish nor Belgian nationality but a Canadian company incorporated in Canada. The Belgian Government has even conceded that it was not concerned with the injury suffered by Barcelona Traction itself, since that was Canada's affair.

75. The Canadian Government itself, which never appears to have doubted its right to intervene on the company's behalf, exercised the protection of Barcelona Traction by diplomatic representation for a number of years, in particular by its note of 27 March 1948, in which it alleged that a denial of justice had been committed in respect of . . . Barcelona Traction . . . , and requested that the bankruptcy judgment be cancelled. It later invoked the Anglo-Spanish treaty of 1922 and the agreement of 1924, which applied to Canada. Further Canadian notes were addressed to the Spanish Government in 1950, 1951 and 1952. Further approaches were made in 1954, and in 1955 the Canadian Government renewed the expression of its deep interest in the affair of Barcelona Traction and its Canadian subsidiaries.

76. In sum, the record shows that from 1948 onwards the Canadian Government made to the Spanish Government numerous representations which cannot be viewed otherwise than as the exercise of diplomatic protection in respect of the Barcelona Traction company. Therefore this was not a case where diplomatic protection was refused or remained in the sphere of fiction. It is also clear that over the whole period of its diplomatic activity the Canadian Government proceeded in full knowledge of the Belgian attitude and activity.

77. It is true that at a certain point the Canadian Government ceased to act on behalf of Barcelona Traction, for reasons which have not been fully revealed, though a statement made in a letter of 19 July 1955 by the Canadian Secretary of State for External Affairs suggests that it felt the matter should be settled by means of private negotiations. The Canadian Government has nonetheless retained its capacity to exercise diplomatic protection; no legal impediment has prevented it from doing so: no fact has arisen to render this protection impossible. It has discontinued its action of its own free will. . . .

83. The Canadian Government's right of protection in respect of the Barcelona Traction company remains unaffected by the present proceedings. The Spanish Government has never challenged the Canadian nationality of the company, either in the diplomatic correspondence with the Canadian Government or before the Court. Moreover it has unreservedly recognized Canada as the national State of Barcelona Traction in both written pleadings and oral statements made in the course of the present proceedings. Consequently, the Court considers that the Spanish Government has not questioned Canada's right to protect the company. . . .

88. It follows from what has already been stated above that, where it is a question of an unlawful act committed against a company representing foreign capital, the general rule of international law authorizes the national State of the company alone to make a claim. . . .

101. For the above reasons, the Court is not of the opinion that, in the particular circumstances of the present case, *jus standi* is conferred on the Belgian Government. . . .

103. Accordingly,

THE COURT

rejects the Belgian Government's claim by fifteen votes to one, twelve votes of the majority being based on the reasons set out in the present Judgment.

Does the Court's extensive examination of the links between the company and Canada in *Barcelona Traction* support the view that corporate nationality depends simply on the place of incorporation or the location of the head office, or does it imply an additional requirement of genuine and effective links between the corporation and the purported state of nationality?

Before leaving this section, reconsider the question posed in the introduction to this section (see Section C(3)(a) above).

4) Passive Personality Principle of Jurisdiction

Like the nationality principle of jurisdiction, the passive personality principle hinges on nationality. Here, however, a state asserts prescriptive jurisdiction not because of the nationality of the person undertaking a particular activity, but because of the nationality of the victim of that activity. Put another way, under the passive personality principle, "jurisdiction is assumed by the state of which the person suffering injury or civil damage is a national."[32]

The passive personality principle as a basis for prescriptive jurisdiction is controversial (unlike the nationality principle), and has not been embraced enthusiastically by countries of the common law tradition. Civil law jurisdictions have, however, been more willing to extend their prescriptive jurisdiction on the basis of the passive personality principle. Consider, for example, the following extract from the German Penal Code:

> *Section 7: Applicability to Acts Abroad in Other Cases*
> (1) German criminal law shall apply to acts, which were committed abroad against a German, if the act is punishable at the place of its commission or the place of its commission is subject to no criminal law enforcement . . . .[33]

Notice the closing language of this provision. What does it suggest in terms of the permissible limits of an assertion of prescriptive jurisdiction on the basis of the passive personality principle?

As another illustration, Canada, in its *Crimes Against Humanity and War Crimes Act*, SC 2000, c 24, also includes a passive personality basis for jurisdiction in relation to crimes of genocide, crimes against humanity and war crimes:

---

32   Shearer, above note 19 at 210.
33   *Penal Code of the Federal Republic of Germany*, 1998, Federal Law Gazette I, s7 at 945 (translation by German Federal Ministry of Justice).

8. A person who is alleged to have committed an offence [covered by the Act] may be prosecuted for that offence if

> (a) at the time the offence is alleged to have been committed . . .
>
> > (iii) the victim of the alleged offence was a Canadian citizen . . . .

Other Canadian *Criminal Code* provisions also extend Canadian criminal jurisdiction to extraterritorial acts where the victim is Canadian.[34] These include sections 7(2.1)(f) (offences against fixed platforms or international maritime navigation); 7(2.31)(a) (offences by crew members of space stations); 7(3.1)(e) (offence of hostage taking); 7(3.7)(d) and 269.1 (offence of torture); and 7(3.73)(g) and 7(3.75)(a) (various terrorism offences). Note that these offences implement Canadian obligations under international crime suppression and anti-terrorism treaties.

5) Protective Principle of Jurisdiction

Pursuant to the protective principle of jurisdiction, "each state may exercise jurisdiction over crimes against its security and integrity or its vital economic interests."[35] One commentator lists the rationale for this source of jurisdiction as follows:

> i. [T]he offences subject to the application of the protective principle are such that their consequences may be of the utmost gravity and concern to the state against which they are directed;
>
> ii. unless the jurisdiction were exercised, many such offences would escape punishment altogether because they did not contravene the law of the place where they were committed (*lex loci delicti*) . . . .[36]

Nearly all states assume jurisdiction over non-nationals for acts committed abroad affecting their security or other vital interests.[37] For example, the Canadian *Criminal Code* extends extraterritorial criminal law jurisdiction in several instances that are suggestive of the protective principle. Thus, without requiring territorial or nationality links (whether of perpetrator or victim), various provisions of section 7 of the *Criminal Code* extend Canadian jurisdiction over hostage taking; offences against UN personnel; offences involving explosives or other lethal devices; and various terrorism offences where these acts are designed to compel a Canadian government to do something or, in some instances, are directed at Canadian government facilities.[38] Note, however, that section 7(7) adds the following caveat: "If the accused is not a Canadian citizen, no proceedings in respect of which courts have jurisdiction by virtue of this section shall be continued unless the consent of the Attorney General of Canada is obtained not later than eight days after the proceedings are commenced." What is the purpose of this provision? What does it suggest about the

---

34 *Criminal Code*, RSC 1985, c C-46, s 7.
35 Shearer, above note 19 at 211.
36 *Ibid* at 212.
37 *Brownlie's Principles*, above note 3 at 462.
38 *Criminal Code*, above note 34, ss 7(3.1)(d), 7(3.71)(f), 7(3.72)(f)–(g), 7(3.73)(e)–(f), and 7(3.75)(b)–(c).

limits imposed by international law on the exercise by states of prescriptive jurisdiction on the basis of the protective principle?

6) Universal Principle of Jurisdiction

The last and perhaps most contentious basis for jurisdiction is known as the universal principle. There are some acts that are of such concern to international law that they are lawfully subject to the prescriptive jurisdiction of *any* state, irrespective of where they may be committed. This underlying rationale was expressed in the following excerpt from the *Eichmann* case:

> *Attorney-General of the Government of Israel v Eichmann* (1961), 36 ILR 5 (Dist Ct Jerusalem)

> 12. The abhorrent crimes defined in this [Israeli] Law [under which Eichmann was charged] are crimes not under Israel law alone. These crimes, which struck at the whole of mankind and shocked the conscience of nations, are grave offences against the law of nations itself (*"delicta juris gentium"*). Therefore, so far from international law negating or limiting the jurisdiction of countries with respect to such crimes, international law is, in the absence of an International Court, in need of the judicial and legislative organs of every country to give effect to its criminal interdictions and to bring the criminals to trial. The jurisdiction to try crimes under international law is *universal*. . . .

> [The Court then engaged in an extensive review of scholarly opinion which supported the proposition that serious international crimes invite universal jurisdiction, at least as long as there is no generally competent international criminal court.]

> 16. We have said that the crimes dealt with in this case are not crimes under Israel[i] law alone, but are in essence offences against the law of nations. Indeed, the crimes in question are not a free creation of the legislator who enacted the Law for the punishment of Nazis and Nazi collaborators, but have been defined in that Law according to a precise pattern of international laws and conventions which define crimes under the law of nations. The "crime against the Jewish people" is defined on the pattern of the crime of genocide defined in the Convention for the Prevention and Punishment of the Crime of Genocide which was adopted by the United Nations Assembly on December 9, 1948. The "crime against humanity" and "war crime" are defined on the pattern of crimes of identical designations defined in the Charter of the International Military Tribunal (which is the Statute of the Nuremberg Court) . . . , and also in Law No. 10 of the Control Council of Germany of December 20, 1945. . . .

> 19. . . . [T]here is no doubt that genocide has been recognized as a crime under international law in the full legal meaning of this term, *ex tunc*; that is to say: the crimes of genocide committed against the Jewish people and other peoples during the period of the Hitler régime were crimes under international law. It follows, therefore, in accordance with the accepted principles of international law, that the jurisdiction to try such crimes is universal. . . .

[The Court continued at length to examine the international legal basis for these crimes. It then considered and dismissed the accused's arguments that he was being prosecuted for retroactively defined crimes, or for "Acts of State" for which only the German state could be responsible.]

39. We should add that the well-known judgment of the Permanent Court of International Justice at The Hague in the "*Lotus Case*" ruled that the principle of territoriality does not limit the power of a State to try crimes and, moreover, that any argument against such power must point to a specific rule in international law which negates that power. We have followed this principle which, so to speak, shifts the "onus of proof" upon him who pleads against jurisdiction, but have preferred to base ourselves on positive reasons for upholding the jurisdiction of the State of Israel.

As one commentator aptly states: "universal jurisdiction is defined by the character of the crime concerned, rather than by the presence of some kind of nexus to the prescribing state."[39] The obvious purpose behind such a permissive basis of jurisdiction is to multiply the chances that the offender's behaviour will be punished, and to address situations where crimes could occur that would otherwise be beyond the jurisdiction of any state. The classic example of behaviour considered to be subject to universal jurisdiction is piracy. Thus, Canada would be within its international legal rights to prosecute, under Canadian law, non-Canadians for piracy committed anywhere on the high seas, regardless of whether the acts of piracy had any effects in Canada or on Canadians. Slavery is another example of behaviour widely considered to be the subject of universal jurisdiction, as are genocide, crimes against humanity, and grave breaches of the laws and customs of war.[40] Torture may also be a crime of universal jurisdiction.[41]

It should be noted that there is a difference between the principle of universal jurisdiction and the treaty obligation to "extradite or prosecute" (*aut dedere aut judicare*), under which states parties must either submit a case for prosecution or extradite a criminal suspect to another state willing to do so.[42] The duty to extradite or prosecute is restricted to parties to treaties containing such an obligation, whereas the universal jurisdiction principle applies to all states. While they are distinct legal concepts, there is a close—though still not clearly defined—relationship between universal jurisdiction and the treaty obli-

---

39 *Brownlie's Principles*, above note 3 at 467.

40 *Ibid* at 468.

41 *Ibid*, although others argue that torture has not yet crystallized as a crime subject to universal jurisdiction in customary international law: Ilias Bantekas, "Criminal Jurisdiction of States under International Law" in Rüdiger Wolfrum, ed, *The Max Planck Encyclopedia of Public International Law*, vol. II (Oxford: Oxford University Press, 2012) at 861–70, para 28.

42 Many multilateral crime suppression treaties contain such an obligation. See International Law Commission, *Survey of multilateral conventions which may be of relevance for the work of the International Law Commission on the topic "The obligation to extradite or prosecute (aut dedere aut judicare)": Study by the Secretariat*, UN Doc A/CN.4/630 (18 June 2010). See also M Cherif Bassiouni & Edward M Wise, *Aut Dedere Aut Judicare: The Duty to Extradite or Prosecute in International Law* (Dordrecht: Martinus Nijhoff, 1995).

gation to extradite or prosecute.[43] It is for this reason that *aut dedere aut judicare* regimes are referred to by some as a form of "quasi universal jurisdiction."[44]

Once it is agreed that a particular crime is subject to universal jurisdiction, it is frequently asserted that the sole connection required between the prosecuting state and the alleged perpetrator is the latter's presence in the territory of the former at the time of prosecution (sometimes referred to as the "presence connection"). An example of this presence connection requirement for the exercise of universal jurisdiction is found in section 8(b) of Canada's *Crimes Against Humanity and War Crimes Act*, SC 2000, c 24:

> 8. A person alleged to have committed an offence [under the Act] may be prosecuted for that offence if:
>
> . . .
>
> (b) after the time the offence is alleged to have been committed, the person is present in Canada.

The presence connection may be considered as largely a practical corollary of the territorial basis of enforcement jurisdiction: while all states' laws may be applicable to a crime subject to universal jurisdiction, only that state with territorial jurisdiction to secure custody of the suspect is in a position to execute any judgment resulting from the exercise of such jurisdiction. Whether it is also a firm requirement for the exercise of prescriptive jurisdiction per se remains a matter of debate, as illustrated in the materials that follow.

Among the most famous examples of laws permitting extraterritorial jurisdiction in relation to serious international crimes is that introduced in 1993 in Belgium, and amended in 1999.[45] Under this law, Belgian courts had jurisdiction to prosecute genocide, crimes against humanity, and war crimes regardless of the place of commission of the crime, the presence of the perpetrator on Belgian territory, the nationality of the perpetrator or the victim, or the date on which the crime was committed. To complain of such a crime, a person did not have to be a Belgian national or resident. This law was amended (again) in 2003, amid some controversy:

Human Rights Watch, "Belgium: Universal Jurisdiction Law Repealed" (2 August 2003)[46]

(Brussels) The Belgian Parliament's repeal of its landmark "universal jurisdiction" statute is a step backwards in the global fight against the worst atrocities, six human rights groups said today . . . .

---

43 The contours of this relationship are a current matter of discussion: *Report of the International Law Commission*, UN GAOR, 67th Sess, Supp No 10 at para 214, UN Doc A/67/10 (2012). The impact of the ICJ's judgment in *Questions Related to the Obligation to Prosecute or Extradite (Belgium v Senegal)*, ICJ General List No 144, 20 July 2012, is also a matter of debate.

44 *Brownlie's Principles*, above note 3 at 469.

45 *Act concerning the Punishment of Grave Breaches of International Humanitarian Law* (Belgium), (1999) 38 ILM 921–25.

46 Online: www.hrw.org/news/2003/08/01/belgium-universal-jurisdiction-law-repealed. See also Luc Reydams, "Belgium Reneges on Universality: The 5 August 2003 Act on Grave Breaches of International Humanitarian Law" (2003) 1 JICJ 679.

Belgium's 1993 universal jurisdiction law, which permitted victims to file complaints in Belgium for atrocities committed abroad, had made Belgium a leader in the struggle for international justice, the groups said. Now, the Belgian law resembles that of other European countries.

"With its universal jurisdiction law, Belgium helped destroy the wall of impunity behind which the world's tyrants had always hidden to shield themselves from justice," said the groups. "It is regrettable that Belgium has now forgotten the victims to whom it gave a hope of justice."

The groups denounced the pressure from the United States which led Belgium to today's action. In June, U.S. Defense Secretary Donald H. Rumsfeld threatened Belgium that it risked losing its status as host to NATO's headquarters if it did not rescind the law. The groups said that the U.S. attack was part of its worldwide campaign against international justice, including the International Criminal Court. The U.S. campaign, as well as the Belgian about-face, go against a growing global trend to hold accountable those accused of the worst crimes, which can be seen in the creation of war crimes tribunals for Rwanda and Yugoslavia, and the International Criminal Court. More than one hundred states have adopted some form of universal jurisdiction, permitting them to pursue the authors of international crimes.

After today, Belgian courts will only have jurisdiction over international crimes if the accused is Belgian or has his primary residence in Belgium; if the victim is Belgian or has lived in Belgium for at least three years at the time the crimes were committed; or if Belgium is required by treaty to exercise jurisdiction over the case. The new law also considerably reduces victims' ability to obtain direct access to the courts—unless the accused is Belgian or has his primary residence in Belgium, the decision whether or not to proceed with any complaint rests entirely with the state prosecutor. Belgium has thus restricted the reach of universal jurisdiction in its courts by adopting a law similar to or more restrictive than most European countries. . . .

Some of the opinions given in the *Arrest Warrant Case* likely influenced Belgium's decision to amend the Act:

Arrest Warrant of 11 April 2000 (Democratic Republic of the Congo v Belgium), Judgment, [2002] ICJ Rep 3

[On 11 April 2000, a Belgian investigating magistrate issued an "international arrest warrant *in absentia*" against Mr. Yerodia, the then foreign affairs minister of the Democratic Republic of the Congo (DRC), alleging that he had committed grave breaches of international humanitarian law and crimes against humanity. Belgium did not claim any connection to the alleged crimes other than a willingness, pursuant to the principle of universal jurisdiction, to prosecute them. The DRC originally claimed that Belgium's actions exceeded the permissible scope of its jurisdiction under international law. However, in its final submissions to the Court, the DRC chose not to pursue that argument, preferring instead to rely on the argument that Belgium's actions violated the sovereign immunity attaching to the acts of its foreign minister. The Court's judgment proceeds on the latter basis. However, a number of judges appended separate opinions addressing the question whether Belgium's actions were consistent with international legal principles of prescriptive jurisdiction, as illustrated in the following excerpts.]

SEPARATE OPINION OF PRESIDENT GUILLAUME:

1. I fully subscribe to the Judgment rendered by the Court. I believe it useful however to set out my position on one question which the Judgment has not addressed: whether the Belgian judge had jurisdiction to issue an international arrest warrant against Mr. Yerodia Ndombasi on 11 April 2000. . . . [T]his is an important and controversial issue, clarification of which would have been in the interest of all States, including Belgium in particular. I believe it worthwhile to provide such clarification here.

2. The Belgian Law of 16 June 1993, as amended by the Law of 10 February 1999, aims at punishing serious violations of international humanitarian law. It covers certain violations of the Geneva Conventions of 12 August 1949 and of Protocols I and II of 8 June 1977 additional to those Conventions. It also extends to crimes against humanity, which it defines in the terms used in the Rome Convention of 17 July 1998. Article 7 of the Law adds that "[t]he Belgian courts shall have jurisdiction in respect of the offences provided for in the present Law, wheresoever they may have been committed."

3. The disputed arrest warrant accuses Mr. Yerodia of grave breaches of the Geneva Conventions and of crimes against humanity. It states that under Article 7 of the Law of 16 June 1993, as amended, perpetrators of those offences "fall under the jurisdiction of the Belgian courts, regardless of their nationality or that of the victims." It adds that "the Belgian courts have jurisdiction even if the accused (Belgian or foreign) is not found in Belgium." . . . It concludes on these bases that the Belgian courts have jurisdiction.

4. In order to assess the validity of this reasoning, the fundamental principles of international law governing States' exercise of their criminal jurisdiction should first be reviewed.

The primary aim of the criminal law is to enable punishment in each country of offences committed in the national territory. That territory is where evidence of the offence can most often be gathered. That is where the offence generally produces its effects. Finally, that is where the punishment imposed can most naturally serve as an example. Thus, the Permanent Court of International Justice observed as far back as 1927 that "in all systems of law the principle of the territorial character of criminal law is fundamental."

The question has, however, always remained open whether States other than the territorial State have concurrent jurisdiction to prosecute offenders. A wide debate on this subject began as early as the foundation in Europe of the major modern States. Some writers, like Covarruvias and Grotius, pointed out that the presence on the territory of a State of a foreign criminal peacefully enjoying the fruits of his crimes was intolerable. They therefore maintained that it should be possible to prosecute perpetrators of certain particularly serious crimes not only in the State on whose territory the crime was committed but also in the country where they sought refuge. In their view, that country was under an obligation to arrest, followed by extradition or prosecution, in accordance with the maxim *aut dedere, aut judicare*.

Beginning in the eighteenth century however, this school of thought favouring universal punishment was challenged by another body of opinion, one opposed to such punishment and exemplified notably by Montesquieu, Voltaire and Jean-Jacques Rousseau. Their views found expression in terms of criminal law in the works of Beccaria, who stated in 1764 that "judges are not the avengers of humankind in general . . . A crime is punishable only in the country where it was committed."

Enlightenment philosophy inspired the lawmakers of the Revolution and nineteenth century law. Some went so far as to push the underlying logic to its conclusion, and in 1831 Martens could assert that "the lawmaker's power [extends] over all persons and property present in the State" and that "the law does not extend over other States and their subjects." A century later, Max Huber echoed that assertion when he stated in 1928, in the Award in the *Island of Palmas* case, that a State has "exclusive competence in regard to its own territory."

In practice, the principle of territorial sovereignty did not permit of any exception in respect of coercive action [i.e., enforcement jurisdiction], but that was not the case in regard to legislative and judicial jurisdiction. In particular, classic international law does not exclude a State's power in some cases to exercise its judicial jurisdiction over offences committed abroad. But as the Permanent Court stated, once again in the "*Lotus*" case, the exercise of that jurisdiction is not without its limits. Under the law as classically formulated, a State normally has jurisdiction over an offence committed abroad only if the offender, or at the very least the victim, has the nationality of that State or if the crime threatens its internal or external security. Ordinarily, States are without jurisdiction over crimes committed abroad as between foreigners.

5. Traditionally, customary international law did, however, recognize one case of universal jurisdiction, that of piracy. . . . [U]niversal jurisdiction is accepted in cases of piracy because piracy is carried out on the high seas, outside all State territory. However, even on the high seas, classic international law is highly restrictive, for it recognizes universal jurisdiction only in cases of piracy and not of other comparable crimes which might also be committed outside the jurisdiction of coastal States, such as trafficking in slaves or in narcotic drugs or psychotropic substances.

6. The drawbacks of this approach became clear at the beginning of the twentieth century in respect of currency counterfeiting, and the Convention of 20 April 1929, prepared within the League of Nations, marked a certain development in this regard. That Convention enabled States to extend their criminal legislation to counterfeiting crimes involving foreign currency. It added that "[f]oreigners who have committed abroad" any offence referred to in the Convention "and who are in the territory of a country whose internal legislation recognises as a general rule the principle of the prosecution of offences committed abroad, should be punishable in the same way as if the offence had been committed in the territory of that country." But it made that obligation subject to various conditions.

A similar approach was taken by the Single Convention on Narcotic Drugs of 30 March 1961 and by the United Nations Convention on Psychotropic Substances of 21 February 1971, both of which make certain provisions subject to "the constitutional limitations of a Party, its legal system and domestic law." There is no provision governing the jurisdiction of national courts in any of these conventions, or for that matter in the Geneva Conventions of 1949.

7. A further step was taken in this direction beginning in 1970 in connection with the fight against international terrorism. To that end, States established a novel mechanism: compulsory, albeit subsidiary, universal jurisdiction.

This fundamental innovation was effected by The Hague Convention for the Suppression of Unlawful Seizure of Aircraft of 16 December 1970. The Convention places an obligation on the State in whose territory the perpetrator of the crime takes refuge to extradite or prosecute him. But this would have been insufficient if the Convention had not at the same time placed the States parties under an obligation to establish their jurisdiction for that purpose. Thus, Article 4, paragraph 2, of the Convention provides:

> Each Contracting State shall . . . take such measures as may be necessary to establish its jurisdiction over the offence in the case where the alleged offender is present in its territory and it does not extradite him pursuant to [the Convention].

This provision marked a turning point, of which The Hague Conference was moreover conscious. From then on, the obligation to prosecute was no longer conditional on the existence of jurisdiction, but rather jurisdiction itself had to be established in order to make prosecution possible.

8. The system as thus adopted was repeated with some minor variations in a large number of conventions. . . .

9. Thus, a system corresponding to the doctrines espoused long ago by Grotius was set up by treaty. Whenever the perpetrator of any of the offences covered by these conventions is found in the territory of a State, that State is under an obligation to arrest him, and then extradite or prosecute. It must have first conferred jurisdiction on its courts to try him if he is not extradited. Thus, universal punishment of the offences in question is assured, as the perpetrators are denied refuge in all States.

By contrast, none of these texts has contemplated establishing jurisdiction over offences committed abroad by foreigners against foreigners when the perpetrator is not present in the territory of the State in question. Universal jurisdiction *in absentia* is unknown to international conventional law.

10. Thus, in the absence of conventional provisions, Belgium, both in its written Memorial and in oral argument, relies essentially on this point on international customary law.

11. In this connection, Belgium cites the development of international criminal courts. But this development was precisely in order to provide a remedy for the deficiencies of national courts, and the rules governing the jurisdiction of international courts as laid down by treaty or by the Security Council of course have no effect upon the jurisdiction of national courts.

12. Hence, Belgium essentially seeks to justify its position by relying on the practice of States and their *opinio juris*. However, the national legislation and jurisprudence cited in the case file do not support the Belgian argument. . . . [T]he only country whose legislation and jurisprudence appear clearly to go the other way is the State of Israel, which in this field obviously constitutes a very special case.

To conclude, I cannot do better than quote what Lord Slynn of Hadley had to say on this point in the first *Pinochet* case:

> It does not seem . . . that it has been shown that there is any State practice or general consensus let alone a widely supported convention that all crimes against international law should be justiciable in National Courts on the basis of the universality of jurisdiction. . . . . That international law crimes should be tried before international tribunals or in the perpetrator's own state is one thing; that they should be impleaded without regard to a long established customary international law rule in the Courts of other states is another. . . . The fact even that an act is recognised as a crime under international law does not mean that the Courts of all States have jurisdiction to try it. . . . There is no universality of jurisdiction for crimes against international law. . . .

In other words, international law knows only one true case of universal jurisdiction: piracy. Further, a number of international conventions provide for the establishment of subsidiary universal jurisdiction for purposes of the trial of certain offenders arrested on national territory and not extradited to a foreign country. Universal jurisdiction *in absentia* as applied in the present case is unknown to international law.

13. Having found that neither treaty law nor international customary law provide a State with the possibility of conferring universal jurisdiction on its courts where the author of the offence is not present on its territory, Belgium contends lastly that, even in the absence of any treaty or custom to this effect, it enjoyed total freedom of action. To this end it cites from the Judgment of the Permanent Court of International Justice in the *"Lotus"* case. . . . Hence, so Belgium claimed, in the absence of any prohibitive rule it was entitled to confer upon itself a universal jurisdiction *in absentia*.

14. This argument is hardly persuasive. Indeed the Permanent Court itself, having laid down the general principle cited by Belgium, then asked itself "whether the foregoing considerations really apply as regards criminal jurisdiction." It held that either this might be the case, or alternatively, that: "the exclusively territorial character of law relating to this domain constitutes a principle which, except as otherwise expressly provided, would, *ipso facto*, prevent States from extending the criminal jurisdiction of their courts beyond their frontiers." In the particular case before it, the Permanent Court took the view that it was unnecessary to decide the point. Given that the case involved the collision of a French vessel with a Turkish vessel, the Court confined itself to noting that the effects of the offence in question had made themselves felt on Turkish territory, and that consequently a criminal prosecution might "be justified from the point of view of this so-called territorial principle."

15. The absence of a decision by the Permanent Court on the point was understandable in 1927, given the sparse treaty law at that time. The situation is different today, it seems to me—totally different. The adoption of the United Nations Charter proclaiming the sovereign equality of States, and the appearance on the international scene of new States, born of decolonization, have strengthened the territorial principle. International criminal law has itself undergone considerable development and constitutes today an impressive legal *corpus*. It recognizes in many situations the possibility, or indeed the obligation, for a State other than that on whose territory the offence was committed to confer jurisdiction on its courts to prosecute the authors of certain crimes where they are present on its territory. International criminal courts have been created. But at no

time has it been envisaged that jurisdiction should be conferred upon the courts of every State in the world to prosecute such crimes, whoever their authors and victims and irrespective of the place where the offender is to be found. To do this would, moreover, risk creating total judicial chaos. It would also be to encourage the arbitrary for the benefit of the powerful, purportedly acting as agent for an ill-defined "international community." Contrary to what is advocated by certain publicists, such a development would represent not an advance in the law but a step backward.

16. States primarily exercise their criminal jurisdiction on their own territory. In classic international law, they normally have jurisdiction in respect of an offence committed abroad only if the offender, or at least the victim, is of their nationality, or if the crime threatens their internal or external security. Additionally, they may exercise jurisdiction in cases of piracy and in the situations of subsidiary universal jurisdiction provided for by various conventions if the offender is present on their territory. But apart from these cases, international law does not accept universal jurisdiction; still less does it accept universal jurisdiction *in absentia*. . . .

JOINT SEPARATE OPINION OF JUDGES HIGGINS, KOOIJMANS AND BUERGENTHAL:

. . . 2. In its Judgment the Court says nothing on the question of whether — quite apart from the status of Mr. Yerodia at the relevant time — the Belgian magistracy was entitled under international law to issue an arrest warrant for someone not at that time within its territory . . .

3. In our opinion it was not only desirable, but indeed necessary, that the Court should have stated its position on this issue of jurisdiction. . . .

19. We therefore turn to the question whether States are entitled to exercise jurisdiction over persons having no connection with the forum State when the accused is not present in the State's territory. . . .

20. Our analysis may begin with national legislation, to see if it evidences a State practice. Save for the Belgian legislation of 10 February 1999, national legislation, whether in fulfilment of international treaty obligations to make certain international crimes offences also in national law, or otherwise, does not suggest a universal jurisdiction over these offences. Various examples typify the more qualified practice. . . .

21. All of these illustrate the trend to provide for the trial and punishment under international law of certain crimes that have been committed extraterritorially. But none of them, nor the many others that have been studied by the Court, represent a classical assertion of a universal jurisdiction over particular offences committed elsewhere by persons having no relationship or connection with the forum State.

22. The case law under these provisions has largely been cautious so far as reliance on universal jurisdiction is concerned. . . .

25. An even more ambiguous answer is to be derived from a study of the provisions of certain important treaties of the last 30 years, and the obligations imposed by the parties themselves.

26. In some of the literature on the subject it is asserted that the great international treaties on crimes and offences evidence universality as a ground for the exercise of jurisdiction recognized in international law. . . . This is doubtful. . . . [The treaties are then reviewed.]

40. This short historical survey may be summarized as follows:

41. The parties to these treaties agreed both to grounds of jurisdiction and as to the obligation to take the measures necessary to establish such jurisdiction. The specified grounds relied on links of nationality of the offender, or the ship or aircraft concerned, or of the victim. . . . These may properly be described as treaty-based broad extraterritorial jurisdiction. But in addition to these were the parallel provisions whereby a State party in whose jurisdiction the alleged perpetrator of such offences is found, shall prosecute him or extradite him. By the loose use of language the latter has come to be referred to as "universal jurisdiction," though this is really an obligatory territorial jurisdiction over persons, albeit in relation to acts committed elsewhere. . . .

44. . . . The assertion that certain treaties and court decisions rely on universal jurisdiction, which in fact they do not, does not evidence an international practice recognized as custom. . . .

45. That there is no established practice in which States exercise universal jurisdiction, properly so called, is undeniable. As we have seen, virtually all national legislation envisages links of some sort to the forum State; and no case law exists in which pure universal jurisdiction has formed the basis of jurisdiction. This does not necessarily indicate, however, that such an exercise would be unlawful. In the first place, national legislation reflects the circumstances in which a State provides in its own law the ability to exercise jurisdiction. But a State is not required to legislate up to the full scope of the jurisdiction allowed by international law. . . . Moreover, while none of the national case law to which we have referred happens to be based on the exercise of a universal jurisdiction properly so called, there is equally nothing in this case law which evidences an *opinio juris* on the illegality of such a jurisdiction. In short, national legislation and case law—that is, State practice—is neutral as to exercise of universal jurisdiction.

46. There are, moreover, certain indications that a universal criminal jurisdiction for certain international crimes is clearly not regarded as unlawful. The duty to prosecute under those treaties which contain the *aut dedere aut prosequi* provisions opens the door to a jurisdiction based on the heinous nature of the crime rather than on links of territoriality or nationality (whether as perpetrator or victim). . . .

47. The contemporary trends, reflecting international relations as they stand at the beginning of the new century, are striking. The movement is towards bases of jurisdiction other than territoriality. "Effects" or "impact" jurisdiction is embraced both by the United States and, with certain qualifications, by the European Union. Passive personality jurisdiction, for so long regarded as controversial, is now reflected not only in the legislation of various countries . . . , [but] today meets with relatively little opposition, at least so far as a particular category of offences is concerned.

48. In civil matters we already see the beginnings of a very broad form of extraterritorial jurisdiction. Under the *Alien Torts Claim Act*, the United States, basing itself on a law

of 1789, has asserted a jurisdiction both over human rights violations and over major violations of international law, perpetrated by non-nationals overseas. Such jurisdiction, with the possibility of ordering payment of damages, has been exercised with respect to torture committed in a variety of countries (Paraguay, Chile, Argentina, Guatemala), and with respect to other major human rights violations in yet other countries. While this unilateral exercise of the function of guardian of international values has been much commented on, it has not attracted the approbation of States generally.

51. . . . At the same time, the international consensus that the perpetrators of international crimes should not go unpunished is being advanced by a flexible strategy, in which newly established international criminal tribunals, treaty obligations and national courts all have their part to play. We reject the suggestion that the battle against impunity is "made over" to international treaties and tribunals, with national courts having no competence in such matters. Great care has been taken when formulating the relevant treaty provisions not to exclude other grounds of jurisdiction that may be exercised on a voluntary basis. . . .

52. We may thus agree with the authors of *Oppenheim's International Law*, 9th Edition, at page 998, that:

> While no general rule of positive international law can as yet be asserted which gives to states the right to punish foreign nationals for crimes against humanity in the same way as they are, for instance, entitled to punish acts of piracy, there are clear indications pointing to the gradual evolution of a significant principle of international law to that effect.

53. This brings us once more to the particular point that divides the Parties in this case: is it a precondition of the assertion of universal jurisdiction that the accused be within the territory?

54. . . . The fact that in the past the only clear example of an agreed exercise of universal jurisdiction was in respect of piracy, *outside of any territorial jurisdiction*, is not determinative. The only prohibitive rule (repeated by the Permanent Court in the "*Lotus*" case) is that criminal jurisdiction should not be exercised, without permission, within the territory of another State. The Belgian arrest warrant envisaged the arrest of Mr. Yerodia in Belgium, or the possibility of his arrest in third States at the discretion of the States concerned. This would in principle seem to violate no existing prohibiting rule of international law. . . .

58. If the underlying purpose of designating certain acts as international crimes is to authorize a wide jurisdiction to be asserted over persons committing them, there is no rule of international law (and certainly not the *aut dedere* principle) which makes illegal co-operative overt acts designed to secure their presence within a State wishing to exercise jurisdiction.

59. If, as we believe to be the case, a State may choose to exercise a universal criminal jurisdiction *in absentia*, it must also ensure that certain safeguards are in place. They are absolutely essential to prevent abuse and to ensure that the rejection of impunity does not jeopardize stable relations between States.

No exercise of criminal jurisdiction may occur which fails to respect the inviolability or infringes the immunities of the person concerned. . . .

A State contemplating bringing criminal charges based on universal jurisdiction must first offer to the national State of the prospective accused person the opportunity itself to act upon the charges concerned. . . .

Further, such charges may only be laid by a prosecutor or juge d'instruction who acts in full independence, without links to or control by the government of that State. Moreover, the desired equilibrium between the battle against impunity and the promotion of good inter-State relations will only be maintained if there are some special circumstances that do require the exercise of an international criminal jurisdiction and if this has been brought to the attention of the prosecutor or juge d'instruction. For example, persons related to the victims of the case will have requested the commencement of legal proceedings.

60. It is equally necessary that universal criminal jurisdiction be exercised only over those crimes regarded as the most heinous by the international community. . . .

65. It would seem (without in any way pronouncing upon whether Mr. Yerodia did or did not perform the acts with which he is charged in the warrant) that the acts . . . do fall within the concept of "crimes against humanity" and would be within that small category in respect of which an exercise of universal jurisdiction is not precluded under international law. . . .

Consider the fundamentally different analytical approaches taken by President Guillaume, on the one hand, and Judges Higgins, Kooijmans, and Buergenthal on the other, when considering the existence and scope of the universal principle of jurisdiction. The former appears to require evidence that international law positively *permits* the exercise of universal jurisdiction, whereas the latter focus on whether any such exercise of jurisdiction is *precluded* by international law. What is the practical significance of this difference of approach in an area where state practice and *opinio juris* may be inconclusive or contested? Which approach is more consistent with the views expressed by the Permanent Court of International Justice when considering the extent of states' prescriptive jurisdiction in the *Lotus Case?*

What advantages and disadvantages are inherent in the exercise of universal jurisdiction? Are some of these advantages and dangers also inherent in other controversial bases of jurisdiction, such as the passive personality principle?

PART III

CONSTRAINTS ON STATE JURISDICTION

INTRODUCTION

In Part II, we explored various international legal doctrines that depict the jurisdiction—essentially, the legalized power—enjoyed by states over territory, persons, conduct, and events. For the most part, those doctrines flow from, and give practical expression to, the somewhat abstract notion of state sovereignty and its corollaries. Perhaps not surprisingly, therefore, they are also essentially descriptive and permissive: they essentially describe the assumed freedoms, powers, and international legal entitlements that attach to states by virtue of their statehood. Recall the starting premise of the Permanent Court of International Justice in the *Lotus* case[1]: that states, as sovereign entities, are assumed to be free to do as they please unless and until a rule of international law limiting their assumed freedom of action is established.

It has become fashionable among some international lawyers to deny the *Lotus* premise, or at least to dismiss it as obsolete in modern international law. According to this view, international law has progressed to the point where it can no longer merely be considered a source of limitations on the inherent freedoms of states; rather, it is the source of both restrictions on *and entitlements of* states. To the extent that this means that international law has rules defining such entitlements, it is undoubtedly true but also hardly a new state of affairs: since its earliest beginnings, international law has sought to give legal expression to both the legal obligations and rights of states. If, however, this view is meant to suggest that states *only* have those powers and capacities that are *positively granted to them* by international law, it is more problematic. Such a position would be inconsistent with the fact that international legal disputes between states are almost never framed and resolved on the assumption that a state's actions are unlawful until a positive source of legal authority for those actions can be established. Quite the contrary: a state's conduct is invariably assumed to be lawful until an applicable legal duty or obligation—a constraint—can be identified which that state has breached.[2]

There is, nevertheless, another sense in which the *Lotus* premise can more defensibly be considered obsolete. In the *Lotus* framework, state freedom is the rule, and restrictions on that freedom are the exceptions. In the eighty or so years since the *Lotus* case was decided, international law has undergone explosive growth, and the great preponderance of this growth has been in the number and extent of legal limitations imposed upon states. As a result, there is today a vast body of international law, in many different subject

---

1   *Case of the SS Lotus (France v Turkey)* (1927), PCIJ (Ser A) No 10.
2   See, for example, *Accordance with International Law of the Unilateral Declaration of Independence in Respect of Kosovo*, Advisory Opinion, [2010] ICJ Rep 403 at para 56.

areas, that significantly narrows a state's powers in relation to persons, conduct, events, and even territory. In this quantitative sense, therefore, the limitations on state jurisdiction have become the rule whereas the freedom of states has become the exception.

It is to the most important of the rules of international law that limit or constrain state jurisdiction — in the broad sense of state power — that we devote this Part. Some of these limiting rules, such as those relating to diplomatic and state immunities, are virtually logical necessities in a world with many equally sovereign states. Others, however, such as those related to human rights, trade, and environmental regimes, represent genuine exercises in "self-denial" by states; that is, they exist not as a matter of logical or structural necessity dictated by the nature and composition of the international legal system, but rather as a result of the voluntary assumption by states of substantive and substantial limitations on their sovereignty. When reviewing these materials, consider the driving factors and circumstances that gave rise to such legal rules and compare the overall robustness of these various legal regimes.

CHAPTER 8

JURISDICTIONAL IMMUNITIES

In Chapter 7, we examined the international legal bases upon which states assert jurisdiction over persons, property, and transactions by applying their domestic law (in the case of prescriptive jurisdiction) or law enforcement (in the case of enforcement jurisdiction). In this chapter, we discuss two distinct but related areas of international law that significantly curtail the extent to which either form of jurisdiction may be exercised by a state, even within its own territory, against foreign state representatives and states themselves: diplomatic immunities and state immunities.

A. DIPLOMATIC IMMUNITIES

A state's ability to exercise its jurisdiction over foreign diplomats within its territory is very limited as a result of a number of strong jurisdictional immunities enjoyed by such diplomats. There is a practical reason for this. Consider the justification for diplomatic immunities, as described by the US Supreme Court:

> [P]rotecting foreign emissaries has a long history and noble purpose. . . The need to protect diplomats is grounded in our Nation's important interest in international relations. As a leading commentator observed in 1844, "it is necessary that nations should treat and hold intercourse together, in order to promote their interests, — to avoid injuring each other, — and to adjust and terminate their disputes." E. Vattel, *The Law of Nations* 452 (J. Chitty ed. 1844). This observation is even more true today given the global nature of the economy and the extent to which actions in other parts of the world affect our own national security. Diplomatic personnel are essential to conduct the international affairs so crucial to the well-being of this Nation. In addition, in light of the concept of reciprocity that governs much of international law in this area . . . we have a more parochial reason to protect foreign diplomats in this country. Doing so ensures that similar protections will be accorded those that we send abroad to represent the United States, and thus serves our national interest in protecting our own citizens. Recent history is replete with attempts, some unfortunately successful, to harass and harm our ambassadors and other diplomatic officials. These underlying purposes combine to make our national interest in protecting diplomatic personnel powerful indeed.[1]

---

1   *Boos v Barry*, 485 US 312 at 323 (1988).

What is the exact scope of these diplomatic immunities? Consider the key provisions of the Vienna Convention on Diplomatic Relations of 1961,[2] which has attracted near universal ratification,[3] but is also widely regarded as a codification of long-standing rules of customary international law. Note that the Vienna Convention on Consular Relations of 1963,[4] discussed later in these materials, contains similar, albeit somewhat less robust, protections for consular officials (for example, those who deal with passports and visas).

Vienna Convention on Diplomatic Relations, 18 April 1961, 500 UNTS 95, in force 24 April 1964

The States Parties to the present Convention,

Recalling that peoples of all nations from ancient times have recognized the status of diplomatic agents,

Having in mind the purposes and principles of the Charter of the United Nations concerning the sovereign equality of States, the maintenance of international peace and security, and the promotion of friendly relations among nations, ...

Realizing that the purpose of such privileges and immunities is not to benefit individuals but to ensure the efficient performance of the functions of diplomatic missions as representing States . . . .

Have agreed as follows: . . . .

Article 2

The establishment of diplomatic relations between States, and of permanent diplomatic missions, takes place by mutual consent.

Article 3

1. The functions of a diplomatic mission consist, *inter alia*, in:

(a) Representing the sending State in the receiving State;
(b) Protecting in the receiving State the interests of the sending State and of its nationals, within the limits permitted by international law;
(c) Negotiating with the Government of the receiving State;
(d) Ascertaining by all lawful means conditions and developments in the receiving State, and reporting thereon to the Government of the sending State;
(e) Promoting friendly relations between the sending State and the receiving State, and developing their economic, cultural and scientific relations.

2. Nothing in the present Convention shall be construed as preventing the performance of consular functions by a diplomatic mission . . . .

Article 9

1. The receiving State may at any time and without having to explain its decision, notify the sending State that the head of the mission or any member of the diplomatic staff of

---

2 Vienna Convention on Diplomatic Relations, 18 April 1961, 500 UNTS 95, Can TS 1966 No 29, in force 24 April 1964.
3 189 parties as of July 2013.
4 Vienna Convention on Consular Relations, 24 April 1963, 596 UNTS 261, Can TS 1974 No 25, in force 19 March 1967 (176 parties as of July 2013).

the mission is *persona non grata* or that any other member of the staff of the mission is not acceptable. In any such case, the sending State shall, as appropriate, either recall the person concerned or terminate his functions with the mission. A person may be declared *non grata* or not acceptable before arriving in the territory of the receiving State.

2. If the sending State refuses or fails within a reasonable period to carry out its obligations under paragraph 1 of this Article, the receiving State may refuse to recognize the person concerned as a member of the mission . . . .

Article 22

1. The premises of the mission shall be inviolable. The agents of the receiving State may not enter them, except with the consent of the head of the mission.

2. The receiving State is under a special duty to take all appropriate steps to protect the premises of the mission against any intrusion or damage and to prevent any disturbance of the peace of the mission or impairment of its dignity.

3. The premises of the mission, their furnishings and other property thereon and the means of transport of the mission shall be immune from search, requisition, attachment or execution.

Article 23

1. The sending State and the head of the mission shall be exempt from all national, regional or municipal dues and taxes in respect of the premises of the mission, whether owned or leased, other than such as represent payment for specific services rendered . . . .

Article 24

The archives and documents of the mission shall be inviolable at any time and wherever they may be . . . .

Article 25

The receiving State shall accord full facilities for the performance of the functions of the mission.

Article 26

Subject to its laws and regulations concerning zones entry into which is prohibited or regulated for reasons of national security, the receiving State shall ensure to all members of the mission freedom of movement and travel in its territory.

Article 27

1. The receiving State shall permit and protect free communication on the part of the mission for all official purposes. In communicating with the Government and the other missions and consulates of the sending State, wherever situated, the mission may employ all appropriate means, including diplomatic couriers and messages in code or cipher. However, the mission may install and use a wireless transmitter only with the consent of the receiving State.

2. The official correspondence of the mission shall be inviolable. Official correspondence means all correspondence relating to the mission and its functions.

3. The diplomatic bag shall not be opened or detained.

. . . 5. The diplomatic courier, who shall be provided with an official document indicating his status and the number of packages constituting the diplomatic bag, shall be protected by the receiving State in the performance of his functions. He shall enjoy personal inviolability and shall not be liable to any form of arrest or detention . . . .

Article 29

The person of a diplomatic agent shall be inviolable. He shall not be liable to any form of arrest or detention. The receiving State shall treat him with due respect and shall take all appropriate steps to prevent any attack on his person, freedom or dignity.

Article 30

1. The private residence of a diplomatic agent shall enjoy the same inviolability and protection as the premises of the mission.

2. His papers, correspondence and, except as provided in paragraph 3 of Article 31, his property, shall likewise enjoy inviolability.

Article 31

1. A diplomatic agent shall enjoy immunity from the criminal jurisdiction of the receiving State. He shall also enjoy immunity from its civil and administrative jurisdiction, except in the case of:

(a) a real action relating to private immovable property situated in the territory of the receiving State, unless he holds it on behalf of the sending State for the purposes of the mission;

(b) an action relating to succession in which the diplomatic agent is involved as executor, administrator, heir or legatee as a private person and not on behalf of the sending State;

(c) an action relating to any professional or commercial activity exercised by the diplomatic agent in the receiving State outside his official functions.

2. A diplomatic agent is not obliged to give evidence as a witness.

3. No measures of execution may be taken in respect of a diplomatic agent except in the cases coming under sub-paragraphs (a), (b) and (c) of paragraph 1 of this Article, and provided that the measures concerned can be taken without infringing the inviolability of his person or of his residence.

4. The immunity of a diplomatic agent from the jurisdiction of the receiving State does not exempt him from the jurisdiction of the sending State.

Article 32

1. The immunity from jurisdiction of diplomatic agents and of persons enjoying immunity under Article 37 may be waived by the sending State.

2. Waiver must always be express.

3. The initiation of proceedings by a diplomatic agent or by a person enjoying immunity from jurisdiction under Article 37 shall preclude him from invoking immunity from jurisdiction in respect of any counter-claim directly connected with the principal claim.

4. Waiver of immunity from jurisdiction in respect of civil or administrative proceedings shall not be held to imply waiver of immunity in respect of the execution of the judgement, for which a separate waiver shall be necessary . . . .

Article 34

A diplomatic agent shall be exempt from all dues and taxes, personal or real, national, regional or municipal, except:

(a) indirect taxes of a kind which are normally incorporated in the price of goods or services;

(b) dues and taxes on private immovable property situated in the territory of the receiving State, unless he holds it on behalf of the sending State for the purposes of the mission;

(c) estate, succession or inheritance duties levied by the receiving State, subject to the provisions of paragraph 4 of Article 39;

(d) dues and taxes on private income having its source in the receiving State and capital taxes on investments made in commercial undertakings in the receiving State;

(e) charges levied for specific services rendered;

(f) registration, court or record fees, mortgage dues and stamp duty, with respect to immovable property, subject to the provisions of Article 23.

Article 35
The receiving State shall exempt diplomatic agents from all personal services, from all public service of any kind whatsoever, and from military obligations such as those connected with requisitioning, military contributions and billeting.

Article 36
1. The receiving State shall, in accordance with such laws and regulations as it may adopt, permit entry of and grant exemption from all customs duties, taxes, and related charges other than charges for storage, cartage and similar services, on:

(a) articles for the official use of the mission;

(b) articles for the personal use of a diplomatic agent or members of his family forming part of his household, including articles intended for his establishment.

2. The personal baggage of a diplomatic agent shall be exempt from inspection, unless there are serious grounds for presuming that it contains articles not covered by the exemptions mentioned in paragraph 1 of this Article, or articles the import or export of which is prohibited by the law or controlled by the quarantine regulations of the receiving State. Such inspection shall be conducted only in the presence of the diplomatic agent or of his authorized representative.

Article 37
1. The members of the family of a diplomatic agent forming part of his household shall, if they are not nationals of the receiving State, enjoy the privileges and immunities specified in Articles 29 to 36 . . . .

Article 39
1. Every person entitled to privileges and immunities shall enjoy them from the moment he enters the territory of the receiving State on proceeding to take up his post or, if already in its territory, from the moment when his appointment is notified to the Ministry for Foreign Affairs or such other ministry as may be agreed.

2. When the functions of a person enjoying privileges and immunities have come to an end, such privileges and immunities shall normally cease at the moment when he leaves the country, or on expiry of a reasonable period in which to do so, but shall subsist until that time, even in case of armed conflict. However, with respect to acts performed

by such a person in the exercise of his functions as a member of the mission, immunity shall continue to subsist.

3. In case of the death of a member of the mission, the members of his family shall continue to enjoy the privileges and immunities to which they are entitled until the expiry of a reasonable period in which to leave the country . . . .

Article 41

1. Without prejudice to their privileges and immunities, it is the duty of all persons enjoying such privileges and immunities to respect the laws and regulations of the receiving State. They also have a duty not to interfere in the internal affairs of that State . . . .

3. The premises of the mission must not be used in any manner incompatible with the functions of the mission as laid down in the present Convention or by other rules of general international law or by any special agreements in force between the sending and the receiving State . . . .

Article 43

The function of a diplomatic agent comes to an end, *inter alia*:

. . .

(b) on notification by the receiving State to the sending State that, in accordance with paragraph 2 of Article 9, it refuses to recognize the diplomatic agent as a member of the mission.

Article 44

The receiving State must, even in case of armed conflict, grant facilities in order to enable persons enjoying privileges and immunities, other than nationals of the receiving State, and members of the families of such persons irrespective of their nationality, to leave at the earliest possible moment. It must, in particular, in case of need, place at their disposal the necessary means of transport for themselves and their property.

Article 45

If diplomatic relations are broken off between two States, or if a mission is permanently or temporarily recalled:

(a) the receiving State must, even in case of armed conflict, respect and protect the premises of the mission, together with its property and archives;

(b) the sending State may entrust the custody of the premises of the mission, together with its property and archives, to a third State acceptable to the receiving State;

(c) the sending State may entrust the protection of its interests and those of its nationals to a third State acceptable to the receiving State.

In considering the potency of diplomatic immunities and the extensive limitations they place on the exercise of host state jurisdiction, note the consensual basis for the establishment of diplomatic relations and the reception of foreign diplomatic staff.[5]

For most practical purposes, a foreign diplomat is immune from application of the receiving state's laws, including most forms of local taxation. Does this mean, in effect, that

---

5 Note too that, in Canada, the decision to declare a foreign diplomat *persona non grata* is not justiciable: *Copello v Canada (Minister of Foreign Affairs)*, 2003 FCA 295.

a foreign diplomat is not subject to local law? Consider Article 41(1) as well as the waiver provisions of Article 32, and reflect upon the distinction between immunity from, and absence of, jurisdiction. What is the distinction between a diplomat's personal "inviolability," provided for in Article 29, and her "immunity from jurisdiction," provided for in Article 31?

Article 31(4) and, to a lesser extent, Article 32 suggest that the sending state has an important role to play in ensuring that diplomatic envoys do not abuse the immunities conferred upon them by international law. What recourse is left to the receiving state if it is not satisfied with the steps taken by the sending state in this regard? Assuming a sending state fails to recall, within a reasonable period, a diplomat who has been declared *persona non grata* by the receiving state, do the Convention's inviolability or immunity provisions continue to constrain the receiving state's jurisdiction over him? Consider the implications of Articles 9(2) and 43(b).

Many of the provisions of the Vienna Convention on Diplomatic Relations (and of the Vienna Convention on Consular Relations) are expressly incorporated into Canadian law by the following enactment:

Foreign Missions and International Organizations Act, SC 1991, c 41

. . . 2. (2) The expression . . . "reasonable period" in paragraph 2 of Article 9 of the Vienna Convention on Diplomatic Relations . . . shall be read as a reference to a period, not exceeding ten days, commencing on the day on which notice is given that a person is *persona non grata* or not acceptable . . . .

3. (1) Articles, 1, 22 to 24 and 27 to 40 of the Vienna Convention on Diplomatic Relations, and Articles 1, 5, 15, 17, 31 to 33, 35, 39 and 40, paragraphs 1 and 2 of Article 41, Articles 43 to 45 and 48 to 54, paragraphs 2 and 3 of Article 55, paragraph 2 of Article 57, paragraphs 1 to 3 of Article 58, Articles 59 to 62, 64, 66 and 67, paragraphs 1, 2, and 4 of Article 70 and Article 71 of the Vienna Convention on Consular Relations, have the force of law in Canada in respect of all foreign states, regardless of whether those states are parties to those Conventions . . . .

LAW IN CONTEXT

Tragedy in Ottawa

In 2001, Mr. Andrei Knyazev, the first secretary of the Russian Embassy in Ottawa, driving while apparently drunk, killed one woman and seriously injured another in Ottawa. In the aftermath, Russia was called upon to waive immunity and allow the diplomat's prosecution under Canadian law. It refused to do so, but a year later, the diplomat was convicted of involuntary manslaughter in a Russian court and received a four-year prison sentence.

Consider one Canadian newspaper's denunciation of diplomatic immunity in the case:

If [Russian ambassador to Canada] Mr. Churkin cares so little for his host country that he insists on maintaining Mr. Knyazev's diplomatic immunity—a form of legal protection that was meant to protect diplomats from being framed or entrapped, not from alleged manslaughter—then John Manley, Canada's Foreign Minister, should make him care.

A woman has died—and the Russians are protecting a suspect for no proper reason. Until Mr. Knyazev is stripped of his immunity and brought back to Canada to face charges, Canada must place diplomatic sanctions on Russia. Mere words are not enough. Perhaps a number of Russian diplomats ought to be expelled. Perhaps Canada's own ambassador ought to be temporarily recalled from Moscow. Whatever Mr. Manley chooses to do, he must ensure that the Knyazev incident does not become a transient diplomatic embarrassment to be swept under the rug the next time Canadian diplomats meet with their Russian counterparts.[6]

Consider also this quite different view, taken by a different newspaper:

Diplomatic immunity does not exist because anyone thinks it's fine for diplomats to break the law. It exists so that the governments of host countries can't harass the emissaries of foreign powers. Canadian diplomats based in a dictatorship, for instance, need safety from what may be the arbitrary and routine abuse of power by that state. To obtain protection from such risks, all countries agree to broad rules of immunity.

If diplomatic immunity applied only to certain offences but not to others, a regime bent on creating trouble would trump up an incident involving one of the unprotected offences.

That does not mean that nothing can be done. Most obviously the Department of Foreign Affairs, in co-operation with Canadian and, particularly, Ottawa police, can track diplomats with a history of legal troubles and, before their next transgression, do the right thing: Expel them. That should have happened to Mr. Knyazev long before last year's tragedy.

While we cannot turn back time with Mr. Knyazev, it is not too late to prevent similar evils. Diplomatic immunity remains a sound institution. The institution that must do better is our ministry of foreign affairs.[7]

Canada subsequently adopted a "zero tolerance" policy, providing for the loss of a diplomat's driving privileges for a first offence of impaired driving, even where charges are not laid by police. After a second offence, or a first offence involving death or injury, the policy provides for the diplomat to be recalled or expelled. According to the Canadian Department of Foreign Affairs, Trade and Development:

This policy is consistent with Canada's international obligations, including those contained in the Vienna Convention on Diplomatic Relations. Since Canada cannot directly sanction diplomats under these international rules, the loss of driving privileges will be effected following a waiver of immunity by the diplomat's state or, alternatively, through a written undertaking by the Head of the Mission pledging that the diplomat will not drive. Should a state refuse to exercise either of these options, the Department will request that the diplomat be recalled or will expel him or her.[8]

---

6   Editorial, "Diplomatic Disgrace" *National Post* (6 February 2001) A15.
7   Editorial, "Immunity Need Not Mean Impunity" *Ottawa Citizen* (18 March 2002) A14.
8   Government of Canada, Foreign Affairs, Trade and Development Canada, "Revised Impaired Driving Policy" (17 March 2010), online: www.international.gc.ca/protocol-protocole/vienna-vienne/idp/index.aspx?view=d.

In addition to the personal inviolability and immunities enjoyed by diplomats and their families, the premises (including diplomatic residences) and means of transport and communication of a diplomatic mission also benefit from the concept of "inviolability" and other significant immunities from receiving state jurisdiction.[9] These provisions are clearly intended as a further inducement to the maintenance of permanent diplomatic contacts between states, again with a view to fostering good international relations.

The inviolability and immunities erected by the Convention around diplomatic premises fall short, however, of the common but misconceived notion that such premises somehow form part of the sovereign territory of the sending state. This is not the case: while diplomatic premises are protected from host state jurisdiction by powerful immunities, they nevertheless ultimately remain subject to the sovereignty of the receiving state. In what ways is this formal distinction significant? Consider, for example, the prohibition in Article 41(3) on using the premises of a diplomatic mission in any manner inconsistent with the functions of the mission. Would there be any basis for such a prohibition if diplomatic premises formed part of the sovereign territory of the sending state?

Note the durability, per Article 45 — even in times of armed conflict — of the receiving state's obligation to respect the premises, property, and archives of a diplomatic mission. Under what limited circumstances would such an obligation lapse?

In addition to obliging receiving states to respect the immunities enjoyed by foreign diplomatic missions, the Convention and customary international law also place certain positive duties on receiving states to protect foreign diplomatic premises and personnel. The following case deals with the legal consequences arising from one of the more spectacular violations, in modern international law, of both types of obligation:

United States Diplomatic and Consular Staff in Tehran (United States of America v Iran), Judgment, [1980] ICJ Rep 3, (1980) 19 ILM 553

[In 1979, Iranian revolutionaries seized and occupied the US Embassy in Tehran and American consulates in Tabriz and Shiraz, with so-called militants detaining some fifty American diplomats as hostages. The United States brought the matter to the International Court of Justice.]

56. . . . The events which are the subject of the United States' claims fall into two phases which it will be convenient to examine separately.

57. The first of these phases covers the armed attack on the United States Embassy by militants on 4 November 1979, the overrunning of its premises, the seizure of its inmates as hostages, the appropriation of its property and archives and the conduct of the Iranian authorities in the face of those occurrences. The attack and the subsequent overrunning, bit by bit, of the whole Embassy premises, was an operation which continued over a period of some three hours without any body of police, any military unit or any Iranian official intervening to try to stop or impede it from being carried through to its completion. The result of the attack was considerable damage to the Embassy premises and property, the forcible opening and seizure of its archives, the confiscation of the

---

9   See, for example, Vienna Convention on Diplomatic Relations, above note 2, arts 22, 27, and 30.

archives and other documents found in the Embassy and, most grave of all, the seizure by force of its diplomatic and consular personnel as hostages, together with two United States nationals.

58. No suggestion has been made that the militants, when they executed their attack on the Embassy, had any form of official status as recognized "agents" or organs of the Iranian State. Their conduct in mounting the attack, overrunning the Embassy and seizing its inmates as hostages cannot, therefore, be regarded as imputable to that State on that basis. Their conduct might be considered as itself directly imputable to the Iranian State only if it were established that, in fact, on the occasion in question the militants acted on behalf on the State, having been charged by some competent organ of the Iranian State to carry out a specific operation. The information before the Court does not, however, suffice to establish with the requisite certainty the existence at that time of such a link between the militants and any competent organ of the State . . . .

61. The conclusion just reached by the Court, that the initiation of the attack on the United States Embassy on 4 November 1979, and of the attacks on the Consulates at Tabriz and Shiraz the following day, cannot be considered as in itself imputable to the Iranian State does not mean that Iran is, in consequence, free of any responsibility in regard to those attacks; for its own conduct was in conflict with its international obligations. By a number of provisions of the Vienna Conventions of 1961 and 1963, Iran was placed under the most categorical obligations, as a receiving State, to take appropriate steps to ensure the protection of the United States Embassy and Consulates, their staffs, their archives, their means of communication and the freedom of movement of the members of their staffs.

62. Thus, after solemnly proclaiming the inviolability of the premises of a diplomatic mission, Article 22 of the 1961 Convention continues in paragraph 2:

> The receiving State is under a special duty to take all appropriate steps to protect the premises of the mission against any intrusion or damage and to prevent any disturbance of the peace of the mission or impairment of its dignity . . . .

So, too, after proclaiming that the person of a diplomatic agent shall be inviolable, and that he shall not be liable to any form of arrest or detention, Article 29 provides:

> The receiving State shall treat him with due respect and shall take all appropriate steps to prevent any attack on his person, freedom or dignity.

The obligation of a receiving State to protect the inviolability of the archives and documents of a diplomatic mission is laid down in Article 24, which specifically provides that they are to be "inviolable at any time and wherever they may be." Under Article 25 it is required to "accord full facilities for the performance of the functions of the mission," under Article 26 to "ensure to all members of the mission freedom of movement and travel in its territory," and under Article 27 to "permit and protect free communication on the part of the mission for all official purposes." Analogous provisions are to be found in the 1963 Convention regarding the privileges and immunities of consular missions and their staffs (Art. 31, para. 3, Arts. 40, 33, 28, 34 and 35). In the view of the Court, the obligations of the Iranian Government here in question are not merely contractual obligations established by the Vienna Conventions of 1961 and 1963, but also obligations under general international law.

63. The facts set out . . . above establish to the satisfaction of the Court that on 4 November 1979 the Iranian Government failed altogether to take any "appropriate steps" to protect the premises, staff and archives of the United States' mission against attack by the militants, and to take any steps either to prevent this attack or to stop it before it reached its completion. They also show that on 5 November 1979 the Iranian Government similarly failed to take appropriate steps for the protection of the United States Consulates at Tabriz and Shiraz. In addition they show, in the opinion of the Court, that the failure of the Iranian Government to take such steps was due to more than mere negligence or lack of appropriate means.

64. The total inaction of the Iranian authorities on that date in face of urgent and repeated requests for help contrasts very sharply with its conduct on several other occasions of a similar kind. Some eight months earlier, on 14 February 1979, the United States Embassy in Tehran had itself been subjected to [an] armed attack . . . , in the course of which the attackers had taken the Ambassador and his staff prisoner. On that occasion, however, a detachment of Revolutionary Guards, sent by the Government, had arrived promptly, together with a Deputy Prime Minister, and had quickly succeeded in freeing the Ambassador and his staff and restoring the Embassy to him. . . On 1 November 1979, only three days before the events which gave rise to the present case, the Iranian police intervened quickly and effectively to protect the United States Embassy when a large crowd of demonstrators spent several hours marching up and down outside it. Furthermore, on other occasions in November 1979 and January 1980, invasions or attempted invasions of other foreign embassies in Tehran were frustrated or speedily terminated . . . .

66. As to the actual conduct of the Iranian authorities when faced with the events of 4 November 1979, the information before the Court establishes that, despite assurances previously given by them to the United States Government and despite repeated and urgent calls for help, they took no apparent steps either to prevent the militants from invading the Embassy or to persuade or to compel them to withdraw. Furthermore, after the militants had forced an entry into the premises of the Embassy, the Iranian authorities made no effort to compel or even to persuade them to withdraw from the Embassy and to free the diplomatic and consular staff whom they had made prisoner.

67. This inaction of the Iranian Government by itself constituted clear and serious violation of Iran's obligations to the United States under the provisions of Article 22, paragraph 2, and Articles 24, 25, 26, 27 and 29 of the 1961 Vienna Convention on Diplomatic Relations, and Articles 5 and 36 of the 1963 Vienna Convention on Consular Relations . . . .

68. The Court is therefore led inevitably to conclude, in regard to the first phase of the events which has so far been considered, that on 4 November 1979 the Iranian authorities:

> (a) were fully aware of their obligations under the conventions in force to take appropriate steps to protect the premises of the United States Embassy and its diplomatic and consular staff from any attack and from any infringement of their inviolability,

and to ensure the security of such other persons as might be present on the said premises;

(b) were fully aware, as a result of the appeals for help made by the United States Embassy, of the urgent need for action on their part;

(c) had the means at their disposal to perform their obligations;

(d) completely failed to comply with these obligations.

Similarly, the Court is led to conclude that the Iranian authorities were equally aware of their obligations to protect the United States Consulates at Tabriz and Shiraz, and of the need for action on their part, and similarly failed to use the means which were at their disposal to comply with their obligations . . . .

69. The second phase of the events which are the subject of the United States' claims comprises the whole series of facts which occurred following the completion of the seizure of the Consulates at Tabriz and Shiraz. . . . [T]he action required of the Iranian Government by the Vienna Conventions and by general international law was manifest. Its plain duty was at once to make every effort, and to take every appropriate step, to bring these flagrant infringements of the inviolability of the premises, archives and diplomatic and consular staff of the United States Embassy to a speedy end, to restore the Consulates at Tabriz and Shiraz to United States control, and in general to re-establish the status quo and to offer reparation for the damage.

70. No such step was, however, taken by the Iranian authorities. At a press conference on 5 November the Foreign Minister, Mr. Yazdi, conceded that "according to international regulations, the Iranian Government is dutybound to safeguard the life and property of foreign nationals." But he made no mention of Iran's obligation to safeguard the inviolability of foreign embassies and diplomats; and he ended by announcing that the action of the students "enjoys the endorsement and support of the government, because America herself is responsible for this incident." . . .

71. In any event expressions of approval of the take-over of the Embassy, and indeed also of the Consulates at Tabriz and Shiraz, by militants came immediately from numerous Iranian authorities. Above all, the Ayatollah Khomeini himself made crystal clear the endorsement by the State both of the takeover of the Embassy and Consulates and of the detention of the Embassy staff as hostages . . . .

73. The seal of official government approval was finally set on this situation by a decree issued on 17 November 1979 by the Ayatollah Khomeini. His decree began with the assertion that the American Embassy was "a centre of espionage and conspiracy" and that "those people who hatched plots against our Islamic movement in that place do not enjoy international diplomatic respect." He went on expressly to declare that the premises of the Embassy and the hostages would remain as they were until the United States had handed over the former Shah for trial and returned his property to Iran . . . .

74. . . . The result of that policy was fundamentally to transform the legal nature of the situation created by the occupation of the Embassy and the detention of its diplomatic and consular staff as hostages. The approval given to these facts by the Ayatollah Khomeini and other organs of the Iranian State, and the decision to perpetuate them, trans-

lated continuing occupation of the Embassy and detention of the hostages into acts of that State . . . .

75. During the six months which have elapsed since the situation just described was created by the decree of the Ayatollah Khomeini, it has undergone no material change . . . .

76. The Iranian authorities' decision to continue the subjection of the premises of the United States Embassy to occupation by militants and of the Embassy staff to detention as hostages, clearly gave rise to repeated and multiple breaches of the applicable provisions of the Vienna Conventions even more serious than those which arose from their failure to take any steps to prevent the attacks on the inviolability of these premises and staff.

77. In the first place, these facts constituted breaches additional to those already committed of paragraph 2 of Article 22 of the 1961 Vienna Convention on Diplomatic Relations which requires Iran to protect the premises of the mission against any intrusion or damage and to prevent any disturbance of its peace or impairment of its dignity. Paragraphs 1 and 3 of that Article have also been infringed, and continue to be infringed, since they forbid agents of a receiving State to enter the premises of a mission without consent or to undertake any search, requisition, attachment or like measure on the premises. Secondly, they constitute continuing breaches of Article 29 of the same Convention which forbids any arrest or detention of a diplomatic agent and any attack on his person, freedom or dignity. Thirdly, the Iranian authorities are without doubt in continuing breach of the provisions of Articles 25, 26 and 27 of the 1961 Vienna Convention and of pertinent provisions of the 1963 Vienna Convention concerning facilities for the performance of functions, freedom of movement and communications for diplomatic and consular staff, as well as of Article 24 of the former Convention and Article 33 of the latter, which provide for the absolute inviolability of the archives and documents of diplomatic missions and consulates. This particular violation has been made manifest to the world by repeated statements by the militants occupying the Embassy, who claim to be in possession of documents from the archives, and by various government authorities, purporting to specify the contents thereof . . . .

80. The facts of the present case, viewed in the light of the applicable rules of law, thus speak loudly and clearly of successive and still continuing breaches by Iran of its obligations to the United States under the Vienna Conventions of 1961 and 1963 . . . .

86. The rules of diplomatic law, in short, constitute a self-contained régime which, on the one hand, lays down the receiving State's obligations regarding the facilities, privileges and immunities to be accorded to diplomatic missions and, on the other, foresees their possible abuse by members of the mission and specifies the means at the disposal of the receiving State to counter any such abuse. These means are, by their nature, entirely efficacious. . . . But the principle of the inviolability of the persons of diplomatic agents and the premises of the diplomatic missions is one of the very foundations of this long-established régime, to the evolution of which the traditions of Islam made a substantial contribution . . . . Even in the case of armed conflict or in the case of a breach in diplomatic relations [Articles 45 and 46 of the Convention] require that both the inviolability of the members of a diplomatic mission and of the premises, property and archives of the mission must be respected by the receiving State . . . .

90. On the basis of the foregoing detailed examination of the merits of the case, the Court finds that Iran, by committing successive and continuing breaches of the obligations laid upon it by the Vienna Conventions of 1961 and 1963 on Diplomatic and Consular Relations . . . and the applicable rules of general international law, has incurred responsibility towards the United States. As to the consequences of this finding, it clearly entails an obligation on the part of the Iranian State to make reparation for the injury thereby caused to the United States . . . .

LAW IN CONTEXT

Other Internationally Protected Persons

Diplomats are not the only officials entitled to immunities from host state jurisdiction. Other classes of such "internationally protected persons" include the following:

- *Consular officials*: The Vienna Convention on Consular Relations extends various immunities to consular premises and officials. Consular officials generally promote a state's commercial activities in a foreign state, and perform various administrative functions such as issuing visas and passports. They are not, however, generally engaged in the higher-level political affairs with which diplomats typically are involved, and are therefore accorded somewhat more limited immunities than those extended to diplomats. Most notably, their immunity from the "jurisdiction of the judicial or administrative authorities of the receiving State" exists only "in respect of acts performed in the exercise of consular functions."[10]
- *Members of special missions*: The Convention on Special Missions of 1969[11] anticipates the sending of "special missions" by one state to another for the purpose of dealing with some specific issue. The members of these special missions are entitled to certain immunities, including from criminal and most forms of civil jurisdiction of the host state. Canada is not a party to this treaty.
- *Officials of international organizations*: Article 105 of the Charter of the United Nations[12] provides that "[t]he Organization shall enjoy in the territory of each of its Members such privileges and immunities as are necessary for the fulfillment of its purposes. . . Representatives of the Members of the United Nations and officials of the Organization shall similarly enjoy such privileges and immunities as are necessary for the independent exercise of their functions in connexion with the Organization." The Convention on the Privileges and Immunities of the United Nations[13] fleshes out these obligations. The International Law Commission added the topic "Immunities of International Organizations" to its long-term programme of work in 2006. A challenge to the immunity from suit accorded to an international organization headquartered in

---

10   Vienna Convention on Consular Relations, above note 4, art 34.
11   Convention on Special Missions, 8 December 1969, 1400 UNTS 231, in force 21 June 1985 (thirty-eight parties as of July 2013).
12   26 June 1945, Can TS 1945 No 7, in force 24 October 1945.
13   13 February 1946, 1 UNTS 15 and 90 UNTS 327, Can TS 1948 No 2, in force 17 September 1946 (159 parties as of July 2013).

Nova Scotia was heard by the Supreme Court of Canada in early 2013 and a decision in the case remained pending at the time of writing.[14]

- *Judges of the International Court of Justice*: Article 19 of the Statute of the International Court of Justice[15] provides that "The members of the Court, when engaged on the business of the Court, shall enjoy diplomatic privileges and immunities."
- *Judges of the International Criminal Court*: The Agreement on Privileges and Immunities of the International Criminal Court[16] also provides various immunities for the judges and other personnel of the International Criminal Court (as well as its premises and assets) from the jurisdiction of states parties.

Also of note, the 1973 Convention on the Prevention and Punishment of Crimes against Internationally Protected Persons, Including Diplomatic Agents[17] obliges states parties to criminalize murder, kidnapping, and other crimes of violence directed at "internationally protected persons." The latter are heads of state and, as indicated in Article 1(1)(b) of the Convention, "any representative or official of a State or any official or other agent of an international organization of an intergovernmental character who . . . is entitled pursuant to international law to special protection from any attack on his person, freedom or dignity, as well as members of his family forming part of his household."

B. STATE IMMUNITIES

1) Nature and Basis of State Immunities

A second category of immunity restricting the exercise of jurisdiction by states, or more specifically, by their courts, is known as "state immunities," or sometimes, "sovereign immunities." These are immunities enjoyed by states themselves and, in some circumstances, their representatives and agents, from proceedings in the courts of other states. Consider the underlying reasons for the existence of such immunities, as expressed in an early, but often cited, US Supreme Court case:

The Schooner Exchange v M'Faddon, 11 US (7 Cranch) 116 (1812)

[Two US citizens owned a ship that was forcibly seized pursuant to decrees issued by Napoleon I, the French emperor. The vessel was pressed into service as a French warship. Thereafter it sailed into an American port and its American owners filed an action in the American courts to reclaim it. At the time, the United States was at peace with France and had permitted the vessel to enter its port as the vessel of a friendly power. At issue was whether the US courts could exercise jurisdiction over the ship. The Court concluded that the ship enjoyed sovereign immunity, and commented as follows:]

---

14 See *Northwest Atlantic Fisheries Organization v Amaratunga*, 2011 NSCA 73, leave to appeal to SCC granted 26 April 2012, appeal heard and judgment reserved 28 March 2013.
15 26 June 1945, Can TS 1945 No 7, in force 24 October 1945.
16 9 September 2002, 2271 UNTS 3, in force 22 July 2004 (seventy-two parties as of July 2013).
17 14 December 1973, 1035 UNTS 167, Can TS 1977 No 43, in force 20 February 1967 (176 parties as of July 2013).

... The jurisdiction of the nation within its own territory is necessarily exclusive and absolute. It is susceptible of no limitation not imposed by itself ....

All exceptions, therefore, to the full and complete power of a nation within its own territories must be traced up to the consent of the nation itself ....

This consent may be either express or implied. In the latter case, it is less determinate, exposed more to the uncertainties of construction; but, if understood, not less obligatory.

The world being composed of distinct sovereignties, possessing equal rights and equal independence, whose mutual benefit is promoted by intercourse with each other, and by an interchange of those good offices which humanity dictates and its wants require, all sovereigns have consented to a relaxation in practice, in cases under certain peculiar circumstances, of that absolute and complete jurisdiction within their respective territories which sovereignty confers.

This consent may, in some instances, be tested by common usage, and by common opinion, growing out of that usage.

A nation would justly be considered as violating its faith, although that faith might not be expressly plighted, which should suddenly and without previous notice, exercise its territorial powers in a manner not consonant to the usages and received obligations of the civilized world.

This full and absolute territorial jurisdiction being alike the attribute of every sovereign ... would not seem to contemplate foreign sovereigns nor their sovereign rights as its objects. One sovereign being in no respect amenable to another; and being bound by obligations of the highest character not to degrade the dignity of his nation, by placing himself or its sovereign rights within the jurisdiction of another, can be supposed to enter a foreign territory only under an express license, or in the confidence that the immunities belonging to his independent sovereign station, though not expressly stipulated, are reserved by implication, and will be extended to him.

This perfect equality and absolute independence of sovereigns, and this common interest impelling them to mutual intercourse, and an interchange of good offices with each other, have given rise to a class of cases in which every sovereign is understood to waive the exercise of a part of that complete exclusive territorial jurisdiction, which has been stated to be the attribute of every nation.

One of these is admitted to be the exemption of the person of the sovereign from arrest or detention within a foreign territory.

If he enters that territory with the knowledge and license of its sovereign, that license, although containing no stipulation exempting his person from arrest, is universally understood to imply such stipulation.

Why has the whole civilized world concurred in this construction? The answer cannot be mistaken. A foreign sovereign is not understood as intending to subject himself to jurisdiction incompatible with his dignity, and the dignity of his nation, and it is to avoid this subjection that the license has been obtained. The character to whom it is given, and the object for which it is granted, equally require that it should be construed to impart full security to the person who has obtained it. This security, however need not be expressed; it is implied from the circumstances of the case ....

In a more modern context, one expert commentator describes the justifications for state immunities as follows:

> State immunity serves three functions: (i) as a method to ensure a 'stand-off' between States where private parties seek to enlist the assistance of the courts of one State to determine their claims made against another State; (ii) as a method of distinguishing between matters relating to public administration of a State and private law claims; (iii) as a method of allocating jurisdiction between States relating to the prosecution of crimes and the settlement of claims by private litigants relating to State activities, in the absence of any international agreement by which to resolve conflicting claims to the exercise of such jurisdiction.[18]

2) The "Restrictive" Doctrine of State Immunities

While sovereign or state immunities have a long and deeply rooted history in customary international law, the extent to which they shield states from the authority of other states' courts has evolved significantly over time. It used to be the case that absent their consent, states enjoyed absolute immunity from all phases of court proceedings in other states. However, twentieth-century state practice and *opinio juris* increasingly departed from this rigid rule, giving rise to a more "restrictive" doctrine of state immunities from foreign judicial process. Key to this evolution was a recognition that the acts of states were not always essentially "sovereign"; sometimes, states acted in essentially "private" capacities such as when engaging in commercial transactions. International law began distinguishing between acts of sovereignty or public authority (*acta jure imperii*) and private acts (*acta jure gestionis*). While the doctrine of sovereign equality certainly justified immunity in respect of acts falling within the former category, it gradually became accepted by states that the same could not be said for acts falling within the latter. There was, however, a degree of variation in the practice of states in terms of distinguishing sovereign from private state acts.

Canada's *State Immunity Act*, first enacted in 1982, was designed to reflect the restrictive approach to the law of state immunities that had then emerged on the international legal plane through changes to state practice.

State Immunity Act, RSC 1985, c S-18, as amended

2. In this Act, . . .

"commercial activity" means any particular transaction, act or conduct or any regular course of conduct that by reason of its nature is of a commercial character . . . .

3. (1) Except as provided by this Act, a foreign state is immune from the jurisdiction of any court in Canada.

(2) In any proceedings before a court, the court shall give effect to the immunity conferred on a foreign state by subsection (1) notwithstanding that the state has failed to take any step in the proceedings.

4. (1) A foreign state is not immune from the jurisdiction of a court if the state waives the

---

18   Hazel Fox, *The Law of State Immunity*, 2d ed (Oxford: Oxford University Press, 2008) at 1–2.

immunity conferred by subsection 3(1) by submitting to the jurisdiction of the court in accordance with subsection (2) or (4).

(2) In any proceedings before a court, a foreign state submits to the jurisdiction of the court where it

(a) explicitly submits to the jurisdiction of the court by written agreement or otherwise either before or after the proceedings commence;

(b) initiates the proceedings in the court; or

(c) intervenes or takes any step in the proceedings before the court . . . .

(4) A foreign state that initiates proceedings in a court or that intervenes or takes any step in proceedings before a court, other than an intervention or step to which paragraph (2)(c) does not apply, submits to the jurisdiction of the court in respect of any third party proceedings that arise, or counter-claim that arises, out of the subject-matter of the proceedings initiated by the state or in which the state has so intervened or taken a step.

5. A foreign state is not immune from the jurisdiction of a court in any proceedings that relate to any commercial activity of the foreign state.

6. A foreign state is not immune from the jurisdiction of a court in any proceedings that relate to

(a) any death or personal or bodily injury, or

(b) any damage to or loss of property

that occurs in Canada. . . .

18. This Act does not apply to criminal proceedings or proceedings in the nature of criminal proceedings.

Consider the following decision of the Court of Appeal for Ontario interpreting some of limitations imposed by the *State Immunity Act* on foreign state immunities:

Bouzari v Iran (2004), 71 OR (3d) 675 (CA), leave to appeal to SCC refused, [2005] 1 SCR vi

The judgment of the Court was delivered by

[1] GOUDGE J.A.: — From June 1993 to January 1994 Houshang Bouzari was abducted, imprisoned and brutally tortured by agents of the Islamic Republic of Iran. Shortly after his release, he escaped from Iran and eventually came to Canada as a landed immigrant in 1998. He now seeks to sue Iran for the damages he suffered.

[2] Swinton J. found that his action is barred by the *State Immunity Act*, R.S.C. 1985, c. S-18 (the "SIA") and that . . . the limited exceptions in the SIA . . . could [not] relieve against this conclusion. She therefore dismissed the action. For the reasons that follow, I agree and would therefore dismiss the appeal . . . .

THE STATE IMMUNITY ACT ISSUE

[39] The appellant brings this action against a foreign state. The action therefore necessarily engages the principle of sovereign immunity or state immunity.

[40] Founded on the concepts of the sovereign equality of states and the non-interference of states in the internal affairs of each other, the principle is rooted in customary international law.

[41] Historically, it provided foreign states with absolute immunity from proceedings in the courts of other states. However, over the years, the dictates of justice have led to some attenuation in the absolute immunity of states, through the evolution of certain specified exceptions to the general rule. Nevertheless, the doctrine of restrictive immunity which has emerged continues to have the general principle of state immunity as its foundation. In *Schreiber v. Canada (Attorney General)* (2002), 216 D.L.R. (4th) 513 (S.C.C.) LeBel J. put it this way at para. 17:

> Despite the increasing number of emerging exceptions, the general principle of sovereign immunity remains an important part of the international legal order, except when expressly stated otherwise, and there is no evidence that an international peremptory norm has been established to suggest otherwise. Indeed, Brownlie [*Principles of Public International Law*, 5th ed. (Oxford: Clarendon Press, 1998)], *supra*, notes at pp. 332–33 that:
>
> > It is far from easy to state the current legal position in terms of customary or general international law. Recent writers emphasize that there is a trend in the practice of states towards the restrictive doctrine of immunity but avoid firm and precise prescriptions as to the present state of the law.
>
> As observed at the outset of these reasons, this principle of international law has been incorporated into the Canadian domestic legal order through the enactment of the federal State Immunity Act.

[42] The SIA reflects this approach. It was passed by Parliament in 1982 and makes foreign states immune from civil suits in Canadian courts unless one of the exceptions in the Act applies. Section 3 is its cornerstone:

> 3. (1) Except as provided by this Act, a foreign state is immune from the jurisdiction of any court in Canada.
>
> (2) In any proceedings before a court, the court shall give effect to the immunity conferred on a foreign state by subsection (1) notwithstanding that the state has failed to take any step in the proceedings.

[43] The appellant relies on three exceptions. The first is found in s. 18 of the Act:

> 18. This Act does not apply to criminal proceedings or proceedings in the nature of criminal proceedings.

[44] The appellant argues that this proceeding is in the nature of a criminal proceeding because he is seeking punitive damages which are in the nature of a fine. The motion judge rejected this argument, concluding that this relief is available only in a civil proceeding after a finding of civil liability and an award of compensatory damages. She found that while the purpose of punitive damages is to deter, they remain a remedy in a civil proceeding. I agree.

[45] Second, the appellant relies on the tort exception found in s. 6 of the Act:

> 6. A foreign state is not immune from the jurisdiction of a court in any proceedings
> that relate to
>> (a) any death or personal or bodily injury, or
>> (b) any damage to or loss of property
>
> that occurs in Canada.

[46] The appellant argues that his suffering continues in Canada and that this constitutes injury occurring in Canada. The motion judge rejected this argument as well, finding that the appellant continues to suffer from physical and psychological injuries inflicted on him not in Canada, but in Iran, because of the acts of torture committed there.

[47] Again I agree. This reasoning conforms with LeBel J.'s discussion of this exception in *Schreiber, supra*. At para. 80 he describes it as reflecting "a legislative intent to create an exception to state immunity which would be restricted to a class of claims arising out of a physical breach of personal integrity." Viewing the exception in this light, the SIA requires that the physical breach of personal integrity giving rise to the claim take place in Canada. The appellant cannot meet that condition. He was tortured in Iran.

[48] The third exception cited by the appellant, and the one he relies on most heavily, is that relating to commercial activity. It is found in s. 5 of the Act:

> 5. A foreign state is not immune from the jurisdiction of a court in any proceedings
> that relate to any commercial activity of the foreign state.

[49] The Act also contains the following definition of "commercial activity":

> "commercial activity" means any particular transaction, act or conduct or any regular
> course of conduct that by reason of its nature is of a commercial character[.]

[50] The appellant argues that this exception applies because the acts of torture on which his claim is based are related to the appellant's commercial activity in connection with the South Pars oil and gas field. The motion judge disagreed, finding that regardless of their purpose, these acts were exercises of the state policing, security and imprisonment powers and therefore were inherently sovereign and not commercial in nature.

[51] I agree with her conclusion that the commercial activity exception does not apply here. Section 5 of the Act requires that the acts to which the proceedings relate (namely the acts of torture) be commercial in nature. It is not enough that the proceedings relate to acts which, in turn, relate to commercial activity of the foreign state. To interpret the exception in this way, as the appellant contends, would broaden the exception beyond the clear language of the SIA.

[52] The issue, then, is whether the acts of torture for which the appellant sues can be said to be commercial in nature. *Re Canada Labour Code*, [1992] 2 S.C.R. 50 is the leading authority on this question. Writing for the majority at 69, LaForest J. set out the two basic questions raised by s. 5: first, whether the acts in question constitute commercial activity and second, whether the proceedings are related to that activity.

[53] LaForest J. found that a consideration of the purpose of the acts is of some, although limited, use in determining both their nature and which facets of the acts in question are truly "related" to the proceedings in issue. Here, apart from their purpose, the acts of torture underpinning the appellant's action cannot be said to have anything to do with commerce. They are nothing more than unilaterally imposed acts of brutality. The appellant believes that they were committed with a purpose of affecting his involvement in the commercial activity of the South Pars project. Even if this is taken to include an intention to affect the commercial activity of Iran, that is not enough to turn the acts of torture themselves into the commercial activity of Iran. The acts of torture are related only by intention to the commercial activity of the South Pars project.

[54] Moreover, the proceedings here are not truly "related" to this aspect of the acts of torture. If the appellant's claim proceeds, the purpose of these acts is of little if any relevance to the appellant's ability to recover damages for them. Damages would flow regardless of the purpose of the acts. In other words, the only aspect of the acts of torture that can be linked in any way to the commercial activity of Iran is their alleged purpose. Since this proceeding is not "related" to this aspect of the acts in question, it cannot be said that these acts relate to any commercial activity of Iran for the purposes of s. 5 of the SIA.

[55] Hence, I conclude that the commercial activity exception in s. 5 of the Act has no application to this case . . . .

The foregoing excerpt from the *Bouzari* case deals with interpretation of the specific exceptions to state immunities set out in the *State Immunity Act*. We will return to this case in the next subsection in order to examine how it addressed a more fundamental question: whether international law recognizes a broader exception to state immunities when the state activity in question amounts to torture or other gross human rights violations. For now, however, consider the "limited" weight given by the Court of Appeal to Iran's purpose when determining whether its acts of torture could be characterized as commercial in nature. Is it possible to determine the nature of a state act without giving due consideration to its purpose? The Supreme Court of Canada has more recently returned to this issue, affirming that an act must be considered in its "full context," including its purpose, in determining whether it is commercial in nature. Consider the contrast between this approach and that taken by other key states, as described in the following excerpt:

Kuwait Airways Corp v Iraq, 2010 SCC 40, [2010] 2 SCR 571

English version of the judgment of the Court delivered by LeBel J:

[2] At the time of [Iraq's 1990] invasion and occupation of Kuwait, the Iraqi government ordered its national airline, the Iraqi Airways Company ("IAC"), to appropriate [Kuwait Airways Corporation's (KAC's)] aircraft, equipment and parts inventory. After the war, . . . KAC brought an action against IAC in the United Kingdom for damages in respect of losses sustained as a result of the appropriation of its property following the invasion. The United Kingdom courts . . . ordered IAC to pay amounts totalling over one billion Canadian dollars to KAC . . . . KAC applied and was granted leave to have the Republic

of Iraq joined as a second defendant in order to claim from it the costs of the actions that had been brought in the United Kingdom, which totalled approximately $84 million in Canadian currency. On July 16, 2008, Steel J. of the [English] High Court of Justice . . . granted the application and ordered Iraq to pay the amount claimed by KAC . . . .

[3] In August 2008, KAC applied for recognition of Steel J.'s judgment in . . . Quebec [where Iraq held property]. Iraq countered these proceedings by filing a motion . . . in which it asked that the application for recognition of the English judgment be dismissed because the impugned acts by Iraq were sovereign acts and because Iraq was entitled to state immunity under Canadian law . . . .

[24] . . . [I turn] to determine whether the commercial activity exception applies in the case at bar. . . .

[29] In the United Kingdom, the courts ask whether the act in question could be performed by a private individual. Lord Goff of Chieveley recommended the use of this test in one of the decisions related to the litigation between KAC and IAC on which the instant case is based. Relying on an earlier opinion of Lord Wilberforce in *I Congreso del Partido*, [1983] A.C. 244, at pp. 262, 267 and 269, he found that the proper test would be not what the state's objective is in performing the act, but whether the act could be performed by a private citizen (*Kuwait Airways Corp. v. Iraqi Airways Co.*, [1995] 3 All E.R. 694, at pp. 704-5). In the United States, the Supreme Court described the sovereign acts protected by state immunity as those performed in the exercise of the powers peculiar to sovereigns:

> Under the restrictive, as opposed to the "absolute," theory of foreign sovereign immunity, a state is immune from the jurisdiction of foreign courts as to its sovereign or public acts (*jure imperii*), but not as to those that are private or commercial in character (*jure gestionis*). . . We explained in *Weltover*. . . that a state engages in commercial activity under the restrictive theory where it exercises "'only those powers that can also be exercised by private citizens,'" as distinct from those "'powers peculiar to sovereigns.'" Put differently, a foreign state engages in commercial activity for purposes of the restrictive theory only where it acts "in the manner of a private player within" the market. (*Saudi Arabia v. Nelson*, 507 U.S. 349 (1993), at pp. 359-60)

[30] Thus, in both U.S. and English law, the characterization of acts for purposes of the application of state immunity is based on an analysis that focusses on their nature. It is therefore not sufficient to ask whether the act in question was the result of a state decision and whether it was performed to protect a state interest or attain a public policy objective. If that were the case, all acts of a state or even of a state-controlled organization would be considered sovereign acts. This would be inconsistent with the restrictive theory of state immunity in contemporary public international law and would have the effect of eviscerating the exceptions applicable to acts of private management, such as the commercial activity exception.

[31] In Canadian law, La Forest J. recommended in *Re Canada Labour Code* [, [1992] 2 S.C.R. 50] that this analytical approach be adopted to resolve the issues related to the application of the *SIA*. But he also made it clear that the Canadian commercial activity

exception requires a court to consider the entire context, which includes not only the nature of the act, but also its purpose:

> It seems to me that a contextual approach is the only reasonable basis of applying the doctrine of restrictive immunity. The alternative is to attempt the impossible—an antiseptic distillation of a "once-and-for-all" characterization of the activity in question, entirely divorced from its purpose. It is true that purpose should not predominate, as this approach would convert virtually every act by commercial agents of the state into an act *jure imperii*. However, the converse is also true. Rigid adherence to the "nature" of an act to the exclusion of purpose would render innumerable government activities *jure gestionis*. [p. 73]

[32] After this, La Forest J. stressed Parliament's intention to confirm the restrictive theory of state immunity expressed in the *SIA* and the need for a contextual analysis focussed on the activity itself:

> I view the Canadian *State Immunity Act* as a codification that is intended to clarify and continue the theory of restrictive immunity, rather than to alter its substance. The relevant provisions of the Act, ss. 2 and 5, focus on the nature and character of the activity in question, just as the common law did. [pp. 7374]

[33] For the purposes of this appeal, therefore, the first step is to review the nature of the acts in issue in KAC's action against Iraq in the English courts in their full context, which includes the purpose of the acts. It is not enough to determine whether those acts were authorized or desired by Iraq, or whether they were performed to preserve certain public interests of that state. The nature of the acts must be examined carefully to ensure a proper legal characterization.

[34] To this end, it is necessary to accept the findings of fact made by Steel J. in the judgment the Quebec court is being asked to recognize . . . . According to him, starting in 1991, Iraq, the sole proprietor of IAC, its state-owned corporation, had controlled and funded IAC's defence throughout the long series of actions for damages brought against IAC in the English courts by the appellant. Iraq had participated throughout this commercial litigation in the hope of protecting its interests in IAC. In doing so, it was responsible for numerous acts of forgery, concealing evidence and lies. . ... These acts misled the English courts and led to other judicial proceedings, including the one in issue . . . .

[35] The Quebec Superior Court and the Quebec Court of Appeal found that, owing to the nature of Iraq's acts, state immunity applies and the commercial activity exception does not. But Steel J.'s findings of fact lead to a different legal characterization. It is true that the acts alleged against Iraq that resulted in the litigation were carried out by a state for the benefit of a state-owned corporation. However, the specific acts in issue here are instead those performed by Iraq in the course of the proceedings in the United Kingdom courts. When all is said and done, the subject of the litigation was the seizure of the aircraft by Iraq. The original appropriation of the aircraft was a sovereign act, but the subsequent retention and use of the aircraft by IAC were commercial acts . . . . The English litigation, in which [Iraq] intervened to defend IAC, concerned the retention of the aircraft. There was no connection between that commercial litigation and the initial

sovereign act of seizing the aircraft. As a result, Iraq could not rely on the state immunity provided for in s. 3 of the *SIA* . . . .

Is the Court of Appeal for Ontario's holding in *Bouzari* that an act's purpose is of "limited use" in determining its commercial nature consistent with the Supreme Court of Canada's approach in *Kuwait Airways*? Is it consistent with La Forest J's statements in *Re Canada Labour Code* quoted at paragraph 31 of *Kuwait Airways*?

In an effort to distill and clarify emerging customary international law on the restrictive nature of state immunities, the International Law Commission prepared a set of draft articles on the topic. This draft formed the basis for a multilateral convention adopted by the UN General Assembly in December 2004 and opened for signature in January 2005. While it remains early in the signature and ratification process,[19] the debates surrounding adoption of the Convention suggest that its provisions conform broadly to existing or emerging rules of customary international law on state immunities and reflect international thinking on the subject.[20] Consider, therefore, the scope of such immunities and their limitations, as defined by the Convention:

United Nations Convention on Jurisdictional Immunities of States and Their Property, 2 December 2004, UN Doc A/59/508 (not yet in force)

Part I
Introduction

Article 1
Scope of the present Convention
The present Convention applies to the immunity of a State and its property from the jurisdiction of the courts of another State.

Article 2
Use of terms
1. For the purposes of the present Convention:
   . . .
   (b) "State" means:
   (i) the State and its various organs of government;
   (ii) constituent units of a federal State or political subdivisions of the State, which are entitled to perform acts in the exercise of sovereign authority, and are acting in that capacity;
   (iii) agencies or instrumentalities of the State or other entities, to the extent that they are entitled to perform and are actually performing acts in the exercise of sovereign authority of the State;
   (iv) representatives of the State acting in that capacity; . . . .

---

19   As of July 2013, there are twenty-eight signatories and fourteen parties to the Convention. According to Article 30(1) of the Convention, thirty parties are required to bring it into force.

20   A Grand Chamber of the European Court of Human Rights, for example, has held that the rule found in Article 11 of the Convention binds non-states-parties as a matter of customary international law: *Sabeh El Leil v France*, No 34869/05, 2011 ECHR, (2012) 51 ILM 4 at paras 53–54.

2. In determining whether a contract or transaction is a "commercial transaction" . . . reference should be made primarily to the nature of the contract or transaction, but its purpose should also be taken into account if the parties to the contract or transaction have so agreed, or if, in the practice of the State of the forum, that purpose is relevant to determining the non-commercial character of the contract or transaction . . . .

Part II
General principles

Article 5
State immunity
A State enjoys immunity, in respect of itself and its property, from the jurisdiction of the courts of another State subject to the provisions of the present Convention . . . .

Article 7
Express consent to exercise of jurisdiction
1. A State cannot invoke immunity from jurisdiction in a proceeding before a court of another State with regard to a matter or case if it has expressly consented to the exercise of jurisdiction by the court with regard to the matter or case . . . .

Article 8
Effect of participation in a proceeding before a court
1. A State cannot invoke immunity from jurisdiction in a proceeding before a court of another State if it has:
    (a) itself instituted the proceeding; or
    (b) intervened in the proceeding or taken any other step relating to the merits. However, if the State satisfies the court that it could not have acquired knowledge of facts on which a claim to immunity can be based until after it took such a step, it can claim immunity based on those facts, provided it does so at the earliest possible moment.

2. A State shall not be considered to have consented to the exercise of jurisdiction by a court of another State if it intervenes in a proceeding or takes any other step for the sole purpose of:
    (a) invoking immunity; or
    (b) asserting a right or interest in property at issue in the proceeding . . . .

Article 9
Counterclaims
1. A State instituting a proceeding before a court of another State cannot invoke immunity from the jurisdiction of the court in respect of any counterclaim arising out of the same legal relationship or facts as the principal claim . . . .

3. A State making a counterclaim in a proceeding instituted against it before a court of another State cannot invoke immunity from the jurisdiction of the court in respect of the principal claim.

Part III
Proceedings in which State immunity cannot be invoked

Article 10
Commercial transactions
1. If a State engages in a commercial transaction with a foreign natural or juridical per-son and, by virtue of the applicable rules of private international law, differences relating to the commercial transaction fall within the jurisdiction of a court of another State, the State cannot invoke immunity from that jurisdiction in a proceeding arising out of that commercial transaction.

2. Paragraph 1 does not apply:
(a) in the case of a commercial transaction between States; or
(b) if the parties to the commercial transaction have expressly agreed otherwise . . . .

Article 11
Contracts of employment
1. Unless otherwise agreed between the States concerned, a State cannot invoke immunity from jurisdiction before a court of another State which is otherwise competent in a pro-ceeding which relates to a contract of employment between the State and an individual for work performed or to be performed, in whole or in part, in the territory of that other State.

2. Paragraph 1 does not apply if:
(a) the employee has been recruited to perform particular functions in the exercise of governmental authority; . . .
(c) the subject-matter of the proceeding is the recruitment, renewal of employment or reinstatement of an individual; . . .

Article 12
Personal injuries and damage to property
Unless otherwise agreed between the States concerned, a State cannot invoke immun-ity from jurisdiction before a court of another State which is otherwise competent in a proceeding which relates to pecuniary compensation for death or injury to the person, or damage to or loss of tangible property, caused by an act or omission which is alleged to be attributable to the State, if the act or omission occurred in whole or in part in the territory of that other State and if the author of the act or omission was present in that territory at the time of the act or omission.

Article 13
Ownership, possession and use of property
Unless otherwise agreed between the States concerned, a State cannot invoke immunity from jurisdiction before a court of another State which is otherwise competent in a pro-ceeding which relates to the determination of:
(a) any right or interest of the State in, or its possession or use of, or any obligation of the State arising out of its interest in, or its possession or use of, immovable property situated in the State of the forum;
(b) any right or interest of the State in movable or immovable property arising by way of succession, gift or *bona vacantia*; or

(c) any right or interest of the State in the administration of property, such as trust property, the estate of a bankrupt or the property of a company in the event of its winding up.

Article 14
Intellectual and industrial property
Unless otherwise agreed between the States concerned, a State cannot invoke immunity from jurisdiction before a court of another State which is otherwise competent in a proceeding which relates to:

(a) the determination of any right of the State in a patent, industrial design, trade name or business name, trademark, copyright or any other form of intellectual or industrial property which enjoys a measure of legal protection, even if provisional, in the State of the forum; or

(b) an alleged infringement by the State, in the territory of the State of the forum, of a right of the nature mentioned in subparagraph (a) which belongs to a third person and is protected in the State of the forum.

Article 15
Participation in companies or other collective bodies
1. A State cannot invoke immunity from jurisdiction before a court of another State which is otherwise competent in a proceeding which relates to its participation in a company or other collective body, whether incorporated or unincorporated . . . .

Article 16
Ships owned or operated by a State
1. Unless otherwise agreed between the States concerned, a State which owns or operates a ship cannot invoke immunity from jurisdiction before a court of another State which is otherwise competent in a proceeding which relates to the operation of that ship if, at the time the cause of action arose, the ship was used for other than government non-commercial purposes.

2. Paragraph 1 does not apply to warships, or naval auxiliaries, nor does it apply to other vessels owned or operated by a State and used, for the time being, only on government non-commercial service . . . .

Part IV
State immunity from measures of constraint in connection with proceedings before a court

Article 18
State immunity from pre-judgment measures of constraint
No pre-judgment measures of constraint, such as attachment or arrest, against property of a State may be taken in connection with a proceeding before a court of another State unless and except to the extent that:

(a) the State has expressly consented to the taking of such measures . . . ; or

(b) the State has allocated or earmarked property for the satisfaction of the claim which is the object of that proceeding.

Article 19

State immunity from post-judgment measures of constraint

No post-judgment measures of constraint, such as attachment, arrest or execution, against property of a State may be taken in connection with a proceeding before a court of another State unless and except to the extent that:

(a) the State has expressly consented to the taking of such measures . . . ; or

(b) the State has allocated or earmarked property for the satisfaction of the claim which is the object of that proceeding; or

(c) it has been established that the property is specifically in use or intended for use by the State for other than government non-commercial purposes . . . .

Article 20

Effect of consent to jurisdiction to measures of constraint

Where consent to the measures of constraint is required under articles 18 and 19, consent to the exercise of jurisdiction under article 7 shall not imply consent to the taking of measures of constraint.

Article 21

Specific categories of property

1. The following categories, in particular, of property of a State shall not be considered as property specifically in use or intended for use by the State for other than government non-commercial purposes under article 19, subparagraph (c):

(a) property, including any bank account, which is used or intended for use in the performance of the functions of the diplomatic mission of the State or its consular posts, special missions, missions to international organizations or delegations to organs of international organizations or to international conferences;

(b) property of a military character or used or intended for use in the performance of military functions;

(c) property of the central bank or other monetary authority of the State;

(d) property forming part of the cultural heritage of the State or part of its archives and not placed or intended to be placed on sale;

(e) property forming part of an exhibition of objects of scientific, cultural or historical interest and not placed or intended to be placed on sale.

2. Paragraph 1 is without prejudice to article 18 and article 19, subparagraphs (a) and (b) . . . .

Note the provisions in both Canada's *State Immunity Act* and the United Nations Convention to the effect that a state may waive, or be deemed to have waived, its state immunities. Consider again, as when considering diplomatic immunities, the importance of the distinction between immunity from, and absence of, jurisdiction. In the next subsection, we will consider a case where waiver of immunity arguably played a significant role in a British court's ability to exercise its jurisdiction over a former Chilean head of state.

Note also how the state immunities recognized in the Convention in respect of pre- and post-judgment execution are much less restrictively defined than those in respect of adjudication on the merits of a claim, an approach also reflected in Canada's *State*

Immunity Act.[21] What is the reason for this distinction? What does it say about the willingness of states to subject themselves to the enforcement jurisdiction of foreign courts in respect of their commercial and other non-sovereign activities?

LAW IN CONTEXT

State Immunity and Visiting Allied Military Forces

Note that the immunity enjoyed by visiting foreign military forces in Canada is governed by a separate statute, the *Visiting Forces Act.*[22] Consider this discussion of immunities extended to allied military forces, prepared by the Canadian Department of Foreign Affairs and International Trade (now Foreign Affairs, Trade and Development):

International law has been unsettled in relation to the amenability of visiting naval and military personnel to the exercise of receiving state criminal jurisdiction . . . . The well-known decision of Chief Justice Marshall in *Schooner Exchange*, prompted American commentators to draw the inference that visiting forces should be considered immune from the exercise of receiving state jurisdiction unless by treaty the sending state waived that immunity.

In *Reference Re: Exemption of United States Forces from Canadian Criminal Law*, [1943] S.C.R. 483, the Supreme Court of Canada considered whether U.S. forces enjoyed immunity from Canadian criminal courts. Duff C.J.C. and Hudson J. held that Canadian criminal courts have full jurisdiction in respect of offenses committed on Canadian soil by U.S. forces except in respect to acts committed within their lines or on board their warships, or of offences against discipline committed by one crew member against another crew member of the same force in which the act or offence does not affect the person or property of a Canadian subject.

Post WWII Canadian law adopted the principle of concurrent jurisdiction. The principle that every sovereign has jurisdiction over criminal acts committed within its territory is embodied in the NATO Status of Forces Agreement of 1951. Article VII of the NATO SOFA envisions three categories of offences to which sovereign immunity attaches to either the sending State or the receiving State. In the first category, the sending State has the right to exclusive jurisdiction over persons subject to its military law when (a) a security offence—treason, espionage, sabotage—is involved; or (b) when the offence is punishable in the sending State but is not a crime in the receiving State. [Article 7, section 2 (a)] In the second category, the receiving State has a right to exclusive jurisdiction because the offence—including security offences—is punishable in that State, but not by the sending State. [Article 7, section 2(b)]

In the third category, the two States have concurrent jurisdiction. [Article 7, section 3(b)] Within the concurrent jurisdiction category, the sending State has the primary right to exercise jurisdiction over their force's personnel if the offence was committed against their own members or if the offence was committed while in the course of official duties. Otherwise, the receiving State shall have primary jurisdiction. Even when the primary

21   *State Immunity Act*, above note 19, s 12.

22   *Visiting Forces Act*, RSC 1985, c V-2.

jurisdiction is held by the sending State, the host state does not lose jurisdiction. A State may waive its primary right and shall notify the other State of its waiver as soon as practicable.

Canada's *Visiting Forces Act* of 1967 implementing the NATO SOFA provides for the extension of concurrent jurisdiction to a list of designated countries including both NATO and non-NATO countries.

The prevailing interpretation of international customary law is that members of foreign warships who happen to be on board are shielded, even where Canada has primary jurisdiction over the matter under the *Visiting Forces Act*. Therefore, Canadian local police cannot enter another country's warship without the permission of the commanding officer, even where there is evidence to believe that the visiting force member committed an offence against a local inhabitant while the visiting force member was not on official duty. The Judge Advocate General Office comments that this immunity is the subject of reciprocal understanding. Our military/naval practice preserves this same practice where Canadian warships are harboured at foreign ports.[23]

3) State Immunities and Serious International Crimes or Other Gross Violations of Human Rights

The shift from an absolute to a restrictive approach to the law of state immunities in the twentieth century was driven mainly by denial of immunities in respect of state acts of a commercial or other private nature. More recently, international focus has shifted to the question whether states do or should enjoy immunities in respect of serious international crimes or other gross violations of human rights committed by them or on their behalf.[24] In this subsection, we review a number of cases that grapple with this contentious issue. They are instructive as to both the nature of state immunities and the ways in which they interact with other fundamental rules of international law.

Before turning to these cases, it is important to note that the approach of courts to this difficult issue depends on the distinctions between two types of state immunity. First, *ratione materiae* immunity attaches to acts, transactions, or conduct of the state itself and its organs, as well as the conduct of government officials, agents, or representatives when acting in their official capacity. In other words, this form of state immunity attaches to particular *conduct* by virtue of its attributability to the state. Second, *ratione personae* immunity attaches to the *person* of certain very senior state officials for so long as they occupy their official position. This is so regardless of whether or not the conduct for which they might otherwise be prosecuted or sued before a foreign court was "official" in nature. Officials enjoying this particular form of state immunity clearly include the head of state

---

23 Michael Leir, "Canadian Practice in International Law at the Department of Foreign Affairs in 1999–2000" (2000) 38 Can YB Int'l Law 331 at 350–52. See also Andrew Dickinson, "Status of Forces under the UN Convention on State Immunity" (2006) 55:2 ICLQ 427.

24 See, for example, Lee M Caplan, "State Immunity, Human Rights and *Jus Cogens*: A Critique of the Normative Hierarchy" (2003) 97 AJIL 741. See also Craig Forcese, "De-Immunizing Torture: Reconciling Human Rights and State Immunity" (2007) 52 McGill LJ 127. For a contrary view, see Xiaodong Yang, "*Jus Cogens* and State Immunity" (2006) 3 NZ YB Int'l L 131; Roger O'Keefe, "State Immunity and Human Rights: Heads and Walls, Hearts and Minds" (2011) 44:4 Vand J Transnat'l L 999.

and/or government and a state's foreign minister, and possibly other key members of the government (but not a state prosecutor or head of national security).[25]

The approach taken by the courts to the issue of state immunities for gross human rights and international humanitarian law violations, such as acts of torture, crimes against humanity, and war crimes, has also varied depending on whether the proceedings in question are criminal or civil. We therefore begin with cases falling within the former category before examining the issue in the context of civil proceedings.

a) Immunities from Criminal Jurisdiction

Consider first the groundbreaking approach taken by the Appellate Committee of the House of Lords (now replaced by the Supreme Court of the United Kingdom) to the issue of state immunities from criminal jurisdiction for acts of torture. In this case, Spain sought from the United Kingdom the extradition of Chile's former head of state, General Augusto Pinochet, in order to try Pinochet in Spain for acts of torture committed in Chile beginning in the 1970s. Spain, the United Kingdom, and Chile are all parties to the Torture Convention, which entered into force in 1987.[26]

> *R v Bow Street Metropolitan Stipendiary Magistrate and others, ex parte Pinochet Ugarte*
> *(Amnesty International and others intervening) (No 3),* [1999] 2 All ER 97 (HL)

LORD BROWNE-WILKINSON. . . .

The facts

On 11 September 1973 a right-wing coup evicted the left-wing regime of President Allende. The coup was led by a military junta, of whom Senator (then General) Pinochet was the leader. At some stage he became head of state. The Pinochet regime remained in power until 11 March 1990 when Senator Pinochet resigned.

There is no real dispute that during the period of the Senator Pinochet regime appalling acts of barbarism were committed in Chile and elsewhere in the world: torture, murder and the unexplained disappearance of individuals, all on a large scale. Although it is not alleged that Senator Pinochet himself committed any of those acts, it is alleged that they were done in pursuance of a conspiracy to which he was a party, at his instigation and with his knowledge. He denies these allegations. None of the conduct alleged was committed by or against citizens of the United Kingdom or in the United Kingdom.

In 1998 Senator Pinochet came to the United Kingdom for medical treatment. The judicial authorities in Spain sought to extradite him in order to stand trial in Spain on a large number of charges. Some of those charges had links with Spain. But most of the charges had no connection with Spain . . . .

---

25 *Certain Questions of Mutual Assistance in Criminal Matters (Djibouti v France)*, Judgment, [1980] ICJ Rep 177 at para 194.

26 United Nations Convention Against Torture and other Cruel, Inhuman or Degrading Treatment or Punishment, 10 December 1984, 1465 UNTS 85, Can TS 1987 No 36, in force 26 June 1987 [Torture Convention].

State immunity

This is the point around which most of the argument turned. It is of considerable general importance internationally since, if Senator Pinochet is not entitled to immunity in relation to the acts of torture alleged to have occurred after 29 September 1988 it will be the first time, so far as counsel have discovered, when a local domestic court has refused to afford immunity to a head of state or former head of state on the grounds that there can be no immunity against prosecution for certain international crimes.

. . . The issue is whether international law grants state immunity in relation to the international crime of torture and, if so, whether the Republic of Chile is entitled to claim such immunity even though Chile, Spain and the United Kingdom are all parties to the Torture Convention and therefore "contractually" bound to give effect to its provisions from 8 December 1988 at the latest.

It is a basic principle of international law that one sovereign state (the forum state) does not adjudicate on the conduct of a foreign state. The foreign state is entitled to procedural immunity from the processes of the forum state. This immunity extends to both criminal and civil liability. State immunity probably grew from the historical immunity of the person of the monarch. In any event, such personal immunity of the head of state persists to the present day: the head of state is entitled to the same immunity as the state itself. The diplomatic representative of the foreign state in the forum state is also afforded the same immunity in recognition of the dignity of the state which he represents. This immunity enjoyed by a head of state in power . . . is a complete immunity attaching to the person of the head of state . . . and rendering him immune from all actions or prosecutions whether or not they relate to matters done for the benefit of the state. Such immunity is said to be granted *ratione personae*.

What then when the ambassador leaves his post or the head of state is deposed? The position of the ambassador is covered by the Vienna Convention on Diplomatic Relations 1961. . . Since he is no longer the representative of the foreign state he merits no particular privileges or immunities as a person. However in order to preserve the integrity of the activities of the foreign state during the period when he was ambassador, it is necessary to provide that immunity is afforded to his official acts during his tenure in post. . . This limited immunity, *ratione materiae*, is to be contrasted with the former immunity *ratione personae* which gave complete immunity to all activities whether public or private.

In my judgment, at common law a former head of state enjoys similar immunities, *ratione materiae*, once he ceases to be head of state. He too loses immunity *ratione personae* on ceasing to be head of state. . . Thus, at common law, the position of the former ambassador and the former head of state appears to be much the same: both enjoy immunity for acts done in performance of their respective functions whilst in office.

. . . Accordingly, in my judgment, Senator Pinochet as former head of state enjoys immunity *ratione materiae* in relation to acts done by him as head of state as part of his official functions as head of state.

The question then which has to be answered is whether the alleged organisation of state torture by Senator Pinochet (if proved) would constitute an act committed by Senator Pinochet as part of his official functions as head of state. It is not enough to say that it cannot be part of the functions of the head of state to commit a crime. Actions which are criminal under the local law can still have been done officially and therefore give rise to immunity *ratione materiae*. The case needs to be analysed more closely.

Can it be said that the commission of a crime which is an international crime against humanity and *jus cogens* is an act done in an official capacity on behalf of the state? I believe there to be strong ground for saying that the implementation of torture as defined by the Torture Convention cannot be a state function . . . .

. . . [I]f the implementation of a torture regime is a public function giving rise to immunity *ratione materiae*, this produces bizarre results. Immunity *ratione materiae* applies not only to ex-heads of state and ex-ambassadors but to all state officials who have been involved in carrying out the functions of the state. . . [I]f the implementation of the torture regime is to be treated as official business sufficient to found an immunity for the former head of state, it must also be official business sufficient to justify immunity for his inferiors who actually did the torturing. Under the convention the international crime of torture can only be committed by an official or someone in an official capacity. They would all be entitled to immunity. It would follow that there can be no case outside Chile in which a successful prosecution for torture can be brought unless the state of Chile is prepared to waive its right to its officials' immunity. Therefore the whole elaborate structure of universal jurisdiction over torture committed by officials is rendered abortive and one of the main objectives of the Torture Convention — to provide a system under which there is no safe haven for torturers — will have been frustrated. In my judgment all these factors together demonstrate that the notion of continued immunity for ex-heads of state is inconsistent with the provisions of the Torture Convention.

For these reasons in my judgment if, as alleged, Senator Pinochet organised and authorised torture after 8 December 1988 he was not acting in any capacity which gives rise to immunity *ratione materiae* because such actions were contrary to international law, Chile had agreed to outlaw such conduct and Chile had agreed with the other parties to the Torture Convention that all signatory states should have jurisdiction to try official torture (as defined in the convention) even if such torture were committed in Chile.

As to the charges of murder and conspiracy to murder, no one has advanced any reason why the ordinary rules of immunity should not apply and Senator Pinochet is entitled to such immunity . . . .

LORD GOFF OF CHIEVELEY. . . .

IV. State immunity

. . . There can be no doubt that the immunity of a head of state, whether *ratione personae* or *ratione materiae*, applies to both civil and criminal proceedings. This is because the immunity applies to any form of legal process . . . .

However, a question arises whether any limit is placed on the immunity in respect of criminal offences. Obviously the mere fact that the conduct is criminal does not of itself exclude the immunity, otherwise there would be little point in the immunity from criminal process; and this is so even where the crime is of a serious character. It follows, in my opinion, that the mere fact that the crime in question is torture does not exclude state immunity. It has however been stated by Sir Arthur Watts (at pp 81-84) that a head of state may be personally responsible: ". . . for acts of such seriousness that they constitute not merely international wrongs (in the broad sense of a civil wrong) but rather international crimes which offend against the public order of the international community." . . . .

So far as torture is concerned, however, there are two points to be made. The first is that it is evident from this passage that Sir Arthur is referring not just to a specific crime as such, but to a crime which offends against the public order of the international community, for which a head of state may be *internationally* (his emphasis) accountable. The instruments cited by him show that he is concerned here with crimes against peace, war crimes and crimes against humanity . . . .

It follows that, if state immunity in respect of crimes of torture has been excluded at all in the present case, this can only have been done by the Torture Convention itself . . . .

It is to be observed that no mention is made of state immunity in the convention. Had it been intended to exclude state immunity, it is reasonable to assume that this would have been the subject either of a separate article, or of a separate paragraph in art 7, introduced to provide for that particular matter. This would have been consistent with the logical framework of the convention, under which separate provision is made for each topic, introduced in logical order . . . .

. . . [I]n accordance both with international law, and with the law of this country which on this point reflects international law, a state's waiver of its immunity by treaty must . . . always be express. Indeed, if this was not so, there could well be international chaos as the courts of different state parties to a treaty reach different conclusions on the question whether a waiver of immunity was to be implied . . . .

However it is, as I understand it, suggested . . . that, for the purposes of the convention, . . . torture does not form part of the functions of public officials or others acting in an official capacity . . . .

In my opinion, the principle which I have described cannot be circumvented in this way. I observe first that the meaning of the word "functions" as used in this context is well established. The functions of, for example, a head of state are governmental functions, as opposed to private acts; and the fact that the head of state performs an act, other than a private act, which is criminal does not deprive it of its governmental character. This is as true of a serious crime, such as murder or torture, as it is of a lesser crime . . . .

. . . Moreover, as I understand it, the only purpose of the proposed implied limitation upon the functions of public officials is to deprive them, or as in the present case a former head of state, of the benefit of state immunity; and in my opinion the policy which requires that such a result can only be achieved in a treaty by express agreement, with the effect that it cannot be so achieved by implication, renders it equally unacceptable that it should be achieved indirectly by means of an implication such as that now proposed.

For the above reasons, . . . Senator Pinochet is entitled to the benefit of state immunity *ratione materiae* as a former head of state . . . .

LORD HOPE OF CRAIGHEAD. . . .

[E]ven in the field of such high crimes as have achieved the status of *jus cogens* under customary international law there is as yet no general agreement that they are outside the immunity to which former heads of state are entitled from the jurisdiction of foreign national courts . . . .

. . . [I]t would be wrong to regard the Torture Convention as having by necessary implication removed the immunity *ratione materiae* from former heads of state in regard to every act of torture of any kind which might be alleged against him falling within the scope of art 1 . . . .

Nevertheless there remains the question whether the immunity can survive Chile's agreement to the Torture Convention if the torture which is alleged was of such a kind or on such a scale as to amount to an international crime. Sir Arthur Watts states (at p. 82) that the idea that individuals who commit international crimes are internationally accountable for them has now become an accepted part of international law . . . .

The allegations which the Spanish judicial authorities have made against Senator Pinochet fall into that category . . . . In my opinion, once the machinery which [the Torture Convention] provides was put in place to enable jurisdiction over such crimes to be exercised in the courts of a foreign state, it was no longer open to any state which was a signatory to the convention to invoke the immunity *ratione materiae* in the event of allegations of systematic or widespread torture committed after that date being made in the courts of that state against its officials or any other person acting in an official capacity.

As Sir Arthur Watts has explained . . . the general principle in such cases is that of individual responsibility for international criminal conduct . . . . [I]t can no longer be doubted that as a matter of general customary international law a head of state will personally be liable to be called to account if there is sufficient evidence that he authorised or perpetrated such serious international crimes. A head of state is still protected while in office by the immunity *ratione personae*, but the immunity *ratione materiae* on which he would have to rely on leaving office must be denied to him.

I would not regard this as a case of waiver. Nor would I accept that it was an implied term of the Torture Convention that former heads of state were to be deprived of their immunity *ratione materiae* with respect to all acts of official torture as defined in art 1. It is just that the obligations which were recognised by customary international law in the case of such serious international crimes by the date when Chile ratified the convention are so strong as to override any objection by it on the ground of immunity *ratione materiae* to the exercise of the jurisdiction over crimes committed after that date which the United Kingdom had made available.

I consider that the date as from which the immunity *ratione materiae* was lost was 30 October 1988, which was the date when Chile's ratification of the Torture Convention on 30 September 1988 took effect . . . . But I am content to accept the view of my noble and learned friend Lord Saville of Newdigate that Senator Pinochet continued to have immunity until 8 December 1988 when the United Kingdom ratified the convention . . . .

LORD HUTTON. . . .

In my opinion [Pinochet] is not entitled to claim [*ratione materiae*] immunity. The Torture Convention 1984 makes it clear that no state is to tolerate torture by its public officials or by persons acting in an official capacity and art. 2 requires that:

1. Each State Party shall take effective legislative, administrative, judicial or other measures to prevent acts of torture in any territory under its jurisdiction.

2. No exceptional circumstances whatsoever, whether a state of war or a threat of

war, internal political instability or any other public emergency, may be invoked as a justification of torture.

Article 4 provides:

1. Each State Party shall ensure that all acts of torture are offences under its criminal law. The same shall apply to an attempt to commit torture and to an act by any person which constitutes complicity or participation in torture.

2. Each State Party shall make these offences punishable by appropriate penalties which take into account their grave nature.

Article 7(1) provides:

The State Party in the territory under whose jurisdiction a person alleged to have committed any offence referred to in article 4 is found shall in the cases contemplated in article 5, if it does not extradite him, submit the case to its competent authorities for the purpose of prosecution.

I do not accept the argument advanced by counsel on behalf of Senator Pinochet that the provisions of the convention were designed to give one state jurisdiction to prosecute a public official of another state in the event of that state deciding to waive state immunity. I consider that the clear intent of the provisions is that an official of one state who has committed torture should be prosecuted if he is present in another state.

Therefore, having regard to the provisions of the Torture Convention, I do not consider that Senator Pinochet or Chile can claim that the commission of acts of torture after 29 September 1988 were functions of the head of state. The alleged acts of torture by Senator Pinochet were carried out under colour of his position as head of state, but they cannot be regarded as functions of a head of state under international law when international law expressly prohibits torture as a measure which a state can employ in any circumstances whatsoever and has made it an international crime . . . .

LORD SAVILLE OF NEWDIGATE. . . .

[T]he immunity [*ratione materiae*] of a former head of state does attach to his conduct whilst in office and is wholly related to what he did in his official capacity.

So far as the states that are parties to the convention are concerned, I cannot see how, so far as torture is concerned, this immunity can exist consistently with the terms of that convention. Each state party has agreed that the other state parties can exercise jurisdiction over alleged official torturers found within their territories, by extraditing them or referring them to their own appropriate authorities for prosecution; and thus, to my mind, can hardly simultaneously claim an immunity from extradition or prosecution that is necessarily based on the official nature of the alleged torture.

Since 8 December 1988 Chile, Spain and this country have all been parties to the Torture Convention. So far as these countries at least are concerned it seems to me that from that date these state parties are in agreement with each other that the immunity *ratione materiae* of their former heads of state cannot be claimed in cases of alleged official torture. In other words, so far as the allegations of official torture against Senator Pinochet are concerned, there is now by this agreement an exception or qualification to the general rule of immunity *ratione materiae.*

I do not reach this conclusion by implying terms into the Torture Convention, but simply by applying its express terms. A former head of state who it is alleged resorted to torture for state purposes falls, in my view, fairly and squarely within those terms and, on the face of it, should be dealt with in accordance with them. Indeed it seems to me that it is those who would seek to remove such alleged official torturers from the machinery of the convention who in truth have to assert that by some process of implication or otherwise the clear words of the convention should be treated as inapplicable to a former head of state, notwithstanding he is properly described as a person who was "acting in an official capacity."

I can see no valid basis for such an assertion. It is said that if it had been intended to remove immunity for alleged official torture from former heads of state there would inevitably have been some discussion of the point in the negotiations leading to the treaty. I am not persuaded that the apparent absence of any such discussions takes the matter any further. If there were states that wished to preserve such immunity in the face of universal condemnation of official torture, it is perhaps not surprising that they kept quiet about it.

It is also said that any waiver by states of immunities must be express, or at least unequivocal. I would not dissent from this as a general proposition, but it seems to me that the express and unequivocal terms of the Torture Convention fulfil any such requirement. To my mind these terms demonstrate that the states who have become parties have clearly and unambiguously agreed that official torture should now be dealt with in a way which would otherwise amount to an interference in their sovereignty . . . .

LORD PHILLIPS OF WORTH MATRAVERS. . . .

[Immunity *ratione materiae* is] an immunity of the state which applies to preclude the courts of another state from asserting jurisdiction in relation to a suit brought against an official or other agent of the state, present or past, in relation to the conduct of the business of the state while in office. While a head of state is serving, his status ensures him immunity. Once he is out of office, he is in the same position as any other state official and any immunity will be based upon the nature of the subject matter of the litigation . . . .

There would seem to be two explanations for immunity *ratione materiae.* The first is that to sue an individual in respect of the conduct of the state's business is, indirectly, to sue the state. The state would be obliged to meet any award of damage made against the individual. This reasoning has no application to criminal proceedings. The second explanation for the immunity is the principle that it is contrary to international law for one state to adjudicate upon the internal affairs of another state . . . .

I reach . . . [my] conclusion on the simple basis that no established rule of international law requires state immunity *ratione materiae* to be accorded in respect of prosecution for an international crime. International crimes and extra-territorial jurisdiction in relation to them are both new arrivals in the field of public international law. I do not believe that state immunity *ratione materiae* can co-exist with them. The exercise of extra-territorial jurisdiction overrides the principle that one state will not intervene in the internal affairs of another. It does so because, where international crime is concerned, that principle cannot prevail. An international crime is as offensive, if not more offensive, to the international community when committed under colour of office. Once extra-territorial jurisdiction is established, it makes no sense to exclude from it acts done in an official capacity.

There can be no doubt that the conduct of which Senator Pinochet stands accused by Spain is criminal under international law. The Republic of Chile has accepted that torture is prohibited by international law and that the prohibition of torture has the character of *jus cogens* and or obligation *erga omnes*. It is further accepted that officially sanctioned torture is forbidden by international law . . . .

The convention is . . . incompatible with the applicability of immunity *ratione materiae*. There are only two possibilities. One is that the state parties to the convention proceeded on the premise that no immunity could exist *ratione materiae* in respect of torture, a crime contrary to international law. The other is that the state parties to the convention expressly agreed that immunity *ratione materiae* should not apply in the case of torture. I believe that the first of these alternatives is the correct one, but either must be fatal to the assertion by Chile and Senator Pinochet of immunity in respect of extradition proceedings based on torture . . . .

LORD MILLETT. . . .

State immunity is not a personal right. It is an attribute of the sovereignty of the state. The immunity which is in question in the present case, therefore, belongs to the Republic of Chile, not to Senator Pinochet. It may be asserted or waived by the state, but where it is waived by treaty or convention the waiver must be express. So much is not in dispute . . . .

Immunity *ratione personae* is a status immunity. An individual who enjoys its protection does so because of his official status. It enures for his benefit only so long as he holds office. While he does so he enjoys absolute immunity from the civil and criminal jurisdiction of the national courts of foreign states. But it is only narrowly available . . . .

This immunity is not in issue in the present case. Senator Pinochet is not a serving head of state. If he were, he could not be extradited. It would be an intolerable affront to the Republic of Chile to arrest him or detain him.

Immunity *ratione materiae* is very different. This is a subject matter immunity. It operates to prevent the official and governmental acts of one state from being called into question in proceedings before the courts of another, and only incidentally confers immunity on the individual. It is therefore a narrower immunity but it is more widely available. It is available to former heads of state and heads of diplomatic missions, and any one whose conduct in the exercise of the authority of the state is afterwards called into question, whether he acted as head of government, government minister, military commander or chief of police, or subordinate public official. The immunity is the same whatever the rank of the office holder. . . It is an immunity from the civil and criminal jurisdiction of foreign national courts, but only in respect of governmental or official acts. The exercise of authority by the military and security forces of the state is the paradigm example of such conduct . . . .

The definition of torture, both in the convention and [the UK implementing legislation], is in my opinion entirely inconsistent with the existence of a plea of immunity *ratione materiae*. The offence can be committed only by or at the instigation of, or with the consent or acquiescence of, a public official or other person acting in an official capacity.

The official or governmental nature of the act, which forms the basis of the immunity, is an essential ingredient of the offence. No rational system of criminal justice can allow an immunity which is co-extensive with the offence.

In my view a serving head of state or diplomat could still claim immunity *ratione personae*... He does not have to rely on the character of the conduct of which he is accused. The nature of the charge is irrelevant; his immunity is personal and absolute. But the former head of state and the former diplomat are in no different position from anyone else claiming to have acted in the exercise of state authority ....

My Lords, the Republic of Chile was a party to the Torture Convention, and must be taken to have assented to the imposition of an obligation on foreign national courts to take and exercise criminal jurisdiction in respect of the official use of torture. I do not regard it as having thereby waived its immunity. In my opinion there was no immunity to be waived. The offence is one which could only be committed in circumstances which would normally give rise to the immunity. The international community had created an offence for which immunity *ratione materiae* could not possibly be available. International law cannot be supposed to have established a crime having the character of a *jus cogens* and at the same time to have provided an immunity which is co-extensive with the obligation it seeks to impose ....

As these extracts indicate, the majority of the Law Lords considered that Pinochet was not entitled to immunity in respect of his alleged role in acts of torture, and could therefore be extradited to Spain. What was the *ratio decidendi* of this case? Was it that no immunity *ratione materiae* could attach to such acts in principle? Or that any such immunity had been waived by Chile when it became a party to the Torture Convention? Would the outcome have been the same had Chile not been a party to the Torture Convention?

Under the law governing extradition between the United Kingdom and Spain at the time, and notwithstanding the decision of the Law Lords, the ultimate decision to surrender an individual wanted for extradition was made by the executive branch of government. After reports were presented suggesting that Pinochet might not be medically fit to stand trial, then UK Home Secretary Jack Straw declined to order the surrender. Pinochet later returned to Chile, where he faced substantial litigation in the Chilean courts, but ultimately died in 2006 at the age of 91 without ever standing trial for his involvement in the enforced disappearance, torture, and murder of thousands of dissidents to his regime.

As Pinochet was no longer Chile's head of state at the time of the UK proceedings, the *Pinochet* judgment turned on the availability of *ratione materiae* immunity. Consider now the approach of the International Court of Justice to a similar type of case, albeit one involving a senior state official still in office:

Arrest Warrant of 11 April 2000 (Democratic Republic of the Congo v Belgium), Judgment, [2002] ICJ Rep 3, 41 ILM 536

THE COURT:

1. On 17 October 2000 the Democratic Republic of the Congo (hereinafter referred to as "the Congo") filed in the Registry of the Court an Application instituting proceedings

against the Kingdom of Belgium (hereinafter referred to as "Belgium") in respect of a dispute concerning an "international arrest warrant issued on 11 April 2000 by a Belgian investigating judge . . . against the Minister for Foreign Affairs in office of the Democratic Republic of the Congo, Mr. Abdulaye Yerodia Ndombasi." . . . .

13. On 11 April 2000 an investigating judge of the Brussels *tribunal de première instance* issued "an international arrest warrant in absentia" against Mr. Abdulaye Yerodia Ndombasi, charging him, as perpetrator or co-perpetrator, with offences constituting grave breaches of the Geneva Conventions of 1949 and of the Additional Protocols thereto [i.e., war crimes], and with crimes against humanity.

At the time when the arrest warrant was issued Mr. Yerodia was the Minister for Foreign Affairs of the Congo . . . .

Article 7 of the Belgian Law provides that "The Belgian courts shall have jurisdiction in respect of the offences provided for in the present Law, wheresoever they may have been committed." In the present case, according to Belgium, the complaints that initiated the proceedings as a result of which the arrest warrant was issued emanated from 12 individuals all resident in Belgium, five of whom were of Belgian nationality. It is not contested by Belgium, however, that the alleged acts to which the arrest warrant relates were committed outside Belgian territory, that Mr. Yerodia was not a Belgian national at the time of those acts, and that Mr. Yerodia was not in Belgian territory at the time that the arrest warrant was issued and circulated. That no Belgian nationals were victims of the violence that was said to have resulted from Mr. Yerodia's alleged offences was also uncontested.

Article 5, paragraph 3, of the Belgian Law further provides that "immunity attaching to the official capacity of a person shall not prevent the application of the present Law." . . . .

47. The Congo maintains that, during his or her term of office, a Minister for Foreign Affairs of a sovereign State is entitled to inviolability and to immunity from criminal process being "absolute or complete," that is to say, they are subject to no exception. Accordingly, the Congo contends that no criminal prosecution may be brought against a Minister for Foreign Affairs in a foreign court as long as he or she remains in office, and that any finding of criminal responsibility by a domestic court in a foreign country, or any act of investigation undertaken with a view to bringing him or her to court, would contravene the principle of immunity from jurisdiction. According to the Congo, the basis of such criminal immunity is purely functional, and immunity is accorded under customary international law simply in order to enable the foreign State representative enjoying such immunity to perform his or her functions freely and without let or hindrance. The Congo adds that the immunity thus accorded to Ministers for Foreign Affairs when in office covers all their acts, including any committed before they took office, and that it is irrelevant whether the acts done whilst in office may be characterized or not as "official acts."

48. The Congo states further that it does not deny the existence of a principle of international criminal law, deriving from the decisions of the Nuremberg and Tokyo international military tribunals, that the accused's official capacity at the time of the acts

cannot, before any court, whether domestic or international, constitute a "ground of exemption from his criminal responsibility or a ground for mitigation of sentence." The Congo then stresses that the fact that an immunity might bar prosecution before a specific court or over a specific period does not mean that the same prosecution cannot be brought, if appropriate, before another court which is not bound by that immunity, or at another time when the immunity need no longer be taken into account. It concludes that immunity does not mean impunity.

49. Belgium maintains for its part that, while Ministers for Foreign Affairs in office generally enjoy an immunity from jurisdiction before the courts of a foreign State, such immunity applies only to acts carried out in the course of their official functions, and cannot protect such persons in respect of private acts or when they are acting otherwise than in the performance of their official functions.

50. Belgium further states that, in the circumstances of the present case, Mr. Yerodia enjoyed no immunity at the time when he is alleged to have committed the acts of which he is accused, and that there is no evidence that he was then acting in any official capacity. It observes that the arrest warrant was issued against Mr. Yerodia personally.

51. The Court would observe at the outset that in international law it is firmly established that, as also diplomatic and consular agents, certain holders of high-ranking office in a State, such as the Head of State, Head of Government and Minister for Foreign Affairs, enjoy immunities from jurisdiction in other States, both civil and criminal. For the purposes of the present case, it is only the immunity from criminal jurisdiction and the inviolability of an incumbent Minister for Foreign Affairs that fall for the Court to consider . . . .

53. In customary international law, the immunities accorded to Ministers for Foreign Affairs are not granted for their personal benefit, but to ensure the effective performance of their functions on behalf of their respective States. In order to determine the extent of these immunities, the Court must therefore first consider the nature of the functions exercised by a Minister for Foreign Affairs. He or she is in charge of his or her Government's diplomatic activities and generally acts as its representative in international negotiations and intergovernmental meetings. Ambassadors and other diplomatic agents carry out their duties under his or her authority. His or her acts may bind the State represented, and there is a presumption that a Minister for Foreign Affairs, simply by virtue of that office, has full powers to act on behalf of the State (see, e.g., Art. 7, para. 2(a), of the 1969 Vienna Convention on the Law of Treaties). In the performance of these functions, he or she is frequently required to travel internationally, and thus must be in a position freely to do so whenever the need should arise. He or she must also be in constant communication with the Government, and with its diplomatic missions around the world, and be capable at any time of communicating with representatives of other States. The Court further observes that a Minister for Foreign Affairs, responsible for the conduct of his or her State's relations with all other States, occupies a position such that, like the Head of State or the Head of Government, he or she is recognized under international law as representative of the State solely by virtue of his or her office. He or she does not have to present letters of credence: to the contrary, it is generally the Minister who

determines the authority to be conferred upon diplomatic agents and countersigns their letters of credence . . . .

54. The Court accordingly concludes that the functions of a Minister for Foreign Affairs are such that, throughout the duration of his or her office, he or she when abroad enjoys full immunity from criminal jurisdiction and inviolability. That immunity and that inviolability protect the individual concerned against any act of authority of another State which would hinder him or her in the performance of his or her duties.

55. In this respect, no distinction can be drawn between acts performed by a Minister for Foreign Affairs in an "official" capacity, and those claimed to have been performed in a "private capacity," or, for that matter, between acts performed before the person concerned assumed office as Minister for Foreign Affairs and acts committed during the period of office. Thus, if a Minister for Foreign Affairs is arrested in another State on a criminal charge, he or she is clearly thereby prevented from exercising the functions of his or her office. The consequences of such impediment to the exercise of those official functions are equally serious, regardless of whether the Minister for Foreign Affairs was, at the time of arrest, present in the territory of the arresting State on an "official" visit or a "private" visit, regardless of whether the arrest relates to acts allegedly performed before the person became the Minister for Foreign Affairs or to acts performed while in office, and regardless of whether the arrest relates to alleged acts performed in an "official" capacity or a "private" capacity. Furthermore, even the mere risk that, by travelling to or transiting another State a Minister for Foreign Affairs might be exposing himself or herself to legal proceedings could deter the Minister from travelling internationally when required to do so for the purposes of the performance of his or her official functions.

56. The Court will now address Belgium's argument that immunities accorded to incumbent Ministers for Foreign Affairs can in no case protect them where they are suspected of having committed war crimes or crimes against humanity. In support of this position, Belgium refers in its Counter-Memorial to various legal instruments creating international criminal tribunals, to examples from national legislation, and to the jurisprudence of national and international courts.

Belgium begins by pointing out that certain provisions of the instruments creating international criminal tribunals state expressly that the official capacity of a person shall not be a bar to the exercise by such tribunals of their jurisdiction.

Belgium also places emphasis on certain decisions of national courts, and in particular on the judgments rendered on 24 March 1999 by the House of Lords in the United Kingdom and on 13 March 2001 by the Court of Cassation in France in the Pinochet and Qaddafi cases respectively, in which it contends that an exception to the immunity rule was accepted in the case of serious crimes under international law. Thus, according to Belgium, the Pinochet decision recognizes an exception to the immunity rule when Lord Millett stated that "international law cannot be supposed to have established a crime having the character of a *jus cogens* and at the same time to have provided an immunity which is co-extensive with the obligation it seeks to impose," or when Lord Phillips of Worth Matravers said that "no established rule of international law requires state immunity *rationae materiae* to be accorded in respect of prosecution for an international crime." As to the French Court of Cassation, Belgium contends that, in holding that, "under international law as it currently stands, the crime alleged [acts of terrorism], irrespective of its gravity, does not come within the exceptions to the principle of immunity from jurisdiction for incumbent foreign Heads of State," the Court explicitly recognized the existence of such exceptions.

57. The Congo, for its part, states that, under international law as it currently stands, there is no basis for asserting that there is any exception to the principle of absolute immunity from criminal process of an incumbent Minister for Foreign Affairs where he or she is accused of having committed crimes under international law.

In support of this contention, the Congo refers to State practice, giving particular consideration in this regard to the Pinochet and Qaddafi cases, and concluding that such practice does not correspond to that which Belgium claims but, on the contrary, confirms the absolute nature of the immunity from criminal process of Heads of State and Ministers for Foreign Affairs. Thus, in the Pinochet case, the Congo cites Lord Browne-Wilkinson's statement that "this immunity enjoyed by a head of state in power and an ambassador in post is a complete immunity attached to the person of the head of state or ambassador and rendering him immune from all actions or prosecutions. . ." According to the Congo, the French Court of Cassation adopted the same position in its Qaddafi judgment, in affirming that "international custom bars the prosecution of incumbent Heads of State, in the absence of any contrary international provision binding on the parties concerned, before the criminal courts of a foreign State."

As regards the instruments creating international criminal tribunals and the latter's jurisprudence, these, in the Congo's view, concern only those tribunals, and no inference can be drawn from them in regard to criminal proceedings before national courts against persons enjoying immunity under international law.

58. The Court has carefully examined State practice, including national legislation and those few decisions of national higher courts, such as the House of Lords or the French Court of Cassation. It has been unable to deduce from this practice that there exists under customary international law any form of exception to the rule according immunity from criminal jurisdiction and inviolability to incumbent Ministers for Foreign Affairs, where they are suspected of having committed war crimes or crimes against humanity . . . .

In view of the foregoing, the Court accordingly cannot accept Belgium's argument in this regard.

59. It should further be noted that the rules governing the jurisdiction of national courts must be carefully distinguished from those governing jurisdictional immunities: jurisdiction does not imply absence of immunity, while absence of immunity does not imply jurisdiction. Thus, although various international conventions on the prevention and punishment of certain serious crimes impose on States obligations of prosecution or extradition, thereby requiring them to extend their criminal jurisdiction, such extension of jurisdiction in no way affects immunities under customary international law, including those of Ministers for Foreign Affairs. These remain opposable before the courts of a foreign State, even where those courts exercise such a jurisdiction under these conventions.

60. The Court emphasizes, however, that the immunity from jurisdiction enjoyed by incumbent Ministers for Foreign Affairs does not mean that they enjoy impunity in respect

of any crimes they might have committed, irrespective of their gravity. Immunity from criminal jurisdiction and individual criminal responsibility are quite separate concepts. While jurisdictional immunity is procedural in nature, criminal responsibility is a question of substantive law. Jurisdictional immunity may well bar prosecution for a certain period or for certain offences; it cannot exonerate the person to whom it applies from all criminal responsibility.

61. Accordingly, the immunities enjoyed under international law by an incumbent or former Minister for Foreign Affairs do not represent a bar to criminal prosecution in certain circumstances.

First, such persons enjoy no criminal immunity under international law in their own countries, and may thus be tried by those countries' courts in accordance with the relevant rules of domestic law.

Secondly, they will cease to enjoy immunity from foreign jurisdiction if the State which they represent or have represented decides to waive that immunity.

Thirdly, after a person ceases to hold the office of Minister for Foreign Affairs, he or she will no longer enjoy all of the immunities accorded by international law in other States. Provided that it has jurisdiction under international law, a court of one State may try a former Minister for Foreign Affairs of another State in respect of acts committed prior or subsequent to his or her period of office, as well as in respect of acts committed during that period of office in a private capacity.

Fourthly, an incumbent or former Minister for Foreign Affairs may be subject to criminal proceedings before certain international criminal courts, where they have jurisdiction . . . .

As in the case of the warrant's issue, its international circulation from June 2000 by the Belgian authorities, given its nature and purpose, effectively infringed Mr. Yerodia's immunity as the Congo's incumbent Minister for Foreign Affairs and was furthermore liable to affect the Congo's conduct of its international relations. Since Mr. Yerodia was called upon in that capacity to undertake travel in the performance of his duties, the mere international circulation of the warrant, even in the absence of "further steps" by Belgium, could have resulted, in particular, in his arrest while abroad. The Court observes in this respect that Belgium itself cites information to the effect that Mr. Yerodia, "on applying for a visa to go to two countries, [apparently] learned that he ran the risk of being arrested as a result of the arrest warrant issued against him by Belgium," adding that "this, moreover, is what the [Congo] . . . hints when it writes that the arrest warrant 'sometimes forced Minister Yerodia to travel by roundabout routes.'" Accordingly, the Court concludes that the circulation of the warrant, whether or not it significantly interfered with Mr. Yerodia's diplomatic activity, constituted a violation of an obligation of Belgium towards the Congo, in that it failed to respect the immunity of the incumbent Minister for Foreign Affairs of the Congo and, more particularly, infringed the immunity from criminal jurisdiction and the inviolability then enjoyed by him under international law . . . .

The *Arrest Warrant* case dealt with the question of *ratione personae* immunity from foreign criminal jurisdiction, concluding that it persists for certain senior state officials in office even where their alleged conduct amounts to serious international crimes. There is even less reason to doubt that such officials also enjoy *ratione personae* immunity from foreign civil jurisdiction.

Note the point made by the Court in paragraph 59 of this judgment, to the effect that "jurisdiction does not imply absence of immunity, while absence of immunity does not imply jurisdiction." What are the implications of this observation for the reasoning of some of the Law Lords in *Pinochet*?

Note too that the International Law Commission commenced its consideration of the topic "Immunity of State Officials from Foreign Criminal Jurisdiction" in 2008. Following early work by a first Special Rapporteur, a new Special Rapporteur appointed in 2012 tabled a preliminary set of draft articles in 2013 providing that: "The immunity from foreign criminal jurisdiction that is enjoyed by Heads of State, Heads of Government and ministers for foreign affairs covers all acts, whether private or official, that are performed by such persons prior to or during their term of office."[27]

Consider also the important limitations on the applicability of state immunities from criminal prosecution recognized by the Court at paragraph 61 of its judgment. As a matter of international law, an official, even while in office, is not immune from the criminal jurisdiction of the courts of her own state (although the domestic laws of some states effectively shield officials from such jurisdiction). Similarly, state immunity has no role to play where the case comes before an *international* criminal tribunal that is duly constituted and granted jurisdiction to consider the matter. The following decision of the Special Court for Sierra Leone, a tribunal established by agreement between the United Nations and Sierra Leone to try crimes against humanity and war crimes committed in that country, turns on this important distinction.

Prosecutor v Taylor, SCSL-2003-01-I, Decision on Immunity from Jurisdiction, Special Court for Sierra Leone, 31 May 2004

I. INTRODUCTION: PROCEDURAL AND FACTUAL HISTORY

1. This is an application by Mr. Charles Taylor, the former President of the Republic of Liberia, to quash his Indictment and to set aside the warrant for his arrest on the grounds that he is immune from any exercise of the jurisdiction of this court. The Indictment and arrest warrant were approved . . . when Mr. Taylor was Head of State of Liberia . . . .

4. Mr. Taylor remained Head of State until August 2003, his tenure of office covering most of the period over which the Special Court has temporal jurisdiction, pursuant to its mandate to try those primarily responsible for the war crimes and crimes against humanity that were committed in Sierra Leone since 30 November 1996.

5. The Indictment against Mr. Taylor contains seventeen counts. It accuses him of the commission of crimes against humanity and grave breaches of the Geneva Conventions, with intent "to obtain access to the mineral wealth of the Republic of Sierra Leone, in

---

27 International Law Commission, "Second Report of the Special Rapporteur, Concepción Escobar Hernández, on the Immunity of State Officials from Foreign Criminal Jurisdiction," UN Doc A/CN.4/661 (2013) at 25, para 74, Draft Article 5(1).

particular the diamond wealth of Sierra Leone, and to destabilise the state." . . . In short, the prosecution maintains that from an early stage and acting in a private rather than an official capacity he resourced and directed rebel forces, encouraging them in campaigns of terror, torture and mass murder, in order to enrich himself from a share in the diamond mines that were captured by the rebel forces . . . .

[Omitting "II. Submissions of the Parties"].

III. CONSIDERATION OF THE MOTION

20. At the time of his indictment (7 March 2003) and of its communication to the authorities in Ghana (4 June 2003) and of this application to annul it (23 July 2003), Mr. Taylor was an incumbent Head of State. As such, he claims entitlement to the benefit of any immunity asserted by that state against exercise of the jurisdiction of this Court. These bare facts raise the issue of law that we are called upon to decide, namely, whether it was lawful for the Special Court to issue an indictment and to circulate an arrest warrant in respect of a serving Head of State. If it was unlawful and the warrant is quashed, the question may then arise as to the extent of Mr. Taylor's immunity as a former Head of state . . . .

IV. IMMUNITY AND JURISDICTION . . . .

. . . 27. The question of sovereign immunity is a procedural question. Shaw is of the opinion that it is one to be taken as a preliminary issue [with the court making reference to Malcolm Shaw, *International Law*, 5th ed (Cambridge: Cambridge University Press, 2003) at 623] . . . .

V. THE LEGAL BASIS OF THE SPECIAL COURT FOR SIERRA LEONE

34. As raised in the submissions of the parties and those of the *amici curiae*, the issues in this motion turn to a large extent on the legal status of the Special Court . . . .

35. The Special Court is established by the Agreement between the United Nations and Sierra Leone which was entered into pursuant to Resolution 1315 (2000) of the Security Council for the sole purpose of prosecuting persons who bear the greatest responsibility for serious violations of international humanitarian law and Sierra Leonean law committed in the territory of Sierra Leone . . . .

VI. IS THE SPECIAL COURT AN INTERNATIONAL CRIMINAL TRIBUNAL?

37. Although the Special Court was established by treaty, unlike the ICTY [International Criminal Tribunal for the Former Yugoslavia] and the ICTR [International Criminal Tribunal for Rwanda] which were each established by resolution of the Security Council in its exercise of powers by virtue of Chapter VII of the UN Charter, it was clear that the power of the Security Council to enter into an agreement for the establishment of the court was derived from the Charter of the United Nations both in regard to the general purposes of the United Nations as expressed in Article 1 of the Charter and the specific powers of the Security Council in Articles 39 and 41. These powers are wide enough to empower the Security Council to initiate, as it did by Resolution 1315, the establishment

of the Special Court by Agreement with Sierra Leone. Article 39 empowers the Security Council to determine the existence of any threat to the peace. In Resolution 1315, the Security Council reiterated that the situation in Sierra Leone continued to constitute a threat to international peace and security in the region.

38. . . . It is to be observed that in carrying out its duties under its responsibility for the maintenance of international peace and security, the Security Council acts on behalf of the members of the United Nations. . . . The Agreement between the United Nations and Sierra Leone is thus an agreement between all members of the United Nations and Sierra Leone. This fact makes the Agreement an expression of the will of the international community. The Special Court established in such circumstances is truly international.

39. By reaffirming in the preamble to Resolution 1315 "that persons who commit or authorize serious violations of international humanitarian law are individually responsible and accountable for those violations and that the international community will exert every effort to bring those responsible to justice in accordance with international standards of justice, fairness and due process of law," it has been made clear that the Special Court was established to fulfil an international mandate and is part of the machinery of international justice . . . .

41. For the reasons that have been given . . . .
    a) The Special Court is not part of the judiciary of Sierra Leone and is not a national court.
    b) The Special Court is established by treaty and has the characteristics associated with classical international organisations (including legal personality; the capacity to enter into agreements with other international persons governed by international law; privileges and immunities; and an autonomous will distinct from that of its members).
    c) The competence and jurisdiction *ratione materiae* and *ratione personae* are broadly similar to that of ICTY and the ICTR and the ICC [International Criminal Court], including in relation to the provisions confirming the absence of entitlement of any person to claim of immunity.
    d) Accordingly, there is no reason to conclude that the Special Court should be treated as anything other than an international tribunal or court, with all that implies for the question of immunity for a serving Head of State . . . .

VII. THE SPECIAL COURT AND JURISDICTIONAL IMMUNITY

. . . 49. . . . The nature of the Tribunals has always been a relevant consideration in the question whether there is an exception to the principle of immunity.

50. More recently, in the [*Arrest Warrant Case*], the International Court of Justice upheld immunities in national courts even in respect of war crimes and crimes against humanity relying on customary international law . . . .

But in regard to criminal proceedings before "certain international criminal courts" it held:

an incumbent or former Minister for Foreign Affairs may be subject to criminal proceedings before certain international criminal courts, where they have jurisdiction . . . .

51. A reason for the distinction, in this regard, between national courts and international courts, though not immediately evident, would appear due to the fact that . . . the principle of state immunity derives from the equality of sovereign states and therefore has no relevance to international criminal tribunals which are not organs of a state but derive their mandate from the international community . . . .

52. Be that as it may, the principle seems now established that the sovereign equality of states does not prevent a Head of State from being prosecuted before an international criminal tribunal or court. We accept the view expressed by Lord Slynn of Hadley [in *Pinochet (No. 1)*, [1998] UKHL 41, [2000] 1 AC 61] that

> there is . . . no doubt that states have been moving towards the recognition of some crimes as those which should not be covered by claims of state or Head of State or other official or diplomatic immunity when charges are brought before international tribunals.

. . . We hold that the official position of the Applicant as an incumbent Head of State at the time when these criminal proceedings were initiated against him is not a bar to his prosecution by this court. The Applicant was and is subject to criminal proceedings before the Special Court for Sierra Leone.

54. Since we have found that the Special Court is not a national court, it is unnecessary to discuss the cases in which immunity is claimed before national courts . . . .

Taylor was arrested and surrendered to the Special Court in 2006. He was found guilty in 2012 of aiding and abetting, as well as planning, some of the most heinous and brutal of crimes, and sentenced to fifty years imprisonment.

What, if any, is the essential difference between an international and a domestic criminal tribunal? Why is it that state immunities that apply to a criminal court established by one state do not apply to a criminal tribunal established by the "international community" of states? Is there a reason for which states acting in the aggregate should not be bound by the same immunities as they are when acting individually? In answering these questions, consider whether there may be a difference in the nature of the jurisdiction exercised by the international community through international criminal tribunals as compared to that exercised by individual states in their domestic criminal courts. After reviewing Chapter 15 on International Criminal Law, consider this issue again.

b) Immunities from Civil Jurisdiction

We return now to the Ontario Court of Appeal's judgment in *Bouzari v Iran*, and, in particular, that part of the case dealing with his claim that international law gave him a right to civil redress for torture that overrode any state immunities that might otherwise be enjoyed by Iran or its agents.

Bouzari v Iran (2004), 71 OR (3d) 675 (CA), leave to appeal to SCC refused, [2005] 1 SCR vi

The judgment of the Court was delivered by

[1] GOUDGE J.A.: . . .

[3] This appeal engages two important principles: the prohibition of torture, which is widely acknowledged as vital to international human rights, and the requirement that sovereign states not be subjected to each other's jurisdiction, which is widely acknowledged as vital to the relations between nations. The balance struck today between these two principles by both Canada's domestic legislation and public international law prohibits a civil claim (though not a criminal prosecution) from being brought in Canada for the torture suffered in Iran by Mr. Bouzari. Hence, Mr. Bouzari's civil action was properly dismissed . . . .

THE PUBLIC INTERNATIONAL LAW ISSUE

a) Introduction

[60] This issue takes the appellant beyond the exceptions to state immunity which are expressly enacted in the SIA [*State Immunity Act*]. He argues that the SIA must be read in conformity with Canada's public international law obligations and that both by treaty and by peremptory norms of customary international law, Canada is bound to permit a civil remedy against a foreign state for torture committed abroad . . . .

b) Canada's treaty obligations

[69] The appellant's argument that Canada has a treaty obligation to provide an exception to state immunity for civil actions for torture committed abroad by a foreign state is based primarily on the Convention Against Torture. . . Canada has ratified this Convention although Iran has not . . . .

[72] . . . [I]t is Article 14 which is the focus of the appellant's argument. It reads as follows:

> 1. Each State Party shall ensure in its legal system that the victim of an act of torture obtains redress and has an enforceable right to fair and adequate compensation including the means for as full rehabilitation as possible. In the event of the death of the victim as a result of an act of torture, his dependants shall be entitled to compensation . . . .

[73] The question is whether this Article creates an obligation on a ratifying state to provide a civil right of redress for torture whether committed at home or abroad or only for torture committed within its own jurisdiction.

[74] The motion judge concluded that the Convention creates no obligation on Canada to provide access to the courts so that a litigant can pursue an action for damages against a foreign state for torture committed outside Canada. Rather, it simply requires Canada to provide a civil remedy for torture committed within its jurisdiction . . . .

[76] The motion judge . . . analyze[d] the text of the Convention and found it to provide no clear guidance on the issue. . . . A full textual analysis of the provisions of the Convention shows that the absence of explicit territorial language does not necessarily mean the absence of territorial limitation. The text of the Convention itself simply provides no answer to the question.

[77] Finally, the motion judge looked to state practice concerning Article 14 . . . .

[78] . . . The motion judge found that no state interprets Article 14 to require it to take civil jurisdiction over a foreign state for acts committed outside the forum state. Indeed, on ratifying the Convention, the United States issued an interpretive declaration indicating that it understood Article 14 to require a state to provide a private right of action for damages only for acts of torture committed within the jurisdiction of that state. Ultimately, the motion judge based her conclusion on . . . evidence of a broad state practice reflecting a shared understanding that Article 14 limits the obligation of a ratifying state to providing the right to a civil remedy only for acts of torture committed within its territory.

[79] While the appellant contests this finding of state practice, particularly that it reaches the level of agreement on the meaning of Article 14, there was ample evidence to sustain this conclusion . . . .

[80] The appellant also argues that the motion judge should have expressly considered the fact that an early draft of Article 14 contained the phrase "committed in any territory under its jurisdiction" and should have drawn the inference that by omitting this phrase from the final draft, the intention was to exclude this concept from the Article. However, [the respondent's expert] Professor Greenwood, whose opinion the motion judge accepted, was of the view that the words were dropped because they were superfluous since this limitation was already implicit in the Article . . . .

[81] In my view, the motion judge correctly concluded on the basis of these various considerations that Canada's treaty obligation pursuant to Article 14 does not extend to providing the right to a civil remedy against a foreign state for torture committed abroad. The appellant's various attacks on her careful analysis all must be dismissed. Canada's treaty obligation under Article 14 simply does not extend to the appellant's case.

[82] In saying that Canada is obliged by treaty to extend a civil remedy for torture to him, the appellant also placed some reliance on Article 14(1) of the International Covenant on Civil and Political Rights . . . by which both Canada and Iran have agreed to be bound. It reads in part:

> *Article 14*
> 1. All persons shall be equal before the courts and tribunals. In the determination of any criminal charge against him, or of his rights and obligations in a suit at law, everyone shall be entitled to a fair and public hearing by a competent, independent and impartial tribunal established by law . . . .

[83] The simple answer to the appellant's position is that the motion judge accepted Professor Greenwood's evidence that Article 14 of this Covenant has not been interpreted to date to require a state to provide access to its courts for sovereign acts committed outside its jurisdiction and his opinion that this provision carries no such obligation. This finding of the motion judge is due deference in this court. Indeed, in my view, it is the right conclusion.

c) Canada's obligations under customary international law

[84] The appellant also argues that Canada is bound by peremptory norms of customary international law to permit a civil claim against a foreign state for torture committed abroad . . . .

[87] The motion judge found that prohibition of torture is a rule of *jus cogens*. For the purpose of this appeal, no one, including the Attorney General of Canada, questions this conclusion. Rather the question is the scope of that norm. In particular, does it extend to a requirement to provide the right to a civil remedy for torture committed abroad by a foreign state?

[88] The motion judge conducted a careful review of the decisions of domestic and international tribunals and state immunity legislation and concluded that the peremptory norm prohibiting torture does not carry with it such an obligation. She put her conclusion succinctly at para. 63 of her reasons:

> An examination of the decisions of national courts and international tribunals, as well as state legislation with respect to sovereign immunity, indicates that there is no principle of customary international law which provides an exception from state immunity where an act of torture has been committed outside the forum, even for acts contrary to *jus cogens*. Indeed, the evidence of state practice, as reflected in these and other sources, leads to the conclusion that there is an ongoing rule of customary international law providing state immunity for acts of torture committed outside the forum state.

[89] The appellant attacks this conclusion primarily on two bases. First, he says that if the prohibition against torture is to be respected, torture cannot be considered a state function and therefore cannot be accorded state immunity. In this he relies on . . . *Pinochet* . . . .

[90] I do not agree. . . . [T]he extent of the prohibition against torture as a rule of *jus cogens* is determined not by any particular view of what is required if it is to be meaningful, but rather by the widespread and consistent practice of states. As the motion judge found, that practice reflects the customary international law principle that state immunity is provided for acts of torture committed outside the forum state, not the obligation contended for by the appellant.

[91] Finally, nothing in *Pinochet* is inconsistent with this. As the motion judge points out, *Pinochet* concerned criminal proceedings against an individual, not civil proceedings against the state of Chile. It is in that context that one of the law lords, Lord Browne-Wilkinson (at 203) offered the view that the commission by an individual of the international crime of torture cannot be considered to be an act done in an official capacity on behalf of the state and therefore is not a state function. However, three of the law lords: Lord Hutton (at 254 and 264), Lord Millett (at 278) and Lord Phillips of Worth Matravers (at 280) expressly discussed the immunity of the state from civil proceedings for torture committed in that state and all accepted that it would apply. Thus, the opinions in *Pinochet* clearly reflect the distinction for state immunity purposes between proceedings seeking a criminal sanction against an individual for acts of torture committed abroad and proceedings seeking a civil remedy against a foreign state for the same acts. In the former case, the sanction can be imposed on the individual without subjecting one state to the jurisdiction of another. That is not so in the latter case.

[92] This distinction is relevant for the appellant's second point. The appellant argues that the prohibition against torture constitutes a right to be free from torture and where there is a right there must be a remedy.

[93] There are two answers to this. The first reflects the distinction drawn in *Pinochet*. As a matter of principle, providing a civil remedy for breach of the prohibition of torture is not the only way to give effect to that prohibition. The criminal prosecution of individual torturers who commit their acts abroad (which is expressly sanctioned by the Convention Against Torture) gives some effect to the prohibition without damaging the principle of state sovereignty on which relations between nations are based.

[94] The second answer is that as a matter of practice, states do not accord a civil remedy for torture committed abroad by foreign states. The peremptory norm of prohibition against torture does not encompass the civil remedy contended for by the appellant.

[95] Thus, I see no basis to depart from the conclusion of the motion judge . . . Both under customary international law and international treaty there is today a balance struck between the condemnation of torture as an international crime against humanity and the principle that states must treat each other as equals not to be subjected to each other's jurisdiction. It would be inconsistent with this balance to provide a civil remedy against a foreign state for torture committed abroad. In the future, perhaps as the international human rights movement gathers greater force, this balance may change, either through the domestic legislation of states or by international treaty. However, this is not a change to be effected by a domestic court adding an exception to the SIA that is not there, or seeing a widespread state practice that does not exist today . . . .

Is the exercise of criminal jurisdiction over a foreign state representative less damaging to the principle of sovereign equality than the exercise of civil jurisdiction over the foreign state itself? Does this explain the difference in outcome between this case and *Pinochet* (see paragraphs 91 and 93 of *Bouzari*, above)?

Mr. Bouzari lost his appeal, an outcome that has prompted significant debate on whether the exceptions to state immunity in the Canadian statute should be expanded to include civil suits seeking damages for gross human rights violations.[28] In 2005, the Committee Against Torture (an expert body established under the Torture Convention), expressed "its concern at . . . the absence [in Canada] of effective measures to provide civil compensation to victims of torture in all cases." While not expressly identified in its report, the Committee was apparently responding to criticisms of the *Bouzari* case. The Committee called upon Canada to "review its position under article 14 of the [Torture] Convention to ensure the provision of compensation through its civil jurisdiction to all victims of torture."[29] At that time, the Committee's wording was somewhat ambiguous in that the Committee did not explicitly call upon Canada to deny state immunity in cases of alleged torture. However, in 2012 the Committee clarified its position, advising Canada that:

---

28   The Quebec and Ontario Courts of Appeal have since confirmed the position taken in *Bouzari*, relying in part on the *Jurisdictional Immunities* judgment discussed overleaf: *Islamic Republic of Iran v Hashemi*, 2012 QCCA 149 at paras 43–60; *Steen v Islamic Republic of Iran*, 2013 ONCA 30, (2013) 114 OR (3d) 206 at paras 29–35. The Supreme Court of Canada granted leave to appeal the *Hashemi* judgment on 7 March 2013.

29   "Conclusions and recommendations of the Committee against Torture: Canada," UN Doc CAT/C/ CR/34/CAN (2005) at paras 4(g), 5(f), reprinted in *Report of the Committee Against Torture*, UN GAOR, 60th Sess, Supp No 44 at 25–28, UN Doc A/60/44 (2005).

15. The Committee remains concerned at the lack of effective measures to provide re-dress, including compensation, through civil jurisdiction to all victims of torture, mainly due to the restrictions under provisions of the State Immunity Act . . . .

The State party should ensure that all victims of torture are able to access remedy and obtain redress, wherever acts of torture occurred and regardless of the nationality of the perpetrator or victim. In this regard, it should consider amending the State Immunity Act to remove obstacles to redress for all victims of torture.[30] [emphasis in original]

Others, however, have expressed opposing views, fearing that, if Canada allows such lawsuits to satisfy the Committee Against Torture's recommendations, Canada will be in breach of its obligations under the international law of state immunity. This is no small conundrum. Torture is obviously a horrific, unprincipled practice for which accountability should lie. On the other hand, jurisdictional immunities are the oil that lubricates inter-national relations. If national courts were empowered to judge other states in a manner not supported by state practice and *opinio juris*, the resulting jurisdictional squabbles could impair diplomatic relations and exacerbate international tensions.

Other national courts have faced similar demands to set aside state immunity in civil claims brought by those who have suffered torture and other gross abuses of human rights at the hands of a foreign state. In *Jones v Ministry of Interior for the Kingdom of Saudi Arabia and others*,[31] the senior Law Lord, Lord Bingham of Cornhill, made reference to the 2005 report by the Committee Against Torture concerning Canada, as follows:

23. . . . I would not wish to question the wisdom of this recommendation, and of course I share the Committee's concern that all victims of torture should be compensated. But the Committee is not an exclusively legal and not an adjudicative body; its power under article 19 [of the Torture Convention] is to make general comments; the Committee did not, in making this recommendation, advance any analysis or interpretation of article 14 of the Convention; and it was no more than a recommendation. Whatever its value in influencing the trend of international thinking, the legal authority of this recommenda-tion is slight . . . .

Lord Hoffman also commented on the Committee's views:

57. . . . Quite why Canada was singled out for this treatment is unclear, but as an inter-pretation of article 14 or a statement of international law, I regard it as having no value. The nearest approach to reasoning in support of the committee's opinion is a remark of Ms Gaer in the course of discussion . . . when she said . . . that "given that there was an exception to State immunity in legislation for business deals, it seemed unclear why an exception could not be considered for torture." The short answer is that an exception for acts *jure gestionis* is recognised by international law and an exception for torture is nei-

---

30 "Concluding Observations of the Committee against Torture: Canada," UN Doc CAT/C/CAN/CO/6 (2012) at para 15, reprinted in *Report of the Committee Against Torture*, UN GAOR, 67th Sess, Supp No 44 at 115–23, UN Doc A/67/44 (2012).

31 [2006] UKHL 26, [2007] 1 AC 270.

ther recognised by international law nor required by article 14. Whether it should be is another matter. The committee has no legislative powers.

58. Ms Gaer's concerns may have been influenced by the existence of the United States *Torture Victim Protection Act 1991*, which establishes civil liability against an individual who "under actual or apparent authority, or color of law, of any foreign nation", subjects an individual to torture (section 2). This represents a unilateral extension of jurisdiction by the United States which is not required and perhaps not permitted by customary international law. It is not part of the law of Canada or any other state.

The ICJ has since expressed its views on the issue:

Jurisdictional Immunities of the State (Germany v Italy; Greece intervening), ICJ General List No 143, 3 February 2012

38. . . . . Germany requests the Court . . . to find that Italy has failed to respect the jurisdictional immunity which Germany enjoys under international law by allowing civil claims to be brought against it in the Italian courts, seeking reparation for injuries caused by violations of international humanitarian law committed by the German Reich during the Second World War. . . .

52. The Court begins by observing that the proceedings in the Italian courts have their origins in acts perpetrated by German armed forces and other organs of the German Reich. Germany has fully acknowledged the "untold suffering inflicted on Italian men and women in particular during massacres, and on former Italian military internees" (Joint Declaration of Germany and Italy, Trieste, 18 November 2008), accepts that these acts were unlawful and stated before this Court that it "is fully aware of [its] responsibility in this regard." The Court considers that the acts in question can only be described as displaying a complete disregard for the "elementary considerations of humanity" [sources omitted] . . . . The Court considers that there can be no doubt that this conduct was a serious violation of the international law of armed conflict applicable in 1943-1945 . . . .

53. However, the Court is not called upon to decide whether these acts were illegal, a point which is not contested. The question for the Court is whether or not, in proceedings regarding claims for compensation arising out of those acts, the Italian courts were obliged to accord Germany immunity . . . .

54. As between Germany and Italy, any entitlement to immunity can be derived only from customary international law, rather than treaty. Although Germany is one of the eight States parties to the European Convention on State Immunity of 16 May 1972 (ETS No. 74, 1495 UNTS 182) . . . Italy is not a party and the Convention is accordingly not binding upon it. Neither State is party to the United Nations Convention on the Jurisdictional Immunities of States and their Property, adopted on 2 December 2004 (hereinafter the "United Nations Convention"), which is not yet in force in any event . . . .

58. The Parties are . . . in broad agreement regarding the validity and importance of State immunity as a part of customary international law. They differ, however, as to whether (as Germany contends) the law to be applied is that which determined the scope and

extent of State immunity in 1943-1945, i.e., at the time that the events giving rise to the proceedings in the Italian courts took place, or (as Italy maintains) that which applied at the time the proceedings themselves occurred . . . . Since the claim before the Court concerns the actions of the Italian courts, it is the international law in force at the time of those proceedings which the Court has to apply. Moreover, as the Court has stated (in the context of the personal immunities accorded by international law to foreign ministers), the law of immunity is essentially procedural in nature (*Arrest Warrant Case*, [2002] ICJ Rep 25, para. 60). It regulates the exercise of jurisdiction in respect of particular conduct and is thus entirely distinct from the substantive law which determines whether that conduct is lawful or unlawful. For these reasons, the Court considers that it must examine and apply the law on State immunity as it existed at the time of the Italian proceedings, rather than that which existed in 1943–1945 . . . .

60. The Court is not called upon to address the question of how international law treats the issue of State immunity in respect of *acta jure gestionis*. The acts of the German armed forces and other State organs which were the subject of the proceedings in the Italian courts clearly constituted *acta jure imperii* . . . . The Court considers that the terms "*jure imperii*" and "*jure gestionis*" do not imply that the acts in question are lawful but refer rather to whether the acts in question fall to be assessed by reference to the law governing the exercise of sovereign power (*jus imperii*) or the law concerning non-sovereign activities of a State, especially private and commercial activities (*jus gestionis*) . . . .

61. Both Parties agree that States are generally entitled to immunity in respect of *acta jure imperii*. That is the approach taken in the United Nations, European and draft Inter-American[32] Conventions, the national legislation in those States which have adopted statutes on the subject and the jurisprudence of national courts. It is against that background that the Court must approach the question raised by the present proceedings, namely whether that immunity is applicable to acts committed by the armed forces of a State (and other organs of that State acting in co-operation with the armed forces) in the course of conducting an armed conflict. Germany maintains that immunity is applicable and that there is no relevant limitation on the immunity to which a State is entitled in respect of *acta jure imperii*. Italy, in its pleadings before the Court, maintains that Germany is not entitled to immunity in respect of the cases before the Italian courts for two reasons: first, that immunity as to *acta jure imperii* does not extend to torts or delicts occasioning death, personal injury or damage to property committed on the territory of the forum State, and, secondly, that, irrespective of where the relevant acts took place, Germany was not entitled to immunity because those acts involved the most serious violations of rules of international law of a peremptory character for which no alternative means of redress was available. The Court will consider each of Italy's arguments in turn . . . .

[The discussion of the "territorial tort" exception to immunity has been omitted. On this issue the Court concluded that, notwithstanding any such exception in general, state immunity continues to apply in the specific case of proceedings for torts allegedly committed by one state's armed forces on the territory of another in the course of an armed conflict.]

---

32 Organization of American States, Inter-American Juridical Committee, "Draft Inter-American Convention on Jurisdictional Immunity of States" (1983) 22 ILM 292.

80. Italy's second argument . . . is that the denial of immunity was justified on account of the particular nature of the acts forming the subject-matter of the claims before the Italian courts and the circumstances in which those claims were made. There are three strands to this argument. First, Italy contends that the acts which gave rise to the claims constituted serious violations of the principles of international law applicable to the conduct of armed conflict, amounting to war crimes and crimes against humanity. Secondly, Italy maintains that the rules of international law thus contravened were peremptory norms (*jus cogens*). Thirdly, Italy argues that the claimants having been denied all other forms of redress, the exercise of jurisdiction by the Italian courts was necessary as a matter of last resort. The Court will consider each of these strands in turn . . . .

A. The gravity of the violations

81. The first strand is based upon the proposition that international law does not accord immunity to a State, or at least restricts its right to immunity, when that State has committed serious violations of the law of armed conflict . . . .

82. At the outset, however, the Court must observe that the proposition that the availability of immunity will be to some extent dependent upon the gravity of the unlawful act presents a logical problem. Immunity from jurisdiction is an immunity not merely from being subjected to an adverse judgment but from being subjected to the trial process. It is, therefore, necessarily preliminary in nature. Consequently, a national court is required to determine whether or not a foreign State is entitled to immunity as a matter of international law before it can hear the merits of the case brought before it and before the facts have been established. If immunity were to be dependent upon the State actually having committed a serious violation of international human rights law or the law of armed conflict, then it would become necessary for the national court to hold an enquiry into the merits in order to determine whether it had jurisdiction. If, on the other hand, the mere allegation that the State had committed such wrongful acts were to be sufficient to deprive the State of its entitlement to immunity, immunity could, in effect be negated simply by skillful construction of the claim.

83. That said, the Court must nevertheless inquire whether customary international law has developed to the point where a State is not entitled to immunity in the case of serious violations of human rights law or the law of armed conflict. Apart from the decisions of the Italian courts which are the subject of the present proceedings, there is almost no State practice which might be considered to support the proposition that a State is deprived of its entitlement to immunity in such a case . . . .

84. In addition, there is a substantial body of State practice from other countries which demonstrates that customary international law does not treat a State's entitlement to immunity as dependent upon the gravity of the act of which it is accused or the peremptory nature of the rule which it is alleged to have violated.

85. That practice is particularly evident in the judgments of national courts. Arguments to the effect that international law no longer required State immunity in cases of allegations of serious violations of international human rights law, war crimes or crimes against humanity have been rejected by the courts in Canada. [The Court cited *Bouzari*

v Iran, as well as cases decided in France, Slovenia, New Zealand, Poland and the United Kingdom.] . . . .

87. The Court does not consider that the United Kingdom judgment in *Pinochet (No. 3)* ([2000] 1 AC 147, 119 ILR 136) is relevant . . . *Pinochet* concerned the immunity of a former head of State from the criminal jurisdiction of another State, not the immunity of the State itself in proceedings designed to establish its liability to damages . . . . Moreover, the rationale for the judgment in *Pinochet* was based upon the specific language of the 1984 United Nations Convention against Torture, which has no bearing on the present case . . . .

91. The Court concludes that, under customary international law as it presently stands, a State is not deprived of immunity by reason of the fact that it is accused of serious violations of international human rights law or the international law of armed conflict. In reaching that conclusion, the Court must emphasize that it is addressing only the immunity of the State itself from the jurisdiction of the courts of other States; the question of whether, and if so to what extent, immunity might apply in criminal proceedings against an official of the State is not in issue in the present case.

B. The relationship between *jus cogens* and the rule of State immunity

92. The Court now turns to the second strand in Italy's argument, which emphasizes the *jus cogens* status of the rules which were violated by Germany during the period 1943-1945. This strand of the argument rests on the premise that there is a conflict between *jus cogens* rules forming part of the law of armed conflict and according immunity to Germany. Since *jus cogens* rules always prevail over any inconsistent rule of international law, whether contained in a treaty or in customary international law, so the argument runs, and since the rule which accords one State immunity before the courts of another does not have the status of *jus cogens*, the rule of immunity must give way.

93. This argument therefore depends upon the existence of a conflict between a rule, or rules, of *jus cogens*, and the rule of customary law which requires one State to accord immunity to another. In the opinion of the Court, however, no such conflict exists. Assuming for this purpose that the rules of the law of armed conflict which prohibit the murder of civilians in occupied territory, the deportation of civilian inhabitants to slave labour and the deportation of prisoners of war to slave labour are rules of *jus cogens*, there is no conflict between those rules and the rules on State immunity. The two sets of rules address different matters. The rules of State immunity are procedural in character and are confined to determining whether or not the courts of one State may exercise jurisdiction in respect of another State. They do not bear upon the question whether or not the conduct in respect of which the proceedings are brought was lawful or unlawful . . . .

94. In the present case, the violation of the rules prohibiting murder, deportation and slave labour took place in the period 1943–1945. The illegality of these acts is openly acknowledged by all concerned. The application of rules of State immunity to determine whether or not the Italian courts have jurisdiction to hear claims arising out of those violations cannot involve any conflict with the rules which were violated. Nor is the argument strengthened by focusing upon the duty of the wrongdoing State to make reparation, rather than upon the original wrongful act. The duty to make reparation is a rule which exists

independently of those rules which concern the means by which it is to be effected. The law of State immunity concerns only the latter; a decision that a foreign State is immune no more conflicts with the duty to make reparation than it does with the rule prohibiting the original wrongful act. Moreover, against the background of a century of practice in which almost every peace treaty or post-war settlement has involved either a decision not to require the payment of reparations or the use of lump sum settlements and set-offs, it is difficult to see that international law contains a rule requiring the payment of full compensation to each and every individual victim as a rule accepted by the international community of States as a whole as one from which no derogation is permitted . . . .

97. Accordingly, the Court concludes that even on the assumption that the proceedings in the Italian courts involved violations of *jus cogens* rules, the applicability of the customary international law on State immunity was not affected.

C. The "last resort" argument

98. The third and final strand of the Italian argument is that the Italian courts were justified in denying Germany the immunity to which it would otherwise have been entitled, because all other attempts to secure compensation for the various groups of victims involved in the Italian proceedings had failed. Germany's response is that in the aftermath of the Second World War it made considerable financial and other sacrifices by way of reparation in the context of a complex series of inter-State arrangements under which, reflecting the economic realities of the time, no Allied State received compensation for the full extent of the losses which its people had suffered. It also points to the payments which it made to Italy under the terms of . . . two 1961 Agreements and to the payments made more recently under the 2000 Federal Law to various Italians who had been unlawfully deported to forced labour in Germany. Italy maintains, however, that large numbers of Italian victims were nevertheless left without any compensation . . . .

101. . . . . [T]he Court cannot accept Italy's contention that the alleged shortcomings in Germany's provisions for reparation to Italian victims, entitled the Italian courts to deprive Germany of jurisdictional immunity. The Court can find no basis in the State practice from which customary international law is derived that international law makes the entitlement of a State to immunity dependent upon the existence of effective alternative means of securing redress. Neither in the national legislation on the subject, nor in the jurisprudence of the national courts which have been faced with objections based on immunity is there any evidence that entitlement to immunity is subjected to such a precondition. States also did not include any such condition in either the European Convention or the United Nations Convention . . . .

103. The Court therefore rejects Italy's argument that Germany could be refused immunity on this basis . . . .

D. The combined effect of the circumstances relied upon by Italy

105. In the course of the oral proceedings, counsel for Italy maintained that the three strands of Italy's second argument had to be viewed together; it was because of the cumulative effect of the gravity of the violations, the status of the rules violated and the absence

of alternative means of redress that the Italian courts had been justified in refusing to accord immunity to Germany.

106. The Court has already held that none of the three strands of the second Italian argument would, of itself, justify the action of the Italian courts. It is not persuaded that they would have that effect if taken together. Nothing in the examination of State practice lends support to the proposition that the concurrent presence of two, or even all three, of these elements would justify the refusal by a national court to accord to a respondent State the immunity to which it would otherwise be entitled . . . .

107. The Court therefore holds that the action of the Italian courts in denying Germany the immunity to which the Court has held it was entitled under customary international law constitutes a breach of the obligations owed by the Italian State to Germany . . . .

Note how the ICJ draws a distinction between substantive law and law that is procedural in nature, in both the *Arrest Warrant* case (at paragraph 60) and *Jurisdictional Immunities of the State* (at paragraph 93). This distinction has also been drawn by scholars[33] and by domestic courts deciding the relationship between *jus cogens* rules and the rules on state immunity. In *Jones v Ministry of the Interior of Saudi Arabia*,[34] Lord Hoffmann opined:

45. To produce a conflict with state immunity, it is therefore necessary to show that the [substantive rule of *jus cogens*, in this case the prohibition on torture], has generated an ancillary procedural rule which, by way of exception to state immunity, entitles or perhaps requires states to assume civil jurisdiction over other states in cases in which torture is alleged. Such a rule may be desirable and, since international law changes, may have developed. But . . . it is not entailed by the [substantive rule of *jus cogens*] . . . .

Could there be room to develop a procedural rule of a *jus cogens* character that would override the rules on state immunity? How could such a development be brought about? Consider the further views of Lord Hoffman in *Jones*:

63. . . . As Professor Dworkin demonstrated in *Law's Empire* (1986), the ordering of competing principles according to the importance of the values which they embody is a basic technique of adjudication. But the same approach cannot be adopted in international law, which is based upon the common consent of nations. It is not for a national court to "develop" international law by unilaterally adopting a version of that law which, however desirable, forward-looking and reflective of values it may be, is simply not accepted by other states.

Notwithstanding these views, should domestic players (whether courts or legislatures) play any role in bringing about desirable, forward-looking, or values-based changes to rules of international law dealing with state immunity? After all, the movement from an absolute to a restrictive approach to matters of state immunity in the latter half of the

---

33   See, for example, Fox, above note 18 at 151.
34   Above note 31.

twentieth century was accomplished largely as a result of the assertion of jurisdiction by domestic courts over the commercial transactions of foreign states, followed or accompanied by the enactment of domestic legislation.

In March 2012, Canada amended its *State Immunity Act* to allow civil actions to be brought in Canadian courts against states considered by Canada to be sponsors of terrorism.[35] The Canadian amendments are similar to those enacted in 1996 by the United States to its *Foreign Sovereign Immunities Act* (FSIA) of 1976.[36]

State Immunity Act, RSC 1985, c S-18, as amended

6.1 (1) A foreign state that is set out on the list referred to in subsection (2) is not immune from the jurisdiction of a court in proceedings against it for its support of terrorism on or after January 1, 1985.

(2) The Governor in Council may, by order, establish a list on which the Governor in Council may, at any time, set out the name of a foreign state if, on the recommendation of the Minister of Foreign Affairs made after consulting with the Minister of Public Safety and Emergency Preparedness, the Governor in Council is satisfied that there are reasonable grounds to believe that the foreign state supported or supports terrorism.

(3) The list must be established no later than six months after the day on which this section comes into force.

. . .

(11) Where a court of competent jurisdiction has determined that a foreign state, set out on the list in subsection (2), has supported terrorism, that foreign state is also not immune from the jurisdiction of a court in proceedings against it, that relate to terrorist activity by the state.

Should these amendments to Canada's *State Immunity Act* be seen as paving the way towards a desirable change in the international law of state immunities? Or alternatively, should they be seen as a breach of the rules of international law on state immunity?

---

35 Canada subsequently designated Iran and Syria as state sponsors of terrorism: *Order Establishing a List of Foreign State Sponsors of Terrorism*, SOR/2012-170 (7 September 2012).

36 *Foreign Sovereign Immunities Act of 1976*, Pub L No 94-583, 90 Stat 2891, as amended by *Anti-Terrorism and Effective Death Penalty Act of 1996*, Pub L No 104-132, 110 Stat 1214. The FSIA as amended is codified at 28 U.S.C. §§1602–611 (see terrorism exception at §1605A).

CHAPTER 9

INTERNATIONAL HUMAN RIGHTS LAW

As a general rule, international law historically regarded a state's treatment of individuals within its borders as a purely domestic matter, even though states have long been obliged to treat specific categories of individuals in particular ways. Take, for example, the protections for religious minorities included in the Treaty of Westphalia, discussed in Chapter 1, or the abolition of slavery and the slave trade in the nineteenth and early twentieth centuries.[1] Nevertheless, arguably the single greatest revolution in international law since its emergence has been the recognition extended since World War II to the rights of the individual, resulting in an enormous body of international human rights law requiring states to act (or not act) in particular ways in their relations with individuals generally.

In this chapter, we provide an overview of international human rights law, with a focus on treaties as the source of international legal obligation. We begin by looking at the key precursors to today's vast international legal framework for the protection of human rights, notably the protection of minorities; the treatment of "aliens" (i.e., foreign nationals); early international labour law; and international humanitarian law. We then focus on how international human rights protections have been codified in treaties developed under the auspices of the United Nations (UN) and several regional organizations. We also examine some of the specific human rights guarantees that have evolved since the end of World War II, as well as the various monitoring and compliance mechanisms that have been put in place to foster domestic implementation of, and state respect for, those guarantees.

A. KEY PRECURSORS TO THE INTERNATIONAL HUMAN RIGHTS REGIMES

1) Protection of Minorities

Even in early international law, various treaties included provisions requiring states parties to protect certain minorities within their borders. In the early modern period, these minorities were often religious rather than ethnic in nature. Examples include Protestants

---

1   See International Slavery Convention, 25 September 1926, 60 LNTS 253, Can TS 1928 No 5, in force 9 March 1927, later amended by the Protocol amending the Slavery Convention, 23 October 1953, 182 UNTS 51, Can TS 1953 No 26, in force 7 December 1953, and expanded upon by the Supplementary Convention on the Abolition of Slavery, the Slave Trade, and Institutions and Practices similar to Slavery, 7 September 1956, 266 UNTS 40, Can TS 1963 No 7, in force 30 April 1957. For an earlier bilateral example, see Treaty Between Great Britain and the United States, to settle and define Boundaries between the Possessions of Her Britannic Majesty in North America, and the Territories of the United States; for the final suppression of the African Slave Trade; and for the Giving up of Criminals and Fugitives from Justice in certain cases, 13 October 1842, 30 *British State Papers* 360, in force 13 October 1842.

in the Westphalia treaty system and Christians in treaties between European powers and the Ottoman Empire in the nineteenth century. In the twentieth century, the League of Nations system included a number of treaties protecting religious, ethnic, and linguistic minorities in Europe, particularly those found in regions of central and Eastern Europe that had been part of the multinational Austro-Hungarian Empire prior to the end of World War I. In the wake of that conflict, the Allied powers redrew many national boundaries but also sought to impose measures to protect such minorities from discrimination or persecution, and to permit them to pursue education in their own languages, in their (sometimes new) countries of residence.

The League of Nations system included a dispute resolution procedure, allowing complaints to be brought to the Council of the League of Nations by wronged minorities. This procedure sometimes led to further referrals on questions of law to the Permanent Court of International Justice (PCIJ). Important PCIJ decisions on minority rights include *Rights of Minorities in Upper Silesia (Minority Schools)*[2] and the advisory opinion on *Minority Schools in Albania*.[3]

The League system of minority protection evaporated prior to World War II, but successor mechanisms exist, including, for example, the High Commissioner on National Minorities within the Organization for Security and Co-operation in Europe (OSCE). The OSCE is a regional intergovernmental organization centred in Europe but with Canada and the United States among its fifty-seven participating states. The office of the High Commissioner on National Minorities was created in 1992 to prevent ethnic conflict, a major source of large-scale violence in modern Europe. The mandate of this office is as follows:

> The High Commissioner on National Minorities' task is to provide "early warning" and, as appropriate, "early action" at the earliest possible stage "in regard to tensions involving national minority issues which have not yet developed beyond an early warning stage, but, in the judgement of the High Commissioner, have the potential to develop into a conflict within the OSCE area."
>
> The High Commissioner on National Minorities (HCNM) thus has a two-fold mission: first, to try to contain and de-escalate tensions and, second, to act as a "tripwire", meaning that he or she is responsible for alerting the OSCE whenever such tensions threaten to develop to a level at which the High Commissioner cannot contain them with the means at his/her disposal.[4]

Another European intergovernmental organization, known as the Council of Europe, has since sponsored the first (and so far only) multilateral convention specifically focused on the protection of the rights of national minorities, giving effect to a desire expressed in the 1990s to transform the political commitments embraced by the OSCE into legal obligations.[5] As for the general international legal position, the rights of ethnic, religious,

---

2   (1928) PCIJ (Ser A) No 15.
3   (1935) PCIJ (Ser A/B) No 64.
4   High Commissioner on National Minorities: About: Mandate, online: www.osce.org/hcnm/43201.
5   Framework Convention for the Protection of National Minorities, 1 February 1995, 2151 UNTS 243, ETS No 157, (1995) 34 ILM 353, in force 1 February 1998.

and linguistic minorities are also recognized by the leading international instrument for the protection of civil and political rights,[6] discussed below (albeit more in the form of individual rather than collective rights). A 1992 declaratory text offers additional guidance.[7]

2) Protection of Foreign Nationals

a) Overview

Foreign nationals within a state are often referred to as "aliens" in international law. International law has long imposed certain constraints on the behaviour of the state in which an alien happens to be. States may not mistreat a foreign national, since to do so is to violate an international legal obligation owed to another state, namely the foreign national's state of nationality. In its starkest form, a state's protection of its nationals abroad was, in the nineteenth century, the pretext for substantial gunboat diplomacy.[8] It has since formed the basis for many claims of international responsibility made by one state against another, often adjudicated before arbitral tribunals.

Exactly what sorts of mistreatment of foreign nationals rise to the level of breaches of international law has been the source of some contention between developing and developed states. In part responding to the concern that the protection of one's nationals abroad was linked to colonialism, and in part due to a sense that it would be unfair to impose the same standard on developing as on developed states, some developing states have sought to set the bar for the treatment of foreign nationals quite low (in the view of some developed states) by advocating a "national treatment" standard. If embraced, a national treatment standard requires that a state treat foreign nationals no worse that it treats its own nationals.[9] As such, national treatment is simply a principle of non-discrimination. It sets no minimum standard of behaviour, leaving foreign nationals vulnerable to abuse where states choose to treat their own citizens equally poorly. To address these concerns, and also motivated by a desire to protect the property rights of their nationals in developing states, developed states have maintained that the treatment of foreign nationals must not fall below an "international minimum standard." It appears

---

6   International Covenant on Civil and Political Rights, 16 December 1966, 999 UNTS 171, Can TS 1976 No 47, (1967) 6 ILM 368, in force 23 March 1976, art 27.

7   *Declaration on the Rights of Persons Belonging to National or Ethnic, Religious or Linguistic Minorities*, GA Res 47/135 (1992), reprinted in UN GAOR, 47th Sess, Supp No 49, vol I at 210–12, UN Doc A/47/49 (1992).

8   Richard B Lillich, *The Human Rights of Aliens in Contemporary International Law* (Manchester: Manchester University Press, 1984) at 14–15.

9   A leading proponent of the national treatment standard was the Argentine diplomat and publicist Carlo Calvo, who argued that aliens have only those rights and privileges extended to nationals, and that they must seek relief for any grievances in national courts. The so-called Calvo Doctrine was influential in Latin America. See also article 9 of the (Montevideo) Convention on the Rights and Duties of States, 26 December 1933, 165 LNTS 19, in force 16 December 1934, discussed in Chapter 3. However, the Calvo doctrine "never has received widespread support elsewhere, primarily because its drastic curtailment of the institution of diplomatic protection would leave aliens without even nominal procedural safeguards under the existing international order": Richard Lillich, "The Current Status of the Law of State Responsibility for Injuries to Aliens" in Richard Lillich, ed, *International Law of State Responsibility for Injuries to Aliens* (Charlottesville: University Press of Virginia, 1983) at 4.

likely that the international minimum standard is in fact a requirement of customary international law.[10]

Exactly how bad a state's behaviour must be to breach the international minimum standard of treatment is somewhat uncertain. The influential *Restatement (Third) of the Foreign Relations Law of the United States* proposes that states violate the requisite standard of conduct where their treatment of foreign nationals transgresses the human rights principles that they are obliged to extend to their own nationals under conventional or customary human rights law.[11] However, states likely also remain obliged to meet some standards in their treatment of foreign nationals that are separate and distinct from their international human rights obligations. For example, the international minimum standard of treatment precludes a "denial of justice" which, in the era prior to the emergence of modern international human rights law, had a broad meaning that included any internationally cognizable injury befalling a foreign national.[12] It captured, for instance, due process violations in criminal proceedings, arbitrary use of force by government actors, and constraints on liberties such as freedom of speech and religion, as well as restrictions on internal travel within a country and the right to marry.[13] Many of these concepts are now covered by international human rights law. "Denial of justice" in the context of alien claims is now defined as an injury "consisting of, or resulting from, denial of access to courts, or denial of procedural fairness and due process in relation to judicial proceedings, whether criminal or civil."[14]

In addition to the "denial of justice" requirements, there may also be a supplemental, more generic standard of conduct that must be met as part of the minimum treatment standard. In *Neer (USA) v Mexico*, a 1926 decision of the Mexico–US General Claims Commission,[15] an American national and mine superintendent (Paul Neer) was killed by Mexican nationals, provoking only a desultory investigation by the Mexican authorities and then a claim by the United States on behalf of the victim's widow and daughter. On the standard to be applied in assessing whether Mexico had breached its international legal obligations relating to the treatment of foreign nationals, the Commission said this:

---

10   James Crawford, *Brownlie's Principles of Public International Law*, 8th ed (Oxford: Clarendon Press, 2012) at 613. See also *Case Concerning Certain German Interests in Polish Upper Silesia*, Merits, (1926), PCIJ (Ser A) No 7, implicitly rejecting the national treatment approach in recognizing "the existence of a common or generally accepted international law respecting the treatment of aliens . . . which is applicable to them despite municipal legislation."

11   American Law Institute, *Restatement of the Law, Third, Foreign Relations Law of the United States* (St Paul, MN: American Law Institute Publishers, 1987) at para 711, comment b & c [*Third Restatement*].

12   *Ibid* at para 711, comment a. See also James L Brierly, *The Law of Nations: An Introduction to the Law of Peace*, 6th ed (New York: Oxford University Press, 1963) at 286 ("[t]he term 'denial of justice' is sometimes loosely used to denote *any* international delinquency towards an alien for which a state is liable to make reparation.")

13   *Third Restatement*, above note 11 at para 711, rep n 2.

14   *Ibid* at comment a. See also Brierly, above note 12 at 286 (a denial of justice in its "more proper sense is an injury involving the responsibility of the state committed by a court of justice").

15   (1926), 4 RIAA 60, 3 ILR 213 [*Neer*].

4. The Commission recognizes the difficulty of devising a general formula for determining the boundary between an international delinquency of this type and an unsatisfactory use of power included in national sovereignty . . . . Without attempting to announce a precise formula, it is in the opinion of the Commission possible . . . to hold (first) that the propriety of governmental acts should be put to the test of international standards, and (second) that the treatment of an alien, in order to constitute an international delinquency, should amount to an outrage, to bad faith, to wilful neglect of duty, or to an insufficiency of governmental action so far short of international standards that every reasonable and impartial man would readily recognize its insufficiency. Whether the insufficiency proceeds from deficient execution of an intelligent law or from the fact that the laws of the country do not empower the authorities to measure up to international standards is immaterial.

Today, the *Neer* threshold of "outrage, bad faith, wilful neglect of duty, or insufficiency of governmental action" may have been strengthened. For example, Article 1105 of the North American Free Trade Agreement (NAFTA)[16] asserts that each state party shall accord to foreign investors "treatment in accordance with international law, including fair and equitable treatment and full protection and security." It is said that this provision on the "Minimum Standard of Treatment" is intended to codify the customary minimum standard of treatment of aliens and not to carve out new rules for NAFTA investors. As explained by the NAFTA states parties, convening as the NAFTA Free Trade Commission: "The concepts of 'fair and equitable treatment' and 'full protection and security' [in Article 1105] do not require treatment in addition to or beyond that which is required by the customary international law minimum standard of treatment of aliens."[17]

Since then, however, some NAFTA arbitrators have found the minimum treatment guaranteed by Article 1105 to be more exacting than the standard set in the *Neer* case. Indeed, in *Mondev International v United States*,[18] a NAFTA Chapter 11 panel rejected the proposition that the *Neer* "outrage" standard reflected the modern measure of minimum treatment, maintaining that the more exacting terms of Article 1105 in fact corresponded to the contemporary customary international legal minimum standard. In the Tribunal's words: "To the modern eye, what is unfair or inequitable need not equate with the outrageous or the egregious. In particular, a State may treat foreign investment unfairly and inequitably without necessarily acting in bad faith."[19] (A word of caution should be voiced here, however. NAFTA tribunals do not bind one another, and a more recent decision seems to revert to the *Neer* "outrage" standard.[20] Nor should it be assumed that develop-

---

16 North American Free Trade Agreement between the Government of Canada, the Government of Mexico and the Government of the United States, 17 December 1992, Can TS 1994 No 2, (1993) 32 ILM 289, in force 1 January 1994 [NAFTA].

17 See NAFTA Free Trade Commission, *Notes of Interpretation of Certain Chapter 11 Provisions* (31 July 2001), (2001) 13:6 *World Trade & Arbitration Materials* 139-40.

18 ICSID Case No ARB(AF)/99/2, Award of 11 October 2002 (2003), 42 ILM 85 (NAFTA Chapter 11 Arbitral Tribunal).

19 *Ibid* at para 116.

20 *Glamis Gold v United States of America*, Award of 8 June 2009, (2009) 48 ILM 1038 at paras 612–16 (NAFTA Chapter 11 Arbitral Tribunal).

ments under the NAFTA regime necessarily reflect standards in other areas where questions of minimum treatment arise.)

Another circumstance in which an international minimum standard of treatment may be required of states is when they expel foreign nationals from their territory. There is jurisprudence to the effect that foreign nationals may only be expelled on a non-discriminatory basis and in a manner that allows them to make provision for their personal or property interests in the expelling state.[21] There is also jurisprudence indicating that an expulsion must not be arbitrary in nature.[22] Nevertheless, there remains controversy regarding the precise contours of these requirements, and the topic remains a subject of ongoing study by the International Law Commission.

b) Consular Protection and the Treatment of Foreign Nationals

The notion that states may act to protect their nationals from mistreatment abroad is one of the oldest doctrines of international law. The protection extended by states may assume several forms. One of these, and our focus in this subsection, is the provision of "consular protection" or "consular services." This form of protection is essentially geared towards the prevention of mistreatment, by foreign states, of one's nationals abroad. The related doctrine of "diplomatic protection" is directed at obtaining redress for mistreatment that has already occurred. As the latter doctrine also applies to violations of international law other than those relating to the treatment of foreign nationals, it will be discussed in Chapter 12, which deals with the responsibility of states for violations of international law generally.

The essence of a state's right to extend consular protection to its nationals is set out in the widely ratified Vienna Convention on Consular Relations (which has 176 states parties). Consider its key provisions:

Vienna Convention on Consular Relations, 24 April 1963, 596 UNTS 261, Can TS 1974 No 25, in force 19 March 1967

Article 5
Consular Functions
Consular functions consist in:

(a) protecting in the receiving State the interests of the sending State and of its nationals, both individuals and bodies corporate, within the limits permitted by international law;

(b) furthering the development of commercial, economic, cultural and scientific relations between the sending State and the receiving State and otherwise promoting friendly relations between them in accordance with the provisions of the present Convention; . . .

(e) helping and assisting nationals, both individuals and bodies corporate, of the sending State; . . .

---

21 *Rankin v Islamic Republic of Iran* (1987), 17 Iran-US CTR 135.
22 *Ahmadou Sadio Diallo (Republic of Guinea v Democratic Republic of the Congo)*, Merits, Judgment, [2010] ICJ Rep 639 at para 65.

(g) safeguarding the interests of nationals, both individuals and bodies corporate, of the sending State in cases of succession mortis causa in the territory of the receiving State, in accordance with the laws and regulations of the receiving State;

(h) safeguarding, within the limits imposed by the laws and regulations of the receiving State, the interests of minors and other persons lacking full capacity who are nationals of the sending State, particularly where any guardianship or trusteeship is required with respect to such persons;

(i) subject to the practices and procedures obtaining in the receiving State, representing or arranging appropriate representation for nationals of the sending State before the tribunals and other authorities of the receiving State, for the purpose of obtaining, in accordance with the laws and regulations of the receiving State, provisional measures for the preservation of the rights and interests of these nationals, where, because of absence or any other reason, such nationals are unable at the proper time to assume the defence of their rights and interests; . . .

(k) exercising rights of supervision and inspection provided for in the laws and regulations of the sending State in respect of vessels having the nationality of the sending State, and of aircraft registered in that State, and in respect of their crews; . . .

Article 36
Communication and Contact with Nationals of the Sending State
1. With a view to facilitating the exercise of consular functions relating to nationals of the sending State:

(a) consular officers shall be free to communicate with nationals of the sending State and to have access to them. Nationals of the sending State shall have the same freedom with respect to communication with and access to consular officers of the sending State;

(b) if he so requests, the competent authorities of the receiving State shall, without delay, inform the consular post of the sending State if, within its consular district, a national of that State is arrested or committed to prison or to custody pending trial or is detained in any other manner. Any communication addressed to the consular post by the person arrested, in prison, custody or detention shall also be forwarded by the said authorities without delay. The said authorities shall inform the person concerned without delay of his rights under this sub-paragraph;

(c) consular officers shall have the right to visit a national of the sending State who is in prison, custody or detention, to converse and correspond with him and to arrange for his legal representation. They shall also have the right to visit any national of the sending State who is in prison, custody or detention in their district in pursuance of a judgment. Nevertheless, consular officers shall refrain from taking action on behalf of a national who is in prison, custody or detention if he expressly opposes such action.

2. The rights referred to in paragraph 1 of this Article shall be exercised in conformity with the laws and regulations of the receiving State, subject to the proviso, however, that the said laws and regulations must enable full effect to be given to the purposes for which the rights accorded under this Article are intended.

Note the precise scope of Article 36(1)(a), which provides that consular officials are "free to communicate with nationals of the sending State and to have access to them." Foreign nationals have a reciprocal freedom to communicate with, and have access to, the consular officers of their state of nationality. Moreover, upon request of such a national, the receiving state must inform "without delay" the relevant consular officials of that national's arrest or detention. Once notified of the detention, consular officials then have a right to visit and converse with the foreign national and arrange for his or her legal representation, unless refused by the national, as set out in Article 36(1)(c).

The obligation to inform detained persons of their rights under Article 36(1)(b) of the Consular Relations Convention has been in issue before two international courts: the International Court of Justice (ICJ)[23] and the Inter-American Court of Human Rights.[24] In the *Avena* case, the ICJ concluded that the obligation to inform arises upon the detaining state learning (or suspecting) that the detained individual is a foreign national.[25] The case resulted in an order that the United States review the convictions and death sentences of fifty-one Mexican prisoners who had not been informed of their rights of consular access after their arrests. Then US President George W Bush announced that the United States would comply with the ICJ's judgment, but the Texas courts ruled that the president had exceeded his powers, resulting eventually in a US Supreme Court ruling that the *Avena* judgment was not binding on US state or federal courts.[26] Mexico subsequently made an unsuccessful request to the ICJ for a reinterpretation of the *Avena* judgment.[27]

LAW IN CONTEXT

An Obligation to Provide Consular Protection?

Once notified of the detention of one its nationals by another state, it is for the state of nationality to determine how it will assist its national and the extent of that assistance. This raises the question of whether a state is *obligated* to extend consular protection to one of its nationals. International law provides for no such general obligation; however, domestic law may be more demanding of particular states.[28] Consider the 2004 decision of Canada's Federal Court concerning the detention of a 17-year-old Canadian national

---

23   See *Avena and other Mexican Nationals (Mexico v United States of America)*, Judgment, [2004] ICJ Rep 12 [*Avena 2004*]. See also *LaGrand Case (Germany v United States of America)*, Judgment, [2001] ICJ Rep 466. On 7 March 2005, the United States withdrew from the treaty that had provided the basis for the ICJ's jurisdiction in both these cases, the Optional Protocol to the Vienna Convention on Consular Relations Concerning the Compulsory Settlement of Disputes, 24 April 1963, 596 UNTS 487, in force 19 March 1967.

24   See *The Right to Information on Consular Assistance in the Framework of the Guarantees of the Due Process of Law*, Advisory Opinion, (1999) Inter-Am Ct HR (Ser A) No 16. Mexico had made the request for this advisory opinion. The Inter-American Commission on Human Rights has also received several complaints of consular access violations, all involving Mexican nationals convicted of crimes in the United States.

25   *Avena 2004*, above note 23 at para 63.

26   *Medellin v Texas*, 525 US 491 (2008). Medellin was subsequently executed on 5 August 2008.

27   *Request for Interpretation of the Judgment of 31 March 2004 in the Case Concerning Avena and Other Mexican Nationals (Mexico v United States of America)*, Judgment, [2009] ICJ Rep 3.

28   See, for example, *R (Abbasi) v Secretary of State for Foreign and Commonwealth Affairs*, [2002] EWCA Civ 1598, [2003] UKHRR 76 (CA) (finding that a legitimate expectation to some form of consular service had been created through previous actions of the British government).

(Omar Khadr) by the US military at its naval base in Guantanamo Bay, Cuba. In that case, Khadr's family sought a court order compelling the Canadian government to extend consular services to Khadr. They argued that, in allegedly failing to provide those services, the minister of foreign affairs had acted contrary to the *Department of Foreign Affairs and International Trade Act* (DFAITA).[29] In a preliminary motion, the government asked the court to dismiss the claim, urging that it had no merit. The court disagreed, stating:

> [T]he language of the DFAITA is quite straightforward. It states that the Minister shall conduct all diplomatic and consular relations on behalf of Canada. There is clearly an obligation to carry out these functions and not merely an authorization to do so . . . . The publication "A Guide for Canadians Imprisoned Abroad" reflects this state of affairs. It asserts that the government will "make every effort to ensure that" a Canadian detained abroad receives "equitable treatment" including ensuring that he or she is not penalized for being a Canadian . . . .
>
> Based upon the foregoing, there is a persuasive case that both the DFAITA and the Guide create a legitimate and reasonable expectation that a Canadian citizen detained abroad will receive many of the services which Omar Khadr has requested. Indeed, Canadians abroad would be surprised, if not shocked, to learn that the provision of consular services in an individual case is left to the complete and unreviewable discretion of the Minister . . . .[30]

3) International Labour Law

The International Labour Organization (ILO) predates the establishment of the UN, having been established in 1919 as an outgrowth of the Versailles peace process that ended World War I.[31] The ILO has since become a UN specialized agency, and remains instrumental in the development of international standards governing matters of labour and employment. Its work has also paved the way for the recognition of a broader international human rights regime that includes not only substantive rules, but also an institutional framework for their advancement.

The ILO has 185 member states and a unique "tripartite" structure that brings together governments, employers' organizations, and workers' organizations. Each member state is represented at the annual International Labour Conference by delegates from each of these three sectors. The Conference establishes and adopts international labour standards, which are often formulated as conventions that are submitted for ratification by member states and later given practical effect through the enactment of domestic legislation.[32]

Indeed, over the years, the ILO has developed 189 conventions for ratification by states. Of these, the ILO has singled out eight as being "fundamental," even for non-states-

---

29 RSC 1985, c E-22.

30 *Khadr v Canada (Minister of Foreign Affairs)*, 2004 FC 1145, [2005] 2 FCR D-25 at paras 20–22.

31 See further, *Treaty of Peace between the Allied Powers and Associated Powers and Germany* (Treaty of Versailles), 28 June 1919, UK TS 1919 No 4, in force 10 January 1920. Part XIII of the Treaty contains the Constitution of the ILO.

32 See, for example, the reference to ILO Convention 187 in the preamble to Part I of the *Canada Labour Code*, RSC 1985, c L-2.

parties. These treaties seek to achieve four strategic objectives of importance, namely: freedom of association and the effective recognition of the right to collective bargaining; the elimination of all forms of forced or compulsory labour; the effective abolition of child labour; and the elimination of discrimination in respect of employment and occupation. Since 1995, the ILO has spearheaded efforts to increase state ratification of conventions covering these four areas. In 1998, the ILO adopted a major declaration calling on its member states to respect and promote the principles and rights embraced in these four areas. This Declaration was considered particularly significant given that the ILO had only adopted one other such declaration previously (at its Philadelphia meeting in 1944). Canada's support for the 1998 Declaration, in addition to its treaty ratifications, has been invoked in a number of domestic Canadian court cases.[33] Consider the text of the 1998 Declaration:

ILO Declaration on Fundamental Principles and Rights at Work, adopted by the International Labour Conference at its 86th Session, Geneva, 18 June 1998, (1998) 37 ILM 1237

Whereas the ILO was founded in the conviction that social justice is essential to universal and lasting peace;

Whereas economic growth is essential but not sufficient to ensure equity, social progress and the eradication of poverty, confirming the need for the ILO to promote strong social policies, justice and democratic institutions;

Whereas the ILO should, now more than ever, draw upon all its standard-setting, technical cooperation and research resources in all its areas of competence, in particular employment, vocational training and working conditions, to ensure that, in the context of a global strategy for economic and social development, economic and social policies are mutually reinforcing components in order to create broad-based sustainable development;

Whereas the ILO should give special attention to the problems of persons with special social needs, particularly the unemployed and migrant workers, and mobilize and encourage international, regional and national efforts aimed at resolving their problems, and promote effective policies aimed at job creation;

Whereas, in seeking to maintain the link between social progress and economic growth, the guarantee of fundamental principles and rights at work is of particular significance in that it enables the persons concerned, to claim freely and on the basis of equality of opportunity, their fair share of the wealth which they have helped to generate, and to achieve fully their human potential;

Whereas the ILO is the constitutionally mandated international organization and the competent body to set and deal with international labour standards, and enjoys universal support and acknowledgement in promoting Fundamental Rights at Work as the expression of its constitutional principles;

---

33   See, for example, *Saskatchewan v Saskatchewan Federation of Labour*, 2012 SKQB 62 at paras 100–13. See also *Health Services and Support — Facilities Subsector Bargaining Assn v British Columbia*, 2007 SCC 27, [2007] 2 SCR 391 at paras 69–79.

Whereas it is urgent, in a situation of growing economic interdependence, to reaffirm the immutable nature of the fundamental principles and rights embodied in the Constitution of the Organization and to promote their universal application;

The International Labour Conference

1. Recalls:

(a) that in freely joining the ILO, all Members have endorsed the principles and rights set out in its Constitution and in the Declaration of Philadelphia, and have undertaken to work towards attaining the overall objectives of the Organization to the best of their resources and fully in line with their specific circumstances;

(b) that these principles and rights have been expressed and developed in the form of specific rights and obligations in Conventions recognized as fundamental both inside and outside the Organization.

2. Declares that all Members, even if they have not ratified the Conventions in question, have an obligation arising from the very fact of membership in the Organization to respect, to promote and to realize, in good faith and in accordance with the Constitution, the principles concerning the fundamental rights which are the subject of those Conventions, namely:

(a) freedom of association and the effective recognition of the right to collective bargaining;

(b) the elimination of all forms of forced or compulsory labour;

(c) the effective abolition of child labour; and

(d) the elimination of discrimination in respect of employment and occupation.

3. Recognizes the obligation on the Organization to assist its Members, in response to their established and expressed needs, in order to attain these objectives by making full use of its constitutional, operational and budgetary resources, including, by the mobilization of external resources and support, as well as by encouraging other international organizations with which the ILO has established relations, pursuant to article 12 of its Constitution, to support these efforts:

(a) by offering technical cooperation and advisory services to promote the ratification and implementation of the fundamental Conventions;

(b) by assisting those Members not yet in a position to ratify some or all of these Conventions in their efforts to respect, to promote and to realize the principles concerning fundamental rights which are the subject of these Conventions; and

(c) by helping the Members in their efforts to create a climate for economic and social development.

4. Decides that, to give full effect to this Declaration, a promotional follow-up, which is meaningful and effective, shall be implemented in accordance with the measures specified in the annex hereto, which shall be considered as an integral part of this Declaration.

5. Stresses that labour standards should not be used for protectionist trade purposes, and that nothing in this Declaration and its follow-up shall be invoked or otherwise used for such purposes; in addition, the comparative advantage of any country should in no way be called into question by this Declaration and its follow-up.

In 2008, the governments, employers, and workers of the ILO adopted a third major declaratory statement of principles and policies, expressing the ILO's approach to social justice issues in the era of globalization.[34] The terms of the 2008 ILO Declaration underscore the need to secure the conditions necessary for the realization of the ILO's four strategic objectives, described above.

4) International Humanitarian Law

International humanitarian law (IHL) also has a long history, dating back at least to the nineteenth century. The rules of IHL govern the conduct of armed conflict, with a particular focus on the treatment of combatants (especially those "hors de combat") and civilians. As such, although IHL has developed as a distinct field of law, the rules of IHL have a close connection with modern international human rights law, which limits the permissible conduct of states vis-à-vis individuals in times of both peace *and* armed conflict. IHL and international human rights law are thus complementary bodies of law.

The international Red Cross movement is closely associated with the development and promotion of this area of international law. Consider this overview prepared by the International Committee of the Red Cross:

> ### *What Is International Humanitarian Law?* (Geneva: International Committee of the Red Cross, July 2004)[35]
>
> International humanitarian law is a set of rules which seek, for humanitarian reasons, *to limit the effects of armed conflict*. It protects persons who are not or are no longer participating in the hostilities and restricts the means and methods of warfare. International humanitarian law is also known as the law of war or the law of armed conflict . . . .
>
> International humanitarian law applies to armed conflicts. It does not regulate whether a State may actually use force; this is governed by an important, but distinct, part of international law set out in the United Nations Charter.
>
> #### Where did international humanitarian law originate?
>
> International humanitarian law is rooted in the rules of ancient civilizations and religions — warfare has always been subject to certain principles and customs. Universal codification of international humanitarian law began in the nineteenth century. Since then, States have agreed to a series of practical rules, based on the bitter experience of modern warfare. These rules strike a careful balance between humanitarian concerns and the military requirements of States. As the international community has grown, an increasing number of States have contributed to the development of those rules. International humanitarian law forms today a universal body of law.

34　ILO Declaration on Social Justice for a Fair Globalization, adopted by the International Labour Conference at its 97th Session, Geneva, 10 June 2008.

35　Available online: www.icrc.org/eng/resources/documents/legal-fact-sheet/humanitarian-law-factsheet.htm.

Where is international humanitarian law to be found?

A major part of international humanitarian law is contained in the four **Geneva Conventions of 1949**. Nearly every State in the world has agreed to be bound by them. The Conventions have been developed and supplemented by two further agreements: the **Additional Protocols of 1977 relating to the protection of victims of armed conflicts**. Other agreements prohibit the use of certain weapons and military tactics and protect certain categories of people and goods. These agreements include:

- the 1954 Convention for the Protection of Cultural Property in the Event of Armed Conflict, plus its two protocols;
- the 1972 Biological Weapons Convention;
- the 1980 Conventional Weapons Convention and its five protocols;
- the 1993 Chemical Weapons Convention;
- the 1997 Ottawa Convention on anti-personnel mines;
- the 2000 Optional Protocol to the Convention on the Rights of the Child on the involvement of children in armed conflict.

Many provisions of international humanitarian law are now accepted as customary law — that is, as general rules by which all States are bound.

When does international humanitarian law apply?

International humanitarian law applies only to armed conflict; it does not cover internal tensions or disturbances such as isolated acts of violence. The law applies only once a conflict has begun, and then equally to all sides regardless of who started the fighting.

International humanitarian law distinguishes between international and non-international armed conflict. **International armed conflicts** are those in which at least two States are involved. They are subject to a wide range of rules, including those set out in the four Geneva Conventions and Additional Protocol I. **Non-international armed conflicts** are those restricted to the territory of a single State, involving either regular armed forces fighting groups of armed dissidents, or armed groups fighting each other. A more limited range of rules apply to internal armed conflicts and are laid down in Article 3 common to the four Geneva Conventions as well as in Additional Protocol II.

It is important to differentiate between international *humanitarian* law and *human rights* law. While some of their rules are similar, these two bodies of law have developed separately and are contained in different treaties. In particular, human rights law — unlike international humanitarian law — applies in peacetime, and many of its provisions may be suspended during an armed conflict.

What does international humanitarian law cover?

International humanitarian law covers two areas:

- the protection of those who are not, or are no longer, taking part in fighting;
- restrictions on the means of warfare — in particular weapons — and the methods of warfare, such as military tactics.

What is "protection"?

International humanitarian law protects those who do not take part in the fighting, such as civilians and medical and religious military personnel. It also protects those who have ceased to take part, such as wounded, shipwrecked and sick combatants, and prisoners of war. These categories of person are entitled to respect for their lives and for their physical and mental integrity. They also enjoy legal guarantees. They must be protected and treated humanely in all circumstances, with no adverse distinction. More specifically: it is forbidden to kill or wound an enemy who surrenders or is unable to fight; the sick and wounded must be collected and cared for by the party in whose power they find themselves. Medical personnel, supplies, hospitals and ambulances must all be protected. There are also detailed rules governing the conditions of detention for prisoners of war and the way in which civilians are to be treated when under the authority of an enemy power. This includes the provision of food, shelter and medical care, and the right to exchange messages with their families.

The law sets out a number of clearly recognizable symbols which can be used to identify protected people, places and objects. The main emblems are the red cross, the red crescent and the symbols identifying cultural property and civil defence facilities.

What restrictions are there on weapons and tactics?

International humanitarian law prohibits all means and methods of warfare which:

- fail to discriminate between those taking part in the fighting and those, such as civilians, who are not, the purpose being to protect the civilian population, individual civilians and civilian property;
- cause superfluous injury or unnecessary suffering;
- cause severe or long-term damage to the environment.

Humanitarian law has therefore banned the use of many weapons, including exploding bullets, chemical and biological weapons, blinding laser weapons and anti-personnel mines.

Is international humanitarian law actually complied with?

Sadly, there are countless examples of violation of international humanitarian law. Increasingly, the victims of war are civilians. However, there are important cases where international humanitarian law has made a difference in protecting civilians, prisoners, the sick and the wounded, and in restricting the use of barbaric weapons.

Given that this body of law applies during times of extreme violence, implementing the law will always be a matter of great difficulty. That said, striving for effective compliance remains as urgent as ever.

What should be done to implement the law?

Measures must be taken to ensure respect for international humanitarian law. States have an obligation to teach its rules to their armed forces and the general public. They must prevent violations or punish them if these nevertheless occur.

In particular, they must enact laws to punish the most serious violations of the Geneva Conventions and Additional Protocols, which are regarded as war crimes. The States must also pass laws protecting the red cross and red crescent emblems.

Measures have also been taken at an international level: tribunals have been created to punish acts committed in two recent conflicts (the former Yugoslavia and Rwanda). An international criminal court, with the responsibility of repressing *inter alia* war crimes, was created by the 1998 Rome Statute.

Whether as individuals or through governments and various organizations, we can all make an important contribution to compliance with international humanitarian law.

As the reference to the tribunals for the former Yugoslavia and Rwanda suggest, IHL is closely tied to recent developments in international criminal law, which is designed in part to enforce IHL. We focus on international criminal law in Chapter 15.

B. OVERVIEW OF THE UN HUMAN RIGHTS SYSTEM

1) The Charter of the United Nations

A universal system of human rights law, more general in scope than its earlier, more specialized precursors, owes its origin to the adoption of the Charter of the United Nations (UN Charter), with its emphasis on non-discrimination and its repeated, though undefined, references to a concept of "human rights." The UN Charter also tasks the UN itself, primarily through two of its principal organs, the General Assembly and the Economic and Social Council (ECOSOC), with the promotion of human rights and fundamental freedoms for all without distinction. Recall that the principal organs of the UN were identified and discussed earlier in Chapter 3, Section B(2)(d).

Charter of the United Nations, 26 June 1945, Can TS 1945 No 7, in force 24 October 1945

Article 1
The Purposes of the United Nations are: . . .

3. To achieve international co-operation in . . . promoting and encouraging respect for human rights and for fundamental freedoms for all without distinction as to race, sex, language, or religion; and

4. To be a centre for harmonizing the actions of nations in the attainment of these common ends . . . .

Article 13
1. The General Assembly shall initiate studies and make recommendations for the purpose of: . . . assisting in the realization of human rights and fundamental freedoms for all without distinction as to race, sex, language, or religion. . . .

Article 55
With a view to the creation of conditions of stability and well-being which are necessary for peaceful and friendly relations among nations based on respect for the principle of equal rights and self-determination of peoples, the United Nations shall promote: . . .

c. universal respect for, and observance of, human rights and fundamental freedoms for all without distinction as to race, sex, language, or religion.

Article 56
All Members pledge themselves to take joint and separate action in co-operation with the Organization for the achievement of the purposes set forth in Article 55 . . . .

Article 62
2. [The Economic and Social Council] may make recommendations for the purpose of promoting respect for, and observance of, human rights and fundamental freedoms for all . . . .

Article 68
The Economic and Social Council shall set up commissions . . . for the promotion of human rights . . . .

Note that the language in the UN Charter has a promotional quality. The treaty does not define, much less impose, a series of binding human rights obligations on states parties. Nevertheless, the UN Charter's provisions provided the springboard for the remarkable codification of international human rights law that followed.

2) The Universal Declaration of Human Rights

The starting point in tracing this evolution is Article 68 of the UN Charter, which empowers ECOSOC to set up "commissions . . . for the promotion of human rights." In 1946, ECOSOC established its first commission, the now defunct Commission on Human Rights (CHR). While the work of that body evolved over time, its initial function was to develop proposals for the articulation of an "international bill of rights."

The Commission met first in 1947, and included in its membership such prominent figures as Eleanor Roosevelt (United States), René Cassin (France), and Charles Malik (Lebanon), with John Humphrey (Canada) assisting as the first director of the human rights division of the UN secretariat.[36] At issue was whether art to proceed with a draft convention that, once ratified by states, would be legally binding, or rather to propose a draft declaration that could be adopted as a resolution of the UN General Assembly pursuant to its Article 13 powers of recommendation. Ultimately, the Commission pursued the latter path. The resolution ultimately adopted by the General Assembly in 1948, with forty-eight votes in favour and eight abstentions, was the Universal Declaration of Human Rights,[37] which included provisions dealing with civil and political rights and also economic, social, and cultural rights.

As a declaratory text adopted by way of a General Assembly resolution, the Universal Declaration has no legal force in its own right. It was, however, intended that the Declaration would provide impetus for the elaboration of a more comprehensive, binding inter-

---

36 See further John P Humphrey, *Human Rights and the United Nations: A Great Adventure* (Dobbs Ferry, NY: Transnational, 1984).

37 *Universal Declaration of Human Rights*, GA Res 217(III), reprinted in UN GAOR, 3d Sess, Part 1 at 71–77, UN Doc A/810 (1948).

national human rights treaty. That objective was ultimately realized in two parts, with the eventual conclusion, in 1966, of the International Covenant on Civil and Political Rights (ICCPR)[38] and the International Covenant on Economic, Social and Cultural Rights (ICESCR).[39] Together, the two Covenants (with Optional Protocols) and the Universal Declaration constitute what is today known within UN circles as the "international bill of human rights."[40]

Progress in the negotiation of the two Covenants was seriously impeded by Cold War politics. Yet during that time period, appreciation also grew for the Universal Declaration, which served as a model for many decolonizing states looking to include a domestic bill of rights within their constitutions. Today, much of the content of the Universal Declaration is considered a reflection of rules of customary international law, although there may be exceptions, such as the Declaration's embrace of a general right to asylum,[41] a human right to property,[42] and a right to rest and leisure.[43] Consider also this summary of the Declaration's significance:

> The Universal Declaration of Human Rights has been the foundation of much of the post-1945 codification of human rights, and the international legal system is replete with global and regional treaties based, in large measure, on the Declaration. Initially adopted only as "a common standard of achievement for all peoples and all nations," the Declaration today exerts a moral, political, and legal influence far beyond the hopes of many of its drafters.
>
> The Universal Declaration has served directly and indirectly as a model for many domestic constitutions, laws, regulations, and policies that protect fundamental human rights. These domestic manifestations include direct constitutional reference to the Universal Declaration or incorporation of its provisions; reflection of the substantive articles of the Universal Declaration in national legislation; and judicial interpretation of domestic laws (and applicable international law) with reference to the Universal Declaration.
>
> Many of the Universal Declaration's provisions also have become incorporated into customary international law, which is binding on all states. This development has been confirmed by states in intergovernmental and diplomatic settings, in arguments submit-

---

38 Above note 6.

39 16 December 1966, 999 UNTS 3, Can TS 1976 No 46, (1967) 6 ILM 360, in force 3 January 1976.

40 See further *Fact Sheet No. 2 (Rev 1): The International Bill of Human Rights* (Geneva: United Nations, 1996).

41 See, however, the widely ratified treaty regime addressing the rights of persons with a well-founded fear of persecution on certain stated grounds: Convention Relating to the Status of Refugees, 28 July 1951, 189 UNTS 150, Can TS 1969 No 6, in force 22 April 1954; and the Protocol relating to the Status of Refugees, 31 January 1967, 606 UNTS 267, Can TS 1969 No 29, (1967) 6 ILM 81, in force 4 October 1967.

42 Property rights are recognized in several regional human rights regimes, including Article 1 of the Protocol to the [European] Convention for the Protection of Human Rights and Fundamental Freedoms, 20 March 1952, 213 UNTS 221, ETS No 9, in force 18 May 1954 [ECHR Protocol No 1]; Article 21 of the American Convention on Human Rights, 21 November 1969, 1144 UNTS 123, OAS TS No 36, (1970) 9 ILM 99, in force 18 July 1978; and Article 14 of the African Charter on Human and Peoples' Rights, 27 June 1981, 1520 UNTS 217, OAU Doc. CAB/LEG/67/3 Rev 5, (1982) 21 ILM 58, in force 21 October 1986.

43 The right of the child to rest and leisure is recognized in Article 31(1) of the widely ratified Convention on the Rights of the Child, 20 November 1989, 1577 UNTS 3, Can TS 1992 No 3, (1989) 28 ILM 1457, in force 2 September 1990.

ted to judicial tribunals, by the actions of intergovernmental organizations, and in the writings of legal scholars . . . .

Despite controversy over many issues, the more than 100 countries which participated in the 1993 UN World Conference on Human Rights reaffirmed "their commitment to the purposes and principles contained in the Charter of the United Nations and the Universal Declaration of Human Rights" and emphasized that the Declaration "is the source of inspiration and has been the basis for the United Nations in making advances in standard setting as contained in the existing international human rights instruments."[44]

3) The Two Leading Multilateral Human Rights Treaties of Universal Application

As noted above, the adoption of the Universal Declaration was followed by the codification of its content in two treaties, both of which came into force in 1976. The Universal Declaration is notable for its inclusion, within one instrument, of civil and political rights, as well as economic, social, and cultural rights. However, in translating the Declaration's content into a more precise, legally binding treaty form, it was thought necessary to recognize differences between these categories of rights. This resulted in the adoption of not one but two treaties, namely the ICCPR[45] and the ICESCR.[46]

This division also reflected, at least in part, differing Cold War-era views among states as to the relative importance of the rights falling into each category. Civil and political rights are readily accepted in the "Western" liberal tradition, and are also considered to impose correlative obligations that are immediate, and prohibitory, in nature (for example, the state shall not torture). Economic, social, and cultural rights have less resonance in liberal democratic thought, but greater appeal for states following other traditions, not least members of the then Soviet Bloc. Economic, social, and cultural rights are also viewed as rights that are progressively realized over time, often requiring positive steps to be taken by the state, as well as a financial commitment, for their realization. The two-treaty approach was the compromise adopted by the contending Cold War camps. Both instruments have now attracted ratifications from a large number of states. As of August 2013, the ICCPR has 167 parties and the ICESCR has 160.

4) Specialized UN-Sponsored Treaties

In addition to the instruments that comprise the "international bill of rights," several more specialized UN-sponsored human rights treaties have also been negotiated and ratified by states. These treaties can be described as belonging to two distinct classes. First are treaties that are broadly "anti-discriminatory" in nature, designed to amplify the non-discrimination guarantee found in the UN Charter and codified in Article 26 of the ICCPR. This class of treaties includes the International Convention on the Elimination of All

---

44   Hurst Hannum, "Status of the Universal Declaration of Human Rights in National and International Law" (1995) 25 Ga J Int'l & Comp L 287 at 289 & 290.

45   Above note 6.

46   Above note 39.

Forms of Racial Discrimination (CERD),[47] the Convention on the Elimination of All Forms of Discrimination against Women (CEDAW),[48] the Convention on the Rights of the Child (CRC),[49] and the Convention on the Rights of Persons with Disabilities (CRPD).[50]

Second are treaties that provide for the criminalization of certain human rights abuses regarded by the international community as particularly egregious. This class includes the Convention on the Prevention and Punishment of the Crime of Genocide (Genocide Convention),[51] the International Convention on the Suppression and Punishment of the Crime of Apartheid (Apartheid Convention),[52] the Convention against Torture and Other Cruel, Inhuman or Degrading Treatment or Punishment (Torture Convention),[53] and the more recent International Convention for the Protection of All Persons from Enforced Disappearance.[54]

For its part, the Rome Statute of the International Criminal Court (Rome Statute)[55] establishes a court with jurisdiction to try certain serious human rights abuses that amount to international crimes: genocide, crimes against humanity, and war crimes. The Rome Statute and the crimes coming within the jurisdiction of the International Criminal Court are addressed in greater detail in Chapter 15.

The party status of the key human rights treaties as of 2013 is set out in the table below.[56]

---

47   21 December 1965, 660 UNTS 195, Can TS 1970 No 28, in force 4 January 1969.

48   18 December 1979, 1249 UNTS 13, Can TS 1982 No 31, in force 3 September 1981.

49   Above note 43.

50   13 December 2006, 2515 UNTS 3, (2007) 46 ILM 443, Can TS 2010 No 8, in force 3 May 2008.

51   9 December 1948, 78 UNTS 277, Can TS 1949 No 27, in force 12 January 1951.

52   30 November 1973, 1015 UNTS 243, in force 18 July 1976 (108 parties). Canada is not a party; however, Canada is a party to the Rome Statute of the International Criminal Court, which includes the crime of apartheid within its provisions on crimes against humanity.

53   10 December 1984, 1465 UNTS 85, Can TS 1987 No 36, in force 26 June 1987.

54   20 December 2006, UN Doc A/61/488 (2006), in force 23 December 2010 [Enforced Disappearance Convention]. Canada is not a party. The UN-sponsored treaty was preceded by a regional instrument, the Inter-American Convention on Forced Disappearance of Persons, 9 June 1994, OAS TS No 68, (1994) 33 ILM 1429, in force 28 March 1996.

55   17 July 1998, 2187 UNTS 90, Can TS 2002 No 13, (1998) 37 ILM 2002, in force 1 July 2002.

56   Designating a human rights treaty as "key" is a subjective exercise, with the UN typically including the Enforced Disappearance Convention, above note 54 (thirty-nine parties), and the International Convention on the Protection of the Rights of All Migrant Workers and their Families, 18 December 1990, 2220 UNTS 3, (1991) 30 ILM 1521, in force 1 July 2003 (forty-six parties). Canada is not a party to either treaty.

Table 9.1 Party Status of Key International Human Rights Treaties

Treaty	Number of Parties	As Percentage of UN Members	Date of Canadian Accession or Ratification*
CEDAW	187	97 percent	10 December 1981
CERD	176	91 percent	14 October 1970
CRPD	132	68 percent	11 March 2010
CRC	193	100 percent**	13 December 1991
ICCPR	167	87 percent	19 May 1976
ICESCR	160	83 percent	19 May 1976
Genocide Convention	142	74 percent	3 September 1952
Torture Convention	153	79 percent	24 June 1987

* Canada usually accedes to a human rights treaty, refraining from signing (and then later ratifying) in recognition of the fact that many international human rights obligations require provincial cooperation (and thus prior consultation) for their implementation within Canada.

** Two UN member states (Somalia and the United States) have signed but not ratified the Convention on the Rights of the Child, while one UN member state has neither signed nor ratified (South Sudan). However, three non-member entities (the Cook Islands, the Holy See, and Niue) have become parties.

C. OVERVIEW OF THE KEY REGIONAL HUMAN RIGHTS SYSTEMS

The universal human rights regime is supplemented by several regional systems, the most significant of which are the European regime, the inter-American regime, and the African regime. The most successful of the three regimes is the European system, which is hosted by the Council of Europe (and not the European Union). It is founded upon the Convention for the Protection of Human Rights and Fundamental Freedoms (also known as the European Convention on Human Rights).[57] The inter-American regime is hosted by the Organization of American States (OAS) and, by contrast, is built upon not one, but two instruments: the American Declaration of the Rights and Duties of Man (American Declaration),[58] and the American Convention on Human Rights (also known as the Pact of San Jose).[59] The African system is the more recently established of the three regimes, hosted initially by the Organization of African Unity and now by the African Union. It is founded upon the African Charter on Human and Peoples' Rights (African Charter).[60]

The inter-American system dates to the adoption of the American Declaration in Bogota, Colombia, in April 1948. Preceding by seven months the adoption of the Universal Declaration of Human Rights,[61] the American Declaration was the first comprehensive international human rights instrument to receive state endorsement. Like the Universal Declaration, the American Declaration was intended as a non-binding, aspirational document. However, the Charter of the Organization of American States[62]—a binding

---

57 4 November 1950, 213 UNTS 221, ETS No 5, in force 3 September 1953.

58 2 May 1948, OAS Doc OEA/Ser.L/V/II.23, doc 21 Rev 6 (1948), reprinted in *Basic Documents Pertaining to Human Rights in the Inter-American System*, Doc OAE/Ser.L/V/I.4 Rev 9 (2003).

59 21 November 1969, 1144 UNTS 123, OAS TS No 36, (1970) 9 ILM 673, in force 18 July 1978.

60 27 June 1981, 1520 UNTS 217, OAU Doc CAB/LEG/67/3 Rev 5, (1982) 21 ILM 58, in force 21 October 1986.

61 Above note 37.

62 30 April 1948, 119 UNTS 3, OAS TS Nos 1-C and 61, Can TS 1990 No 23, in force 13 December 1951, in force for Canada 8 January 1990, as amended by the Protocol of Buenos Aires of 27 February 1967, the

treaty also adopted in 1948—makes reference to the promotion and protection of human rights. In 1989, the Inter-American Court of Human Rights (discussed in greater detail below) declared in an advisory opinion that: "For the member states of the Organization, the Declaration is the text that defines the human rights referred to in the Charter."[63] Thus the provisions of the Declaration have, through the Charter, gained legal effect.

The American Declaration was followed in 1969 by the adoption of an American Convention on Human Rights,[64] which came into force in 1978. As with the European system, which has been supplemented by the adoption of a European Social Charter,[65] an Additional Protocol to the American Convention on Human Rights in the Area of Economic, Social and Cultural Rights (also known as the Protocol of San Salvador) was subsequently adopted in 1988.[66]

LAW IN CONTEXT

Canada's Relationship with the Inter-American Human Rights System

In 2003, the Standing Senate Committee on Human Rights studied the question of Canada's participation in the inter-American human rights system. While Canada, as an OAS member state since 1990, is subject to the American Declaration of the Rights and Duties of Man and the petition process it has fostered before the Inter-American Commission on Human Rights, Canada has not acceded to the American Convention on Human Rights and does not accept the jurisdiction of the Inter-American Court of Human Rights. The text of the American Convention was negotiated before Canada was an OAS member, and several provisions are thought to pose difficulties for Canada, including Article 14 which provides for a "right to reply" for anyone injured by inaccurate or offensive statements published by the press.[67]

The right to life provision in Article 4 of the American Convention is also problematic. Article 4 reflects the Catholic tradition of Latin America and provides that: "Every person has the right to have his life respected. This right shall be protected by law and, in general, from the moment of conception. No one shall be arbitrarily deprived of his life." In the past, Canada has argued that Article 4 conflicts with Canadian law on access to abortion. Although Canada could ratify the Convention with a reservation to this Article, and possibly others, such a reservation would contradict Canada's stated opposition to the mak-

---

Protocol of Cartagena de Indias of 5 December 1985, the Protocol of Washington of 14 December 1992, and the Protocol of Managua of 10 June 1993.

63 *Interpretation of the American Declaration of the Rights and Duties of Man within the Framework of Article 64 of the American Convention on Human Rights*, Advisory Opinion, (1989) Inter-Am Ct HR (Ser A) No 10 at para 45.

64 Above note 59.

65 European Social Charter, 18 October 1961, 529 UNTS 90, ETS No 35, in force 26 February 1965, but see European Social Charter (Revised), 3 May 1996, 2151 UNTS 277, ETS No 163, (1997) 36 ILM 34, in force 1 July 1999.

66 17 November 1988, OAS TS No 69, (1989) 28 ILM 161, in force 16 November 1999.

67 See further, Michael Leir, "Canadian Practice in International Law: At the Department of Foreign Affairs in 1998–99" (1999) 37 Can YB Int'l Law 317 at 327.

ing of reservations to human rights treaties. The Senate Committee made the following observations:

> Canada has been a member of the Organization of American States since January of 1990. We have developed strong relationships with the Americas and we have been active in promoting human rights issues in the region. However, Canada has not yet ratified the principal treaty with respect to the protection of human rights in the Americas: the American Convention on Human Rights. Many wonder why Canada is so reluctant to ratify the Convention and therefore be fully part of the OAS Human Rights System.
>
> Over the course of our hearings, we have found that there are in fact no compelling reasons for Canada not to ratify the Convention. While legitimate concerns were raised before the Committee, both by government and non-government witnesses, concerning the compatibility of Canadian law with some provisions of the Convention, none of these concerns constitute insurmountable obstacles. Witnesses, including legal experts, human rights groups, representatives from NGOs, all have suggested solutions to overcome the obstacles highlighted by the Government of Canada. Support for Canadian ratification of the Convention, with at least one reservation and some statements of understanding has been unanimous among witnesses.
>
> The Committee has heard from a variety of experts. During its first mandate, it traveled to the seat of the Inter-American Court of Human Rights, in San José, Costa Rica. Members of the Committee met with the President and judges of the Inter-American Court and were able to witness first hand how the Court functions by attending hearings. While in Costa Rica, Committee members also had an opportunity to meet with the Inter-American Commission on Human Rights . . . . All have expressed their hope that Canada will ratify the American Convention on Human Rights so as to play an even greater role than the one it currently plays in the promotion and protection of human rights in the hemisphere.
>
> In short, through its study, the Committee has found that the Inter-American Commission and Court would like to see Canada ratify the Convention. Civil society in Canada would like to see our government ratify the Convention. The Committee has been told that the Canadian provinces have concerns but none of them agreed to share them with the Committee. Witnesses, including legal experts, have suggested solutions to address specific issues of compatibility between Canadian domestic law and the Convention.[68]

The Senate renewed its call for a thorough review of Canada's approach to the American Convention in a May 2005 report.[69] In response, the government was positive, but cautious, making these observations:

> . . . we are pleased to inform the Senate that we agree that the American Convention is an important human rights instrument for the Americas. The Government further agrees that Canada should give all due consideration to adherence. In considering adherence

---

68 Standing Senate Committee on Human Rights, *Enhancing Canada's Role in the OAS: Canadian Adherence to the American Convention on Human Rights* (Ottawa: Parliament of Canada, 2003).

69 Standing Senate Committee on Human Rights, *Canadian Adherence to the American Convention on Human Rights: It is Time to Proceed* (Ottawa: Parliament of Canada, 2005).

however, care must be taken to ensure that domestic law and policy, and other international legal obligations are in compliance with the obligations of the Convention. Careful consideration will have to be given to issues that were identified in the past, many of which were examined by the Committee, as well as any new issues that may have arisen since then.[70]

The European Convention on Human Rights (ECHR)[71] dates back to 1950 and, so far, has generated the most successful international human rights regime, backed by an international court—the European Court of Human Rights.[72] The ECHR was concluded by states under the aegis of the Council of Europe, a regional organization established in 1949 with a mandate to promote human rights, democracy, and the rule of law. Initially a western European organization, over time, membership in the Council of Europe has expanded to include states in both central and eastern Europe, resulting in a mandate to promote the adoption of continent-wide agreements to standardize social and legal practices and promote awareness of a European identity based upon a set of shared values.[73] The ECHR entered into force in 1953 and has been amended by a number of protocols. While all forty-seven member-states of the Council of Europe are parties to the ECHR, the rate of ratification varies in respect of the sixteen protocols.

The African Charter of Human and Peoples' Rights[74] was concluded in 1981 and entered into force in 1986. It is often considered unique among the instruments underpinning the key regional systems in that it aims to protect the entire range of human rights—civil, political, social, cultural, and economic—in one treaty (although the American Declaration also does this to some extent). The African Charter is also unique in that it supplements individual human rights with wider societal rights such as "a right to national and international peace and security" (Article 23) and "a right to a generally satisfactory environment" (Article 24). As its title indicates, the African Charter also recognizes certain collective or "peoples" rights, a concept not addressed as directly in other human rights instruments (although it must be noted that the right of self-determination discussed in Chapter 4, the right to be free from genocide, and the rights of minorities are rights that are collective in nature).

The parties to the key regional instruments are set out in the table on the next page.

---

70 Government of Canada, *Canadian Adherence to the American Convention on Human Rights: It is Time to Proceed: Government Response to the Eighteenth Report of the Standing Senate Committee on Human Rights* (25 November 2005) (on file with authors).

71 Above note 57.

72 The Court operated on a part-time basis until 1998, with the former European Commission on Human Rights coming to an end in 1999.

73 "The aim of the Council of Europe is to achieve a greater unity between its members for the purpose of safeguarding and realizing the ideals and principles which are their common heritage and facilitating their economic and social progress": Statute of the Council of Europe, 5 May 1949, 87 UNTS 104, ETS No 1, in force 3 August 1949, art 1.

74 Above note 60.

Table 9.2 Party Status to Key Regional Human Rights Instruments

Instrument	States Parties as of 2013
American Declaration	(Via party status to the Charter of the Organization of American States): Antigua and Barbuda, Bahamas, Belize, Canada, Cuba, Guyana, Saint Kitts and Nevis, Saint Lucia, Saint Vincent and the Grenadines, Trinidad and Tobago, United States, Venezuela
American Convention on Human Rights	Argentina, Barbados, Bolivia, Brazil, Chile, Colombia, Costa Rica, Dominica, Ecuador, El Salvador, Grenada, Guatemala, Haiti, Honduras, Jamaica, Mexico, Nicaragua, Panama, Paraguay, Peru, Dominican Republic, Suriname, Uruguay
European Convention on Human Rights	Albania, Andorra, Armenia, Austria, Azerbaijan, Belgium, Bosnia and Herzegovina, Bulgaria, Croatia, Cyprus, Czech Republic, Denmark, Estonia, Finland, France, Georgia, Germany, Greece, Hungary, Iceland, Ireland, Italy, Latvia, Liechtenstein, Lithuania, Luxembourg, Malta, Moldova, Monaco, Montenegro, Netherlands, Norway, Poland, Portugal, Romania, Russia, San Marino, Serbia, Slovakia, Slovenia, Spain, Sweden, Switzerland, the former Yugoslav Republic of Macedonia, Turkey, Ukraine, United Kingdom
African Charter on Human and Peoples' Rights	Algeria, Angola, Benin, Botswana, Burkina Faso, Burundi, Cameroon, Cape Verde, Central African Republic, Chad, Comoros, Congo, Côte d'Ivoire, Democratic Republic of the Congo, Djibouti, Egypt, Equatorial Guinea, Eritrea, Ethiopia, Gabon, Gambia, Ghana, Guinea, Guinea-Bissau, Kenya, Lesotho, Liberia, Libya, Madagascar, Malawi, Mali, Mauritania, Mauritius, Mozambique, Namibia, Niger, Nigeria, Rwanda, Saharawi Arab Democratic Republic*, Sao Tome and Principe, Senegal, Seychelles, Sierra Leone, Somalia, South Africa, Sudan, Swaziland, Togo, Tunisia, Uganda, United Republic of Tanzania, Zambia, Zimbabwe

*   A non-member entity with respect to the UN.

With respect to the inter-American regime, all OAS member states are subject to the American Declaration by virtue of their adherence to the OAS Charter, but for those OAS states that are party to the American Convention on Human Rights, the latter takes precedence. Two states (Trinidad and Tobago, and Venezuela) have denounced the American Convention, but remain subject to the American Declaration.

D. SUBSTANTIVE HUMAN RIGHTS CONTENT

We turn now to an overview of the substantive content of international human rights law. First we examine the nature of the obligations imposed by international human rights law on states and then we turn to some of the specific rights guaranteed by the various international human rights instruments, focusing on the two treaties of universal application — the ICCPR and the ICESCR. Throughout the discussion, it should be kept in mind that the object and purpose of a treaty for the protection of human rights requires that its provisions be interpreted and applied so that its safeguards are practical and effective,[75] and not theoretical or illusory. It is often said by human rights advocates that a state party

---

75   See *Soering v United Kingdom*, App No 14038/88, (1989) ECHR (Ser A) No 161, (1989) 11 EHRR 439, (1989) 28 ILM 1063 at para 87.

to a human rights treaty undertakes a duty to respect, protect, promote, and fulfill the rights recognized therein.

1) Nature of Obligations Imposed

We have already noted arguments that the Universal Declaration reflects, at least in part, customary international law. To the extent it does, the commitments enumerated in that instrument are binding by way of custom on all states. In contrast, the nature and extent of the obligations states must observe in relation to international human rights treaties depend on the terms found in those treaties. It is often argued that human rights are indivisible, in the sense that all are equally important. Consider the view expressed in the Vienna Declaration and Programme of Action, which emanated from the 1993 World Conference on Human Rights:

> All human rights are universal, indivisible and interdependent and interrelated. The international community must treat human rights globally in a fair and equal manner, on the same footing, and with the same emphasis. While the significance of national and regional particularities and various historical, cultural and religious backgrounds must be borne in mind, it is the duty of States, regardless of their political, economic and cultural systems, to promote and protect all human rights and fundamental freedoms.[76]

On the other hand, the *de jure* extent of a state's treaty-based human rights obligations does vary according to whether the right falls within the civil and political or, rather, the economic, social, and cultural categories.

a) The Obligation to Respect and Ensure Civil and Political Rights

A treaty concerned with the protection of civil and political rights typically imposes a general obligation on its states parties to "respect and ensure" the rights recognized within that particular treaty text. This obligation is of an immediate nature, triggered by a state's consent to be bound by the treaty (or the treaty's coming into force, whichever comes later), and requires the state party to ensure the performance of its treaty obligations through either existing or new legislation, administrative action, policies, and education. While we will focus on Article 2 of the ICCPR to illustrate this point, a similar obligation is found in Articles 1 and 2 of the American Convention on Human Rights[77] and Article 1 of the European Convention on Human Rights.[78] (Article 1 of the African Charter on Human and Peoples' Rights[79] will be mentioned separately below.)

---

76   Vienna Declaration and Programme of Action, UN Doc A/CONF.157/23 (1993) at para 5.
77   Above note 59.
78   Above note 57.
79   Above note 60.

International Covenant on Civil and Political Rights, 16 December 1966, 999 UNTS 171, Can TS 1976 No 47, (1967) 6 ILM 368, in force 23 March 1976

Article 2

1. Each State Party to the present Covenant undertakes to respect and to ensure to all individuals within its territory and subject to its jurisdiction the rights recognized in the present Covenant, without distinction of any kind, such as race, colour, sex, language, religion, political or other opinion, national or social origin, property, birth or other status.

2. Where not already provided for by existing legislative or other measures, each State Party to the present Covenant undertakes to take the necessary steps, in accordance with its constitutional processes and with the provisions of the present Covenant, to adopt such laws or other measures as may be necessary to give effect to the rights recognized in the present Covenant.

3. Each State Party to the present Covenant undertakes:

(a) To ensure that any person whose rights or freedoms as herein recognized are violated shall have an effective remedy, notwithstanding that the violation has been committed by persons acting in an official capacity;

(b) To ensure that any person claiming such a remedy shall have his right thereto determined by competent judicial, administrative or legislative authorities, or by any other competent authority provided for by the legal system of the State, and to develop the possibilities of judicial remedy;

(c) To ensure that the competent authorities shall enforce such remedies when granted.

Further guidance on the nature of the obligation to respect and ensure civil and political rights has been offered by the Human Rights Committee, the treaty monitoring body established by states pursuant to the ICCPR:

Human Rights Committee, *General Comment No 31: Nature of the General Legal Obligation on States Parties to the Covenant,* **UN Doc CCPR/C/21/Rev.1/Add.13 (2004)**[80]

3. Article 2 defines the scope of the legal obligations undertaken by States Parties to the Covenant. A general obligation is imposed on States Parties to respect the Covenant rights and to ensure them to all individuals in their territory and subject to their jurisdiction (see paragraph 10 below). Pursuant to the principle articulated in article 26 of the Vienna Convention on the Law of Treaties, States Parties are required to give effect to the obligations under the Covenant in good faith.

4. The obligations of the Covenant in general and article 2 in particular are binding on every State Party as a whole. All branches of government (executive, legislative and judicial), and other public or governmental authorities, at whatever level—national, regional or local—are in a position to engage the responsibility of the State Party. The executive branch that usually represents the State Party internationally, including before the

---

80 Reprinted in *Compilation of General Comments and General Recommendations made by Human Rights Treaty Bodies,* UN Doc HRI/GEN/1/Rev.9 (2008), vol I at 243–47.

Committee, may not point to the fact that an action incompatible with the provisions of the Covenant was carried out by another branch of government as a means of seeking to relieve the State Party from responsibility for the action and consequent incompatibility. This understanding flows directly from the principle contained in article 27 of the Vienna Convention on the Law of Treaties, according to which a State Party "may not invoke the provisions of its internal law as justification for its failure to perform a treaty." Although article 2, paragraph 2, allows States Parties to give effect to Covenant rights in accordance with domestic constitutional processes, the same principle operates so as to prevent States parties from invoking provisions of the constitutional law or other aspects of domestic law to justify a failure to perform or give effect to obligations under the treaty. In this respect, the Committee reminds States Parties with a federal structure of the terms of article 50, according to which the Covenant's provisions "shall extend to all parts of federal states without any limitations or exceptions."

5. The article 2, paragraph 1, obligation to respect and ensure the rights recognized by the Covenant has immediate effect for all States parties. Article 2, paragraph 2, provides the overarching framework within which the rights specified in the Covenant are to be promoted and protected. . . .

6. The legal obligation under article 2, paragraph 1, is both negative and positive in nature. States Parties must refrain from violation of the rights recognized by the Covenant, and any restrictions on any of those rights must be permissible under the relevant provisions of the Covenant. Where such restrictions are made, States must demonstrate their necessity and only take such measures as are proportionate to the pursuance of legitimate aims in order to ensure continuous and effective protection of Covenant rights. In no case may the restrictions be applied or invoked in a manner that would impair the essence of a Covenant right.

7. Article 2 requires that States Parties adopt legislative, judicial, administrative, educative and other appropriate measures in order to fulfil their legal obligations. The Committee believes that it is important to raise levels of awareness about the Covenant not only among public officials and State agents but also among the population at large.

8. The article 2, paragraph 1, obligations are binding on States [Parties] and do not, as such, have direct horizontal effect as a matter of international law. The Covenant cannot be viewed as a substitute for domestic criminal or civil law. However the positive obligations on States Parties to ensure Covenant rights will only be fully discharged if individuals are protected by the State, not just against violations of Covenant rights by its agents, but also against acts committed by private persons or entities that would impair the enjoyment of Covenant rights in so far as they are amenable to application between private persons or entities. There may be circumstances in which a failure to ensure Covenant rights as required by article 2 would give rise to violations by States Parties of those rights, as a result of States Parties' permitting or failing to take appropriate measures or to exercise due diligence to prevent, punish, investigate or redress the harm caused by such acts by private persons or entities. States are reminded of the interrelationship between the positive obligations imposed under article 2 and the need to provide effective remedies in the event of breach under article 2, paragraph 3 . . . .

9. The beneficiaries of the rights recognized by the Covenant are individuals . . . .

10. States Parties are required by article 2, paragraph 1, to respect and to ensure the Covenant rights to all persons who may be within their territory and to all persons subject to their jurisdiction. This means that a State party must respect and ensure the rights laid down in the Covenant to anyone within the power or effective control of that State Party, even if not situated within the territory of the State Party. As indicated in General Comment 15 adopted at the twenty-seventh session (1986),[81] the enjoyment of Covenant rights is not limited to citizens of States Parties but must also be available to all individuals, regardless of nationality or statelessness, such as asylum seekers, refugees, migrant workers and other persons, who may find themselves in the territory or subject to the jurisdiction of the State Party. This principle also applies to those within the power or effective control of the forces of a State Party acting outside its territory, regardless of the circumstances in which such power or effective control was obtained, such as forces constituting a national contingent of a State Party assigned to an international peace-keeping or peace-enforcement operation . . . .

12. Moreover, the article 2 obligation requiring that States Parties respect and ensure the Covenant rights for all persons in their territory and all persons under their control entails an obligation not to extradite, deport, expel or otherwise remove a person from their territory, where there are substantial grounds for believing that there is a real risk of irreparable harm . . . .

13. Article 2, paragraph 2, requires that States Parties take the necessary steps to give effect to the Covenant rights in the domestic order. It follows that, unless Covenant rights are already protected by their domestic laws or practices, States Parties are required on ratification to make such changes to domestic laws and practices as are necessary to ensure their conformity with the Covenant. Where there are inconsistencies between domestic law and the Covenant, article 2 requires that the domestic law or practice be changed to meet the standards imposed by the Covenant's substantive guarantees. Article 2 allows a State Party to pursue this in accordance with its own domestic constitutional structure and accordingly does not require that the Covenant be directly applicable in the courts, by incorporation of the Covenant into national law. The Committee takes the view, however, that Covenant guarantees may receive enhanced protection in those States where the Covenant is automatically or through specific incorporation part of the domestic legal order. The Committee invites those States Parties in which the Covenant does not form part of the domestic legal order to consider incorporation of the Covenant to render it part of domestic law to facilitate full realization of Covenant rights as required by article 2.

14. The requirement under article 2, paragraph 2, to take steps to give effect to the Covenant rights is unqualified and of immediate effect. A failure to comply with this obligation cannot be justified by reference to political, social, cultural or economic considerations within the State.

---

81 Reprinted in *Compilation of General Comments and General Recommendations made by Human Rights Treaty Bodies*, UN Doc HRI/GEN/1/Rev.9 (2008), vol I at 189–91.

15. Article 2, paragraph 3, requires that in addition to effective protection of Covenant rights States Parties must ensure that individuals also have accessible and effective remedies to vindicate those rights. Such remedies should be appropriately adapted so as to take account of the special vulnerability of certain categories of person, including in particular children. The Committee attaches importance to States Parties' establishing appropriate judicial and administrative mechanisms for addressing claims of rights violations under domestic law. The Committee notes that the enjoyment of the rights recognized under the Covenant can be effectively assured by the judiciary in many different ways, including direct applicability of the Covenant, application of comparable constitutional or other provisions of law, or the interpretive effect of the Covenant in the application of national law. Administrative mechanisms are particularly required to give effect to the general obligation to investigate allegations of violations promptly, thoroughly and effectively through independent and impartial bodies. National human rights institutions, endowed with appropriate powers, can contribute to this end. A failure by a State Party to investigate allegations of violations could in and of itself give rise to a separate breach of the Covenant. Cessation of an ongoing violation is an essential element of the right to an effective remedy.

16. Article 2, paragraph 3, requires that States Parties make reparation to individuals whose Covenant rights have been violated. Without reparation to individuals whose Covenant rights have been violated, the obligation to provide an effective remedy, which is central to the efficacy of article 2, paragraph 3, is not discharged . . . . The Committee notes that, where appropriate, reparation can involve restitution, rehabilitation and measures of satisfaction, such as public apologies, public memorials, guarantees of non-repetition and changes in relevant laws and practices, as well as bringing to justice the perpetrators of human rights violations . . . .

b) The Progressive Realization of Economic, Social, and Cultural Rights

As noted earlier, during the negotiations aimed at converting the rights recognized in the Universal Declaration into a legally binding treaty (and later two treaties), it was recognized that economic, social, and cultural rights need to be treated differently than civil and political rights. Compare the "respect and ensure" language of the ICCPR with that used in Article 2 of the ICESCR:

International Covenant on Economic, Social and Cultural Rights, 16 December 1966, 993 UNTS 3, Can TS 1976 No 46, (1967) 6 ILM 360, in force 3 January 1976

Article 2
1. Each State Party to the present Covenant undertakes to take steps, individually and through international assistance and co-operation, especially economic and technical, to the maximum of its available resources, with a view to achieving progressively the full realization of the rights recognized in the present Covenant by all appropriate means, including particularly the adoption of legislative measures.

2. The States Parties to the present Covenant undertake to guarantee that the rights enunciated in the present Covenant will be exercised without discrimination of any kind

as to race, colour, sex, language, religion, political or other opinion, national or social origin, property, birth or other status.

3. Developing countries, with due regard to human rights and their national economy, may determine to what extent they would guarantee the economic rights recognized in the present Covenant to non-nationals.

Compare the undertaking to take steps "with a view to achieving progressively" the rights set out in the ICESCR with the much more emphatic and immediate obligation stated in the ICCPR. The Committee on Economic, Social and Cultural Rights, the body established by ECOSOC to perform a monitoring role under the ICESCR, has offered the following interpretation of this progressive realization standard:

Committee on Economic, Social and Cultural Rights, *General Comment No 3: The Nature of States Parties Obligations*, UN Doc E/1991/23 at 83–87 (1990)[82]

1. Article 2 is of particular importance to a full understanding of the Covenant and must be seen as having a dynamic relationship with all of the other provisions of the Covenant. It describes the nature of the general legal obligations undertaken by States parties to the Covenant . . . . [W]hile the Covenant provides for progressive realization and acknowledges the constraints due to the limits of available resources, it also imposes various obligations which are of immediate effect . . . .

2. [One of these] is the undertaking in article 2(1) "to take steps," which in itself, is not qualified or limited by other considerations . . . . Thus while the full realization of the relevant rights may be achieved progressively, steps towards that goal must be taken within a reasonably short time after the Covenant's entry into force for the States concerned. Such steps should be deliberate, concrete and targeted as clearly as possible towards meeting the obligations recognized in the Covenant.

3. The means which should be used in order to satisfy the obligation to take steps are stated in article 2(1) to be "all appropriate means, including particularly the adoption of legislative measures." The Committee recognizes that in many instances legislation is highly desirable and in some cases may even be indispensable. For example, it may be difficult to combat discrimination effectively in the absence of a sound legislative foundation for the necessary measures. In fields such as health, the protection of children and mothers, and education, as well as in respect of the matters dealt with in articles 6 to 9, legislation may also be an indispensable element for many purposes.

4. The Committee . . . wishes to emphasize, however, that the adoption of legislative measures, as specifically foreseen by the Covenant, is by no means exhaustive of the obligations of States parties. Rather, the phrase "by all appropriate means" must be given its full and natural meaning. . . .

---

82 Reprinted in *Compilation of General Comments and General Recommendations made by Human Rights Treaty Bodies*, UN Doc HRI/GEN/1/Rev.9 (2008), vol I at 7–10.

5. Among the measures which might be considered appropriate, in addition to legislation, is the provision of judicial remedies with respect to rights which may, in accordance with the national legal system, be considered justiciable. The Committee notes, for example, that the enjoyment of the rights recognized, without discrimination, will often be appropriately promoted, in part, through the provision of judicial or other effective remedies. Indeed, those States parties which are also parties to the International Covenant on Civil and Political Rights are already obligated (by virtue of arts. 2 (paras. 1 and 3), 3 and 26) of that Covenant to ensure that any person whose rights or freedoms (including the right to equality and non-discrimination) recognized in that Covenant are violated, "shall have an effective remedy" (art. 2 (3)(a)). In addition, there are a number of other provisions in the International Covenant on Economic, Social and Cultural Rights, including articles 3, 7(a)(i), 8, 10(3), 13(2)(a), (3) and (4) and 15(3) which would seem to be capable of immediate application by judicial and other organs in many national legal systems. Any suggestion that the provisions indicated are inherently non-self-executing would seem to be difficult to sustain. . . .

7. Other measures which may also be considered "appropriate" for the purposes of article 2(1) include, but are not limited to, administrative, financial, educational and social measures.

8. The Committee notes that the undertaking "to take steps . . . by all appropriate means including particularly the adoption of legislative measures" neither requires nor precludes any particular form of government or economic system being used as the vehicle for the steps in question, provided only that it is democratic and that all human rights are thereby respected. Thus, in terms of political and economic systems the Covenant is neutral and its principles cannot accurately be described as being predicated exclusively upon the need for, or the desirability of a socialist or a capitalist system, or a mixed, centrally planned, or laisser-faire economy, or upon any other particular approach. In this regard, the Committee reaffirms that the rights recognized in the Covenant are susceptible of realization within the context of a wide variety of economic and political systems, provided only that the interdependence and indivisibility of the two sets of human rights, as affirmed *inter alia* in the preamble to the Covenant, is recognized and reflected in the system in question. The Committee also notes the relevance in this regard of other human rights and in particular the right to development.

9. The principal obligation of result reflected in article 2 (1) is to take steps "with a view to achieving progressively the full realization of the rights recognized" in the Covenant. The term "progressive realization" is often used to describe the intent of this phrase. The concept of progressive realization constitutes a recognition of the fact that full realization of all economic, social and cultural rights will generally not be able to be achieved in a short period of time. In this sense the obligation differs significantly from that contained in article 2 of the International Covenant on Civil and Political Rights which embodies an immediate obligation to respect and ensure all of the relevant rights. Nevertheless, the fact that realization over time, or in other words progressively, is foreseen under the Covenant should not be misinterpreted as depriving the obligation of all meaningful content. It is on the one hand a necessary flexibility device, reflecting the realities of the

real world and the difficulties involved for any country in ensuring full realization of economic, social and cultural rights. On the other hand, the phrase must be read in the light of the overall objective, indeed the raison d'être, of the Covenant which is to establish clear obligations for States parties in respect of the full realization of the rights in question. It thus imposes an obligation to move as expeditiously and effectively as possible towards that goal. Moreover, any deliberately retrogressive measures in that regard would require the most careful consideration and would need to be fully justified by reference to the totality of the rights provided for in the Covenant and in the context of the full use of the maximum available resources . . . .

11. The Committee wishes to emphasize, however, that even where the available resources are demonstrably inadequate, the obligation remains for a State party to strive to ensure the widest possible enjoyment of the relevant rights under the prevailing circumstances. Moreover, the obligations to monitor the extent of the realization, or more especially of the non-realization, of economic, social and cultural rights, and to devise strategies and programmes for their promotion, are not in any way eliminated as a result of resource constraints . . . .

The ICESCR's weaker language on state obligations is replicated in some, but not all, of the other instruments covering economic, social, and cultural rights. Thus, in the inter-American system, the American Convention's strong language in relation to civil and political rights is not included in the Additional Protocol to the American Convention on Human Rights in the Area of Economic, Social and Cultural Rights.[83] The latter instrument reads, in part:

Article 1
Obligation to Adopt Measures
The States Parties to this Additional Protocol to the American Convention on Human Rights undertake to adopt the necessary measures, both domestically and through international cooperation, especially economic and technical, to the extent allowed by their available resources, and taking into account their degree of development, for the purpose of achieving progressively and pursuant to their internal legislations, the full observance of the rights recognized in this Protocol.

Article 2
Obligation to Enact Domestic Legislation
If the exercise of the rights set forth in this Protocol is not already guaranteed by legislative or other provisions, the States Parties undertake to adopt, in accordance with their constitutional processes and the provisions of this Protocol, such legislative or other measures as may be necessary for making those rights a reality.

The distinction between civil and political and economic, social, and cultural rights is also reflected in the Convention on the Rights of the Child, a UN-sponsored treaty that recognizes both types of rights:

---

83 Protocol of San Salvador, above note 66.

Article 4

States Parties shall undertake all appropriate legislative, administrative, and other measures for the implementation of the rights recognized in the present Convention. With
regard to economic, social and cultural rights, States Parties shall undertake such measures to the maximum extent of their available resources and, where needed, within the
framework of international co-operation.

But not every instrument is as preoccupied with the distinction between civil and
political rights and economic, social, and cultural rights. The African Charter is unusual
among comprehensive human rights instruments in that it does not differentiate between the obligations states have in relation to these different types of rights:

Article 1

The Member States of the Organization of African Unity parties to the present Charter shall recognize the rights, duties and freedoms enshrined in this Chapter and shall
undertake to adopt legislative or other measures to give effect to them.

c) Limitation Provisions

Another consideration of importance in understanding most human rights treaties is the
extent to which the rights in a particular treaty are qualified or limited, recognizing that
few human rights obligations are absolute. These limitations govern the very definition of
the rights recognized within the treaty, with many rights being limited in order to secure
the rights of others or to meet the "just requirements of morality, public order and the
general welfare in a democratic society." This phrasing is taken from the general limitation clause found in Article 29(2) of the Universal Declaration of Human Rights[84] (which
later inspired the adoption of a general limitation provision for the *Canadian Charter of
Rights and Freedoms*). A similar approach is taken in Article 28 of the American Declaration of the Rights and Duties of Man,[85] Article 5 of the Additional Protocol to the American
Convention on Human Rights in the Area of Economic, Social and Cultural Rights,[86] and
Article 4 of the ICESCR.[87] The latter reads as follows:

Article 4

The States Parties to the present Covenant recognize that, in the enjoyment of those
rights provided by the State in conformity with the present Covenant, the State may subject such rights only to such limitations as are determined by law only in so far as this
may be compatible with the nature of these rights and solely for the purpose of promoting the general welfare in a democratic society.

Other human rights instruments, beginning with the European Convention on Human
Rights[88] in 1950, have eschewed the use of a general limitation clause in favour of a more

---

84 Above note 37.
85 Above note 58.
86 Protocol of San Salvador, above note 66.
87 Above note 39.
88 Above note 57.

tailored approach that builds the relevant limitations, where applicable, into each right, thus ensuring that some rights are absolute (such as the prohibition on torture or slavery), some rights are strictly qualified (such as the rights to liberty and a fair trial), and some rights are limited out of consideration for the rights of others and the general interests of society (such as the rights to freedom of expression and peaceful assembly). A similar approach is taken with respect to the rights codified in the ICCPR.

Fear that the internal limitations in the ICCPR may open the door to interpretations that would undermine the vitality of the rights themselves led to the convening of a conference in Siracusa, Italy, in 1984, where thirty-one international law experts formulated the following guidance for the Human Rights Committee's consideration:[89]

Siracusa Principles on the Limitation and Derogation Provisions in the International Covenant on Civil and Political Rights, as presented in a *Note Verbale dated 24 August 1985 from the Permanent Representative of the Netherlands to the United Nations Office at Geneva*, UN Doc E/CN.4/1985/4 (1985)

I. LIMITATION CLAUSES

A. General Interpretative Principles Relating to the Justification of Limitations

1. No limitations or grounds for applying them to rights guaranteed by the Covenant are permitted other than those contained in the terms of the Covenant itself.

2. The scope of a limitation referred to in the Covenant shall not be interpreted so as to jeopardize the essence of the right concerned.

3. All limitation clauses shall be interpreted strictly and in favour of the rights at issue.

4. All limitations shall be interpreted in the light and context of the particular right concerned.

5. All limitations on a right recognized by the Covenant shall be provided for by law and be compatible with the objects and purposes of the Covenant.

6. No limitation referred to in the Covenant shall be applied for any purpose other than that for which it has been prescribed.

7. No limitation shall be applied in an arbitrary manner.

8. Every limitation imposed shall be subject to the possibility of challenge to and remedy against its abusive application.

9. No limitation on a right recognized by the Covenant shall discriminate contrary to Article 2, paragraph 1.

10. Whenever a limitation is required in the terms of the Covenant to be "necessary," this term implies that the limitation:

---

89 Domestic courts may also find the Siracusa Principles to be of interpretive assistance, as suggested in *Re Charkaoui*, 2009 FC 342, [2010] 3 FCR 67 at para 57. See also *A and others v Secretary of State for the Home Department* (2004), [2004] UKHL 56, [2005] 2 AC 68.

(a) is based on one of the grounds justifying limitations recognized by the relevant article of the Covenant,

(b) responds to a pressing public or social need,

(c) pursues a legitimate aim, and

(d) is proportionate to that aim.

Any assessment as to the necessity of a limitation shall be made on objective considerations.

11. In applying a limitation, a state shall use no more restrictive means than are required for the achievement of the purpose of the limitation.

12. The burden of justifying a limitation upon a right guaranteed under the Covenant lies with the state.

13. The requirement expressed in Article 12 of the Covenant, that any restrictions be consistent with other rights recognized in the Covenant, is implicit in limitations to the other rights recognized in the Covenant.

14. The limitation clauses of the Covenant shall not be interpreted to restrict the exercise of any human rights protected to a greater extent by other international obligations binding upon the state.

B. Interpretative Principles Relating to Specific Limitation Clauses

i. "prescribed by law"

15. No limitation on the exercise of human rights shall be made unless provided for by national law of general application which is consistent with the Covenant and is in force at the time the limitation is applied.

16. Laws imposing limitations on the exercise of human rights shall not be arbitrary or unreasonable.

17. Legal rules limiting the exercise of human rights shall be clear and accessible to everyone.

18. Adequate safeguards and effective remedies shall be provided by law against illegal or abusive imposition or application of limitations on human rights.

ii. "in a democratic society"

19. The expression "in a democratic society" shall be interpreted as imposing a further restriction on the limitation clauses it qualifies.

20. The burden is upon a state imposing limitations so qualified to demonstrate that the limitations do not impair the democratic functioning of the society.

21. While there is no single model of a democratic society, a society which recognizes and respects the human rights set forth in the United Nations Charter and the Universal Declaration of Human Rights may be viewed as meeting this definition. . . .

iii. "public order (ordre public)"

22. The expression "public order (ordre public)" as used in the Covenant may be defined as the sum of rules which ensure the functioning of society or the set of fundamental

principles on which society is founded. Respect for human rights is part of public order (ordre public).

23. Public order (ordre public) shall be interpreted in the context of the purpose of the particular human right which is limited on this ground.

24. State organs or agents responsible for the maintenance of public order (ordre public) shall be subject to controls in the exercise of their power through the parliament, courts, or other competent independent bodies.

iv. "public health"

25. Public health may be invoked as a ground for limiting certain rights in order to allow a state to take measures dealing with a serious threat to the health of the population or individual members of the population. These measures must be specifically aimed at preventing disease or injury or providing care for the sick and injured.

26. Due regard shall be had to the international health regulations of the World Health Organization.

v. "public morals"

27. Since public morality varies over time and from one culture to another, a state which invokes public morality as a ground for restricting human rights, while enjoying a certain margin of discretion, shall demonstrate that the limitation in question is essential to the maintenance of respect for fundamental values of the community.

28. The margin of discretion left to states does not apply to the rule of non-discrimination as defined in the Covenant. . . .

vi. "national security"

29. National security may be invoked to justify measures limiting certain rights only when they are taken to protect the existence of the nation or its territorial integrity or political independence against force or threat of force.

30. National security cannot be invoked as a reason for imposing limitations to prevent merely local or relatively isolated threats to law and order.

31. National security cannot be used as a pretext for imposing vague or arbitrary limitations and may only be invoked when there exists adequate safeguards and effective remedies against abuse.

32. The systematic violation of human rights undermines true national security and may jeopardize international peace and security. A state responsible for such violation shall not invoke national security as a justification for measures aimed at suppressing opposition to such violation or at perpetrating repressive practices against its population.

vii. "public safety"

33. Public safety means protection against danger to the safety of persons, to their life or physical integrity, or serious damage to their property.

34. The need to protect public safety can justify limitations provided by law. It cannot be used for imposing vague or arbitrary limitations and may only be invoked when there exist adequate safeguards and effective remedies against abuse.

viii. "rights and freedoms of others" or the "rights or reputations of others"

35. The scope of the rights and freedoms of others that may act as a limitation upon rights in the Covenant extends beyond the rights and freedoms recognized in the Covenant.

36. When a conflict exists between a right protected in the Covenant and one which is not, recognition and consideration should be given to the fact that the Covenant seeks to protect the most fundamental rights and freedoms. In this context especial weight should be afforded to rights not subject to limitations in the Covenant.

37. A limitation to a human right based upon the reputation of others shall not be used to protect the state and its officials from public opinion or criticism.

ix. "restrictions on public trial"

38. All trials shall be public unless the Court determines in accordance with law that:
    (a) the press or the public should be excluded from all or part of a trial on the basis of specific findings announced in open court showing that the interest of the private lives of the parties or their families or of juveniles so requires; or
    (b) the exclusion is strictly necessary to avoid publicity prejudicial to the fairness of the trial or endangering public morals, public order (ordre public), or national security in a democratic society.

d) Derogations

Times of public emergency (such as armed conflict, major terrorist threats, and natural disasters) may also justify a specific kind of limitation on the performance of some international human rights obligations, known as a derogation. Unlike limitation provisions, derogations are temporary measures, allowing for the suspension of certain specified human rights guarantees for so long as it is not possible for the state to secure respect for these rights. However, not all human rights guarantees permit derogation, with the treaty text indicating which rights are non-derogable. In the most recent of the three key regional human rights treaties discussed above, there is no derogation provision, although the provisions of the African Charter permit the limitation of almost all rights under certain conditions.[90] The ICCPR, for its part, contains the following derogation provision:

Article 4

1. In time of public emergency which threatens the life of the nation and the existence of which is officially proclaimed, the States Parties to the present Covenant may take measures derogating from their obligations under the present Covenant to the extent strictly required by the exigencies of the situation, provided that such measures are not inconsistent with their other obligations under international law and do not involve discrimination solely on the ground of race, colour, sex, language, religion or social origin.

2. No derogation from articles 6 [right to life], 7 [torture and cruel, inhuman and degrading treatment and punishment], 8 (paragraphs I and 2) [slavery and servitude], 11 [imprisonment for debt], 15 [non-retroactivity of criminal law], 16 [recognition as a person before the law] and 18 [freedom of thought, conscience and religion] may be made under this provision.

---

90 See the African Charter on Human and Peoples' Rights, above note 60.

3. Any State Party to the present Covenant availing itself of the right of derogation shall immediately inform the other States Parties to the present Covenant, through the intermediary of the Secretary-General of the United Nations, of the provisions from which it has derogated and of the reasons by which it was actuated. A further communication shall be made, through the same intermediary, on the date on which it terminates such derogation.

Concerned that this derogation provision may be abused, the Human Rights Committee has offered this interpretation of Article 4:

Human Rights Committee, *General Comment No 29: Article 4: Derogations during a State of Emergency,* **UN Doc CCPR/C/21/Rev.1/Add.11 (2001)**[91]

1. Article 4 of the Covenant is of paramount importance for the system of protection for human rights under the Covenant. On the one hand, it allows for a State party unilaterally to derogate temporarily from a part of its obligations under the Covenant. On the other hand, article 4 subjects both this very measure of derogation, as well as its material consequences, to a specific regime of safeguards. The restoration of a state of normalcy where full respect for the Covenant can again be secured must be the predominant objective of a State party derogating from the Covenant . . . .

2. Measures derogating from the provisions of the Covenant must be of an exceptional and temporary nature. Before a State moves to invoke article 4, two fundamental conditions must be met: the situation must amount to a public emergency which threatens the life of the nation, and the State party must have officially proclaimed a state of emergency. The latter requirement is essential for the maintenance of the principles of legality and rule of law at times when they are most needed. When proclaiming a state of emergency with consequences that could entail derogation from any provision of the Covenant, States must act within their constitutional and other provisions of law that govern such proclamation and the exercise of emergency powers; it is the task of the Committee to monitor the laws in question with respect to whether they enable and secure compliance with article 4 . . . .

3. Not every disturbance or catastrophe qualifies as a public emergency which threatens the life of the nation, as required by article 4, paragraph 1. During armed conflict, whether international or non-international, rules of international humanitarian law become applicable and help, in addition to the provisions in article 4 and article 5, paragraph 1, of the Covenant, to prevent the abuse of a State's emergency powers. The Covenant requires that even during an armed conflict measures derogating from the Covenant are allowed only if and to the extent that the situation constitutes a threat to the life of the nation. If States parties consider invoking article 4 in other situations than an armed conflict, they should carefully consider the justification and why such a measure is necessary and legitimate in the circumstances . . . .

---

91 Reprinted in *Compilation of General Comments and General Recommendations made by Human Rights Treaty Bodies,* UN Doc HRI/GEN/1/Rev.9 (2008), vol I at 234–41.

4. A fundamental requirement for any measures derogating from the Covenant, as set forth in article 4, paragraph 1, is that such measures are limited to the extent strictly required by the exigencies of the situation. This requirement relates to the duration, geographical coverage and material scope of the state of emergency and any measures of derogation resorted to because of the emergency . . . .

5. The issues of when rights can be derogated from, and to what extent, cannot be separated from the provision in article 4, paragraph 1, of the Covenant according to which any measures derogating from a State party's obligations under the Covenant must be limited "to the extent strictly required by the exigencies of the situation." This condition requires that States parties provide careful justification not only for their decision to proclaim a state of emergency but also for any specific measures based on such a proclamation. If States purport to invoke the right to derogate from the Covenant during, for instance, a natural catastrophe, a mass demonstration including instances of violence, or a major industrial accident, they must be able to justify not only that such a situation constitutes a threat to the life of the nation, but also that all their measures derogating from the Covenant are strictly required by the exigencies of the situation. In the opinion of the Committee, the possibility of restricting certain Covenant rights under the terms of, for instance, freedom of movement (article 12) or freedom of assembly (article 21) is generally sufficient during such situations and no derogation from the provisions in question would be justified by the exigencies of the situation.

6. The fact that some of the provisions of the Covenant have been listed in article 4 (paragraph 2), as not being subject to derogation does not mean that other articles in the Covenant may be subjected to derogations at will, even where a threat to the life of the nation exists. The legal obligation to narrow down all derogations to those strictly required by the exigencies of the situation establishes both for States parties and for the Committee a duty to conduct a careful analysis under each article of the Covenant based on an objective assessment of the actual situation.

7. Article 4, paragraph 2, of the Covenant explicitly prescribes that no derogation from the following articles may be made: article 6 (right to life), article 7 (prohibition of torture or cruel, inhuman or degrading punishment, or of medical or scientific experimentation without consent), article 8, paragraphs 1 and 2 (prohibition of slavery, slave-trade and servitude), article 11 (prohibition of imprisonment because of inability to fulfil a contractual obligation), article 15 (the principle of legality in the field of criminal law, i.e. the requirement of both criminal liability and punishment being limited to clear and precise provisions in the law that was in place and applicable at the time the act or omission took place, except in cases where a later law imposes a lighter penalty), article 16 (the recognition of everyone as a person before the law), and article 18 (freedom of thought, conscience and religion). The rights enshrined in these provisions are non-derogable by the very fact that they are listed in article 4, paragraph 2 . . . .

8. According to article 4, paragraph 1, one of the conditions for the justifiability of any derogation from the Covenant is that the measures taken do not involve discrimination solely on the ground of race, colour, sex, language, religion or social origin. Even though article 26 or the other Covenant provisions related to non-discrimination (articles 2, 3, 14,

paragraph 1, 23, paragraph 4, 24, paragraph 1, and 25) have not been listed among the non-derogable provisions in article 4, paragraph 2, there are elements or dimensions of the right to non-discrimination that cannot be derogated from in any circumstances. In particular, this provision of article 4, paragraph 1, must be complied with if any distinctions between persons are made when resorting to measures that derogate from the Covenant.

9. Furthermore, article 4, paragraph 1, requires that no measure derogating from the provisions of the Covenant may be inconsistent with the State party's other obligations under international law, particularly the rules of international humanitarian law . . . .

14. Article 2, paragraph 3, of the Covenant requires a State party to the Covenant to provide remedies for any violation of the provisions of the Covenant. This clause is not mentioned in the list of non-derogable provisions in article 4, paragraph 2, but it constitutes a treaty obligation inherent in the Covenant as a whole. Even if a State party, during a state of emergency, and to the extent that such measures are strictly required by the exigencies of the situation, may introduce adjustments to the practical functioning of its procedures governing judicial or other remedies, the State party must comply with the fundamental obligation, under article 2, paragraph 3, of the Covenant to provide a remedy that is effective.

15. It is inherent in the protection of rights explicitly recognized as non-derogable in article 4, paragraph 2, that they must be secured by procedural guarantees, including, often, judicial guarantees. The provisions of the Covenant relating to procedural safeguards may never be made subject to measures that would circumvent the protection of non-derogable rights. Article 4 may not be resorted to in a way that would result in derogation from non-derogable rights. Thus, for example, as article 6 of the Covenant is non-derogable in its entirety, any trial leading to the imposition of the death penalty during a state of emergency must conform to the provisions of the Covenant, including all the requirements of articles 14 and 15.

16. Safeguards related to derogation, as embodied in article 4 of the Covenant, are based on the principles of legality and the rule of law inherent in the Covenant as a whole. As certain elements of the right to a fair trial are explicitly guaranteed under international humanitarian law during armed conflict, the Committee finds no justification for derogation from these guarantees during other emergency situations. The Committee is of the opinion that the principles of legality and the rule of law require that fundamental requirements of fair trial must be respected during a state of emergency. Only a court of law may try and convict a person for a criminal offence. The presumption of innocence must be respected. In order to protect non-derogable rights, the right to take proceedings before a court to enable the court to decide without delay on the lawfulness of detention, must not be diminished by a State party's decision to derogate from the Covenant.

17. In paragraph 3 of article 4, States parties, when they resort to their power of derogation under article 4, commit themselves to a regime of international notification. A State party availing itself of the right of derogation must immediately inform the other States parties, through the United Nations Secretary-General, of the provisions it has derogated from and of the reasons for such measures. Such notification is essential not only for the discharge of the Committee's functions, in particular in assessing whether the measures

taken by the State party were strictly required by the exigencies of the situation, but also to permit other States parties to monitor compliance with the provisions of the Covenant . . . . These obligations have not always been respected: States parties have failed to notify other States parties, through the Secretary-General, of a proclamation of a state of emergency and of the resulting measures of derogation from one or more provisions of the Covenant, and States parties have sometimes neglected to submit a notification of territorial or other changes in the exercise of their emergency powers . . . .

LAW IN CONTEXT

The "War on Terror" and Derogations under the European Convention on Human Rights

The European Convention on Human Rights contains a derogation provision that is similar in purpose, theory, and criteria to that of the ICCPR,[92] with terrorism being the main trigger for European states to invoke derogation. In fact, the very first case before the European Court of Human Rights concerned a derogation by Ireland.[93] Turkey has also derogated from the European Convention in respect of terrorism in its southeast region, and from the 1970s on, the United Kingdom also derogated from the European Convention in connection with terrorism related to Northern Ireland.

After the September 11 terrorist attacks on the United States, the United Kingdom amended its law to allow for the indefinite detention of foreign nationals suspected of international terrorism, but who could not be deported because they would likely be tortured in the country to which they would be removed. Indefinite detention, and detention pending unreasonably delayed deportation, offend the right to liberty and security recognized in Article 5(1) of the European Convention; however, the Convention also permits derogations from this right "[i]n time of war or other public emergency threatening the life of the nation . . . to the extent strictly required by the exigencies of the situation, provided that such measures are not inconsistent with other obligations under international law."

Thus, in preparation for the anticipated passage of the new law, the United Kingdom claimed a derogation from the European Convention (as well as the domestic legislation incorporating the European Convention into British law)[94] on the basis that:

There exists a terrorist threat to the United Kingdom from persons suspected of involvement in international terrorism. In particular, there are foreign nationals present in the United Kingdom who are suspected of being concerned in the commission, preparation or instigation of acts of international terrorism, of being members of organisations or groups which are so concerned or of having links with members of such organisations or groups, and who are a threat to the national security of the United Kingdom.[95]

The legality of the UK measures was addressed by the House of Lords in *A and others v Secretary of State for the Home Department*. That case concerned a challenge brought by

---

92 Compare ICCPR, above note 6, art 4 with European Convention on Human Rights, above note 57, art 15.
93 *Lawless v Ireland (No 3)*, App No 332/57, (1961) ECHR (Ser A) No 3, 1 EHRR 15.
94 *The Human Rights Act 1998 (Designated Derogation) Order 2001*, SI 2001 No 3644.
95 *Ibid.*

several non-UK nationals, each of whom was detained but faced no criminal charge and no prospect of a forthcoming trial.[96] The Law Lords rejected the government's approach. While most of the judges upheld the government's conclusion that there was a "public emergency threatening the life of the nation," they concluded that there was no reason to presume that foreign nationals (as opposed to UK nationals) presented the greatest threat. There was, therefore, no rational link between the law and the security concern, and thus the measure was not "strictly required by the exigencies of the situation."

In response, the United Kingdom withdrew its derogation in 2005, but it did not relinquish its assertion that there is a public emergency threatening the life of the nation. The UK Parliament later enacted legislation permitting "control orders" directed at the activities of both foreign and UK nationals suspected of terrorist activity.[97] This legislation was repealed in 2011, with the enactment of new counter-terrorism legislation.[98]

e) Concept of Duties

In addition to recognizing the rights of individuals and the obligations of states to respect those rights (often limited by the need to respect the rights of others), a handful of human rights instruments also include express mention of duties that individuals are expected to observe. The earliest examples of such provisions can be found in the American Declaration,[99] although none of the duties recognized there provide a basis for complaint and they are thus viewed as exhortations rather than justiciable obligations. Examples include a duty to protect minor children (Article 30), a duty to acquire at least an elementary education (Article 31), a duty to obey the law (Article 33), a duty to render service to the state when required (Article 34), a duty to cooperate with the state and community with respect to social security and welfare (Article 35), a duty to pay taxes (Article 36), a duty to work (Article 37), a duty to refrain from certain political activities (Article 38), and a duty imposed on children to honour their parents (Article 30). By contrast, the American Convention on Human Rights does not contain such an extensive list of duties but instead simply states that: "Every person has responsibilities to his family, his community and mankind."[100] The African Charter, however, does contain specific provisions on individual duties, including duties towards one's family and society, one's community, and the state.[101] The African Charter also contains express provisions on the duty to work, the duty to pay taxes, and the duty to "preserve and strengthen positive African cultural values."[102]

2) Specific Human Rights Guarantees

We turn now to an examination of some of the human rights protected by the key human rights instruments, focusing on the two leading multilateral treaties intended to have universal application: the ICCPR and the ICESCR. Reference will also be made to the key

---

96 *A and others v Secretary of State for the Home Department* (2004), [2004] UKHL 56, [2005] 2 AC 68.

97 *Prevention of Terrorism Act 2005*, 2005, c 2.

98 *Terrorism Prevention and Investigation Measures Act 2011*, 2011, c 23.

99 Above note 58.

100 American Convention on Human Rights, above note 59, art 32(1).

101 African Charter on Human and Peoples' Rights, above note 60, art 27(1).

102 *Ibid*, art 29.

regional treaties, as well as to the supporting network of more specific UN treaties, such as the CEDAW, the CERD, the CRC, and the CRPD. We also include mention of the Torture Convention and the Genocide Convention. This section is organized according to the nature of the rights protected, from rights of an absolute or near-absolute nature; to rights that are qualified or limited by a need to protect the rights of others; followed by rights of an economic, social, and cultural nature. We also mention the special protections provided for the rights of minors and for other vulnerable groups, which leads, finally, to an examination of the overarching right to be free from discrimination.

a) Absolute and Near-Absolute Rights

i) The Right to be Free from Torture and Cruel, Inhuman and Degrading Treatment or Punishment

The right to be free from torture and other forms of serious ill treatment is an example of an absolute right, where no social goal or emergency can limit the right. Building upon Article 5 of the Universal Declaration, Article 7 of the ICCPR provides that: "No one shall be subjected to torture or to cruel, inhuman or degrading treatment or punishment. In particular, no one shall be subjected without his free consent to medical or scientific experimentation." A similar prohibition is found in Article 3 of the ECHR, Article 26 of the American Declaration, Article 5 of the American Convention on Human Rights, Article 5 of the African Charter, and Article 37 of the CRC.

These prohibitions are supplemented by regional treaties emphasizing the need to take preventive measures, such as the European Convention for the Prevention of Torture and Inhuman or Degrading Treatment or Punishment[103] and the Inter-American Convention to Prevent and Punish Torture.[104] However, the most important supplemental treaty is the Torture Convention, which is intended to be of universal application and complements the pre-existing prohibitions with the addition of a definition. Consider the following excerpt:

> **Convention against Torture and Other Cruel, Inhuman or Degrading Treatment or Punishment, 10 December 1984, 1465 UNTS 85, Can TS 1987 No 36, in force 26 June 1987**
>
> PART I
>
> *Article 1*
> 1. For the purposes of this Convention, the term "torture" means any act by which severe pain or suffering, whether physical or mental, is intentionally inflicted on a person for such purposes as obtaining from him or a third person information or a confession, punishing him for an act he or a third person has committed or is suspected of having committed, or intimidating or coercing him or a third person, or for any reason based on discrimination of any kind, when such pain or suffering is inflicted by or at the instigation of or with the consent or acquiescence of a public official or other person acting in

---

103 26 November 1987, 1561 UNTS 363, ETS No 126, (1988) 27 ILM 1154, in force 1 February 1989.
104 9 December 1985, OAS TS No 67, (1992) 25 ILM 519, in force 28 February 1987.

an official capacity. It does not include pain or suffering arising only from, inherent in or incidental to lawful sanctions.

2. This article is without prejudice to any international instrument or national legislation which does or may contain provisions of wider application.

Article 2

1. Each State Party shall take effective legislative, administrative, judicial or other measures to prevent acts of torture in any territory under its jurisdiction.

2. No exceptional circumstances whatsoever, whether a state of war or a threat of war, internal political instability or any other public emergency, may be invoked as a justification of torture.

3. An order from a superior officer or a public authority may not be invoked as a justification of torture.

Article 3

1. No State Party shall expel, return ("refouler") or extradite a person to another State where there are substantial grounds for believing that he would be in danger of being subjected to torture.

2. For the purpose of determining whether there are such grounds, the competent authorities shall take into account all relevant considerations including, where applicable, the existence in the State concerned of a consistent pattern of gross, flagrant or mass violations of human rights.

Article 4

1. Each State Party shall ensure that all acts of torture are offences under its criminal law. The same shall apply to an attempt to commit torture and to an act by any person which constitutes complicity or participation in torture.

2. Each State Party shall make these offences punishable by appropriate penalties which take into account their grave nature.

Article 5

1. Each State Party shall take such measures as may be necessary to establish its jurisdiction over the offences referred to in article 4 in the following cases:
   (a) When the offences are committed in any territory under its jurisdiction or on board a ship or aircraft registered in that State;
   (b) When the alleged offender is a national of that State;
   (c) When the victim is a national of that State if that State considers it appropriate.

2. Each State Party shall likewise take such measures as may be necessary to establish its jurisdiction over such offences in cases where the alleged offender is present in any territory under its jurisdiction and it does not extradite him pursuant to article 8 to any of the States mentioned in paragraph 1 of this article.

3. This Convention does not exclude any criminal jurisdiction exercised in accordance with internal law.

Article 6

1. Upon being satisfied, after an examination of information available to it, that the circumstances so warrant, any State Party in whose territory a person alleged to have committed any offence referred to in article 4 is present shall take him into custody or take other legal measures to ensure his presence. The custody and other legal measures shall be as provided in the law of that State but may be continued only for such time as is necessary to enable any criminal or extradition proceedings to be instituted . . . .

4. When a State, pursuant to this article, has taken a person into custody, it shall immediately notify the States referred to in article 5, paragraph 1, of the fact that such person is in custody and of the circumstances which warrant his detention. The State which makes the preliminary inquiry contemplated in paragraph 2 of this article shall promptly report its findings to the said States and shall indicate whether it intends to exercise jurisdiction.

Article 7

1. The State Party in the territory under whose jurisdiction a person alleged to have committed any offence referred to in article 4 is found shall in the cases contemplated in article 5, if it does not extradite him, submit the case to its competent authorities for the purpose of prosecution . . . .

Article 10

1. Each State Party shall ensure that education and information regarding the prohibition against torture are fully included in the training of law enforcement personnel, civil or military, medical personnel, public officials and other persons who may be involved in the custody, interrogation or treatment of any individual subjected to any form of arrest, detention or imprisonment.

2. Each State Party shall include this prohibition in the rules or instructions issued in regard to the duties and functions of any such person.

Article 11

Each State Party shall keep under systematic review interrogation rules, instructions, methods and practices as well as arrangements for the custody and treatment of persons subjected to any form of arrest, detention or imprisonment in any territory under its jurisdiction, with a view to preventing any cases of torture.

Article 12

Each State Party shall ensure that its competent authorities proceed to a prompt and impartial investigation, wherever there is reasonable ground to believe that an act of torture has been committed in any territory under its jurisdiction.

Article 13

Each State Party shall ensure that any individual who alleges he has been subjected to torture in any territory under its jurisdiction has the right to complain to, and to have his case promptly and impartially examined by, its competent authorities. Steps shall be taken to ensure that the complainant and witnesses are protected against all ill-treatment or intimidation as a consequence of his complaint or any evidence given.

Article 14

1. Each State Party shall ensure in its legal system that the victim of an act of torture obtains redress and has an enforceable right to fair and adequate compensation, including the means for as full rehabilitation as possible. In the event of the death of the victim as a result of an act of torture, his dependants shall be entitled to compensation.

2. Nothing in this article shall affect any right of the victim or other persons to compensation which may exist under national law.

Article 15

Each State Party shall ensure that any statement which is established to have been made as a result of torture shall not be invoked as evidence in any proceedings, except against a person accused of torture as evidence that the statement was made.

Article 16

1. Each State Party shall undertake to prevent in any territory under its jurisdiction other acts of cruel, inhuman or degrading treatment or punishment which do not amount to torture as defined in article 1, when such acts are committed by or at the instigation of or with the consent or acquiescence of a public official or other person acting in an official capacity. In particular, the obligations contained in articles 10, 11, 12 and 13 shall apply with the substitution for references to torture of references to other forms of cruel, inhuman or degrading treatment or punishment.

2. The provisions of this Convention are without prejudice to the provisions of any other international instrument or national law which prohibits cruel, inhuman or degrading treatment or punishment or which relates to extradition or expulsion.

Inspired by the European system of preventative visits, an Optional Protocol to the Torture Convention[105] allows for a team of experts to visit any place of detention within a consenting state party and to report on the conditions found. Note that other forms of serious ill treatment falling short of torture are also prohibited by the various human rights treaties, as emphasized by Article 16 of the Torture Convention.

ii) The Right to be Free from Slavery, Servitude, and Forced and Compulsory Labour
As for other examples of absolute rights, Article 8 of the ICCPR recognizes the long-standing prohibition on slavery and involuntary servitude, and further confirms the extension of the prohibition to forced and compulsory labour. Similar prohibitions are found in Article 4 of the ECHR, Article 6 of the American Convention on Human Rights, and Article 5 of the African Charter, while the prohibition on forced and compulsory labour is bolstered by a series of specialized treaties developed under the auspices of the ILO. These include Convention (No 29) concerning Forced or Compulsory Labour,[106] Convention (No 105) concerning the Abolition of Forced Labour,[107] and Convention (No 182)

---

105 Optional Protocol to the Convention against Torture and Other Cruel, Inhuman or Degrading Treatment or Punishment, 18 December 2002, 2375 UNTS 237, (2003) 42 ILM 26, in force 22 June 2006 (sixty-nine states parties as of July 2013). Canada is not a party.
106 28 June 1930, 39 UNTS 55, Can TS 2012 No 15, in force 1 May 1932 (in force for Canada 13 June 2012).
107 25 June 1957, 320 UNTS 291, Can TS 1960 No 21, in force 17 January 1959.

concerning the Prohibition and Immediate Action for the Elimination of the Worst Forms of Child Labour.[108] Also relevant are the treaties addressing trafficking in persons and their exploitation, specifically the Convention for the Suppression of the Traffic in Persons and of the Exploitation of the Prostitution of Others,[109] the Protocol to Prevent, Suppress and Punish Trafficking in Persons, Especially Women and Children, Supplementing the United Nations Convention Against Transnational Organized Crime,[110] and, at the regional level, the Council of Europe Convention on Action against Trafficking in Human Beings.[111] The CRC also has an optional protocol aimed at obliging states parties to criminalize the sale of children and child prostitution.[112]

iii) The Right to Life

Contrary to popular opinion, the right to life is not an absolute right as there are certain circumstances, strictly interpreted, in which the state is permitted to take life. Building on the declaration that "Everyone has the right to life, liberty and security of the person" in Article 3 of the Universal Declaration, the drafters of the ICCPR confirmed that every human being has the inherent right to life; but the drafters also made clear that there are circumstances when the state may need to take life, such as when necessary to protect the life of another, provided the deprivation of life is not arbitrary.

International Covenant on Civil and Political Rights, 16 December 1966, 999 UNTS 171, Can TS 1976 No 47, (1967) 6 ILM 368, in force 23 March 1976

Article 6

1. Every human being has the inherent right to life. This right shall be protected by law. No one shall be arbitrarily deprived of his life.

2. In countries which have not abolished the death penalty, sentence of death may be imposed only for the most serious crimes in accordance with the law in force at the time of the commission of the crime and not contrary to the provisions of the present Covenant and to the Convention on the Prevention and Punishment of the Crime of Genocide. This penalty can only be carried out pursuant to a final judgement rendered by a competent court.

3. When deprivation of life constitutes the crime of genocide, it is understood that nothing in this article shall authorize any State Party to the present Covenant to derogate in any way from any obligation assumed under the provisions of the Convention on the Prevention and Punishment of the Crime of Genocide.

---

108 17 June 1999, 2133 UNTS 161, Can TS 2001 No 2, (1999) 38 ILM 1207, in force 19 November 2000.

109 2 December 1949, 96 UNTS 271, in force 25 July 1951.

110 15 November 2000, 2237 UNTS 319, Can TS 2002 No 25, (2001) 40 ILM 335, in force 25 December 2003.

111 16 May 2005, 2569 UNTS 33, CETS No 197, (2006) 45 ILM 21, in force 1 February 2008.

112 Optional Protocol to the Convention on the Rights of the Child on the Sale of Children, Child Prostitution and Child Pornography, 25 May 2000, 2171 UNTS 227, (2000) 39 ILM 1285, in force 18 January 2002. See also Council of Europe Convention on the Protection of Children against Sexual Exploitation and Sexual Abuse, 25 October 2007, CETS No 201, in force 1 July 2010.

4. Anyone sentenced to death shall have the right to seek pardon or commutation of the sentence. Amnesty, pardon or commutation of the sentence of death may be granted in all cases.

5. Sentence of death shall not be imposed for crimes committed by persons below eighteen years of age and shall not be carried out on pregnant women.

6. Nothing in this article shall be invoked to delay or to prevent the abolition of capital punishment by any State Party to the present Covenant.

The right to life is also guaranteed by Article 2 of the ECHR and Article 4 of the American Convention on Human Rights, although the former qualifies the right by making specific reference to the state's use of force to defend another, to effect an arrest, or to quell an insurrection or riot; and the latter (as discussed earlier) protects the right to life "in general, from the moment of conception." In contrast to the ECHR, the right to life in Article 4 of the African Charter is codified in general terms, without specific exceptions, but nevertheless clearly permits non-arbitrary deprivations. The jurisprudence of the European Court of Human Rights makes clear that the right to life not only imposes an obligation on a state not to take life unless absolutely necessary, but also imposes a positive duty on states to protect liarfe. This positive duty entails an obligation on the state party to ensure an effective investigation into any loss of life and to train all police and security forces to exercise strict control over the planning and execution of any operation so as to minimize, as much as possible, the use of lethal force.[113]

As to the interaction between the right to life and the death penalty, it must be remembered that many of the leading human rights treaties were drafted at a time when the death penalty was still imposed in many states, including several western European states. Separate protocols have since been developed to provide for the extension of the right to life so as to prohibit the use of capital punishment, first in peacetime and then also in war.[114] In 1989, a "Second Optional Protocol to the International Covenant on Civil and Political Rights, aiming at the abolition of the death penalty"[115] was adopted, reflecting a growing international movement to abolish the death penalty. Its key provisions read as follows:

Article 1
1. No one within the jurisdiction of a State Party to the present Protocol shall be executed.

---

113 See, for example, *McCann v United Kingdom*, App No 18984/91, (1996) 21 EHRR 97 (E Ct HR).
114 See Protocol No 6 to the Convention on the Protection of Human Rights and Fundamental Freedoms concerning the Abolition of the Death Penalty, 18 April 1983, 1496 UNTS 281, ETS No 114, (1983) 22 ILM 538, in force 1 March 1985, and Protocol No 13 to the Convention on the Protection of Human Rights and Fundamental Freedoms, concerning the Abolition of the Death Penalty in all Circumstances, 3 May 2002, 2246 UNTS 110, ETS No 187, (2002) 41 ILM 515, in force 1 July 2003. See also Protocol to the American Convention on Human Rights to Abolish the Death Penalty, 8 June 1990, OAS TS No 73, in force upon ratification.
115 15 December 1989, 1642 UNTS 414, Can TS 2006 No 25, (1990) 29 ILM 1466, in force 11 July 1991 (seventy-seven states parties as of July 2013).

2. Each State Party shall take all necessary measures to abolish the death penalty within its jurisdiction . . . .

Article 2

1. No reservation is admissible to the present Protocol, except for a reservation made at the time of ratification or accession that provides for the application of the death penalty in time of war pursuant to a conviction for a most serious crime of a military nature committed during wartime.

One particularly egregious form of the death penalty is so-called extra-judicial execution. These summary executions are performed without benefit of a fair trial or due process. Extra-judicial executions clearly violate Article 6 of the ICCPR, and equivalent provisions in other treaties, and must be considered a violation of customary international law. This practice has also prompted the elaboration of a number of normative or soft law instruments to provide additional guidance, most notably the Principles on the Effective Prevention and Investigation of Extra-Legal, Arbitrary and Summary Executions recommended by ECOSOC in 1989.[116] The principles call on states to:

> . . . prohibit by law all extra-legal, arbitrary and summary executions and . . . ensure that any such executions are recognized as offences under their criminal laws, and are punishable by appropriate penalties which take into account the seriousness of such offences. Exceptional circumstances including a state of war or threat of war, internal political instability or any other public emergency may not be invoked as a justification of such executions. Such executions shall not be carried out under any circumstances including, but not limited to, situations of internal armed conflict, excessive or illegal use of force by a public official or other person acting in an official capacity or by a person acting at the instigation, or with the consent or acquiescence of such person, and situations in which deaths occur in custody. This prohibition shall prevail over decrees issued by governmental authority.[117]

iv) The Right to be Free from Genocide

Genocide is a fundamental violation of the right to life, one closely associated with the Holocaust and other horrors of World War II as well as, more recently, the Rwandan massacres of 1994. The mass murder of the Holocaust prompted the international community to prohibit genocide in the first post-war human rights treaty of universal application, the Genocide Convention. Consider its key substantive terms:

---

116 ECOSOC Res 1989/65, reprinted in *Resolutions and Decisions of the Economic and Social Council*, UN Doc. E/1989/89 at 52–53 (1989).

117 For a discussion of the legal framework applicable to state policies permitting the use of targeted killings, including the use of unmanned aerial vehicles (UAVs) (also known as drones), see *Report of the Special Rapporteur on extrajudicial, summary or arbitrary executions, Philip Alston: Study on Targeted Killings*, UN Doc A/HRC/14/24/Add.6 (28 May 2010). In 2013, the UN Special Rapporteur on counterterrorism and human rights, Ben Emmerson QC, launched an investigation into the civilian impact of the use of drones and other forms of targeted killing.

Convention for the Prevention and Punishment of the Crime of Genocide, 9 December 1948, 78 UNTS 277, Can TS 1949 No 27, in force 12 January 1951

Article I

The Contracting Parties confirm that genocide, whether committed in time of peace or in time of war, is a crime under international law which they undertake to prevent and to punish.

Article II

In the present Convention, genocide means any of the following acts committed with intent to destroy, in whole or in part, a national, ethnical, racial or religious group, as such:
    (a) Killing members of the group;
    (b) Causing serious bodily or mental harm to members of the group;
    (c) Deliberately inflicting on the group conditions of life calculated to bring about its physical destruction in whole or in part;
    (d) Imposing measures intended to prevent births within the group;
    (e) Forcibly transferring children of the group to another group.

Article III

The following acts shall be punishable:
    (a) Genocide;
    (b) Conspiracy to commit genocide;
    (c) Direct and public incitement to commit genocide;
    (d) Attempt to commit genocide;
    (e) Complicity in genocide.

Article IV

Persons committing genocide or any of the other acts enumerated in article III shall be punished, whether they are constitutionally responsible rulers, public officials or private individuals.

Article V

The Contracting Parties undertake to enact, in accordance with their respective Constitutions, the necessary legislation to give effect to the provisions of the present Convention, and, in particular, to provide effective penalties for persons guilty of genocide or any of the other acts enumerated in article III.

Article VI

Persons charged with genocide or any of the other acts enumerated in article III shall be tried by a competent tribunal of the State in the territory of which the act was committed, or by such international penal tribunal as may have jurisdiction with respect to those Contracting Parties which shall have accepted its jurisdiction . . . .

Given the very specific intention requirement incorporated into the definition of genocide in Article II, whether any given atrocity qualifies as a genocide or rather, a crime against humanity, is often a contested issue. Consider this discussion from the Legal Affairs Bureau of Canada's Department of Foreign Affairs and International Trade on whether mistreatment of ethnic Albanians in Kosovo in 1999 constituted "genocide":

Michael Leir, "Canadian Practice in International Law: At the Department of Foreign Affairs in 1998–99" (1999) 37 Can YB Int'l Law 317 at 327–30

This definition [of genocide in the Genocide Convention] (which has been imported without changes into the statutes for the International Criminal Tribunals for the Former Yugoslavia and for Rwanda, as well as that of the International Criminal Court) contains two essential elements for the purposes of the Kosovo situation: targeting on the basis of ethnicity; intent to destroy.

In the case of the Kosovar Albanians, the first element of the threshold test is being met, namely, that they are a group targeted on the basis of ethnicity. Subparagraphs 2 (a) and (b) describe acts currently being carried out against this group. It is worth noting that lay usage of the term "genocide" erroneously tends to look to the scale of killings to make out a charge of genocide, without reference to the threshold test of the nationality, ethnicity, race or religion of the group targeted.

However, the crux of the Kosovo case is in the second element, the criminal intent necessary to constitute the crime of genocide. The required intent (*mens rea*) element is "to destroy, in whole or in part . . . ." Whether that test is being met in the present case is not nearly as clearly cut as it might appear.

"Ethnic cleansing" as such is not an express form of genocide as per the definition in the Convention. Indeed, in the 1948 negotiations of the Convention, a proposal to include as a formal act of genocide "[i]mposing measures intended to oblige members of a group to abandon their homes in order to escape the threat of subsequent ill-treatment" was rejected.

While ethnic cleansing—a term that acquired international legal currency only in the early days (1991) of the Balkan conflict—is clearly a crime against humanity (a term which itself has the flexibility to accommodate any emerging form of barbarity not covered by express treaty law), it shows an intent somewhat different from the "intent to destroy."

Ethnic Albanians are being killed and injured in *order to drive them from their homes* not in order to *destroy them as a group, in whole or in part*. That said, one could argue that killing ethnic Albanians in order to drive the group out of Kosovo has the result of destroying the sub-group of Kosovar Albanians. In addition, if the evidence discloses that Albanian males are being killed specifically, an argument could be made that there is an intent to destroy the group in part, i.e., the male portion of the population.

While such an argument is not without merit, in our experience the tendency of international tribunals is for a narrow interpretation of provisions contained in treaties (see, for example, the International Criminal Tribunal for the Former Yugoslavia's (ICTFY) lengthy decision on the non-applicability of the "grave breaches provisions of the Geneva Conventions in the *Tadić* case). Genocide being a treaty term, we would expect a tribunal to resist expansion of the definition to include a reference to "subgroups," especially in the light of the rejected provision from the *travaux préparatoires* and the fact that the more general—and legally less questionable—charge of crimes against humanity can be made out based on the same facts.

What is clear, however, is that the actions of the Mlgoslav leadership in Kosovo constitute a crime against humanity . . . .

Our view, with the facts currently available to us, is that although the actions of the Government of the FRY appear to amount to genocide, it is doubtful that a charge of genocide against members of the FRY leadership would be sustained by an international tribunal. It would, therefore, be advisable to refer to Yugoslav actions in Kosovo with the more generic reference of "crimes against humanity," rather than the very specific—and legally limited—term of "genocide."

[Reprinted with permission of the Publisher from Canadian Yearbook of International Law, Volume 37 edited by Don McRae © University of British Columbia Press 1999. All rights reserved by the Publisher.]

b) Qualified Rights

i) *The Right to Liberty and Security of the Person*

The Universal Declaration embraces a "right to life, liberty and security of the person" (Article 3) as well as a prohibition on "arbitrary arrest, detention or exile" (Article 9). The legally binding text of the ICCPR adds further detail to the recognition of these and related rights. This detail makes clear that such rights are qualified, either because non-arbitrary interferences with them are not prohibited or because they are subject to specific limitations that take into account the rights of others and general societal goals.

International Covenant on Civil and Political Rights, 16 December 1966, 999 UNTS 171, Can TS 1976 No 47, (1967) 6 ILM 368, in force 23 March 1976

Article 9

1. Everyone has the right to liberty and security of person. No one shall be subjected to arbitrary arrest or detention. No one shall be deprived of his liberty except on such grounds and in accordance with such procedure as are established by law.

2. Anyone who is arrested shall be informed, at the time of arrest, of the reasons for his arrest and shall be promptly informed of any charges against him.

3. Anyone arrested or detained on a criminal charge shall be brought promptly before a judge or other officer authorized by law to exercise judicial power and shall be entitled to trial within a reasonable time or to release. It shall not be the general rule that persons awaiting trial shall be detained in custody, but release may be subject to guarantees to appear for trial, at any other stage of the judicial proceedings, and, should occasion arise, for execution of the judgement.

4. Anyone who is deprived of his liberty by arrest or detention shall be entitled to take proceedings before a court, in order that that court may decide without delay on the lawfulness of his detention and order his release if the detention is not lawful.

5. Anyone who has been the victim of unlawful arrest or detention shall have an enforceable right to compensation.

Article 10

1. All persons deprived of their liberty shall be treated with humanity and with respect for the inherent dignity of the human person.

2. (a) Accused persons shall, save in exceptional circumstances, be segregated from convicted persons and shall be subject to separate treatment appropriate to their status as unconvicted persons; (b) Accused juvenile persons shall be separated from adults and brought as speedily as possible for adjudication.

3. The penitentiary system shall comprise treatment of prisoners the essential aim of which shall be their reformation and social rehabilitation. Juvenile offenders shall be segregated from adults and be accorded treatment appropriate to their age and legal status.

Article 11

No one shall be imprisoned merely on the ground of inability to fulfil a contractual obligation.

Article 12

1. Everyone lawfully within the territory of a State shall, within that territory, have the right to liberty of movement and freedom to choose his residence.

2. Everyone shall be free to leave any country, including his own.

3. The above-mentioned rights shall not be subject to any restrictions except those which are provided by law, are necessary to protect national security, public order (ordre public), public health or morals or the rights and freedoms of others, and are consistent with the other rights recognized in the present Covenant.

4. No one shall be arbitrarily deprived of the right to enter his own country.

The right to liberty and security of the person is recognized, with similarly tailored qualifications, in Article 5 of the ECHR (with Article 1 of Protocol No 4 adding a prohibition similar to that found in Article 11 of the ICCPR), and in Articles 5 and 7 of the American Convention on Human Rights.[118] The African Charter also recognizes the right to liberty and security of the person (Article 6), but lacks the additional guidance provided by the more detailed drafting of the other treaties. The special attention given to the rights and needs of juvenile offenders, reflected in Article 10 of the ICCPR, is supplemented by Article 37 of the CRC.

Remarkably, the only universal convention focusing specifically on women's rights — the CEDAW — contains no language on women's right to life and security of the person (including freedom from violence against women). Certainly, these rights are equally protected for women and men in the key human rights instruments, as underscored by the UN General Assembly.[119] However, the inter-American system has gone further than the adoption of declaratory statements with the conclusion of the Inter-American Convention on the Prevention, Punishment, and Eradication of Violence Against Women, which came into force in 1995.[120] This treaty defines violence against women as "any act or conduct, based on gender, which causes death or physical, sexual or psychological harm or suffering to women, whether in the public or the private sphere." Among others, it includes the following rights:

---

118 See also article 25 of the American Declaration, above note 58.

119 *Declaration on the Elimination of Violence against Women*, GA Res 48/104 (1993), reprinted in UN GAOR, 48th Sess, Supp No 49 at 217–19, UN Doc A/48/49 (1994).

120 9 June 1994, OAS TS No A-61, (1994) 33 ILM 1534, in force 3 May 1995. All OAS member states are parties to this treaty, with the exception of Canada, Cuba, and the United States.

Inter-American Convention on the Prevention, Punishment, and Eradication of Violence Against Women, 9 June 1994, OAS TS No A-61, (1994) 33 ILM 1534, in force 3 May 1995

Article 3
Every woman has the right to be free from violence in both the public and private spheres.

Article 4
Every woman has the right to the recognition, enjoyment, exercise and protection of all human rights and freedoms embodied in regional and international human rights instruments. These rights include, among others:
  a. The right to have her life respected;
  b. The right to have her physical, mental and moral integrity respected;
  c. The right to personal liberty and security;
  d. The right not to be subjected to torture;
  e. The right to have the inherent dignity of her person respected and her family protected;
  f. The right to equal protection before the law and of the law;
  g. The right to simple and prompt recourse to a competent court for protection against acts that violate her rights;
  h. The right to associate freely;
  i. The right of freedom to profess her religion and beliefs within the law; and
  j. The right to have equal access to the public service of her country and to take part in the conduct of public affairs, including decision-making.

Article 5
Every woman is entitled to the free and full exercise of her civil, political, economic, social and cultural rights, and may rely on the full protection of those rights as embodied in regional and international instruments on human rights. The States Parties recognize that violence against women prevents and nullifies the exercise of these rights.

Article 6
The right of every woman to be free from violence includes, among others:
  a. The right of women to be free from all forms of discrimination; and
  b. The right of women to be valued and educated free of stereotyped patterns of behavior and social and cultural practices based on concepts of inferiority or subordination.

In 2011, the member states of the Council of Europe also adopted a convention specifically aimed at preventing and combating violence against women and domestic violence.[121]

ii) The Right to a Fair Trial
Another fundamental right that is subject to certain qualifications is the right to a fair trial. The core of the right is expressed in Article 10 of the Universal Declaration: "Everyone is entitled to a fair and public hearing by an independent and impartial tribunal, in the deter-

---

121 Council of Europe Convention on Preventing and Combating Violence against Women and Domestic Violence, 11 May 2011, CETS No 210 (not yet in force).

mination of his rights and obligations and of any criminal charge against him." Article 26 of the American Declaration similarly states that: "Every person accused of an offence has the right to be given an impartial and public hearing, and to be tried by courts previously established in accordance with pre-existing laws . . . ." Although both declarations also confirm the right of an accused to be presumed innocent,[122] qualifications were added when the right to a fair trial was codified in legally-binding treaty texts, as illustrated by this excerpt from the ICCPR:

International Covenant on Civil and Political Rights, 16 December 1966, 999 UNTS 171, Can TS 1976 No 47, (1967) 6 ILM 368, in force 23 March 1976

Article 14

1. All persons shall be equal before the courts and tribunals. In the determination of any criminal charge against him, or of his rights and obligations in a suit at law, everyone shall be entitled to a fair and public hearing by a competent, independent and impartial tribunal established by law. The press and the public may be excluded from all or part of a trial for reasons of morals, public order (*ordre public*) or national security in a democratic society, or when the interest of the private lives of the parties so requires, or to the extent strictly necessary in the opinion of the court in special circumstances where publicity would prejudice the interests of justice; but any judgement rendered in a criminal case or in a suit at law shall be made public except where the interest of juvenile persons otherwise requires or the proceedings concern matrimonial disputes or the guardianship of children.

2. Everyone charged with a criminal offence shall have the right to be presumed innocent until proved guilty according to law.

3. In the determination of any criminal charge against him, everyone shall be entitled to the following minimum guarantees, in full equality:
    (a) To be informed promptly and in detail in a language which he understands of the nature and cause of the charge against him;
    (b) To have adequate time and facilities for the preparation of his defence and to communicate with counsel of his own choosing;
    (c) To be tried without undue delay;
    (d) To be tried in his presence, and to defend himself in person or through legal assistance of his own choosing; to be informed, if he does not have legal assistance, of this right; and to have legal assistance assigned to him, in any case where the interests of justice so require, and without payment by him in any such case if he does not have sufficient means to pay for it;
    (e) To examine, or have examined, the witnesses against him and to obtain the attendance and examination of witnesses on his behalf under the same conditions as witnesses against him;
    (f) To have the free assistance of an interpreter if he cannot understand or speak the language used in court;
    (g) Not to be compelled to testify against himself or to confess guilt.

---

122 See article 11 of the Universal Declaration, above note 37, and article 26 of the American Declaration, above note 58.

4. In the case of juvenile persons, the procedure shall be such as will take account of their age and the desirability of promoting their rehabilitation.

5. Everyone convicted of a crime shall have the right to his conviction and sentence being reviewed by a higher tribunal according to law.

6. When a person has by a final decision been convicted of a criminal offence and when subsequently his conviction has been reversed or he has been pardoned on the ground that a new or newly discovered fact shows conclusively that there has been a miscarriage of justice, the person who has suffered punishment as a result of such conviction shall be compensated according to law, unless it is proved that the non-disclosure of the unknown fact in time is wholly or partly attributable to him.

7. No one shall be liable to be tried or punished again for an offence for which he has already been finally convicted or acquitted in accordance with the law and penal procedure of each country.

Article 15
1. No one shall be held guilty of any criminal offence on account of any act or omission which did not constitute a criminal offence, under national or international law, at the time when it was committed. Nor shall a heavier penalty be imposed than the one that was applicable at the time when the criminal offence was committed. If, subsequent to the commission of the offence, provision is made by law for the imposition of the lighter penalty, the offender shall benefit thereby.

2. Nothing in this article shall prejudice the trial and punishment of any person for any act or omission which, at the time when it was committed, was criminal according to the general principles of law recognized by the community of nations.

Similarly tailored codifications of the right to a fair trial can be found in Article 6 of the ECHR and Article 8 of the American Convention on Human Rights, with a somewhat shorter version found in Article 7 of the African Charter. The right to a fair trial for children is supplemented by Article 40 of the CRC.

c) Fundamental Freedoms

The leading human rights treaties also extend protection to the classic fundamental freedoms recognized in Western liberal democracies, namely the freedoms of peaceful assembly and association; opinion and expression; and thought, conscience, and religion. The exercise of these freedoms is subject to restrictions designed to protect the rights of others and to achieve certain societal goals. A right to privacy is also recognized in international human rights law. Building upon Articles 12 and 18–20 of the Universal Declaration, the ICCPR provides as follows:

International Covenant on Civil and Political Rights, 16 December 1966, 999 UNTS 171, Can TS 1976 No 47, (1967) 6 ILM 368, in force 23 March 1976

Article 17
1. No one shall be subjected to arbitrary or unlawful interference with his privacy, family, home or correspondence, nor to unlawful attacks on his honour and reputation.

2. Everyone has the right to the protection of the law against such interference or attacks.

Article 18

1. Everyone shall have the right to freedom of thought, conscience and religion. This right shall include freedom to have or to adopt a religion or belief of his choice, and freedom, either individually or in community with others and in public or private, to manifest his religion or belief in worship, observance, practice and teaching.

2. No one shall be subject to coercion which would impair his freedom to have or to adopt a religion or belief of his choice.

3. Freedom to manifest one's religion or beliefs may be subject only to such limitations as are prescribed by law and are necessary to protect public safety, order, health, or morals or the fundamental rights and freedoms of others.

4. The States Parties to the present Covenant undertake to have respect for the liberty of parents and, when applicable, legal guardians to ensure the religious and moral education of their children in conformity with their own convictions.

Article 19

1. Everyone shall have the right to hold opinions without interference.

2. Everyone shall have the right to freedom of expression; this right shall include freedom to seek, receive and impart information and ideas of all kinds, regardless of frontiers, either orally, in writing or in print, in the form of art, or through any other media of his choice.

3. The exercise of the rights provided for in paragraph 2 of this article carries with it special duties and responsibilities. It may therefore be subject to certain restrictions, but these shall only be such as are provided by law and are necessary:
   (a) For respect of the rights or reputations of others;
   (b) For the protection of national security or of public order (*ordre public*), or of public health or morals.

Article 20

1. Any propaganda for war shall be prohibited by law.

2. Any advocacy of national, racial or religious hatred that constitutes incitement to discrimination, hostility or violence shall be prohibited by law.

Article 21

The right of peaceful assembly shall be recognized. No restrictions may be placed on the exercise of this right other than those imposed in conformity with the law and which are necessary in a democratic society in the interests of national security or public safety, public order (*ordre public*), the protection of public health or morals or the protection of the rights and freedoms of others.

Article 22

1. Everyone shall have the right to freedom of association with others, including the right to form and join trade unions for the protection of his interests.

2. No restrictions may be placed on the exercise of this right other than those which are prescribed by law and which are necessary in a democratic society in the interests of national security or public safety, public order (*ordre public*), the protection of public health or morals or the protection of the rights and freedoms of others. This article shall not prevent the imposition of lawful restrictions on members of the armed forces and of the police in their exercise of this right . . . .

Countries with domestic bills of rights, whether statutory or with constitutional status, often ensure the implementation of their international human rights treaty obligations through the provisions of these bills of rights. Considering the content of the *Canadian Charter of Rights and Freedoms*, has Canada ensured the implementation of all of its ICCPR obligations? Must Canada also rely on ordinary legislation and the common law for implementation?

Comparable provisions can be found in the key regional human rights regimes, such as Articles 8–11 of the ECHR,[123] Articles 3–5, 9–10, and 21–22 of the American Declaration, and Articles 11–16 of the American Convention on Human Rights. It must, however, be noted that the balance struck between respecting the right to freedom of expression and the rights of others may differ, with the inter-American system embracing a "right of reply" when one's reputation and honour are put in issue.[124] By contrast, the African Charter does not recognize a right to privacy, reputation, and honour, but does recognize the freedoms of assembly, association, expression, and the practice of religion (Articles 8–11). Several ILO conventions protect the right to unionize in the workplace, including Convention (No 87) concerning Freedom of Association and Protection of the Right to Organise.[125] Fundamental freedoms guarantees are also bolstered in respect of children by Articles 12–17 of the CRC.

A declaratory text adopted by the UN General Assembly in 1981 provides further guidance with respect to the right to freedom of thought, conscience, and religion,[126] while another declaratory text adopted by the General Assembly in 1999 reminds states that individuals who advocate on behalf of human rights, known as human rights defenders, also have free association rights.[127] Article 5 of this declaration provides:

Article 5

For the purpose of promoting and protecting human rights and fundamental freedoms, everyone has the right, individually and in association with others, at the national and international levels: (a) To meet or assemble peacefully; (b) To form, join and participate

---

123 Freedom of association is further bolstered in Europe by articles 5 and 6 of the European Social Charter (Revised), above note 65.

124 An early effort to establish a so-called universal right of correction to address false news reports has garnered little support: Convention on the International Right of Correction, 31 March 1953, 435 UNTS 191, in force 24 August 1962 (seventeen states parties).

125 9 July 1948, 68 UNTS 17, Can TS 1973 No 14, in force 4 July 1950.

126 *Declaration on the Elimination of All Forms of Intolerance and of Discrimination Based on Religion or Belief*, GA Res 36/55 (1981), reprinted in UN GAOR, 36th Sess, Supp No 51 at 171–72, UN Doc A/36/51 (1982).

127 *Declaration on the Right and Responsibility of Individuals, Groups and Organs of Society to Promote and Protect Universally Recognized Human Rights and Fundamental Freedoms*, GA Res 53/144 (1998), reprinted in UN GAOR, 53rd Sess, Supp No 49, vol I at 269–72, UN Doc A/53/49 (1999).

in non-governmental organizations, associations or groups; (c) To communicate with non-governmental or intergovernmental organizations.

d) Participation Rights

Citizen voting rights and the right to take part in the conduct of public affairs, whether directly or through freely chosen representatives, are also recognized as fundamental human rights under international law, with Article 21 of the Universal Declaration having inspired Article 25 of the ICCPR:

> **International Covenant on Civil and Political Rights, 16 December 1966, 999 UNTS 171, Can TS 1976 No 47, (1967) 6 ILM 368, in force 23 March 1976**
>
> *Article 25*
> Every citizen shall have the right and the opportunity, without any of the distinctions mentioned in article 2 and without unreasonable restrictions:
>> (a) To take part in the conduct of public affairs, directly or through freely chosen representatives;
>> (b) To vote and to be elected at genuine periodic elections which shall be by universal and equal suffrage and shall be held by secret ballot, guaranteeing the free expression of the will of the electors;
>> (c) To have access, on general terms of equality, to public service in his country.

Further recognition of participation rights can be found in Article 20 of the American Declaration, Article 23 of the American Convention on Human Rights, Article 13 of the African Charter, and in the first Protocol to the ECHR (adopted soon after the drafting of the ECHR itself).[128] A number of UN-sponsored treaties further emphasize the need for states parties to eliminate discrimination in the public and political life of the state, including Article 7 of CEDAW and Article 5 of CERD.

e) Economic, Social, and Cultural Rights

i) *Economic, Social, and Cultural Rights Recognized in the ICESCR*

As previously noted, both the American Declaration and the Universal Declaration extend recognition to economic, social, and cultural rights, as well as civil and political rights. The division between the two categories is not always clear, with the right of free association, for example, included as a civil and political right, and the right to form trade unions recognized as an economic right. Nonetheless, rights often recognized as economic, social, or cultural in character include the right to work, the right to social security, the right to education, the right to an adequate standard of living, as well as the right to participate in the cultural life of the community. These rights have been codified in the widely ratified ICESCR:

---

128 ECHR Protocol No 1, above note 42.

International Covenant on Economic, Social and Cultural Rights, 16 December 1966, 999 UNTS 3, Can TS 1976 No 46, (1967) 6 ILM 360, in force 3 January 1976

Part III

Article 6

1. The States Parties to the present Covenant recognize the right to work, which includes the right of everyone to the opportunity to gain his living by work which he freely chooses or accepts, and will take appropriate steps to safeguard this right.

2. The steps to be taken by a State Party to the present Covenant to achieve the full realization of this right shall include technical and vocational guidance and training programmes, policies and techniques to achieve steady economic, social and cultural development and full and productive employment under conditions safeguarding fundamental political and economic freedoms to the individual.

Article 7

The States Parties to the present Covenant recognize the right of everyone to the enjoyment of just and favourable conditions of work which ensure, in particular:
(a) Remuneration which provides all workers, as a minimum, with:
(i) Fair wages and equal remuneration for work of equal value without distinction of any kind, in particular women being guaranteed conditions of work not inferior to those enjoyed by men, with equal pay for equal work;
(ii) A decent living for themselves and their families in accordance with the provisions of the present Covenant;
(b) Safe and healthy working conditions;
(c) Equal opportunity for everyone to be promoted in his employment to an appropriate higher level, subject to no considerations other than those of seniority and competence;
(d) Rest, leisure and reasonable limitation of working hours and periodic holidays with pay, as well as remuneration for public holidays.

Article 8

1. The States Parties to the present Covenant undertake to ensure:
(a) The right of everyone to form trade unions and join the trade union of his choice, subject only to the rules of the organization concerned, for the promotion and protection of his economic and social interests. No restrictions may be placed on the exercise of this right other than those prescribed by law and which are necessary in a democratic society in the interests of national security or public order or for the protection of the rights and freedoms of others;
(b) The right of trade unions to establish national federations or confederations and the right of the latter to form or join international trade-union organizations;
(c) The right of trade unions to function freely subject to no limitations other than those prescribed by law and which are necessary in a democratic society in the interests of national security or public order or for the protection of the rights and freedoms of others;
(d) The right to strike, provided that it is exercised in conformity with the laws of the particular country.

2. This article shall not prevent the imposition of lawful restrictions on the exercise of these rights by members of the armed forces or of the police or of the administration of the State. . . .

Article 9

The States Parties to the present Covenant recognize the right of everyone to social security, including social insurance.

Article 10

The States Parties to the present Covenant recognize that:

1. The widest possible protection and assistance should be accorded to the family, which is the natural and fundamental group unit of society, particularly for its establishment and while it is responsible for the care and education of dependent children. Marriage must be entered into with the free consent of the intending spouses.

2. Special protection should be accorded to mothers during a reasonable period before and after childbirth. During such period working mothers should be accorded paid leave or leave with adequate social security benefits.

3. Special measures of protection and assistance should be taken on behalf of all children and young persons without any discrimination for reasons of parentage or other conditions. Children and young persons should be protected from economic and social exploitation. Their employment in work harmful to their morals or health or dangerous to life or likely to hamper their normal development should be punishable by law. States should also set age limits below which the paid employment of child labour should be prohibited and punishable by law.

Article 11

1. The States Parties to the present Covenant recognize the right of everyone to an adequate standard of living for himself and his family, including adequate food, clothing and housing, and to the continuous improvement of living conditions. The States Parties will take appropriate steps to ensure the realization of this right, recognizing to this effect the essential importance of international co-operation based on free consent.

2. The States Parties to the present Covenant, recognizing the fundamental right of everyone to be free from hunger, shall take, individually and through international co-operation, the measures, including specific programmes, which are needed:
    (a) To improve methods of production, conservation and distribution of food by making full use of technical and scientific knowledge, by disseminating knowledge of the principles of nutrition and by developing or reforming agrarian systems in such a way as to achieve the most efficient development and utilization of natural resources;
    (b) Taking into account the problems of both food-importing and food-exporting countries, to ensure an equitable distribution of world food supplies in relation to need.

Article 12

1. The States Parties to the present Covenant recognize the right of everyone to the enjoyment of the highest attainable standard of physical and mental health.

2. The steps to be taken by the States Parties to the present Covenant to achieve the full realization of this right shall include those necessary for:

(a) The provision for the reduction of the stillbirth-rate and of infant mortality and for the healthy development of the child;

(b) The improvement of all aspects of environmental and industrial hygiene;

(c) The prevention, treatment and control of epidemic, endemic, occupational and other diseases;

(d) The creation of conditions which would assure to all medical service and medical attention in the event of sickness.

Article 13

1. The States Parties to the present Covenant recognize the right of everyone to education. They agree that education shall be directed to the full development of the human personality and the sense of its dignity, and shall strengthen the respect for human rights and fundamental freedoms. They further agree that education shall enable all persons to participate effectively in a free society, promote understanding, tolerance and friendship among all nations and all racial, ethnic or religious groups, and further the activities of the United Nations for the maintenance of peace.

2. The States Parties to the present Covenant recognize that, with a view to achieving the full realization of this right:

(a) Primary education shall be compulsory and available free to all;

(b) Secondary education in its different forms, including technical and vocational secondary education, shall be made generally available and accessible to all by every appropriate means, and in particular by the progressive introduction of free education;

(c) Higher education shall be made equally accessible to all, on the basis of capacity, by every appropriate means, and in particular by the progressive introduction of free education;

(d) Fundamental education shall be encouraged or intensified as far as possible for those persons who have not received or completed the whole period of their primary education;

(e) The development of a system of schools at all levels shall be actively pursued, an adequate fellowship system shall be established, and the material conditions of teaching staff shall be continuously improved.

3. The States Parties to the present Covenant undertake to have respect for the liberty of parents and, when applicable, legal guardians to choose for their children schools, other than those established by the public authorities, which conform to such minimum educational standards as may be laid down or approved by the State and to ensure the religious and moral education of their children in conformity with their own convictions.

4. No part of this article shall be construed so as to interfere with the liberty of individuals and bodies to establish and direct educational institutions, subject always to the observance of the principles set forth in paragraph I of this article and to the requirement that the education given in such institutions shall conform to such minimum standards as may be laid down by the State.

Article 14

Each State Party to the present Covenant which, at the time of becoming a Party, has not been able to secure in its metropolitan territory or other territories under its jurisdiction compulsory primary education, free of charge, undertakes, within two years, to work out and adopt a detailed plan of action for the progressive implementation, within a reasonable number of years, to be fixed in the plan, of the principle of compulsory education free of charge for all.

Article 15

1. The States Parties to the present Covenant recognize the right of everyone:
    (a) To take part in cultural life;
    (b) To enjoy the benefits of scientific progress and its applications;
    (c) To benefit from the protection of the moral and material interests resulting from any scientific, literary or artistic production of which he is the author.

2. The steps to be taken by the States Parties to the present Covenant to achieve the full realization of this right shall include those necessary for the conservation, the development and the diffusion of science and culture.

3. The States Parties to the present Covenant undertake to respect the freedom indispensable for scientific research and creative activity.

4. The States Parties to the present Covenant recognize the benefits to be derived from the encouragement and development of international contacts and co-operation in the scientific and cultural fields.

The European, inter-American, and African regional human rights instruments, as well as treaties sponsored by the ILO, also recognize various rights of an economic, social, and cultural nature. In addition, a network of specialized treaties sponsored by the UN is aimed at eradicating discrimination in the enjoyment of such rights. Some of these protections are found within the main treaty, while others are found in additional protocols.[129]

Several civil and political rights have provided a basis for inferring additional rights of an economic, social, and cultural nature. For example, the African Commission on Human and Peoples' Rights has inferred a right to food from the African Charter's recognition of the rights to life, health, and development.[130] In the European system, the European Court of Human Rights has recognized that what might be described as a right to a clean and safe environment is implied by the ECHR's rights to life, privacy, and the enjoyment of one's home.[131]

---

129 The rights to work, health and education are protected in articles 15–17 of the African Charter, above note 60, while the American Convention on Human Rights is supplemented by an additional protocol on economic, social, and cultural rights, the Protocol of San Salvador, above note 66. In Europe, economic, social, and cultural rights are addressed by a regime separate from the ECHR known as the European Social Charter (Revised), above note 65; however, some rights, such as the right to education, are recognized in the ECHR's additional protocols (see article 2 of ECHR Protocol No 1, above note 42).

130 *Social and Economic Rights Action Centre (SERAC) v Nigeria*, Communication No 155/96, (2001) AHRLR 60 (African Comm Hum Rts).

131 *Lopez Ostra v Spain* (1994), ECHR (Ser A) No 303-C, (1994) 20 EHRR 277 (ECHR).

Some domestic bills of rights also recognize economic, social, and cultural rights alongside civil and political rights, with the associated jurisprudence demonstrating that, at the very least, the obligation "to take steps" with respect to the enjoyment of economic, social, and cultural rights is justiciable in relation to such matters as healthcare.[132]

ii) The Right to Development

There is some debate as to whether international human rights law also includes a general "right to development." Article 22 of the African Charter is the only codification of an express "right to economic, social and cultural development" among the existing human rights treaties. The UN General Assembly has urged that such a right exists universally, most notably in a 1986 declaratory text that provides as follows:

Declaration on the Right to Development, GA Res 41/128 (1986), reprinted in UN GAOR, 41st Sess, Supp No 53 at 186–87, UN Doc A/41/53 (1986)

Article 1

1. The right to development is an inalienable human right by virtue of which every human person and all peoples are entitled to participate in, contribute to, and enjoy economic, social, cultural and political development, in which all human rights and fundamental freedoms can be fully realized . . . .

Article 2

1. The human person is the central subject of development and should be the active participant and beneficiary of the right to development . . . .

3. States have the right and the duty to formulate appropriate national development policies that aim at the constant improvement of the well-being of the entire population and of all individuals, on the basis of their active, free and meaningful participation in development and in the fair distribution of the benefits resulting therefrom.

Article 3

. . . 3. States have the duty to co-operate with each other in ensuring development and eliminating obstacles to development. States should realize their rights and fulfil their duties in such a manner as to promote a new international economic order based on sovereign equality, interdependence, mutual interest and co-operation among all States, as well as to encourage the observance and realization of human rights.

Article 4

1. States have the duty to take steps, individually and collectively, to formulate international development policies with a view to facilitating the full realization of the right to development . . . .

Article 8

1. States should undertake, at the national level, all necessary measures for the realization of the right to development and shall ensure, *inter alia*, equality of opportunity for all in their access to basic resources, education, health services, food, housing, employment

---

132 *Minister of Health v Treatment Action Campaign*, Case CCT 8/02, 2002 (5) SALR 721 (S Africa Const Ct).

and the fair distribution of income. Effective measures should be undertaken to ensure that women have an active role in the development process. Appropriate economic and social reforms should be carried out with a view to eradicating all social injustices.

2. States should encourage popular participation in all spheres as an important factor in development and in the full realization of all human rights.

This resolution on the right to development was adopted by a recorded vote of 146 votes in favour, one against (the United States), and eight abstentions (Denmark, Finland, Germany, Iceland, Israel, Japan, Sweden, and the United Kingdom).[133] Nevertheless, at the World Conference on Human Rights in 1993, a declaration was adopted by consensus that reaffirmed "the right to development, as established in the Declaration on the Right to Development, as a universal and inalienable right and an integral part of fundamental human rights."[134]

In 2000, heads of state and government meeting at the UN in New York pledged to meet eight "millennium development goals."[135] The Office of the UN High Commissioner for Human Rights has drawn a link between these goals and a number of the rights found in the UN-sponsored human rights treaties, as follows:[136]

Goal 1: Eradicate extreme poverty and hunger	Right to adequate standard of living; right to work; right to food
Goal 2: Achieve universal primary education	Right to education
Goal 3: Promote gender equality and empower women	Women's right to equality
Goal 4: Reduce child mortality	Right to life
Goal 5: Improve maternal health	Women's right to life and health
Goal 6: Combat HIV/AIDS, malaria, and other diseases	Right to health
Goal 7: Ensure environmental sustainability	Right to environmental health; right to water and sanitation; right to adequate housing
Goal 8: Develop a global partnership for development	Right to development; economic, social, and cultural rights; right to health

f) Special Protections for Minors

As we have seen, certain vulnerable groups are accorded special human rights protections by international human rights law. The best established of these regimes is that applicable to minors, and the CRC is the pre-eminent treaty expression of such protections. Its opening articles specify the following:

---

133 UN Doc A/41/PV.97 at 64.
134 Vienna Declaration and Programme of Action, above note 76.
135 *United Nations Millennium Declaration*, GA Res 55/2 (2000), reprinted in UN GAOR, 55th Sess, Supp No 49, vol I at 4–9, UN Doc A/55/49 (2001).
136 Office of the United Nations High Commissioner for Human Rights, "Millennium Development Goals and Human Rights Standards," online: www.ohchr.org/EN/Issues/MDG/Pages/MDGsStandards.aspx.

Convention on the Rights of the Child, 20 November 1989, 1577 UNTS 3, Can TS 1992 No 3, in force 2 September 1990

Article 3

1. In all actions concerning children, whether undertaken by public or private social welfare institutions, courts of law, administrative authorities or legislative bodies, the best interests of the child shall be a primary consideration.

2. States Parties undertake to ensure the child such protection and care as is necessary for his or her well-being, taking into account the rights and duties of his or her parents, legal guardians, or other individuals legally responsible for him or her, and, to this end, shall take all appropriate legislative and administrative measures.

3. States Parties shall ensure that the institutions, services and facilities responsible for the care or protection of children shall conform with the standards established by competent authorities, particularly in the areas of safety, health, in the number and suitability of their staff, as well as competent supervision . . . .

Article 5

States Parties shall respect the responsibilities, rights and duties of parents or, where applicable, the members of the extended family or community as provided for by local custom, legal guardians or other persons legally responsible for the child, to provide, in a manner consistent with the evolving capacities of the child, appropriate direction and guidance in the exercise by the child of the rights recognized in the present Convention . . . .

The CRC then requires special application of many civil, political, economic, social, and cultural rights to minors. In recent years, special provision has also been made for the protection of minors in circumstances of armed conflict, building upon the existing protections found in Article 38 of the CRC, which provides:

Article 38

1. States Parties undertake to respect and to ensure respect for rules of international humanitarian law applicable to them in armed conflicts which are relevant to the child.

2. States Parties shall take all feasible measures to ensure that persons who have not attained the age of fifteen years do not take a direct part in hostilities.

3. States Parties shall refrain from recruiting any person who has not attained the age of fifteen years into their armed forces. In recruiting among those persons who have attained the age of fifteen years but who have not attained the age of eighteen years, States Parties shall endeavour to give priority to those who are oldest.

4. In accordance with their obligations under international humanitarian law to protect the civilian population in armed conflicts, States Parties shall take all feasible measures to ensure protection and care of children who are affected by an armed conflict.

These obligations are now supplemented by the Optional Protocol to the Convention on the Rights of the Child on the Involvement of Children in Armed Conflicts,[137] which

---

137 25 May 2000, 2173 UNTS 222, Can TS 2002 No 5, (2000) 39 ILM 1285, in force 12 February 2002.

entered into force in 2002. This treaty raises the age for compulsory military recruitment and participation in combat as follows:

Article 1

States Parties shall take all feasible measures to ensure that members of their armed forces who have not attained the age of 18 years do not take a direct part in hostilities.

Article 2

States Parties shall ensure that persons who have not attained the age of 18 years are not compulsorily recruited into their armed forces . . . .

g) Protections for Other Vulnerable Groups

International human rights law also extends certain protections to vulnerable groups other than children. For instance, Article 18(4) of the African Charter provides that: "The aged and the disabled shall also have the right to special measures of protection in keeping with their physical or moral needs." Elder rights and the rights of the disabled are also recognized in Articles 15 and 23 of the European Social Charter (Revised),[138] and in more detail in the inter-American human rights regime. The following provisions provide an illustration of the latter:

Additional Protocol to the American Convention on Human Rights in the Area of Economic, Social and Cultural Rights (Protocol of San Salvador), 17 November 1988, OAS TS No 69, (1989) 28 ILM 161, in force 16 November 1999

Article 17: Protection of the Elderly

Everyone has the right to special protection in old age. With this in view the States Parties agree to take progressively the necessary steps to make this right a reality and, particularly, to:

a. Provide suitable facilities, as well as food and specialized medical care, for elderly individuals who lack them and are unable to provide them for themselves;

b. Undertake work programs specifically designed to give the elderly the opportunity to engage in a productive activity suited to their abilities and consistent with their vocations or desires;

c. Foster the establishment of social organizations aimed at improving the quality of life for the elderly.

Article 18: Protection of the Handicapped

Everyone affected by a diminution of his physical or mental capacities is entitled to receive special attention designed to help him achieve the greatest possible development of his personality. The States Parties agree to adopt such measures as may be necessary for this purpose and, especially, to:

a. Undertake programs specifically aimed at providing the handicapped with the resources and environment needed for attaining this goal, including work programs consistent with their possibilities and freely accepted by them or their legal representatives, as the case may be;

---

138 Above note 65.

b. Provide special training to the families of the handicapped in order to help them solve the problems of coexistence and convert them into active agents in the physical, mental and emotional development of the latter;

c. Include the consideration of solutions to specific requirements arising from needs of this group as a priority component of their urban development plans;

d. Encourage the establishment of social groups in which the handicapped can be helped to enjoy a fuller life.

In more recent years, success has been achieved in concluding treaty texts devoted to the rights of persons with disabilities, starting with the Inter-American Convention on the Elimination of All Forms of Discrimination Against Persons With Disabilities,[139] and then the Convention on the Rights of Persons with Disabilities (CRPD), a treaty of universal application.[140] The CRPD entered into force in 2008 and aims to ensure that states parties take the necessary measures to remove the various barriers that hinder the full and effective participation in society of those who have long-term physical, mental, intellectual, or sensory impairments. The CRPD also works with Article 23 of the CRC, which recognizes special rights for children with disabilities.

h) Non-Discrimination and the Right to Equality

As indicated above, one of the very purposes of the UN is "[t]o achieve international co-operation . . . in promoting and encouraging respect for human rights and for fundamental freedoms for all without distinction as to race, sex, language, or religion."[141] A similar prohibition of discrimination on enumerated grounds was also included in the Universal Declaration, with the list of enumerated grounds expanded to include "race, colour, sex, language, religion, political or other opinion, national or social origin, property, birth or other status," as well as "the political, jurisdictional or international status of the country or territory to which a person belongs, whether it be independent, trust, non-self-governing or under any other limitation of sovereignty."[142] Since then, all human rights treaties have included a prohibition of discrimination, including the two Covenants:

International Covenant on Civil and Political Rights, 16 December 1966, 999 UNTS 171, Can TS 1976 No 47, (1967) 6 ILM 368, in force 23 March 1976

Article 2

1. Each State Party to the present Covenant undertakes to respect and to ensure to all individuals within its territory and subject to its jurisdiction the rights recognized in the present Covenant, without distinction of any kind, such as race, colour, sex, language, religion, political or other opinions, national or social origin, property, birth or other status . . . .

---

139 7 June 1999, OAS TS No A65, in force 14 September 2001.

140 Above note 50.

141 Charter of the United Nations, 26 June 1945, Can TS 1945 No 7, 24 October 1945, art 1(3).

142 Universal Declaration, above note 37, art 2.

International Covenant on Economic, Social and Cultural Rights, 16 December 1966, 999 UNTS 3, Can TS 1976 No 46, (1967) 6 ILM 360, in force 3 January 1976

Article 2

1. . . .

2. The States Parties to the present Covenant undertake to guarantee that the rights enunciated in the present Covenant will be exercised without discrimination of any kind as to race, colour, sex, language, religion, political or other opinion, national or social origin, property, birth or other status. . . .

Article 26 of the ICCPR further provides that: "All persons are equal before the law and are entitled without any discrimination to the equal protection of the law. In this respect, the law shall prohibit any discrimination and guarantee to all persons equal and effective protection against discrimination on any ground such as race, colour, sex, language, religion, political or other opinion, national or social origin, property, birth or other status." This guarantee of a free-standing right to equality, distinct from the enjoyment of other rights and freedoms, is supplemented by several specific UN-sponsored treaties intended to correct the historic disadvantages imposed on women, racialized groups, children, and, most recently, persons with disabilities. These specialized treaties further assist by providing a definition of discrimination, as illustrated in these excerpts from CERD and CEDAW:

International Convention on the Elimination of All Forms of Racial Discrimination, 21 December 1965, 660 UNTS 195, Can TS 1970 No 28, in force 4 January 1969

Article 1

1. In this Convention, the term "racial discrimination" shall mean any distinction, exclusion, restriction or preference based on race, colour, descent, or national or ethnic origin which has the purpose or effect of nullifying or impairing the recognition, enjoyment or exercise, on an equal footing, of human rights and fundamental freedoms in the political, economic, social, cultural or any other field of public life.

2. This Convention shall not apply to distinctions, exclusions, restrictions or preferences made by a State Party to this Convention between citizens and non-citizens.

3. Nothing in this Convention may be interpreted as affecting in any way the legal provisions of States Parties concerning nationality, citizenship or naturalization, provided that such provisions do not discriminate against any particular nationality.

4. Special measures taken for the sole purpose of securing adequate advancement of certain racial or ethnic groups or individuals requiring such protection as may be necessary in order to ensure such groups or individuals equal enjoyment or exercise of human rights and fundamental freedoms shall not be deemed racial discrimination, provided, however, that such measures do not, as a consequence, lead to the maintenance of separate rights for different racial groups and that they shall not be continued after the objectives for which they were taken have been achieved.

Convention on the Elimination of All Forms of Discrimination Against Women, 18 December 1979, 1249 UNTS 13, Can TS 1982 No 31, in force 3 September 1981

Article 1

For the purposes of the present Convention, the term "discrimination against women" shall mean any distinction, exclusion or restriction made on the basis of sex which has the effect or purpose of impairing or nullifying the recognition, enjoyment or exercise by women, irrespective of their marital status, on a basis of equality of men and women, of human rights and fundamental freedoms in the political, economic, social, cultural, civil or any other field. . . .

Article 4

1. Adoption by States Parties of temporary special measures aimed at accelerating de facto equality between men and women shall not be considered discrimination as defined in the present Convention, but shall in no way entail as a consequence the maintenance of unequal or separate standards; these measures shall be discontinued when the objectives of equality of opportunity and treatment have been achieved.

2. Adoption by States Parties of special measures, including those measures contained in the present Convention, aimed at protecting maternity shall not be considered discriminatory.

As for similar protections in the regional human rights regimes, it is worth noting that the ECHR has, for many years, lacked a free-standing right to equality provision. Rather, Article 14 of the original text of the ECHR indicates that its right to equality is an accessory provision, requiring any alleged discrimination to be claimed in tandem with "the enjoyment of the rights and freedoms set forth in the Convention." An attempt to address this weakness in the European human rights regime has been made with the adoption of a protocol to amend the ECHR so as to provide for a more robust equality provision, but less than half of the states parties to the ECHR have ratified the protocol.[143] A provision similar to Article 14 of the ECHR is found in Article 1 of the American Convention on Human Rights (albeit bolstered by a guarantee of equality before the law in Article 24), and in Article 2 of the African Charter. However, Article 18(3) of the African Charter further requires the state to "ensure the elimination of every discrimination against women and also ensure the protection of the rights of the woman and the child as stipulated in international declarations and conventions."

E. ENCOURAGING COMPLIANCE: KEY HUMAN RIGHTS INSTITUTIONS AND THEIR OUTPUTS

A state party to a human rights treaty, as with any other treaty, has an obligation to ensure the performance of its treaty obligations in good faith, although with a human rights treaty the beneficiaries of the obligation are the individuals within the territory and juris-

---

143 Protocol No 12 to the Convention on the Protection of Human Rights and Fundamental Freedoms, 4 November 2000, ETS No 177, in force 1 April 2005 (eighteen states parties as of July 2013).

diction of the state party. The obligation to perform a treaty that is in force, and to which a state has given its consent to be bound, is discussed in Chapter 2, Section B(6)(a).

General rules of international law do not specify the means by which a human rights treaty is to be implemented domestically. Accordingly, absent express provisions to the contrary, a state is free to implement its human rights treaty obligations in the manner it chooses — although usually this occurs through a combination of existing and new legislation, administrative action, policy measures, and educational activities. While many states with domestic bills of rights rely on such instruments for the domestic implementation of their international human rights obligations, there is no general obligation under international law that requires states to accord constitutional legal status to any or all of its human rights treaty obligations. There is, however, an obligation to ensure that any person whose civil and political rights are violated has an effective remedy, although it need not be a judicial remedy.[144] This obligation is enhanced for violations caused by unlawful arrests and detentions, as well as miscarriages of justice, which result in a right to compensation.[145]

At the international level, the usual method of promoting compliance is a process of "naming and shaming" to encourage change and improvement through publicity and a state's concern for its international reputation. The states parties to the various international human rights treaties at the UN level have, through their consent to the relevant treaties or associated protocols, created several treaty-monitoring bodies. These bodies typically have the task of periodically reviewing states parties' performance of their obligations of domestic implementation, as well as providing guidance to states parties in this regard. In this section, we will review the work of the principal such treaty-monitoring bodies in encouraging state compliance, before discussing the activities of other bodies created under the UN Charter to promote the protection of human rights. We end the section with a brief review of the regional mechanisms used to encourage state compliance within the key regional human rights regimes.

1) The Treaty-Monitoring Bodies

Each of the major human rights treaties developed under the auspices of the UN has a body that monitors performance of the treaty obligations by states parties. Each treaty-monitoring body consists of independent experts elected to serve on a part-time basis by states parties, and is serviced by the UN secretariat in Geneva.

There are currently ten human rights treaty-monitoring bodies at the UN level, including the Human Rights Committee (which monitors compliance with the ICCPR), and the Committee on Economic, Social and Cultural Rights (which monitors compliance with the ICESCR). The specialized UN human rights treaties each have their own treaty-monitoring bodies as well, aptly named the Committee on the Elimination of Racial Discrimination, the

---

144 ICCPR, above note 6, art 2(3). See also article 8 of the Universal Declaration, above note 37; articles 8 and 24 of the American Declaration, above note 58; and article 24 of the American Convention on Human Rights above, note 59.

145 ICCPR, above note 6, art 9(5). See also article 5(5) of the ECHR, above note 57, and article 10 of the American Convention on Human Rights, above note 59.

Committee on the Elimination of Discrimination Against Women, the Committee Against Torture, the Committee on the Rights of the Child, and the Committee on the Rights of Persons with Disabilities, respectively, with an additional Subcommittee on the Prevention of Torture for states parties to the Optional Protocol to the Torture Convention.[146] There is also a Committee on Migrant Workers, a Committee on Enforced Disappearances for states parties to the Migrant Workers Convention,[147] and the Enforced Disappearance Convention,[148] respectively.

Consider the following description of the work of these treaty-monitoring bodies, keeping in mind that Canada has agreed to report periodically to seven of the ten committees and accepts the right of individual petition to three of the committees, specifically the Human Rights Committee, the Committee Against Torture, and the Committee on the Elimination of Discrimination Against Women (in addition to the Inter-American Commission on Human Rights at the regional level):

> **Mark Freeman & Gibran van Ert,** *International Human Rights Law* (Toronto: Irwin Law, 2004) at 385–97[149]
>
> Four kinds of procedures fall within the jurisdiction of various of the treaty bodies:
>
> 1) review of periodic reports submitted by states parties;
> 2) investigation of systematic violations;
> 3) review of petitions filed by one state against another; and
> 4) review of petitions made by individuals against states parties.[150] . . .
>
> ### 2) State Reporting Procedures
>
> All the major human rights treaties establish a mandatory reporting system under which states parties submit periodic reports regarding the measures they have taken to meet the treaty's requirements. Treaty bodies typically require reports at two- to five-year intervals. They may also request states parties to submit information on an urgent basis regarding situations of particular concern. States are expected to make their reports widely available to the public.
>
> Each treaty body has adopted "general comments" (sometimes called "general recommendations") which serve as interpretive aids for states parties in drafting their reports. General comments are often quite detailed, leaving little doubt as to the conclusions a treaty body will ultimately reach on many issues . . . .[151]

---

146 Above note 105.

147 Above note 56.

148 Above note 54.

149 Copyright Irwin Law, Inc. Reprinted with permission. Original footnotes omitted (footnotes appearing in the following excerpt are by the present authors).

150 The Committee on the Elimination of Racial Discrimination also has an early warning procedure, designed to draw attention to situations that require immediate attention, as a preventative measure aimed at avoiding serious violations.

151 Note that "Canada does not consider . . . the General Comments . . . to be authoritative interpretations of Covenant obligations, legal or otherwise. Rather the General Comments merely represent the views or interpretations of Committee members in their independent capacities. The General Comments

The typical reporting procedure is as follows. First, the state party submits a report. The report may be accompanied by a "core document" applicable to reports before all treaty bodies. The treaty body then examines the report, along with information obtained from UN and other sources. Great reliance is placed on information received from NGOs and other civil society organizations, which increasingly prepare their own parallel reports known as "shadow reports." Next the treaty body prepares a "list of issues" which it sends to the state. The issues can be quite specific and demanding at times. The state then has an opportunity to submit a written reply. Later a formal public session, generally lasting one day, is held at UN offices in Geneva . . . at which the state's report and any subsequent clarifications it has made are questioned and discussed. Finally, the treaty body meets in private and adopts "concluding observations" for submission to the state and inclusion in its annual report to the General Assembly. A few treaty bodies have reviewed state parties' performances even in the absence of a report.

Many states produce very thorough reports. But some states treat the process of drafting reports as an exercise in disingenuous self-assessment done without consulting the most closely concerned NGOS. Some states have included only constitutional and statutory quotations in their reports. There have been serious delays by states in fulfilling their treaty reporting obligations, sometimes in good faith and other times not. States with bad human rights records are often responsible for the most severe delays, and there are many states that have never submitted a report to any treaty body. Yet if states did start to fulfill their reporting obligations in a timely manner, it is far from clear that the treaty bodies could cope with the extra caseload.

All of the treaty bodies' concluding observations contain a section on "positive aspects" of a state party's performance prior to a concluding section on "principal areas of concern and recommendations." Most concluding observations on Canada have praised its general commitment to human rights. But treaty bodies have also criticized Canada on many issues. The most frequent criticisms relate to Canada's treatment of Aboriginal peoples. For example, the Committee on Economic, Social and Cultural Rights recently expressed concern at the "gross disparity" between Aboriginals and the majority of Canadians with respect to the enjoyment of ICESCR rights:

> There has been little or no progress in the alleviation of social and economic deprivation among aboriginal people. In particular, the Committee is deeply concerned at the shortage of adequate housing, the endemic mass unemployment and the high rate of suicide, especially among youth, in the aboriginal communities. Another concern is the failure to provide safe and adequate drinking water to aboriginal communities on reserves. The delegation of the State party conceded that almost a quarter of aboriginal household dwellings required major repairs and lacked basic amenities.

Rates of female and child poverty have been another subject of concern. The Committee on the Elimination of Discrimination against Women recently stated:

---

have not been endorsed by Canada or other States Parties to the Covenant and they do not enjoy any status in law": Colleen Swords, "Canadian Practice in International Law: At the Department of Foreign Affairs and International Trade in 2002–3" (2003) 41 Can YB Int'l Law 443 at 467.

> While appreciating the federal Government's various anti-poverty measures, the Committee is concerned about the high percentage of women living in poverty, in particular elderly women living alone, female lone parents, aboriginal women, older women, women of colour, immigrant women and women with disabilities, for whom poverty persists or even deepens, aggravated by the budgetary adjustments made since 1995 and the resulting cuts in social services. The Committee is also concerned that those strategies are mostly directed towards children and not towards these groups of women.

Another subject of concern has been Canada's treatment of refugee claimants and their families. The Committee against Torture recently urged Canada to enhance the effectiveness of the remedies to protect the rights granted by CAT article 3(1):

> Noting the assurances that the proposed new Immigration and Refugee Act provides for a pre-removal risk assessment "available to all persons under a removal order," the Committee encourages the State party to ensure that the proposed new legislation permits in-depth examination by an independent entity of claims, including those from persons already assessed as security risks. The Committee urges the State party to ensure that obstacles to the full implementation of article 3 are removed, so that an opportunity is given to the individual concerned to respond before a security risk decision is made, and that assessments of humanitarian and compassionate grounds are made without demanding a fee from a person who seeks protection.

Many treaty bodies have also expressed concern about the ability of the federal government to ensure comprehensive domestic implementation of its treaty obligations. But these are only examples . . . .

3) Investigation of Systematic Violations

The . . . [Torture Convention (CAT), the Optional Protocol to CEDAW (CEDAW-OP), and the Optional Protocol to the Torture Convention (CAT-OP)][152] provide unique in-country investigative powers to their respective treaty bodies. Article 20 of the CAT gives the Committee Against Torture the power to initiate confidential investigations of a state party when there is reliable information that torture is being "systematically practiced" by that state party. The Committee will first invite the state to reply to the allegations. Thereafter, it may undertake a further confidential inquiry that can include an on-site, consensual visit to the state, and the transmission of findings to that state. The whole process is confidential unless the state consents to publication of a summary account of the investigation in the Committee's annual report. CAT article 28 permits states parties to opt out of the article 20 procedure by making a formal declaration to that effect. In practice, the Committee only has enough funds to conduct one in-country visit per year. By contrast, the European Committee for the Prevention of Torture is able to conduct

---

152 An inquiry procedure is also available in relation to the Disability Rights Convention (CRPD) and the ICESCR with the coming into force of their respective optional protocols: Optional Protocol to the Convention on the Rights of Persons with Disabilities, 13 December 2006, UN Doc A/61/611, in force 3 May 2008; Optional Protocol to the International Covenant on Economic, Social and Cultural Rights, 10 December 2008, UN Doc A/63/435, (2009) 48 ILM 262, in force 5 May 2013. Canada is not a party to either protocol.

approximately twenty visits per year. It has a budget almost twenty-five times that of the UN Committee Against Torture.

CEDAW-OP article 8 creates a similar procedure to CAT article 20. The procedure allows the Committee on the Elimination of Discrimination against Women to initiate confidential investigations in cases of "grave or systematic violations" of the CEDAW. As with the CAT procedure, the Committee first invites the state party to submit observations on the allegations before considering whether to conduct a further inquiry that could include an in-country visit. Following any such inquiry and/or visit, the Committee forwards its findings to the state party, which has six months to respond. All information remains confidential unless the state party consents to its publication. States parties may opt out of the article 8 procedure by making an appropriate declaration under CEDAW-OP article 10 at the time of ratification or accession.

The CAT-OP was inspired by the detention centre inspection mechanisms of the International Committee of the Red Cross and the European Committee for the Prevention of Torture. The treaty opened for signature on 1 January 2003 and [entered into force in June 2006]. The core purpose of the CAT-OP is to prevent torture and other cruel, inhuman or degrading treatment or punishment. Article 2(1) establishes the Sub-Committee on Prevention, an independent subcommittee of the Committee against Torture composed of ten elected independent experts, while article 3 requires states parties to maintain at the domestic level one or more "national preventive mechanisms." The Sub-Committee on Prevention . . . [has] the authority to conduct in-country inspections of detention facilities and provide assistance and recommendations to national preventive mechanisms and states parties. Articles 12 and 14 of the CAT-OP require states parties to fully co-operate with the Sub-Committee on Prevention before, during, and after any in-country visit. Article 13 requires the Sub-Committee to establish a programme of regular visits, which are to be conducted by at least two Sub-Committee members and any experts they may invite from a pre-established roster. Recommendations and observations of the Sub-Committee must be communicated confidentially to the state party; but states parties may also consent to publication. If a state party refuses to fully co-operate with the Sub-Committee on Prevention or fails to act on its recommendations, the Committee against Torture (acting on the advice of the Sub-Committee) may bring the matter to public attention after the state party has had an opportunity to explain its actions.

The national preventive mechanisms under the CAT-OP are to be accorded powers to make unannounced visits to detention centres and examine persons held there, to make recommendations to the state party, and to submit proposals and observations on relevant legislation. Article 20 requires states parties to provide national preventive mechanisms full access and co-operation in fulfilling their mandate, including the right to meet and share information directly with the Sub-Committee on Prevention. Article 22 requires states parties to publish and disseminate the annual reports issued by national preventive mechanisms. States parties may, however, make a declaration upon joining the treaty that would allow their treaty obligations to be postponed for up to a maximum of five years (article 24). The mandatory nature of the visits by national mechanisms could raise constitutional concerns for federal states like Canada, since the CAT-OP extends to all parts of a federal state without any limitation or exception and reservations to the protocol are barred.

4) Individual Petition Procedures

The Human Rights Committee, the Committee Against Torture, the Committee on the Elimination of Racial Discrimination, the Committee on the Elimination of Discrimination against Women, and the Committee on the Protection of the Rights of All Migrant Workers and Members of Their Families all operate individual petition procedures. [Provision is also made for individual petitions to the Committee on the Rights of Persons with Disabilities, the Committee on Enforced Disappearances, the Committee on Economic, Social and Cultural Rights, and (when the relevant provisions enter into force) the Committee on the Rights of the Child.] Victims, family members, and NGOs are permitted to present petitions (known as "communications"). . . . The Human Rights Committee has received by far the most individual petitions.

There are generally two stages to a treaty body's treatment of an individual petition: admissibility and consideration on the merits. Most petitions are rejected at the admissibility stage. The burden of proof of admissibility rests, naturally, on the applicant. For a petition to be admissible, a number of criteria must be satisfied. First, there is typically a bar on anonymous submissions. Second, the petition must be in writing and must involve facts that occurred after the date when the petition procedure came into force against the concerned state. Third, the petition must not have been previously examined by the treaty body in question. Fourth, consideration of any matter that is being examined under another international procedure of investigation or settlement is generally barred. Fifth, the petition must not be manifestly ill-founded nor constitute an abuse of the rules of procedure for submission. Finally, and most importantly, all available and sufficient domestic remedies must have been exhausted. The purpose of this rule is to allow states an adequate opportunity to resolve the matter internally, since treaty body procedures are not intended to replace domestic mechanisms. The burden of proof of exhaustion of domestic remedies falls upon the applicant, who must make a *prima facie* case as to domestic exhaustion or alternatively as to why exhaustion is not possible in the particular state. Thereafter the burden passes to the state to establish that an effective domestic remedy was, and remains, available. The exhaustion requirement is generally interpreted in a liberal and flexible manner, and may be waived explicitly or implicitly (as by failure to reply in a timely manner) by the responding state.

Upon receipt of an admissible complaint, the treaty body will review it in private. Letters and documentation submitted by the complainant will remain confidential. In some cases, interim measures may be granted to avoid "irreparable damage" to the complainant. Treaty bodies do not conduct oral hearings between the individual applicant and the respondent state, but instead forward the complaint to the state, permitting it three to six months to respond. The treaty body then makes a final determination on the matter in closed session, whether or not the state chose to contest the complaint. The "views" (that is, the conclusions) of the body are then forwarded to the state party and the complainant, and eventually to the UN General Assembly. The views of a treaty body are not binding but merely hortatory; treaty bodies have no power to order specific remedies for violations but only to make general findings and recommendations. Actions recommended by the Human Rights Committee have included conducting a full public investigation, bringing the perpetrators to justice, paying compensation, providing restitution, providing medical treatment, ensuring non-repetition of the violation, changing legislation, and ensuring various case-specific forms of remedy such as release from jail or commutation of a death sentence. Some treaty bodies have established a Special Rapporteur for the Follow-up of Views, to monitor the implementation of their recommendations, but they only have the power to shame. Unless domestic law provides otherwise, the views of treaty bodies are not enforceable as judgments before domestic courts.

Several dozen complaints have been made against Canada before the Human Rights Committee for violations of the ICCPR. About half of these were deemed inadmissible. Of the admissible cases, there have been several findings against Canada, most of which have involved multiple breaches of the ICCPR. Canada's record of compliance with the Committee's recommendations has been mixed. Just over a dozen complaints against Canada have been filed with the Committee Against Torture for alleged violations of the CAT. Most were found inadmissible. Of the admissible cases, only one finding has been made in favour of the applicant [dealing with the removal of a refugee claimant to possible torture].

A surprisingly high number of states have never been the subject of individual complaint under any of the relevant treaty body procedures. What's more, where complaints are made, in many cases treaty bodies receive insufficient cooperation from the state party. On the whole, however, individual petition procedures have been reasonably effective mechanisms and their potential for enhanced enforcement remains great. The Human Rights Committee, in particular, has developed a useful jurisprudence that has deepened understanding of many human rights.

LAW IN CONTEXT

The Effect of the Human Rights Committee's Views in Canada

The Human Rights Committee is not a court and it does not have the power to issue legally binding judgments. Instead, the Human Rights Committee (as with the other treaty-monitoring bodies) relies on the reputation and expertise of its members, and the potentially persuasive force of its views, to encourage states parties to comply with its interpretation of their ICCPR obligations. Past members of the Human Rights Committee include Thomas Buergenthal and Rosalyn Higgins, former judges of the International Court of Justice, as well as former Ontario Court of Appeal Justice Walter Tarnopolsky.

The individual petition procedure allows for the examination of individual cases by the Human Rights Committee. If found admissible,[153] the Human Rights Committee will consider an individual's complaint in light of all written information made available by the individual and the state concerned, and then come to a "view" that is later published. This right of individual petition has been exercised in over 1,000 cases since the Human Rights Committee began operations in 1976, leading to the development of an extensive body of "jurisprudence" consisting of the Committee's views on the application and interpretation of the ICCPR in a variety of factual situations.[154]

---

153 The grounds for admissibility are set out in the Optional Protocol to the International Covenant on Civil and Political Rights, 16 December 1966, 999 UNTS 171, Can TS 1976 No 47, in force 23 March 1976, entry into force for Canada 19 August 1976. These include the requirement that all available domestic remedies be exhausted before proceeding to the international forum.

154 The Office of the UN High Commissioner for Human Rights has established a treaty body database to provide free access to this jurisprudence, along with access to state reports, concluding observations

A number of individual complaints lodged with the Human Rights Committee have concerned Canada's performance of its ICCPR obligations. Probably the most well-known complaint against Canada was that brought by Sandra Lovelace, now a member of Canada's Senate, who successfully claimed that Canada was in breach of the ICCPR in requiring Aboriginal women who married non-Aboriginal men to relinquish their status under the *Indian Act* and, consequently, to lose their right to live on an Indian reserve.[155] Canada remedied the breach of its international obligations identified by the Human Rights Committee by enacting legislation, and further explained in its response to the Human Rights Committee's findings that the coming into force of section 15 of the *Canadian Charter of Rights and Freedoms* would, in future, provide an effective domestic remedy.[156] Canada has not, however, been as responsive in other cases, particularly where the breach of the ICCPR has been found in an extradition or deportation context. These Committee views also received no mention in subsequent Canadian judicial proceedings.[157]

Individuals bringing complaints before the Human Rights Committee may also seek the issuance of interim measures of protection where needed to avoid irreparable harm to their rights while consideration of their complaint is pending. Such measures are common in litigation before various international courts, commissions, and committees, in recognition of the need to protect the interests of parties while a case is under consideration. However, in the 2002 case of *Ahani v Canada*,[158] Canada refused to comply with a Human Rights Committee interim measures request to refrain from deporting a complainant who claimed that his deportation to face torture would violate Canada's international obligations. When Canada signalled its intention to continue with the desired deportation, it was not prevented from doing so by the Ontario Court of Appeal, which held that the Committee's request was not legally binding:

> In signing[159] the [Optional] Protocol [to the ICCPR permitting individual communications], Canada did not agree to be bound by the final views of the Committee, nor did it even agree that it would stay its own domestic proceedings until the Committee gave its views. In other words, neither the Committee's views nor its interim measures requests are binding on Canada as a matter of international law, much less as a matter of domestic

---

and general comments. The database is available online: http://tb.ohchr.org/default.aspx. Committee views of note may also be reported in the *International Human Rights Reports*, *International Legal Materials*, and *International Law Reports*.

155 *Lovelace v Canada*, Communication No 24/1977 (views adopted 30 July 1981), UN Doc CCPR/C/13/D/24/1977, reprinted in *Report of the Human Rights Committee*, UN GAOR, 36th Sess, Supp No 40, annex XVIII, UN Doc A/36/40 (1981); 68 ILR 17; (1981) 2 HRLJ 158. See also Anne F Bayefsky, "The Human Rights Committee and the Case of Sandra Lovelace" (1982) 20 Can YB Int'l Law 244.

156 *An Act to Amend the Indian Act*, SC 1985, c 27. See also "Response of Canada to the Views of the Human Rights Committee" in *Report of the Human Rights Committee*, UN GAOR, 38th Sess, Supp No 40 at 249, UN Doc A/38/40 (1983).

157 See further, Joanna Harrington, "The Absent Dialogue: Extradition and the International Covenant on Civil and Political Rights" (2006) 32:1 Queen's LJ 82–134. By contrast, the Committee's views dismissing a complaint of racial discrimination against Canada were cited in subsequent Canadian proceedings: see *Canada (Human Rights Commission) v Taylor*, [1990] 3 SCR 892.

158 *Ahani v Canada* (2002), 58 OR (3d) 107 (CA), leave to appeal to SCC refused, [2002] SCCA No 62.

159 Canada did not, in fact, "sign" either the ICCPR or its Optional Protocol. Canada acceded to both treaties after consultations with the provinces.

law. The party states that ratified the Covenant and the Optional Protocol turned their minds to the question of whether they should agree to be bound by the Committee's views, or whether they should at least agree to refrain from taking any action against an individual who had sought the Committee's views until they were known. They decided as a matter of policy that they should not, leaving each party state, on a case-by-case basis, free to accept or reject the Committee's final views, and equally free to accede to or not accede to an interim measures request.[160]

By contrast, a very different position has been embraced by the Judicial Committee of the Privy Council, acting as the highest appellate court for Jamaica. The Privy Council, by four votes to one, recognized that an individual has a right to a stay of proceedings under domestic law when his or her petition is pending before the Human Rights Committee (or the Inter-American Commission on Human Rights). According to this ruling, when a state chooses to give its consent to an international petition process, the petitioner gains a right to complete that process and obtain the views of the treaty body on grounds of due process and protection of the law.[161]

For its part, the Human Rights Committee considers its interim measures requests to be necessary to avert irreparable harm to alleged victims of human rights violations, and is critical of states that ignore such requests.

Mark Freeman & Gibran van Ert, *International Human Rights Law* (Toronto: Irwin Law, 2004) at 397[162]

5) Inter-State Petition Procedure

. . . Inter-state complaint procedures typically operate as follows: a state party makes an allegation against another state party (assuming both have recognized the competence of the particular treaty body to handle inter-state petitions); the responding state is given a few months to reply; if the states fail to resolve the question in an amicable manner, the case is referred to the relevant treaty body; which can appoint, with the states' consent, a conciliation mechanism to make non-binding findings. To date, no state has filed an inter-state complaint with a treaty body; and thus the relevance of these procedures is questionable. Possible reasons for the non-use of these procedures include fear that a complaint against another state will adversely affect diplomatic relations, concern that it will incite retaliation by the other state, and doubt that the procedures are effective.

2) UN Charter-Based Institutions

a) UN Human Rights Council

As noted earlier, ECOSOC is empowered by Article 68 of the UN Charter to "set up commissions . . . for the promotion of human rights." To assist with its tasks, ECOSOC cre-

---

160 *Ahani v Canada*, above note 158 at para 32.
161 *Lewis v Jamaica (Attorney General)*, [2001] 2 AC 50, [2000] UKPC 35, [2000] 3 WLR 1785 (PC). See further, Joanna Harrington, "Punting Terrorists, Assassins and Other Undesirables: Canada, the Human Rights Committee and Requests for Interim Measures of Protection" (2003) 48:1 McGill LJ 55–87.
162 Copyright Irwin Law, Inc. Reprinted with permission.

ated the Commission on Human Rights in 1946, which played an important role in setting new standards and generating new conceptual understandings of human rights for the next sixty years.[163] Unfortunately, in its later years, the Commission was also a subject of criticism, particularly when its membership included states with very poor human rights records,[164] and in 2006, the Commission on Human Rights was replaced with a "Human Rights Council" at the behest of the General Assembly. As a result, the Human Rights Council is a subsidiary body of the General Assembly, rather than of ECOSOC.

The Human Rights Council is the main intergovernmental body within the UN responsible for promoting universal respect for human rights and the effective coordination and mainstreaming of human rights protection within the UN system. The Council comprises forty-seven states, with Canada having served as a member of the Council from 2006–2009.[165] It meets in regular and special sessions in Geneva for approximately ten weeks each year. The Council serves as a forum for dialogue among states on thematic issues of human rights, and a body within which resolutions may be adopted calling attention to human rights concerns. The Council has also gained several functions that used to be carried out by the former Commission on Human Rights. For example, the Council may address consistent patterns of gross and reliably attested systematic human rights violations through the adoption of recommendations.[166] The Council is also responsible for the appointment of a number of independent experts, who serve voluntarily as special rapporteurs and members of working groups, to focus attention on specific human rights issues or country-specific human rights situations.[167] An Advisory Committee of eighteen experts, replacing the former Sub-commission on the Promotion and Protection of Human Rights, also supports the Council in its work.

Since its creation in 2006, the Council has also been responsible for conducting a periodic review of the performance of all UN member states with respect to the fulfillment of their human rights commitments and obligations. This mechanism is known as "universal periodic review." Canada underwent its first review in February 2009 and its second in April 2013.[168] An excerpt concerning Canada's most recent review follows the examination below of the Council's creation.

i)   The Creation of the Human Rights Council

The proposal to replace the Commission on Human Rights with a more effective and credible intergovernmental body gained support in the lead-up to the 2005 World Summit on UN reform, and soon thereafter. For some, the hope had been to create a new Council with

---

163 See further, Philip Alston, "The Commission on Human Rights" in Philip Alston, ed, *The United Nations and Human Rights: A Critical Appraisal* (Oxford: Oxford University Press, 1992) at 126–210.

164 Among the most notorious examples were the election of Sudan in 2002 and the Libyan chairmanship of the Commission in 2003.

165 For an appraisal, see Joanna Harrington, "Canada and the United Nations Human Rights Council: Dissent and Division" (2010) 60 UNBLJ 78–115.

166 *Human Rights Council*, GA Res 60/251 (2006), reprinted in UN GAOR, 60th Sess, Supp No 49, vol III at 2–5, UN Doc A/60/49 (2006), para 3.

167 Examples include the special rapporteur on the right to food and the working group on arbitrary detention.

168 For an appraisal of Canada's first review, see Joanna Harrington, "Canada, the United Nations Human Rights Council, and Universal Periodic Review" (2009) 18:2 *Constitutional Forum* 79–93.

a standing comparable to the other Councils within the UN—a proposal championed by then UN Secretary-General Kofi Annan in his 2005 report to member states:

In Larger Freedom: Towards Development, Security and Human Rights For All: Report of the Secretary-General, UN Doc A/59/2005 (21 March 2005)[169]

165. Its founders endowed the United Nations with three Councils, each having major responsibilities in its own area: the Security Council, the Economic and Social Council and the Trusteeship Council. Over time, the division of responsibilities between them has become less and less balanced: the Security Council has increasingly asserted its authority and, especially since the end of the cold war, has enjoyed greater unity of purpose among its permanent members but has seen that authority questioned on the grounds that its composition is anachronistic or insufficiently representative; the Economic and Social Council has been too often relegated to the margins of global economic and social governance; and the Trusteeship Council, having successfully carried out its functions, is now reduced to a purely formal existence.

166. I believe we need to restore the balance, with three Councils covering respectively, (a) international peace and security, (b) economic and social issues, and (c) human rights, the promotion of which has been one of the purposes of the Organization from its beginnings but now clearly requires more effective operational structures. These Councils together should have the task of driving forward the agenda that emerges from summit and other conferences of Member States, and should be the global forms in which the issues of security, development and justice can be properly addressed. The first two Councils, of course, already exist but need to be strengthened. The third requires a far-reaching overhaul and upgrading of our existing human rights machinery . . . .

Proposed Human Rights Council

181. The Commission on Human Rights has given the international community a universal human rights framework, comprising the Universal Declaration on Human Rights, the two International Covenants and other core human rights treaties. During its annual session, the Commission draws public attention to human rights issues and debates, provides a forum for the development of United Nations human rights policy and establishes a unique system of independent and expert special procedures to observe and analyse human rights compliance by theme and by country. The Commission's close engagement with hundreds of civil society organizations provides an opportunity for working with civil society that does not exist elsewhere.

182. Yet the Commission's capacity to perform its tasks has been increasingly undermined by its declining credibility and professionalism. In particular, States have sought membership of the Commission not to strengthen human rights but to protect themselves against criticism or to criticize others. As a result, a credibility deficit has developed, which casts a shadow on the reputation of the United Nations system as a whole.

---

169 Reprinted with the permission of United Nations Publications.

183. If the United Nations is to meet the expectations of men and women everywhere—and indeed, if the Organization is to take the cause of human rights as seriously as those of security and development—then Member States should agree to replace the Commission on Human Rights with a smaller standing Human Rights Council. Member States would need to decide if they want the Human Rights Council to be a principal organ of the United Nations or a subsidiary body of the General Assembly, but in either case its members would be elected directly by the General Assembly by a two-thirds majority of members present and voting. The creation of the Council would accord human rights a more authoritative position, corresponding to the primacy of human rights in the Charter of the United Nations. Member States should determine the composition of the Council and the term of office of its members. Those elected to the Council should undertake to abide by the highest human rights standards.

The idea of creating a new Human Rights Council was endorsed by states in the General Assembly at the 2005 World Summit,[170] but several more months were needed to negotiate the Council's more specific details. Eventually, in March 2006, a resolution creating the Human Rights Council was adopted by the General Assembly by a recorded vote of 170 to four with three abstentions, with Israel, the Marshall Islands, Palau, and the United States voting against:

Human Rights Council, GA Res 60/251 (2006), UN Doc A/RES/60/251, reprinted in UN GAOR, 60th Sess, Supp No 49, vol III at 2–5, UN Doc. A/60/49 (2006)

The General Assembly,

Reaffirming the purposes and principles contained in the Charter of the United Nations, including developing friendly relations among nations based on respect for the principle of equal rights and self-determination of peoples, achieving international cooperation in solving international problems of an economic, social, cultural or humanitarian character and in promoting and encouraging respect for human rights and fundamental freedoms for all,

Reaffirming also the Universal Declaration of Human Rights, and the Vienna Declaration and Programme of Action, and recalling the International Covenant on Civil and Political Rights, the International Covenant on Economic, Social and Cultural Rights and other human rights instruments,

Reaffirming further that all human rights are universal, indivisible, interrelated, interdependent and mutually reinforcing and that all human rights must be treated in a fair and equal manner, on the same footing and with the same emphasis,

Reaffirming that while the significance of national and regional particularities and various historical, cultural and religious backgrounds must be borne in mind, all States, regardless of their political, economic and cultural systems, have the duty to promote and protect all human rights and fundamental freedoms,

---

170 *2005 World Summit Outcome*, GA Res 60/1 (2005), UN Doc A/RES/60/1, reprinted in UN GAOR, 60th Sess, Supp No 49, vol I at 3–25, UN Doc A/60/49 (2006), paras 157–59.

Emphasizing the responsibilities of all States, in conformity with the Charter, to respect human rights and fundamental freedoms for all, without distinction of any kind as to race, colour, sex, language or religion, political or other opinion, national or social origin, property, birth or other status,

Acknowledging that peace and security, development and human rights are the pillars of the United Nations system and the foundations for collective security and well-being, and recognizing that development, peace and security and human rights are interlinked and mutually reinforcing,

Affirming the need for all States to continue international efforts to enhance dialogue and broaden understanding among civilizations, cultures and religions, and emphasizing that States, regional organizations, non-governmental organizations, religious bodies and the media have an important role to play in promoting tolerance, respect for and freedom of religion and belief,

Recognizing the work undertaken by the United Nations Commission on Human Rights and the need to preserve and build on its achievements and to redress its shortcomings,

Recognizing also the importance of ensuring universality, objectivity and non-selectivity in the consideration of human rights issues, and the elimination of double standards and politicization,

Recognizing further that the promotion and protection of human rights should be based on the principles of cooperation and genuine dialogue and aimed at strengthening the capacity of Member States to comply with their human rights obligations for the benefit of all human beings,

Acknowledging that non-governmental organizations play an important role at the national, regional and international levels, in the promotion and protection of human rights,

Reaffirming the commitment to strengthen the United Nations human rights machinery, with the aim of ensuring effective enjoyment by all of all human rights, civil, political, economic, social and cultural rights, including the right to development, and to that end, the resolve to create a Human Rights Council,

1. Decides to establish the Human Rights Council, based in Geneva, in replacement of the Commission on Human Rights, as a subsidiary organ of the General Assembly; the Assembly shall review the status within five years;

2. Decides that the Council will be responsible for promoting universal respect for the protection of all human rights and fundamental freedoms for all, without distinction of any kind and in a fair and equal manner;

3. Also decides that the Council should address situations of violations of human rights, including gross and systematic violations, and make recommendations thereon. It should also promote effective coordination and the mainstreaming of human rights within the United Nations system;

4. Further decides that the work of the Council shall be guided by the principles of universality, impartiality, objectivity and non-selectivity, constructive international dialogue and cooperation, with a view to enhancing the promotion and protection of all human rights, civil, political, economic, social and cultural rights, including the right to development;

5. Decides that the Council will, *inter alia*:

(a) Promote human rights education and learning as well as advisory services, technical assistance and capacity-building, to be provided in consultation with and with the consent of Member States concerned;

(b) Serve as a forum for dialogue on thematic issues on all human rights;

(c) Make recommendations to the General Assembly for the further development of international law in the field of human rights;

(d) Promote the full implementation of human rights obligations undertaken by States and follow-up to the goals and commitments related to the promotion and protection of human rights emanating from United Nations conferences and summits;

(e) Undertake a universal periodic review, based on objective and reliable information, of the fulfilment by each State of its human rights obligations and commitments in a manner which ensures universality of coverage and equal treatment with respect to all States; the review shall be a cooperative mechanism, based on an interactive dialogue, with the full involvement of the country concerned and with consideration given to its capacity-building needs; such a mechanism shall complement and not duplicate the work of treaty bodies; the Council shall develop the modalities and necessary time allocation of the universal periodic review mechanism within one year after the holding of its first session;

(f) Contribute, through dialogue and cooperation, towards the prevention of human rights violations and respond promptly to human rights emergencies;

(g) Assume the role and responsibilities of the Commission on Human Rights relating to the work of the Office of the United Nations High Commissioner for Human Rights, as decided by the General Assembly in its resolution 48/141 of 20 December 1993;

(h) Work in close cooperation in the field of human rights with Governments, regional organizations, national human rights institutions and civil society;

(i) Make recommendations with regard to the promotion and protection of human rights;

(j) Submit an annual report to the General Assembly;

6. Decides also that the Council will assume, review and, where necessary, improve and rationalize all mandates, mechanisms, functions and responsibilities of the Commission on Human Rights in order to maintain a system of special procedures, expert advice and complaint procedure; the Council shall complete this review within one year after the holding of its first session;

7. Decides further that the Council shall consist of 47 Member States, which shall be elected directly and individually by secret ballot by the majority of the members of the General Assembly; the membership shall be based on equitable geographical distribution and seats shall be distributed as follows among regional groups: African Group, thirteen; Asian Group, thirteen; Eastern European Group, six; Latin American and Caribbean Group, eight; and Western European and Others Group, seven; the members of the Council will serve for a period of three years and shall not be eligible for immediate re-election after two consecutive terms;

8. Decides that the membership in the Council shall be open to all Member States of the United Nations; when electing members of the Council, Member States shall take into

account the contribution of candidates to the promotion and protection of human rights and their voluntary pledges and commitments made thereto; the General Assembly, by a two-thirds majority of the members present and voting, may suspend the rights of membership in the Council of a member of the Council that commits gross and systematic violations of human rights;

9. Decides also that members elected to the Council shall uphold the highest standards in the promotion and protection of human rights, fully cooperate with the Council and be reviewed under the universal periodic review mechanism during their term of membership;

10. Decides further that the Council shall meet regularly throughout the year and schedule not fewer than three sessions per year, including a main session, for a total duration of no less than ten weeks, and shall be able to hold special sessions, when needed, at the request of a member of the Council with the support of one third of the membership of the Council;

11. Decides that the Council shall apply the rules of procedure established for committees of the General Assembly, as applicable, unless subsequently otherwise decided by the Assembly or the Council, and also decides that the participation of and consultation with observers, including States that are not members of the Council, the specialized agencies, other intergovernmental organizations and national human rights institutions, as well as non-governmental organizations, shall be based on arrangements, including Economic and Social Council resolution 1996/31 of 25 July 1996 and practices observed by the Commission on Human Rights, while ensuring the most effective contribution of these entities;

12. Decides also that the methods of work of the Council shall be transparent, fair and impartial and enable genuine dialogue, be result-oriented, allow subsequent follow-up discussions to recommendations and their implementation and also allow for substantive interaction with special procedures and mechanisms;

13. Recommends the Economic and Social Council to request the Commission on Human Rights to conclude its work at its sixty-second session and to abolish the Commission on 16 June 2006;

14. Decides to elect the new members of the Council; the terms of membership shall be staggered and such decision will be taken for the first election by the drawing of lots, taking into consideration equitable geographical distribution;

15. Decides also that the elections of the first members of the Council shall take place on 9 May 2006 and that the first meeting of the Council shall be convened on 19 June 2006;

16. Decides further that the Council shall review its work and functioning five years after its establishment and report to the General Assembly.

The election of members to the first Human Rights Council was held in May 2006 and its inaugural session was held in June 2006. During its first year of operation, the Council was required by paragraph 6 of General Assembly resolution 60/251, excerpted above, to "assume, review and, where necessary, improve and rationalize all mandates, mechanisms, functions and responsibilities of the Commission on Human Rights in order to maintain a system of special procedures, expert advice and complaint procedure; the Council shall complete this review within one year after the holding of its first session." After a year of intense behind-the-scenes negotiations, a last minute deal was finally reached in June 2007 on an "institution-building package" that added certain refinements to the Council's mandate.

In this institution-building package, one finds the details governing the universal periodic review mechanism and the advisory committee, as well as the details concerning functions once carried out by the former Commission on Human Rights and now assumed by the Council, such as the use of special procedures. The term "special procedures" refers to the mechanisms established by the Commission, now assumed by the Council, to address either country-specific situations or thematic issues in all parts of the world. As of August 2013, there are twelve country-specific mandates and thirty-six thematic mandates, including Special Rapporteurs examining such issues as the right to adequate housing, the independence of judges and lawyers, and the right to food. Various activities are undertaken by the independent experts appointed to carry out the special procedures, including the receipt of specific complaints, the provision of technical assistance, and the conducting of studies and outreach activities.[171]

Institution-building of the United Nations Human Rights Council, HRC Res 5/1 (2007), reprinted in ***Report of the Human Rights Council***, UN GAOR, 62nd Sess, Supp No 53 at 48–83, UN Doc A/62/53 (2007)

II. SPECIAL PROCEDURES

A. Selection and appointment of mandate-holders

39. The following general criteria will be of paramount importance while nominating, selecting and appointing mandate-holders: (a) expertise; (b) experience in the field of the mandate; (c) independence; (d) impartiality; (e) personal integrity; and (f) objectivity.

40. Due consideration should be given to gender balance and equitable geographic representation, as well as to an appropriate representation of different legal systems. . . .

42. The following entities may nominate candidates as special procedures mandate-holders: (a) Governments; (b) Regional Groups operating within the United Nations human rights system; (c) international organizations or their offices (e.g. the Office of the High Commissioner for Human Rights); (d) non-governmental organizations; (e) other human rights bodies; (f) individual nominations.

43. The Office of the High Commissioner for Human Rights shall immediately prepare, maintain and periodically update a public list of eligible candidates in a standardized format, which shall include personal data, areas of expertise and professional experience. Upcoming vacancies of mandates shall be publicized.

---

171 See further, *Manual of Operations of the Special Procedures of the Human Rights Council* (Geneva: UN Office of Human Rights, 2008).

44. The principle of non-accumulation of human rights functions at a time shall be respected.

45. A mandate-holder's tenure in a given function, whether a thematic or country mandate, will be no longer than six years (two terms of three years for thematic mandate-holders).

46. Individuals holding decision-making positions in Government or in any other organization or entity which may give rise to a conflict of interest with the responsibilities inherent to the mandate shall be excluded. Mandate-holders will act in their personal capacity. . . .

B. Review, rationalization and improvement of mandates

54. The review, rationalization and improvement of mandates, as well as the creation of new ones, must be guided by the principles of universality, impartiality, objectivity and nonselectivity, constructive international dialogue and cooperation, with a view to enhancing the promotion and protection of all human rights, civil, political, economic, social and cultural rights, including the right to development.

55. The review, rationalization and improvement of each mandate would take place in the context of the negotiations of the relevant resolutions. An assessment of the mandate may take place in a separate segment of the interactive dialogue between the Council and special procedures mandate-holders.

56. The review, rationalization and improvement of mandates would focus on the relevance, scope and contents of the mandates, having as a framework the internationally recognized human rights standards, the system of special procedures and General Assembly resolution 60/251.

57. Any decision to streamline, merge or possibly discontinue mandates should always be guided by the need for improvement of the enjoyment and protection of human rights.

58. The Council should always strive for improvements:
   (a) Mandates should always offer a clear prospect of an increased level of human rights protection and promotion as well as being coherent within the system of human rights;
   (b) Equal attention should be paid to all human rights. The balance of thematic mandates should broadly reflect the accepted equal importance of civil, political, economic, social and cultural rights, including the right to development;
   (c) Every effort should be made to avoid unnecessary duplication;
   (d) Areas which constitute thematic gaps will be identified and addressed, including by means other than the creation of special procedures mandates, such as by expanding an existing mandate, bringing a cross-cutting issue to the attention of mandate-holders or by requesting a joint action to the relevant mandate-holders;
   (e) Any consideration of merging mandates should have regard to the content and predominant functions of each mandate, as well as to the workload of individual mandate-holders;

(f) In creating or reviewing mandates, efforts should be made to identify whether the structure of the mechanism (expert, rapporteur or working group) is the most effective in terms of increasing human rights protection;

(g) New mandates should be as clear and specific as possible, so as to avoid ambiguity.

59. It should be considered desirable to have a uniform nomenclature of mandate-holders, titles of mandates as well as a selection and appointment process, to make the whole system more understandable.

60. Thematic mandate periods will be of three years. Country mandate periods will be of one year. . . .

62. Current mandate-holders may continue serving, provided they have not exceeded the six-year term limit . . . . On an exceptional basis, the term of those mandate-holders who have served more than six years may be extended until the relevant mandate is considered by the Council and the selection and appointment process has concluded.

63. Decisions to create, review or discontinue country mandates should also take into account the principles of cooperation and genuine dialogue aimed at strengthening the capacity of Member States to comply with their human rights obligations.

64. In case of situations of violations of human rights or a lack of cooperation that require the Council's attention, the principles of objectivity, non-selectivity, and the elimination of double standards and politicization should apply.

HRC resolution 5/1 also confirmed that the Council would have a complaint procedure "to address consistent patterns of gross and reliably attested violations of all human rights and all fundamental freedoms occurring in any part of the world and under any circumstances," building upon what was known as the "1503 Procedure" of the former Commission on Human Rights.[172]

ii) Canada and the Universal Periodic Review Mechanism

The universal periodic review mechanism, introduced in 2006, is a state-driven process, occurring on a cyclical basis, with every UN member state undergoing a review of its human rights record once every four years. No other universal mechanism of this kind exists, with the treaty-monitoring bodies only able to review the human rights records of those states that are treaty parties.

The output of the treaty-monitoring bodies may, however, be considered by states in preparing for the universal periodic review, along with the views of stakeholders. The state under review also presents a written report on the actions it has taken to improve its human rights record. The actual review takes place orally, during a three-hour process of "interactive dialogue" that allows states to make various recommendations to the state under review for the improvement of its human rights record. At the conclusion of the process, a report is made available, summarizing the recommendations made and asking the state for its response.

---

172 With reference to ECOSOC resolution 1503 (XLVIII) of 27 May 1970, as revised by resolution 2000/3 of 19 June 2000.

During its first review in February 2009, Canada received sixty-eight recommendations, some of which were accepted while others were not. A similar number of recommendations were made during Canada's second review in April 2013. Canada used the latter opportunity to draw attention to developments that had taken place since the first review, focusing on five specific areas of its human rights record, namely: the relationship with Aboriginal peoples; violence against women and children; Canada's social protection framework; immigration and refugee protection; and national security and public safety. Canada's opening statement at its 2013 review is recorded as follows:

Report of the Working Group on the Universal Periodic Review: Canada, UN Doc A/HRC/ 24/11 (2013)

6. Human rights are protected by constitutional and legislative measures, and advanced through policies and programmes. All levels of government cooperate to ensure protections are in place across the country. Where Canadians consider themselves to be subject to a rights violation, avenues for redress are well established and openly accessible.

7. She [the head of the Canadian delegation] outlined some developments since the last universal periodic review, reporting that Canada ratified the Convention on the Rights of Persons with Disabilities (CRPD) in 2010.

8. Efforts to strengthen the relationship between Aboriginal peoples and other Canadians are fundamental to reconciliation and to paving the way for the full participation of Aboriginal people in the social, economic and cultural prosperity of Canada.

9. Equality between men and women is central to Canada's foreign and domestic policies. The rights of women and girls are firmly entrenched in Canada's Constitution and Canada is committed to improving their lives, particularly ending all forms of violence against women.

10. Canada's approach includes a combination of responses to prevent and reduce violence against women and children; provide health and social assistance to those affected by it; and hold the perpetrators accountable. Addressing violence against Aboriginal women and girls is an important priority and Canada continues to take concrete steps to address this complex issue.

11. Canada continues to strengthen its comprehensive social protection framework and advance social innovation so that all individuals and communities can reach their full potential. Addressing disparity focuses on providing individuals with the opportunity to achieve independence and find long-term solutions through appropriate employment, income, housing, education and health supports.

12. Canada's generous system provides asylum to persons in need of international protection. Persons that obtain the status of refugees can become permanent residents and apply for Canadian citizenship. A network of assistance and religious organizations assists their integration.

13. Canada's police, correctional services and institutions responsible for national security and public safety are firmly committed to ensuring safety with due respect for human rights. Oversight is available to ensure that public security activities are in line with na-

tional and international obligations, and redress is available for upheld complaints. Canada believes that public outreach awareness and the active participation of all its citizens on national security issues, are important.

Canada's response to the various recommendations made by states during its second universal periodic review was due in September 2013.

b) Other UN Charter-Based Bodies

The Human Rights Council is one among several UN Charter-based bodies with a human rights focus. There are, for example, other commissions created by ECOSOC, such as the UN Commission on the Status of Women; or, within the UN Secretariat, there is the Office of the UN High Commissioner for Human Rights.

> **Mark Freeman & Gibran van Ert,** *International Human Rights Law* (Toronto: Irwin Law, 2004) at 407–10[173]
>
> 2) The Commission on the Status of Women
>
> ECOSOC created the Commission on the Status of Women in 1946 and mandated it to "prepare recommendations and reports to ECOSOC on promoting women's rights in political, economic, social and educational fields" and "make recommendations to ECOSOC on urgent problems." The Commission is composed of forty-five states, each elected by ECOSOC according to criteria of equitable geographical representation.
>
> The Commission meets in regular session once a year. Since 1995, the Commission has focused on enhancing the follow-up process to the Fourth World Conference on Women (1995), by regularly reviewing and reporting on the level of implementation of the Beijing Declaration and Platform for Action that was adopted at the Conference. The Commission's focus has tended to be on standard-setting rather than on responding to specific violations of women's human rights. Since 1984, however, the Commission has operated a procedure to handle complaints relating to violations of women's human rights. The procedure, which is entirely confidential, is similar in many respects to the Commission on Human Rights' 1503 procedure. The UN Division for the Advancement of Women conducts the initial screen of relevant communications, and provides an opportunity for the implicated state to reply to the allegations. Original communications and state replies are then forwarded to the Commission's Working Group on Communications, which prepares and submits a report to the full Commission. The Commission may then make recommendations to ECOSOC aimed at identifying and responding to the situations revealed by the communications. No decisions are taken on the merits of any individual case . . . .

C. OFFICE OF THE HIGH COMMISSIONER FOR HUMAN RIGHTS

1) Establishment of the OHCHR

On 25 June 1993, at the [United Nation's] Second World Conference on Human Rights, the representatives of 171 states with pressure and encouragement from hundreds of

---

173 Copyright Irwin Law, Inc. Reprinted with permission.

NGOs—adopted by consensus the Vienna Declaration and Programme of Action 1993. The Declaration was intended to serve as a global agenda for enhancing human rights norms and procedures. Perhaps the most important of the Declaration's recommendations was the creation of the Office of the High Commissioner for Human Rights (OHCHR). The following December, General Assembly Resolution 48/141 established the High Commissioner as the UN official with principal responsibility for human rights activities, albeit "under the direction and authority of the Secretary-General" and "within the framework of the overall competence, authority and decisions of the General Assembly, the Economic and Social Council and the Commission on Human Rights."

The OHCHR is based in Geneva. It is part of the UN Secretariat. Functions of the OHCHR include: providing substantive support to treaty bodies, the Commission on Human Rights, the Sub-Commission on the Promotion and Protection of Human Rights, and related bodies; preparing research and reports; reviewing complaints of human rights violations; providing advisory services and technical assistance to governments; and supporting human rights field presences and missions.

2) Role of the High Commissioner

The UN Secretary-General, with the approval of the General Assembly, appoints the High Commissioner for a four-year term [with the possibility of extensions]. The High Commissioner has the rank of an Under Secretary-General of the UN. The first High Commissioner, Jose Ayala Lasso, formerly Ecuador's Permanent Representative to the UN, assumed office in the spring of 1994. Mary Robinson, a former President of Ireland, succeeded him in 1997. Sergio Vieira de Mello, a Brazilian with significant prior UN experience, succeeded her in 2002. Vieira de Mello was killed in a bomb attack in Iraq in August 2003 while he was serving as Special Representative of the Secretary-General in Iraq. Louise Arbour, formerly the lCTY's Chief Prosecutor and most recently a justice of the Supreme Court of Canada, was appointed as the new High Commissioner in February 2004 and took up her post in July 2004. [Justice Arbour completed her term as UN High Commissioner in 2008 and was succeeded by former ICTR and ICC Judge Navanethem Pillay of South Africa.]

The High Commissioner runs the OHCHR under the authority and direction of the Secretary-General. He or she also engages in dialogue with governments to secure respect for human rights. Commissioners serve in their personal capacity and not on behalf of any particular government or state. At their most influential, they can have something close to the profile of the UN Secretary-General, in effect speaking and acting as the voice and conscience of human rights victims around the world. High Commissioners can also work more discretely, for example, by inquiring about political prisoners to government officials in the course of official visits. The position requires a strong combination of advocacy and diplomacy skills.

3) OHCHR Technical Cooperation

Technical co-operation is one of the key areas of OHCHR human rights activity. The UN Technical Co-operation Programme in the Field of Human Rights helps states build and strengthen domestic human rights mechanisms such as human rights commissions. The Programme also works on the incorporation of human rights standards into domestic laws and policies and the formulation of national plans of action for the promotion and protection of human rights. Technical co-operation takes the form of expert advisory services, training courses, workshops, fellowships, grants, provision of information and documentation, and assessment of domestic human rights needs. At present, the OHCHR operates dozens of technical co-operation projects, primarily in the developing world.

4) Human Rights Field Presences

The OHCHR maintains or supports a number of field offices and operations responsible for monitoring human rights situations and capacity building in particular countries. The earliest human rights field presences were created prior to the establishment of the OHCHR by UN political departments (for example, El Salvador in 1991) and regional bodies like the OAS (for example, Haiti in 1992). Following its inauguration in 1994, the OHCHR began to establish its own human rights field presences independent of UN peacekeeping, peacemaking, and peacebuilding missions. The first one was established in Rwanda in late 1994 shortly after the genocide there. Since then, human rights field operations have been established by various procedures, including at the initiative of the Security Council (for example, Angola), at the initiative of the UN General Assembly (for example, the civilian mission in Guatemala), at the request of the Commission on Human Rights (for example, the former Yugoslavia), or within the framework of bilateral agreements between the OHCHR and individual states (for example, Colombia). As a rule, the tasks of a UN human rights field operation include monitoring, investigating, and reporting on the human rights situation on the ground, and improving local capacity in human rights protection. Because they are nearer to victims, field operations may constitute the most important and effective human rights activities carried out by the UN. There is, however, an ongoing challenge to ensure greater use of the information and experience gained in the field for purposes of decision-making at UN headquarters. Also, the effectiveness of UN human rights field operations is often hampered by vague mandates and unstable funding arrangements.

3) Regional Bodies

In addition to the institutions at the UN level for the promotion and protection of human rights, there are several more institutions at the regional level aimed at encouraging compliance with human rights obligations. For example, Canada has consented to a right of individual petition before the Inter-American Commission on Human Rights through its membership in the Organization of American States (OAS).[174] These regional institutions

---

174 Although Canada became a member of the OAS in 1990, it was not until October 2003 that a petition lodged against Canada within the inter-American system was declared admissible: see *Grand Chief Michael Mitchell v Canada*, Report No 74/03, Petition 790/01 (22 October 2003), reported in *Annual Report of the Inter-American Commission on Human Rights 2003*, OAS Doc OEA/Ser.L/V/II.118, Doc 5 Rev 2 (2003) at III.C.2. The Commission's final decision on the merits, finding that it was not proven that the petitioners' cultural rights under article 13 of the American Declaration had been violated, is recorded in *Grand Chief Michael Mitchell v Canada*, Report No 61/08, Case 12.435, reproduced in *Annual Report of the Inter-American Commission on Human Rights 2008*, OAS Doc OEA/Ser.L/V/II.134, Doc 5 rev 1 (2009) at III.C.5.

may also serve as a source of comparative guidance, given the similarities among the rights protected by the UN and regional instruments. Canadian courts, for example, have shown some interest in the jurisprudence of the European Court of Human Rights, albeit as a source of comparative constitutional law, rather than international law per se, given the incorporation of the ECHR[175] into the domestic law of its states parties. We close this chapter with the following discussion of the institutional frameworks erected under the inter-American, European, and African human rights systems:

Mark Freeman & Gibran van Ert, *International Human Rights Law* **(Toronto: Irwin Law, 2004) at 425–37, 438–42, and 447–52**[176]

A. THE INTER-AMERICAN SYSTEM

The OAS is the oldest of all regional organizations. All thirty-five independent states in the Western hemisphere—almost all of them democratically governed—are OAS members. Canada became a Permanent Observer to the OAS in 1972, and has been a full member since 1990. Shortly after becoming a member, Canada took a lead role on various human rights issues within the OAS.

The OAS consists of two main bodies: the General Assembly and Permanent Council. The Assembly meets annually in a regularly scheduled session, but also on an *ad hoc* basis as necessary. It is responsible for setting most OAS policy and is roughly equivalent to the UN General Assembly. The Council is the chief decision-making branch of the organization, especially when the General Assembly is not in session. It is the OAS equivalent to the UN Security Council. Both the OAS General Assembly and Permanent Council have authority to deal with human rights issues . . . .

The primary OAS mechanisms for the promotion and protection of human rights are the Inter-American Commission on Human Rights and the Inter-American Court of Human Rights. The Inter-American Commission on Human Rights has jurisdiction to receive cases based on the AmDR [American Declaration of the Rights and Duties of Man] and the ACHR [American Convention on Human Rights], while the Inter-American Court of Human Rights has jurisdiction to receive cases based exclusively on the ACHR. Unlike the UN system, the OAS does not establish a separate treaty body for each of its human rights treaties, but rather situates them within the existing authority and procedures of the Inter-American Court and Commission, as the case may be. This is a far more efficient arrangement.

1) The Inter-American Commission on Human Rights

The Inter-American Commission on Human Rights was established in 1959 by the OAS Permanent Council, a decade before the ACHR was adopted. In 1965, OAS member states authorized it to examine communications regarding alleged human rights violations. The Commission functioned as an "autonomous entity" of the OAS until the Protocol of Bue-

---

175 Above note 57.
176 Copyright Irwin Law, Inc. Reprinted with permission. Original footnotes omitted (footnotes appearing in the following excerpt are by the present authors).

nos Aires 1967 came into effect in 1970, making it an official OAS Charter organ with responsibility for the promotion and protection of human rights.

Today the Commission, which is based in Washington, D.C., reviews alleged violations of the OAS Charter and the AmDR by OAS member states, and of the ACHR by its states parties. Thus, it has two distinct if overlapping roles: one as a "Charter organ" vis-à-vis all OAS member states and one as a "Convention organ" in respect of ACHR states parties. The Commission has seven members. They are elected by the member states of the OAS and serve in their personal capacity. Commissioners are assisted by a small permanent staff and perform their duties in two annual sessions of three weeks' duration each.

The Commission has played a significant role in the promotion and protection of human rights in the Americas, particularly in the last twenty years. Among other things, it has conducted important on-site investigations and published damning reports on the state of human rights in particular countries. Today most of its work is focused on individual petitions. There have been no inter-state petitions submitted to the Commission thus far. And unlike the UN treaty body system, there is no obligatory state reporting procedure contemplated by the OAS Charter or the ACHR.

a) The Commission as a Charter Organ

The Commission has a number of functions in its capacity as a Charter organ, including assisting in the development of human rights instruments, providing advice *to* the OAS Permanent Council and General Assembly, mediating human rights issues in contexts of war *or* internal tensions, and preparing special resolutions and reports on specific regional issues. It also undertakes country studies and in-country investigations in the event of serious concerns about a general *or* particular human rights situation in an OAS member state.

The Commission has created its own robust Rules of Procedure to govern in-country missions. Missions are conditional upon receipt of an invitation from the government in question or its prior consent in "serious and urgent cases." In some cases, the Commission may publish a report based on investigations conducted outside the concerned state where that state refuses an in-country mission. Article 54 of the Rules of Procedure compels governments to assist the members of a visiting mission, and to refrain from adverse measures against those who co-operate with it. Article 55 of the Rules allows mission members to travel freely within the host country and to meet anyone, including prisoners. It also requires the host country to co-operate with requests for information and ensure the mission's safety during the investigation. Following the conclusion of an in-country investigation, the mission presents a draft report for confidential comment by the concerned government. If the government fails to respond, the Commission must publish the report; if there is a response then publication of the report is optional. To date, Canada has only been the subject of one in-country investigation by the Inter-American Commission on Human Rights [dealing with asylum and the refugee system].

In its capacity as a Charter organ, the Commission is also authorized to receive individual petitions under article 20 of its Statute. Petitions may be resolved by friendly settlement or decided on the merits. The procedure for handling individual petitions is very similar to the procedure for handling ACHR-based petitions, discussed immediately below. The major difference is that Charter-based petitions may not be referred to the Inter-American Court of Human Rights. The Commission simply publishes its conclusions and recommendations and forwards them to the parties and the OAS General Assembly . . . .

b) The Commission as a Convention Organ

In its capacity as a Convention organ, the Commission exercises many of the same functions as it does in its capacity as a Charter organ. It participates in the development of human rights instruments, assists the OAS Permanent Council and General Assembly, mediates human rights crises, and carries out in-country investigations.

However, ACHR articles 44–51 establish a distinct individual and inter-state complaints procedure before the Commission for states parties to the ACHR. Article 44 permits any individual, group, or recognized NGO to submit an individual complaint to the Commission regarding a violation by any ACHR state party. Article 45 permits a state party to submit a complaint against another state party, provided that both states have accepted the Commission's jurisdiction over inter-state complaints. Articles 46 and 47 provide a standard set of rules of admissibility applicable to individual and inter-state complaints. In contrast to UN treaty body rules of admissibility, ACHR article 46(1)(b) requires a complaint to be filed with the Commission "within a period of six months from the date on which the party alleging violation of his rights was notified of the final judgment" at the domestic level. Provisional measures are available in particularly serious and urgent cases to prevent irreparable harm.

ACHR articles 48–51 govern complaint resolution. The Commission reviews and investigates the facts alleged in an admissible complaint and then holds hearings in which both parties participate. If a friendly settlement is reached, the Commission draws up a report setting out the facts and the solution. Friendly settlements have often provided for multiple remedies, including significant compensatory damages. Where a friendly settlement is not achieved, the Commission may give the respondent state its conclusions and recommendations in private in the form of a preliminary report, permitting the state a brief time to comply or contest. When the time runs out, the Commission may do one of two things: deliver a final report which, in the event of further non-compliance, the Commission will usually make public; or take the case to the Inter-American Court of Human Rights, provided that it does so within three months of the delivery of its preliminary report and provided that the state has declared its acceptance of the Court's jurisdiction. Individual complainants may not refer cases to the Court; only the Commission or a state party may do so. Where the Commission refers a case to the Court, it must appear before the Court. Its function there is much like a *Ministerio Publico* in a civil law system; the Commission strives to protect the integrity of the legal order and to ensure the proper application of the ACHR, and not to advance the interests of any party.

The conclusions and recommendations of the Commission in contentious cases carry significant weight, but do not bind states in the judicial sense. The Inter-American Court of Human Rights has, however, stated that

> in accordance with the principle of good faith . . . . if a State signs and ratifies an international treaty, especially one concerning human rights, such as the American Convention, it has the obligation to make every effort to comply with the recommendations of a protection organ such as the Inter-American Commission . . . .

c) The Commission and other OAS Human Rights Treaties

The Inter-American Commission on Human Rights also plays an important supervisory role concerning other OAS human rights treaties. For instance, pursuant to article 13 of the Inter-American Convention on the Forced Disappearance of Persons 1994, individuals may submit complaints to the Commission alleging the forced disappearance of persons. The complaints are subject to the same procedures established in the ACHR and in the Commission's and Court's respective statutes, regulations, and rules of procedure. Article 12 of the Inter-American Convention on the Prevention, Punishment and Eradication of Violence against Women 1994 provides much the same. By contrast, individual petitions before the Commission are not possible under the Inter-American Convention to Prevent and Punish Torture 1985, although there is a state reporting obligation and a corresponding supervisory function for the Commission.

The Additional Protocol to the ACHR in the area of Economic, Social, and Cultural Rights 1988 (ACHR-OPl) also requires state parties to submit periodic performance reports. It authorizes the Inter-American Commission on Human Rights to make observations and recommendations on those reports and on state performance generally. ACHR-OPI article 19(6) authorizes the Commission (and when applicable, the Court) to process individual petitions, but only with respect to the right to unionize (article 8(l)(a)) and the right to education (article 13). These petitions are handled according to the same procedures applicable to complaints under the ACHR.

To date, Canada is not party to any of these treaties and hence is not subject to such procedures.

d) Special Rapporteurs of the Commission

In 1994, the Commission established the permanent office of the Rapporteurship on the Rights of Women. The Rapporteurship publishes thematic studies, assists in developing the Commission's jurisprudence concerning the rights of women, and examines issues affecting women's rights in specific countries through in-country missions and reports. In 2002, the Rapporteurship conducted its first independent in-country mission, for the purpose of investigating the situation in Ciudad Juarez, Mexico where hundreds of women have been killed or disappeared in recent years.

In 1998, the Commission created the permanent office of the Special Rapporteur for Freedom of Expression. The Special Rapporteur provides legal assistance to the Commission and to OAS member states, carries out promotion and protection activities concerning freedom of expression, conducts visits to member states, and publishes thematic, country, and annual reports.

2) The Inter-American Court of Human Rights

The Inter-American Court of Human Rights was established in 1979 under the ACHR. Today, it has its own Statute and Rules of Procedure. The Court is composed of seven judges elected by ACHR states parties. It is based in San Jose, Costa Rica. Nationals of any OAS member state may sit on the Court, whether or not their state is party to the ACHR. To date, no Canadians have served as judges on the Court. The judges sit on a part-time basis only; as the Court is only in session for approximately ten weeks each year. The Court is assisted by the Inter-American Institute for Human Rights, an autonomous human rights education and research centre based, like the Court, in San Jose.

The Court only has jurisdiction over ACHR states parties that have accepted its compulsory jurisdiction under ACHR articles 48 and 50. Like most supranational tribunals, the Inter-American Court of Human Rights exercises both advisory and contentious jurisdiction. In contrast to the European Court of Human Rights [of today], however, individuals and NGOs may not submit petitions before the Court. Instead, contentious cases may only be initiated by ACHR states parties or by the Inter-American Commission on Human Rights. To date, no ACHR state party has submitted a case to the Court against another state party. Thus, all of the contentious judgments rendered by the Court so far have been initiated by the Commission. Advisory cases may be initiated by any OAS member state (including non-parties to the ACHR like Canada) or by certain OAS organs. The cases may relate to the ACHR or to "other treaties concerning the protection of human rights in the American states." ACHR article 63(1) permits the Court broad discretion to impose remedies. It provides:

> If the Court finds that there has been a violation of a right or freedom protected by this Convention, the Court shall rule that the injured party be ensured the enjoyment of his right or freedom that was violated. It shall also rule, if appropriate, that the consequences of the measure or situation that constituted the breach of such right or freedom be remedied and that fair compensation be paid to the injured party.

Among other things, the Court has required states to change legislation to make it compatible with the ACHR. It has ordered a wide variety of non-monetary remedies including orders for restitution of rights or property; acknowledgment of wrongdoing, public investigation, punishment of the perpetrator, medical treatment for the victim, and measures to guarantee non-repetition of the violation. The Court has also ordered payment of specific damages for pecuniary and non-pecuniary injuries. As a rule, the question of damages is handled in a second phase of proceedings following judgment on the merits. Where possible, the Court allows the parties to settle the quantum among themselves, limiting its role to verification of the fairness of any settlement. In a number of recent cases brought by the Inter-American Commission on Human Rights, states have conceded responsibility for violations of the ACHR and left it to the Court to determine the quantum of damages to be awarded to victims. At any stage of its proceedings, the Court may also order provisional measures.

In making its judgments, the Court is at liberty to reverse the Commission's findings of fact or law: Since there is no appeals chamber, all of the Court's judgments are final and not subject to appeal. The Court is required to inform the OAS General Assembly of cases of non-compliance with its decisions, but there is no mechanism to ensure enforcement of the Court's decisions. As a result, the Court keeps cases open until the state party in question has fully complied with the judgment. During the last ten years, the record of state compliance with adverse judgments has been encouraging.

In contrast to the Commission — which has rendered hundreds of findings in individual cases — the Court has rendered relatively few judgments to date. While the Court's caseload remains quite small, it is growing, due largely to the active human rights NGO movement in Latin America. The most significant contentious judgments rendered by the Court remain its early judgments in the so-called "Honduran Disappearance Cases." These were the first international judgments dealing with forced disappearance and led to groundbreaking rulings on the nature of state obligations. Since then, the Court has rendered major judgments on issues such as *habeas corpus* guarantees in states of emergency, the death penalty, and the abduction, torture, and murder of street children by police officers.

While the jurisprudence of the Court is somewhat underdeveloped in comparison to that of the European Court of Human Rights, it has greater expertise in human rights matters that have arisen more frequently in OAS member states than in Europe, such as forced disappearances and amnesty laws. It has also developed a much richer jurisprudence of remedies. Today, as democratic practices consolidate throughout the Americas, the Court's docket is starting to focus on less extreme types of violations ranging from wrongful dismissal of judges to film censorship.

B.   EUROPEAN SYSTEMS

. . .

a)   The European Court of Human Rights

. . . The European Court of Human Rights is currently the only supranational human rights tribunal in the world that permits individuals to make direct claims against member states. In contrast to the Inter-American Court, the jurisdiction of the European Court is compulsory for all ECHR states parties. The Court's . . . [47] judges are elected for renewable six-year terms from a list of nominees submitted by ECHR states parties. Nominees do not need to be nationals of a Council of Europe member state. Unlike the Inter-American Court, the European Court of Human Rights sits on a permanent rather than part-time basis. . . . [It generally sits in committees of three and chambers of seven judges, with special provision made for the use of a Grand Chamber of 17 judges in certain circumstances.] The Court has jurisdiction over all aspects of a case, including admissibility, fact-finding, and decisions on the merits. Like other supranational courts, it exercises both contentious and advisory jurisdiction. By most accounts, its jurisprudence has had a powerful influence on European states.

Both individuals and states have the right to bring contentious cases before the Court. In inter-state cases the applicant state does not need to have a relationship to the actual victim of the violation to bring the case. The only admissibility requirement for such cases is exhaustion of domestic remedies. States parties rarely invoke the inter-state complaint mechanism.

In petitions brought by private parties against states, ECHR article 34 provides that the Court may receive petitions from "any person, non-governmental organization or group of individuals," including legal persons, claiming to be a victim of a violation by an ECHR state party. An individual need not file claims against the state of his or her nationality; claims can be made against any ECHR state party. Thus, a national of state A can file an application against state B if the latter was the state responsible for the alleged violation. The admissibility requirements for bringing a case before the Court are virtually the same as those for UN treaty bodies.

Once a claim is deemed admissible, it is the responsibility of the Court to "pursue the examination of the case," including if necessary by investigation. If a friendly settlement is reached, the Court must issue a decision setting out the facts and the solution reached in order to facilitate the Committee of Ministers' enforcement of the settlement. Failing a friendly settlement, a hearing may be held. The hearing must be held in public, other than in "exceptional circumstances." Decisions of Chambers may be appealed to the Grand Chamber at its discretion within three months of judgment, but only if the case involves "a serious question affecting the interpretation or application of the Convention or the protocols thereto, or a serious issue of general importance" (article 43(2)).

While there is no rule of *stare decisis* (binding precedent) applicable to the judgments of the European Court of Human Rights, the Court nevertheless tends to follow its own case law. The largest share of cases has involved claims arising under ECHR articles 5 (right to liberty and security of the person) and 6 (right to a fair hearing). Upon a finding of violation, the Court may afford "just satisfaction" (article 41) to the injured party. This may include a declaration or finding of breach (a moral remedy) or compensation for pecuniary and non-pecuniary harm (a material remedy). The Court cannot reverse national judicial decisions or annul national laws but it can declare a national law in conflict with the ECHR and call for the adoption of new legislation. In deciding whether there has been a violation at all, the Court allows states parties a "margin of appreciation" (that is, a degree of deference to local standards and approaches).

Concerning its advisory jurisdiction, only the Committee of Ministers may request advisory opinions from the Court [although a protocol adopted in 2013 will allow the highest courts and tribunals of states parties to request that the Court give advisory opinions].[177] Such opinions may not deal with

> any question relating to the content or scope of the rights or freedoms defined in Section I of the Convention and the protocols thereto, or with any other question which the European Court of Human Rights or the Committee of Ministers might have to consider in consequence of any such proceedings as could be instituted in accordance with the Convention.

Although the Court lacks a formal mechanism for enforcement of its decisions, to date the record of compliance with its judgments has been exemplary. In the event of non-compliance with a judgment of the Court, the matter goes onto the agenda of the [Council of Europe's] Committee of Ministers within six months. The [Council of Europe's] Parliamentary Assembly assists with the enforcement of judgments via its Assembly Monitoring Committee, which may adopt adverse resolutions and remove a state delegation's credentials.

The current challenge for the Court is dealing with the backlog of cases that resulted from the enormous expansion in its caseload. . . . The Court receives more than 30,000 petitions every year, almost half of which indicate a *prima facie* case. Although the Court manages to render hundreds of final judgments each year, and thousands of decisions on admissibility, the situation is not sustainable. As a consequence, the Committee of Ministers established a Steering Committee for Human Rights to propose changes. It recommended urgent reforms that were quickly endorsed by the Committee of Ministers.

---

177 Protocol No 16 to the Convention for the Protection of Human Rights and Fundamental Freedoms, 2 October 2013 (not yet in force).

b) The European Committee of Social Rights

Because it only examines cases involving violations of the ECHR and its protocols, the European Court of Human Rights does not have jurisdiction over violations of economic and social rights. Instead, the EurSC [European Social Charter], the primary Council of Europe treaty dealing with economic, social and cultural rights, established a separate supervisory body, the European Committee of Social Rights. It consists of thirteen independent experts elected by the Committee of Ministers for renewable terms of six years.

The Committee oversees a state party reporting procedure and, since the entry into force of the Additional Protocol Providing for a System of Collective Complaints 1995, a "collective complaints" procedure. Every two years, states parties to the EurSC and its protocols must submit a report on their performance. The Committee then publishes its own "conclusions." If the concerned state fails to address any matter covered in the Committee's conclusions, the Committee of Ministers may issue a "recommendation" to that state calling upon it to do so. The Committee of Ministers' work is prepared by a "Governmental Committee" comprising representatives of the states parties to the EurSC and its protocols, assisted by observers representing European employers' and workers' organizations.

In the collective complaints procedure, certain organizations—notably eligible NGOs and employers' and workers' organizations—are permitted to file complaints with the Committee. Once a complaint has been deemed admissible, there follows an exchange of memorials between the parties, followed by a possible public hearing. Decisions on the merits are communicated to the parties and to the Committee of Ministers, which may ultimately recommend specific measures to remedy any proven violation. The Parliamentary Assembly also receives the decision and makes it public . . . .

C. THE AFRICAN UNION

. . .

1) The . . . African Court on Human and Peoples' Rights

In 1998, the Protocol to the African Charter on Human and Peoples' Rights on the Establishment of an African Court on Human and Peoples' Rights 1998 was adopted. [The Protocol entered into force on 25 January 2004, after attracting the required 15 ratifications, and currently has 26 states parties.] . . . The models for the . . . African Court are the European Court of Human Rights and the Inter-American Court of Human Rights. The Court . . . [is] composed of eleven judges serving for a maximum of two six-year terms. It will exercise contentious and advisory jurisdiction. In contentious cases, only the African Commission on Human and Peoples' Rights, states parties, and "African Intergovernmental Organizations" will have the right to submit cases. NGOs with observer status before the Commission will also be able to submit cases, provided their state has made an appropriate enabling declaration upon becoming a party to the Protocol. The Court will be able to make declaratory judgments and order compensation and reparation. It will also be authorized to issue provisional measures in cases of "extreme gravity and urgency." Judgments will be binding and final since there will be no appeals chamber. The AU [African Union] Council of Ministers will enforce the Court's judgments. In advisory cases, only AU organs, AU member states, and African organizations recognized by the AU will have the authority to request such opinions. The African Court will be able to render advisory opinions

> on any legal matter relating to the [AfrCHPR] or any other relevant human rights instruments, provided that the subject matter of the opinion is not related to a matter being examined by the [African Commission on Human and Peoples' Rights].

The Court's relationship to the African Commission on Human and Peoples' Rights will be much like the relationship between the Inter-American Commission on Human Rights and the Inter-American Court of Human Rights. [Ed note: The African Court on Human and People's Rights officially started its operations in 2006, dealing with operational and administrative issues, including relocation, until 2008. The Court's first judgment was issued in 2009.]

2) The African Commission on Human and Peoples' Rights

. . . [T]he African Commission on Human and Peoples' Rights remains the principal human rights body in the AU system. Established in 1987 and based in Banjul, The Gambia, the Commission is composed of eleven members elected to six-year terms and serving in their personal capacities. Like its counterpart in the Americas, the African Commission has adopted its own Rules of Procedure. It is in session only twice a year and lacks sufficient funding and staff.

The Commission has a very broad promotional mandate. Article 45(1)(a) of the African Charter on Human and Peoples' Rights 1981 (AfrCHPR) includes the following among the functions of the Commission:

> to collect documents, undertake studies and researches on African problems in the field of human and peoples' rights, organize seminars, symposia and conferences, disseminate information, encourage national and local institutions concerned with human and peoples' rights, and should the case arise, give its views or make recommendations to Governments . . . .

In fulfilment of this promotional mandate, the Commission grants "affiliated status" to national human rights commissions or institutions that conform to the Principles relating to the Status of National Institutions (also known as the Paris Principles) adopted in 1993 by the UN General Assembly. Affiliated status entitles national institutions to be invited to sessions of the Commission, to participate without voting rights in Commission deliberations, and to submit proposals which may be put to vote at the request of any Commission member.

The Commission also has jurisdiction to review bi-annual reports submitted by states (AfrCHPR article 62). The examination of reports takes place in a public forum, and only the Commission can put questions to the state. The procedure, which is modelled on the UN treaty body reporting process, suffers from chronic delays in the submission of reports and grudging co-operation by states. About half of all states parties to the AfrCHPR have failed to submit any report at all since 1991 when the procedure was established.

The Commission has jurisdiction to handle both inter-state complaints (AfrCHPR articles 47–54) and individual complaints (AfrCHPR articles 55–56). The inter-state procedure has been invoked only once. Like its regional equivalents, the African inter-state complaints procedure begins when one state delivers a complaint to another state, with a copy to the AU Secretary-General and the Commission. If the matter is not resolved within three months, then the Commission may privately investigate the matter and receive further submissions from each state, before ultimately preparing a report for delivery to the states involved and to the AU Assembly.

The Commission's individual complaints procedure differs from its UN and Inter-American equivalents. On paper, it does not resemble an individual petition procedure at all, but rather something more like the Commission on Human Rights' 1503 Procedure described in Chapter Fourteen. Article 58(1) of the AfrCHPR provides that the Commission can only act upon "special cases which reveal the existence of a series of serious or massive violations of human and peoples' rights," suggesting that a single human rights violation is not enough to trigger the Commission's jurisdiction. In practice the Commission has tended to ignore this language. It has relied on AfrCHPR article 55(2) to justify its consideration of petitions that do not meet the "special case" test.

The Commission can receive communications from individuals and from NGOs with observer status. The Commission will examine complaints regarding violations of any AfrCHPR right. Its rules of admissibility resemble those of UN treaty bodies and other regional equivalents. Upon certifying a complaint as admissible, the Commission will seek an amicable resolution of the matter, failing which it will provide a report of its findings and recommendations to the AU Assembly: There is a requirement of confidentiality throughout the proceedings up until the time the Commission completes its conclusions and recommendations. Officially, decisions of the Commission are to remain confidential until the AU Assembly decides otherwise. However, the Commission now regularly publishes its findings. To date, the Commission has rendered a handful of significant decisions. These have concerned issues such as the criteria for a fair trial, the right to self-determination, and the right to a generally satisfactory environment.

The Commission can also issue something close to advisory opinions on AfrCHPR norms. Specifically; AfrCHPR article 45(3) lists as one of the Commission's functions to "[i]nterpret all the provisions of the present Charter at the request of a State party, an institution of the OAU or an African Organization recognized by the OAU . . . ."

The Commission also has a unique quasi-legislative function. Article 45(1)(b) authorizes it to "formulate and lay down, principles and rules aimed at solving legal problems relating to human and peoples' rights and fundamental freedoms upon which African Governments may base their legislation."

Under AfrCHPR articles 60 and 61, the Commission is permitted to rely on a uniquely broad range of sources in carrying out its tasks, including all significant human rights instruments adopted by the UN and by the AU and, as "subsidiary measures," any relevant African human rights practices.

Overall, the African Commission on Human and Peoples' Rights and the AU human rights system as a whole is notably weaker than its UN and regional equivalents. Yet the Commission is gradually becoming more effective. Among other things, it has begun to undertake fact-finding missions to countries in which there are systematic violations, and to appoint special rapporteurs on key topics including prisons and conditions of detention, arbitrary and summary executions, and the rights of women.

3) The Committee of Experts on the Rights and Welfare of the Child

Article 32 of the African Charter on the Rights and Welfare of the Child 1990 establishes an African Committee of Experts on the Rights and Welfare of the Child. The Committee, which has only recently begun work, consists of eleven independent expert members elected by states parties. States parties are required to provide reports to the Committee every three years concerning their implementation of the treaty (article 43). Individuals, groups, and recognized NGOs may submit confidential communications to the Committee for its consideration (article 44), and the Committee may investigate using "appropriate" methods (article 45).

CHAPTER 10

CONSTRAINTS ON STATE REGULATION OF ECONOMIC ACTIVITY

An essential aspect of a state's sovereignty is the power to determine its own economic system and to regulate economic activity within its territory. Recall that the General Assembly's influential Declaration on Principles of International Law concerning Friendly Relations and Co-operation among States in accordance with the Charter of the United Nations indicates that: "Every State has an inalienable right to choose its . . . economic . . . system, without interference in any form by another State."[1] This is, however, only a starting point. While in theory a state might attempt to insulate its economy from all outside influences by barring all foreign economic activity within its borders and, conversely, forbidding all extraterritorial economic activity by its nationals, in practice, international economic activity is the norm. The international legal issue that therefore arises is the extent to which, and how, states may lawfully exercise jurisdiction over such economic activity. We have already addressed some aspects of this issue in our examination of the general rules of state jurisdiction over persons, property, and transactions (Chapter 7) and of state immunities (Chapter 8). In this chapter, we focus on specific, additional, jurisdictional constraints that states have imposed upon themselves in two main areas of international economic activity: foreign investment and the transborder movement of goods and services.

A. TREATMENT OF FOREIGN INVESTORS

A controversial set of international legal constraints on state jurisdiction over economic activity concerns state expropriation of property owned by foreigners. These limitations form part of a broader body of international law relating to what historically was called the "treatment of aliens," other aspects of which we examine elsewhere.[2]

There is a political dimension to the controversy surrounding the international law governing state expropriation of foreign-owned property: the property in question has usually been located in developing states but owned by investors from developed states. Such "property investments" were a common feature of the colonial period, and often persisted following decolonization. This continuing foreign ownership, along with additional investments following decolonization, has frequently been perceived by newly independent and other developing states as a form of "neo-colonialism." The response of such states has therefore frequently taken the form of nationalization, referring to the

---

1   GA Res 2625 (XXV), UN Doc A/RES/2625/XXV, reprinted in UN GAOR, 25th Sess, Supp No 28 at 121–24, UN Doc A/8028 Corr 1 (1970); (1970) 9 ILM 1292 [Friendly Relations Declaration].
2   See Chapter 9, "Respect for International Human Rights," and Chapter 12, "State Responsibility."

national expropriation of these investments in a bid by the expropriating state to regain control over its natural resources and economic activity.

Given the developed-developing state dimension to the issue, it is no surprise that the international legal rules governing state expropriation of foreign-owned property have been a key point of contention between developed and developing states. Motivated by a desire to create a "New International Economic Order" (NIEO),[3] the UN General Assembly—dominated at that time by newly independent states and confronted with the consequences of the OPEC crisis—adopted a resolution embracing a new Charter of Economic Rights and Duties of States in December 1974.[4] Although a non-legally binding declaratory text, and therefore not a source of international law, the new Charter did reflect clearly the developing world's view of economic sovereignty. Consider the key provisions of Chapter II of the Charter:

Charter of Economic Rights and Duties of States, GA Res 3281 (XXIX) (1974)

Article 1
Every State has the sovereign and inalienable right to choose its economic system as well as its political, social and cultural systems in accordance with the will of its people, without outside interference, coercion or threat in any form whatsoever.

Article 2
1. Every State has and shall freely exercise full permanent sovereignty, including possession, use and disposal, over all its wealth, natural resources and economic activities.

2. Each State has the right:
   (a) To regulate and exercise authority over foreign investment within its national jurisdiction in accordance with its laws and regulations and in conformity with its national objectives and priorities. No State shall be compelled to grant preferential treatment to foreign investment;
   (b) To regulate and supervise the activities of transnational corporations within its national jurisdiction and take measures to ensure that such activities comply with its laws, rules and regulations and conform with its economic and social policies. Transnational corporations shall not intervene in the internal affairs of a host State. Every State should, with full regard for its sovereign rights, cooperate with other States in the exercise of the right set forth in this subparagraph;
   (c) To nationalize, expropriate or transfer ownership of foreign property, in which case appropriate compensation should be paid by the State adopting such measures, taking into account its relevant laws and regulations and all circumstances that the State considers pertinent. In any case where the question of compensation gives rise

---

3 *Declaration on the Establishment of a New International Economic Order*, GA Res 3201 (S-VI), UN Doc A/RES/3201/S-VI, reprinted in UN GAOR, 6th Special Sess, Supp No 1 at 3–5, UN Doc A/9559 (1974). See further, Margot E Salomon, "From NIEO to Now and the Unfinishable Story of Economic Justice" (2013) 62:1 ICLQ 31.

4 GA Res 3281 (XXIX), UN Doc A/RES/3281/XXIX, reprinted in UN GAOR, 29th Sess, Supp No 31 at 50–55, UN Doc A/9631 (1974). See further, SK Chatterjee, "The Charter of Economic Rights and Duties of States: An Evaluation After 15 Years" (1991) 40 ICLQ 669.

to a controversy, it shall be settled under the domestic law of the nationalizing State and by its tribunals, unless it is freely and mutually agreed by all States concerned that other peaceful means be sought on the basis of the sovereign equality of States and in accordance with the principle of free choice of means.

The Charter claimed substantial state freedom to expropriate foreign-owned property within its territory and to decide on the measure of compensation to be paid for such property according to its own laws, policies, and procedures. This approach was and is, however, unattractive to many developed, capital-exporting states. Consider the assertion of a more robust set of customary international rules governing expropriation and compensation in the following arbitral decision of the Iran-United States Claims Tribunal. This arbitral Tribunal was established in 1981 by agreement between Iran and the United States to adjudicate financial claims arising against Iran in the aftermath of the Tehran hostages crisis of 1979, although its jurisprudence is of wider interest than to just the two parties.[5]

Amoco v Iran (1987), 15 Iran-US CTR 189

1. The present claim arises out of the Khemco Agreement, entered into on 12 July 1966 between Amoco and NPC, pursuant to which the parties thereto agreed to form a joint venture company, Khemco, for the purpose of building and operating a plant for the production and marketing of sulfur, natural gas liquids and liquified petroleum gas derived from natural gas.

2. The Claimant, AIFC, contends that the Government of the Islamic Republic of Iran ("Iran"), independently and through its agencies and instrumentalities, deprived AIFC of its 50 percent property interest in Khemco. AIFC now seeks recovery of the value of its property interest in Khemco . . . .

4.   Lawfulness or Unlawfulness of the Expropriation

a)   The Applicable Law
87. Both Parties contend, and the Tribunal agrees, that the lawfulness of the expropriation must be decided by reference to international law. The Claimant maintains that the expropriation was unlawful because it was contrary to the . . . [1955 Treaty of Amity, Economic Relations, and Consular Rights between the United States and Iran], which in any case incorporates the rules of customary international law as a minimum standard. For their part, the Respondents contend that any expropriation was made in conformity with international law, since it was the legitimate exercise of Iran's right to nationalize, such right being recognized by customary international law . . . .

(ii) Customary International Law
. . . 113. . . . A leading expression of [the] rules [of customary international law] is the judgment of the Permanent Court of International Justice in the *Case Concerning Certain*

---

5   See further, George H Aldrich, *The Jurisprudence of the Iran-United States Claims Tribunal* (Oxford: Clarendon Press, 1996).

German Interests in Polish Upper Silesia (Germany v. Poland), 1926 P.C.I.J., Ser. A, No. 7 (Judgment of 25 May 1926). As reflected in this case, the principles of international law generally accepted some sixty years ago in regard to the treatment of foreigners recognized very few exceptions to the principle of respect for vested rights. The Court listed among such exceptions only "expropriation for reasons of public utility, judicial liquidation and similar measures." Id. at 22. A very important evolution in the law has taken place since then, with the progressive recognition of the right of States to nationalize foreign property for a public purpose. This right is today unanimously accepted, even by States which reject the principle of permanent sovereignty over natural resources, considered by a majority of States as the legal foundation of such a right.

114. The importance of this evolution derives from the fact that nationalization is generally defined as the transfer of an economic activity from private ownership to the public sector. It is realized through expropriation of the assets of an enterprise or of its capital stock, with a view to maintaining such enterprise as a going concern under State control. Modern nationalization often brings into State ownership a number of enterprises of the same kind and may even be applied to all enterprises in a particular industry. It may result, therefore, in a taking of private property of much greater magnitude than the traditional expropriation for reasons of public utility, and is also of a very different nature, since it is always linked to determined political choices. For these reasons, and because it applies to going concerns, taken as such, modern nationalization raises specific legal problems, notably in relation to the issue of compensation . . . .

116. . . . While a few recent resolutions of international bodies or conferences, including the General Assembly of the United Nations, have cast doubts on the existence of an international rule [on compensation] (see especially the Charter of the Economic Rights and Duties of States, G.A. Res. 3281 (XXIX) (12 December 1974)), other less controversial resolutions, such as G.A. Res. 1803 (XVII) (14 December 1962) on the Permanent Sovereignty over Natural Resources, confirm the existence of the rule. Furthermore, the rule is generally recognized and applied by international tribunals and reflected in the practice of States, notably in numerous conventions relating to the treatment of foreign property or to the settlement of disputes arising from nationalizations. A number of such awards and conventions were referred to by both Parties in their pleadings . . . .

117. The rules of customary international law relating to the determination of the nature and amount of the compensation to be paid, as well as of the conditions of its payment, are less well settled. They were, and still are, the object of heated controversies, the outcome of which is rather confused. Terms such as "prompt, adequate and effective," "full," "just," "adequate," "adequate in taking account of all pertinent circumstances," "equitable," and so on, are currently used in order to qualify the compensation due, and are construed with broadly divergent meanings . . . .

191. By and large, both Parties refer to the same authorities in the discussion of their respective theses [on compensation], but give them opposite interpretations. They agree that the leading case in this context is *Case Concerning the Factory at Chorzow (Germany v. Poland)*, 1928 P.C.I.J., Ser. A. No. 17 (Judgment of 13 September 1928) ("Chorzow Factory"), decided by the Permanent Court of International Justice in 1928. The Tribunal

shares this view. In spite of the fact that it is nearly sixty years old, this judgment is widely regarded as the most authoritative exposition of the principles applicable in this field, and is still valid today. It must be recognized, however, that its treatment of compensation is fairly complex and must be carefully analyzed.

192. Undoubtedly, the first principle established by the Court is that a clear distinction must be made between lawful and unlawful expropriations, since the rules applicable to the compensation to be paid by the expropriating State differ according to the legal characterization of the taking . . . .

193. According to the Court in Chorzow Factory, an obligation of reparation of all the damages sustained by the owner of expropriated property arises from an unlawful expropriation. The rules of international law relating to international responsibility of States apply in such a case. They provide for *restitutio in integrum*: restitution in kind or, if impossible, its monetary equivalent. If need be, "damages for loss sustained which would not be covered by restitution" should also be awarded. See Chorzow Factory, supra, at 47. On the other hand, a lawful expropriation must give rise to "the payment of fair compensation," id. at 46, or of "the just price of what was expropriated." Id. at 47 . . . .

Summarizing the applicable international customary rules of expropriation, one commentator has advised:

Practice, doctrine and case law unite in showing that, to be valid under international law, an expropriation of foreign private property must:

1. be for a public purpose in accordance with a declared national policy;
2. not discriminate between aliens and citizens, or as between different foreign nationalities;
3. not involve the commission of an unjustified irregularity;
4. be accompanied by a payment of appropriate compensation.

 . . . Nothing less than *restitutio in integrum*, or its monetary equivalent, is held to be the appropriate level of reparation in the case of unlawful takings. Where monetary compensation in lieu of restitution is deemed appropriate, the amount will include not only the market value of the assets (*damnum emergens*) but also damages representing the loss of expected profits (*lucrum cessans*). For lawful takings the standard of compensation is less easy to state authoritatively, as it has varied in state practice and arbitral opinion . . . . It seems that the adequacy [of compensation] tends now to be influenced by the negative measure of what would be unjust enrichment to the expropriating state if the taking were uncompensated, and to be assessed against other equitable criteria.[6]

In practice, much of the modern law on the expropriation of foreign-owned property is governed by so-called bilateral investment treaties (BITs), also known as foreign investment promotion and protection agreements (FIPAs) in Canada. Numbering over 2,500 and linking states around the world, BITs regulate the parties' treatment of investments

---

6   Ivan A Shearer, ed, *Starke's International Law*, 11th ed (Toronto: Butterworths, 1994) at 272.

by one another's nationals.[7] Free trade agreements (FTAs) may also include investment protections, with Chapter 11 of the North American Free Trade Agreement (NAFTA)[8] being one example. Recall that we have observed in Chapter 9 that NAFTA includes a minimum treatment standard in Article 1105, as follows:

Article 1105: Minimum Standard of Treatment

1. Each Party shall accord to investments of investors of another Party treatment in accordance with international law, including fair and equitable treatment and full protection and security.

2. Without prejudice to paragraph 1 and notwithstanding Article 1108(7)(b), each Party shall accord to investors of another Party, and to investments of investors of another Party, non-discriminatory treatment with respect to measures it adopts or maintains relating to losses suffered by investments in its territory owing to armed conflict or civil strife . . . .

Consider also NAFTA's provisions on expropriation:

Article 1110: Expropriation and Compensation

1. No Party may directly or indirectly nationalize or expropriate an investment of an investor of another Party in its territory or take a measure tantamount to nationalization or expropriation of such an investment ("expropriation"), except:

    (a) for a public purpose;

    (b) on a non-discriminatory basis;

    (c) in accordance with due process of law and Article 1105(1); and

    (d) on payment of compensation in accordance with paragraphs 2 through 6.

2. Compensation shall be equivalent to the fair market value of the expropriated investment immediately before the expropriation took place ("date of expropriation"), and shall not reflect any change in value occurring because the intended expropriation had become known earlier. Valuation criteria shall include going concern value, asset value including declared tax value of tangible property, and other criteria, as appropriate, to determine fair market value.

3. Compensation shall be paid without delay and be fully realizable.

Chapter 11 of NAFTA, along with equivalent provisions in many BITs, create investor-state dispute settlement systems. One such mechanism, known as the International Centre for the Settlement of Investment Disputes (ICSID), is established under the Convention on the Settlement of Investment Disputes Between States and Nationals of Other States.[9] ICSID, an autonomous international institution with close links to the World

---

7   Rudolf Dolzer & Christoph Schreuer, *Principles of International Investment Law* (Oxford: Oxford University Press, 2008) at 2.

8   North American Free Trade Agreement between the Government of Canada, the Government of the United Mexican States and the Government of the United States of America, 17 December 1992, Can TS 1994 No 2, (1993) 32 ILM 289, in force 1 January 1994 [NAFTA].

9   Convention on the Settlement of Investment Disputes Between States and Nationals of Other States, 18 March 1965, 575 UNTS 159, in force 14 October 1966. Canada is not yet a party to this convention.

Bank, currently has 147 member states. It provides facilities for the voluntary settlement of investment disputes between member states and their nationals by means of conciliation and arbitration. It, and other, investor-state dispute settlement systems essentially allow foreign investors to make claims against states where certain economic rights are impaired—typically, where an asset is expropriated or the state violates a standard of minimum treatment. Decisions issued by these arbitral bodies are binding on the parties and subject only to limited rights of appeal in domestic courts.

LAW IN CONTEXT

NAFTA Chapter 11 and Environmental Regulation

As noted, modern customary international law permits expropriation of foreign-owned property, but generally only where done for a public purpose, on a non-discriminatory basis, and upon payment of adequate compensation. Article 1110 of NAFTA echoes these basic requirements, barring states parties from expropriating or taking "a measure tantamount to nationalization or expropriation" except for a public purpose, on a non-discriminatory basis, on payment of compensation, and in accordance with due process of law and the minimum treatment guarantees in Article 1105.

Where NAFTA appears to break with general customary international law is on the question of what constitutes an expropriation. While the issue is not without controversy, customary international law has tended to address outright takings or dispossession of foreign-owned property,[10] whether direct or indirect. Less certain is whether it also applies to regulatory takings: expropriation in the sense of diminishment of an investment's value stemming from a law directed at; for instance, environmental protection.[11] In comparison, NAFTA has been interpreted to extend to this form of expropriation. As the Tribunal in the *Metalclad* case put it:

> . . . [E]xpropriation under NAFTA includes not only open, deliberate and acknowledged takings of property, such as outright seizure or formal or obligatory transfer of title in favor of the host State, but also covert or incidental interference with the use of property which has the effect of depriving the owner, in whole or in significant part, of the use or reasonably-to-be-expected economic benefit of property even if not necessarily to the obvious benefit of the host State.[12]

---

10   M Sornarajah, *The International Law on Foreign Investment*, 3d ed (Cambridge: Cambridge University Press, 2010) at 363.

11   See Jon A Stanley, "Comment: Keeping Big Brother out of Our Backyard: Regulatory Takings As Defined in International Law and Compared to American Fifth Amendment Jurisprudence" (2001) 15 Emory Int'l L Rev 349 at 372 (urging that in the right circumstances, "state legislation is capable of surpassing the current line between police power and expropriation, and gives rise to a compensable taking" in customary international law but also observing that: "International courts and tribunals have afforded states a large, and almost impenetrable, amount of deference in applying their 'police powers.'").

12   *Metalclad Corp v United Mexican States* (30 August 2000), Case No Arb (AF)/97/1, (2001) 40 ILM 36 at para 103 [*Metalclad*], online: https://icsid.worldbank.org/ICSID/FrontServlet?requestType=CasesRH& actionVal=showDoc&docId=DC542_En&caseId=C155.

In *Metalclad v Mexico*, the Tribunal found that a government decree creating an ecological reserve in the area in which the investor sought to site its landfill was an act "tantamount to an expropriation."[13]

This approach to Article 1110 has opened the door to repeated claims of regulatory takings in Chapter 11 cases. To date, however, most of these efforts have been unsuccessful. In the *Methanex* case, the Tribunal rejected the investor's argument that a legislated ban on its fuel additive amounted to an expropriation. In so doing, it appeared to draw a line that might apply in many other cases alleging regulatory takings:

> [A]s a matter of general international law, a non-discriminatory regulation for a public purpose, which is enacted in accordance with due process and which affects, *inter alia*, a foreign investor or investment is not deemed expropriatory and compensable unless specific commitments had been given by the regulating government to the then putative foreign investor contemplating investment that the government would refrain from such regulation.[14]

Put another way, expropriation by regulatory taking may be confined to circumstances where the alleged regulation runs counter to a foreign investor's expectation attributable to the government. No expropriation existed where there was no such government commitment and where:

> Methanex entered a political economy in which it was widely known, if not notorious, that governmental environmental and health protection institutions at the federal and state level, operating under the vigilant eyes of the media, interested corporations, non-governmental organizations and a politically active electorate, continuously monitored the use and impact of chemical compounds and commonly prohibited or restricted the use of some of those compounds for environmental and/or health reasons.[15]

The decision—if reflective of the Chapter 11 standard—may defuse many of the concerns flowing from *Metalclad* on the application of Article 1110 to environmental regulations. Consider this summary of the international arbitral jurisprudence on regulatory takings:

> In assessing whether a regulatory taking will amount to an expropriation, the character, purpose, and effect of the measure will be relevant. In this regard, a tribunal will likely consider (1) the degree of interference with the investment; (2) the investor's legitimate expectations in relation to the use and enjoyment of its investment; and (3) the character of the state's regulatory measure, including its purpose .... [T]he greater the interference with the investment, the more likely the tribunal will find that a given regulatory act is expropriatory. It should be noted that most bona fide regulatory actions of general application will not result in the degree of interference necessary to constitute an expropriation. It is more likely that specifically targeted acts of a state, tailored to one particular

---

13   *Ibid* at para 111. This finding was upheld on judicial review: *United Mexican States v Metalclad Corp*, 2001 BCSC 664 at para 100, with supplementary reasons for judgment, 2001 BCSC 1529.

14   *Methanex Corporation v United States of America*, Final Award, 3 August 2005, Part IV, Chapter D at para 7, online: www.state.gov/documents/organization/51052.pdf(NAFTA Ch 11 Panel) [*Methanex*].

15   *Ibid* at para 9.

investor, will constitute the degree of interference necessary for an expropriation. On the other hand, if the government is found to be legitimately adopting certain regulations within its police powers, including for health and environmental reasons, its actions will be less likely to be found expropriatory. This proportionality analysis must be done with the legitimate expectation of the investor in mind. Indeed, any investor should expect the host state to adopt legitimate and proportionate regulatory measures in the general public's interest. On the other hand, if specific commitments have been made to an investor, tribunals will expect that those commitments will be kept.[16]

B. STATE TREATMENT OF THE TRANSBORDER MOVEMENT OF GOODS AND SERVICES

Since the mid-twentieth century, states have increasingly entered into a series of bilateral, regional, and multilateral treaties that restrict in various ways the extent to which they may control the movement of goods and services across their borders. They have done so largely as a means of putting into operation economic doctrines favouring the maximization of international trade as a driver of global economic development. Consider the following discussion:

> **World Trade Organization, *Understanding the WTO: Basics—The Case for Open Trade*** (undated), online: www.wto.org/english/thewto_e/whatis_e/tif_e/fact3_e.htm
>
> The economic case for an open trading system based on multilaterally agreed rules is simple enough and rests largely on commercial common sense. But it is also supported by evidence: the experience of world trade and economic growth since the Second World War. Tariffs on industrial products have fallen steeply and now average less than 5% in industrial countries. During the first 25 years after the war, world economic growth averaged about 5% per year, a high rate that was partly the result of lower trade barriers. World trade grew even faster, averaging about 8% during the period.
>
> The data show a definite statistical link between freer trade and economic growth. Economic theory points to strong reasons for the link. All countries, including the poorest, have assets—human, industrial, natural, financial—which they can employ to produce goods and services for their domestic markets or to compete overseas. Economics tells us that we can benefit when these goods and services are traded. Simply put, the principle of "comparative advantage" says that countries prosper first by taking advantage of their assets in order to concentrate on what they can produce best, and then by trading these products for products that other countries produce best.
>
> In other words, liberal trade policies—policies that allow the unrestricted flow of goods and services—sharpen competition, motivate innovation and breed success. They multiply the rewards that result from producing the best products, with the best design, at the best price.
>
> But success in trade is not static. The ability to compete well in particular products can shift from company to company when the market changes or new technologies make

---

16 Rahim Moloo & Justin M Jacinto, "Environmental and Health Regulation: Assessing Liability under Investment Treaties" (2011) 29 Berkeley J Int'l L 1 at 24.

cheaper and better products possible. Producers are encouraged to adapt gradually and in a relatively painless way. They can focus on new products, find a new "niche" in their current area or expand into new areas.

Experience shows that competitiveness can also shift between whole countries. A country that may have enjoyed an advantage because of lower labour costs or because it had good supplies of some natural resources, could also become uncompetitive in some goods or services as its economy develops. However, with the stimulus of an open economy, the country can move on to become competitive in some other goods or services. This is normally a gradual process.

Nevertheless, the temptation to ward off the challenge of competitive imports is always present. And richer governments are more likely to yield to the siren call of protectionism, for short term political gain — through subsidies, complicated red tape, and hiding behind legitimate policy objectives such as environmental preservation or consumer protection as an excuse to protect producers.

Protection ultimately leads to bloated, inefficient producers supplying consumers with outdated, unattractive products. In the end, factories close and jobs are lost despite the protection and subsidies. If other governments around the world pursue the same policies, markets contract and world economic activity is reduced. One of the objectives that governments bring to WTO negotiations is to prevent such a self-defeating and destructive drift into protectionism.

As noted, in pursuit of these economic policies, many regional trade regimes have been established, including NAFTA. However, the same policies have also been pursued at the multilateral, global level, beginning with the 1947 General Agreement on Tariffs and Trade (GATT),[17] later renewed and expanded by various agreements, eventually leading to the establishment of the World Trade Organization (WTO).[18] The WTO, with its 157 members, can be described as follows:

World Trade Organization, *Understanding the WTO: Basics — What is the World Trade Organization* **(undated), online: www.wto.org/english/thewto_e/whatis_e/tif_e/fact1_e.htm**

Simply put: the World Trade Organization (WTO) deals with the rules of trade between nations at a global or near-global level. But there is more to it than that. . . . There are a number of ways of looking at the WTO. It's an organization for liberalizing trade. It's a forum for governments to negotiate trade agreements. It's a place for them to settle trade disputes. It operates a system of trade rules . . . .

Above all, it's a negotiating forum . . . Essentially, the WTO is a place where member governments go, to try to sort out the trade problems they face with each other. The first step is to talk. The WTO was born out of negotiations, and everything the WTO does is the result of negotiations. The bulk of the WTO's current work comes from the 1986–94 ne-

---

17 General Agreement on Tariffs and Trade, 30 October 1947, 55 UNTS 194, Can TS 1948 No 31, in force 1 January 1948.

18 See Marrakesh Agreement establishing the World Trade Organization, 15 April 1994, 1867 UNTS 14, (1994) 33 ILM 1144, in force 1 January 1995 [WTO Agreement].

gotiations called the Uruguay Round and earlier negotiations under the General Agreement on Tariffs and Trade (GATT). The WTO is currently the host to new negotiations, under the "Doha Development Agenda" launched in 2001.

Where countries have faced trade barriers and wanted them lowered, the negotiations have helped to liberalize trade. But the WTO is not just about liberalizing trade, and in some circumstances its rules support maintaining trade barriers—for example to protect consumers or prevent the spread of disease.

It's a set of rules . . . At its heart are the WTO agreements, negotiated and signed by the bulk of the world's trading nations. These documents provide the legal ground-rules for international commerce. They are essentially contracts, binding governments to keep their trade policies within agreed limits. Although negotiated and signed by governments, the goal is to help producers of goods and services, exporters, and importers conduct their business, while allowing governments to meet social and environmental objectives.

The system's overriding purpose is to help trade flow as freely as possible—so long as there are no undesirable side-effects—because this is important for economic development and well-being. That partly means removing obstacles. It also means ensuring that individuals, companies and governments know what the trade rules are around the world, and giving them the confidence that there will be no sudden changes of policy. In other words, the rules have to be "transparent" and predictable.

And it helps to settle disputes . . . This is a third important side to the WTO's work. Trade relations often involve conflicting interests. Agreements, including those painstakingly negotiated in the WTO system, often need interpreting. The most harmonious way to settle these differences is through some neutral procedure based on an agreed legal foundation. That is the purpose behind the dispute settlement process written into the WTO agreements.

Born in 1995, but not so young
The WTO began life on 1 January 1995, but its trading system is half a century older. Since 1948, the General Agreement on Tariffs and Trade (GATT) had provided the rules for the system . . . .

It did not take long for the General Agreement to give birth to an unofficial, de facto international organization, also known informally as GATT. Over the years GATT evolved through several rounds of negotiations.

The last and largest GATT round, was the Uruguay Round which lasted from 1986 to 1994 and led to the WTO's creation. Whereas GATT had mainly dealt with trade in goods, the WTO and its agreements now cover trade in services, and in traded inventions, creations and designs (intellectual property).

It would be very difficult in an introductory casebook on public international law to review exhaustively the nature and operation of the WTO and the content of its numerous agreements, much less those of the many regional trade regimes such as the NAFTA. We confine our discussion, therefore, to three common, driving principles of these international trade law regimes: non-discrimination; free trade (an expression with several legal meanings); and binding dispute settlement.

1) Non-Discrimination

World Trade Organization, *Understanding the WTO: Principles of the trading system* (undated), online: www.wto.org/english/thewto_e/whatis_e/tif_e/fact2_e.htm

Trade without discrimination

1. Most-favoured-nation (MFN): treating other people equally
Under the WTO agreements, countries cannot normally discriminate between their trading partners. Grant someone a special favour (such as a lower customs duty rate for one of their products) and you have to do the same for all other WTO members. This principle is known as most-favoured-nation (MFN) treatment . . . . It is so important that it is the first article of the General Agreement on Tariffs and Trade (GATT), which governs trade in goods. MFN is also a priority in the General Agreement on Trade in Services (GATS) (Article 2) and the Agreement on Trade-Related Aspects of Intellectual Property Rights (TRIPS) (Article 4), although in each agreement the principle is handled slightly differently. Together, those three agreements cover all three main areas of trade handled by the WTO.

Some exceptions are allowed. For example, countries can set up a free trade agreement that applies only to goods traded within the group — discriminating against goods from outside. Or they can give developing countries special access to their markets. Or a country can raise barriers against products that are considered to be traded unfairly from specific countries. And in services, countries are allowed, in limited circumstances, to discriminate. But the agreements only permit these exceptions under strict conditions. In general, MFN means that every time a country lowers a trade barrier or opens up a market, it has to do so for the same goods or services from all its trading partners — whether rich or poor, weak or strong.

2. National treatment: Treating foreigners and locals equally
Imported and locally produced goods should be treated equally — at least after the foreign goods have entered the market. The same should apply to foreign and domestic services, and to foreign and local trademarks, copyrights and patents. This principle of "national treatment" (giving others the same treatment as one's own nationals) is also found in all the three main WTO agreements (Article 3 of GATT, Article 17 of GATS and Article 3 of TRIPS), although once again the principle is handled slightly differently in each of these.

National treatment only applies once a product, service or item of intellectual property has entered the market. Therefore, charging customs duty on an import is not a violation of national treatment even if locally-produced products are not charged an equivalent tax . . . .

Consider the following decision of the WTO Appellate Body discussing the national treatment concept and contextualizing the WTO agreements within the broader rules of international treaty law:

Japan—Taxes on Alcoholic Beverages, WTO Appellate Body, AB-1996-2 (4 October 1996)

Article 3.2 of the DSU [Dispute Settlement Understanding, annexed to the WTO Agreement] directs the Appellate Body to clarify the provisions of GATT 1994 and the other "covered agreements" of the WTO Agreement "in accordance with customary rules of interpretation of public international law." Following this mandate, . . . we [have in past cases] stressed the need to achieve such clarification by reference to the fundamental rule of treaty interpretation set out in Article 31(1) of the Vienna Convention [on the Law of Treaties]. We [have] stressed . . . that this general rule of interpretation "has attained the status of a rule of customary or general international law." There can be no doubt that Article 32 of the Vienna Convention, dealing with the role of supplementary means of interpretation, has also attained the same status . . . .

Article 31 of the Vienna Convention provides that the words of the treaty form the foundation for the interpretive process: "interpretation must be based above all upon the text of the treaty." The provisions of the treaty are to be given their ordinary meaning in their context. The object and purpose of the treaty are also to be taken into account in determining the meaning of its provisions. A fundamental tenet of treaty interpretation flowing from the general rule of interpretation set out in Article 31 is the principle of effectiveness (*ut res magis valeat quam pereat*). In *United States—Standards for Reformulated and Conventional Gasoline*, we noted that "[o]ne of the corollaries of the 'general rule of interpretation' in the Vienna Convention is that interpretation must give meaning and effect to all the terms of the treaty. An interpreter is not free to adopt a reading that would result in reducing whole clauses or paragraphs of a treaty to redundancy or inutility.". . .

F. Interpretation of Article III

The WTO Agreement is a treaty—the international equivalent of a contract. It is self-evident that in an exercise of their sovereignty, and in pursuit of their own respective national interests, the Members of the WTO have made a bargain. In exchange for the benefits they expect to derive as Members of the WTO, they have agreed to exercise their sovereignty according to the commitments they have made in the WTO Agreement.

One of those commitments is Article III of the GATT 1994, which is entitled "National Treatment on Internal Taxation and Regulation." For the purpose of this appeal, the relevant parts of Article III read as follows:

Article III
National Treatment on Internal Taxation and Regulation
1. The contracting parties recognize that internal taxes and other internal charges, and laws, regulations and requirements affecting the internal sale, offering for sale, purchase, transportation, distribution or use of products, and internal quantitative regulations requiring the mixture, processing or use of products in specified amounts or proportions, should not be applied to imported or domestic products so as to afford protection to domestic production.

2. The products of the territory of any contracting party imported into the territory of any other contracting party shall not be subject, directly or indirectly, to internal taxes

or other internal charges of any kind in excess of those applied, directly or indirectly, to like domestic products. Moreover, no contracting party shall otherwise apply internal taxes or other internal charges to imported or domestic products in a manner contrary to the principles set forth in paragraph 1.

Ad Article III
Paragraph 2
A tax conforming to the requirements of the first sentence of paragraph 2 would be considered to be inconsistent with the provisions of the second sentence only in cases where competition was involved between, on the one hand, the taxed product and, on the other hand, a directly competitive or substitutable product which was not similarly taxed.

The broad and fundamental purpose of Article III is to avoid protectionism in the application of internal tax and regulatory measures. More specifically, the purpose of Article III "is to ensure that internal measures 'not be applied to imported or domestic products so as to afford protection to domestic production.'" Toward this end, Article III obliges Members of the WTO to provide equality of competitive conditions for imported products in relation to domestic products. "[T]he intention of the drafters of the Agreement was clearly to treat the imported products in the same way as the like domestic products once they had been cleared through customs. Otherwise indirect protection could be given." Moreover, it is irrelevant that "the trade effects" of the tax differential between imported and domestic products, as reflected in the volumes of imports, are insignificant or even non-existent; Article III protects expectations not of any particular trade volume but rather of the equal competitive relationship between imported and domestic products. Members of the WTO are free to pursue their own domestic goals through internal taxation or regulation so long as they do not do so in a way that violates Article III or any of the other commitments they have made in the WTO Agreement . . . .

2) Free Trade

World Trade Organization, *Understanding the WTO: Basics — Principles of the trading system* **(undated), online: www.wto.org/english/thewto_e/whatis_e/tif_e/fact2_e.htm**

Freer trade: gradually, through negotiation
Lowering trade barriers is one of the most obvious means of encouraging trade. The barriers concerned include customs duties (or tariffs) and measures such as import bans or quotas that restrict quantities selectively. From time to time other issues such as red tape and exchange rate policies have also been discussed.

Since GATT's creation in 1947–48 there have been eight rounds of trade negotiations. A ninth round, under the Doha Development Agenda, is now underway. At first these focused on lowering tariffs (customs duties) on imported goods. As a result of the negotiations, by the mid-1990s industrial countries' tariff rates on industrial goods had fallen steadily to less than 4%.

But by the 1980s, the negotiations had expanded to cover non-tariff barriers on goods, and to the new areas such as services and intellectual property.

Opening markets can be beneficial, but it also requires adjustment. The WTO agreements allow countries to introduce changes gradually, through "progressive liberalization". Developing countries are usually given longer to fulfil their obligations.

Predictability: through binding and transparency

Sometimes, promising not to raise a trade barrier can be as important as lowering one, because the promise gives businesses a clearer view of their future opportunities. With stability and predictability, investment is encouraged, jobs are created and consumers can fully enjoy the benefits of competition — choice and lower prices. The multilateral trading system is an attempt by governments to make the business environment stable and predictable. . . .

[Table omitted]

In the WTO, when countries agree to open their markets for goods or services, they "bind" their commitments. For goods, these bindings amount to ceilings on customs tariff rates. Sometimes countries tax imports at rates that are lower than the bound rates. Frequently this is the case in developing countries. In developed countries the rates actually charged and the bound rates tend to be the same.

A country can change its bindings, but only after negotiating with its trading partners, which could mean compensating them for loss of trade. One of the achievements of the Uruguay Round of multilateral trade talks was to increase the amount of trade under binding commitments . . . .

The system tries to improve predictability and stability in other ways as well. One way is to discourage the use of quotas and other measures used to set limits on quantities of imports — administering quotas can lead to more red-tape and accusations of unfair play. Another is to make countries' trade rules as clear and public ("transparent") as possible. Many WTO agreements require governments to disclose their policies and practices publicly within the country or by notifying the WTO. The regular surveillance of national trade policies through the Trade Policy Review Mechanism provides a further means of encouraging transparency both domestically and at the multilateral level.

Promoting fair competition

The WTO is sometimes described as a "free trade" institution, but that is not entirely accurate. The system does allow tariffs and, in limited circumstances, other forms of protection. More accurately, it is a system of rules dedicated to open, fair and undistorted competition.

The rules on non-discrimination — MFN and national treatment — are designed to secure fair conditions of trade. So too are those on dumping (exporting at below cost to gain market share) and subsidies. The issues are complex, and the rules try to establish what is fair or unfair, and how governments can respond, in particular by charging additional import duties calculated to compensate for damage caused by unfair trade . . . .

World Trade Organization, *Understanding the WTO: The Agreements — Anti-dumping, subsidies, safeguards: Contingencies, etc.* (undated), online: www.wto.org/english/thewto_e/whatis_e/tif_e/agrm8_e.htm

Anti-dumping actions

If a company exports a product at a price lower than the price it normally charges on its own home market, it is said to be "dumping" the product. Is this unfair competition? Opinions differ, but many governments take action against dumping in order to defend their domestic industries. The WTO agreement does not pass judgement. Its focus is on how governments can or cannot react to dumping—it disciplines anti-dumping actions, and it is often called the "Anti-Dumping Agreement." . . .

The legal definitions are more precise, but broadly speaking the WTO agreement allows governments to act against dumping where there is genuine ("material") injury to the competing domestic industry. In order to do that the government has to be able to show that dumping is taking place, calculate the extent of dumping (how much lower the export price is compared to the exporter's home market price), and show that the dumping is causing injury or threatening to do so.

GATT (Article 6) allows countries to take action against dumping. The Anti-Dumping Agreement clarifies and expands Article 6, and the two operate together. They allow countries to act in a way that would normally break the GATT principles of binding a tariff and not discriminating between trading partners—typically anti-dumping action means charging extra import duty on the particular product from the particular exporting country in order to bring its price closer to the "normal value" or to remove the injury to domestic industry in the importing country.

There are many different ways of calculating whether a particular product is being dumped heavily or only lightly. The agreement narrows down the range of possible options. It provides three methods to calculate a product's "normal value." The main one is based on the price in the exporter's domestic market. When this cannot be used, two alternatives are available—the price charged by the exporter in another country, or a calculation based on the combination of the exporter's production costs, other expenses and normal profit margins. And the agreement also specifies how a fair comparison can be made between the export price and what would be a normal price.

Calculating the extent of dumping on a product is not enough. Anti-dumping measures can only be applied if the dumping is hurting the industry in the importing country. Therefore, a detailed investigation has to be conducted according to specified rules first. The investigation must evaluate all relevant economic factors that have a bearing on the state of the industry in question. If the investigation shows dumping is taking place and domestic industry is being hurt, the exporting company can undertake to raise its price to an agreed level in order to avoid anti-dumping import duty.

Detailed procedures are set out on how anti-dumping cases are to be initiated, how the investigations are to be conducted, and the conditions for ensuring that all interested parties are given an opportunity to present evidence. Anti-dumping measures must expire five years after the date of imposition, unless an investigation shows that ending the measure would lead to injury.

Anti-dumping investigations are to end immediately in cases where the authorities determine that the margin of dumping is insignificantly small (defined as less than 2% of the export price of the product). Other conditions are also set. For example, the investigations also have to end if the volume of dumped imports is negligible . . . .

The agreement says member countries must inform the Committee on Anti-Dumping Practices about all preliminary and final anti-dumping actions, promptly and in detail. They must also report on all investigations twice a year. When differences arise, members are encouraged to consult each other. They can also use the WTO's dispute settlement procedure.

Subsidies and countervailing measures

[The Agreement on Subsidies and Countervailing Measures] does two things: it disciplines the use of subsidies, and it regulates the actions countries can take to counter the effects of subsidies. It says a country can use the WTO's dispute settlement procedure to seek the withdrawal of the subsidy or the removal of its adverse effects. Or the country can launch its own investigation and ultimately charge extra duty (known as "countervailing duty") on subsidized imports that are found to be hurting domestic producers.

The agreement contains a definition of subsidy. It also introduces the concept of a "specific" subsidy—i.e. a subsidy available only to an enterprise, industry, group of enterprises, or group of industries in the country (or state, etc.) that gives the subsidy. The disciplines set out in the agreement only apply to specific subsidies. They can be domestic or export subsidies.

The agreement defines two categories of subsidies: prohibited and actionable . . . .

- **Prohibited subsidies**: subsidies that require recipients to meet certain export targets, or to use domestic goods instead of imported goods. They are prohibited because they are specifically designed to distort international trade, and are therefore likely to hurt other countries' trade. They can be challenged in the WTO dispute settlement procedure where they are handled under an accelerated timetable. If the dispute settlement procedure confirms that the subsidy is prohibited, it must be withdrawn immediately. Otherwise, the complaining country can take counter measures. If domestic producers are hurt by imports of subsidized products, countervailing duty can be imposed.
- **Actionable subsidies**: in this category the complaining country has to show that the subsidy has an adverse effect on its interests. Otherwise the subsidy is permitted. The agreement defines three types of damage they can cause. One country's subsidies can hurt a domestic industry in an importing country. They can hurt rival exporters from another country when the two compete in third markets. And domestic subsidies in one country can hurt exporters trying to compete in the subsidizing country's domestic market. If the Dispute Settlement Body rules that the subsidy does have an adverse effect, the subsidy must be withdrawn or its adverse effect must be removed. Again, if domestic producers are hurt by imports of subsidized products, countervailing duty can be imposed.

Some of the disciplines are similar to those of the Anti-Dumping Agreement. Countervailing duty (the parallel of anti-dumping duty) can only be charged after the importing country has conducted a detailed investigation similar to that required for anti-dumping action. There are detailed rules for deciding whether a product is being subsidized (not always an easy calculation), criteria for determining whether imports of subsidized products are hurting ("causing injury to") domestic industry, procedures for initiating and conducting investigations, and rules on the implementation and duration (normally five years) of countervailing measures. The subsidized exporter can also agree to raise its export prices as an alternative to its exports being charged countervailing duty.

Subsidies may play an important role in developing countries and in the transformation of centrally-planned economies to market economies. Least-developed countries and developing countries with less than $1,000 per capita GNP are exempted from disciplines on prohibited export subsidies . . . .

The most controversial trade dispute involving Canada concerns the export of Canadian softwood lumber to the United States. Canada-US disputes over trade in Canadian softwood lumber date to the period prior to Confederation and have reoccurred throughout Canadian history. The most recent round commenced in 2001, upon expiry of a 1996 Canada-US memorandum of understanding that had managed the lumber trade by imposing certain quotas on softwood exports. The 2001 dispute, labelled "Lumber IV," was initiated by a coalition of US lumber producers filing complaints with US trade authorities concerning alleged Canadian subsidization and dumping of softwood. Among other things, the subsidy allegation singled out the "stumpage" rates charged by Canadian provinces to lumber companies for timber harvesting, alleging that these fees were unjustifiably low and constituted a subsidy.

In 2002, the US government concluded that both subsidization and dumping existed, and imposed significant duties on Canadian softwood exports in response. Canada challenged these determinations in several cases at the WTO, focusing on whether the US actions complied with the many technical rules found in the Anti-Dumping Agreement and Agreement on Subsidies and Countervailing Measures found within the WTO Agreement. Canada's record of success in these challenges has been mixed.

As the case below suggests, Canada failed to persuade the WTO that the United States acted wrongly in holding that provincial stumpage programmes constituted subsidies. Under the WTO Agreement on Subsidies and Countervailing Measures, a subsidy exists if the government provides a financial contribution to the trading entity and a benefit is thereby conferred. The extract that follows focuses on the WTO Appellate Body's findings as to whether stumpage programmes truly constituted a financial contribution. Note that references to the "Panel" refer to the WTO dispute resolution body of first instance.

United States — Final Countervailing Duty Determination With Respect To Certain Softwood Lumber From Canada, WTO Appellate Body, AB-2003-6 (19 January 2004)

B. General Interpretation of the Requirements of Article 1.1(a)(1)(iii) of the SCM Agreement

50. We begin our analysis of this issue with the text of the relevant provision. Article 1 sets out a definition of "subsidy" for the purposes of the SCM [Subsidies and Countervailing Measures] Agreement. It reads as follows:

Definition of a Subsidy
1.1 For the purpose of this Agreement, a subsidy shall be deemed to exist if:

(a)(1) there is a financial contribution by a government or any public body within the territory of a Member (referred to in this Agreement as "government"), i.e. where:

> (i) a government practice involves a direct transfer of funds (e.g., grants, loans, and equity infusion), potential direct transfers of funds or liabilities (e.g., loan guarantees);
> (ii) government revenue that is otherwise due is foregone or not collected (e.g., fiscal incentives such as tax credits);
> (iii) a government provides goods or services other than general infrastructure, or purchases goods;

(iv) a government makes payments to a funding mechanism, or entrusts or directs a private body to carry out one or more of the type of functions illustrated in (i) to (iii) above which would normally be vested in the government and the practice, in no real sense, differs from practices normally followed by governments;

or

(a)(2) there is any form of income or price support in the sense of Article XVI of GATT 1994;

and

(b) a benefit is thereby conferred. (emphasis added, footnote omitted)

51. The concept of subsidy defined in Article 1 of the SCM Agreement captures situations in which something of economic value is transferred by a government to the advantage of a recipient. A subsidy is deemed to exist where two distinct elements are present. First, there must be a financial contribution by a government, or income or price support. Secondly, any financial contribution, or income or price support, must confer a benefit. Canada's appeal focuses on the Panel's finding with respect to the first element, namely the existence of a financial contribution.

52. An evaluation of the existence of a financial contribution involves consideration of the nature of the transaction through which something of economic value is transferred by a government. A wide range of transactions falls within the meaning of "financial contribution" in Article 1.1(a)(1). According to paragraphs (i) and (ii) of Article 1.1(a)(1), a financial contribution may be made through a direct transfer of funds by a government, or the foregoing of government revenue that is otherwise due. Paragraph (iii) of Article 1.1(a)(1) recognizes that, in addition to such monetary contributions, a contribution having financial value can also be made in kind through governments providing goods or services, or through government purchases. Paragraph (iv) of Article 1.1(a)(1) recognizes that paragraphs (i)–(iii) could be circumvented by a government making payments to a funding mechanism or through entrusting or directing a private body to make a financial contribution. It accordingly specifies that these kinds of actions are financial contributions as well. This range of government measures capable of providing subsidies is broadened still further by the concept of "income or price support" in paragraph (2) of Article 1.1(a).

53. Article 1.1(a)(1)(iii) of the SCM Agreement, the specific provision at issue in Canada's appeal, sets forth that a financial contribution exists where a government "provides goods or services other than general infrastructure, or purchases goods." As such, the Article contemplates two distinct types of transaction. The first is where a government provides goods or services other than general infrastructure. Such transactions have the potential to lower artificially the cost of producing a product by providing, to an enterprise, inputs having a financial value. The second type of transaction falling within Article 1.1(a)(1)(iii) is where a government purchases goods from an enterprise. This type of transaction has the potential to increase artificially the revenues gained from selling the product.

54. Canada's appeal requires us to focus upon one element of the first type of transaction contemplated by Article 1.1(a)(1)(iii), namely, whether, through stumpage programs,

provincial governments provide goods. Canada takes issue with the Panel's interpretation of each of the two words in this expression. With respect to the meaning of the term "goods" in Article 1.1(a)(1)(iii) of the SCM Agreement, Canada submits that the Panel erred in finding that "standing timber" falls within the meaning of that term. Canada advances two arguments in support of this aspect of its appeal. First, it argues that, in the context of Article 1.1(a)(1)(iii) of the SCM Agreement, the term "goods" is limited to "tradable items with an actual or potential tariff classification." Secondly, even if we were to find that the Panel's interpretation of the term "goods" is correct, Canada argues that the Panel erred in its legal characterization of the facts before it, because standing timber does not fall within the definition proposed by the Panel, which defines goods, inter alia, by reference to the concept of "personal property."

55. Canada further argues that the Panel erred in its interpretation of the term "provides." In particular, Canada submits that the Panel incorrectly found that standing timber was "provided" to harvesters merely by virtue of the conferral, through stumpage arrangements, of an intangible right to harvest . . . .

C. Do Provincial Stumpage Programs "Provide Goods" in the Sense of Article 1.1(a)(1)(iii) of the SCM Agreement?

57. With this in mind, we turn to Canada's argument that standing timber does not fall within the meaning of the term "goods" in the phrase "provides goods or services other than general infrastructure." At the outset, we note that there is no dispute that trees are goods once they are harvested. The question raised by Canada's appeal is, rather, whether the term "goods" in Article 1.1(a)(1)(iii) captures trees before they are harvested, that is, standing timber attached to the land (but severable from it) and incapable of being traded across borders as such.

58. The meaning of a treaty provision, properly construed, is rooted in the ordinary meaning of the terms used. The Panel adopted a definition of the term "goods," drawn from *Black's Law Dictionary*, put forward in the submissions of both Canada and the United States, that the term "goods" includes "tangible or movable personal property other than money." In particular, the Panel noted that this definition set out in *Black's Law Dictionary* contemplates that the term "goods" could include "growing crops, and other identified things to be severed from real property." We observe that the *Shorter Oxford English Dictionary* offers a more general definition of the term "goods" as including "property or possessions" especially—but not exclusively—"movable property."

59. These definitions offer a useful starting point for discerning the ordinary meaning of the word "goods." In particular, we agree with the Panel that the ordinary meaning of the term "goods," as used in Article 1.1(a)(1)(iii), includes items that are tangible and capable of being possessed. We note, however, as we have done on previous occasions, that dictionary definitions have their limitations in revealing the ordinary meaning of a term. This is especially true where the meanings of terms used in the different authentic texts of the WTO Agreement are susceptible to differences in scope. We note that the European Communities, in its third participant's submission, observed that in the French version of the SCM Agreement, Article 1.1(a)(1)(iii) addresses, *inter alia*, the provision

of "biens." In the Spanish version, the term used is "bienes." The ordinary meanings of these terms include a wide range of property, including immovable property. As such, they correspond more closely to a broad definition of "goods" that includes "property or possessions" generally, than with the more limited definition adopted by the Panel. As we have observed previously, in accordance with the customary rule of treaty interpretation reflected in Article 33(3) of the Vienna Convention on the Law of Treaties (the "Vienna Convention"), the terms of a treaty authenticated in more than one language-like the WTO Agreement are presumed to have the same meaning in each authentic text. It follows that the treaty interpreter should seek the meaning that gives effect, simultaneously, to all the terms of the treaty, as they are used in each authentic language. With this in mind, we find that the ordinary meaning of the term "goods" in the English version of Article 1.1(a)(1)(iii) of the SCM Agreement should not be read so as to exclude tangible items of property, like trees, that are severable from land.

60. We find that terms that accompany the word "goods" in Article 1.1(a)(1)(iii) support this interpretation. In Article 1.1(a)(1)(iii), the only explicit exception to the general principle that the provision of "goods" by a government will result in a financial contribution is when those goods are provided in the form of "general infrastructure." In the context of Article 1.1(a)(1)(iii), all goods that might be used by an enterprise to its benefit — including even goods that might be considered infrastructure — are to be considered "goods" within the meaning of the provision, unless they are infrastructure of a general nature . . . .

65. In seeking to exclude "standing timber" from the definition of "goods" in Article 1.1(a)(1)(iii), Canada contends . . . that, even if we find that the term is not limited to "tradable items with an actual or potential tariff classification," standing timber is still not "goods" as the Panel has defined them, because it is neither "personal property" nor an "identified thing to be severed from real property." The concepts of "personal" and "real" property are, in the context Canada raises them, creatures of municipal law that are not reflected in Article 1.1(a)(1)(iii) itself. As we have said above, the manner in which the municipal law of a WTO Member classifies an item cannot, in itself, be determinative of the interpretation of provisions of the WTO covered agreements. As such, we do not believe that the distinction drawn by Canada is dispositive of the issues raised in this appeal.

66. Similarly, we reject Canada's argument that specific trees are not "identified" in stumpage contracts and therefore cannot fall within the scope of "goods" within the meaning of the dictionary definition relied upon by the Panel. We disagree that trees must be specifically and individually "identified" in order to constitute "goods" for purposes of Article 1.1(a)(1)(iii) of the SCM Agreement. As the Panel found, stumpage contracts concern a specified area of land containing a predictable quantity of timber that may be harvested under certain conditions. Harvesters pay a volumetric "stumpage fee" only for that volume of timber actually harvested. In these circumstances, we do not see the relevance, for an assessment of whether trees are goods, of the fact that each individual tree within the specified area of land covered by a stumpage contract may not be identified at the time the contract is made. Indeed, the identification of trees by reference to a general area of forest renders the situation of the timber growing in that area similar to

that of fungible goods. Fungible goods are goods even though they are identifiable only by number, volume, value or weight. We see no reason why disciplines on subsidies that regulate the provision of non-monetary resources should focus on identifiable physical objects and not on tangible, but fungible, input material . . . .

67. In sum, nothing in the text of Article 1.1(a)(1)(iii), its context, or the object and purpose of the SCM Agreement, leads us to the view that tangible items — such as standing, un-felled trees — that are not both tradable as such and subject to tariff classification, should be excluded, as Canada suggests, from the coverage of the term "goods" as it appears in that Article. It follows that we agree with the Panel that standing timber — trees — are "goods" within the meaning of Article 1.1(a)(1)(iii) of the SCM Agreement.

68. Having considered the meaning of the term "goods," we now turn to consider what it means to "provide" goods, for purposes of Article 1.1(a)(1)(iii) of the SCM Agreement. Canada argues that stumpage arrangements do not "provide" standing timber. According to Canada, all that is provided by these arrangements is an intangible right to harvest. At best, this intangible right "makes available" standing timber. But, in Canada's submission, the connotation "makes available" is not an appropriate reading of the term "provides" in Article 1.1(a)(1)(iii). In contrast, the United States argues that the Panel's interpretation that stumpage arrangements "provide" standing timber is correct. The United States contends that, where a government transfers ownership in goods by giving enterprises a right to take them, the government "provides" those goods, within the meaning of Article 1.1(a)(1)(iii).

69. Again, we begin with the ordinary meaning of the term. Before the Panel, the United States pointed to a definition of the term "provides," which suggested that the term means, *inter alia*, to "supply or furnish for use; make available." This definition is the same as that relied upon by USDOC in making its determination that "regardless of whether the Provinces are supplying timber or making it available through a right of access, they are providing timber" within the meaning of the provision of United States countervailing duty law that corresponds to Article 1.1(a)(1)(iii) of the SCM Agreement. We note that another definition of "provides" is "to put at the disposal of." . . .

75. Turning to the Panel's finding regarding what is provided by provincial stumpage programs, we note that the Panel found that stumpage arrangements give tenure holders a right to enter onto government lands, cut standing timber, and enjoy exclusive rights over the timber that is harvested. Like the Panel, we conclude that such arrangements represent a situation in which provincial governments provide standing timber. Thus, we disagree with Canada's submission that the granting of an intangible right to harvest standing timber cannot be equated with the act of providing that standing timber. By granting a right to harvest, the provincial governments put particular stands of timber at the disposal of timber harvesters and allow those enterprises, exclusively, to make use of those resources. Canada asserts that governments do not supply felled trees, logs, or lumber through stumpage transactions. In our view, this assertion misses the point, because felled trees, logs and lumber are all distinct from the "standing timber" on which the Panel based its conclusions. Moreover, what matters, for purposes of determining whether a government "provides goods" in the sense of Article 1.1(a)(1)(iii), is the conse-

quence of the transaction. Rights over felled trees or logs crystallize as a natural and inevitable consequence of the harvesters' exercise of their harvesting rights. Indeed, as the Panel indicated, the evidence suggests that making available timber is the raison d'être of the stumpage arrangements. Accordingly, like the Panel, we believe that, by granting a right to harvest standing timber, governments provide that standing timber to timber harvesters. We therefore agree with the Panel that, through stumpage arrangements, the provincial governments "provide" such goods, within the meaning of Article 1.1(a)(1)(iii) of the SCM Agreement.

76. For these reasons, we uphold the Panel's finding, in paragraph 7.30 of the Panel Report, that [the U.S. Department of Commerce] "[d]etermination that the Canadian provinces are providing a financial contribution in the form of the provision of a good by providing standing timber to timber harvesters through the stumpage programmes" is not inconsistent with Article 1.1(a)(1)(iii) of the SCM Agreement.

Canada has also used the NAFTA to challenge the US softwood tariffs. But its NAFTA challenges have turned on different considerations than its WTO appeals. Unlike the WTO, NAFTA does not include special international rules on dumping and subsidies. Each NAFTA party applies its own domestic dumping and subsidy trade rules (which, in any event, must be consistent with WTO rules since the three NAFTA parties are also WTO members). What Chapter 19 of NAFTA does, however, is introduce an international review mechanism for determinations made by each party applying its own laws: "[E]ach Party shall replace judicial review of final antidumping and countervailing duty determinations with binational panel review." These "binational panels" examine whether the party has applied its domestic law properly: "An involved Party may request that a panel review . . . a final antidumping or countervailing duty determination of a competent investigating authority of an importing Party to determine whether such determination was in accordance with the antidumping or countervailing duty law of the importing Party."[19]

In Lumber IV, Canada brought several NAFTA cases under Chapter 19, urging that the US government had failed to adhere to US law in assessing duties against Canadian softwood lumber. Canada was largely successful in these cases. However, the mix of WTO and NAFTA challenges launched in the Lumber IV dispute confused the question as to whether the United States had acted legally in imposing duties on Canadian softwood lumber. The WTO decisions have been more accommodating of the US position. Thus, while Canada has pointed to NAFTA rulings to press its argument that the United States has acted inconsistently with its trade agreements, the United States has sought solace in the WTO rulings. Consider the following discussion:

> While both sides claim victory, confusion prevails on the implications of these seemingly contradictory rulings. According to Canadian trade lawyer Lawrence Herman, the WTO and NAFTA rulings should not be seen as contradictory, but rather as "mutually exclusive." He noted that NAFTA panels evaluate compliance with domestic laws while the WTO Dispute Settlement Body assesses Members' adherence to international trade laws.

---

19 NAFTA, above note 8, art 1904.

The ensuing debate has also drawn attention to the logic of a country's engagement in overlapping trade agreements. Canada has been fighting U.S. duties under both trade pacts with the hopes that a win from either body would bolster their case. However, the findings that have emerged call this strategy into question. Indeed, with multiple rulings emerging from multiple trade panels on multiple issues, a gloss of confusion appears to have washed across the debate. While the WTO and NAFTA rulings do not address the same exact issue, they conflict on the key issue of whether U.S. duties on Canadian softwood — regardless of the set amount — are justified. Thus, both parties are pointing to the respective trade bodies' findings as proof of their vindication.[20]

In mid-2006 both countries negotiated a settlement of the lumber dispute.[21]

3) Binding Dispute Settlement

As the discussion in this chapter has already suggested, the international trade law regime includes sophisticated dispute settlement mechanisms. Consider the dispute settlement system of the WTO:

> World Trade Organization, *Understanding the WTO: Settling Disputes — A Unique Contribution* (undated), online: www.wto.org/english/thewto_e/whatis_e/tif_e/disp1_e.htm

> Dispute settlement is the central pillar of the multilateral trading system, and the WTO's unique contribution to the stability of the global economy. Without a means of settling disputes, the rules-based system would be less effective because the rules could not be enforced. The WTO's procedure underscores the rule of law, and it makes the trading system more secure and predictable. The system is based on clearly-defined rules, with timetables for completing a case. First rulings are made by a panel and endorsed (or rejected) by the WTO's full membership. Appeals based on points of law are possible.

> However, the point is not to pass judgement. The priority is to settle disputes, through consultations if possible. By January 2008, only about 136 of the nearly 369 cases had reached the full panel process. Most of the rest have either been notified as settled "out of court" or remain in a prolonged consultation phase — some since 1995.

> *Principles: equitable, fast, effective, mutually acceptable*
> Disputes in the WTO are essentially about broken promises. WTO members have agreed that if they believe fellow-members are violating trade rules, they will use the multilateral system of settling disputes instead of taking action unilaterally. That means abiding by the agreed procedures, and respecting judgements.

> A dispute arises when one country adopts a trade policy measure or takes some action that one or more fellow-WTO members considers to be breaking the WTO agreements,

---

20 International Centre for Trade and Sustainable Development, "NAFTA, WTO Panels Issue Seemingly Contradictory Rulings On Softwood Lumber" (2005) 9:29 *Bridges Weekly Trade Digest* 6 at 7, online: http://ictsd.org/news/bridgesweekly.

21 Softwood Lumber Agreement between the Government of Canada and the Government of the United States of America, 12 September 2006, Can TS 2006 No. 23, in force 12 October 2006.

or to be a failure to live up to obligations. A third group of countries can declare that they have an interest in the case and enjoy some rights.

A procedure for settling disputes existed under the old GATT, but it had no fixed timetables, rulings were easier to block, and many cases dragged on for a long time inconclusively. The Uruguay Round agreement introduced a more structured process with more clearly defined stages in the procedure. It introduced greater discipline for the length of time a case should take to be settled, with flexible deadlines set in various stages of the procedure. The agreement emphasizes that prompt settlement is essential if the WTO is to function effectively. It sets out in considerable detail the procedures and the timetable to be followed in resolving disputes. If a case runs its full course to a first ruling, it should not normally take more than about one year — 15 months if the case is appealed. The agreed time limits are flexible, and if the case is considered urgent (e.g., if perishable goods are involved), it is accelerated as much as possible.

The Uruguay Round agreement also made it impossible for the country losing a case to block the adoption of the ruling. Under the previous GATT procedure, rulings could only be adopted by consensus, meaning that a single objection could block the ruling. Now, rulings are automatically adopted unless there is a consensus to reject a ruling — any country wanting to block a ruling has to persuade all other WTO members (including its adversary in the case) to share its view.

Although much of the procedure does resemble a court or tribunal, the preferred solution is for the countries concerned to discuss their problems and settle the dispute by themselves. The first stage is therefore consultations between the governments concerned, and even when the case has progressed to other stages, consultation and mediation are still always possible . . . . [Chart omitted]

How are disputes settled?

Settling disputes is the responsibility of the Dispute Settlement Body (the General Council in another guise), which consists of all WTO members. The Dispute Settlement Body has the sole authority to establish "panels" of experts to consider the case, and to accept or reject the panels' findings or the results of an appeal. It monitors the implementation of the rulings and recommendations, and has the power to authorize retaliation when a country does not comply with a ruling.

- **First stage**: consultation (up to 60 days). Before taking any other actions the countries in dispute have to talk to each other to see if they can settle their differences by themselves. If that fails, they can also ask the WTO director-general to mediate or try to help in any other way.
- **Second stage**: the panel (up to 45 days for a panel to be appointed, plus 6 months for the panel to conclude). If consultations fail, the complaining country can ask for a panel to be appointed. The country "in the dock" can block the creation of a panel once, but when the Dispute Settlement Body meets for a second time, the appointment can no longer be blocked (unless there is a consensus against appointing the panel).

Officially, the panel is helping the Dispute Settlement Body make rulings or recommendations. But because the panel's report can only be rejected by consensus in the Dispute Settlement Body, its conclusions are difficult to overturn. The panel's findings have to be based on the agreements cited.

The panel's final report should normally be given to the parties to the dispute within six months. In cases of urgency, including those concerning perishable goods, the deadline is shortened to three months.

The agreement describes in some detail how the panels are to work. The main stages are:

- **Before the first hearing**: each side in the dispute presents its case in writing to the panel.
- **First hearing: the case for the complaining country and defence**: The complaining country (or countries), the responding country, and those that have announced they have an interest in the dispute, make their case at the panel's first hearing.
- **Rebuttals**: The countries involved submit written rebuttals and present oral arguments at the panel's second meeting.
- **Experts**: If one side raises scientific or other technical matters, the panel may consult experts or appoint an expert review group to prepare an advisory report.
- **First draft**: The panel submits the descriptive (factual and argument) sections of its report to the two sides, giving them two weeks to comment. This report does not include findings and conclusions.
- **Interim report**: The panel then submits an interim report, including its findings and conclusions, to the two sides, giving them one week to ask for a review.
- **Review**: The period of review must not exceed two weeks. During that time, the panel may hold additional meetings with the two sides.
- **Final report**: A final report is submitted to the two sides and three weeks later, it is circulated to all WTO members. If the panel decides that the disputed trade measure does break a WTO agreement or an obligation, it recommends that the measure be made to conform with WTO rules. The panel may suggest how this could be done.
- **The report becomes a ruling**: The report becomes the Dispute Settlement Body's ruling or recommendation within 60 days unless a consensus rejects it. Both sides can appcal the report (and in some cases both sides do).

Appeals

Either side can appeal a panel's ruling. Sometimes both sides do so. Appeals have to be based on points of law such as legal interpretation—they cannot reexamine existing evidence or examine new issues.

Each appeal is heard by three members of a permanent seven-member Appellate Body set up by the Dispute Settlement Body and broadly representing the range of WTO membership. Members of the Appellate Body have four-year terms. They have to be individuals with recognized standing in the field of law and international trade, not affiliated with any government.

The appeal can uphold, modify or reverse the panel's legal findings and conclusions. Normally appeals should not last more than 60 days, with an absolute maximum of 90 days.

The Dispute Settlement Body has to accept or reject the appeals report within 30 days—and rejection is only possible by consensus.

The case has been decided: what next?

... If a country has done something wrong, it should swiftly correct its fault. And if it continues to break an agreement, it should offer compensation or suffer a suitable penalty that has some bite.

Even once the case has been decided, there is more to do before trade sanctions (the conventional form of penalty) are imposed. The priority at this stage is for the losing "defendant" to bring its policy into line with the ruling or recommendations. The dispute settlement agreement stresses that "prompt compliance with recommendations or rulings of the DSB [Dispute Settlement Body] is essential in order to ensure effective resolution of disputes to the benefit of all Members."

If the country that is the target of the complaint loses, it must follow the recommendations of the panel report or the appeals report. It must state its intention to do so at a Dispute Settlement Body meeting held within 30 days of the report's adoption. If complying with the recommendation immediately proves impractical, the member will be given a "reasonable period of time" to do so. If it fails to act within this period, it has to enter into negotiations with the complaining country (or countries) in order to determine mutually-acceptable compensation — for instance, tariff reductions in areas of particular interest to the complaining side.

If after 20 days, no satisfactory compensation is agreed, the complaining side may ask the Dispute Settlement Body for permission to impose limited trade sanctions ("suspend concessions or obligations") against the other side. The Dispute Settlement Body must grant this authorization within 30 days of the expiry of the "reasonable period of time" unless there is a consensus against the request.

In principle, the sanctions should be imposed in the same sector as the dispute. If this is not practical or if it would not be effective, the sanctions can be imposed in a different sector of the same agreement. In turn, if this is not effective or practicable and if the circumstances are serious enough, the action can be taken under another agreement. The objective is to minimize the chances of actions spilling over into unrelated sectors while at the same time allowing the actions to be effective.

In any case, the Dispute Settlement Body monitors how adopted rulings are implemented. Any outstanding case remains on its agenda until the issue is resolved.

CHAPTER 11

INTERNATIONAL ENVIRONMENTAL LAW

A. INTRODUCTION

International environmental law comprises substantive, procedural, and institutional rules of international law that have the primary objective of protecting of the environment.[1] That said, "the legal underpinnings of the protection of the environment continue to be institutions of general international law," such as the principles of state responsibility (which we examine in Chapter 12).[2] Environmental issues touch directly or indirectly upon almost every aspect of legal regulation, and the breadth of international environmental law is correspondingly wide. Consider how environmental concerns have already been implicated in previous chapters, such as in our discussions of the law of the sea and the legal regime of Antarctica.

There is no single international legal definition of the "environment," but it is generally agreed that the concept is broader than natural habitats or ecosystems and includes artificial and human environments. Some treaties that use the term "environment" simply do not define it.[3] Others have adopted varying definitions. For example, the 1979 Convention on Long-range Transboundary Air Pollution defines "environment" as including "agriculture, forestry, materials, aquatic and other natural ecosystems and visibility."[4] The more recent 1991 Convention on Environmental Impact Assessment in a Transboundary Context defines "environment" to include "human health and safety, flora, fauna, soil, air, water, climate, landscape and historical monuments or other physical structures or the interaction among these factors."[5] The International Court of Justice (ICJ) has observed

---

1 Philippe Sands & Jacqueline Peel, *Principles of International Environmental Law*, 3d ed (New York: Cambridge University Press, 2012) at 13.

2 James Crawford, *Brownlie's Principles of Public International Law*, 8th ed (Oxford: Oxford University Press, 2012) at 353 [*Brownlie's Principles*].

3 See, for example, United Nations Convention on the Law of the Sea, 10 December 1982, 1833 UNTS 3, (1982) 21 ILM 1261, in force 16 November 1994 [UNCLOS], which does not define the term "marine environment" used in articles 194(3)(d) and (4). See also the 2013 Minamata Convention on Mercury in *Report of the Intergovernmental Negotiating Committee to Prepare a Global Legally Binding Instrument on Mercury on the Work of its Fifth Session*, UN Doc UNEP (DTIE)/Hg/INC.5/7 (14 March 2013), which does not define "environment" but uses the word throughout (for example, in arts 1–3, 5–14, 17–19, and 22–24).

4 Convention on Long-range Transboundary Air Pollution, 13 November 1979, 1302 UNTS 217, Can TS 1983 No 34, (1979) 18 ILM 1442, in force 16 March 1983, art 7(d) [Long-range Transboundary Air Pollution Convention].

5 Convention on Environmental Impact Assessment in a Transboundary Context (Espoo Convention), 25 February 1991, 1989 UNTS 309, Can TS 1998 No 11, (1991) 30 ILM 800, in force 10 September 1997, art 1(vii) [Espoo Convention]. See further, Neil Craik, *The International Law of Environmental Impact Assessment: Process, Substance and Integration* (New York: Cambridge University Press, 2008).

that "the environment is not an abstraction but represents the living space, the quality of life and the very health of human beings, including generations unborn."[6]

The development of international environmental law is often regarded as falling into three periods.[7] In the first period, environmental issues were viewed as bilateral "side" issues relating to the larger issue of economic development. The 1941 *Trail Smelter*[8] arbitral award excerpted below falls into this phase. The second period was characterized by significantly increased focus on the environmental impact of pollution and its effect on wildlife and habitat. In this phase, a large number of multilateral treaties were adopted, often in response to specific incidents of environmental degradation. For example, the 1986 Vienna Convention on Early Notification of a Nuclear Accident was adopted following the Chernobyl nuclear disaster.[9] Thus, this period was largely reactive. The current period is characterized by an understanding that environmental degradation is a worldwide issue that concerns not just individual states, but humankind as a whole. Treaties such as the 1992 United Nations Framework Convention on Climate Change[10] and its 1997 Kyoto Protocol[11] are illustrative of legal developments during this phase. This chapter begins by examining international environmental law's general legal principles, and then turns to those that may be emerging or evolving. It next explores international legal protections relating to specific environmental concerns: protection of the atmosphere against transboundary air pollution, ozone depletion, and global climate change; activities involving nuclear, toxic, and hazardous substances; marine pollution; and the protection of biodiversity and conservation of living resources.

B. GENERAL PRINCIPLES OF INTERNATIONAL ENVIRONMENTAL LAW

The late international law professor Antonio Cassese noted that there are four general legal principles that underpin international environmental law: first, states must not allow their territory to be used in such a manner as to damage the environment of other states; second, states must cooperate to protect the environment; third, states must immediately notify other states of a risk to the environment; and fourth, states must refrain from massive pollution of the atmosphere or the seas.[12]

---

6 *Legality of the Threat or Use of Nuclear Weapons*, Advisory Opinion, [1996] ICJ Rep 226 at para 29 [*Nuclear Weapons Advisory Opinion*].

7 See, for example, Catherine Redgwell, "International Environmental Law" in Malcolm D Evans, ed, *International Law*, 3d ed (New York: Oxford University Press, 2010) at 687.

8 *Trail Smelter Arbitration (United States v Canada)*, (1931–1941) 3 RIAA 1905.

9 Vienna Convention on Early Notification of a Nuclear Accident, 26 September 1986, 1439 UNTS 276, Can TS 1990 No 21, (1986) 25 ILM 1370, in force 27 October 1986.

10 9 May 1992, 1771 UNTS 107, Can TS 1994 No 7, (1992) 31 ILM 849, in force 21 March 1994 [Climate Change Convention].

11 Kyoto Protocol to the United Nations Framework Convention on Climate Change, 11 December 1997, 2303 UNTS 214, (1998) 37 ILM 22, in force 16 February 2005 (entry into force for Canada 17 December 2002, withdrawal effective 15 December 2012) [Kyoto Protocol].

12 Antonio Cassese, *International Law*, 2d ed (New York: Oxford University Press, 2005) at 487.

1) States Must Not Allow Their Territory to Be Used in a Manner that Damages the Environment of Other States

The ICJ, in its 1996 advisory opinion on the *Legality of the Threat or Use of Nuclear Weapons*, observed: "The existence of the general obligation of States to ensure that activities within their jurisdiction and control respect the environment of other States or of areas beyond national control is now part of the corpus of international law relating to the environment."[13] One of the earliest applications of this general principle was in the well-known 1941 *Trail Smelter* arbitration.

Trail Smelter Arbitration (United States v Canada), (1931–1941) 3 RIAA 1905

[Beginning in 1896, a smelter was operated at Trail, British Columbia. As of 1906, this smelter was owned and operated by the Consolidated Mining and Smelting Company of Canada. The United States claimed that the sulphur dioxide emissions from the smelter had caused environmental damage, at least during the period 1925 to 1937, including to land used for cattle grazing and growing of crops, and to trees that were crucial to the logging industry. Canada and the United States asked the International Joint Commission to resolve this issue. When that attempt failed, Canada and the United States agreed to arbitration of the following issues:

1) Whether damage caused by the Trail Smelter in the State of Washington has occurred since the first day of January 1932, and, if so, what indemnity should be paid therefor?
2) In the event of the answer to the first part of the preceding question being in the affirmative, whether the Trail Smelter should be required to refrain from causing damage in the State of Washington in the future and, if so, to what extent?
3) In the light of the answer to the preceding question, what measures or regime, if any, should be adopted or maintained by the Trail Smelter?
4) What indemnity or compensation, if any, should be paid on account of any decision or decisions rendered by the Tribunal pursuant to the first two questions?

In its interim decision of 1938, the Tribunal found that the Trail Smelter had caused damage in the United States from 1 January 1932 to 1 October 1937 and that Canada should pay $78,000 plus interest in compensation. In its 1941 final decision, the Tribunal addressed the issue of how states must govern the use of their territory:]

The second question under Article III of the Convention is as follows:

> In the event of the answer to the first part of the preceding question being in the affirmative, whether the Trail Smelter should be required to refrain from causing damage in the State of Washington in the future and, if so, to what extent?

> Damage has occurred since January 1, 1932, as fully set forth in the previous decision. To that extent, the first part of the preceding question has thus been answered in the affirmative.

---

13   *Nuclear Weapons Advisory Opinion*, above note 6.

As has been said above, the report of the International Joint Commission . . . contained a definition of the word "damage" excluding "occasional damage that may be caused by SO_2 fumes being carried across the international boundary in air pockets or by reason of unusual atmospheric conditions," as far, at least, as the duty of the Smelter to reduce the presence of that gas in the air was concerned . . . .

As Professor Eagleton puts in (*Responsibility of States in International Law*, 1928, p. 80): "A State owes at all times a duty to protect other States against injurious acts by individuals from within its jurisdiction." A great number of such general pronouncements by leading authorities concerning the duty of a State to respect other States and their territory have been presented to the Tribunal. These and many others have been carefully examined. International decisions, in various matters, from the *Alabama* case onward, and also earlier ones, are based on the same general principle, and, indeed, this principle, as such, has not been questioned by Canada. But the real difficulty often arises rather when it comes to determine what, *pro subjecta materie*, is deemed to constitute an injurious act . . . .

No case of air pollution dealt with by an international tribunal has been brought to the attention of the Tribunal nor does the Tribunal know of any such case. The nearest analogy is that of water pollution. But, here also, no decision of an international tribunal has been cited or has been found.

There are, however, as regards both air pollution and water pollution, certain decisions of the Supreme Court of the United States which may legitimately be taken as a guide in this field of international law, for it is reasonable to follow by analogy, in international cases, precedents established by that court in dealing with controversies between States of the Union or with other controversies concerning the quasi-sovereign rights of such States, where no contrary rule prevails in international law and no reason for rejecting such precedents can be adduced from the limitations of sovereignty inherent in the Constitution of the United States . . . .

The Tribunal . . . finds that [these US Supreme Court] decisions, taken as a whole, constitute an adequate basis for its conclusions, namely, that, under the principles of international law, as well as of the law of the United States, no State has the right to use or permit the use of its territory in such a manner as to cause injury by fumes in or to the territory of another or the properties or persons therein, when the case is of serious consequence and the injury is established by clear and convincing evidence.

The decisions of the Supreme Court of the United States which are the basis of these conclusions are decisions in equity and a solution inspired by them, together with the régime hereinafter prescribed, will, in the opinion of the Tribunal, be "just to all parties concerned", as long, at least, as the present conditions in the Columbia River Valley continue to prevail.

Considering the circumstances of the case, the Tribunal holds that the Dominion of Canada is responsible in international law for the conduct of the Trail Smelter. Apart from the undertakings in the Convention, it is, therefore, the duty of the Government of the Dominion of Canada to see to it that this conduct should be in conformity with the obligation of the Dominion under international law as herein determined.

The Tribunal, therefore, answers Question No. 2 as follows: (2) So long as the present conditions in the Columbia River Valley prevail, the Trail Smelter shall be required to refrain from causing any damage through fumes in the State of Washington; the damage herein referred to and its extent being such as would be recoverable under the decisions of the courts of the United States in suits between private individuals. The indemnity for such damage should be fixed in such manner as the Governments, acting under Article XI of the Convention, should agree upon.

The obligation of states not to allow their territory to be used in such a manner as to damage the environment of other states is generally considered to be a well-established rule of customary international law.[14]

2) States Must Cooperate to Protect the Environment

Consider the general principle of cooperation for the protection of the environment recited in Principle 24 of the 1972 Stockholm Declaration of the United Nations Conference on the Human Environment:

> International matters concerning the protection and improvement of the environment should be handled in a cooperative spirit by all countries, big and small, on an equal footing. Co-operation through multilateral or bilateral arrangements or other appropriate means is essential to effectively control, prevent, reduce and eliminate adverse environmental effects resulting from activities conducted in all spheres, in such a way that due account is taken of the sovereignty and interests of all States.[15]

While the principle of cooperation is implicit in most international environmental law treaties, Article 197 of the United Nations Convention on the Law of the Sea refers to the principle explicitly: "States shall cooperate on a global basis and, as appropriate, on a regional basis, directly or through competent international organizations, in formulating and elaborating international rules, standards and recommended practices and procedures consistent with this Convention, for the protection and preservation of the marine environment . . . ."

This principle is based on the assumption that the environment is a matter of concern to all states, and that all states must cooperate for the protection of this asset regardless of whether or not their own environment has been or may be harmed.[16] Cassese, however, has noted that, due to the vagueness of this general principle, it must be applied jointly with the customary international legal norm of good faith: "every State must in good faith endeavour to co-operate with other States with a view to protecting the environment."[17]

---

14 See, for example, Michael B Akehurst, "International Liability for Injurious Consequences Arising Out of Acts Not Prohibited by International Law" (1985) Nethl YB Int'l Law 3 at 5. See also Sands & Peel, above note 1 at 191.

15 The official text of the *Declaration of the United Nations Conference on the Human Environment* can be found in *Report of the United Nations Conference on the Human Environment: Stockholm, 5–16 June 1972*, UN Doc A/CONF.48/14/Rev.1 (1973) at 3–5.

16 Cassese, above note 12 at 489.

17 *Ibid.*

3) States Must Immediately Notify Other States of a Risk to the Environment

The obligation to notify other states of risks to the environment largely developed during international environmental law's second period described in the introduction. This obligation was invoked in the aftermath of the 1986 Chernobyl nuclear accident in Ukraine, during which the then Soviet Union failed to inform other states of the accident in a timely fashion. That same year, states adopted the following convention:

Convention on Early Notification of a Nuclear Accident, 26 September 1986, 1439 UNTS 276, Can TS 1990 No 21, (1986) 25 ILM 1370, in force 27 October 1986

The States Parties to this Convention,

. . .

Convinced of the need for States to provide relevant information about nuclear accidents as early as possible in order that transboundary radiological consequences can be minimized, . . .

Have agreed as follows:

Article 1
Scope of application
1. This Convention shall apply in the event of any accident involving facilities or activities of a State Party or of persons or legal entities under its jurisdiction or control, referred to in paragraph 2 below, from which a release of radioactive material occurs or is likely to occur and which has resulted or may result in an international transboundary release that could be of radiological safety significance for another State.

2. The facilities and activities referred to in paragraph 1 are the following:
(a) any nuclear reactor wherever located;
(b) any nuclear fuel cycle facility;
(c) any radioactive waste management facility;
(d) the transport and storage of nuclear fuels or radioactive wastes;
(e) the manufacture, use, storage, disposal and transport of radioisotopes for agricultural, industrial, medical and related scientific and research purposes; and
(f) the use of radioisotopes for power generation in space objects.

Article 2
Notification and information
In the event of an accident specified in article 1 (hereinafter referred to as a "nuclear accident"), the State Party referred to in that article shall:
(a) forthwith notify, directly or though the International Atomic Energy Agency (hereinafter referred to as the "Agency"), those States which are or may be physically affected as specified in article 1 and the Agency of the nuclear accident, its nature, the time of its occurrence and its exact location where appropriate; and
(b) promptly provide the States referred to in sub-paragraph (a), directly or through the Agency, and the Agency with such available information relevant to minimizing the radiological consequences in those States, as specified in article 5.

Article 3

Other Nuclear Accidents

With a view to minimizing the radiological consequences, States Parties may notify in the event of nuclear accidents other than those specified in article 1.

Article 4

Functions of the Agency

The Agency shall:

(a) forthwith inform States Parties, Member States, other States which are or may be physically affected as specified in article 1 and relevant international intergovernmental organizations (hereinafter referred to as "international organizations") of a notification received pursuant to sub-paragraph (a) of article 2; and

(b) promptly provide any State Party, Member State or relevant international organization, upon request, with the information received pursuant to sub-paragraph (b) of article 2.

Article 5

Information to be provided

1. The information to be provided pursuant to sub-paragraph (b) of article 2 shall comprise the following data as then available to the notifying State Party:

(a) the time, exact location where appropriate, and the nature of the nuclear accident;

(b) the facility or activity involved;

(c) the assumed or established cause and the foreseeable development of the nuclear accident relevant to the transboundary release of the radioactive materials;

(d) the general characteristics of the radioactive release, including, as far as is practicable and appropriate, the nature, probable physical and chemical form and the quantity, composition and effective height of the radioactive release;

(e) information on current and forecast meteorological and hydrological conditions, necessary for forecasting the transboundary release of the radioactive materials;

(f) the results of environmental monitoring relevant to the transboundary release of the radioactive materials;

(g) the off-site protective measures taken or planned;

(h) the predicted behaviour over time of the radioactive release.

2. Such information shall be supplemented at appropriate intervals by further relevant information on the development of the emergency situation, including its foreseeable or actual termination.

3. Information received pursuant to sub-paragraph (b) of article 2 may be used without restriction, except when such information is provided in confidence by the notifying State Party.

Article 6

Consultations

A State Party providing information pursuant to sub-paragraph (b) of article 2 shall, as far as is reasonably practicable, respond promptly to a request for further information or consultations sought by an affected State Party with a view to minimizing the radiological consequences in that State . . . .

The principle of early notification was reiterated in Principles 18 and 19 of the declaration adopted at the United Nations Conference on Environment and Development held in Rio de Janeiro in June 1992:

Rio Declaration on Environment and Development, UN Doc A/CONF.151/26/Rev.1 (vol 1) (1993) at 3–8, (1992) 31 ILM 876

Principle 18

States shall immediately notify other States of any natural disasters or other emergencies that are likely to produce sudden harmful effects on the environment of those States. Every effort shall be made by the international community to help States so afflicted.

Principle 19

States shall provide prior and timely notification and relevant information to potentially affected States on activities that may have a significant adverse transboundary environmental effect and shall consult with those States at an early stage and in good faith . . . .

Some commentators now argue that this duty to notify of potential transboundary harm has become a rule of customary international law.[18]

4) States Must Refrain from Massive Pollution of the Atmosphere or the Seas

The general principle that states must refrain from massive pollution of the atmosphere or the seas has evolved under the influence of the United Nations Convention on the Law of the Sea and other treaties addressing protection of the marine environment, as well as through international conventions relating to the ozone layer, global warming, climate change, and transboundary air pollution. These conventions are discussed in Section D below.

C. EMERGING OR EVOLVING PRINCIPLES OF INTERNATIONAL ENVIRONMENTAL LAW

There are a number of apparently emerging or evolving principles that are also important to an understanding of the framework of international environmental law. These are the principles of prevention; sustainable development; the rights of future generations; common but differentiated responsibilities; the precautionary approach; and the polluter pays. Each of these emerging or evolving principles will be examined in turn.

1) Prevention

The principle of prevention embraces the common sense position in favour of "timely prevention of environmental damage to the greatest extent possible, particularly when it is likely to be irreversible or too insidious or diffuse to be effectively dealt with through

---

18 Redgwell, above note 7 at 695.

civil liability or when reparation would be extremely expensive."[19] Prevention is frequently the goal of environmental law treaties because it is often impossible to remedy environmental harm once it has occurred.

In 2001, the International Law Commission adopted draft articles on the Prevention of Transboundary Harm from Hazardous Activities and recommended to the UN General Assembly that a convention be negotiated on the basis of these draft articles. The draft articles have been described as "provid[ing] an authoritative statement on the scope of a state's international legal obligation to prevent a risk of transboundary harm,"[20] although there is "uncertainty regarding their future formal status."[21] Consider some key articles from that document:

Draft Articles on Prevention of Transboundary Harm from Hazardous Activities in
Report of the International Law Commission, **UN GAOR, 56th Sess, Supp No 10 at 370–77, UN Doc A/56/10 (2001)**

Article 3
Prevention
The State of origin shall take all appropriate measures to prevent significant transboundary harm or at any event to minimize the risk thereof.

Article 4
Cooperation
States concerned shall cooperate in good faith and, as necessary, seek the assistance of one or more competent international organizations in preventing significant transboundary harm or at any event in minimizing the risk thereof.

Article 5
Implementation
States concerned shall take the necessary legislative, administrative or other action, including the establishment of suitable monitoring mechanisms to implement the provisions of the present articles.

Article 6
Authorization
1. The State of origin shall require its prior authorization for:
    (a) any activity within the scope of the present articles carried out in its territory or otherwise under its jurisdiction or control;
    (b) any major change in an activity referred to in subparagraph (a);
    (c) any plan to change an activity which may transform it into one falling within the scope of the present articles. . . .

---

19 Nicolas de Sadeleer, *Environmental Principles: From Political Slogans to Legal Rules* (New York: Oxford University Press, 2002) at 61. This approach was also noted by the ICJ in *Gabčíkovo-Nagymaros Project (Hungary/Slovakia)*, [1997] ICJ Rep 7 at 78 [*Gabčíkovo-Nagymaros*].
20 *Brownlie's Principles*, above note 2 at 357.
21 Günther Handl, "Transboundary Impacts" in Daniel Bodansky, Jutta Brunnée, & Ellen Hey, eds, *The Oxford Handbook of International Environmental Law* (New York: Oxford University Press, 2007) 531 at 540 [*Oxford Handbook*].

Article 7

Assessment of risk

Any decision in respect of the authorization of an activity within the scope of the present articles shall, in particular, be based on an assessment of the possible transboundary harm caused by that activity, including any environmental impact assessment.

Article 8

Notification and information

1. If the assessment referred to in article 7 indicates a risk of causing significant transboundary harm, the State of origin shall provide the State likely to be affected with timely notification of the risk and the assessment and shall transmit to it the available technical and all other relevant information on which the assessment is based.

2. The State of origin shall not take any decision on authorization of the activity pending the receipt, within a period not exceeding six months, of the response from the State likely to be affected.

Article 9

Consultations on preventive measures

1. The States concerned shall enter into consultations, at the request of any of them, with a view to achieving acceptable solutions regarding measures to be adopted in order to prevent significant transboundary harm or at any event to minimize the risk thereof. The States concerned shall agree, at the commencement of such consultations, on a reasonable time frame for the consultations.

2. The States concerned shall seek solutions based on an equitable balance of interests in the light of article 10.

3. If the consultations referred to in paragraph 1 fail to produce an agreed solution, the State of origin shall nevertheless take into account the interests of the State likely to be affected in case it decides to authorize the activity to be pursued, without prejudice to the rights of any State likely to be affected.

Article 10

Factors involved in an equitable balance of interests

In order to achieve an equitable balance of interests as referred to in paragraph 2 of article 9, the States concerned shall take into account all relevant factors and circumstances, including:

(a) the degree of risk of significant transboundary harm and of the availability of means of preventing such harm, or minimizing the risk thereof or repairing the harm;

(b) the importance of the activity, taking into account its overall advantages of a social, economic and technical character for the State of origin in relation to the potential harm for the State likely to be affected;

(c) the risk of significant harm to the environment and the availability of means of preventing such harm, or minimizing the risk thereof or restoring the environment;

(d) the degree to which the State of origin and, as appropriate, the State likely to be affected are prepared to contribute to the costs of prevention;

(e) the economic viability of the activity in relation to the costs of prevention and to the possibility of carrying out the activity elsewhere or by other means or replacing it with an alternative activity;

(f) the standards of prevention which the State likely to be affected applies to the same or comparable activities and the standards applied in comparable regional or international practice.

Article 11
Procedures in the absence of notification
1. If a State has reasonable grounds to believe that an activity planned or carried out in the State of origin may involve a risk of causing significant transboundary harm to it, it may request the State of origin to apply the provision of article 8. The request shall be accompanied by a documented explanation setting forth its grounds.

2. In the event that the State of origin nevertheless finds that it is not under an obligation to provide a notification under article 8, it shall so inform the requesting State within a reasonable time, providing a documented explanation setting forth the reasons for such finding. If this finding does not satisfy that State, at its request, the two States shall promptly enter into consultations in the manner indicated in article 9.

3. During the course of the consultations, the State of origin shall, if so requested by the other State, arrange to introduce appropriate and feasible measures to minimize the risk and, where appropriate, to suspend the activity in question for a reasonable period . . . .

The prevention principle is implemented primarily through the use of environmental impact assessments, which are meant to determine whether a particular activity will result in environmental damage within a state or to other states.[22] Principle 17 of the 1992 Rio Declaration states that: "Environmental impact assessment, as a national instrument, shall be undertaken for proposed activities that are likely to have a significant adverse impact on the environment and are subject to a decision of a competent national authority."[23] Consider how environmental impact assessment is used as a method of implementing the principle of prevention in Article 14 of the 1992 Convention on Biological Diversity:

Convention on Biological Diversity, 5 June 1992, 1760 UNTS 79, Can TS 1993 No 24, (1992) 31 ILM 818, in force 29 December 1993

Article 14
Impact Assessment and Minimizing Adverse Impacts
1. Each Contracting Party, as far as possible and as appropriate, shall:
    (a) Introduce appropriate procedures requiring environmental impact assessment of its proposed projects that are likely to have significant adverse effects on biological

---

22 The best known treaty-based iteration of the requirement to conduct environmental impact assessments is found in the Espoo Convention, above note 5.

23 *Rio Declaration on Environment and Development* in *Report of the United Nations Conference on Environment and Development: Rio de Janeiro, 3–14 June 1992*, UN Doc A/CONF.151/26/Rev.1 (1993) (vol I) at 3–8, (1992) 31 ILM 876 [1992 Rio Declaration].

diversity with a view to avoiding or minimizing such effects and, where appropriate, allow for public participation in such procedures;

(b) Introduce appropriate arrangements to ensure that the environmental consequences of its programmes and policies that are likely to have significant adverse impacts on biological diversity are duly taken into account;

(c) Promote, on the basis of reciprocity, notification, exchange of information and consultation on activities under their jurisdiction or control which are likely to significantly affect adversely the biological diversity of other States or areas beyond the limits of national jurisdiction, by encouraging the conclusion of bilateral, regional or multilateral arrangements, as appropriate;

(d) In the case of imminent or grave danger or damage, originating under its jurisdiction or control, to biological diversity within the area under jurisdiction of other States or in areas beyond the limits of national jurisdiction, notify immediately the potentially affected States of such danger or damage, as well as initiate action to prevent or minimize such danger or damage; and

(e) Promote national arrangements for emergency responses to activities or events, whether caused naturally or otherwise, which present a grave and imminent danger to biological diversity and encourage international cooperation to supplement such national efforts and, where appropriate and agreed by the States or regional economic integration organizations concerned, to establish joint contingency plans.

The ICJ has recently commented on the use of environmental impact assessments, finding:

[A] practice, which in recent years has gained so much acceptance among States that it may now be considered a requirement under general international law to undertake an environmental impact assessment where there is a risk that the proposed industrial activity may have a significant adverse impact in a transboundary context, in particular, on a shared resource. Moreover, due diligence, and the duty of vigilance and prevention which it implies, would not be considered to have been exercised, if a party planning works liable to affect the régime of the river or the quality of its waters did not undertake an environmental impact assessment on the potential effects of such works.[24]

However, the ICJ also noted that international law does not define either the required scope or substantive content of an environmental impact assessment:

Consequently, it is the view of the Court that it is for each State to determine in its domestic legislation or in the authorization process for the project, the specific content of the environmental impact assessment required in each case, having regard to the nature and magnitude of the proposed development and its likely adverse impact on the environment as well as to the need to exercise due diligence in conducting such an assessment. The Court also considers that an environmental impact assessment must be conducted prior to the implementation of a project. Moreover, once operations have started and,

---

24   *Pulp Mills on the River Uruguay (Argentina v Uruguay)*, Judgment, [2010] ICJ Rep 14 at para 204.

where necessary, throughout the life of the project, continuous monitoring of its effects on the environment shall be undertaken.[25]

Professor Crawford, in his revision of *Brownlie's Principles of Public International Law*, points out that this hybrid obligation — under which international law requires an environmental impact assessment, but domestic law determines its content and scope — is problematic, in particular for the evaluation of transboundary harm.[26]

The principle of prevention is attended by many uncertainties in its current state of development. Is full knowledge of the risk of the potential injuries required before the principle is engaged? Should the principle be acted upon at the moment any injury is detected, or can it be implemented later? Does the principle apply to the source of the environmental damage, or to the effect of the damage?[27]

2) Sustainable Development

Sustainable development has become an integral part of the conceptual framework of international environmental law,[28] although it is also emerging as a distinct legal field.[29] In 1987, the World Commission on Environment and Development issued its well-known report, *Our Common Future*, which defines "sustainable development" as "development that meets the needs of the present without compromising the ability of future generations to meet their own needs."[30] That report concluded that development (including that of the least developed countries) and environmental protection need not be considered mutually incompatible. Economic growth is both desirable and possible within a context of sustainable development. Indeed, "[d]evelopment, a process of change toward improving quality of life for human beings and their communities, is said to be sustainable when it is achieved by the integration of social, economic, and environmental considerations in a way that provides for and protects the long-term well-being of populations."[31]

The term "sustainable development" appears several times in the 1992 Rio Declaration. For example, Principle 4 states: "In order to achieve sustainable development, environmental protection shall constitute an integral part of the development process and cannot be considered in isolation from it."[32] Sustainable development was also recognized and defined by Vice President Weeramantry in his separate opinion in the *Gabčíkovo-Nagymaros* case:

---

25   *Ibid* at para 205.

26   *Brownlie's Principles*, above note 2 at 360.

27   See further, De Sadeleer, above note 19 at 80–82 and 89–90.

28   Sands & Peel, above note 1 at 206, refer to sustainable development as an "international legal concept"; Crawford (and Brownlie before him), in *Brownlie's Principles*, above note 2 at 356 and 358, consider it an "emergent legal principle"; and Cassese, above note 12 at 492, described it as a "general guideline" laid down in soft law documents.

29   *Brownlie's Principles*, above note 2 at 358.

30   Gro Harlem Bruntland, ed, *Our Common Future: The World Commission on Environment and Development* (Oxford: Oxford University Press, 1987) at 43 [*Our Common Future*].

31   *Brownlie's Principles*, above note 2 at 358.

32   1992 Rio Declaration, above note 23, Principle 4.

[I]t has been recognized that development cannot be pursued to such a point as to result in substantial damage to the environment within which it is to occur. Therefore development can only be prosecuted in harmony with the reasonable demands of environmental protection . . . .

The principle of sustainable development is . . . a part of modern international law by reason not only of its inescapable logical necessity, but also by reason of its wide and general acceptance by the global community.[33]

More recently, sustainable development was the focus of the 2012 United Nations Rio+20 Conference on Sustainable Development. The outcome document, contained in Resolution I adopted by that conference and entitled *The Future We Want*, defined sustainable development in a roundabout manner:

[P]overty eradication, changing unsustainable and promoting sustainable patterns of consumption and production and protecting and managing the natural resource base of economic and social development are the overarching objectives of and essential requirements for sustainable development. [Heads of State and Government and high level representatives] also reaffirm the need to achieve sustainable development by promoting sustained, inclusive and equitable economic growth, creating greater opportunities for all, reducing inequalities, raising basic standards of living, fostering equitable social development and inclusion, and promoting the integrated and sustainable management of natural resources and ecosystems that supports, inter alia, economic, social and human development while facilitating ecosystem conservation, regeneration and restoration and resilience in the face of new and emerging challenges.[34]

While sustainable development has become an important concept, "because of its changeable content and scope, [it] has to be assigned to the sphere of mere political ideals," although the same commentators recognize that "it is an important source from which subsequent legal norms can flow."[35] Others agree that the principle does not form part of customary international law, but for different reasons: "sustainable development is better understood as a collection, or collation, of different legal categories," such as those relating to human rights and trade.[36]

What does the concept of sustainable development contribute to international environmental law? Does this concept help to reconcile the views of developing and developed states regarding the balance to be struck between development and environmental protection?

---

33   *Gabčíkovo-Nagymaros*, above note 19 at 92–95.

34   "Outcome document: 'The Future We Want'" in *Report of the United Nations Conference on Sustainable Development: Rio de Janeiro, 20–22 June 2012*, UN Doc A/CONF.216/16 (2012) 1 at para 4 [*The Future We Want*].

35   Ulrich Beyerlin & Jenny Grote Stoutenburg, "Environment, International Protection" in Rüdiger Wolfrum, ed, *Max Planck Encyclopedia of Public International Law*, vol III (New York: Oxford University Press, 2012) 461 at para 27.

36   *Brownlie's Principles*, above note 2 at 358.

3) Rights of Future Generations

Principle 3 of the 1992 Rio Declaration states: "The right to development must be fulfilled so as to equitably meet developmental and environmental needs of present and future generations."[37] This principle may well have been inspired by Article 4 of the 1972 World Heritage Convention, which provides that "[e]ach State Party to this Convention recognizes that the duty of ensuring the identification, protection, conservation, presentation and transmission to future generations of the cultural and natural heritage . . . situated on its territory, belongs primarily to that State."[38] In addition, Article 3(1) of the Climate Change Convention provides that "[t]he Parties should protect the climate system for the benefit of present and future generations of humankind."[39]

Judge Weeramantry's dissenting opinion with respect to an order granted in the 1995 *Nuclear Tests Case* commented on intergenerational equity, noting that it is "an important and rapidly developing principle of contemporary environmental law."[40] The principle of intergenerational equity has also been described in the following way:

> Inter-generational equity is based upon the recognition of two key facts: (1) that human life emerged from, and is dependent upon, the Earth's natural resource base, including its ecological processes, and is thus inseparable from environmental conditions; and (2) that human beings have a unique capacity to alter the environment upon which life depends. From these facts emerges the notion that humans [who] are alive today have a special obligation as custodians or trustees of the planet to maintain its integrity to ensure the survival of the human species. Those living have received a heritage from their forbears in which they have beneficial rights of use that are limited by the interests and needs of future generations. This limitation requires each generation to maintain the corpus of the trust and pass it on in no worse condition than it was received.[41]

How does the principle of intergenerational equity relate to the principle of sustainable development?

4) Common but Differentiated Responsibilities

Fundamental differences of opinion between developed and developing states on how to share the environmental protection burden have been translated into the idea of "com-

---

37 1992 Rio Declaration, above note 23, Principle 3.

38 Convention for the Protection of the World Cultural and Natural Heritage, 16 November 1972, 1037 UNTS 152, Can TS 1976 No 45, (1972) 11 I.L.M. 1358, in force 17 December 1975, art 4.

39 Climate Change Convention, above note 10, art 3(1).

40 *Request for an Examination of the Situation in Accordance with Paragraph 63 of the Court's Judgement of 20 December 1974 in the Nuclear Tests Case (New Zealand v France)*, Order of 22 September 1995, [1995] ICJ Rep 288 (dissenting opinion of Judge Weeramantry, 317 at 341) [*Order in the Nuclear Tests Case*]. See also Cassese, above note 12 at 491, categorizing this as a "soft law" guideline, explaining that "the environment is an asset belonging to mankind, to be safeguarded for the benefit of everybody including future generations."

41 Dinah Shelton, "Equity" in *Oxford Handbook*, above note 21, 639 at 643.

mon but differentiated responsibilities."[42] Also referred to as "differential treatment," the principle of common but differentiated responsibilities "refers to instances where, because of pervasive differences or inequalities among states, the principle of sovereign equality is sidelined to accommodate extraneous factors, such as divergences in levels of economic development or unequal capacities to tackle a given problem."[43] The concept of common but differentiated responsibilities is articulated in the following way in Principle 7 of the 1992 Rio Declaration:

> States shall cooperate in a spirit of global partnership to conserve, protect and restore the health and integrity of the Earth's ecosystem. In view of the different contributions to global environmental degradation, States have common but differentiated responsibilities. The developed countries acknowledge the responsibility that they bear in the international pursuit of sustainable development in view of the pressures their societies place on the global environment and of the technologies and financial resources they command.[44]

The concept of common but differentiated responsibilities was reaffirmed in the outcome document of the United Nations Rio+20 Conference on Sustainable Development held in June 2012.[45] It is also reflected in many treaties. For example, the 1992 Climate Change Convention provides as follows:

United Nations Framework Convention on Climate Change, 9 May 1992, 1771 UNTS 107, Can TS 1994 No 7, (1992) 31 ILM 849, in force 21 March 1994

Article 3
In their actions to achieve the objective of the Convention and to implement its provisions, the Parties shall be guided, *inter alia*, by the following:

(1) The Parties should protect the climate system for the benefit of present and future generations of humankind, on the basis of equity and in accordance with their common but differentiated responsibilities and respective capabilities. Accordingly, the developed country Parties should take the lead in combating climate change and the adverse effects thereof.

(2) The specific needs and special circumstances of developing country parties, especially those that are particularly vulnerable to the adverse effects of climate change, and of those Parties, especially developing country Parties, that would have to bear a disproportionate or abnormal burden under the Convention, should be given full consideration . . . .

There are several mechanisms used in treaties to create common but differentiated responsibilities. First, developed states may be obligated to meet stricter standards than

---

42 Lavanya Rajamani, *Differential Treatment in International Environmental Law* (New York: Oxford University Press, 2006) at 88.
43 Philippe Cullet, *Differential Treatment in International Environmental Law* (Aldershot, Hants: Ashgate, 2003) at 15.
44 1992 Rio Declaration, above note 23, Principle 7.
45 *The Future We Want*, above note 34 at para 15.

developing states.[46] Second, developed states may be obligated to transfer technology or provide financial assistance to less-developed states.[47] Finally, different timelines may be used: developed states may be required to implement treaty obligations immediately, whereas developing states may be required to implement these obligations at a later date.[48] Some question whether this is "wise environmental policy in the long run."[49]

Beyond treaty law, however, some feel that a generally applicable principle of differentiated responsibilities "is not evident."[50] The Seabed Disputes Chamber of the International Tribunal on the Law of the Sea, in its advisory opinion on *Responsibilities and Obligations of States*, considered arguments that developing states had less stringent environmental protection obligations with respect to the deep seabed, and replied:

> Equality of treatment between developed and developing states is consistent with the need to prevent commercial enterprises based in developed States from setting up companies in developing States, acquiring their nationality and obtaining their sponsorship in the hope of being subjected to less burdensome regulations and control .... [This would] jeopardize uniform application of the highest standards of protection of the marine environment, the safe development of activities in the Area and protection of the common heritage of mankind.[51]

How does the concept of common but differentiated responsibilities interact with the concept of intergenerational equity?

5) Precautionary Approach

The precautionary approach would require the avoidance of environmental harm by taking action even before there is full scientific certainty that a particular thing (for example, a chemical), process, or method will lead to serious or irreversible environmental damage. This approach is articulated as follows in Principle 15 of the 1992 Rio Declaration: "In order to protect the environment, the precautionary approach shall be widely applied by States according to their capabilities. Where there are threats of serious or irreversible damage, lack of full scientific certainty shall not be used as a reason for postponing cost-effective measures to prevent environmental degradation."[52]

---

46 See, for example, Kyoto Protocol, above note 11, art 10.

47 See, for example, Basel Convention on the Control of Transboundary Movements of Hazardous Wastes and Their Disposal, 22 March 1989, 1673 UNTS 126, Can TS 1992 No 19, (1989) 28 ILM 657, in force 5 May 1992, art 10(2) [Basel Convention]; Convention on Biological Diversity, 5 June 1992, 1760 UNTS 79, Can TS 1993 No 24, (1992) 31 ILM 818, in force 29 December 1993, arts 16, 20, & 21; Climate Change Convention, above note 10, art 4.

48 See, for example, Montreal Protocol on Substances that Deplete the Ozone Layer, 16 September 1987, 1522 UNTS 3, Can TS 1989 No 42, (1987) 26 ILM 1550, in force 1 January 1990, art 5 [Montreal Protocol].

49 Beyerlin & Stoutenberg, above note 35 at para 26.

50 Sands & Peel, above note 1 at 236.

51 *Responsibilities and Obligations of States Sponsoring Persons and Entities with Respect to Activities in the Area*, Case No 17, Advisory Opinion, (2011) 50 ILM 458 at 481 at para 159 (Seabed Disputes Chamber of the International Tribunal for the Law of the Sea).

52 1992 Rio Declaration, above note 23, Principle 15.

The Climate Change Convention includes a reference to the precautionary approach:

United Nations Framework Convention on Climate Change, 9 May 1992, 1771 UNTS 107, Can TS 1994 No 7, (1992) 31 ILM 849, in force 21 March 1994

Article 3
In their actions to achieve the objective of the Convention and to implement its provisions, the Parties art shall be guided, *inter alia*, by the following: . . .

(3) The Parties should take precautionary measures to anticipate, prevent or minimize the causes of climate change and mitigate its adverse effects. Where there are threats of serious or irreversible damage, lack of full scientific certainty should not be used as a reason for postponing such measures, taking into account that policies and measures to deal with climate change should be cost-effective so as to ensure global benefits at the lowest possible cost. To achieve this, such policies and measures should take into account different socio-economic contexts, be comprehensive, cover all relevant sources, sinks and reservoirs of greenhouse gases and adaptation, and comprise all economic sectors. Efforts to address climate change may be carried out cooperatively by interested Parties.

How does the 1992 Rio Declaration's articulation of the precautionary approach differ from that of the Climate Change Convention? Which aspects of the precautionary approach may already be encompassed within the regime of state responsibility described in Chapter 12?

The precautionary approach has also been considered in an advisory opinion of the Seabed Disputes Chamber of the International Tribunal for the Law of the Sea examining deep seabed mining:

Responsibilities and Obligations of States Sponsoring Persons and Entities with Respect to Activities in the Area, Case No 17, Advisory Opinion, (2011) 50 ILM 458 (Seabed Disputes Chamber)

125. The Nodules Regulations and the Sulphides Regulations [with respect to deep seabed mining] contain provisions that establish a direct obligation for sponsoring States. This obligation is relevant for implementing the "responsibility to ensure" that sponsored contractors meet the obligations set out in . . . regulation 31, paragraph 2, of the Nodules Regulations and regulation 33, paragraph 2, of the Sulphides Regulations, both of which state that sponsoring States (as well as the [International Seabed] Authority) "shall apply a precautionary approach, as reflected in Principle 15 of the Rio Declaration" in order "to ensure effective protection for the marine environment from harmful effects which may arise from activities in the Area".

. . .

127. The provisions of the aforementioned Regulations transform [the] non-binding statement of the precautionary approach in the Rio Declaration into a binding obligation. The implementation of the precautionary approach as defined in these Regulations is one of the obligations of sponsoring States.

128. It should be noted that while the first sentence of Principle 15 seems to refer in general terms to the "precautionary approach", the second sentence limits its scope to threats of "serious or irreversible damage" and to "cost-effective" measures adopted in order to prevent "environmental degradation".

129. Moreover, by stating that the precautionary approach shall be applied by States "according to their capabilities", the first sentence of Principle 15 introduces the possibility of differences in application of the precautionary approach in light of the different capabilities of each State . . . .

130. The reference to the precautionary approach as set out in the two Regulations applies specifically to the activities envisaged therein, namely, prospecting and exploration for polymetallic nodules and polymetallic sulphides. It is to be expected that the Authority will either repeat or further develop this approach when it regulates exploitation activities and activities concerning other types of minerals.

131. Having established that under the Nodules Regulations and the Sulphides Regulations, both sponsoring States and the Authority are under an obligation to apply the precautionary approach in respect of activities in the Area, it is appropriate to point out that the precautionary approach is also an integral part of the general obligation of due diligence of sponsoring States, which is applicable even outside the scope of the Regulations. The due diligence obligation of the sponsoring States requires them to take all appropriate measures to prevent damage that might result from the activities of contractors that they sponsor. This obligation applies in situations where scientific evidence concerning the scope and potential negative impact of the activity in question is insufficient but where there are plausible indications of potential risks. A sponsoring State would not meet its obligation of due diligence if it disregarded those risks. Such disregard would amount to a failure to comply with the precautionary approach.

132. The link between an obligation of due diligence and the precautionary approach is implicit in the Tribunal's Order of 27 August 1999 in the *Southern Bluefin Tuna Cases (New Zealand v. Japan; Australia v. Japan)*. This emerges from the declaration of the Tribunal that the parties "should in the circumstances act with prudence and caution to ensure that conservation measures are taken . . ." (*ITLOS Reports 1999*, p. 274, at paragraph 77), and is confirmed by the further statements that "there is scientific uncertainty regarding measures to be taken to conserve the stock of southern bluefin tuna" (paragraph 79) and that "although the Tribunal cannot conclusively assess the scientific evidence presented by the parties, it finds that measures should be taken as a matter of urgency" (paragraph 80).

133. It should be further noted that the Sulphides Regulations, Annex 4, section 5.1, in setting out a "standard clause" for exploration contracts, provides that:

> The Contractor shall take necessary measures to prevent, reduce and control pollution and other hazards to the marine environment arising from its activities in the Area as far as reasonably possible applying a precautionary approach and best environmental practices.

Thus, the precautionary approach (called "principle" in the French text of the standard clause just mentioned) is a contractual obligation of the sponsored contractors whose compliance the sponsoring State has the responsibility to ensure.

134. In the parallel provision of the corresponding standard clauses for exploration contracts in the Nodules Regulations, Annex 4, section 5.1, no reference is made to the precautionary approach. However, under the general obligation illustrated in paragraph 131, the sponsoring State has to take measures within the framework of its own legal system in order to oblige sponsored entities to adopt such an approach.

135. The Chamber observes that the precautionary approach has been incorporated into a growing number of international treaties and other instruments, many of which reflect the formulation of Principle 15 of the Rio Declaration. In the view of the Chamber, this has initiated a trend towards making this approach part of customary international law. This trend is clearly reinforced by the inclusion of the precautionary approach in the Regulations and in the "standard clause" contained in Annex 4, section 5.1, of the Sulphides Regulations. So does the following statement in paragraph 164 of the ICJ Judgment in *Pulp Mills on the River Uruguay* that "a precautionary approach may be relevant in the interpretation and application of the provisions of the Statute" (i.e., the environmental bilateral treaty whose interpretation was the main bone of contention between the parties). This statement may be read in light of article 31, paragraph 3(c), of the Vienna Convention, according to which the interpretation of a treaty should take into account not only the context but "any relevant rules of international law applicable in the relations between the parties".

Some commentators view the precautionary approach as a principle of customary international law,[53] while others see it merely as an emerging soft law principle.[54] As can be seen immediately above, the Seabed Disputes Chamber of the International Tribunal for the Law of the Sea has referred to a "trend toward making this approach part of customary international law." In 1999, the Legal Affairs Bureau of the then Canadian Department of Foreign Affairs and International Trade took the following view:

[T]he evidence presented does not support the conclusion that the precautionary approach has attained the status of a rule of customary law or that there is agreement as to its content. Neither does it support the conclusion that the approach has crystallized as a general principle of law . . . . Canada has not accepted that the precautionary approach has attained the status of a legal rule or principle in international law.[55]

---

53 Judge Ad Hoc Palmer, in his dissenting opinion in the 1995 *Order in the Nuclear Tests Case*, above note 40 at 412, stated that "the norm involved in the precautionary principle has developed rapidly and may now be a principle of customary international law relating to the environment." De Sadeleer, above note 19 at 100, states: "Owing to its near universality and to the development of certain State practices that recognize its validity, the precautionary principle should be considered a rule of international law, although this position does not yet enjoy unanimous support." Beyerlin & Stoutenburg, above note 35 at para 24, lean towards the conclusion that it is custom.

54 Judge Weeramantry in the *Order in the Nuclear Tests Case*, above note 40 at 342, stated in his dissenting opinion that this is a "principle which is gaining increasing support as part of the international law of the environment." See also *Brownlie's Principles*, above note 2 at 356.

55 Michael Leir, "Canadian Practice in International Law at the Department of Foreign Affairs in 1998–1999"

6) The Polluter Pays

Under the "polluter pays" principle, an entity that harms the environment would be held responsible for the costs of remedying that harm. Principle 16 of the 1992 Rio Declaration states: "National authorities should endeavour to promote the internalization of environmental costs and the use of economic instruments, taking into account the approach that the polluter should, in principle, bear the cost of pollution, with due regard to the public interest and without distorting international trade and investment."[56]

Notice the hortatory language of this principle. Its exact status in international law is not clear. The preamble to a 1990 convention on oil pollution preparedness, response, and cooperation states that "polluter pays" is "a general principle of international environmental law."[57] However, several scholars are more cautious in their characterization. Some refer to the concept as a general guideline or emergent principle,[58] and others argue that it "cannot supply guidance on the content of national or international liability without further definition."[59] Professors Sands and Peel observe that "a number of states, both developed and developing, [view] the polluter pays principle [as] applicable at the domestic level but [consider that it] does not govern relations or responsibilities between states at the international level."[60] Given the weak language of Principle 16 of the 1992 Rio Declaration, the vague content of the principle,[61] the fact that most references to it are found in conventions of regional application or conventions entered into only by industrialized nations,[62] and differing views of the principle's status, it is likely that the "polluter pays" concept has not yet become a rule of customary international law.

D. SECTORAL PROTECTIONS UNDER INTERNATIONAL ENVIRONMENTAL LAW

Professor Crawford describes the multilateral standard-setting conventions devoted to particular environmental problems as a "significant development in international law."[63] There are many such "sectoral" conventions, each covering one or more specific aspects of the environment. Indeed, so many international environmental law treaties have been

---

(1999) 37 Can YB Int'l Law 317 at 320–21. But see *114957 Canada Ltée (Spraytech, Société d'arrosage) v Hudson (Town)*, 2001 SCC 40, [2001] 2 SCR 241 at para 32 for judicial expression of a different viewpoint.

56 1992 Rio Declaration, above note 23, Principle 16.

57 International Convention on Oil Pollution Preparedness, Response and Cooperation, 30 November 1990, 1891 UNTS 78, (1991) 30 ILM 733, in force 13 May 1995, preamble [Oil Pollution Convention].

58 Cassese, above note 12 at 492; *Brownlie's Principles*, above note 2 at 359.

59 Patricia W Birnie, Alan E Boyle, & Catherine Redgwell, *International Law and the Environment*, 3d ed (New York: Oxford University Press, 2009) at 326.

60 Sands & Peel, above note 1 at 229.

61 *Brownlie's Principles*, above note 2 at 359.

62 See, for example, Convention on the Protection of the Marine Environment of the Baltic Sea Area, 9 April 1992, 2099 UNTS 197, in force 17 January 2000, art 3(4); Convention on the Protection and Use of Transboundary Watercourses and International Lakes, 17 March 1992, 1936 UNTS 269, (1992) 31 ILM 1312, in force 6 October 1996, art 2(5)(b).

63 *Brownlie's Principles*, above note 2 at 360.

adopted since the 1970s that some fear the field is subject to "treaty congestion."[64] In this section, we explore key international environmental conventions in thematic groups.

1) Protection of the Atmosphere: Transboundary Air Pollution, Ozone Depletion, and Global Climate Change

a) Transboundary Air Pollution

Transboundary air pollution was the first type of atmospheric pollution to be regulated internationally. The *Trail Smelter* arbitration, excerpted above, was one of the earliest cases of an international claim for atmospheric damage—in that case, relating to the smelter's sulphur dioxide emissions. In the 1970s and 1980s, the problem of acid deposition, commonly called "acid rain," was identified. Acid rain occurs when sulphur dioxide and nitrogen oxides combine to form acidic particles and vapours, such as sulphuric acid, ammonium nitrate, and nitric acid, which are deposited through rain, snow, sleet, hail, or dry particulates. The relevant particles and vapours can be transported through the atmosphere over great distances (often many thousands of kilometres) before they are deposited. This acid deposition can change the pH of the soil and water, leading to the death of plant and animal species.

Canada has been particularly concerned about acid deposition, initially in eastern Canada, and now also in western Canada, that originates from the United States.[65] The concern led to the signature of a Memorandum of Intent Concerning Transboundary Air Pollution in 1980 and the conclusion of a bilateral Canada-US agreement on air quality in 1991.

> **Agreement between the Government of Canada and the Government of the United States of America on Air Quality, 13 March 1991, Can TS 1991 No 3, (1991) 30 ILM 676, in force 13 March 1991**
>
> The Government of the United States of America and the Government of Canada, hereinafter referred to as "the Parties", . . .
>
> Desiring that emissions of air pollutants from sources within their countries not result in significant transboundary air pollution;
>
> Convinced that transboundary air pollution can effectively be reduced through cooperative or coordinated action providing for controlling emissions of air pollutants in both countries; . . .
>
> Reaffirming Principle 21 of the Stockholm Declaration, which provides that "States have, in accordance with the Charter of the United Nations and the principles of inter-

---

64 See further, Donald K Anton, "Treaty Congestion in Contemporary International Environmental Law" in Shawcat Alam et al, eds, *Routledge Handbook of International Environmental Law* (New York: Routledge, 2012) at 651.

65 The Canadian Council of Ministers of the Environment (CCME) has adopted a "Canada-wide Acid Rain Strategy for Post-2000," which has led to the gathering and sharing of scientific studies. See further, *Five-year Review of The Canada-Wide Acid Rain Strategy for Post-2000* (Ottawa: Canadian Council of Ministers of the Environment, 2006). Provincial governments are also developing strategies to cope with acid deposition, with Alberta, for example, adopting an Acid Deposition Management Framework that prescribes a regular assessment cycle. See further, *2004 Acid Deposition Assessment for Alberta: A Report of the Acid Deposition Assessment Group* (Edmonton: Alberta Environment, 2006).

national law, the sovereign right to exploit their own resources pursuant to their own environmental policies, and the responsibility to ensure that activities within their jurisdiction or control do not cause damage to the environment of other States or of areas beyond the limits of national jurisdiction"; . . .

Have agreed as follows:

Article I — Definitions

For the purposes of this Agreement:

1. "Air pollution" means the introduction by man, directly or indirectly, of substances into the air resulting in deleterious effects of such a nature as to endanger human health, harm living resources and ecosystems and material property and impair or interfere with amenities and other legitimate uses of the environment, and "air pollutants" shall be construed accordingly;

2. "Transboundary air pollution" means air pollution whose physical origin is situated wholly or in part with the area under the jurisdiction of one Party and which has adverse effects, other than effects of a global nature, in the area under the jurisdiction of the other Party; . . .

Article II — Purpose

The purpose of the Parties is to establish, by this Agreement, a practical and effective instrument to address shared concerns regarding transboundary air pollution.

Article III — General Air Quality Objective

1. The general objective of the Parties is to control transboundary air pollution between the two countries.

2. To this end, the Parties shall:
    (a) in accordance with Article IV, establish specific objectives for emissions limitations or reductions of air pollutants and adopt the necessary programs and other measures to implement such specific objectives;
    (b) in accordance with Article V, undertake environmental impact assessment, prior notification, and, as appropriate, mitigation measures;
    (c) carry out coordinated or cooperative scientific and technical activities, and economic research, in accordance with Article VI, and exchange information, in accordance with Article VII;
    (d) establish institutional arrangements, in accordance with Articles VIII and IX; and
    (e) review and assess progress, consult, address issues of concern, and settle disputes, in accordance with Articles X, XI, XII and XIII.

Article IV — Specific Air Quality Objectives

1. Each Party shall establish specific objectives, which it undertakes to achieve, for emissions limitations or reductions of such air pollutants as the Parties agree to address. Such specific objectives will be set forth in annexes to this Agreement.

2. Each Party's specific objectives for emissions limitations or reductions of sulphur dioxide and nitrogen oxides, which will reduce transboundary flows of these acidic deposition precursors, are set forth in Annex 1. Specific objectives for such other air pollutants as

the Parties agree to address should take into account, as appropriate, the activities undertaken pursuant to Article VI.

3. Each Party shall adopt the programs and other measures necessary to implement its specific objectives set forth in any annexes.

4. If either Party has concerns about the programs or other measures of the other Party referred to in paragraph 3, it may request consultations in accordance with Article XI.

Article V — Assessment, Notification, and Mitigation

1. Each Party shall, as appropriate and as required by its laws, regulations and policies, assess those proposed actions, activities and projects within the area under its jurisdiction that, if carried out, would be likely to cause significant transboundary air pollution, including consideration of appropriate mitigation measures.

2. Each Party shall notify the other Party concerning a proposed action, activity or project subject to assessment under paragraph 1 as early as practicable in advance of a decision concerning such action, activity or project and shall consult with the other Party at its request in accordance with Article XI.

3. In addition, each Party shall, at the request of the other Party, consult in accordance with Article XI concerning any continuing actions, activities or projects that may be causing significant transboundary air pollution, as well as concerning changes to its laws, regulation or policies that, if carried out, would be likely to affect significantly transboundary air pollution.

4. Consultations pursuant to paragraphs 2 and 3 concerning actions, activities or projects that would be likely to cause or may be causing significant transboundary air pollution shall include consideration of appropriate mitigation measures.

5. Each Party shall, as appropriate, take measures to avoid or mitigate the potential risk posed by actions, activities or projects that would be likely to cause or may be causing significant transboundary air pollution.

6. If either Party becomes aware of an air pollution problem that is of joint concern and requires an immediate response, it shall notify and consult the other Party forthwith . . . .

Article VIII — The Air Quality Committee

1. The Parties agree to establish and maintain a bilateral Air Quality Committee to assist in the implementation of this Agreement . . . .

2. The Committee's responsibilities shall include:
(a) reviewing progress made in the implementation of this Agreement, including its general and specific objectives;
(b) preparing and submitting to the Parties a progress report within a year after entry into force of this Agreement and at least every two years thereafter;
(c) referring each progress report to the International Joint Commission [created under the Boundary Waters Treaty] for action in accordance with Article IX of this Agreement; and
(d) releasing each progress report to the public after its submission to the Parties . . . .

Article IX—Responsibilities of the International Joint Commission

1. The International Joint Commission is hereby given, by a Reference pursuant to Article IX of the Boundary Waters Treaty, the following responsibilities for the sole purpose of assisting the Parties in the implementation of this Agreement:

(a) to invite comments, including through public hearings as appropriate, on each progress report prepared by the Air Quality Committee pursuant to Article VIII;

(b) to submit to the Parties a synthesis of the views presented pursuant to sub-paragraph (a), as well as the record of such views if either Party so requests; and

(c) to release the synthesis of views to the public after its submission to the Parties.

2. In addition, the Parties shall consider such other joint references to the International Joint Commission as may be appropriate for the effective implementation of this Agreement . . . .

Article XIII—Settlement of Disputes

1. If, after consultations in accordance with Article XI, a dispute remains between the Parties over the interpretation or the implementation of this Agreement, they shall seek to resolve such dispute by negotiations between them. Such negotiations shall commence as soon as practicable, but in any event not later than ninety days from the date of receipt of the request for negotiation, unless otherwise agreed by the Parties.

2. If a dispute is not resolved through negotiation, the Parties shall consider whether to submit that dispute to the International Joint Commission in accordance with either Article IX or Article X of the Boundary Waters Treaty. If, after such consideration, the Parties do not elect either of these options, they shall, at the request of either Party, submit the dispute to another agreed form of dispute resolution . . . .

What are the strengths and weaknesses of the Canada-US Agreement on Air Quality? While the issue of acid rain has not been addressed by a convention at the global level, it has been addressed at the European and North American levels through the 1979 Convention on Long-range Transboundary Air Pollution and its Protocols.[66] Canada and the United States are both parties to this treaty regime,[67] which defines "air pollution" as "the introduction by man, directly or indirectly, of substances or energy into the air resulting in deleterious effects of such a nature as to endanger human health, harm living re-

---

66 Long-range Transboundary Air Pollution Convention, above note 4, as amended by the 1999 Protocol to Abate Acidification, Eutrophication and Ground-level Ozone, in force 17 May 2005 (itself amended in 2012); the 1998 Protocol on Persistent Organic Pollutants, in force 23 October 2003; the 1998 Protocol on Heavy Metals, in force 29 December 2003; the 1994 Protocol on Further Reduction of Sulphur Emissions, in force 5 August 1998; the 1991 Protocol concerning the Control of Emissions of Volatile Organic Compounds or their Transboundary Fluxes, in force 29 September 1997; the 1988 Protocol concerning the Control of Nitrogen Oxides or their Transboundary Fluxes, in force 14 February 1991; the 1985 Protocol on the Reduction of Sulphur Emissions or their Transboundary Fluxes by at least 30 percent, in force 2 September 1987; and the 1984 Protocol on Long-term Financing of the Cooperative Programme for Monitoring and Evaluation of the Long-range Transmission of Air Pollutants in Europe, in force 28 January 1988 [collectively, the Air Pollution Protocols].

67 The United States lodged its acceptance on 30 November 1981 while Canada ratified the convention on 15 December 1981.

sources and ecosystems and material property and impair or interfere with amenities and other legitimate uses of the environment."[68] "Long-range transboundary air pollution" is defined as "air pollution . . . [the] physical origin [of which] is situated wholly or in part within the area under the national jurisdiction of one State and which has adverse effects in the area under the jurisdiction of another State at such a distance that it is not generally possible to distinguish the contribution of individual emission sources or groups of sources."[69] The Long-range Transboundary Air Pollution Convention is essentially a framework agreement providing for the development of policies and strategies, exchange of information, and research and development relating to air pollution, including such pollution caused by sulphur dioxide.[70] It does not set specific limits on transboundary air pollution emissions. However, in the context of its protocols, limits have been agreed upon with respect to, *inter alia*, sulphur emissions, nitrogen oxides, and persistent organic pollutants.[71]

b)   Ozone Depletion

The first treaty adopted to address ozone depletion was the 1985 Vienna Convention for the Protection of the Ozone Layer.[72] This convention is a framework agreement that provides the institutional structure, including a secretariat and dispute settlement mechanism, for coordinated action as determined through several protocols. The first protocol adopted was the 1987 Montreal Protocol on Substances that Deplete the Ozone Layer, which provided for a moratorium on the use of halons and a reduction over time of the use of chlorofluorocarbons (CFCs).[73] Subsequently, the parties to the main treaty and this protocol adopted the 1989 Helsinki Declaration on the Protection of the Ozone Layer, under which they agreed to end the production and use of CFCs by 2000, as well as to end the use of halons and control the use of other ozone-depleting substances.[74] The parties made adjustments and amendments to the Montreal Protocol in 1990, 1992, 1997, 1999, and 2007.[75] The Montreal Protocol (as adjusted and amended) has been hailed for introducing extensive control measures and a relatively fast phase-out of CFCs and other ozone-depleting substances.

c)   Global Climate Change

The climate of any given region on Earth is a function of innumerable factors. However, the planet's overall climate system exists largely because of the Earth's atmosphere, a combination of gases that slows the dissipation of solar energy striking the Earth and thereby facilitates the existence of a reasonable range of temperatures on the planet's

---

68   Long-range Transboundary Air Pollution Convention, above note 4, art 1(a).

69   *Ibid*, art 1(b).

70   *Ibid*, arts 6–9.

71   Air Pollution Protocols, above note 66.

72   22 March 1985, 1513 UNTS 323, Can TS 1988 No 23, (1987) 26 ILM 1529, in force 22 September 1988.

73   Montreal Protocol, above note 48.

74   Helsinki Declaration on the Protection of the Ozone Layer, adopted 2 May 1989 by the Governments and the European Communities represented at the 1st Meeting of the Parties to the Vienna Convention and the Montreal Protocol, reprinted in (1989) 28 ILM 1335.

75   See further, United Nations Environment Programme, Ozone Secretariat, "The Montreal Protocol on Substances that Deplete the Ozone Layer" (undated), online: ozone.unep.org/new_site/en/montreal_protocol. php.

surface. Changing the relative concentration of these so-called greenhouse gases alters the rate at which this energy dissipates, prompting changes in climatic temperatures. All else being equal, where the concentration of greenhouse gases increases, temperatures rise.[76] The overwhelming and resounding view of climatic scientists is that human emissions of greenhouse gases are having, and will continue to have, an impact on the Earth's climate system.[77]

In 1983, the UN General Assembly established the World Commission on Environment and Development. The Commission was chaired by Prime Minister Gro Harlem Brundtland of Norway. Its 1987 report, *Our Common Future*, called for, *inter alia*, research into the origins and effects of climate change, scientific study and monitoring of the climate, international negotiations for a climate change treaty, and international policies on the reduction of greenhouse gas emissions.[78] In 1988, the General Assembly adopted resolution 43/53, which recognized that "climate change is a common concern of mankind" and urged "[g]overnments, intergovernmental and non-governmental organizations and scientific institutions to treat climate change as a priority issue."[79] The resolution also urged the convening of an international conference on global warming.[80]

In 1990, scientific alarm over the threat of anthropogenic (human-induced) climate change prompted the UN-sponsored Intergovernmental Panel on Climate Change to issue its first Assessment Report, labeling climate change a threat and calling for an international treaty on the issue.[81] In response to this call, and to that made by the Second World Climate Conference in the fall of 1990, the UN General Assembly adopted resolution 45/212 in December 1990, launching negotiations on a climate change framework agreement.[82] After more than a year of negotiations, the United Nations Framework Convention on Climate Change was opened for signature at the "Earth Summit" in Rio de Janeiro, Brazil on 4 June 1992, and came into force on 21 March 1994.

Establishing a framework for intergovernmental efforts to reduce greenhouse gas emissions, the objective of the Climate Change Convention is to achieve stabilization of atmospheric concentrations of greenhouse gases at levels that would prevent dangerous anthropogenic interference with the climate system.[83] The convention recognizes that states have varying obligations to contribute to the goal of greenhouse gas reduction, depending on their level of development. Thus, the convention specifies two key classes of parties: so-called Annex I parties, comprising forty-two developed states and the

---

76 For a more detailed discussion of climate change science, see Environment Canada, "Climate Change Science and Research" (undated), online: www.ec.gc.ca/sc-cs/Default.asp?lang=En&n=56010B41-1.

77 See Intergovernmental Panel on Climate Change, *Climate Change 2007: The Physical Science Basis: Summary for Policymakers* (Cambridge & New York: Cambridge University Press, 2007).

78 *Our Common Future*, above note 30.

79 *Protection of the Global Climate for Present and Future Generations of Mankind*, GA Res 43/53, UN Doc A/RES/43/53 (1988), reprinted in UN GAOR, 43rd Sess, Supp No 49 at 133–34, UN Doc A/43/49 (1989), at paras 1 and 6.

80 *Ibid* at para 8.

81 Intergovernmental Panel on Climate Change, *First Assessment Report* (1990) at 51 and 60.

82 *Protection of global climate for present and future generations of mankind*, GA Res 45/212, UN Doc A/RES/45/212 (1990), reprinted in UN GAOR, 45th Sess, Supp No 49 at 147–49, UN Doc A/45/49 (1991).

83 Climate Change Convention, above note 10, art 2.

European Union; and non-Annex I parties, consisting of 154 developing states.[84] Annex I parties were expected to meet the non-legally binding aim of reducing carbon dioxide emissions to 1990 levels by 2000.

Note, however, that despite its "framework" nomenclature, the convention does contain some legal obligations:

United Nations Framework Convention on Climate Change, 9 May 1992, 1771 UNTS 107, Can TS 1994 No 7, (1992) 31 ILM 849, in force 21 March 1994

Article 4—Commitments
1. All Parties, taking into account their common but differentiated responsibilities and their specific national and regional development priorities, objectives and circumstances, shall:

(a) Develop, periodically update, publish and make available to the Conference of the Parties, in accordance with Article 12, national inventories of anthropogenic emissions by sources and removals by sinks of all greenhouse gases not controlled by the Montreal Protocol, using comparable methodologies to be agreed upon by the Conference of the Parties;

(b) Formulate, implement, publish and regularly update national and, where appropriate, regional programmes containing measures to mitigate climate change by addressing anthropogenic emissions by sources and removals by sinks of all greenhouse gases not controlled by the Montreal Protocol, and measures to facilitate adequate adaptation to climate change;

(c) Promote and cooperate in the development, application and diffusion, including transfer, of technologies, practices and processes that control, reduce or prevent anthropogenic emissions of greenhouse gases not controlled by the Montreal Protocol in all relevant sectors, including the energy, transport, industry, agriculture, forestry and waste management sectors;

(d) Promote sustainable management, and promote and cooperate in the conservation and enhancement, as appropriate, of sinks and reservoirs of all greenhouse gases not controlled by the Montreal Protocol, including biomass, forests and oceans as well as other terrestrial, coastal and marine ecosystems;

(e) Cooperate in preparing for adaptation to the impacts of climate change; develop and elaborate appropriate and integrated plans for coastal zone management, water resources and agriculture, and for the protection and rehabilitation of areas, particularly in Africa, affected by drought and desertification, as well as floods;

(f) Take climate change considerations into account, to the extent feasible, in their relevant social, economic and environmental policies and actions, and employ appropriate methods, for example impact assessments, formulated and determined nationally, with a view to minimizing adverse effects on the economy, on public health and on the quality of the environment, of projects or measures undertaken by them to mitigate or adapt to climate change;

---

84 *Ibid* at Annex I, as amended in 1998, 2010, and 2013. There is also an "Annex II" class comprising the Organization for Economic Cooperation and Development (OECD) members of Annex I.

(g) Promote and cooperate in scientific, technological, technical, socio-economic and other research, systematic observation and development of data archives related to the climate system and intended to further the understanding and to reduce or eliminate the remaining uncertainties regarding the causes, effects, magnitude and timing of climate change and the economic and social consequences of various response strategies;

(h) Promote and cooperate in the full, open and prompt exchange of relevant scientific, technological, technical, socio-economic and legal information related to the climate system and climate change, and to the economic and social consequences of various response strategies;

(i) Promote and cooperate in education, training and public awareness related to climate change and encourage the widest participation in this process, including that of non-governmental organizations; and

(j) Communicate to the Conference of the Parties information related to implementation, in accordance with Article 12.

2. The developed country Parties and other Parties included in annex I commit themselves specifically as provided for in the following:

(a) Each of these Parties shall adopt national policies and take corresponding measures on the mitigation of climate change, by limiting its anthropogenic emissions of greenhouse gases and protecting and enhancing its greenhouse gas sinks and reservoirs. These policies and measures will demonstrate that developed countries are taking the lead in modifying longer-term trends in anthropogenic emissions consistent with the objective of the Convention, recognizing that the return by the end of the present decade to earlier levels of anthropogenic emissions of carbon dioxide and other greenhouse gases not controlled by the Montreal Protocol would contribute to such modification, and taking into account the differences in these Parties' starting points and approaches, economic structures and resource bases, the need to maintain strong and sustainable economic growth, available technologies and other individual circumstances, as well as the need for equitable and appropriate contributions by each of these Parties to the global effort regarding that objective. These Parties may implement such policies and measures jointly with other Parties and may assist other Parties in contributing to the achievement of the objective of the Convention and, in particular, that of this subparagraph; . . .

3. The developed country Parties and other developed Parties included in annex II shall provide new and additional financial resources to meet the agreed full costs incurred by developing country Parties in complying with their obligations under Article 12, paragraph 1. They shall also provide such financial resources, including for the transfer of technology, needed by the developing country Parties to meet the agreed full incremental costs of implementing measures that are covered by paragraph 1 of this Article and that are agreed between a developing country Party and the international entity or entities referred to in Article 11, in accordance with that Article. The implementation of these commitments shall take into account the need for adequacy and predictability in the flow of funds and the importance of appropriate burden sharing among the developed country Parties.

4. The developed country Parties and other developed Parties included in annex II shall also assist the developing country Parties that are particularly vulnerable to the adverse effects of climate change in meeting costs of adaptation to those adverse effects.

5. The developed country Parties and other developed Parties included in annex II shall take all practicable steps to promote, facilitate and finance, as appropriate, the transfer of, or access to, environmentally sound technologies and know-how to other Parties, particularly developing country Parties, to enable them to implement the provisions of the Convention. In this process, the developed country Parties shall support the development and enhancement of endogenous capacities and technologies of developing country Parties. Other Parties and organizations in a position to do so may also assist in facilitating the transfer of such technologies.

6. In the implementation of their commitments under paragraph 2 above, a certain degree of flexibility shall be allowed by the Conference of the Parties to the Parties included in Annex I undergoing the process of transition to a market economy, in order to enhance the ability of these Parties to address climate change, including with regard to the historical level of anthropogenic emissions of greenhouse gases not controlled by the Montreal Protocol chosen as a reference.

7. The extent to which developing country Parties will effectively implement their commitments under the Convention will depend on the effective implementation by developed country Parties of their commitments under the Convention related to financial resources and transfer of technology and will take fully into account that economic and social development and poverty eradication are the first and overriding priorities of the developing country Parties.

8. In the implementation of the commitments in this Article, the Parties shall give full consideration to what actions are necessary under the Convention, including actions related to funding, insurance and the transfer of technology, to meet the specific needs and concerns of developing country Parties arising from the adverse effects of climate change and/or the impact of the implementation of response measures, especially on:
   (a) Small island countries;
   (b) Countries with low-lying coastal areas;
   (c) Countries with arid and semi-arid areas, forested areas and areas liable to forest decay;
   (d) Countries with areas prone to natural disasters;
   (e) Countries with areas liable to drought and desertification;
   (f) Countries with areas of high urban atmospheric pollution;
   (g) Countries with areas with fragile ecosystems, including mountainous ecosystems;
   (h) Countries whose economies are highly dependent on income generated from the production, processing and export, and/or on consumption of fossil fuels and associated energy-intensive products; and
   (i) Land-locked and transit countries.

Further, the Conference of the Parties may take actions, as appropriate, with respect to this paragraph.

9. The Parties shall take full account of the specific needs and special situations of the least developed countries in their actions with regard to funding and transfer of technology.

10. The Parties shall, in accordance with Article 10, take into consideration in the implementation of the commitments of the Convention the situation of Parties, particularly developing country Parties, with economies that are vulnerable to the adverse effects of the implementation of measures to respond to climate change. This applies notably to Parties with economies that are highly dependent on income generated from the production, processing and export, and/or consumption of fossil fuels and associated energy-intensive products and/or the use of fossil fuels for which such Parties have serious difficulties in switching to alternatives.

Concerned that the commitments established by the Climate Change Convention would not suffice, governments launched a new round of talks in 1995, designed to establish binding carbon emission targets for developed states. The result, several years later, was the Kyoto Protocol. Annex I parties[85] that also became parties to this Protocol committed themselves to specific targets and timetables for the reduction of certain greenhouse gases. The core commitments are found in Article 3:

Kyoto Protocol to the United Nations Framework Convention on Climate Change, 11 December 1997, 2303 UNTS 214, (1998) 37 ILM 22, in force 16 February 2005

Article 3
1. The Parties included in Annex I shall, individually or jointly, ensure that their aggregate anthropogenic carbon dioxide equivalent emissions of the greenhouse gases listed in Annex A do not exceed their assigned amounts, calculated pursuant to their quantified emission limitation and reduction commitments inscribed in Annex B and in accordance with the provisions of this Article, with a view to reducing their overall emissions of such gases by at least 5 per cent below 1990 levels in the commitment period 2008 to 2012.

2. Each Party included in Annex I shall, by 2005, have made demonstrable progress in achieving its commitments under this Protocol.

3. The net changes in greenhouse gas emissions by sources and removals by sinks resulting from direct human-induced land use change and forestry activities, limited to afforestation, reforestation and deforestation since 1990, measured as verifiable changes in carbon stocks in each commitment period, shall be used to meet the commitments under this Article of each Party included in Annex I. The greenhouse gas emissions by sources and removals by sinks associated with those activities shall be reported in a transparent and verifiable manner and reviewed in accordance with Articles 7 and 8.

---

85 Annex I parties are Australia, Austria, Belarus, Belgium, Bulgaria, Canada, Croatia, Czech Republic, Denmark, European Economic Community (now known as the European Union), Estonia, Finland, France, Germany, Greece, Hungary, Iceland, Ireland, Italy, Japan, Latvia, Liechtenstein, Lithuania, Luxembourg, Malta, Monaco, Netherlands, New Zealand, Norway, Poland, Portugal, Romania, Russian Federation, Slovakia, Slovenia, Spain, Sweden, Switzerland, Turkey, Ukraine, United Kingdom, and United States.

4. Prior to the first session of the Conference of the Parties serving as the meeting of the Parties to this Protocol, each Party included in Annex I shall provide, for consideration by the Subsidiary Body for Scientific and Technological Advice, data to establish its level of carbon stocks in 1990 and to enable an estimate to be made of its changes in carbon stocks in subsequent years. The Conference of the Parties serving as the meeting of the Parties to this Protocol shall, at its first session or as soon as practicable thereafter, decide upon modalities, rules and guidelines as to how, and which, additional human-induced activities related to changes in greenhouse gas emissions by sources and removals by sinks in the agricultural soils and the land use change and forestry categories shall be added to, or subtracted from, the assigned amounts for Parties included in Annex I, taking into account uncertainties, transparency in reporting, verifiability, the methodological work of the Intergovernmental Panel on Climate Change, the advice provided by the Subsidiary Body for Scientific and Technological Advice in accordance with Article 5 and the decisions of the Conference of the Parties. Such a decision shall apply in the second and subsequent commitment periods. A Party may choose to apply such a decision on these additional human-induced activities for its first commitment period, provided that these activities have taken place since 1990.

5. The Parties included in Annex I undergoing the process of transition to a market economy whose base year or period was established pursuant to decision 9/CP.2 of the Conference of the Parties at its second session shall use that base year or period for the implementation of their commitments under this Article. Any other Party included in Annex I undergoing the process of transition to a market economy which has not yet submitted its first national communication under Article 12 of the Convention may also notify the Conference of the Parties serving as the meeting of the Parties to this Protocol that it intends to use an historical base year or period other than 1990 for the implementation of its commitments under this Article. The Conference of the Parties serving as the meeting of the Parties to this Protocol shall decide on the acceptance of such notification.

6. Taking into account Article 4, paragraph 6, of the Convention, in the implementation of their commitments under this Protocol other than those under this Article, a certain degree of flexibility shall be allowed by the Conference of the Parties serving as the meeting of the Parties to this Protocol to the Parties included in Annex I undergoing the process of transition to a market economy.

7. In the first quantified emission limitation and reduction commitment period, from 2008 to 2012, the assigned amount for each Party included in Annex I shall be equal to the percentage inscribed for it in Annex B of its aggregate anthropogenic carbon dioxide equivalent emissions of the greenhouse gases listed in Annex A in 1990, or the base year or period determined in accordance with paragraph 5 above, multiplied by five. Those Parties included in Annex I for whom land-use change and forestry constituted a net source of greenhouse gas emissions in 1990 shall include in their 1990 emissions base year or period the aggregate anthropogenic carbon dioxide equivalent emissions by sources minus removals by sinks in 1990 from land-use change for the purposes of calculating their assigned amount.

8. Any Party included in Annex I may use 1995 as its base year for hydrofluorocarbons,

perfluorocarbons and sulphur hexafluoride, for the purposes of the calculation referred to in paragraph 7 above.

9. Commitments for subsequent periods for Parties included in Annex I shall be established in amendments to Annex B to this Protocol, which shall be adopted in accordance with the provisions of Article 20, paragraph 7. The Conference of the Parties serving as the meeting of the Parties to this Protocol shall initiate the consideration of such commitments at least seven years before the end of the first commitment period referred to in paragraph 1 above.

10. Any emission reduction units, or any part of an assigned amount, which a Party acquires from another Party in accordance with the provisions of Article 6 or of Article 16 shall be added to the assigned amount for the acquiring Party.

11. Any emission reduction units, or any part of an assigned amount, which a Party transfers to another Party in accordance with the provisions of Article 6 or of Article 16 shall be subtracted from the assigned amount for the transferring Party.

12. Any certified emission reductions which a Party acquires from another Party in accordance with the provisions of Article 12 shall be added to the assigned amount for the acquiring Party.

13. If the emissions of a Party included in Annex I in a commitment period are less than its assigned amount under this Article, this difference shall, on request of that Party, be added to the assigned amount for that Party for subsequent commitment periods.

14. Each Party included in Annex I shall strive to implement the commitments mentioned in paragraph 1 above in such a way as to minimize adverse social, environmental and economic impacts on developing country Parties . . . .

Until recently, the Kyoto Protocol had attracted near universal participation, with 192 states parties. The Protocol entered into force in February 2005, ninety days after at least fifty-five states parties to the Climate Change Convention, including Annex I parties accounting for at least 55 percent of the total 1990 carbon dioxide emissions from that group, deposited their instruments of ratification, acceptance, approval, or accession.[86]

Canada ratified the Protocol in 2002 and, as a result, was required to reduce specified greenhouse gas emissions by 6 percent by the commitment period 2008–2012.[87] In 2006, Canada's federal minister of the environment publicly stated that Canada would not reach this target, a position reiterated in later years. Immediately after the conclusion of the 17th United Nations Climate Change Conference of the Parties in Durban, South Africa, on 12 December 2011, Canada announced its intention to withdraw from the Kyoto Protocol. The environment minister explained Canada's position as follows:

. . . As we said from the outset, the Kyoto Protocol did not represent the path forward for Canada. The Durban Platform is a way forward that builds on our work at Copenhagen and Cancun. Before this week, the Kyoto Protocol covered less than 30% of global emis-

---

86 Kyoto Protocol, above note 11, art 25.
87 *Ibid*, Annex B.

sions. Now it covers less than 13%—and that number is only shrinking. The Kyoto Protocol does not cover the world's two largest emitters—the United States and China—and
therefore will not work. It is now clear that Kyoto is not the path forward for a global solution to climate change; instead, it is an impediment. We believe that a new agreement,
with legally binding commitments for all major emitters, that allows us as a country to
continue to generate jobs and economic growth, represents the path forward.

Increasingly, support is growing for Canada's position—from the EU, to the United
States, Australia, New Zealand, least developed countries and the group of 43 small island states. Canada will work towards a legally binding agreement to address global emissions that allows us to continue creating jobs and economic growth in Canada.

. . . As we have said, Kyoto—for Canada—is in the past. As such, we are invoking our
legal right to formally withdraw from Kyoto. This decision formalizes what we have said
since 2006 that we will not implement the Kyoto Protocol. We remain committed to negotiating an international climate change agreement that works. That means getting a pact
that involves all the major emitters. We will work toward this in the coming weeks and
months. It will not be easy but it is important. And Canada will continue to be willing
partner with those looking to address Kyoto's many failings, while also ensuring major
emitters live up to binding commitments to reduce greenhouse gases.[88]

As a result, Canada became the first state to withdraw from the Kyoto Protocol.
Canada's withdrawal took effect as of 15 December 2012. Not long after, Canada also
gave notice of its intention to withdraw from the United Nations Convention to Combat
Desertification (a treaty that enjoyed universal ratification until Canada's withdrawal).[89]

The Kyoto Protocol has not been followed by another treaty regime. Rather, states have
opted for soft law arrangements, specifically the 2007 Bali Roadmap (which includes the
Bali Action Plan),[90] the 2009 Copenhagen Accord,[91] the 2010 Cancun Agreements,[92] and

---

88   "Statement by Minister Kent" (12 December 2011), online: www.ec.gc.ca/default.asp?lang=En&n=
FFE36B6D-1&news=6B04014B-54FC-4739-B22C-F9CD9A840800. See also UN Treaty Section depositary notification C.N.1313.2002.TREATIES-56 of 17 December 2002, UN Treaty Registration No A-30822.

89   United Nations Convention to Combat Desertification in Countries Experiencing Serious Drought and/
or Desertification, Particularly in Africa, 14 October 1994, 1954 UNTS 3, in force 26 December 1996.
Canada's notice of withdrawal (UN Treaty Registration No. I-33480) will take effect on 28 March 2014.
For reaction, see Mike Blanchfield, "Canada Quits UN Drought Convention" Globe and Mail (28 March
2013) A18; Mike Blanchfield, "Canada's Move 'Regrettable,' UN Says" Globe and Mail (30 March 2013) A9.

90   Report of the Conference of the Parties on its Thirteenth Session, held in Bali from 3 to 15 December 2007,
Part Two: Action Taken by the Conference of Parties at its Thirteenth Session, UN Doc FCCC/CP/2007/6/
Add.1 (14 March 2008) at 3.

91   Report of the Conference of the Parties on its Fifteenth Session, held in Copenhagen from 7 to 19 December
2009, Part Two: Action Taken by the Conference of the Parties at its Fifteenth Session, UN Doc FCCC/
CP/2009/11/Add.1 (30 March 2010) at 4.

92   Report of the Conference of the Parties on its Sixteenth Session, held in Cancun from 29 November–10
December 2010, Part Two: Action Taken by the Conference of the Parties at its Sixteenth Session, UN Doc
FCCC/CP/2010/7/Add.1 (15 March 2011) at 2; and Report of the Conference of the Parties Serving as the
Meeting of the Parties to the Kyoto Protocol on its Sixth Session, held in Cancun from 29 November to 10
December 2010, Part 2: Action Taken by the Conference of the Parties Serving as the Meeting of the Parties
to the Kyoto Protocol at its Sixth Session, UN Doc FCCC/KP/CMP/2010/12/Add.2 (15 March 2011) at 22.

the 2011 Durban Platform for Enhanced Action.[93] At the 2011 meeting in Durban, states agreed to launch a new round of negotiations under the Climate Change Convention with the goal of concluding, by 2015, a new, universal greenhouse gas reduction protocol or other legally binding outcome covering the period beyond 2020.[94] In 2012, meeting in Doha, states agreed on a timetable for the adoption of a universal climate agreement by 2015, to come into effect in 2020.[95] All of these developments, considered together, represent the future of the climate change regime.

2) Nuclear, Toxic, and Hazardous Substances

Nuclear activities can have profoundly devastating global or regional environmental impacts. It is for this reason that nuclear activities are considered ultrahazardous[96] and several international conventions have been adopted to govern these activities. Being ultrahazardous, nuclear activities typically attract strict liability under these conventions, such that the state where the activity takes place is liable regardless of fault.[97] Apart from conventions on nuclear testing and weapons, conventions have been adopted to govern the transport and use of peacetime nuclear materials, as well as responses to nuclear emergencies. In 1980, the Convention on the Physical Protection of Nuclear Material was adopted in order to protect nuclear materials in transit.[98] The 1986 Convention on Early Notification of a Nuclear Accident, which stemmed from the Chernobyl nuclear accident, is described above. Also in 1986, the Convention on Assistance in the Case of a Nuclear Accident or Radiological Emergency was adopted.[99] Both of these 1986 conventions were concluded under the auspices of the International Atomic Energy Agency (IAEA), and formed the basis of the IAEA's emergency response to the 2011 Fukushima Daiichi nu-

---

93 *Report of the Conference of the Parties serving as the Meeting of the Parties to the Kyoto Protocol on its Seventh Session, held in Durban from 28 November to 11 December 2011, Part 2: Action Taken by the Conference of the Parties Serving as the Meeting of the Parties to the Kyoto Protocol at its Seventh Session*, UN Doc FCCC/KP/CMP/2011/10/Add.1 (15 March 2012) at 2.

94 *Report of the Conference of the Parties on its Seventeenth Session, held in Durban from 28 November to 11 December 2011, Part Two: Action Taken by the Conference of the Parties at its Seventeenth Session*, UN Doc FCCC/CP/2011/9/Add.1 (15 March 2012) at 4.

95 *Report of the Conference of the Parties on its Eighteenth Session, held in Doha from 26 November to 8 December 2012, Part Two: Action Taken by the Conference of the Parties at its Eighteenth Session*, UN Doc FCCC/CP/2012/8/Add.1 (28 February 2013) at 19–20.

96 Redgwell, above note 7 at 705.

97 See, for example, Vienna Convention on Civil Liability for Nuclear Damage, 21 May 1963, 1063 UNTS 266, (1963) 2 ILM 727, in force 12 November 1977, and the Protocol to Amend the 1963 Vienna Convention on Civil Liability for Nuclear Damage, 12 September 1997, 2241 UNTS 302, (1997) 36 ILM 1454, in force 4 October 2003. A 1997 effort to amend these treaties has not attracted support: Convention on Supplementary Compensation for Nuclear Damage, 12 September 1997, (1997) 36 ILM 1461 (not in force).

98 Convention on the Physical Protection of Nuclear Material, 3 March 1980, 1456 UNTS 124, (1979) 18 ILM 1419, in force 8 February 1987.

99 Convention on Assistance in the Case of a Nuclear Accident or Radiological Emergency, 26 September 1986, 1457 UNTS 134, (1994) 33 ILM 1514, in force 26 February 1987. This convention has been signed, but not ratified, by Canada.

clear disaster in Japan.[100] In 1994, the Convention on Nuclear Safety was also adopted to regulate the safe use of nuclear energy.[101]

Other hazardous activities and materials have also been the subject of international treaties. The 1989 Basel Convention on the Transboundary Movement of Hazardous Wastes and their Disposal was the first convention of its kind.[102] The hazardous wastes covered by this convention include clinical, pharmaceutical, cyanide-containing heat treatment, and explosive wastes.[103] The convention has a dual focus, ensuring safe transboundary movement of hazardous waste and proper environmental management of its disposal. This convention affirms that states may prohibit the importation of hazardous wastes and this prohibition must be respected by other parties.[104]

The 1998 Rotterdam Convention on Prior Informed Consent subjects hazardous chemicals and pesticides to a regime of prior informed consent by the importing party.[105] Thus the convention does not ban the use of hazardous chemicals or fertilizers, but simply controls their trade. The 2001 Stockholm Convention on Persistent Organic Pollutants aims to eliminate or limit the release of persistent organic pollutants (POPs).[106] Article 1 of the Stockholm Convention provides: "Mindful of the precautionary approach as set forth in Principle 15 of the Rio Declaration on Environment and Development, the objective of this Convention is to protect human health and the environment from persistent organic pollutants." POPs are chemicals such as polychlorinated biphenyls (PCBs) that can remain in the environment for long periods of time, accumulate in fatty tissue, and be toxic to humans.

In January 2013, states adopted the text of the Minamata Convention on Mercury, the object of which is "to protect human health and the environment from anthropogenic emissions and releases of mercury and mercury compounds."[107] The treaty will provide controls, and require reductions, across a range of products, processes, and industries where mercury is used, released, or emitted.[108] It was named after a city in Japan where serious health damage occurred as a result of mercury pollution in the mid-twentieth century.[109]

---

100 On 11 March 2011, a major earthquake and tsunami seriously damaged the Fukushima Daiichi nuclear power plant in Japan, causing a nuclear meltdown and release of radioactive material. The IAEA was actively involved in monitoring the situation and keeping states parties to the two conventions informed: *IAEA Activities in Response to the Fukushima Accident: Report of the Director General*, IAEA Doc GOV/INF/2011/8 (3 June 2011).

101 Convention on Nuclear Safety, 17 June 1994, 1963 UNTS 293, Can TS 1996 No 44, (1994) 33 ILM 1518, in force 24 October 1996.

102 Basel Convention, above note 47.

103 *Ibid*, Annex 1.

104 *Ibid*, art 4.

105 Rotterdam Convention on the Prior Informed Consent Procedure for Certain Hazardous Chemicals and Pesticides in International Trade, 10 September 1998, 2244 UNTS 337, (1999) 38 ILM 1, in force 24 February 2004.

106 Stockholm Convention on Persistent Organic Pollutants, 22 May 2001, 2256 UNTS 119, (2001) 40 ILM 532, in force 17 May 2004.

107 Minamata Convention, above note 3, art 1. The treaty will be opened for signature in October 2013.

108 United Nations Environment Programme, "Minamata Convention Agreed by Nations" (19 January 2013), online: www.unep.org/newscentre/default.aspx?DocumentID=2702&ArticleID=9373.

109 *Ibid*.

3) Marine Pollution

Marine pollution can occur in a variety of ways: through the operation of, or accidents involving, vessels; deliberate or accidental dumping from vessels; and activities involving the seabed (such as oil drilling). Marine pollution can also occur from land-based sources such as rivers and pipelines.

The main source of international environmental law on marine pollution is the 1982 United Nations Convention on the Law of the Sea (UNCLOS), specifically Part XII concerning the protection and preservation of the marine environment. Under this Part, states have an obligation to protect and preserve the marine environment, including when exploiting their own natural resources.[110] Consider the specific measures they are required to take:

United Nations Convention on the Law of the Sea, 10 December 1982, 1833 UNTS 3, (1982) 21 ILM 1261, in force 16 November 1994

Article 194 — Measures to prevent, reduce and control pollution of the marine environment
1. States shall take, individually or jointly as appropriate, all measures consistent with this Convention that are necessary to prevent, reduce and control pollution of the marine environment from any source, using for this purpose the best practicable means at their disposal and in accordance with their capabilities, and they shall endeavour to harmonize their policies in this connection.

2. States shall take all measures necessary to ensure that activities under their jurisdiction or control are so conducted as not to cause damage by pollution to other States and their environment, and that pollution arising from incidents or activities under their jurisdiction or control does not spread beyond the areas where they exercise sovereign rights in accordance with this Convention.

3. The measures taken pursuant to this Part shall deal with all sources of pollution of the marine environment. These measures shall include, *inter alia*, those designed to minimize to the fullest possible extent:
   (a) the release of toxic, harmful or noxious substances, especially those which are persistent, from land-based sources, from or through the atmosphere or by dumping;
   (b) pollution from vessels, in particular measures for preventing accidents and dealing with emergencies, ensuring the safety of operations at sea, preventing intentional and unintentional discharges, and regulating the design, construction, equipment, operation and manning of vessels;
   (c) pollution from installations and devices used in exploration or exploitation of the natural resources of the seabed and subsoil, in particular measures for preventing accidents and dealing with emergencies, ensuring the safety of operations at sea, and regulating the design, construction, equipment, operation and manning of such installations or devices;
   (d) pollution from other installations and devices operating in the marine environment, in particular measures for preventing accidents and dealing with emergencies,

---

110 UNCLOS, above note 3, arts 192–93.

ensuring the safety of operations at sea, and regulating the design, construction, equipment, operation and manning of such installations or devices.

4. In taking measures to prevent, reduce or control pollution of the marine environment, States shall refrain from unjustifiable interference with activities carried out by other States in the exercise of their rights and in pursuance of their duties in conformity with this Convention.

5. The measures taken in accordance with this Part shall include those necessary to protect and preserve rare or fragile ecosystems as well as the habitat of depleted, threatened or endangered species and other forms of marine life.

Article 195 — Duty not to transfer damage or hazards or transform one type of pollution into another
In taking measures to prevent, reduce and control pollution of the marine environment, States shall act so as not to transfer, directly or indirectly, damage or hazards from one area to another or transform one type of pollution into another.

Article 196 — Use of technologies or introduction of alien or new species
1. States shall take all measures necessary to prevent, reduce and control pollution of the marine environment resulting from the use of technologies under their jurisdiction or control, or the intentional or accidental introduction of species, alien or new, to a particular part of the marine environment, which may cause significant and harmful changes thereto.

2. This article does not affect the application of this Convention regarding the prevention, reduction and control of pollution of the marine environment.

UNCLOS also contains a duty of notification of imminent or actual damage by pollution to the marine environment,[111] and an obligation to create contingency plans for pollution incidents.[112] In addition, the convention contains detailed provisions requiring states to adopt national legislation addressing pollution from land-based sources,[113] seabed activities subject to national jurisdiction,[114] pollution by dumping,[115] pollution from vessels,[116] and pollution through the atmosphere.[117]

Additional conventions governing marine pollution include the 1969 International Convention relating to Intervention on the High Seas in Cases of Oil Pollution Casualties;[118] the 1973 Convention and its 1978 Protocol concerning the prevention of pollution from

---

111 *Ibid*, art 198.
112 *Ibid*, art 199.
113 *Ibid*, art 207. See also art 213 on enforcement.
114 *Ibid*, art 208. See also art 214 on enforcement.
115 *Ibid*, art 210. See also art 216 on enforcement.
116 *Ibid*, art 211. See also arts 217–21 on enforcement.
117 *Ibid*, art 212. See also art 222 on enforcement.
118 29 November 1969, 970 UNTS 212, (1970) 9 ILM 25, in force 6 May 1975, as amended by the Protocol relating to Intervention on the High Seas in Cases of Pollution by Substances Other Than Oil, 2 November 1973, 1313 UNTS 4, in force 30 March 1983.

ships;[119] and the 1990 Convention on Oil Pollution Preparedness, Response and Co-operation.[120]

4) Biodiversity and Conservation of Living Resources

Among the earliest international environmental law treaties were those focused upon conserving wildlife.[121] This section will focus on two conventions considered to be central to the conservation of living resources: the 1973 Convention on International Trade in Endangered Species of Wild Fauna and Flora (CITES Convention),[122] and the 1992 Convention on Biological Diversity.[123]

The CITES Convention prohibits or restricts trade in species or in products derived from species that are in danger of extinction. It currently accords varying degrees of protection to 34,000 species of animals and plants.[124] For example, in 2013, states parties to the treaty regime agreed to regulate the trade of five species of sharks in response to declining shark populations due to the harvesting of shark fins and meat for human consumption.[125] The CITES Convention provides for three kinds of trade control. Appendix I forbids trade in listed species threatened with extinction, subject to certain "exceptional circumstances."[126] Appendix II permits restricted trade in listed species that are not currently threatened with extinction but could be if trade is not subject to strict regulation.[127] Appendix III covers species subject to national regulation but for which states seek international cooperation in controlling trade in order to prevent or restrict exploitation.[128]

As with other treaties, the success of the CITES Convention depends heavily on domestic enforcement by states:

---

119 Protocol of 1978 relating to the International Convention for the Prevention of Pollution from Ships (MARPOL Convention), 2 November 1973, 1313 UNTS 4, in force 30 March 1983, as amended.

120 Oil Pollution Convention, above note 57.

121 See, for example, Paris Convention on the Protection of Birds Useful to Agriculture, 19 March 1902, 30 de Martens (2d ed) 686. See also the Pan-American Convention on Nature Protection and Wild Life Preservation in the Western Hemisphere, 12 October 1940, 161 UNTS 193, in force 30 April 1942, and the International Convention on the Protection of Birds, 18 October 1950, 638 UNTS 138, in force 17 January 1963.

122 3 March 1973, 993 UNTS 244, Can TS 1975 No 32, (1973) 12 ILM 1055, in force 1 July 1975, as amended [CITES Convention].

123 Convention on Biological Diversity, above note 47.

124 CITES, "The CITES Species" (21 November 2011), online: www.cites.org/eng/disc/species.php.

125 CITES, "Press Release: CITES Conference Takes Decisive Action to Halt Decline of Tropical Timber, Sharks, Manta Rays and a Wide Range of Other Plants and Animals" (14 March 2013), online: www.cites.org/eng/news/pr/2013/20130314_cop16.php.

126 CITES Convention, above note 122, art II(1).

127 *Ibid*, art II(2).

128 *Ibid*, art II(3).

Convention on International Trade in Endangered Species of Wild Flora and Fauna, 3 March 1973, 993 UNTS 244, Can TS 1975 No 32, (1973) 12 ILM 1085, in force 1 July 1975, as amended

Article VIII
Measures to be Taken by the Parties
1. The Parties shall take appropriate measures to enforce the provisions of the present Convention and to prohibit trade in specimens in violation thereof. These shall include measures:

(a) to penalize trade in, or possession of, such specimens, or both; and

(b) to provide for the confiscation or return to the State of export of such specimens.

2. In addition to the measures taken under paragraph 1 of this Article, a Party may, when it deems it necessary, provide for any method of internal reimbursement for expenses incurred as a result of the confiscation of a specimen traded in violation of the measures taken in the application of the provisions of the present Convention.

3. As far as possible, the Parties shall ensure that specimens shall pass through any formalities required for trade with a minimum of delay. To facilitate such passage, a Party may designate ports of exit and ports of entry at which specimens must be presented for clearance. The Parties shall ensure further that all living specimens, during any period of transit, holding or shipment, are properly cared for so as to minimize the risk of injury, damage to health or cruel treatment.

4. Where a living specimen is confiscated as a result of measures referred to in paragraph 1 of this Article:

(a) the specimen shall be entrusted to a Management Authority of the State of confiscation;

(b) the Management Authority shall, after consultation with the State of export, return the specimen to that State at the expense of that State, or to a rescue centre or such other place as the Management Authority deems appropriate and consistent with the purposes of the present Convention; and

(c) the Management Authority may obtain the advice of a Scientific Authority, or may, whenever it considers it desirable, consult the Secretariat in order to facilitate the decision under sub-paragraph (b) of this paragraph, including the choice of a rescue centre or other place.

5. A rescue centre as referred to in paragraph 4 of this Article means an institution designated by a Management Authority to look after the welfare of living specimens, particularly those that have been confiscated.

6. Each Party shall maintain records of trade in specimens of species included in Appendices I, II and III which shall cover:

(a) the names and addresses of exporters and importers; and

(b) the number and type of permits and certificates granted; the States with which such trade occurred; the numbers or quantities and types of specimens, names of species as included in Appendices I, II and III and, where applicable, the size and sex of the specimens in question.

7. Each Party shall prepare periodic reports on its implementation of the present Convention and shall transmit to the Secretariat:

(a) an annual report containing a summary of the information specified in sub-paragraph (b) of paragraph 6 of this Article; and

(b) a biennial report on legislative, regulatory and administrative measures taken to enforce the provisions of the present Convention.

8. The information referred to in paragraph 7 of this Article shall be available to the public where this is not inconsistent with the law of the Party concerned.

Compliance with the CITES Convention is monitored through infraction reports submitted by the Secretariat to the Conference of Parties.[129] If a state party is found to be non-compliant, a recommendation may be issued to suspend trade with that state in CITES-listed species. In 2006, for example, Haiti was deemed non-compliant with respect to the export of Queen conch (*strombus gigas*) and therefore all parties were asked to suspend the import of Queen conch from Haiti.[130] These recommended trade suspensions have proven to be "a potent tool for ensuring proper national implementation of CITES' obligations to enact legislation, develop work plans, control legal/illegal trade, and/or improve the basis for government decision-making."[131]

Canada ratified the CITES Convention in 1975 and has implemented the treaty through domestic legislation.[132]

As for the broader issue of biological diversity, the 1992 Convention on Biological Diversity has filled a gap in international environmental law by establishing a system for regulating biological diversity as a whole, as opposed to specific aspects of such diversity. Like the Climate Change Convention, this treaty was also adopted at the UN Conference on Environment and Development held in Rio de Janeiro in 1992.

Convention on Biological Diversity, 5 June 1992, 1760 UNTS 79, Can TS 1993 No 24, (1992) 31 ILM 818, in force 29 December 1993

The Contracting Parties,

Conscious of the intrinsic value of biological diversity and of the ecological, genetic, social, economic, scientific, educational, cultural, recreational and aesthetic values of biological diversity and its components,

Conscious also of the importance of biological diversity for evolution and for maintaining life sustaining systems of the biosphere,

---

129 *Ibid*, arts XII & XIII.

130 *Notification to the Parties Concerning Implementation of Resolution Conf 12.8 (Rev CoP13): Recommendations of the Standing Committee*, No 2006/034 (12 May 2006), online: www.cites.org/eng/notif/2006/E034.pdf.

131 Marceil Yeater & Juan Vasquez, "Demystifying the Relationship between CITES and the WTO" (2001) 10 RECIEL 271 at 274–75, as cited in Redgwell, above note 7 at 713.

132 See *Wild Animal and Plant Protection and Regulation of International and Interprovincial Trade Act*, SC 1992, c 52 as amended; *Export and Import Permits Act*, RSC 1985, c E-19, as amended, with its export control list.

Affirming that the conservation of biological diversity is a common concern of humankind,

Reaffirming also that States are responsible for conserving their biological diversity and for using their biological resources in a sustainable manner, . . .

Have agreed as follows:

Article 1. Objectives

The objectives of this Convention, to be pursued in accordance with its relevant provisions, are the conservation of biological diversity, the sustainable use of its components and the fair and equitable sharing of the benefits arising out of the utilization of genetic resources, including by appropriate access to genetic resources and by appropriate transfer of relevant technologies, taking into account all rights over those resources and to technologies, and by appropriate funding.

Article 2. Use of Terms

For the purposes of this Convention:

"Biological diversity" means the variability among living organisms from all sources including, inter alia, terrestrial, marine and other aquatic ecosystems and the ecological complexes of which they are part; this includes diversity within species, between species and of ecosystems.

"Biological resources" includes genetic resources, organisms or parts thereof, populations, or any other biotic component of ecosystems with actual or potential use or value for humanity.

"Biotechnology" means any technological application that uses biological systems, living organisms, or derivatives thereof, to make or modify products or processes for specific use.

"Country of origin of genetic resources" means the country which possesses those genetic resources in *in-situ* conditions.

"Country providing genetic resources" means the country supplying genetic resources collected from *in-situ* sources, including populations of both wild and domesticated species, or taken from *ex-situ* sources, which may or may not have originated in that country.

"Domesticated or cultivated species" means species in which the evolutionary process has been influenced by humans to meet their needs.

"Ecosystem" means a dynamic complex of plant, animal and micro-organism communities and their non-living environment interacting as a functional unit.

"*Ex-situ* conservation" means the conservation of components of biological diversity outside their natural habitats.

"Genetic material" means any material of plant, animal, microbial or other origin containing functional units of heredity.

"Genetic resources" means genetic material of actual or potential value.

"Habitat" means the place or type of site where an organism or population naturally occurs.

"*In-situ* conditions" means conditions where genetic resources exist within ecosystems and natural habitats, and, in the case of domesticated or cultivated species, in the surroundings where they have developed their distinctive properties.

"*In-situ* conservation" means the conservation of ecosystems and natural habitats and the maintenance and recovery of viable populations of species in their natural surroundings and, in the case of domesticated or cultivated species, in the surroundings where they have developed their distinctive properties.

"Protected area" means a geographically defined area which is designated or regulated and managed to achieve specific conservation objectives . . . .

"Sustainable use" means the use of components of biological diversity in a way and at a rate that does not lead to the long-term decline of biological diversity, thereby maintaining its potential to meet the needs and aspirations of present and future generations.

"Technology" includes biotechnology.

Article 3. Principle
States have, in accordance with the Charter of the United Nations and the principles of international law, the sovereign right to exploit their own resources pursuant to their own environmental policies, and the responsibility to ensure that activities within their jurisdiction or control do not cause damage to the environment of other States or of areas beyond the limits of national jurisdiction.

Article 4. Jurisdictional Scope
Subject to the rights of other States, and except as otherwise expressly provided in this Convention, the provisions of this Convention apply, in relation to each Contracting Party:
(a) In the case of components of biological diversity, in areas within the limits of its national jurisdiction; and
(b) In the case of processes and activities, regardless of where their effects occur, carried out under its jurisdiction or control, within the area of its national jurisdiction or beyond the limits of national jurisdiction.

Article 5. Cooperation
Each Contracting Party shall, as far as possible and as appropriate, cooperate with other Contracting Parties, directly or, where appropriate, through competent international organizations, in respect of areas beyond national jurisdiction and on other matters of mutual interest, for the conservation and sustainable use of biological diversity.

Article 6. General Measures for Conservation and Sustainable Use
Each Contracting Party shall, in accordance with its particular conditions and capabilities:
(a) Develop national strategies, plans or programmes for the conservation and sustainable use of biological diversity or adapt for this purpose existing strategies, plans or programmes which shall reflect, *inter alia*, the measures set out in this Convention relevant to the Contracting Party concerned; and
(b) Integrate, as far as possible and as appropriate, the conservation and sustainable use of biological diversity into relevant sectoral or cross-sectoral plans, programmes and policies.

Article 7. Identification and Monitoring

Each Contracting Party shall, as far as possible and as appropriate, in particular for the purposes of Articles 8 and 10:

(a) Identify components of biological diversity important for its conservation and sustainable use having regard to the indicative list of categories set down in Annex I;

(b) Monitor, through sampling and other techniques, the components of biological diversity identified pursuant to subparagraph (a) above, paying particular attention to those requiring urgent conservation measures and those which offer the greatest potential for sustainable use;

(c) Identify processes and categories of activities which have or are likely to have significant adverse impacts on the conservation and sustainable use of biological diversity, and monitor their effects through sampling and other techniques; and

(d) Maintain and organize, by any mechanism data, derived from identification and monitoring activities pursuant to subparagraphs (a), (b) and (c) above.

Article 8. In-situ Conservation

Each Contracting Party shall, as far as possible and as appropriate:

(a) Establish a system of protected areas or areas where special measures need to be taken to conserve biological diversity;

(b) Develop, where necessary, guidelines for the selection, establishment and management of protected areas or areas where special measures need to be taken to conserve biological diversity;

(c) Regulate or manage biological resources important for the conservation of biological diversity whether within or outside protected areas, with a view to ensuring their conservation and sustainable use;

(d) Promote the protection of ecosystems, natural habitats and the maintenance of viable populations of species in natural surroundings;

(e) Promote environmentally sound and sustainable development in areas adjacent to protected areas with a view to furthering protection of these areas;

(f) Rehabilitate and restore degraded ecosystems and promote the recovery of threatened species, *inter alia*, through the development and implementation of plans or other management strategies;

(g) Establish or maintain means to regulate, manage or control the risks associated with the use and release of living modified organisms resulting from biotechnology which are likely to have adverse environmental impacts that could affect the conservation and sustainable use of biological diversity, taking also into account the risks to human health;

(h) Prevent the introduction of, control or eradicate those alien species which threaten ecosystems, habitats or species;

(i) Endeavour to provide the conditions needed for compatibility between present uses and the conservation of biological diversity and the sustainable use of its components;

(j) Subject to its national legislation, respect, preserve and maintain knowledge, innovations and practices of indigenous and local communities embodying traditional lifestyles relevant for the conservation and sustainable use of biological diversity and promote their wider application with the approval and involvement of the holders of such knowledge, innovations and practices and encourage the equitable sharing of the benefits arising from the utilization of such knowledge, innovations and practices;

(k) Develop or maintain necessary legislation and/or other regulatory provisions for the protection of threatened species and populations;

(l) Where a significant adverse effect on biological diversity has been determined pursuant to Article 7, regulate or manage the relevant processes and categories of activities; and

(m) Cooperate in providing financial and other support for *in-situ* conservation outlined in subparagraphs (a) to (l) above, particularly to developing countries.

Article 9. Ex-situ Conservation

Each Contracting Party shall, as far as possible and as appropriate, and predominantly for the purpose of complementing *in-situ* measures:

(a) Adopt measures for the *ex-situ* conservation of components of biological diversity, preferably in the country of origin of such components;

(b) Establish and maintain facilities for *ex-situ* conservation of and research on plants, animals and micro-organisms, preferably in the country of origin of genetic resources;

(c) Adopt measures for the recovery and rehabilitation of threatened species and for their reintroduction into their natural habitats under appropriate conditions;

(d) Regulate and manage collection of biological resources from natural habitats for *ex-situ* conservation purposes so as not to threaten ecosystems and *in-situ* populations of species, except where special temporary *ex-situ* measures are required under subparagraph (c) above; and

(e) Cooperate in providing financial and other support for *ex-situ* conservation outlined in subparagraphs (a) to (d) above and in the establishment and maintenance of *ex-situ* conservation facilities in developing countries.

Article 10. Sustainable Use of Components of Biological Diversity

Each Contracting Party shall, as far as possible and as appropriate:

(a) Integrate consideration of the conservation and sustainable use of biological resources into national decision-making;

(b) Adopt measures relating to the use of biological resources to avoid or minimize adverse impacts on biological diversity;

(c) Protect and encourage customary use of biological resources in accordance with traditional cultural practices that are compatible with conservation or sustainable use requirements;

(d) Support local populations to develop and implement remedial action in degraded areas where biological diversity has been reduced; and

(e) Encourage cooperation between its governmental authorities and its private sector in developing methods for sustainable use of biological resources.

Article 11. Incentive Measures

Each Contracting Party shall, as far as possible and as appropriate, adopt economically and socially sound measures that act as incentives for the conservation and sustainable use of components of biological diversity . . . .

Article 15. Access to Genetic Resources
1. Recognizing the sovereign rights of States over their natural resources, the authority to determine access to genetic resources rests with the national governments and is subject to national legislation.

2. Each Contracting Party shall endeavour to create conditions to facilitate access to genetic resources for environmentally sound uses by other Contracting Parties and not to impose restrictions that run counter to the objectives of this Convention . . . .

4. Access, where granted, shall be on mutually agreed terms and subject to the provisions of this Article.

5. Access to genetic resources shall be subject to prior informed consent of the Contracting Party providing such resources, unless otherwise determined by that Party . . . .

7. Each Contracting Party shall take legislative, administrative or policy measures, as appropriate . . . with the aim of sharing in a fair and equitable way the results of research and development and the benefits arising from the commercial and other utilization of genetic resources with the Contracting Party providing such resources. Such sharing shall be upon mutually agreed terms . . . .

Annex I. Identification and Monitoring
1. Ecosystems and habitats: containing high diversity, large numbers of endemic or threatened species, or wilderness; required by migratory species; of social, economic, cultural or scientific importance; or, which are representative, unique or associated with key evolutionary or other biological processes;

2. Species and communities which are: threatened; wild relatives of domesticated or cultivated species; of medicinal, agricultural or other economic value; or social, scientific or cultural importance; or importance for research into the conservation and sustainable use of biological diversity, such as indicator species; and

3. Described genomes and genes of social, scientific or economic importance.

Note that the Convention on Biological Diversity has a dual focus on conservation and sustainable use. What is the nature of the obligations found in this convention as compared with those of the CITES Convention? Are they narrower or broader, weaker or stronger? How does this convention fit within the concept of sustainable development outlined above? How does the convention attempt to balance economic development (including with respect to genetic resources) and preservation of ecosystems?

PART IV

RECOURSE FOR VIOLATIONS OF INTERNATIONAL LAW

INTRODUCTION

In this Part, we concentrate on steps open to states or the international community in response to violations of international law. In discussing substantive international law throughout these materials, we have already incidentally touched upon a number of fora which may be in a position to grant remedies for such violations, including the International Court of Justice and other international tribunals or arbitral bodies, the UN Security Council, the various human rights bodies, and, in limited circumstances, domestic civil and criminal courts. Our focus here, however, is on a number of specific international legal regimes that *define* the remedies that may be available in these and other fora.

Thus, in Chapter 12, we examine the concept of "state responsibility" — essentially, a generalized theory of state liability for conduct contrary to international law. In Chapter 13, we consider economic sanctions as a response to state violations of international law. In Chapter 14, we examine the limited circumstances in which armed force may still be used, and by whom, to secure or restore compliance with international law. Lastly, in Chapter 15, we shift our focus from the state to the individual in examining international criminal law as a system of accountability for individual perpetrators of international crimes.

CHAPTER 12

STATE RESPONSIBILITY

A. NATURE OF STATE RESPONSIBILITY

One jurist has described state responsibility as follows: "Frequently action taken by one state results in injury to, or outrage on, the dignity or prestige of another state. The rules of international law as to state responsibility concern the circumstances in which, and the principle whereby, the injured state becomes entitled to redress for the damage suffered."[1] In other words, state responsibility is a general set of rules governing the international legal consequences of violations, by states, of their international legal obligations.

As there is currently no multilateral treaty exhaustively setting out the rules of state responsibility, these are found principally in customary international law.[2] However, articulating a comprehensive series of articles on state responsibility was on the agenda of the International Law Commission (ILC) for forty-five years. In 2001, the ILC at last adopted a final set of "Draft Articles on the Responsibility of States for Internationally Wrongful Acts" (ILC Articles on State Responsibility).[3] Governments are still considering whether to develop these articles into a multilateral convention, but all indications to date are that the ILC Articles on State Responsibility have generally been embraced in their current form as a useful and reliable restatement of the rules of customary international law on the subject.[4]

---

1   Ivan A Shearer, ed, *Starke's International Law*, 11th ed (Toronto: Butterworths, 1994) at 264.

2   See further James Crawford, *The Law of International Responsibility* (Oxford: Oxford University Press, 2010).

3   Draft Articles on the Responsibility of States for Internationally Wrongful Acts in *Report of the International Law Commission*, UN GAOR, 56th Sess, Supp No 10 at c IV, para 76, UN Doc A/56/10 (2001) [ILC Articles on State Responsibility]. Ten years later, the ILC adopted a set of articles addressing the related issue of responsibility of international organizations, the terms of which largely echo those of the ILC Articles on State Responsibility, subject, of course, to adaptations reflecting the specific nature and role of international organizations: see Draft Articles on the Responsibility of International Organizations in *Report of the International Law Commission*, UN GAOR, 66th Sess, Supp No 10 at c 5, para 87, UN Doc A/66/10 (2011). The General Assembly has requested the views of governments on these articles and will next consider them during its 2014 session: see *Responsibility of International Organizations*, GA Res 66/100, UN Doc A/RES/66/100, reprinted in UN GAOR, 66th Sess, Supp No 49, vol I at 580–89, UN Doc A/66/49 (2011).

4   See *Responsibility of States for Internationally Wrongful Acts*, GA Res 65/19, UN Doc A/RES/65/19, reprinted in UN GAOR, 65th Sess, Supp No 49, vol I at 608, UN Doc A/65/49 (2010), commending again the articles to the attention of governments and deciding to reconsider the question of whether to prepare a convention based on the articles during its 2013 session.

As a result, we organize our review of the law of state responsibility around the ILC Articles on State Responsibility and the ILC's commentaries that accompany them.[5]

B. GENERAL PRINCIPLES OF STATE RESPONSIBILITY

To a domestic lawyer, the idea that breach of a legal obligation necessarily entails responsibility to remedy that breach may seem self-evident. However, in an international legal system that was, until relatively recently, largely devoid of peaceful law enforcement or adjudicative mechanisms, this principle was not clearly established as a matter of state practice and *opinio juris* prior to the twentieth century. Witness the need for the Permanent Court of International Justice (PCIJ) to address this issue by relying on general principles of law in the following 1928 decision:

> *Case Concerning the Factory at Chorzów (Claim for Indemnity) (Germany v Poland),* Merits, (1928), PCIJ (Ser A) No 17 at 29
>
> [As part of the peace settlements following World War I, Upper Silesia was transferred from Germany to Poland. Thereafter the Polish government expropriated a factory, located at Chorzów in Upper Silesia, which had been established by a German company under contract to the German government. Germany sought reparations for losses caused by the Polish takeover of the factory.]
>
> . . . It follows from the foregoing that the application is designed to obtain, in favour of Germany, reparation the amount of which is determined by the damage suffered by the Oberschlesische and Bayerische. Three fundamental questions arise:
>
> (1) The existence of the obligation to make reparation.
> (2) The existence of the damage which must serve as a basis for the calculation of the amount of the indemnity.
> (3) The extent of this damage.
>
> As regards the first point. The Court observes that it is a principle of international law, and even a general conception of law, that any breach of an engagement involves an obligation to make reparation . . . . [T]he Court has already said that reparation is the indispensable complement of a failure to apply a convention, and there is no necessity for this to be stated in the convention itself. The existence of the principle establishing the obligation to make reparation, as an element of positive international law, has moreover never been disputed in the course of the proceedings in the various cases concerning the Chorzów factory . . . .

The ILC Articles on State Responsibility are founded on this general principle: *secondary* rules of responsibility and reparation are triggered whenever a *primary* international legal obligation of any sort is breached. This is so regardless of whether the primary obligation expressly provides for a system of responsibility and remedies, although such a "tailor-made" system will generally prevail in cases of conflict with the general rules of state responsibility:

---

5   "Text of the draft articles with commentaries thereto" in *Report of the International Law Commission,* UN GAOR, 56th Sess, Supp No 10 at c IV, para 77, UN Doc A/56/10 [Commentaries].

ILC Articles on State Responsibility for Internationally Wrongful Acts, 2001

Article 1
Responsibility of a State for its internationally wrongful acts
Every internationally wrongful act of a State entails the international responsibility of that State.

Commentary
. . . The term "international responsibility" covers the new legal relations which arise under international law by reason of the internationally wrongful act of a State . . . . That every internationally wrongful act of a State entails the international responsibility of that State, and thus gives rise to new international legal relations additional to those which existed before the act took place, has been widely recognized . . . . [T]he term "international responsibility" . . . covers the relations which arise under international law from the internationally wrongful act of a State, whether such relations are limited to the wrong-doing State and one injured State or whether they extend also to other States or indeed to other subjects of international law, and whether they are centred on obligations of restitution or compensation or also give the injured State the possibility of responding by way of countermeasures . . . .

Article 2
Elements of an internationally wrongful act of a State
There is an internationally wrongful act of a State when conduct consisting of an action or omission:
   (a) is attributable to the State under international law; and
   (b) constitutes a breach of an international obligation of the State.

Commentary
Article 2 specifies the conditions required to establish the existence of an internationally wrongful act of the State, i.e., the constituent elements of such an act . . . . For particular conduct to be characterized as an internationally wrongful act, it must first be attributable to the State. The State is a real organized entity, a legal person with full authority to act under international law. But to recognize this is not to deny the elementary fact that the State cannot act of itself . . . . States can act only by and through their agents and representatives . . . . The second condition for the existence of an internationally wrongful act of the State is that the conduct attributable to the State should constitute a breach of an international obligation of that State . . . . In international law the idea of breach of an obligation has often been equated with conduct contrary to the rights of others [for example, a treaty obligation] . . . .

Article 55
Lex specialis
These articles do not apply where and to the extent that the conditions for the existence of an internationally wrongful act or the content or implementation of the international responsibility of a State are governed by special rules of international law.

Commentary
When defining the primary obligations that apply between them, States often make special provision for the legal consequences of breaches of those obligations, and even for

determining whether there has been such a breach. The question then is whether those provisions are exclusive, i.e. whether the consequences which would otherwise apply under general international law, or the rules that might otherwise have applied for determining a breach, are thereby excluded . . . . [A]rticle 55 makes it clear that the present articles operate in a residual way. It will depend on the special rule to establish the extent to which the more general rules on State responsibility set out in the present articles are displaced by that rule. In some cases it will be clear from the language of a treaty or other text that only the consequences specified are to flow . . . . In other cases, one aspect of the general law may be modified, leaving other aspects still applicable . . . . For the *lex specialis* principle to apply it is not enough that the same subject matter is dealt with by two provisions; there must be some actual inconsistency between them, or else a discernible intention that one provision is to exclude the other . . . .

C. ATTRIBUTION OF CONDUCT TO THE STATE

1) Conduct of State Organs and Entities Empowered to Exercise Governmental Authority

As suggested by Article 2, states can only be held responsible for conduct that is attributable to them. This seemingly straightforward requirement is complicated by the fact that states are, in reality, politico-legal abstractions which can only truly act through human actors. The attribution of conduct to a state therefore depends on rules defining the range of actors for whose conduct the state may be considered responsible as a matter of international law. The obvious starting point is the state's own, formally defined, organs, as well as those individuals and entities which it has empowered to exercise elements of governmental authority on its behalf:

ILC Articles on State Responsibility for Internationally Wrongful Acts, 2001

Article 4
Conduct of organs of a State
1. The conduct of any State organ shall be considered an act of that State under international law, whether the organ exercises legislative, executive, judicial or any other functions, whatever position it holds in the organization of the State, and whatever its character as an organ of the central Government or of a territorial unit of the State.

2. An organ includes any person or entity which has that status in accordance with the internal law of the State.

Commentary
. . . In theory, the conduct of all human beings, corporations or collectivities linked to the State by nationality, habitual residence or incorporation might be attributed to the State, whether or not they have any connection to the Government. In international law, such an approach is avoided, both with a view to limiting responsibility to conduct which engages the State as an organization, and also so as to recognize the autonomy of persons acting on their own account and not at the instigation of a public authority. Thus, the

general rule is that the only conduct attributed to the State at the international level is that of its organs of government, or of others who have acted under the direction, instigation or control of those organs, i.e., as agents of the State . . . .

In determining what constitutes an organ of a State for the purposes of responsibility, the internal law and practice of each State are of prime importance . . . . It is a matter for each State to decide how its administration is to be structured and which functions are to be assumed by government. But while the State remains free to determine its internal structure and functions through its own law and practice, . . . the conduct of certain institutions performing public functions and exercising public powers (e.g. the police) is attributed to the State even if those institutions are regarded in internal law as autonomous and independent of the executive government . . . .

It does not matter . . . whether the territorial unit in question is a component unit of a federal State or a specific autonomous area, and it is equally irrelevant whether the internal law of the State in question gives the federal parliament power to compel the component unit to abide by the State's international obligations . . . .

Article 5
Conduct of persons or entities exercising elements of governmental authority
The conduct of a person or entity which is not an organ of the State under article 4 but which is empowered by the law of that State to exercise elements of the governmental authority shall be considered an act of the State under international law, provided the person or entity is acting in that capacity in the particular instance.

Commentary
. . . The article is intended to take account of the increasingly common phenomenon of para-statal entities, which exercise elements of governmental authority in place of State organs, as well as situations where former State corporations have been privatized but retain certain public or regulatory functions . . . . The generic term "entity" reflects the wide variety of bodies which, though not organs, may be empowered by the law of a State to exercise elements of governmental authority. They may include public corporations, semi-public entities, public agencies of various kinds and even, in special cases, private companies, provided that in each case the entity is empowered by the law of the State to exercise functions of a public character normally exercised by State organs, and the conduct of the entity relates to the exercise of the governmental authority concerned. For example in some countries private security firms may be contracted to act as prison guards and in that capacity may exercise public powers such as powers of detention and discipline pursuant to a judicial sentence or to prison regulations. Private or State-owned airlines may have delegated to them certain powers in relation to immigration control or quarantine . . . .

The fact that an entity can be classified as public or private according to the criteria of a given legal system, the existence of a greater or lesser State participation in its capital, or, more generally, in the ownership of its assets, the fact that it is not subject to executive control—these are not decisive criteria for the purpose of attribution of the entity's conduct to the State. Instead, article 5 refers to the true common feature, namely that these entities are empowered, if only to a limited extent or in a specific context, to exercise specified elements of governmental authority . . . .

Article 7

Excess of authority or contravention of instructions

The conduct of an organ of a State or of a person or entity empowered to exercise elements of the governmental authority shall be considered an act of the State under international law if the organ, person or entity acts in that capacity, even if it exceeds its authority or contravenes instructions.

Commentary

. . . The State cannot take refuge behind the notion that, according to the provisions of its internal law or to instructions which may have been given to its organs or agents, their actions or omissions ought not to have occurred or ought to have taken a different form. This is so even where the organ or entity in question has overtly committed unlawful acts under the cover of its official status or has manifestly exceeded its competence. It is so even if other organs of the State have disowned the conduct in question . . . .

The central issue to be addressed in determining the applicability of article 7 to unauthorized conduct of official bodies is whether the conduct was performed by the body in an official capacity or not. Cases where officials acted in their capacity as such, albeit unlawfully or contrary to instructions, must be distinguished from cases where the conduct is so removed from the scope of their official functions that it should be assimilated to that of private individuals, not attributable to the State . . . .

[T]he conduct referred to comprises only the actions and omissions of organs purportedly or apparently carrying out their official functions, and not the private actions or omissions of individuals who happen to be organs or agents of the State. In short, the question is whether they were acting with apparent authority . . . .

Note that internal law is not determinative of whether any particular entity is an "organ" of the state. How is this position reflected in Article 4 of the ILC Articles on State Responsibility? Consider the following clarification, by the International Court of Justice, of the circumstances in which an entity may be deemed an organ of the state notwithstanding the provisions of internal law on the matter:

Application of the Convention on the Prevention and Punishment of the Crime of Genocide (Bosnia and Herzegovina v Serbia and Montenegro), Merits, [2007] ICJ Rep 43

[This case arises, in part, from the Bosnian Serb (Republika Srpska) takeover of the UN "safe area" of Srebrenica in Bosnia and Herzegovina in July 1995. After seizing Srebrenica, units of the Bosnian Serb army (VRS) massacred thousands of military-aged Bosnian Muslim men from the town. Bosnia and Herzegovina sought a declaration that Serbia and Montenegro, or its predecessor, the Federal Republic of Yugoslavia (FRY), was responsible for genocide in connection with the massacres. The ICJ found, based in part on factual findings previously made by the International Criminal Tribunal for the Former Yugoslavia, that the massacres amounted to genocide. The ICJ then proceeded to consider whether those acts of genocide were attributable to the FRY.]

(3) The Question of Attribution of the Srebrenica Genocide to the Respondent on the Basis of the Conduct of Its Organs

385. The first [question] relates to the well-established rule, one of the cornerstones of the law of State responsibility, that the conduct of any State organ is to be considered an act of the State under international law . . . . This rule, which is one of customary international law, is reflected in Article 4 of the ILC Articles on State Responsibility . . . .

386. When applied to the present case, this rule first calls for a determination whether the acts of genocide committed in Srebrenica were perpetrated by "persons or entities" having the status of organs of the Federal Republic of Yugoslavia (as the Respondent was known at the time) under its internal law, as then in force. It must be said that there is nothing which could justify an affirmative response to this question. It has not been shown that the FRY army took part in the massacres, nor that the political leaders of the FRY had a hand in preparing, planning or in any way carrying out the massacres. It is true that there is much evidence of direct or indirect participation by the official army of the FRY, along with the Bosnian Serb armed forces, in military operations in Bosnia and Herzegovina in the years prior to the events at Srebrenica . . . . It has however not been shown that there was any such participation in relation to the massacres committed at Srebrenica . . . . Further, neither the Republika Srpska, nor the VRS were *de jure* organs of the FRY, since none of them had the status of organ of that State under its internal law.

387. The Applicant has however claimed that all officers in the VRS, including General Mladić, remained under FRY military administration, and that their salaries were paid from Belgrade right up to 2002, and accordingly contends that these officers "were *de jure* organs of [the FRY], intended by their superiors to serve in Bosnia and Herzegovina with the VRS." . . .

388. The Court notes first that no evidence has been presented that either General Mladić or any of the other officers . . . were, according to the internal law of the Respondent, officers of the army of the Respondent . . . . There is no doubt that the FRY was providing substantial support, *inter alia*, financial support, to the Republika Srpska . . . , and that one of the forms that support took was payment of salaries and other benefits to some officers of the VRS, but this did not automatically make them organs of the FRY . . . . The expression "State organ," as used in customary international law and in Article 4 of the ILC Articles, applies to one or other of the individual or collective entities which make up the organization of the State and act on its behalf (cf. ILC Commentary to Art. 4, para. (1)). The functions of the VRS officers, including General Mladić, were however to act on behalf of the Bosnian Serb authorities, in particular the Republika Srpska, not on behalf of the FRY; they exercised elements of the public authority of the Republika Srpska . . . .

390. The argument of the Applicant however goes beyond mere contemplation of the status, under the Respondent's internal law, of the persons who committed the acts of genocide; it argues that Republika Srpska and the VRS . . . must be deemed, notwithstanding their apparent status, to have been "*de facto* organs" of the FRY, in particular at the time in question, so that all of their acts, and specifically the massacres at Srebrenica, must be considered attributable to the FRY, just as if they had been organs of that State under its internal law; reality must prevail over appearances . . . .

391. The first issue raised by this argument is whether it is possible in principle to at-tribute to a State conduct of persons—or groups of persons—who, while they do not have the legal status of State organs, in fact act under such strict control by the State that they must be treated as its organs for purposes of the necessary attribution leading to the State's responsibility for an internationally wrongful act. The Court has in fact already addressed this question, and given an answer to it in principle, in its Judgment of 27 June 1986 in the case concerning *Military and Paramilitary Activities in and against Nicaragua (Nicaragua v. United States of America) (Merits, Judgment, I.C.J. Reports 1986*, pp. 62–64). In paragraph 109 of that Judgment the Court stated that it had to

> "determine . . . whether or not the relationship of the *contras* to the United States Gov-ernment was so much one of dependence on the one side and control on the other that it would be right to equate the *contras*, for legal purposes, with an organ of the United States Government, or as acting on behalf of that Government" (p. 62).

Then, examining the facts in the light of the information in its possession, the Court observed that "there is no clear evidence of the United States having actually exercised such a degree of control in all fields as to justify treating the *contras* as acting on its be-half" (para. 109), and went on to conclude that "the evidence available to the Court . . . is insufficient to demonstrate [the *contras*'] complete dependence on United States aid", so that the Court was "unable to determine that the *contra* force may be equated for legal purposes with the forces of the United States" (pp. 62–63, para. 110).

392. The passages quoted show that, according to the Court's jurisprudence, persons, groups of persons or entities may, for purposes of international responsibility, be equated with State organs even if that status does not follow from internal law, provided that in fact the persons, groups or entities act in "complete dependence" on the State, of which they are ultimately merely the instrument. In such a case, it is appropriate to look beyond legal status alone, in order to grasp the reality of the relationship between the person taking action, and the State to which he is so closely attached as to appear to be nothing more than its agent: any other solution would allow States to escape their international responsibility by choosing to act through persons or entities whose supposed indepen-dence would be purely fictitious.

393. However, so to equate persons or entities with State organs when they do not have that status under internal law must be exceptional, for it requires proof of a particularly great degree of State control over them, a relationship which the Court's Judgment quot-ed above expressly described as "complete dependence." It remains to be determined in the present case whether, at the time in question, the persons or entities that committed the acts of genocide at Srebrenica had such ties with the FRY that they can be deemed to have been completely dependent on it . . . .

394. The Court can only answer this question in the negative. At the relevant time, July 1995, neither the Republika Srpska nor the VRS could be regarded as mere instruments through which the FRY was acting, and as lacking any real autonomy. While the politi-cal, military and logistical relations between the federal authorities in Belgrade and the authorities in Pale, between the Yugoslav army and the VRS, had been strong and close

in previous years . . . , and these ties undoubtedly remained powerful, they were, at least at the relevant time, not such that the Bosnian Serbs' political and military organizations should be equated with organs of the FRY. It is even true that differences over strategic options emerged at the time between Yugoslav authorities and Bosnian Serb leaders; at the very least, these are evidence that the latter had some qualified, but real, margin of independence. Nor, notwithstanding the very important support given by the Respondent to the Republika Srpska, without which it could not have "conduct[ed] its crucial or most significant military and paramilitary activities" (*[Nicaragua,]* I.C.J. *Reports 1986*, p. 63, para. 111), did this signify a total dependence of the Republika Srpska upon the Respondent . . . .

The Court therefore finds that the acts of genocide at Srebrenica cannot be attributed to the Respondent as having been committed by its organs or by persons or entities wholly dependent upon it, and thus do not on this basis entail the Respondent's international responsibility . . . .

Considering Article 5, is there any meaningful difference between attribution to the state of the conduct of its organs and that of entities it has empowered to exercise elements of governmental authority? In answering this question, consider whether it is possible for a state organ to act other than "in that capacity."

What threat to the viability of the system of state responsibility is avoided by the rule set out in Article 7? Consider its practical importance as illustrated in the following case from the human rights context:

Velásquez Rodríguez Case, [1988] Inter-Am Ct HR (Ser C) No 4, (1988) 28 ILM 294

[In this decision of the Inter-American Court on Human Rights, petitioners made claims against the Honduran government after several students were "disappeared" by armed men in civilian clothing. At issue, in part, was whether these men were state agents for whose conduct the Honduran state was responsible. In addressing this question, the Court focused on the implications of Article 1(1) of the American Convention on Human Rights,[6] which reads in part: "The States Parties to this Convention undertake to respect the rights and freedoms recognized herein and to ensure to all persons subject to their jurisdiction the free and full exercise of those rights and freedoms."]

169. According to Article 1(1), any exercise of public power that violates the rights recognized by the Convention is illegal. Whenever a State organ, official or public entity violates one of those rights, this constitutes a failure of the duty to respect the rights and freedoms set forth in the Convention.

170. This conclusion is independent of whether the organ or official has contravened provisions of internal law or overstepped the limits of his authority: under international law a State is responsible for the acts of its agents undertaken in their official capacity and for their omissions, even when those agents act outside the sphere of their authority or violate internal law.

---

6   22 November 1969, 144 UNTS 123, OAS TS No 36, in force 18 July 1978.

171. This principle suits perfectly the nature of the Convention, which is violated whenever public power is used to infringe the rights recognized therein. If acts of public power that exceed the State's authority or are illegal under its own laws were not considered to compromise that State's obligations under the treaty, the system of protection provided for in the Convention would be illusory.

172. Thus, in principle, any violation of rights recognized by the Convention carried out by an act of public authority or by persons who use their position of authority is imputable to the State . . . .

2) Conduct of Other Entities

The international law of state responsibility also recognizes a number of circumstances in which a state may be accountable for the conduct of persons not formally affiliated with it in the sense of Articles 4 and 5.

a) Persons Acting Under State Instructions, Direction, or Control

Even a private person can, in some circumstances, engage the responsibility of the state:

ILC Articles on State Responsibility for Internationally Wrongful Acts, 2001

Article 8
Conduct directed or controlled by a State
The conduct of a person or group of persons shall be considered an act of a State under international law if the person or group of persons is in fact acting on the instructions of, or under the direction or control of, that State in carrying out the conduct.

Commentary
As a general principle, the conduct of private persons or entities is not attributable to the State under international law. Circumstances may arise, however, where such conduct is nevertheless attributable to the State because there exists a specific factual relationship between the person or entity engaging in the conduct and the State. Article 8 deals with two such circumstances . . . .

. . . In . . . cases [involving state instructions] it does not matter that the person or persons involved are private individuals nor whether their conduct involves "governmental activity." . . .

More complex issues arise in determining whether conduct was carried out "under the direction or control" of a State. Such conduct will be attributable to the State only if it directed or controlled the specific operation and the conduct complained of was an integral part of that operation. The principle does not extend to conduct which was only incidentally or peripherally associated with an operation and which escaped from the State's direction or control . . . .

. . . In any event it is a matter for appreciation in each case whether particular conduct was or was not carried out under the control of a State, to such an extent that the conduct controlled should be attributed to it.

The International Law Commission adverts to an apparent difference in the stringency of the attributability considerations applicable to persons acting on instructions and to persons acting "under the direction or control" of a state. Consider how each form of attributability was engaged in the following decision of the International Court of Justice dealing with US activities in Nicaragua in the 1980s:

Military and Paramilitary Activities in and against Nicaragua (Nicaragua v United States of America), Merits, Judgment, [1986] ICJ Rep 14

[Nicaragua claimed that the United States had engaged in a campaign to destabilize its government, first by undertaking certain acts of sabotage against Nicaraguan port and oil facilities, and second, by supporting and directing the activities of an armed rebel group in Nicaragua known as the "*contras*." At issue in the following passages is whether the United States was responsible in international law for the attacks on the port and oil facilities, as well as for the acts of the *contras*.]

75. Before examining the complaint of Nicaragua against the United States that the United States is responsible for the military capacity, if not the very existence, of the *contra* forces, the Court will first deal with events which, in the submission of Nicaragua, involve the responsibility of the United States in a more direct manner. These are the mining of Nicaraguan ports or waters in early 1984; and certain attacks on, in particular, Nicaraguan port and oil installations in late 1983 and early 1984 . . . . Those directly concerned in the acts were, it is claimed, . . . either United States military personnel or persons of the nationality of unidentified Latin American countries, paid by, and acting on the direct instructions of, United States military or intelligence personnel. (These persons were apparently referred to in the vocabulary of the CIA as "UCLAs" — "Unilaterally Controlled Latino Assets", and this acronym will be used, purely for convenience, in what follows.) Furthermore, Nicaragua contends that such United States personnel, while they may have refrained from themselves entering Nicaraguan territory or recognized territorial waters, directed the operations and gave very close logistic, intelligence and practical support . . . . These complaints will now be examined . . . .

80. . . . . [T]he Court finds it established that, on a date in late 1983 or early 1984, the President of the United States authorized a United States government agency to lay mines in Nicaraguan ports; that in early 1984 mines were laid in or close to the ports of El Bluff, Corinto and Puerto Sandino, either in Nicaraguan internal waters or in its territorial sea or both, by persons in the pay and acting on the instructions of that agency, under the supervision and with the logistic support of United States agents . . . .

86. [T]he Court finds [other] incidents . . . to be established. The general pattern followed by these attacks appears to the Court, on the basis of that evidence and of press reports quoting United States administration sources, to have been as follows. A "mother ship" was supplied (apparently leased) by the CIA; whether it was of United States registry does not appear. Speedboats, guns and ammunition were supplied by the United States administration, and the actual attacks were carried out by "UCLAs". Helicopters piloted by Nicaraguans and others piloted by United States nationals were also involved on some occasions. According to one report the pilots were United States civilians under contract

to the CIA. Although it is not proved that any United States military personnel took a direct part in the operations, agents of the United States participated in the planning, direction, support and execution of the operations. The execution was the task rather of the "UCLAs," while United States nationals participated in the planning, direction and support. The imputability to the United States of these attacks appears therefore to the Court to be established . . . .

106. [Turning to the actions of the contras, i]n the light of the evidence and material available to it, the Court is not satisfied that all the operations launched by the *contra* force, at every stage of the conflict, reflected strategy and tactics wholly devised by the United States. However, it is in the Court's view established that the support of the United States authorities for the activities of the *contras* took various forms over the years, such as logistic support, the supply of information on the location and movements of the Sandinista troops, the use of sophisticated methods of communication, the deployment of field broadcasting networks, radar coverage, etc. The Court finds it clear that a number of military and paramilitary operations by this force were decided and planned, if not actually by United States advisers, then at least in close collaboration with them, and on the basis of the intelligence and logistic support which the United States was able to offer, particularly the supply aircraft provided to the *contras* by the United States.

107. To sum up, . . . the financial support given by the Government of the United States to the military and paramilitary activities of the *contras* in Nicaragua is a fully established fact . . . .

108. Despite the large quantity of documentary evidence and testimony which it has examined, the Court has not been able to satisfy itself that the respondent State "created" the *contra* force in Nicaragua . . . . Nor does the evidence warrant a finding that the United States gave "direct and critical combat support," at least if that form of words is taken to mean that this support was tantamount to direct intervention by the United States combat forces, or that all contra operations reflected strategy and tactics wholly devised by the United States. On the other hand, the Court holds it established that the United States authorities largely financed, trained, equipped, armed and organized the FDN.

[On these facts, the Court found that the *contras* were not so completely dependent on the United States that they should be equated with United States forces; that is, an organ of the United States. The Court nevertheless went on to consider whether the acts of the *contras* could be said to have been carried out under the direction or control of the United States:]

115. The Court has taken the view . . . that United States participation, even if preponderant or decisive, in the financing, organizing, training, supplying and equipping of the *contras*, the selection of its military or paramilitary targets, and the planning of the whole of its operation, is still insufficient in itself, on the basis of the evidence in the possession of the Court, for the purpose of attributing to the United States the acts committed by the *contras* in the course of their military or paramilitary operations in Nicaragua. All the forms of United States participation mentioned above, and even the general control by the respondent State over a force with a high degree of dependency on it, would not in themselves mean, without further evidence, that the United States directed or enforced

the perpetration of the acts contrary to human rights and humanitarian law alleged by the applicant State. Such acts could well be committed by members of the *contras* without the control of the United States. For this conduct to give rise to legal responsibility of the United States, it would in principle have to be proved that that State had effective control of the military or paramilitary operations in the course of which the alleged violations were committed.

116. The Court does not consider that the assistance given by the United States to the *contras* warrants the conclusion that these forces are subject to the United States to such an extent that any acts they have committed are imputable to that State. It takes the view that the *contras* remain responsible for their acts, and that the United States is not responsible for the acts of the *contras*, but for its own conduct vis-à-vis Nicaragua, including conduct related to the acts of the *contras*. What the Court has to investigate is not the complaints relating to alleged violations of humanitarian law by the *contras*, regarded by Nicaragua as imputable to the United States, but rather unlawful acts for which the United States may be responsible directly in connection with the activities of the *contras*. The lawfulness or otherwise of such acts of the United States is a question different from the violations of humanitarian law of which the *contras* may or may not have been guilty . . . .

In the result, the United States was responsible for the conduct of the "UCLAs" acting under its instructions, as well as its own acts of supporting the *contras*—to the extent these acts violated international law. It was not, however, responsible for the wrongs committed by the *contras* themselves.

The ICJ's exacting "effective control" test subsequently elicited negative commentary by the Appeals Chamber of the International Criminal Tribunal for the Former Yugoslavia in the following case:

Prosecutor v Duško Tadić, [1995] ICTY App Ch Case No IT-94-1-A, (1995) 35 ILM 32

[Tadić, a member of a Bosnian Serb militia, was charged with twelve counts of grave breaches of the 1949 Geneva Conventions (among other offences). The applicable provisions of the Convention applied only to international—as opposed to internal—armed conflict. At issue, therefore, was whether there was a sufficient link between the Federal Republic of Yugoslavia (FRY) and the Bosnian Serb militia to render the conflict to which the latter was a party international. In answering this question, the Appeals Chamber considered the degree of authority or control that must be wielded by a State over armed forces before they can be considered to be fighting on its behalf. On this issue, the Appeals Chamber took issue with the approach adopted by the ICJ in *Nicaragua*, as follows:]

116. A first ground on which the *Nicaragua* test as such may be held to be unconvincing is based on the very logic of the entire system of international law on State responsibility.

117. . . . . States are not allowed on the one hand to act *de facto* through individuals and on the other to disassociate themselves from such conduct when these individuals breach international law. The requirement of international law for the attribution to States of acts performed by private individuals is that the State exercises control over the individuals. The *degree of control* may, however, vary according to the factual circumstances

of each case. The Appeals Chamber fails to see why in each and every circumstance international law should require a high threshold for the test of control. Rather, various situations may be distinguished . . . .

120. One should distinguish the situation of individuals acting on behalf of a State without specific instructions, from that of individuals making up *an organised and hierarchically structured group*, such as a military unit or, in case of war or civil strife, armed bands of irregulars or rebels. Plainly, an organised group differs from an individual in that the former normally has a structure, a chain of command and a set of rules as well as the outward symbols of authority. Normally a member of the group does not act on his own but conforms to the standards prevailing in the group and is subject to the authority of the head of the group. Consequently, for the attribution to a State of acts of these groups it is sufficient to require that the group as a whole be under the overall control of the State . . . .

122. . . . . In the case of an organised group, the group normally engages in a series of activities. If it is under the overall control of a State, it must perforce engage the responsibility of that State for its activities, *whether or not each of them was specifically imposed, requested or directed by the State* . . . .

124. There is a second ground—of a similarly general nature as the one just expounded—on which the *Nicaragua* test as such may be held to be unpersuasive. This ground is determinative of the issue. The "effective control" test propounded by the International Court of Justice as an exclusive and all-embracing test is at variance with international judicial and State practice: such practice has envisaged State responsibility in circumstances where a lower degree of control than that demanded by the *Nicaragua* test was exercised. In short, as shall be seen, this practice has upheld the *Nicaragua* test with regard to individuals or unorganised groups of *individuals* acting on behalf of States. By contrast, it has applied a different test with regard to *military or paramilitary groups*.

125. In cases dealing with members of *military or paramilitary groups*, courts have clearly departed from the notion of "effective control" set out by the International Court of Justice (i.e., control that extends to the issuance of specific instructions concerning the various activities of the individuals in question) . . . .

130. Precisely what measure of State control does international law require for organised military groups? Judging from international case law and State practice, it would seem that for such control to come about, it is not sufficient for the group to be financially or even militarily assisted by a State. This proposition is confirmed by the international practice concerning national liberation movements. Although some States provided movements such as the PLO, SWAPO or the ANC with a territorial base or with economic and military assistance (short of sending their own troops to aid them), other States, including those against which these movements were fighting, did not attribute international responsibility for the acts of the movements to the assisting States. *Nicaragua* also supports this proposition, since the United States, although it aided the contras financially, and otherwise, was not held responsible for their acts . . . .

131. In order to attribute the acts of a military or paramilitary group to a State, it must be proved that the State wields overall control over the group, not only by equipping and

financing the group, but also by coordinating or helping in the general planning of its military activity. Only then can the State be held internationally accountable for any misconduct of the group. However, it is not necessary that, in addition, the State should also issue, either to the head or to members of the group, instructions for the commission of specific acts contrary to international law.

132. It should be added that courts have taken a different approach with regard to *individuals or groups not organised into military structures*. With regard to such individuals or groups, courts have not considered an overall or general level of control to be sufficient, but have instead insisted upon specific instructions or directives aimed at the commission of specific acts, or have required public approval of those acts following their commission . . . .

137. In sum, the Appeals Chamber holds the view that international rules do not always require the same degree of control over armed groups or private individuals for the purpose of determining whether an individual not having the status of a State official under internal legislation can be regarded as a *de facto* organ of the State. The extent of the requisite State control varies. [C]ontrol by a State over subordinate *armed forces or militias or paramilitary units* may be of an overall character (and must comprise more than the mere provision of financial assistance or military equipment or training). This requirement, however, does not go so far as to include the issuing of specific orders by the State, or its direction of each individual operation. Under international law it is by no means necessary that the controlling authorities should plan all the operations of the units dependent on them, choose their targets, or give specific instructions concerning the conduct of military operations and any alleged violations of international humanitarian law. The control required by international law may be deemed to exist when a State (or, in the context of an armed conflict, the Party to the conflict) *has a role in organising, coordinating or planning the military actions* of the military group, in addition to financing, training and equipping or providing operational support to that group. Acts performed by the group or members thereof may be regarded as acts of *de facto* State organs regardless of any specific instruction by the controlling State concerning the commission of each of those acts . . . .

In *Nicaragua*, did the ICJ in fact require "effective control" of the *contras* in the sense of "control that extends to the issuance of specific instructions concerning the various activities of the individuals in question" or issuance of "instructions for the commission of specific acts contrary to international law" (see paragraphs 125 and 131 of *Tadić* above)? Compare these characterizations of the ICJ's judgment with the last sentence of paragraph 115 of *Nicaragua*.

The ICJ has since returned to this issue:

Application of the Convention on the Prevention and Punishment of the Crime of Genocide (Bosnia and Herzegovina v Serbia and Montenegro), Merits, [2007] ICJ Rep 43

[The facts and issues were summarized in the excerpt of this case found in the preceding section. After concluding that Republika Sprska and the VRS were not organs of the Respondent, the Court continued:]

(4) The Question of Attribution of the Srebrenica Genocide to the Respondent on the Basis of Direction or Control

396. . . . . [T]he Court must now determine whether the massacres at Srebrenica were committed by persons who, though not having the status of organs of the Respondent, nevertheless acted on its instructions or under its direction or control, as the Applicant argues in the alternative; the Respondent denies that such was the case.

397. The Court must emphasize, at this stage in its reasoning, that the question just stated is not the same as those dealt with thus far. It is obvious that it is different from the question whether the persons who committed the acts of genocide had the status of organs of the Respondent under its internal law; nor however, and despite some appearance to the contrary, is it the same as the question whether those persons should be equated with State organs *de facto*, even though not enjoying that status under internal law. The answer to the latter question depends, as previously explained, on whether those persons were in a relationship of such complete dependence on the State that they cannot be considered otherwise than as organs of the State, so that all their actions performed in such capacity would be attributable to the State for purposes of international responsibility. Having answered that question in the negative, the Court now addresses a completely separate issue: whether, in the specific circumstances surrounding the events at Srebrenica the perpetrators of genocide were acting on the Respondent's instructions, or under its direction or control. An affirmative answer to this question would in no way imply that the perpetrators should be characterized as organs of the FRY, or equated with such organs. It would merely mean that the FRY's international responsibility would be incurred owing to the conduct of those of its own organs which gave the instructions or exercised the control resulting in the commission of acts in breach of its international obligations. In other words, it is no longer a question of ascertaining whether the persons who directly committed the genocide were acting as organs of the FRY, or could be equated with those organs — this question having already been answered in the negative. What must be determined is whether FRY organs — incontestably having that status under the FRY's internal law — originated the genocide by issuing instructions to the perpetrators or exercising direction or control, and whether, as a result, the conduct of organs of the Respondent, having been the cause of the commission of acts in breach of its international obligations, constituted a violation of those obligations.

398. On this subject the applicable rule, which is one of customary law of international responsibility, is laid down in Article 8 of the ILC Articles on State Responsibility . . . .

399. This provision must be understood in the light of the Court's jurisprudence on the subject, particularly that of the 1986 Judgment in the case concerning *Military and Paramilitary Activities in and against Nicaragua* . . . . [The Court then referred to the "effective control" test it articulated in paragraph 115 of *Nicaragua*.]

400. The test thus formulated differs in two respects from the test . . . to determine whether a person or entity may be equated with a State organ even if not having that status under internal law. First, in this context it is not necessary to show that the persons who performed the acts alleged to have violated international law were in general in a re-

lationship of "complete dependence" on the respondent State; it has to be proved that they acted in accordance with that State's instructions or under its "effective control". It must however be shown that this "effective control" was exercised, or that the State's instructions were given, in respect of each operation in which the alleged violations occurred, not generally in respect of the overall actions taken by the persons or groups of persons having committed the violations.

401. The Applicant has, it is true, contended that the crime of genocide has a particular nature, in that it may be composed of a considerable number of specific acts separate, to a greater or lesser extent, in time and space. According to the Applicant, this particular nature would justify, among other consequences, assessing the "effective control" of the State allegedly responsible, not in relation to each of these specific acts, but in relation to the whole body of operations carried out by the direct perpetrators of the genocide. The Court is however of the view that the particular characteristics of genocide do not justify the Court in departing from the criterion elaborated in [*Nicaragua*]. The rules for attributing alleged internationally wrongful conduct to a State do not vary with the nature of the wrongful act in question in the absence of a clearly expressed *lex specialis*. Genocide will be considered as attributable to a State if and to the extent that the physical acts constitutive of genocide that have been committed by organs or persons other than the State's own agents were carried out, wholly or in part, on the instructions or directions of the State, or under its effective control. This is the state of customary international law, as reflected in the ILC Articles on State Responsibility.

402. The Court notes however that the Applicant has further questioned the validity of applying, in the present case, the criterion adopted in the *Military and Paramilitary Activities* Judgment. It has drawn attention to the Judgment of the ICTY Appeals Chamber in the *Tadić* case (IT-94-1-A, Judgment, 15 July 1999). In that case the Chamber did not follow the jurisprudence of the Court in the *Military and Paramilitary Activities* case . . . . [T]he Appeals Chamber took the view that acts committed by Bosnian Serbs could give rise to international responsibility of the FRY on the basis of the overall control exercised by the FRY over the Republika Srpska and the VRS, without there being any need to prove that each operation during which acts were committed in breach of international law was carried out on the FRY's instructions, or under its effective control.

403. The Court has given careful consideration to the Appeals Chamber's reasoning in support of the foregoing conclusion, but finds itself unable to subscribe to the Chamber's view. First, the Court observes that the ICTY was not called upon in the *Tadić* case, nor is it in general called upon, to rule on questions of State responsibility, since its jurisdiction is criminal and extends over persons only . . . . As stated above, the Court attaches the utmost importance to the factual and legal findings made by the ICTY in ruling on the criminal liability of the accused before it . . . . The situation is not the same for positions adopted by the ICTY on issues of general international law which do not lie within the specific purview of its jurisdiction . . . .

404. This is the case of the doctrine laid down in the *Tadić* Judgment. Insofar as the "overall control" test is employed to determine whether or not an armed conflict is international, which was the sole question which the Appeals Chamber was called upon to decide, it may

well be that the test is applicable and suitable . . . . On the other hand, the ICTY presented the "overall control" test as equally applicable under the law of State responsibility for the purpose of determining—as the Court is required to do in the present case—when a State is responsible for acts committed by paramilitary units, armed forces which are not among its official organs. In this context, the argument in favour of that test is unpersuasive.

405. It should first be observed that logic does not require the same test to be adopted in resolving the two issues, which are very different in nature: the degree and nature of a State's involvement in an armed conflict on another State's territory which is required for the conflict to be characterized as international, can very well, and without logical inconsistency, differ from the degree and nature of involvement required to give rise to that State's responsibility for a specific act committed in the course of the conflict.

406. It must next be noted that the "overall control" test has the major drawback of broadening the scope of State responsibility well beyond the fundamental principle governing the law of international responsibility: a State is responsible only for its own conduct, that is to say the conduct of persons acting, on whatever basis, on its behalf . . . . [A] State's responsibility can be incurred for acts committed by persons or groups of persons—neither State organs nor to be equated with such organs—only if, assuming those acts to be internationally wrongful, they are attributable to it under the rule of customary international law reflected in Article 8 cited above . . . . In this regard the "overall control" test is unsuitable, for it stretches too far, almost to breaking point, the connection which must exist between the conduct of a State's organs and its international responsibility.

407. Thus it is on the basis of its settled jurisprudence that the Court will determine whether the Respondent has incurred responsibility under the rule of customary international law set out in Article 8 of the ILC Articles on State Responsibility.

[The Court then proceeded to consider the available evidence and concluded that, while there was evidence of FRY "influence" over the Republika Sprska and VRS, it had "not been established that [the] massacres were committed on the instructions, or under the direction of organs of the Respondent State, nor that the Respondent exercised effective control over the operations in the course of which those massacres . . . were perpetrated."]

Notwithstanding the ICJ's rejection of the ICTY Appeals Chamber's purported reformulation of the "effective control" test, does the above excerpt from the *Tadić* decision nevertheless suggest differences between the attributability rules applicable to persons acting under a state's "instructions" and those applicable to persons acting under the "direction or control" of states? What is the significance of the ICJ's conclusion (in the 2007 *Genocide* case) that it had not been established that "*massacres* were committed on the instructions, or under the direction of organs of the Respondent State, nor that the Respondent exercised effective control over the *operations* in the course of which those massacres . . . were perpetrated"? [Emphasis added.]

b) State Adoption of Non-State Conduct

A state may also unilaterally adopt the conduct of persons or entities with which it has no prior legal or factual connection whatsoever:

ILC Articles on State Responsibility for Internationally Wrongful Acts, 2001

Article 11
Conduct acknowledged and adopted by a State as its own
Conduct which is not attributable to a State under the preceding articles shall nevertheless be considered an act of that State under international law if and to the extent that the State acknowledges and adopts the conduct in question as its own.

Commentary
All the bases for attribution covered [above] assume that the status of the person or body as a State organ, or its mandate to act on behalf of the State, are established at the time of the alleged wrongful act. Article 11, by contrast, provides for the attribution to a State of conduct that was not or may not have been attributable to it at the time of commission, but which is subsequently acknowledged and adopted by the State as its own . . . .

The phrase "acknowledges and adopts the conduct in question as its own" is intended to distinguish cases of acknowledgement and adoption from cases of mere support or endorsement . . . . [A]s a general matter, conduct will not be attributable to a State under article 11 where a State merely acknowledges the factual existence of conduct or expresses its verbal approval of it. In international controversies States often take positions which amount to "approval" or "endorsement" of conduct in some general sense but do not involve any assumption of responsibility. The language of "adoption," on the other hand, carries with it the idea that the conduct is acknowledged by the State as, in effect, its own conduct . . . . [T]he term "acknowledges and adopts" . . . makes it clear that what is required is something more than a general acknowledgement of a factual situation, but rather that the State identifies the conduct in question and makes it its own . . . .

[T]he act of acknowledgment and adoption, whether it takes the form of words or conduct, must be clear and unequivocal . . . .

Consider how the ICJ applied this concept of attribution in the *Tehran Hostages* case:

United States Diplomatic and Consular Staff in Tehran (United States of America v Iran), Judgment, [1980] ICJ Rep 3

[In 1979, Iranian "militants" seized and occupied the US Embassy in Tehran, detaining American diplomatic staff as hostages and prompting the United States to bring this case to the International Court of Justice. The events leading up to and following the initial occupation of the Embassy were described in the excerpt of the case reproduced in Chapter 8, in our discussion of diplomatic immunities. Only those facts relevant to the attribution issue discussed by the ICJ are reproduced here.]

26. From the outset of the attack upon its Embassy in Tehran, the United States protested to the Government of Iran both at the attack and at the seizure and detention of the hostages. On 7 November a former Attorney-General of the United States, Mr. Ramsey Clark, was instructed to go with an assistant to Iran to deliver a message from the President of the United States to the Ayatollah Khomeini . . . . While he was en route, Tehran radio broadcast a message from the Ayatollah Khomeini dated 7 November, solemnly forbidding members of the Revolutionary Council and all the responsible officials to meet

the United States representatives. In that message it was asserted that "the U.S. Embassy in Iran is our enemies' centre of espionage against our sacred Islamic movement," and the message continued:

> "Should the United States hand over to Iran the deposed shah . . . and give up espionage against our movement, the way to talks would be opened on the issue of certain relations which are in the interest of the nation."

Subsequently, despite the efforts of the United Sates Government to open negotiations, it became clear that the Iranian authorities would have no direct contact with representatives of the United States Government concerning the holding of the hostages . . . .

56. . . . . [The Court] must determine how far, legally, the acts in question may be regarded as imputable to the Iranian State . . . .

58. No suggestion has been made that the militants, when they executed their attack on the Embassy, had any form of official status as recognized "agents" or organs of the Iranian State. Their conduct in mounting the attack, overrunning the Embassy and seizing its inmates as hostages cannot, therefore, be regarded as imputable to that State on that basis. Their conduct might be considered as itself directly imputable to the Iranian State only if it were established that, in fact, on the occasion in question the militants acted on behalf of the State, having been charged by some competent organ of the Iranian State to carry out a specific operation. The information before the Court does not, however, suffice to establish with the requisite certainty the existence at that time of such a link between the militants and any competent organ of the State.

59. Previously, it is true, the religious leader of the country, the Ayatollah Khomeini, had made several public declarations inveighing against the United States as responsible for all his country's problems. In so doing, it would appear, the Ayatollah Khomeini was giving utterance to the general resentment felt by supporters of the revolution at the admission of the former Shah to the United States. The information before the Court also indicates that a spokesman for the militants, in explaining their action afterwards, did expressly refer to a message issued by the Ayatollah Khomeini, on 1 November 1979. In that message the Ayatollah Khomeini had declared that it was "up to the dear pupils, students and theological students to expand with all their might their attacks against the United States and Israel, so they may force the United States to return the deposed and criminal shah, and to condemn this great plot" (that is, a plot to stir up dissension between the main streams of Islamic thought). In the view of the Court, however, it would be going too far to interpret such general declarations of the Ayatollah Khomeini to the people or students of Iran as amounting to an authorization from the State to undertake the specific operation of invading and seizing the United States Embassy. To do so would, indeed, conflict with the assertions of the militants themselves who are reported to have claimed credit for having devised and carried out the plan to occupy the Embassy. Again, congratulations after the event, such as those reportedly telephoned to the militants by the Ayatollah Khomeini on the actual evening of the attack, and other subsequent statements of official approval, though highly significant in another context shortly to be considered, do not alter the initially independent and unofficial character of the militants' attack on the Embassy . . . .

71. In any event expressions of approval of the take-over of the Embassy . . . by militants came immediately from numerous Iranian authorities, including religious, judicial, executive, police and broadcasting authorities. Above all, the Ayatollah Khomeini himself made crystal clear the endorsement by the State both of the take-over of the Embassy and Consulates and of the detention of the Embassy staff as hostages. At a reception in Qom on 5 November, the Ayatollah Khomeini left his audience in no doubt as to his approval of the action of the militants in occupying the Embassy, to which he said they had resorted "because they saw that the shah was allowed in America." Saying that he had been informed that the "centre occupied by our young men . . . has been a lair of espionage and plotting," he asked how the young people could be expected "simply to remain idle and witness all these things." Furthermore he expressly stigmatized as "rotten roots" those in Iran who were "hoping we would mediate and tell the young people to leave this place". The Ayatollah's refusal to order "the young people" to put an end to their occupation of the Embassy . . . must have appeared the more significant when, on 6 November, he instructed "the young people" who had occupied the Iraqi Consulate in Kermanshah that they should leave it as soon as possible. The true significance of this was only reinforced when, next day, he expressly forbade members of the Revolutionary Council and all responsible officials to meet the special representatives sent by President Carter to try and obtain the release of the hostages and evacuation of the Embassy.

72. At any rate, thus fortified in their action, the militants at the Embassy at once went one step farther. On 6 November they proclaimed that the Embassy, which they too referred to as "the U.S. centre of plots and espionage", would remain under their occupation, and that they were watching "most closely" the members of the diplomatic staff taken hostage whom they called "U.S. mercenaries and spies".

73. The seal of official government approval was finally set on this situation by a decree issued on 17 November 1979 by the Ayatollah Khomeini. His decree began with the assertion that the American Embassy was "a centre of espionage and conspiracy" and that "those people who hatched plots against our Islamic movement in that place do not enjoy international diplomatic respect". He went on expressly to declare that the premises of the Embassy and the hostages would remain as they were until the United States had handed over the former Shah for trial and returned his property to Iran. This statement of policy the Ayatollah qualified only to the extent of requesting the militants holding the hostages to "hand over the blacks and the women, if it is proven that they did not spy, to the Ministry of Foreign Affairs so that they may be immediately expelled from Iran". As to the rest of the hostages, he made the Iranian Government's intentions all too clear:

> "The noble Iranian nation will not give permission for the release of the rest of them. Therefore, the rest of them will be under arrest until the American Government acts according to the wish of the nation."

74. The policy thus announced by the Ayatollah Khomeini, of maintaining the occupation of the Embassy and the detention of its inmates as hostages for the purpose of exerting pressure on the United States Government was complied with by other Iranian authorities and endorsed by them repeatedly in statements made in various contexts. The result of that policy was fundamentally to transform the legal nature of the situation cre-

ated by the occupation of the Embassy and the detention of its diplomatic and consular staff as hostages. The approval given to these facts by the Ayatollah Khomeini and other organs of the Iranian State, and the decision to perpetuate them, translated continuing occupation of the Embassy and detention of the hostages into acts of that State. The militants, authors of the invasion and jailers of the hostages, had now become agents of the Iranian State for whose acts the State itself was internationally responsible. On 6 May 1980, the Minister for Foreign Affairs, Mr. Ghotbzadeh, is reported to have said in a television interview that the occupation of the United States Embassy had been "done by our nation". Moreover, in the prevailing circumstances the situation of the hostages was aggravated by the fact that their detention by the militants did not even offer the normal guarantees which might have been afforded by police and security forces subject to the discipline and the control of official superiors.

75. During the six months which have elapsed since the situation just described was created by the decree of the Ayatollah Khomeini, it has undergone no material change . . . .

76. The Iranian authorities' decision to continue the subjection of the premises of the United States Embassy to occupation by militants and of the Embassy staff to detention as hostages, clearly gave rise to repeated and multiple breaches of the applicable provisions of the Vienna Conventions even more serious than those which arose from their failure to take any steps to prevent the attacks on the inviolability of these premises and staff . . . .

90. On the basis of the foregoing detailed examination of the merits of the case, the Court finds that Iran, by committing successive and continuing breaches of the obligations laid upon it by the Vienna Conventions of 1961 and 1963 on Diplomatic and Consular Relations, the Treaty of Amity, Economic Relations, and Consular Rights of 1955, and the applicable rules of general international law, has incurred responsibility towards the United States. As to the consequences of this finding, it clearly entails an obligation on the part of the Iranian State to make reparation for the injury thereby caused to the United States. Since however Iran's breaches of its obligations are still continuing, the form and amount of such reparation cannot be determined at the present date . . . .

c) Absence or Displacement of Governmental Authority

Consider, finally, the treatment given to the conduct of non-state actors in two extraordinary circumstances: first, where such actors "step in" for governmental authorities that are absent or that fail to act; and second, where they forcibly displace the existing governmental authorities:

ILC Articles on State Responsibility for Internationally Wrongful Acts, 2001

Article 9
Conduct carried out in the absence or default of the official authorities
The conduct of a person or group of persons shall be considered an act of a State under international law if the person or group of persons is in fact exercising elements of the governmental authority in the absence or default of the official authorities and in circumstances such as to call for the exercise of those elements of authority.

Commentary

. . . The exceptional nature of the circumstances envisaged in th[is] article is indicated by the phrase "in circumstances such as to call for". Such cases occur only rarely, such as during revolution, armed conflict or foreign occupation, where the regular authorities dissolve, are disintegrating, have been suppressed or are for the time being inoperative. They may also cover cases where lawful authority is being gradually restored, e.g., after foreign occupation . . . .

. . . [T]he person or group acting must be performing governmental functions, though they are doing so on their own initiative. In this respect, the nature of the activity performed is given more weight than the existence of a formal link between the actors and the organization of the State. It must be stressed that the private persons covered by article 9 are not equivalent to a general *de facto* Government. The cases envisaged by article 9 presuppose the existence of a Government in office and of State machinery whose place is taken by irregulars or whose action is supplemented in certain cases. This may happen on part of the territory of a State which is for the time being out of control, or in other specific circumstances. A general *de facto* Government, on the other hand, is itself an apparatus of the State, replacing that which existed previously. The conduct of the organs of such a Government is covered by article 4 rather than article 9.

Article 10
Conduct of an insurrectional or other movement
1. The conduct of an insurrectional movement which becomes the new Government of a State shall be considered an act of that State under international law.

2. The conduct of a movement, insurrectional or other, which succeeds in establishing a new State in part of the territory of a pre-existing State or in a territory under its administration shall be considered an act of the new State under international law . . . .

Commentary
. . . At the outset, the conduct of the members of the [insurrectional] movement presents itself purely as the conduct of private individuals . . . . The general principle in respect of the conduct of such movements, committed during the continuing struggle with the constituted authority, is that it is not attributable to the State under international law. In other words, the acts of unsuccessful insurrectional movements are not attributable to the State, unless under some other article of [the ILC Articles on State Responsibility] . . . .

In contrast, where the movement achieves its aims and either installs itself as the new Government of the State or forms a new State in part of the territory of the pre-existing State or in a territory under its administration, it would be anomalous if the new regime or new State could avoid responsibility for conduct earlier committed by it . . . . The basis for the attribution of conduct of a successful insurrectional or other movement to the State under international law lies in the continuity between the movement and the eventual Government . . . . In such a case, the State does not cease to exist as a subject of international law. It remains the same State, despite the changes, reorganizations and adaptations which occur in its institutions. Moreover it is the only subject of international law to which responsibility can be attributed . . . .

Where the insurrectional or other movement succeeds in establishing a new State, either in part of the territory of the pre-existing State or in a territory which was previously under its administration, the attribution to the new State of the conduct of the insurrectional or other movement is again justified by virtue of the continuity between the organization of the movement and the organization of the State to which it has given rise . . . .[7]

Note the curious retroactive effect of the rules in Article 10: acts by insurrectional movements that subsequently gain power or establish a new state are deemed to have been acts of the state all along. What is the purpose of such rules?

D. ESTABLISHING THE BREACH OF AN INTERNATIONAL OBLIGATION

Recall the second element of an internationally wrongful act by a state as defined in Article 2: the breach of an international obligation of the state. Consider the following Articles enlarging upon this requirement.

ILC Articles on State Responsibility for Internationally Wrongful Acts, 2001

Article 3
Characterization of an act of a State as internationally wrongful
The characterization of an act of a State as internationally wrongful is governed by international law. Such characterization is not affected by the characterization of the same act as lawful by internal law.

Commentary
Article 3 makes explicit a principle already implicit in article 2 . . . . There are two elements to this. First, an act of a State cannot be characterized as internationally wrongful unless it constitutes a breach of an international obligation, even if it violates a provision of the State's own law. Secondly and most importantly, a State cannot, by pleading that its conduct conforms to the provisions of its internal law, escape the characterization of that conduct as wrongful by international law. An act of a State must be characterized as internationally wrongful if it constitutes a breach of an international obligation, even if the act does not contravene the State's internal law — even if, under that [domestic] law, the State was actually bound to act in that way . . . .

Article 12
Existence of a breach of an international obligation
There is a breach of an international obligation by a State when an act of that State is not in conformity with what is required of it by that obligation, regardless of its origin or character.

Commentary
It must be stressed . . . that the articles do not purport to specify the content of the primary rules of international law, or of the obligations thereby created for particular States.

---

7   For criticism, see Jean d'Aspremont, "Rebellion and State Responsibility: Wrongdoing by Democratically Elected Insurgents" (2009) 58 ICLQ 427.

In determining whether given conduct attributable to a State constitutes a breach of its international obligations, the principal focus will be on the primary obligation concerned. It is this which has to be interpreted and applied to the situation, determining thereby the substance of the conduct required, the standard to be observed, the result to be achieved, etc. There is no such thing as a breach of an international obligation in the abstract, and [the ILC Articles on State Responsibility] can only play an ancillary role in determining whether there has been such a breach, or the time at which it occurred, or its duration . . . .

. . . The formula "regardless of its origin" refers to all possible sources of international obligations, that is to say, to all processes for creating legal obligations recognized by international law . . . . Thus there is no room in international law for a distinction, such as is drawn by some legal systems, between the regime of responsibility for breach of a treaty and for breach of some other rule . . . . As far as the origin of the obligation breached is concerned, there is a single general regime of State responsibility. Nor does any distinction exist between the "civil" and "criminal" responsibility as is the case in internal legal systems . . . .

Article 13
International obligation in force for a State

An act of a State does not constitute a breach of an international obligation unless the State is bound by the obligation in question at the time the act occurs.

Commentary

. . . This [Article] is but the application in the field of State responsibility of the general principle of intertemporal law, as stated by Judge Huber in another context in the *Island of Palmas* case:

> [A] juridical fact must be appreciated in the light of the law contemporary with it, and not of the law in force at the time when a dispute in regard to it arises or falls to be settled.

Article 13 provides an important guarantee for States in terms of claims of responsibility. Its formulation ("does not constitute . . . unless . . .") is in keeping with the idea of a guarantee against the retrospective application of international law in matters of State responsibility . . . .

In international law, the principle stated in article 13 is not only a necessary but also a sufficient basis for responsibility. In other words, once responsibility has accrued as a result of an internationally wrongful act, it is not affected by the subsequent termination of the obligation, whether as a result of the termination of the treaty which has been breached or of a change in international law.[8]

Is the rule in Article 13 consistent with those set out in Article 10?
Notice that the ILC Articles on State Responsibility are silent as to any general requirement of "fault" on the part of the state before its conduct can be considered internation-

---

8   Note that article 13 was cited with approval by the International Court of Justice in *Jurisdictional Immunities of the State (Germany v Italy; Greece intervening)*, Judgment of 3 February 2012 at para 58.

ally wrongful. All that is required is a breach of an international legal obligation, whether or not such breach is the result of negligence, recklessness, or intentional wrongdoing. It is true that some international legal obligations have their own "built-in" mental element—for example, states' obligations of due diligence in protecting foreign diplomatic missions. However, the silence of the ILC Articles on the issue of fault likely reflects the sometimes disputed (but nevertheless preponderant) view that state responsibility does not generally require that breaches of international legal obligations be accompanied by a culpable "state of mind" before they can be considered internationally wrongful acts of the state. As the ILC observed in its commentary to Article 2, which, as seen above, sets out the elements of an internationally wrongful act of a state:

> Whether there has been a breach of a rule may depend on the intention or knowledge of relevant State organs or agents and in that sense may be "subjective". For example, article II of the Convention on the Prevention and Punishment of the Crime of Genocide[9] states that: "In the present Convention, genocide means any of the following acts committed with intent to destroy, in whole or in part, a national, ethnical, racial or religious group, as such . . ." In other cases, the standard for breach of an obligation may be "objective", in the sense that the advertence or otherwise of relevant State organs or agents may be irrelevant. Whether responsibility is "objective" or "subjective" in this sense depends on the circumstances, including the content of the primary obligation in question. The articles lay down no general rule in that regard. The same is true of other standards, whether they involve some degree of fault, culpability, negligence or want of due diligence. Such standards vary from one context to another for reasons which essentially relate to the object and purpose of the treaty provision or other rule giving rise to the primary obligation. Nor do the articles lay down any presumption in this regard as between the different possible standards. Establishing these is a matter for the interpretation and application of the primary rules engaged in the given case. . . .
>
> . . . In the absence of any specific requirement of a mental element in terms of the primary obligation, it is only the act of a State that matters, independently of any intention.[10]

Consider also an early affirmation of this view in the following arbitral decision:

Estate of Jean-Baptiste Caire (France v United Mexican States) (1929), 5 RIAA 516

[Caire, a French national, was killed in Mexico by officers and soldiers of the Mexican armed forces after refusing their demands for money. The issue was whether Mexico could be held responsible for these unauthorized and illegal acts of its armed personnel. The following excerpt from the arbitral award has been translated from the French by the authors.]

Commissioner Verzijl:

. . . The issues in contention can only be resolved in the light of general principles governing the conditions under which States may as a rule be held internationally responsible for the acts of their public officials . . . .

---

9 9 December 1948, 78 UNTS 277, Can TS 1949 No 27, in force 12 January 1951.

10 Commentaries, above note 5 at 34 and 36.

At the outset of my consideration of these issues . . . in the light of the general principles to which I have just referred, I intend in the first instance to interpret said principles
in accordance with the authorities that assert, in this connection, the "objective responsibility" of the State—that is, the responsibility imposed upon a State for acts committed by its officials or organs notwithstanding the absence of any "fault" on its part. It is
notable that, in this area, theory has evolved considerably in recent years, in particular
through the ground-breaking work of [Italian jurist and judge] Dionisio Anzilotti who
has cleared the road for new ideas according to which the responsibility of a State for the
acts of its officials is not dependent on any "fault" on its part. Without venturing here
into an examination of the question whether these new ideas, perhaps overly rigid, may
require some refinements . . . , I consider them in any case to be perfectly correct insofar
as they tend to attach international responsibility to a State for all acts committed by its
officials or organs that constitute breaches of the law of nations, regardless of whether the
official or organ in question acted within or beyond the limits of his, her, or its authority. "There is unanimous agreement," says M. Bourquin rightly, "that acts committed by
officials and agents of the State engage its international responsibility, even where their
author had no authority to so act . . . . [This is because] international relations would become too difficult, too complicated and too uncertain if we required foreign States to keep
track of the legal provisions, often complex, that establish the limits of [official] authority
in internal law. It is therefore plain that . . . the international responsibility of a State is of
a purely objective character and that it rests on the idea of indemnity, in respect of which
the subjective notion of fault plays no role." . . .

[The Commissioner concluded that even if Mexico were not "at fault" for the fact that
its soldiers had acted beyond their authority in these circumstances, it still bore international responsibility for their acts.]

E. DEFENCES

In articulating a general regime of responsibility by states for breaches of their international legal obligations, the International Law Commission also had to take into account that
some such breaches are not considered wrongful, in customary international law, in certain specific circumstances. Consider the following enumeration of such circumstances:

ILC Articles on State Responsibility for Internationally Wrongful Acts, 2001

Commentary
. . . [The ILC Articles on State Responsibility] set[] out six circumstances precluding the
wrongfulness of conduct that would otherwise not be in conformity with the international obligations of the State concerned. The existence in a given case of a circumstance
precluding wrongfulness in accordance with [the Articles] provides a shield against an
otherwise well-founded claim for the breach of an international obligation . . . .
. . . [These] circumstances precluding wrongfulness are of general application. Unless otherwise provided, they apply to any internationally wrongful act whether it involves
the breach by a State of an obligation arising under a rule of general international law,
a treaty, a unilateral act or from any other source. They do not annul or terminate the

obligation; rather they provide a justification or excuse for non-performance while the circumstance in question subsists . . . .

Article 20
Consent

Valid consent by a State to the commission of a given act by another State precludes the wrongfulness of that act in relation to the former State to the extent that the act remains within the limits of that consent.

Commentary

. . . In order to preclude wrongfulness, consent dispensing with the performance of an obligation in a particular case must be "valid." Whether consent has been validly given is a matter addressed by international law rules outside the framework of State responsibility. Issues include whether the agent or person who gave the consent was authorized to do so on behalf of the State (and if not, whether the lack of that authority was known or ought to have been known to the acting State), or whether the consent was vitiated by coercion or some other factor. Indeed there may be a question whether the State could validly consent at all . . . .

Article 21
Self-defence

The wrongfulness of an act of a State is precluded if the act constitutes a lawful measure of self-defence taken in conformity with the Charter of the United Nations.

Article 22
Countermeasures in respect of an internationally wrongful act

The wrongfulness of an act of a State not in conformity with an international obligation towards another State is precluded if and to the extent that the act constitutes a countermeasure taken against the latter State in accordance with [these Articles].

Commentary

In certain circumstances, the commission by one State of an internationally wrongful act may justify another State injured by that act in taking non-forcible countermeasures in order to procure its cessation and to achieve reparation for the injury. Article 22 deals with this situation from the perspective of circumstances precluding wrongfulness. [The Articles dealing with remedies] regulate[] countermeasures in further detail . . . .

Article 23
Force majeure

1. The wrongfulness of an act of a State not in conformity with an international obligation of that State is precluded if the act is due to *force majeure,* that is the occurrence of an irresistible force or of an unforeseen event, beyond the control of the State, making it materially impossible in the circumstances to perform the obligation.

2. Paragraph 1 does not apply if:
    (a) the situation of *force majeure* is due, either alone or in combination with other factors, to the conduct of the State invoking it; or
    (b) the State has assumed the risk of that situation occurring.

Commentary

Force majeure . . . involves a situation where the State in question is in effect compelled to act in a manner not in conformity with the requirements of an international obligation incumbent upon it. *Force majeure* differs from a situation of distress (art. 24) or necessity (art. 25) because the conduct of the State which would otherwise be internationally wrongful is involuntary or at least involves no element of free choice . . . .

. . . The adjective "irresistible" qualifying the word "force" emphasizes that there must be a constraint which the State was unable to avoid or oppose by its own means. To have been "unforeseen" the event must have been neither foreseen nor of an easily foreseeable kind. Further the "irresistible force" or "unforeseen event" must be causally linked to the situation of material impossibility . . . . Subject to paragraph 2, where these elements are met the wrongfulness of the State's conduct is precluded for so long as the situation of *force majeure* subsists.

. . . *Force majeure* does not include circumstances in which performance of an obligation has become more difficult, for example due to some political or economic crisis. Nor does it cover situations brought about by the neglect or default of the State concerned, even if the resulting injury itself was accidental and unintended.

Article 24

Distress

1. The wrongfulness of an act of a State not in conformity with an international obligation of that State is precluded if the author of the act in question has no other reasonable way, in a situation of distress, of saving the author's life or the lives of other persons entrusted to the author's care.

2. Paragraph 1 does not apply if:
   (a) the situation of distress is due, either alone or in combination with other factors, to the conduct of the State invoking it; or
   (b) the act in question is likely to create a comparable or greater peril.

Commentary

. . . Th[is] article precludes the wrongfulness of conduct adopted by the State agent in circumstances where the agent had no other reasonable way of saving life. Unlike situations of *force majeure* dealt with in article 23, a person acting under distress is not acting involuntarily, even though the choice is effectively nullified by the situation of peril. Nor is it a case of choosing between compliance with international law and other legitimate interests of the State, such as characterize situations of necessity under article 25. The interest concerned is the immediate one of saving people's lives, irrespective of their nationality . . . .

Article 25

Necessity

1. Necessity may not be invoked by a State as a ground for precluding the wrongfulness of an act not in conformity with an international obligation of that State unless the act:
   (a) is the only way for the State to safeguard an essential interest against a grave and imminent peril; and
   (b) does not seriously impair an essential interest of the State or States towards which the obligation exists, or of the international community as a whole.

2. In any case, necessity may not be invoked by a State as a ground for precluding wrongfulness if:

(a) the international obligation in question excludes the possibility of invoking necessity; or

(b) the State has contributed to the situation of necessity . . . .

Commentary

. . . The plea of necessity is exceptional in a number of respects. Unlike consent (art. 20), self-defence (art. 21) or countermeasures (art. 22), it is not dependent on the prior conduct of the injured State. Unlike *force majeure* (art. 23), it does not involve conduct which is involuntary or coerced. Unlike distress (art. 24), necessity consists not in danger to the lives of individuals in the charge of a State official but in a grave danger either to the essential interests of the State or of the international community as a whole. It arises where there is an irreconcilable conflict between an essential interest on the one hand and an obligation of the State invoking necessity on the other. These special features mean that necessity will only rarely be available to excuse non-performance of an obligation and that it is subject to strict limitations to safeguard against possible abuse . . . .

Article 27

Consequences of invoking a circumstance precluding wrongfulness

The invocation of a circumstance precluding wrongfulness in accordance with this chapter is without prejudice to:

(a) compliance with the obligation in question, if and to the extent that the circumstance precluding wrongfulness no longer exists;

(b) the question of compensation for any material loss caused by the act in question.

Of the six defences recognized in the ILC Articles on State Responsibility, "necessity" gives rise to the greatest number of controversies given the inherently subjective notion of a state's "essential interests."[11] Consider the following application of the necessity defence by the International Court of Justice:

Gabčíkovo-Nagymaros Project (Hungary/Slovakia), Judgment, [1997] ICJ Rep 7

. . . The present case arose out of the signature, on 16 September 1977, by the Hungarian People's Republic and the Czechoslovak People's Republic, of a treaty "concerning the construction and operation of the Gabčíkovo-Nagymaros System of Locks" (hereinafter called the "1977 Treaty") . . . . The 1977 Treaty entered into force on 30 June 1978. It provides for the construction and operation of a System of Locks by the parties as a "joint investment" . . . . The joint investment was . . . essentially aimed at the production of hydroelectricity, the improvement of navigation on the relevant section of the Danube and the protection of the areas along the banks against flooding. At the same time, by the terms of the Treaty, the contracting parties undertook to ensure that the quality of water in the Danube was not impaired as a result of the Project, and that compliance with the

---

11   See Robert D Sloane, "On the Use and Abuse of Necessity in the Law of State Responsibility" (2012) 106 Am J Int'l L 447.

obligations for the protection of nature arising in connection with the construction and operation of the System of Locks would be observed . . . .

As a result of intense criticism which the Project had generated in Hungary, the Hungarian Government decided on 13 May 1989 to suspend the works at Nagymaros pending the completion of various studies which the competent authorities were to finish before 31 July 1989. On 21 July 1989, the Hungarian Government extended the suspension of the works at Nagymaros until 31 October 1989, and, in addition, suspended the works at Dunakiliti until the same date. Lastly, on 27 October 1989, Hungary decided to abandon the works at Nagymaros and to maintain the status quo at Dunakiliti.

During this period, negotiations . . . continued between the two parties but to no avail, and, on 19 May 1992, the Hungarian Government transmitted to the Czechoslovak Government a Note Verbale terminating the 1977 Treaty with effect from 25 May 1992 . . . .

On 1 January 1993 Slovakia became an independent State . . . .

The two Parties to this case concur in recognizing that the 1977 Treaty [was] validly concluded and . . . duly in force when the facts recounted above took place. Further, they do not dispute the fact that, however flexible [it] may have been, [the 1977 Treaty] did not envisage the possibility of the signatories unilaterally suspending or abandoning the work provided for therein, or even carrying it out according to a new schedule not approved by the two partners.

Throughout the proceedings, Hungary contended that, although it did suspend or abandon certain works, on the contrary, it never suspended the application of the 1977 Treaty itself. To justify its conduct, it relied essentially on a "state of ecological necessity" . . . . According to Hungary, the principal ecological dangers which would have been caused by [the Gabčíkovo-Nagymaros System of Locks] were as follows . . . . In the long term, the quality of water would have been seriously impaired . . . . The fluvial fauna and flora . . . would have been condemned to extinction . . . . [T]he yield of the bank-filtered wells providing two-thirds of the water supply of the city of Budapest would have appreciably diminished . . . . From all these predictions, in support of which it quoted a variety of scientific studies, Hungary concluded that a "state of ecological necessity" did indeed exist in 1989 . . . .

[T]he Court need [not] dwell upon the question of the relationship between the law of treaties and the law of State responsibility, to which the Parties devoted lengthy arguments, as those two branches of international law obviously have a scope that is distinct. A determination of whether a convention is or is not in force, and whether it has or has not been properly suspended or denounced, is to be made pursuant to the law of treaties. On the other hand, an evaluation of the extent to which the suspension or denunciation of a convention, seen as incompatible with the law of treaties, involves the responsibility of the State which proceeded to it, is to be made under the law of State responsibility. Thus the Vienna Convention of 1969 on the Law of Treaties confines itself to defining—in a limitative manner—the conditions in which a treaty may lawfully be denounced or suspended; while the effects of a denunciation or suspension seen as not meeting those conditions are, on the contrary, expressly excluded from the scope of the Convention by operation of Article 73. It is moreover well established that, when a State has committed an internationally wrongful act, its international responsibility is likely to be involved whatever the nature of the obligation it has failed to respect . . . .

The Court will now consider the question of whether there was, in 1989, a state of necessity which would have permitted Hungary, without incurring international responsibility, to suspend and abandon works that it was committed to perform in accordance with the 1977 Treaty and related instruments.

In the present case, the Parties are in agreement in considering that the existence of a state of necessity must be evaluated in the light of the criteria laid down by the International Law Commission . . . . [The Court set out the equivalent of Article 25 of the ILC Articles on State Responsibility.] In its Commentary, the Commission defined the "state of necessity" as being "the situation of a State whose sole means of safeguarding an essential interest threatened by a grave and imminent peril is to adopt conduct not in conformity with what is required of it by an international obligation to another State" . . . . It concluded that "the notion of state of necessity is . . . deeply rooted in general legal thinking" . . . .

The Court considers, first of all, that the state of necessity is a ground recognized by customary international law for precluding the wrongfulness of an act not in conformity with an international obligation. It observes moreover that such ground for precluding wrongfulness can only be accepted on an exceptional basis. The International Law Commission was of the same opinion when it explained that it had opted for a negative form of words in Article [25] of its Draft "in order to show, by this formal means also, that the case of invocation of a state of necessity as a justification must be considered as really constituting an exception—and one even more rarely admissible than is the case with the other circumstances precluding wrongfulness . . . ." Thus, according to the Commission, the state of necessity can only be invoked under certain strictly defined conditions which must be cumulatively satisfied; and the State concerned is not the sole judge of whether those conditions have been met.

In the present case, the following basic conditions set forth in Draft Article [25] are relevant: it must have been occasioned by an "essential interest" of the State which is the author of the act conflicting with one of its international obligations; that interest must have been threatened by a "grave and imminent peril"; the act being challenged must have been the "only means" of safeguarding that interest; that act must not have "seriously impair[ed] an essential interest" of the State towards which the obligation existed; and the State which is the author of that act must not have "contributed to the occurrence of the state of necessity." Those conditions reflect customary international law. The Court will now endeavour to ascertain whether those conditions had been met at the time of the suspension and abandonment, by Hungary, of the works that it was to carry out in accordance with the 1977 Treaty.

The Court has no difficulty in acknowledging that the concerns expressed by Hungary for its natural environment in the region affected by the Gabčíkovo-Nagymaros Project related to an "essential interest" of that State, within the meaning given to that expression in Article [25] of the Draft of the International Law Commission. The Commission, in its Commentary, indicated that one should not, in that context, reduce an "essential interest" to a matter only of the "existence" of the State, and that the whole question was, ultimately, to be judged in the light of the particular case . . . ; at the same time, it included among the situations that could occasion a state of necessity, "a grave danger to . . . the ecological preservation of all or some of [the] territory [of a State]" . . . ;

and specified, with reference to State practice, that "It is primarily in the last two decades that safeguarding the ecological balance has come to be considered an 'essential interest' of all States." . . . The Court recalls that it has recently had occasion to stress, in the following terms, the great significance that it attaches to respect for the environment, not only for States but also for the whole of mankind:

> "the environment is not an abstraction but represents the living space, the quality of life and the very health of human beings, including generations unborn. The existence of the general obligation of States to ensure that activities within their jurisdiction and control respect the environment of other States or of areas beyond national control is now part of the corpus of international law relating to the environment."
> (*Legality of the Threat or Use of Nuclear Weapons, Advisory Opinion, I.C.J. Reports 1996,* pp. 241–42, para. 29.)

The verification of the existence, in 1989, of the "peril" invoked by Hungary, of its "grave and imminent" nature, as well as of the absence of any "means" to respond to it, other than the measures taken by Hungary to suspend and abandon the works, are all complex processes. As the Court has already indicated . . . , Hungary on several occasions expressed, in 1989, its "uncertainties" as to the ecological impact of putting in place the Gabčíkovo-Nagymaros barrage system, which is why it asked insistently for new scientific studies to be carried out. The Court considers, however, that, serious though these uncertainties might have been they could not, alone, establish the objective existence of a "peril" in the sense of a component element of a state of necessity. The word "peril" certainly evokes the idea of "risk"; that is precisely what distinguishes "peril" from material damage. But a state of necessity could not exist without a "peril" duly established at the relevant point in time; the mere apprehension of a possible "peril" could not suffice in that respect. It could moreover hardly be otherwise, when the "peril" constituting the state of necessity has at the same time to be "grave" and "imminent". "Imminence" is synonymous with "immediacy" or "proximity" and goes far beyond the concept of "possibility". As the International Law Commission emphasized in its commentary, the "extremely grave and imminent" peril must "have been a threat to the interest at the actual time." . . . That does not exclude, in the view of the Court, that a "peril" appearing in the long term might be held to be "imminent" as soon as it is established, at the relevant point in time, that the realization of that peril, however far off it might be, is not thereby any less certain and inevitable. The Hungarian argument on the state of necessity could not convince the Court unless it was at least proven that a real, "grave" and "imminent" "peril" existed in 1989 and that the measures taken by Hungary were the only possible response to it . . . .

The Court will begin by considering the situation at Nagymaros. As has already been mentioned . . . , Hungary maintained that, if the works at Nagymaros had been carried out as planned, the environment—and in particular the drinking water resources—in the area would have been exposed to serious dangers on account of problems linked to the upstream reservoir on the one hand and, on the other, the risks of erosion of the riverbed downstream. The Court notes that the dangers ascribed to the upstream reservoir were mostly of a long-term nature and, above all, that they remained uncertain. [A]ny dangers associated with the putting into service of the Nagymaros portion of the Project would have been closely linked to the extent to which it was operated in peak mode and to the modalities of such operation. It follows that, even if it could have been established—which, in the Court's appreciation of the evidence before it, was not the case—that the reservoir would ultimately have constituted a "grave peril" for the environment in the area, one would be bound to conclude that the peril was not "imminent" at the time at which Hungary suspended and then abandoned the works relating to the dam. With regard to the lowering of the riverbed downstream of the Nagymaros dam, the danger could have appeared at once more serious and more pressing, in so far as it was the supply of drinking water to the city of Budapest which would have been affected . . . . The Court would stress, however, that, even supposing, as Hungary maintained, that the construction and operation of the dam would have created serious risks, Hungary had means available to it, other than the suspension and abandonment of the works, of responding to that situation. It could for example have proceeded regularly to discharge gravel into the river downstream of the dam. It could likewise, if necessary, have supplied Budapest with drinking water by processing the river water in an appropriate manner. The two Parties expressly recognized that that possibility remained open even though—and this is not determinative of the state of necessity—the purification of the river water, like the other measures envisaged, clearly would have been a more costly technique.

The Court now comes to the Gabčíkovo sector. It will recall that Hungary's concerns in this sector related on the one hand to the quality of the surface water . . . with its effects on the quality of the groundwater in the region, and on the other hand, more generally, to the . . . effects on the fauna and flora in the alluvial plain of the Danube . . . . [T]he Court finds here again, that the peril claimed by Hungary was to be considered in the long term, and, more importantly, remained uncertain. As Hungary itself acknowledges, the damage that it apprehended had primarily to be the result of some relatively slow natural processes, the effects of which could not easily be assessed . . . . The report dated 23 June 1989 by the *ad hoc* Committee of the Hungarian Academy of Sciences . . . does not express any awareness of an authenticated peril—even in the form of a definite peril, whose realization would have been inevitable in the long term . . . . The Court also notes that, in these proceedings, Hungary acknowledged that, as a general rule, the quality of the Danube waters had improved over the past 20 years, even if those waters remained subject to hypertrophic conditions. However "grave" it might have been, it would accordingly have been difficult, in the light of what is said above, to see the alleged peril as sufficiently certain and therefore "imminent" in 1989. The Court moreover considers that Hungary could, in this context also, have resorted to other means in order to respond to the dangers that it apprehended. In particular, within the framework of the original Project, Hungary seemed to be in a position to control at least partially the distribution of the water between the bypass canal, the old bed of the Danube and the side-arms . . . .

The Court concludes from the foregoing that, with respect to both Nagymaros and Gabčíkovo, the perils invoked by Hungary, without prejudging their possible gravity, were not sufficiently established in 1989, nor were they "imminent"; and that Hungary had available to it at that time means of responding to these perceived perils other than the suspension and abandonment of works with which it had been entrusted. What is more, negotiations were under way which might have led to a review of the Project and the extension of some of its time-limits, without there being need to abandon it. The Court infers from this that the respect by Hungary, in 1989, of its obligations under the terms of the 1977 Treaty would not have resulted in a situation "characterized so aptly by the maxim *summum jus summa injuria*" . . . .

Moreover, the Court notes that Hungary decided to conclude the 1977 Treaty, a Treaty which—whatever the political circumstances prevailing at the time of its conclusion—was treated by Hungary as valid and in force until the date declared for its termination in May 1992. As can be seen from the material before the Court, a great many studies of a scientific and technical nature had been conducted at an earlier time, both by Hungary and by Czechoslovakia. Hungary was, then, presumably aware of the situation as then known, when it assumed its obligations under the Treaty. Hungary contended before the Court that those studies had been inadequate and that the state of knowledge at that time was not such as to make possible a complete evaluation of the ecological implications of the Gabčíkovo-Nagymaros Project. It is nonetheless the case that although the principal object of the 1977 Treaty was the construction of a System of Locks for the production of electricity, improvement of navigation on the Danube and protection against flooding, the need to ensure the protection of the environment had not escaped the parties . . . .

What is more, the Court cannot fail to note the positions taken by Hungary after the entry into force of the 1977 Treaty. In 1983, Hungary asked that the works under the Treaty should go forward more slowly, for reasons that were essentially economic but also, subsidiarily, related to ecological concerns. In 1989, when, according to Hungary itself, the state of scientific knowledge had undergone a significant development, it asked for the works to be speeded up, and then decided, three months later, to suspend them and subsequently to abandon them. The Court is not however unaware that profound changes were taking place in Hungary in 1989, and that, during that transitory phase, it might have been more than usually difficult to co-ordinate the different points of view prevailing from time to time.

The Court infers from all these elements that, in the present case, even if it had been established that there was, in 1989, a state of necessity linked to the performance of the 1977 Treaty, Hungary would not have been permitted to rely upon that state of necessity in order to justify its failure to comply with its treaty obligations, as it had helped, by act or omission to bring it about . . . .

F. REMEDIES

1) Cessation, Non-Repetition, and Reparation

The whole point of the doctrine of state responsibility is the imposition, by operation of law, of an obligation on a wrongdoing state to remedy its wrong. While the international law of remedies bears similarities to that of many domestic legal systems, it also has features that reflect the peculiar nature of the main subjects of the international legal system—sovereign states. Consider the codification of this law of remedies in the ILC Articles on State Responsibility:

ILC Articles on State Responsibility for Internationally Wrongful Acts, 2001

Article 30

Cessation and non-repetition

The State responsible for the internationally wrongful act is under an obligation:

(a) to cease that act, if it is continuing;

(b) to offer appropriate assurances and guarantees of non-repetition, if circumstances so require.

Commentary

. . . Cessation of conduct in breach of an international obligation is the first requirement in eliminating the consequences of wrongful conduct. With reparation, it is one of the two general consequences of an internationally wrongful act. Cessation is often the main focus of the controversy produced by conduct in breach of an international obligation . . . . By contrast reparation, important though it is in many cases, may not be the central issue in a dispute between States as to questions of responsibility . . . .

The question of cessation often arises in close connection with that of reparation, and particularly restitution. The result of cessation may be indistinguishable from restitution, for example in cases involving the freeing of hostages or the return of objects or premises seized. Nonetheless the two must be distinguished. Unlike restitution, cessation is not subject to limitations relating to proportionality. It may give rise to a continuing obligation, even when literal return to the *status quo ante* is excluded or can only be achieved in an approximate way . . . .

Assurances or guarantees of non-repetition may be sought by way of satisfaction (e.g., the repeal of the legislation which allowed the breach to occur), and there is thus some overlap between the two in practice. However they are better treated as an aspect of the continuation and repair of the legal relationship affected by the breach. Where assurances and guarantees of non-repetition are sought by an injured State, the question is essentially the reinforcement of a continuing legal relationship and the focus is on the future, not the past . . . .

Article 31

Reparation

1. The responsible State is under an obligation to make full reparation for the injury caused by the internationally wrongful act.

2. Injury includes any damage, whether material or moral, caused by the internationally wrongful act of a State.

Commentary

The obligation placed on the responsible State by article 31 is [in the words of the Permanent Court of International Justice in] the *Factory at Chorzów* [case,] . . . to "wipe out all the consequences of the illegal act and re-establish the situation which would, in all probability, have existed if that act had not been committed." . . .

"Material" damage here refers to damage to property or other interests of the State and its nationals which is assessable in financial terms. "Moral" damage includes such items as individual pain and suffering, loss of loved ones or personal affront associated with an intrusion on one's home or private life . . . .

[T]here is no general requirement, over and above any requirements laid down by the relevant primary obligation, that a State should have suffered material harm or damage before it can seek reparation for a breach. The existence of actual damage will be highly relevant to the form and quantum of reparation. But there is no general requirement of material harm or damage for a State to be entitled to seek some form of reparation . . . .

Article 34
Forms of reparation
Full reparation for the injury caused by the internationally wrongful act shall take the form of restitution, compensation and satisfaction, either singly or in combination . . . .

Article 35
Restitution
A State responsible for an internationally wrongful act is under an obligation to make restitution, that is, to re-establish the situation which existed before the wrongful act was committed, provided and to the extent that restitution:
    (a) is not materially impossible;
    (b) does not involve a burden out of all proportion to the benefit deriving from restitution instead of compensation.

Commentary
. . . [B]ecause restitution most closely conforms to the general principle that the responsible State is bound to wipe out the legal and material consequences of its wrongful act by re-establishing the situation that would exist if that act had not been committed, it comes first among the forms of reparation . . . . Restitution may take the form of material restoration or return of territory, persons or property, or the reversal of some juridical act, or some combination of them . . . . The term "juridical restitution" is sometimes used where restitution requires or involves the modification of a legal situation either within the legal system of the responsible State or in its legal relations with the injured State. Such cases include the revocation, annulment or amendment of a constitutional or legislative provision enacted in violation of a rule of international law . . . .

Under article 35, subparagraph (a), restitution is not required if it is "materially impossible". This would apply where property to be restored has been permanently lost or destroyed, or has deteriorated to such an extent as to be valueless. On the other hand, restitution is not impossible merely on grounds of legal or practical difficulties, even though the responsible State may have to make special efforts to overcome these . . . .

[R]estitution may not be required if it would "involve a burden out of all proportion to the benefit deriving from restitution instead of compensation." This applies only where there is a grave disproportionality between the burden which restitution would impose on the responsible State and the benefit which would be gained, either by the injured State or by any victim of the breach. It is thus based on considerations of equity and reasonableness, although with a preference for the position of the injured State in any case where the balancing process does not indicate a clear preference for compensation as compared with restitution . . . .

Article 36
Compensation

1. The State responsible for an internationally wrongful act is under an obligation to compensate for the damage caused thereby, insofar as such damage is not made good by restitution.

2. The compensation shall cover any financially assessable damage including loss of profits insofar as it is established.

Commentary

Article 36 deals with compensation for damage caused by an internationally wrongful act, to the extent that such damage is not made good by restitution. The notion of "damage" is defined inclusively in article 31, paragraph 2 as any damage whether material or moral. Article 36, paragraph 2 develops this definition by specifying that compensation shall cover any financially assessable damage including loss of profits so far as this is established in the given case. The qualification "financially assessable" is intended to exclude compensation for what is sometimes referred to as "moral damage" to a State, i.e., the affront or injury caused by a violation of rights not associated with actual damage to property or persons: this is the subject matter of satisfaction, dealt with in article 37 . . . .

Of the various forms of reparation, compensation is perhaps the most commonly sought in international practice . . . . Restitution, despite its primacy as a matter of legal principle, is frequently unavailable or inadequate. It may be partially or entirely ruled out either on the basis of the exceptions expressed in article 35, or because the injured State prefers compensation or for other reasons. Even where restitution is made, it may be insufficient to ensure full reparation. The role of compensation is to fill in any gaps so as to ensure full reparation for damage suffered . . . .

. . . Compensation corresponds to the financially assessable damage suffered by the injured State or its nationals. It is not concerned to punish the responsible State, nor does compensation have an expressive or exemplary character. Thus compensation generally consists of a monetary payment, though it may sometimes take the form, as agreed, of other forms of value . . . .

As to the appropriate heads of compensable damage and the principles of assessment to be applied in quantification, these will vary, depending upon the content of particular primary obligations, an evaluation of the respective behaviour of the parties and, more generally, a concern to reach an equitable and acceptable outcome . . . .

Article 37
Satisfaction

1. The State responsible for an internationally wrongful act is under an obligation to give satisfaction for the injury caused by that act insofar as it cannot be made good by restitution or compensation.

2. Satisfaction may consist in an acknowledgement of the breach, an expression of regret, a formal apology or another appropriate modality.

3. Satisfaction shall not be out of proportion to the injury and may not take a form humiliating to the responsible State . . . .

Commentary

Satisfaction is the third form of reparation which the responsible State may have to provide in discharge of its obligation to make full reparation for the injury caused by an internationally wrongful act. It is not a standard form of reparation, in the sense that in many cases the injury caused by an internationally wrongful act of a State may be fully repaired by restitution and/or compensation. The rather exceptional character of the remedy of satisfaction, and its relationship to the principle of full reparation, are emphasized by the phrase "insofar as [the injury] cannot be made good by restitution or compensation." . . . Satisfaction . . . is the remedy for those injuries, not financially assessable, which amount to an affront to the State. These injuries are frequently of a symbolic character, arising from the very fact of the breach of the obligation, irrespective of its material consequences for the State concerned . . . . Examples include situations of insults to the symbols of the State, such as the national flag, violations of sovereignty or territorial integrity, attacks on ships or aircraft, ill-treatment of or deliberate attacks on heads of State or Government or diplomatic or consular representatives or other protected persons and violations of the premises of embassies or consulates or of the residences of members of the mission . . . .

Paragraph 2 of article 37 provides that satisfaction may consist in an acknowledgement of the breach, an expression of regret, a formal apology or another appropriate modality. The forms of satisfaction listed in the article are no more than examples. The appropriate form of satisfaction will depend on the circumstances and cannot be prescribed in advance. Many possibilities exist, including due inquiry into the causes of an accident resulting in harm or injury, a trust fund to manage compensation payments in the interests of the beneficiaries, disciplinary or penal action against the individuals whose conduct caused the internationally wrongful act or the award of symbolic damages for non-pecuniary injury. Assurances or guarantees of non-repetition, which are dealt with in the articles in the context of cessation, may also amount to a form of satisfaction . . . . One of the most common modalities of satisfaction provided in the case of moral or non-material injury to the State is a declaration of the wrongfulness of the act by a competent court or tribunal . . . . Another common form of satisfaction is an apology, which may be given verbally or in writing by an appropriate official or even the head of State . . . .

Excessive demands made under the guise of "satisfaction" in the past suggest the need to impose some limit on the measures that can be sought by way of satisfaction to prevent abuses, inconsistent with the principle of the equality of States. In particular, satisfaction is not intended to be punitive in character, nor does it include punitive damages. Paragraph 3 of article 37 places limitations on the obligation to give satisfaction by setting out two criteria: first, the proportionality of satisfaction to the injury; and secondly, the requirement that satisfaction should not be humiliating to the responsible State. It is true that the term "humiliating" is imprecise, but there are certainly historical examples of demands of this kind . . . .

Article 40
[Serious breaches of peremptory norms]
1. [Articles 40 and 41] appl[y] to the international responsibility which is entailed by a serious breach by a State of an obligation arising under a peremptory norm of general international law.

2. A breach of such an obligation is serious if it involves a gross or systematic failure by the responsible State to fulfil the obligation.

Article 41
Particular consequences of a serious breach of [a peremptory norm]
1. States shall cooperate to bring to an end through lawful means any serious breach within the meaning of article 40.

2. No State shall recognize as lawful a situation created by a serious breach within the meaning of article 40, nor render aid or assistance in maintaining that situation.

3. This article is without prejudice to the other consequences referred to in this Part and to such further consequences that a breach to which this chapter applies may entail under international law . . . .

Commentary
. . . [T]he present Articles do not recognize the existence of any distinction between State "crimes" and "delicts." . . . On the other hand, it is necessary for the Articles to reflect that there are certain *consequences* flowing from the basic concepts of peremptory norms of general international law and obligations to the international community as a whole within the field of State responsibility . . . . What is called for in the face of serious breaches is a joint and coordinated effort by all States to counteract the effects of these breaches. It may be open to question whether general international law at present prescribes a positive duty of cooperation, and paragraph 1 [of Article 41] in that respect may reflect the progressive development of international law. But in fact such cooperation, especially in the framework of international organizations, is carried out already in response to the gravest breaches of international law and it is often the only way of providing an effective remedy. Paragraph 1 seeks to strengthen existing mechanisms of cooperation, on the basis that all States are called upon to make an appropriate response to the serious breaches referred to in article 40 . . . .

Pursuant to paragraph 2 of article 41, States are under a duty of abstention, which comprises two obligations, first, not to recognize as lawful situations created by serious breaches in the sense of article 40, and, second, not to render aid or assistance in maintaining that situation . . . . The first of these two obligations refers to the obligation of collective non-recognition by the international community as a whole of the legality of situations resulting directly from serious breaches in the sense of article 40. The obligation applies to "situations" created by these breaches, such as, for example, attempted acquisition of sovereignty over territory through the denial of the right of self-determination of peoples. It not only refers to the formal recognition of these situations, but also prohibits acts which would imply such recognition . . . .

An example of the practice of non-recognition of acts in breach of peremptory norms is provided by the reaction of the Security Council to the Iraqi invasion of Kuwait in 1990. Following the Iraqi declaration of a "comprehensive and eternal merger" with Kuwait, the Security Council, in resolution 662 (1990) of 9 August 1990, decided that the annexation had "no legal validity, and is considered null and void," and called upon all States, international organizations and specialized agencies not to recognize that annexation and to refrain from any action or dealing that might be interpreted as a recognition of it, whether direct or indirect. In fact no State recognized the legality of the purported annexation, the effects of which were subsequently reversed . . . .

The second obligation contained in paragraph 2 prohibits States from rendering aid or assistance in maintaining the situation created by a serious breach in the sense of article 40. This goes beyond the provisions dealing with aid or assistance in the commission of an internationally wrongful act, which are covered by article 16. It deals with conduct "after the fact" which assists the responsible State in maintaining a situation "opposable to all States in the sense of barring *erga omnes* the legality of a situation which is maintained in violation of international law." . . .

As suggested in the ILC Commentaries, reparation frequently requires resorting to more than one method of "wiping out the consequences" of the internationally wrongful act. Moreover, in cases where a state has espoused a claim on behalf of its nationals but also presses a claim for violation of international legal obligations owed directly to it, several remedies may be in order. Consider the following cases illustrating the need for multiple remedies to provide full reparation for the consequences of the internationally wrongful acts of the respondent states:

Claim of the British Ship "I'm Alone" v United States (1933), 3 RIAA 1609 at 1617–618, (1935) 29 Am J Int'l L 326

[The *I'm Alone* was a Canadian registered vessel that was sunk on the high seas by an American Coast Guard vessel after two days of hot pursuit that began 12 nautical miles from the American coast. An arbitration Commission was established by the parties to deal with the resulting international claims.]

It will be recalled that the *I'm Alone* was sunk on the 22nd day of March, 1929, on the high seas, in the Gulf of Mexico, by the United States revenue cutter *Dexter* . . . . The Commissioners [have found that the sinking of the vessel] could not be justified by any principle of international law.

The vessel was a British ship of Canadian registry; after her construction she was employed for several years in rum running, the cargo being destined for illegal introduction into, and sale in, the United States. In December, 1928, and during the early months of 1929, down to the sinking of the vessel on the 22nd of March, of that year, she was engaged in carrying liquor from Belize, in British Honduras, to an agreed point or points in the Gulf of Mexico, in convenient proximity to the coast of Louisiana, where the liquor was taken from her in smaller craft, smuggled into the United States, and sold there.

We find as a fact that, from September, 1928, down to the date when she was sunk, the *I'm Alone*, although a British ship of Canadian registry, was *de facto* owned, controlled, and at the critical times, managed, and her movements directed and her cargo dealt with and disposed of, by a group of persons acting in concert who were entirely, or nearly so, citizens of the United States, and who employed her for the purposes mentioned. The possibility that one of the group may not have been of United States nationality we regard as of no importance in the circumstances of this case.

The Commissioners consider that, in view of the facts, no compensation ought to be paid in respect of the loss of the ship or the cargo.

The act of sinking the ship, however, by officers of the United States Coast Guard, was, as we have already indicated, an unlawful act; and the Commissioners consider that the United States ought formally to acknowledge its illegality, and to apologize to His Majesty's Canadian Government therefor; and, further, that as a material amend in respect of the wrong the United States should pay the sum of $25,000 to His Majesty's Canadian Government; and they recommend accordingly.

The Commissioners have had under consideration the compensation which ought to be paid by the United States to His Majesty's Canadian Government for the benefit of the captain and members of the crew, none of whom was a party to the illegal conspiracy to smuggle liquor into the United States and sell the same there. The Commissioners recommend that compensation be paid as follows:

For the captain, John Thomas Randell, the sum of $7,906.00

For John Williams, deceased, to be paid to his proper representatives 1,250.50

For Jens Jansen 1,098.00

For James Barrett 1,032.00

For William Wordsworth, deceased, to be paid to his proper representatives 907.00

For Eddie Young 999.50

For Chesley Hobbs 1,323.50

For Edward Fouchard 965.00

For Amanda Mainguy, as compensation in respect of the death of Leon Mainguy, for the benefit of herself and the children of Leon Mainguy (Henriette Mainguy, Jeanne Mainguy and John Mainguy) the sum of 10,185.00 . . . .

Arrest Warrant of 11 April 2000 (Democratic Republic of the Congo v Belgium), Judgment, [2002] ICJ Rep 3

[On 11 April 2000, a Belgian investigating magistrate issued an "international arrest warrant *in absentia*" against the then foreign affairs minister of the Congo, Mr. Yerodia, alleging that he had committed grave breaches of the Geneva Conventions of 1949 and their Additional Protocols, as well as crimes against humanity. The Court found that, by issuing the arrest warrant, Belgium had violated its international legal obligations and made these findings regarding the remedy for such violation:]

75. The Court has already concluded . . . that the issue and circulation of the arrest warrant of 11 April 2000 by the Belgian authorities failed to respect the immunity of the incumbent Minister for Foreign Affairs of the Congo and, more particularly, infringed the immunity from criminal jurisdiction and the inviolability then enjoyed by Mr. Yerodia under international law. Those acts engaged Belgium's international responsibility. The Court considers that the findings so reached by it constitute a form of satisfaction which will make good the moral injury complained of by the Congo.

76. . . . In the present case, [quoting the Permanent Court of International Justice's *Factory of Chorzów* case] "the situation which would, in all probability have existed if [the

illegal act] had not been committed" cannot be re-established merely by a finding by the Court that the arrest warrant was unlawful under international law. The warrant is still extant, and remains unlawful, notwithstanding the fact that Mr. Yerodia has ceased to be Minister for Foreign Affairs. The Court accordingly considers that Belgium must, by means of its own choosing, cancel the warrant in question and so inform the authorities to whom it was circulated.

77. The Court sees no need for further remedy . . .

Consider, however, the restraint signalled by the International Court of Justice in responding to the applicant's request for multiple remedies in the following case:

Pulp Mills on the River Uruguay (Argentina v Uruguay), Judgment, [2010] ICJ Rep 14

[The boundary between Argentina and Uruguay follows, in part, the Uruguay River. In this case, Argentina claimed that Uruguay, in allowing construction of a pulp mill (the "Orion (Botnia) mill") on the river, had breached a treaty between the two states (the "1975 Statute") governing permissible uses of the river. The ICJ concluded that, while Uruguay had breached various procedural obligations under the 1975 Statute (such as the duty to negotiate with Argentina prior to allowing construction of the mill), Uruguay was under no obligation to refrain from allowing construction when those negotiations failed and had not otherwise breached any substantive obligations under the 1975 Statute. The ICJ then considered the question of appropriate remedies for Uruguay's procedural breaches:]

267. Having concluded that Uruguay breached its procedural obligations under the 1975 Statute . . . it is for the Court to draw the conclusions following from these internationally wrongful acts giving rise to Uruguay's international responsibility and to determine what that responsibility entails . . . .

269. The Court considers that its finding of wrongful conduct by Uruguay in respect of its procedural obligations per se constitutes a measure of satisfaction for Argentina. As Uruguay's breaches of the procedural obligations occurred in the past and have come to an end, there is no cause to order their cessation.

270. Argentina nevertheless argues that a finding of wrongfulness would be insufficient as reparation . . . . Argentina contends that Uruguay is under an obligation to "re-establish on the ground and in legal terms the situation that existed before [the] internationally wrongful acts were committed". To this end, the Orion (Botnia) mill should be dismantled. According to Argentina, *restitutio in integrum* is the primary form of reparation for internationally wrongful acts. Relying on Article 35 of the International Law Commission's Articles on the Responsibility of States for Internationally Wrongful Acts, Argentina maintains that restitution takes precedence over all other forms of reparation except where it is "materially impossible" or involves "a burden out of all proportion to the benefit deriving from restitution instead of compensation". It asserts that dismantling the mill is not materially impossible and would not create for the Respondent State a burden out of all proportion, since the Respondent has . . . assume[d] the risk of having to dismantle the mills in the event of an adverse decision by the Court . . . . Argentina adds that whether or not restitution is disproportionate must be determined at the latest as of

the filing of the Application instituting proceedings, since as from that time Uruguay, knowing of Argentina's request to have the work halted and the *status quo ante* re-established, could not have been unaware of the risk it ran in proceeding with construction of the disputed mill . . . .

273. The Court recalls that customary international law provides for restitution as one form of reparation for injury, restitution being the re-establishment of the situation which existed before occurrence of the wrongful act. The Court further recalls that, where restitution is materially impossible or involves a burden out of all proportion to the benefit deriving from it, reparation takes the form of compensation or satisfaction, or even both . . . .

274. Like other forms of reparation, restitution must be appropriate to the injury suffered, taking into account the nature of the wrongful act having caused it . . . . What constitutes 'reparation in an adequate form' clearly varies depending upon the concrete circumstances surrounding each case and the precise nature and scope of the injury, since the question has to be examined from the viewpoint of what is the 'reparation in an adequate form' that corresponds to the injury . . . .

275. . . . . [T]he procedural obligations under the 1975 Statute did not entail any ensuing prohibition on Uruguay's building of the Orion (Botnia) mill, failing consent by Argentina, after the expiration of the period for negotiation. The Court has however observed that construction of that mill began before negotiations had come to an end, in breach of the procedural obligations laid down in the 1975 Statute. Further, as the Court has found, on the evidence submitted to it, the operation of the Orion (Botnia) mill has not resulted in the breach of substantive obligations laid down in the 1975 Statute . . . . As Uruguay was not barred from proceeding with the construction and operation of the Orion (Botnia) mill after the expiration of the period for negotiation and as it breached no substantive obligation under the 1975 Statute, ordering the dismantling of the mill would not, in the view of the Court, constitute an appropriate remedy for the breach of procedural obligations.

276. As Uruguay has not breached substantive obligations arising under the 1975 Statute, the Court is likewise unable, for the same reasons, to uphold Argentina's claim in respect of compensation for alleged injuries suffered in various economic sectors, specifically tourism and agriculture.

277. Argentina further requests the Court to adjudge and declare that Uruguay must "provide adequate guarantees that it will refrain in future from preventing the Statute of the River Uruguay of 1975 from being applied, in particular the consultation procedure established by Chapter II of that Treaty".

278. The Court fails to see any special circumstances in the present case requiring the ordering of a measure such as that sought by Argentina. As the Court has recently observed [in *Dispute regarding Navigational and Related Rights (Costa Rica v. Nicaragua)*, Judgment, [2009] I.C.J. Rep. 13 at para. 150]: "[W]hile the Court may order, as it has done in the past, a State responsible for internationally wrongful conduct to provide the injured State with assurances and guarantees of non-repetition, it will only do so if the

circumstances so warrant, which it is for the Court to assess. As a general rule, there is no reason to suppose that a State whose act or conduct has been declared wrongful by the Court will repeat that act or conduct in the future, since its good faith must be presumed . . . . There is thus no reason, except in special circumstances . . . to order [the provision of assurances and guarantees of non-repetition]."

What important qualification to the obligation to make restitution, not expressly set out in Article 35 of the ILC Articles, does the ICJ apply in denying the restitutionary and compensatory remedies sought by Argentina in this case? Does paragraph 273 of the judgment affirm or deny a hierarchy among the different forms of reparation? Note also the ICJ's indication that assurances and guarantees of non-repetition will only exceptionally be ordered. Is it appropriate to presume the good faith of a state that has already been found in breach of its international legal obligations? Is such a presumption likely to be more, or less, conducive to future respect of the offending state's obligations than an explicit judicial order to that effect?

2) Countermeasures

Long before rules of state responsibility, judicial remedies, and peaceful dispute settlement mechanisms were well-entrenched features of international law, states aggrieved by the internationally wrongful conduct of other states essentially had to rely on various forms of self-help in order to obtain redress. A common form of such self-help was the "reprisal" — basically, an act directed by one state against another that would be internationally wrongful but for the fact that it was in response to a prior internationally wrongful act of the target state. The modern international legal requirement that states seek to resolve their disputes by peaceful means has rendered much of the old law of reprisals obsolete. However, this is not generally so of reprisals falling short of the use of force contrary to the UN Charter or those that would not be violations of fundamental human rights, certain rules of international humanitarian law, and peremptory norms of international law.

The modern term for reprisals is "countermeasures." As discussed above, a finding that an act is a genuine and permissible countermeasure precludes a finding of wrongfulness for that act and thus works as a sort of defence against claims arising out of it. Countermeasures remain a form of self-help remedy available to states that are the victims of the internationally wrongful acts of other states. Consider the following codification of the limits placed by modern international law upon such acts of self-help:

ILC Articles on State Responsibility for Internationally Wrongful Acts, 2001

Article 49
Object and limits of countermeasures
1. An injured State may only take countermeasures against a State which is responsible for an internationally wrongful act in order to induce that State to comply with its obligations under Part Two [that is, those relating to cessation, non-repetition, and reparation].

2. Countermeasures are limited to the non-performance for the time being of international obligations of the State taking the measures towards the responsible State.

3. Countermeasures shall, as far as possible, be taken in such a way as to permit the resumption of performance of the obligations in question.

Commentary

Countermeasures are a feature of a decentralized system by which injured States may seek to vindicate their rights and to restore the legal relationship with the responsible State which has been ruptured by the internationally wrongful act . . . . It is recognized both by governments and by the decisions of international tribunals that countermeasures are justified under certain circumstances . . . . Like other forms of self-help, countermeasures are liable to abuse and this potential is exacerbated by the factual inequalities between States . . . .

Countermeasures are to be contrasted with retorsion, i.e., unfriendly conduct which is not inconsistent with any international obligation of the State engaging in it even though it may be a response to an internationally wrongful act. Acts of retorsion may include the prohibition of or limitations upon normal diplomatic relations or other contacts, embargoes of various kinds or withdrawal of voluntary aid programs. Whatever their motivation, so long as such acts are not incompatible with the international obligations of the States taking them towards the target State, they do not involve countermeasures and they fall outside the scope of the present Articles . . . .

Countermeasures may only be taken by an injured State in order to induce the responsible State to comply with its obligations under Part Two, namely, to cease the internationally wrongful conduct, if it is continuing, and to provide reparation to the injured State. Countermeasures are not intended as a form of punishment for wrongful conduct but as an instrument for achieving compliance with the obligations of the responsible State under Part Two . . . .

A State taking countermeasures acts at its peril, if its view of the question of wrongfulness turns out not to be well founded. A State which resorts to countermeasures based on its unilateral assessment of the situation does so at its own risk and may incur responsibility for its own wrongful conduct in the event of an incorrect assessment. In this respect there is no difference between countermeasures and other circumstances precluding wrongfulness . . . .

Article 50
Obligations not affected by countermeasures
1. Countermeasures shall not affect:
    (a) the obligation to refrain from the threat or use of force as embodied in the Charter of the United Nations;
    (b) obligations for the protection of fundamental human rights;
    (c) obligations of a humanitarian character prohibiting reprisals;
    (d) other obligations under peremptory norms of general international law.

2. A State taking countermeasures is not relieved from fulfilling its obligations:
    (a) under any dispute settlement procedure applicable between it and the responsible State;
    (b) to respect the inviolability of diplomatic or consular agents, premises, archives and documents.

Commentary

. . . The obligations dealt with in article 50 fall into two basic categories. Paragraph 1 deals with certain obligations which by reason of their character must not be the subject of countermeasures at all. Paragraph 2 deals with certain obligations relating in particular to the maintenance of channels of communication between the two States concerned, including machinery for the resolution of their disputes . . . .

Article 51

Proportionality

Countermeasures must be commensurate with the injury suffered, taking into account the gravity of the internationally wrongful act and the rights in question.

Commentary

Proportionality is a well-established requirement for taking countermeasures, being widely recognized in State practice, doctrine and jurisprudence . . . . Proportionality is concerned with the relationship between the internationally wrongful act and the countermeasure. In some respects proportionality is linked to the requirement of purpose specified in article 49: a clearly disproportionate measure may well be judged not to have been necessary to induce the responsible State to comply with its obligations but to have had a punitive aim and to fall outside the purpose of countermeasures enunciated in article 49. Proportionality is, however, a limitation even on measures which may be justified under article 49. In every case a countermeasure must be commensurate with the injury suffered, including the importance of the issue of principle involved and this has a function partly independent of the question whether the countermeasure was necessary to achieve the result of ensuring compliance . . . .

Article 52

Conditions relating to resort to countermeasures

1. Before taking countermeasures, an injured State shall:

   (a) call upon the responsible State . . . to fulfil its obligations under Part Two [i.e., those relating to cessation, non-repetition and reparation];

   (b) notify the responsible State of any decision to take countermeasures and offer to negotiate with that State.

2. Notwithstanding paragraph 1 (b), the injured State may take such urgent countermeasures as are necessary to preserve its rights.

3. Countermeasures may not be taken, and if already taken must be suspended without undue delay if:

   (a) the internationally wrongful act has ceased; and

   (b) the dispute is pending before a court or tribunal which has the authority to make decisions binding on the parties.

4. Paragraph 3 does not apply if the responsible State fails to implement the dispute settlement procedures in good faith.

Commentary

Overall, article 52 seeks to establish reasonable procedural conditions for the taking of countermeasures in a context where compulsory third party settlement of disputes may not be available, immediately or at all. At the same time it needs to take into account the possibility that there may be an international court or tribunal with authority to make decisions binding on the parties in relation to the dispute. Countermeasures are a form of self-help, which responds to the position of the injured State in an international system in which the impartial settlement of disputes through due process of law is not yet guaranteed. Where a third party procedure exists and has been invoked by either party to the dispute, the requirements of that procedure, e.g. as to interim measures of protection, should substitute as far as possible for countermeasures. On the other hand, even where an international court or tribunal has jurisdiction over a dispute and authority to indicate interim measures of protection, it may be that the responsible State is not cooperating in that process. In such cases the remedy of countermeasures necessarily revives.

Article 53
Termination of countermeasures
Countermeasures shall be terminated as soon as the responsible State has complied with its obligations under Part Two in relation to the internationally wrongful act.

Article 54
Measures taken by States other than an injured State
This chapter does not prejudice the right of any State, entitled under article 48, paragraph 1 to invoke the responsibility of another State, to take lawful measures against that State to ensure cessation of the breach and reparation in the interest of the injured State or of the beneficiaries of the obligation breached.

Commentary
. . . . At present, there appears to be no clearly recognized entitlement of States referred to in article 48 to take countermeasures in the collective interest. Consequently it is not appropriate to include in the present articles a provision concerning the question whether other States, identified in article 48, are permitted to take countermeasures in order to induce a responsible State to comply with its obligations. Instead [Article 54] includes a saving clause which reserves the position and leaves the resolution of the matter to the further development of international law . . . . Article 54 accordingly provides that the chapter on countermeasures does not prejudice the right of any State, entitled under article 48, paragraph 1 to invoke the responsibility of another State, to take lawful measures against the responsible State to ensure cessation of the breach and reparation in the interest of the injured State or the beneficiaries of the obligation breached. The article speaks of "lawful measures" rather than "countermeasures" so as not to prejudice any position concerning measures taken by States other than the injured State in response to breaches of obligations for the protection of the collective interest or those owed to the international community as a whole.

Should there still be room for lawful countermeasures in modern international law? In answering this question, recall the consensual basis of jurisdiction of the International Court of Justice in contentious cases. Do the ILC Articles on State Responsibility posit a clear obligation to resort to other dispute resolution mechanisms before having recourse to countermeasures? Should they?

G. INVOKING STATE RESPONSIBILITY

1) Standing

In Section C above, we examined the range of actors for whose conduct a state may be held responsible in international law. The converse of this issue is: which actors are able to make an international claim against a state for its internationally wrongful acts? In other words, who has standing to invoke the responsibility of states?

We have already presaged this issue in a general way in examining the international legal personality of states and international organizations in Chapter 3. One of the key attributes of being an "international legal person" is the capacity to make claims against other such persons. In principle, therefore, any state has the legal capacity to bring an international claim against any other state. Whether the same is true of an international organization depends, as we have seen, on the degree of international legal personality — in particularly the legal capacities — expressly or impliedly conferred upon that organization by its member states through its constitutive treaty. As we saw in the *Reparations* case,[12] the United Nations has been conferred sufficient international legal personality by its Charter to be able to assert international claims against states (whether members of the organization or not).

There are, however, several further layers of complexity to the issue of standing. For example, the legal rules pursuant to which any particular international dispute resolution forum is established will often determine which classes of entities have standing to bring claims before it. Thus, standing before the International Court of Justice in contentious cases is expressly limited, by the Court's Statute, to states; whereas advisory opinions can only be requested of the Court by certain United Nations organs and specialized agencies.

Further, even when the classes of entities entitled to bring an international claim against a state in any particular forum are established, the question becomes: which particular entities falling within an eligible class in fact have standing to press the specific claim in question? As states in general have capacity to invoke the international responsibility of other states, the ILC Articles address this issue by focusing on *which* states may invoke the responsibility of another state that has breached one of its international legal obligations:

ILC Articles on State Responsibility for Internationally Wrongful Acts, 2001

Article 42
Invocation of responsibility by an injured State
A State is entitled as an injured State to invoke the responsibility of another State if the obligation breached is owed to:
    (a) that State individually; or
    (b) a group of States including that State, or the international community as a whole, and the breach of the obligation:
        (i) specially affects that State; or

---

12 *Reparation for Injuries Suffered In the Service of the United Nations*, Advisory Opinion, [1949] ICJ Rep 174 [*Reparations*].

(ii) is of such a character as radically to change the position of all the other States to which the obligation is owed with respect to the further performance of the obligation.

Commentary

Article 42 . . . defines ["injured state"] in a relatively narrow way, drawing a distinction between injury to an individual State or possibly a small number of States and the legal interests of several or all States in certain obligations established in the collective interest. The latter are dealt with in article 48 . . . .

Subparagraph (b) deals with injury arising from violations of collective obligations, i.e. obligations that apply between more than two States and whose performance in the given case is not owed to one State individually, but to a group of States or even the international community as a whole. The violation of these obligations only injures any particular State if additional requirements are met . . . .

Subparagraph (b)(i) stipulates that a State is injured if it is "specially affected" by the violation of a collective obligation . . . . Even in cases where the legal effects of an internationally wrongful act extend by implication to the whole group of States bound by the obligation or to the international community as a whole, the wrongful act may have particular adverse effects on one State or on a small number of States . . . . For a State to be considered injured it must be affected by the breach in a way which distinguishes it from the generality of other States to which the obligation is owed . . . .

In contrast, subparagraph (b)(ii) deals with a special category of obligations, breach of which must be considered as affecting per se every other State to which the obligation is owed . . . . [T]hey must all be considered as individually entitled to react to a breach. This is so whether or not any one of them is particularly affected; indeed they may all be equally affected . . . . [However,] a State is only considered injured under subparagraph (b) (ii) if the breach is of such a character as radically to affect the enjoyment of the rights or the performance of the obligations of all the other States to which the obligation is owed . . . .

Article 46
Plurality of Injured States

Where several States are injured by the same internationally wrongful act, each injured State may separately invoke the responsibility of the State which has committed the internationally wrongful act . . . .

Article 48
Invocation of responsibility by a State other than an injured State

1. Any State other than an injured State is entitled to invoke the responsibility of another State in accordance with paragraph 2 if:

(a) the obligation breached is owed to a group of States including that State, and is established for the protection of a collective interest of the group; or

(b) the obligation breached is owed to the international community as a whole.

2. Any State entitled to invoke responsibility under paragraph 1 may claim from the responsible State:

(a) cessation of the internationally wrongful act, and assurances and guarantees of non-repetition . . . ; and

(b) performance of the obligation of reparation . . . in the interest of the injured State or of the beneficiaries of the obligation breached . . . .

Commentary

Article 48 is based on the idea that in case of breaches of specific obligations protecting the collective interests of a group of States or the interests of the international community as a whole, responsibility may be invoked by States which are not themselves injured in the sense of article 42 . . . .

Obligations coming within the scope of subparagraph (1) (a) have to be "collective obligations," i.e. they must apply between a group of States and have been established in some collective interest. They might concern, for example, the environment or security of a region (e.g. a regional nuclear-free zone treaty or a regional system for the protection of human rights) . . . . [T]heir principal purpose will be to foster a common interest, over and above any interests of the States concerned individually . . . .

Under *paragraph 1*(b), States other than the injured State may invoke responsibility if the obligation in question was owed "to the international community as a whole." The provision intends to give effect to the statement by the ICJ in the *Barcelona Traction* case, where the Court drew "an essential distinction" between obligations owed to particular States and those owed "towards the international community as a whole" . . . . Each State is entitled, as a member of the international community as a whole, to invoke the responsibility of another State for breaches of such obligations . . . .

Paragraph 2 specifies the categories of claim which States may make when invoking responsibility under article 48. The list given in the paragraph is exhaustive, and invocation of responsibility under article 48 gives rise to a more limited range of rights as compared to those of injured States under article 42. In particular, the focus of action by a State under article 48 — such State not being injured in its own right and therefore not claiming compensation on its own account — is likely to be on the very question whether a State is in breach and on cessation if the breach is a continuing one . . . .

As one commentator has noted, Article 42 "is far from being a masterpiece of clarity."[13] Nonetheless, reviewing the wording of Article 42, is it necessary, for standing purposes, for a state to show that it has suffered any adverse impact as a result of the breach of an obligation owed to it? In what sense is a state that has suffered no adverse impact as a result of the breach of such an obligation an "injured" state? Why should the rule be different for members of a group of states in the case of breach of an obligation owed to that group? To what extent does subparagraph 1(a) of Article 48 close the gap between the requirements of paragraphs (a) and (b) of Article 42?

Considering the types of claims that may be advanced by a state under paragraph 2 of Article 48, how likely is it that states will assert such standing? Are there any practical reasons for which states might in fact be very wary of doing so? Consider the following example of just such a claim, successfully asserted by Belgium against Senegal:

---

13 Pierre-Marie Dupuy, "Back to the Future of a Multilateral Dimension of the Law of State Responsibility for Breaches of 'Obligations Owed to the International Community as a Whole'" (2012) 23 EJIL 1059 at 1060.

Questions Related to the Obligation to Prosecute or Extradite (Belgium v Senegal), ICJ
General List No 144, 20 July 2012

[Hissène Habré became president of Chad in 1982 following an armed revolution. He
was similarly ousted from power in 1990, whereupon he sought, and was granted, asylum in Senegal. During Habré's eight years in power, large-scale violations of human
rights, including torture, were committed in Chad. In 2005, acting on complaints filed
by Chadian and Belgian nationals, a Belgian investigating judge issued an international
arrest warrant for Habré on charges of serious violations of international humanitarian law, torture, genocide, and crimes against humanity. Senegal declined Belgium's
subsequent request for Habré's extradition on these charges and failed to take steps to
investigate or prosecute him within its own penal system, leading Belgium to bring this
claim against Senegal.]

49. Belgium ... contends that Senegal breached its obligations under Article 6, paragraph 2, and Article 7, paragraph 1, of the Convention against Torture.[14] These provisions
respectively require a State party to the Convention, when a person who has allegedly
committed an act of torture is found on its territory, to hold "a preliminary inquiry into
the facts" and, "if it does not extradite him", to "submit the case to its competent authorities for the purpose of prosecution" ....

64. Senegal objects to the admissibility of Belgium's claims. It maintains that "Belgium
is not entitled to invoke the international responsibility of Senegal for the alleged breach
of its obligation to submit the H[issène] Habré case to its competent authorities for the
purpose of prosecution, unless it extradites him". In particular, Senegal contends that
none of the alleged victims of the acts said to be attributable to Mr. Habré was of Belgian
nationality at the time when the acts were committed.

65. Belgium does not dispute the contention that none of the alleged victims was of
Belgian nationality at the time of the alleged offences. However, it noted in its Application that "[a]s the present jurisdiction of the Belgian courts is based on the complaint
filed by a Belgian national of Chadian origin, the Belgian courts intend to exercise passive personal jurisdiction" .... In the oral proceedings, Belgium also claimed to be in a
"particular position" since "it has availed itself of its right under Article 5 to exercise its
jurisdiction and to request extradition". Moreover, Belgium argued that "[u]nder the Convention, every State party, irrespective of the nationality of the victims, is entitled to claim
performance of the obligation concerned, and, therefore, can invoke the responsibility
resulting from the failure to perform".

66. The divergence of views between the Parties concerning Belgium's entitlement to
bring its claims against Senegal before the Court with regard to the application of the
Convention in the case of Mr. Habré raises the issue of Belgium's standing. For that
purpose, Belgium based its claims not only on its status as a party to the Convention but
also on the existence of a special interest that would distinguish Belgium from the other
parties to the Convention and give it a specific entitlement in the case of Mr. Habré.

14 [Convention against Torture and Other Forms of Cruel, Inhuman and Degrading Treatment or Punishment, 10 December 1984, 1465 UNTS 85, Can TS 1987 No 36, in force 26 June 1987.]

67. The Court will first consider whether being a party to the Convention is sufficient for a State to be entitled to bring a claim to the Court concerning the cessation of alleged violations by another State party of its obligations under that instrument.

68. As stated in its Preamble, the object and purpose of the Convention is "to make more effective the struggle against torture . . . throughout the world". The States parties to the Convention have a common interest to ensure, in view of their shared values, that acts of torture are prevented and that, if they occur, their authors do not enjoy impunity. The obligations of a State party to conduct a preliminary inquiry into the facts and to submit the case to its competent authorities for prosecution are triggered by the presence of the alleged offender in its territory, regardless of the nationality of the offender or the victims, or of the place where the alleged offences occurred. All the other States parties have a common interest in compliance with these obligations by the State in whose territory the alleged offender is present. That common interest implies that the obligations in question are owed by any State party to all the other States parties to the Convention. All the States parties "have a legal interest" in the protection of the rights involved (*Barcelona Traction, Light and Power Company, Limited, Judgment, I.C.J. Reports 1970*, p. 32, para. 33). These obligations may be defined as "obligations *erga omnes partes*" in the sense that each State party has an interest in compliance with them in any given case. In this respect, the relevant provisions of the Convention against Torture are similar to those of the Convention on the Prevention and Punishment of the Crime of Genocide, with regard to which the Court observed that

> "In such a convention the contracting States do not have any interests of their own; they merely have, one and all, a common interest, namely, the accomplishment of those high purposes which are the *raison d'être* of the Convention." (*Reservations to the Convention on the Prevention and Punishment of the Crime of Genocide, Advisory Opinion, I.C.J. Reports 1951*, p. 23.)

69. The common interest in compliance with the relevant obligations under the Convention against Torture implies the entitlement of each State party to the Convention to make a claim concerning the cessation of an alleged breach by another State party. If a special interest were required for that purpose, in many cases no State would be in the position to make such a claim. It follows that any State party to the Convention may invoke the responsibility of another State party with a view to ascertaining the alleged failure to comply with its obligations *erga omnes partes*, such as those under Article 6, paragraph 2, and Article 7, paragraph 1, of the Convention, and to bring that failure to an end.

70. For these reasons, the Court concludes that Belgium, as a State party to the Convention against Torture, has standing to invoke the responsibility of Senegal for the alleged breaches of its obligations under Article 6, paragraph 2, and Article 7, paragraph 1, of the Convention in the present proceedings. Therefore, the claims of Belgium based on these provisions are admissible.

As a consequence, there is no need for the Court to pronounce on whether Belgium also has a special interest with respect to Senegal's compliance with the relevant provisions of the Convention in the case of Mr. Habré.

[The Court proceeded to find that Senegal was in breach of articles 6(2) and 7(1) of the Convention against Torture, and then turned to the question of appropriate remedies:]

121. The Court emphasizes that, in failing to comply with its obligations under Article 6, paragraph 2, and Article 7, paragraph 1, of the Convention, Senegal has engaged its international responsibility. Consequently, Senegal is required to cease this continuing wrongful act, in accordance with general international law on the responsibility of States for internationally wrongful acts. Senegal must therefore take without further delay the necessary measures to submit the case to its competent authorities for the purpose of prosecution, if it does not extradite Mr. Habré.

2) Espousal of Claims

If standing to bring international claims against states is in principle limited to international legal persons — that is, states and some international organizations — this is not to say that individuals or corporations have no international legal recourse against states which may injure their interests. How are claims in respect of such injuries advanced at the international level?

Treaties may establish exactly when and how a state may make claims on behalf of an injured national. In the economic area, many investment treaties — including the North American Free Trade Agreement[15] — enable injured investors themselves to bring claims against states in special international tribunal or arbitral proceedings.

More generally, however, individuals and corporations must rely on what is called "diplomatic protection." Diplomatic protection is a doctrine of customary international law that permits, but does not require, states to extend "protection" to their nationals when the latter have suffered injuries as a result of the wrongful acts of other states. We have already seen, for example, that international law imposes constraints on the treatment of foreign nationals, and there are innumerable other ways in which the conduct of states may violate the rights of individuals or corporations. As the ICJ observed in 2007, in connection with a claim advanced by the Republic of Guinea on behalf of one of its nationals against the Democratic Republic of Congo: "Owing to the substantive development of international law over recent decades in respect of the rights it accords to individuals, the scope *ratione materiae* of diplomatic protection, originally limited to alleged violations of the minimum standard of treatment of aliens, has subsequently widened to include, *inter alia*, internationally guaranteed human rights."[16]

The forms of protection which may be so extended range from informal state-to-state contact in an effort to resolve the matter amicably, to more formal diplomatic representations asserting injury and requiring redress, and ultimately to "espousal" and formal assertion of the claim in some international forum with jurisdiction to resolve the matter.

---

15   North American Free Trade Agreement Between the Government of Canada, the Government of Mexico and the Government of the United States, 17 December 1992, Can TS 1994 No 2, in force 1 January 1994.

16   *Ahmadou Sadio Diallo (Republic of Guinea v Democratic Republic of the Congo)*, Preliminary Objections, Judgment, [2007] 2 ICJ Rep 582 at para 39.

It is the latter process—the espousal of the claim of an individual or a corporation by a state—that is our focus here.

LAW IN CONTEXT

An Obligation to Espouse?

Is a state *obligated* to extend diplomatic protection to one of its nationals? Not as a matter of international law. It is true that in 1758, Emmerich de Vattel claimed, in his treatise *The Law of Nations*, that "whoever uses a citizen ill indirectly offends the State, which is *bound to protect this citizen*."[17] However, more contemporary authorities reject this view. For example, in *Barcelona Traction*, the International Court of Justice noted that "[t]he State must be viewed as the sole judge to decide whether its protection will be granted, to what extent it is granted, and when it will cease. It retains in this respect a discretionary power the exercise of which may be determined by considerations of a political or other nature, unrelated to the particular case."[18] The Court did, however, recognize that the discretionary nature of the right to exercise diplomatic protection does not prevent the state from committing itself to its nationals to exercise such a right, and a few Eastern European states have enacted domestic laws recognizing their nationals' right to receive diplomatic protection from their governments.[19]

In 2009, a young Canadian national being held in an American military detention facility in Guantanamo Bay, Cuba, succeeded in convincing a Canadian trial judge, and then the majority of a Canadian Federal Court of Appeal panel, to order the Government of Canada to request his immediate repatriation from the United States on the basis of a breach of the *Canadian Charter of Rights and Freedoms*: see *Khadr v Canada (Prime Minister)*, 2009 FC 405, [2010] 1 FCR 34 and *Canada (Prime Minister) v Khadr*, 2009 FCA 246, [2010] 1 FCR 73. However, on further appeal, the Supreme Court of Canada modified the order, confirming that the *Charter* had been breached, but allowing the Canadian government a measure of discretion in deciding how best to remedy that breach: *Canada (Prime Minister) v Khadr*, 2010 SCC 3, [2010] 1 SCR 44.

Consider the following early case discussing the fundamental transformation in the nature of a claim that takes place when a state chooses to espouse it:

---

17 Emmerich de Vattel, *Law of Nations* (Philadelphia: T & JW Johnson, 1833) at 161 [emphasis added].
18 *Barcelona Traction, Light and Power Company Limited (Belgium v Spain)*, [1970] ICJ Rep 3 at para 79 [*Barcelona Traction*]. See also Richard B Lillich, *The Human Rights of Aliens in Contemporary International Law* (Manchester: Manchester University Press, 1984) at 9 ("The doctrine as it actually developed was that the State was entitled to protect its citizens abroad if it so chose. However, it was under no duty, domestically or internationally, to do so.")
19 *Barcelona Traction, ibid* at para 78 ("The municipal legislator may lay upon the State an obligation to protect its citizens abroad and may also confer upon the national a right to demand the performance of that obligation, and clothe the right with corresponding sanction.")

Case of the Mavrommatis Palestine Concessions (Greece v United Kingdom) (1924), PCIJ (Ser A) No 2 at 11–12

. . . [Greece] is asserting its own rights by claiming from His Britannic Majesty's Government an indemnity on the ground that M. Mavrommatis, one of its subjects, has been treated by the Palestine or British authorities in a manner incompatible with certain international obligations which they were bound to observe.

In the case of the Mavrommatis concessions it is true that the dispute was at first between a private person and a State—i.e., between M. Mavrommatis and Great Britain. Subsequently, the Greek Government took up the case. The dispute then entered upon a new phase; it entered the domain of international law, and became a dispute between two States . . . .

. . . It is an elementary principle of international law that a State is entitled to protect its subjects, when injured by acts contrary to international law committed by another State, from whom they have been unable to obtain satisfaction through the ordinary channels. By taking up the case of one of its subjects and by resorting to diplomatic action or international judicial proceedings on his behalf, a State is in reality asserting its own rights—its right to ensure, in the person of its subjects, respect for the rules of international law.

The question, therefore, whether the present dispute originates in an injury to a private interest, which in point of fact is the case in many international disputes, is irrelevant from this standpoint. Once a State has taken up a case on behalf of one of its subjects before an international tribunal, in the eyes of the latter the State is sole claimant. The fact that Great Britain and Greece are the opposing Parties to the dispute arising out of the Mavrommatis concessions is sufficient to make it a dispute between two States . . . .

The notion that espousal of a claim is tantamount to an assertion by the espousing state of "its own rights" has been the subject of criticism. But the idea that such espousal transforms the claim into an international one in respect of which the espousing state has standing has not. Espousing the claim of an individual or corporation effectively amounts to a state asserting standing in circumstances in which the indirect interests of the state itself are engaged. It is not surprising, therefore, that a state's right to do so is often hotly contested by the state against which the claim is brought. The result is a set of customary international rules limiting the circumstances in which states may validly espouse such claims. While the ILC Articles on State Responsibility do not attempt to codify these rules,[20] the International Law Commission adopted, in 2006, a set of Draft Articles on Diplomatic Protection with commentaries.[21] It has also recommended the elaboration of a convention on the basis of these Draft Articles.[22] Consider their key provisions:

---

20   Article 44 of the ILC Articles on State Responsibility is non-committal on the topic, providing merely that: "The responsibility of a State may not be invoked if: (a) the claim is not brought in accordance with any applicable rule relating to the nationality of claims; (b) the claim is one to which the rule of exhaustion of local remedies applies and any available and effective local remedy has not been exhausted."

21   Reprinted in *Report of the International Law Commission*, UN GAOR, 61st Sess, Supp No 10 at c IV, para 49, UN Doc A/61/10 (2006).

22   See further *Diplomatic protection*, GA Res 65/27, UN Doc A/RES/65/27, reprinted in UN GAOR, 65th Sess, Supp No 49, vol I at 620–21, UN Doc A/65/49 (2010), commending once again the articles on diplomatic protection to states and deciding to further examine in 2013 the question whether to elaborate

ILC Draft Articles on Diplomatic Protection, 2006

Article 1
Definition and scope
For the purposes of the present draft articles, diplomatic protection consists of the invocation by a State, through diplomatic action or other means of peaceful settlement, of the responsibility of another State for an injury caused by an internationally wrongful act of that State to a natural or legal person that is a national of the former State with a view to the implementation of such responsibility . . . .

Article 3
Protection by the State of nationality
1. The State entitled to exercise diplomatic protection is the State of nationality.

2. Notwithstanding paragraph 1, diplomatic protection may be exercised by a State in respect of a person that is not its national in accordance with draft article 8 . . . .

Article 5
Continuous nationality of a natural person
1. A State is entitled to exercise diplomatic protection in respect of a person who was a national of that State continuously from the date of injury to the date of the official presentation of the claim. Continuity is presumed if that nationality existed at both these dates.

2. Notwithstanding paragraph 1, a State may exercise diplomatic protection in respect of a person who is its national at the date of the official presentation of the claim but was not a national at the date of injury, provided that the person had the nationality of a predecessor State or lost his or her previous nationality and acquired, for a reason unrelated to the bringing of the claim, the nationality of the former State in a manner not inconsistent with international law.

3. Diplomatic protection shall not be exercised by the present State of nationality in respect of a person against a former State of nationality of that person for an injury caused when that person was a national of the former State of nationality and not of the present State of nationality.

4. A State is no longer entitled to exercise diplomatic protection in respect of a person who acquires the nationality of the State against which the claim is brought after the date of the official presentation of the claim.

Article 6
Multiple nationality and claim against a third State
1. Any State of which a dual or multiple national is a national may exercise diplomatic protection in respect of that national against a State of which that person is not a national.

2. Two or more States of nationality may jointly exercise diplomatic protection in respect of a dual or multiple national.

---

a convention on the basis of the articles. For criticism of the ILC's work, see Allain Pellet, "The Second Death of Euripide Mavrommatis? Notes on the International Law Commission's Draft Articles on Diplomatic Protection" (2008) 7 Law and Practice of International Courts and Tribunals 33.

Article 7

Multiple nationality and claim against a State of nationality

A State of nationality may not exercise diplomatic protection in respect of a person against a State of which that person is also a national unless the nationality of the former State is predominant, both at the date of injury and at the date of the official presentation of the claim.

Article 8

Stateless persons and refugees

1. A State may exercise diplomatic protection in respect of a stateless person who, at the date of injury and at the date of the official presentation of the claim, is lawfully and habitually resident in that State.

2. A State may exercise diplomatic protection in respect of a person who is recognized as a refugee by that State, in accordance with internationally accepted standards, when that person, at the date of injury and at the date of the official presentation of the claim, is lawfully and habitually resident in that State.

3. Paragraph 2 does not apply in respect of an injury caused by an internationally wrongful act of the State of nationality of the refugee . . . .

Article 10

Continuous nationality of a corporation

1. A State is entitled to exercise diplomatic protection in respect of a corporation that was a national of that State, or its predecessor State, continuously from the date of injury to the date of the official presentation of the claim. Continuity is presumed if that nationality existed at both these dates.

2. A State is no longer entitled to exercise diplomatic protection in respect of a corporation that acquires the nationality of the State against which the claim is brought after the presentation of the claim . . . .

Article 12

Direct injury to shareholders

To the extent that an internationally wrongful act of a State causes direct injury to the rights of shareholders as such, as distinct from those of the corporation itself, the State of nationality of any such shareholders is entitled to exercise diplomatic protection in respect of its nationals . . . .

Article 14

Exhaustion of local remedies

1. A State may not present an international claim in respect of an injury to a national or other person referred to in draft article 8 before the injured person has, subject to draft article 15, exhausted all local remedies.

2. "Local remedies" means legal remedies which are open to an injured person before the judicial or administrative courts or bodies, whether ordinary or special, of the State alleged to be responsible for causing the injury . . . .

Article 15

Exceptions to the local remedies rule

Local remedies do not need to be exhausted where:

(a) There are no reasonably available local remedies to provide effective redress, or the local remedies provide no reasonable possibility of such redress;

(b) There is undue delay in the remedial process which is attributable to the State alleged to be responsible;

(c) There was no relevant connection between the injured person and the State alleged to be responsible at the date of injury;

(d) The injured person is manifestly precluded from pursuing local remedies; or

(e) The State alleged to be responsible has waived the requirement that local remedies be exhausted.

We have already considered, in discussing the nationality principle of jurisdiction in Chapter 7, the international rules governing the nationality of individuals and corporations. In light of the rules governing the espousal of claims, consider again the importance of the limitations placed by customary international law on the obligation of states to recognize grants of nationality by other states.

On the issue of one state of nationality espousing a claim against another state of nationality, note that Article 4 of the 1930 Hague Convention on the Conflict of Nationality Laws[23] provides that: "A State may not afford diplomatic protection to one of its nationals against a State whose nationality such person also possesses." Article 4 is of incidental relevance in its own right, as only a handful of states have ratified the Hague Convention. However, the provision was long considered to reflect customary international law. If customary international law is so exacting, it represents an uncomfortable exception to the general ability of a state to espouse the claims of its nationals.

Canada was, at one time, a party to the Hague Convention on Conflict of Nationality Laws. However, it withdrew from the treaty in 1996, reportedly due to dissatisfaction with Article 4.

In 2003, Canada's foreign policy establishment was rocked by the detention, torture, and murder of a Canadian citizen by a foreign government. On 23 June 2003, Zahra (Ziba) Kazemi, a 54-year-old photojournalist with dual Canadian-Iranian nationality, was arrested by Iranian authorities in Iran. Branded a spy after photographing a local prison, Ms. Kazemi was severely beaten by her interrogators and suffered a brain haemorrhage as a result. She died from her injuries in Iran in early July 2003. In response to the resulting protests from Canada, Iran asserted that, as Ms. Kazemi was born in Iran and remained, under Iranian law, an Iranian national, Canada had no standing to intervene in the affair. Ms. Kazemi's son Stephen (Salman) Hashemi has pursued a civil action against Iran in the Canadian courts, but he has been unsuccessful on state immunity grounds.[24]

---

23 Convention on Certain Questions relating to the Conflict of Nationality Laws, 12 April 1930, 179 LNTS 89, Can TS 1937 No 7, (1930) 24 Am J Int'l L Supp 192, in force 1 July 1937, denunciated by Canada 15 May 1996.

24 *Islamic Republic of Iran v Hashemi*, 2012 QCCA 1449.

The Kazemi case raises the question: Can a government adequately protect its citizens who are also dual nationals of other countries?[25] Some observers have concluded that, as a practical, diplomatic matter, the answer to this question is probably "no," and that dual nationals from all but the most powerful countries are without effective protection while visiting the states from which they may have emigrated years before. The legal response is, however, apparently evolving, as indicated by the International Law Commission's adoption of Article 7 of the ILC Draft Articles on Diplomatic Protection. In justifying Draft Article 7, then Special Rapporteur Professor John Dugard urged that:

> The weight of authority supports the dominant nationality principle in matters involving dual nationals. Moreover, both judicial decisions and scholarly writings have provided clarity on the factors to be considered in making such a determination. The principle contained in article [7] therefore reflects the current position in customary international law and is consistent with developments in international human rights law, which accords legal protection to individuals even against the State of which they are nationals.[26]

The requirement that the individual or corporation "exhaust local remedies" before their claim may be espoused is relatively easy to state in theory but very difficult to apply in practice, as suggested by the broad language used to describe exceptions to the rule in Draft Article 15. Consider the following cases which illustrate some of the practical difficulties in applying the exhaustion of local remedies rule:

The Ambatielos Claim (Greece v United Kingdom) (1956), 12 RIAA 83 at 118–20

[Ambatielos entered into contracts with the United Kingdom with respect to the supply of ships. When Ambatielos's action against the United Kingdom for breach of contract failed in the English courts, Greece espoused his claim and the dispute was submitted to a commission of arbitration.]

. . . In countering the claim of the Greek Government the Government of the United Kingdom relies on the non-exhaustion by Mr. Ambatielos of the legal remedies which English law put at his disposal . . . .

The rule thus invoked by the United Kingdom Government is well established in international law. Nor is its existence contested by the Greek Government. It means that the State against which an international action is brought for injuries suffered by private individuals has the right to resist such an action if the persons alleged to have been injured have not first exhausted all the remedies available to them under the municipal law of that State. The defendant State has the right to demand that full advantage shall have been taken of all local remedies before the matters in dispute are taken up on the international level by the State of which the persons alleged to have been injured are nationals.

In order to contend successfully that international proceedings are inadmissible, the defendant State must prove the existence, in its system of internal law, of remedies which

25 See further Craig Forcese, "The Capacity to Protect: Diplomatic Protection of Dual Nationals in the 'War on Terror'" (2006) 17 EJIL 369–94.

26 C John R Dugard, Special Rapporteur, *First Report on Diplomatic Protection*, UN Doc A/CN.4/506 and Add 1, reprinted in [2000] 2 ILC Ybk 205–46 at para 160.

have not been used. The views expressed by writers and in judicial precedents, however, coincide in that the existence of remedies which are obviously ineffective is held not to be sufficient to justify the application of the rule. Remedies which could not rectify the situation cannot be relied upon by the defendant State as precluding an international action.

The Greek Government contends that in the present case the remedies which English law offered to Mr. Ambatielos were ineffective and that, accordingly, the rule is not applicable.

The ineffectiveness of local remedies may result clearly from the municipal law itself. That is the case, for example, when a Court of Appeal is not competent to reconsider the judgment given by a Court of first instance on matters of fact, and when, failing such reconsideration, no redress can be obtained. In such a case there is no doubt that local remedies are ineffective.

Furthermore, however, it is generally considered that the ineffectiveness of available remedies, without being legally certain, may also result from circumstances which do not permit any hope of redress to be placed in the use of those remedies. But in a case of that kind it is essential that such remedies, if they had been resorted to, would have proved to be *obviously futile*.

Here a question of considerable practical importance arises.

If the rule of exhaustion of local remedies is relied upon against the action of the claimant State, what is the test to be applied by an international tribunal for the purpose of determining the applicability of the rule? As the arbitrator ruled in the *Finnish Vessels* Case of 9th May, 1934, the only possible test is to assume the truth of the facts on which the claimant State bases its claim. As will be shown below, any departure from this assumption would lead to inadmissible results . . . .

In the *Ambatielos Case*, failure to use certain means of appeal is . . . relied upon by the United Kingdom Government, but reliance is also placed on the failure of Mr. Ambatielos to adduce before Mr. Justice Hill evidence which it is now said would have been essential to establish his claims. There is no doubt that the exhaustion of local remedies requires the use of the means or procedure which are essential to redress the situation complained of by the person who is alleged to have been injured . . . .

The rule requires that "local remedies" shall have been exhausted before an international action can be brought. These "local remedies" include not only reference to the courts and tribunals, but also the use of the procedural facilities which municipal law makes available to litigants before such courts and tribunals. It is the whole system of legal protection, as provided by municipal law, which must have been put to the test before a State, as the protector of its nationals, can prosecute the claim on the international plane . . . .

It is clear, however, that it cannot be strained too far. Taken literally, it would imply that the fact of having neglected to make use of some means of procedure—even one which is not important to the defence of the action—would suffice to allow a defendant State to claim that local remedies have not exhausted, and that, therefore, an international action cannot be brought. This would confer on the rule of the prior exhaustion of local remedies a scope which is unacceptable.

In the view of the Commission the non-utilisation of certain means of procedure can be accepted as constituting a gap in the exhaustion of local remedies only if the use of these means of procedure were essential to establish the claimant's case before the municipal courts.

It is on the assumption that the statements of the claimant Government are correct that the international tribunal will be able to say whether the non-utilisation of this or that method of procedure makes it possible to raise against a claim a plea of inadmissibility on the ground of non-exhaustion of local remedies . . . .

[The Commission ruled that Ambatielos had failed to exhaust local remedies by failing to call key witnesses during the trial of his action in the English courts, and in thereafter failing to appeal the negative result obtained at trial in the English appellate courts.]

Elettronica Sicula SpA (ELSI) (United States of America v Italy), Judgment, [1989] ICJ Rep 15

[ELSI was an Italian corporation whose shares were wholly owned by Raytheon and Machlett, two American corporations. Raytheon and Machlett had intended to liquidate ELSI due to financial difficulties, but the Italian government stepped in and "requisitioned" (expropriated) ELSI before they could do so. Pursuant to a Treaty of Friendship, Commerce and Navigation between Italy and the United States (the "FCN" treaty), the United States claimed compensation on behalf of Raytheon and Machlett against Italy, given that the expropriation had dramatically reduced the return that the two corporations would have received had ELSI been liquidated as planned. Although Raytheon and Machlett had pursued litigation in respect of Italy's actions in the Italian courts, Italy objected to the United States' espousal of their claim on the basis that they had failed to exhaust local remedies.]

58. [I]t is . . . apparent that the substance of the claim brought to the adjudication of the Italian courts is essentially the claim which the United States now brings before this Chamber. The arguments were different, because the municipal court was applying Italian law, whereas this Chamber applies international law; and, of course, the parties were different. Yet it would seem that the municipal courts had been fully seized of the matter which is the substance of the Applicant's claim before the Chamber. For both claims turn on the allegation that the requisition, by frustrating the orderly liquidation, triggered the bankruptcy, and so caused the alleged losses.

59. With such a deal of litigation in the municipal courts about what is in substance the claim now before the Chamber, it was for Italy to demonstrate that there was nevertheless some local remedy that had not been tried; or at least, not exhausted. This burden Italy never sought to deny. It contended that it was possible for the matter to have been brought before the municipal courts, citing the provisions of the treaties themselves, and alleging their violation. This was never done. In the actions brought before the Court of Palermo, and subsequently the Court of Appeal of Palermo, and the Court of Cassation, the FCN Treaty and its Supplementary Agreement were never mentioned. This is not surprising, for, as Italy recognizes, the way in which the matter was pleaded before the courts of Palermo was not for Raytheon and Machlett to decide but for the trustee. Furthermore, the local remedies rule does not, indeed cannot, require that a claim be presented to the municipal courts in a form, and with arguments, suited to an international tribunal, ap-

plying different law to different parties: for an international claim to be admissible, it is sufficient if the essence of the claim has been brought before the competent tribunals and pursued as far as permitted by local law and procedures, and without success.

60. The question, therefore, reduces itself to this: ought Raytheon and Machlett, suing in their own right, as United States corporations allegedly injured by the requisition of property of an Italian company whose shares they held, have brought an action in the Italian courts, within the general limitation-period (five years), alleging violation of certain provisions of the FCN Treaty between Italy and the United States; this mindful of the fact that the very question of the consequences of the requisition was already in issue in the action brought by its trustee in bankruptcy, and that any damages that might there be awarded would pass into the pool of realized assets, for an appropriate part of which Raytheon and Machlett had the right to claim as creditors?

61. Italy contends that Raytheon and Machlett could have based such an action before the Italian courts on Article 2043 of the Italian Civil Code, which provides that "Any act committed either wilfully or through fault which causes wrongful damages to another person implies that the wrongdoer is under an obligation to pay compensation for those damages." According to Italy, this provision is frequently invoked by individuals against the Italian State, and substantial sums have been awarded to claimants where appropriate. If Raytheon and Machlett suffered damage caused by violations by Italian public authorities of the FCN Treaty and the Supplementary Agreement, an Italian court would, it was contended, have been bound to conclude that the relevant acts of the public authorities were wrongful acts for the purposes of Article 2043. It is common ground between the Parties that implementing legislation (*"ordini di esecuzione"*) was enacted (Law No. 385 of 15 June 1949 and Law No. 910 of 1 August 1960), to give effect in Italy to the FCN Treaty and Supplementary Agreement, but that their provisions cannot be invoked in protection of individual rights before the Italian courts unless those provisions are regarded by the courts as self-executing. In order to show that the relevant provisions would be so regarded, decisions of the Court of Cassation have been cited by Italy in which provisions of the FCN Treaty (not the provisions relied on in the present case) have been applied for the benefit of United States nationals who have invoked them before Italian courts, and a provision of a treaty between Italy and the Federal Republic of Germany, said to be comparable with Article V of the FCN Treaty, was given effect.

62. However, those decisions were not based on Article 2043 of the Italian Civil Code; and the treaty provisions applied were given effect in conjunction with municipal legislation or the provisions of other treaties, through the mechanism of a most-favoured-nation provision. In none of the cases cited was the FCN Treaty provision relied on to establish the wrongfulness of conduct of Italian public officials. When in 1971 Raytheon consulted two Italian jurists on the question of local remedies for the purposes of a diplomatic claim, it apparently did not occur to either of them to refer even as a possibility to action under Article 2043 in conjunction with the FCN Treaty. It thus appears to the Chamber to be impossible to deduce, from the recent jurisprudence cited, what the attitude of the Italian courts would have been had Raytheon and Machlett brought an action, some 20 years ago, in reliance on Article 2043 of the Civil Code in conjunction with the provisions of

the FCN Treaty and the Supplementary Agreement. Where the determination of a question of municipal law is essential to the Court's decision in a case, the Court will have to weigh the jurisprudence of the municipal courts, and "If this is uncertain or divided, it will rest with the Court to select the interpretation which it considers most in conformity with the law" (*Brazilian Loans, P.C.I.J., Series A, Nos. 20/21*, p. 124). In the present case, however, it was for Italy to show, as a matter of fact, the existence of a remedy which was open to the United States stockholders and which they failed to employ. The Chamber does not consider that Italy has discharged that burden.

63. It is never easy to decide, in a case where there has in fact been much resort to the municipal courts, whether local remedies have truly been "exhausted." But in this case Italy has not been able to satisfy the Chamber that there clearly remained some remedy which Raytheon and Machlett, independently of ELSI, and of ELSI's trustee in bankruptcy, ought to have pursued and exhausted. Accordingly, the Chamber will now proceed to consider the merits of the case . . . .

CHAPTER 13

ECONOMIC SANCTIONS

In this chapter, we discuss economic sanctions as a tool used by states, acting either multilaterally or alone, for responding to violations of international law.

A. MANDATORY SANCTIONS IMPOSED BY THE UN SECURITY COUNCIL

Recall that Article 41 of the Charter of the United Nations[1] provides that:

> The Security Council may decide what measures not involving the use of armed force are to be employed to give effect to its decisions, and it may call upon the Members of the United Nations to apply such measures. These may include complete or partial interruption of economic relations and of rail, sea, air, postal, telegraphic, radio, and other means of communication, and the severance of diplomatic relations.

The measures short of force authorized by the UN Security Council pursuant to Article 41 have typically focused on the "complete or partial interruption of economic relations," or, in more common parlance, economic "sanctions." Economic sanctions usually impose constraints on the exchange of goods and services with, and on investment in, a state considered by the Security Council to be in violation of its international obligations in a manner that poses a threat to international peace and security. Such sanctions may be very broad in nature, prohibiting most forms of economic exchange with the target state, or may be more tailored in scope, limiting, for example, trade in arms or commodities suspected of fuelling local or regional conflict. When adopted as a decision pursuant to Article 41, respect for such sanctions is mandatory for all UN member states by operation of Articles 25 and 103 of the UN Charter.

Consider the following summary of Canadian practice with respect to the implementation of mandatory sanctions imposed by the Security Council:

Alan H Kessel, "Canadian Practice in International Law at the Department of Foreign Affairs and International Trade in 2008–9" (2009) 47 Can YB Int'l Law 411 at 429–30

. . . As a member of the UN, Canada has the international legal obligation to implement into domestic law the binding provisions of United Nations Security Council Resolutions [UNSCRs]. In some cases, no action is required as the substance of the binding provision has already been implemented into Canadian law (i.e. in *Export and Import Permits Act ("EIPA")*, *Criminal Code*, *Immigration and Refugee Protection Act ("IRPA")* etc.). For example, Canada need not take further steps to implement the travel bans required by

---

1   26 June 1945, Can TS 1945 No 7, in force 24 October 1945 [UN Charter].

certain UNSCRs as they are already assured by provisions of the *IRPA*. However, if the terms of the UNSCR create a binding obligation upon Canada that is not already implemented in Canadian domestic law, it has an international obligation to act. It is in these cases it turns to the *UN Act* [*United Nations Act*, RSC 1985, c U-2].

Article 2 of the *UN Act* states:

> When, in pursuance of Article 41 of the Charter of the United Nations, set out in the schedule, the Security Council of the United Nations decides on a measure to be employed to give effect to any of its decisions and calls on Canada to apply the measure, the Governor in Council may make such orders and regulations as appear to him to be necessary or expedient for enabling the measures to be effectively applied.
>
> . . .

The *UN Act* is limited to these circumstances and cannot be used to implement controls in excess of what the UNSC [UN Security Council] has mandated.

As there is no clear external authority to interpret the UNSC resolutions, Member States must determine themselves whether the provisions are "binding" and thus require domestic implementation. This is generally done by analyzing the language of the provision itself:

> The question as to whether the Council has imposed an obligation binding under articles 24 and 25 should be determined from the Council's actual language in any given situation [and]. . . in most cases, the Council does use relatively clear language in its operative paragraphs. For example, it can be clearly established that by using "urges" and "invites," as opposed to "decides," the paragraph is intended to be exhortatory and not binding. [Security Council Report—Special Research Report, *Security Council Action Under Chapter VII*, 2008, No 1, 23 June 2008, at 12.]

The language "decides" clearly indicates that the UNSC deemed this provision to be binding . . . .

[Reprinted with permission of the Publisher from Canadian Yearbook of International Law, Volume 47 edited by Don McRae © University of British Columbia Press 2009. All rights reserved by the Publisher.]

As discussed in Chapter 3, the effective functioning of the Security Council suffers from significant political and legal obstacles. Recall that decisions of the Council on non-procedural matters require the affirmative support of a "super-majority" of nine out of fifteen Council members. Moreover, each of the five permanent members, wielding the veto provided by Article 27(3) of the UN Charter, is in a position to derail Security Council action.

As a consequence, the Security Council imposed only two mandatory non-military sanctions regimes prior to the collapse of the eastern bloc and the Gulf War in 1990: the Southern Rhodesia sanctions regime initiated in 1966,[2] and the South Africa arms embargo beginning in 1977.[3] With the end of the Cold War, Security Council resolutions imposing such sanctions have become more commonplace.[4] However, notwithstanding the un-

---

2   SC Resolution 232 (1966), adopted 16 December 1966, UN Doc S/RES/232 (1966) and SC Resolution 253 (1968), adopted 29 May 1968, UN Doc S/RES/253 (1968).
3   SC Resolution 418 (1977), adopted 4 November 1977, UN Doc S/RES/418 (1977).
4   During the 1990s, UN measures of one sort or another were applied against various countries, including: **Iraq**: SC Resolution 661 (1990); the **former Yugoslavia**: SC Resolutions 713 (1992), 757 (1992), 820 (1993),

precedented level of cooperation exhibited during the 1990s and early 2000s,[5] the Council remains vulnerable to changing political fortunes. Council members, for instance, are clearly divided on the best way to approach Iran's possible intent to build a nuclear weapon, although the Council has imposed increasingly strict economic sanctions on that country since 2006.[6] Consider this Government of Canada summary of those UN sanctions:

- a prohibition on the export to Iran of certain items, materials, equipment, goods and technology which could contribute to Iran's uranium enrichment-related, reprocessing or heavy water-related activities, or to the development of nuclear weapon delivery systems . . . ;
- a prohibition on the provision to any person in Iran of technical assistance, financial services, brokerage or other services related to the supply, sale, transfer, manufacture or use of any of the products subject to the export ban;
- a prohibition on making available to any person in Iran any property, financial assistance or investment, related to the supply, sale, transfer, manufacture or use of any of the products subject to the export ban;
- a prohibition on making property or financial services available to Iran for the purpose of investing in specified nuclear-related activities;
- a prohibition on providing any technology in respect of any activity related to ballistic missiles capable of delivering nuclear weapons; and;
- a prohibition on the export to Iran of any battle tanks, armored combat vehicles, large caliber artillery systems, combat aircrafts, attack helicopters, warships, missiles or missile systems;
- a prohibition on the import from Iran of arms and related material and items related to proliferation-sensitive nuclear activities or to the development of nuclear weapon delivery systems . . . ;
- an assets freeze against persons and entities engaged in Iran's uranium enrichment-related, reprocessing or heavy water-related activities, or in the development of nuclear weapon delivery systems, who have been listed by the Security Council or the Committee established pursuant to paragraph 18 of resolution 1737 (2006) ("the 1737 Committee");
- a travel ban against persons listed by the Security Council or the 1737 Committee as being involved in Iran's nuclear program; and

---

942 (1994), and 1160 (1998); **Somalia**: SC Resolution 733 (1992); **Libya**: SC Resolutions 748 (1992) and 883 (1993); **Liberia**: SC Resolution 788 (1992); **Haiti**: SC Resolutions 841 (1993) and 917 (1996); **Angola**: SC Resolutions 864 (1993), 1127 (1997), and 1173 (1998); **Rwanda**: SC Resolution 918 (1994); **Sierra Leone**: SC Resolution 1132 (1997); **Sudan**: SC Resolution 1054 (1996); and **Afghanistan**: SC Resolution 1267 (1999). See further, the helpful summaries of UN sanctions regimes in Jeremy Matam Farrall, *United Nations Sanctions and the Rule of Law* (Cambridge: Cambridge University Press, 2007), Appendix 2.

5   See **Eritrea and Ethiopia**: SC Resolution 1298 (2000); **Liberia**: SC Resolution 1343 (2001); **Democratic Republic of the Congo**: SC Resolutions 1493 (2003) and 1533 (2004); **Liberia**: SC Resolution 1521 (2003); **Sudan**: SC Resolutions 1556 (2004) and 1591 (2005); **Côte d'Ivoire**: SC Resolution 1572 (2004); and **North Korea**: SC Resolution 1718 (2006), as modified by Resolution 1879 (2009), and SC Resolution 2094 (2013).

6   See SC Resolution 1737 (2006), adopted 23 December 2006, UN Doc S/RES/1737 (2006). See also SC Resolutions 1747 (2007), 1803 (2008), and 1929 (2010).

- a prohibition against claims by Iran or designated persons in relation to any trans-actions prevented by reason of the sanctions imposed against Iran.[7]

However, there have been other situations where the Security Council has failed to act, prompting states to impose sanctions unilaterally, without Security Council author-ization, or plurilaterally, along with other like-minded states (sometimes in response to a call for sanctions from a regional body). Some states may also wish to go further than the Security Council, such as the Canadian sanctions against Iran, which are in excess of what is required by the Security Council. As described by the Canadian prime minister: "[Canadian] sanctions bar dealings with designated individuals and entities involved in nuclear or WMD proliferation, including key members of the Islamic Revolutionary Guard Corps. They ban new investments in Iran's oil and gas sector and the export of goods to Iran that could contribute to nuclear proliferation. They also prohibit Iranian financial institutions from establishing a presence in Canada and vice versa."[8]

We examine legal issues related to unilateral (and plurilateral) sanctions in the next two sections: first, by discussing the rules of international law that may affect a state's ability to impose such sanctions, and second, by surveying the Canadian approach to economic sanctions not mandated by the Security Council under Chapter VII of the UN Charter.

B. ECONOMIC SANCTIONS OTHER THAN THOSE IMPOSED BY THE UN SECURITY COUNCIL

1) International Legal Considerations

There is no rule of customary international law obliging states to trade with one an-other.[9] Thus, economic sanctions generally constitute a form of "retorsion" rather than a countermeasure (or, as it is sometimes called, a reprisal). As noted in Chapter 12 on state responsibility, a countermeasure is a *prima facie* internationally wrongful action that is nevertheless justified as a response to the failure of the target state to conform to its international legal obligations. Retorsion, by contrast, is a response that would not, in any case, be a violation of international law. In other words, as a matter of general cus-tomary international law, economic sanctions imposed by states need not be limited to responses to internationally wrongful acts of other states (although that is, in practice, the context in which they are most commonly invoked).

This situation has, however, been substantially modified by the General Agreement on Tariffs and Trade (GATT)[10] and the establishment of the World Trade Organization

---

7 Government of Canada, Department of Foreign Affairs and International Trade, *Canadian Economic Sanctions: Iran*, online: www.international.gc.ca/sanctions/iran.aspx?lang=eng&menu_id=60&view=d.

8 Government of Canada, *Statement of the Prime Minister of Canada on the implementation of further sanctions against Iran through the Special Economic Measures Act* (26 July 2010), online: www.pm.gc.ca/eng/media.asp?category=3&featureId=6&pageId=49&id=3553.

9 Royal Gardner, "Taking the Principle of Just Compensation Abroad: Private Property Rights, National Sovereignty, and the Cost of Environmental Protection" (1997) 65 U Cin L Rev 539 at 581.

10 General Agreement on Tariffs and Trade 1994, Annex 1A to the Marrakesh Agreement establishing the World Trade Organization, 15 April 1994, 1867 UNTS 154, (1994) 33 ILM 1144, in force 1 January 1995 [GATT]. The GATT incorporates by reference the provisions of the General Agreement on Tariffs and Trade, 30 October 1947, 55 UNTS 187, Can TS 1948 No 31, in force 1 January 1948.

(WTO),[11] at least insofar as trade in goods between WTO member states is concerned. Article XI, paragraph 1, of the GATT prohibits any restrictions other than duties, taxes, or other permissible charges on goods imported from, or exported to, any other member state:

> No prohibitions or restrictions other than duties, taxes or other charges, whether made effective through quotas, import or export licences or other measures, shall be instituted or maintained by any contracting party on the importation of any product of the territory of any other contracting party or on the exportation or sale for export of any product destined for the territory of any other contracting party.

The exceptions to this rule, set out in Article XI(2), do not include reference to any consideration of relevance in the application of economic sanctions. In addition, although there is not universal agreement on this issue, the general exemptions to the GATT, established in Article XX, are narrowly phrased and are likely of limited utility in defending sanctions imposed, for instance, on human rights grounds:

> Subject to the requirement that such measures are not applied in a manner which would constitute a means of arbitrary or unjustifiable discrimination between countries where the same conditions prevail, or a disguised restriction on international trade, nothing in this Agreement shall be construed to prevent the adoption or enforcement by any contracting party of measures:
>
> (a) necessary to protect public morals;
>
> (b) necessary to protect human, animal or plant life or health;
>
> (c) relating to the importations or exportations of gold or silver;
>
> (d) necessary to secure compliance with laws or regulations which are not inconsistent with the provisions of this Agreement, including those relating to customs enforcement, the enforcement of monopolies . . . , the protection of patents, trade marks and copyrights, and the prevention of deceptive practices;
>
> (e) relating to the products of prison labour;
>
> (f) imposed for the protection of national treasures of artistic, historic or archaeological value;
>
> (g) relating to the conservation of exhaustible natural resources if such measures are made effective in conjunction with restrictions on domestic production or consumption;
>
> (h) undertaken in pursuance of obligations under any intergovernmental commodity agreement . . . ;
>
> (i) involving restrictions on exports of domestic materials necessary to ensure essential quantities of such materials to a domestic processing industry during periods when the domestic price of such materials is held below the world price as part of a governmental stabilization plan . . . ;
>
> (j) essential to the acquisition or distribution of products in general or local short supply . . . .

Article XXI includes other general exemptions. For instance, it is clear that the GATT/WTO does not impede states in responding to a UN Security Council resolution requiring

---

11 Marrakesh Agreement establishing the World Trade Organization, above note 10.

the imposition of sanctions. Further, under Article XXI, unilateral sanctions might well be justified on national security grounds. Consider the language of Article XXI:

> Nothing in this Agreement shall be construed
>
> (a) to require any contracting party to furnish any information the disclosure of which it considers contrary to its essential security interests; or
>
> (b) to prevent any contracting party from taking any action which it considers necessary for the protection of its essential security interests
>
> (i) relating to fissionable materials or the materials from which they are derived;
>
> (ii) relating to the traffic in arms, ammunition and implements of war and to such traffic in other goods and materials as is carried on directly or indirectly for the purpose of supplying a military establishment;
>
> (iii) taken in time of war or other emergency in international relations; or
>
> (c) to prevent any contracting party from taking any action in pursuance of its obligations under the United Nations Charter for the maintenance of international peace and security.

Notably, interpretation of the national security provision has proven fairly elastic in the past.[12]

LAW IN CONTEXT

Sanctions and Foreign Policy Considerations

There is extensive literature on economic sanctions and their utility in influencing "rogue" regimes. Much of it has been critical of sanctions, suggesting that sanctions have been ineffective[13] and can often be counterproductive.[14] One study focusing on the utility of sanctions for middle powers argues that "sanctions are, on balance, a normatively bad policy

---

12   See Riyaz Dattu & John Boscariol, "GATT Article XXI, Helms-Burton and Continuing Abuse" (1997) 28 Can Business LJ 198.

13   For example, between 1914 and 1990, countries imposed (mostly unilateral) sanctions 115 times. These sanctions have been characterized as effective in 34 percent of the cases, with effectiveness in the post-1973 period being significantly lower than between 1914 and 1973. See Kimberly Ann Elliot, "Factors Affecting the Success of Sanctions" in David Cortright & George A Lopez, eds, *Economic Sanctions: Panacea or Peacebuilding in a Post-Cold War World?* (Boulder, CO: Westview Press, 1995) at 51.

14   A policy brief by Richard Haass of the Brookings Institution makes a number of observations on the effectiveness of US sanctions: First, "sanctions alone are unlikely to achieve desired results if the aims are large or time is short." Unilateral sanctions, in particular, are unlikely to be successful. In addition, "[s]anctions tend to be easier to introduce than to lift" and "[s]anctions fatigue tends to settle in over time and international compliance tends to diminish." Finally, "[s]anctions are blunt instruments that often produce unintended and undesirable consequences." In particular, "sanctions can have the perverse effect of bolstering authoritarian, statist societies. By creating scarcity, they enable governments to better control distribution of goods. The danger is both moral, in that innocents are affected, as well as practical, in that sanctions that harm the population at large can bring about undesired effects that include bolstering the regime, triggering large scale emigration, and retarding the emergence of a middle class and civil society." Richard N Haass, *Economic Sanctions: Too Much of a Bad Thing* (Washington, DC: Brookings Institution, 1998), online: www.brookings.edu/research/papers/1998/06/sanctions-haass.

instrument: not only are they generally ineffective in producing political change in the target nation, but they also are a violent, blunt, and gendered tool of statecraft."[15] Political scientist Kim Richard Nossal has described sanctions introduced by middle powers like Canada and Australia as "rain dances": measures satisfying domestic constituencies without having appreciable impact on the political behaviour of the sanctioned country. More than ineffective, say some commentators, sanctions have a discernable, negative impact on the most vulnerable populations in the target states, leaving the political elite untouched.

Responding to the collateral consequences of economic sanctions, the now abolished UN Sub-Commission on the Promotion and Protection of Human Rights, comprising human rights specialists from various regions, appealed to the now abolished Commission on Human Rights in 2000 to recommend "to all competent organs, bodies and agencies of the United Nations system that they observe and implement all relevant provisions of human rights and international humanitarian law" in their sanctioning activities.[16] Similarly, the Committee on Economic, Social and Cultural Rights, established by states parties to the International Covenant on Economic, Social and Cultural Rights,[17] has advised that sanctioning parties are obliged by virtue of their treaty obligations "to take steps, individually and through international assistance and co-operation, especially economic and technical" to mitigate human suffering prompted by sanctions.[18] For their part, the five permanent members of the Security Council themselves have reflected on the detrimental impacts of sanctions, concluding in a 1995 non-paper on the humanitarian impact of sanctions that "further collective actions in the Security Council within the context of any future sanctions regime should be directed to minimize unintended adverse side-effects of sanctions on the most vulnerable segments of targeted countries."[19]

On the other hand, "sanctions can on occasion achieve (or help to achieve) various foreign policy goals ranging from the modest to the fairly significant."[20] In this regard, sanctions introduced after the (first) Gulf War are said to have increased Iraqi compliance with resolutions requiring that Iraq rid itself of weapons of mass destruction. Sanctions are also said to have contributed to Serbia's assent to the Dayton Peace Accords in August

---

15 Kim Richard Nossal, *Rain Dancing: Sanctions in Canadian and Australian Foreign Policy* (Toronto: University of Toronto Press, 1994) at 252.

16 United Nations, Economic and Social Council, Sub-Commission on the Promotion and Protection of Human Rights, *Human Rights and Humanitarian Consequences of Sanctions, Including Embargoes*, Sub-Commission on Human Rights Resolution 2000/1 at para 1(a), UN Doc E/CN.4/SUB.2/RES/2000/1 (11 August 2000).

17 16 December 1966, 993 UNTS 3, Can TS 1976 No 46, in force 3 January 1976.

18 Committee on Economic, Social, and Cultural Rights, *General Comment No. 8: The relationship between economic sanctions and respect for economic, social and cultural rights*, UN Doc E/C.12/1997/8 (1997), reprinted in *Compilation of General Comments and General Recommendations Adopted by Human Rights Treaty Bodies*, UN Doc HRI/GEN/1/Rev.9 (vol I) (2008) at 43–46, para 14. The Committee on Economic, Social and Cultural Rights has expressly reminded states parties of General Comment No. 8 in General Comments 12, 14, and 15, adopted in 1999, 2000 and 2002 respectively, and reprinted in the *Compilation of General Comments* (*ibid*) at 55–62, 78–96, and 97–113.

19 *Letter dated 13 April 1995 from the Permanent Representatives of China, France, the Russian Federation, the United Kingdom of Great Britain and Northern Ireland, and the United States of America to the United Nations Addressed to the President of the Security Council*, UN Doc S/1995/300 (13 April 1995) at 2.

20 Haass, above note 14.

1995.[21] One study suggests that sanctions are most likely to be successful where the goal is relatively modest, the target is much smaller than the country applying the sanctions, there is substantial trade between the two nations, the sanctions are imposed rapidly and decisively, and the cost to the sanctioning country is low.[22]

These conclusions were echoed by the International Peace Academy in a 2000 study on "smart sanctions." As the Academy noted, comprehensive sanctions represent the bluntest form of economic coercion, often with unpredictable and devastating humanitarian and political side effects. Conversely, "[m]ore selective, targeted sanctions resulted in fewer humanitarian difficulties."[23] These findings led the authors to favour narrowly tailored measures and to argue "not that targeted or selective sanctions are ineffective, but that policy steps necessary to enhance the impact of these more limited measures have not been taken."[24]

The Academy established a sophisticated analytical framework for assessing the viability of sanctions. Rather than endorsing a "naïve theory" that envisages political change flowing directly from the economic pain caused by sanctions, the study suggested that the "political impact of sanctions ultimately depends on internal political dynamics within the targeted country."[25] Specifically:

> Sanctions succeed when targeted decision-makers change their calculation of costs and benefits and determine that the advantages of cooperation with Security Council resolutions outweigh the costs of continued defiance of expressed global norms. One of the key considerations in a leadership's calculation of costs is the degree of opposition from domestic political constituencies. To the extent that sanctions strengthen or encourage these opposition constituencies, they are more likely to achieve success.[26]

Put another way, sanctions might be most appropriate when directed against states experiencing some domestic opposition.

In terms of specific economic sanctions measures, the study called financial sanctions "the centerpiece of a targeted sanctions strategy."[27] The effectiveness of these measures depends, in the study's words, "on the ability to identify and target specific individuals and entities whose assets are to be frozen."[28] Similarly, arms embargoes were regarded as a "potentially effective form . . . of targeted sanctions," one "intended to deny wrongdoers the resources needed for repression and military aggression."[29] The effectiveness of arms embargoes depends, of course, on the cooperation of the international community, particularly frontline states likely to see growth in arms smuggling.

The International Peace Academy report coincided with a serious rethinking of sanc-

---

21 *Ibid* (with reference to the General Framework Agreement for Peace in Bosnia and Herzegovina, 14 December 1995, (1996) 35 ILM 75, in force 14 December 1995, also known as the Dayton Peace Accords).

22 Elliot, above note 13.

23 David Cortright & George A Lopez, *The Sanctions Decade: Assessing UN Strategies in the 1990s* (Boulder, CO: Lynne Rienner, 2000) at 213.

24 *Ibid* at 209.

25 *Ibid* at 22.

26 *Ibid.*

27 *Ibid* at 241.

28 *Ibid.*

29 *Ibid* at 242.

tions policy at the United Nations. In April 2000, the Security Council established (on a temporary basis) an informal working group "to develop general recommendations on how to improve the effectiveness of United Nations sanctions."[30] In keeping with the conclusions of the Academy's report, the focus of recent UN sanctions activity is now placed on limited sanctions measures that target governing elites rather than states, or that name certain individuals and entities involved in activities that pose a threat to international peace and security, such as global terrorism.[31] Note however that labelling sanctions as "targeted" does not guarantee that the sanctions are hitting their targets, as several reports have noted.[32]

While preferable to comprehensive or broad-based economic sanctions, the use of targeted financial and travel sanctions to "blacklist" named individuals raises other concerns, including due process concerns, which need to be addressed.[33] These targeted sanctions regimes use lists of designated individuals and entities who are subject to extensive asset freezes and travel bans, with the resolutions being in effect directed at banks and airlines. While the effort to suppress international terrorism provides a public policy rationale for these Security Council regulatory regimes, mistakes can be made, the effect of which is compounded by the absence of an in-built judicial review procedure by which individuals may challenge the taking of property or denial of passage that flow from being listed. Several court challenges have raised the human rights implications of such sanctions,[34] including the Abdelrazik case in Canada.[35] The Security Council has responded to critiques of what is now known as the "Al-Qaida Sanctions List" by creating a de-listing procedure,[36] as well as an independent and impartial Office of the Ombudsperson,[37] to handle complaints.[38] The first Ombudsperson is Judge Kimberly Prost of Canada.

---

30 See *Note by the President of the Security Council*, UN Doc S/2000/319 at para 3 (17 April 2000).

31 SC Resolution 1267 (1999), adopted on 15 October 1999, UN Doc S/RES/1267 (1999), subsequently extended by SC Resolution 1333 (2000), adopted 19 December 2000, UN Doc S/RES/1333 (2000). See also SC Resolution 1390 (2002), adopted 28 June 2002, UN Doc S/RES/1390 (2002). While critiques have focused on the 1267 sanctions regime, the Security Council first used economic sanctions targeting individuals involved in terrorism in 1997: SC Resolution 1127 (1997), adopted 28 August 1997, UN Doc S/RES/1127 (1997).

32 See, for example, United Kingdom, House of Lords, Select Committee on Economic Affairs, *The Impact of Economic Sanctions*, 2d Report of Session 2006–07, online: http://www.publications.parliament.uk/pa/ld200607/ldselect/ldeconaf/96/96i.pdf.

33 See paragraph 109 of the *2005 World Summit Outcome*, GA Res 60/1, UN Doc A/RES/60/1, reprinted in UN GAOR, 60th Sess, Supp No 49, vol I at 3–25, UN Doc A/60/49 (vol I) (2005) ("We also call upon the Security Council . . . to ensure that fair and clear procedures exist for placing individuals and entities on sanctions lists and for removing them, as well as for granting humanitarian exemptions.") See also Bardo Fassbender, *Targeted Sanctions and Due Process* (20 March 2006), online: www.un.org/law/counsel/Fassbender_study.pdf.

34 See, for example, *Yassin Abdullah Kadi and al-Barakaat Foundation v Council of the European Union and Commission of the European Communities*, Joined Cases C-402/05 P and C-415/05 P, [2008] ECR I-6351 (Court of Justice of the European Communities).

35 *Abdelrazik v Canada (Minister of Foreign Affairs)* (2009), 2009 FC 580, [2010] 1 FCR 267.

36 See section 7 of the *Guidelines of the Committee for the Conduct of Its Work* by the Security Council Committee pursuant to Resolutions 1267 (1999) and 1989 (2011) concerning Al-Qaida and Associated Individuals and Entities (30 November 2011), online: www.un.org/sc/committees/1267/pdf/1267_guidelines.pdf.

37 SC Resolution 1904 (2009), adopted 17 December 2009, UN Doc S/RES/1904 (2009).

38 For the current mandate, see SC Resolution 2083 (2012), adopted 17 December 2012, UN Doc S/RES/2083 (2012).

2) Canadian Sanctions Law

Historically, Canada has not been an enthusiastic proponent of unilateral economic sanctions. Consider this 1990 discussion of economic sanctions by the Legal Bureau of what was then Canada's Department of External Affairs:

> ### Edward G Lee QC, "Canadian Practice in International Law" (1990) 28 Can YB Int'l Law 471 at 493
>
> In a memorandum dated February 16, 1990, the Legal Bureau wrote:
>
> The legality of economic countermeasures that States may employ in retaliation against conduct of which they disapprove depends on the circumstances. If the countermeasure is applied in a manner consistent with the international legal obligations of the State (for example, putting a tariff on an unbound item or applying restrictions to a service not governed by the GATT or other agreement), it is technically legal, but it may well give rise to retaliation by the country against whom the countermeasure is applied. Furthermore, the constraints of ensuring that the countermeasures are consistent with international legal obligations make the usefulness of economic countermeasures doubtful.
>
> International law allows an affected State to take countermeasures that are otherwise unlawful, but only in limited circumstances when certain conditions are fully met. These conditions are: the offending conduct must be a clear breach of international law, the countermeasures must be proportional to the breach, and must be preceded by a demand for redress. If the countermeasure involves the breach of an international agreement that contains a dispute settlement mechanism, the grounds for breaching the agreement by way of countermeasure are then further circumscribed under international law.
>
> Given the likelihood of differing interpretations of the legality of the impugned conduct and the proportionality of the countermeasure, taking any countermeasures that violate international agreements exposes the State taking the measure to retaliation and a possible challenge of the measure through the relevant dispute settlement proceedings. In summary, using trade measures to coerce other States into specific action should be approached with caution. The question of their legality may well be outweighed by the economic consequences of the action.
>
> Canada has resorted to economic sanctions on very few occasions in recognition of the limited circumstances in which such action is merited. Canada imposed economic sanctions against Rhodesia pursuant to a Security Council decision. We have also joined with other States in imposing sanctions against Iran for the holding of American hostages, against the USSR and Poland for the state of martial law in Poland and against Argentina during the Falklands war.
>
> Given the strong preference for the peaceful settlement of disputes in international law, the unilateral imposition of trade sanctions is not welcomed.
>
> [Reprinted with permission of the Publisher from Canadian Yearbook of International Law, Volume 28 edited by CB Bourne © University of British Columbia Press 1990. All rights reserved by the Publisher.]

At present, there are four Canadian statutes governing the manner in which the Canadian government may impose economic sanctions:

- As seen above, the *United Nations Act*, RSC 1985, c U-2, is a short statute empowering the federal Cabinet to make orders and regulations that appear to it "to be necessary or expedient" to implement a measure called for by the UN Security Council under Article 41 of the UN Charter. For instance:

. . . [O]n May 2, 2005, the *Regulations Amending the United Nations Sudan Regulations* (P.C. 2005-692; SOR 2005-122) entered into force to implement the assets freeze under Canadian domestic law. Canadian implementation of the travel ban is ensured under existing provisions of the *Immigration and Refugee Protection Act*.

These latest *Regulations* also introduce new exemptions to the arms embargo, which were also decided by the Security Council in Resolution 1591 (2005), namely to enable the supply of material in support of the Comprehensive Peace Accord, signed between the Government of Sudan and the Sudan People's Liberation Movement/Army in January 2005, and to allow movement of material otherwise subject to embargo into the Darfur region only if the movement is approved by the Security Council sanctions committee at the request of the Sudanese government.

On May 3, 2005, the *United Nations Cote d'Ivoire Regulations* (P.C. 2005-699; SOR 2005-127) entered into force to implement the measures decided by the United Nations Security Council in its Resolution 1572 of November 15, 2004 concerning the situation in Cote d'Ivoire. The Council decided that:

1. all States shall, for an initial period of 13 months from the date of the resolution, prevent the supply of arms and technical assistance related to military activities to Cote d'Ivoire; and that

2. all States shall impose, for a 12-month period starting one month after the date of the resolution, a travel ban and a freeze of assets against those who are deemed to constitute a threat to the peace and national reconciliation process in Cote d'Ivoire, as well as those responsible for serious violations of human rights and international humanitarian law in Cote d'Ivoire. A sanctions committee established pursuant to Resolution 1572 is charged with designating those who are to be targeted by these measures.

The *Regulations* give effect to the assets freeze in Canadian domestic law and to the arms and military assistance embargo, the latter in conjunction with Canada's *Export and Import Permits Act*. Implementation of the travel ban is ensured in Canada pursuant to the *Immigration and Refugee Protection Act*.[39]

- The *Customs Tariff*, SC 1997, c 36, empowers the federal Cabinet to extend a special tariff rate, known under Canadian law as the General Preferential Tariff (GPT), to developing countries. While these tariff benefits are not formally conditioned on human rights performance, the law permits Cabinet to remove the tariff at its discretion.[40] GPT benefits have been removed, for instance, from Myanmar (previously known as Burma) in response to that country's poor human rights record.
- The *Export and Import Permits Act*, RSC 1985, c E-19, is a complex statute regulating various aspects of Canada's trade relations and serving as an important tool of trade

---

39 Government of Canada, Department of Foreign Affairs and International Trade, Legal Affairs Bureau, *Examples of Current Issues of International Law of Particular Importance to Canada* (October 2005) at 14–15 [copy on file with the authors].

40 *Customs Tariff*, SC 197, c 36, s 34.

policy. The Act includes an "Export Control List," an "Import Control List," and an "Area Control List," all of which are capable of restricting trade for certain enumerated reasons. In particular, the grounds for placing goods on an Export Control List include instances where goods having "a strategic nature or value" might be used in a fashion detrimental to national security.[41] Similarly, many of the bases for placing goods on the Import Control list are arguably grounded in national security justifications.[42] Further, goods may also be placed on both lists "to implement an intergovernmental arrangement or commitment."[43]

The Area Control list allows Cabinet to "establish a list of countries" with respect to which it deems "it necessary to control the export of any goods."[44] This appears to be a discretionary power unconnected with the Export or Import Control lists, and thus unfettered by any conditions. As one observer has stated, the Area Control List mechanism "assumes that the destination of the good is per se a reason for the restriction of its export, regardless of the nature of the good and its potential applications under any circumstance."[45] Belarus and North Korea are currently subject to the Area Control List.

Where goods are placed on either the Export or Import Control lists or are destined for a country on the Area Control List, international trade in these goods is illicit in the absence of ministerial permits.

- The *Special Economic Measures Act*, SC 1992, c 17 (SEMA), is Canada's most recent sanctions law, designed to fill the gaps left by older legislation. Consider its key provisions:

Special Economic Measures Act, SC 1992, c 17

4.(1) The Governor in Council may, for the purpose of implementing a decision, resolution or recommendation of an international organization of states or association of states, of which Canada is a member, that calls on its members to take economic measures against a foreign state, or where the Governor in Council is of the opinion that a grave breach of international peace and security has occurred that has resulted or is likely to result in a serious international crisis,

(a) make such orders or regulations with respect to the restriction or prohibition of any of the activities referred to in subsection (2) in relation to a foreign state as the Governor in Council considers necessary; and

(b) by order, cause to be seized, frozen or sequestrated in the manner set out in the order any property situated in Canada that is held by or on behalf of

(i) a foreign state,

(ii) any person in that foreign state, or

(iii) a national of that foreign state who does not ordinarily reside in Canada.

---

41 *Export and Import Permits Act*, RSC 1985, c E-19, s 3.
42 *Ibid*, s 5.
43 *Ibid*, ss 3(d) and 5(e).
44 *Ibid*, s 4.
45 Selma M Lussenburg, "The Collision of Canadian and U.S. Sovereignty in the Area of Export Controls" (1994) 20 Can-USLJ 145 at 157.

(2) Orders and regulations may be made pursuant to paragraph (1)(a) with respect to the restriction or prohibition of any of the following activities, whether carried out in or outside Canada, in relation to a foreign state:

(a) any dealing by any person in Canada or Canadian outside Canada in any property wherever situated held by or on behalf of that foreign state, any person in that foreign state, or a national of that foreign state who does not ordinarily reside in Canada;

(b) the exportation, sale, supply or shipment by any person in Canada or Canadian outside Canada of any goods wherever situated to that foreign state or any person in that foreign state, or any other dealing by any person in Canada or Canadian outside Canada in any goods wherever situated destined for that foreign state or any person in that foreign state;

(c) the transfer, provision or communication by any person in Canada or Canadian outside Canada of any technical data to that foreign state or any person in that foreign state;

(d) the importation, purchase, acquisition or shipment by any person in Canada or Canadian outside Canada of any goods that are exported, supplied or shipped from that foreign state after a date specified in the order or regulations, or any other dealing by any person in Canada or Canadian outside Canada in any such goods;

(e) the provision or acquisition by any person in Canada or Canadian outside Canada of financial services or any other services to, from or for the benefit of or on the direction or order of that foreign state or any person in that foreign state;

(f) the docking in that foreign state of ships registered or licensed, or for which an identification number has been issued, pursuant to any Act of Parliament;

(g) the landing in that foreign state of aircraft registered in Canada or operated in connection with a Canadian air service licence;

(h) the docking in or passage through Canada by ships registered in that foreign state or used, leased or chartered, in whole or in part, by or on behalf of or for the benefit of that foreign state or a person in that foreign state; and

(i) the landing in or flight over Canada by aircraft registered in that foreign state or used, leased or chartered, in whole or in part, by or on behalf of or for the benefit of that foreign state or any person in that foreign state.

Note that the SEMA empowers the federal Cabinet to impose sanctions unilaterally where it is of the opinion that a grave breach of international peace and security has occurred that has resulted, or is likely to result, in a serious international crisis. Clearly, this is a discretionary power that does not require formal action by the United Nations Security Council, as is the case under the *United Nations Act*. Further, the government can act in concert with other states for the purpose of implementing a decision, resolution, or recommendation of an international organization of states or association of states (of which Canada is a member) that calls on its members to take economic measures against a foreign state. These would include, but would not be limited to, binding UN Security Council resolutions under Article 41 of the UN Charter.

In addition, the range of sanctions available to the Government of Canada under the SEMA is quite potent. While the language of the Act itself is somewhat less than clear on this issue, it has been used to prohibit investment in Yugoslavia[46] and in Myanmar.[47] Further, subsection 4(2) refers to both "restrictions" and "prohibitions," implying that the Government of Canada is able both to bar the activities enumerated in subsection 4(2) and to restrict and regulate them. As a consequence, the SEMA is the only instrument available to the Government of Canada that can be used to oblige, for instance, Canadian companies to cease operations in a foreign country. It also appears to be an instrument that allows the government to restrict the nature and conduct of that overseas activity. Consider the following summary of Government of Canada practice under SEMA:

Alan H Kessel, "Canadian Practice in International Law at the Department of Foreign Affairs and International Trade in 2008–9" (2009) 47 Can YB Int'l Law 411 at 430–31

There are two mechanisms by which the Canadian government may impose economic sanctions: the *United Nations Act* ("UN Act") and the *Special Economic Measures Act* ("SEMA"). In the absence of a United Nations Security Council decision that requires all Member States to impose sanctions, Canada may unilaterally impose sanctions under

---

46 See *Special Economic Measures (Federal Republic of Yugoslavia) Regulations*, SOR/98-397 of 28 July 1998, repealed on 1 August 2001. The relevant provisions read as follows:

> 3. (1) Subject to subsection (2), no person in Canada and no Canadian outside Canada shall make an investment in Serbia.

> (2) Subsection (1) does not apply to the acquisition of an investment from a person who ordinarily resides in Canada.

> "Investment" was defined in the order as follows:

> "investment" means acquiring, directly or indirectly, ownership or control of any of the following properties:
> (a) assets of an organization;
> (b) an equity security of an organization;
> (c) a debt security of an organization
>   (i) where the organization is an affiliate of the investor, or
>   (ii) where the original term of the debt security is at least 180 days;
> (d) a loan to an organization
>   (i) where the organization is an affiliate of the investor, or
>   (ii) where the original term of the loan is at least 180 days;
> (e) an interest or a right in an organization that entitles the owner to share in income or profits of the organization;
> (f) an interest or a right in an organization that entitles the owner to share in the assets of that organization on termination or dissolution;
> (g) property used or intended to be used for the purpose of economic benefit or other benefits; or
> (h) interests or rights arising from the commitment of capital or other resources, including
>   (i) contracts involving an investor's property, turnkey construction contracts, and concessions, and
>   (ii) contracts where remuneration depends principally on the production, revenues or profits of an organization.

47 See section 7 of the *Special Economic Measures (Burma) Regulations*, SOR/2007-285, in force 13 December 2007, but note that the sanctions set out in this regulation were substantially scaled back in April 2012 in response to the improving human rights situation in Myanmar (Burma): see *Regulations Amending the Special Economic Measures (Burma) Regulations*, SOR/2012-85, in force 24 April 2012.

the SEMA. The SEMA provides the Government of Canada the discretionary authority to impose sanctions against a foreign nation if the triggers it sets out in section 4(1) have been met . . . .

The Governor in Council may, for the purpose of implementing a decision, resolution or recommendation of an international organization of states or association of states, of which Canada is a member, that calls on its members to take economic measures against a foreign state, or where the Governor in Council is of the opinion that a grave breach of international peace and security has occurred that has resulted or is likely to result in a serious international crisis. . . .

The first trigger enables Canada to impose sanctions in response to a call of an international organization or association of states of which Canada is a member. Were Canada in its consultations with various international fora to receive a call for additional sanctions from an appropriate international body then this trigger would be satisfied.

Under SEMA's second trigger, sanctions can be imposed outside of a multilateral scheme when a "grave breach of international peace and security has occurred that has resulted or is likely to result in a serious international crisis". This may be a more legally onerous standard than that which appears in the UN Charter for Security Council action. Article 39 of the Charter of the United Nations enables sanctions action in situations of threats to the peace only. The Security Council has found actual breaches (as opposed to threats) in few instances . . . . In addition, the second trigger of the SEMA must not only constitute a grave breach but that breach must have "resulted or is likely to result in a serious international crisis".

Canada has invoked sanctions under the SEMA four times. Sanctions have been imposed under the call from an international body in the cases of Haiti (a call from the OAS) and the Former Republic of Yugoslavia (a call from the G8). The second trigger was used for the first time with the sanctions imposed against Burma in December 2007, and was used again with sanctions imposed against Zimbabwe in September 2008.

The SEMA allows Canada to impose various measures against a foreign State, including:

- A prohibition to import all or specified goods from that foreign State;
- A prohibition to export all or specified goods to that foreign State or any person in that foreign State;
- An assets freeze against designated individuals and/or entities;
- A prohibition on the transfer of technical data to that foreign State or any person in that foreign State;
- A prohibition on the provision or acquisition of financial services or other services to, from or for the benefit of, or on the direction or order of that foreign State or any person in that foreign State;
- A prohibition on Canadian-registered ships or aircraft from docking/landing in a foreign State; and
- A prohibition on foreign State-registered ships or aircraft from docking/landing in Canada.

In addition to the four instances of SEMA sanctions identified above, the Government of Canada has imposed SEMA sanctions on Iran,[48] Libya,[49] the Democratic People's Republic of Korea (North Korea),[50] and Syria.[51] It would thus appear that Canada's historical reluctance to resort to unilateral economic sanctions has evolved considerably.

---

48 *Special Economic Measures (Iran) Regulations*, SOR/2010-165, in force 22 July 2010, as amended by the *Regulations Amending the Special Economic Measures (Iran) Regulations*, SOR/2011-225, in force 17 October 2011, the *Regulations Amending the Special Economic Measures (Iran) Regulations*, SOR/2011-268, in force 21 November 2011, the *Regulations Amending the Special Economic Measures (Iran) Regulations*, SOR/2012-7, in force 31 January 2012, and the *Regulations Amending the Special Economic Measures (Iran) Regulations*, SOR/2012-283, in force 1 December 2012.

49 *Regulations Implementing the United Nations Resolution on Libya and Taking Special Economic Measures*, SOR/2011-51, in force 27 February 2011, as amended by the *Regulations Amending the Regulations Implementing the United Nations Resolution on Libya and Taking Special Economic Measures*, SOR/2011-172, in force 31 August 2011, and the *Regulations Amending the Regulations Implementing the United Nations Resolutions on Libya and Taking Special Economic Measures*, SOR/2011-198, in force 22 September 2011.

50 *Special Economic Measures (Democratic People's Republic of Korea) Regulations*, SOR/2011-167, in force 11 August 2011.

51 *Special Economic Measures (Syria) Regulations*, SOR/2011-114, in force 24 May 2011, as amended by the *Regulations Amending the Special Economic Measures (Syria) Regulations*, SOR/2011-166, in force 11 August 2011, the *Regulations Amending the Special Economic Measures (Syria) Regulations*, SOR/2011-220, in force 3 October 2011, the *Regulations Amending the Special Economic Measures (Syria) Regulations*, SOR/2011-330, in force 23 December 2011, the *Regulations Amending the Special Economic Measures (Syria) Regulations*, SOR/2012-6, in force 25 January 2012, the *Regulations Amending the Special Economic Measures (Syria) Regulations*, SOR/2012-35, in force 5 March 2012, the *Regulations Amending the Special Economic Measures (Syria) Regulations*, SOR/2012-74, in force 30 March 2012, the *Regulations Amending the Special Economic Measures (Syria) Regulations*, SOR/2012-107, in force 18 May 2012, the *Regulations Amending the Special Economic Measures (Syria) Regulations*, SOR/2012-145, in force 5 July 2012, the *Regulations Amending the Special Economic Measures (Syria) Regulations*, SOR/2012-166, in force 29 August 2012, and the *Regulations Amending the Special Economic Measures (Syria) Regulations*, SOR/2012-249, in force 28 November 2012.

CHAPTER 14

THE USE OF FORCE

A. INTRODUCTION

In this chapter, we consider the extent to which international law permits states to use military force against one another (and possibly against non-state actors). We discuss this as a matter of international law enforcement because the circumstances in which states may still lawfully use such force have effectively been narrowed to those in which the target state is in breach of certain of its international legal obligations.

This is not to suggest, however, that the use of force is generally available as a response to the violation by a state of any of its international legal obligations. As previously noted in Chapter 3, modern international law as a general rule outlaws resort to force by states against other states, subject only to certain narrowly defined exceptions. We therefore begin with a review of the scope of the general prohibition on the use of force in interstate relations, followed by an examination of the limited exceptions to that general prohibition. We will see that the exceptions are conceived as necessary means — when all other options have been exhausted or are otherwise unavailable — of securing respect by states of their more fundamental international legal obligations.

B. THE GENERAL PROHIBITION OF THE THREAT OR USE OF FORCE

Recall the basic prohibition set out in Article 2(4) of the Charter of the United Nations:[1] "All Members shall refrain in their international relations from the threat or use of force against the territorial integrity or political independence of any state, or in any other manner inconsistent with the Purposes of the United Nations." The corollary obligation is found in Article 2(3) of the UN Charter: "All Members shall settle their international disputes by peaceful means . . . ." Recall also the General Assembly's elaboration of the Article 2(4) principle in the Friendly Relations Declaration:

Declaration on Principles of International Law Concerning Friendly Relations and Co-operation in accordance with the Charter of the United Nations, GA Res 2625 (XXV), UN Doc A/RES/2625/XXV, reprinted in UN GAOR, 25th Sess, Supp No 28 at 121–24, UN Doc A/8028 Corr 1 (1970); (1970) 9 ILM 1292

The principle that States shall refrain in their international relations from the threat or use of force against the territorial integrity or political independence of any State, or in any other manner inconsistent with the purpose of the United Nations:

---

1   Charter of the United Nations, 26 June 1945, Can TS 1945 No 7, in force 24 October 1945 [UN Charter].

Every State has the duty to refrain in its international relations from the threat or use of force against the territorial integrity or political independence of any State, or in any other manner inconsistent with the purposes of the United Nations. Such a threat or use of force constitutes a violation of international law and the Charter of the United Nations and shall never be employed as a means of settling international issues.

A war of aggression constitutes a crime against the peace, for which there is responsibility under international law.

In accordance with the purposes and principles of the United Nations, States have the duty to refrain from propaganda for wars of aggression.

Every State has the duty to refrain from the threat or use of force to violate the existing international boundaries of another State or as a means of solving international disputes, including territorial disputes and problems concerning frontiers of States . . . .

States have a duty to refrain from acts of reprisal involving the use of force.

Every State has the duty to refrain from any forcible action which deprives peoples referred to in the elaboration of the principle of equal rights and self-determination of their right to self-determination and freedom and independence.

Every State has the duty to refrain from organizing or encouraging the organization of irregular forces or armed bands including mercenaries, for incursion into the territory of another State.

Every State has the duty to refrain from organizing, instigating, assisting or participating in acts of civil strife or terrorist acts in another State or acquiescing in organized activities within its territory directed towards the commission of such acts, when the acts referred to in the present paragraph involve a threat or use of force.

The territory of a State shall not be the object of military occupation resulting from the use of force in contravention of the provisions of the Charter. The territory of a State shall not be the object of acquisition by another State resulting from the threat or use of force. No territorial acquisition resulting from the threat or use of force shall be recognized as legal. Nothing in the foregoing shall be construed as affecting:

(a) Provisions of the Charter or any international agreement prior to the Charter regime and valid under international law; or

(b) The powers of the Security Council under the Charter . . . .

Nothing in the foregoing paragraphs shall be construed as enlarging or diminishing in any way the scope of the provisions of the Charter concerning cases in which the use of force is lawful.

While not a formal source of international law in its own right, the Friendly Relations Declaration (also referred to as General Assembly Resolution 2625 (XXV)) is generally accepted to be an expression of customary international law. Consider the significance accorded to its provisions by the International Court of Justice (ICJ) in the course of its discussion of the scope and nature of the prohibition on the use of force in the following case:

Military and Paramilitary Activities in and against Nicaragua (Nicaragua v United States of America), Merits, Judgment, [1986] ICJ Rep 14

[Recall that, in this case, Nicaragua claimed that the United States had used force unlawfully against it, contrary to Article 2(4) of the UN Charter. The following excerpts of the case set out the Court's reasoning on this issue.]

188. The Court . . . finds that both Parties take the view that the principles as to the use of force incorporated in the United Nations Charter correspond, in essentials, to those found in customary international law. The Parties thus both take the view that the fundamental principle in this area is expressed in the terms employed in Article 2, paragraph 4, of the United Nations Charter . . . . The Court has however to be satisfied that there exists in customary international law an *opinio juris* as to the binding character of such [a principle]. This *opinio juris* may, though with all due caution, be deduced from, *inter alia*, the attitude of the Parties and the attitude of States towards certain General Assembly resolutions, and particularly resolution 2625 (XXV) entitled "Declaration on Principles of International Law concerning Friendly Relations and Co-operation among States in accordance with the Charter of the United Nations". The effect of consent to the text of such resolutions cannot be understood as merely that of a "reiteration or elucidation" of the treaty commitment undertaken in the Charter. On the contrary, it may be understood as an acceptance of the validity of the rule or set of rules declared by the resolution by themselves. The principle of non-use of force, for example, may thus be regarded as a principle of customary international law . . . .

190. A further confirmation of the validity as customary international law of the principle of the prohibition of the use of force expressed in Article 2, paragraph 4, of the Charter of the United Nations may be found in the fact that it is frequently referred to in statements by State representatives as being not only a principle of customary international law but also a fundamental or cardinal principle of such law. The International Law Commission, in the course of its work on the codification of the law of treaties, expressed the view that "the law of the Charter concerning the prohibition of the use of force in itself constitutes a conspicuous example of a rule in international law having the character of *jus cogens*" (paragraph (1) of the commentary of the Commission to Article 50 of its draft Articles on the Law of Treaties, *ILC Yearbook*, 1966-II, p. 247). Nicaragua . . . in the present case states that the principle prohibiting the use of force embodied in Article 2, paragraph 4, of the Charter of the United Nations "has come to be recognized as *jus cogens*". The United States . . . found it material to quote the views of scholars that this principle is a "universal norm", a "universal international law", a "universally recognized principle of international law", and a "principle of *jus cogens*" . . . .

227. The Court will appraise the facts in the light of the principle of the non-use of force . . . . What is unlawful, in accordance with that principle, is recourse to either the threat or the use of force against the territorial integrity or political independence of any State. For the most part, the complaints by Nicaragua are of the actual use of force against it by the United States. Of the acts which the Court has found imputable to the Government of the United States, the following are relevant in this respect:
– the laying of mines in Nicaraguan internal or territorial waters in early 1984 . . . ;
– certain attacks on Nicaraguan ports, oil installations and a naval base . . . .

These activities constitute infringements of the principle of the prohibition of the use of force, defined earlier, unless they are justified by circumstances which exclude their unlawfulness, a question now to be examined. The Court has also found . . . the exist-ence of military manoeuvres held by the United States near the Nicaraguan borders; and Nicaragua has made some suggestion that this constituted a "threat of force", which is equally forbidden by the principle of non-use of force. The Court is however not satisfied that the manoeuvres complained of, in the circumstances in which they were held, con-stituted on the part of the United States a breach, as against Nicaragua, of the principle forbidding recourse to the threat or use of force.

228. Nicaragua has also claimed that the United States has violated Article 2, paragraph 4, of the Charter, and has used force against Nicaragua in breach of its obligation under customary international law in as much as it has engaged in "recruiting, training, arm-ing, equipping, financing, supplying and otherwise encouraging, supporting, aiding, and directing military and paramilitary actions in and against Nicaragua" [by the con-tras] . . . . As to [this claim], the Court finds that . . . the United States has committed a prima facie violation of that principle by its assistance to the *contras* in Nicaragua, by "organizing or encouraging the organization of irregular forces or armed bands . . . for incursion into the territory of another State", and "participating in acts of civil strife . . . in another State", in the terms of General Assembly resolution 2625 (XXV). According to that resolution, participation of this kind is contrary to the principle of the prohibition of the use of force when the acts of civil strife referred to "involve a threat or use of force". In the view of the Court, while the arming and training of the *contras* can certainly be said to involve the threat or use of force against Nicaragua, this is not necessarily so in respect of all the assistance given by the United States Government. In particular, the Court considers that the mere supply of funds to the *contras*, while undoubtedly an act of intervention in the internal affairs of Nicaragua, as will be explained below, does not in itself amount to a use of force. . . .

Notice the Court's emphasis that even the "threat" of force is an "equally forbidden" violation of the principle set out in Article 2(4) of the UN Charter. The precise bounds of what would constitute such a threat were the subject of more detailed examination by the Court in its advisory opinion on the legality of the threat or use of nuclear weapons:

Legality of the Threat or Use of Nuclear Weapons, Advisory Opinion, [1996] ICJ Rep 226

[The General Assembly requested an advisory opinion from the Court on the question: "Is the threat or use of nuclear weapons in any circumstances permitted under inter-national law?" In the course of giving its opinion, the Court made the following com-ments concerning the prohibition of the use of force in international relations.]

37. The Court will now address the question of the legality or illegality of recourse to nuclear weapons in the light of the provisions of the Charter relating to the threat or use of force.

38. The Charter contains several provisions relating to the threat and use of force. In Article 2, paragraph 4, the threat or use of force against the territorial integrity or political independence of another State or in any other manner inconsistent with the purposes of the United Nations is prohibited . . . .

39. These provisions do not refer to specific weapons. They apply to any use of force, regardless of the weapons employed. The Charter neither expressly prohibits, nor permits, the use of any specific weapon, including nuclear weapons. A weapon that is already unlawful *per se*, whether by treaty or custom, does not become lawful by reason of its being used for a legitimate purpose under the Charter . . . .

47. In order to lessen or eliminate the risk of unlawful attack, States sometimes signal that they possess certain weapons to use in self-defence against any State violating their territorial integrity or political independence. Whether a signalled intention to use force if certain events occur is or is not a "threat" within Article 2, paragraph 4, of the Charter depends upon various factors. If the envisaged use of force is itself unlawful, the stated readiness to use it would be a threat prohibited under Article 2, paragraph 4. Thus it would be illegal for a State to threaten force to secure territory from another State, or to cause it to follow or not follow certain political or economic paths. The notions of "threat" and "use" of force under Article 2, paragraph 4, of the Charter stand together in the sense that if the use of force itself in a given case is illegal—for whatever reason—the threat to use such force will likewise be illegal. In short, if it is to be lawful, the declared readiness of a State to use force must be a use of force that is in conformity with the Charter. For the rest, no State—whether or not it defended the policy of deterrence—suggested to the Court that it would be lawful to threaten to use force if the use of force contemplated would be illegal.

48. Some States put forward the argument that possession of nuclear weapons is itself an unlawful threat to use force. Possession of nuclear weapons may indeed justify an inference of preparedness to use them. In order to be effective, the policy of deterrence, by which those States possessing or under the umbrella of nuclear weapons seek to discourage military aggression by demonstrating that it will serve no purpose, necessitates that the intention to use nuclear weapons be credible. Whether this is a "threat" contrary to Article 2, paragraph 4, depends upon whether the particular use of force envisaged would be directed against the territorial integrity or political independence of a State, or against the Purposes of the United Nations or whether, in the event that it were intended as a means of defence, it would necessarily violate the principles of necessity and proportionality. In any of these circumstances the use of force, and the threat to use it, would be unlawful under the law of the Charter . . . .

What is the effect of the Court's reasoning that the legality of a threat to use force must be evaluated in connection with the legality of the contemplated use of force itself? Does this mean that the legality of a threat can only be reliably evaluated once the threat has been carried out? If not, what challenges are posed for evaluating the legality of a threat of force based on the legality of a future, hypothetical use of force? What does all this mean for the utility of the prohibition of the *threat* of force, as distinct from the *use* of force itself? Consider the role played by the legal concept of a threat of force in the following award of an arbitral tribunal constituted under Annex VII of the United Nations Convention on the Law of the Sea:

Guyana v Suriname, **Award of the Arbitral Tribunal of 17 September 2007, (2008) 47 ILM 166**

[Guyana and Suriname, previously colonies of the United Kingdom and the Netherlands respectively, are two small adjacent states in northern South America. This arbitral award concerned the disputed location of the maritime boundary dividing their respective territorial seas, exclusive economic zones, and continental shelves.]

150. Among the concessions issued by Guyana for oil exploration in the disputed area of the continental shelf was a concession granted in 1998 to CGX Resources Inc. ("CGX"), a Canadian company. In 1999, CGX arranged for seismic testing to be performed over the entire concession area . . . . On 11 and 31 May 2000, Suriname demanded through diplomatic channels that Guyana cease all oil exploration activities in the disputed area [and] ordered CGX to immediately cease all activities [there] . . . .

151. On 3 June 2000, two patrol boats from the Surinamese navy approached CGX's oil rig and drill ship, the *C.E. Thornton*, [in the disputed area]. The Surinamese patrol boats ordered the ship and its service vessels to leave the area within twelve hours. The crew members aboard the *C.E. Thornton* detached the oil rig from the sea floor and withdrew from the concession area. The Surinamese patrol boats followed them throughout their departure. CGX has not since returned to the concession area . . . .

263. Guyana claims that Suriname's actions in June 2000 represented a breach of . . . Article 2(3) of the UN Charter requiring Member States to settle international disputes by peaceful means . . . and . . . Article 2(4) of the UN Charter in using or threatening to use force in its international relations against the territorial integrity of Guyana, which it argues remains applicable in the context of territorial or maritime boundary disputes . . . .

270. Suriname submits that Guyana exaggerates the nature of its naval operation and characterizes it as a law enforcement measure of no greater force than was strictly necessary to achieve legitimate objectives. Suriname further submits that the circumstances surrounding the action, including, *inter alia*, its instructions not to use or threaten force, are consistent with law enforcement under its domestic legislation and consistent with the type of force considered acceptable on arrest of a ship. Suriname denies that a use or threat of force has been proven or that any action was directed at Guyana because of the foreign nationality of the flag and crew of the vessel, and takes the position that exercise of coastal jurisdiction does not amount to armed force . . . .

432. With respect to the question of whether the CGX incident constituted a threat of force, the Tribunal considers it helpful to examine the statements of some of the main participants in that incident.

433. Mr Edward Netterville, the Rig Supervisor on the *C.E. Thornton*, described the incident in these terms in his witness statement:

> Shortly after midnight on 4 June 2000, while this coring process (drilling for core samples) was underway, gunboats from the Surinamese Navy arrived at our location. The gunboats established radio contact with the C.E. Thornton and its service vessels, and ordered us to "leave the area in 12 hours," warning that if we did not comply

"the consequences will be yours." The Surinamese Navy repeated this order several times. I understood this to mean that if the C.E. Thornton and its support vessels did not leave the area within twelve hours, the gunboats would be unconstrained to use armed force against the rig and its service vessels . . . .

435. Mr. Graham Barber, who served as Reading & Bates Area Manager for the project and had overall responsibility for its rig and shore-based operations, gave similar testimony. He stated that:

> After midnight on 3 June 2000, during the jacking-up process, two gunboats from the Surinamese Navy approached us and shined their search lights on the rig. A Surinamese naval officer informed us by radio that we "were in Surinamese waters" and that we had 12 hours to leave the area or "face the consequences." He repeated this phrase, or variations of it, several times . . . . Faced with these threats from the Surinamese Navy, in the early morning hours of 4 June 2003, I convened a meeting with other persons in authority aboard the C.E. Thornton. We decided that we had no alternative other than to evacuate the rig from the Eagle location.

436. Major J.P. Jones, Commander Staff Support of the LUMAR (the Suriname Air Force and Navy), recorded this exchange between himself and the drilling platform:

> This is the Suriname navy. You are in Suriname waters without authority of the Suriname Government to conduct economic activities here. I order you to stop immediately with these activities and leave the Suriname waters.
>
> The answer to this from the platform was: "we are unaware of being in Suriname waters". I persisted saying that they were in Suriname waters and that they had to leave these waters within 12 hours. And if they would not do so, the consequences would be theirs. They then asked where they should move to. I said that they should retreat to Guyanese waters. He reacted by saying that they needed time to start up their departure. I then allowed them 24 hours to leave the Suriname waters. We then hung around for some time and after about one hour we left . . . .

437. Major Jones added:

> If the platform had not left our waters voluntarily, I would definitely not have used force. I had no instructions to that effect and anyhow I did not have the suitable weapons to do so. I even had no instructions to board the drilling platform and also I did not consider that.

438. The captains of the two Surinamese patrol boats, Mr. M. Galong and Mr. R.S. Bhola, both confirmed that the drilling platform was ordered to leave Suriname waters within 12 hours and if this order was not complied with, the consequences would be theirs. With respect to what the consequences would be, both Captain Galong and Captain Bhola noted that they had no instructions with regard to the use of force. Captain Bhola stated that:

> In the periods May 1989–1990 and 1997 up to now I have performed at least 30 patrol missions off the coast of Suriname. These patrol missions also involved the sea area between 10° and 30° North which is disputed between Suriname and Guyana. The patrols had mainly to do with expelling fishermen without a licence from Suriname

waters. This has always been achieved by issuing summons. In such cases the commander of the vessel is in command of the operation. My instructions never imply that I may use force and I have never used force. All things considered the course of the removal of the drilling platform, as far as I am concerned, does not differ essentially from the course taken during other patrols.

439. The testimony of those involved in the incident clearly reveals that the rig was ordered to leave the area and if this demand was not fulfilled, responsibility for unspecified consequences would be theirs. There was no unanimity as to what these "consequences" might have been. The Tribunal is of the view that the order given by Major Jones to the rig constituted an explicit threat that force might be used if the order was not complied with. The question now arises whether this threat of the use of force breaches the terms of . . . the UN Charter and general international law . . . .

[The Tribunal then referred to passages from the ICJ's *Nuclear Weapons* and *Nicaragua* cases, excerpted above, before continuing:]

445. The Tribunal accepts the argument that in international law force may be used in law enforcement activities provided that such force is unavoidable, reasonable and necessary. However in the circumstances of the present case, this Tribunal is of the view that the action mounted by Suriname on 3 June 2000 seemed more akin to a threat of military action rather than a mere law enforcement activity. This Tribunal has based this finding primarily on the testimony of witnesses to the incident, in particular the testimony of Messrs Netterville and Barber. Suriname's action therefore constituted a threat of the use of force in contravention of the Convention [on the Law of the Sea], the UN Charter and general international law.

How would you draw the line between a threat of force used in law enforcement activities and a threat of military action? Note that, as seen in Chapter 12, resort to countermeasures in response to an internationally wrongful act does not relieve the responding state from its obligation to refrain from the threat or use of force.

Recall that the Friendly Relations Declaration refers, in the context of the prohibition on the threat or use of force, to the illegality of a "war of aggression." "Aggression" is also referred to in Article 39 of the UN Charter, which provides that the "Security Council shall determine the existence of any threat to the peace, breach of the peace, or act of aggression and shall make recommendations, or decide what measures shall be taken . . . to maintain or restore international peace and security." The exact definition of "aggression" in international law has been the source of long-standing controversy in the international community. Consider the UN General Assembly's approach to the issue, expressed by way of a resolution adopted some four years after the Friendly Relations Declaration:

Definition of Aggression, GA Res 3314 (XXIX), UN Doc A/RES/3314/XXIX, reprinted in UN GAOR, 29th Sess, Supp No 31 at 142–44, UN Doc A/9631 (1974)

Article 1
Aggression is the use of armed force by a State against the sovereignty, territorial integrity or political independence of another State, or in any other manner inconsistent with the Charter of the United Nations, as set out in this Definition . . . .

Article 2

The first use of armed force by a State in contravention of the Charter shall constitute *prima facie* evidence of an act of aggression although the Security Council may, in conformity with the Charter, conclude that a determination that an act of aggression has been committed would not be justified in the light of other relevant circumstances, including the fact that the acts concerned or their consequences are not of sufficient gravity.

Article 3

Any of the following acts, regardless of a declaration of war, shall, subject to and in accordance with the provisions of article 2, qualify as an act of aggression:

(a) The invasion or attack by the armed forces of a State of the territory of another State, or any military occupation, however temporary, resulting from such invasion or attack, or any annexation by the use of force of the territory of another State or part thereof;

(b) Bombardment by the armed forces of a State against the territory of another State or the use of any weapons by a State against the territory of another State;

(c) The blockade of the ports or coasts of a State by the armed forces of another State;

(d) An attack by the armed forces of a State on the land, sea or air forces, or marine and air fleets of another State;

(e) The use of armed forces of one State which are within the territory of another State with the agreement of the receiving State, in contravention of the conditions provided for in the agreement or any extension of their presence in such territory beyond the termination of the agreement;

(f) The action of a State in allowing its territory, which it has placed at the disposal of another State, to be used by that other State for perpetrating an act of aggression against a third State;

(g) The sending by or on behalf of a State of armed bands, groups, irregulars or mercenaries, which carry out acts of armed force against another State of such gravity as to amount to the acts listed above, or its substantial involvement therein.

Article 4

The acts enumerated above are not exhaustive and the Security Council may determine that other acts constitute aggression under the provisions of the Charter.

Article 5

1. No consideration of whatever nature, whether political, economic, military or otherwise, may serve as a justification for aggression.

2. A war of aggression is a crime against international peace. Aggression gives rise to international responsibility.

3. No territorial acquisition or special advantage resulting from aggression is or shall be recognized as lawful.

Article 6

Nothing in this Definition shall be construed as in any way enlarging or diminishing the scope of the Charter, including its provisions concerning cases in which the use of force is lawful.

Article 7

Nothing in this Definition, and in particular article 3, could in any way prejudice the right to self-determination, freedom and independence, as derived from the Charter, of peoples forcibly deprived of that right and referred to in the Declaration on Principles of International Law concerning Friendly Relations and Cooperation among States in accordance with the Charter of the United Nations, particularly peoples under colonial and racist regimes or other forms of alien domination: nor the right of these peoples to struggle to that end and to seek and receive support, in accordance with the principles of the Charter and in conformity with the above-mentioned Declaration.

Article 8

In their interpretation and application the above provisions are interrelated and each provision should be construed in the context of the other provisions.

Thirty-six years later, states adopted amendments to the Rome Statute of the International Criminal Court (ICC) that would extend the ICC's jurisdiction to a new "crime of aggression."[2] As discussed in Chapter 15, the primary significance of those amendments is that individuals may someday be held individually accountable for acts of aggression. While only five states have ratified the amendments at the time of writing, it is nevertheless significant that, in drafting them, states parties to the Rome Statute relied virtually *verbatim* on the General Assembly's 1974 text as an accurate definition of the *act* of aggression — a key element of the *crime* of aggression.

Based on the provisions of the 1974 Definition of Aggression, is "aggression" simply any unjustified violation of the principle articulated in Article 2(4) of the UN Charter? Note the subtle textual differences between Article 1 of the Definition above and Article 2(4) of the UN Charter. Do these differences necessarily mean that one provision articulates a broader, more comprehensive prohibition than the other? Notice also the references to "gravity" in Articles 2 and 3 of the Definition above. Do these imply that acts of aggression are only those unjustified violations of Article 2(4) of the UN Charter that exceed a certain "gravity" threshold? The answer to this question may be clearer following consideration of the law of self-defence, below.

C. EXCEPTIONS TO THE PROHIBITION OF FORCE

1) Overview

The materials reviewed in the preceding section clearly imply that not all threats or uses of force contrary to Article 2(4) of the UN Charter are necessarily unlawful. The Charter itself explicitly recognizes two exceptions to the general prohibition set out in Article 2(4): collective military action authorized by the UN Security Council, and self-defence. Key to understanding each exception is an appreciation of their common underlying premise: that resort to force is, ultimately and in certain exceptional circumstances, a necessary

---

2   "The Crime of Aggression (Amendments to the Rome Statute of the International Criminal Court)," 11 June 2010, Resolution RC/Res.6, (2010) 49 ILM 1334, Annex I, art 2.

feature of the international legal system. Consider the following summary of the applicable rules, which refers to this underlying premise and the difficulties it poses:

A More Secure World: Our Shared Responsibility: Report of the Secretary-General's High-level Panel on Threats, Challenges and Change, UN Doc A/59/565 at 8–99 (2 December 2004)[3]

183. The framers of the Charter of the United Nations recognized that force may be necessary for the "prevention and removal of threats to the peace, and for the suppression of acts of aggression or other breaches of the peace". Military force, legally and properly applied, is a vital component of any workable system of collective security, whether defined in the traditional narrow sense or more broadly as we would prefer. But few contemporary policy issues cause more difficulty, or involve higher stakes, than the principles concerning its use and application to individual cases.

184. The maintenance of world peace and security depends importantly on there being a common global understanding, and acceptance, of when the application of force is both legal and legitimate. One of these elements being satisfied without the other will always weaken the international legal order—and thereby put both State and human security at greater risk . . . .

185. The Charter of the United Nations, in Article 2.4, expressly prohibits Member States from using or threatening force against each other, allowing only two exceptions: self-defence under Article 51, and military measures authorized by the Security Council under Chapter VII . . . in response to "any threat to the peace, breach of the peace or act of aggression".

186. For the first 44 years of the United Nations, Member States often violated these rules and used military force literally hundreds of times, with a paralysed Security Council passing very few Chapter VII resolutions and Article 51 only rarely providing credible cover. Since the end of the cold war, however, the yearning for an international system governed by the rule of law has grown. There is little evident international acceptance of the idea of security being best preserved by a balance of power, or by any single—even benignly motivated—superpower.

187. But in seeking to apply the express language of the Charter, three particularly difficult questions arise in practice: first, when a State claims the right to strike preventively, in self-defence, in response to a threat which is not imminent; secondly, when a State appears to be posing an external threat, actual or potential, to other States or people outside its borders, but there is disagreement in the Security Council as to what to do about it; and thirdly, where the threat is primarily internal, to a State's own people.

We consider these difficult questions in examining the exceptions to the prohibition of the use of force in the materials that follow.

---

3   Reprinted with permission.

2) Collective Action Authorized by the UN Security Council

a) The Power of the Security Council to Authorize the Use of Force

Recall that Article 42 of the UN Charter provides as follows:

> Should the Security Council consider that measures provided for in Article 41 [that is, those "not involving the use of armed force"] would be inadequate or have proved to be inadequate, it may take such action by air, sea, or land forces as may be necessary to maintain or restore international peace and security. Such action may include demonstrations, blockade, and other operations by air, sea, or land forces of Members of the United Nations.

The original scheme of the UN Charter contemplated, in Articles 43 to 47, that a standing military force would be placed at the disposal of the Security Council by member states to permit it to fulfill its functions under Article 42 directly. For reasons largely tied to the Cold War, however, such a standing force was never established. The practice that emerged in its stead was to read Article 42 as permitting the Security Council to authorize member states to use force on its behalf in appropriate circumstances.[4] Thus, in 1950, the Security Council "recommend[ed]" that member states "furnish such assistance to the Republic of Korea as may be necessary to repel the armed attack [by forces from North Korea] and to restore international peace and security in the area."[5] Similarly, in 1990 the Security Council "authorize[d]" member states to use "all necessary means" to secure the withdrawal of Iraqi occupying forces from Kuwait.[6] The words "all necessary means," or substantially similar wording, have become the accepted formulation used by the Security Council when it is authorizing the use of armed force by member states. A state using force against another state pursuant to such an authorization is presumed to be acting lawfully.[7]

This practice of the Security Council of "reading between the lines" of its Article 42 powers, and using euphemisms when authorizing the use of force, has tempted some states to take liberties of their own with the collective security regime of Chapter VII of the UN Charter. Perhaps most controversially, some states have resorted to strained interpretations of Security Council resolutions in order to glean legal cover for their use of force in particular circumstances. For example, the United States and the United Kingdom failed to secure express Security Council authorization for their invasion of Iraq in 2003. Nevertheless, efforts were made by both countries to justify their actions in part by relying on a series of past resolutions concerning Iraq, including the 1990 resolution authoriz-

---

4   An alternative explanation of this practice is that it is an exercise of the Security Council's powers of "recommendation" under Article 39 of the UN Charter, which provides that the "Security Council shall determine the existence of any threat to the peace, breach of the peace or act of aggression and shall make recommendations . . . to maintain or restore international peace and security." Little appears to turn on whether the *locus* of the power being exercised by the Security Council in such cases is Article 39 or 42, as both come within Chapter VII of the UN Charter and in no such cases has the Security Council purported to *compel* (rather than authorize) states to use force to restore international peace and security.

5   SC Resolution 83 (1950), adopted 27 June 1950, UN Doc S/RES/83 (1950).

6   SC Resolution 678 (1990), adopted 29 November 1990, UN Doc S/RES/678 (1990).

7   Yoram Dinstein, *War, Aggression and Self-Defence*, 5th ed (Cambridge: Cambridge University Press, 2011) at paras 814 and 838; Robert Kolb, "Does Article 103 of the Charter of the United Nations Apply Only to Decisions or Also to Authorizations Adopted by the Security Council?" (2004) 64 ZaöRV 21 at 25–28.

ing the liberation of Kuwait mentioned above. Consider the following legal memorandum from Attorney General Lord Peter Goldsmith to Prime Minister Tony Blair:

Attorney General's Advice on the Iraq War, 7 March 2003[8]

Iraq: Resolution 1441

1. You have asked me for advice on the legality of military action against Iraq without a further resolution of the Security Council . . . .

Possible legal bases for the use of force
. . . 5. Force may be used where this is authorised by the UN Security Council acting under Chapter VII of the UN Charter. The key question is whether [Security Council] resolution 1441 has the effect of providing such authorisation.

Resolution 1441
6. As you are aware, the argument that resolution 1441 itself provides the authorisation to use force depends on the revival of the express authorisation to use force given in 1990 by Security Council resolution 678. This in turn gives rise to two questions:
(a) is the so-called "revival argument" a sound legal basis in principle?
(b) is resolution 1441 sufficient to revive the authorisation in resolution 678?

I deal with these questions in turn. It is a trite, but nonetheless relevant observation given what some commentators have been saying, that if the answer to these two questions is "yes," the use of force will have been authorised by the United Nations and not in defiance of it.

The revival argument
7. Following its invasion and annexation of Kuwait, the Security Council authorised the use of force against Iraq in resolution 678 (1990). This resolution authorised coalition forces to use all necessary means to force Iraq to withdraw from Kuwait and to restore international peace and security in the area. The resolution gave a legal basis for Operation Desert Storm, which was brought to an end by the cease-fire set out by the Council in resolution 687 (1991). The conditions for the cease-fire in that resolution (and subsequent resolutions) imposed obligations on Iraq with regard to the elimination of WMD and monitoring of its obligations. Resolution 687 suspended, but did not terminate, the authority to use force in resolution 678. Nor has any subsequent resolution terminated the authorisation to use force in resolution 678. It has been the UK's view that a violation of Iraq's obligations under resolution 687 which is sufficiently serious to undermine the basis of the cease-fire can revive the authorisation to use force in resolution 678.

8. In reliance on this argument, force has been used on certain occasions. I am advised by the Foreign Office Legal Advisers that this was the basis for the use of force between 13 and 18 January 1993 following UN Presidential Statements on 8 and 11 January 1993 condemning particular failures by Iraq to observe the terms of the cease-fire resolution. The revival argument was also the basis for the use of force in December 1998 by the US

---

8   Reprinted in (2005) 54:3 ICLQ 767–78.

and UK (Operation Desert Fox). This followed a series of Security Council resolutions, notably, resolution 1205 (1998).

9. Law Officers have advised in the past that, provided the conditions are made out, the revival argument does provide a sufficient justification in international law for the use of force against Iraq. That view is supported by an opinion given in August 1992 by the then UN Legal Counsel, Carl-August Fleischauer. However, the UK has consistently taken the view (as did the Fleischauer opinion) that, as the cease-fire conditions were set by the Security Council in resolution 687, it is for the Council to assess whether any such breach of those obligations has occurred. The US have a rather different view: they maintain that the fact of whether Iraq is in breach is a matter of objective fact which may therefore be assessed by individual Member States. I am not aware of any other state which supports this view. This is an issue of critical importance when considering the effect of resolution 1441.

10. The revival argument is controversial. It is not widely accepted among academic commentators. However, I agree with my predecessors' advice on this issue. Further, I believe that the arguments in support of the revival argument are stronger following adoption of resolution 1441. That is because of the terms of the resolution and the course of the negotiations which led to its adoption. Thus, preambular paragraphs 4, 5 and 10 recall the authorisation to use force in resolution 678 and that resolution 687 imposed obligations on Iraq as a necessary condition of the cease-fire. Operative paragraph (OP) 1 provides that Iraq has been and remains in material breach of its obligations under relevant resolutions, including resolution 687. OP13 recalls that Iraq has been warned repeatedly that "serious consequences" will result from continued violations of its obligations. The previous practice of the Council and statements made by Council members during the negotiation of resolution 1441 demonstrate that the phrase "material breach" signifies a finding by the Council of a sufficiently serious breach of the cease-fire conditions to revive the authorisation in resolution 678 and that "serious consequences" is accepted as indicating the use of force.

11. I disagree, therefore, with those commentators and lawyers, who assert that nothing less than an explicit authorisation to use force in a Security Council resolution will be sufficient.

Sufficiency of resolution 1441
12. In order for the authorisation to use force in resolution 678 to be revived, there needs to be a determination by the Security Council that there is a violation of the conditions of the cease-fire and that the Security Council considers it sufficiently serious to destroy the basis of the cease-fire. Revival will not, however, take place, notwithstanding a finding of violation, if the Security Council has made it clear either that action short of the use of force should be taken to ensure compliance with the terms of the cease-fire, or that it intends to decide subsequently what action is required to ensure compliance. Notwithstanding the determination of material breach in OP1 of resolution 1441, it is clear that the Council did not intend that the authorisation in resolution 678 should revive immediately following the adoption of resolution 1441, since OP2 of the resolution affords Iraq a "final opportunity" to comply with its disarmament obligations under previous

resolutions by cooperating with the enhanced inspection regime described in OPs 3 and 5-9. But OP2 also states that the Council has determined that compliance with resolution 1441 is Iraq's last chance before the cease-fire resolution will be enforced. OP2 has the effect therefore of suspending the legal consequences of the OP1 determination of material breach which would otherwise have triggered the revival of the authorisation in resolution 678. The narrow but key question is: on the true interpretation of resolution 1441, what has the Security Council decided will be the consequences of Iraq's failure to comply with the enhanced regime.

13. The provisions relevant to determining whether or not Iraq has taken the final opportunity given by the Security Council are contained in OPs 4, 11 and 12 of the resolution.

- OP4 provides that false statements or omissions in the declaration to be submitted by Iraq under OP3 and failure by Iraq at any time to comply with and cooperate fully in the implementation of resolution 1441 will constitute a further material breach of Iraq's obligations and will be reported to the Council for assessment under paragraphs 11 and 12 of the resolution.

- OP11 directs the Executive Chairman of UNMOVIC and the Director-General of the IAEA to report immediately to the Council any interference by Iraq with inspection activities, as well as any failure by Iraq to comply with its disarmament obligations, including the obligations regarding inspections under resolution 1441.

- OP12 provides that the Council will convene immediately on receipt of a report in accordance with paragraphs 4 or 11 "in order to consider the situation and the need for compliance with all of the relevant Council resolutions in order to secure international peace and security."

It is clear from the text of the resolution, and is apparent from the negotiating history, that if Iraq fails to comply, there will be a further Security Council discussion. The text is, however, ambiguous and unclear on what happens next . . . .

Summary

26. To sum up, the language of resolution 1441 leaves the position unclear and the statements made on adoption of the resolution suggest that there were differences of view within the Council as to the legal effect of the resolution. Arguments can be made on both sides. A key question is whether there is in truth a need for an assessment of whether Iraq's conduct constitutes a failure to take the final opportunity or has constituted a failure fully to cooperate within the meaning of OP 4 such that the basis of the cease-fire is destroyed. If an assessment is needed of that sort, it would be for the Council to make it. A narrow textual reading of the resolution suggests that sort of assessment is not needed, because the Council has pre-determined the issue. Public statements, on the other hand, say otherwise.

27. In these circumstances, I remain of the opinion that the safest legal course would be to secure the adoption of a further resolution to authorise the use of force. I have already advised that I do not believe that such a resolution need be explicit in its terms. The key point is that it should establish that the Council has concluded that Iraq has failed to take the final opportunity offered by resolution 1441, as in the draft which has already been tabled.

28. Nevertheless, having regard to the information on the negotiating history which I have been given and to the arguments of the US Administration which I heard in Washington, I accept that a reasonable case can be made that resolution 1441 is capable in principle of reviving the authorisation in 678 without a further resolution.

29. However, the argument that resolution 1441 alone has revived the authorisation to use force in resolution 678 will only be sustainable if there are strong factual grounds for concluding that Iraq has failed to take the final opportunity. In other words, we would need to be able to demonstrate hard evidence of non-compliance and non-cooperation. Given the structure of the resolution as a whole, the views of UNMOVIC and the IAEA will be highly significant in this respect. In the light of the latest reporting by UNMOVIC, you will need to consider extremely carefully whether the evidence of non-cooperation and non-compliance by Iraq is sufficiently compelling to justify the conclusion that Iraq has failed to take its final opportunity.

30. In reaching my conclusions, I have taken account of the fact that on a number of previous occasions, including in relation to Operation Desert Fox in December 1998 and Kosovo in 1999, UK forces have participated in military action on the basis of advice from my predecessors that the legality of the action under international law was no more than reasonably arguable. But a "reasonable case" does not mean that if the matter ever came before a court I would be confident that the court would agree with this view. I judge that, having regard to the arguments on both sides, and considering the resolution as a whole in the light of the statements made on adoption and subsequently, a court might well conclude that OPs 4 and 12 do require a further Council decision in order to revive the authorisation in resolution 678. But equally I consider that the counter view can be reasonably maintained. However, it must be recognised that on previous occasions when military action was taken on the basis of a reasonably arguable case, the degree of public and Parliamentary scrutiny of the legal issue was nothing like as great as it is today.

31. The analysis set out above applies whether a second resolution fails to be adopted because of a lack of votes or because it is vetoed. As I have said before, I do not believe that there is any basis in law for arguing that there is an implied condition of reasonableness which can be read into the power of veto conferred on the permanent members of the Security Council by the UN Charter. So there are no grounds for arguing that an "unreasonable veto" would entitle us to proceed on the basis of a presumed Security Council authorisation. In any event, if the majority of world opinion remains opposed to military action, it is likely to be difficult on the facts to categorise a French veto as "unreasonable." The legal analysis may, however, be affected by the course of events over the next week or so, e.g. the discussions on the draft second resolution. If we fail to achieve the adoption of a second resolution, we would need to consider urgently at that stage the strength of our legal case in the light of circumstances at that time.

Possible consequences of acting without a second resolution

32. In assessing the risks of acting on the basis of a reasonably arguable case, you will wish to take account of the ways in which the matter might be brought before a court. There are a number of possibilities. First, the General Assembly [GA] could request an advisory opinion on the legality of the military action from the International Court of Justice (ICJ).

A request for such an opinion could be made at the request of a simple majority of the States within the GA, so the UK and US could not block such action. Second, given that the United Kingdom has accepted the compulsory jurisdiction of the ICJ, it is possible that another State which has also accepted the Court's jurisdiction might seek to bring a case against us. This, however, seems a less likely option since Iraq itself could not bring a case and it is not easy to see on what basis any other State could establish that it had a dispute with the UK. But we cannot absolutely rule out that some State strongly opposed to military action might try to bring such a case. If it did, an application for interim measures to stop the campaign could be brought quite quickly (as it was in the case of Kosovo).

33. The International Criminal Court [ICC] at present has no jurisdiction over the crime of aggression and could therefore not entertain a case concerning the lawfulness of any military action. The ICC will however have jurisdiction to examine whether any military campaign has been conducted in accordance with international humanitarian law. Given the controversy surrounding the legal basis for action, it is likely that the Court will scrutinise any allegations of war crimes by UK forces very closely . . . . The ICC would only be able to exercise jurisdiction over UK personnel if it considered that the UK prosecuting authorities were unable or unwilling to investigate and, if appropriate, prosecute the suspects themselves . . . .

35. In short, there are a number of ways in which the opponents of military action might seek to bring a legal case, internationally or domestically, against the UK . . . . Some of these seem fairly remote possibilities, but given the strength of opposition to military action against Iraq, it would not be surprising if some attempts were made to get a case of some sort off the ground. We cannot be certain that they would not succeed. The GA route may be the most likely, but you are in a better position than me to judge whether there are likely to be enough States in the GA who would be willing to vote for such a course of action in present circumstances.

Proportionality

36. Finally, I must stress that the lawfulness of military action depends not only on the existence of a legal basis, but also on the question of proportionality. Any force used pursuant to the authorisation in resolution 678 (whether or not there is a second resolution):

- must have as its objective the enforcement of the terms of the cease-fire contained in resolution 687 (1990) and subsequent relevant resolutions;
- be limited to what is necessary to achieve that objective; and
- must be a proportionate response to that objective, i.e., securing compliance with Iraq's disarmament obligations.

That is not to say that action may not be taken to remove Saddam Hussein from power if it can be demonstrated that such action is a necessary and proportionate measure to secure the disarmament of Iraq. But regime change cannot be the objective of military action. This should be borne in mind in considering the list of military targets and in making public statements about any campaign.

As is well known, the United States, United Kingdom, and some other states proceeded with an invasion of Iraq in 2003. They did so even though they had failed to secure a Security Council resolution clearly endorsing this course of action, and notwithstanding vehement protests by France and other Security Council members that Resolution 1441 (2002)[9] had not been intended to authorize force without further Security Council action on the matter. An inquiry into the United Kingdom's involvement in the Iraq conflict, chaired by Sir John Chilcot, was launched in 2009 and is expected to report in 2014.

As is usual for such resolutions, the final operative paragraph of Resolution 1441 (2002) states that the Security Council "[d]ecides to remain seized of the matter." What is the effect of interpreting this resolution as effectively authorizing "all necessary measures" against Iraq? Given that the states willing to give Resolution 1441 (2002) such an interpretation included some permanent members of the Security Council, would it have been possible for the Security Council to contradict this interpretation in a subsequent, clarifying resolution? If not, in what sense did the Security Council "remain seized of the matter"? Would any international body have been in a position to clarify the scope of Resolution 1441 (2002)? Consider the UK attorney general's discussion of the possibility of a General Assembly request for an advisory opinion from the International Court of Justice. Consider also the recognition of a potential role for the International Criminal Court and domestic courts on a rather different issue, that is, compliance by UK actors with international humanitarian law governing conduct in armed conflict (as distinct from compliance by the United Kingdom with international legal limits on its ability to resort to armed conflict in the first place).

b) A Security Council *Responsibility* to Authorize the Use of Force?

For reasons related to the veto possessed by the five permanent members, a general indifference to particular conflicts, or both, the Security Council has often failed to authorize the use of force in circumstances where critics say it would not only have been warranted but essential. This has been particularly so in cases of mass atrocities committed in the course of internal armed conflict. Recent examples include Rwanda, Kosovo, Sudan, and Syria.

This repeated failure by the Security Council to act prompted significant debate in the late 1990s as to whether there is (or should be) a right for states to intervene forcibly in the territory of other states, without Security Council authorization, to prevent mass atrocities. Whether such a "right of humanitarian intervention" exists as a matter of international law remains a contentious issue. Consider the position taken by Belgium in the following case:

Legality of Use of Force (Yugoslavia v Belgium), **Provisional Measures, [1999] ICJ Rep 124: Oral argument of the Kingdom of Belgium, 10 May 1999, Doc CR/99/15 [translation]**

[In 1999, NATO commenced a bombing campaign against the then Federal Republic of Yugoslavia, provoked by fears of mass atrocities in Kosovo. This use of force had not been clearly sanctioned by the Security Council, as Russia had threatened to veto any proposed resolution that purported to do so. In response to the NATO bombing campaign, Yugoslavia (later Serbia and Montenegro) instituted proceedings against ten member states of NATO in the International Court of Justice, claiming violations of the prohibition on the use of force. Yugoslavia sought provisional measures from the Court to secure a halt to the ongoing bombing campaign. Most respondent states confined their submissions

---

9   SC Resolution 1441 (2002), adopted 8 November 2002, UN Doc S/RES/1441 (2002).

at this stage to matters of jurisdiction, but Belgium proceeded to make submissions on the underlying merits of Yugoslavia's claim, pleading that it had acted on the basis of humanitarian considerations.]

... NATO, and the Kingdom of Belgium in particular, felt obliged to intervene to forestall an ongoing humanitarian catastrophe, acknowledged in Security Council resolutions. To safeguard what? To safeguard, Mr. President, essential values which also rank as *jus cogens*. Are the right to life, physical integrity, the prohibition of torture, are these not norms with the status of *jus cogens*? They undeniably have this status, so much so that international instruments on human rights ... protect them in a waiver clause (the power of suspension in case of war of all human rights except right to life and integrity of the individual): thus they are absolute rights, from which we may conclude that they belong to the *jus cogens*. Thus, NATO intervened to protect fundamental values enshrined in the *jus cogens* and to prevent an impending catastrophe recognized as such by the Security Council. There is another important feature of NATO's action: NATO has never questioned the political independence and the territorial integrity of the Federal Republic of Yugoslavia—the Security Council's resolutions, the NATO decisions, and the press releases have, moreover, consistently stressed this. Thus this is not an intervention against the territorial integrity or independence of the former Republic of Yugoslavia. The purpose of NATO's intervention is to rescue a people in peril, in deep distress. For this reason the Kingdom of Belgium takes the view that this is an armed humanitarian intervention, compatible with Article 2, paragraph 4, of the Charter, which covers only intervention against the territorial integrity or political independence of a State.

There is no shortage of precedents. India's intervention in Eastern Pakistan; Tanzania's intervention in Uganda; Vietnam in Cambodia, the West African countries' interventions first in Liberia and then in Sierra Leone. While there may have been certain doubts expressed in the doctrine, and among some members of the international community, these interventions have not been expressly condemned by the relevant United Nations bodies .... Allow me to remind the Court of the three features of the intervention which have been noted by the international authorities, in this case the Security Council; there was a humanitarian catastrophe, recognised by the Security Council, imminent danger, i.e., a situation constituting a threat to peace as noted by the Security Council resolution; and the power responsible for this—as is made clear in the three Security Council resolutions—is the Federal Republic of Yugoslavia.

The intervention is of a quite exceptional character, prompted by entirely objective criteria. In the circumstances do we need to add another consideration, the tendency in contemporary international law towards a steadily greater protection of minorities? We are accused of encroaching on sovereignty, but the Government of the Kingdom of Belgium would like to quote a passage from a speech given by Mr. Kofi Annan, United Nations Secretary-General, on 30 April last, at the University of Michigan. Mr. Annan said "no Government has the right to hide behind national sovereignty in order to violate the human rights or fundamental freedoms of its peoples", and [made] a very important point, "Emerging slowly, but I believe surely is an international norm against the violent repression of minorities that will and must take precedence over concerns of State sovereignty".

NATO's action has had and still has a further dimension. The aim is to protect a distressed population in the throes of a humanitarian catastrophe, but there is also a need to safeguard the stability of an entire region, for the Security Council resolutions have also noted that the behaviour of the Federal Republic of Yugoslavia in Kosovo was generating a threat to international peace and security by impairing the stability of the whole area. This is a case of a lawful armed humanitarian intervention for which there is a compelling necessity. And, Mr. President, Members of the Court, if we have failed to convince you that what has been taking place is armed humanitarian intervention justified by international law, the Government of the Kingdom of Belgium will also plead, in the alternative, that there is a state of necessity.

The state of necessity

The notion of a state of necessity, which is enshrined in all branches of the law, is unquestionably acknowledged in international law; and the draft Article 33 [concerning state responsibility] proposed by the International Law Commission reflects this.

Allow me to suggest a definition to the Court: what is a state of necessity? A state of necessity is the cause which justifies the violation of a binding rule in order to safeguard, in face of grave and imminent peril, values which are higher than those protected by the rule which has been breached. Let me review the elements of this definition one at a time and set them against the case we are dealing with today.

First, what rule has been breached? We do not accept that any rule has been breached. However, for the sake of argument, let us say that it is the rule prohibiting the use of force. Where is the imminent peril, the grave and imminent peril? There it was—no doubt about it—at the time of the armed intervention; there it is still, the humanitarian catastrophe recorded in the resolutions of the Security Council—an impending peril. What are the higher values which this intervention attempts to safeguard? They are rights of *jus cogens*. It is the collective security of an entire region. And the final element of a state of necessity, I almost forgot, is that the acts must be proportionate; the intervention must be proportional to the threat. The intervention is wholly in proportion to the gravity of the peril; it is limited to aerial bombardments directed solely and exclusively against the war machine of the aggressor and against its military-industrial complex.

The Court will see that this is a use of force which is utterly unlike the parallel drawn this morning by one of my esteemed opponents; a parallel with what was the *diktats* of the Nazi régime to its peaceful neighbours. The Kingdom of Belgium regrets to have to say that it finds such a parallel totally unacceptable, and apt to shock the civilized legal conscience. The situation is the total reverse. It is we, the member countries of NATO, democratic countries with freely elected governments, who find ourselves confronted by a régime which rejects the most fundamental values of humanity . . . .

The Court declined the request for provisional measures and made only inconclusive references to issues affecting the merits of the case. Ultimately, the cases against all the NATO members, including Canada, were dismissed on jurisdictional grounds (Yugoslavia not having been a party to the Statute of the Court at the time the proceedings were instituted).[10] Had the case proceeded to the merits, the Court would have had an oppor-

---

10 *Legality of Use of Force (Serbia and Montenegro v Belgium)*, Preliminary Objections, [2004] ICJ Rep 279;
   Legality of Use of Force (Serbia and Montenegro v Canada), Preliminary Objections, [2004] ICJ Rep 429;
   Legality of Use of Force (Serbia and Montenegro v France), Preliminary Objections, [2004] ICJ Rep 575;

tunity to pronounce on the existence of the alleged international legal right of humanitarian intervention.

Notwithstanding the humanitarian appeal of the Belgian arguments, the preponderance of international legal opinion is that a right of unilateral "humanitarian intervention" is not presently established in international law. For example, in the *Nicaragua* case,[11] the ICJ had this to say, in response to an argument by the United States that its use of armed force in Nicaragua was justified on humanitarian grounds:

> 268. . . . [W]hile the United States might form its own appraisal of the situation as to respect for human rights in Nicaragua, the use of force could not be the appropriate method to monitor or ensure such respect. With regard to the steps actually taken, the protection of human rights, a strictly humanitarian objective, cannot be compatible with the mining of ports, the destruction of oil installations, or again with the training, arming and equipping of the *contras*. The Court concludes that the argument derived from the preservation of human rights in Nicaragua cannot afford a legal justification for the conduct of the United States . . . .

A literal approach to the UN Charter—one that does not permit humanitarian intervention that is not authorized by the Security Council—sits poorly with many people preoccupied with the atrocities that force, motivated by good intentions, might forestall. On this basis, many international lawyers took the view that the intervention in Kosovo was perhaps illegal, but still "legitimate"—a perplexing distinction suggesting moral rectitude in the face of illegality. Consider, for example, the following, somewhat self-contradictory, views on the Kosovo intervention articulated before the UK House of Commons Select Committee on Foreign Affairs:

Kosovo, Select Committee on Foreign Affairs, Fourth Report, 1999–2000 Session, House of Commons, United Kingdom, HC 28-I, 23 May 2000[12]

INTRODUCTION

124. The Government has consistently asserted that the military action taken in the Kosovo campaign has been lawful, and that NATO would not have acted outside the principles of international law. [Two] Ministers told us that states had the right to use force

---

Legality of Use of Force (Serbia and Montenegro v Germany), Preliminary Objections, [2004] ICJ Rep 720; *Legality of Use of Force (Serbia and Montenegro v Italy)*, Preliminary Objections, [2004] ICJ Rep 865; *Legality of Use of Force (Serbia and Montenegro v Netherlands)*, Preliminary Objections, [2004] ICJ Rep 1011; *Legality of Use of Force (Serbia and Montenegro v Portugal)*, Preliminary Objections, [2004] ICJ Rep 1160; *Legality of Use of Force (Serbia and Montenegro v United Kingdom)*, Preliminary Objections, [2004] ICJ Rep 1307.

11   *Military and Paramilitary Activities in and against Nicaragua (Nicaragua v United States of America)*, Merits, Judgment, [1986] ICJ Rep 14 [*Nicaragua*].

12   See also *Fourth Report of the Foreign Affairs Committee, 1999–2000 Session, Kosovo, Response of the Secretary of State for Foreign and Commonwealth Affairs*, Cm 4825 (August 2000). The memoranda prepared by Professors Brownlie, Chinkin, Greenwood, and Lowe are reprinted in (2000) 49:4 ICLQ 876–943. See also Bruno Simma, "NATO, the UN and the Use of Force: Legal Aspects" (2000) 1 EJIL 22. [Bolding in original.]

in the case of "overwhelming humanitarian necessity where, in the light of all the circumstances, a limited use of force is justifiable as the only way to avert a humanitarian catastrophe." A number of difficult questions of law (as well as difficult questions of fact) arise. In considering these questions, the Committee benefited greatly from oral evidence from three international lawyers . . . . Our oral legal witnesses were Professor Christopher Greenwood QC of the London School of Economics, Mr Mark Littman QC (author of *Kosovo: Law and Diplomacy*) and Professor Vaughan Lowe of Oxford University. Most useful written evidence was also received from Professor Ian Brownlie QC (Oxford University), Professor Christine Chinkin (University of Michigan), Professor Peter Rowe (Lancaster University) and Professor Bruno Simma (Ludwig-Maximilians-Universität, Munich). The Committee also sought the opinion of the Attorney General, but the Attorney declined to give evidence on what he described as a "matter as sensitive as this," citing the convention of the confidentiality of the Law Officers' advice to Government.

125. These legal questions are not arcane. There is a need for a system of law governing the conduct of states, just as the internal affairs of states should be governed by the rule of law. An agreed system of law is particularly important where the use of force is concerned. It is in the national interest of the United Kingdom that an international order based on law should exist, and that individual states, or groups of states, should not be able to interpret the law perversely in their immediate interest. When the law is clear, there can be a consensus; when there is ambiguity, international stability and the mechanisms of collective security set up through the United Nations are threatened.

Was military intervention legal?

UNITED NATIONS APPROVAL

126. . . . The Charter prohibits the threat or use of force except in self defence or when the Security Council determines that there is a threat to peace, breach of the peace or act of aggression, in which case the Security Council may determine (under Chapter VII) that force should be employed "to maintain or restore international peace and security." The NATO military intervention was patently not an act of self defence, nor was there any specific Security Council authorisation for the operation . . . . The FCO [Foreign and Commonwealth Office] told us that it had been clear since June 1998 that China and Russia would veto any authorisation of Chapter VII intervention in Kosovo in the Security Council . . . .

127. There were certainly many actions at the United Nations which could properly be interpreted as supportive of the NATO allies' position:

- UNSCR [UN Security Council Resolution] 1199 of September 1998 was agreed under Chapter VII, though it did not authorise "all necessary means." It called for a cease-fire, recognised "the impending humanitarian catastrophe," and affirmed that there was a threat to peace and security;
- UNSCR 1203, adopted in October 1998 after the agreement signed in Belgrade following the NATO threat of force, does not condemn the threat of force (and indeed welcomed the agreement secured), and can therefore be taken tacitly to support its use. It again affirms the existence of a threat to peace;
- the Security Council rejected (by 12 votes to 3) a draft resolution proposed by Russia on 26 March 1999 which would have condemned NATO military action. The rejection of a

proposition that military action should be condemned could be interpreted as approval of that action;

- UNSCR 1244 of 10 June 1999 authorised the international security presence in Kosovo to exercise "all necessary means" to fulfill its responsibilities. Again, this could be taken to imply post facto approval of the military action.

As Professor Chinkin put it:

"Arguments for the legality of NATO's actions in the FRY are strengthened by taking all these actions together: the Security Council recognised the situation in Kosovo as warranting Chapter VII action; it imposed such measures as it could get agreement on; prior to the bombing it affirmed the on-going actions of various European organisations, the EU, the OSCE and NATO, that did not involve the use of force; when it could take no stronger measures itself it did not condemn the regional agency that did so act; and subsequent to the action it endorsed the political agreement."

But she remains dubious that these were sufficient grounds to regard NATO's actions as lawful.

UNITING FOR PEACE

128. There is a procedure at the United Nations known as "Uniting for Peace" [GA Res. 377 A (V), reprinted in UN GAOR, 5th Sess., Supp. No. 20 at 10-12, UN Doc. A/1775 (1950)]. This can help a blockage in the Security Council to be bypassed by reference to the General Assembly. Uniting for Peace is relevant only when a peace-and-security issue is on the Security Council agenda and the Council is prevented from exercising its "primary responsibility" to deal with it by veto of one of its permanent members. Though Article 12 of the UN Charter bars the General Assembly from making any recommendation in respect of any dispute or situation where the Security Council is exercising its functions, except at Security Council request, a procedural vote to refer a matter to the General Assembly requires the affirmative vote of nine members of the Security Council and is not subject to veto. The Uniting for Peace procedure was used against the United Kingdom and France over their intervention in Suez in 1956. In the case of Kosovo, the General Assembly could have been called into special session and could, by two-thirds majority, have supported military action. [Nevertheless], though a resolution of the General Assembly would have been particularly persuasive, the UN Charter still specified that military action required Security Council endorsement. Moreover, in some ways a bare two thirds majority would have been less persuasive than the majority (of 12 to three) actually secured in the Security Council on 26 March 1999. There was thus no ready means at the United Nations of securing direct approval for the NATO action in Kosovo. **Our conclusion is that *Operation Allied Force* was contrary to the specific terms of what might be termed the basic law of the international community—the UN Charter, although this might have been avoided if the Allies had attempted to use the Uniting for Peace procedures.**

CUSTOMARY INTERNATIONAL LAW: INTERVENTION FOR HUMANITARIAN PURPOSES (HUMANITARIAN INTERVENTION)

129. International law is not, however, static. It develops both through the agreement of new treaties and other international instruments, and through the evolution of customary law. The Charter of the United Nations has been interpreted in different ways in the

half century since it was written. As Professor Greenwood pointed out, some parts of the Charter have been conveniently ignored, while, since the end of the Cold War, the provisions of Article 2(7) which forbid intervention in internal affairs of states have been widened to allow such intervention on the grounds that what is happening internally in the state threatens international peace and security. Moreover, it is at least arguable that the preponderant will of the international community ought not to be held to ransom by the exercise of the veto (or threat of the exercise of the veto) by a minority, or indeed only one, of the permanent members of the Security Council. As Professor Greenwood put it, "an interpretation of international law which would forbid intervention to prevent something as terrible as the Holocaust, unless a permanent member could be persuaded to lift its veto, would be contrary to the principles on which modern international law is based as well as flying in the face of the developments of the last fifty years." We also note the fact that a veto by China on 25 February 1999 prevented the Security Council from authorising a six month extension of the term of the UN Preventive Deployment Force (UNPREDEP) in Macedonia. It was commonly believed that this veto was cast because of the establishment of diplomatic relations with Taiwan by Macedonia. One country's veto should not force the international community to sit on the sidelines and watch appalling human rights violations continue unchecked. We discuss the issue of the morality of the intervention, as distinct from its legality, below.

130. Supporters of NATO's position argue that a new right has developed in customary international law—the right of humanitarian intervention. The argument in favour of the existence of this right was set out by Professor Greenwood. First he asserted that states' rights did not take priority over human rights. Second he argued that there was increasing evidence of the exercise of intervention in defence of human rights. Third he pointed to recognition by the Security Council that human rights violations could be a threat to international security. He concluded that "modern customary international law does not exclude all possibility of military intervention on humanitarian grounds by states, or by an organisation like NATO," though he qualified his opinion by saying that two criteria had to be met: the existence, or immediate threat, of "the most serious humanitarian emergency involving large scale loss of life" and military intervention being "the only practicable means by which that loss of life can be ended or prevented." Dame Pauline Neville-Jones [of the FCO] was clear that NATO action had been lawful, and Professor Lowe told us that NATO action (if a breach of a fifty year old Charter) was "consonant with the way international customary law is developing." Professor Reisman put it thus: "when human rights enforcement by military means is required, it should, indeed be the responsibility of the Security Council acting under the Charter. But when the Council cannot act, the legal requirement continues to be to save lives."

131. Professor Greenwood conceded that the right of humanitarian intervention was based on state practice, but that this was state practice which had evolved in the past 10 years since the end of the Cold War. Although the interventions of India in East Pakistan (1971), Vietnam in Cambodia (1978), and Tanzania in Uganda (1979) had the effect of putting an end to massive human rights violations in each case, the intervening states relied ultimately on arguments of self-defence to justify their actions, even if reference was also made to the humanitarian situation. Only the interventions of ECOWAS

in Liberia (1990) and the intervention by the USA, the United Kingdom and France in northern Iraq (1992) seem to have been unambiguously humanitarian in their stated aims. Professor Greenwood told us that the very short time scale over which the new practice had been apparent was unsurprising in international law, where a custom could develop much more quickly than in domestic law. Moreover, he argued that customary law formed a much more important part of international law than it did of domestic law.

132. An entirely contrary view is taken by Professor Brownlie, who provided the Committee with an exhaustive review of the authorities, including jurists of twelve nationalities, three of whom had been President of the International Court of Justice. He concluded that "there is very little evidence to support assertions that a new principle of customary law legitimating humanitarian intervention has crystallised." Professor Brownlie's view that the right of humanitarian intervention was at least doubtful was also held by Professor Lowe (who told us that "few lawyers would claim that the 'right' is at present clearly established in international law") and Professor Chinkin (who wrote that she did "not think that state practice is sufficient to conclude definitively that the right to use force for humanitarian reasons has become part of customary international law"). We are persuaded that Professor Greenwood was too ambitious in saying that a new customary right has developed. **We conclude that, at the very least, the doctrine of humanitarian intervention has a tenuous basis in current international customary law, and that this renders NATO action legally questionable.**

HUMANITARIAN INTERVENTION IN SUPPORT OF THE SECURITY COUNCIL

133. Circumvention of the Security Council is a step which cannot be taken lightly, especially when, as Professor Lowe argued, the Security Council has begun to act since the end of the Cold War as it was always intended to act, with Chapter VII invoked over 120 times and few vetos cast. Mr Littman told us of his view that acting without Security Council approval was also contrary to public policy since to do so might lead to more conflict; because the precedent was likely to be abused; and because such action would only be taken by powerful states against less powerful states. To sideline the Council would, in his view, be foolish. But as we have already described, there were many indications of Security Council support for NATO's actions, even if no resolution specifically authorised the use of force.

134. To justify its action the British Government relied not just upon a defence of humanitarian intervention, but a defence of humanitarian intervention in support of the Security Council, if not specifically endorsed by the Council. The Government's position on the legality of *Operation Allied Force* was in this way clearly set out by the then Defence Secretary on 25 March 1999. He told the House that the Government was "in no doubt that NATO is acting within international law" and that "the use of force . . . can be justified as an exceptional measure in support of purposes laid down by the UN Secretary, but without the Council's express authorisation, where that is the only means to avert an immediate and overwhelming humanitarian catastrophe." Identical wording was used in evidence to the Committee. This legal justification was described by Professor Lowe as "one of some subtlety" because it wrapped up two separate issues—the criteria on which it might be lawful to intervene, and the manner in which it can be determined whether those criteria

have been met. We conclude that, faced with the threat of veto in the Security Council by Russia and China, the NATO allies did all that they could to make the military intervention in Kosovo as compliant with the tenets of international law as possible . . . .

INTERNATIONAL COURT OF JUSTICE

136. It would have been possible for the legality of the intervention to have been subject to the judgement of the International Court of Justice. Yugoslavia brought proceedings against several members of NATO, including the United Kingdom, in April 1999. The United Kingdom, decided, however, not to contest the substantive issue but to argue the procedural point that Yugoslavia had accepted the Court's compulsory jurisdiction too late for the United Kingdom to be required to deal with the substantive issue. Dr Jones Parry agreed that this was "a legal technicality." Mr Littman was very critical of this decision because it had, in his view, deprived the world of an authoritative judgement on the legality of humanitarian intervention. Professor Lowe, however, argued that the United Kingdom should not accept jurisdiction in this case because the law in the area was in a state of development, and the International Court might arrest that development. The decision to rely on a technicality to prevent the International Court from deciding the issue does suggest a concern that the judgement would not have been favourable, though this was specifically denied by FCO witnesses, who instead said that the Government had been unwilling to allow the "capricious" use of the Court by the Yugoslavs.

LAW AND MORALITY

137. Disputes about international law are not ones which this Committee can resolve, but there is a separate question of morality. Philosophers since Aquinas have wrestled with the issue of when a war is a just war, and many of the issues raised by the Kosovo campaign are germane to that debate. Whether NATO action was lawful is a very different question from whether NATO action was right . . . . Professor Simma pointed out that there is a moral, as well as a legal issue at stake:

> "Humanitarian interventions involving the threat or use of armed force and undertaken without the mandate or the authorisation of the Security Council will, as a matter of principle, remain in breach of international law. But such a general statement cannot be the last word. Rather, in any instance of humanitarian intervention a careful assessment will have to be made of how heavily such illegality weighs against all the circumstances of a particular concrete case, and of the efforts, if any, undertaken by the parties involved to get 'as close to the law' as possible. Such analyses will influence not only the moral but also the legal judgement in such cases."

As Professor Chinkin put it, "the actions have a legitimacy, if not strict legality under international law." Professor Reisman, while upholding the importance of the rule of law, and clearly discomforted by some aspects of the legality of the Kosovo campaign, pointed to US Supreme Court Justice Holmes's dictum that "a constitution is not a suicide pact." We believe that, while legal questions in international relations are important, law cannot become a means by which universally acknowledged principles of human rights are undermined.

138. To determine whether NATO's action was morally justified, and legally justified under the criteria which NATO set itself, we have to ask whether a humanitarian emer-

gency existed before NATO intervened, and whether a humanitarian catastrophe would have occurred—perhaps over a number of years, rather than being concentrated within the 78 days of the NATO campaign—if intervention had not taken place. We have dealt with these issues elsewhere, and concluded that the answer to both questions is "yes". That being the case, **we conclude that NATO's military action, if of dubious legality in the current state of international law, was justified on moral grounds.**

THE DEVELOPMENT OF THE LAW

139. Professor Lowe told us that it was now much more important to develop international law so that actions such as *Operation Allied Force* would in future be legally acceptable. Ideally, the international community should agree [to] a treaty which would set out the conditions under which humanitarian intervention should be permissible. However, Professor Lowe believed that there was no likelihood of consensus on a treaty text on humanitarian intervention, but that the parameters for action set by NATO as expressed by the then Defence Secretary should become the basis of new customary law principles. Mr Littman believed that Professor Lowe's view that there was no prospect of a new treaty text indicated that there was no consensus as to the principles of humanitarian intervention, and for that reason it could not be argued that a new custom of international law had arisen. In his view, "a custom can only exist by the general consent of mankind." Professor Greenwood repudiated this argument, pointing to the past failure to agree on the definition of terrorism. He told us that "the fact that states are not prepared to agree on a form of words does not mean that they do not support the principle of humanitarian intervention."

140. Professor Lowe set out his principles for humanitarian intervention as follows:

"• prior determination by the Security Council of a grave crisis, threatening international peace and security;
• articulation by the Security Council of specific policies for the resolution of the crisis, the implementation of which can be secured or furthered by armed intervention;
• an imminent humanitarian catastrophe which it is believed can be averted by the use of force and only by the use of force;
• intervention by a multinational force."

A considerable problem for these criteria is the involvement of the Security Council. As Mr Littman pointed out, if "the passing of the non-force resolution would legally open the door to forceful intervention, the states which were opposed to the latter would veto the former." It is certainly likely that China and Russia might not be prepared to allow the Security Council to determine that a country's internal problems were a threat to peace if they felt that a resolution to this effect gave a green light to the use of force somewhere down the line. Professor Lowe's desire to keep the Security Council involved was shared by Professor Greenwood who told us that it was "obviously desirable, where possible" for the Security Council to take action. But the dilemma remains of balancing the problem of potential Security Council paralysis with the danger of having too few hurdles to prevent states from asserting a right of intervention on specious humanitarian grounds. In a subsequent memorandum, Professor Lowe conceded that, if the use of the veto in the

Security Council led to stalemate, "the possibility of proceeding on the basis of a similar determination made by a regional organisation might have to be considered."

141. Alternative criteria were set out by Professor Chinkin. These were that:
    (i) a gross violation of human rights occurring in the targeted state
    (ii) the UN is unable or unwilling to act
    (iii) an overwhelming necessity to act
    (iv) the intervention must be proportionate . . . .

143. Of course, NATO's action in Kosovo is itself a precedent. As Professor Greenwood told us, customary international law develops through actions by states. Professor Lowe pointed out that "new rules of customary law emerge when a consistent practice is followed or acquiesced in by states in general", and that if NATO states assert that *Operation Allied Force* was the exercise of a legal right, "they help to lay the foundations of a legal rule that would entitle all states to act similarly in comparable situations." He amplified his view in a supplementary memorandum. Mr Littman told us that the precedent was not valid because the Kosovo action was not regarded as lawful, but in this view he appears to argue against the whole principle of evolving customary law.

144. The international community will not be *obliged* to intervene for humanitarian reasons even if it were legally possible for it to do so. As in the case of Rwanda, drawn to our attention by Professor Greenwood, or Chechnya, it may choose not to do so for reasons of practicality or *realpolitik*. The Government's formulation of "likely to achieve its objective" would cover the case of Chechnya. It will certainly be important that strict criteria such as those set out by the Government are applied before any humanitarian intervention is deemed desirable. Mr Littman quoted a FCO document of 1986 which argues against the right of humanitarian intervention "on prudential grounds" because "the scope for abusing such a right argues strongly against its creation." Professor Greenwood argued that this is not persuasive, because "all rights are capable of being abused." Professor Lowe did not believe that "objective criteria can ever be used to establish without doubt that a particular instance of humanitarian intervention is justifiable", and he conceded that "the danger of abuse is evident." Nevertheless, what will be important is that criteria are devised which would establish with as little doubt as possible when humanitarian intervention is justifiable and when it is not, and that these criteria must not be so flexible as to legitimise one state's intervention in another's internal affairs simply because of an assertion of humanitarian grounds for doing so. **We support the FCO in its aim of establishing in the United Nations new principles governing humanitarian intervention.**

What does it mean to be "as compliant with the tenets of international law as possible"? Should such a characterization play any role in assessing the legality of a state's actions under international law?

What would be the principal danger of recognizing a right for states to intervene militarily in other states, without Security Council authorization, on humanitarian grounds?

Note the Report's recommendation that the UK FCO support the establishment "in the United Nations" of new principles governing humanitarian intervention. This presages the way in which the debate over humanitarian intervention has in fact evolved since the Kosovo crisis. Rather than focusing on whether states may have a unilateral right to intervene on humanitarian grounds, discussion has centred around the responsibilities incumbent upon the Security Council as a result of its unique role under the UN Charter. Thus, considerable energy in UN reform discussions has been devoted to the question of when force *should be* authorized by the Security Council—that is, when it should discharge its "responsibility to protect."

Canada also responded to the challenge by creating and resourcing an independent twelve-member body, known as the International Commission on Intervention and State Sovereignty (ICISS), which pioneered the "responsibility-to-protect" concept. Consider some of its key conclusions:

The Responsibility to Protect: Report of the International Commission on Intervention and State Sovereignty **(Ottawa: International Development Research Centre, 2001) at xi**

(1) BASIC PRINCIPLES
A. State sovereignty implies responsibility, and the primary responsibility for the protection of its people lies with the state itself.
B. Where a population is suffering serious harm, as a result of internal war, insurgency, repression or state failure, and the state in question is unwilling or unable to halt or avert it, the principle of non-intervention yields to the international responsibility to protect.

(2) FOUNDATIONS
The foundations of the responsibility to protect, as a guiding principle for the international community of states, lie in:
A. obligations inherent in the concept of sovereignty;
B. the responsibility of the Security Council, under Article 24 of the UN Charter, for the maintenance of international peace and security;
C. specific legal obligations under human rights and human protection declarations, covenants and treaties, international humanitarian law and national law;
D. the developing practice of states, regional organizations and the Security Council itself.

(3) ELEMENTS
The responsibility to protect embraces three specific responsibilities:
A. **The responsibility to prevent:** to address both the root causes and direct causes of internal conflict and other man-made crises putting populations at risk.
B. **The responsibility to react:** to respond to situations of compelling human need with appropriate measures, which may include coercive measures like sanctions and international prosecution, and in extreme cases military intervention.
C. **The responsibility to rebuild:** to provide, particularly after a military intervention, full assistance with recovery, reconstruction and reconciliation, addressing the causes of the harm the intervention was designed to halt or avert.

(4) PRIORITIES
A. **Prevention is the single most important dimension of the responsibility to protect:** prevention options should always be exhausted before intervention is contemplated, and more commitment and resources must be devoted to it.

B. The exercise of the responsibility to both prevent and react should always involve less intrusive and coercive measures being considered before more coercive and intrusive ones are applied.

THE RESPONSIBILITY TO PROTECT: PRINCIPLES FOR MILITARY INTERVENTION

(1) THE JUST CAUSE THRESHOLD

Military intervention for human protection purposes is an exceptional and extraordinary measure. To be warranted, there must be serious and irreparable harm occurring to human beings, or imminently likely to occur, of the following kind:

A. **large scale loss of life**, actual or apprehended, with genocidal intent or not, which is the product either of deliberate state action, or state neglect or inability to act, or a failed state situation; or

B. **large scale 'ethnic cleansing'**, actual or apprehended, whether carried out by killing, forced expulsion, acts of terror or rape.

(2) THE PRECAUTIONARY PRINCIPLES

A. **Right intention:** The primary purpose of the intervention, whatever other motives intervening states may have, must be to halt or avert human suffering. Right intention is better assured with multilateral operations, clearly supported by regional opinion and the victims concerned.

B. **Last resort:** Military intervention can only be justified when every non-military option for the prevention or peaceful resolution of the crisis has been explored, with reasonable grounds for believing lesser measures would not have succeeded.

C. **Proportional means:** The scale, duration and intensity of the planned military intervention should be the minimum necessary to secure the defined human protection objective.

D. **Reasonable prospects:** There must be a reasonable chance of success in halting or averting the suffering which has justified the intervention, with the consequences of action not likely to be worse than the consequences of inaction.

(3) RIGHT AUTHORITY

A. There is no better or more appropriate body than the United Nations Security Council to authorize military intervention for human protection purposes. The task is not to find alternatives to the Security Council as a source of authority, but to make the Security Council work better than it has.

B. Security Council authorization should in all cases be sought prior to any military intervention action being carried out. Those calling for an intervention should formally request such authorization, or have the Council raise the matter on its own initiative, or have the Secretary-General raise it under Article 99 of the UN Charter.

C. The Security Council should deal promptly with any request for authority to intervene where there are allegations of large scale loss of human life or ethnic cleansing. It should in this context seek adequate verification of facts or conditions on the ground that might support a military intervention.

D. The Permanent Five members of the Security Council should agree not to apply their veto power, in matters where their vital state interests are not involved, to obstruct the passage of resolutions authorizing military intervention for human protection purposes for which there is otherwise majority support.

E. If the Security Council rejects a proposal or fails to deal with it in a reasonable time, alternative options are:

    I. consideration of the matter by the General Assembly in Emergency Special Session under the "Uniting for Peace" procedure; and

    II. action within area of jurisdiction by regional or sub-regional organizations under Chapter VIII of the Charter, subject to their seeking subsequent authorization from the Security Council.

F. The Security Council should take into account in all its deliberations that, if it fails to discharge its responsibility to protect in conscience-shocking situations crying out for action, concerned states may not rule out other means to meet the gravity and urgency of that situation — and that the stature and credibility of the United Nations may suffer thereby.

(4) OPERATIONAL PRINCIPLES

A. Clear objectives; clear and unambiguous mandate at all times; and resources to match.

B. Common military approach among involved partners; unity of command; clear and unequivocal communications and chain of command.

C. Acceptance of limitations, incrementalism and gradualism in the application of force, the objective being protection of a population, not defeat of a state.

D. Rules of engagement which fit the operational concept; are precise; reflect the principle of proportionality; and involve total adherence to international humanitarian law.

E. Acceptance that force protection cannot become the principal objective.

F. Maximum possible coordination with humanitarian organizations . . . .

The ICISS report had a profound impact on the shape and thrust of subsequent discussions. Three years after its release, its central theme had entered the wider lexicon of UN reform and the concept of a responsibility to protect received endorsement in the preparatory work for the UN World Summit of 2005, as seen in the following excerpts from the report of the UN Secretary-General's High-level Panel on Threats, Challenges and Change:

A More Secure World: Our Shared Responsibility, Report of the Secretary-General's High-level Panel on Threats, Challenges and Change, UN Doc A/59/565 at 8–99 (2 December 2004)[13]

193. In the case of a State posing a threat to other States, people outside its borders or to international order more generally, the language of Chapter VII is inherently broad enough, and has been interpreted broadly enough, to allow the Security Council to approve any coercive action at all, including military action, against a State when it deems this "necessary to maintain or restore international peace and security". That is the case whether the threat is occurring now, in the imminent future or more distant future; whether it involves the State's own actions or those of non-State actors it harbours or supports; or whether it takes

---

13 Reprinted with permission. [Bolding in original.]

the form of an act or omission, an actual or potential act of violence or simply a challenge to the Council's authority . . . .

195. Questions of legality apart, there will be issues of prudence, or legitimacy, about whether such preventive action *should* be taken: crucial among them is whether there is credible evidence of the reality of the threat in question (taking into account both capability and specific intent) and whether the military response is the only reasonable one in the circumstances. We address these issues further below.

196. It may be that some States will always feel that they have the obligation to their own citizens, and the capacity, to do whatever they feel they need to do, unburdened by the constraints of collective Security Council process. But however understandable that approach may have been in the cold war years, when the United Nations was manifestly not operating as an effective collective security system, the world has now changed and expectations about legal compliance are very much higher.

197. One of the reasons why States may want to bypass the Security Council is a lack of confidence in the quality and objectivity of its decision-making. The Council's decisions have often been less than consistent, less than persuasive and less than fully responsive to very real State and human security needs. But the solution is not to reduce the Council to impotence and irrelevance: it is to work from within to reform it, including in the ways we propose in the present report.

198. **The Security Council is fully empowered under Chapter VII of the Charter of the United Nations to address the full range of security threats with which States are concerned. The task is not to find alternatives to the Security Council as a source of authority but to make the Council work better than it has** . . . .

199. The Charter of the United Nations is not as clear as it could be when it comes to saving lives within countries in situations of mass atrocity. It "reaffirm(s) faith in fundamental human rights" but does not do much to protect them, and Article 2.7 prohibits intervention "in matters which are essentially within the jurisdiction of any State". There has been, as a result, a long-standing argument in the international community between those who insist on a "right to intervene" in man-made catastrophes and those who argue that the Security Council, for all its powers under Chapter VII to "maintain or restore international security", is prohibited from authorizing any coercive action against sovereign States for whatever happens within their borders.

200. Under the Convention on the Prevention and Punishment of the Crime of Genocide (Genocide Convention), States have agreed that genocide, whether committed in time of peace or in time of war, is a crime under international law which they undertake to prevent and punish. Since then it has been understood that genocide anywhere is a threat to the security of all and should never be tolerated. The principle of non-intervention in internal affairs cannot be used to protect genocidal acts or other atrocities, such as large-scale violations of international humanitarian law or large-scale ethnic cleansing, which can properly be considered a threat to international security and as such provoke action by the Security Council.

201. The successive humanitarian disasters in Somalia, Bosnia and Herzegovina, Rwanda, Kosovo and now Darfur, Sudan, have concentrated attention not on the immunities

of sovereign Governments but their responsibilities, both to their own people and to the wider international community. There is a growing recognition that the issue is not the "right to intervene" of any State, but the "responsibility to protect" of *every* State when it comes to people suffering from avoidable catastrophe—mass murder and rape, ethnic cleansing by forcible expulsion and terror, and deliberate starvation and exposure to disease. And there is a growing acceptance that while sovereign Governments have the primary responsibility to protect their own citizens from such catastrophes, when they are unable or unwilling to do so that responsibility should be taken up by the wider international community—with it spanning a continuum involving prevention, response to violence, if necessary, and rebuilding shattered societies. The primary focus should be on assisting the cessation of violence through mediation and other tools and the protection of people through such measures as the dispatch of humanitarian, human rights and police missions. Force, if it needs to be used, should be deployed as a last resort.

202. The Security Council so far has been neither very consistent nor very effective in dealing with these cases, very often acting too late, too hesitantly or not at all. But step by step, the Council and the wider international community have come to accept that, under Chapter VII and in pursuit of the emerging norm of a collective international responsibility to protect, it can always authorize military action to redress catastrophic internal wrongs if it is prepared to declare that the situation is a "threat to international peace and security", not especially difficult when breaches of international law are involved.

203. **We endorse the emerging norm that there is a collective international responsibility to protect, exercisable by the Security Council authorizing military intervention as a last resort, in the event of genocide and other large-scale killing, ethnic cleansing or serious violations of international humanitarian law which sovereign Governments have proved powerless or unwilling to prevent** . . . .

204. The effectiveness of the global collective security system, as with any other legal order, depends ultimately not only on the legality of decisions but also on the common perception of their legitimacy—their being made on solid evidentiary grounds, and for the right reasons, morally as well as legally.

205. If the Security Council is to win the respect it must have as the primary body in the collective security system, it is critical that its most important and influential decisions, those with large-scale life-and-death impact, be better made, better substantiated and better communicated. In particular, in deciding whether or not to authorize the use of force, the Council should adopt and systematically address a set of agreed guidelines, going directly not to whether force *can* legally be used but whether, as a matter of good conscience and good sense, it *should* be.

206. The guidelines we propose will not produce agreed conclusions with pushbutton predictability. The point of adopting them is not to guarantee that the objectively best outcome will always prevail. It is rather to maximize the possibility of achieving Security Council consensus around when it is appropriate or not to use coercive action, including armed force; to maximize international support for whatever the Security Council decides; and to minimize the possibility of individual Member States bypassing the Security Council.

207. In considering whether to authorize or endorse the use of military force, the Security Council should always address—whatever other considerations it may take into account—at least the following five basic criteria of legitimacy:

(a) *Seriousness of threat.* Is the threatened harm to State or human security of a kind, and sufficiently clear and serious, to justify prima facie the use of military force? In the case of internal threats, does it involve genocide and other large-scale killing, ethnic cleansing or serious violations of international humanitarian law, actual or imminently apprehended?

(b) *Proper purpose.* Is it clear that the primary purpose of the proposed military action is to halt or avert the threat in question, whatever other purposes or motives may be involved?

(c) *Last resort.* Has every non-military option for meeting the threat in question been explored, with reasonable grounds for believing that other measures will not succeed?

(d) *Proportional means.* Are the scale, duration and intensity of the proposed military action the minimum necessary to meet the threat in question?

(e) *Balance of consequences.* Is there a reasonable chance of the military action being successful in meeting the threat in question, with the consequences of action not likely to be worse than the consequences of inaction?

208. The above guidelines for authorizing the use of force should be embodied in declaratory resolutions of the Security Council and General Assembly.

209. We also believe it would be valuable if individual Member States, whether or not they are members of the Security Council, subscribed to them.

In March 2005, with only a few months to go before the UN World Summit in September, the "responsibility-to-protect" concept, as embraced by the High-level Panel, received the endorsement of then Secretary-General Kofi Annan:

In Larger Freedom: Towards Development, Security and Human Rights for All: Report of the Secretary-General, UN Doc A/59/2005 (21 March 2005)

7. I urge Heads of State and Government to recommit themselves to supporting the rule of law, human rights and democracy—principles at the heart of the Charter of the United Nations and the Universal Declaration of Human Rights. To this end, they should:

. . .

(b) Embrace the "responsibility to protect" as a basis for collective action against genocide, ethnic cleansing and crimes against humanity, and agree to act on this responsibility, recognizing that this responsibility lies first and foremost with each individual State, whose duty it is to protect its population, but that if national authorities are unwilling or unable to protect their citizens, then the responsibility shifts to the international community to use diplomatic, humanitarian and other methods to help protect civilian populations, and that if such methods appear insufficient the Security Council may out of necessity decide to take action under the Charter, including enforcement action, if so required; . . . .

126. The task is not to find alternatives to the Security Council as a source of authority but to make it work better. When considering whether to authorize or endorse the use of mil-

itary force, the Council should come to a common view on how to weigh the seriousness of the threat; the proper purpose of the proposed military action; whether means short of the use of force might plausibly succeed in stopping the threat; whether the military option is proportional to the threat at hand; and whether there is a reasonable chance of success. By undertaking to make the case for military action in this way, the Council would add transparency to its deliberations and make its decisions more likely to be respected, by both Governments and world public opinion. **I therefore recommend that the Security Council adopt a resolution setting out these principles and expressing its intention to be guided by them when deciding whether to authorize or mandate the use of force . . . .**

135. The International Commission on Intervention and State Sovereignty and more recently the High-level Panel on Threats, Challenges and Change, with its 16 members from all around the world, endorsed what they described as an "emerging norm that there is a collective responsibility to protect" (see A/59/565, para. 203). While I am well aware of the sensitivities involved in this issue, I strongly agree with this approach. **I believe that we must embrace the responsibility to protect, and, when necessary, we must act on it.** This responsibility lies, first and foremost, with each individual State, whose primary raison d'être and duty is to protect its population. But if national authorities are unable or unwilling to protect their citizens, then the responsibility shifts to the international community to use diplomatic, humanitarian and other methods to help protect the human rights and well-being of civilian populations. When such methods appear insufficient, the Security Council may out of necessity decide to take action under the Charter of the United Nations, including enforcement action, if so required . . . . [Bolding in original.]

A period of intense negotiations followed, resulting in the inclusion of the concept of a responsibility to protect in the General Assembly's 2005 World Summit Outcome document in these terms:

2005 World Summit Outcome, **GA Res 60/1, UN Doc A/RES/60/1, reprinted in UN GAOR, 60th Sess, Supp No 49, vol I at 3–25, UN Doc A/60/49 (vol I) (2005)**

138. Each individual State has the responsibility to protect its populations from genocide, war crimes, ethnic cleansing and crimes against humanity. This responsibility entails the prevention of such crimes, including their incitement, through appropriate and necessary means. We accept that responsibility and will act in accordance with it. The international community should, as appropriate, encourage and help States to exercise this responsibility and support the United Nations in establishing an early warning capability.

139. The international community, through the United Nations, also has the responsibility to use appropriate diplomatic, humanitarian and other peaceful means, in accordance with Chapters VI and VIII of the Charter, to help to protect populations from genocide, war crimes, ethnic cleansing and crimes against humanity. In this context, we are prepared to take collective action, in a timely and decisive manner, through the Security Council, in accordance with the Charter, including Chapter VII, on a case-by-case basis and in cooperation with relevant regional organizations as appropriate, should peaceful means be inadequate and national authorities are manifestly failing to protect their populations from genocide, war crimes, ethnic cleansing and crimes against humanity.

We stress the need for the General Assembly to continue consideration of the responsibility to protect populations from genocide, war crimes, ethnic cleansing and crimes against humanity and its implications, bearing in mind the principles of the Charter and international law. We also intend to commit ourselves, as necessary and appropriate, to helping States build capacity to protect their populations from genocide, war crimes, ethnic cleansing and crimes against humanity and to assisting those which are under stress before crises and conflicts break out.

140. We fully support the mission of the Special Adviser of the Secretary-General on the Prevention of Genocide.

The 2005 conception of the responsibility-to-protect concept was subsequently "reaffirmed" by the Security Council in a 2006 resolution on the protection of civilians in armed conflict.[14] To what extent does the responsibility-to-protect principle endorsed by the General Assembly and Security Council respond to the concerns that gave rise to the humanitarian intervention debate in the 1990s? Is it consistent with the concept originally articulated by the ICISS, excerpted above? Should it be?

If the responsibility-to-protect principle as endorsed by the General Assembly and Security Council were to acquire customary international legal status, would it allow individual states to use force against one another without Security Council authorization, even in extreme humanitarian crises? Would it add anything to the legal powers of the Security Council already articulated in the UN Charter? Even if not, the concept of a responsibility to protect may play a potentially useful political role in exhorting the Security Council—and particularly its permanent members—to interpret the "maintenance of international peace and security" as a responsibility that occasionally requires the subordination of state sovereignty—and their own national interests—to greater humanitarian imperatives. Consider the following resolution adopted by the Security Council in response to the humanitarian crisis attending Libya's civil war in 2011:

Resolution 1973 (2011), adopted on 17 March 2011, UN Doc S/RES/1973 (2011)[15]

The Security Council, . . .

Reiterating the responsibility of the Libyan authorities to protect the Libyan population and *reaffirming* that parties to armed conflicts bear the primary responsibility to take all feasible steps to ensure the protection of civilians,

---

14   SC Resolution 1674 (2006), adopted on 28 April 2006, UN Doc S/RES/1674 (2006) at para 4. The Security Council subsequently authorized the UN Mission in Sudan (UNMIS) "to use all necessary means . . . to prevent disruption of the implementation of the Darfur Peace Agreement by rebel groups, without prejudice to the responsibility of the Government of Sudan, to protect civilians under threat of physical violence": see SC Resolution 1706 (2006), adopted on 31 August 2006, UN Doc S/RES/1706 (2006) at para 12(a).

15   See also SC Resolution 1970 (2011), adopted on 26 February 2011, UN Doc S/RES/1970 (2011) at preamb para 9; SC Resolution 1975 (2011), adopted on 30 March 2011, UN Doc S/RES/1975 (2011) at preamb para 9 (regarding escalating violence in Côte d'Ivoire). See further Catherine Powell, "Libya: A Multilateral Constitutional Moment? (2012) 106 Am J Int'l L 298. But for the view that "the legal significance of Libya is minimal," see Simon Chesterman, "'Leading from Behind': The Responsibility to Protect, the Obama Doctrine, and Humanitarian Intervention after Libya" (2011) 25:3 Ethics & International Affairs 279.

Condemning the gross and systematic violation of human rights, including arbitrary detentions, enforced disappearances, torture and summary executions, . . .

Considering that the widespread and systematic attacks currently taking place in the Libyan Arab Jamahiriya against the civilian population may amount to crimes against humanity, . . .

Expressing its determination to ensure the protection of civilians and civilian populated areas and the rapid and unimpeded passage of humanitarian assistance and the safety of humanitarian personnel, . . .

Considering that the establishment of a ban on all flights in the airspace of the Libyan Arab Jamahiriya constitutes an important element for the protection of civilians as well as the safety of the delivery of humanitarian assistance and a decisive step for the cessation of hostilities in Libya, . . .

Reaffirming its strong commitment to the sovereignty, independence, territorial integrity and national unity of the Libyan Arab Jamahiriya,

Determining that the situation in the Libyan Arab Jamahiriya continues to constitute a threat to international peace and security,

Acting under Chapter VII of the Charter of the United Nations,

1. *Demands* the immediate establishment of a cease-fire and a complete end to violence and all attacks against, and abuses of, civilians; . . .

4. *Authorizes* Member States . . . , acting nationally or through regional organizations or arrangements . . . to take all necessary measures . . . to protect civilians and civilian populated areas under threat of attack in the Libyan Arab Jamahiriya, including Benghazi, while excluding a foreign occupation force of any form on any part of Libyan territory, and *requests* the Member States concerned to inform the Secretary-General immediately of the measures they take pursuant to the authorization conferred by this paragraph which shall be immediately reported to the Security Council; . . .

6. *Decides* to establish a ban on all flights in the airspace of the Libyan Arab Jamahiriya in order to help protect civilians;

7. *Decides further* that the ban imposed by paragraph 6 shall not apply to flights whose sole purpose is humanitarian, such as delivering or facilitating the delivery of assistance, including medical supplies, food, humanitarian workers and related assistance, or evacuating foreign nationals from the Libyan Arab Jamahiriya, nor shall it apply to flights authorised by paragraphs 4 or 8, nor other flights which are deemed necessary by States acting under the authorisation conferred in paragraph 8 to be for the benefit of the Libyan people . . . ;

8. *Authorizes* Member States . . . , acting nationally or through regional organizations or arrangements, to take all necessary measures to enforce compliance with the ban on flights imposed by paragraph 6 above, as necessary[;] . . .

29. *Decides* to remain actively seized of the matter.

Does Security Council Resolution 1973 (2011) constitute a precedent that sets the responsibility to protect on a more solid international legal footing than that conferred by its endorsement by the General Assembly in the 2005 World Summit Outcome document? Do the criticisms made by some states that Resolution 1973 (2011) was misused or overextended by Western states to provide a UN mandate for regime change alter your view?

Recall the final paragraph in the UK attorney general's memorandum, excerpted above. If Resolution 1973 (2011) does constitute a precedent, what is the effect of the Security Council's repeated failure in 2012 to adopt resolutions that would address the humanitarian crisis then unfolding in Syria? What does such selectivity in Security Council action mean for the international legal status, and meaning, of the responsibility to protect? What is the significance, if any, of the 2013 intervention in Mali with the approval of the Security Council and the Malian Government?[16]

Notwithstanding the concept's endorsement in 2005, the UN Secretary-General has recognized the need to encourage further discussion among states in order to allay fears held by some about the concept's scope and application. In an early 2009 report seeking to broaden support for putting the concept into action, the Secretary-General proposed a three-pillar structure for its implementation.[17] The first pillar emphasizes that the primary responsibility for protecting a population from mass atrocities rests with the state itself.[18] With the state thus firmly established as the primary bearer of the responsibility to protect, the second pillar envisages that the international community will assume a supportive role, particularly by way of international assistance and capacity-building. The third pillar then contemplates, as a measure of last resort, the use of collective action to protect populations at risk in accordance with the UN Charter. The General Assembly continues to explore and refine its understanding of the responsibility to protect through annual informal and interactive dialogues, based in part on this three-pillar approach as well as further annual reports prepared by the Secretary-General designed to clarify the measures coming within, and the actors affected by, the concept.[19]

3) Self-Defence

a) General Principles

If the performance of the Security Council in authorizing the use of force under Chapter VII has sparked controversy, the use of force by states in self-defence has proven even more controversial. That states may use force in self-defence, without prior Security Council authorization, is expressly anticipated in the UN Charter. Article 51 reads:

> Nothing in the present Charter shall impair the inherent right of individual or collective self-defence if an armed attack occurs against a Member of the United Nations, until the Security Council has taken measures necessary to maintain international peace and security. Measures taken by Members in the exercise of this right of self-defence shall be immediately reported to the Security Council and shall not in any way affect the authority

---

16   SC Resolution 2085 (2012), adopted on 20 December 2012, UN Doc S/RES/2085 (2012) at paras 9 and 13.

17   *Implementing the Responsibility to Protect: Report of the Secretary-General*, UN Doc A/63/677 (12 January 2009).

18   See for example SC Resolution 2085 (2012), *ibid* at preamb para 13 and para 12.

19   See *Early Warning, Assessment and the Responsibility to Protect: Report of the Secretary-General*, UN Doc A/64/864 (14 July 2010); *The Role of Regional and Subregional Arrangements in Implementing the Responsibility to Protect: Report of the Secretary-General*, UN Doc A/65/877-S/2011/393 (27 June 2011); *Responsibility to Protect: Timely and Decisive Response: Report of the Secretary-General*, UN Doc A/66/874-S/2012/578 (25 July 2012); and *Responsibility to Protect: State Responsibility and Prevention: Report of the Secretary-General*, UN Doc A/67/929-S/2013/399 (9 July 2013).

and responsibility of the Security Council under the present Charter to take at any time such action as it deems necessary in order to maintain or restore international peace and security.

The reference in Article 51 to an "inherent" right is generally taken as a signal that the full scope of the right of states to use force in self-defence is defined in customary international law. For example, the *Caroline* incident (discussed below in Section C(3)(c)) is generally recognized as an early source for such guiding principles as proportionality and necessity. Consider the following opinion and judgment of the International Court of Justice in which the applicability of the right of self-defence, and the conditions under which it may lawfully be invoked, are discussed:

Legality of the Threat or Use of Nuclear Weapons, **Advisory Opinion, [1996] ICJ Rep 226**

[The General Assembly requested an advisory opinion from the Court on the question: "Is the threat or use of nuclear weapons in any circumstances permitted under international law?" In the course of giving its opinion, the Court made the following comments concerning the right of self-defence.]

40. The entitlement to resort to self-defence under Article 51 is subject to certain constraints. Some of these constraints are inherent in the very concept of self-defence. Other requirements are specified in Article 51.

41. The submission of the exercise of the right of self-defence to the conditions of necessity and proportionality is a rule of customary international law. As the Court stated in the case concerning *Military and Paramilitary Activities in and against Nicaragua (Nicaragua v. United States of America)*: there is a "specific rule whereby self-defence would warrant only measures which are proportional to the armed attack and necessary to respond to it, a rule well established in customary international law" (*I.C.J. Reports 1986*, p. 94, para. 176). This dual condition applies equally to Article 51 of the Charter, whatever the means of force employed.

42. The proportionality principle may thus not in itself exclude the use of nuclear weapons in self-defence in all circumstances. But at the same time, a use of force that is proportionate under the law of self-defence, must, in order to be lawful, also meet the requirements of the law applicable in armed conflict which comprise in particular the principles and rules of humanitarian law.

43. Certain States have in their written and oral pleadings suggested that in the case of nuclear weapons, the condition of proportionality must be evaluated in the light of still further factors. They contend that the very nature of nuclear weapons, and the high probability of an escalation of nuclear exchanges, mean that there is an extremely strong risk of devastation. The risk factor is said to negate the possibility of the condition of proportionality being complied with. The Court does not find it necessary to embark upon the quantification of such risks; nor does it need to enquire into the question whether tactical nuclear weapons exist which are sufficiently precise to limit those risks: it suffices for the Court to note that the very nature of all nuclear weapons and the profound risks associated therewith are further considerations to be borne in mind by States believing they

can exercise a nuclear response in self-defence in accordance with the requirements of proportionality.

44. Beyond the conditions of necessity and proportionality, Article 51 specifically requires that measures taken by States in the exercise of the right of self-defence shall be immediately reported to the Security Council; this article further provides that these measures shall not in any way affect the authority and responsibility of the Security Council under the Charter to take at any time such action as it deems necessary in order to maintain or restore international peace and security. These requirements of Article 51 apply whatever the means of force used in self-defence . . . .

Military and Paramilitary Activities in and against Nicaragua (Nicaragua v United States of America), Merits, Judgment, [1986] ICJ Rep 14

[Recall that in this case, Nicaragua claimed that the United States had unlawfully used force against it contrary to Article 2(4) of the UN Charter. One of the justifications advanced by the United States for its behaviour was that it was acting in "collective self-defence" of Nicaragua's neighbouring states El Salvador, Honduras, and Costa Rica, which it alleged had been subject to prior unlawful uses of force and intervention by Nicaragua. The following excerpts from the case set out the Court's reasoning with respect to this argument.]

193. The general rule prohibiting force allows for certain exceptions. In view of the arguments advanced by the United States to justify the acts of which it is accused by Nicaragua, the Court must express a view on the content of the right of self-defence, and more particularly the right of collective self-defence. First, with regard to the existence of this right, it notes that in the language of Article 51 of the United Nations Charter, the inherent right (or "droit naturel") which any State possesses in the event of an armed attack, covers both collective and individual self-defence. Thus, the Charter itself testifies to the existence of the right of collective self-defence in customary international law. Moreover, just as the wording of certain General Assembly declarations adopted by States demonstrates their recognition of the principle of the prohibition of force as definitely a matter of customary international law, some of the wording in those declarations operates similarly in respect of the right of self-defence (both collective and individual). Thus, in the declaration quoted above on the Principles of International Law concerning Friendly Relations and Co-operation among States in accordance with the Charter of the United Nations, the reference to the prohibition of force is followed by a paragraph stating that:

"nothing in the foregoing paragraphs shall be construed as enlarging or diminishing in any way the scope of the provisions of the Charter concerning cases in which the use of force is lawful".

This resolution demonstrates that the States represented in the General Assembly regard the exception to the prohibition of force constituted by the right of individual or collective self-defence as already a matter of customary international law.

194. With regard to the characteristics governing the right of self-defence, since the Parties consider the existence of this right to be established as a matter of customary international law, they have concentrated on the conditions governing its use. In view of the

circumstances in which the dispute has arisen, reliance is placed by the Parties only on the right of self-defence in the case of an armed attack which has already occurred, and the issue of the lawfulness of a response to the imminent threat of armed attack has not been raised. Accordingly the Court expresses no view on that issue. The Parties also agree in holding that whether the response to the attack is lawful depends on observance of the criteria of the necessity and the proportionality of the measures taken in self-defence. Since the existence of the right of collective self-defence is established in customary international law, the Court must define the specific conditions which may have to be met for its exercise, in addition to the conditions of necessity and proportionality to which the Parties have referred.

195. In the case of individual self-defence, the exercise of this right is subject to the State concerned having been the victim of an armed attack. Reliance on collective self-defence of course does not remove the need for this. There appears now to be general agreement on the nature of the acts which can be treated as constituting armed attacks. In particular, it may be considered to be agreed that an armed attack must be understood as including not merely action by regular armed forces across an international border, but also "the sending by or on behalf of a State of armed bands, groups, irregulars or mercenaries, which carry out acts of armed force against another State of such gravity as to amount to" (*inter alia*) an actual armed attack conducted by regular forces, "or its substantial involvement therein". This description, contained in Article 3, paragraph (g), of the Definition of Aggression annexed to General Assembly resolution 3314 (XXIX), may be taken to reflect customary international law. The Court sees no reason to deny that, in customary law, the prohibition of armed attacks may apply to the sending by a State of armed bands to the territory of another State, if such an operation, because of its scale and effects, would have been classified as an armed attack rather than as a mere frontier incident had it been carried out by regular armed forces. But the Court does not believe that the concept of "armed attack" includes not only acts by armed bands where such acts occur on a significant scale but also assistance to rebels in the form of the provision of weapons or logistical or other support. Such assistance may be regarded as a threat or use of force, or amount to intervention in the internal or external affairs of other States. It is also clear that it is the State which is the victim of an armed attack which must form and declare the view that it has been so attacked. There is no rule in customary international law permitting another State to exercise the right of collective self-defence on the basis of its own assessment of the situation. Where collective self-defence is invoked, it is to be expected that the State for whose benefit this right is used will have declared itself to be the victim of an armed attack.

196. The question remains whether the lawfulness of the use of collective self-defence by the third State for the benefit of the attacked State also depends on a request addressed by that State to the third State . . . .

199. At all events, the Court finds that in customary international law, whether of a general kind or that particular to the inter-American legal system, there is no rule permitting the exercise of collective self-defence in the absence of a request by the State which regards itself as the victim of an armed attack. The Court concludes that the requirement of a request by the State which is the victim of the alleged attack is additional to the requirement that such a State should have declared itself to have been attacked.

200. At this point, the Court may consider whether in customary international law there is any requirement corresponding to that found in the treaty law of the United Nations Charter, by which the State claiming to use the right of individual or collective self-defence must report to an international body, empowered to determine the conformity with international law of the measures which the State is seeking to justify on that basis. Thus Article 51 of the United Nations Charter requires that measures taken by States in exercise of this right of self-defence must be "immediately reported" to the Security Council . . . . Whatever influence the Charter may have had on customary international law in these matters, it is clear that in customary international law it is not a condition of the lawfulness of the use of force in self-defence that a procedure so closely dependent on the content of a treaty commitment and of the institutions established by it, should have been followed. On the other hand, if self-defence is advanced as a justification for measures which would otherwise be in breach both of the principle of customary international law and of that contained in the Charter, it is to be expected that the conditions of the Charter should be respected. Thus for the purpose of enquiry into the customary law position, the absence of a report may be one of the factors indicating whether the State in question was itself convinced that it was acting in self-defence . . . .

229. The Court must thus consider whether, as the Respondent claims, the acts in question of the United States are justified by the exercise of its right of collective self-defence against an armed attack. The Court must therefore establish whether the circumstances required for the exercise of this right of self-defence are present and, if so, whether the steps taken by the United States actually correspond to the requirements of international law. For the Court to conclude that the United States was lawfully exercising its right of collective self-defence, it must first find that Nicaragua engaged in an armed attack against El Salvador, Honduras or Costa Rica.

230. As regards El Salvador, the Court has found . . . that it is satisfied that between July 1979 and the early months of 1981, an intermittent flow of arms was routed via the territory of Nicaragua to the armed opposition in that country. The Court was not however satisfied that assistance has reached the Salvadorian armed opposition, on a scale of any significance, since the early months of 1981, or that the Government of Nicaragua was responsible for any flow of arms at either period. Even assuming that the supply of arms to the opposition in El Salvador could be treated as imputable to the Government of Nicaragua, to justify invocation of the right of collective self-defence in customary international law, it would have to be equated with an armed attack by Nicaragua on El Salvador. As stated above, the Court is unable to consider that, in customary international law, the provision of arms to the opposition in another State constitutes an armed attack on that State. Even at a time when the arms flow was at its peak, and again assuming the participation of the Nicaraguan Government, that would not constitute such armed attack.

231. Turning to Honduras and Costa Rica, the Court has also stated . . . that it should find established that certain transborder incursions into the territory of those two States, in 1982, 1983 and 1984, were imputable to the Government of Nicaragua. Very little information is however available to the Court as to the circumstances of these incursions or their possible motivations, which renders it difficult to decide whether they may be treated for legal purposes as amounting, singly or collectively, to an "armed attack" by

Nicaragua on either or both States . . . . There are however other considerations which justify the Court in finding that neither these incursions, nor the alleged supply of arms to the opposition in El Salvador, may be relied on as justifying the exercise of the right of collective self-defence.

232. The exercise of the right of collective self-defence presupposes that an armed attack has occurred; and it is evident that it is the victim State, being the most directly aware of that fact, which is likely to draw general attention to its plight. It is also evident that if the victim State wishes another State to come to its help in the exercise of the right of collective self-defence, it will normally make an express request to that effect. Thus in the present instance, the Court is entitled to take account, in judging the asserted justification of the exercise of collective self-defence by the United States, of the actual conduct of El Salvador, Honduras and Costa Rica at the relevant time, as indicative of a belief by the State in question that it was the victim of an armed attack by Nicaragua, and of the making of a request by the victim State to the United States for help in the exercise of collective self-defence.

233. The Court has seen no evidence that the conduct of those States was consistent with such a situation, either at the time when the United States first embarked on the activities which were allegedly justified by self-defence, or indeed for a long period subsequently. So far as El Salvador is concerned, it appears to the Court that while El Salvador did in fact officially declare itself the victim of an armed attack, and did ask for the United States to exercise its right of collective self-defence, this occurred only on a date much later than the commencement of the United States activities which were allegedly justified by this request . . . .

234. As to Honduras and Costa Rica, they also were prompted by the institution of proceedings in this case to address communications to the Court; in neither of these is there mention of armed attack or collective self-defence . . . .

235. There is also an aspect of the conduct of the United States which the Court is entitled to take into account as indicative of the view of that State on the question of the existence of an armed attack. At no time, up to the present, has the United States Government addressed to the Security Council, in connection with the matters the subject of the present case, the report which is required by Article 51 of the United Nations Charter in respect of measures which a State believes itself bound to take when it exercises the right of individual or collective self-defence . . . . [T]his conduct of the United States hardly conforms with the latter's avowed conviction that it was acting in the context of collective self-defence as consecrated by Article 51 of the Charter. This fact is all the more noteworthy because, in the Security Council, the United States has itself taken the view that failure to observe the requirement to make a report contradicted a State's claim to be acting on the basis of collective self-defence . . . .

237. Since the Court has found that the condition *sine qua non* required for the exercise of the right of collective self-defence by the United States is not fulfilled in this case, the appraisal of the United States activities in relation to the criteria of necessity and proportionality takes on a different significance. As a result of this conclusion of the Court, even if the United States activities in question had been carried on in strict compliance with the canons of necessity and proportionality, they would not thereby become

lawful. If however they were not, this may constitute an additional ground of wrongful-ness. On the question of necessity, the Court observes that the United States measures taken in December 1981 . . . cannot be said to correspond to a "necessity" justifying the United States action against Nicaragua on the basis of assistance given by Nicaragua to the armed opposition in El Salvador. First, these measures were only taken, and began to produce their effects, several months after the major offensive of the armed opposition against the Government of El Salvador had been completely repulsed (January 1981), and the actions of the opposition considerably reduced in consequence. Thus it was possible to eliminate the main danger to the Salvadorian Government without the United States embarking on activities in and against Nicaragua. Accordingly, it cannot be held that these activities were undertaken in the light of necessity. Whether or not the assistance to the *contras* might meet the criterion of proportionality, the Court cannot regard the United States activities . . . relating to the mining of the Nicaraguan ports and the attacks on ports, oil installations, etc., as satisfying that criterion. Whatever uncertainty may exist as to the exact scale of the aid received by the Salvadorian armed opposition from Nicaragua, it is clear that these latter United States activities in question could not have been proportionate to that aid. Finally on this point, the Court must also observe that the reaction of the United States in the context of what it regarded as self-defence was continued long after the period in which any presumed armed attack by Nicaragua could reasonably be contemplated.

238. Accordingly, the Court concludes that the plea of collective self-defence against an alleged armed attack on El Salvador, Honduras or Costa Rica, advanced by the United States to justify its conduct toward Nicaragua, cannot be upheld; and accordingly that the United States has violated the principle prohibiting recourse to the threat or use of force by the acts listed . . . above, and by its assistance to the *contras* to the extent that this as-sistance "involve[s] a threat or use of force" . . . .

Note the distinction drawn by the Court in *Nicaragua* between an "armed attack" and a "mere frontier incident." The distinction implies that the use of force in response to a "mere frontier incident" or other uses of force falling short of an "armed attack" would not be justified in self-defence. What recourse is available to a state that is subject to low-level uses of force, falling short of an "armed attack," by another state?

Note also the Court's somewhat cryptic reference to "motivations" of the state against which the act of self-defence is directed as a potentially relevant factor in determining whether an armed attack has occurred. Consider the following case, which sheds some light on the legal relevance of such motivations, as well as the importance of directing one's acts in self-defence against a state demonstrably responsible for an armed attack:

Oil Platforms (Islamic Republic of Iran v United States of America), Merits, [2003] ICJ Rep 161

[During the Iran-Iraq War of 1980–88, both states engaged in a series of attacks on ship-ping, including foreign-flagged oil tankers, in international waters in the Persian Gulf. In response, a number of third party states, including the United States, sent naval forces to protect their commercial shipping from such attacks. This case arose out of two incidents causing loss to American-flagged vessels. In the first incident, the *Sea Isle City*, a commercial vessel flying the American flag was hit by a missile which the United States suspected had been launched by Iran. Three days later, on 19 October 1987, American naval forces attacked an Iranian offshore oil production installation, the Reshadat complex, nearly destroying it. In the second incident, an American naval vessel struck and was damaged by a mine, which the United States again suspected had been laid by Iran. Four days later, on 18 April 1988, the United States attacked and almost completely destroyed two more Iranian oil production complexes (the Salman and Nasr complexes). Iran brought this claim against the United States pursuant to a 1955 Treaty of Amity between the two states, which the Court found essentially reiterated the use of force and self-defence provisions of the UN Charter. The United States defended its actions on the basis that it had acted, in both instances, in self-defence.]

43. The Court will thus examine first the application of Article XX, paragraph 1 *(d)*, of the 1955 Treaty, which in the circumstances of this case, as explained above, involves the principle of the prohibition in international law of the use of force, and the qualification to it constituted by the right of self-defence. On the basis of that provision, a party to the Treaty may be justified in taking certain measures which it considers to be "necessary" for the protection of its essential security interests. As the Court emphasized, in relation to the comparable provision of the 1956 United States/Nicaragua Treaty in the case concerning *Military and Paramilitary Activities in and against Nicaragua*, "the measures taken must not merely be such as tend to protect the essential security interests of the party taking them, but must be 'necessary' for that purpose"; and whether a given measure is "necessary" is "not purely a question for the subjective judgment of the party" (*I.C.J. Reports 1986*, p. 141, para. 282), and may thus be assessed by the Court. In the present case, the question whether the measures taken were "necessary" overlaps with the question of their validity as acts of self-defence. As the Court observed in its decision of 1986 the criteria of necessity and proportionality must be observed if a measure is to be qualified as self-defence (see *ibid.*, p. 103, para. 194, and paragraph 74 below).

44. In this connection, the Court notes that it is not disputed between the Parties that neutral shipping in the Persian Gulf was caused considerable inconvenience and loss, and grave damage, during the Iran-Iraq war. It notes also that this was to a great extent due to the presence of mines and minefields laid by both sides. The Court has no jurisdiction to enquire into the question of the extent to which Iran and Iraq complied with the international legal rules of maritime warfare. It can however take note of these circumstances, regarded by the United States as relevant to its decision to take action against Iran which it considered necessary to protect its essential security interests. Nevertheless, the legality of the action taken by the United States has to be judged by reference to Article XX, paragraph 1 *(d)*, of the 1955 Treaty, in the light of international law on the use of force in self-defence.

45. The United States has never denied that its actions against the Iranian platforms amounted to a use of armed force. Some of the details of the attacks, so far as established by the material before the Court, may be pertinent to any assessment of the lawfulness of those actions. As already indicated, there were attacks on two successive occasions, on 19

October 1987 and on 18 April 1988. The Court will examine whether each of these met the conditions of Article XX, paragraph 1 *(d)*, as interpreted by reference to the relevant rules of international law.

46. The first installation attacked, on 19 October 1987, was the Reshadat complex, which consisted of three drilling and production platforms — R-3, R-4 and R-7 — linked to a total of 27 oil wells . . . .

47. On 19 October 1987, four destroyers of the United States Navy, together with naval support craft and aircraft, approached the Reshadat R-7 platform. Iranian personnel was warned by the United States forces via radio of the imminent attack and abandoned the facility. The United States forces then opened fire on the platform; a unit later boarded and searched it, and placed and detonated explosive charges on the remaining structure. The United States ships then proceeded to the R-4 platform, which was being evacuated; according to a report of a Pentagon spokesman, cited in the press and not denied by the United States, the attack on the R-4 platform had not been included in the original plan, but it was seen as a "target of opportunity." After having conducted reconnaissance fire and then having boarded and searched the platform, the United States forces placed and detonated explosive charges on this second installation. As a result of the attack, the R-7 platform was almost completely destroyed and the R-4 platform was severely damaged. While the attack was made solely on the Reshadat complex, it affected also the operation of the Resalat complex. Iran states that production from the Reshadat and Resalat complexes was interrupted for several years . . . .

50. The Court will . . . first concentrate on the facts tending to show the validity or otherwise of the claim to exercise the right of self-defence. In its communication to the Security Council, cited above, the United States based this claim on the existence of

> "a series of unlawful armed attacks by Iranian forces against the United States, including laying mines in international waters for the purpose of sinking or damaging United States flag ships, and firing on United States aircraft without provocation";

it referred in particular to a missile attack on the *Sea Isle City* as being the specific incident that led to the attack on the Iranian platforms. Before the Court, it has based itself more specifically on the attack on the *Sea Isle City*, but has continued to assert the relevance of the other attacks (see paragraph 62 below). To justify its choice of the platforms as target, the United States asserted that they had "engaged in a variety of actions directed against United States flag and other non-belligerent vessels and aircraft". Iran has denied any responsibility for (in particular) the attack on the *Sea Isle City*, and has claimed that the platforms had no military purpose, and were not engaged in any military activity.

51. . . . [I]n order to establish that it was legally justified in attacking the Iranian platforms in exercise of the right of individual self-defence, the United States has to show that attacks had been made upon it for which Iran was responsible; and that those attacks were of such a nature as to be qualified as "armed attacks" within the meaning of that expression in Article 51 of the United Nations Charter, and as understood in customary law on the use of force. As the Court observed in the case concerning *Military and Paramilitary Activities in and against Nicaragua*, it is necessary to distinguish "the most grave forms of

the use of force (those constituting an armed attack) from other less grave forms" (*I.C.J. Reports 1986*, p. 101, para. 191), since "In the case of individual self-defence, the exercise of this right is subject to the State concerned having been the victim of an armed attack" (*ibid.*, p. 103, para. 195). The United States must also show that its actions were necessary and proportional to the armed attack made on it, and that the platforms were a legitimate military target open to attack in the exercise of self-defence.

52. Since it was the missile attack on the *Sea Isle City* that figured most prominently in the United States contentions, the Court will first examine in detail the evidence relating to that incident. The *Sea Isle City* was a Kuwaiti tanker reflagged to the United States; on 16 October 1987 it had just ended a voyage under "Operation Earnest Will" (see paragraph 24 above), when it was hit by a missile near Kuwait's Al-Ahmadi Sea Island (or Mina al-Ahmadi) terminal. This incident, which caused damage to the ship and injury to six crew members, was claimed by the United States to be the seventh involving Iranian anti-ship cruise missiles in the area in the course of 1987. The United States asserts that the missile that struck the *Sea Isle City* was launched by Iran from a facility located in the Fao area. It recalls that in February 1986 Iran had taken control of a large part of the Fao peninsula and had captured three formerly Iraqi missile sites in the area, which it held at the time of the attack. It also maintains that there was an additional active cruise missile staging facility on Iranian territory near the Fao peninsula . . . .

57. For present purposes, the Court has simply to determine whether the United States has demonstrated that it was the victim of an "armed attack" by Iran such as to justify it using armed force in self-defence; and the burden of proof of the facts showing the existence of such an attack rests on the United States. The Court does not have to attribute responsibility for firing the missile that struck the *Sea Isle City*, on the basis of a balance of evidence, either to Iran or to Iraq; if at the end of the day the evidence available is insufficient to establish that the missile was fired by Iran, then the necessary burden of proof has not been discharged by the United States.

58. As noted above, the United States claims that the missile that struck the *Sea Isle City* was a ground-launched HY-2 anti-ship missile of the type known as the "Silkworm", but it has not been able to produce physical evidence of this, for example in the form of recovered fragments of the missile. The Court will however examine the other evidence on the hypothesis that the missile was of this type. The United States contends that the missile was fired from Iranian-held territory in the Fao area, and it has offered satellite pictures and expert evidence to show that there was, at the time, Iranian missile-firing equipment present there. Even with the assistance of the expert reports offered by both Parties, the Court does not however find the satellite images sufficiently clear to establish this point. The evidence that the particular missile came from the Fao direction is the testimony, mentioned above, of a Kuwaiti military officer, who claims to have observed the flight of the missile overhead, and thus to be able to identify the approximate bearing on which it was travelling. However, this testimony was given ten years after the reported events; and the officer does not state that he observed the launch of the missile (and the alleged firing point was too remote for this to have been possible), nor that he saw the missile strike the *Sea Isle City*, but merely that he saw a missile passing "overhead", and

that that vessel was struck by a missile "minutes later". In sum, the witness evidence cannot be relied upon. Furthermore, the Court notes that there is a discrepancy between the English and Arabic texts of the statement produced before the Court, both of which were signed by the witness; the Arabic version lacks any indication of the bearing on which the observed missile was travelling.

59. There is a conflict of evidence between the Parties as to the characteristics of the Silkworm missile, in particular its maximum range, and whether or not when fired it always follows a straight-line course. According to the United States, the maximum range of the missile is of the order of 105 km, and this type of missile always follows a straight course until it approaches its objective, when its on-board guidance equipment causes it to lock on to a target which may be up to 12 degrees on either side of its course. Iran however contends that the missile may also be set to follow either a curved or dog-leg path, and that its maximum range is less, 95 km at the most. The Court does not consider that it is necessary for it to decide between the conflicting expert testimony. It appears that at the time different models of the missile existed, with differing programming characteristics and maximum ranges. There is however no direct evidence at all of the type of missile that struck the *Sea Isle City*; the evidence as to the nature of other missiles fired at Kuwaiti territory at this period is suggestive, but no more. In considering whether the United States has discharged the burden of proof that Iranian forces fired the missile that struck the *Sea Isle City*, the Court must take note of this deficiency in the evidence available.

60. In connection with its contention that the *Sea Isle City* was the victim of an attack by Iran, the United States has referred to an announcement by President Ali Khameini of Iran some three months earlier, indicating that Iran would attack the United States if it did not "leave the region". This however is evidently not sufficient to justify the conclusion that any subsequent attack on the United States in the Persian Gulf was indeed the work of Iran. The United States also observes that, at the time, Iran was blamed for the attack by "Lloyd's Maritime Information Service, the General Council of British Shipping, *Jane's Intelligence Review* and other authoritative public sources". These "public sources" are by definition secondary evidence; and the Court has no indication of what was the original source, or sources, or evidence on which the public sources relied. In this respect the Court would recall the caveat it included in its Judgment in the case concerning *Military and Paramilitary Activities in and against Nicaragua*, that "Widespread reports of a fact may prove on closer examination to derive from a single source, and such reports, however numerous, will in such case have no greater value as evidence than the original source." (*I.C.J. Reports 1986*, p. 41, para. 63.)

61. In short, the Court has examined with great care the evidence and arguments presented on each side, and finds that the evidence indicative of Iranian responsibility for the attack on the *Sea Isle City* is not sufficient to support the contentions of the United States. The conclusion to which the Court has come on this aspect of the case is thus that the burden of proof of the existence of an armed attack by Iran on the United States, in the form of the missile attack on the *Sea Isle City*, has not been discharged.

62. . . . . [T]he United States has however not relied solely on the *Sea Isle City* incident as constituting the "armed attack" to which the United States claimed to be responding.

It asserted that that incident was "the latest in a series of such missile attacks against United States flag and other non-belligerent vessels in Kuwaiti waters in pursuit of peaceful commerce" . . . .

64. On the hypothesis that all the incidents complained of are to be attributed to Iran, and thus setting aside the question, examined above, of attribution to Iran of the specific attack on the *Sea Isle City*, the question is whether that attack, either in itself or in combination with the rest of the "series of . . . attacks" cited by the United States can be categorized as an "armed attack" on the United States justifying self-defence. The Court notes first that the *Sea Isle City* was in Kuwaiti waters at the time of the attack on it, and that a Silkworm missile fired from (it is alleged) more than 100 km away could not have been aimed at the specific vessel, but simply programmed to hit some target in Kuwaiti waters . . . . There is no evidence that the minelaying alleged to have been carried out by the *Iran Ajr*, at a time when Iran was at war with Iraq, was aimed specifically at the United States; and similarly it has not been established that the mine struck by the *Bridgeton* was laid with the specific intention of harming that ship, or other United States vessels. Even taken cumulatively, and reserving, as already noted, the question of Iranian responsibility, these incidents do not seem to the Court to constitute an armed attack on the United States, of the kind that the Court, in the case concerning *Military and Paramilitary Activities in and against Nicaragua*, qualified as a "most grave" form of the use of force (see paragraph 51 above).

65. The second occasion on which Iranian oil installations were attacked was on 18 April 1988, with the action against the Salman and Nasr complexes. The Salman offshore oil complex consisted of seven interconnected platforms, including one drilling and two production platforms . . . . The Nasr complex comprised one central platform, one flaring point, and six oil-producing platforms grouped around the central platform . . . .

66. United States naval forces attacked the Salman and Nasr complexes on 18 April 1988. Two destroyers and a supply ship were involved in the attack on the Salman complex: shortly before 8 a.m., local time, the United States forces warned the personnel on the platforms that the attack was due to begin; some of them began to evacuate the installation, while others opened fire. A few minutes later, shelling on the complex commenced from United States ships, warplanes and helicopters. United States forces then boarded some of the platforms (but not that containing the control centre), and placed and detonated explosives. Iran states that the attack caused severe damage to the production facilities of the platforms, and that the activities of the Salman complex were totally interrupted for four years, its regular production being resumed only in September 1992, and reaching a normal level in 1993.

The central platform of the Nasr complex was attacked at around 8.15 a.m. by three United States warships and a number of helicopters. After having been warned of the imminent military action, Iranian personnel evacuated the platform. The United States forces bombarded the installation and almost completely destroyed it; the platform was not boarded, since it was considered unsafe due to secondary explosions and fire. According to Iranian accounts, activities in the whole Nasr complex (including oil production and water injection) were interrupted as a consequence of the attack and did not resume until nearly four years later . . . .

68. The Court notes that the attacks on the Salman and Nasr platforms were not an isolated operation, aimed simply at the oil installations, as had been the case with the attacks of 19 October 1987; they formed part of a much more extensive military action, designated "Operation Praying Mantis", conducted by the United States against what it regarded as "legitimate military targets"; armed force was used, and damage done to a number of targets, including the destruction of two Iranian frigates and other Iranian naval vessels and aircraft.

69. The USS *Samuel B. Roberts* was a warship returning to Bahrain on 14 April 1988, after escorting a convoy of United States-flagged merchant ships in the context of "Operation Earnest Will", when it hit a mine near Shah Allum Shoal in the central Persian Gulf. The United States reports that, in the days following the attack, Belgian and Dutch mine-clearing forces and its own navy discovered several mines bearing Iranian serial numbers in the vicinity and it concludes therefore that the mine struck by the USS *Samuel B. Roberts* was laid by Iran. It also adduces other discoveries of Iranian mining activities at the time . . . , contemporary statements by Iranian military leaders and conclusions of the international shipping community (see paragraph 60 above), all allegedly demonstrating that Iran made a general practice of using mines to attack neutral shipping . . . .

71. As in the case of the attack on the *Sea Isle City*, the first question is whether the United States has discharged the burden of proof that the USS *Samuel B. Roberts* was the victim of a mine laid by Iran. The Court notes that mines were being laid at the time by both belligerents in the Iran-Iraq war, so that evidence of other minelaying operations by Iran is not conclusive as to responsibility of Iran for this particular mine. In its communication to the Security Council in connection with the attack of 18 April 1988, the United States alleged that "The mines were laid in shipping lanes known by Iran to be used by US vessels, and intended by them to damage or sink such vessels" . . . . Iran has claimed that it laid mines only for defensive purposes in the Khor Abdullah Channel, but the United States has submitted evidence suggesting that Iran's mining operations were more extensive. The main evidence that the mine struck by the USS *Samuel B. Roberts* was laid by Iran was the discovery of moored mines in the same area, bearing serial numbers matching other Iranian mines . . . . This evidence is highly suggestive, but not conclusive.

72. The Court notes further that, as on the occasion of the earlier attack on oil platforms, the United States in its communication to the Security Council claimed to have been exercising the right of self-defence in response to the "attack" on the USS *Samuel B. Roberts*, linking it also with "a series of offensive attacks and provocations Iranian naval forces have taken against neutral shipping in the international waters of the Persian Gulf" (paragraph 67 above). Before the Court, it has contended, as in the case of the missile attack on the *Sea Isle City*, that the mining was itself an armed attack giving rise to the right of self-defence and that the alleged pattern of Iranian use of force "added to the gravity of the specific attacks, reinforced the necessity of action in self-defense, and helped to shape the appropriate response" (see paragraph 62 above). No attacks on United States-flagged vessels (as distinct from United States-owned vessels), additional to those cited as justification for the earlier attacks on the Reshadat platforms, have been brought to the Court's attention, other than the mining of the USS *Samuel B. Roberts* itself. The question is therefore whether that incident sufficed in itself to justify action in self-de-

fence, as amounting to an "armed attack." The Court does not exclude the possibility that the mining of a single military vessel might be sufficient to bring into play the "inherent right of self-defence"; but in view of all the circumstances, including the inconclusiveness of the evidence of Iran's responsibility for the mining of the USS *Samuel B. Roberts*, the Court is unable to hold that the attacks on the Salman and Nasr platforms have been shown to have been justifiably made in response to an "armed attack" on the United States by Iran, in the form of the mining of the USS *Samuel B. Roberts*.

73. As noted above (paragraph 43), in the present case a question of whether certain action is "necessary" arises both as an element of international law relating to self-defence and on the basis of the actual terms of Article XX, paragraph 1 *(d)*, of the 1955 Treaty, already quoted, whereby the Treaty does "not preclude . . . measures . . . necessary to protect [the] essential security interests" of either party. In this latter respect, the United States claims that it considered in good faith that the attacks on the platforms were necessary to protect its essential security interests, and suggests that "A measure of discretion should be afforded to a party's good faith application of measures to protect its essential security interests." Iran was prepared to recognize some of the interests referred to by the United States—the safety of United States vessels and crew, and the uninterrupted flow of maritime commerce in the Persian Gulf—as being reasonable security interests of the United States, but denied that the United States actions against the platforms could be regarded as "necessary" to protect those interests. The Court does not however have to decide whether the United States interpretation of Article XX, paragraph 1 *(d)*, on this point is correct, since the requirement of international law that measures taken avowedly in self-defence must have been necessary for that purpose is strict and objective, leaving no room for any "measure of discretion". The Court will therefore turn to the criteria of necessity and proportionality in the context of international law on self-defence.

74. In its decision in the case concerning *Military and Paramilitary Activities in and against Nicaragua*, the Court endorsed the shared view of the parties to that case that in customary law "whether the response to the [armed] attack is lawful depends on observance of the criteria of the necessity and the proportionality of the measures taken in self-defence" (*I.C.J. Reports 1986*, p. 103, para. 194). One aspect of these criteria is the nature of the target of the force used avowedly in self-defence. In its communications to the Security Council, . . . the United States indicated the grounds on which it regarded the Iranian platforms as legitimate targets for an armed action in self-defence. In the present proceedings, the United States has continued to maintain that they were such, and has presented evidence directed to showing that the platforms collected and reported intelligence concerning passing vessels, acted as a military communication link co-ordinating Iranian naval forces and served as actual staging bases to launch helicopter and small boat attacks on neutral commercial shipping. The United States has referred to documents and materials found by its forces . . . allegedly establishing that the Reshadat platforms served as military communication facilities. It has also affirmed that the international shipping community at the time was aware of the military use of the platforms, as confirmed by the costly steps commercial vessels took to avoid them, and by various witness reports describing Iranian attacks. The United States has also submitted expert analysis of the conditions and circumstances surrounding these attacks, examining their

pattern and location in the light of the equipment at Iran's disposal. Finally, the United States has produced a number of documents, found on the Reshadat complex when it was attacked, allegedly corroborating the platforms' military function. In particular, it contends that these documents prove that the Reshadat platforms had monitored the movements of the *Sea Isle City* on 8 August 1987. On the other hand, the forces that attacked the Salman and Nasr complexes were not able to board the platforms containing the control centres, and did not therefore seize any material (if indeed such existed) tending to show the use of those complexes for military purposes.

75. Iran recognizes the presence of limited military personnel and equipment on the Reshadat platforms, but insists that their purpose was exclusively defensive and justified by previous Iraqi attacks on its oil production facilities. Iran further challenges the evidence adduced by the United States in this regard. It alleges that documents found aboard the *Iran Ajr* and the Reshadat platforms are read out of their proper context, incorrectly translated and actually consistent with the platforms' purely defensive role; and that military expert analysis relied on by the United States is hypothetical and contradictory. Iran asserts further that reports and testimony referred to by the United States are mostly non-specific about the use of the platforms as staging bases to launch attacks, and that the equipment at its disposal could be used from mainland and offshore islands, without any need to have recourse to the platforms.

76. The Court is not sufficiently convinced that the evidence available supports the contentions of the United States as to the significance of the military presence and activity on the Reshadat oil platforms; and it notes that no such evidence is offered in respect of the Salman and Nasr complexes. However, even accepting those contentions, for the purposes of discussion, the Court is unable to hold that the attacks made on the platforms could have been justified as acts of self-defence. The conditions for the exercise of the right of self-defence are well settled: as the Court observed in its Advisory Opinion on *Legality of the Threat or Use of Nuclear Weapons*, "The submission of the exercise of the right of self-defence to the conditions of necessity and proportionality is a rule of customary international law" (*I.C.J. Reports 1996 (I)*), p. 245, para. 41); and in the case concerning *Military and Paramilitary Activities in and against Nicaragua*, the Court referred to a specific rule "whereby self-defence would warrant only measures which are proportional to the armed attack and necessary to respond to it" as "a rule well established in customary international law" (*I.C.J. Reports 1986*, p. 94, para. 176). In the case both of the attack on the *Sea Isle City* and the mining of the USS *Samuel B. Roberts*, the Court is not satisfied that the attacks on the platforms were necessary to respond to these incidents. In this connection, the Court notes that there is no evidence that the United States complained to Iran of the military activities of the platforms, in the same way as it complained repeatedly of minelaying and attacks on neutral shipping, which does not suggest that the targeting of the platforms was seen as a necessary act. The Court would also observe that in the case of the attack of 19 October 1987, the United States forces attacked the R-4 platform as a "target of opportunity", not one previously identified as an appropriate military target . . . .

77. As to the requirement of proportionality, the attack of 19 October 1987 might, had the Court found that it was necessary in response to the *Sea Isle City* incident as an armed

attack committed by Iran, have been considered proportionate. In the case of the attacks of 18 April 1988, however, they were conceived and executed as part of a more extensive operation entitled "Operation Praying Mantis" (see paragraph 68 above). The question of the lawfulness of other aspects of that operation is not before the Court, since it is solely the action against the Salman and Nasr complexes that is presented as a breach of the 1955 Treaty; but the Court cannot assess in isolation the proportionality of that action to the attack to which it was said to be a response; it cannot close its eyes to the scale of the whole operation, which involved, *inter alia*, the destruction of two Iranian frigates and a number of other naval vessels and aircraft. As a response to the mining, by an unidentified agency, of a single United States warship, which was severely damaged but not sunk, and without loss of life, neither "Operation Praying Mantis" as a whole, nor even that part of it that destroyed the Salman and Nasr platforms, can be regarded, in the circumstances of this case, as a proportionate use of force in self-defence.

78. The Court thus concludes from the foregoing that the actions carried out by United States forces against Iranian oil installations on 19 October 1987 and 18 April 1988 cannot be justified, under Article XX, paragraph 1 *(d)*, of the 1955 Treaty, as being measures necessary to protect the essential security interests of the United States, since those actions constituted recourse to armed force not qualifying, under international law on the question, as acts of self-defence, and thus did not fall within the category of measures contemplated, upon its correct interpretation, by that provision of the Treaty . . . .

Consider the significance of the Court's search, in paragraph 64 above, for evidence of a specific intent by Iran to direct attacks against the United States. In the Court's view, would such a specific intent be a prerequisite to characterizing such attacks as an "armed attack" that would give rise to a US right of self-defence against Iran?

b) Self-Defence against Non-State Actors

The importance of attributing an armed attack to the state against which force in self-defence is directed (critical to the outcome in *Oil Platforms*) raises a related issue: Does the right to use force in self-defence extend to responding to armed attacks by *non-state* actors? The traditional self-defence analysis assumes that the armed attack that gives rise to a right of self-defence has been perpetrated by, or is at least attributable to, another state. In reality, however, states may be subject to attacks launched by non-state actors, sometimes operating from the territory of neighbouring or even distant states (the September 11 attacks by al-Qaida against the United States are a notorious example of this). Consider the following opinion of the International Court of Justice on this difficult issue:

Legal Consequences of the Construction of a Wall in the Occupied Palestinian Territory, Advisory Opinion, [2004] ICJ Rep 136

[Recall that in 2003, the UN General Assembly asked the Court for an advisory opinion as follows: "What are the legal consequences arising from the construction of the wall being built by Israel, the occupying Power, in the Occupied Palestinian Territory, including in and around East Jerusalem, as described in the report of the Secretary-General, considering the rules and principles of international law . . . ?" In answering this question, the

Court considered whether the construction of the wall could be justified as a measure in self-defence.]

138. The Court has thus concluded that the construction of the wall constitutes action not in conformity with various international legal obligations incumbent upon Israel. However, Annex I to the report of the Secretary-General states that, according to Israel: "the construction of the Barrier is consistent with Article 51 of the Charter of the United Nations, its inherent right to self-defence and Security Council resolutions 1368 (2001) and 1373 (2001)". More specifically, Israel's Permanent Representative to the United Nations asserted in the General Assembly on 20 October 2003 that "the fence is a measure wholly consistent with the right of States to self-defence enshrined in Article 51 of the Charter"; the Security Council resolutions referred to, he continued, "have clearly recognized the right of States to use force in self-defence against terrorist attacks", and therefore surely recognize the right to use non-forcible measures to that end (A/ES10/PV.21, p. 6).

139. Under the terms of Article 51 of the Charter of the United Nations:

> "Nothing in the present Charter shall impair the inherent right of individual or collective self-defence if an armed attack occurs against a Member of the United Nations, until the Security Council has taken measures necessary to maintain international peace and security."

Article 51 of the Charter thus recognizes the existence of an inherent right of self-defence in the case of armed attack by one State against another State. However, Israel does not claim that the attacks against it are imputable to a foreign State.

The Court also notes that Israel exercises control in the Occupied Palestinian Territory and that, as Israel itself states, the threat which it regards as justifying the construction of the wall originates within, and not outside, that territory. The situation is thus different from that contemplated by Security Council resolutions 1368 (2001) and 1373 (2001), and therefore Israel could not in any event invoke those resolutions in support of its claim to be exercising a right of self-defence.

Consequently, the Court concludes that Article 51 of the Charter has no relevance in this case . . . .

141. The fact remains that Israel has to face numerous indiscriminate and deadly acts of violence against its civilian population. It has the right, and indeed the duty, to respond in order to protect the life of its citizens. The measures taken are bound nonetheless to remain in conformity with applicable international law.

142. In conclusion, the Court considers that Israel cannot rely on a right of self-defence or on a state of necessity in order to preclude the wrongfulness of the construction of the wall resulting from the considerations mentioned in paragraphs 122 and 137 above. The Court accordingly finds that the construction of the wall, and its associated régime, are contrary to international law . . . .

Part of the Court's reasoning in concluding that Article 51 "has no relevance" in the case of the wall being built by Israel was that the threats to which it is responding come from within territory it controls. Is this a decisive factor in assessing the relevance of

Article 51 to responses to armed attacks by non-state actors? Consider the Court's approach to such attacks coming from the territory of another state:

Armed Activities on the Territory of the Congo (Democratic Republic of the Congo v Uganda), Merits, [2005] ICJ Rep 168

[This case is a product of the complex and violent situation that has existed in the Great Lakes region of Africa for many years. In 1997, when President Kabila came to power in the Democratic Republic of the Congo (DRC), he invited Uganda and Rwanda to provide military assistance to the DRC in suppressing various insurgent groups operating in the DRC's eastern provinces. In 1998, the DRC reversed this policy and terminated its consent to the presence of Ugandan and Rwandan forces on its territory. However, rather than leave the territory of the DRC, Uganda increased its troop presence and military activities in the DRC as part of so-called operation "Safe Haven." The DRC claimed that this amounted to an unlawful use of force contrary to Article 2(4) of the UN Charter, whereas Uganda claimed that it was acting in self-defence.]

109. The Court finds it useful at this point to reproduce in its entirety the Ugandan High Command document [which] provides the basis for the operation known as operation "Safe Haven". The document reads as follows:

> "WHEREAS for a long time the DRC has been used by the enemies of Uganda as a base and launching pad for attacks against Uganda;
>
> AND
>
> WHEREAS the successive governments of the DRC have not been in effective control of all the territory of the Congo; . . .
>
> Now THEREFORE the High Command sitting in Kampala this 11th day of September, 1998, resolves to maintain forces of the UPDF in order to secure Uganda's legitimate security interests which are the following:
>
> 1. To deny the Sudan opportunity to use the territory of the DRC to destabilize Uganda.
> 2. To enable UPDF to neutralize Uganda dissident groups which have been receiving assistance from the Government of the DRC and the Sudan.
> 3. To ensure that the political and administrative vacuum, and instability caused by the fighting between the rebels and the Congolese Army and its allies do not adversely affect the security of Uganda.
> 4. To prevent the genocidal elements, namely, the Interahamwe, and ex-FAR [Rwandan Armed Forces], which have been launching attacks on the people of Uganda from the DRC, from continuing to do so.
> 5. To be in position to safeguard the territory integrity of Uganda against irresponsible threats of invasion from certain forces." . . .

119. The Court first observes that the objectives of operation "Safe Haven", as stated in the Ugandan High Command document . . . , were not consonant with the concept of self-defence as understood in international law . . . .

121. Uganda claimed that there was a tripartite conspiracy in 1998 between the DRC, the ADF [an anti-Ugandan rebel group] and the Sudan; . . . and that the DRC encouraged and facilitated stepped-up cross border attacks from May 1998 onwards . . . .

130. The Court observes that it has not been presented with evidence that can safely be relied on in a court of law to prove that there was an agreement between the DRC and the Sudan to participate in or support military action against Uganda . . . .

[The Court went on to conclude that, at most, the available evidence suggested some Sudanese support for the ADF's activities. By contrast, the evidence did not disclose a Congolese policy of supporting the ADF, but rather suggested that the DRC was simply unable to control events along its border.]

141. In the light of this assessment of all the relevant evidence, the Court is now in a position to determine whether the use of force by Uganda within the territory of the DRC could be characterized as self-defence . . . .

145. The Court would first observe that in August and early September 1998 Uganda did not report to the Security Council events that it had regarded as requiring it to act in self-defence.

146. It is further to be noted that, while Uganda claimed to have acted in self-defence, it did not ever claim that it had been subjected to an armed attack by the armed forces of the DRC. The "armed attacks" to which reference was made came rather from the ADF. The Court has found above . . . that there is no satisfactory proof of the involvement in these attacks, direct or indirect, of the Government of the DRC. The attacks did not emanate from armed bands or irregulars sent by the DRC or on behalf of the DRC, within the sense of Article 3 (g) of General Assembly resolution 3314 (XXIX) on the definition of aggression, adopted on 14 December 1974. The Court is of the view that, on the evidence before it, even if this series of deplorable attacks could be regarded as cumulative in character, they still remained non-attributable to the DRC.

147. For all these reasons, the Court finds that the legal and factual circumstances for the exercise of a right of self-defence by Uganda against the DRC were not present . . . .

148. . . . Article 51 of the Charter may justify a use of force in self-defence only within the strict confines there laid down. It does not allow the use of force by a State to protect perceived security interests beyond these parameters. Other means are available to a concerned State, including, in particular, recourse to the Security Council . . . .

300. As to the question of whether the DRC breached its duty of vigilance by tolerating anti-Ugandan rebels on its territory, the Court notes that this is a different issue from the question of active support for the rebels, because the Parties do not dispute the presence of the anti-Ugandan rebels on the territory of the DRC as a factual matter. The DRC recognized that anti-Ugandan groups operated on the territory of the DRC from at least 1986. Under the Declaration on Friendly Relations, "every State has the duty to refrain from . . . acquiescing in organized activities within its territory directed towards the commission of such acts" (e.g., terrorist acts, acts of internal strife) and also "no State shall . . . tolerate subversive, terrorist or armed activities directed towards the violent overthrow of the regime of another State . . .". As stated earlier, these provisions are declaratory of customary international law . . . .

301. The Court has noted that, according to Uganda, the rebel groups were able to operate "unimpeded" in the border region between the DRC and Uganda "because of its mountainous terrain, its remoteness from Kinshasa (more than 1,500 km), and the almost complete absence of central government presence or authority in the region during President Mobutu's 32-year term in office".

During the period under consideration both anti-Ugandan and anti-Zairean rebel groups operated in this area. Neither Zaire [the predecessor to the DRC] nor Uganda were in a position to put an end to their activities. However, in the light of the evidence before it, the Court cannot conclude that the absence of action by Zaire's Government against the rebel groups in the border area is tantamount to "tolerating" or "acquiescing" in their activities . . . .

The reference above to the September 11 terrorist attacks on the United States raises a question about whether a terrorist attack by a terrorist group can amount to an "armed attack" within the meaning of Article 51. It was widely accepted, even before September 11, that an act of terrorism could give rise to an Article 51 right of self-defence if the nexus between the terrorist act and another state was sufficiently close. The difficulty lies in defining the required connection. Based on the above excerpts from the ICJ's decision in *Democratic Republic of the Congo v Uganda*, what are the minimum requirements of this connection?

This issue was engaged by the 1986 response of the United States to the bombing of a Berlin discotheque in Germany, killing two US military personnel and a Turkish civilian. That bombing was greeted enthusiastically by Libya's then leader, Colonel Qaddafi. The United States claimed that there was also conclusive evidence of direct Libyan involvement in the bombing, and launched air strikes against Libya. In justifying this course of action, the US ambassador to the United Nations argued that the United States had acted in self-defence against Libya's "continued policy of terrorist threats and the use of force, in violation of . . . Article 2(4) of the Charter."[20] This justification failed to convince most UN member states, a fact illustrated most starkly by condemnation of the US attacks in a General Assembly resolution.[21] A resolution disapproving the US actions was also proposed in the Security Council, but vetoed by the United States, the United Kingdom, and France.[22] One scholar suggests that the poor reception given to the US claim of self-defence stemmed in part from a "perceived lack of evidence tying the West Berlin discotheque bombing and other terrorist activities to Libya."[23]

More recently, US armed responses (in Sudan and Afghanistan) to the 1998 US embassy bombings in Kenya and Tanzania—again explained by the United States as acts of self-defence[24]—provoked less sweeping criticism. Those states critical of the United States tended to focus their objections on the proportionality and necessity of the US

---

20   *Letter from the Acting Permanent Representative of the United States of America, to the United Nations Addressed to the President of the Security Council*, UN Doc S/17990 (19 April 1986).

21   *Declaration of the Assembly of Heads of State and Governments of the Organization of African Unity on the aerial and naval military attack against the Socialist People's Libyan Arab Jamahiriya by the present United States Administration in April 1986*, GA Res 41/38, UN Doc A/RES/41/85, reprinted in UN GAOR, 41st Sess, Supp No 53, UN Doc A/41/53 at 34 (1986).

22   *Provisional Verbatim Records of the 2682d Meeting*, UN Doc S/PV.2682 at 43 (21 April 1986).

23   Jack M Beard, "America's New War on Terror: The Case for Self-Defense Under International Law" (2002) 25 Harv JL & Pub Pol'y 559 at 564.

24   See *Letter to Congressional Leaders Reporting on Military Action Against Terrorist Sites in Afghanistan and Sudan*, 34 Weekly Comp Pres Doc 1650 (21 August 1998), reported in Sean D Murphy, "Contemporary Practice of the United States Relating to International Law" (1999) 93 Am J Int'l L 161 at 162–63.

armed response (to the extent they raised legal issues at all).[25] These more muted reactions in the 1990s to force deployed in response to terrorism suggest a gradual, albeit hesitant, expansion of the circumstances in which the actions of non-state actors may be considered an "armed attack" within the meaning of Article 51.

In fact, the text of Article 51 does not exclude the possibility that violence by non-state actors against a state can constitute an "armed attack,"[26] a fact underlined by the reaction to the September 11 terrorist attacks. Given the shocking scale of those attacks and the fact that they were so evidently directed against the territory of the United States, the international community quickly embraced the view that a right of self-defence arose in the circumstances. The UN Security Council, for instance, invoked the right to self-defence in condemning the terrorist acts.[27] For its part, the North Atlantic Treaty Organization declared that the September 11 acts satisfied the requirements of an "armed attack" under Article 5 of the North Atlantic Treaty,[28] triggering a collective response from NATO.[29] The Organization of American States arrived at a similar conclusion, invoking Article 3 of the Inter-American Treaty of Reciprocal Assistance.[30]

These responses, and the widespread reaction of individual states offering assistance to the United States, support the conclusion that al-Qaida's terrorist act on September 11 reached the level of an "armed attack." Yet it remains significant that, in its Article 51 letter to the Security Council reporting its use of force against al-Qaida in Afghanistan in self-defence, the United States explicitly claimed that the Taliban (then the government of Afghanistan) had "supported" al-Qaida, and that the September 11 attacks had been "made possible" by the Taliban's decision to allow al-Qaida to use Afghan territory as a base of operations.[31] Similarly, in its Article 51 letter to the Security Council, the United Kingdom relied on the "close alliance" between al-Qaida and the Taliban, and asserted that the latter

---

25 See discussion in Tal Becker, *Terrorism and the State: Rethinking the Rules of State Responsibility* (Oxford: Hart Publishing, 2006) at 203–4.

26 See, for example, Major Darren C Huskisson, "The Air Bridge Denial Program and the Shootdown Of Civil Aircraft Under International Law" (2005) 56 AFL Rev 109 at 144: "The concept of an armed attack was left deliberately open to the interpretation of Member States and UN Organs, and the wording is broad enough to include the acts of non-State actors as 'armed attacks.'" See also Carsten Stahn, "'Nicaragua is Dead, Long Live Nicaragua' — The Right to Self-defence under Art. 51" in Christian Walter et al, *Terrorism as a Challenge for National and International Law: Security versus Liberty* (Berlin: Springer, 2003) at 830.

27 Resolution 1368 (2001), adopted by the Security Council on 12 September 2001, UN Doc S/RES/1368 (2001); Resolution 1373 (2001), adopted by the Security Council on 28 September 2001, UN Doc S/RES/1373 (2001).

28 4 April 1949, 34 UNTS 244, Can TS 1949 No 7, in force 24 August 1949.

29 NATO Press Release, "Invocation of Article 5 Confirmed" (2 October 2001).

30 2 September 1847, 21 UNTS 77, in force 30 December 1948, art 3 of which reads: "an armed attack by any State against an American State shall be considered as an attack against all the American States and, consequently, each one of the said Contracting Parties undertakes to assist in meeting the attack in the exercise of the inherent right of individual or collective self-defense recognized by Article 51 of the Charter of the United Nations." See also Twenty-fourth Meeting of Consultation of Ministers of Foreign Affairs, *Terrorist Threat to the Americas*, OAS Doc RC.24/Res.1/01 (21 September 2001).

31 *Letter dated 7 October 2001 from the Permanent Representative of the United States of America to the United Nations Addressed to the President of the Security Council*, UN Doc S/2001/946 (7 October 2001).

had "supported" the former.[32] In other words, the right of self-defence against a terrorist group was again predicated on the existence of a connection between that group and the state in whose territory the acts of self-defence were to occur. Under these circumstances, a common (although not unanimous) view is that the ensuing armed response against al-Qaida in Afghanistan was compliant with international law, insofar as other elements of the law of self-defence, such as proportionality and necessity, were observed.[33]

c) "Anticipatory" and "Pre-emptive" Self-Defence

The ICJ cases reviewed above focus in particular on whether a given action constitutes an "armed attack," which triggers a right to self-defence. A hotly debated issue is whether a right of self-defence may also be invoked where an attack has not actually yet happened, but is anticipated. This issue was famously raised in the *Caroline* incident, a dispute between the United States and Great Britain involving an American ship. The British believed that this vessel—the *Caroline*—would be used by American nationals to support the 1837 uprising in Upper Canada. The vessel was therefore destroyed by British forces on the American side of the border. In a series of letters between the US and UK governments attempting to resolve the resulting dispute, the US secretary of state expressed the view, apparently shared by both sides, that anticipatory actions in self-defence were only warranted where the "necessity of that self-defence is instant, overwhelming, and leaving no choice of means, and no moment for deliberation."[34]

Whether anticipatory self-defence in the face of an imminent attack of the *Caroline* sort is permitted is a point of contention among international lawyers. There are no authoritative rulings by international tribunals on the matter. States themselves have been remarkably reticent to rely on a right of anticipatory self-defence, preferring instead to go to great lengths to characterize their uses of force in self-defence as being reactions to prior armed attacks. Scholars are also divided on the issue, some taking the view that there is insufficient state practice accompanied by *opinio juris* to evidence any right of anticipatory self-defence,[35] while others rely on the necessity of such a doctrine in an era of long-range weapons of mass destruction.[36] Still others take a middle position: "where there is convincing evidence not merely of threats and potential danger but of *an attack being actually mounted*, then an armed attack may be said to have begun to occur, though it has not passed the frontier."[37]

---

32 *Letter dated 7 October 2001 from the Chargé d'Affaires a.i. of the Permanent Mission of the United Kingdom of Great Britain and Northern Ireland to the United Nations Addressed to the President of the Security Council*, UN Doc S/2001/947 (7 October 2001).

33 See, for example, Jordan Paust, "Use of Armed Force against Terrorists in Iraq, Afghanistan and Beyond" (2002) 35 Cornell Int'l LJ 533.

34 See RY Jennings, "The Caroline and the McLeod Cases" (1938) Am J Int'l L 82.

35 See, for example, Christine Gray, *International Law and the Use of Force*, 3d ed (Oxford: Oxford University Press, 2008) at 160–65 and 208–27.

36 See, for example, Derek Bowett, *Self-Defence in International Law* (Manchester: Manchester University Press, 1958); Anthony Arend & Robert Beck, *International Law and the Use of Force: Beyond the UN Charter Paradigm* (London: Routledge, 1993).

37 CHM Waldock, *The Regulation of the Use of Force by Individual States in International Law*, (1952-II) 81 Hague Recueil 451, 498 [emphasis added]. See also Yoram Dinstein, *War, Aggression and Self-Defence*, above note 7 at 203–5.

More contentious still is whether international law recognizes a right of "pre-emptive self-defence," one not responsive to imminent but rather potential threats. The argument that such an expansive right of self-defence exists is sometimes referred to as the "Bush Doctrine," given its first clear articulation as a plank of US national security policy in the wake of the September 11 terrorist attacks against the World Trade Centre and Pentagon:

National Security Strategy of the United States of America, 17 September 2002[38]

. . . Defending our Nation against its enemies is the first and fundamental commitment of the Federal Government. Today, that task has changed dramatically. Enemies in the past needed great armies and great industrial capabilities to endanger America. Now, shadowy networks of individuals can bring great chaos and suffering to our shores for less than it costs to purchase a single tank. Terrorists are organized to penetrate open societies and to turn the power of modern technologies against us . . . .

It has taken almost a decade for us to comprehend the true nature of this new threat. Given the goals of rogue states and terrorists, the United States can no longer solely rely on a reactive posture as we have in the past. The inability to deter a potential attacker, the immediacy of today's threats, and the magnitude of potential harm that could be caused by our adversaries' choice of weapons, do not permit that option. We cannot let our enemies strike first . . . .

For centuries, international law recognized that nations need not suffer an attack before they can lawfully take action to defend themselves against forces that present an imminent danger of attack. Legal scholars and international jurists often conditioned the legitimacy of preemption on the existence of an imminent threat—most often a visible mobilization of armies, navies, and air forces preparing to attack.

We must adapt the concept of imminent threat to the capabilities and objectives of today's adversaries. Rogue states and terrorists do not seek to attack us using conventional means. They know such attacks would fail. Instead, they rely on acts of terror and, potentially, the use of weapons of mass destruction—weapons that can be easily concealed, delivered covertly, and used without warning.

The targets of these attacks are our military forces and our civilian population, in direct violation of one of the principal norms of the law of warfare. As was demonstrated by the losses on September 11, 2001, mass civilian casualties is the specific objective of terrorists and these losses would be exponentially more severe if terrorists acquired and used weapons of mass destruction.

The United States has long maintained the option of preemptive actions to counter a sufficient threat to our national security. The greater the threat, the greater is the risk of inaction—and the more compelling the case for taking anticipatory action to defend ourselves, even if uncertainty remains as to the time and place of the enemy's attack. To forestall or prevent such hostile acts by our adversaries, the United States will, if necessary, act preemptively.

---

38 Reprinted in (2002) 41 ILM 1478–479.

The United States will not use force in all cases to preempt emerging threats, nor should nations use preemption as a pretext for aggression. Yet in an age where the enemies of civilization openly and actively seek the world's most destructive technologies, the United States cannot remain idle while dangers gather. We will always proceed deliberately, weighing the consequences of our actions . . . .

The purpose of our actions will always be to eliminate a specific threat to the United States or our allies and friends. The reasons for our actions will be clear, the force measured, and the cause just . . . .

The American-led invasion of Iraq in 2003 was justified in part by the Bush Administration as a necessary response to an alleged Iraqi weapons of mass destruction program. The subsequent failure of United States and allied forces to unearth such weapons brought the dangers of the doctrine of pre-emptive self-defence into sharp focus. Consider the UN High-level Panel's discussion of the right of pre-emptive self-defence, and the problems it raises, in its 2004 report:

A More Secure World: Our Shared Responsibility: Report of the Secretary-General's High-level Panel on Threats, Challenges and Change, UN Doc A/59/565 at 8-99 (2 December 2004)[39]

188. The language of . . . article [51] is restrictive: "Nothing in the present Charter shall impair the inherent right of individual or collective self-defense if an armed attack occurs against a member of the United Nations, until the Security Council has taken measures to maintain international peace and security". However, a threatened State, according to long established international law, can take military action as long as the threatened attack is *imminent*, no other means would deflect it and the action is proportionate. The problem arises where the threat in question is not imminent but still claimed to be real: for example the acquisition, with allegedly hostile intent, of nuclear weapons-making capability.

189. Can a State, without going to the Security Council, claim in these circumstances the right to act, in anticipatory self-defence, not just pre-emptively (against an imminent or proximate threat) but preventively (against a non-imminent or non-proximate one)? Those who say "yes" argue that the potential harm from some threats (e.g., terrorists armed with a nuclear weapon) is so great that one simply cannot risk waiting until they become imminent, and that less harm may be done (e.g., avoiding a nuclear exchange or radioactive fallout from a reactor destruction) by acting earlier.

190. The short answer is that if there are good arguments for preventive military action, with good evidence to support them, they should be put to the Security Council, which can authorize such action if it chooses to. If it does not so choose, there will be, by definition, time to pursue other strategies, including persuasion, negotiation, deterrence and containment—and to visit again the military option.

---

39 Reprinted with permission. [Emphasis in original.]

191. For those impatient with such a response, the answer must be that, in a world full of perceived potential threats, the risk to the global order and the norm of non-intervention on which it continues to be based is simply too great for the legality of unilateral preventive action, as distinct from collectively endorsed action, to be accepted. Allowing one to so act is to allow all.

192. **We do not favour the rewriting or reinterpretation of Article 51.**

The revised National Security Strategy of the United States released in May 2010 by the Obama Administration makes no further mention of pre-emption of "emerging threats" or pre-emptive self-defence, apparently signalling abandonment of the doctrine. Rather, it states that "[t]he United States must reserve the right to act unilaterally if necessary to defend our nation and our interests, yet we will also seek to adhere to standards that govern the use of force."[40]

---

40 *National Security Strategy*, May 2010, online: http://www.whitehouse.gov/sites/default/files/rss_viewer/national_security_strategy.pdf.

CHAPTER 15

INTERNATIONAL CRIMINAL LAW

A. INTRODUCTION

International criminal law is a body of international rules designed both to proscribe crimes of sufficient gravity to be of international concern and to impose criminal liability on those persons who engage in such conduct.[1] This body of rules either authorizes states, or imposes upon them an obligation, to submit certain acts for prosecution or punishment. It also regulates prosecutions of persons suspected of these crimes before international criminal tribunals.[2] Substantively, international criminal law is concerned primarily with genocide, crimes against humanity, and war crimes (often referred to as the "core crimes," along with the crime of aggression), but as it evolves, the field may also address such crimes as torture and terrorism. The core crimes tend to be those in respect of which international prosecutorial mechanisms have been put in place; whereas other crimes of international concern with a cross-border element tend to be addressed by establishing rules that enhance the reach and effectiveness of domestic mechanisms of prevention, investigation, prosecution, and punishment. This distinction is underscored by referring to the latter body of rules as "transnational"—rather than "international"—criminal law.[3]

Issues addressed by international criminal law range from the definition of international crimes and the modes of participation therein; to jurisdiction over such crimes and immunities from prosecution; to international and national procedures for investigating, prosecuting, and punishing such crimes. Given its scope, international criminal law overlaps with a number of other areas of public international law as well as national criminal law. For example, the definition of war crimes used in international criminal law is taken directly from international humanitarian law, introduced in Chapter 9. International criminal law does not, however, encompass all of international humanitarian law, as the latter contains a vast number of rules unrelated to the prohibition or prosecution of war crimes as such.

This chapter will concentrate on the development of the international law and institutions relating to the prosecution of genocide, crimes against humanity, and war crimes,

---

1   Antonio Cassese et al, *Cassese's International Criminal Law*, 3d ed (New York: Oxford University Press, 2013) at 3.

2   *Ibid.*

3   Robert J Currie, *International & Transnational Criminal Law* (Toronto: Irwin Law, 2010) at 19–21. See also Neil Boister, *An Introduction to Transnational Criminal Law* (New York: Oxford University Press, 2012) at 13 ("Transnational criminal law is the law that suppresses crime that transcends national frontiers; it can be defined as 'the indirect suppression by international law through domestic penal law of criminal activities that have actual or potential trans-boundary effects.'")

as well as key issues surrounding the crime of terrorism. It will consider the establishment, during the past two decades, of the International Criminal Tribunals for the Former Yugoslavia and Rwanda; the International Criminal Court; and "internationalized" tribunals such as the Special Court for Sierra Leone, the Extraordinary Chambers in the Courts of Cambodia, and the Special Tribunal for Lebanon. We begin this chapter with a brief history of precursors to the current international criminal tribunals, to illustrate that the impetus behind the creation of these tribunals, and particularly the International Criminal Court, is not new. We will also see, however, that the vision of establishing a permanent international criminal tribunal has evolved considerably over time.

B. PRECURSORS TO THE INTERNATIONAL CRIMINAL COURT

1) Immediate Post–World War I Proposals

In January 1919, at the end of World War I, a peace conference was convened in Paris to draft the terms of peace with the defeated Central Empire powers. In the course of doing so, the conference struck a Commission on the Responsibility of the Authors of the War and on Enforcement of Penalties. The Commission's mandate was to investigate the possible international criminal liability for war crimes of enemy officers and leaders.[4] The Commission opined that each Allied power was empowered by international law to prosecute enemy accused suspected of violating the laws and customs of war and that enemy officials suspected of committing outrages against citizens of several Allied nations should be tried before an amalgamated high tribunal.[5] In scrutinizing the activities of enemy accused, this tribunal would apply "the principles of the law of nations as they result from the usages established among civilized peoples, from the laws of humanity and from the dictates of public conscience."[6] Convicts were to be sentenced to punishments consistent with those that might be imposed for similar offences in the convict's own country or in Allied states represented on the tribunal.[7] The surrendering Central Empire powers would be obliged to endorse this tribunal as part of the peace treaty process.[8]

The difficulties of prosecuting war criminals before an international tribunal in the absence of a justiciable codification of international crimes was not lost on the Allied nations, particularly the United States. The problem posed by the fundamental principle of *nullum crimen sine lege*—there can be no crime that is not defined in law—galvanized the American response to the Commission's proposal. Concerned with preserving a stable peace and already more preoccupied with events in Russia than with Central

---

4 "Commission on the Responsibility of the Authors of the War and on Enforcement of Penalties: Report Presented to the Preliminary Peace Conference, March 29, 1919" reprinted in (1920) 14 Am J Int'l L 95. The Commission concluded (at 115 and 117) that Germany and Austria, along with their Turkish and Bulgarian allies, had waged war through "barbarous and illegitimate methods" and that military personnel and civilians who had sanctioned or participated in these acts should be prosecuted.

5 Matthew Lippman, "Towards an International Criminal Court" (1995) 3 *San Diego Justice Journal* 1 at 14.

6 "Commission on the Responsibility of the Authors of the War and on Enforcement of Penalties," above note 4 at 122.

7 *Ibid.*

8 Lippman, above note 5 at 15.

Empire war criminals,[9] American experts on the Commission argued, *inter alia*, that the "laws of humanity" remained an ill-defined notion difficult to apply in a prosecutorial setting. Further, no international instrument existed that contemplated the existence of an international criminal court or that defined violations of the laws and customs of war or the laws of humanity as international crimes with specific sanctions.[10]

In the end, Article 228 of the Treaty of Versailles committed the German government to recognizing the rights of Allied military courts to prosecute German suspects and to sentence them — if convicted — to punishment "laid down by law."[11] Under Article 229, where an accused had perpetrated crimes against nationals of more than one Allied power, mixed courts "composed of members of the military tribunals of the Powers concerned" were to be established. Germany was to extradite accused persons to the Allies for trial, "notwithstanding any proceedings or prosecution before a tribunal in Germany or in the territory of her allies."

The Versailles formula did represent a turning point in international law, in that no general amnesty was granted to the vanquished, and violations of the laws of war were to culminate in criminal liability. At the same time, Articles 228 and 229 reflected a mere extension of the domestic jurisdiction of Allied courts to Germans who had engaged in actions injurious to citizens of Allied countries. The only truly international tribunal contemplated by the Treaty of Versailles, in Article 227, was one intended to "publicly arraign William II of Hohenzollern [the German Kaiser] . . . for a supreme offence against international morality and the sanctity of treaties." While such an arraignment would have represented an important erosion of the notion of the sovereign immunity of heads of state, the tribunal's grounds for proceeding were very vaguely worded. In this regard, Article 227 indicated that the tribunal was to be "guided by the highest motives of international policy, with a view to vindicating the solemn obligation of international undertakings and the validity of international morality."

In practice, little came of Articles 227, 228, and 229. Within a month of its ratification, Germany repudiated the treaty as a harsh settlement unilaterally imposed (or *diktat*), and refused to honour its provisions.[12] The Netherlands, meanwhile, granted asylum to the Kaiser, effectively placing him beyond the reach of the tribunal contemplated in Article 227. Further, none of the 1,580 German accused pursued by the Allies were ever extradited by Germany and only forty-five were prosecuted before the German Reichsgericht (Supreme Court).[13]

---

9   *Ibid.*

10   See "Annex II: Memorandum of Reservations Presented by the Representatives of the United States to the Report of the Commission on Responsibilities, April 4, 1919") in "Commission on the Responsibility of the Authors of the War and on Enforcement of Penalties," above note 4 at 127–51.

11   Treaty of Peace between the Allied Powers and Associated Powers and Germany (Treaty of Versailles), 28 June 1919, UK TS 1919 No 4, (1919) 13 AJIL Supp 151, in force 10 January 1920.

12   Benjamin Ferencz, *An International Criminal Court, A Step Toward World Peace: A Documentary History And Analysis*, vol 1 (London: Oceana Publications, 1980) at 32.

13   Lippman, above note 5 at 20. The sentences handed down by the Reichsgericht in those cases that were not dismissed by the court were extremely lenient and were later annulled. All war crimes proceedings were eventually quashed when Hitler came to power in 1933.

The attempt to bring accused Turkish war criminals to trial was even more perfunctory. The original treaty of peace between Turkey and the Allies—the Treaty of Sèvres—envisaged the handover of Turks who had committed "crimes against humanity," including the forced displacement and massacre of large segments of the Armenian population of the Ottoman Empire.[14] The treaty—signed in 1920—was never implemented and its replacement, the 1923 Treaty of Lausanne, followed upon the granting of a general amnesty and contained no mention of accountability for war crimes.[15]

2) Subsequent Inter-War Proposals

The notion of an international criminal tribunal did not die with the failure of the immediate post–World War I efforts. In 1920, the League of Nations established an Advisory Committee of Jurists to draft the statute for the Permanent Court of International Justice (the predecessor to today's International Court of Justice). During the debate surrounding the draft statute, Baron Deschamps of Belgium argued forcefully for the inclusion of another international court system—a "High Court of International Justice"—that would try "crimes against international public order and against the universal law of nations" that were referred to it by the Assembly or Council of the League of Nations.[16]

The Baron's proposal met significant resistance from other committee members who felt that the issue of an international criminal court fell outside their mandate and who were troubled by the vague invocation of "universal law" and "crimes against international public order." While the committee eventually recommended that the League of Nations create a High Court of International Justice, the League's Legal Committee ultimately rejected this proposal, noting that "there is not yet any international penal law recognized by all nations" and preferring to rely on the Permanent Court of International Justice to adjudicate those international crimes that were extant at the time.[17] The Assembly of the League of Nations ended discussion of an international criminal court, deciding it was premature.[18]

Despite the League's inaction, international legal scholars continued to advocate the creation of an international criminal court, with critiques becoming more pointed as the inadequacies of the processes envisaged in the Treaty of Versailles became increasingly evident. In the 1920s, proposals for such a court were made by the International Law Association and the Inter-Parliamentary Union, but were again not implemented by the League of Nations. The concept of an international criminal court remained a dead letter until revived once again in 1934. In October of that year, a Croatian nationalist assassinated King Alexander I of Yugoslavia and French Foreign Minister Louis Barthou in Marseilles. The alleged assassin escaped to Italy, which refused to extradite the suspect. In December, France called for a convention on terrorism that would include an inter-

---

14 Treaty of Peace Between the Allies and Associated Powers and Turkey, 10 August 1920, UKTS 1920 No 11, (1921) 15 AJIL Supp. 179, not in force.

15 Ferencz, above note 12 at 39; Treaty of Peace signed at Lausanne, 24 July 1923, 28 LNTS 11, (1924) 18 AJIL Supp 1, in force 6 August 1924.

16 Ferencz, above note 12 at 193, citing Advisory Committee of Jurists, Procès-Verbaux of the Proceedings of the Committee, 16–24 July 1920.

17 *Ibid* at 228.

18 *Ibid* at 38.

national court competent to try accused terrorists. The international court would have jurisdiction when the state on whose territory the accused was found did not wish to extradite or prosecute.[19]

The Council of the League of Nations appointed a Committee for the International Repression of Terrorism to examine the issue and devise a draft convention. The Committee ultimately drafted two separate conventions—one on the prevention and punishment of terrorism and the other on the creation of an international criminal court.[20] States could enter into the former without ratifying the later, although membership in the international criminal court convention was contingent on acceptance of the convention on terrorism. Both conventions were received coolly by the international community: when they were eventually opened for signature and ratification, only one state (India) ratified the Convention for the Prevention and Punishment of Terrorism[21] and no state ratified the Convention for the Creation of an International Criminal Court.[22]

3) World War II and the Nuremburg and Far East Tribunals

By the onset of World War II, the global community had progressed no further towards establishing a permanent international criminal tribunal than it had in the immediate post–World War I era. At the same time, the Allied powers—who as early as 1942 were contemplating the prosecution of Axis war criminals—recognized that, based on their experiences in the aftermath of World War I, the pursuit of accused persons could not be left up to Germany or the other Axis powers themselves.[23]

In June 1943, the London International Assembly—the unofficial successor to the League of Nations, comprising governments of Allied states—prepared a report advocating the creation of an international criminal court to prosecute Nazis accused of war crimes. The latter were defined as "any grave outrages violating the general principles of criminal law as recognised by civilised nations and committed in wartime or connected with the preparation, the waging or the prosecution of war, or perpetrated with a view to preventing the restoration of peace."[24] The court was to have jurisdiction only when no domestic court of a member of the future United Nations had jurisdiction over an accused that it was willing to exercise, or when two or more states having jurisdiction over the accused agreed to have the accused brought before the court.[25] Further, the London International Assembly's proposal sidestepped the problems that had stymied the terrorism conventions by defining the court as a "Criminal Court common to all nations." As a

---

19 Lippman, above note 5 at 38.

20 Ferencz, above note 12 at 376.

21 (1934) *League of Nations Official Journal* 23–34.

22 (1934) *League of Nations Official Journal* 37–51. See further Ferencz, above note 12 at 54; Geoffrey Marston, "Early Attempts to Suppress Terrorism: The Terrorism and International Criminal Court Conventions of 1937" (2002) 73:1 Brit. YB Int'l L 293–313.

23 Lippman, above note 5 at 45.

24 *Draft Convention for the Creation of an International Criminal Court* (London International Assembly, 1943) reprinted in *Historical Survey of the Question of the International Criminal Jurisdiction: Memorandum Submitted by the Secretary-General*, UN Doc A/CN.4/7/Rev.1 at 97–112 (1949).

25 *Ibid*, art 3.

consequence, "justice administered by this court shall not be considered as foreign" and "[t]he handing over of an accused person to the prosecuting authority of the [International Criminal Court] is not an extradition."[26]

Subsequently, in 1944, the United Nations War Crimes Commission, established to compile lists of war crimes, went somewhat beyond its original mandate and prepared a draft Convention for the Establishment of a United Nations War Crimes Court. The court was to prosecute war criminals, defined in Article 1(2) as "any person—irrespective of rank or position—who has committed or attempted to commit, or has ordered, caused, aided, abetted or incited another person to commit, or by his failure to fulfil a duty incumbent upon him has himself committed, an offence against the laws and customs of war."[27] The court was to have jurisdiction over war crimes committed by a person of any state "engaged in war or armed hostilities with any of the High Contracting Parties, or in hostile occupation of any of the High Contracting Parties."[28]

In the end, the major Allied powers, after debating whether they should simply execute summarily German war crimes suspects, opted to create an international military tribunal. The agreement reached by the four major Allied powers in London on 8 August 1945, for the prosecution and punishment of the major war criminals of the European Axis, also contained a Charter for the desired International Military Tribunal (IMT). The IMT, based in Nuremberg, had jurisdiction over crimes against peace, war crimes, and crimes against humanity. These crimes were defined in some detail in Article 6 of what became known as the Nuremberg Charter:

> **Agreement by the Government of the United Kingdom of Great Britain and Northern Ireland, the Government of the United States of America, the Provisional Government of the French Republic and the Government of the Union of Soviet Socialist Republics for the Prosecution and Punishment of the Major War Criminals of the European Axis (Nuremberg Charter), 8 August 1945, 82 UNTS 279, (1945) 39 AJIL Supp 258, in force 8 August 1945**

II. JURISDICTION AND GENERAL PRINCIPLES

Article 6

The Tribunal established by the Agreement referred to in Article 1 hereof for the trial and punishment of the major war criminals of the European Axis countries shall have the power to try and punish persons who, acting in the interests of the European Axis countries, whether as individuals or as members of organizations, committed any of the following crimes.

The following acts, or any of them, are crimes coming within the jurisdiction of the Tribunal for which there shall be individual responsibility:

---

26 *Ibid*, art 5.
27 United Nations War Crimes Commission, *Draft Convention for the Establishment of a United Nations War Crimes Court with an Explanatory Memorandum* (1944) reprinted in *Historical Survey of the Question of the International Criminal Jurisdiction*, above note 24 at 112–19.
28 *Ibid*, art 1(3).

(a) CRIMES AGAINST PEACE: namely, planning, preparation, initiation or waging of a war of aggression, or a war in violation of international treaties, agreements or assurances, or participation in a common plan or conspiracy for the accomplishment of any of the foregoing;

(b) WAR CRIMES: namely, violations of the laws or customs of war. Such violations shall include, but not be limited to, murder, ill-treatment or deportation to slave labor or for any other purpose of civilian population of or in occupied territory, murder or ill-treatment of prisoners of war or persons on the seas, killing of hostages, plunder of public or private property, wanton destruction of cities, towns or villages, or devastation not justified by military necessity;

(c) CRIMES AGAINST HUMANITY: namely, murder, extermination, enslavement, deportation, and other inhumane acts committed against any civilian population, before or during the war; or persecutions on political, racial or religious grounds in execution of or in connection with any crime within the jurisdiction of the Tribunal, whether or not in violation of the domestic law of the country where perpetrated.

Leaders, organizers, instigators and accomplices participating in the formulation or execution of a common plan or conspiracy to commit any of the foregoing crimes are responsible for all acts performed by any persons in execution of such plan.

Twenty-four Nazi accused were indicted in October 1945 and tried pursuant to Article 6. On 30 September 1946, in rendering judgment, the IMT noted that: "The Charter is not an arbitrary exercise of power on the part of the victorious Nations, but in the view of the Tribunal . . . it is the expression of international law existing at the time of its creation; and to that extent is itself a contribution to international law."[29] Ten of the accused were convicted and sentenced to death. Three others were acquitted, and several others were partially acquitted and sentenced to terms of imprisonment.[30] The IMT ruled that the principle of *nullum crimen sine lege* did not prevent convictions since the accused must have known that they were in breach of treaty obligations and been aware of international prohibitions on the aggressive use of force.[31]

In deciding whether the accused had committed crimes against peace, the Tribunal preferred not to define a "war of aggression," instead merely indicating that twelve of the defendants had indeed "planned and waged aggressive wars against twelve nations, and were therefore guilty of this series of crimes."[32]

With regard to war crimes, the IMT ruled that the acts attributed to the Nazi accused and defined in Article 6(b) were clearly violations of international law and the customs of war as recognized by all civilized nations by 1939.[33] To convict, the Tribunal required evi-

---

29 Trial of the Major War Criminals Before the International Military Tribunal, Nuremberg, 14 November 1945–1 October 1946 (Secretariat of the IMT, Allied Control Authority for Germany, 1948) [IMT Trial Judgment].
30 Ferencz, above note 12 at 74.
31 IMT Trial Judgment, above note 29.
32 *Ibid.*
33 Ferencz, above note 12 at 485–86.

dence connecting the accused to the planning, ordering, inciting, or commission of war crimes. Simple knowledge of crimes, transmission of orders, or failure to prevent commission of the acts was held not to be sufficient grounds for a conviction.[34]

On the charges of crimes against humanity, the IMT noted that inhumane acts committed after the commencement of the war that could not be considered war crimes were crimes against humanity "since they were all committed in execution of, or in connection with, the aggressive war."[35] Months after the introduction of the Nuremberg Charter, the law establishing the jurisdictional basis for Allied prosecutions of German war criminals in national military tribunals defined crimes against humanity as "atrocities and offenses, including but not limited to murder, extermination, enslavement, deportation, imprisonment, torture, rape, or other inhumane acts committed against any civilian population, or persecutions on political, racial or religious grounds."[36]

A Tribunal similar to the IMT, the International Military Tribunal for the Far East (IMTFE), was established to try Japanese accused. The Charter of the IMTFE was drafted by the United States and essentially copied the Nuremberg Charter.[37] Twenty-eight Japanese leaders and politicians were tried by the IMTFE for crimes against peace, murder, war crimes, and conspiracy to commit these crimes.[38] The indictments were submitted to the Tribunal on 29 April 1946; thereafter the Tribunal convened on 3 May 1946, adjourned on 16 April 1948, and rendered judgment in November 1948.[39] Two accused died during the proceedings and one was declared unfit to stand trial.[40] Seven were sentenced to death by hanging and were executed shortly after their conviction. Sixteen were sentenced to life imprisonment: three died in prison, while the other thirteen were paroled in 1955. Two were sentenced to finite sentences.[41]

4) Post–World War II Proposals

The findings of the IMT and IMTFE did not go completely unchallenged. The decisions were criticized as victors' justice poorly grounded in international law and thus amounting

---

34   IMT Trial Judgment, above note 29.

35   Ferencz, above note 12 at 486. The Tribunal concluded that, because the definition of crimes against humanity in Article 6(c) included the caveat that the impugned acts were to be committed "in execution of or in connection with any crime within the jurisdiction of the Tribunal," and because the only other crimes the Tribunal dealt with were those occurring at and during war, pre-war acts that would otherwise be considered crimes against humanity could not be considered by the Tribunal: IMT Trial Judgment, above note 29.

36   Control Council Law No 10, Punishment of Persons Guilty of War Crimes, Crimes Against Peace and Against Humanity, 20 December 1945, (1946) 3 *Official Gazette Control Council for Germany* 50–55.

37   Statute of the International Military Tribunal for the Far East, reprinted in Robert Cryer & Neil Boister, eds, *Documents on the Tokyo International Military Tribunal: Charter, Indictment and Judgments* (New York: Oxford University Press, 2008) at 7.

38   Robert Cryer, "Tokyo International Military Tribunal" in Antonio Cassese, ed, *The Oxford Companion to International Criminal Justice* (New York: Oxford University Press, 2009) at 535.

39   *Ibid* at 536.

40   *Ibid*.

41   *Ibid* at 537; Robert Cryer et al, *An Introduction to International Criminal Law and Procedure*, 2d ed (New York: Cambridge University Press, 2010) at 116.

to *ex post facto* criminalization. Partly in response to these criticisms, one of the first tasks undertaken by the newly established United Nations was to seek to further codify international criminal law and reinvigorate work on a permanent international criminal court.

In 1948, genocide was codified as an international crime in the Genocide Convention.[42] During the negotiation of the Genocide Convention, much of the debate over its content centred on enforcement. The UN Secretary-General's original draft would have required the contracting states to "pledge themselves to punish any offender under this Convention within any territory under their jurisdiction, irrespective of the nationality of the offender or of the place where the offence has been committed."[43] States not prosecuting offenders or those complicit in the act of genocide were to remit that person for trial before an international court.[44] In the months that followed, delegates debated whether to include provisions for the establishment of an international criminal court within the Genocide Convention.[45] Ultimately, a detailed criminal court proposal was deleted from the draft convention in favour of a generally worded allusion in Article VI to an "international penal tribunal" to have jurisdiction "with respect to those Contracting Parties which shall have accepted its jurisdiction." Otherwise, those accused of genocide were to be tried by "a competent tribunal of the State in the territory of which the act was committed."[46]

At about the same time, the UN General Assembly asked the International Law Commission (ILC) to consider formulating a comprehensive code of international crimes and to re-examine the idea of establishing a permanent international court. From that point forward, progress on the international criminal court would be hampered by complications inherent in the elaboration of an international code of crimes, with UN delegates unwilling to proceed with the former until the latter was concluded.

In 1950, the ILC proposed a draft code reaffirming the Nuremberg crimes of aggression ("crimes against peace"), war crimes, and crimes against humanity.[47] Yet, in 1951, the General Assembly suspended consideration of the draft Code of Offences against the Peace and Security of Mankind until the ILC was able to decide upon an acceptable definition of the crime of aggression. In 1954, following inability on the part of the ILC to agree on such a definition, and with the Cold War well underway, active work on the Code effectively ceased. Though the Code would be revisited periodically in subsequent years, no real progress would be made for a least another quarter century[48] (with a consensus General Assembly resolution defining aggression — though not necessarily the *crime* of aggression — eventually reached in 1974, as discussed in Chapter 14). In 1957, the General Assembly postponed consideration of the international criminal court pending movement

---

42 Convention on the Prevention and Punishment of the Crime of Genocide, 9 December 1948, 78 UNTS 277, Can TS 1949 No 27, in force 12 January 1951 [Genocide Convention].

43 *Draft Convention on the Crime of Genocide*, UN Doc E/447 (26 June 1947), art VII.

44 *Ibid*, art IX.

45 See *Ad Hoc Committee on Genocide: Summary Record of the Eighth Meeting*, UN Doc E/AC.25/SR.8 (17 April 1948), for the arguments marshalled by various delegates. See also Ferencz, above note 12, and Lippman, above note 5.

46 Genocide Convention, above note 42, art VI.

47 Benjamin B Ferencz, "An International Criminal Code and Court: Where They Stand and Where They're Going" (1992) 30 Colum J Transnat'l L 375 at 375.

48 Ferencz, above note 12, vol 2 at 48.

on the Code, thereby "effectively ending attempts to establish such a tribunal."[49] From the late 1950s through to the late 1980s, scholars nevertheless continued to advocate the creation of an international criminal tribunal.[50]

In the international arena, the notion of an international criminal tribunal surfaced next in the context of the International Convention on the Suppression and Punishment of the Crime of Apartheid.[51] Echoing Article VI of the Genocide Convention, Article V of the Apartheid Convention provided that jurisdiction over violators could be tried "by a competent tribunal of any State Party to the Convention which may acquire jurisdiction over the person of the accused or by an international penal tribunal having jurisdiction with respect to those States Parties which shall have accepted its jurisdiction."

Subsequently, in 1979, the UN General Assembly approved the planned undertaking of a study, by an Ad Hoc Working Group of Experts on Southern Africa, "on ways and means of implementing international instruments" such as the Apartheid Convention, including "the establishment of the international jurisdiction envisaged by the Convention."[52] The experts unanimously adopted a draft statute for an international criminal court that would have jurisdiction over grave breaches of the convention such as murder; torture; cruel, inhuman, or degrading treatment or punishment; and arbitrary arrest and detention.[53] States parties could also agree to allow the court to scrutinize international crimes proscribed by other conventions.[54] States, UN organs, and other international bodies, as well as individuals, could all file complaints with a Procuracy, which would evaluate whether the claims were "manifestly unfounded." However, the UN General Assembly took no further action on the basis of the report and proposed draft statute.[55]

The international criminal court project thus lay dormant for another decade. In the late 1980s, however, the possibility of establishing an international criminal court was reinvigorated in light of the end of the Cold War and subsequent events in Yugoslavia and Rwanda.

---

49   Lippman, above note 5 at 89.
50   See, for example, John W Bridge, "The Case for an International Criminal Justice and the Formulation of International Criminal Law" (1964) 13 Int'l & Comp LQ 1255; Maynard B Golt, "The Necessity of an International Court of Criminal Justice" (1966–1967) 6 Washburn LJ 13; Julius Stone & Robert K Woetzel, eds, *Toward a Feasible International Criminal Court* (Geneva: World Peace Through Law Centre, 1970); M Cherif Bassiouni & Ved P Nanda, eds, *A Treatise on International Criminal Law* (Springfield, IL: Charles C Thomas Publisher, 1973); M Cherif Bassiouni, ed, *International Terrorism and Political Crimes* (Springfield, IL: Charles C Thomas Publisher, 1975).
51   30 November 1973, 1015 UNTS 243, in force 18 July 1976 [Apartheid Convention].
52   See paragraph 20 of the *Programme of Activities to be Undertaken during the Second Half of the Decade for Action to Combat Racism and Racial Discrimination* annexed to *Implementation of the Programme for the Decade of Action to Combat Racism and Racial Discrimination*, GA Res 34/24, reprinted in UN GAOR, 34th Sess, Supp No 46 at 162–64, UN Doc A/34/46 (1980).
53   See M Cherif Bassiouni & Daniel H Derby, "Final Report on the Establishment of an International Criminal Court for the Implementation of the Apartheid Convention and Other Relevant International Instruments" (1980–81) 9 Hofstra L Rev 523 at 548, art IV(1).
54   *Ibid*, art IV(2).
55   Lippman, above note 5 at 93.

5) The Ad Hoc Tribunals for the Former Yugoslavia and Rwanda

On 22 February 1993, the UN Security Council adopted Resolution 808 (1993) establishing an international tribunal for the prosecution of serious violations of international law committed in the territory of the former Yugoslavia since 1991.[56] The Statute of the International Criminal Tribunal for the Former Yugoslavia[57] gives that body jurisdiction over individuals accused of genocide, crimes against humanity, violations of the laws and customs of war, and grave breaches of the Geneva Conventions of 1949.[58] The International Criminal Tribunal for the Former Yugoslavia (ICTY) has no jurisdiction over breaches of the 1977 Additional Protocols to the Geneva Conventions of 1949 or over the crime of aggression.[59] However, its jurisdiction to try breaches of the laws and customs of war enables it to apply the substance of the Additional Protocols to the extent that they reflect customary international law.[60]

On 8 November 1994, the Security Council adopted Resolution 955 (1994) creating the International Criminal Tribunal for Rwanda (ICTR) and establishing a similar Statute to govern that Tribunal's work.[61] The ICTR is mandated by Article 1 of its Statute to "prosecute persons responsible for serious violations of international humanitarian law committed in the territory of Rwanda and Rwandan citizens responsible for such violations committed in the territory of neighbouring states between 1 January 1994 and 31 December 1994 . . . ." Such violations are defined in the Statute as acts of genocide, crimes against humanity, breaches of Common Article 3 of the Geneva Conventions of 1949, and violations of the second Additional Protocol of 1977 governing non-international conflicts (Additional Protocol II).[62] The ICTR's Statute essentially replicates that of the ICTY, while differing in certain respects. For example, the Security Council concluded that the events in Rwanda qualified as an internal (as opposed to international) armed conflict, which is why the ICTR's jurisdiction is phrased in terms of Common Article 3

---

56 SC Resolution 808 (1993), adopted 22 February 1993, UN Doc S/RES/808 (1993). For discussion, see Daniel B Pickard, "Security Council Resolution 808: A Step Toward A Permanent International Court for the Prosecution of International Crimes and Human Rights Violations" (1995) 25 Golden Gate UL Rev 435.

57 Approved by the Security Council, SC Resolution 827 (1993), adopted 25 May 1993, UN Doc S/RES/827 (1993) at para 2.

58 *Report of the Secretary-General Pursuant to Paragraph 2 of Security Council Resolution 808 (1993)*, UN Doc S/25704 (3 May 1993), Annex, arts 2–5. The definition of crimes against humanity expands upon the Nuremberg principles in being acts of murder, extermination, enslavement, deportation, imprisonment, torture, and rape; persecutions on political, racial, and religious grounds; and other inhumane acts directed against a civilian population during an armed internal or international conflict. Notably, France, the United States, and Russia "expressed the understanding that to constitute crimes against humanity, acts must be committed within the context of a widespread or systematic attack against a civilian population for national, political, ethnic, racial, or religious reasons." See Caroline D Krass, "Bringing the Perpetrators of Rape in the Balkans to Justice: Time for an International Criminal Court" (1993–94) 22 Denv J Int'l L & Pol'y 317 at 340, summarizing UN Doc S/PV.3217 (25 May 1993) at 11, 16, and 45.

59 See discussion in Kim Carter, "The International Criminal Tribunal: Current Realities and Future Prospects" for *The Agenda for Change Series: Perspectives on UN Reform: Prepared for the Canadian Committee for the Fiftieth Anniversary of the United Nations* (November 1994).

60 *Ibid* at 4.

61 SC Resolution 955 (1994), adopted 8 November 1994, UN Doc S/RES/955 (1994).

62 *Ibid*, Annex, arts 2–4.

of the 1949 Geneva Conventions and Additional Protocol II (which apply in cases of non-international armed conflict).

The Statutes of these ad hoc Tribunals, negotiated within the Security Council, are more detailed than those of the International Military Tribunals established following World War II and impose specific obligations of assistance and cooperation on states. The provisions of the ICTY's Statute, for example, reflect developments in international criminal law since the end of World War II: the definition of genocide was taken from the 1948 Genocide Convention, the definition of crimes against humanity from the caselaw developed in post–World War II trials, and the definition of war crimes (grave breaches and violations of the laws and customs of war) from the 1949 Geneva Conventions. Consider the following excerpt from the ICTY's Statute, which focuses on the ICTY's jurisdiction with respect to crimes and criminal responsibility:

Statute of the International Criminal Tribunal for the Former Yugoslavia, adopted 25 May 1993 by Security Council Resolution 827 (1993), UN Doc S/RES/827 (1993), as subsequently amended

Having been established by the Security Council acting under Chapter VII of the Charter of the United Nations, the International Tribunal for the Prosecution of Persons Responsible for Serious Violations of International Humanitarian Law Committed in the Territory of the Former Yugoslavia since 1991 (hereinafter referred to as "the International Tribunal") shall function in accordance with the provisions of the present Statute.

Article 1
Competence of the International Tribunal

The International Tribunal shall have the power to prosecute persons responsible for serious violations of international humanitarian law committed in the territory of the former Yugoslavia since 1991 in accordance with the provisions of the present Statute.

Article 2
Grave breaches of the Geneva Conventions of 1949

The International Tribunal shall have the power to prosecute persons committing or ordering to be committed grave breaches of the Geneva Conventions of 12 August 1949, namely the following acts against persons or property protected under the provisions of the relevant Geneva Convention:

(a) wilful killing;
(b) torture or inhuman treatment, including biological experiments;
(c) wilfully causing great suffering or serious injury to body or health;
(d) extensive destruction and appropriation of property, not justified by military necessity and carried out unlawfully and wantonly;
(e) compelling a prisoner of war or a civilian to serve in the forces of a hostile power;
(f) wilfully depriving a prisoner of war or a civilian of the rights of fair and regular trial;
(g) unlawful deportation or transfer or unlawful confinement of a civilian;
(h) taking civilians as hostages.

Article 3
Violations of the laws or customs of war

The International Tribunal shall have the power to prosecute persons violating the laws or customs of war. Such violations shall include, but not be limited to:

(a) employment of poisonous weapons or other weapons calculated to cause unnecessary suffering;

(b) wanton destruction of cities, towns or villages, or devastation not justified by military necessity;

(c) attack, or bombardment, by whatever means, of undefended towns, villages, dwellings, or buildings;

(d) seizure of, destruction or wilful damage done to institutions dedicated to religion, charity and education, the arts and sciences, historic monuments and works of art and science;

(e) plunder of public or private property.

Article 4
Genocide

1. The International Tribunal shall have the power to prosecute persons committing genocide as defined in paragraph 2 of this article or of committing any of the other acts enumerated in paragraph 3 of this article.

2. Genocide means any of the following acts committed with intent to destroy, in whole or in part, a national, ethnical, racial or religious group, as such:

(a) killing members of the group;

(b) causing serious bodily or mental harm to members of the group;

(c) deliberately inflicting on the group conditions of life calculated to bring about its physical destruction in whole or in part;

(d) imposing measures intended to prevent births within the group;

(e) forcibly transferring children of the group to another group.

3. The following acts shall be punishable:

(a) genocide;

(b) conspiracy to commit genocide;

(c) direct and public incitement to commit genocide;

(d) attempt to commit genocide;

(e) complicity in genocide.

Article 5
Crimes against humanity

The International Tribunal shall have the power to prosecute persons responsible for the following crimes when committed in armed conflict, whether international or internal in character, and directed against any civilian population:

(a) murder;

(b) extermination;

(c) enslavement;

(d) deportation;

(e) imprisonment;

(f) torture;

(g) rape;

(h) persecutions on political, racial and religious grounds;

(i) other inhumane acts.

Article 6
Personal jurisdiction

The International Tribunal shall have jurisdiction over natural persons pursuant to the provisions of the present Statute.

Article 7
Individual criminal responsibility

1. A person who planned, instigated, ordered, committed or otherwise aided and abetted in the planning, preparation or execution of a crime referred to in articles 2 to 5 of the present Statute, shall be individually responsible for the crime.

2. The official position of any accused person, whether as Head of State or Government or as a responsible Government official, shall not relieve such person of criminal responsibility nor mitigate punishment.

3. The fact that any of the acts referred to in articles 2 to 5 of the present Statute was committed by a subordinate does not relieve his superior of criminal responsibility if he knew or had reason to know that the subordinate was about to commit such acts or had done so and the superior failed to take the necessary and reasonable measures to prevent such acts or to punish the perpetrators thereof.

4. The fact that an accused person acted pursuant to an order of a Government or of a superior shall not relieve him of criminal responsibility, but may be considered in mitigation of punishment if the International Tribunal determines that justice so requires.

Article 8
Territorial and temporal jurisdiction

The territorial jurisdiction of the International Tribunal shall extend to the territory of the former Socialist Federal Republic of Yugoslavia, including its land surface, airspace and territorial waters. The temporal jurisdiction of the International Tribunal shall extend to a period beginning on 1 January 1991.

Article 9
Concurrent jurisdiction

1. The International Tribunal and national courts shall have concurrent jurisdiction to prosecute persons for serious violations of international humanitarian law committed in the territory of the former Yugoslavia since 1 January 1991.

2. The International Tribunal shall have primacy over national courts. At any stage of the procedure, the International Tribunal may formally request national courts to defer to the competence of the International Tribunal in accordance with the present Statute and the Rules of Procedure and Evidence of the International Tribunal . . . .

The ICTY and ICTR have rendered numerous influential decisions and judgments relating to the *mens rea* and *actus reus* required for genocide, crimes against humanity, and war crimes. These judgments also address a number of other issues, such as standards of sentencing at the international level, rules of evidence in cases of sexual violence, the right of the accused to counsel of his or her choosing, and individual responsibility versus the responsibility of a commander or a superior for the actions of his or her subordinates. The excerpt below from a judgment of the ICTY's Appeals Chamber addresses the difficult issues involved in proving the elements of genocide:

Prosecutor v Radislav Krstić, Case No IT-98-33-A, Judgment of 19 April 2004, (2004) 43 ILM 1301 (ICTY Appeals Chamber)

[The facts of this case relate mainly to events which took place in Srebrenica, in eastern Bosnia and Herzegovina, in July 1995, when Bosnian women, children, and elderly men were removed from the enclave, and 7,000–8,000 Bosnian Muslim men were systematically murdered. Srebrenica is located in the area for which the Drina Corps of the Bosnian Serb Army (VRS) was responsible. Radislav Krstić was a Major-General in the VRS and Commander of the Drina Corps at the time the crimes at issue were committed. The Trial Chamber found Krstić guilty of genocide; crimes against humanity in the form of persecution through murders, cruel and inhumane treatment, terrorizing the civilian population, forcible transfer, and destruction of personal property; and murder as a violation of the laws or customs of war. The Trial Chamber sentenced Krstić to forty-six years' imprisonment. The defence appealed, alleging, *inter alia*, both factual and legal errors on the part of the Trial Chamber in entering the conviction for genocide. Recall the definition of genocide in Article 4(2) of the ICTY Statute, set out above.]

II. THE TRIAL CHAMBER'S FINDING THAT GENOCIDE OCCURRED IN SREBRENICA

5. The Defence appeals Radislav Krstić's conviction for genocide committed against Bosnian Muslims in Srebrenica. The Defence argues that the Trial Chamber both misconstrued the legal definition of genocide and erred in applying the definition to the circumstances of this case. With respect to the legal challenge, the Defence's argument is two-fold. First, Krstić contends that the Trial Chamber's definition of the part of the national group he was found to have intended to destroy was unacceptably narrow. Second, the Defence argues that the Trial Chamber erroneously enlarged the term "destroy" in the prohibition of genocide to include the geographical displacement of a community.

A. The Definition of the Part of the Group

6. Article 4 of the Tribunal's Statute, like the Genocide Convention, covers certain acts done with "intent to destroy, in whole or in part, a national, ethnical, racial or religious group, as such." The Indictment in this case alleged, with respect to the count of genocide, that Radislav Krstić "intend[ed] to destroy a part of the Bosnian Muslim people as a national, ethnical, or religious group." The targeted group identified in the Indictment, and accepted by the Trial Chamber, was that of the Bosnian Muslims. The Trial Chamber determined that the Bosnian Muslims were a specific, distinct national group, and therefore covered by Article 4. This conclusion is not challenged in this appeal.

7. As is evident from the Indictment, Krstić was not alleged to have intended to destroy the entire national group of Bosnian Muslims, but only a part of that group. The first question presented in this appeal is whether, in finding that Radislav Krstić had genocidal intent, the Trial Chamber defined the relevant part of the Bosnian Muslim group in a way which comports with the requirements of Article 4 and of the Genocide Convention.

8. It is well established that where a conviction for genocide relies on the intent to destroy a protected group "in part," the part must be a substantial part of that group. The aim of the Genocide Convention is to prevent the intentional destruction of entire human groups, and the part targeted must be significant enough to have an impact on the group as a whole. Although the Appeals Chamber has not yet addressed this issue, two Trial Chambers of this Tribunal have examined it. In *Jelisic*, the first case to confront the question, the Trial Chamber noted that, "[g]iven the goal of the [Genocide] Convention to deal with mass crimes, it is widely acknowledged that the intention to destroy must target at least a *substantial* part of the group." The same conclusion was reached by the *Sikirica* Trial Chamber: "This part of the definition calls for evidence of an intention to destroy a substantial number relative to the total population of the group." As these Trial Chambers explained, the substantiality requirement both captures genocide's defining character as a crime of massive proportions and reflects the Convention's concern with the impact the destruction of the targeted part will have on the overall survival of the group.

9. The question has also been considered by Trial Chambers of the ICTR, whose Statute contains an identical definition of the crime of genocide. These Chambers arrived at the same conclusion. In *Kayishema*, the Trial Chamber concluded, after having canvassed the authorities interpreting the Genocide Convention, that the term "'in part' requires the intention to destroy a considerable number of individuals who are part of the group." This definition was accepted and refined by the Trial Chambers in *Bagilishema* and *Semanza*, which stated that the intent to destroy must be, at least, an intent to destroy a substantial part of the group.

10. This interpretation is supported by scholarly opinion. The early commentators on the Genocide Convention emphasized that the term "in part" contains a substantiality requirement. Raphael Lemkin, a prominent international criminal lawyer who coined the term "genocide" and was instrumental in the drafting of the Genocide Convention, addressed the issue during the 1950 debate in the United States Senate on the ratification of the Convention. Lemkin explained that "the destruction in part must be of a substantial nature so as to affect the entirety." He further suggested that the Senate clarify, in a statement of understanding to accompany the ratification, that "the Convention applies only to actions undertaken on a mass scale." Another noted early commentator, Nehemiah Robinson, echoed this view, explaining that a perpetrator of genocide must possess the intent to destroy a substantial number of individuals constituting the targeted group. In discussing this requirement, Robinson stressed, as did Lemkin, that "the act must be directed toward the destruction of a *group*," this formulation being the aim of the Convention.

11. Recent commentators have adhered to this view. The International Law Commission, charged by the UN General Assembly with the drafting of a comprehensive code

of crimes prohibited by international law, stated that "the crime of genocide by its very nature requires the intention to destroy at least a substantial part of a particular group." The same interpretation was adopted earlier by the 1985 report of Benjamin Whitaker, the Special Rapporteur to the United Nations Sub-Commission on Prevention of Discrimination and Protection of Minorities.

12. The intent requirement of genocide under Article 4 of the Statute is therefore satisfied where evidence shows that the alleged perpetrator intended to destroy at least a substantial part of the protected group. The determination of when the targeted part is substantial enough to meet this requirement may involve a number of considerations. The numeric size of the targeted part of the group is the necessary and important starting point, though not in all cases the ending point of the inquiry. The number of individuals targeted should be evaluated not only in absolute terms, but also in relation to the overall size of the entire group. In addition to the numeric size of the targeted portion, its prominence within the group can be a useful consideration. If a specific part of the group is emblematic of the overall group, or is essential to its survival, that may support a finding that the part qualifies as substantial within the meaning of Article 4.

13. The historical examples of genocide also suggest that the area of the perpetrators' activity and control, as well as the possible extent of their reach, should be considered. Nazi Germany may have intended only to eliminate Jews within Europe alone; that ambition probably did not extend, even at the height of its power, to an undertaking of that enterprise on a global scale. Similarly, the perpetrators of genocide in Rwanda did not seriously contemplate the elimination of the Tutsi population beyond the country's borders. The intent to destroy formed by a perpetrator of genocide will always be limited by the opportunity presented to him. While this factor alone will not indicate whether the targeted group is substantial, it can—in combination with other factors—inform the analysis.

14. These considerations, of course, are neither exhaustive nor dispositive. They are only useful guidelines. The applicability of these factors, as well as their relative weight, will vary depending on the circumstances of a particular case.

15. In this case, having identified the protected group as the national group of Bosnian Muslims, the Trial Chamber concluded that the part the VRS Main Staff and Radislav Krstić targeted was the Bosnian Muslims of Srebrenica, or the Bosnian Muslims of Eastern Bosnia. This conclusion comports with the guidelines outlined above. The size of the Bosnian Muslim population in Srebrenica prior to its capture by the VRS forces in 1995 amounted to approximately forty thousand people. This represented not only the Muslim inhabitants of the Srebrenica municipality but also many Muslim refugees from the surrounding region. Although this population constituted only a small percentage of the overall Muslim population of Bosnia and Herzegovina at the time, the importance of the Muslim community of Srebrenica is not captured solely by its size. As the Trial Chamber explained, Srebrenica (and the surrounding Central Podrinje region) were of immense strategic importance to the Bosnian Serb leadership. Without Srebrenica, the ethnically Serb state of Republika Srpska they sought to create would remain divided into two disconnected parts, and its access to Serbia proper would be disrupted. The capture

and ethnic purification of Srebrenica would therefore severely undermine the military efforts of the Bosnian Muslim state to ensure its viability, a consequence the Muslim leadership fully realized and strove to prevent. Control over the Srebrenica region was consequently essential to the goal of some Bosnian Serb leaders of forming a viable political entity in Bosnia, as well as to the continued survival of the Bosnian Muslim people. Because most of the Muslim inhabitants of the region had, by 1995, sought refuge within the Srebrenica enclave, the elimination of that enclave would have accomplished the goal of purifying the entire region of its Muslim population.

16. In addition, Srebrenica was important due to its prominence in the eyes of both the Bosnian Muslims and the international community. The town of Srebrenica was the most visible of the "safe areas" established by the UN Security Council in Bosnia. By 1995 it had received significant attention in the international media. In its resolution declaring Srebrenica a safe area, the Security Council announced that it "should be free from armed attack or any other hostile act." This guarantee of protection was re-affirmed by the commander of the UN Protection Force in Bosnia (UNPROFOR) and reinforced with the deployment of UN troops. The elimination of the Muslim population of Srebrenica, despite the assurances given by the international community, would serve as a potent example to all Bosnian Muslims of their vulnerability and defenselessness in the face of Serb military forces. The fate of the Bosnian Muslims of Srebrenica would be emblematic of that of all Bosnian Muslims.

17. Finally, the ambit of the genocidal enterprise in this case was limited to the area of Srebrenica. While the authority of the VRS Main Staff extended throughout Bosnia, the authority of the Bosnian Serb forces charged with the take-over of Srebrenica did not extend beyond the Central Podrinje region. From the perspective of the Bosnian Serb forces alleged to have had genocidal intent in this case, the Muslims of Srebrenica were the only part of the Bosnian Muslim group within their area of control.

18. In fact, the Defence does not argue that the Trial Chamber's characterization of the Bosnian Muslims of Srebrenica as a substantial part of the targeted group contravenes Article 4 of the Tribunal's Statute. Rather, the Defence contends that the Trial Chamber made a further finding, concluding that the part Krstić intended to destroy was the Bosnian Muslim men of military age of Srebrenica. In the Defence's view, the Trial Chamber then engaged in an impermissible sequential reasoning, measuring the latter part of the group against the larger part (the Bosnian Muslims of Srebrenica) to find the substantiality requirement satisfied. The Defence submits that if the correct approach is properly applied, and the military age men are measured against the entire group of Bosnian Muslims, the substantiality requirement would not be met.

19. The Defence misunderstands the Trial Chamber's analysis. The Trial Chamber stated that the part of the group Radislav Krstić intended to destroy was the Bosnian Muslim population of Srebrenica. The men of military age, who formed a further part of that group, were not viewed by the Trial Chamber as a separate, smaller part within the meaning of Article 4. Rather, the Trial Chamber treated the killing of the men of military age as evidence from which to infer that Radislav Krstić and some members of the VRS Main Staff had the requisite intent to destroy all the Bosnian Muslims of Srebrenica, the only part of the protected group relevant to the Article 4 analysis.

20. In support of its argument, the Defence identifies the Trial Chamber's determination that, in the context of this case, "the intent to kill the men [of military age] amounted to an intent to destroy a substantial part of the Bosnian Muslim group." The Trial Chamber's observation was proper. As a specific intent offense, the crime of genocide requires proof of intent to commit the underlying act and proof of intent to destroy the targeted group, in whole or in part. The proof of the mental state with respect to the commission of the underlying act can serve as evidence from which the fact-finder may draw the further inference that the accused possessed the specific intent to destroy.

21. The Trial Chamber determined that Radislav Krstić had the intent to kill the Srebrenica Bosnian Muslim men of military age. This finding is one of intent to commit the requisite genocidal act — in this case, the killing of the members of the protected group, prohibited by Article 4(2)(a) of the Statute. From this intent to kill, the Trial Chamber also drew the further inference that Krstić shared the genocidal intent of some members of the VRS Main Staff to destroy a substantial part of the targeted group, the Bosnian Muslims of Srebrenica.

22. It must be acknowledged that in portions of its Judgement, the Trial Chamber used imprecise language which lends support to the Defence's argument. The Trial Chamber should have expressed its reasoning more carefully. As explained above, however, the Trial Chamber's overall discussion makes clear that it identified the Bosnian Muslims of Srebrenica as the substantial part in this case.

23. The Trial Chamber's determination of the substantial part of the protected group was correct. The Defence's appeal on this issue is dismissed.

B. The Determination of the Intent to Destroy

24. The Defence also argues that the Trial Chamber erred in describing the conduct with which Radislav Krstić is charged as genocide. The Trial Chamber, the Defence submits, impermissibly broadened the definition of genocide by concluding that an effort to displace a community from its traditional residence is sufficient to show that the alleged perpetrator intended to destroy a protected group. By adopting this approach, the Defence argues, the Trial Chamber departed from the established meaning of the term genocide in the Genocide Convention — as applying only to instances of physical or biological destruction of a group — to include geographic displacement.

25. The Genocide Convention, and customary international law in general, prohibit only the physical or biological destruction of a human group. The Trial Chamber expressly acknowledged this limitation, and eschewed any broader definition. The Chamber stated: "[C]ustomary international law limits the definition of genocide to those acts seeking the physical or biological destruction of all or part of the group. [A]n enterprise attacking only the cultural or sociological characteristics of a human group in order to annihilate these elements which give to that group its own identity distinct from the rest of the community would not fall under the definition of genocide."

26. Given that the Trial Chamber correctly identified the governing legal principle, the Defence must discharge the burden of persuading the Appeals Chamber that, despite

having correctly stated the law, the Trial Chamber erred in applying it. The main evidence underlying the Trial Chamber's conclusion that the VRS forces intended to eliminate all the Bosnian Muslims of Srebrenica was the massacre by the VRS of all men of military age from that community. The Trial Chamber rejected the Defence's argument that the killing of these men was motivated solely by the desire to eliminate them as a potential military threat. The Trial Chamber based this conclusion on a number of factual findings, which must be accepted as long as a reasonable Trial Chamber could have arrived at the same conclusions. The Trial Chamber found that, in executing the captured Bosnian Muslim men, the VRS did not differentiate between men of military status and civilians. Though civilians undoubtedly are capable of bearing arms, they do not constitute the same kind of military threat as professional soldiers. The Trial Chamber was therefore justified in drawing the inference that, by killing the civilian prisoners, the VRS did not intend only to eliminate them as a military danger. The Trial Chamber also found that some of the victims were severely handicapped and, for that reason, unlikely to have been combatants. This evidence further supports the Trial Chamber's conclusion that the extermination of these men was not driven solely by a military rationale.

27. Moreover, as the Trial Chamber emphasized, the term "men of military age" was itself a misnomer, for the group killed by the VRS included boys and elderly men normally considered to be outside that range. Although the younger and older men could still be capable of bearing arms, the Trial Chamber was entitled to conclude that they did not present a serious military threat, and to draw a further inference that the VRS decision to kill them did not stem solely from the intent to eliminate them as a threat. The killing of the military aged men was, assuredly, a physical destruction, and given the scope of the killings the Trial Chamber could legitimately draw the inference that their extermination was motivated by a genocidal intent.

28. The Trial Chamber was also entitled to consider the long-term impact that the elimination of seven to eight thousand men from Srebrenica would have on the survival of that community. In examining these consequences, the Trial Chamber properly focused on the likelihood of the community's physical survival. As the Trial Chamber found, the massacred men amounted to about one fifth of the overall Srebrenica community. The Trial Chamber found that, given the patriarchal character of the Bosnian Muslim society in Srebrenica, the destruction of such a sizeable number of men would "inevitably result in the physical disappearance of the Bosnian Muslim population at Srebrenica." Evidence introduced at trial supported this finding, by showing that, with the majority of the men killed officially listed as missing, their spouses are unable to remarry and, consequently, to have new children. The physical destruction of the men therefore had severe procreative implications for the Srebrenica Muslim community, potentially consigning the community to extinction.

29. This is the type of physical destruction the Genocide Convention is designed to prevent. The Trial Chamber found that the Bosnian Serb forces were aware of these consequences when they decided to systematically eliminate the captured Muslim men. The finding that some members of the VRS Main Staff devised the killing of the male prisoners with full knowledge of the detrimental consequences it would have for the physical survival of the Bosnian Muslim community in Srebrenica further supports the Trial

Chamber's conclusion that the instigators of that operation had the requisite genocidal intent.

30. The Defence argues that the VRS decision to transfer, rather than to kill, the women and children of Srebrenica in their custody undermines the finding of genocidal intent. This conduct, the Defence submits, is inconsistent with the indiscriminate approach that has characterized all previously recognized instances of modern genocide.

31. The decision by Bosnian Serb forces to transfer the women, children and elderly within their control to other areas of Muslim-controlled Bosnia could be consistent with the Defence argument. This evidence, however, is also susceptible of an alternative interpretation. As the Trial Chamber explained, forcible transfer could be an additional means by which to ensure the physical destruction of the Bosnian Muslim community in Srebrenica. The transfer completed the removal of all Bosnian Muslims from Srebrenica, thereby eliminating even the residual possibility that the Muslim community in the area could reconstitute itself. The decision not to kill the women or children may be explained by the Bosnian Serbs' sensitivity to public opinion. In contrast to the killing of the captured military men, such an action could not easily be kept secret, or disguised as a military operation, and so carried an increased risk of attracting international censure.

32. In determining that genocide occurred at Srebrenica, the cardinal question is whether the intent to commit genocide existed. While this intent must be supported by the factual matrix, the offence of genocide does not require proof that the perpetrator chose the most efficient method to accomplish his objective of destroying the targeted part. Even where the method selected will not implement the perpetrator's intent to the fullest, leaving that destruction incomplete, this ineffectiveness alone does not preclude a finding of genocidal intent. The international attention focused on Srebrenica, combined with the presence of the UN troops in the area, prevented those members of the VRS Main Staff who devised the genocidal plan from putting it into action in the most direct and efficient way. Constrained by the circumstances, they adopted the method which would allow them to implement the genocidal design while minimizing the risk of retribution.

33. The Trial Chamber—as the best assessor of the evidence presented at trial—was entitled to conclude that the evidence of the transfer supported its finding that some members of the VRS Main Staff intended to destroy the Bosnian Muslims in Srebrenica. The fact that the forcible transfer does not constitute in and of itself a genocidal act does not preclude a Trial Chamber from relying on it as evidence of the intentions of members of the VRS Main Staff. The genocidal intent may be inferred, among other facts, from evidence of "other culpable acts systematically directed against the same group."

34. The Defence also argues that the record contains no statements by members of the VRS Main Staff indicating that the killing of the Bosnian Muslim men was motivated by genocidal intent to destroy the Bosnian Muslims of Srebrenica. The absence of such statements is not determinative. Where direct evidence of genocidal intent is absent, the intent may still be inferred from the factual circumstances of the crime. The inference that a particular atrocity was motivated by genocidal intent may be drawn, moreover, even where the individuals to whom the intent is attributable are not precisely identified. If the crime committed satisfies the other requirements of genocide, and if the evidence

supports the inference that the crime was motivated by the intent to destroy, in whole or in part, a protected group, a finding that genocide has occurred may be entered.

35. In this case, the factual circumstances, as found by the Trial Chamber, permit the inference that the killing of the Bosnian Muslim men was done with genocidal intent. As already explained, the scale of the killing, combined with the VRS Main Staff's awareness of the detrimental consequences it would have for the Bosnian Muslim community of Srebrenica and with the other actions the Main Staff took to ensure that community's physical demise, is a sufficient factual basis for the finding of specific intent. The Trial Chamber found, and the Appeals Chamber endorses this finding, that the killing was engineered and supervised by some members of the Main Staff of the VRS. The fact that the Trial Chamber did not attribute genocidal intent to a particular official within the Main Staff may have been motivated by a desire not to assign individual culpability to persons not on trial here. This, however, does not undermine the conclusion that Bosnian Serb forces carried out genocide against the Bosnian Muslims.

36. Among the grievous crimes this Tribunal has the duty to punish, the crime of genocide is singled out for special condemnation and opprobrium. The crime is horrific in its scope; its perpetrators identify entire human groups for extinction. Those who devise and implement genocide seek to deprive humanity of the manifold richness its nationalities, races, ethnicities and religions provide. This is a crime against all of humankind, its harm being felt not only by the group targeted for destruction, but by all of humanity.

37. The gravity of genocide is reflected in the stringent requirements which must be satisfied before this conviction is imposed. These requirements—the demanding proof of specific intent and the showing that the group was targeted for destruction in its entirety or in substantial part—guard against a danger that convictions for this crime will be imposed lightly. Where these requirements are satisfied, however, the law must not shy away from referring to the crime committed by its proper name. By seeking to eliminate a part of the Bosnian Muslims, the Bosnian Serb forces committed genocide. They targeted for extinction the forty thousand Bosnian Muslims living in Srebrenica, a group which was emblematic of the Bosnian Muslims in general. They stripped all the male Muslim prisoners, military and civilian, elderly and young, of their personal belongings and identification, and deliberately and methodically killed them solely on the basis of their identity. The Bosnian Serb forces were aware, when they embarked on this genocidal venture, that the harm they caused would continue to plague the Bosnian Muslims. The Appeals Chamber states unequivocally that the law condemns, in appropriate terms, the deep and lasting injury inflicted, and calls the massacre at Srebrenica by its proper name: genocide. Those responsible will bear this stigma, and it will serve as a warning to those who may in future contemplate the commission of such a heinous act.

38. In concluding that some members of the VRS Main Staff intended to destroy the Bosnian Muslims of Srebrenica, the Trial Chamber did not depart from the legal requirements for genocide. The Defence appeal on this issue is dismissed.

The International Court of Justice (ICJ) relied upon many of the factual and legal findings of the ICTY in the proceedings concerning Radislav Krstić, among other cases, in reaching the conclusion that a state may be found to have committed genocide within the meaning of the Genocide Convention.[63] The ICJ was nevertheless careful to clarify that this would not entail the imposition of criminal responsibility upon a state.[64] Rather, the state would be responsible for acts of genocide committed by individuals or other entities if those acts were attributable to it, applying the usual rules of state responsibility. For further discussion, see Sections C(1) and C(2)(a) in Chapter 12.

At the time of writing, the ICTY and ICTR have been in existence for about two decades. The ICTY has indicted 161 individuals and concluded proceedings in 136 of these cases, with ongoing proceedings in twenty-five cases.[65] The concluded cases have resulted in sixty-nine individuals sentenced, eighteen acquitted, thirteen referrals to national jurisdictions, twenty withdrawn indictments, and sixteen cases in which the accused died.[66] There are no outstanding fugitives for the ICTY. The ICTR has issued fifty-five trial judgments against seventy-five accused, referred four cases against four accused to national authorities in Rwanda and France, and indicted nine others who are fugitives.[67]

The net budget for the ICTY exceeds US$100 million per year, standing at $250,814,300 for the 2012–2013 biennium.[68] The ICTR's net budget is considerably less, at US$159,535,800 for the 2012–2013 biennium, largely because it has nearly finished its mandate and is therefore handling fewer cases.[69] These budget amounts are funded by assessed contributions from UN member states.

The size of the budgets has led to waning enthusiasm among some states for the work of the Tribunals. In 2003, the Security Council adopted a "completion strategy" for each Tribunal, pursuant to which the ICTY and ICTR were to have completed their investiga-

---

63 *Application of the Convention on the Prevention and Punishment of the Crime of Genocide (Bosnia and Herzegovina v Serbia and Montenegro)*, Judgment, [2007] ICJ Rep 43. The Court concluded that it had not been established on the facts of that case that either Serbia and Montenegro or its predecessor, the Federal Republic of Yugoslavia, was responsible for acts of genocide. However, the state was found to have failed in its duty to prevent and punish genocide.

64 *Ibid* at para 170.

65 *Letter dated 23 May 2013 from the President of the International Tribunal for the Prosecution of Persons Responsible for Serious Violations of International Humanitarian Law Committed in the Territory of the Former Yugoslavia since 1991, addressed to the President of the Security Council*, UN Doc S/2013/308 (23 May 2013), Annex I at 4.

66 International Criminal Tribunal for the Former Yugoslavia, "Key Figures for the Cases," online: www.icty. org/sid/24.

67 *Letter dated 23 May 2013 from the President of the International Criminal Tribunal for Rwanda addressed to the President of the Security Council*, UN Doc S/2013/310 (23 May 2013), Annexes I–III [*ICTR Completion Strategy Report* (May 2013)].

68 *Financing of the International Tribunal for the Prosecution of Persons Responsible for Serious Violations of International Humanitarian Law Committed in the Territory of the Former Yugoslavia since 1991*, GA Res 66/239, UN Doc A/RES/66/239 (2011), reprinted in UN GAOR, 66th Sess, Supp No 49, vol I at 533–34, UN Doc A/66/49 (2012) at para 10.

69 *Financing of the International Criminal Tribunal for the Prosecution of Persons Responsible for Genocide and Other Serious Violations of International Humanitarian Law Committed in the Territory of Rwanda and Rwandan Citizens Responsible for Genocide and Other Such Violations Committed in the Territory of Neighbouring States between 1 January and 31 December 1994*, GA Res 66/238, UN Doc A/RES/66/238 (2012), reprinted in UN GAOR, 66th Sess, Supp No 49, vol I at 531–33, UN Doc A/66/49 at para 9.

tions in 2004 and finished first-instance trials by 2008 and appeals by 2010.[70] In reality, the completion strategies have taken longer to fulfill. With the arrest of such high profile accused as Radovan Karadžić (former president of Republika Srpska) in July 2008, Ratko Mladić (former commander of the Bosnian Serb Army) in May 2011, and Goran Hadžić (former president of the Republic of Serbian Krajina) in July 2011, the ICTY was only able to begin these complex cases relatively late in its mandate. In May 2013, the ICTY estimated that the Karadžić trial would finish in 2014, the Hadžić trial by the end of 2015, and the Mladić trial by mid-2016.[71] The ICTR finished all of its trials in 2012 and has estimated that all appeals will be completed before the end of 2014, save for one, which should finish by July 2015.[72]

There are, however, a number of issues that must be addressed after the closure of the ICTY and ICTR, such as ongoing protection of victims and witnesses, tracking of ICTR fugitives, preservation of Tribunal archives, and monitoring of convicts serving sentences. The UN Security Council therefore established the Mechanism for International Criminal Tribunals (MICT) to carry out these essential functions.[73] The MICT comprises two branches: an Arusha branch and a Hague branch. The Arusha branch covers functions related to the ICTR and is located in Arusha, Tanzania. It commenced operations on 1 July 2012.[74] The Hague branch covers functions related to the ICTY and began operating on 1 July 2013.[75]

The initial period of the MICT's work will overlap with that of the ICTR and the ICTY as the Tribunals complete outstanding work on trial and appeal proceedings. In his second progress report to the UN Security Council, the MICT's president summarized the work undertaken by the Arusha branch in its first ten months of operation:

> It has been actively providing support and protection for witnesses who have testified in completed cases before the International Criminal Tribunal for Rwanda. The Arusha branch is also engaged in monitoring the cases referred by the Tribunal to national jurisdictions and has assumed responsibility over issues related to the enforcement of sentences handed down by it [by, for example, granting requests for early release]. The branch has sought, and will continue to seek, the cooperation of States on a variety of matters, including the critically important issue of the arrest and surrender of the remaining fugitives indicted by the Tribunal. In addition, it is providing assistance to States in their domestic investigations and prosecutions of individuals charged in relation to the genocide in Rwanda.[76]

70　See SC Resolution 1503 (2003), adopted 28 August 2003, UN Doc S/RES/1503 (2003) and SC Resolution 1534 (2004), adopted 26 March 2004, UN Doc S/RES/1534 (2006).

71　UN Doc S/2013/308, above note 65 at 42.

72　*ICTR Completion Strategy Report* (May 2013), above note 67 at para 80.

73　SC Resolution 1966 (2010), adopted 22 December 2010, UN Doc S/RES/1966 (2010).

74　*Letter dated 23 May 2013 from the President of the International Residual Mechanism for Criminal Tribunals addressed to the President of the Security Council*, UN Doc S/2013/309 (23 May 2013) at para 3.

75　*Ibid.*

76　*Ibid* at para 4. See also paras 29–30 on the granting of requests for early release of two convicted individuals.

In sum, the ICTY and ICTR have shown that international tribunals equipped with sufficiently clear mandates and well-defined bodies of substantive and procedural international criminal law can dispense international criminal justice relatively successfully. By the same token, the costs and challenges associated with establishing temporary, situation-specific criminal tribunals have provided states with powerful incentives to seek other solutions to the problem of impunity for serious international crimes. It is not particularly surprising, therefore, that the experience of the ad hoc Tribunals led directly to the reinvigoration of proposals for the establishment of a permanent international criminal court.

C. THE INTERNATIONAL CRIMINAL COURT

1) Background

As noted above, discussions concerning the creation of a permanent international criminal tribunal stalled during the Cold War. However, in 1989, Trinidad and Tobago proposed that the United Nations consider establishing a permanent international criminal court as a means of combatting international drug trafficking and other transnational criminal activities. In 1990, the UN General Assembly invited the International Law Commission (ILC) to examine this proposal within the framework of its ongoing project of preparing a Draft Code of Crimes Against the Peace and Security of Mankind, and in 1993 asked the ILC to give priority to the preparation of a draft statute for an international criminal court.

The ILC duly prepared a draft statute for an international criminal court in 1994, and followed this with a Draft Code of Crimes against the Peace and Security of Mankind. This Draft Code defined international crimes and criminal responsibility in even more detail than the Statutes of the ICTY and ICTR. For example, it contained a more fulsome list of acts amounting to crimes against humanity:

Draft Code of Crimes against the Peace and Security of Mankind in *Report of the International Law Commission,* **UN GAOR, 51st Sess, Supp No 10 at 93–94, UN Doc A/51/10 (1996)**

Article 18
Crimes Against Humanity
A crime against humanity means any of the following acts, when committed in a systematic manner or on a large scale and instigated or directed by a Government or by any organization or group:

    (a) murder;
    (b) extermination;
    (c) torture;
    (d) enslavement;
    (e) persecution on political, racial, religious or ethnic grounds;
    (f) institutionalized discrimination on racial, ethnic or religious grounds involving the violation of fundamental human rights and freedoms and resulting in seriously disadvantaging a part of the population;
    (g) arbitrary deportation or forcible transfer of population;
    (h) arbitrary imprisonment;

(i) forced disappearance of persons;

(j) rape, enforced prostitution and other forms of sexual abuse;

(k) other inhumane acts which severely damage physical or mental integrity, health or human dignity, such as mutilation and severe bodily harm.

2) The Rome Statute of the International Criminal Court

While the ILC's Draft Code remains just that—a draft—its content clearly influenced (though did not determine) the scope of the jurisdictional provisions of the Rome Statute of the International Criminal Court.[77] The Rome Statute was adopted in July 1998, following years of negotiations, and is the most detailed instrument on international criminal law ever adopted—far more detailed than the charters of the post–World War II international military tribunals and the statutes of the ICTY and ICTR. Assuming the form of a treaty, it is a product of intense multilateral negotiations, with each of its 128 articles reflecting the views of numerous UN member states.[78] Its adoption was heralded by then UN Secretary-General Kofi Annan as "one of the finest moments in the history of the United Nations."[79]

Sixty states had become parties to the Rome Statute by April 2002, triggering its entry into force soon after on 1 July 2002. Since that time, the International Criminal Court (ICC) has become a functioning reality, with the ICC Prosecutor launching eighteen cases involving twenty-five individuals focused on eight situations in the Central African Republic, Côte d'Ivoire, the Democratic Republic of the Congo, Kenya, Libya, Mali, Sudan (Darfur region), and Uganda. As of August 2013, the Rome Statute had attracted 122 states parties.

The ICC has jurisdiction over genocide, crimes against humanity, war crimes, and the crime of aggression,[80] although it will only be able to exercise its jurisdiction over the crime of aggression in the future, once a complex state acceptance requirement is met.[81] Under the Rome Statute, proceedings may be initiated by any state party, by the Security Council, or by the prosecutor.[82] To date, proceedings have been initiated by states parties themselves (Central African Republic, the Democratic Republic of the Congo, Mali, and Uganda), the Security Council (regarding the situations in Libya and Sudan), a non-party state that has accepted the exercise of jurisdiction by the ICC (Côte d'Ivoire), and by the prosecutor (Kenya). The Rome Statute provides for consultation with the states concerned and allows them to challenge jurisdiction.[83]

---

77 17 July 1998, 2187 UNTS 90, Can TS 2002 No 13, (1998) 37 ILM 2002, in force 1 July 2002 [Rome Statute].

78 See Philippe Kirsch & Valerie Oosterveld, "Negotiating an Institution for the 21st Century: Multilateral Diplomacy and the International Criminal Court" (2001) 46 McGill LJ 1141–160.

79 Kofi Annan, "Preface" in Roy S Lee, ed, *The International Criminal Court: The Making of the Rome Statute: Issues, Negotiations, Results* (Boston: Kluwer Law International, 1999) at ix.

80 Rome Statute, above note 77, arts 6–8.

81 In 2010, a Review Conference of the Rome Statute adopted a definition of the crime of aggression, although the ICC will not be able to exercise its jurisdiction over that crime until two-thirds of states parties decide to activate jurisdiction after 1 January 2017 and at least thirty states parties ratify or accept the amendments: *Review Conference of the Rome Statute of the International Criminal Court Official Records*, ICC Doc RC/11 at Resolution RC/Res.6, Annex I.

82 Rome Statute, above note 77, arts 13–15.

83 *Ibid*, arts 18–19.

Moreover, before the ICC can exercise criminal jurisdiction over any particular individual, some form of state acceptance is required. When the Security Council refers a situation to the ICC, this acceptance flows from the obligation of UN member states (to which they have consented by becoming parties to the UN Charter) to carry out decisions of the Security Council. In the absence of a Security Council referral, acceptance must be provided by either the state of nationality of the accused or the state in the territory of which the crime was allegedly committed.[84] Those states that are parties to the Rome Statute are automatically deemed to have so consented, although consent can also be given by a relevant non-party state on an ad hoc basis.[85]

The Court's jurisdiction is also said to be "complementary" to that of national judicial systems, in the sense that it may only exercise its jurisdiction when relevant national legal systems are unwilling or unable genuinely to investigate or prosecute individuals suspected of having committed relevant crimes.[86]

The Rome Statute also contains provisions reflecting general principles of international criminal law, such as:

- non-retroactivity (the Statute applies only in a prospective fashion);[87]
- the exclusion from the jurisdiction of the ICC of children under 18 years of age at the time of alleged commission of the crime;[88]
- the irrelevance of a person's official capacity, such that individuals cannot escape criminal liability on the basis of their title or official position;[89]
- the non-application of statutes of limitations to the crimes within the jurisdiction of the ICC;[90]
- individual criminal responsibility for aiding and abetting, ordering, or inducing the commission of crimes; and[91]
- command responsibility, whereby a commander or superior can be held liable for crimes committed by his or her subordinates.[92]

The Court is composed of three main bodies: the Office of the Prosecutor, the Registry, and the judiciary (comprising Pre-Trial, Trial, and Appeals Chambers).[93] The eighteen judges, the prosecutor and deputy prosecutor(s), and the registrar are elected by states parties to the Rome Statute.[94] The seat of the Court is in The Hague, the Netherlands.[95]

The Rome Statute contains detailed provisions governing investigation, indictment and arrest, prosecution, sentencing and penalties, appeals, rights of the accused, protection

---

84 *Ibid*, art 12.
85 *Ibid*, art 12(3).
86 *Ibid*, art 17.
87 *Ibid*, arts 11 and 24.
88 *Ibid*, art 26.
89 *Ibid*, art 27.
90 *Ibid*, art 29.
91 *Ibid*, art 25.
92 *Ibid*, art 28.
93 *Ibid*, art 34.
94 *Ibid*, arts 36, 42, & 43.
95 *Ibid*, art 3.

and participation of victims and witnesses, and obligations of ratifying states to cooperate fully with the ICC. The ICC does not have its own police or armed force and therefore relies entirely on state cooperation to carry out its enforcement functions.[96] States parties provide management oversight to the ICC, including the power to determine its budget.[97] The ICC is financed by assessed contributions by states parties.[98] No reservations may be made to the Rome Statute.[99]

Consider the following extracts from the Rome Statute, describing the jurisdictional reach of the ICC:

Rome Statute of the International Criminal Court, 17 July 1998, 2187 UNTS 90, Can TS 2002 No 13, (1998) 37 ILM 2002, in force 1 July 2002[100]

Article 5
Crimes within the jurisdiction of the Court
1. The jurisdiction of the Court shall be limited to the most serious crimes of concern to the international community as a whole. The Court has jurisdiction in accordance with this Statute with respect to the following crimes:
(a) The crime of genocide;
(b) Crimes against humanity;
(c) War crimes;
(d) The crime of aggression.

2. The Court shall exercise jurisdiction over the crime of aggression once a provision is adopted in accordance with articles 121 and 123 defining the crime and setting out the conditions under which the Court shall exercise jurisdiction with respect to this crime. Such a provision shall be consistent with the relevant provisions of the Charter of the United Nations.

Article 6
Genocide
For the purpose of this Statute, "genocide" means any of the following acts committed with intent to destroy, in whole or in part, a national, ethnical, racial or religious group, as such:
(a) Killing members of the group;
(b) Causing serious bodily or mental harm to members of the group;
(c) Deliberately inflicting on the group conditions of life calculated to bring about its physical destruction in whole or in part;
(d) Imposing measures intended to prevent births within the group;
(e) Forcibly transferring children of the group to another group.

---

96 *Ibid*, art 86.
97 *Ibid*, art 112.
98 *Ibid*, art 115.
99 *Ibid*, art 120.
100 We have reproduced the original, unamended text of the Rome Statute because the great majority of states parties have not ratified or accepted the 2010 amendments relating to the crime of aggression.

Article 7

Crimes against humanity

1. For the purpose of this Statute, "crime against humanity" means any of the following acts when committed as part of a widespread or systematic attack directed against any civilian population, with knowledge of the attack:

(a) Murder;

(b) Extermination;

(c) Enslavement;

(d) Deportation or forcible transfer of population;

(e) Imprisonment or other severe deprivation of physical liberty in violation of fundamental rules of international law;

(f) Torture;

(g) Rape, sexual slavery, enforced prostitution, forced pregnancy, enforced sterilization, or any other form of sexual violence of comparable gravity;

(h) Persecution against any identifiable group or collectivity on political, racial, national, ethnic, cultural, religious, gender as defined in paragraph 3, or other grounds that are universally recognized as impermissible under international law, in connection with any act referred to in this paragraph or any crime within the jurisdiction of the Court;

(i) Enforced disappearance of persons;

(j) The crime of apartheid;

(k) Other inhumane acts of a similar character intentionally causing great suffering, or serious injury to body or to mental or physical health.

2. For the purpose of paragraph 1:

(a) "Attack directed against any civilian population" means a course of conduct involving the multiple commission of acts referred to in paragraph 1 against any civilian population, pursuant to or in furtherance of a State or organizational policy to commit such attack;

(b) "Extermination" includes the intentional infliction of conditions of life, inter alia the deprivation of access to food and medicine, calculated to bring about the destruction of part of a population;

(c) "Enslavement" means the exercise of any or all of the powers attaching to the right of ownership over a person and includes the exercise of such power in the course of trafficking in persons, in particular women and children;

(d) "Deportation or forcible transfer of population" means forced displacement of the persons concerned by expulsion or other coercive acts from the area in which they are lawfully present, without grounds permitted under international law;

(e) "Torture" means the intentional infliction of severe pain or suffering, whether physical or mental, upon a person in the custody or under the control of the accused; except that torture shall not include pain or suffering arising only from, inherent in or incidental to, lawful sanctions;

(f) "Forced pregnancy" means the unlawful confinement of a woman forcibly made pregnant, with the intent of affecting the ethnic composition of any population or carrying out other grave violations of international law. This definition shall not in any way be interpreted as affecting national laws relating to pregnancy;

(g) "Persecution" means the intentional and severe deprivation of fundamental rights contrary to international law by reason of the identity of the group or collectivity;

(h) "The crime of apartheid" means inhumane acts of a character similar to those referred to in paragraph 1, committed in the context of an institutionalized regime of systematic oppression and domination by one racial group over any other racial group or groups and committed with the intention of maintaining that regime;

(i) "Enforced disappearance of persons" means the arrest, detention or abduction of persons by, or with the authorization, support or acquiescence of, a State or a political organization, followed by a refusal to acknowledge that deprivation of freedom or to give information on the fate or whereabouts of those persons, with the intention of removing them from the protection of the law for a prolonged period of time.

3. For the purpose of this Statute, it is understood that the term "gender" refers to the two sexes, male and female, within the context of society. The term "gender" does not indicate any meaning different from the above.

Article 8
War crimes[101]

1. The Court shall have jurisdiction in respect of war crimes in particular when committed as part of a plan or policy or as part of a large-scale commission of such crimes.

2. For the purpose of this Statute, "war crimes" means:

(a) Grave breaches of the Geneva Conventions of 12 August 1949, namely, any of the following acts against persons or property protected under the provisions of the relevant Geneva Convention:

    (i)   Wilful killing;

    (ii) Torture or inhuman treatment, including biological experiments;

    (iii) Wilfully causing great suffering, or serious injury to body or health;

    (iv) Extensive destruction and appropriation of property, not justified by military necessity and carried out unlawfully and wantonly;

    (v) Compelling a prisoner of war or other protected person to serve in the forces of a hostile Power;

    (vi) Wilfully depriving a prisoner of war or other protected person of the rights of fair and regular trial;

    (vii) Unlawful deportation or transfer or unlawful confinement;

    (viii) Taking of hostages.

(b) Other serious violations of the laws and customs applicable in international armed conflict, within the established framework of international law, namely, any of the following acts:

    (i)   Intentionally directing attacks against the civilian population as such or against individual civilians not taking direct part in hostilities;

---

101 This article was amended by resolution RC/Res.5 of 11 June 2010 (adding paragraphs 2(e)(xiii) to 2(e)(xv)). These read: "2(e)(xiii) Employing poison or poisoned weapons; (xiv) Employing asphyxiating, poisonous or other gases, and all analogous liquids, materials or devices; (xv) Employing bullets which expand or flatten easily in the human body, such as bullets with a hard envelope which does not entirely cover the core or is pierced with incisions."

(ii)   Intentionally directing attacks against civilian objects, that is, objects which are not military objectives;

(iii)   Intentionally directing attacks against personnel, installations, material, units or vehicles involved in a humanitarian assistance or peacekeeping mission in accordance with the Charter of the United Nations, as long as they are entitled to the protection given to civilians or civilian objects under the international law of armed conflict;

(iv)   Intentionally launching an attack in the knowledge that such attack will cause incidental loss of life or injury to civilians or damage to civilian objects or widespread, long-term and severe damage to the natural environment which would be clearly excessive in relation to the concrete and direct overall military advantage anticipated;

(v)   Attacking or bombarding, by whatever means, towns, villages, dwellings or buildings which are undefended and which are not military objectives;

(vi)   Killing or wounding a combatant who, having laid down his arms or having no longer means of defence, has surrendered at discretion;

(vii)   Making improper use of a flag of truce, of the flag or of the military insignia and uniform of the enemy or of the United Nations, as well as of the distinctive emblems of the Geneva Conventions, resulting in death or serious personal injury;

(viii) The transfer, directly or indirectly, by the Occupying Power of parts of its own civilian population into the territory it occupies, or the deportation or transfer of all or parts of the population of the occupied territory within or outside this territory;

(ix)   Intentionally directing attacks against buildings dedicated to religion, education, art, science or charitable purposes, historic monuments, hospitals and places where the sick and wounded are collected, provided they are not military objectives;

(x)   Subjecting persons who are in the power of an adverse party to physical mutilation or to medical or scientific experiments of any kind which are neither justified by the medical, dental or hospital treatment of the person concerned nor carried out in his or her interest, and which cause death to or seriously endanger the health of such person or persons;

(xi)   Killing or wounding treacherously individuals belonging to the hostile nation or army;

(xii)   Declaring that no quarter will be given;

(xiii) Destroying or seizing the enemy's property unless such destruction or seizure be imperatively demanded by the necessities of war;

(xiv)   Declaring abolished, suspended or inadmissible in a court of law the rights and actions of the nationals of the hostile party;

(xv)   Compelling the nationals of the hostile party to take part in the operations of war directed against their own country, even if they were in the belligerent's service before the commencement of the war;

(xvi)   Pillaging a town or place, even when taken by assault;

(xvii) Employing poison or poisoned weapons;

(xviii) Employing asphyxiating, poisonous or other gases, and all analogous liquids, materials or devices;

(xix) Employing bullets which expand or flatten easily in the human body, such as bullets with a hard envelope which does not entirely cover the core or is pierced with incisions;

(xx) Employing weapons, projectiles and material and methods of warfare which are of a nature to cause superfluous injury or unnecessary suffering or which are inherently indiscriminate in violation of the international law of armed conflict, provided that such weapons, projectiles and material and methods of warfare are the subject of a comprehensive prohibition and are included in an annex to this Statute, by an amendment in accordance with the relevant provisions set forth in articles 121 and 123;

(xxi) Committing outrages upon personal dignity, in particular humiliating and degrading treatment;

(xxii) Committing rape, sexual slavery, enforced prostitution, forced pregnancy, as defined in article 7, paragraph 2 (f), enforced sterilization, or any other form of sexual violence also constituting a grave breach of the Geneva Conventions;

(xxiii) Utilizing the presence of a civilian or other protected person to render certain points, areas or military forces immune from military operations;

(xxiv) Intentionally directing attacks against buildings, material, medical units and transport, and personnel using the distinctive emblems of the Geneva Conventions in conformity with international law;

(xxv) Intentionally using starvation of civilians as a method of warfare by depriving them of objects indispensable to their survival, including wilfully impeding relief supplies as provided for under the Geneva Conventions;

(xxvi) Conscripting or enlisting children under the age of fifteen years into the national armed forces or using them to participate actively in hostilities.

(c) In the case of an armed conflict not of an international character, serious violations of article 3 common to the four Geneva Conventions of 12 August 1949, namely, any of the following acts committed against persons taking no active part in the hostilities, including members of armed forces who have laid down their arms and those placed hors de combat by sickness, wounds, detention or any other cause:

(i) Violence to life and person, in particular murder of all kinds, mutilation, cruel treatment and torture;

(ii) Committing outrages upon personal dignity, in particular humiliating and degrading treatment;

(iii) Taking of hostages;

(iv) The passing of sentences and the carrying out of executions without previous judgement pronounced by a regularly constituted court, affording all judicial guarantees which are generally recognized as indispensable.

(d) Paragraph 2 (c) applies to armed conflicts not of an international character and thus does not apply to situations of internal disturbances and tensions, such as riots, isolated and sporadic acts of violence or other acts of a similar nature.

(e) Other serious violations of the laws and customs applicable in armed conflicts not of an international character, within the established framework of international law, namely, any of the following acts:

   (i)   Intentionally directing attacks against the civilian population as such or against individual civilians not taking direct part in hostilities;

   (ii)   Intentionally directing attacks against buildings, material, medical units and transport, and personnel using the distinctive emblems of the Geneva Conventions in conformity with international law;

   (iii)   Intentionally directing attacks against personnel, installations, material, units or vehicles involved in a humanitarian assistance or peacekeeping mission in accordance with the Charter of the United Nations, as long as they are entitled to the protection given to civilians or civilian objects under the international law of armed conflict;

   (iv)   Intentionally directing attacks against buildings dedicated to religion, education, art, science or charitable purposes, historic monuments, hospitals and places where the sick and wounded are collected, provided they are not military objectives;

   (v)   Pillaging a town or place, even when taken by assault;

   (vi)   Committing rape, sexual slavery, enforced prostitution, forced pregnancy, as defined in article 7, paragraph 2 (f), enforced sterilization, and any other form of sexual violence also constituting a serious violation of article 3 common to the four Geneva Conventions;

   (vii)   Conscripting or enlisting children under the age of fifteen years into armed forces or groups or using them to participate actively in hostilities;

   (viii) Ordering the displacement of the civilian population for reasons related to the conflict, unless the security of the civilians involved or imperative military reasons so demand;

   (ix)   Killing or wounding treacherously a combatant adversary;

   (x)   Declaring that no quarter will be given;

   (xi)   Subjecting persons who are in the power of another party to the conflict to physical mutilation or to medical or scientific experiments of any kind which are neither justified by the medical, dental or hospital treatment of the person concerned nor carried out in his or her interest, and which cause death to or seriously endanger the health of such person or persons;

   (xii)   Destroying or seizing the property of an adversary unless such destruction or seizure be imperatively demanded by the necessities of the conflict; [*Note: see note 101 for text of additional subparagraphs*]

(f) Paragraph 2 (e) applies to armed conflicts not of an international character and thus does not apply to situations of internal disturbances and tensions, such as riots, isolated and sporadic acts of violence or other acts of a similar nature. It applies to armed conflicts that take place in the territory of a State when there is protracted armed conflict between governmental authorities and organized armed groups or between such groups.

3. Nothing in paragraph 2 (c) and (e) shall affect the responsibility of a Government to maintain or re-establish law and order in the State or to defend the unity and territorial integrity of the State, by all legitimate means . . . .

Article 12
Preconditions to the exercise of jurisdiction

1. A State which becomes a Party to this Statute thereby accepts the jurisdiction of the Court with respect to the crimes referred to in article 5.

2. In the case of article 13, paragraph (a) or (c), the Court may exercise its jurisdiction if one or more of the following States are Parties to this Statute or have accepted the jurisdiction of the Court in accordance with paragraph 3:
(a) The State on the territory of which the conduct in question occurred or, if the crime was committed on board a vessel or aircraft, the State of registration of that vessel or aircraft;
(b) The State of which the person accused of the crime is a national.

3. If the acceptance of a State which is not a Party to this Statute is required under paragraph 2, that State may, by declaration lodged with the Registrar, accept the exercise of jurisdiction by the Court with respect to the crime in question. The accepting State shall cooperate with the Court without any delay or exception in accordance with Part 9.

Article 13
Exercise of jurisdiction

The Court may exercise its jurisdiction with respect to a crime referred to in article 5 in accordance with the provisions of this Statute if:
(a) A situation in which one or more of such crimes appears to have been committed is referred to the Prosecutor by a State Party in accordance with article 14;
(b) A situation in which one or more of such crimes appears to have been committed is referred to the Prosecutor by the Security Council acting under Chapter VII of the Charter of the United Nations; or
(c) The Prosecutor has initiated an investigation in respect of such a crime in accordance with article 15.

Article 14
Referral of a situation by a State Party

1. A State Party may refer to the Prosecutor a situation in which one or more crimes within the jurisdiction of the Court appear to have been committed requesting the Prosecutor to investigate the situation for the purpose of determining whether one or more specific persons should be charged with the commission of such crimes.

2. As far as possible, a referral shall specify the relevant circumstances and be accompanied by such supporting documentation as is available to the State referring the situation.

Article 15
Prosecutor

1. The Prosecutor may initiate investigations *proprio motu* on the basis of information on crimes within the jurisdiction of the Court . . . .

Article 25
Individual criminal responsibility
1. The Court shall have jurisdiction over natural persons pursuant to this Statute.

2. A person who commits a crime within the jurisdiction of the Court shall be individually responsible and liable for punishment in accordance with this Statute.

3. In accordance with this Statute, a person shall be criminally responsible and liable for punishment for a crime within the jurisdiction of the Court if that person:
(a) Commits such a crime, whether as an individual, jointly with another or through another person, regardless of whether that other person is criminally responsible;
(b) Orders, solicits or induces the commission of such a crime which in fact occurs or is attempted;
(c) For the purpose of facilitating the commission of such a crime, aids, abets or otherwise assists in its commission or its attempted commission, including providing the means for its commission;
(d) In any other way contributes to the commission or attempted commission of such a crime by a group of persons acting with a common purpose. Such contribution shall be intentional and shall either:
  (i) Be made with the aim of furthering the criminal activity or criminal purpose of the group, where such activity or purpose involves the commission of a crime within the jurisdiction of the Court; or
  (ii) Be made in the knowledge of the intention of the group to commit the crime;
(e) In respect of the crime of genocide, directly and publicly incites others to commit genocide;
(f) Attempts to commit such a crime by taking action that commences its execution by means of a substantial step, but the crime does not occur because of circumstances independent of the person's intentions. However, a person who abandons the effort to commit the crime or otherwise prevents the completion of the crime shall not be liable for punishment under this Statute for the attempt to commit that crime if that person completely and voluntarily gave up the criminal purpose.

4. No provision in this Statute relating to individual criminal responsibility shall affect the responsibility of States under international law . . . .

Article 27
Irrelevance of official capacity
1. This Statute shall apply equally to all persons without any distinction based on official capacity. In particular, official capacity as a Head of State or Government, a member of a Government or parliament, an elected representative or a government official shall in no case exempt a person from criminal responsibility under this Statute, nor shall it, in and of itself, constitute a ground for reduction of sentence.

2. Immunities or special procedural rules which may attach to the official capacity of a person, whether under national or international law, shall not bar the Court from exercising its jurisdiction over such a person.

Article 28

Responsibility of commanders and other superiors

In addition to other grounds of criminal responsibility under this Statute for crimes within the jurisdiction of the Court:

(a) A military commander or person effectively acting as a military commander shall be criminally responsible for crimes within the jurisdiction of the Court committed by forces under his or her effective command and control, or effective authority and control as the case may be, as a result of his or her failure to exercise control properly over such forces, where:

   (i) That military commander or person either knew or, owing to the circumstances at the time, should have known that the forces were committing or about to commit such crimes; and

   (ii) That military commander or person failed to take all necessary and reasonable measures within his or her power to prevent or repress their commission or to submit the matter to the competent authorities for investigation and prosecution.

(b) With respect to superior and subordinate relationships not described in paragraph (a), a superior shall be criminally responsible for crimes within the jurisdiction of the Court committed by subordinates under his or her effective authority and control, as a result of his or her failure to exercise control properly over such subordinates, where:

   (i) The superior either knew, or consciously disregarded information which clearly indicated, that the subordinates were committing or about to commit such crimes;

   (ii) The crimes concerned activities that were within the effective responsibility and control of the superior; and

   (iii) The superior failed to take all necessary and reasonable measures within his or her power to prevent or repress their commission or to submit the matter to the competent authorities for investigation and prosecution . . . .

Article 33

Superior orders and prescription of law

1. The fact that a crime within the jurisdiction of the Court has been committed by a person pursuant to an order of a Government or of a superior, whether military or civilian, shall not relieve that person of criminal responsibility unless:

(a) The person was under a legal obligation to obey orders of the Government or the superior in question;

(b) The person did not know that the order was unlawful; and

(c) The order was not manifestly unlawful.

2. For the purposes of this article, orders to commit genocide or crimes against humanity are manifestly unlawful . . . .

The ICC has been in existence for over a decade. It has issued one trial judgment, in the case of Thomas Lubanga Dyilo, a former leader of a militia group in the Democratic Republic of the Congo known as the *Union des patriotes congolais*. Lubanga was charged with the war crimes of enlisting and conscripting children under fifteen years of age and using them to participate actively in hostilities.[102] In March 2012, he was found guilty and was later sentenced to a total of fourteen years' imprisonment.[103] This judgment is on appeal at the time of writing.

The ICC has had some success in securing custody of its indictees — for example, it has Laurent Gbagbo, former president of Côte d'Ivoire, in detention — but it has been frustrated in obtaining custody of such high-profile indictees as President Omar Al Bashir of Sudan and Saif Al-Islam Gaddafi, the son of former Libyan leader Muammar Gaddafi. President Al Bashir, in particular, has been able to enter the territory of certain ICC states parties with impunity, despite their obligations under the Rome Statute to execute ICC arrest warrants. This failure by some ICC states parties to fulfill their obligations has resulted in judicial orders such as this:

Prosecutor v Omar Hassan Ahmad Al Bashir, **Case No ICC-02/05-01/09, Decision Regarding Omar Al Bashir's Visit to the Federal Republic of Nigeria (15 July 2013) (ICC Pre-Trial Chamber II)**

. . .

5. On 15 July 2013, the Chamber received the Prosecutor's Notification, in which she contends that, on the basis of media reports, Omar Al-Bashir has arrived in the Nigerian capital, Abuja, to participate in the Special Summit of the African Union on HIV/AIDS, Tuberculosis and Malaria, scheduled to take place from 12 to 16 July 2013.[7] The Prosecutor further contends that the spokesperson of the Nigerian President has stated that "[t]he Sudanese president came for an AU event and the AU has taken a position on the ICC arrest order, so Nigeria has not taken action different from the AU stand" . . . .

7. The Chamber observes that the Federal Republic of Nigeria is a State Party to the Statute since 27 September 2001 and, accordingly, it is under the obligation pursuant to articles 86 and 89 of the Statute, to execute the pending Court's decisions concerning the arrest and surrender of Omar Al-Bashir. The Chamber expects the Federal Republic of Nigeria to immediately arrest Omar Al-Bashir and surrender him to the Court.

8. The Chamber further notes that according to article 87(7) of the Statute "[w]here a State Party fails to comply with a request to cooperate by the Court contrary to the provisions of this Statute [. . .] the Court may make a finding to that effect and refer the matter to the Assembly of States Parties or, where the Security Council referred the matter to the Court, to the Security Council."

FOR THESE REASONS, THE CHAMBER HEREBY

a) *requests* the Federal Republic of Nigeria to immediately arrest Omar Al-Bashir and surrender him to the Court;

---

102 *Prosecutor v Thomas Lubanga Dyilo*, Case No ICC-01/04-01/06, Warrant of Arrest (10 February 2006) (ICC Pre-Trial Chamber I).

103 *Prosecutor v Thomas Lubanga Dyilo*, Case No ICC-01/04-01/06, Judgment Pursuant to Article 74 of the Statute (14 March 2012) (ICC Trial Chamber I); *Prosecutor v Thomas Lubanga Dyilo*, Case No ICC-01/04-01/06, Decision on Sentence Pursuant to Article 76 of the Statute (10 July 2012) (ICC Trial Chamber I).

b) *instructs* the Registry to immediately transmit the present decision to the Federal Republic of Nigeria;

c) *orders* the Registry to prepare a report to the Chamber concerning Omar Al-Bashir's visit to the Federal Republic of Nigeria.

State cooperation is undoubtedly crucial to the ICC's long-term success, but is also, potentially, its greatest weakness.

D. HYBRID COURTS

The jurisdiction of the ICC is limited to crimes occurring after 1 July 2002, and, being treaty-based, is not universal. Thus, certain so-called hybrid or internationalized tribunals have, from time to time, been established to fill some of the gaps not covered by the ICC, ICTY, and ICTR. These tribunals are referred to as internationalized or hybrid tribunals because they incorporate elements of the domestic criminal justice systems of the affected states into the international structure of the tribunals. This section will discuss three of these hybrid tribunals: the Special Court for Sierra Leone (SCSL), the Extraordinary Chambers in the Courts of Cambodia (ECCC), and the Special Tribunal for Lebanon (STL).

In 2000, hundreds of UN peacekeepers were taken hostage by rebel forces in Sierra Leone. That country had ostensibly ended a brutal, decade-long civil war with the signing of the 1999 Lomé Peace Agreement, which provided a blanket amnesty for all those involved in the conflict.[104] The hostage taking prompted the UN Security Council to take action to end the cycle of impunity in Sierra Leone and, at the request of the government of Sierra Leone, to hold to account those bearing the greatest responsibility for crimes against humanity and war crimes during the civil war.[105] Canada was a member of the Security Council at the time and was heavily involved in the creation of a new tribunal called the Special Court for Sierra Leone.

However, the SCSL was not created by the Security Council (and therefore does not benefit from Chapter VII enforcement powers as do the ICTY and ICTR), but is, rather, the result of an agreement between the United Nations and Sierra Leone.[106] The Security Council was heavily involved in drafting the Statute of the SCSL and putting into place the modalities to ensure its operation. The SCSL was explicitly directed, in its Statute, to focus on "persons who bear the greatest responsibility" for crimes against humanity and war crimes committed in the territory of Sierra Leone since 30 November 1996.[107]

The seat of the SCSL was intentionally located in the capital of Sierra Leone, Freetown, in order to ensure that it would be as accessible as possible to those individuals most af-

---

104 Peace Agreement Between the Government of Sierra Leone and the Revolution United Front of Sierra Leone (7 July 1999), art IX ("Pardon and Amnesty").

105 *Report of the Secretary-General on the Establishment of a Special Court for Sierra Leone*, UN Doc S/2000/915 (4 October 2000); SC Resolution 1315 (2000), adopted 14 August 2000, UN Doc S/RES/1315 (2000).

106 Agreement between the United Nations and the Government of Sierra Leone on the Establishment of a Special Court for Sierra Leone, 16 January 2002, 2178 UNTS 138, in force 12 April 2002 [SCSL Agreement]. Note that the Statute of the Special Court of Sierra Leone [SCSL Statute] is annexed to the SCSL Agreement.

107 SCSL Statute, above note 106 at art 1(1).

fected by the conflict.[108] The Court's Statute also provided for other links to Sierra Leone, such as trial and appeals judges appointed by the Government of Sierra Leone, a Sierra Leonean deputy prosecutor, Sierra Leonean prosecutorial staff, assistance by Sierra Leonean authorities, references to Sierra Leonean law, and imprisonment of convicted persons in Sierra Leone.[109] The court, which operates with a yearly budget that is significantly less than that of the ICTY or ICTR, has been lauded by many as a success for its effectiveness, efficiency, and relevance to Sierra Leoneans. However, the SCSL, which is funded through voluntary contributions by interested states — creating unreliable funding levels from year to year — has faced ongoing financial crises throughout its lifespan as it has proceeded with its work.

The following are excerpts from the SCSL's Statute with respect to the crimes covered and criminal responsibility. Note that, under Article 7, the SCSL may try children who were between 15 and 18 years of age at the time of their alleged commission of a crime. While this departs from the position adopted under the Statutes of the ICTY, the ICTR, and the ICC, the Special Court's prosecutor decided, in the exercise of his prosecutorial discretion, not to charge anyone this young. Article 10 also clarifies that the amnesty contemplated in the Lomé Peace Agreement does not apply to the international crimes covered by this Statute.

Statute of the Special Court for Sierra Leone, 16 January 2002, 2178 UNTS 137, in force 12 April 2002

Article 1
Competence of the Special Court
1. The Special Court shall, except as provided in subparagraph (2), have the power to prosecute persons who bear the greatest responsibility for serious violations of international humanitarian law and Sierra Leonean law committed in the territory of Sierra Leone since 30 November 1996, including those leaders who, in committing such crimes, have threatened the establishment of and implementation of the peace process in Sierra Leone.

2. Any transgressions by peacekeepers and related personnel present in Sierra Leone pursuant to the Status of Mission Agreement in force between the United Nations and the Government of Sierra Leone or agreements between Sierra Leone and other Governments or regional organizations, or, in the absence of such agreement, provided that the peacekeeping operations were undertaken with the consent of the Government of Sierra Leone, shall be within the primary jurisdiction of the sending State.

3. In the event the sending State is unwilling or unable genuinely to carry out an investigation or prosecution, the Court may, if authorized by the Security Council on the proposal of any State, exercise jurisdiction over such persons.

---

108 SCSL Agreement, above note 106 at art 10.
109 SCSL Statute, above note 106 at arts 5, 12(1), 15(2), 15(4), 19(1), 20(3), and 22.

Article 2
Crimes against humanity
The Special Court shall have the power to prosecute persons who committed the following crimes as part of a widespread or systematic attack against any civilian population:

a. Murder;
b. Extermination;
c. Enslavement;
d. Deportation;
e. Imprisonment;
f. Torture;
g. Rape, sexual slavery, enforced prostitution, forced pregnancy and any other form of sexual violence;
h. Persecution on political, racial, ethnic or religious grounds;
i. Other inhumane acts.

Article 3
Violations of Article 3 common to the Geneva Conventions and of Additional Protocol II
The Special Court shall have the power to prosecute persons who committed or ordered the commission of serious violations of article 3 common to the Geneva Conventions of 12 August 1949 for the Protection of War Victims, and of Additional Protocol II thereto of 8 June 1977. These violations shall include:

a. Violence to life, health and physical or mental wellbeing of persons, in particular murder as well as cruel treatment such as torture, mutilation or any form of corporal punishment;
b. Collective punishments;
c. Taking of hostages;
d. Acts of terrorism;
e. Outrages upon personal dignity, in particular humiliating and degrading treatment, rape, enforced prostitution and any form of indecent assault;
f. Pillage;
g. The passing of sentences and the carrying out of executions without previous judgement pronounced by a regularly constituted court, affording all the judicial guarantees which are recognized as indispensable by civilized peoples;
h. Threats to commit any of the foregoing acts.

Article 4
Other serious violations of international humanitarian law
The Special Court shall have the power to prosecute persons who committed the following serious violations of international humanitarian law:

a. Intentionally directing attacks against the civilian population as such or against individual civilians not taking direct part in hostilities;
b. Intentionally directing attacks against personnel, installations, material, units or vehicles involved in a humanitarian assistance or peacekeeping mission in accordance with the Charter of the United Nations, as long as they are entitled to the protection given to civilians or civilian objects under the international law of armed conflict;

    c. Conscripting or enlisting children under the age of 15 years into armed forces or groups or using them to participate actively in hostilities.

Article 5
Crimes under Sierra Leonean law

The Special Court shall have the power to prosecute persons who have committed the following crimes under Sierra Leonean law:

    a. Offences relating to the abuse of girls under the Prevention of Cruelty to Children Act, 1926 (Cap. 31):
        i. Abusing a girl under 13 years of age, contrary to section 6;
        ii. Abusing a girl between 13 and 14 years of age, contrary to section 7;
        iii. Abduction of a girl for immoral purposes, contrary to section 12.

    b. Offences relating to the wanton destruction of property under the Malicious Damage Act, 1861:
        i. Setting fire to dwelling-houses, any person being therein, contrary to section 2;
        ii. Setting fire to public buildings, contrary to sections 5 and 6;
        iii. Setting fire to other buildings, contrary to section 6.

Article 6
Individual criminal responsibility

1. A person who planned, instigated, ordered, committed or otherwise aided and abetted in the planning, preparation or execution of a crime referred to in articles 2 to 4 of the present Statute shall be individually responsible for the crime.

2. The official position of any accused persons, whether as Head of State or Government or as a responsible government official, shall not relieve such person of criminal responsibility nor mitigate punishment.

3. The fact that any of the acts referred to in articles 2 to 4 of the present Statute was committed by a subordinate does not relieve his or her superior of criminal responsibility if he or she knew or had reason to know that the subordinate was about to commit such acts or had done so and the superior had failed to take the necessary and reasonable measures to prevent such acts or to punish the perpetrators thereof.

4. The fact that an accused person acted pursuant to an order of a Government or of a superior shall not relieve him or her of criminal responsibility, but may be considered in mitigation of punishment if the Special Court determines that justice so requires.

5. Individual criminal responsibility for the crimes referred to in article 5 shall be determined in accordance with the respective laws of Sierra Leone.

Article 7
Jurisdiction over persons of 15 years of age

1. The Special Court shall have no jurisdiction over any person who was under the age of 15 at the time of the alleged commission of the crime. Should any person who was at the time of the alleged commission of the crime between 15 and 18 years of age come before the Court, he or she shall be treated with dignity and a sense of worth, taking into account his or her young age and the desirability of promoting his or her rehabilitation,

reintegration into and assumption of a constructive role in society, and in accordance with international human rights standards, in particular the rights of the child.

2. In the disposition of a case against a juvenile offender, the Special Court shall order any of the following: care guidance and supervision orders, community service orders, counselling, foster care, correctional, educational and vocational training programmes, approved schools and, as appropriate, any programmes of disarmament, demobilization and reintegration or programmes of child protection agencies . . . .

Article 10
Amnesty
An amnesty granted to any person falling within the jurisdiction of the Special Court in respect of the crimes referred to in articles 2 to 4 of the present Statute shall not be a bar to prosecution . . . .

One of the major difficulties faced by all international and internationalized tribunals is obtaining custody of indictees. The prosecutor of the SCSL indicted Charles Taylor in 2003 when he was still president of Liberia.[110] Instead of being turned over to the SCSL, however, Charles Taylor was permitted to live in exile in Nigeria. Amid accusations that he was violating the terms of his exile, international pressure grew and Taylor was ultimately arrested in Nigeria and turned over to the SCSL in 2006.[111] The SCSL's indictment was challenged by Taylor's lawyers on the basis that he is entitled to head of state immunity. The precedent-setting decision of the SCSL's Appeals Chamber, denying such immunity, is reproduced in Chapter 8. In a high-profile trial that was conducted in The Hague due to security concerns, Taylor was accused of receiving "blood diamonds" from rebels in Sierra Leone in exchange for arms and ammunition.[112] In April 2012, the SCSL convicted Taylor of aiding, abetting, and planning crimes against humanity and war crimes during the conflict in Sierra Leone.[113] He was sentenced to fifty years imprisonment.[114] The Appeals Chamber of the SCSL upheld Taylor's conviction and sentence on 26 September 2013, and he was subsequently transferred to the United Kingdom to serve his sentence.[115] Following this appeal judgment, the SCSL will close and its continuing obligations — maintaining its archives, providing for witness protection, responding to requests for access to evidence from national authorities, and supervising the enforcement of sen-

---

110 *Prosecutor v Charles Taylor*, Case No SCSL-03-01-PT, Prosecution's Second Amended Indictment (29 May 2007) (SCSL Trial Chamber II).

111 *Prosecutor v Charles Taylor*, Case No SCSL-03-01-T, Judgment (18 May 2012) at paras 9–10 (SCSL Trial Chamber II) [*Taylor* Trial Judgment].

112 *Prosecutor v Charles Taylor*, Case No SCSL-03-01-T, Prosecution Final Trial Brief (8 April 2011) at paras 18–21 and 34182 (SCSL Office of the Prosecutor).

113 *Taylor* Trial Judgment, above note 111 at Disposition.

114 *Prosecutor v Charles Taylor*, Case No SCSL-03-01-T, Sentencing Judgment (30 May 2012) (SCSL Trial Chamber II).

115 *Prosecutor v Charles Taylor*, Case No SCSL-03-01-A, Judgment (26 September 2013) (SCSL Appeals Chamber); Confidential Order Designating State in which Charles Ghankay Taylor is to Serve His Sentence (Reclassified as Public), Document No SCSL-03-01-1391 (10 October 2013).

tences—will be assumed by an institution to be known as the Residual Special Court for Sierra Leone and funded by voluntary contributions.[116]

Other internationalized criminal tribunals have been established in recent years, although each is unique in the manner in which it has been established, its degree of internationalization, and its precise jurisdiction. For example, the Extraordinary Chambers in the Courts of Cambodia for the Prosecution of Crimes Committed during the Period of Democratic Kampuchea (the Extraordinary Chambers or the ECCC) were established in Phnom Penh pursuant to a 2003 agreement between the United Nations and Cambodia.[117] Their purpose is to prosecute acts of genocide, crimes against humanity, and war crimes committed in Cambodia during the Khmer Rouge era (1975–79).[118] Although formally part of the Cambodian judicial system, the Extraordinary Chambers are, in reality, a hybrid Tribunal with judicial and prosecutorial positions held by both Cambodians and non-Cambodians. The Extraordinary Chambers follow the inquisitorial model of criminal justice, adapted to incorporate aspects of an international tribunal: for example, the process is led by two co-investigating judges and two co-prosecutors (one Cambodian and one international in each case).[119] UN officials feared interference by the government of Cambodia in the work of the Tribunal, which is why the agreement creating the Extraordinary Chambers provides that, although each level of the Tribunal has a majority of Cambodian judges, any decision must be made by an affirmative vote of a supermajority (the majority plus one, the latter to be an international judge in the case of a majority of Cambodian judges).[120] However, this structure has not prevented claims of interference.[121] That said, the ECCC has issued one trial and one appeals judgment—in the case of Kaing Guek Eav (alias Duch)—and is in the midst of its second case, which involves senior leaders of the Khmer Rouge.[122]

The Special Tribunal for Lebanon (STL) was established in 2007 with very different jurisdiction than that of the SCSL and the ECCC. Its mandate is to "prosecute persons responsible for the attack of 14 February 2005 resulting in the death of former Lebanese Prime Minister Rafiq Hariri and in the death or injury of other persons."[123] As such, the STL is the first internationalized terrorism Tribunal. Located in Leidschendam, the Netherlands,

---

116 Special Court for Sierra Leone, *Ninth Annual Report of the President of the Special Court for Sierra Leone: June 2011–May 2012* at 38–39.

117 Agreement between the United Nations and the Royal Government of Cambodia Concerning the Prosecution under Cambodian Law of Crimes Committed During the Period of Democratic Kampuchea, 6 June 2003, 2329 UNTS 117, in force 29 April 2005.

118 *Ibid*, art 1.

119 *Ibid*, arts 5–6.

120 *Ibid*, arts 3, 4, and 7.

121 See, for example, Robert Petit, "Lawfare and International Tribunals: A Question of Definition? A Reflection on the Creation of the 'Khmer Rouge Tribunal'" (2010) 43 Case W Res J Int'l L 189.

122 *Prosecutor v Kaing Guek Eav* (alias Duch), 001/18-07-2007/ECCC/TC, Judgment (26 July 2010) (Extraordinary Chambers in the Courts of Cambodia, Trial Chamber); *Prosecutor v Kaing Guek Eav* (alias Duch), 001/18-07-2007/ECCC/AC, Appeal Judgment (3 February 2012) (Extraordinary Chambers in the Courts of Cambodia, Supreme Court Chamber); *Prosecutor v Khieu Samphan and Nuon Chea*, 002/19-09-2007/ECCC/TC, Decision on Severance of Case 002 Following Supreme Court Chamber Decision of 8 February 2013 (26 April 2013) (Extraordinary Chambers in the Courts of Cambodia, Trial Chamber).

123 Agreement between the United Nations and the Lebanese Republic on the establishment of a Special Tribunal for Lebanon, Annex to SC Resolution 1757 (2007), adopted 30 May 2007, UN Doc S/RES/1757 (2007), art 1. Attached to the Agreement is the Statute of the Special Tribunal for Lebanon.

the STL came into being as a result of an agreement between the Lebanese Republic and the UN brought into force by way of a resolution of the UN Security Council.[124] The STL is considered a hybrid Tribunal because its Chambers comprise both Lebanese and international judges and staff, and because the crimes it may prosecute, while restricted to those under the Lebanese Criminal Code, include acts of terrorism.[125] Consider the STL's subject-matter jurisdiction:

Statute of the Special Tribunal for Lebanon, Attachment to Annex to SC Resolution 1757 (2007), adopted 30 May 2007, UN Doc S/RES/1757 (2007)

Article 1: Jurisdiction of the Special Tribunal
The Special Tribunal shall have jurisdiction over persons responsible for the attack of 14 February 2005 resulting in the death of former Lebanese Prime Minister Rafiq Hariri and in the death or injury of other persons. If the Tribunal finds that other attacks that occurred in Lebanon between 1 October 2004 and 12 December 2005, or any later date decided by the Parties and with the consent of the Security Council, are connected in accordance with the principles of criminal justice and are of a nature and gravity similar to the attack of 14 February 2005, it shall also have jurisdiction over persons responsible for such attacks. This connection includes but is not limited to a combination of the following elements: criminal intent (motive), the purpose behind the attacks, the nature of the victims targeted, the pattern of the attacks (modus operandi) and the perpetrators.

Article 2: Applicable criminal law
The following shall be applicable to the prosecution and punishment of the crimes referred to in article 1, subject to the provisions of this Statute:
(a) The provisions of the Lebanese Criminal Code relating to the prosecution and punishment of acts of terrorism, crimes and offences against life and personal integrity, illicit associations and failure to report crimes and offences, including the rules regarding the material elements of a crime, criminal participation and conspiracy; and
(b) Articles 6 and 7 of the Lebanese law of 11 January 1958 on "Increasing the penalties for sedition, civil war and interfaith struggle".

Of all the international and hybrid criminal tribunals, the STL has had the most difficulty securing the arrest and detention of its accused: to date, no indictees are in custody. This has led the STL to consider using its powers, available under its Statute and in accordance with Lebanese law, to hold trials *in absentia*.[126] In February 2012, the Trial Chamber agreed to the trial *in absentia* of four accused—Salim Ayyash, Mustafa Badreddine, Hussein Oneissi, and Assad Sabra—after they failed to appear before the Tribunal.[127] The

---

124 Statute of the Special Tribunal for Lebanon, *ibid.*
125 *Ibid*, arts 2, 8, and 11.
126 *Ibid*, art 22.
127 *Prosecutor v Salim Ayyash, Mustafa Badreddine, Hussein Oneissi and Assad Sabra*, Case No STL-11-01, Decision to Hold Trial *In Absentia* (1 February 2012) (STL Trial Chamber).

Appeals Chamber approved this decision in November 2012.[128] Those trials are expected to begin in early 2014.[129]

LAW IN CONTEXT

Modern International Anti-terrorism Law

Terrorism is considered a serious crime of international concern. Even so, many states "still feel on practical grounds [that] terrorism is better investigated and prosecuted at the state level by individual or joint enforcement and judicial action."[130] This approach is affirmed in the thirteen multilateral anti-terrorism treaties currently in force, detailed in the chart below. All but two of these conventions define terrorism-related offences and oblige states parties to criminalize these acts in their domestic penal codes. Another common feature of all but one of these treaties is the obligation imposed on each state party to extradite or prosecute persons suspected of committing the relevant offences and found within the territory of that state. Thus, where a state party does not extradite, it is obliged to submit the case for prosecution. Assuming widespread ratification of such treaties, a perpetrator should ultimately end up in a state with both the jurisdiction and the obligation to try him or her. Note, however, that there is some nuance in the standard treaty requirement that a state "submit the case without undue delay to its competent authorities for the purpose of prosecution, through proceedings in accordance with the laws of that State." Submission of a case for prosecution is not the same thing as actual prosecution. The treaty language therefore accommodates the exercise of prosecutorial discretion, including assessment of whether the evidence is sufficient to submit the matter to trial.[131] However, it also potentially opens the door to impunity for terrorist actions. As one scholar notes, "[i]f the criminal justice system lacks integrity, the risk of political intervention in the prosecution or at the trial exists. Such intervention may prevent the trial, a conviction, or the appropriate punishment of the accused."[132]

For some, the great failing of this body of anti-terrorism law is, however, the absence of a comprehensive anti-terrorism treaty. The thirteen treaties in force are piecemeal in their coverage, targeting certain forms of violence and terrorism-related activities, but without denouncing terrorism writ large. This patchwork coverage is no accident. Terrorism is a

---

128 *Prosecutor v Salim Ayyash, Mustafa Badreddine, Hussein Oneissi and Assad Sabra*, Case No STL-11-01, Appeals Decision to Hold Trial *In Absentia* (1 November 2012) (STL Appeals Chamber).

129 Special Tribunal for Lebanon, Press Release, "Pre-Trial Judge Sets Tentative Date for Start of Trial" (2 August 2013), online: www.stl-tsl.org/en/media/press-releases/02-08-2013-pre-trial-judge-sets-tentative-date-for-start-of-trial.

130 Cassese, above note 1 at 146.

131 See, for example, Christopher C Joyner, "International Extradition and Global Terrorism: Bringing International Terrorists to Justice" (2002–2003) 25 Loy LA Int'l & Comp LJ 493 at 512–13 ("this language preserves for the alleged offender the rights of due process, a fair trial, and guarantees the concept of innocent until proven guilty. Presumably, an investigation into the facts of the allegation against an accused offender determines whether to proceed to the trial phase. If the investigation produces sufficient evidence, the offender may be prosecuted").

132 John Murphy, "The Control of International Terrorism," in John Norton Moore & Robert Turner, eds, *National Security Law*, 2d ed (Durham: Carolina Academic Press, 2005) 457 at 466.

tactic, monopolized by no single political, religious, or ideological cause. As such, it attracts condemnation or support according to the sympathies generated by the cause of those who practice or espouse it. Acts of politically motivated violence undertaken as part of an anti-colonial struggle for self-determination, for instance, have been evaluated very differently than similar acts of violence committed in other contexts. It has, therefore, been notoriously difficult for the international community to agree on a general definition of "terrorism."[133]

The problem of definition persists even after September 11. As one scholar has noted, "terrorism is a loaded term that is often used as a politically convenient label by which to deny legitimacy to an adversary while claiming it for oneself."[134] In these circumstances, not everyone is prepared to condemn unequivocally every act of political violence, although the world community emphatically denounces terrorism in the abstract. Key international instruments, such as UN Security Council Resolution 1373 (2001), appear to reflect this apparent contradiction: on the one hand, Resolution 1373 requires that "terrorist acts [be] established as serious criminal offences in domestic laws and regulations and that the punishment duly [reflect] the seriousness of such terrorist acts."[135] Yet on the other, it fails to define terrorism or terrorist acts.

In 2011, the STL stepped into the fray, holding that:

> [A] number of treaties, UN resolutions, and the legislative and judicial practice of States evince the formation of a general *opinio juris* in the international community, accompanied by a practice consistent with such opinion, to the effect that a customary rule of international law regarding the international crime of terrorism, at least in times of peace, has indeed emerged. This customary rule requires the following three key elements: (i) the perpetration of a criminal act (such as murder, kidnapping, hostage-taking, arson, and so on), or threatening such and act; (ii) the intent to spread fear among the population (which would generally entail the creation of public danger) or directly or indirectly coerce a national or international authority to take some action, or to refrain from taking it; (iii) when the act involves a transnational element.[136]

The ICTY and the SCSL have also considered the definition of terrorism, albeit in the specific context of defining the scope of certain war crimes.[137] The SCSL has held, for example, that the war crime of committing acts of terror includes widespread "rape, sexual slavery, forced marriages and outrages on personal dignity, when committed against a civilian population with the specific intent to terrorize."[138]

---

133 See further Ben Saul, *Defining Terrorism in International Law* (New York: Oxford University Press, 2008).

134 Tal Becker, *Terrorism and the State: Rethinking the Rules of State Responsibility* (Oxford: Hart Publishing, 2006) at 85.

135 SC Resolution 1373 (2001), adopted 28 September 2001, UN Doc S/RES/1373 (2001) at para 2(e).

136 *Prosecutor v Salim Ayyash, Mustafa Badreddine, Hussein Oneissi and Assad Sabra*, Case No STL-11-01, Interlocutory Decision on the Applicable Law (16 February 2011) at para 85 (STL Appeals Chamber).

137 *Prosecutor v Stanislav Galić*, Case No IT-98-29-A, Judgment (30 November 2006) at paras 70–109 (ICTY Appeals Chamber).

138 *Taylor* Trial Judgment, above note 111 at para 2035.

As well, terrorist acts of the magnitude of those perpetrated on September 11, may also amount to crimes against humanity. As discussed in Section C, above, the Rome Statute defines "crimes against humanity" as, *inter alia*:

> any of the following acts when committed as part of a widespread or systematic attack directed against any civilian population, with knowledge of the attack:
> (a) Murder; . . .
> (k) Other inhumane acts of a similar character intentionally causing great suffering, or serious injury to body or to mental or physical health.[139]

In a legal opinion prepared for the Government of Canada, the Legal Bureau of the then Department of Foreign Affairs and International Trade concluded that the attacks of September 11 met this definition. That day's events obviously constituted murder and caused great suffering. Moreover, they were "widespread and systematic":

> The September 11 attack involved four virtually simultaneous hijackings from different airports by different teams, all designed to bring the planes to specifically targeted buildings within a one-half to one hour period. At least some of the hijackers had undergone pilot training in the months prior to the attack. In addition, if other attacks are also considered, such as those on the U.S. embassies in 1998, then the September 11 acts may be seen as part of a larger systematic plan to target U.S. citizens, interests and buildings . . . . There is a strong argument that the September 11 attack was numerically widespread, as thousands of people died.[140]

Terrorist acts of this gravity are, therefore, amenable to prosecution before the ICC, assuming the Rome Statute's jurisdictional requirements are otherwise met.[141]

Despite the decisions of the Special Tribunal for Lebanon and other tribunals, and UN Security Council guidance,[142] many still consider that a general definition of terrorism remains elusive.

---

139 Rome Statute, above note 77, art 7.

140 Colleen Swords, "Canadian Practice in International Law at the Department of Foreign Affairs in 2001–2002" (2002) 40 Can YB Int'l Law 469 at 470–71.

141 For example, the accused must be a national of a state party or the crime must have taken place on the territory of a state party. Alternatively, the prosecution could be authorized by the Security Council.

142 The Security Council partially corrected its definitional omission by offering its understanding of terrorism in 2004 as comprising: "criminal acts, including against civilians, committed with the intent to cause death or serious bodily injury, or taking of hostages, with the purpose to provoke a state of terror in the general public or in a group of persons or particular persons, intimidate a population or compel a government or an international organization to do or to abstain from doing any act, which constitute offences within the scope of and as defined in the international conventions and protocols relating to terrorism." See SC Resolution 1566 (2004), adopted 8 October 2004, UN Doc S/RES/1566 (2004) at para 3.

Table 15.1 Anti-terrorism Conventions in Force (as of August 2013)*

Convention	Content
A. Conventions Banning Certain Terrorist Techniques and Practices	
1. Terrorism against Transportation and Infrastructure	
Convention on Offences and Certain Other Acts Committed on Board Aircraft (Tokyo Convention), 14 September 1963, 704 UNTS 220, Can TS 1970 No 5, in force 4 December 1969	Authorizes aircraft commanders to take steps to protect an in-flight aircraft from acts which are penal offences, or may (or do) jeopardize the safety of the aircraft or of persons or property in it, or jeopardize good order and discipline on board. Requires states parties to take into custody a person performing these acts upon disembarkation and to restore control of the aircraft to its commander.
Convention for the Suppression of Unlawful Seizure of Aircraft (Hague Convention), 16 December 1970, 860 UNTS 106, Can TS 1972 No 23, in force 14 October 1971 (amended by a 2010 Protocol)	Requires states parties to criminalize the offence of unlawfully—by force or threat thereof, or by any other form of intimidation—seizing, or exercising control of an in-flight aircraft; or of attempting to perform or being an accomplice to any such act.
Convention for the Suppression of Unlawful Acts Against the Safety of Civil Aviation (Montreal Convention), 23 September 1971, 974 UNTS 178, Can TS 1973 No 6, in force 26 January 1973	Requires states parties to criminalize the following offences (and attempting and being an accomplice to such offences): • performing an act of violence against a person on board an aircraft in flight if that act is likely to endanger the safety of that aircraft; • destroying an aircraft in service or causing damage to such an aircraft which renders it incapable of flight, or which is likely to endanger its safety in flight; • placing or causing to be placed on an aircraft in service, by any means whatsoever, a device or substance which is likely to destroy that aircraft, or to cause damage to it which renders it incapable of flight, or to cause damage to it which is likely to endanger its safety in flight; • destroying or damaging air navigation facilities or interfering with their operation, if any such act is likely to endanger the safety of aircraft in flight; and • communicating information which the perpetrator knows to be false, thereby endangering the safety of an aircraft in flight.
Protocol for the Suppression of Unlawful Acts of Violence at Airports Serving International Aviation, 24 February 1988, 1589 UNTS 474, Can TS 1993 No 8, in force 6 August 1989	Extends the scope of the Montreal Convention to require states parties to criminalize: • performance of an act of violence against a person at an airport serving international civil aviation which causes or is likely to cause serious injury or death; and • destruction or serious damage to the facilities of an airport serving international civil aviation or aircraft not in service located there, or disrupting the services of the airport, if such an act endangers or is likely to endanger safety at that airport.

Convention	Content
Convention for the Suppression of Unlawful Acts against the Safety of Maritime Navigation, 10 March 1998, 1678 UNTS 222, Can TS 1993 No 10, in force 1 March 1992 (Maritime Convention, 1988)	Requires states parties to criminalize the following offences: • seizing or exercising control over a ship by force or threat thereof or any other form of intimidation; • performing an act of violence against a person on board a ship if that act is likely to endanger the safe navigation of that ship; • destroying a ship or causing damage to a ship or to its cargo which is likely to endanger the safe navigation of that ship; • placing or causing to be placed on a ship, by any means whatsoever, a device or substance which is likely to destroy that ship, or causing damage to that ship or its cargo which endangers or is likely to endanger the safe navigation of that ship; • destroying or seriously damaging maritime navigational facilities or seriously interfering with their operation, if any such act is likely to endanger the safe navigation of a ship; • communicating information which the person knows to be false, thereby endangering the safe navigation of a ship; • threatening aimed at compelling a physical or juridical person to do or refrain from doing any act, to commit any of the offences in the second, third, and fifth bullets above, if that threat is likely to endanger the ship's safe navigation; • using on, or from, a ship, or transporting on a ship, various radioactive or nuclear materials, or nuclear or chemical or biological weapons to intimidate a population, or to compel a government or an international organization to do or to abstain from doing any act. State parties are also to criminalize attempts; participating as an accomplice; organizing or directing others to commit an above-listed offence; and intentionally contributing in any other way to the commission of one or more offences by a group of persons acting with a common purpose with the aim of furthering the general criminal activity or purpose of the group, or made in the knowledge of the intention of the group to commit the offence or offences concerned.
Protocol for the Suppression of Unlawful Acts Against the Safety of Fixed Platforms Located on the Continental Shelf, 10 March 1998, 1678 UNTS 304, Can TS 1993 No 9, in force 1 March 1992 (Maritime Convention Protocol, 1998)	Requires states parties to criminalize the following offences (and attempting, aiding, and being an accomplice to such offences): • seizing or exercising control over a fixed platform by force or threat thereof or any other form of intimidation; • performing an act of violence against a person on board a fixed platform if that act is likely to endanger its safety; • destroying a fixed platform or causing damage to it which is likely to endanger its safety; • placing or causing to be placed on a fixed platform, by any means whatsoever, a device or substance which is likely to destroy that fixed platform or likely to endanger its safety;

Convention	Content
Protocol for the Suppression of Unlawful Acts Against the Safety of Fixed Platforms Located on the Continental Shelf (continued)	• threatening aimed at compelling a physical or juridical person to do or refrain from doing any act, to commit any of the offences in the second and third bullets above, if that threat is likely to endanger the safety of the fixed platform; and • using on or from a fixed platform (or threatening to do so) various radioactive or nuclear materials, or nuclear or chemical or biological weapons to intimidate a population, or to compel a government or an international organization to do or to abstain from doing any act. State parties are also to criminalize attempts; participating as an accomplice; organizing or directing others to commit an above-listed offence; and intentionally contributing in any other way to the commission of one or more offences by a group of persons acting with a common purpose with the aim of furthering the general criminal activity or purpose of the group, or made in the knowledge of the intention of the group to commit the offence or offences concerned.
2. Terrorism against Protected Persons	
Convention on the Prevention and Punishment of Crimes against Internationally Protected Persons, including Diplomatic Agents, 14 December 1973, 1035 UNTS 167, Can TS 1977 No 43, in force 20 February 1977	Requires states parties to criminalize the intentional commission of (and attempts, threats, or being an accomplice to) murder, kidnapping, or other attack upon the person or liberty of an internationally protected person or a violent attack upon the official premises, the private accommodation, or the means of transport of an internationally protected person likely to endanger his or her person or liberty. "Internationally protected person" is defined as: • a head of state, including any member of a collegial body performing the functions of a head of state under the constitution of the state concerned, a head of government, or a minister for foreign affairs, whenever any such person is in a foreign state, as well as members of her family who accompany her; • any representative or official of a state, or any official or other agent of an international organization of an intergovernmental character who, at the time when and in the place where a crime against him, his official premises, his private accommodation, or his means of transport is committed, is entitled pursuant to international law to special protection from any attack on his person, freedom or dignity, as well as members of his family forming part of his household.
3. Nuclear Terrorism	
International Convention for the Suppression of Acts of Nuclear Terrorism, 13 April 2005, 2445 UNTS 89, in force 7 July 2007 (Nuclear Terrorism Convention 2005)	Requires states parties to criminalize: • possession of radioactive material or making or possessing a nuclear or radiological explosive device with the intent to cause death or serious bodily injury; or with the intent to cause substantial damage to property or to the environment; and

Convention	Content
International Convention for the Suppression of Acts of Nuclear Terrorism (continued)	• using in any way radioactive material or a device, or using or damaging a nuclear facility in a manner which releases or risks the release of radioactive material with the intent to cause death or serious bodily injury; or with the intent to cause substantial damage to property or to the environment; or with the intent to compel a natural or legal person, an international organization or a state to do or refrain from doing an act. The above noted offences include attempts. States parties are also to criminalize: • threats, under circumstances which indicate the credibility of the threat, to commit an offence listed in the second bullet point above; and • demanding, unlawfully and intentionally, radioactive material, a nuclear or radiological device, or a nuclear facility by threat, under circumstances which indicate the credibility of the threat, or by use of force. State parties are also to criminalize participating as an accomplice; organizing or directing others to commit an above-listed offence; and intentionally contributing in any other way to the commission of one or more offences by a group of persons acting with a common purpose with the aim of furthering the general criminal activity or purpose of the group, or made in the knowledge of the intention of the group to commit the offence or offences concerned.
4. Certain Other Forms of Terrorist Violence	
International Convention Against the Taking of Hostages, 17 December 1979, 1316 UNTS 205, Can TS 1986 No 45, in force 3 June 1983	Requires states parties to criminalize the seizing or detention and threat to kill, to injure, or to continue to detain a person ("hostage") in order to compel a third party, namely, a state, an international intergovernmental organization, a natural or juridical person, or a group of persons, to do or abstain from doing any act as an explicit or implicit condition for the release of the hostage.
International Convention for the Suppression of Terrorist Bombings, 15 December 1997, 2149 UNTS 256, Can TS 2002 No 8, in force 23 May 2001	Requires states parties to criminalize the unlawful and intentional delivery, placement, discharge, or detonation of an explosive or other lethal device in, into, or against a place of public use, a state or government facility, a public transportation system, or an infrastructure facility with the intent to cause death or serious bodily injury; or with the intent to cause extensive destruction of such a place, facility, or system, where such destruction results in or is likely to result in major economic loss. State parties are also to criminalize attempts; participating as an accomplice; organizing or directing others to commit an above-listed offence; and intentionally contributing in any other way to the commission of one or more offences by a group of persons acting with a common purpose with the aim of furthering the general criminal activity or purpose of the group, or made in the knowledge of the intention of the group to commit the offence or offences concerned.

Convention	Content
B. Conventions Relating to Terrorist Material	
Convention on the Physical Protection of Nuclear Material, 3 March 1980, 1456 UNTS 125, Can TS 1987 No 35, in force 8 February 1987 (Nuclear Material Convention, 1980)	Requires states parties to criminalize the intentional commission (and attempted commission) of: • an act without lawful authority which constitutes the receipt, possession, use, transfer, alteration, disposal, or dispersal of nuclear material and which causes or is likely to cause death or serious injury to any person or substantial damage to property; • a theft or robbery of nuclear material; • an embezzlement or fraudulent obtaining of nuclear material; • an act constituting a demand for nuclear material by threat or use of force, or by any other form of intimidation; and • a threat to use nuclear material to cause death or serious injury to any person or substantial property damage, or to use nuclear material in order to compel a natural or legal person, international organization, or state to do or to refrain from doing any act.
Convention on the Marking of Plastic Explosives for the Purpose of Detection, 1 March 1991, 2122 UNTS 374, Can TS 1998 No 54, in force 21 June 1998	Each state party shall take the necessary and effective measures to prohibit and prevent the manufacture in its territory of unmarked explosives. Each state party shall take the necessary and effective measures to prohibit and prevent the movement into or out of its territory of unmarked explosives. Marking means introducing a detection agent into an explosive.
International Convention for the Suppression of the Financing of Terrorism, 9 December 1999, 2178 UNTS 197, Can TS 2002 No 9, in force 10 April 2002	Requires states parties to criminalize the following offence: directly or indirectly, unlawfully and willfully, providing or collecting funds with the intention that they should be used or in the knowledge that they are to be used, in full or in part, in order to carry out: (a) An act which constitutes an offence within the scope of and as defined in most of the treaties listed in this table; or (b) Any other act intended to cause death or serious bodily injury to a civilian, or to any other person not taking an active part in the hostilities in a situation of armed conflict, when the purpose of such act, by its nature or context, is to intimidate a population, or to compel a government or an international organization to do or to abstain from doing any act. State parties are also to criminalize attempts; participating as an accomplice; organizing or directing others to commit this offence; and intentionally contributing to the commission of one or more offences by a group of persons acting with a common purpose, with the aim of furthering the general criminal activity or purpose of the group, or made in the knowledge of the intention of the group to commit the offence or offences concerned.

* Note that there is one anti-terrorism convention not listed above, as it is not yet in force: the Convention on the Suppression of Unlawful Acts relating to International Civil Aviation (Beijing Convention), 10 September 2010, ICAO Doc 9960. When in force, this convention will criminalize the act of using civil aircraft as a weapon to cause death, injury, or damage, as well as the act of using civil aircraft to discharge biological, chemical, and nuclear weapons or similar substances to cause death, injury, or damage. It will also ensure that a cyber attack on air navigation facilities constitutes an offence.

E. CANADIAN IMPLEMENTATION OF INTERNATIONAL CRIMINAL LAW

In 2000, Canada's *Crimes Against Humanity and War Crimes Act*[143] came into force. This Act, which implements Canada's obligations under the Rome Statute (and was the first such implementing legislation adopted in the world), criminalizes acts of genocide, crimes against humanity, and war crimes, and imposes, in some circumstances, criminal responsibility on military commanders and civilian superiors for such acts committed by their subordinates. The Act defines genocide, crimes against humanity, and war crimes in accordance with customary, conventional, or general principles of international law. Under the Act, individuals suspected of committing these crimes in Canada can be prosecuted in Canada or surrendered to the International Criminal Court. Those suspected of committing such offences outside Canada can also be tried in Canada, provided that certain jurisdictional requirements are met.[144]

Consider the following key provisions of the Act:

Crimes Against Humanity and War Crimes Act, SC 2000, c 24

OFFENCES WITHIN CANADA

4.(1) Every person is guilty of an indictable offence who commits

(*a*) genocide;

(*b*) a crime against humanity; or

(*c*) a war crime.

(1.1) Every person who conspires or attempts to commit, is an accessory after the fact in relation to, or counsels in relation to, an offence referred to in subsection (1) is guilty of an indictable offence.

(2) Every person who commits an offence under subsection (1) or (1.1)

(*a*) shall be sentenced to imprisonment for life, if an intentional killing forms the basis of the offence; and

(*b*) is liable to imprisonment for life, in any other case.

(3) The definitions in this subsection apply in this section.

"crime against humanity" means murder, extermination, enslavement, deportation, imprisonment, torture, sexual violence, persecution or any other inhumane act or omission that is committed against any civilian population or any identifiable group and that, at the time and in the place of its commission, constitutes a crime against humanity according to customary international law or conventional international law or by virtue of its being criminal according to the general principles of law recognized by the community of nations, whether or not it constitutes a contravention of the law in force at the time and in the place of its commission.

---

143 *Crimes Against Humanity and War Crimes Act*, SC 2000, c 24.
144 *Ibid*, s 8.

"genocide" means an act or omission committed with intent to destroy, in whole or in part, an identifiable group of persons, as such, that, at the time and in the place of its commission, constitutes genocide according to customary international law or conventional international law or by virtue of its being criminal according to the general principles of law recognized by the community of nations, whether or not it constitutes a contravention of the law in force at the time and in the place of its commission.

"war crime" means an act or omission committed during an armed conflict that, at the time and in the place of its commission, constitutes a war crime according to customary international law or conventional international law applicable to armed conflicts, whether or not it constitutes a contravention of the law in force at the time and in the place of its commission.

(4) For greater certainty, crimes described in Articles 6 and 7 and paragraph 2 of Article 8 of the Rome Statute are, as of July 17, 1998, crimes according to customary international law. This does not limit or prejudice in any way the application of existing or developing rules of international law.

5. (1) A military commander commits an indictable offence if
    (a) the military commander
        (i) fails to exercise control properly over a person under their effective command and control or effective authority and control, and as a result the person commits an offence under section 4, or
        (ii) fails, after the coming into force of this section, to exercise control properly over a person under their effective command and control or effective authority and control, and as a result the person commits an offence under section 6;
    (b) the military commander knows, or is criminally negligent in failing to know, that the person is about to commit or is committing such an offence; and
    (c) the military commander subsequently
        (i) fails to take, as soon as practicable, all necessary and reasonable measures within their power to prevent or repress the commission of the offence, or the further commission of offences under section 4 or 6, or
        (ii) fails to take, as soon as practicable, all necessary and reasonable measures within their power to submit the matter to the competent authorities for investigation and prosecution.

(2) A superior commits an indictable offence if
(a) the superior
        (i) fails to exercise control properly over a person under their effective authority and control, and as a result the person commits an offence under section 4, or
        (ii) fails, after the coming into force of this section, to exercise control properly over a person under their effective authority and control, and as a result the person commits an offence under section 6;
(b) the superior knows that the person is about to commit or is committing such an offence, or consciously disregards information that clearly indicates that such an offence is about to be committed or is being committed by the person;

(c) the offence relates to activities for which the superior has effective authority and control; and

(d) the superior subsequently

(i) fails to take, as soon as practicable, all necessary and reasonable measures within their power to prevent or repress the commission of the offence, or the further commission of offences under section 4 or 6, or

(ii) fails to take, as soon as practicable, all necessary and reasonable measures within their power to submit the matter to the competent authorities for investigation and prosecution.

(2.1) Every person who conspires or attempts to commit, is an accessory after the fact in relation to, or counsels in relation to, an offence referred to in subsection (1) or (2) is guilty of an indictable offence.

(3) Every person who commits an offence under subsection (1), (2) or (2.1) is liable to imprisonment for life.

(4) The definitions in this subsection apply in this section.

"military commander" includes a person effectively acting as a military commander and a person who commands police with a degree of authority and control comparable to a military commander.

"superior" means a person in authority, other than a military commander.

OFFENCES OUTSIDE CANADA

6. (1) Every person who, either before or after the coming into force of this section, commits outside Canada

(a) genocide,

(b) a crime against humanity, or

(c) a war crime,

is guilty of an indictable offence and may be prosecuted for that offence in accordance with section 8.

(1.1) Every person who conspires or attempts to commit, is an accessory after the fact in relation to, or counsels in relation to, an offence referred to in subsection (1) is guilty of an indictable offence.

(2) Every person who commits an offence under subsection (1) or (1.1)

(a) shall be sentenced to imprisonment for life, if an intentional killing forms the basis of the offence; and

(b) is liable to imprisonment for life, in any other case.

(3) The definitions in this subsection apply in this section.

"crime against humanity" means murder, extermination, enslavement, deportation, imprisonment, torture, sexual violence, persecution or any other inhumane act or omission that is committed against any civilian population or any identifiable group and that, at the time and in the place of its commission, constitutes a crime against humanity according to customary international law or conventional international law or by virtue of its being criminal according to the general principles of law recognized by the community of nations, whether or not it constitutes a contravention of the law in force at the time and in the place of its commission.

"genocide" means an act or omission committed with intent to destroy, in whole or in part, an identifiable group of persons, as such, that at the time and in the place of its commission, constitutes genocide according to customary international law or conventional international law or by virtue of its being criminal according to the general principles of law recognized by the community of nations, whether or not it constitutes a contravention of the law in force at the time and in the place of its commission.

"war crime" means an act or omission committed during an armed conflict that, at the time and in the place of its commission, constitutes a war crime according to customary international law or conventional international law applicable to armed conflicts, whether or not it constitutes a contravention of the law in force at the time and in the place of its commission.

(4) For greater certainty, crimes described in articles 6 and 7 and paragraph 2 of article 8 of the Rome Statute are, as of July 17, 1998, crimes according to customary international law, and may be crimes according to customary international law before that date. This does not limit or prejudice in any way the application of existing or developing rules of international law.

(5) For greater certainty, the offence of crime against humanity was part of customary international law or was criminal according to the general principles of law recognized by the community of nations before the coming into force of either of the following:
(a) the Agreement for the prosecution and punishment of the major war criminals of the European Axis, signed at London on August 8, 1945; and
(b) the Proclamation by the Supreme Commander for the Allied Powers, dated January 19, 1946.

7. (1) A military commander commits an indictable offence if
(a) the military commander, outside Canada,
(i) fails to exercise control properly over a person under their effective command and control or effective authority and control, and as a result the person commits an offence under section 4, or
(ii) fails, before or after the coming into force of this section, to exercise control properly over a person under their effective command and control or effective authority and control, and as a result the person commits an offence under section 6;
(b) the military commander knows, or is criminally negligent in failing to know, that the person is about to commit or is committing such an offence; and
(c) the military commander subsequently
(i) fails to take, as soon as practicable, all necessary and reasonable measures within their power to prevent or repress the commission of the offence, or the further commission of offences under section 4 or 6, or

(ii) fails to take, as soon as practicable, all necessary and reasonable measures within their power to submit the matter to the competent authorities for investigation and prosecution.

(2) A superior commits an indictable offence if

(a) the superior, outside Canada,

(i) fails to exercise control properly over a person under their effective authority and control, and as a result the person commits an offence under section 4, or

(ii) fails, before or after the coming into force of this section, to exercise control properly over a person under their effective authority and control, and as a result the person commits an offence under section 6;

(b) the superior knows that the person is about to commit or is committing such an offence, or consciously disregards information that clearly indicates that such an offence is about to be committed or is being committed by the person;

(c) the offence relates to activities for which the superior has effective authority and control; and

(d) the superior subsequently

(i) fails to take, as soon as practicable, all necessary and reasonable measures within their power to prevent or repress the commission of the offence, or the further commission of offences under section 4 or 6, or

(ii) fails to take, as soon as practicable, all necessary and reasonable measures within their power to submit the matter to the competent authorities for investigation and prosecution.

(2.1) Every person who conspires or attempts to commit, is an accessory after the fact in relation to, or counsels in relation to, an offence referred to in subsection (1) or (2) is guilty of an indictable offence.

(3) A person who is alleged to have committed an offence under subsection (1), (2) or (2.1) may be prosecuted for that offence in accordance with section 8.

(4) Every person who commits an offence under subsection (1), (2) or (2.1) is liable to imprisonment for life.

(5) Where an act or omission constituting an offence under this section occurred before the coming into force of this section, subparagraphs (1)(a)(ii) and (2)(a)(ii) apply to the extent that, at the time and in the place of the act or omission, the act or omission constituted a contravention of customary international law or conventional international law or was criminal according to the general principles of law recognized by the community of nations, whether or not it constituted a contravention of the law in force at the time and in the place of its commission.

(6) The definitions in this subsection apply in this section.

"military commander" includes a person effectively acting as a military commander and a person who commands police with a degree of authority and control comparable to a military commander.

"superior" means a person in authority, other than a military commander.

8. A person who is alleged to have committed an offence under section 6 or 7 may be prosecuted for that offence if

(a) at the time the offence is alleged to have been committed,

(i) the person was a Canadian citizen or was employed by Canada in a civilian or military capacity,

(ii) the person was a citizen of a state that was engaged in an armed conflict against Canada, or was employed in a civilian or military capacity by such a state,

(iii) the victim of the alleged offence was a Canadian citizen, or

(iv) the victim of the alleged offence was a citizen of a state that was allied with Canada in an armed conflict; or

(b) after the time the offence is alleged to have been committed, the person is present in Canada.

PROCEDURE AND DEFENCES

9. . . .

(3) No proceedings for an offence under any of sections 4 to 7 of this Act . . . may be commenced without the personal consent in writing of the Attorney General or Deputy Attorney General of Canada, and those proceedings may be conducted only by the Attorney General of Canada or counsel acting on their behalf.

The first charges under the *Crimes Against Humanity and War Crimes Act* were laid in 2005. On 19 October 2005, the RCMP arrested Désiré Munyaneza in Toronto on seven charges of genocide, crimes against humanity, and war crimes under the Act. Munyaneza was alleged to have committed these crimes in Butare, Rwanda, in 1994.[145] In 2009, Munyaneza was convicted on all counts and sentenced to life imprisonment.[146] At the time of writing, his case was on appeal. The *Munyaneza* case illustrates the challenges associated with holding a trial in Canada on the basis of universal jurisdiction, and the difficulties inherent in proving international crimes. The trial began on 27 March 2007 in Montreal and lasted until 19 December 2008, when Justice Denis took the case under advisement.[147] Prior to the start of the trial proceedings in Canada, the trial judge presided over a rogatory commission in Kigali, Rwanda, during which time he heard from the first fourteen prosecution witnesses who could not travel to Canada.[148] In Canada, the prosecution called an additional sixteen witnesses.[149] In 2008, the trial judge presided over further rogatory commissions in Paris, France; Kigali, Rwanda; and Dar es Salaam, Tanzania to hear twenty-four defence witnesses who could not travel to Canada.[150] The defence

---

145 *R v Munyaneza*, [2009] QCCS 2201, [2009] RJQ 1432 at s 7.8 [*Munyaneza* Trial Judgment].

146 *R v Munyaneza*, [2009] QCCS 4865 [*Munyaneza* Sentencing Judgment]. For an analysis of the *Munyaneza* judgments, see Fannie Lafontaine, "Canada's Crimes Against Humanity and War Crimes Act on Trial: An Analysis of the Munyaneza Case" (2010) 8:1 J Int'l Crim Justice 269.

147 *Munyaneza* Trial Judgment, above note 145 at paras 12 and 29.

148 *Ibid* at para 15.

149 *Ibid* at para 18.

150 *Ibid* at paras 20–22.

presented twelve additional witnesses in Canada.[151] The parties also filed close to 200 exhibits and submitted more than 1,200 pages of pleadings as well as "tens of thousands of pages of jurisprudence and various authorities."[152] Justice Denis specifically mentioned that the organization of the four rogatory commissions was "a colossal undertaking" and that the entire case was "demanding."[153]

The complicated nature of cases involving international crimes was again demonstrated in the second set of charges brought under Canada's *Crimes Against Humanity and War Crimes Act*. On 6 November 2009, RCMP officers arrested Jacques Mungwarere in Windsor, Ontario.[154] He was charged with one count of genocide and one count of crimes against humanity, on suspicion of involvement in the 1994 genocide in Rwanda. On 5 July 2013, after twenty-six weeks of trial, Mungwarere was acquitted. The trial judge found that the Crown had not proven its case beyond a reasonable doubt.[155] Justice Charbonneau indicated that the central problem with the case was the reliability of the witnesses on both sides.[156] While the Crown has indicated that it intends to appeal, the judgment undoubtedly represents a setback for Canada's War Crimes Program, which is tasked with deciding which actions to take in cases involving genocide, crimes against humanity and war crimes.[157]

---

151 *Ibid* at para 24.

152 *Ibid* at paras 26–27.

153 *Ibid* at paras 23 and 31.

154 Steven Chase, "Man charged in Rwandan Genocide," *Globe and Mail* (9 November 2009) A9.

155 CBC News, "Ontario Judge Clears 'Probably Guilty' Rwandan of War Crimes" (5 July 2013) online: www.cbc.ca/news/canada/story/2013/07/04/pol-rwanda-mungwarere-verdict.html.

156 *Ibid*; Chloé Fedio, "Mungwarere Not Guilty of Genocide; Ottawa Judge Rules Evidence Not Credible in Case against Rwandan," *The Ottawa Citizen* (6 July 2013) A6.

157 Department of Justice, "War Crimes Program" online: canada.justice.gc.ca/eng/cj-jp/wc-cdg/prog.html.

TABLE OF CASES

INTERNATIONAL CASES

OTHER JURISDICTIONS

TABLE OF INTERNATIONAL INSTRUMENTS

Please note: bolded page references indicate where documents have been reproduced within the text.

TREATIES

UN GENERAL ASSEMBLY RESOLUTIONS

UN SECURITY COUNCIL RESOLUTIONS

UN ECONOMIC AND SOCIAL COUNCIL RESOLUTIONS

INTERNATIONAL LAW COMMISSION TEXTS

OTHER INSTRUMENTS

ABOUT THE AUTHORS

John H. Currie is a professor in the Faculty of Law at the University of Ottawa, where he teaches, *inter alia*, public international law, the use of force by states, and the law of armed conflict. He is also an adjunct research professor in the Norman Paterson School of International Affairs at Carleton University. The holder of degrees in astronomy and physics from the University of Toronto, and in law from the universities of Ottawa and Cambridge, Professor Currie is editor-in-chief of *The Canadian Yearbook of International Law* and the author or co-author of several books. His research and writing interests include various aspects of public international law, with a particular focus on its reception in domestic legal systems. He has been scholar-in-residence in the Legal Affairs Bureau of Canada's Department of Foreign Affairs and International Trade, advising on matters of international criminal and humanitarian law and representing Canada before a number of UN bodies (including the International Criminal Tribunal for the Former Yugoslavia). He is also a past president of the Canadian Council on International Law; has designed and taught courses on public international law for the Canadian Foreign Service Institute; and served as a member of the Canadian delegation to the 2010 Review Conference of the Rome Statute of the International Criminal Court.

Craig Forcese is vice dean and associate professor in the Faculty of Law (Common Law Section) at the University of Ottawa, where he teaches public international law, national security law, administrative law, and public law and legislation, and runs the annual foreign policy practicum. Much of his present research and writing relates to international law, national security, and democratic accountability. Prior to joining the law school faculty, he practiced law with the Washington DC office of Hughes Hubbard & Reed LLP, specializing in international trade law. Craig has law degrees from the University of Ottawa and Yale University, a BA from McGill, and an MA in international affairs from the Norman Paterson School of International Affairs, Carleton University. He is a member of the bars of Ontario, New York, and the District of Columbia.

Joanna Harrington is a professor in the Faculty of Law at the University of Alberta, where she teaches public international law and international criminal law, as well as constitutional law when not serving as an associate dean with the Faculty of Graduate Studies and Research. She has degrees from the universities of British Columbia (BA), Victoria (JD), and Cambridge (PhD), and an Academy of European Law Diploma in Human Rights Law from the European University Institute in Italy. Her research and writings often focus on the interplay between international and domestic law, including the interplay between international human rights law and domestic bills of rights. From 2006 to 2008, she served as the scholar-in-residence with the Legal Affairs Bureau of Canada's then Department of Foreign Affairs and International Trade, participating in the negotiation of new human rights instruments at the United Nations and the Organization of American States. Before becoming a law professor, she served as the legal officer to a member of Britain's House of Lords during a period of significant constitutional reform.

Valerie Oosterveld is an associate professor in the Faculty of Law at the University of Western Ontario, where she teaches public international law, the law of international organizations, and international criminal law. She has degrees from the universities of Ottawa (BSocSc), Toronto (LLB), and Columbia (LLM and JSD). Her research and writings focus on gender issues within international criminal justice. Before joining the faculty in 2005, Valerie served in the Legal Affairs Bureau of Canada's then Department of Foreign Affairs and International Trade. In this role, she provided legal advice on international criminal accountability for genocide, crimes against humanity, and war crimes. She was a member of the Canadian delegation to the International Criminal Court (ICC) negotiations, as well as the subsequent ICC Assembly of States Parties and the 2010 Review Conference of the Rome Statute of the ICC.